# PLATO AND PAUL;

OR,

# PHILOSOPHY AND CHRISTIANITY.

## AN EXAMINATION

OF THE

TWO FUNDAMENTAL FORCES OF COSMIC AND HUMAN
HISTORY, WITH THEIR CONTENTS, METHODS,
FUNCTIONS, RELATIONS, AND
RESULTS COMPARED.

BY

## J. W. MENDENHALL, PH. D., D. D.,

AUTHOR OF "ECHOES FROM PALESTINE," ETC.

"Plato is philosophy, and philosophy, Plato."—R. W. EMERSON.
"Christianity is the philosophy of the people."—VICTOR COUSIN.
"Πάντα δοκιμάζετε· τὸ καλὸν κατέχετε."—THE APOSTLE PAUL.

CINCINNATI:
JENNINGS & GRAHAM
NEW YORK:
EATON AND MAINS.

# INTRODUCTION.

PHILOSOPHY is Speculation; Christianity is Truth. So far forth as the subject-matter of the one is related to, or is identical with, the subject-matter of the other, the range of the one is equal to the range of the other. The realm of speculation is in the philosophic sense illimitable because the realm of truth is without bounds. Speculation concerns itself with truth, not as knowing it, but as seeking it, and as being ready to investigate it when found, or when it is assumed that it has been found. Both are engaged with the same problems, employing different and sometimes opposite methods in the attempt to solve them, but anticipating in their final rehearsal a vindication of the same truths, or the same forms of truth.

Philosophy, self-guided and self-reliant, speculates with enthusiastic purpose on the accepted or assumed verities of Christianity. Without knowledge, or waiving the use of Revelation as a source of knowledge, it can do nothing but speculate. It can assume nothing, it must prove every thing; it knows nothing, it must inquire as it goes along. It not infrequently happens that, dazed by the magnitude of its tasks, or discouraged by reason of the incompleteness of its discoveries, philosophy merely drifts along the routes of inquiry, marking the distances traveled by the mile-posts of its successive leaders, seemingly unconscious of the fact that the ages have waited for a settlement of the highest problems, and that it should promote a settlement or abandon its position as guide to truth. It often lags in its self-burdened efforts, and sometimes despairs of reaching the goal. From this uncertain and paralyzing condition, however, it usually recovers, apparently inspired with a conviction of duty it can not shake off, and proceeds with patient steps to the development of issues closely akin to those that have their life and power in the bosom of Christianity.

In the nature of the case philosophy is under restraint in the prosecution of its endeavors, but there is no help for it so long as its fundamental idea is in opposition to the idea of Revelation.

Dealing with *data*, whose explanation is impossible without the recognition of the supernatural as the *initial force* of all things, it aims to establish the all-sufficiency of things themselves, which, however absurd in appearance, engages its loftiest efforts, and constitutes a concept of modern philosophic thought. The beginning of speculation is a simple interrogation; its intermediate stage is an anxious and complex inquiry, looking to final results; its end is sometimes *doubt*, sometimes *knowledge*, sometimes *faith*, sometimes the *theistic notion*. Whatever the outcome or emergence philosophy is a wanderer in the wilderness of thought, piloting itself by its own compass, anxious all the while for rescue, but uncertain all the time as to the issue.

On the other hand, Christianity, designating the supernatural as its starting-point, and accepting revelation as the constituent idea of religion, descends to the natural realm, with an explanation of its phenomena by the laws of the higher realm, thereby reversing the method of inquiry adopted by philosophy, and illuminates all truth by its self-enkindled light, to the satisfaction of the reason, and the comfort of the doubting and perplexed inquirer. The immediate effect of Revelation is *knowledge*, which philosophy, unaided and rejecting the auxiliaries of religion, fails to impart.

The extent and limitations of metaphysical research are defined, not so much by the principles it seeks to maintain, which are identical with the ultimate facts of religion, as by the methods of investigation it voluntarily and in the end necessarily adopts. Empirical, or absolutely logical methods, adequate enough in the pursuit of scientific facts, are lamentably inadequate to the ascertainment of truth in the higher realms of thought; but other methods are unknown to the philosopher, or if known are by the terms of his purpose unavailable. He undertakes to pronounce the *reason* of things, or *explain them by themselves*, than which in the lower realm no higher pursuit is possible or more profitable; but as he attempts to *reason concerning the reason of things* he suddenly discovers his instrument defective and insufficient. The instrument is by no means valueless, but it is imperfect, and serves him only in primary investigation. Reason is the *ratio of truths* or *things*, and the discovery of reason is the discovery of the hidden ratio of truths, or the exposition of truth in its relation to the source of final truth. The discovery of reason, bound up in things, or secreted in the highest truth, is the key to the universe, which philosophy is persistently striving to find. That its seeking has been in vain it were injudicious to assert; but that it has been successful no one acquainted with its history of failure will claim. No disparagement of philosophical labor, no ridicule of scientific discoveries, no misrepresentations of materialistic thinkers, but a justifiable depreciation of philosophical results in the field of ultimate inquiry and the evident embarrassments of all classes of speculatists in the realm of higher thought, will be exhibited in this treatise. The limitations of philosophic inquiries, and the weaknesses of philosophic methods for the determination of final, that is, *absolute*, truth, as contrasted with the defensible and transparent methods of Christianity and the adequacy of its truths to the accomplishment of the divine ideals respecting man and the universe, constitute the primary and pregnant thought of this volume.

In comparing the two methods and the results obtained by their use, the radical contents, both of philosophy and Christianity, as systems of truth, must not only be submitted, but they must be analyzed and tested by the methods themselves, and as thoroughly as the purposes of the investigation require. A superficial reference to these systems would not enable the reader to discover the failure of the one or the success of the other, and, what is more important, it would not enable him to understand the *reason of failure* in the one instance or the *reason of success* in the other. Hence, a full schedule of the systems themselves, both as to what each is in itself, and what they contain in common, we have undertaken to furnish, and trust the result will be satisfactory to the students of speculative forms. Beginning with Brucker, the father of historians of philosophy, and wandering among the nations and following the footsteps of the thinkers in search of answers to fundamental questions, we have sought to ascertain the original ideas of philosophic leaders, and always to compare their judgments and indoctrinations with the engrossed revelations of the Sacred Teacher, in the belief that the superiority of the latter will be clearly manifest. The extent to which this has been done the reader must determine for himself.

Evidently enfeebled as philosophy is by its necessary and constitutional methods, it may surprise the reader to be informed that the author's aim is in part to establish that Christianity may be amply justified by the philosophical method, and that its philosophical basis is as impregnable as the more common historical basis on which it supposedly and safely rests. It is altogether probable, therefore, that it will be inferred that if the philosophical method is insufficient for philosophical purposes, it must also be inadequate in the hands of the Christian investigator for his purposes. Such a conclusion must not be hastily drawn. Christianity has its Theological argument—an argument strong, robust, granitic; its argument from Experience, the more decisive because in form the more philosophical; its argument from History, a running fire burning up the wild guesses of materialism in its path, and illuminating the heavens as it spreads over the earth, its latest work the best because the most destructive and the most complete. While the Theological, the Experiential, and the Historical arguments are involved one in another, and constitute an all-sufficient defense of religious truth, the Philosophical Argument for Christianity is as important as these, and as unanswerable, because *Christianity is true philosophy*, or the *philosophy of truth* in a religious form; and, to meet the demands of the present day, this argument is emphasized in this volume more than any other, being rendered in such form as to make Christianity appear quite as much a philosophy as a religion, or that the two are inseparable in Christianity. On this basis—the *scientific complexion of the highest religion*—we hold that Christianity may successfully assail the naïve materialism and popular agnosticism of the times. The conflict now raging is not so much a conflict between Christianity and another phase of religion, as it is a conflict between Christianity and some form of philosophy. Even in India and in pagan lands generally a contest of religions is rarely witnessed, but a contest of primordial religious truth with a current philosophic idea is constantly going on. In appearance the contest is exclusively religious, but at bottom it is the striving of religious truth with philosophic error. In Christian lands little or no attention has been given to the *philosophical character of Christianity*, its defense being largely historical or in form theological; hence, the philosophic thinker, finding his method abjured, has been led to conclude against the philosophical value of religion, and has pronounced it a superstition. To acquaint him with the primordial ideas of religion, vindicating them from the philosophical standpoint, and to re-impress the image of truth upon the mind of man, the mistakes of materialism, and the insufficiency and frigidity of a godless philosophy, and the deep, pervasive, and unquenchable spirit of Christianity, with the authority of its truths, and the sufficiency of its revelations, must be fully aud comprehensively shown, and this is attempted in the volume here presented.

In theological treatises a distinction is observed between mathematical certainty and moral certainty, or evidence of a mathematical cast or force and evidence moral in its content and conditional in its power of persuasion, and this distinction is applied in the enforcement of religious truth, not only to the discredit of the Christian stand-point, but also to the weakening of the supports of faith in such truth. That the distinction itself is correct must be admitted, for evidence differs in its degree of certainty, the positive and demonstrative being properly styled "mathematical," and the probable or conjectural, but undemonstrative, being called "moral." Moral evidence may be as convincing to the unprejudiced intellect as the mathematical, and the truth supported by it may be as transparent as an axiom, but many minds, unaccustomed to the balancing of probabilities or the weighing of evidence in other than the scales of exact mathematical dimensions, hesitate to receive for truth that which the theologian offers, because he urges in its behalf only a moral argument, and that in an apologetic form and without data to confirm it. It is time to consider if a mistake has not been made in advancing Christianity as *probably*, but not positively, true, in conceding that its truths are not demonstrations, and can not be demonstrated, in granting that its evidences are not mathematical in spirit or form, and can not assume a more precise and satisfactory character, and in insisting that it must be received from a moral conviction of its verity, and alone on moral grounds of its absolute sufficiency and truthfulness. The mistake appears all the greater when it is remembered that the theologian is willing to concede that physical science and philosophic truth appeal with mathematical force to human judgment, and encircle themselves with evidences indisputable and of universal authority. In his view it is enough if Christianity, inasmuch as it is a system of moral truth, is urged as a moral certainty, and accepted on moral evidence, however uncertain the certainty and unsatisfactory the evidence. To be sure, he will not accept physical truth on moral grounds, or subscribe to a system of philosophic thought, because moral arguments alone support it; he can not be persuaded to accept gravitation, or chemical affinity on moral evidence; but he accepts monotheism, incarnation, atonement, regeneration, resurrection, and the doctrines of heaven and hell on grounds of moral certainty, as if incapable of a mathematical demonstration. The philosopher, seeing the theologian repudiate moral evidence as applied to physical facts, and mathematical evidence as applied to moral facts, translates the certainties of religion into uncertainties, regarding his own stand-point as preferable because positive and assuring.

In this way theology unwittingly surrenders the argument that belongs to it, loses its hold upon the intellectual truth-seeker, and invalidates nearly all that it has gained in its conflict with error. Verily, *we are inclined to reverse the order of the argument.* Philosophy is the uncertain, *because only morally certain,* if at all certain, system of truth; *Christiantity is the mathematically certain form of the highest truth, the* GEOMETRICAL PROOF OF ETERNAL RATIOS. Spinoza ventured to affirm that theological truth can be proved from a mathematical standpoint, but this canon was in the interest of pantheism. We subsidize the thought in the interest of Christianity, declaring that, as a system of truth, it is susceptible of mathematical demonstration; that is, that its truths may be as authentically and as satisfactorily vindicated as any truth in geology, chemistry, geometry, astronomy, biology, or psychology, and by precisely those methods which science regards inalienable and conclusive. The old way was to enforce the Gospel by the exercise of authority—not the authority of truth, but the authority of force. In those days the fagot, the dungeon, the thumbscrew, and the sword were fashioned into arguments that seldom appealed in vain. Behold, there is a more excellent way, and that is, to present Christianity in its wholeness, and as inherently, and, therefore, *philosophically,* true.

The defense of Christianity on the sole ground of its *inspiration,* however justifiable in theology, is not resorted to here, since the doctrine of inspiration itself is undergoing a change of meaning and a modification of expression in Christian circles that forbid its employment as a philosophical instrument in the support of the highest truth. Dogmatic Inspiration, or that inspiration which Theology maintains, has now all it can do to maintain itself, while Philosophical Inspiration, or that inspiration which is inherent in Truth and logically affirms itself, is potent in the strengthening of one's faith in such truth. The integrity of truth is not determined by its so-called inspiration, for truth is truth, inspired or uninspired. Christianity as *truth*, not as inspired but as philosophical truth, is the object of our inquiry. Conceding only a conditional value to the dogmatic doctrine of inspiration, at the same time it must be affirmed that in an unquestionable sense *Christianity is an inspiration*, and by so much as it is an inspiration its truth must be larger than that truth whose source is natural or uninspired. Inspired truth, however, is not *more reliable* than uninspired—that is, philosophical truth. An algebraic equation is as complete and reliable as the doctrine of the Incarnation of Jesus Christ, but it is all-important to show that the doctrine of the incarnation is as authoritative and self-luminous as the algebraic equation. This can not be done on the ground of its alleged inspiration, because that is a matter of faith, but it can be done on the ground of its philosophical inherency and perfection, because such perfection is a matter of demonstration. Inspiration itself is philosophical, quite as philosophical as incarnation, atonement, or any other Biblical truth, and so far as it is considered at all in these pages, it is considered in its philosophical value and aspects. As a theological dogma it has provoked criticism ; as a philosophical doctrine it will stand any test applied to it. Thus Christianity is presented rather as the philosophy than the inspiration of truth.

Plato and Paul are the exponents of the two antagonistic systems of thought, and of the two methods of demonstration. Each stands first in his relation to his system, the one to philosophy, the other to Christianity. From the one we trace the stream of philosophic inquiry through its tortuous course along the ages, developing as it goes into cataracts, lakes, and oceans, to its present bubbling currents in materialism, evolution, and agnosticism, at last losing sight of Plato in the mysterious depths of metaphysical seas, and hearing only the tumultuous roar of many waters. Than Plato no one better represents the philosophic spirit in man. From the other we trace the historic march of truth from the first morning's dawn, through the intervening periods of progress and opposition, noting its administration in all lands and among all peoples, recounting its long and patient struggles with ignorant and embittered foes, and observing its quaint and unfortunate embarrassments with sincere and undisciplined friends, tarrying often to point out its internal deficiencies and external advantages, acknowledging meanwhile its evident defeats and positive successes, and finally prefiguring the joy with which it surveys the Past and the calmness with which it omnisciently contemplates the Future. Paul introduces Christianity in its completeness, but soon disappears in the richer history of Christianity itself.

Holding fast to the conviction that religion will demonstrate its superiority to metaphysics, and on grounds occupied by the latter, and anticipating the final triumph of Christianity in our growing world, both through philosophic and religious methods of activity, this volume is sent forth on an independent errand, and as an aid to the consummation.

J. W. MENDENHALL.

DELAWARE, OHIO, April 15, 1886.

# CONTENTS.

## CHAPTER I.

PAGE.

PLATO, . . . . . . . . . . . . . . . . . . . . . . . . . . . . . . 15

## CHAPTER II.

THE CORNER-STONES OF PHILOSOPHY, . . . . . . . . . . . . 70

## CHAPTER III.

THE PROVINCE OF PHILOSOPHY, . . . . . . . . . . . . . . 108

## CHAPTER IV.

NATURE, OR AN EXEGESIS OF MATTER, . . . . . . . . . . . 128

## CHAPTER V.

THE DANCE OF THE ATOMS, . . . . . . . . . . . . . . . . . 143

## CHAPTER VI.

THE GROUND OF LIFE, . . . . . . . . . . . . . . . . . . . . 155

## CHAPTER VII.

MAN, OR ANTHROPOLOGY, . . . . . . . . . . . . . . . . . . 168

## CHAPTER VIII.

MIND AN INTEGER, . . . . . . . . . . . . . . . . . . . . . . 189

## CHAPTER IX.

THE AREA OF HUMAN KNOWLEDGE, . . . . . . . . . . . . . 210

## CHAPTER X.

PAGE.

THE LAW OF CAUSALITY, OR EFFICIENT CAUSE, . . . . . . 234

## CHAPTER XI.

THE CONTENT OF FORCE, . . . . . . . . . . . . . . . . . . 247

## CHAPTER XII.

THE FIRST CAUSE, . . . . . . . . . . . . . . . . . . . . . . 255

## CHAPTER XIII.

THE FINAL CAUSE, . . . . . . . . . . . . . . . . . . . . . . 286

## CHAPTER XIV.

THE BREAK-DOWN OF PHILOSOPHY, . . . . . . . . . . . . 307

## CHAPTER XV.

THE RELATION OF PHILOSOPHY TO CHRISTIANITY, . . . . 328

## CHAPTER XVI.

THE RELIGIOUS CONCEPT, . . . . . . . . . . . . . . . . . . 343

## CHAPTER XVII.

THE APOSTLE PAUL, . . . . . . . . . . . . . . . . . . . . . 355

## CHAPTER XVIII.

THE PROVINCE OF CHRISTIANITY, . . . . . . . . . . . . . 408

## CHAPTER XIX.

THE TWO CHRISTIANITIES, . . . . . . . . . . . . . . . . . 425

## CHAPTER XX.

PHILOSOPHICAL GERMS IN CHRISTIANITY, . . . . . . . . 438

## CHAPTER XXI.

PAGE.

CHRISTIANITY THE KEY TO THE PHENOMENAL WORLD, . 456

## CHAPTER XXII.

THE THEODICY OF CHRISTIANITY, . . . . . . . . . . . . . 478

## CHAPTER XXIII.

THE IDEAL SOCIETY, OR THE RELATION OF CHRISTIANITY
    TO SOCIETY, . . . . . . . . . . . . . . . . . . . . . . 493

## CHAPTER XXIV.

THE PERFECTION OF MAN THE IDEAL OF CHRISTIANITY, . 519

## CHAPTER XXV.

THE FRUITS OF CHRISTIANITY, . . . . . . . . . . . . . . 535

## CHAPTER XXVI.

THE NEW IN CHRISTIANITY, . . . . . . . . . . . . . . . 557

## CHAPTER XXVII.

THE ESCHATOLOGY OF CHRISTIANITY, . . . . . . . . . . . 577

## CHAPTER XXVIII.

THE DYNAMICS OF CHRISTIANITY, . . . . . . . . . . . . . 619

## CHAPTER XXIX.

THE MAGNETISM OF CHRISTIANITY, . . . . . . . . . . . . 636

## CHAPTER XXX.

THE PSEUDODOX IN CHRISTIANITY, . . . . . . . . . . . . 652

## CHAPTER XXXI.

PAGE.

THE DIAGNOSTIC OF CHRISTIANITY, OR EXPERIENCE THE
  PHILOSOPHIC TEST OF RELIGION, . . . . . . . . . . . . 670

## CHAPTER XXXII.

COMMON GROUNDS OF PHILOSOPHY AND CHRISTIANITY, . 687

## CHAPTER XXXIII.

THE PROSPECTUS OF THE FUTURE OF CHRISTIANITY, . . . 707

## CHAPTER XXXIV.

CHRISTIANITY A PHILOSOPHIC AND RELIGIOUS FINALITY, 725

## CHAPTER XXXV.

PRESENT TASKS OF CHRISTIANITY, . . . . . . . . . . . . . . 741

# PHILOSOPHY AND CHRISTIANITY.

## CHAPTER I.

### PLATO.

MYTHOLOGY ascribes to Plato a human and divine parentage; human, in that Perictione, a lady of culture and relative of Solon, was his mother; divine, in that the god Apollo was his father. The story of his birth is very like that recorded of the birth of One greater than Plato in the first chapter of the Gospel according to Matthew.

Does philosophy begin with an incarnation? Must Plato be regarded as a divine man? Was the greatest philosopher, like the greatest religionist, a divine teacher, manifesting a divine idea to the world? The background of Christianity is incarnation, inspiration; the sole figure is Christ. The background of philosophy—does it glow with inspiration? Does it flash an incarnate figure on our vision? Is the one altogether the product of inspiration, and the other wholly the product of human reason? or does the latter share somewhat the munificent equipment and impelling force of the former? Is philosophy an inert, phlegmatic, uninspired mass of crudities, and are its representatives equally impassive and impenetrable?

Is there no inspiration outside of the Bible? Aristotle asserts that God governs all things on earth in proportion to their sympathy with the heavenly bodies. Inspiration in its final form is the measure of human sympathy with God, or human sympathy with things divine, intelligent, beautiful, good, and true, is the measure of the inspiring force received. By this rule there is more than one kind of inspiration, which, differentiating itself in many forms, is actualized in the strifes, industries, aspirations, and activities of men, and gives tone and direction to human history. The lowest inspiration is physical, exhibited in Jael, Samson, and David, as they overcome men or beasts; in Joshua, Cyrus, and Nehemiah, resisting national foes; in the world's armies, battling for human liberty; and in earth's grim toilers, awakening the secret hope of deliverance and victory. The

(15)

pioneer, the sailor, the mechanic, the victim of circumstance, possessed at times by a strange spirit, suddenly accomplishes that which is not possible in his ordinary sphere, and illustrates endurance, integrity, and the power of performance that puts to shame the routine of existence. Usually the unexpected achievances in human life are ascribed to patriotism, bravery, stoicism, love of fame; rather are they the result of heroic latencies divinely incited to activity.

In like manner there is an intellectual inspiration, of which Wilberforce, Webster, Newton, Franklin, Angelo, Stevenson, and Stanley are good examples. Inventions, discoveries, the products of genius, literature, oratory, art, and music are instances of the results of an intellectual afflatus, not always native to the human mind. Intellectual triumphs we are prone to attribute to native genius; but God is in the world governing its history, marking out its lines of progress, endowing and calling men to loftiest endeavor and highest service. Hence, it is true to say, God is in the genius of the world; he is in music, art, poetry, and literature; he is in every invention, every discovery; he is the presiding Spirit, the informing *Νοῦς* of the universe.

These inspirations, physical and intellectual, are not the highest, because they are not redemptive, and they, therefore, are not religious in their content or purpose. Even wicked men are moved physically and intellectually, that is, to physical deeds of grandeur and intellectual achievements of permanent value, by the divine Spirit; but such inspiration is for temporal ends, and is not religiously redemptive. A spiritual inspiration, begetting reformation, repentance, regeneration, raising up reformers, martyrs, ministers, Christians—this is the highest, this is redemptive. Christianity, so far forth as it is a revelation of truth, is the product of the spiritual inspiration of the writers of the sacred books.

Conceding inspiration to philosophy, the word must be used in a very guarded, or qualified, sense. The inspiration of Socrates, Plato, Descartes, and Locke can only be of an intellectual type, of a kind like that which attaches to art, music, oratory, invention, and discovery. God was in Angelo, Beethoven, Irving, and Shakespeare as much as in Anaxagoras, Parmenides, and Plato. The fruits of an intellectual inspiration are visible in the intellectual realm of life; they can be only approximately or relatively spiritual.

Philosophic truth, it may be said, is in its content similar to religious truth; the philosophic purpose also is a religious purpose; hence philosophy, unlike art, music, poetry, and invention, is related to religion. The inspiration of the one is like that of the inspiration of the other; Plato is on a level with Paul. The relation of philosophic ideas to revealed truths, because similar in contents, may be acknowledged without involving the admission of the spiritual inspiration of both. All truth, scientific, physical, æsthetic, artistic, poetic, is related to revealed truth, is to some extent an illustration, or foreshadowing of it, and has back of it the restraining or stimulating influence of inspiration. Philosophic truth supposedly sustains only a closer relation because it deals specifically with the same problems of religion. Seneca, Confucius, Socrates, and Plato stand out more like theologians than Angelo, Charlemagne, Palissy, and Bacon, because they deal with the truths that had expansion in Moses, Christ, and Paul. Handling the same truths, they appear like similar teachers; but the point of divergence is in the source and method of teaching. Inspiration relates not alone to the nature of truth to be taught, but to the method by which the truth is communicated. In general, the method of philosophy is rationalistic; the method of religion is supernaturalistic. One is the product of the human mind, the other the product of the divine Spirit. Greek philosophy was the rational adumbration of Christianity, reflecting incarnation, atonement, resurrection, eternal judgment, prayer, and the rites of worship. It was a reflection, not a revelation; it was a prototype, not a fulfillment.

Plato can not be enrolled among the prophets or apostles; philosophy is not revelation, as it is not inspiration. Like some distant towering peak, Plato rises from the obscurity of the past, dim by reason of the distance, yet evidently visible by reason of his greatness. He is more than the figure-head of his age, more than a teacher of philosophy. He is the representative of the culture of his times, of the aristocratic sense of the higher classes, of the best philosophical elements possible among a people given to inquiry; he stands for government, for social ideas, for ethical education, for religious teaching. In him whatever is good in his age reaches high-water mark; education, the governmental idea, the philosophic purpose, ascends to a height beyond which, among the Greeks, it never went. In some things even our modern life has not superseded Plato.

The outward history or the biographical facts of Plato may be briefly given. Of leaders in religion or philosophy, the biography is often obscure or the data incomplete. Like Elijah they come, and like him they go, mysterious heralds of Providence, giving little account of themselves to history, save as they report truth, unfurl an idea, or reveal law. Several biographies of Plato, of which Zenocrates's was the best, but which has disappeared, have been written; but the details as given are contradictory, or written evidently in a spirit of unfairness or without reference to the truth. As to his birth, it is agreed that it occurred about the time of the death of Pericles,

Grote fixing it at B. C. 427. Athens was then in its glory as respects art, architecture, literature, and general culture. Pericles had beautified it with the products of art, expending his wealth in its ornamentation; orators, rhetoricians, grammarians, mathematicians, poets, dramatists, and philosophers made the city their home or rendezvous; academies, the sites of which are still known, flourished; the government was aristocratic and tyrannical; the military spirit was intense, and the people were ambitious for all the glory that success in arms could give them. To be born then was a privilege; it brought opportunity; it almost conferred honor. Plato's parents were Athenians. Born on the island of Ægina, he was reared amid Athenian culture, inheriting the polish, improving the advantages, and sharing the literary spirit of the city, returning to it in later life more than he had received in the fruits of a philosophic spirit and the products of vast literary labor. The reports of his genius, of the alighting of bees on his lips, his aptitude to learning, his versatile talents, his delight in athletic sports, his fondness for music, his love of poetry, his preference for political affairs, and finally, his taste for philosophy, are doubtless authentic, showing how broad his intellectual basis, how great his possibilities, how high his aspirations, and indicating the achievements of his future. First named Aristocles, his parents soon substituted Plato, a word signifying "broad," but whether it meant broad-browed, or broad-shouldered, or a broad style, the critics have not settled. If Plato stood for the broad thinker, the broad observer, the broad scholar, the broad man, it will aptly represent the philosopher of whom we are now writing, who was indeed the broadest of men in the qualities of mind, insight, and love of truth.

In moral character he was comparatively blameless, for no blemishes, no vices, are reported against him. This can not be said of the Cynics, Sophists, or Stoics of his time. He was of a melancholy disposition, perhaps the outgrowth of a pensive habit of mind. Lewes charges him with a want of amiability. If he means the coldness of greatness, perhaps he is correct; but if he means that Plato was a misanthrope, he does him injustice. Gifted with an aristocratic sense, accustomed to refinement, disgusted with political affairs, he retired to the academy, where, undisturbed by politics or the multitude, he solaced himself with those investigations of truth which place him above his times and give him rank among the thinkers of all ages. Of his childhood life little is known, save that in its intellectual graspings it was prophetic of the life that grew out of it. He is introduced to the world at the age of twenty years, when, exhibiting an eagerness for knowledge and an investigating spirit, he became the pupil of Socrates, an arrangement that proved advantageous to both master and disciple. Socrates was the conversing philosopher of Athens—a thinker on ethical subjects, roaming about, talking and disputing with individuals as he might meet them; a man who never wrote a book or a line, but whose method of reasoning, and whose conversations embodying his principles, have been transmitted to us by Plato; a man who never addressed a public assembly save when on trial for his life, but whose auditor was the single individual; a man who never traveled, so given was he to reflection rather than observation. Quaint in dress, ugly in face, his nose having been broken when he was nine years old, and going about pretending to know nothing, but inquiring of every body what he knew, how he knew, and testing his answers by the most skillful dialectical analysis, he became a well-known figure in the literary and social circles of Athens. Young men were amused at his appearance and enjoyed his irony, while the elders dreaded or respected him, as he had taught them or overwhelmed them with his satire.

Instinctively, young Plato comprehended the motive of Socrates, and, inquiring for his method of reasoning, soon discerned its adequacy, and began himself to apply it to the great questions which philosophy superinduced. Socrates bequeathed to Plato more than the dialectical spirit; he awakened in him a philosophic conception of the universe which, in its developed form, eclipsed the conceptions of Socrates. Logical, he became philosophical; logical in method, philosophical in subject. Socrates's dream of the swan was fulfilled in Plato. A swan flies from the altar in the academy, alighting on Socrates's breast; then, spreading its wings, it flies toward heaven, enticing by its voice gods and men. Plato appearing in his presence, Socrates pronounced him the swan of the dream.

Thus an unbroken and profitable friendship was the result of the mutual faith of tutor and pupil, the latter true to the former even unto death, and advancing his philosophic teachings by still broader inquiries and deeper answers. Plato and Socrates, says Emerson, were a "double star," certainly a fine putting of their relations. This relationship continued for eight years, when Socrates drank the hemlock, and Plato was left alone, ripening into the independent philosopher, and standing for truth as if it were all his own.

Plato never married. Like Adam Smith, Swedenborg, Macaulay, Washington Irving, and Humboldt, he lived without knowing any thing of the conjugal relation. His appreciation of woman was not remarkable; he advocated the "community" idea with earnestness, supporting it by exclusive philosophical considerations. This makes against him—if not against him, then against his philosophy. He was not wanting in genuine patriotism; he enlisted in the military

service of his country in the time of her danger; in peace he sought
to serve the state by devotion to public interests. He was a patriot
as well as philosopher. Political rather than military affairs he preferred; and, when the Thirty Tyrants came into power, Plato,
through the courtesy of one of them, who was his cousin, obtained a
civil position, which enabled him to study the science of government,
the necessity of reforms, and the relation of laws to civil progress
and individual happiness. This fitted him for a philosophic contemplation of government, which found expression afterward in two
volumes, entitled the *Republic* and the *Laws*. Plato was a tyrant
himself, the result of his surroundings, education, and position.
Thoroughly opposed to democracy, he welcomed the change to
tyranny, advocating severe governmental discipline; he also advocated caste, and secluded himself from the crowd as beneath him.
Naturally, he became obnoxious to the people, sometimes because he
was the friend of Socrates, sometimes because of his aristocracy,
sometimes because of his socialism, sometimes because of his politics.
During his early years he was in and out of Athens, as public feeling
was hostile or friendly to him.

Unlike Socrates, he became a traveler, driven abroad by the hostilities he himself had invoked; but it proved to be providential, as
it broadened him still more, and prepared him, as he was not prepared when Socrates vanished, for the vindication of the philosophic
pursuit. He visited Megara, absorbing mathematics and philosophy;
he saw Italy, and drafted its sunshine into his meditations; he jour-
neyed into Egypt, plucking religious ideas from temples and priests;
it is said he visited Palestine, and extended his travels eastward as
far as Persia, taking knowledge of religion, history, art, science, and
philosophy. Nearly ten years were given to travel. He returned to
Athens at forty years of age with mind richly stored, intellectual impulses quickened, personal hostilities extinct, and with disciples from
many lands ready to receive instruction. Having studied mathematics, poetry, music, grammar, logic, religions, and philosophies;
having been a soldier, a politician, and a civil officer; having been a
traveler, a reformer, a statesman; he settles down, thus equipped
and experienced, into his life-work, founding an academy, and making his name imperishable by the imperishable truths he communicates
to men. For forty years he teaches in this academy, dying, as some
assert, at the advanced age of eighty-one years, with pen in hand
and writing. The academy building was located one mile north of
the city, on a level spot just beyond a ridge which now separates the
modern city from the country. Over the doorway was the inscrip-
tion, "Let none but geometricians enter here." This is the dialectical

spirit in a mathematical form, and the key to Plato's mind. All that remains of the ancient academy are a few marble pillars, which our own eyes looked upon a few years since. A modern house occupies the grounds, but the family within is without the spirit of Plato. Not far away is the famous, well-worn path of the Peripatetics. Here Plato builded better than he knew. In the atmosphere of the academy let us study its founder, his teachings, and the far-reaching effects of what he taught. As an academician must Plato be estimated; all else is preliminary, preparatory.

Plato, the philosopher! Plato, the coefficient of universal thought! Such he is; as such he must be contemplated, namely, as an individual philosopher and the representative of all philosophy. As Emerson says, "he is the arrival of accuracy and intelligence," speaking with that self-command which profound insight inspires. He follows his inner light sufficiently to be original. Little is found in outside philosophies not found in him; he is philosophy, as Christ is Christianity.

At the very threshold of this study a question presents itself for settlement which Plato himself ought to have disposed of, but he did not, leaving to his admirers and the students of his works a perplexing and never-ceasing mystery. The ability, genius, and education of Plato are conceded; that he founded an academy and taught philosophy are accepted as facts; that his literary labors were immense is established by the works attributed to him; but it is not yet determined just what Plato believed and taught respecting the great problems of philosophy. It is not clear that Plato, while he founded a *school* of philosophy, instituted a *system* of philosophy, or that Platonism definitely means any philosophic truth. This implies mysticism in thought, ambiguity in teaching, poetic driftings, imaginative musings, and unsettled opinions, the value of which is uncertain and obscure. Emerson, a competent and an admiring critic, declares that Plato is without system, and that no one can define Platonism. The same may be said of Aristotle, also. Of modern philosophy this certainly is true. It lacks system; it abounds in contradictions; it is a house divided against itself. This, then, would appear to be the beginning of high-toned, reverential philosophy—a systemless system of thought; a miscellany of discussions, without regard to order, consistency, or harmony. Schleiermacher is not alone in affirming a philosophic scheme in Plato, but when he attempts to point it out it is more of the German's scheme than the Athenian's. Grote assails the idea of scheme; the majority of students reject the German conception of a system in Plato.

A kindred difficulty arises with every attempt to classify his writings, which furnish few traces of a chronological order, or an order of thought. Not even Aristophanes was able to arrange the books of Plato in a satisfactory manner. Some critics assume that the *Phædrus* was the earliest written dialogue and the *Laws* the latest, basing the conclusion on internal evidence; but the maturity or immaturity of thought in these dialogues will not assist in determining the historical order of their composition, inasmuch as both exhibit the mature and the immature intellect of the philosopher. One reader will refer the *Laws* to an early period in Plato's life; another sees the signs of superannuation in the book. Many German critics are of the opinion that Plato wrote all of his books before he established the academy, but this is a wild conjecture, for it leaves him nothing to do in the academy but repeat what he had written. At times Plato is thoroughly dialectical in method and subject, as in the *Sophist* and *Statesman*, teaching the art of reasoning or thinking; at another ethical subjects, as in the *Meno*, engross his attention; at another cosmogony and physical themes, as in the *Timæus*, are supreme. Hence, it is natural to divide his philosophy into dialectics, ethics, and physics. But this is not comprehensive enough, as all readers agree. Schleiermacher, insisting upon an inner connection among the dialogues, divides them according to their subject-matter into three classes: 1. *Elementary* Dialogues, embracing the Apology, Crito, Phædrus, Parmenides, Protagoras, Ion, Lysis, Hippias Minor, Laches, Euthyphron, and Charmides; 2. *Progressive* Dialogues, embracing the Cratylus, Theætetus, Menon, Gorgias, Sophistes, Politicus, Euthydemus, Philebus, Phædo, the Symposium, the first Alcibiades, Menexenus, and the Hippias Major; 3. *Constructive* Dialogues, embracing the Timæus, the Republic, the Critias, the Laws, and the thirteen Epistles.

Henry Davis, a modern translator of Plato, arranges the books into three classes, according to their relation to the period the philosopher spent in travel: 1. About thirteen books were written before he traveled; 2. About ten books were written on his return to Athens; 3. The others were written in advanced life.

Thrasyllus simplified the subject by dividing the treatises into two classes: 1. Inquisitory; 2. Expository. Some writers style some of the books dramatic, others narrative, others mixed; but Diogenes Laertius says this is a theatrical rather than a philosophical division. Laertius speaks of his dialogues as logical, ethical, political, "midwife description," tentative, and demonstrative.

From the analysis of Plato's writings, as made by both ancient and modern writers, the difficulty of interpreting them as expressive of a single thought or of but few ideas, and of building out of them a philosophic system, becomes apparent. Had he left a system, complete in outline or in parts, the historians of philosophy had found it long before now. The failure to find the system raises the suspicion that he did not intend to suggest any ; but our conjecture must rest upon something more than our own failure in investigation. Perhaps an explanation of this unfortunate omission of Plato lies along the path we are traveling.

In his seventh Epistle he expresses an aversion to writing as a means of communicating or preserving philosophy, declaring that there never shall be a treatise of Plato; and in the *Phœdrus* he explains at great length his contempt for the written argument, or what we would call a printed book. He says a published argument, like a painting, will be criticised without any power to answer back ; it must be subject to ridicule and injury without the means of defense or explanation. Hence he undoubtedly opposed the publication of his philosophy in the sense of committing it to the world. This has given rise to the opinion which Tennemann adopts, that his real philosophy was *esoteric*, or confined to the academy, and that it is impossible to conjecture the whole of it. If, however, he meant not his philosophy for the public, he did mean it for his disciples, one of whom—Aristotle—makes so many allusions to the printed works which pass for Plato's that it is impossible not to believe that they are the products of his academic teaching. We scarcely believe that Plato's philosophy was *esoteric*, but if it was, he formulated it in his books, which, without doubt, have come down to us. He may have held to speculations which do not appear in the books. Aristotle admits as much ; but they were not fundamental. To the books we must, therefore, look for his philosophy; we shall not, perhaps, find a system of philosophy, but philosophic truth, more or less, accurately expressed, is in them.

The books, as Plato's readers know, are written in the form of dialogues, in which Plato hides himself under the names of the disputants; so that it is not always easy to detect his own opinion, or whether he expresses any at all or not. The impersonal form of discourse which Plato adopts, besides relieving him of personal responsibility, accounts for the difficulty of interpreting him. In this impersonal way Plato is an esoteric philosopher. The chief interlocutor in these dialogues is Socrates, who at times appears to be Plato's master, and at other times it is evident that he is an imaginary person, leaving us in doubt whether Plato is reporting Socrates's opinion or expressing his own. Is Plato Socrates's correspondent or an original author?

If he hides himself in his dialogues, does he hide his teaching? Some there are who assert that Plato is dogmatic, but this is incapable of proof, for the affirmations of Plato are in the form of inferences, sometimes expressed, but often implied. Borrowing the dialogistic style from Socrates, he wrote the thirty-six works attributed to him in this form, save the *Apology*, which is a single discourse. He questions the Eleatic stranger, the Athenian poet, or Alcibiades or Theodorus or Meno; he reasons by interrogation; he is an inquirer after truth; he seeks; he is painfully anxious for knowledge. He assumes the duty of a midwife, ready to deliver the new-born thought of the pregnant mind; he stands ready to nurse the infant into life and form. He enounces little; he does not demonstrate, like Aristotle; it is not demonstration that Plato wants; it is discovery. This may be philosophic, but it is misleading and evasive, showing that the philosopher, feeling his way, is not certain of the ground under his feet. On great problems, therefore, he is often obscure; mysteries are mysteries still; doctrines are unexplained; as in the *Euthyphron*, he leaves holiness undefined, and often he contradicts himself, as his discussion of fortitude in the *Laches* does not harmonize with allusions to it in the *Republic*. Either because of incertitude and ambiguity, or because of direct espousal of error, both Christians and pagans have alternately claimed Plato, and it is confessed that at times it is difficult to assign him his true place.

With obscurities and ambiguities attaching to Plato, Schwegler insists "that the Platonic philosophy is essentially a development;" that viewed in reference to the influence which at different stages controlled in its expression, it might be divided into three periods, viz.: the Socratic, the Heraclitic-Eleatic, and the Pythagorean; or viewed with reference to its substance, it might be divided into the antisophistic-ethic, the dialectic or mediating, and the systematic or constructive periods. The development proposed by Schwegler is open to the objection that lies against all suggested schemes; it is artificial, not natural, exhibiting a mixed and not an orderly or progressive arrangement. The Socratic element in Plato's philosophy belongs to all its periods of development, and the Pythagorean influence was felt even before the establishment of the academy. In truth, Plato had entered upon the philosophical inheritance, appropriating such teachings from the masters as commended themselves to his judgment, and rejecting those inconsistent with his preferences, before his return to Athens from his extensive travels in other lands. His acquisitions from the philosophers were made prior to the endowment of the academy. The itinerant period of Plato's life represents his accumulation of philosophic material; the academy represents his use of the material or his own personal philosophic development. During the forty years of academic teaching, the influence of Socrates, Heraclitus, the Eleatics, and Pythagoras was simultaneously effective, and can not be divided into periods.

Equally unsatisfactory is Schwegler's second classification of the contents of Plato's philosophy. In the beginning the dialectic spirit is manifest in Plato, and he never parts with it. It permeates his ethics, and aids in systematic apprehension of the truth. It occupies no subordinate place; Plato stands as the dialectician, rigidly employing the analytic method in the search for truth. If there is any development in Plato, it is a dialectical development, which, however, is without historical inherence; it can not be traced; it is without beginning; it is without stages; it is without a specific end.

Others have ventured to suggest that Plato's work was critical and not creative; that he had in view the refutation of error, and not the establishment of truth. In such dialogues as the *Sophist* and the *Gorgias* it is apparent that the motive of Plato is the annihilation of sophistical methods, and the extinction of sophistical conclusions, which passed for philosophic truths. In these, however, it must be noted that the conflict in Plato's mind is the conflict of method rather than the conflict of truth and error. The Socratic method is pitched against the Sophistic method; the latter succumbs. The result is the overthrow of method, not the establishment of truth. Without doubt such encounters have led students to estimate Plato as a critical philosopher, a refuter of error; but the basis of the estimate is insufficient, for he was rather a refuter of method. In other dialogues, however, as in the *Phædo*, he appears as the creative philosopher, establishing the truth, or at least pointing to it with the finger of faith. He confutes ignorant opinion; he analyzes scientific notions; he reaches out after the beautiful, as in the *Phædrus*, and declares for science, as in the *Theætetus*. Still, one feels, as he reads him, that Plato is a groper, a seeker, a devout inquirer, but not altogether a revealer. He is a pathfinder, but not a truth-finder. Plato abounds in investigations, thinkings, inquirings, but falls short of positive revelation. He stood on the threshold of truth, as Eusebius observes, but the temple-door did not swing open at his touch. This is the secret of his systemless philosophy. Affirmations, not interrogations; results, not inquiries; truths, not refuted errors, constitute the elements of a system. Results, he cautiously declared; his whole system is an interrogation point.

Not a system-maker, Plato nevertheless was a thinker, an original thinker, heralding thoughts or throwing out signs of truths that were new to his generation, whose value the retreating centuries have not impaired. Borrowing from other philosophers, he went beyond them in the use of their own theories, applying logic with a dexterous hand to the tearing down of the false and the building of the true, as he understood it. In his theologic conceptions of the universe, in his representation of the divine being, in his ethical data, he surpassed his contemporaries, and trenched on a true Biblical revelation. In some particulars he so harmonizes with the Old Testament, as in allusions to the deluge, that his familiarity with it must almost be accepted; and yet he never alludes to Moses or the Jewish cosmogony. No, Plato was not inspired; but these high intellectual reachings indicate original power, original thought, which gives him the right to be heard.

Lewes is emphatic in the belief that Plato's philosophy consists wholly in its *method*, not in its results, not in its relation to truth; that he sacrificed all subjects to method; that method of thinking, or the true process of thought, is the only valuable product of Plato's labors. This is a too confined interpretation, for, rigidly dialectical as is Plato, he had in view more than the establishment of the art of reasoning. If not, he is little more than a rhetorician; but he is a theologian, a psychologist, an ethical teacher, a cosmogonist, a scientist. Surely he sacrificed not all these problems to the art of rhetoric or a style of logic. Method was the instrument, not the end, of investigation. Plato was an investigator, not a mere method-maker.

His method must not be depreciated. Essentially Socratic, he improved it, but it was left to Aristotle to perfect it, showing that Plato gave more attention to the subjects of investigation than to the method of investigation. Socrates initiated a new style of thinking, which led to far-reaching results in his day. He was the first to insist on *definitions*, and then, as Aristotle reports, he introduced *inductive* or analogical reasoning, which gave order to thought. Definition and Induction constitute the Socratic system. Plato finding it inadequate added Analysis or Classification, or " Seeing the One in the Many." Aristotle added Demonstration, or the Syllogism. Definition, Induction, Analysis, and Demonstration constitute a perfect method of thinking or reasoning. Evidently Plato's method, an improvement on Socrates, was behind that of Aristotle; it lacked completeness. A faulty method of reasoning and an unknown system of philosophy we discover in Plato, but this does not compel a withdrawal of admiration for his dialectical attempts, or of faith in the trend of his philosophy.

Lewes also depreciates Plato by asserting that he introduced no new elements into the philosophy of his age, making him a tinker of other men's ideas. Why not call him a compiler, a plagiarist, a historian, any thing but a philosopher? Lewes is an extremist, an iconoclast, an antagonist of philosophy, purposing to undermine the whole by dethroning Plato. Plato did introduce analysis into the philosophical method of reasoning; he did originate the theory of *ideas* in explanation of the creation of the universe; his theory of being was entirely foreign to the conceptions of his day; his psychology, Socratic in spirit, was a development, a reduction to scientific form, of what his master taught; his theology bears the marks of intellectual bravery; and his ethics, bating the self-evident frailties in it, was superior to his age.

These different departments of his philosophy we shall now undertake to examine, without reference to any classification proposed by other writers. The order we here follow grows out of a careful reading of all the works attributed to Plato, the spurious as well as the genuine, and the inferences drawn are based on the verified texts of the various editions and translations of Plato.

Pre-eminently attractive in Plato is what properly may be styled his *theology*. He is not a dogmatic theologian, nor a dogmatist in any sense; but he discusses theological problems, aiding the theologians, and serving his own purpose as well. He is more conservative than radical, except in the application of certain principles to certain ends, as explanatory of fundamental facts and teachings. In this department the dogmatism, if any, is concealed; it is not offensive. Without a thought of becoming a theologian, like Homer he has set forth a theology or opinions relative to the formation of the world, the existence of God, and the character of man, which, organized into an orderly system, would relieve Plato somewhat of the charge of indefiniteness and obscurity. He has something to say on ontology, cosmology, and psychology, which, whether re-said by others or not, is worth hearing. The fundamental truth of philosophy, as of theology, is God. Philosophy searches, religion reveals. Plato posits the divine existence as the essential of the universe, differing from those who posit the divine existence as essential to philosophy, and proving that he was more anxious to find the truth than to establish a method of finding it. Not philosophy, but philosophic truth, Plato sought. Hence no system, hence adumbrations of truth.

As to the substance of his teaching, he is a theologian; as to the method of teaching, he is a philosopher. There are two revelations of God—the one written, the other unwritten; the latter only was open to the searching gaze of Plato. The written revelation is the subject of interpretation; it contains truths, the explanation of which rests with the theologian. Dealing in truths furnished, he is not a discoverer of truth; he is only an interpreter. The unwritten revelation of God is nature, or the physical universe, from whose forms of matter and systems of operating forces flash the suggestions of infinite power and wisdom, the keys to the nature of the absolute God. The theologian of nature is more than an interpreter; he is a discov-

erer of truth hidden in the shell of the universe.  Nature is a product;
the producer must be found.  Thus the task of the theologian merges
into that of the philosopher, and Plato, double-winged, was both theologian and philosopher.  Seems not his task greater than that of
Paul, who only interpreted revealed truth, and was aided in interpretation by inspiration?  Plato was a Columbus seeking a new continent; Paul stood still and the continent came to him, and then
he described it.  Plato was a seeker, Paul a finder.  Influenced, as
we have seen, by the Eleatics and Pythagoreans, there came an hour
in his mental journeyings when, saying farewell to his guides, he
piloted himself into the regions of the unknown, returning with the
evidences of a new discovery.  This was brave, but it was imperative,
the measure of success attending Plato demonstrating not merely his
greatness, but the possibility of the human mind evolving the highest
truth without the aid of inspiration.

The theology of Plato, in its fragmentary form, scattered through
his various works, resembles the theology of the Bible.  The Bible
writers were not system-makers; they were truth-tellers, writing
without order, and with no thought of unity; they were unconscious
of theological harmonies, and never framed a creed.  Plato precipitates
thoughts in the same disorderly, systemless way, trusting to the skill
of others to classify, formulate, and build them into a system.  But
this carelessness of method is not a sign of inspiration; it is a sign
that method is not the chief ambition of Plato.

However, many of his dialogues are devoted to the elucidation of
special subjects, as the *Second Alcibiades* to prayer, the *Charmides* to
temperance, the *Phœdo* to the immortality of the soul, the *Euthyphron*
to holiness, the *Banquet* to love, the *Theœtetus* to science, the *Meno* to
virtue, and the *Parmenides* to idealities.  In the treatment of any
single subject, he is sure to make observations on other subjects quite
as valuable as those that pertain to the subject under discussion;
hence, every dialogue emits more than a single ray of light.

The theism of Plato is not always on the surface, but sometimes
is vague and indefinite, reaching back into or beginning with the
mysterious conception of being as the ground of all that is or appears.
Here is the influence of the Eleatics on Plato.  He distinguished between the being and the non-being, avoiding the mistake of Zeno
by recognizing the reality of non-being, or the phenomenal world.
In the *Sophist* he clearly defines the separation between entity and
non-entity, asserting that entity is the "one", and that existences are
to be regarded as powers.  This hint modern philosophy has appropriated in its definition of being as "activity."  In the *Cratylus* Plato affirms that some things have a "certain firm existence of their own,"

attributing to them the distinguishing mark of power, stability, eternity. Groping forward, but declaring a little more with each step, he enounces the doctrine of "the one" in its fullness, establishing it with consummate dialectical skill in the *Parmenides*, a dialogue surpassing all others in metaphysical subtlety and intrinsic development of a single idea. Plato is not particular as to "the many," but holds to "the one," averring an "essence existing itself by itself," and pronouncing it "infinite." Accidents of time do not belong to it; it does not participate in "the many," but in being; it is being. If being, it always was, it always will be; hence, Plato defines "the one" to be that which "was, is, and will be," language like unto John's in his praise of the Almighty. "If one is not," says Plato summarily, "nothing is." Thus the philosopher, establishing the idea of being as separate from non-being, prepares the way for the final assertion of God as the centralization of being, or the essence of "the one." Being, undefined, vague, infinite, is the foundation-stone upon which rises faith in a personal God. Being is not one thing and God another; God is being, being is God.

In a compromising spirit the philosopher conceded the existence of gods, thus ministering to the polytheistic faith of the people, and sustaining the old religion. He speaks of the gods and their quarrelsome dispositions in the *Euthyphron*, but more especially in the *Laws*, where he eulogizes them, encouraging festivals in their honor and the offering of prayers and sacrifices in the temples. He even attributes to them creative powers, and assigns them a share in the government of the world. Man is the creation of one of these subordinate gods. Two explanations of this mythological corruption of his theism may be given: 1. Such mythology was prevalent in his day; he must recognize it. 2. He may have believed in the gods. The latter supposition we reject, for the philosophers were not, as a class, believers in the accepted religion, and Plato in the *Republic* traces faith in the gods "to tradition" alone. One of the accusations against Socrates was that he denied the gods, and Plato must have shared the opinion of his master, but through fear of popular tumult he spoke reverently of the popular faith, always counseling obedience and holiness.

Out of mythology he quickly arose into the clearer faith of the existence of a personal God, the Creator, Preserver, and Governor of the universe, affirming it repeatedly, sometimes inquiringly, but rarely doubtfully. Monotheism is a Platonic doctrine, asserted dimly in the *Philebus*, where Plato refers to the "really existing," and to the *science of the Eternal*; but openly in the *Republic*, where God's goodness and God's reality are the subjects of thought; clearly in the first *Alcibiades*, where the Deity is spoken of as a guide; discriminatingly

in the *Theætetus*, where God's attributes are proclaimed; personally
in the *Minos*, where Zeus converses with men; and positively in the
*Laws*, where God is declared as "having the beginning, the end, and
middle of all things." In addition to these fragmentary proofs of the
monotheism of Plato, we find a comprehensive theistic conception,
especially in the *Republic*, the *Timæus*, and the *Laws*, forever relieving him of the suspicion of inconsistency and of a wavering faith in
God. In the *Laws* he insists that the Deity is "worthy of blessed
attention," and, resisting the dictum of Protagoras that "man is the
measure of all things," he enounces that the Deity is the measure of
all things, a sublime doctrine, elevating and true. To measure the
universe from the divine standpoint, to measure man from God, not
God from man, is a very high conception, first promulgated by Plato.
In the *Republic* God is represented as good, the author of good, and
not the author of evil; his immutability is also fairly taught; and as
in the *Timæus*, here also he declares retribution for the wicked and
reward for the virtuous, both administered by the justice-loving God.
Between appearance and reality he draws a definite distinction, regarding the phenomenal world as an appearance and God as the great
reality. In the *Cratylus* he avows that Zeus is rightly named, since
he is the *cause of the living*.

Judged by themselves, these Platonic or monotheistic representations of God, incomplete as they are, but unaccompanied with tradition or superstition, are more satisfactory than the uninspired theologies
of the East, and justify the theistic hypothesis from the rationalistic
base. Incomplete, they show the necessity of revelation; they prepare the way for revelation; they help to comprehend revelation.
St. Augustine said, "Plato made me know the true God." Plato
declared God; Christ revealed him. Plato assures us that God exists;
Christ showeth us the Father. Plato believes; Christ knows. Philosophy is faith; Christianity is truth.

Closely associated with the monotheistic conception of God is
Plato's cosmological account of the universe, which, excepting the
Mosaic revelation of world-building, is superior to any thing ever
framed by theology or philosophy. His theology and cosmogony are
inseparable, as they involve each other; an understanding of one
requires an understanding of the other. Plato, in the *Timæus*, says:
"Let us declare on what account the framing Artificer settled
the formation of this universe." He also says: "Let us consider
respecting it whether it always existed, having no beginning, or
was generated, beginning from some certain commencement. It is
generated: for this universe is palpable and has a body." Here is
the recognition of a difference between the maker and the thing

made, a discrimination between subject and object, or mind and matter; hence Plato is not a pantheist, or an Eleatic. Spinoza did not borrow his doctrine of one substance from Plato. There are two substances, which a wise philosophy will recognize. Plato's starting-point is the difference between, and not the identity of, being and non-being. This starting-point, fundamental to a correct theological or philosophical representation, both of God and the universe, Plato consistently maintains in all his works, as if, whether in doubt respecting other things, he entertained no doubt respecting this truth. In the *Parmenides* he draws the line between the two substances when he affirms, "all is said when 'the one' and 'the others' are said." "The one," and "the others"—between them there is nothing in common. In like manner the Eleatic guest in the *Sophist* reports adversely the opinion of the multitude that "nature generates from some *self-acting* fortuitous cause, and without a generating intellect," signifying the impossibility of a self-producing universe; and in the *Laws* he condemns materialism as a "stupid opinion." Plato characterizes creation in the *Banquet* as "a thing of extensive meaning," but the meaning is not fully interpreted in this dialogue; we find it elsewhere, as in the *Philebus*, where he discusses the presence of mind in nature, "arranging things and governing throughout," and in the *Theœtetus*, where he insists that no one must be allowed to say "that any thing exists" or "is produced of itself." Here, as elsewhere, the doctrine of causation, or a created universe, he accepts and maintains as a first principle, without which a true cosmogony is impossible. In the *Philebus* he defines the "limitless," and "the limit," representing God and the universe by these singularly expressive words, and insisting that the "limit" is the product of the "limitless."

Plato's idea of the universe was a growth, not a suddenly developed conception, as he himself tells in the *Phœdo*. It seems that, attracted by the theory of Anaxagoras, which attributed the cause of things to intelligence, he became dissatisfied with it, owing to its superficial application of intelligence in the creation of worlds, and its explanation or "final cause" of things, and he rejected it; or, rather, advanced beyond it. Real, self-operating cause, Plato sought; and this, he affirmed, the senses could not grasp or apprehend; only the soul may know the "limitless," the "producing," the "regulating" cause. Likewise in the *Laws* he insists on *searching* for the cause, as not at all impious but in the direction of intelligence; and in his sixth *Epistle* he teaches that the "cause" may be "clearly known." Most emphatically he shows in the *Hippias Major* that "the produced is one thing, and the producer is another;" while in the *Phædrus* he teaches that "every thing that is created must necessarily be created from a beginning," but the beginning force or creator is "uncreate;" that is, the initial moving force, or mover, is without beginning, or eternal.

Summarizing these teachings from Plato, it is easy to see that he accepts the *difference between being and non-being; that he holds to the idea of causality, as afterward expanded by Aristotle into efficient and final causes, as the underlying doctrine of cosmology, and implying radical discriminations between God and the universe; that he embraces the thought that there was a time when the universe was not, and it, therefore, had a beginning; that he discourages the theory of a self-originating universe; and that he declares that the originating mind or cause may be known.*

This is an upheaval of ideas, and goes far toward the vindication of philosophic inquiry; whatever is charged against modern philosophy, Plato can not be charged in his cosmological starting-point with puerility, intellectual weakness, or materialistic tendency.

Gladly granting the above, Plato seems uncertain at a very vital point in the unwritten history of creation, which no one since his time has adequately settled. The co-eternity of matter is foreshadowed in the discussions in the *Theætetus*, and really declared in the *Timæus;* but the co-eternity of the universe he rejects. Matter he regards in its original condition as something rude, unformed, lawless, roaming aimlessly in space when it is arrested and organized into the universe. Given the four elements, earth, air, fire, and water, God built the worlds, according to the *Timæus,* using fire and earth at first, but adding air and water afterward; fire made it visible, earth gave it solidity, air and water "are indispensable to keep the solid bodies in due proportion to one another," and secure unity. He is obscure, however, as to the origin of the elements, really does not account for them. Prior to the formation of the universe, "three distinct things existed, *being, place,* and *generation,*" or God, space, and the generating process, or the idea of world-building. The actual generation of the universe was the product of the mutual motion of the elements, a mechanical sifting and combination under divine direction—a sentiment that suggests the dance of the atoms, or the modern theory of world-building. Singularly, too, these elements were convertible, air into fire, and earth into water, a view suggesting the modern doctrine of the *conservation of forces.* Reading this from Plato, we can indorse Emerson's eulogy: "Great havoc makes he among our originalities." His mathematical conception of the universe; his idea that the proportion of original elements remained ever the same; his thought that ideas and numbers governed in world-building, have not been eclipsed by any modern discovery or teaching. In cosmology Plato stands at the head.

We characterize, however, the obscurity or failure to account for the elements, and for original matter, as a weakness. What original matter was, or how much there was, Plato does not intimate; but, avowing this doctrine, he furnishes support to the atomists and materialists of our day, who, going farther than he would allow, assert the all-sufficient potency of matter for its own organization and development. If original matter were uncreated, the Creator turns out to be an organizer merely; but this is fatal both to theology and a divine cosmogony, since original matter may have had the inherent tendency to organization, which would displace the reign of a creative intellect in the universe. Countenance is given to the doctrine of organization, as a substitute for creation, in the *Statesman*, where the Deity is represented as changing "the heavens unto the present figure," endowing the heavenly bodies with circular motion; in the *Laws*, where he speaks of a "well-arranged universe;" and in the *Phœdo*, where the philosopher indulges in a lengthy description of the earth and its assignment in the heavens. God an organizer! The universe an organization! This is Platonism, yet not essentially inconsistent even with the doctrine of causation, or the doctrine of one substance, for Plato conceded no power, no life, no originating principle, in unformed matter.

However, he made almost a redeeming use of the doctrine of the co-eternity of matter in that he affirmed that in it was embedded the antagonistic principle of evil, now operating in the universe. In the *Banquet* he explains the presence of the two principles, the rational and the irrational, which, without doubt, he borrowed from the poets and Empedocles, and interprets organization as a triumph over the antagonistic principle. Organization was a reduction of antagonism to order, form, beauty, energy; it was a resurrection from death to life, it was the impartation of "good" to matter, which appears quite fully in the *Cratylus*.

Somewhat contradictory of the doctrine of the co-eternity of matter is the Heraclitic doctrine of the "becoming," or the flux of nature, which Plato accepted, as may be seen in the discussions in the *Cratylus*, where the universe is spoken of as "marching," and as having in it the *spirit of going*, which is the organ of nature's motions. He fully believed in the reality of the phenomenal world, confuting the doctrine of Protagoras in the *Theœtetus*, that "nothing ever is but always becoming." This is the doctrine of Heraclitus, but Plato went not so far. Persistently opposed to the idea of *permanency* in nature, he nevertheless held to its *reality*, which saved him from Eleaticism; and, distinguishing between the two realities, the finite and the infinite, he saved himself from pantheism. The effect of motion on nature he discusses as "removal" and "change," the former signifying a going from one place to another, and the latter a transformation of quality, as sweet into bitter; the former is the substitute of *place*, the latter the substitute of *quality*. But he classifies motion producing these effects as original and subsidiary; original motion is self-motion, the highest, belonging to soul, to God; subsidiary motion is derived motion, or dependent power. In the *Laws* he enumerates ten kinds of motions, as follows: "1. Revolution around a center; 2. Locomotion from place to place; 3. Condensation; 4. Rarefaction; 5. Increase; 6. Decrease; 7. Generation; 8. Destruction; 9. Change produced in another by another; 10. Change produced by a thing itself, both in itself and in another." The tenth motion is the motion of the soul; it is the motion of God, the power manifest in the universe. Through self-existent motion the universe was begotten; the motion of God was communicated to unformed and motionless matter, which, as it yielded to the communicating impulse, emerged into systems of worlds, such as now occupy the heavens; and they are as real as he is real. Call it "becoming;" it is the reality of becoming.

The core of Plato's cosmogonal conception, however, has not been revealed; it remains for consideration. In his analytic observations of nature Plato always proceeded from the inner to the outer; from the subjective to the objective; from himself to God; from himself to the universe. Mind, thought, idea, constituted the chief corner-stone in every superstructure. In some way thought entered into the construction of the universe; God first thought the universe before he made it. It existed in God in the intellectual sense before it stood forth as a completed physical fact. The idea of the world preceded its execution. God is a being of ideas; the divine mind is pregnant with ideas; *it is an idea*. Divine ideas are contingent, relative, or unchangeable and necessary. Ideas of truth, goodness, beauty are eternal, governing divine movements in their loftiest manifestations. According to preconceived, necessary ideas, which served as patterns or rules, God made all things, impregnating unformed matter with them, and so giving shape and comeliness to the universe. Nature is the receptacle of the divine ideas; nature is the concreted idea; nature is an idea, the idea of God. The universe is a congregation of ideas in visible forms; it is little else than God going out of himself and crystallizing in the universe.

An admirable conception of the universe is this, but marked by weaknesses which show the marvelous struggles of the great thinker in his search for the truth. One of the objections to this theory of ideas is its ambiguity, for it is not certain whether Plato held that these ideas were abstract merely, or that they had a separate, individual existence. Were they real existences which the divine mind appropriated, and according to which he formed the universe, or were they the products of the divine intelligence, native to it as the idea of causation is native to the human mind? Cousin, in defending Plato, insists that he did not assume for ideas an independent existence; but Aristotle assailed him on the ground that he did maintain the independent vitality of the idea, and annihilated the Platonic system by clearly showing that while the idea had a *subjective*, it had not an *objective*, existence. Aristotle ridicules them as " immortalized things of sense;" but in so doing he leaves room for the play of " ideas " in the universe. But did even Aristotle assail the Platonic idea by the strongest argument? The argument was effective, but it was not comprehensive of the idea itself. Aristotle's idea is correct, but he admits the existence of Plato's idea by making it subjective instead of objective. Plato located it without, giving it independence; Aristotle located it within, making it dependent on the originating mind. In this way only did Aristotle annihilate the Platonic *system* of ideas; he did not annihilate the ideas.

The value of the ideas is a separate question; the system goes, the ideas remain. But the ideas are not vital, sovereign existences; they remain as abstract patterns and guides. An abstract idea has no being, no life, no form. Malebranche says ideas are little beings not to be despised, but this can not be allowed; otherwise the Platonic system must be accepted. An idea is as lifeless or beingless as a grain of sand. It derives its existence only from the being that originates it. Aristotle did not assail the idea itself; but it is assailable on the ground that possibly Plato, in advocating its existence, also intended to signify that it had being. He leaves us in doubt as to the origin of the ideas, whether they are eternal or derivative; whether they governed God as vitally eternalizing forces or God governed them. Plato likewise involves the subject in mystery by the manner in which he presents it. In creation he conceives that the idea " participated " in matter, as a vital force, as the inspiration of matter, instead of the model of material forms. The fact is, Plato's ideas are of three kinds: (*a*) subjective, or the divine idea in the mind of God; (*b*) objective, or independent ideas, either as abstract or as having being; (*c*) material, *i. e.*, the participating idea. The last introduces a troublesome element in the classification, for it is difficult to separate the notion of a participating idea from a pantheistic conception of the universe, which Plato himself repudiates.

The Platonic idea has another signification which involves it in trouble. The philosopher, drawing a distinction between the universal and the particular, conceived that the universal is general, invisible, abstract, and the particular is individual, visible, and concrete, and that the particular is modeled after the universal. Pointing to a table, he speaks of it as the " particular," back of which is the universal, table or general idea of tables. So horse is particular, but back of horses there is a universal horse. This distinction is a philosophical hallucination, for there is no such thing as a universal table, or a universal tree, or a universal horse. Such universals do not exist; they do not exist as ideas even. The idea of a table can not be universal in any rational sense. It is particular if it exist both in the divine mind and in its actual form. This is the weakness of rationalism, that it abstracts the particular reason of the human mind, converting it into an independent reality, segregated from all mind, human and divine, and making it the universal reason. There is no such reason. This is the weakness of Schopenhauer's idealistic notion of God, that he .is impersonal, universal will. There is no such will. Will, reason, thought, idea can not be impersonal, universal, abstract; they all imply personality or mind. Plato's idea points to mind; Plato himself delivered it from all relation, and endowed it with independence, which is absurdity.

These are some of the weaknesses of the Platonic system of ideas, but the great Platonic idea that God built the universe according to a preconceived pattern is not only beautiful, but also imperishable; theology can not improve it, philosophy should be content with it. This is Platonic idealism.

From his cosmogony we pass to the consideration of Plato's *psychology*, a department of study abounding in discoveries, teachings, and suppositions as wonderful and instructive as any to be found in the philosopher's writings. At the same time he equally abounds in errors, fragments of thought, and great misconceptions in the treatment of some of the psychological problems which he investigated and discussed. His psychology, as a whole, marks the rising and falling of intellectual apprehension, the fluctuation of the dialectical force of Plato.

Beginning with the question, What is man? Plato answers it with extreme caution, considering his physical origin first, and his spiritual character and intellectual framework afterward. Usually free from the mythological spirit, he rehearses the tales of the ancients respecting an early race of gods and heroes on the earth, from which descended the human race to which we belong. The early race, according to the *Statesman*, was " earth-born, and not begotten from each other;" the people lived a spontaneous life, guarded by the

Deity, nature offering to them her fruits without toil, and a spirit of sedition was absent from them. It was a golden period, not destined to continue, for revolution is the order of progress on the earth. The generations died; nature itself became cold and unproductive, and an uninhabited planet was the result. In due time the Deity is moved to re-people the abandoned world, which is easily done by resurrections, transmigrations, or creations; and after many revolutions of this kind, man as we know him appeared, the lord of creation. These old tales Plato abandons in the *Banquet* for another, which recites that at one time there were three kinds of human beings on the earth—man, woman, and a man-woman, a being partaking of the character of both. At length Jupiter devised a plan for the formation of a race which should consist of two sexes, the third disappearing. The surgical process by which this was accomplished Plato relates in its disgusting details, showing at once the need of a true account of man's creation. In the *Philebus* reference is made to the superiority of the ancestors of the present race, a fiction in which the Greek mind was wont to indulge.

Respecting the present man, Plato, in the *Protagoras*, recalls the fable of his creation by the gods, who fashioned the race within the earth, "composing them of earth and fire," and "commanded Prometheus and Epimetheus to adorn them, and to distribute to each such faculties as were proper for them;" Prometheus, stealing "the artificial wisdom of Vulcan and Minerva," confers it upon the mortal race, and man is thus equipped for an earth-life.

Fables in Plato: is it any wonder that, as in the *Phædrus*, he should inquire whether man is a beast, "with more folds and more furious than Typhon," or "a more mild and simple animal, naturally partaking of a certain divine and modest condition?" An expounder of the degeneracy of the races, a believer in the greatness of ancestors, he yet affirms a god-like origin of the present man. But gods, not God, created him.

As to the physical body of man, Plato writes elaborately, showing, however, little knowledge of its construction, or the uses of its prominent organs. He is not much of a physiologist. He discourses on pathology, describes fevers, and their antidote, and even reveals the *fact* of the circulation of the blood; but, after reading the *Timæus*, the physician will prefer modern medical science to its suggestions. Of the liver Plato knows nothing more than that it is the seat of the *mortal* part of the soul! The bile is a "vicious secretion." Of the difference between veins and arteries, of the relation of the lungs and viscera, he has no true conception, and of the formation of bones and flesh he is only approximately satisfactory.

Of the soul, which is "glued" to the body, he is specific; specific as to its origin, its character, its possibilities, its immortality, its destiny; he is a theologian, a psychologist, a great teacher. The duty of self-knowledge he emphasizes and explains in the *Charmides*, and in other dialogues he insists on the study of the soul as the only condition of progress from depravity to purity, and as a preparation for the highest immortality.

The first or initial doctrine in Plato's psychology is the *pre-existence* of the soul, supported and enforced by reasonings the most plausible, and by arguments singularly effective and difficult to overthrow in the absence of Scripture truth, which some, however, have affirmed does not absolutely determine the question of the origin of souls. Adam's soul was the breath of God which pre-existed, but it pre-existed as breath, not as a soul. The breathing into Adam's nostrils was the creation of the soul; and if a creation, its pre-existence is impeached. Modern theology rejects the doctrine of pre-existence, and wisely.

To Plato's arguments, however. In the *Phædo* the philosopher demonstrates that knowledge is reminiscence; an act of memory is the recalling of knowledge in a previous state; the memory is a waxen tablet, containing eternal impressions; what modern psychology styles "innate ideas" is proof of previous knowledge; the soul knows some things on its own account, and by itself, which is evidence of its pre-existent state. These arguments are expanded in the *Theætetus*, and repeated in the *Phædrus* and the *Meno;* in the former, rejecting the theory of sense-knowledge, he interprets soul-knowledge as reminiscence, and reminiscence is the sign of pre-existence; in the latter he insists on the purity of soul-knowledge, and a like interpretation is irresistible. He even goes further, and describes the process of soul-knowledge, or the acquisition of beauty and truth, as the swelling of the wings of the soul; "the whole boils and throbs violently" in the eagerness to recall "the most blessed of all mysteries," a knowledge of the truth it lost by union with the body.

The error of this psychology is the confounding of reminiscence and the intuitional facts of consciousness, which, instead of supporting the doctrine of pre-existence, supports the doctrine of immortality, pointing forward instead of backward. Aristotle opposed the doctrine of reminiscence. The soul, Plato divides, in the *Republic*, into three parts; viz., the rational, the concupiscent, and the irascible. The rational or reasoning part, which is immortal, he locates in the head; the concupiscent or affectional part, and the irascible or passionate part, both of which are mortal, he locates in the heart and liver. Aristotle located the mortal part in the heart only. Repugnant as is this division to our Christian sense, and self-contradictory in its contents as it is, for it is subversive of the idea of the unity of the soul, Plato nevertheless holds to the doctrine of immortality for the intellectual part of the soul. The intellect is immortal; the intellect, therefore, alone pre-existed, if the doctrine of pre-existence be true. The affectional and passionate elements of the soul must be the products of the bodily organization, or, at the least, the results of the intellectual and physical union, either of which being true, the modern theory of life as the product of organization has some justification. It has a foothold in Plato. The soul is either immortal or mortal, not both; if immortal, then it is not the product of the bodily organization; if mortal, it may be the result of organized matter, as is the eye.

More of the immortality of the soul a little later; just now let us listen to Plato concerning its nature. " What it is"—see the *Phœdrus*—"would in every way require a divine and lengthened exposition to tell, but what it is like, a human and a shorter one." From this he proceeds to liken it "to the combined power of a pair of winged steeds and a charioteer," describing its activities by the conduct of the steeds, and its government by the wisdom of the charioteer. Sometimes the steeds are of noble extraction—then the soul is virtuous, good; sometimes they are of the "opposite extraction," and drag the soul down to the earth. In this metaphorical way Plato represents the moral character of the soul, confessing that it has suffered loss by union with the body, which loads it with corruptions, and clips its wings so that it falls to the ground. In the *Laws* he affirms that the soul is "most divine;" that it is a leader in the heavens; that it has received some of the properties of the gods; that it is "altogether superior to the body;" and that it is the "oldest" of all things, and "rules over all bodies." Magnificent conjectures, equal to revelations, are these.

Conceding greatness to the soul, and affirming its godlike character, Plato preaches depravity as emphatically as John Calvin or Paul. In the *Cratylus* the body is spoken of as the sepulcher of the soul, and the "mark" of the soul. The soul makes its mark with the body. It is in the *Republic*, however, that he dilates upon the "four depravities," dividing the soul into mortal and immortal, and assigning to the mortal part the lusts, affections, appetites, and angers of human nature. Its degradation is affirmed as the result of the union of body and intellect. Plato declares his conviction that very many men are "profoundly wicked," and in representing ours as an iron race, he means that it is a fallen race; fallen from the golden period; fallen from purity; fallen from knowledge. In the *Laws* he affirms that, " of all evils, the greatest is implanted in the souls of a major part of mankind," and pitifully exclaims that, while each one is anxious for a pardon, no one devises a plan for avoiding evil. The soul of a slave, he asserts, is unhealthy, and the soul of a woman is more vicious than that of a man. Speaking of the pains of the soul, he enumerates in the *Philebus* "anger, fear, desire, lamentation, love, emulation, envy, and all other such passions;" and argues in the *Meno* that virtue must be communicated, if at all, by a certain "divine fate," or the favor of the deity.

Depravity implies something more than positive impulses to evil; it implies what is more serious, what Plato is constantly teaching and in manifold ways striving to impress upon his disciples, and that is, that the soul is ignorant of itself. Ignorance is the greatest depravity.

Of this ignorance he speaks in the *Laws* thus: "Almost all men appear to have been nearly ignorant of what the soul happens to be, and what power it possesses with respect to other things belonging to it, and its generation besides—how that it is amongst the first of substances and before all, and that more than any thing else it rules over the change and altered arrangement of bodies." Elsewhere he repeats the sentiment when he says that, whether man is a "plaything of the gods" or the result of a "serious act," we can not tell.

In these statements concerning the soul, especially the references to depravity, we recognize familiar truth; not the truth in a Scriptural form, but the truth to which all men bear witness. Plato wrote from observation, experience, history, reflection—sources of knowledge always to be respected. Rejecting the mythology woven with the study of the origin of the soul, it must be allowed that he has represented its character as a whole in a masterful manner; and, rejecting his three-fold classification of soul, it is granted that it almost accurately represents the manifestations of soul life. He was ever on the border of truth; in these instances he well-nigh expressed experimental facts.

Remembering that, according to Plato, the intellect alone is immortal, it will be profitable to note his explanations of intellect, or the mental processes, and the limits he assigns to intellectual inquiry; for he considers all these questions, furnishing in his conclusions many psychological hints which modern philosophy might appropriate to its advantage. The ancients compared intellect to water, because it is "sober;" but Plato in the *Philebus* observes that, "mind is either the same thing as truth, or of all things the most like to it." No material thing resembles or suggests the nature of mind. It is *truth*, or, as in the *Cratylus*, it is *power*, unmixed power, which is a better definition than the other, in that it is not so abstract, nor so indefinable. Mind is *power*, or as again in the *Philebus*, it "is a relation to cause, and is nearly of that genus;" that is, mind is cause or *causal power*, an exact definition, a true conception of its operations; mind an *unmixed, independent, originating, truth-inspiring*, CAUSAL POWER.

This is Plato's starting-point, from which he advances to the study of the sources of knowledge, or how it is obtained; and here he is explicit, counteracting the empiricism of his day by defending the mind against all attacks, by exhibiting its power to know some things on its own account, by examining the theory of sensuous knowledge, and by insisting on the superior value of moral and philosophical truth. Whence is knowledge? From within, or from without, or from both within and without? There is room here for extremes— the extreme of empiricism, the extreme of subjective idealism, or Eleaticism. In its answers philosophy has vibrated to the one or the other, whereas a true psychology will recognize the double source of knowledge, a mixed or *empirico-idealistic* source of sensations appropriated by and intermingled with the facts of consciousness, thus giving employment in the acquisition of knowledge to both senses and intellect. Plato avoided the extreme of empiricism; he did not entirely avoid the extreme of idealism. He was an idealist; he was a rationalist; his psychology was a reaction from the Sophists, who insisted that man could not know any thing, and from the floating sensualism of the materialists. He defined the mind, explained and vindicated its processes, justified its deductions, and announced its empire to be the universe of being. He enthroned mind, and dethroned the senses, making them subordinate and tributary to intellect.

He relates in the *Phædrus* the temple tale that " the first prophetic words issued from an oak," and remarks that men in the ancient days, in their simplicity, listened to an oak and a stone, "if only they spoke the truth;" but, evidently, this is an ironical swording of empiricism. Knowledge is not in the oak or stone. In the same dialogue Plato also considers the fable that traces the sciences to the revelations of the gods, but this is unsatisfactory. If knowledge springs neither from nature nor the gods, what is its source? Let it be conceded that the senses are avenues of communication between the outer world of matter and the inner world of mind; what of sense-knowledge? What is its character? What its value? In the *Philebus* Plato represents the sciences as rushing into the mind through the senses, and in the *Theætetus*, that they possess it, or the science-possessed mind is like an "aviary of birds." But the crowding of the mind with the sciences is not true knowledge; it is not ample knowledge; it is not satisfying knowledge. All such knowledge Plato underrated and in a sense rejected, compelled so to do by the lofty view he entertained of mind.   The mind is not sense-bound; it is not dependent on the senses.   Sight and hearing, he affirms in the *Phædo*, do not convey truth to men, and "if these bodily senses are neither accurate nor clear, much less can the others be so, for they are all inferior to these."   Again, he writes that the soul, "when it employs the body to examine any thing, is drawn by the body to things that never continue the same, and wanders, and is confused, and reels as if intoxicated through coming into contact with things of this kind."   In the *Theætetus* he defines the senses as instruments of the mind, but imperfect; and again, in the *Phædo*, characterizes them as "full of deception," and cautions against a great reliance upon them.   Gorgias having taught, in vindication of sense-knowledge, that the qualities of things might be perceived by the senses, Plato annihilates the position in the *Meno*, and in the *Theætetus* he shows that sight and science are by no means the same.

Without referring further, it is clear that Plato uprooted empiricism, and prepared the way for a very radical but rational psychology. His primary question in the *Theætetus* is, *what is it to know?*   Is it to "have" science?   This he repudiates, as also many other things which the parties in the dialogue submit as answers.   Unfortunately, the dialogue closes without a satisfactory settlement of the question; but fortunately, in the *Cratylus*, he defines thought as the "looking-into and agitating a begetting," or a bringing forth of ideas and truths, and that the "soul marches along with things;" and here he defines man as "contemplating what he sees."   In the *Philebus* the soul's act in the acquisition of knowledge is represented as the writing of a speech; the soul produces speeches within itself.   From these fragments we learn that Plato's idea of man is that he is a contemplator, a reflector, a thinker; a begetter of thoughts; an inquirer, a marcher; a speech-maker.   Knowledge is not science, but thought. Knowledge is acquired, not through the senses, but by the mind.

Easily and consistently Plato passes from the nature of knowledge to the power of mind itself, asserting, as in the *Theætetus*, that the soul in thinking discourses with itself; that it beholds things by itself; and, as in the *Phædrus*, that it is nourished by and thrives upon the truth.   Truth, not nature, is the food of the soul.   The soul can shut itself up with truth, or be content with its own facts, not regarding the outer world at all.   He asserts in the *Phædo* that if one should "approach a subject by means of the mental faculties, neither employing the sight in conjunction with the reflective faculty, nor introducing any other sense together with reasoning," but, "using pure reflection by itself" in the search of pure essence, he "will arrive, if any one can, at the knowledge of that which is."   Expanding this proposition, he concludes that " if we are ever to know any thing purely, we must be separated from the body, and contemplate the things themselves by the mere soul." Surely this is a revelation of soul-power which empirical psychology has not understood, and against which it has virtually arrayed itself by the emphasis with which it defends the theory of sensuous knowledge. According to Plato, the bodily senses are hindrances to pure knowledge; according to the empiricists, knowledge is impossible without their aid—they are the only sources or avenues of knowledge. Between the two, the difference is that between the highest idealism and the grossest materialism; as between the Platonic conception of mind, and the associationalist's conception, one must accept the former, since it dignifies the soul, gives it independence, and foreshadows its immortality.

Announcing the independent, truth-acquiring propensity of the soul, Plato foresees certain limits to human knowledge, arising out of the combination of soul and body, which suffocates aspiration and blockades advance. Self-stimulating as the mind is, it gropes amid outward things, seeing and knowing them at first only superficially, and grows slowly into correct apprehension of phenomena. He illustrates in the *Theætetus* the gradual process of mind-opening by the fact that one sees letters without knowing their meaning, and hears the language of a barbarian without understanding it; he sees and hears without knowing; sense-perception, sense-knowledge, must be followed by mind-perception and mind-knowledge. As if relating a dream, Plato then teaches that the first elements can not be explained by reason; that an element can not be defined; but things compounded of them may be explained and understood. He illustrates by the following example : the word *Socrates* is composed of syllables, and the syllables of elements, or sounds ; *so*, a syllable, is composed of *s* and *o* ; but *s* is a consonant, a sound, and can not be defined. Compounds, therefore, we may understand ; *elements are indefinable*. Applying this to nature, or the universe, it is clear that it may be understood only in its component relations ; as a product of elemental principles, forces, or facts, it may be analyzed; but the original elements, named, pointed out, discovered, yet elude significant interpretation. In the *Statesman* it is shown that the soul, suffering thus respecting the elements, fluctuates sometimes respecting all things, even the " comminglings," or the combinations of the elements, and that it arrives only at a small portion of truth. Catching up the Heraclitic idea of the " becoming," he applies it in the *Cratylus* to our knowledge of beauty, saying it is always " secretly going away," that even " while we are speaking about it, it becomes immediately something else; " so that it can not be known by any one. This is a leaning toward the Eleatic principle of the " one," which, however, Plato guarded against by asserting the reality of the " manifold," a knowledge of which is limited to compounds.

Confessing the limitations of knowledge, how just the rebuke he administers in the *Euthydemus* to Dionysiodorus, who held that if one knew any thing he knew all things! Man is not all-ignorant, nor all-knowing; he knows some things; the soul knows truth when it sees it; it knows the outer world; but it knows not completely in this present state.

The subject of limitation is renewed in the *Seventh Epistle*, in the discussion of the steps to progressive knowledge, Plato stating the first requisite to be the *name* of a thing; second, its definition; third, its resemblance; fourth, its science; but, proceeding in this order in the analysis of a truth, or a thing, the philosopher adds that it is of uncertain value. For there is no *fixed* name for any thing, as a round thing might be called straight; there is nothing in a name as men use names; and " the same assertion is true of a definition." Human knowledge is a speculation.

From this extreme concession or morbid surrender, Plato rebounds both in the *Philebus* and the *Banquet*, carrying us back to the heights of soul-knowledge, to knowledge of the abstract, of being, of essence, and showing that his compromises of the powers of mind were incidental only. In the *Philebus* he declares the substance of good to consist of beauty, symmetry, and truth, the " bounds of the intelligible," a knowledge of which it is in the power of mind to obtain. It must hunt for them; it may find them. In a most elegant manner he speaks in the *Banquet* of the process of knowledge as an " ascending," a march by one's self, going " from the beauty of bodies (to the beauty of soul, and from the beauty of soul) to that of pursuits; from the beauty of pursuits to that of doctrines; until he arrives at length from the beauty of doctrines (generally) to that single one relating to nothing else than beauty in the abstract (and he knows at last what is the beautiful itself)." The steps, please observe: body, soul, pursuit, doctrine, the *abstract*. This is an intellectual ascension, which modern psychology would do well to embrace.

Nor is this all. Plato defines *logos* in the *Theœtetus* to be the *science of the difference;* that is, it implies the elimination from a thing of all qualities common to other things, and the discovery of that particular quality, element, function, or prerogative which, remaining, separates it from all other things, and distinguishes it as an independent and individual object. This process of elimination, separation, winnowing, or whatever it may be called, is the province of dialectics, in which Plato was a master, and which he demonstrated to be possible in the study of truth.

This is the summit of Plato's psychology—a knowledge of the abstract, a knowledge of the *logos* of truth, of all things; a knowledge of soul; self-knowledge, truth-knowledge. Heights, these; beyond them, only the heights of the eternal.

With the psychological conception of man the purely ethical branch of Plato's philosophy is closely related. Ethics he could not avoid; philosophy can not avoid it. In this department it demonstrates its utility to the race, or exposes its insufficiency, in either case determining the value of philosophy as a practical pursuit. In its theological bearings, it may be speculative; in its psychological revelations, it may be abstract and concrete; in its ethics, it is concrete.

Plato's *Republic* is a miniature of ethical principles, both as they respect the State and the individual, while his *Laws* are the details of practical, social, moral, and civil life. However, the ethical beliefs, sanctions, and discriminations of Plato are reflected, like his psychology, in all his dialogues, sometimes as mere hints, then as open declarations; sometimes in dialectical form, then as prescriptive statements; but always sufficiently transparent and sufficiently positive, though not always essentially sound. To his theory of the *origin of evil* we take exception on philosophic, historic, and religious grounds. It is philosophically erroneous, historically contradictory, religiously absurd. Of evil, as the antagonistic principle in the universe, located in inert matter, we have already spoken, but we recall it in this connection. To this remote origin Plato traces it.

That man is a partaker of vice, degraded, contaminated, Plato unequivocally asserts; that he is not good by nature, he teaches in the *Meno;* that he is ignorant of virtue, he shows both in the *Laches* and the *Meno,* and proves in the latter that it can neither be taught nor acquired as science; that the soul is burdened with baseness and injustice, he declares and establishes in the *Gorgias,* and re-affirms its ignorance and diseases in the *Sophist;* that evil is a deep disease is manifest in the *Lysis;* that the major part of mankind are wrecks, and that, in comparison with the gods, every man is vile, that passion is inherent and man the most savage of animals, Plato confesses in the *Laws.* Let this testimony to "total depravity" be sufficient.

His condemnation of evil is explicit, strong, wrathful. In the *Crito* it is declared that it is not right to do evil; in the *Gorgias,* that "to act unjustly is the greatest of evils," that intemperance is disorder, that it is dreadful to be discordant with "myself," that an "insatiable and intemperate" life is reprehensible; in the *Minos,* that intoxication must be forbidden; in the *Banquet,* that drunkenness is a crime, and "shame for bad acts" is the glory of a man; in the *Laws*, that to live without justice is not good, that intoxicatlon is not of a "trifling nature," and man drunk is again a child, and that idleness, slander, theft, murder, profane oaths, and human sacrifices are crimes in the sight of gods and men.

Equally strong is he in his encouragements and persuasions to seek the good and avoid the evil. Man, as in the *Crito*, should not be anxious about living, but about *living well;* an unjust person or an unhealthy soul, as in the *Gorgias*, is miserable; good is the end of all actions; the depraved soul should be restrained; he is happy who has no vice in his soul; as in the *Protagoras*, the soul needs training and healing; justice "bears the nearest possible resemblance to holiness," therefore practice it; the safety of life consists in the right choice of pleasure and pain; as in the *Cratylus*, the soul that moves badly, or in a "restrained and shackled manner," is depraved, it needs freedom; as in the *Philebus*, pleasure is not the chief good, nor even intellect, but the mixed life of intellect and pleasure; as in the *Charmides*, "temperance is the practice of things good;" as in the *Menexenus*, "knowledge separated from justice appears to be knavery;" as in the *Minos*, "right is a royal law," it has science in it; as in the *Second Epistle*, evil must be removed if the soul meet with truth; as in the *Ninth Epistle*, "each is not born for himself alone," but must recognize the claims of country, parents, and friends; as in the *Laws*, children should reverence parents, making images to their memory, and old men should not do shameless things before children; and crystallizes the whole in these: virtue is the basis of all honor; "*truth is the leader of every good.*" What lofty instructions here!

Recognizing the depravity of soul, condemning evil, and postulating the necessity of virtue, what remedy does Plato offer for depravity? What is the impulsive ethical force of his philosophy? Let us not expect too much from one piloting himself in a new region. He leads; let us follow. He recognizes the difficulty, wrestling with it in no uncertain, but, as we shall find, in an insufficient manner. In the *Protagoras* he points out the difficulty of becoming a good man, "square as to his hands and feet and mind, fashioned without fault;" but in the *Banquet* he exhorts to obtain the good, and in the *Euthydemus* he exclaims with the vehemence of a seeker, "*Let him destroy me, and, if he will, boil me, or do whatever else he pleases with me, if he does but render me a good man.*" Could spiritual yearning go farther?

The acquisition of good, according to Plato, is conditional upon self-knowledge and a knowledge of good, both of which may be obtained by the pursuit of both in a philosophical manner. This is the kernel of the ethical theory of Plato. In the *First Alcibiades* he insists that we must know ourselves before we can make ourselves better, illustrating it in this way, that if one does not know what a finger-ring is, he can not make better finger-rings. Self-knowledge is the primary condition of improvement; this results in the exposure of the concupiscent soul, and all the depravities of the irascible nature. No one will dispute Plato at this point; but when, as in the *Protagoras*, he undertakes to show that "no man errs willingly," and, as in the *Banquet*, that all men desire good to be present, we suspend judgment a moment to inquire what he means. He reveals the depravity of the soul, but are we to understand that it is an *involuntary depravity?* If so, he is in perfect accord with the Biblical representation of man's original corruption; but he departs from it if he means that evil, as a manifested product in the life, is equally involuntary. The inner man may be involuntarily depraved, the outer man is voluntarily depraved. Nature is involuntary in its contents; conduct is wholly voluntary. Plato is not discerning at this point, or he is too lenient in the interpretation of wrong in man's history. Self-knowledge leads to the discovery of the voluntary as well as the involuntary in human history, and one can not be ignored any more than the other. Strong as the involuntary principle of evil is, the world suffers more from voluntary evils, or the free exercise of the involuntary principle. Crime is the voluntary manifestation of the involuntary principle; sin is the voluntary disturbance of God's order in the universe. The involuntary excites sympathy; the voluntary, approval or condemnation, as it embraces right or wrong. The one is authoritative; the other is within control, and may be directed or suppressed. Plato's sentiment is an apology for evil, internal and external; it is, therefore, ethically unsound.

The knowledge of good precedes the acquisition of good. This Platonic condition we accept. What is the good? What are its essentials, its signs, its functions? With these questions Plato struggles in the *Philebus*, announcing that beauty, symmetry, and truth prevail in the form of good; in the *Laches*, teaching that fortitude is related to the good; in the *Laws*, showing the difference between divine and human good, mentioning as elements of the latter the four virtues, prudence, temperance, fortitude, and justice. As if not quite satisfied with these attempts at definition, he adds in the *Laws* that the perfect man is the reflective man, or reason is a quality of goodness, and that the good man governs himself, or is capable of self-control; in his *Seventh Epistle* he advises Dionysius to be in accord with himself, as if *self-harmony* were the content of goodness; and in the *Charmides* he discusses the problem of "living scientifically," which he finally resolves into a knowledge of the science of good and evil.

The sum of these fragments is that good is a complex content, consisting of truth, symmetry, beauty, prudence, temperance, fortitude, justice, reason, harmony, and scientific order; a catalogue of noble virtues, possessing which, the soul will not be "barren nor unfruitful" in the things that make for righteousness and peace.

How may they be secured? How may the good be obtained? This is the crucial question of theology, of philosophy, of Plato, who fancies that he has prescribed a sufficient remedy for evil, and suggested a way for the attainment of good. His answer is three-fold, theological, religious, and philosophical, the merits of which will be seen when the answer is fully given. The *theological answer* relates to the infallibility of conscience as a guide into all truth, Plato, especially in the *First Alcibiades*, referring to it as a sufficient monitor and helper. The "dæmon" of Socrates has furnished a topic for many an essay and discussion, some writers finding it difficult to reconcile it with the conscience; but it seems to us very difficult to reconcile it with any thing else, unless we identify it with the Holy Spirit, which we are not prepared to do. The power of conscience, as a prompting influence in morals, as an inspiration toward the right, we fully grant; but the world needs something more than a conscience. It needs truth, which will enable the conscience properly to act, for it is an indisputed fact that the unenlightened conscience, if it does not reprove, does not always restrain from wrong-doing, especially if such wrong-doing is sanctioned by religious teaching. The conscience may be guided or become a guide, in proportion to its knowledge of right and wrong. In itself, it is without such knowledge; it needs truth, therefore. The Bible represents the need of the Holy Spirit as a reprover, a teacher, a guide, a comforter, inasmuch as man's conscience will not always reprove, or teach, or guide. According to the Bible, man can not guide himself into the truth; he needs truth, and he needs God to guide him into the truth. Of the "dæmon" of Socrates and Plato, we do not find that it was an illuminator, or *guide into truth*, but a restraining influence in conduct, checking the disposition to evil, the purpose to do wrong. In the *Theages* Plato clearly distinguishes between the conscience as a restraining and inciting power, affirming that it "dissuades and does not suffer me to do" wrong, "but it never at any time incites me" to do right. Evidently, then, the inciting power, the guiding influence to truth, is not in the conscience. Plato's theological answer is incomplete.

The *religious answer* relates to the utility of prayer as an agency in the world's moral elevation. Plato is a believer in prayer; he prays to the gods; he recommends sacrifices and festivals in their honor; but he *records no answers to his prayers.* This has been over-looked by the students of Plato; its announcement is now made for the first time. At the close of the *Phædrus,* Socrates is made to offer the following beautiful prayer: "O, beloved Pan, and all ye other gods of this place, grant me to become beautiful in the inner man, and that whatever outward things I have may be at peace with those within." What a prayer! Was it genuine, or a mere concession to the polytheism of the country? A genuine heart-yearning for good Plato possessed, but he trusted neither to the restraining conscience nor unanswered prayer for its acquisition.

The great remedy for evil, the chief agency in the acquisition of good, is *education;* this is Plato's philosophical answer, it is the answer of modern philosophy. Both in the *Meno* and the *Sophist* he teaches the value of correct opinion, and that confutation is the greatest of purifications. Both in the *Protagoras* and the *Lysis* he enforces the duty of education. In the *Rivals* he shows that to be ignorant of one's self is to be of unsound mind. He labors in the *Laws* espe-cially to prove that ignorance is the cause of crime, which leads him to recommend education as a preventive; but the disease is not fairly stated, hence the remedy is inadequate. The principle that vice is a mental disease is erroneous in fact, and in contradiction of the natu-ral depravity which the philosopher attributes to the mortal part of the soul. Vice is a spiritual disease, to be overcome by a spiritual remedy; but Plato did not diagnose correctly; hence did not pre-scribe accurately or sufficiently. A disease may be determined by its remedy, and the remedy required may be indicated by the disease. Consumption requires complicated treatment; a pin-scratch scarcely any notice. If the evil taint is interpreted as a misfortune or weak-ness that may easily be overcome; if its deadly spirit is not recog-nized; if it is pronounced, on the one hand, a superficial blemish, or, on the other, an incradicable bent, the philosophical remedies for it will be educational, social, legislative, philanthropic, but neither spirit-ual nor divine. If, as Theodore Parker held, sin is but the tripping of a child, a blunder, a mistake, an unfortunate step, then, indeed, its bad effects are within personal control. From Plato to Parker, through all the various evolutions of transcendentalism, there has been no adequate interpretation of the evil principle, no solution of the evil germ, either as to its origin or character, and no discovery of a satis-factory antidote. All along the line the failure has been complete. Plato's remedy—education—is the best that philosophy has ever sug-gested, the best outside of a divine religion. Let it be known as Plato's *patent-right remedy* for evil; it is not original with Herbert Spencer, therefore, or with modern thought.

4

The potency of culture, the civilizing influence of education, the intellectual improvement that man has made within twenty centuries, justifies the establishment of schools, colleges, the press, the publication of books, and all the efforts now making to emancipate the race from the thralldom of ignorance. Education is a universal necessity, but it is not an adequate remedy for sin. Even Athens, with its superior culture, decayed; and Greece, with philosophers in all its cities, declined in morals, because there was no impelling force behind philosophic teaching. Valuable as is culture, it is wanting in the moral power to deliver from evil, especially to eradicate it from the nature.

The education prescribed by Plato was not of a character to inspire a love of the beautiful, or to incline the soul to righteousness. He speaks often of a " liberal education," but the curriculum embraced gymnastics, equestrian skill, as in the *Laches*, dancing, music, arithmetic, and astronomy, as in the *Laws*. He mourns over the " slave-like cut of hair " in the souls of men, talks freely of popular education among the Persians, as in the *First Alcibiades*, but, while suggesting philosophy to the few as the cure for their evils, he orders the above, both for boys and girls, as a sufficient preparation for life, and an adequate security against depravity. In the *Republic* he prescribes four virtues for the ideal man ; viz., wisdom, temperance, fortitude, and justice, the strong pillars of human character; but these are the products of individual endeavor, the results of philosophic study, of a persevering purpose, and of the observance of a rigid asceticism. The weakness of the educational method, consisting in part in a superficial estimate of evil, is evident in this, that it attributes the power of moral change or moral elevation wholly to the individual. He regenerates himself by the force of education ; the sources and agencies of moral change are within himself. This Plato taught; this modern philosophy teaches ; and it all grows out of the theory of evil as a superficial hindrance to the development of character, to be removed by self-effort, by the educational process.

Of some evils Plato has a deep abhorrence, as drunkenness, gluttony, unchaste pleasures, and laziness ; and for this reason he excludes the poets from his *Republic*, especially Homer, whose falsehoods, fables, and immoralities, as given in the Iliad, he exposes with a merciless hand, insisting that the literature of the poets excites the predisposition to evil, and is contaminating in every respect. At the same time, evil-hater as he was, he permits the governors in his *Republic* to lie under given circumstances ; and in his *Laws* a person is permitted to steal pears, apples, and pomegranates, if he does it " secretly," that is, if not caught at it. Such are some of the inconsistencies in Plato's educational method, involving a hatred of some evils, but a superficial estimate of *evil*, as the ruining force in the world.

In this connection it is all-important to inquire what relation he assigns to religion in his ethical economy. Has religion, as a principle, as an office, or prerogative, any recognition in Plato? The term "religion" embraces a multiple of ideas, more or less fundamental, which appear in crude or developed forms in religious structures and institutions, being prominent in permanent religions and obscure in the transient. Plato's religious conceptions, lifted out of their polytheistic environment, have a fundamental value, and are the organic ideas, so far as they go, of the best religions, if not of the divine. The paganism of Plato is not ultra; rather is it the accidental glamour of the popular faith.

Respecting the existence of God, having already spoken of his belief, it is enough now to recall the fact that he is a monotheist; but Plato's monotheism included a broad, circumstantial view of a divine government, manifesting itself in the providential, and, therefore, minutely careful, supervision of this world. This feature of a divinely governing influence in human affairs Plato develops in the *Laws*, discussing the origin of the prevailing doubt respecting it, and conclusively establishing that the small no less than the great affairs in this world are under divine supervision. Wonderfully inspiring is the thought that God has a particular plan for each individual, and that, however small the plan, it stretches "its view to the whole," is related to a universal plan; and equally faith-inspiring is the thought that God has a *plan* for the ultimate triumph of virtue. Virtue will gain the victory in the universe. This is evangelical philosophy; its failure is in not pointing out the "plan." Just here, however, the religion and ethics of Plato unite.

Believing in God, worship, sacrifices, temples, prayers, Plato does not hesitate to enjoin religious duties, consistently recognizing the spontaneous activities of the religious nature of man in these directions. In the *Republic* he says temples should be erected to the Delphian Apollo, and sacrifices should be offered to the gods who know, see, and hear all things; but this is suggested in a faint-hearted way, as if some recognition must be made to the popular religion. In the *Laws*, however, Plato is undisguisedly an advocate of the polytheistic institutions, denouncing impiety, sacrilege, and atheism, and prescribing punishments therefor. No one, he affirms, should be elevated to the position of guardian of the laws who denies the existence of the gods.

As to prayers, he continually orders them in the *Laws;* in the *Eighth Epistle* he says "it is meet to begin from the gods in every thing ;" in the *Philebus* he speaks of the presence of a favoring deity, and intimates the helpfulness of prayer in study ; and the *Second Alcibiades* is a dialogue almost wholly devoted to the consideration of the utility of prayer. Carefulness in prayer, a study of what the gods are likely to grant, he assumes, will restrain the praying spirit, and prevent the utterance of intemperate requests, while a study of the prayers of the Lacedæmonians will show that the gods prefer a "good-omened address" to a multitude of meaningless sacrifices. The dialogue leaves the impression that prayer is, on the whole, of doubtful value.

Is the doctrine of *spiritual influence* recognized by Plato? Not frequently, nor even thoroughly, and yet somewhat beautifully, causing us to suspect that Plato does not record all his experiences, or express definitely all his convictions respecting the communicating influence of God's spirit. In the *Apology* Socrates is made to say that the Deity *called* him to philosophize, a call analogous to that which every evangelical minister claims as having been extended to him ; and in the *Phœdrus* he confesses that he is "moved by some divine influence" which envelops even the place where he is sitting, and *makes it divine.* This means wonderful illumination, attributed by Plato to a divine source. Discoursing on the prophetic art, he pronounces it a divine madness, and as to its result he says that which comes from God is nobler than that which proceeds from men.

In respect to spiritual living, Plato teaches in the *Second Alcibiades* that the mist must be removed by the divine being from the soul, as Minerva removed it from the eyes of Diomede, that he might see gods and men ; and in the *Laws* he strictly enjoins that one must live after the manner of the gods, saying that similarity to the deity is pleasing in his sight. Depravity must be cured; this he urges in the *Laws.* He intimates the existence of a cure, without describing it, in the *Charmides,* as an incantation which restores body and soul to health and purity ; but, alas! where or what is the incantation? Shall we turn to the *Euthyphron* and listen to Plato as he discourses on holiness? What is holiness? asks the interlocutor. This is a fundamental question ; Plato's answer is not fundamental, for he does not know. Definitions, many and bordering on a true conception of holiness, are given, but each is unsatisfactory, because incomplete, and lacking a divine element or force. Holiness is the prosecution of injustice; "that which is pleasing to the gods is holy;" "that which the gods love is holy;" holiness is a part of justice ; it is a knowledge of sacrifice and praying. Such are the humdrum definitions in the dialogue, but all are finally abandoned by Plato himself, without a settlement of the question, What is holiness? In the *Phi-*

*lebus* he brings forward the subject of purity, and really expands it satisfactorily in the guise of an illustration. The purity of white, says Plato, is that " in which there is no portion of any other color." Admirable, but he fails in the application ; indeed, he makes no application. Holiness is that in which there is no portion of any thing unlike it, but Plato does not say this ; he did not grasp it ; he had not experienced it. His holiness was abstract, not concrete—localized, if at all, in matter, not in men.

The religion of Plato included more than sacrifices, prayers, faith, temples, and conformity to a god-like life. In some respects he may be viewed as a doctrinal teacher, or expounder of certain eschatological truths, fundamental to all religions, mythological as well as the truly historical and real. These truths Plato does not shun; he seeks them, uses them as the instrument of persuasion to a holy life, drawing arguments from heaven and hell to impress men to follow the deity. The question of the future life was then as vital, as absorbing, as it is now. Belief in it was universal. The thought of the immortality of the soul, vaguely accepted, exerted a potent influence on the conduct, and often subdued men into respect for righteousness. Plato was the first to elaborate the doctrine, to establish it by unanswerable proof, succeeding better than our own Emerson, who reduces it to a hope, or a belief in it to a guess.

Of the spirituality of the soul, we have sufficiently spoken ; of the proofs of its immortality, we may now rehearse those of Plato, premising that, studying them in their fullness, they appear incontrovertible. Gleaning the dialogues, we hear him say in the *Banquet* that men "have a yearning for immortality ;" in the *Philebus*, that the soul is full of expectations, making speeches to itself of the future; in the *Republic*, that evil can not destroy the soul as disease the body, but that it is immortal ; in the *Phœdo*, that "there are two species of things, the one visible, the other invisible ;" the invisible always continues the same, but "the visible never the same ;" and the soul being invisible, must always be the same, and therefore immortal. Again, in the *Banquet*, that while the body is " being perpetually altered," and even manners, morals, opinions, and sciences change, the soul abideth forever ; in the *First Alcibiades*, that as the user of tools and the tools are different, so soul and body are different ; in the *Phœdrus*, declaring " every soul is immortal ;" in the *Phœdo* again, that pre-existence, which he taught, is the proof of immortality, and that future punishment, being necessary, could not be experienced without future existence; and also that there are two kinds of things, the one compounded, the other simple. The compounded may be dissolved, but the simple is indissoluble ; the soul, being an uncompounded unit, is necessarily immortal.  Again, that the soul can not admit the "contrary of life," which is death; and in the *Crito*, that Socrates dreamed that a beautiful woman approached him and said, "Three days hence you will reach fertile Phthia," and Socrates's almost last words, "Catch me, if you can." These are the merest fragments from Plato, but sufficient in their amplified form to justify faith in immortality.

With the faith of Plato there was mingled some doubt, which is another weakness of a purely philosophic religion.  In the *Phædo* the parties to the dialogue appear dissatisfied with Socrates's argument for immortality, from the fact that the soul has pre-existed, and Socrates does not remove the doubt.  Again, the analogy between a weaver's garments and the weaver existing long after they have perished, and the soul existing long after the body has rotted, Socrates himself acknowledges inconclusive; and yet Plato is decidedly committed to the doctrine of immortality.  The tenth book of his *Laws* carries one far toward a convincing and intelligent faith in the doctrine.  Without such a doctrine there is no room for any eschatology; one falls with the other, it is the other.

Plato introduces the subject of future rewards and punishments in the *Phædo* by saying, "I entertain a good hope that something awaits those who die, and that, as was said long since, it will be *far better for the good than the evil.*"  On future rewards he is not altogether definite, saying he hopes "to go amongst good men, though I would not positively assert it; that, however, I shall go amongst gods, who are perfectly good masters, be assured I can positively assert this, if I can any thing of the kind."  Concerning future retributions, he is decisive; he writes like a divine judge, holding them over the guilty as the penalty of crime, and threatening them for inferiority, baseness, ignorance, and stupidity.  Plato borrows the doctrine of transmigration from Pythagoras, and incorporates it with his eschatology. He speaks of Hades and the invisible world, but has a preference for transmigration; and in the *Phædo* he writes of transmigrated souls loving impurity while in the flesh, wandering like shadowy phantoms "amongst monuments and tombs," and others, who had given themselves to "gluttony and drinking," are spoken of as "clothed in the form of asses and brutes."  Both in the *Phædrus* and *Theætetus* the doctrine of transmigration is clearly announced, somewhat in detail, as a soul passes into the life of a beast, a man passes into a man again, or into the nature of woman; and in any event, whatever the extremely wicked soul's lot is, in beast or man, it remains with wings cut off for ten thousand years, and can have no hope of improvement until the expiration of that period.  Others, less wicked and with more aspiration, may escape the imprisonment at the end of three thousand or even one thousand years. In the *Laws* he insists that the wicked after death "shall come back hither to suffer punishment according to nature," going into animals or men, as they were beastly and depraved.

Accepting transmigration as a form of retribution, Plato logically veered toward a most pernicious doctrine, which, considerably modified or expanded in these days, passes by the name of *spiritualism.* He did not formulate Spiritualism, but its germ is in Transmigration, and in more than one instance Plato relates spiritualistic phenomena. In the *Second Epistle* he declares that the dead perceive what is going on here, and in the *Seventh Epistle* he teaches that the unjust after death rove upon the earth and get into animals and persons. In the *Eighth Epistle* he speaks the speech of the departed Dion, as if inspired by him to speak it; and the dialogue entitled *Menexenus* is virtually a proclamation of Spiritualism. The seed of the modern delusion is in the Platonic system.

In addition to transmigration Plato refers to the judgment of the departed, especially in the *Gorgias,* before Minos, Rhadamanthus, and Æacus, who sentence the good to the "isles of the blessed," and the wicked to Tartarus; and in the *Phœdo* he relates the old fable of the four rivers on the earth, among them the River Styx, and alludes to lakes and Tartarus as the abode of the incurably wicked. Of those whose wickedness is curable deliverance from Tartarus may be expected. This is the *purgatory* of Plato, the seed of the Catholic doctrine, and the germ of the "second-probation" idea mooted in certain quarters in these days. *Transmigration* and *Tartarus*—these are the sign-words of the eschatology of Plato.

In view of the future Plato exhorts in the *Gorgias* to holy living while on the earth with an emphasis, a persuasion, an enthusiasm equal to any thing the pulpit ever uttered, and not less earnest is he in the *Phœdo* in urging an immediate care of the soul. The doctrine that the future life will be determined by the life here is also announced in the *Republic.* Plato was a great preacher, an exhorter to righteousness, as necessary to a happy future.

To what a banquet of religious ideas Plato invites us! Providence, sacrifices, prayers, worships, holiness, spiritual influence, immortality—there is inspiration in these, the trend thereof is upward; transmigration, spiritualism, purgatory, second probation, Tartarus—these are the attenuated extremes of philosophical dreaming, a mixture of fable, superstition, and invention, to be banished both from religion and philosophy. The ethical system of Plato, in its conceptions, provisions, and suggestions, is a combination of truth and error; the religious system is akin to it.

Plato's *socialism*, or the governmental idea, is as distinct and well articulated as his psychology and religion, and as it is referred to oftener than either, it deserves more than a passing notice. Full credit has not been given to all his teachings on a subject of such vast importance; he has been censured because misunderstood, and not condemned sufficiently when understood. This department of his philosophy, unlike all others, is eminently practical; it is a reduction of the abstract to the concrete, or an application of principles to common life; it is the framework of a new system of sociology. He rises high enough to say in the *First Alcibiades* that States possessing virtue do not need walls, ships, and docks, a sentiment almost parallel with that more ancient one, that "righteousness exalteth a nation, but sin is a reproach to any people." Similar is his utterance in the *Laws*, that virtue should be the end of law; and emphatic is his opposition to foreign war, and that more deadly internal contagion—sedition. Order, harmony, obedience to law, philosophical truth, education, and virtue he considers essential to good government, subordinating every thing to their attainment. Such is his notion of the importance of the State that he exalts it above individual right, regulating human liberty, personal aims and ambitions, and all things belonging to the individual, in the interest of the government, submerging individualism in the governmental purpose. He says in the *Laws*, "Neither yourselves are your own property, nor this substance of yours," but yourselves, substance and families belong to the State. Paul echoes Plato's sentiment so far as to say, "Ye are not your own," but he differs in placing the owner's life of man not in the State, but in God. God owns every man; the State owns nobody. This is the difference between them, a difference that will strikingly manifest itself in the elucidation of socialistic philosophy and Christianity, for it is the key-note of both.

Plato's *Republic* is interpreted as an ideal State, in contrast with the then existing government of Athens, which the philosopher conceived to be corrupt, and which he thoroughly hated. Discovering the weaknesses of popular government, whether as a tyranny or democracy, he assigned himself the task of framing a government which should embody the best political conceptions, and be a model to the nations after him. The *Republic* was accordingly written, ostensibly as an ideal conception, but as a covert rebuke of the prevailing city government. Later in life the *Laws* appeared, as a supplemental development of the *Republic*. The *Republic* is ideal; the *Laws* are concrete, practical. The one deals in moral principles; the other in legal forms and penalties. The one is the constitution; the other the statute-book. To these we must look for principles, laws, and expositions of the governmental idea, which in Plato is a singular conglomeration of ethical virtues and social aberrations, a mixture of health and disease in the body politic.

Of first importance is the form of political government. He enumerates in the *Statesman* three definite polities—monarchy, aristocracy, and democracy—out of which, bisecting, he produces six; but, whatever the bisected form, he leans in his preferences toward monarchy "as the best of the six polities." The same preference, is expressed in his *Fifth Epistle*, in which he says: "There is a voice from each form of polity, as it were from certain animals, one from a democracy, another from an oligarchy, and another again from a monarchy. Very many persons assert that they understand these voices; but except a few, they are very far from understanding them." The "voice" of the monarchy is pleasant in his ears. "There are," he says in the *Laws*, "two mothers of polities," from which all others are produced, monarchy and democracy; but he criticises the extreme form of each, adding that a mixture of both forms is preferable. Notwithstanding this advocacy of a milder monarchy than appears in the *Statesman* and *Republic*, certain it is his leanings were toward a high-toned government, either as an aristocracy or monarchy; for it was his repudiation of democracy in Athens, and the indorsement of the reign of the Tyrants, that made him unpopular and compelled his exile.

It is in the *Republic* that, quoting an old fable, he intimates that in the forming of men the Deity mixed gold with some, fitting them for governors: silver with others, intending them to be soldiers; iron and brass with others, designing them to be craftsmen and husbandmen. This is a square affirmation of the natural inequality of men, on which is predicated the righteousness of caste, which Plato emphasized with earnestness, and introduced into the ideal State. The higher and the lower must be recognized in humanity; society must be organized, not on the unities or resemblances even, but on the *differences* in men. Inequality in a sense is admitted, but in Plato's sense it is the essence of inextinguishable social dissonance, the fixing of permanent barriers or walls of partition, that ought to be broken down. In the *Menexenus*, relaxing the caste spirit, Plato espouses the thought of equality in a masterly manner, affirming that all are born as brethren, having "one mother," and that they are "neither the slaves nor the lords of each other." But he was in a tender mood while writing this humane sentiment, for he was thinking of the dead, and the shadow of the sepulcher was upon him. The grave always hallows the doctrine of equality. He is in another mood while framing laws.

Holding to caste, it is not surprising that he excludes diseased men from his ideal State; he insists that they ought to die. Christianity would introduce the physician, the nurse, the hospital, the asylum, but none of these auxiliaries to human comfort are wanted in his republic. Herodicus he censures for propping himself with drugs, lengthening out his life, and procuring a *lingering death.* Healthy men, who die of extreme old age, are wanted in his republic. This offends the sympathetic spirit in man, paralyzes philanthropy, suppresses aspiration, and strikes at a majority of mankind. The doctrine is as odious as it is unfraternal, and pernicious as it is unkind.

Neither aristocracy nor caste is the worst feature in the socialism of Plato; neither constitutes the *esprit de corps* of socialism. Both, however, are preparatory steps to it. Plato locates the ideal republic outside of Athens, in a beautiful country, with a single city at its center, the whole being walled, and safe from attack, both from without and within. The number of families within the walls must not exceed five thousand and forty, all of whom shall be loyal to the governmental purpose, and in sympathy with ideal ends. In view of death and immigration, the exact number of families may be difficult to preserve, but it must be attempted at all hazards, as Plato considers a small republic more likely to fulfill its mission than a large one. In this protected city certain governmental conditions, primary to all governments, must be observed; as the conditions of suffrage, the tenure of office-holding, the number of offices, the duties of officers, which Plato enumerates with appropriate circumstantiality. As the subject of foreign relations can not be ignored, since other nations exist, and some are contiguous, Plato establishes laws relating to naturalization, and the surceasing of citizenship, and enacts free trade *in extenso* by forbidding the payment of duty on imports and exports; that is, no revenue whatever shall be obtained from international trade.

Touching internal social relations, the *core of the socialistic spirit,* he advocates compulsory marriage for the sake of the immortality of the race, a not inconsequential consideration; but in the ideal society marriage is abandoned for the good of the State. What is called free-loveism in these days supersedes the sacred idea of marriage; home is blotted out; parental and filial relations are unknown; children are foundlings, handed over to the care of the State; and the family perishes. Plato quotes the communism of birds and animals, as chaste and safe, in defense of the idea as applied to human society, and insists that it will result in the procreation of a higher generation of men and women.

The advocacy of the communism of property naturally follows. The assignment of land to the individual is by the government, for the sake of the government; title to land is not acquired; shares in profits are forbidden; each lives, labors, suffers, and dies for the whole. Abnegation of proprietary rights is the imperative condition of mutual support and general prosperity. Without further elucidation, this is Plato's social idealism. Among its best elements, it includes order, education, virtue; on the other side are state-ownership, monarchy, caste, free trade, community of women, and community of property. Both elements can not co-exist; education and caste are antagonistic, virtue and extinct homes do not abide together. The socialism of Plato means the dismemberment of society; the ideal State means the degradation of man.

In Athens his governmental ideas were never enforced; in Sicily he undertook a reformation of the government, but failed.

Having considered Plato's philosophy in its details, it remains to consider his relation to philosophy in general, or to estimate Plato's place in history and his services to mankind. What is permanent in Plato and what transient, what superior or imperishable, and what inferior or evanescent, whether he was born for his age or all ages; this is an inquiry that can not be omitted. Without controversy, he was abundant in labor, and lived to propagate ideas that are fundamental, and which have entered into the philosophies and religions of the world. To understand these ideas, it is not absolutely necessary to understand the times in which he lived, or the philosophies that prevailed, or the religions that held sway over the common mind, for they are not the product of his age, but belong to all ages. Other ideas, not fundamental or universal, take their coloring from his age, and belong to it. To understand these the age must be understood. That is to say, what is accidental, inferior, evanescent, in Plato, is the result of the influence of the age on Plato; what is permanent and imperishable is outside of that influence. In many respects he stood out from his age, because he stood against it and condemned it.

As a man, he had his weaknesses; he lacked the fortitude with which he clothes the ideal man; he authorized the worship of the gods without having a personal faith in them; he was aristocratic in instinct; he hated democracy; he retired from public affairs, and virtually abjured his citizenship.

His philosophy is burdened with weaknesses, plain and palpable; its effects in some directions have been injurious, undermining the order of society; its virtues are of definite value, and worthy of renown. To specify the varied results of Plato's career, we shall consider, first, Plato as a writer; second, Plato as a philosopher; third,

Plato as a moral teacher; fourth, Plato as a socialist; fifth, Plato as a forerunner of Christianity; sixth, the need of Christianity demonstrated by the Platonic system.

As a *writer, composer,* and *thinker,* Plato had not an equal among his contemporaries, and it is doubtful if, since his day, any one has appeared who has excelled him in the art of composition. Both in the art of thinking and the art of expression he certainly is a model. For intensity of thought, subtlety of apprehension, sublimity of inquiry, persistence in analysis, accuracy of dialectical statement, and elegance in representation, he is both superior and inspiring. It is not the dialogue form of discourse which he preferred that is commended, but the style itself, which is clear, definite, logical, illustrative, and conclusive. He wrote in Attic Greek, the language of Pericles and Demosthenes, itself a pure and finished language, a vehicle for sublime thoughts and inquiries. He was an earnest inquirer for truth, definitely expressing what he desired to know, if he failed in finding the knowledge itself. He asked questions—he was sometimes slow to affirm until the foundations of an answer had been well laid in investigation and comparison. He does not write, therefore, in a positive and affirmative way, but as if searching for a path for his feet; walking along, at times, as if his lantern had gone out, as it had. Besides the perspicuity, the elegance, and the logical strength of his compositions, there is a *personal tone* in every dialogue that wins the sympathy of the reader. He does not write as if building a system of truth for others, but as if in eager search for the truth for himself. He is not a revealer, he is a seeker, and writes accordingly. Understanding Plato's purpose, it is easy to understand his style.

Lewes, always underrating Plato, pronounces him a " very difficult and somewhat repulsive writer;" and Jowett, so far as the *Timæus* is concerned, reiterates the criticism. To Plato, as a writer, the criticism does not apply; it is crudely unjust. A paragraph now and then, as in the *Phædrus* or *Euthydemus,* may be open to such objection, but what writer has not produced objectionable paragraphs? Shakespeare is not exempt from such criticism. Not Plato's paragraphs, but Plato's *works,* must afford the basis for critical judgment; and on that basis the critics must be silent. Lewes likewise insinuates that Plato is indefinite, confirming his report by the statement of Cicero that he leaves many questions undetermined. No one disputes that many discussions in Plato are inconclusive, that he does not answer serious inquiries, as that concerning holiness; but Plato failed on such subjects because he did not know the truth. He is inconclusive, but not indefinite. He seeks, but, as Schleiermacher points out, does not arrive at truth. When Diogenes Laertius reports that Plato is unintelligible to the ignorant, the statement can not be contradicted; but Kepler's astronomical researches, Bacon's scientific data, and Kant's rational criticisms, are even more unintelligible to the ignorant than Plato's cosmogony or ethics.

It may be truly charged against Plato that he is an inconsistent writer, contradicting in one dialogue what he affirms in another, thereby confusing and unsettling the mind of the reader. The following are examples : in the *Meno* he holds that virtue can not be taught, but in the *Clitopho* he expresses an opposite opinion; in the *Phædo* he proves the doctrine of reminiscence, but in the *Statesman* he speaks of ancestors who "had no recollection of former events," a virtual denial of pre-existence; again, in the *Statesman* he both advises and condemns written statutes and customs, leaving it undetermined which is better for the State; in the *Timæus* he vindicates the freedom of the will, while in the *Hippias Minor* he appears like a fatalist. These, however, are examples of inconsistency in thinking, not contradictions in writing; they are not blemishes of composition.

The same answer may be made with respect to the charge that there is a want of method in Plato's literary work; even if true, it does not apply to style of expression or composition; if true, it applies to Plato's conception of his work, not to its execution. Plato's literary thought is one thing, the literary execution is another. Moreover, as want of method, or absence of system, has been charged against his philosophy, it is possible that the critic has transferred the objection to the literary work of Plato; but whatever objection is made to his philosophy, or to his literary plans and methods, it does not apply to Plato as a writer.

Singularly enough, Plato condemned writing, but only in a philosophical sense, saying that it is the "grave of thought," which Talleyrand metamorphosed into the form that language is employed by men for the purpose of concealing their ideas. Practically, Plato believed in writing; he wrote—and died with pen in hand.

We next estimate Plato as a philosopher. Compared with the philosophers of his own time, or from the time of Thales to that of Christ, there was none greater. None dealt with so many problems, and none elaborated more fully or saw so deeply into divine mysteries. Of the ancient philosophies, we must accept Plato's as superior to all others, whether we consider his theology, which was in advance of others; or his cosmogony, which was clearer than any; or his ethics, which, however defective, partook of the spirit of the times, and had been better had the public religion been different. In these particulars Plato, like Saul of old, is head and shoulders above the academicians.

However, it is not so much with reference to the comparative value of his teachings in that day, as it is with reference to their value compared with modern philosophy, that his philosophy is now considered. Is Plato of any value now, or has he been superseded by philosophers who, in the light of discovery and Christianity, see farther and deeper into divine mysteries? The death-knell of nearly all the old philosophies Christianity sounded, as soon as it was preached, and they were rolled up as a scroll, and laid away. Plato's for the time went the way of all the rest. Epicurus and Zeno—the philosophy of the porch—superseded that of the academy, showing that the rationalism of Plato had not changed the public faith, or rooted itself in civil affairs. Mythology reigned in Athens when Paul visited the city, and the Epicurean philosophy was in the ascendant. The Stoics Paul mentions; of Plato he says nothing. Neoplatonism was the attempt to unite Christianity and Platonism, or Christ and Plato, but it failed.

Until the sixteenth century of our era Plato is unknown as an intellectual force, his philosophy is without influence, idealism has perished. With the revival of letters, he rallies from the grave, and asks again to be heard, and is heard. Whatever is good in Plato, as well as whatever is evil, whether idealism or agnosticism, rationalism or materialism, theology or ethical science, is re-echoed in the circles of modern thinkers, modified, abbreviated, or amplified, as the thinkers prefer, but retaining the spirit of the old academy. Sometimes the Platonism in modern philosophy assumes a disguised appearance, but it is there, the core of modern philosophic thought, in one form or another. Nothing new has been announced by the peripatetics of the nineteenth century. Take idealism as the highest type of philosophy. Neither Hegel nor Kant, nor any philosopher of modern times, has improved on Plato, either in beauty or originality of idea, or clearness and fitness of expression. To be sure, the idealism of Plato is not without blemish, but with all its weaknesses, it carries unaided human thought up to the heights of belief in a personal God, which is sufficient atonement for its mistakes. Of modern idealism, not so much can be said in its favor. Leibnitz is not as rational an idealist as Plato. Plato gives us a lofty idea of God. Kant tells us that, by the theoretical reason alone, God's existence can not be demonstrated; Plato annuls the Kantian presumption by demonstrating the existence of God. Plato may not have apprehended the two reasons as Kant discriminates them, but he saw the way to God through the total reason of the soul, and proclaimed him. In him the idea of God as a being of goodness, holiness, and immortality is expanded into beautiful proportions, proving that a rational philosopher may go farther than to conclude that there is a divine being; he may declare his attributes. The Eleatics pronounced in favor of being, but it was left to Plato to distinguish between unchangeable being and changeable phenomena or non-being. Separating the two, Plato assigned to each a specific character; the study of being leading him to the thought of the divine attributes, of providence, of government, and of the spiritual sphere; the study of non-being leading to the investigation of natural principles, and the relation of God and the universe. From the thought of God, Plato passed to an inquiry respecting the soul, which he distinguished from the body, pronouncing it both spiritual and immortal. Plato was the *first philosopher to demonstrate the immortality of the soul,* as he was the *first to demonstrate the existence of a personal God, or the Creator of the universe.*

As respects the Platonic cosmogony, what modern philosopher has excelled it? Some there are who, like Comte, have denied the evidence of design or final cause in nature, but Plato reduces the whole subject to this form: *motion implies a mover;* and all modern expressions, such as design implies a designer, and contrivance a contriver, are built upon the Platonic apothegm. Not half as mysterious as Heraclitus, with his theory of flux, which he illuminates and accepts, nor half as confusing as the moderns, with their theories of bioplasm and atomic revolutions, he reduces the primitive elements to four: earth, air, fire, and water, with which the Creator builds the universe. The moderns talk of the convertibility of one thing into another, as heat into light and light into heat, a theory that Plato announced in the *Timæus* with as much clearness as it is now declared.

The theory of evolution Plato anticipates in the *Laws,* and Swedenborg found "contraries" and "similars," or the theory of corespondence, in the same volumes. In these particulars Plato is the original philosopher, the discoverer of first cosmological principles, which the moderns have appropriated and wrested to their destruction. Aristotle assailed the political opinions of Plato; his ethical system we assail as thoroughly weak and inadequate; but his philosophical conceptions of God and the universe are almost invulnerable; as speculations, they are apparently divine. As respects philosophy itself, Plato divided it into dialectics, metaphysics, and ethics, a division comprehending all the subjects which should engage the philosopher's attention.

He was the first to make such a classification; it is not clear that it has been improved by any subsequent attempt. It assigned special tasks and definite limits to the philosophical pursuit, having illustration in Plato himself.

Prior to Plato, philosophy was without a language of its own; but it needs a language as much as chemistry or physiology, and he was the first to suggest a form of sound words, to which the ages have contributed their stock, and a philosophical language is the result. In the *Cratylus* he discusses the propriety of names, answering that common question, what is in a name? He shows that the name must be the sign of the idea, that the name should have value, and that great truths must have proper expression. In this respect he is both a nominalist and a realist, believing in realities and in names suited to them. He is not a nominalist in the sense that there is nothing in a name, but that it represents value, or truth, or fact, in this way showing the importance of a philosophical language and laying the foundations for such a language.

As a psychologist he was the first to announce the spirit of identity and contradiction as a law of thought, than which a more important discovery he did not make; he also distinguished between sensation and perception, sensation and cognition, sensation and volition, regarding sensation as an external preliminary to internal intellectual movement, but not as absolutely essential; he distinguished, likewise, between analysis and synthesis as modes of investigation, employing both himself, but evidently preferring the former; he distinguished between the universal and the particular, the contingent and the necessary, applying these especially in cosmological and theological discussions. The elder Mill was captivated by these classifications, and Bacon was aided in scientific pursuit by observing them. He is a rational, in opposition to the empirical, psychologist. In this sense he is a rationalist: he believes in the *dominion of the reason*; he reasons, but the idea is the product of the reason. Hence, he is an ideologist. Psychology is the mother of ideology. Coleridge was inspired by the idealities of Plato, and Hegel became fanatical over them. From Plato, psychology, rationalism, and idealism emerged, as the necessary products of his system.

Plato was a sincere investigator of truth. Sometimes spoken of as an "ironical philosopher," since he employed irony in the refutation of an error, one of his chief characteristics was the intense sincerity of his purpose to find the truth. With Plato, sophistry in reasoning ended. He brought the Sophists to a stand-still; more, he annihilated the brood. He compelled seriousness in investigation, and made truth the object of investigation. He gave aim to philosophy. Earnest, sensitive to knowledge, acutely anxious for truth himself, he stimulated others to inquiry; he excited thought, and then directed it into proper channels. Sincerity and stimulation are among the effects of Plato's teaching.

The philosophical Plato, whether studied as a theologian or cosmologist, as a classifier of philosophy, as an originator of philosophical language, as a psychologist, or as a sincere and stimulating investigator, is reproducing himself in the philosophies of modern times, affecting the speculative spirit, and stimulating inquiry more than all the ancients combined. In him is the root of philosophical truth. Along with the truths he announced, half-truths and errors also made an appearance, and these also are bearing fruit in the speculative systems of the thinkers. Thus both the weakness and the strength of Plato have shared the immortality which properly belongs to truth alone.

Next, his influence as an ethical teacher must be considered. His data of ethics are clearly insufficient for a system of ethics. He advocates the principles of justice, denounces the poets for their falsehoods, and forbids drunkenness in his republic; but, notwithstanding the high ethical aim of some of his teachings, he holds to views that in their very nature prevent the attainment of good, and so the whole system falls to the ground. In a spirit of self-flattery, he concedes to man a voluntary love of good and a natural abhorrence of evil, and appoints education as the remedy for the world's evil. The unfitness of the remedy grows out of an ignorance of the disease. The disease is spiritual; the remedy must be spiritual also, but Plato's is intellectual. It is as if a remedy for defective hearing were prescribed for defective eyes. Plato regarded vice as an intellectual aberration, and ignorance as the great disease, for the cure of which intellectual development is sufficient.

Without discussing this further, and yet insisting that in any system of ethics the remedy must be proportioned to the disease, we are warranted in saying that Plato's voice is still heard in the modern systems of philosophic ethics. The *remedy for evil is education.* Herbert Spencer has not advanced beyond Plato in his ethical teaching. Spencer is in favor of scientific, in opposition to supernaturalistic, morality; he advocates a rational, not a religious, basis, for ethics. Plato's scheme failed, and Spencer's is the stupendous failure of the nineteenth century.

As a social teacher, or a socialist, Plato stands in a condemnatory attitude, having given birth to theories and proclaimed ideas which are re-appearing in the socialism, nihilism, and communism that now threaten the existence of public order, if not of society itself. All the dangerous social doctrines impregnating and agitating modern society are the echoes of the Platonic system, which, however, was ideal and never put into practice. One would scarcely believe that a philosopher like Plato would be found on the side of what is evidently corrupting, disintegrating, and abhorrent; but it is so. In the *Republic* he is the open advocate of a community of women, guarded by certain restrictions and established for ideal or philosophic ends. To these *ends* we call special attention. He holds that the guardians or rulers in his republic are the best men in it; physically they are without a blemish, having subjected themselves to hygienic discipline; intellectually, they are scholars, statesmen, philosophers, and represent the highest manhood. It is equally important that certain women, well-endowed and handsome, shall pass through the same preparatory experiences and discipline, becoming healthy, intellectual, and the fit associates for the best men. These two best classes he would throw together promiscuously for the procreation of the *best* children in the republic, securing a generation of noblest men and women, but at the expense of conjugal and filial relations. He would permit marriage between the upper classes, but not as a necessity, and, when a marriage has been celebrated, the children of such parents are not to know their parents, nor the parents the children. It is a community organized for the State, in which personality is undefined and relationship obscured.

Now, the *end* may appear good, but the means are too expensive. It is the end that controls in the breeding of sporting dogs, birds, and horses, just as Plato cites; and he would establish society upon a similar— that is, an animal—basis. The following facts we quote against it:

1. In Europe royal families have confined marriages within their limits, or if the high contracting parties go outside, and a morganatic marriage is established, it is held in disrepute, and the royal descendant suffers disinheritance and social penalty. What has been the consequence? Are the children of kings any better than others? Lunacy and imbecility, the dreadful fruits of violated consanguinity and intemperance and crime, make up a not inconsiderable portion of the history of royal families, overthrowing the royal principle of Plato, which, carried out in its details as he has prescribed, is only another name for free-loveism.

2. As a matter of fact, the best men and women may be found outside the royal lines. Reformers, poets, philosophers, physicians, theologians, and statesmen, eminent and useful, have emerged from poverty, obscurity, and degradation. Often the jewel is found in a pig-sty. God lifts one from the dunghill to the throne. In the round-about way of marriage between lower and higher classes the world's gradual elevation will be secured; if at times the blood of the best is vitiated by this method, the blood of the base is purified. Already the signs of a race-improvement are visible; it is a historic fact that the man of the nineteenth century is in advance of the man of

the first century. Ours is not a race of prize-fighters or Olympic run-ners, but in longevity, beauty of form, health, physical skill, and all the essentials of physical nobleness, the race is far in advance of what it was in Plato's time; and this improvement and prophecy of still larger development is the result of evolution, through the intermin-gling and wedding of all classes, rather than their separation. Plato's plan must result in the fixed division of the race into upper and lower classes, the best and the worst, with no hope of advance for the latter, but rather a continuous decline, while the providential, historically working plan is resulting in the perceptible elevation of the whole race. Plato was legislating for the few; God has his eye upon all.

Besides the unwisdom of Plato's plan—a plan that must fail in itself—what mischief has it wrought in modern society! With the revival of interest in Plato all his theories, socialistic as well as phil-osophical, were reannounced and found supporters, to the discredit of the age in which they lived.

The laxity of the marriage bond in civilized states; the reign of the doctrine of " Platonic affinity " in higher circles; the relation of spiritualism and free-loveism in this country; the multiplication of divorces and the assaults upon the home—are directly or indirectly the offspring of the Platonic philosophy. It strikes, therefore, at the foundations of society; it impairs faith in the most sacred relations, and turns the family into a nest of harlots; it abrogates the social tie, and converts government into anarchy. Besides these direful re-sults, it is the parent of those socialistic theories which are endan-gering social order and mocking civil law throughout the world. Carried out to its full extent, socialism will subvert human society. It is not believed that Plato contemplated such far-reaching and rev-olutionary catastrophes, but they logically follow his teachings, and are already actualized in organized attempts against society. A com-munity of goods, or communism, nihilism, socialism, and a community of women, or abrogation of the family idea, Plato advocated with not a little conviction and enthusiasm; but in all fairness it must be ad-mitted that he estimated the theories he advocated as purely philo-sophical, and never attempted to organize a society with these theories as a basis. The modern socialist is not a philosopher, but the admin-istrator of the philosophical idea, which reduces him to a destruction-ist, who goes forth with dynamite or the dagger to execute the plan and reorganize society. Socialism as a philosophical idea is absurd, and, put into practical operation, it is ruinous to both the family and the state. As the exponent of the idea, Plato must be condemned.

The task is not unpleasant to estimate Plato in his relations to Christianity; that is, to ask and attempt to answer the question,

What were his services to religion, and did he to any degree prepare the way for the introduction of Christianity to the East? Too much must not be allowed to philosophy in general or to Plato in particular; but, on the other hand, the preliminary work of each should be recognized, and the points of union and departure, or resemblance and dissimilarity, between philosophy and Christianity should be declared. The advent of the divine religion was preceded by a long-continued series of preparation—religious, philosophical, moral, and political preparations—without which its appearance would have been attended with withering resistances and retrograding revolutions. An example of precedent steps to the sway of the Gospel India furnishes in her long history. First, Brahminism looms large, spreading all over the land, and ruling with exclusive authority; then Buddhism protests and stalks like a reformer from the mountains to the sea; then Mohammedanism penetrates the two colossal creeds, dividing again the thinking of the people; then Christianity shoots a solitary ray across the religious horizon, and India wonders and pauses; then the English occupation involves the old faiths in restraint; then the universities of India beget in thousands of young men a doubt of the old religion; then Rationalism invades the land, and superstition trembles; then Protestantism plants churches, and echoes Calvary in the ears of the millions; then Chunder Sen preaches Christ, and mysticism takes the place of tradition; and at last India opens her gates to the dawn of the Gospel day. A slow process, involving centuries of time and the burdens of ages, but it illustrates the preparation needed for the admission and appreciation of Gospel truth. In like manner philosophy, in its manifold phases, had something to do in preparing the public mind for the new religion; it was related to the religious idea, and portended its development. Paganism, corrupt and insufficient, was a religious idea, and as such demonstrated the necessity of another religion, in which the idea might have complete development. Philosophy, weak, anxious, and helpless, made the same demonstration; it was the prophecy of religion. If Plato's voice is still ringing in the socialism of modern times; if his ethical system has been reproduced in Herbert Spencer; if his rationalism reappears in modern idealism—surely the whole philosophy of Plato must have had a potent influence in his day in preparing the people for a religion higher than his philosophy, and infinitely better than paganism.

The specific work of philosophy as a service to or preparation for Christianity may be indicated as follows:

1. The undermining of faith in mythology was the sign of the reign of reason in religion. The fable withered under the exegetical

analysis of the academy. The gods of Plato are the gods of tradition, not the gods of the reason. Plato says he had a "searching spirit" which prompted him to inquire into the reasonableness of the popular religion, which he secretly rejected. Philosophy broke with mythology—this was a step toward religious freedom and the annihilation of error.

2. The monotheism of Plato was an antecedent sign of the monotheism of Christianity. The origin of philosophic monotheism is to many a mystery, inasmuch as theology has insisted that the theistic hypothesis can not be a product of the reason, but must be a matter of revelation. Richard Watson holds that the ground of revelation is the inability of the human intellect to discover God in his character and relations; but the theological basis is no longer tenable. The facts are against it. The power of the reason in concluding for the existence of God, and in apprehending him in part, is exemplified in the monotheism of Plato; either this must be allowed or Plato was inspired. To make known the will, purposes, and plans of God, a revelation is a necessity. Plato announces the existence of God, associating certain necessary attributes as belonging to him; but he does not unfold divine plans, though he hints their existence. These plans the Scriptures unfold; to a Scriptural revelation Plato undoubtedly pointed.

3. Respecting man, Plato taught his immortality and the doctrine of responsibility, which involved the two-fold idea of future rewards and retributions. Obscure and even repulsive as is his eschatology, it has its value as a prefigurement of the clearer and more rational eschatology of the New Testament. The eschatological idea of Plato is the antecedent sign of the eschatological details of Christianity.

4. The incompleteness of the Platonic system, the essential emasculation of philosophy, was an indirect demonstration of the necessity of religious truth as a substitute for speculation; in this respect it rendered unintended service to Christianity, and prepared the public mind to receive it. Had Plato taught all that Christ taught, or anticipated every truth of the Gospel, what need of the Master? It was because his pen lagged, his reason faltered, his eye grew dim, and error appeared like truth, that the divine teacher must appear and reveal the truth. Plato was the morning-star; Christ the noonday sun. Plato was the forerunner of Christ; philosophy was the preparation for Christianity. With its defects it had virtues: with its falsehoods, celestial truths; with its aberrations, it was a steady, rational blaze; with its puerilities, it had enduring substance; walking with the staff of reason, it climbed the stairway to the stars. Christianity, beginning with the stars, ascended to the eternal throne.

The total impression that Plato makes is that of an appointed inquirer for truth, a searcher of the deep things of God. In all the wanderings, questionings, and conclusions of Plato, embracing all the problems of being and non-being, with their innumerable relations, he exhibits the humble, patient, and teachable spirit of a truth-seeker. Nowhere does he assume to be a final teacher; at no time does he offer *his* philosophy as the panacea for the world's angry ills; never does he pronounce the limit reached. Beyond the philosopher, beyond the rationalism, the idealism, the ethical system, the eschatology of the academician, must the world go; and upon another system of thought, even the truth, as it is in Jesus, must the heart of man lean for comfort in sorrow, knowledge in ignorance, light in darkness.

## CHAPTER II.

### THE CORNER=STONES OF PHILOSOPHY.

EMPEDOCLES, a disciple of Pythagoras, and an apologist of the doctrine of transmigration, delighted in declaring that, before becoming a man, he had been a boy, a girl, a bird, a fish, and a shrub, and that he had a complete remembrance of all his pre-existent experiences.

Viewed in its historical stages and connections, philosophy furnishes a transparent illustration of the Pythagorean doctrine, for it has passed through many transformations, and is undergoing at the present time a many-phased development. In its vibrations between empiricism and idealism, materialism and theism, it presents a variety of forms and beliefs, theories and interpretations, without, however, conducting to well-settled conclusions, or to the decision of questions in which the race has been, is, and ever will be permanently interested. Now and then a philosophical suggestion, as the idealism of Hegel, has risen like an island out of the sea of thought around it and attracted attention; while other ideas, like islands in the Pacific Ocean, have, from internal weaknesses, disappeared from sight. Belonging to these extinct philosophies, however, there were truths, discovered by the patient inquiry of genius, that were transferred to later and more vital economies, the perpetuity of which will be determined by the excess of truth over error they contain. For twenty-five centuries, this coming and going of philosophical ideas, this rising and falling of philosophical systems, this questioning and answering, only to be repeated by succeeding generations, has been a marked fact in human progress, and a proof of the instability of finite, and, consequently, imperfect thought.

To trace the births and deaths of philosophies, to ascend the heights and sink into the depths of the mysteries of speculative research, we deem necessary, since a knowledge of the attempts of philosophy will prepare us to understand both the approximate truth in it and the causes of its decline, to comprehend both its purpose and the failure of its realization. The task before us is not small, for in order to understand one system we must have a knowledge of all, and to comprehend the whole we must analyze its several parts. Like all things in human history, philosophy had its birthday, its birthplace; it had an individual character, and also a prophetic destiny. To Judea belongs the supreme honor of introducing, framing, and postulating a permanent religion; from Rome emerge in permanent form the principles of jurisprudence; the first alphabetic language acknowledges its paternity in the Phœnician mind; but none of these gave to the world the first *system* of philosophy. We say *system*, for long before a systematic philosophy appeared, there were in existence adumbrations of doctrines and ideas, the germs of philosophical thought, just as before the Christian religion was developed there were religious ideas in the world, and as before Roman law was enacted there were laws in human society, and as before a Phœnician alphabet was constructed there were spoken languages among men. Our search is not for adumbrations or germs, but systems, the formulated expression of consecutive inquiry, with definitely uttered beliefs, and integral and tangible results.

In the south of Europe is a small country, with sides indented by gulfs and bays, with its southern shore washed by a sea, with its interior partly punctuated by mountain peaks and partly flattened into plains, a country of classical renown and historic fame. To the student Greece is known as the birthplace of philosophy. Twenty-five hundred years ago, amid the roar of the echoing sea, and, perhaps, as an indigenous product of sea, sky, air, rock, mountain, and plain, the first genuine philosophic system was declared, from which, not in a regular, synthetic series, have all future systems sprung, but which was the beginning of all that followed. However far beyond the crude, insufficient, and materialistic inquiry of that period the world may have gone, and whatever were the originating influences of the philosophic impulse, certain it is that, going back six centuries before Christ among the Hellenes, we reach a *day-breaking epoch* in the history of the race. Original questions were then asked in a sincere philosophic form, and original answers were returned in an equally sincere philosophic manner. Hellenic philosophy was original philosophy, the birth-form of the philosophic idea, the visible setting up of an interrogation point on the highway of thought, the first exclamation of philosophic formalism. Brucker's attempt to find a primitive philosophic people before the Deluge is a failure. The Grecian mind is the exponent of philosophic inquiry.

In our inspection or analysis of these actual philosophies, the study of which can not fail to evoke special interest, we shall not find systems essentially complete, or in all cases exactly rational, for in its experimental or rudimentary stages, philosophy assumed singular and even grotesque forms, often declaring for axiomatic doctrines statements that afterward were abandoned. Nor were the Hellenic systems of philosophy, however distinct enough in their enunciations, related to one another by sympathetic bonds; that is, one was not necessarily the forerunner of another. They were not genealogical systems like father and son, the disciple sometimes projecting a philosophy from the standpoint of the teacher, as Parmenides developed the Eleaticism of Zenophanes, but sometimes it happened that the disciple rejected the system of his master, as Aristotle was charged with repudiating Platonism. The pre-Socratic schools did not follow in regular order, but several rose simultaneously, the dividing line often being indistinct. A walk from Thales to Aristotle, or from Zeno's porch to Plato's academy is not the making of perpendicular steps up a mountain side, getting nearer the summit with every step, but rather like a winding trail around the slope, now evidently making a forward movement, then descending toward the bottom again; now rising into the clear atmosphere that plays about great heights, then sinking into the shadows of cave-like crevices or dull forests; now seeing the philosopher on a run toward the top, then turning and gliding downward toward the abysses.

Simplicity characterizes the earliest betrayal of the philosophic spirit. There are no profound generalizations, no laborious gathering of facts from which inductive results issue; the philosophy is simple, based on one idea, or fact, or principle, instead of being an aggregation or combination of ideas and principles, distinguishing itself very markedly in this respect from the complex systems of Kant, Hegel, and Hamilton. However, complexity in philosophy is not a bad sign—it is the sign of an advance, that the shell is broken, and flight has commenced. The naïve simplicities, the one-idea systems of the Ionic philosophers, are a mark of childhood, a beginning, a promise of something to come.

The first philosophic inquiries were grounded in an attentive observation of the facts and forms of nature, or the activities, conditions, envelopments, and developments of the physical world. The external was the range of observation ; the objective, therefore, constituted the limitation of speculative analysis. Without doubt, climate, geographical environment, nature in form and force, subtly affects a people, tinging their civilization, influencing customs, institutions, literature, government, and religion. Buckle carries this to an extreme when he intimates that nature dictates the essentials of civilization, and that governments and religions are the products of physical suggestion and have no independent source. Evidently, however, the climatic or physical influence was felt more in earlier times than it is now in all the spheres of life ; man was in greater bondage to the elements, to the laws and changes of the physical world, than he is now. Not yet entirely free from natural influence, it is patent that, as he rises in the scale of intelligence, he subordinates nature to his will, and thinks independently of her presence. Theories, philosophies, and religions, grounded solely in the phenomena of nature, or the result of physical dictation, must be wanting in intellectual independence and spiritual tone. Logically, the first thinking of man would concern external things ; his problems would be physical problems ; historically, we find the first thinking *was* external, the first problems were physical. Philosophy is first external, afterward internal ; first material or physical, second intellectual or metaphysical. Materialism is the first product of philosophic thought, to be superseded by something different as the reflective faculties are opened and employed, and philosophic inquiry becomes subjective or internal. Materialism is infantile, the sign of childhood philosophy, a beginning ; internal thought is robust, the sign of intellectual emancipation, the forerunner of the culmination of philosophic inquiry. This distinction is true, as applied to modern as well as ancient philosophy. Modern materialism may be labeled childish quite as appropriately as Ionic philosophy, for the former has advanced in its logical conclusion not one cubit beyond the latter.

The naturalness of Ionic materialism, arising from climatic environment and the tendency of inquiry into external facts, is clearly demonstrated. We can not expect from the Grecian mind, in its incipient strugglings with original problems, any thing except *raw materialism*, a philosophy with a physical basis, a thinking grounded in empiricism, with corresponding implied negations of higher theological truth. Original philosophy is a climatic, geographical, sea-born, sky-infected, mountain-tinged, speculative hypothesis ; a philosophy, not the result of comparison, analysis, reason, but of the sight of the eyes, taking its color from the hues of the external world. An external, not an internal philosophy, it is; a sense-philosophy, not a reason-philosophy; a material, not an intellectual, philosophy. If we pronounce it the lowest grade of thought, a rudiment, it is because it begins in earthi. ness and settles in the supposed realities of natural phenomena.

In order easily to comprehend the course of philosophy, and to. avoid burdening the mind with a too minute classification of its varied forms, or indulging in manifold divisions and subdivisions, it may be divided into epochs or cycles, as follows:

I. The Ancient or Hellenic Epoch, beginning with Thales, and ending with the new academy. While some of the early philosophers were not born in Greece, among the number Thales himself, it is believed the generic title of the epoch will be received as sufficiently accurate and inclusive of all the sects and schools that arose in Europe and the islands in the vicinity of Greece prior to the Christian era. During this epoch philosophy appeared in the phases of materialism, idealism, empiricism, and skepticism, four marked and decisive developments that have their counterparts in the modern systems of speculative thought.

Justifiably, and according to custom, we exclude from considera. tion the mythologies and religions of the Roman Empire and the Eastern World, since in no true sense were they philosophies. Ram Chandra Bose, of India, will challenge this statement, but Hindu metaphysics are without recognition. Not even Grecian mythology is accorded a place in the history of Grecian philosophy. The Hindu religions, with their philosophical adumbrations, may be properly analyzed and studied as religions; so mythologies, as such, may be investigated and estimated. Philosophy, pure and distinct, neither mythology nor religion, interwoven with philosophy, is the object of this chapter.

For other reasons we exclude from historical consideration the uprising of Roman philosophy, which was legitimate enough in its sphere, and exercised a powerful effect on the public mind, undermining the public religion and aiding the introduction of Christianity into the empire. The Romans were borrowers; the poets, dramatic writers, historians, mathematicians, scientists, rhetoricians, sculptors and philosophers, were indebted to the Greeks for models, ideas, plans, plots, systems—every thing in the literary sense. No original philosophy emerges from Roman history. What we find is a duplication of Grecian thought, with little variation and no advanced suggestions. Lucretius, like Epicurus, denied immortality, and was a pantheist in his conception of nature. Even Cicero was in doubt as to the immortality of the soul, and regarded God as the soul of the world. A devout admirer of Plato, he should have accepted immortality and God as fundamental truths. Seneca is noted as the ethical Roman philosopher, but is not in advance of Socrates. Epictetus honored the conscience and taught the virtue of suicide; but this was not an improvement on Zeno, the Stoic. M. Aurelius Antoninus insisted on the purity of the conscience; Maximus Tyrius inclined to Platonism ; Galen was an Empiricist, attributing knowledge to experience.

In none of the Roman philosophers is there an original philosophic suggestion beyond what grew out of the Grecian systems. Separate recognition of their labors is, therefore, unnecessary.

II. The Interregnum, or Middle Epoch, a period of philosophic quietism, disturbed only by the appearance of Neo-Platonism, and still later by the suicidal theories of Scholasticism.

III. The Modern Epoch, embracing European, English, and American endeavors in the fields of inquiry.

As has been intimated, the Ionic sect of philosophers, headed by Thales, was the first to grapple with the problem of causality, applying the principle to nature in the belief that it was either self-caused or that one element or force of nature was the primal cause of all that exists. It is scarcely in point to introduce the theology of the Ionics who, believing in a self-centered, personal, eternal, infinite and absolute God, the father of all things, undertook to solve nature by nature, as one would explain history by history, or poetry by poetry, without robbing the Deity of any attribute or excellence. On being asked for a definition of God, Thales answered, "That which has neither beginning nor end;" in other words, he is the eternal, uncaused cause. Recognizing a divine principle if not a divine personalty, the "wise men" were not intentionally atheistic, though their systems are sentimentally atheistic. What they at bottom proposed to discover without complicating their systems or beliefs, and without involving divine power in the creative realm, was a causal principle of life, purely objective and material, in the physical world itself; a self-creating, self-propagating and self-sustaining power *in*, not outside of, nature. Committing themselves, *ab initio*, to this theory, they were confined in their searchings to physical origins, above which they did not think it important to go until a new sect contested the integrity of their theories and demanded another basis of investigation.

Thales, born B. C. 640, appears as the founder of the Ionic sect, and as such must be accepted as the first accredited philosopher in human history. Reported by Diogenes Laërtius, he was "the first to converse about natural philosophy," or the philosophy of nature, inquiring into its origin. A great traveler, having visited Egypt,

Phœnicia, Crete, and many other countries, observing forms of governments and systems of religion, he was prepared to formulate a philosophical belief which, being new and original and supported by his great learning, was received with favor by the multitudes, and made a channel for itself among those whose education was almost as liberal as his own.

What was the first genuine philosophic, oracular utterance? Nothing more, nothing less than that *water* is in some way the principal of life in the natural world, the acting substitutional cause of all existence or phenomena. It is the *prima materia*, to use a phrase of Lewes, of all things. In this we see the naturalness of the philosophy of Thales; it is climatic, maritime, the outbirth of the surrounding sea of gulfs, bays, rivers, mists, and rains. By what processes this dogmatic conclusion was reached, and with what boldness it was proclaimed as the explanation of the mystery of the universe, it is not important to inquire. Perhaps the philosopher discovered what no observer will deny, that moisture is essential to, or an accompaniment of, physical existence; that without it man, animal, plant, and leaf would perish; and then Thales concluded that, as it is a *condition* of life, it must therefore be the *principle* of life. The inner weakness of the philosophy is in the want of discrimination between condition and cause, between principles of life and the necessary supports of life, a failure that is made by Spencer as well as Thales. It is the philosophy of material conditions, not of causal principles; it is a *water-born*, not a rational, philosophic conjecture. It is *liquid* in antithesis to *dirt* philosophy, but kindred to it.

Equally materialistic, equally earth-born, a mere diversion from the original solution of Thales, and perhaps an inhalation of it, was the subsequent hypothesis of Anaximenes, who, in the calm of sincerity, proclaimed *air* to be the life-giving source of all things. This conclusion was deduced from the relation of the air to life. That which is essential to life must be the principle of life. So reasoned, if they reasoned at all, the ancestors of philosophy. Thales's is a sea-philosophy; Anaximenes's is a wind-philosophy; each was founded on observation, and a knowledge of some of the conditions of life; each was defective at the same point and in the same manner, namely: it attributed to matter an omnipotent, originating energy, the property of creative force, the original element of production.

The Ionics were led to cosmogonies; they interpreted the world by physiological principles, just as Buckle and Draper in our day interpret civilization; but neither the universe nor civilization yields to the interpretation. Natural philosophy alone is an insufficient explanation of either. One century after Thales, Pythagoras, the founder of the Italic sect, the forerunner of a new era, the champion of a new philosophy, appeared. Like Thales he was an extensive traveler; he was also devoted to the mathematical sciences, especially arithmetic and geometry; moreover, he was an ardent lover of music. Music and mathematics enter into his mystical philosophy. He held that the universe is the product of the harmonious co-operation of forces and factors, the harmony which he conceived to exist being expressed by the word *number*, which has confused those who have not inquired into its origin. Lewes asserts that Anaximander, who held to the abstract rather than the concrete, influenced Pythagoras; we believe he was as original as any Grecian philosopher, and a product of all his predecessors. He held to a mathematico-musical theory; mathematical in that proportion is strictly observed in the physical plan of the universe; musical in that concord, not antagonism, is the result. It differs from materialism in that it attributes no creative energy either to the mathematical or musical principle, but that both principles were observed in the building of the world; it suggests a plan of creation, with the Planner back of it, and is anti-materialistic. From this period or division in philosophy the real struggle for supremacy in speculative thought begins, and continues down the ages, assuming a variety of forms, and precipitating schools, systems, and sects, without number for investigation and analysis. Henceforth, philosophy is neither Thalic, *i. e*, wholly and intrinsically materialistic or physiological, nor Pythagorean, *i. e.*, mystical, musical, mathematical, but a *complex, self-clashing, dissolving, and surviving system or systems*, bordering at times on correct interpretations, and desperate at all times in its purpose to approach the truth.

Back from materialism, or nature, as if driven from it by a supernatural whirlwind of revelation, the Eleatics stood in defense of the one-sided thought that there is only one reality, which is *being*, and that it is the ground of all *not-being;* that the not-being is the phenomenal, without positive existence; that it is an appearance only, and must be referred to being. It is not clear that Zenophanes, the founder of this sect, meant by "being" the one true God, although he said, "all is one," and "God is the one." He certainly believed in one God, in opposition to the popular polytheism, which owed its origin to the theological poets, Homer and Hesiod, but he was more interested in philosophy than in theology, and concerned himself more with principles than personalities. The principle of being, and the non-existence of not-being, or the phenomenal world, characterized his thinking, and gave form to his philosophic utterances. This was an extreme reaction from the early materialism, and a midway departure from Pythagoreanism, which could not be maintained, since a denial of the existence of the physical world was sure to subject the philosophical systems built upon the denial to great wrenching, and the philosophers themselves to personal embarrassment. Yet was the new philosophy preferred to any thing that preceded it, and had it succeeded in reconciling itself to the not-being, or interpreting it in harmony with being, it had not so soon or readily dissolved, or lost its grip on the Grecian mind. Under Parmenides Eleaticism reached its highest development; and under Zeno it began to decline.

As exhibiting the tendency to mutation in philosophical study, we now consider another phase of materialism in the theory of Heraclitus, which, akin to the theories of the physiologists, did not appear until Pythagoreanism and Eleaticism had expressed themselves. It is a swing of the pendulum back to the starting-point. His fundamental principle was that of the *becoming*, the not-being, the phenomenal, which had been rejected by the Eleatics. "All is and is not," said the philosopher; " for though in truth it does come into being, yet it forthwith ceases to be." Nature is a *flux*, ever in motion, ever changing, like a river, and hence never the same. Zeno denied *motion*; Heraclitus rejected the theory of *rest* or inertia. The principle of nature is *fire*, self-enkindled and self-extinguished. Nature is always becoming but never is. From its ceaseless flow, nature is responsible to itself, and has within itself an acting or efficient cause in fire.

From this epoch of inquiry the philosophic struggle is simplified, being reduced to Eleaticism—*alias* idealism—on the one hand, and Heraclitic formalism, or realism, on the other; it comprehends the relation of the being and the not-being, and the possibility of their unity, or a common ground of interpretation. Whatever *revolutions subsequently occur in ancient philosophy are the resultant of the conflict of these two higher principles of speculative knowledge.* This is the dividing line, the battle-field of philosophy, viz. : the determination of the existence of being and non-being, and their relations, a modern as well as an ancient question, for Kant, Hamilton, Cousin, Comte, and others, have found the problem quite as perplexingly mysterious as did Parmenides and Heraclitus.

Philosophy, fastening its prongs in the *becoming*, i. e., the phenomenal, and returning to materialism, gravitated to a lower depth than at any previous time under the direction of Democritus (who had imbibed some atheistic conceptions from Leucippus), who sought to eliminate the causal principle from existence and the universe. Like other philosophers, he traveled extensively, laughing at every thing, as Heraclitus had wept over every thing, denying the evidence of the senses, and resolving historic events and natural phenomena into chance or accident. He gave prominence to what is known as the atomic theory, namely, that in ages past there were original atoms which by their own affinities were drawn toward one another, and by combinations, various and singular, the earth and every thing on it appeared. The atomic theory, though ancient, has tinctured the philosophy of the moderns, exhibiting itself in the motion-theory of Hobbes, and not remotely in the nerve-source of mental action, as advocated by Bain and Spencer. The philosophy entirely dispenses with an external power, or supervising intelligent force or principle; it banishes God from the universe, a result that the positivism of Comte announces with unhesitating constancy. This sepulchral philosophy came from one who lived in a tomb, proving that the philosophies of the ancients were suggested by, or took their form and color from their surroundings. Thales saw the sea, and lo! water is the first cause; Anaximenes breathed the air, and it is the principle of life; Heraclitus lived in a mountain, and the principle of the becoming, the solid, the phenomenal, is announced; Democritus inhabited a tomb, and the *philosophy of death* emanated and was accepted. This last was Thalism degenerated into atheism; it was a state philosophy in shrouds, decorated with flowers that bloom only in snows. To a greater depth philosophic thinking could not descend; indeed, its next movement must be upward, away from tombs, out into the world, up above the mountain, beyond air, cloud, sea, sky. Eleaticism ventured into the highest regions, but unfortunately it had but one wing; its flight was therefore circular, ill-balanced, one-sided, and it fell. Then, by a very natural process, it returned to original materialism, sinking deeper than ever in the darkness of its contemplations, until it was evident that it must have a resurrection into a better form, or perish in the tomb whence it came.

Afflicted, as it were, with a self-remorse which included a repentance of all past materialism and atheism, and weighed down with a consciousness of failure, it threw off its load, and announced a new career for itself. This came in the form of the philosophy of Anaxagoras, who, perceiving marks of design in nature, concluded that it was not self-originative, but that it had a governing and order-arranging νους or mind, without which, whether it was personal or not, the universe was impossible. He was not an Eleatic in that he believed both in the being and the non-being, and associated them together, not in the act of creation but in the act of arrangement, or methodizing nature. The *nous* in philosophy, whether it was divine, or had personation in being, or only represented an unconscious intellectual process and order, was so far in advance of the materialism of Thales, the number-theory of Pythagoras, the being of Zenophanes, the becoming of Heraclitus, and the chance theory of Democritus, that it was the sign of day in Greece.   Before him no one had discovered the teleological principle in nature, nor did he himself carry it, as Paley did centuries afterward, to its logical termination of establishing the existence of a Designer.   Believing in God, he did not employ the philosophy of the *nous* in the vindication of a theistic faith, but turned it over to his successors.

Still, considering the fluctuations of philosophic thought in two centuries, the flowing and ebbing of inquiry, the development and retrogression of speculative truth from Thales to Anaxagoras, it is gratifying that it progressed even so far as from water to *nous*, from matter to mind, as the controlling principle and informing power, substance, and cause, in the universe.   This is the result of the first period, commonly called pre-Socratic, of Grecian philosophy, which, concerning itself chiefly with nature, and yet with ultimate facts and principles, advanced, through mutations many and serious, to a final assertion in Anaxagoras.   Beginning in cosmological conceptions, vibrating to unsafe forms of idealism, and then sinking into the abysses of atheism, it rises, glorified in the principle, if not personality, of mind—this is progress, not regular, methodical progress, but in its final form an advance.   And this unsettling and settling, this series of downward and upward step-taking, occurs within two centuries, preparing the Grecian mind for a rapid and a still higher flight into regions whose boundaries are not space and time, and in which philosophy may find the sole center, the infinite substance, the first cause—*God.*

But the first period did not close with Anaxagoras.   Between him and those who introduced a more decisive ethical and dialectical form of thought appeared the Sophists, a class of men renowned for their learning, but not exactly philosophic in their genius or attainments ; wise, shrewd, intellectual, apparently discursive, but superficial, after all, in the treatment of the grave problems of life.   Protagoras held that " man is the measure of all things," a doctrine that Plato annihilated ; Gorgias, an Eleatic in principle, talked of nature as the non-existent ; Hippias and Prodicus, men of wonderful mathematical and grammatical attainments, defended their master with singular plausibility, but were always defeated by Plato.

The Sophists mark a period in the speculative thought of Greece. They influenced the culture and contributed to the learning of the age, preparing it for the subtle and transparent polemics of the Socratic philosophers who soon appeared.   Learned as they were, they yet denied the truths of physical science or natural philosophy, supporting the denials with evasive and sophistical arguments, which enhanced their reputation for dialectical skill and wisdom. But the imputations they cast upon science precipitated a period in which the affirmations of science had a hearing.

The *second period* of Hellenic philosophy signalized its advent by an immediate break with the first, making use only of its facts, but ignoring its conclusions. Cousin, setting aside the first period, assigns to Socrates the position of founder of ancient philosophy. Back of him he finds no genuine philosophic discernment, no philosophic guidance, through the mysteries of thought. He dates ancient philosophy with the birth of Socrates. In this he forgets the history of philosophy, which can not be thus ignored. However, the Socratic spirit is the only genuine philosophic spirit in the ancient world; from it alone has come the highest philosophic form.

*Natural* philosophy preceded Socrates; he investigated it, affirmed its truth, and then went beyond; he introduced *moral philosophy*, finally eschewing astronomy, geometry, and the whole brood of sciences, as sufficient for man, preferring a philosophy that had for its base moral truth, rather than physical fact. The first period was essentially physical, materialistic, atheistic; the second period was ethical, sentimental, intellectual. Neither the laws of nature nor the origin of nature—not the facts, forms, or methods of nature—did Socrates seek to know, but moral ideas, moral principles, which may be applied to civil government, the family institution, and human society. Hitherto there had been no application of philosophy to society, the family, the State, partly because it was in its infancy, but more especially because it was barren of ethical principles. Without moral ideas it could suggest nothing to rulers, legislators, parents, or the individual. This weakness of the pre-Socratic schools Socrates discovered; and, abjuring the old scientific philosophies, he invested inquiry with a new and practical interest, going about bareheaded and barefooted in the streets of Athens, and teaching in the shops and market-places the highest moral duties, and man's relation to his fellow-man. The materialists spoke of nature; Socrates spoke of man. Cosmogony characterizes the one; psychology the other. The personality of man, the immortality of the soul, human responsibility, the duties of reciprocity, the love of justice, the practice of virtue, outward, if not inward, holiness, constituted the tenets of the Socratic system, so far forth as he was the author of a system. This implies self-knowledge, a knowledge of mind, a knowledge of God, all of which he taught by the dialectic method of question and answer, impressing moral truth in its wholeness upon the conscience of his age, and lifting it out of the slough of materialism.

According to Diogenes Laertius, Socrates would say there is only one good—namely, knowledge; and only one evil—namely, ignorance. Socrates laid the foundations; Plato built the superstructure. Ethical was Plato; theological also. The pre-Socratics studied nature; Socrates, man; Plato, man and God. Progressive stages, these, but the highest development is in Plato, as he not only includes nature and man, but comprehends to a degree the divine character and the method of divine working. Platonism, whether a system or fragmentary ideas is intended, is the summit of ancient philosophy; all other philosophies, however related to it, are beneath it, being less comprehensive and less divine.

Aristotle, the pupil of Plato, and teacher of Alexander, founded the Lyceum, or peripatetic school of philosophers, which accepted the Platonic theory of ideas in outline, but obtained them differently, and made a different use of them. With Plato human ideas had their source in the mind's free activity; with Aristotle they are the product of sensations. With the one their origin is inward; with the other, their origin is outward. Plato advocated innate ideas; Aristotle, empirical or sensational ideas. Plato began with ideas and proceeded to facts, as their symbols or exponents, deducting and constructing systems or principles, while Aristotle gathered the facts and then inferred the principles. By this method of investigation Aristotle finally developed the method of inductive reasoning, which established his fame forever. A trained mind will reason inductively; long before Aristotle induction was an intellectual habit, but he formulated it into a system, declaring its laws and giving form and direction to intellectual pursuits. This was the dialectical fruit of his study.

In the physical department of philosophy he was quite as rigid as, and perhaps more penetrating than, Plato, for he reduced the universe to four primary principles, viz.: matter, form, efficient cause, and end. Ethically, he was not as discursive or as rational as Plato, though he regarded man as a "political animal," and taught that the institutions of the family, society, and government should be maintained upon the basis of righteousness and in the interest of the race.

It would not be unprofitable to contrast these three philosophers of the second period of ancient philosophy; they resembled and differed from one another, and were actuated by one purpose, weaker in Socrates, stronger in Plato, to ascertain the unascertained answers to ultimate inquiry. Socrates was the street and conversational philosopher; Plato the academic and dialogue philosopher; Aristotle the prose-writing and voluminous philosopher. In the measure of their influence Socrates and Plato were chiefly Hellenic or national, being inspired with a love of country, while Aristotle was cosmopolitan or universal, regarding mankind as of more consequence than the Grecians alone. Socrates taught for his age; Plato for his country; Aristotle for the world. Socrates was the ethico-practical philosopher, the persuasive moralist; Plato was the idealist, not such as Parmenides, whose idealism, excluding the phenomenal, defeated itself, but such as comprehended being and not-being in their correlations and ultimate and hidden sources; Aristotle was the empirical philosopher, seeking solutions by an entirely different method.

Plato and Aristotle, bent on one achievement, so differed in method of procedure, representation of thought, and style of expression that the opinion prevailed that Aristotle was an antagonist of the Platonic system. Plato was a poetically expressing philosopher; Aristotle, discarding and even condemning poetic dress, introduced passionless prose to his readers. Plato indulged in imaginative flights, soaring toward the sun, while Aristotle preferred to burrow toward the center of the earth. Both were sincere, both contributed to the cultivation of the philosophic spirit.

Like the first, the second period of Grecian philosophy ends better than it began, though its commencement constitutes the brightest epoch in Grecian speculative endeavor, none of the succeeding philosophers rivaling in genius, research, philosophic acumen and illumination this triad of teachers—Socrates, Plato, and Aristotle. In truth, ancient philosophy had in these representatives its culmination of greatness, for they gave to the world independently, and yet in a sense connectedly, systems of logic, physics, natural theology, jurisprudence, and individual morality, that succeeding ages have not improved, and which may be studied to-day with no little advantage by students of humanity and worshipers of God.

As from the first to the second period of Grecian culture was an ascending movement, so from the second to the third is a descending movement, in respect both to the character and ability of the philosophic teachers, and to the vitality and duration of the systems they inaugurated. Stoicism, the first system of the post-Aristotelian epoch, had for its founder Zeno, who was an empirical psychologist, teaching the doctrine, inherited from Aristotle, that knowledge is derived from the senses, and so contradicting the idea-philosophy of Platonism. The Stoics had the reputation of being great scholars and ingenious reasoners; but, theologically, they taught that matter was pre-existent, and God merely organized it into worlds; and, ethically, they dictated no higher code than that of nature. They had ideas of what constituted the supreme good; they believed in virtue in general, were insensible to pain, and applauded heroism, or courage in bearing evil, as the highest duty of man. Zeno committed suicide.

Thus Stoicism was a degeneracy, compared dialectically, ethically, and theologically, with Platonism.

Nor was Epicureanism, a simultaneous philosophy, originated by Epicurus, any better; rather has it fewer commendable features. It is said by Rollin that the Epicureans were the only natural philosophers of Greece; that they pursued science methodically, and sought to ascertain the facts of nature and systematize them; but the historian's statement is too sweeping. The science of Epicurus is atomic and atheistic. To be sure, he avowed faith in God, but denied that he exercised any paternal care over men, or had any interest in the affairs of this world—a theological view no better than atheism itself. He revived the atomic theory of the universe, elaborated by Democritus, and dispensed with a Creator.

Accepting the sensational philosophy of the Stoics as a correct theory of knowledge, he went beyond them in the declaration that men see things as they are, the senses in no case deceiving or misrepresenting. For instance, the moon, he said, is no larger than it seems, and every thing is as it seems to us.

Ethically, while Cleanthus, speaking for the Stoics, had said, "Pleasure is not an end of nature," Epicurus announced that pleasure is the supreme good, and made it the measure of human activity and morality. He denied the immortality of man, and rejected the doctrine of responsibility.

Theologically, philosophically, ethically, Epicureanism descended to the lowest depths. Its value has not been demonstrated. In what the supreme good consisted, whether in virtue, as the Stoics chanted, or in pleasure, as the Epicureans declared, was not only the line of difference between the two sects, but it also became the inquiry, and, therefore, the actual spirit of the post-Aristotleian philosophy. Other questions, such as man's nature, and his relation to the infinite and the phenomenal, received occasional attention, but the absorbing theme was not the ultimate of things, nor the ground of existence, but how to make existence comfortable and happy. Hence, one reads of the pleasure-seeking, the luxury-loving spirit, and the voluptuousness of the Epicureans. Epicurean philosophy was the philosophy of pleasure, amusement, jollification, eating and drinking, and proposed to introduce an era of good feeling, fellowship, and hospitality among men. This being the end of philosophy, it was fitting to paint the scene of a barbecue at the entrance of its temple, and make it the symbol of its purpose. From Plato to Epicurus is a stepping out of the study into the dining-room, a going from the writing-desk to the table, an exchange of books for vegetables and meats. This is a supreme and fatal degeneracy.

Nor is it surprising that, with Stoicism on the one hand, and Epicureanism on the other, mongrel systems of philosophy, some based on doubt, others without any discoverable basis, should arise, and that the Athenian mind, once united on Plato, should now be divided and shivered into fragments. The ancient academy is no longer in the ascendant, but Pyrrho steps forth, announcing as a leading principle of philosophy the necessity of *indifference* to all things, to all philosophies, theories, governments, and religions. Not being certain of any thing, he neither affirmed nor denied; he held to no opinion, considering it probably, as Plato phrases it, a "sacred disease." This is skepticism reduced to a science. Pyrrhonism passed for a philosophy.

Skepticism, or the denial of certainty in knowledge, was the organic doctrine of the new academy, under the leadership of Arcesilaus and his successors. The third period of Greek philosophy, beginning with sensuous experience as the capital doctrine or central fact of both Stoicism and Epicureanism, descends into a denial of sense-knowledge, then of all knowledge, and, finally, of all truth.

Having traced original philosophic inquiry through its three stages of development, we find the salient doctrine, or *esprit de corps*, of each to be: 1. That of the first period, *materialism*; 2. That of the second, *idealism*; 3. That of the third, *empiricism*, ending in radical skepticism.

From this bird's-eye view of the ancient struggle, the rise and fall of philosophy, it is seen that modern philosophy has not only combated the questions that disturbed the Hellenic mind, but also has essayed their solution from the same standpoints of materialism, idealism, and empiricism, and therefore has made essentially very little progress.

What followed the Hellenic forms of philosophic thought? In other words, what were the results of that fermenting period of inquiry and speculation? What systems, if any, were carried over into the Christian era, and embodied themselves in the civilization, literature, and moral progress of mankind? Or did any survive the wreck of the general break-up of Grecian life? To one who has hoped for permanent things from that original period, the fact of the decadence of nearly every school of thought and every system of philosophy is painful, and he looks over the weary waste of the great struggle with a mournful interest and a deep sympathy of regret. Save the better part of Platonism and the dialectics of Aristotle, very little of absolute worth has been transmitted from that pre-Christian epoch to our day. Intensely acute as was the Grecian mind, it must also be said that it failed to perpetuate the philosophic spirit in the race; its own philosophy died without immediate succession or issue. It had no heirs and left its estate in the tomb. Cousin writes that the Socratic spirit survived for ten centuries, but it then disappeared in the mysticism of Neoplatonism. For nearly sixteen centuries the philosophic impulse was quiet; no great questions, save those of religion and sectarian forms, agitated the public mind; wars were numerous, dividing history into eras; the people sank into darkness, and an interregnum, so to speak, prevailed in the philosophic realm from Christ to Bacon.

Of this *interregnum,* or *middle epoch,* we shall now speak. To us it seems a misfortune that during the rise of the Church the intellectual giants of Southern Europe, seizing the philosophic truths of Plato and Aristotle, did not appropriate them to the service of religion; but the world seemed shut up as in a cave, the people were like fishes without eyes; and so the long roll of centuries passed before the philosophic spirit returned. However, let us not be understood as implying that no attempts were made anywhere or by any one for the revival of interest in the themes formerly discussed by the Greek academicians; there were inquiries, but they were sporadic; speculations, but without majesty; and an occasional philosophy, but it ended in mysticism or religious eccentricity.

Neoplatonism, or Alexandrian mysticism, arising in the third century through the dialectical theology of Plotinus, was an attempt to revive Platonism, or to unite Greek philosophy and Christianity; but it either added or subtracted so much from both that the result was a mystical religion and an indefinable philosophy. It proposed visions and miracles on the one side, and abstraction and Platonic platitude on the other. It espoused inspiration as a possible experience; extra mental illumination, spiritual ecstasy, and absorption for the time into the life of the Deity, constituted one of its doctrinal points; it was somewhat of a religion and somewhat of a philosophy, but exclusively neither.

Cousin affirms that it was the final assertion of Greek philosophy, in which form it expired, Justinian closing the schools of philosophy in Athens, A. D. 529; but it is not evident which produced it, Christianity or Platonism. In our judgment, Greek philosophy terminated, not in mysticism, but in skepticism, as we have shown. It expired, not by contact with religion, but by descending into nothingness. For three hundred years Neoplatonism swayed the East, but arraying itself against Christianity, it at last decayed and perished.

Centuries now pass without mental quickening, or illumination of the grave Hellenic problems; no one asks questions, no answers are framed. Finally the sluggish mind of man is stirred, not to any great depth, but it is stirred. Scotus Erigena, standing on the edge of the ninth century and looking backward, perceived the merit of Neoplatonism, and, appropriating it, he sought to combine it with Christianity and present to the world both a new religion and a new philosophy. But Christianity, true to its inner life, refused to enter into any combination, and especially to suffer Neoplatonization. Whatever religious kinship there was between them, the one was stiff in death, while the other was the vital force of mankind; hence, no partnership, no union, doctrinal or otherwise, was contracted.

Nearly two centuries pass, and Anselm is born, A. D. 1035. A new era is at once apparent. Philosophical palpitations characterize the three succeeding centuries. Scholasticism, inaugurated by Anselm, is perpetuated by such rare minds as Thomas Aquinas, Duns Scotus, John of Salisbury, Roger Bacon, and others, exciting enthusiasm in the Church, and reviving the philosophic spirit in society. It was a type of Christian philosophy, not a Platonic religion. Hitherto the Church had been engrossed with theology, the refutation of errors, the settlement of doctrines, but the time was fully ripe for the consideration of analytic thought. Intense as were the schoolmen, they erred in the following manner: John of Salisbury, discarding speculative thought, raised the standard of *utility* as the measure of all things; Thomas Aquinas, most learned and devout, exalted the *understanding* above the moral sense; Duns Scotus, a profound reasoner, exalted the *will* as the instrument of character, and all affirmed the explanation of divine truth by rational and even dogmatic processes. The unity of faith and knowledge, or the scientific apprehension of supernatural mysteries, was the backbone idea of scholasticism; but it was not strong enough to support either philosophy or religion. Its persistence was its destruction. It developed into nominalism, or the application of names, denying realities and realism, or the affirmation of objective realities. With William of Occam, the latest and strongest schoolman who espoused nominalism in its most radical form, scholasticism ceased to exist as an independent or systematic philosophy.

Thus ended the interregnum.

As great movements in nature, such as earthquakes and revolutions or reformations in history, are frequently preceded by outward and anticipatory signs, so the *modern epoch of philosophy*, fruitful in philosophic experiments, was preceded by signs of preparation, and was at length precipitated by an exhibition of the scientific spirit. Usually, the religious spirit has preceded philosophic speculation, and has often followed it, either in mysticism or some other form; modern philosophy was introduced by the scientific spirit, which has pervaded, and even dictated, the philosophic course, materializing, corrupting, and undermining it.   Scholasticism extinct, a love of letters revived, America was discovered, and a new interest in the natural sciences was generated; but the intellectual activity of the period revived also a genuine philosophic purpose.   Francis Bacon, born A. D. 1561, reported himself as the apostle of a new era by submitting new methods of reasoning and inciting a spirit of investigation such as had never been felt by man.   Partaking of the scientific spirit of Roger Bacon, the schoolman, he plunged into the work of original discovery, adopting as guiding principles the following: 1. Abandonment of the past in so far as to reject its influence; he declined to be prejudiced by ancient teachings, or enter upon investigation with preconceived views.   2. He affirmed that knowledge is the result of experience. 3. He reinstated the inductive method of reasoning which had been handed down from Socrates, Plato, and Aristotle, but which had been obscured and ignored by the schoolmen.

An intellectual quickening was the result; love of knowledge and a scientific eagerness dominated the public mind.   In a much less degree, but with a similar purpose, Jacob Boehme was arousing the German mind from a scientific and philosophic lethargy, preparing it for an upheaval, a revolution, indeed; yea, more, for that patient study of the greatest problems in philosophy which has distinguished that country down to this day.

Let it not be supposed, however, from their relation to modern thought, that either Bacon or Boehme was the founder of modern philosophy.   Lord Verulam, it is true, was the instrumental inspirer of the intellectual life of modern times, on which account it is almost like robbing him of a well-earned glory to assign the beginning of the philosophic epoch to a later period, and to name another thinker as its founder.   Yet Bacon was not a philosopher; he was a scientist, an investigator of physical facts, formulating no philosophic system, and leaving none to the generations following.   Like Magellan, who, beholding the broad Pacific, did not venture to navigate it, Bacon may have cast his eye over the philosophic sea, but he did not sail on its waters; he clung to earth, its facts, realities, laws, and forces.

Fifty years later, Descartes, a Frenchman, assumed a philosophic attitude and indulged in philosophic utterances which history justly acknowledges as the beginning of modern speculative thought, the tracing of which through its manifold stages of development, its obscurities and transparencies, its orthodoxies and heterodoxies, its materialism and idealism, must now engage our attention.   Admitting that other classifications are possible, we propose to consider modern philosophy under the following general heads, without subdivisions: 1. Dualism; 2. Spinozism; 3. Empiricism; 4. Common-sense Truism; 5. Idealism; 6. Emotionalism; 7. Pessimism; 8. Positivism; 9. Rationalism; 10. Evolution; 11. Ideal Realism; 12. Theologic Dogmatism; 13. Christian Philosophy.

With this outline before us, and remembering what is beyond it, we exclaim with the poet, only changing the view to philosophy—

> "But these attained, we tremble to survey
> The growing labors of the lengthened way;
> The increasing prospect tires our wandering eyes,
> Hills peep o'er hills, and Alps on Alps arise."

Descartes, imbibing the Baconian spirit of indifference to the past, intensified it to absolute doubt of all teaching, a phase of Pyrrhonism justified by the solemn and sublime purpose that dictated it. The starting-point of investigation is *doubt.* Accept nothing, not for skeptical ends, but for truth's sake. Yet was this rather an incidental than an essential principle. It was not the end, only the beginning of philosophy; it was not the result of, but an inducement to, inquiry.

Beginning thus, Descartes faithfully and laboriously took up the great problems of philosophy; viz., matter, mind, knowledge, and God, wrestling with the difficulties that inhered in the problems themselves, and declaring certain principles to be fundamental to their solution. The famous philosophic apothegm, *"Cogito, ergo sum,"* he originated, and insisted upon its sufficiency and authority in the discussion of the problem of existence. From the power to think, from thinking as a distinct act, he inferred existence. He did not see that, reversing the proposition, the truth he meant to convey would have been declared in a statelier and more logical form. Thought is proof of existence, says Descartes; *existence is proof of thought,* say we. He believed in both; he believed in matter and being, distinguishing them as follows: the essence of matter is extension, the essence of mind is thought. The Cartesian definitions and discriminations, subjected to keen analysis, required modification before they could be accepted; but the destructive weakness of the system was the interpretation of the relation, or rather non-relation, of the two substances, as he designated mind and matter. They exist without the possibility of interaction or mutual influence; the mind does not influence the body, the body affects not the mind. This is dualism, the corner-stone of modern philosophy, the first product of the modern philosophic spirit.

Himself undisturbed by the dualistic conclusion, the pupils and successors of Descartes, recognizing that mediation between the two distinct, non-interacting substances was a necessity, undertook to affect it. Geulinex and Malebranche, especially, espying the inconsistency of dualism, were greatly exercised to bring about a reconciliation, and at last affirmed that the interacting union of mind and matter is possible with God.

Vulnerable as is the Cartesian philosophy from its dualism, it is clear in its enunciation of the difference between thought and matter, or being and not-being; but, striking the difference, it did not solve the problem of existence, it really added difficulties to the solution.

Spinoza appeared A. D. 1632, a man destined to exert a potential influence in philosophy, but who did not succeed even as well as Descartes, in the settlement of the problem of being. He agreed with Descartes in interpreting God as the infinite substance, with this difference: Descartes interpreted God to be a personal being; Spinoza pronounced God to be the universe. Spinozism is pantheism, or as Jacobi said, it is fatalism and atheism. The belief in one infinite substance, as the source of all things, is Christian in form, but its interpretation is the essence of atheism. Of this one substance Spinoza affirmed that mind and matter are mere accidents; that is, they are not the properties but the emanations of the one substance, as according to the nebular hypothesis, the worlds are the emanations of one central orb. The dualism of Descartes was thus swallowed up in the monism of Spinoza, which was unsatisfactory in the extreme. Dualism was not a solution; hence, it was unsatisfactory. Spinozism was a solution; but it was even more unsatisfactory than dualism, for it contained the worst elements, namely, pantheism, atheism, and fatalism; while dualism recognized mind and matter as essentially distinct, and God as infinite mind, as absolute personality. In the hands of Spinoza philosophy came to a standstill, if it did not retrograde into a barbarism.

The year that gave Spinoza to the world also witnessed the birth of John Locke, who early appeared as an investigator and original thinker. Descartes incited him to thought; Spinoza, being contemporaneous, did not affect him. His mission was to consider the mind, its original constitution, the laws of thought, and the sources of knowledge, and, devoting himself most carefully to these inquiries, he embodied the results in his famous essay on the "Human Understanding." As a starting-point Mr. Locke held, contrary to Plato, that there are no innate ideas, that the mind at birth is a void, a blank space, a *tabula rasa*, containing nothing, originating nothing. It is a receiver of impressions and ideas, not an originator of thought. It derives all it knows from without; it *knows nothing of itself.* Sensation is the source of knowledge. Subsequently driven by unanswerable criticism into a philosophic relenting, he added reflection, as a means of knowledge, but the materials for reflection he insisted sensation or experience furnished, so that he drifted into an empirical, realistic, and materialistic philosophy.

Respecting being, his sensationalism logically compelled a denial of all knowledge of the divine substance, or the character of God. How different this from the dualism of Descartes and the monism of Spinoza! Descartes interprets mind and matter in their differentiation; Spinoza, in their pantheistic unity; Locke estimates mind as 'a substance without quality, subordinated in its activities to foreign influence, *i. e.*, to external impression. Descartes denies all interaction; Spinoza merges interaction into unity of action; Locke denies to mind independent action, but allows it an externally forced activity. Both dualism and monism are perplexingly mysterious; sensationalism is a transparent dogmatism. While Locke's theory of mind has been exploded, and although Morell characterizes his philosophy as ephemeral, it is indisputable that it has had a marked influence on the philosophic thought of two centuries. Not upon dualism or Spinozism, but upon Locke's empiricism, philosophic systems have been reared which exist to-day, contaminating speculative thought and reducing all inquiry to the level of materialism. Hume, taking up Locke's theory, fashioned a skeptical philosophy whose influence has been pernicious to the last degree. If sensation is the source of knowledge, then knowledge is mere impression, it is not a mental reality; and, reasoning after the manner of Berkeley, who denied reality to matter, he virtually denied reality to mind. This was the outcome of the philosophy of Locke, a skepticism that was followed in due time and inevitably by all the consequences natural to it, as looseness in morals, a decline of the doctrine of human responsibility, and an abandonment of religious belief and rules.

The greatest mischief, as the logical result of empiricism, occurred in France, expressing itself in a variety of theories, but all ended in the maelstrom of naked materialism. For instance, Condillac, denying that the sources of knowledge are sensation and reflection, reduced them to one and became the founder of the school of sensualism; Helvetius became the apostle of altruism; Diderot disposed by logical processes of morality and God; La Mettrie overthrew faith in the immortality of the soul; and so philosophy, instead of lifting man up to the knowledge of the one substance which had been proclaimed by Descartes and even pantheistically represented by Spinoza, degenerated into a skepticism that well-nigh ruined a nation and threatened the submergence of the Christian faith in its downfall.

This realism, eventuating in skeptical disaster, could not long prevail. It was a negativism; the mind requires affirmation. Reaction was inevitable.

Empiricism, or Locke's theory of knowledge, was formidably antagonized by Reid, a Scottish philosopher, who, adopting the psychological method, not only counteracted the dangerous tendencies of sensationalism, but prepared the way for the idealism that followed. Locke, having declared that the "mind knows not things immediately, but by the intervention of the ideas it has of them," Reid proceeded to show the contrary, namely, that our perceptions are not dependent upon intermediate ideas, but are immediate. This he established by the facts of consciousness, or the common sense of the race, which in his judgment weighed more than the most brilliant abstraction. The term "common sense" has, therefore, been applied to his philosophy, as embracing intuitions, beliefs, spontaneous convictions, the universal judgments of men. Whether the philosophy itself is sound or not, it was a step in the right direction, since it negatived empiricism. It was also Socratic in spirit in that it rested on a psychological birthright to authority. Dugald Stewart, possibly more learned than Reid, amplified and classified the philosophy of "common sense," but really originated no independent philosophy. Brown antagonized Reid, and Abercrombie was more of a critic of all philosophic ideas than a philosopher. Reid stands at the head of Scottish philosophers, with weaknesses that later schools have detected. He did not quite annihilate empiricism.

Another period was at hand; it had dawned with the dawning of sensationalism in the idealism of Leibnitz, but did not attain meridian strength until Kant, Fitche, Schelling, and Hegel had applied their master forces to its development. Over against the empiricism of Locke, Hume, and others, idealism appeared, contesting the right of dominion in the realm of philosophy. As in the past, so now, the contests in philosophy have been chiefly between these two schools, empiricism and idealism, which will continue until a higher philosophy appears which shall supersede both.

It is conceded that on the whole, Germany, beginning with Leibnitz, furnishes for more than one century the leading philosophic minds of the world. Heine says the English control the sea, the French the land, the Germans the air; hence, metaphysics and moral philosophy in Germany.

Leibnitz was born A. D. 1646, fourteen years later than Locke and Spinoza, and, detecting the vulnerability of monism, he at once assailed it. He held to the individuality of mind, a vague conception of the personality of God, and the separate substance of matter. Pantheism he rejected as violative of faith in the immortality of the soul.

His cosmological views separated him still more from Spinoza, and placed him upon the pedestal of an independent thinker. His cosmology was a monadology, the theory of monads applied to the interpretation of the universe. Such was the apparent resemblance between the atomic theory of Democritus and the monadology of Leibnitz that the latter was compelled to frame a definition of the monad, or endow it with properties and functions which did not inhere in original atoms. Accordingly, each monad is distinguished by its individuality, independence, and unlikeness to every other monad : the atoms of Democritus were uniform in size, form, function, and appearance. This is a broad distinction, but not so broad as that which, allowing the atom to be potentially active, conferred on the monad the properties of soul, making it a self-subsistent, normal substance and an intelligent, acting reality. The monad is a soul. While this monadic idealism is not free from objection, it accomplished much toward the cancellation of Spinozism. It, therefore, had a mission. Monadism resisted, if it did not overthrow, monism.

Monadism, however, is not the height of idealism. George Berkeley, an Irish philosopher, reveling in the transcendentalism of his own genius, became infatuated with the idea that he was to reveal a new principle in philosophy, and, by a singular dialectic process, plunged the theorists into the wildest antagonisms, and imperiled some well-established conclusions of philosophy. By a course of reasoning plausible, apposite, and captivating, he arrived at the conclusion that the natural or phenomenal world does not exist, that it is an illusion, a mere appearance—a doctrine not new, since the Eleatics, especially Parmenides, and the Sophists, had rejected the existence of matter—but the argument was new, and the world was agitated. The other half of his principle, that mind alone exists, led to the exaltation of man's character, and the glorification of the eternal Spirit ; but, as a principle, it is as defective as that of the Eleatics, and could not be sustained. Hume, employing Berkeley's argument, soon demonstrated the non-existence of mind, a conclusion more dangerous than, but as logical as, that of the non-existence of matter. To such irrational conclusions did philosophical speculation conduct the speculators. Evidently, idealism had not reached its culmination, and waited for a truer exponent and defender.

In the appearance of Kant idealism had a protagonist of profound wisdom, a thinker of acute understanding, and a framer of an original philosophical view of existence, and its various problems. Hume's conclusion aroused the philosophical spirit in him. He began to question the power of reason ; he examined it as one would an instrument, and sought to ascertain its relation to the problems of Hume, Berkeley, and Descartes. What is the range or content of the reason? What are the limitations, if any, to rational conception? Fundamentally, Kant held that the world can not be known, since space and time intervene; what he calls the "thing-in-itself," *i. e.*, the substance or reality of things, we can not know, but only phenomena and their relations. This principle of necessary limited knowledge, though fundamental to the Kantian creed, and its greatest weakness, for it virtually abandons the chief end of philosophy, namely, the search for the *noumenon*, is not permitted, with evident inconsistency, to interfere with the successful attempt of the practical reason to demonstrate one ultimate cause, and all other truths of theology or philosophy. Reason has two hemispheres, or cerebral functions; the one he calls Pure or Theoretical Reason, which, subtle, penetrating, and exceedingly sensitive to the presence of thought, is yet unable to establish the immortality of the soul, the moral freedom of man, or the existence of God. In his "Critique of Pure Reason," his greatest work, after showing that pure reason deals with three ideas, or the greatest in philosophy; viz., the psychological, the cosmological, and the theological, he confesses that the ideas are unsustained by Pure Reason; that is, that while the contents of Pure Reason are these ideas, it will not vindicate them, because it abounds in antinomies and paralogisms, and the ideas themselves have, therefore, not a constitutional authority, but only a regulative force. This is not going over to Locke's denial of innate ideas, but it is in that direction, from which, however, Kant himself recoiled. His real estimate of these ideas is seen in the demonstrating power of the Practical Reason, which vindicates them beyond successful assault from any quarter. The Pure Reason is the "nay" of Kant; the Practical reason the "yea" and "amen." By the one the indemonstrableness of the greatest truths is apparent; by the other their demonstration is self-evident, clear, and convincing. A close examination, however, of the two reasons, does not satisfy us that they exist, or, existing, that a philosophy can possibly be maintained upon both. The universal consciousness of the race furnishes no testimony in proof of their existence, nor is it possible in psychological classification to assign definite functions to two kinds of reason. If two reasons, why not two memories, two imaginations, two wills, two consciences? Besides, admitting the two reasons, the Pure ought to be the stronger, unfallen, unbiased reason, while the Practical ought to be the fallen, imperfect, and, therefore, unsafe and inconclusive reason. But Kant insists that the Pure, or stronger reason, is the infirm, unhealthy, self-contradicting reason, unable to vindicate its own ideas, while the fallen, Practical reason is able to demonstrate the highest truth. This is the essence of antinomy itself. Far preferable is Cousin's division of the reason into intuitional or spontaneous, and reflective or voluntary, the value of which for theological or philosophical purposes he defines clearly and satisfactorily. By the spontaneous reason God is immediately and universally recognized, since it is absolute reason which is in harmony with God. Spontaneous reason is theistic, concluding reason. It is reliable because intuitional. Reflective reason is somewhat uncertain.

Guilty of bad and unwarrantable distinctions as he was, Kant was not one-sided, as was Berkeley ; nor skeptical, as was Hume ; nor monadic, as was Leibnitz ; nor dualistic, as was Descartes ; nor pantheistic, as was Spinoza ; but his subjective idealism was orthodoxically rational in its intent, looking toward the infinite with the eye of a quickened, rational judgment, and inspired rational research with the promise of reward. Great was the immediate influence of the Kantian philosophy ; it is great still, though its positions are undergoing modification, and a gradual change of base in inquiry is apparent.

Not long after Kant, philosophy assumed a new phase, not in contradiction of Kant, but in advance of it—a kind of tangent from the circle of thought in which the thinkers had moved, bringing them to a pause, if nothing more. Jacobi heralded a new revelation, and claimed that he had found the true path to ultimate knowledge, supporting the claim with learning, and dialectic, not to say metaphysical, plausibility ; and, had he not weakened his conclusions by self-confessions, he possibly had pioneered philosophy through the wilderness of doubt and darkness into the broad sunlight of truth. Taking up Spinozism, he showed that it was the result of a demonstrative philosophical attempt ; that is, it necessarily followed from certain accepted data, or the categories of reason, though in its essence it was atheistic and fatalistic. Considering the theoretical reason of Kant, he showed that it must sustain, or at least can not contradict, the three ideas which constitute the estate of a prime philosophy. Rising from this stand-point, he pointed out that the supersensible can be known only by supersensible means, not by the reason alone, but by the *principle of faith*, or feeling, a "direct apprehension, without proof, of the True, the supersensuous, the Eternal." Thus "faith-philosophy," or emotionalism, had its introduction, but Jacobi was ridiculed, as preaching theology in disguise, and he admitted, from what motive is not clear, that while his heart embraced his conclusions, his head or reason condemned them.

Nevertheless, Emotionalism anchored itself in the deep sea of speculative thought, stirring up the waters of inquiry, and even intrenching on the distant, rock-rooted shores of the holiest truth. It could not be ignored. It was not annihilated. It still exists. Schleiermacher, aroused and embracing its fundamental conceptions, relieved it of its theological aspects, and endowed it with a more legitimate or acceptable philosophic form. Charging the Reason with incapacity to discover ultimate truth, he declared it could be known only through the consciousness, or the intuition of feeling. This knowing, truth-searching consciousness has two sides, viz. : there is in man a "God-consciousness," from which a feeling of dependence on the Infinite arises, and there is a Christian consciousness, which inspires communion with God through Jesus Christ. Out of the former arises the thought of dependence, which implies its correlative—a being independent, or upon whom man depends. Hence, from the spiritual feeling, rather than the reason, springs the ontological conception—long searched for and believed in—of God.

Mansel, discovering in man a sense of moral obligation to the independent being, conclusively establishes the existence of such a being, carrying the faith-philosophy over in still clearer form to the support of the theistic conception. However, contrary to Schleiermacher, he does not see in the sense of dependence a *consciousness* of the Absolute, but only an implication of the infinite. The distinction is clear, but the result is the same.

But this philosophy, exciting amusement on the one hand, and deep seriousness on the other, has not fully satisfied even Christian thinkers, as it seems to rely too exclusively upon the uncertain and perturbed emotions of consciousness. The contents of consciousness are proleptic of ultimate truth, but while philosophy will accept rational intuitions, it is slow to accept the conclusions of feeling, or to be guided by the various indexes of consciousness. Evidently wanting in some particulars, there may be hidden in this new philosophy the leaven that will leaven the whole lump. Ignoring the Kantian basis, it has perhaps perpetrated a suicidal act, but there may be in it a guiding principle which, in other hands, will be developed and purified.

Meanwhile, idealism, temporarily eclipsed, or rather suspending its aggressive purpose, soon reappears in a form kindred to, but different from, the Kantian idea. As in Nevada there are streams which, running for miles, suddenly sink out of sight and then reappear, so idealism, sinking for a brief time into obscurity, again presents itself in the utterances of Fitche, Schelling, and Hegel, changing its complexion, but retaining its spirit, with each thinker.

Fitche is the exponent of a strict subjective idealism, which, defined, has exclusive respect to the ego as the only substance. Between the ego-in-itself and the object-in-itself we must choose; one must be rejected. He cast his vote in favor of the ego. Yet there is a non-ego which he regarded as the limitation or hindrance of the ego, so that the non-ego is a part of, or the umbration of, the ego. The Ego, therefore, is all in all. In later years he interpreted the ego as God, which, including the non-ego, savored of Spinozism, or a mild and unintended form of pantheism. Hence, subjective idealism was in peril; it needed correction, purification.

Schelling, born thirteen years after Fitche, passed through many mental vicissitudes, being captivated at first with Fitche and becoming an idealist, but, charmed by other theories, he drifted from one to another, until he developed a form of philosophy known as objective idealism, the contrary of Fitche's. He began by recognizing the same absolute in nature as in mind: "Nature is visible mind, and mind is invisible nature;" but this species of subjective idealism did not satisfy him. From this point his struggles multiply and his driftings commence. He is anxious to formulate the absolute, and, vibrating between subject and object, or the ego and the non-ego, he concludes that the Absolute is neither subject nor object, but the root of both. However, the spell of this objective idealism was soon broken, and, imbibing Spinozism, he rejected both subjective and objective idealism, announcing as a philosophic dictum the *indifference of the real and the ideal*, and the reason as the only Absolute. With this conclusion this restless thinker is soon dissatisfied, and drifts into the latitude of Neo-Platonism, discarding nature and all finite things, and looking to the Absolute as the only Real. Being and not the "becoming" (a touch of pure Eleaticism) absorbs his thought and receives his homage. Even this high-toned conception brings him no comfort, nor had philosophy the power to comfort him. In all its various stages philosophy had given to Schelling only an *idea* of God, not God himself. He yearned for a knowledge of the absolute, and, driven by intellectual impulses and instructive entreaties, he went on, trying, testing, accepting, and rejecting philosophies, one after another, until in despair of soul he turns from philosophy to Johannean Christianity, which reveals to him the everlasting God, and he is satisfied. In passing, we note that this is the cure for all speculation.

Idealism again appears, attaining an absolute and final character in Hegel who affirms the existence of the Absolute, but the Absolute is every thing. In his logic he discusses the doctrine of being, the doctrine of essence, and the doctrine of notion, positing that being is, *per se*, the one, but the one is the manifold; that is, there are no distinctions between thought and being, subject and object; all are one and the one is all. "The Absolute is, with him, not the infinite substance, as with Spinoza; nor the infinite subject, as with Fitche;

nor the infinite mind, as with Schelling; it is a perpetual process, an eternal thinking, without beginning and without end." This God is the unity of all things, the finite and the infinite, the natural and the supernatural, the temporal and the eternal, involving the stupendous paralogism of the identity of Being and Nothing; a pantheism illogical for Hegel's law of logic is the identity of contraries or contradictions, while from Aristotle to our day the law of contradiction has been considered unassailable; a pantheism more intense than any Grecian form of it; a pantheism absurd, anti-Christian, unphilosophic, atheistic.

While Hegel threw up a mountain range at the front, defending his position with force, his philosophy, or the philosophy of idealism, as he had generalized it, was bound to decline, and with it idealism in an absolute form. If idealism were constructively a disguised pantheism, or if its final determinations were the overthrow of the Kantian postulates of reason, in either case it must be abandoned; and Hegel did much to aggravate both of these possible accusations. Absolute idealism, therefore, rose and fell with Hegel. From the decline of Hegelianism philosophy degenerates from its lofty purpose to find the ultimate cause and contents itself with becoming largely a negativism; there is a general breaking up; there is no uniformity of method in investigation; unity of purpose in pursuit is visibly absent.

Schopenhauer is the first representative of the universal decline, for, espousing subjective idealism, and accepting Fitche's interpretation of the absolute, he reduces the subject to a state of passivity, and so transfigures idealism into realism. He retains the "thing-in-itself," not with Kant's explanations, but asserts that it is the *will*, a blind, necessary force, moving and regulating all existence. The world is both real and ideal; the Will is the real world; the ideal is that which each person represents to himself. "The world is my representation and I am only when I represent," says this teacher. Here is idealistic-realism, or realistic-idealism, of a beautiful type, but which is singularly defective in its physical, not to say psychological elements, for it not only denies objectivity to the world, as such, but it locates the subject in the object, a poetic confusion of distinct conceptions rather than positive truth. Yet Schopenhauer admits the existence of the natural world, as the product of will, which actualizes itself, (a), in the organic world; (b), in the vegetable kingdom; (c), in animals. Its highest object-form is the human brain. Contending that Will is the thing-in-itself, the moving, universal force, he likewise contends for the contradiction that physical causation is identical with matter, and causality itself is the law of sufficient reason. This transfer of causation from the will to the substance or matter, prepares the way for the ethical representation of the world, or the outcome of Schopenhauer's hard realism. Logically, and emotionally, he is a pessimist; without belief in a personal God, attributing so-called providential government to an impersonal and necessary will, he muses in despair over existence, sees in history only the worst regulating principles, discovers nothing alleviating or redemptive in natural agencies, and mingles his meditations with the Buddhists, accepting the doctrine of *nirvana*, as the only final relief from a conscious life. His philosophy, so Schwegler writes, is a "union of the transcendentalism of Kant and Fitche, the empiricism of Locke, the pantheism of Spinoza and Schelling, the idealism of Plato, and the pessimism of the Buddhists"—a conglomeration truly, with little of originality or independence of philosophical assertion. Pessimism is the first step downward from absolute idealism.

Its very recent advocate is Hartmann, of Germany, who departed from Schopenhauer in the enlargement of philosophic distinctions, and the clearness of philosophic definitions. Hartmann says Schopenhauer's Will can only be an efficient cause; there must also be a final cause, which implies an act of the reason. The Will is an efficient but not final cause; Reason is a final but not efficient cause; therefore, the two, Will and Reason, constitute the substance and ground of all being. But the acting Reason is a mechanically acting, and therefore, unconscious reason; hence, the Absolute is the union of unconscious intelligence and the will in *unconscious force*. With Schopenhauer, God is blind, impersonal will; with Hartmann, God is the unconscious force of reason and will; hence, the world is badly constructed, and man is the victim of a hopeless government.

How different this from Platonism! How differen. from Descartes, Leibnitz, Kant, Jacobi, Fitche, Schelling, and Hegel!

Comte introduces another retrograding phase of philosophy, called Positivism, whose logical termination is atheism. He achieved notoriety in suggesting that the mind in its natural development passes through three successive stages, as follows: 1. The theological, or fictitious; 2. The metaphysical, or abstract; 3. The positive, or scientific. Asserting that the mind unfolded in this order, it followed that it outgrew the theological or religious, and the metaphysical or philosophical, and attained in its higher development a positive or scientific state. Psychologists, however, immediately rejected this discrimination, it having been established that the mind grows in the reverse order, attaining to a normal theological condition last. Atheistic as is the spirit of positivism, Comte admitted the necessity of religion, and actually prepared a creed and ordinances, but the purpose was ethical, not religious in the highest sense. Can philosophy go lower than pessimism and positivism? Reactions usually follow extremes. Comte has been overthrown; Hartmann is without followers; yet in these days of modern inquiry, it can not be said that philosophy is recovering an idealistic tone; or that it is solving the problem of the ultimate.

Along with the materialistic and self-contradictory philosophic ideas of the early part of the nineteenth century there appeared an eclectic spirit which, prudently surveying the field, ventured to suggest a new basis for philosophic investigation. Rejecting materialism, it also parted company with theology, as such, and made psychology or the reason the starting-point of philosophic endeavor, a hopeful sign of progress as well as a barrier to the atheism of the period. This is Rationalism, or Eclecticism, V. Cousin, an able, eloquent, sincere investigator of the great problems of life, being its exponent. In insisting on the reason, or subjective experience, as the foundation of all investigation, he coincides with Socrates, who was the first to introduce the subjective method in philosophic pursuits; in insisting on the infallibility or inspiration of the spontaneous reason we find a ground for fatal criticism, since even the spontaneous reason of man is supposed to be affected somewhat by his inherited degeneracy. Rationalism assigns to the reason *hyper-functional powers*. The objection of Dr. B. F. Cocker that Cousin does not rely upon revealed truth, or the Scriptures, is not well taken, since philosophy undertakes to pilot itself without the aid of religion to the shores of the eternal. Guided by revealed religion, philosophy will have no trouble, but in that event the strength or weakness of philosophy, as such, will not be manifest.

Rationalism, without its extremes, occupies a right footing, being preferable to idealism, and certainly is superior to the foggy atmosphere of pessimism or positivism. The starting-point of materialism is nature; of theology, God; of rationalism, *man*.

In historic order we have reached the so-called Associational school of psychologists, who, sensitive to the charge of atheism and quick to repel it, have advanced explanatory theories of the mind and its action which logically justify the unenviable accusation of materialism. The psychological principle of the school is that the laws of thought, which we distinguish by specific names, are reducible to one universal law, namely, *association*, without which the mind is inert and productionless. To John Stuart Mill and Alexander Bain, the one dead, the other living, the doctrine is indebted for advocates. Mr. Mill inherited the doctrine of utilitarianism through his father from Jeremy Bentham; he was also most profoundly influenced by Dr. David Hartley, whose physiological explanation of mental action deprived the mind of intuitional and original character. It is well known that the elder Mill very early determined to mold the son according to his philosophical theories, to give him no religious education, to foster in him no reverential sentiments, to make him just what he desired; the son, therefore, was a singular character, a machine-made man; and it is no wonder that his philosophy is faulty, inadequate, materialistic, and inherited, *i. e., borrowed* rather than original. In his published works J. S. Mill holds that knowledge is the product of sensation; hence, phenomena alone are knowable; being is unknowable. Thus far he had traveled along the familiar track of philosophy from the days of Aristotle, but he took a step in advance in his proclamation of causation as an example of succession in nature; that is, that there is no necessary connection between cause and effect, but only a sequence. This was destructive of all Ætiology, threw mystery over all the operations of nature, blotted out accepted conclusions of philosophy, and inaugurated the *drift* period in speculative thought. Foundations were shaken; anchorage was impossible; the ultimate could no longer be reached *a posteriori,* or by the frequented steps of causation.

In keeping with this physical theory, he taught that the mind is a "series of feelings," or an association of emotions, without causal connection. Eliminating causation from the natural world, it was easy to eliminate it from mental activity, which conclusion became the essence of associationalism.

The step to evolution, or the last type of modern philosophy, is a short one. Herbert Spencer is its sponsor. If one's education has any thing to do with one's philosophy, then in the fact that Spencer's education was largely confined to physical studies we find an explanation of the mechanical hypothesis of creation he finally adopted and has to the present hour emphasized. Respecting the universe, he holds that it is the product of evolutionary forces; respecting God, he holds that he is ignoscible, unthinkable; respecting the human mind, he is an associationalist, teaching that consciousness is a nervous sensation and thought a product of organization. He distinguishes between the nature of mind, which is unknowable, and the phenomena of mind, which are knowable, affirming that there is a science, but not a philosophy, of mind. The process of evolution is expressed as the "redistribution of matter and motion," by which mental states are produced and succeed one another. The nervous structure is double-faced, being objective and subjective; objective activity is unknowable; subjective experience, consisting of conscious or phenomenal states, is recognized, and, therefore, knowable. Intellectual activity is refined nervousness.

Following this reduction of mental phenomena to nervous states, Mr. Spencer had little difficulty in pronouncing the limitations of human knowledge. Conceptions he divides into three classes, viz.: 1. Complete; 2. Symbolic; 3. Pseud-ideas. On the complete and symbolic conceptions, inasmuch as they are knowable, positive science may securely rest; but such ideas as God, immortality, or religions, or necessary moral truths, inasmuch as they are unknowable, are denominated pseud-ideas, to be entertained as speculations or abstractions only. In these conclusions Spencer draws the curtains of midnight around us, and turns the earth away from the sun. To ignore necessary truths, as does Mr. Spencer, is as if one carrying a lighted lamp should forget about it and let it fall, occasioning an explosion and consuming his person. To this it may be replied that Mr. Spencer's lamp is not lit, and there is no danger if he let it fall. Perhaps this is the trouble. Necessary, religious truths ought to flame in and around heart and intellect; then the notion of pseud-ideas would be extinguished in the brilliant blaze of truth. The observer will discover that Spencer, forgetting necessary truth, confines himself to *his conceptions of truths in general*; but a genuine philosophy deals with the former and ignores the latter, or considers them as incidental forms. The philosophy of Herbert Spencer is sensational, negative; phenomenal, not ultra-phenomenal; dealing with appearances, not causes; with matter, not mind; with physical activity, not a personal God.

Ethically, the philosophy is defective in contents and pernicious in effect, for if intellectual manifestation can be reduced to nervous action, moral emotions, convictions, aspirations, and sentiments may be considered a display of the nervous sensibilities. And so we find it. The ethics of Spencer is the sum of physiological, psychological, and sociological influences; that is, the result of the suggestions of nature, the convenience and expediency of communities, the comparison of wants, the study of the issues of virtue and vice. Ethical teaching is not grounded in philosophical, religious, or ultimate truth; there is no immutable standard of right and wrong; so said Epicurus; so said Aristotle; so echoes Spencer. In the language of Spencer, conduct is the adjustment of the inner relations of life to the outer relations, *i. e.*, the world. Conduct is a struggle toward this adjustment; if one succeed in realizing the adjustment, he has perfected his conduct; otherwise, he is a wreck. Success, then, or *survival*, is the standard of right. This is the ethical side of the physical theory of mind, the essence of the philosophy of Spencer, the latest expression of the character of man.

To omit all reference to American philosophers would be unjust to them as a class, and render this survey incomplete. Really there is no American philosophy, *per se*, but the "Concord School" still exists, representing a form of Hegelianism, a phase of pantheism, and the nobler edition of Emersonianism. Perhaps the philosophy taught by the school should be characterized as *ideal realism*, a mixture of the high and low, carrying both sides of the great problems, and emphasizing to-day what seems to be in the ascendant, but at liberty to change to-morrow. In this we do it no injustice.

Happily, we may now speak of a philosophy of an entirely different character from any of the preceding, the chief objection to it being its theologic trend, or whether it is philosophic at all in its method and spirit. We refer to theological dogmatism, whose purpose is the vindication of the very problems which have exercised a controlling influence on speculative thought, and whose solutions have not yet been wrought out in the name of philosophy. James Arminius and John Calvin properly represent the theologic school of dogmatics, who, assuming the Scriptures to be inspired of God, demonstrate by both *a priori* and *a posteriori* methods the existence of God, and interpret both nature and man as an easy task. The aid of revelation is not considered indispensable to philosophy; but the day will dawn when philosophy will be warranted in appropriating all the aids at hand, religion being one of them. If dogmatic theology be rejected as a philosophical conception, then surely there is room for a school of Christian philosophers, just as there has been room for atheistic and pessimistic philosophers; that is, the philosopher may be justified in establishing theistic conclusions without peril to his reputation. To this the world is fast coming. Emerging from the philosophical wrecks is, what the ages have waited for, but which is, as yet, undeveloped, namely, a Christian philosophy, or the *philosophy of being from the Christian standpoint.* Lotze, of Germany, and Bowne and McCosh, of the United States, may be taken as the representatives of the religious element in philosophy, without which there is no true philosophy. Philosophy, without the pilotage of religion, runs into pessimism, atheism, materialism; with it, there is transparency, because there is revelation. But, as this phase of philosophy will hereafter receive attention, we do no more at present than mention it.

We have traveled a long distance from Thales to Lotze, having gone over mountains, crossed the seas, wandered through wildernesses of thought, tarried in schools and academies, looked up into the sky, down into the soul, and beyond all things, for the face of God. Philosophy is a weary and weird traveler, ever journeying on foot, provided only with scrip, crackers, and staff; a beggar, asking of every thing, but receiving doubtful answers and unsatisfactory aid. During this long period of twenty-five hundred years, philosophy has not found the ultimate; the problem of *being* is still unsolved; and though at times, as in Plato, it has gone up to Pisgah's heights, from which the Holy Land of thought was seen, it has, as in Mill, drifted toward the North Pole, and, as in Spencer, gone down to the center of the earth. In Plato, an eagle; in Mill, a bear; in Spencer, a mole.

In these twenty-five centuries there have been progress as well as decline, approximate solutions, lacking only the full tide of inspiration to make them entirely correct, and give them complete and authoritative validity, as well as self-acknowledged or universally perceived failures. It can not, therefore, be said that the progress, whatever its character and extent, has been direct and methodical, or that it can be easily traced from system to system, or school to school, for it has receded and flowed like the tides, rising and falling with no uniformity, and under no visible law of development. Vico taught that history repeated itself, or that life revolved in a *circle;* Goethe taught that the world moved in *spirals;* Hegel taught that the history of philosophy is a "united process," a gradual unfolding of principles, a constant advancement toward the truth. Reviewing the historic struggles of philosophy, one is almost ready to affirm that it is a *repeating* process, a circle of ideas; or, if progressive, that its method is spiral; but that its progress has been regular, each system an improvement on the preceding, each age nearer the truth than a former age, seems inconsistent with the facts. Progress is the law of nature, language, science, music, mind; as Cocker says, "the present, both in nature and history and civilization, is, so to speak, the aggregate and sum total of the past;" but philosophy has not followed the law of evolution, either in its general course or in its outcome, for idealism is superior to materialism, and Plato is a safer philosopher than Herbert Spencer. There has been no steady, uniform progress in philosophical discovery, nor even a gradual advancement toward a knowledge of the absolute and everlasting God. The line of progress, if we allow it at all, is a zigzag line, exceedingly irregular and unsatisfactory. Putting the eye on the historical order of philosophic development, we often see two or more systems opposed in their fundamental conceptions, as the "fire" philosophy of Heraclitus and the atomic theory of Democritus in ancient times, and the pantheism of Spinoza and the empiricism of Locke in modern times, arise almost simultaneously, the one not quenching the other, but modified by a future teacher and discoverer. The historical order is illogical; the logical order is unhistorical. One system does not grow out of another. Each springs up like Jonah's gourd in the darkness, and withers away because of its inner and excessive weaknesses, abominations, and inaptitudes.

By this we do not mean that there is no connection whatever among the various schools or systems of thought, for this would be to overlook the confessed relation of Socrates and Plato, Locke and Hume, Spencer and Hamilton, Fitche and Schelling, Schopenhauer and Hartmann, Hartley and Mill. But, adopting Mill's interpretation of causation, we say the connection of philosophical systems is not causal, but formal and accidental; the history thereof is the history of succession, not of necessary relation.

That this interpretation of the historic order of philosophy is correct, we place in columnar array the names of the principal philosophers of the ancient period, designating their systems, and the time of their birth, or the period when they flourished—a schedule of the entire history.

| PHILOSOPHERS. | PERIOD OR BIRTH. | PHILOSOPHY. |
|---|---|---|
| Thales, . . . . . | B. C. 640–550, . | Materialism, or the Physical Principle. |
| Anaximander, . | B. C. 610, . . . | "            "            " |
| Anaximenes, . . | B. C. 529–480, . | "            "            " |
| Heraclitus, . . . | B. C. 503–420, . | "            "            " |
| Pythagoras, . . | B. C. 605, . . . | Mathematical Principle. |
| Zenophanes, . . | B. C. 616–516, . | Idealism, or the Intelligent Principle. |
| Parmenides, . . | B. C. 536, . . . | "            "            " |
| Zeno, . . . . . | B. C. 500, . . . | "            "            " |
| Anaxagoras, . . | B. C. 500–428, . | Mental Principle. |
| Leucippus, . . . | B. C. 500–400, . | Atomic Principle. |
| Democritus, . . | B. C. 460–357, . | "            " |
| Empedocles, . . | B. C. 440, . . . | Eclecticism. |
| Protagoras, . . . | B. C. 440, . . . | Nescience. |
| Gorgias, . . . . | B. C. 427, . . . | Idealism. |
| Socrates, . . . . | B. C. 469–399, . | " |
| Plato, . . . . . | B. C. 430–347, . | " |
| Aristotle, . . . . | B. C. 384, . . . | Sensationalism. |
| Epicurus, . . . | B. C. 342–270, . | Epicureanism. |
| Zeno, . . . . . | B. C. 340, . . . | Stoicism. |
| Arcesilaus, . . . | B. C. 316–241, . | Skepticism. |

The above is Grecian philosophy in outline, a zigzag line, truly, its systems unconnected, and its last state worse than the first. Beginning with a materialistic assumption, which changes its form and phraseology, but not its spirit, with every succeeding teacher, it rises to an incipient or anticipatory idealism in Pythagoras, attains to a one-sided or absolute idealism in the Eleatics, especially in Parmenides, assumes philosophic dignity in the *nous* or mental principle of Anaxagoras, and then, with melted wings, sinks down into the atomic theory, or another phase of materialism, of Democritus—the atheism and chance-philosophy of Greece. Materialism, idealism, atheism, are the successive but irregular steps thus far of the early philosophy.

Springing back like the released bow, it betakes itself again to idealism, reaching its profoundest culmination in Socrates and Plato, Socrates being the flower and Plato the fruit of a dialectical system that has never been surpassed. This is the summit, the highest water-mark of ancient philosophy, from which it descends first in Aristotle to empiricism, then in Zeno to spiritualistic pantheism, and in Epicurus to the logical termination of the mechanical hypothesis— atheism. From this is but a single step to skepticism, which the New Academy, in Arcesilaus, maintained.

In these successive movements of the ancient systems it is impossible to discover an inner connection, or a periodic progress, or any type of evolution. Reactions, reformations, upheavals, disguises, interrogations, summits, abysses—these belong to the philosophic period of four hundred years, but an orderly or even final progress is not visible.

Passing through the interregnum, which furnished little genuine philosophy, we arrive at the modern period; a period full of inquiry, persevering in its research, teeming with results in systems without number, and opening new paths for the feet of future travelers. Its history may be tabulated about as follows:

| PHILOSOPHERS. | BIRTH. | PHILOSOPHY. |
| --- | --- | --- |
| Bacon, | A. D. 1561, | Science. |
| Boehme, | A. D. 1575, | Mysticism. |
| Descartes, | A. D. 1596, | Dualism. |
| Spinoza, | A. D. 1632, | Pantheism. |
| Locke, | A. D. 1632, | Sensationalism. |
| Leibnitz, | A. D. 1646, | Idealism. |
| Berkeley, | A. D. 1685, | " |
| Reid, | A. D. 1710, | Common Sense. |
| Hume, | A. D. 1711, | Skepticism. |
| Kant, | A. D. 1724, | Idealism. |
| Jacobi, | A. D. 1743, | Faith-philosophy. |
| Stewart, | A. D. 1753, | Common Sense. |
| Fitche, | A. D. 1762, | Subjective Idealism. |
| Schelling, | A. D. 1775, | Objective " |
| Herbart, | A. D. 1776, | Sensationalism. |
| Hegel, | A. D. 1770, | Absolute Idealism. |
| Brown, | A. D. 1778, | Representationism. |
| Hamilton, | A. D. 1788, | Nescience. |
| Schopenhauer, | A. D. 1788, | Pessimism. |
| Comte, | A. D. 1798, | Positivism. |
| J. S. Mill, | A. D. 1806, | Associationalism. |
| Spencer, | A. D. 1820, | Evolution. |
| Hartmann, | A. D. 1842, | Pessimism. |
| Lotze, | A. D. 1817, | Monotheism. |

One has only to glance at this historic representation of modern philosophy to be able to decide whether it has regularly progressed or declined, and what its last state is compared with the first. Beginning with Bacon, it dealt chiefly with the facts and problems of natural science, together with a review of the methods of reasoning, or dialectics. Bacon was a scientist, a pioneer, paving the way for philosophy, and really summoned it to its rightful tasks. Following him it appeared according to the above schedule. In Descartes it lost or did not find the idea of unity; in Spinoza it lost God; in Locke it declared for an empty mind; over Leibnitz the idealistic spirit broods, and monadology is the result; in Berkeley a form of Eleaticism reappears; in Hume the mind is without recognition. Reactions follow, and Kant strikes for idealism. There is a rising again; the wings begin to grow. Jacobi declares for faith in God; Fitche, Schelling, and Hegel wheel into the direct line of idealism, ascending higher than their predecessors, but compelled to halt if not beat a retreat. Idealism broke its bow by over-straining.

Idealism lost caste, being followed rapidly by the pessimism of Schopenhauer, the positivism of Comte, the associationalism of Mill, and the evolution of Spencer, checked only a trifle by the intermediate systems of Hamilton, Stewart, and Reid.

Spanning the period from the idealism of Descartes to the evolution of Spencer, and recollecting the manifold forms of pantheism, sensationalism, skepticism, idealism, pessimism, and atheism, which it has assumed, we can not concede a regular order in philosophic history, nor is progress noticeable, save in the general results of research and the study of mind. Modern philosophy ends as did ancient philosophy, with sensationalism, a physical conception of the universe, and an atheistic sentiment respecting its Maker. In these results modern has repeated the story of ancient philosophy, only varying the form. The old philosophy was the archetype of the new, the ancient of the modern; *there is little new in the new.* Eleaticism was the forerunner of Idealism; Pythagoras was the Descartes of his age; Parmenides repeats himself in Spinoza; Zeno is transformed in Hegel. This is not progress.

But the end is not yet. Such words as pessimism, atheism, evolution, ring in our ears, disturbing our slumber with nightmare, and filling life's activity with anxiety and fear; but the new words, soul, God, immortality, heaven, taken up by Lotze, have gone out into all the world to inspire the sons of men. Are they deceptions, or are they real? We shall see.

## CHAPTER III.

### THE PROVINCE OF PHILOSOPHY.

IN the Loggia of Raphael, in the Vatican at Rome, are four pictures, which the visitor is sure to observe with considerable interest, both because the artist produced them at the early age of twenty-five years, and also because they represent the departments of theology, poetry, philosophy, and justice. One has no difficulty in finding "philosophy," which rises as a vaulted hall, with outside marble steps, on which sits lazy Diogenes, clothed in a single garment; in the hall Plato and Aristotle are conversing, Plato pointing *upward*, and Aristotle pointing *forward*. Raphael's conception of the historic career of philosophy, and, equally, of its prophetic mission, is perhaps as correct as any that has had expression, either in art, or history, or philosophy. Diogenes represents the slow, plodding thinker, careless of this world, being occupied with thoughts that the multitude do not understand, or in which they have invested but a little interest; Plato represents its highest aspirations; Aristotle, its spirit of progress.

Has philosophy a mission? Is there a field for the philosopher? Lewes insists that its mission has been fulfilled, and its reign in thought, research, and history, is over. Acknowledging that it initiated positive science, he declares that positive science has supplanted it, and that philosophy must disappear. Reviewing the past, he sees that the one has made no progress in the study of its problems, while the other is revealing facts and the laws that govern the material universe. For effete, worn-out philosophical speculations, he substitutes the facts of positive science, declaring its empire established. Prejudging the subject in this way, he undertakes to write a history of philosophy, making good use of the facts as he finds them, and turning them against the citadel itself.

Mr. Lewes, however, is not supreme authority, notwithstanding the positive discrimination he makes between philosophy and science, and his evident preference for the latter. When he writes that philosophy initiated science, he forgets that Thales was a natural philosopher, *i. e.*, a scientist before he became a speculatist. Physics preceded metaphysics. So in modern times Bacon, the scientist, preceded Descartes, the philosopher. Science has given birth to philosophy, not philosophy to science. The declaration that there has been no progress in speculation and that "philosophy moves in the same endless circle," is more than an assumption; it is a perversion of fact. Mind, matter, and God are better understood to-day because of philosophical inquiry; better understood negatively, perhaps, than affirmatively, but it is *Platonic* to consider all sides of a subject before announcing a conclusion. The final conclusions of philosophy have not been reached; the partial conclusions heralded are in some respects unsatisfactory, disturbing and incomplete. The declaration that philosophy is neglected and abandoned is about as true as would be the assertion that science, poetry, art, and religion are neglected. England rarely produces a philosophical mind; Germany is still able to furnish a philosophical thinker. The scientific spirit is always productive of the philosophic spirit; and this inquiring age must produce scientists and philosophers. The facts of science are the materials of the philosopher. Philosophy is impossible without science. The universe is the shadow of an infinite thought, to be deciphered by the slow process of philosophic inquiry. Understanding the universe the infinite thinker is understood. This is the process of thought; hence, Cousin is correct in affirming that philosophy is *last* in the order of thought, overturning the assertion of Lewes that it was historically *first*. Inasmuch as philosophy is last, it has a future, waiting for science to do its duty as an investigator of facts and laws, and it can not go forward until science has prepared the way for it. Its future, therefore, is a contingency; it follows science.

Mr. Lewes again contends that philosophy is engaged in a search after the *impossible!* Essences, causes can never be known. This is the dictum of modern science; but is it not presumptive in a scientist to declare that causes are unknowable because science can not and does not undertake to demonstrate them? It is the old spirit of scientific antagonism to higher knowledge, a settlement of the limitations of human inquiry by the *ipse dixit* of a class whose business it is not to go beyond phenomena, who can not by their methods ascertain causes.

In his statement that philosophy proceeds altogether from *a priori* premises, he asserts what can not be maintained, for all methods are open to philosophy.

Schlegel, having a scheme of his own to defend, pronounces the philosophy of the schools *unintelligible*, and advises an abandonment of the "fine-spun webs of dialectics" for a more practical philosophy of life. The objection is not well taken, for, with few exceptions, such as the abstract ideas of Anaximander and the monadology of Leibnitz, the student has no difficulty in separating one system from another, or in detailing the tenets of the philosophers from the Ionic school to Emerson. Besides, such an objection, if fatal in its content, will dispense with much that passes for science, which in these days utters unintelligible theories without number, and is always incomplete in its data and uncertain in its conclusions. That the history of philosophy abounds in systems inharmonious and contradictory, no one will deny ; but science, transitional, progressive, ever finding new facts, ever discovering new laws, must be open to the same objection. The severest charge against philosophy is that in its aberrations it resembles science, building up and tearing down, enlightening to-day but confusing to-morrow, and so leaving the world in perplexity, mystery, and misery. Science furnishes the example, and philosophy imitates it.

Antisthenes, the Cynic, in eulogy of philosophy boasted that it had enabled him to live with himself, which is the very highest end of life. The Cynic compromised the force of his statement by leading an impure and worthless life, but in proportion as it contributes to right principles it lays the foundation for right living.

Schelling observed that the end of philosophy is to make an intelligence out of nature, or a nature out of intelligence ; succeeding in doing either, and especially in doing both, it will justify its place in history.

At all events, the relation of philosophical pursuits to the practical life of man and the world's intelligence is intimate enough to secure them a place in the curriculum of the world's studies and activities.

Some Christian thinkers have innocently espoused the belief that inspired truth is all-sufficient in itself, and that what is not revealed can not be known, and, therefore, philosophical inquiry touching the unrevealed is forbidden by the terms of revelation itself. Philosophy aspires not to the character of a revelation ; but, like theology, it does venture its explanations of what is revealed. It deals with revelations, cosmological, psychological, spiritual, and written revelations, attempting to harmonize them in the unity of thought and being, in all of which it goes no farther than the revelations themselves. Its purpose is to understand revelation. It does not reveal, only as explanation is revelation.

This brings us definitely to consider what is philosophy in its generic spirit and function, without a knowledge of which it will be impossible to decide if there is any room for it. Dividing and subdividing after the manner of Plato, we should say philosophy is not dialectic ; or mathematics ; or psychology ; or metaphysic ; or science ; or religion ; not these taken singly or wholly, but embracing a not inconsiderable part of all. Aristotle called metaphysic "first philosophy," and physics "second philosophy." The "second philosophy" we relegate to the physicists. Prof. Bowne assigns to psychology the task of explaining the genesis of ideas, reserving to philosophy the duty of explaining the grounds of belief. It is not clear that the distinction is valid or that the tasks of psychology and philosophy are sufficiently apportioned ; for philosophy deals with *origins;* the origin of ideas, not the ideas themselves; the origin of beliefs, not beliefs alone. Psychology is an assistant to, not a usurper of, philosophy. The invalidity of the distinction, or the separateness of the tasks Prof. Bowne assigns to these departments will appear if the philosophical method of investigation be considered. Two methods obtain in philosophy, viz. : the psychological and the empirical. Aristotle, Locke, Condillac, Hume, and the associationalists, adopting the empirical method, constitute that class of philosophers known as materialists; while Socrates, Plato, Kant, Cousin, Fitche, and Hegel, adopting the psychological method, are known as idealists, rationalists, or metaphysicians. In recent years both methods have been adopted by the same philosopher, creating a school of empirical psychologists, represented by Alexander Bain ; but it is the spirit of empiricism overshadowing psychology, and not harmonizing with it. Its purpose is the destruction of psychology. Prof. Bowne seems opposed to the empirico-psychological method, as preliminary to, or an aid in, metaphysical inquiry ; but while the opposition to both methods joined together is not the same as opposition to either method taken by itself, he impresses the reader that the psychological method is insufficient in itself for metaphysics. Cousin, however, has demonstrated the insufficiency of the empirical method, and exalted the other. Both methods, therefore, are deprived of application in philosophy.

But if psychology is justified in undertaking one of the tasks of philosophy, the psychological method may be properly appropriated by philosophy, without damage to the former, and with some advantage to the latter. The tasks and methods of psychology border closely on those of philosophy ; but, beyond those of the former, the latter must finally go if it work out an independent mission. A point of separation must finally be reached.

In like manner, philosophy is not dialectic, but *dialectical;* nor is it science, but scientific; nor religion, but religious. Its methods are those of religion, science, psychology, and dialectics; it searches the truth, now by *a priori*, and then by *a posteriori* methods; like science, it may employ the empirical method; like psychology, the rational; like theology, the theistic; that is, it may start from nature, mind, or God, or from the known or the unknown; it has no method of its own, as distinguished from these. Hence, its alliance with all things.

Kindred to science and religion in method, its aims are specific, being above the one and alongside those of the other. Without a difference of aim, it is without a reason for being. The justification of philosophy is that it has in hand a problem which the scientist does not admit into his realm, and which the theologian can not solve without his aid. The specific task of philosophy, therefore, remains to be stated.

Schwegler says, to philosophize is to reflect, but the *subject* of reflection should be included. Socrates insisted on the value of definitions, and was skillful himself in separating the accidental from the essential elements of things. To define philosophy is the first duty. A variety of definitions the philosophers have made, each an approximate statement of the trend of philosophical discovery. To say that it is the "science of wholes," or the science of the absolute, is not a bad definition, save that it reduces philosophy to a science, which, however, ought to insure its favorable reception among the scientists; to say that it is an inquiry into realities, or a search for causes, or a feeling after being, is an improved representation of its purpose. Schlegel defines philosophy to be the "science of consciousness alone," which leads into the rationalism of Cousin. Plato states that the "end of philosophy is the intuition of unity," an abstract definition, which, thoroughly analyzed, will be found to contain the true idea of philosophy; but its occult meaning renders it unsatisfactory as a definition. The definition in this case must be defined. According to Epicurus, philosophy is an activity related to human happiness. The definition is practical, not philosophical. According to Diogenes Laertius, Pythagoras was the "first person who invented the term philosophy, and who called himself a philosopher." Dissatisfied with the name *wisdom*, which had been applied to scientific and metaphysical pursuits, he originated the word philosophy to express the *love of wisdom*, or a state of mind that delighted in philosophic speculation. The word, as thus used, is faulty in that it does not signify the kind of wisdom to be loved or pursued; it may include a love of lower or higher truth; if the former, it would be science; if the latter, philosophy. As a word for the pursuit of the highest truth, it is wanting in explicitness; still, as it has been baptized by so worthy a thinker as Pythagoras, it should retain its place in speculation, and signify the pursuit of the highest truth.

What is the highest truth? This must be settled before the duty of pursuit can be enforced. The aim of philosophy has been to get back to first principles, without exactly knowing what they are, and without knowing the shortest route to their discovery. The struggle of every thinker since the days of Plato, the mental travail of every investigator, metaphysical and scientific, has been to penetrate through the visible into the invisible. The universal faith that the limit of knowledge has not been reached stimulates every seeker to press on, in the hope that he may be able to open a new door into the infinite mysteries, and declare the last secret solved. The effort to reach original principles, powers, or personalities, to give them name, describe their form, analyze their nature, is stupendous in itself, and, when sincerely made, is heroic and deserving of applause. No easy task, it is confessed, is his who in this day takes up a problem still unsolved, and which modern science has the effrontery to declare insoluble. True philosophy, embracing the fundamentals in the dark, sets its face pastward, depthward, and bidding good-bye to the visible, plunges into the invisible as the diver into the Arabian Sea, and is lost in the splendors of its own explorations.

That there are first principles, or highest truths, must be conceded, for not only is philosophy impossible without such concession, but also the universe can neither be explained nor maintained without them. The idea of substratum, source, foundation, can not be repudiated without danger to whatever is; belief in originals is not more the imperative of consciousness than the imperative of science. The existent has been produced by another existent, or it produced itself; from this alternative there is no escape. *Self-existence,* or *caused existence*—this is the final form of the philosophical problem.

A cedar receiving collateral support from air, sunshine, moisture, is yet dependent upon soil, and can not flourish without it. An imperfect scheme will content itself with an examination of the collateral supports or adjuncts of life, but a genuine philosophy seeks the basal elements, without which the collateral elements would be powerless. Neither the drapery of existence, nor the flourishing and magnificent material forms about us, nor the visible realities which attract the eye, are the only or chief objects of philosophic inquiry; but back of all these, back of all that is, are the sources, the images, the originating and manifesting forces. The uncovering of the foundations, the exposing of the olden mysteries, the compelling the First to answer the Second—this is the first, the last, interrogation of genuine philosophy. Plato more clearly than before declares the purpose of philosophy to be, "that it may ascend as far as the unconditioned, and, having grasped this, may then lay hold of the principles next adjacent to it, and so go down to the end, terminating in forms." The *unconditioned;* the *conditioned*—these philosophy must interrogate and examine, and then report the results. If it be thought that the realm of philosophy is enlarged by this epitome of its purpose beyond the possibility of a thorough survey of all it contains or proposes, and that to restrict it to the sensible or phenomenal will be in keeping with the spirit of the age, we reply that we have neither assigned arbitrary boundaries to it, nor broken down old and existing limitations of former philosophic purposes. Philosophy itself, not the writer, establishes its own boundaries, expunges all horizons from the mental vision, and points to the illimitable as the theater of the mind's free activity, as the field of the inquiring spirit of man. In the days of Athenian splendor, its chief purpose was an exploration of the illimitable; but nineteenth century philosophy has arrogantly erected barriers around the philosophic spirit, muttering, as to oceanic tides, "thus far and no farther." Beyond the sensible, the phenomenal, the explainable, the modern investigator proposes not even to attempt to go, and balustrades thought with rock and ocean and sky and nerves and molecules.

In respect to boundaries, modern thought contrasts with the philosophy of Plato's day. The latter grasped the conception of the genesis of things, but could not actualize it in a philosophic form; the former repudiates the idea of genesis in self-subsisting, original creative spirit, to which both consciousness and religion, both nature and history, most surely point. The Hellenic spirit was a pioneer; the modern spirit is an heir to all the revelations of the history of humanity and the developments of religion. One preceded inquiry; the other follows it. One fore-glimpsed the unknown God; the other refuses recognition of the known God. One, beginning at the bottom, ascended for a moment the perilous heights of vision, only to fall back into darkness again; the other, born near the summits, descends into abysses of doubt and shadow, reversing the order of the academicians. The one soared from the earth; the other has fallen from the heavens. Plato is the one; Lucifer is the other.

As to its realm, philosophy is quite independent of the philosopher, just as botany is quite independent of the botanist. His task is to explore the province as he finds it; he can not construct boundaries, and define the frontier of his inquiry, for the field is the infinite. If he is narrow in conception it is because he has gone to the tops of the mountains, or planted himself in the stars, the outer courts of the invisible. What he must do is to approach the invisible Center of all things, inquiring for his steps in the fields of creation, and rising beyond all into the very presence of the power that made all. To that Center he must go, and from it he must start in his quest of truth. Neither ancient nor modern philosophy fixed their point of departure from the great Center—the one because it could not, the other because it would not—nor has the objective point of the latter been the discovery of primary truth, or the foundation of existence. A strange perversion of philosophy, indeed, which neither starts from nor returns to the first, the outlying, eternal Cause of all things! Yet to this philosophy must come if it retain its name and place in the esteem of mankind.

The philosophic pursuit implies a specific purpose. Its general purpose must be absorbed by the special. Broadly speaking, the successive systems of philosophic inquiry, which both ancient and modern times have produced, may be interpreted as so many attempts of the human mind to unravel eternal mysteries, to explore incomprehensible realities, and definitely to fix the limits of human knowledge. In a narrower sense, it appears as if philosophy has had, for its animating principle, the determination of the infinite, and a study of the exact relations of the infinite and the finite, together with the cognate questions they suggest. While seeking to examine the foundations of the universe, it covets also a knowledge of remotest being, or the ultimate facts of existence. This is tearing away the veil that separates the natural from the supernatural, and discovering the invisible—a high undertaking, but not impious. From the days of Thales until now, philosophy has been characterized by a purpose to ascertain the unknown, exhibiting in its pursuit no trifling or chaotic spirit, but an intellectual zeal in harmony with the high end that inspired it. Ancient philosophy sought only in darkness. Unaided and alone, it sallied forth in quest of truth, but failed to find it.

Again, Plato says: "The problem of philosophy is, for all that exists conditionally, to find a ground unconditioned and absolute." Involved in this search of the unconditioned is a knowledge of the conditioned, implying a wide range of intellectual research, and a devout comprehension of the universe in all its manifold relations. Plato understood the problem, therefore. Among the Ionic philosophers the inquiry was of a similar nature, a seeking of the original cause of things; but, locating the cause in the things themselves, they sunk into materialism. From Homer's theology of the gods as the originators of the universe, they turned with dissatisfaction, and, in a reactionary mood, attributed to the physical elements, fire, air, and water, certain creative powers and impulses, ending in their depersonification, thus exchanging mythological beings for visible forces, as the first causes of phenomena. Whether in this there was an advance many may hesitate to allow; but it was the death-knell of mythology as a philosophical or religious explanation of the physical universe, and rendered in this respect excellent service to the cause of truth. In this vibration from Platonic idealism to Ionic materialism, the extremes of ancient philosophic research are manifest; but modern philosophy swings between the same extremes, seemingly unable to go beyond them.

Looking to conclusions alone, ancient philosophy asserts the unconditioned, modern philosophy the conditioned; in its highest mood the former was theistic, in its lowest mood the latter is atheistic. Between the theistic and the atheistic conception of the universe; between a supernaturally-caused and a self-originating universe, philosophy must at last decide, for the truth is in one or the other. To creation's picture there is a background, which is reflected in light and shadow upon the picture itself. The Causer is not in the foreground, but in the background, blushing over his works, and suffusing them with the hues of his unseen face. To reveal the unseen Causer is the manifest duty of philosophy. It must fearlessly tread along the boundaries of creation, touching the edges of the infinite, and grasping the hand of the eternal; this is its province, or it has nothing to do. Plainly is it seen that its functional career is above that of science. Pure science concerns itself with facts, laws, methods; philosophy with causes and ends. Science is fact-seeking; philosophy, principle-seeking. The one deals with experience; the other, with thought. Science embraces physiology, psychology, astronomy, chemistry, botany, zoölogy; philosophy inquires for the originating principle of all things. The province of the one is the visible; that of the other, the invisible. Science may conclude that the First Cause is undiscoverable; philosophy must discover such cause.

In this assignment of specific business to philosophy, it will be observed that it trenches upon the sphere of theology, with this difference, however: theology is the concretion of divine truths, as found in verbal revelations; philosophy is the concretion of similar truths, as found in physical revelations. Between science and religion it is the bridge. To science, the Causer is unknowable; to philosophy, *knowable*; to religion, KNOWN.

Is it the prerogative of philosophy to doubt, and that of religion to believe? Pyrrho introduced the spirit of doubt in ancient philosophy, which was rather a contamination than an inspiration. His followers were called skeptics, and "ephetics," *i. e.*, men who suspended judgment and never reached a conclusion. The spirit of doubt dominated at the introduction of modern philosophy, Bacon refusing to accept scientific data until he had investigated them, and Descartes refusing all philosophical principles until he had demonstrated them. Hume created the aphorism, "To doubt is the sum of knowledge." Hence, philosophy is branded as the doubter; but it is a seeker, also. It doubts in order to seek. Doubt is the stimulus of investigation. Montaigne's skepticism was intended to be the inspiration of inquiry. The inspiring doubt of Bacon and Descartes has given place to the dead doubt of Spencer, Bain, and the whole brood of empiricists and materialists. Under this load philosophy staggers.

Jacobi, a "faith-philosopher," held that Spinozism, or a pantheistic conception of the universe, must be the issue of pure philosophizing; but it is clear that the result may be neither atheism nor pantheism, but theism. In examining the philosophical contests of the last three centuries, however, we must confess that philosophy has been unsuccessful in its attemps to vindicate the existence of an original Causer; and, instead of rising to the religious height of the known, it has fallen down to the scientific level of the unknowable, and declares the Causer not only unknowable but unthinkable.

Is the ultimate incognizable by philosophy? Its own melancholy answer, echoing through history, is that it can not decipher the all-mystery, it can not measure the infinite, its plumb-line is too short for the depths of being. Accepting this account of itself, it furnishes a strong argument for the necessity of a supernatural revelation of God, for if it is not in the power of the human mind to conceive of the original Causer, and announce him in his attributes, if man can not predetermine the existence of a Creator, either ignorance or revelation of a Creator must ensue. Relying upon itself, philosophy gravitates to ignorance, proclaiming the idea of a first cause speculative and beyond demonstration. From the declaration of an unknown and unknowable God, the step is a short one to the declaration that mind and matter are beyond the pale of knowledge. Such step it has already taken, in that it has declared that phenomena only may be known. It is a question, however, if it requires more mind to know things than phenomena, to know substance than qualities, to know being than attributes, for there are no qualities without substance, and no attributes without being. *The problem of Plato the nineteenth century unhesitatingly declares can not be solved.* In its latest aspects, philosophy seems incapable of any thing except to pull down the temple of truth on its own head. Making the unproven assumption that God, mind, and matter are unknowable, it has degenerated into a series of ignorant platitudes, as the apology for its imbecility, and wrestles no longer with the inquiry of the ancients. Modern philosophy is the *philosophy of ignorance*, intellectual agnosticism, nineteenth century charlatanry. The hint of Shakespeare that matter presents a "false seeming," or it is not what it seems to be, has been converted into the dictum of philosophy, and all things, not excepting the first cause, have been clothed with masks.

Kant, thundering opinions that have shaken more than one system from its pedestal, originated the philosophic aphorism that the "thing-in-itself," which is objective, can not be known, but only phenomena and their relations may be known.   Implying a noumenon, an objective somewhat, it is phenomenon only we can know ; it is the *noumenon*, however, we are most anxious to know.   To limit knowledge to phenomena is to limit inquiry to superficial ends, and to paralyze the spirit of pursuit, for it is the somewhat, and not the manifestations thereof, the mind seeks to understand.   The " thing-in-itself," however, is only a captious phrase, or, as Prof. Bowne pronounces it, one of the " insanities of idealism."

As if with a purpose to exceed Kant in absurd philosophizing, Reid announces that, not only are phenomena alone known, but also that they are known incompletely, and, of necessity, superficially. Upham joins the philosophers in the general view of the incompetency of the human mind to penetrate the nature or understand the substance of matter, for he says, " we are altogether ignorant of the subjective or real essence of matter ; our knowledge embraces merely its qualities or properties, and nothing more."   Here the delusion of separateness between properties and substance, or belonging and being, has outspoken representation.   Herbert Spencer voices in clearest tones the creed of modern philosophy in the statement that *knowledge is relational*, not *absolute*.   Agreeing with predecessors and contemporaries that phenomena only are knowable, he imposes limitation on the knowledge of phenomena by reducing it to a cognition of relations. The *real* in matter and spirit is absolutely unknowable.

This is modern philosophy—the philosophy of cultivated self-complacent, self-atoning ignorance.   The effort of three thousand years to open a pathway for the human mind toward the infinite results in the paralyzing conviction that fore-glimpses of God, except through meager manifestations, and these expressive only of relations, are impossible.   Forever closed to man's best gaze is the infinite.   The ascertainment by any philosophical process, or a demonstration of the existence of a First Cause and an acquaintance with his attributes, is declared null and void by the moderns.   To mankind, the colossal ultimate must be, if not a myth, a stupendous, unthinkable, unexplainable mystery, to be forgotten as an empty abstraction, to be eliminated from human history, and no longer to constitute a force in religion.   To this conclusion does the " guarded or qualified materialism" of modern thinkers lead.

To reverse this conclusion is the specific business of philosophy. The problem of ontology is its first problem, which, once solved, prepares the way for the solution of all other problems.   To refuse to grapple with the problem of the unconditioned is a sign of cowardice or imbecility ; to go forward is neither irreverence nor presumption. Just what the philosophic inquirer may finally discover by a persistent search after the infinite, whether he will find God or merely find proofs of God, it is too soon to determine; no one can affirm in advance of discovery what will be discovered. It is a plunge into the unknown, with a faith that it will be less unknown, though not completely known, after the plunge than before. "The office of philosophy," says Mansel, "is not to give us a knowledge of the absolute nature of God, but to teach us to know ourselves and the limits of our faculties." This is a specific limitation of philosophic research into humanity, forbidding the higher inquiry into ontology. The "office of philosophy" is to find out what it can both concerning God and man, and to restrict it to one is a very incomplete view of what ought to be done. It is a surrender of the question before a beginning has been made. A knowledge of God will lead to a knowledge of man; a knowledge of man will be helpful to a knowledge of God; they are reciprocal, not antagonistic. Moreover, the outside universe, or the conditioned world, is a testimony to the infinite; what the testimony is, to what extent we can read it and understand it, and whether a conception of the infinite based on natural revelations, the oldest in point of time, will be sufficient, or at least helpful, in a final conception of the infinite, must in its place and time have due consideration.

The final conception of the unconditioned is, therefore, complex, partaking of a certain apriorism, or sense of the infinite, which is the product of the infinite itself, the testimony of human consciousness, and the testimony of the physical universe, a trinity of proofs resulting in a unity of notion, or the abstract idea of an infinite and unconditioned personality. Surely such glimmerings of the infinite the philosophic spirit may observe, and, observing, it may decide some things respecting the infinite. To know the infinite is to know God. Mansel, discriminating entirely too finely, says, "men may believe in an absolute and infinite without in any proper sense believing in God;" but such a belief in an absolute is a pure abstraction. The idea of the infinite is the idea of God. It may be an incomplete idea, a superstitious idea, but it is a species of theism inseparable from the idea itself. When the thought seizes the notion of an absolute, it expands into a theistic conception, either by virtue of the idea itself or the tendency of the mind to go in that direction. A close analysis of the genesis of the idea of the infinite will bring to light the fact that the idea itself, lodged in mind, is self-expansive. It is not exactly the "God-consciousness" of Schleiermacher, but an *a priori* unfolding of the idea-divine in the mind, independently of mental process or rational deduction. This apriorism, or primary output of the infinite by its own spirit, is the legitimate demonstration of the existence of the infinite, which philosophy is bound to regard. "The manifestation of the Spirit is given to every man to profit withal," says Paul. He is in the world, and always has been. He was in Socrates; he is in the heathen. The universal search is for the infinite spirit, which, if found at all, must first be found, not in man, nor in nature, but outside of both, as inherent, complete, absolute, and as only the more maturely reflected by both. This *a priori* conception of God is extra-transcendental, but it is required by the philosophic spirit. God in man is one mode of manifestation; God in nature is another; but God manifest in spirit is the highest manifestation. To deal with the highest is the first duty. The spirit of the infinite is abroad and may be found. *What* the infinite is becomes a secondary question in philosophy, not unimportant, however; perhaps, in practical life, it is more important even than the first.

It is enough, however, that philosophy may detect the infinite spirit, since the infinite is a self-acting, self-manifesting spirit. Inaccessible he is in his own region, but not without manifestation in our sphere. The condition of spirit is activity; activity implies manifestation; manifestation may be by direct methods, or indirect, that is, through the forms of consciousness, or the forms of matter.

Of the scintillations of the infinite in human consciousness, or the reflection of God in man, the proofs are not wanting, they are not obscure. This reflection of the infinite we denominate a maturer reflection than that of pure spirit, since it is within our reach, and susceptible of a partial analysis. The aprioristic proof of God is a sensible revelation of his spirit; but it is not a full revelation of his character. This is the next demand. The testimony of the human consciousness to the existence of the infinite, is at the least assuring, and as to the character of God it speaks to some purpose. The origin of consciousness is not now in dispute; its revelations alone concerns us. In the depths of human consciousness Cousin clearly foresaw the signs of the infinite, tracing them in those intuitional forms which constitute the frame-work of rational psychology. Reason, like the magnet, points in one direction only; unerringly does it indicate the infinite. By reason, Cousin means the universal, untaught, primary race-consciousness of God which no degradation can smother and no ignorance annihilate. Descartes projecting the psychological method had an apt follower in Cousin, who emphasized the method beyond its author in the proof of the existence of God. The substratum of thought is the infinite; the foundations of conscious existence are laid in the absolute. "In him we live;" in us he lives also. The contents of the consciousness, or of reason may be embraced in at least three terms, which understood in their relations, may be finally reduced to a single term. Without education, without development, the deeply laid reason of man concedes, recognizes, and in its spontaneities operates with, the correlated ideas of the infinite and the finite, unity and multiplicity, causation and its consequence; with the inevitable relation of one to the other; and any apparent after-acquirement of these ideas is but the expansion of ideas original with the human consciousness. The condition of consciousness is the constant but unstudied recognition of finite and infinite, from which may be predicted the existence of both. A dependent pair of ideas is suggestive of the independent existence of the objective forms they represent. So the intuitional thought of finite and infinite is a proclamation of the existence of both in objective forms and relations. This much the consciousness affirms if it affirm any thing. How it affirms any thing is not involved in the investigation; that it affirms the infinite what is called the race-consciousness will allow. And in affirming the infinite, it immediately affirms it in relation which is a step toward the solution of character. Pure, unrelated spirit, manifesting itself by pressure only, may not be analyzed; but pure related spirit, active and manifested in action, *i. e.*, in relation, the mind may the more clearly discern, and to a degree comprehend. Hence, a related infinite is preferable to an unrelated infinite. An *unrelated infinite does not exist;* it is an abstraction, and philosophy is unphilosophical in so far as it confines itself to the unconditioned. The related infinite is a true philosophical infinite, which the rational spirit in man at once recognizes and worships. True, this is an anthropomorphic infinite, an infinite constructed by the consciousness; this is the trend of intuitionalism, but it can not be avoided. Socrates drifted into anthropomorphism; all rational, psychological, intuitional philosophy is carried over into a recognition of such an infinite. The only question is, is the infinite predicated by the reason, the true infinite? To this we reply that as there can not be two infinites, any infinite predicated on a ground that can account for itself must be the true infinite. A false infinite is never predicated by any thing. A true infinite only is foreshadowed, dimly it may be, but not uncertainly. Hence, an anthropomorphic infinite is as reliable as a spirit or *a priori* infinite, or any other manifested or unmanifested infinite. Prof. Bowne seriously questions the force of intuitionalism, so-called, in the realm of ontology. Styling innate ideas the "raw rudiments of consciousness," he makes vigorous war upon them in order to relieve intuitionalism from some of its absurdities; but it is evident that in avoiding one extreme he has swung over to its opposite. In answering Mill's allusion to the innate ideas of children, he scorns the thought of making a babe a pope in philosophy; but he at length accords to the "latencies" of consciousness which develop in the reflective mind the value of convictions respecting the infinite. The spontaneous consciousness is insignificant in its determination of the absolute; the reflective consciousness is voiceful of the infinite. In outcome, what is the difference between raw intuitionalism and the developed reason? And if the developed reason intimates the infinite, the spontaneous reason must contain the intimation, just as the acorn contains the tree. The pope in philosophy is either a babe or a man; in either case it is consciousness. Bowne is, therefore, an intuitionalist, vindicating the infinite from himself, an irresistible argument, put either in the old way, or the new.

Mansel, examining the conditions of human consciousness, finds in it no absolutely clear adumbration of the infinite; on the contrary, he sees in its conditions the contradictions of attributes which are allowed to belong to the infinite. This is a gun which in its recoil destroys the man that fires it. In an act of consciousness, one object is distinguished from another which implies limitation; but limitation can not belong to the absolute. Again, consciousness implies relation between subject and object; but the absolute is unrelated. Again, consciousness implies succession and duration in time, or the finite; but the infinite is not finite. Lastly, consciousness implies personality; but personality implies limitation and relation; hence, it can not represent the infinite.

The weakness of this representation is two-fold: 1. Its implications of consciousness; 2. Its assumptions of the infinite. Initial or "raw" consciousness has but a single term, the infinite. From the single term emerges another term, the finite, and from both another, or relation. Relations, succession, limitations, are the products of the single term. The only idea in the consciousness is God. All others are subordinate or correlated. Mansel, selecting the subordinate ideas of the consciousness, proceeds to demolish the structure of rational theology, thus affording aid and comfort to materialism.

His assumptions respecting the infinite are even more glaring than his weak analysis of consciousness. To deny personality to the infinite is to leave us Hartmann's *unconscious* deity, or no deity at all. To assert that the absolute is unrelated, is to assert what a finite mind can not know. To assert that the infinite is without any limitation whatever is equally a matter beyond human knowledge. Evidently, Mansel's infinite is not anthropomorphic; it is not a rational, conscious, personal being. But this is drifting. God's foundations are in man as man's foundation is in the dust; a psychological infinite is the demand of the reason, as a physiological finite is the demand of the senses. To deny to reason the power to apprehend the infinite from its own processes of thought, to deny to consciousness the power to index the absolute is to leave God without a witness of himself in his greatest work, and will require a theology on a basis entirely foreign to human instincts and human life. Such a theology the human race has not as yet demanded.

Mansel asserts that "we have no immediate intuitions of the divine attributes, even as phenomena;" but this is straining the case beyond warrant. No intuitionalist claims that through the consciousness alone a knowledge of the divine attributes, taken singly, is possible; all that he claims is a satisfactory assurance of the existence of an absolute being, whose attributes are vaguely inferred by subsequent acts of the reflective reason. In the subsequent work of attribute-building there may be mistakes, but in the original conception of the Absolute there is no mistake. Discovery of the infinite precedes description. Theology, revelation, psychology, may be necessary to the latter; apriorism and consciousness are necessary to the former.

Sir William Hamilton, prior to Mansel, going over the same ground, characterized the anthropomorphic infinite as a mere abstraction, and rejected its identity with the true infinite. Breaking loose from rational testimony, he constructs an infinite, unconditioned, unrelated, unknowable, unthinkable. His conclusion is logical. To posit a rational infinite, or an unthinkable infinite, or no infinite at all, is the only alternative. An irrational infinite is inconceivable; a supra-rational infinite is possible, but it is unthinkable, because above reason. Hamilton, unrestrained in imagination, exalts the unthinkable infinite, and Mansel echoes the baneful philosophy.

In these flights to supra-rationalism the ordinary methods of reasoning have been abandoned, and necessarily so. The psychological method, so instrumental in the hands of Cousin, is opposed to supra-rationalism; the empirical method, in the hands of the associationalists, only leads to an irrational infinite, or no infinite at all; the theological method conducts to a rational infinite; but the supra-rational method leads to a supra-rational infinite, in which man can have no practical or permanent interest.

The answer to supra-rationalism is the consciousness itself, the contents of which, having been analyzed, need not be repeated.

The remaining item in our conception of the infinite is the testimony of the physical universe, which not only encourages belief in the divine existence, but also reflects somewhat of the divine character, two points necessary to a comprehensive understanding of the infinite. The fact of God is of primary importance. Does the natural world re-declare him with the emphasis that attends the declaration of the human consciousness? Clearly, the answer turns upon the meaning philosophy gives to the natural world. If, as Mill suggested, the outer world is only a projection of subjective elements, an argument from it is of the nature of that drawn from the consciousness, and is a reinforcement. If, as Berkeley insisted, matter does not exist, no argument is possible from that quarter. If, as Fitche held, the non-ego is a limitation of the ego, or a part of the ego, then indeed a divine argument emerges, but at the expense of the idea of absolute and independent personality. If, as Descartes taught, the subject and object, or mind and matter, are entirely distinct, with no impulse to interaction, then it is possible to frame an argument from each which shall join in the general conclusion. If the implicit teaching of materialists that the universe is eternal be correct, then the question of an infinite God is open for discussion. If the implicit faith of humanity that the objective is the result of creation be well-founded, then an argument for a Creator is irresistible.

From these and other standpoints nature may be viewed in its relation to the problem of the infinite, adding its testimony to the common faith, or bewildering, and possibly overthrowing it. All idealistic views aside, the conflict in the testimony springs from the empirical conception of the universe as infinite or eternal, in contrast with the rational conception that it is finite, and, therefore, a product of the infinite. Between these reason must decide. Revelation apart, the reason must spell the infinite in the characters of the finite; or, denying the finite, accept the pantheistic conception of the unity of God and the universe—a conception which, failing to distinguish one from the other, virtually destroys both. The "eternity of matter" is in conflict with the eternity of God. In an apologetic spirit, Leibnitz leaned toward the materialistic assumption of an eternal universe, yet so as not to compromise the idea of the absolute infinity of God. This he did by distinguishing between a relative infinity, as applied to the universe, and an absolute infinity, as applied to God; but the thought of two kinds of infinity is not rational. If a relative infinity is less than infinite, it is not infinity at all; if equal to it, it is divine. One or other it is. Some there are who say space is infinite and time eternal, meaning a relative infinity as applied to one, and a relative eternity as applied to the other; but the language is used in an accommodated sense to express incomputable vastness, and practically limitless duration. The philosopher, however, rarely speaks in an accommodated sense. His business is with absolute truth, which will not admit an easy, or elastic phraseology. A relative infinity is suggestive of a relative infinite, from which the mind recoils. The suspicion that the universe is in any sense infinite or eternal is a compromise of the basal idea of the infinity and eternity of God.

Hamilton struggled with the alternative of an infinite non-commencement or an absolute commencement of the universe, deciding that it is impossible to conceive of either, and yet that he must believe in the latter. This is only one of a number of paralogisms for which that philosopher is so eminently noted. If both are inconceivable, then the universe is inconceivable; but, as the universe is conceivable, an absolute commencement is conceivable, since an infinite non-commencement is in itself absurd. But absolute commencement is the logical basis of the common faith in a Creator. Thus, from the alternative of Hamilton emerges a theistic conclusion as satisfactory as theology would require; and though he phrases the unconditioned and absolute as inconceivable, he yet demands faith in it, as he finally does in a finite universe. This is the testimony of the universe: it is finite, it reflects the infinite; it had a beginning, it reflects the eternal; it is conditioned, it reflects the unconditioned. Beyond such testimony we need not go. As to its revelations of the infinite God, in his character, government, and purposes, this is not the place for a free estimate; in subsequent pages the divine character will be exhibited, as it is revealed.

The primary question of philosophy relates to the possibility of a knowledge of the existence of God by the reason. Evidently, such knowledge may be attained in this way. Employing *a priori* convictions, the sentiments of the consciousness, and the testimony of the universe, the reason is able to satisfy itself as to the existence of a divine being; and this justifies the philosophic attempt at investigation. Philosophy has a mission, since God is cognizable by the reason. The philosopher's occupation is not ended; it is but begun.

Nor is the problem of the infinite the only problem of philosophy. Man is a stupendous mystery, and asks for self-explanation. God interpreted, the interpretation of man must follow; hence, God and man are one in the solution. Still, secondary as man is, he is warranted in making an independent self-examination, in order the more completely to understand God in his relations to man. A knowledge of being; a knowledge of soul; a knowledge of relations; enter into the final conception of man. The history of humanity is as imperative as the history of the idea of God, for the human idea is as patent in civilization and history as the divine. Ignoring not the higher, it is incumbent on the philosopher carefully to inquire into the lower, and beginning with God to terminate in man, or beginning with man to terminate in God, linking the two into unity.

The necessity for a searching self-examination or a study of the contents of human history, grows chiefly out of recent philosophic interpretations of man, both as respects his physical origin and physical character. The old question, "What is man?" is as philosophical as it is Scriptural, to be answered philosophically as well as Scripturally. Evolutionists like Häckel and Spencer pronounce man's appearance to be the result of the animal development in the world; and psychologists like Alexander Bain, abrogating the essential difference between matter and spirit, declare mental action to be the result of physical organization, and the mind, therefore, to be a refined form of matter. The common faith respecting man's creation and the immortality of the soul is in direct conflict with evolution as expressed or formulated and with psychology as perverted in the interest of materialism. The conflict is fundamental. It involves character, destiny; involving character, it involves God; involving destiny, it involves the highest self-interest. Hence, philosophy in its secondary work becomes physiological and psychological, as in its first work it is eminently theological. Nor can it suspend its task until, sinking lower, and yet rationally, it undertakes to estimate the visible or phenomenal world, interpreting it in its essence and in its relations to being. A lower task, but parallel in one sense with the higher, for the solution of the non-ego will materially aid in the understanding of the ego, as the solution of the ego will certainly result in a comprehension of the non-ego. In a previous paragraph it is hinted that philosophy tends sometimes to pantheism, or Spinozism, or Eleaticism, or subjective idealism, either to an amalgamation of the finite and infinite, or a total denial of the finite, all of which is subversive of true knowledge. As in the case of man, the universe must have a separate and independent treatment, or confusion will follow in the human understanding respecting things that otherwise might be partially understood.

Conceding separate treatment, which is conceding separate reality to nature, we confront certain philosophic theories respecting our knowledge of nature that destroys the value not only of separate treatment but also of any treatment at all of nature. For example: Hamilton precipitates his doctrine of the *relativity of knowledge*, confining inquiry to mere relations, or phenomena in their relations, and forbidding any scrutiny back of forms or qualities. This is a blockade to intelligent inquiry, compelling it to cease at the very point where it is anxious to press for answer. Superior to Hamilton in defining the limitations of knowledge, Kant declares the phenomenal alone knowable, shrouding the "thing-in-itself," or essence of matter, with the blackness of mystery, and inculpating the intellect with an inability to penetrate beyond the visible. This is in conflict with the Christian conception of nature and with a true theory of knowledge, both of which will be stated and enforced at the proper time. In its interpretation of the universe philosophy descends into geology for facts, and roams over psychology for principles. Thus is it a scientific seeker, or philosophy with a scientific spirit.

Philosophy in its search for the unconditioned is strictly theological; in its study of man it is semi-scientific; in its estimate of the universe it is wholly scientific. It embraces all knowledge, outside of Revelation, and is itself a continual revelation of truth, combining the study of God, mind, and matter, as neither theology nor science, if confined to their specific tasks, can do.

What is the province of philosophy? Is it to dwell in caves, lit up by the feeble torchlights of the senses? or is it to seek the transfigured heights of truth, and, discovering the long-lost and long-sought knowledge, pilot the race through the avenues of darkness to the jeweled throne of God?

The province of philosophy, as apprehended by philosophers themselves, as sketched in these pages, is the discovery or declaration of the uncaused personality in the universe, as the cause of all actuality, of the phenomenal world. This is its first duty. Personality, not law; being, not manifestation; substance, not qualities; God, not atomic principles; it must seek to understand and proclaim. Philosophy must not discrown God.

The province of philosophy is to understand man chiefly as a *mind-being*. Psychology and physiology, if twins, are not Siamese twins; they are not a unit; they cling not together; they perish not together. The distinction between mind and matter must be clearly drawn, and man must be ennobled, not degraded, by self-knowledge. Philosophy must not discrown man.

The province of philosophy is to comprehend the universe. This it is essaying to do, but its failure is manifest. Philosophy must be emancipated from the fiction that the universe is a self-creating, self-preserving, self-executing mechanism. Nor in the emancipation will it swing to a pantheistic conception of the universe, an equally dangerous fiction, as it confuses personality with universality. Philosophy, linking the phenomenal to its chariot, as the conquering Roman generals did their prisoners, may ride around the world amid the plaudits of the multitudes; but, clinging like Stephen to the divine throne, it may ascend amid a mob of stones into the presence of God.

The initial fact of philosophy is—*Nature.*

The intermediate term of philosophy is—*Man.*

The ultimate word of philosophy is—*God.*

# CHAPTER IV.

### NATURE; OR AN EXEGESIS OF MATTER.

SO absorbed with rational inquiry and moral speculation was Socrates that he formed no acquaintance with nature; he never addressed her in any form, and she never impressed him, notwithstanding her beauty and power. From the trees, the rocks, the fields, he learned nothing, but drifted into an idealistic conception of things that extinguished all interest in them. How far the absence of cordial sympathy with the physical world is a disqualification for philosophic insight into its contents may not be pointed out, but if one would exhaustively contemplate phenomenal appearances and activities, one must be *en rapport* with the phenomenal spirit, or the essence of things. Sir Walter Scott loved the trees; Cromwell was at home in the fields; Audubon drew the birds to his hand; Hugh Miller traced in the rocks the hand-marks of an unseen power; and David shouted, "The heavens declare the glory of God." Rousseau was a worshiper of the material universe, and Häckel proposes the religion of nature as a substitute for Christianity. The philosophic indifference of Socrates and the philosophic devotion of Häckel are extremes to be avoided, for nature, as the arcanum of truth, should be studied, probed, questioned, and yet not be regarded as supreme, since both philosophy and religion agree that its existence is a mutation, and its final fate a dissolution. Nature is possessed of charms that poets have embalmed in verse; laws that scientists have framed in words; relationships that naturalists have reduced to systems; interactions, homologies and adaptations that have excited the admiration of observers; moral hints and suggestions that theologians have eagerly turned to account; evidences of superintending power that atheists have not overthrown; and exhibitions of divine wisdom that should thrill alike the inquirer and believer.

Wide is the field of nature; hidden are some of its forces; occult is its ultimate purpose; problematical is its destiny; and difficult is the task of searching and finding the spirit that dwells in it. Such a task philosophy imposes, such a task the philosopher must assume. That difficulties lie before the investigator of nature is self-evident; that a satisfactory conclusion touching all points involved in the investigation should not be expected in our present state of knowledge concerning matter, all must agree.

To be comprehensive, one's study of nature should embrace three points of view: viz., the common representation, the philosophic interpretation, and the religious conception, each being distinct in itself but taken together affording a progressive and complete idea of the physical universe.

By the common representation is meant the uneducated, universal view of the race which, gross in some particulars, and superstitious in others, has in it certain traditional elements of truth upon which the race has acted with singular uniformity from the beginning. The practical sagacity of mankind, never rising to the height of a critical or close observation, and never going behind what it sees, hears, and touches, has led to the discovery of specific facts and principles in the economy of nature which have been applied to agriculture, navigation, architecture, and the general sphere of man's civil and social life, to his advantage and development. In other words, nature has been made tributary to the race's history and happiness. The appropriation of nature's laws, facts, and forms in man's history has been superficial since man himself has been slow to inquire, discover, adapt, and employ the resources of nature. However, out of the crude and artless utilization of nature in the civilization of the world have issued a knowledge of nature, and a purpose to find out more than is now known.

To interpret nature according to a religious creed, or in the religious spirit, is the specific enterprise of those charged with the defense and propagation of Christian doctrine; but philosophy itself can not proceed by entirely ignoring the Biblical exegesis, or even the crude conceptions of the unlettered multitude.

The philosophic interpretation will appear to better advatage as its relations to the common and the Christian conceptions are conceded; but for the purposes of this chapter it may be considered apart from both.

As a preparation for a philosophic understanding of nature, we oblige ourselves to consider it in its wholeness, and not in its parts, only as they shall serve to illustrate the fundamental principles at issue. The law of analysis binds us to a descent from the universal to the particular, or, holding us to the universal conception of nature, permits its application to the individualizations of that conception in the concrete forms of matter. As painting may be studied in its abstract principles, and no particular product of an artist be under inspection; as music and oratory may be historically contemplated without regard to particular compositions—so nature may be viewed in its entirety without a minute analysis of any particular form of it. The topaz is not the open door into the mineral kingdom; the geranium is not the sponsor for the vegetable world; the mastodon, the lynx, the eagle, or the horse represents not the animal kingdom; that is, the part is not the key to the whole, but the whole is the key to all the parts. From the height of the whole the interactions, the relations, and the individuality of the parts may be detected, expressed, and understood.

From this view it is easy to see that what will explain one world will explain the universe, and what will interpret the earth will interpret all that is upon it. What will account for the ocean will account for every drop in it. If we can not account for the whole, we can not account for the parts, The whole includes the parts.

Out of the reduction of many views to one, and from this gaze in the beginning at the universal instead of the particular, arises the suspicion that nature is one, and is to be philosophically interpreted from the standpoint of unity. The conclusion of a unity in nature is not new to the religious mind, for it is a Biblical doctrine, but philosophy has slowly advanced toward it, and is now compelled to embrace it. Plato was on the right track when he said, " The end of all philosophy is the intuition of unity," but his was a unity of cause rather than a unity of effect—a unity of the infinite intelligence rather than a unity of the manifested universe. Both conceptions—the unity of God and the unity of nature—are legitimate philosophic deductions, with only the latter of which we are at present concerned.

Worshipers of the idea of the unity of nature are not confined to theologians; the most eminent scientists and philosophers bow down before it, as they are affected by the religious spirit, or as pure science compels its acknowledgment, or as they discover that it apparently contributes to the support of their particular hypothesis. Whatever the motive, the unity of nature is now accepted by all classes of thinkers as a demonstrated fact. Häckel is very loud in its praise, but with evident purpose to rob nature of a teleological authorship, and to honor it as a self-made product. Humboldt was firmly persuaded that " one indissoluble chain of affinity binds together all nature." Sir W. R. Grove refers the causation of all " material affections," such as light, heat, electricity, magnetism, and motion to " one omnipresent influence ;" while Hume admits that " one design prevails throughout the whole " universe, and that all things in it are " evidently of a piece." Linnæus urged that the animal world sprang from a single pair, and that the spirit of oneness is in nature. Hermann Lotze intimates that the essence of " things " is unity ; hence the essence of nature is the spirit of unity that pervades it.

Without qualifying the opinions of the scientists and philosophers, or attempting to separate the true from the false, it is clear that the conviction that nature is, in an extraordinary sense, a unit, is universal. Materialists, evolutionists, associationalists, psychologists, physiologists, naturalists, have at last surrendered to the Biblical conception of the unity of the universe. The scientific dogma of unity may be expressed in phrases different from the form of the Biblical dogma, but the two agree in one. The basis of the former is scientific demonstration; the basis of the latter is revealed truth. In what the unity consists—whether of substance, form, origin, use, or destiny—is a primary question; but it is gratifying that the scientific dogma and the Biblical representation are almost identical on all these points. Whatever difference exists is incidental.

Respecting the substance of matter, it has been demonstrated that the same gross constituents enter the composition of all planetary bodies, and that matter is, so far as determined, the same everywhere. By means of the spectroscope it has been ascertained that the sun and the earth are composed of the same materials, from which it is inferred that the planetary bodies constitute a brotherhood, bearing the same image, made in the same way, and appointed to the same destiny. The unity of substance is therefore the first declaration of the scientific dogma establishing the unity of the authorship of the physical universe.

Quite as expository of the scientific dogma is the admitted fact of the simplicity of matter, by which is meant that nature is a compound reducible in the last analysis to a few essential elements. The chemist is bold enough to announce that at the most there are not more than seventy elements that compose the earth, but of these only thirteen are prominent, or used freely in the forms and combinations of nature. Of the thirteen elements, only three or four, namely, oxygen, carbon, silicon, and nitrogen, are universally active, and of these oxygen constitutes about one-half. Professor Huxley reduces every material substance to water, ammonia, and carbonic acid, but this is a complex reduction, susceptible to a more minute subdivision. Oxygen is the great world-builder—a single element. Back of oxygen, however, it may finally be possible to go, for as a simple element, it may be ascertained to be compound; and so of all other so-called simple elements. Under a more incisive and penetrating analysis, the simple may appear compound and the compound simple, until, going back to the final limit, all matter may be reduced to one element, of which the others are but diversified manifestations. In the immature stages of Physics voltaic electricity, thermo-electricity, and animal electricity were designated as different *kinds* of electricity, but electricity is a unit divisible into these different forms. So the seventy elements may be the metamorphosis of one element. Indeed, Dr. Prout, attributing a certain numerical value to chemical substances, which he called the atomic weight of the substance, found in nearly all cases that it was an exact multiple of the atomic weight of hydrogen, and was disposed, therefore, to regard *hydrogen as unity, or the starting-point of the material universe.* To be sure, oxygen or carbon, or any other element, might be taken as the unit of weight, but in such a case it would be arbitrary, whereas hydrogen appears like nature's own unit, and chemists generally now recognize it as the standard of atomic measurement. This system of weights or values has been assailed, but it is remarkable that it has not been overthrown.

With slight variations in the system to meet certain exceptions, it may be used to prove that all substances are but multiples or manifestations of primary substances, or a single original element, leading back to a unit never before dreamed of in philosophy. Thales traced all things to water ; but modern chemistry traces the atomic unit to hydrogen. If the worlds are but multiples of the atomic unit, how simple the whole universe, and what a demonstration of its unity ! The diversity of nature-forms in no sense stands in the way of, or qualifies the objective oneness of, world-life, for, given the single element, it is possible to explain all nature from it. An endless number of forms do not perplex any more than a limited number. Three thousand stars do not introduce any more new problems than a single orb ; the explanation of one is the explanation of all. We are not, then, at the mercy of diversity ; it has its explanation.

Vast is the animal kingdom, including more than twenty thousand species, and yet the whole is comprehended in the usual zoölogical system, which divides them into Vertebrata, Articulata, Mollusca, and Radiata, four great divisions, suggestive of the four elements which prominently appear in the inorganic world ; and, as the four elements have been reduced to an atomic unit, so the four zoölogical branches may be reduced to a single beginning. This is, indeed, the theory of "descent," a contribution to the doctrine of the world's unity, but warped in the support of a materialistic hypothesis of the world's origin and development.

Scientists have been troubled not a little over the subject of species, Linnæus insisting that the animal kingdom originated from a single pair, while nearly all the later scientists have consented to a limited number of fixed types or original species in the beginning. Even granting that the theory of Linnæus is unacceptable, the doctrine of fixed types is sufficiently efficient in its support of the doctrine of unity.

Moreover, from the homological principle which seems to pervade the animal kingdom, a singularly striking proof of the scientific dogma of unity may be obtained. Zoölogists agree that there is a correspondence, not, perhaps, complete, but sufficiently close to be observable, among the vertebrates in the general construction of their organs and the arrangement of their parts, pointing to a general plan in their history and development. For instance, the hands and feet of a man, the paws of a lion, the feet of a horse, and the fins of a whale, are homologous, demonstrating a common idea, and really establishing an animalic relationship. The parallelism is by no means incidental; its prominence in nature materialists employ as the proof of the unity of the world, or that one general idea pervades the one kingdom. Accepting the scientific discovery of the homological principle, it furnishes irresistible proof of the philosophic and theistic notion of a world-wide unity, centering in a common divine authorship.

In like manner the vegetable world may be divided and subdivided, and, under the homological principle, reduced to a single plan, and possibly to a single element. The inorganic world likewise submits to a similar reduction, pointing unmistakably to one plan and to one source. Evidently, science is pushing back toward the fewest elements in the process of world-building, and is priding itself on the discovery of the law of atomic unity in nature, grounding all its forms into multiples of a unit, invested with the capabilities of a manifold life.

Philosophy may readily embrace the doctrine of unity when so thoroughly supported by facts; yet, if Häckel's view of nature be sustained, namely, that it is a physico-chemical process, without a personal author, and that it is a history of false suggestions, then deductions are unreliable; but, on the whole, science gravitates to the view of the unity of nature in the sense explained. Häckel applies the word "cenogeny" to nature, meaning by it a "history of falsifications," as if nature were untrue to itself or its own laws; but this is in the interest of the grossest materialism. The scientific presentation of the hypothesis of unity is not always what a philosopher may approve, and the philosophic elaboration of a scientific fact may be repugnant to a true or theistic conception of unity; nevertheless, the idea of unity is congenial to science, philosophy, and religion.

Planck undertakes to solve the unity of nature by a principle of "inner concentration," which is impulsive enough to reach out in all directions, producing in its activity the great and the small, and man as well as the insect. Just what the principle is, beyond its ideal character, it is a little difficult to gather, but, rationalizing it into a practical force, he attributes to it more than it actually possesses. St. George Mivart hints of an innate force, or internal powers, but his is a scientific utterance, while Planck's is a metaphysical illusion that really accounts for nothing. Its break-down is in its application to man, who, instead of being the product of an inner impulse of nature, is verily the image of a power outside of nature. The attempt of Planck, however inconclusive and unsatisfactory, is yet in harmony with the general idea; it presupposes that idea, and undertakes its solution.

That mystical religious teacher, Swedenborg, was charmed with the scientific idea of unity, but went entirely beyond the limits of science for an explanation, and so his theory has suffered the usual fate of such adventures. Reduced to an aphoristic form, "nature is always self-similar." This is another phrase for the homology of nature extended to plants as well as animals. In the botanical realm the plant proceeds from leaf to leaf, ascending to something higher, but always carrying the mark of the lower; it is a process of repetition as the condition of enlargement. The great is the repetition of the small. In the animal kingdom the same law has constant illustration, as in vertebrates, beginning with the spine, hands, feet, and spines multiply, and at last man emerges. *Man is a spine!* Nature is an ascending scale of unities and homologies, or a series of repetitions and enlargements, working along a line of anticipations of something higher, a foreshadowing of evolution, mystically, rather than scientifically, presented.

Concentrating his thought upon the doctrine of unity, Swedenborg surmised that each unity, so to speak, is a compound of unities, the simple is the sign of the complex, as the unity of the heart is made up of the unities of small hearts, and the unity of the eye consists of the unities of small eyes. A rational scientific order proceeds from the complex to the simple, but Swedenborg's mystical order ascends from the simple to the complex, rising from the finite to the infinite; but it is confusing, because it is not transparent. Besides, its scientific accuracy may well be doubted. The eye is not a combination of eyes; the hand is not a combination of hands; a leaf is not a combination of leaves. At least the scientific proof is wanting. Notwithstanding the mystical idea of Swedenborg is mythical, and the theory of unity within unities is untenable, he held to the primary thought of wholeness in nature that pointed to a single governmental administration, having all power and all wisdom, and therefore sufficient for all things.

Goethe speculated with rare philosophical ingenuity on nature, discerning in it a unity based on the correlation of its parts, and suggesting the latter-day doctrine of the correlation of forces. Emerson's statement that "he has said the best things about nature that ever were said," we can not accept fully, for he has denied some of the most patent scientific principles or facts, as the prismatic colors. Concerning unity, the leaf, in his judgment, is the key to the botanical kingdom, and the spine to the vertebrates; that is, the leaf is the unit in the one kingdom, and the spine the unit in the other. He affirms that the plant is a transformed leaf, and that the leaf may be converted into any organ of the plant, and any organ of a plant may be converted into a leaf. As clearly does he declare that the head is the spine transformed, and it would follow that the head might be converted into spines, or a spine into any organ of the head. This theory of " transformation" implies an involved relationship that borders closely on the chemical idea of correlation, as motion is a form of heat, and heat a form of motion. It is a question if Goethe's idea, rescued from a scientific form, will not appear more speculative than practical or real, and if he did not borrow a little hallucination from Swedenborg. Even if the doctrine of correlation of forces has an indisputable basis in fact, it may not be true as applied to the organs of plants, or the forms of matter, that is, the products of these forces. The homology of organs does not imply the convertibility of organs into one another. A leaf may be the figure of a tree in the mind's eye, but it is not clear that the tree is a transformed leaf. Goethe looked at nature, not in its wholeness, but in its parts, and proceeded in his theorizing from the particular to the universal, a mistaken order, resulting in a mistaken interpretation of nature. Like all other theories, however, it confirms the doctrine of unity in nature, which is the chief point under consideration.

Humboldt, prying into the deep secrets of the world as if they must throw off their disguises in his presence, imbibed as a foundation-idea of his cosmical beliefs the conception of a world-wide unity, which was the inspiration of all his discoveries and the root of all his labors. In him the conviction was profound that throughout nature one plan prevails by which order and development can be explained, and which had behind it the principle of an efficient and final causation. Swedenborg is mystical; Goethe, speculative; Humboldt is rigidly scientific, and therefore the most accurate and the most conclusive.

The option of the student is that, while accepting unity as a scientific and philosophic doctrine, he may choose the materialistic solution of the doctrine as enunciated by Häckel, the mystical as avowed by Swedenborg, the correlative as proclaimed by Goethe, or the scientific as clearly presented by Humboldt. The trend of science, speculation, and philosophy is toward the doctrine of unity in nature. Except the most deformed and irrational pessimisms, all science, all philosophy, all religions, all materialisms, *unite in proclaiming the regnancy of an absolute monistic principle in the realm of nature.* On any other hypothesis science is impossible, and along this line of accepted doctrine there is the possibility of reconciliation between systems hitherto roughly antagonistic and productive of discord in circles that ought to agree. The first right view of nature, then, is that which so many divergent systems of thinking combine in maintaining, namely, *the unity of the physical world.*

Agreeing to the doctrine of unity, the problem of the origin of nature, which now introduces itself, is somewhat simplified, for, if there are two or more kinds of matter, one origin might be insufficient to account for them. As it is, in the solution of the origin of an atom of matter, or the discovery of a physiological or initial unit, lies the solution of the universe, and, conversely, the solution of the universe involves the solution of all that it contains.

In its search after solutions the reason is confined to one of three theories, all of which have been ably expounded, but only one of which can be entertained as true.

(*a*). The theory of the pre-existence of matter which the Stoics espoused and which does not require personal agency to account for it. Personal agency may be necessary to the organization of matter into forms, but by this theory divine intervention in the institution of matter is eliminated. Seneca taught that God organized matter, but did not create it. Anaxagoros said "all things had been produced at the same time, and then intellect had come and arranged them all in order." Intellect is an organizer, but not a creator.

(*b*). The theory that matter created itself. This is absurd, but recent scientists have held that the world organized itself without divine agency. Even Kant conceded that while God created matter and endowed it with laws, the universe developed without his personal supervision. Seneca and Kant occupy opposite grounds. Cicero conclusively disposes of the theory of a self-made universe by remarking that it is as sensible to suppose the Iliad was written by shaking letters in a bag as to suppose that the universe made itself.

(*c*). The theory of the divine creation of matter. This solves every difficulty and in itself is the most rational conception of the origin of the universe. Given an intelligent Creator, and the end is reached, the dilemma is solved. Middle ground is impossible here. Between a self-made and a created universe there is no room even for thought. By its very constitution the mind demands not only a cause for every thing, but the cause must be sufficient to produce the effect. The Greeks fancied that every tree had its Dryad, which inspired it with life and died with the tree. The Dryad is represented as a cause, but it is not a sufficient cause. The mind refuses to be satisfied with inadequate causes, even though they are causes and come to us in stately forms and are dressed in philosophic beauty. The cause must not only be a cause, but it must be adequate. Atomism is inadequate, for the atomist is unable to account for the atom. Atomism explains nothing; the most that it does is to remove the problem so far back that the mind loses sight of it, but vagueness is not solution. In the present stage of scientific research mystery impends over all problems, but it is incumbent on the scientist to avoid absurdities, contradictions, and false shows, and either suspend judgment until all the facts are obtained, or provisionally accept that theory which contains the fewest antinomies, and is freest from internal difficulties.

Reference to the mechanical theory of the world is unsatisfactory, for it deals with a developing world, or one in process of organic structure from pre-existing substances and by virtue of pre-existing forces and laws, and goes not back to primary or original sources. Reaching secondary causes it labels them primary, but the deception is apparent. Even should it contract the universe into a single atom, with a potentiality equal to the production of the universe, it is incumbent that it show where and how the first atom originated and whence it derived its sovereign vitality. What was the first throb of power that resulted in a potential atom, an atom that had a world or system of worlds rolled up in its invisible boundaries? Mechanical philosophy stares wildly as it searches for the beginning of the atomic movement.

Musæus, an Athenian, taught that "all things originated in one thing and when dissolved returned to the same thing;" but the *one thing*, as source of all things, he does not name or describe, and had he described it, its origin had still been a problem. Simplification of a problem is desirable, but it is not equivalent to a solution. Germs, physiological units, protoplasm, atoms, cells, eggs,—these do not contain the whole truth, the omitted portion being more important than what is declared. Atomism, monism, mechanism, words these that vindicate the doctrine of unity, but the origin of unity, the origin of atoms, cells, eggs, still remains unanswered.

The nebular hypothesis if true may explain the origin of planets but not the origin of matter; that is, mechanical theories may be useful in determining the origin of the forms of matter without giving the least hint of the origin of matter. Between substance and form, or the spirit and body of matter, the difference is as great as that between memory and the brain. Once insure the existence of formless matter and its subsequent formal assertion follows. In this connection Kant perpetrates the following: "Give me matter, and I will explain the formation of a world; but give me matter only, and I can not explain the formation of a caterpillar." Formless matter is the prophecy of formal matter only because a Former exists and superintends the form. First the Former, second formless matter, third formal matter; these steps are philosophical because necessary and rational. Spinoza accords to matter three potencies, gravity, light, and organization, but these are the potencies of law, for the organizing process is quite as much a legal procedure as the reign of gravity in nature. In no sense are these self-endowed potencies, but on the contrary, they are the expression of an intelligent supervision of the nature-world, by which it is perpetuated and controlled. Organization, or form, is the manner in which substance chooses to express itself; it is the way in which substance behaves. Original or formless matter, the "world-stuff," may have been independent of government; if so, its only law was *inertia*; it existed with scarcely a property; it was potential, not actual; but in process of time the organizing spirit being imparted to it, it took permanent shape through the avenues of gravitation, chemical affinity, crystallization, and by means of the entire catalogue of nature's laws. By this change from the formless to the formal, matter advanced to a state of becoming something and is distinguished from being by being styled the *becoming*, or the non-being. It is not being, but it seems to strive after being, and comes as near to it as one substance can be like another. It has reality, but its visible reality consists in its forms; its hidden reality is the spirit that dwells in it. Both the form and the spirit we shall now consider.

The forms of matter are not the accidental results of the attrition of unguided forces, but the careful expression of geometrical ideas, evincing a plan in the history and development of nature. Nature is geometry crystallized. Not a single physical form can be pointed out that is not the embodiment of a geometrical principle or figure. The circle and the ellipse are embodied in the orbits of the spheres, and in the spheres themselves; and angles of every name are illustrated in crystals, ores, and the physiological construction of animals and plants. Music, painting, sculpture can be reduced to a mathematical process. *Number is the ideal of the universe.* Pythagoras discerned the ideal plan, but did not elaborate it perfectly. Agreeing to a plan and then ascertaining what it is, it goes far toward confirming the theistic conception of the origin of the world, for a plan that involves geometric law is implicit with divine intelligence and points directly to a supervising Creator.

So closely related is the subject of form to that of substance, that the passage from one to the other is not difficult; and as form can not be explained without substance, the latter must receive careful attention. The interpretations of nature, or those theoretical readings of the spirit of nature which obtain in philosophy, compel the conclusion that a solution of matter except by the theistic suggestion is improbable. To reach the theistic suggestion, however, certain logical steps must be taken, beginning with the objective or formal realities of matter, and proceeding until the subjective side or inner light of nature is discerned.

Every one sees the world differently; but this is not because the world is absolutely different to every individual, but because every individual is different. Epicurus taught that the world is actually what it appears to be; an absurd idea, for to no two persons does it appear the same. Yet it is the same world, and it is the *actual*, not the appearing, world, that the mind seeks to understand. Beneath its appearance is the substantial, manipulating spirit that gives its form; this unseen power, this invisible substance, the mind desires to know. Schopenhauer considered the world as his representation, or the product of his idea, a not uninteresting conception, however far from absolute truth it is. It is not one's idea of the world, but rather the absolute world, that philosophy must deal with and reveal. Not appearances, not representations, not ideas, not forms, but substance, absolute spirit, internal reality, philosophy must find and declare.

The idealistic interpretation of nature is not without friends in these modern days, as it was not wanting in advocates in the palmy days of Greece. Its danger lies in its tendency to fanaticism, for it is idealism that raises the question, does matter really exist? With this extreme we have no sympathy. Nature is a sublime reality, whose polarity or opposite is spirit. Non-being is as real as being; the phenomenal as patent as the substantial. Bishop Berkeley developed idealism into a philosophic fanaticism, which received a philosophic thrashing at the hands of Hume.

Purified of the fanatical tendency, and restrained by the realistic spirit, idealism, as a logical system, tends to the denial of the existence of matter, and is therefore repugnant to the common sense of mankind. However, philosophy does not, and perhaps ought not to, ask the opinion of the majority concerning its teachings; for its purpose is truth, which the majority may at first be inclined to reject. The apology for the fanatical content of idealism is in the plausible statement that the only reality is being, and that nature is *becoming*, but never is, and so is an illusion. To this transcendental interpretation, which reduces the visible to nothingness, Emerson commits himself, justifying it quite as much on Christian as on philosophic grounds; for he insists that Christianity, by its denunciation of the world, by its declaration that it is perishable, and that it will finally perish, suggests an idealism identical with that of philosophy. But the idealism of Christianity does not deny the existence of matter;

it puts upon it the ban of perishability, and declares that, as compared with truth, spirit, knowledge, redemption, the world is valueless, is nothing.    Christian idealism is productive of contempt for matter as such, because immortal things are in the foreground of the soul, and belong to it as its rightful inheritance.

The old view of Heraclitus, that nature is involved in a process of flux or constant change, Plato accepted; and, as a philosophic principle, it certainly is not wanting for demonstration.    Seneca says no man bathes in the same river twice.    Nature is a miracle of mutation—ever changing, yet ever remaining.    The instability of nature is not an instability of geometric ideals, for these are fixed; nor an instability of inherent laws, for these abide, but an instability of phenomena; the details, the products, the forms, perish, revive, and perish again.    An inquiry into nature will be incomplete, therefore, that does not probe for stable elements, for fixed principles; it is the *fixed*, and not the *fluxing*, that really constitutes nature.    An explanation of nature is not in a revelation of a flux in nature, but of something which, producing the flux, remains itself unfluxed, unchangeable.

Oersted, a Danish philosopher, was convinced that the world has a soul, but this is more fictitious than real, unless it be conceded that by soul is meant the law by which nature exists; for our final analysis of nature conducts to the belief that it is impregnated by a legal spirit, which is the essence of its reality.    There is something in nature which the eye can not see.    It is the soul of law.    To the eye of man nature is full of facts; to the mind of man nature is full of laws; *nature is law in execution.*

Prof. Morris holds that the life of nature is the life of spirit, which may be accepted with the qualification that the spirit-life manifests itself through law, otherwise he must affirm that nature is spirit, abolishing the primal distinctions between matter and spirit, or verging on the idealistic denial of the existence of matter.    In the very highest sense it is true to say that God is in nature, and that its life is the life of God; but in a critical or philosophic sense it is equally true to affirm that nature is the product of the laws of God, and so reducing nature to law.

Horace Bushnell defines nature to be that "created realm of being or substance which has an acting, a going on, or process from within itself, under and by its own laws."    Nature is an "acting from within itself," or a process of law, as we prefer to phrase it.

Herbart reduces the essence of a thing to a "simple quality;" but, as he can not designate the quality, his theory is a bundle of words.

John Stuart Mill defines matter to be a "permanent possibility of sensations," but this is no definition at all. Matter a possibility! Matter is a certainty, a reality, whose existence is in no sense dependent on human consciousness, or its relation to sensation.

Herbert Spencer is equally airy in his definition, which is as follows: "Our conception of matter reduced to its simplest shape is that of co-existent positions that offer resistance." Matter a position! This only states *where* matter is, not *what* it is.

The familiar definition of Alexander Bain, that matter is a "double-faced somewhat, having a spiritual and a physical side," is readily recalled in this connection. Without dissecting his application of the definition, but using it in our own way, we confess that it represents the truth respecting matter, whose physical side is its form, together with its properties, and whose spiritual side is the law, the life of its activity or existence.

Hermann Lotze, sweeping away the mists, settles down to the conclusion that a Thing is law; the essence of matter is not a simple quality, as Herbart holds, nor an aggregation of qualities, nor is it a "possibility" or "position," but it is the spirit of law, or the law of its activity or existence. Nature is the form of law; law is in nature. He says: "Laws never exist *outside, between, beside,* or *above* the things that are to obey them." "Law or truth is," with which Plato agrees when he defines law to be the *discovery of that which is.* Law is the great reality, the ruling spirit, the life of the world.

Prof. Bowne, seeing that activity is involved in the nature of things, and going behind the scenes of the phenomenal world, amplifies the law of activity into the law of being, which means that law accounts for reality, or phenomena. In the law by which a thing exists is the secret of existence. A thing may therefore be defined, not by properties or its form, but by the law by which it is produced.

Plato taught that ideas "participated" in the formal appearance of matter, which philosophy has either perverted or innocently misunderstood; for, stripped of its mystical guise, the meaning is that law, which is a divine idea, not alone became incorporated with matter, but instrumentally originated it. Without law matter is impossible. Law originated and participated in matter, and abides there. It is the only thing that does abide. Forms perish, but the geometric ideals, which are the signs of geometric law, abide forever. Forms, appearances, possibilities, properties, positions, all are lost sight of in the radical idea of law, as the essence of things, as the spirit of the life of nature, as the revealed secret of the universe.

Going back to the source of things, the explanation of material phenomena, as respects their origin, development, history, and destiny, is not so difficult a task as has been imagined.

Creation may be interpreted as the outgoing of law. By "creation" is meant not alone the physical universe, which is properly the result of creative energy, but the act or process of creation itself. If at one time the universe was involved in an atom, it is rational to conceive of the atom as constituted in its prophetic fullness by law. Just what was the first act of Deity when he resolved upon creation is not known, but it is quite conceivable that motion or action itself was the first sensation of the divine being. As motion is convertible into heat, light, electricity, so the first motion of the Deity contained potentially the life of the universe. It is possible that the first divine act resulted in non-living matter, for the historic order of the phenomenal world, according to science, is from the non-living to the living, and this is also according to the Mosaic cosmogony. Matter first, life afterwards. The non-living first, that the Deity might behold his crude work; the living next, that he might glorify himself in it. If motion were the first act of the Deity, it was also the first law, or the law of activity, by which all things finally appeared.

This leads out into the broader arena of the universe as a created product, or the result of a Being whose first law is motion, and whose condition is activity. The universe was created according to law. This means method or order in the process of creation. What that order was, geology attempts in part to explain, while Moses gives it in full; it was a scientific order, a progress from the non-living toward the living, a methodical development of physical history. It is clear, therefore, that the highest as well as the lowest types of existence, the crudest as well as the most finished forms of matter, are the results of the *law of motion*, which, distributed throughout the limitless field of being, and applied by infinite wisdom, produced trees, crystals, birds, fishes, worlds, men.

Every thing—matter, mind, soul—came into existence by virtue of a legal, that is, an orderly and methodical, process, since law is life, and life is the spirit of law. Our conclusions respecting nature are as follows:

1st. Nature is the embodiment of the principle of unity; it is a unit in its physical substance, whether the substance is hydrogen, protoplasm, bioplasm, or any undetermined substance. The differences in matter are largely the differences of form, for all things may finally be reduced to the same thing. The correlation of substances is a standing proof of the unity of substance. Nature is one, not two. This demonstrates the singleness of its authorship, and points to one Supreme Being, the maker of all things.

2d. Respecting its origin, nature is proof of the necessity of a Creator; the theistic conception is fundamental to an explanation of the existence of nature. No materialistic theory can account for an atom; God is a necessity.

3d. The substance, the spirit, of matter, is the law by which it exists. Nature is law in form; nature can not exist without law, but the law may exist without nature. Hence nature may perish and the law remain. The substance, the spirit, is immortal; the form or nature is mortal. As law is immortal, so God, from whom it came, is immortal.

The unity, the form, the substance of nature join in an affidavit to the necessity of the theistic conception as alone adequate to the existence of a phenomenal world.

## CHAPTER V.

### THE DANCE OF THE ATOMS.

IN the year 1599 Sir John Davies published a poem entitled " *Nosce Te ipsum*," in which he describes the original movements of matter under the figure of a dance. All space is at the disposal of the dancers; plants, animals, men, stars, and angels engage in the mazy scene, the movements being alternately gentle and violent, quiet and demonstrative, graceful and awkward, solemn and gay, as the parties are absorbed with the business-like amusement before them. Going back of these, the poet fancies that he sees the elements, fire, air, water, and earth, engaged in a revolving motion, now embracing, then separating, now combining, then each standing apart, and so proceeding until a world of order and beauty is the result.

John Dryden likewise embalms in verse the idea of the world's creation by atomic movement, as follows:

> " From harmony, from heav'nly harmony,
>   This universal frame began,
> When Nature underneath a heap
>   Of jarring atoms lay,
>   And could not heave her head,
> The tuneful voice was heard from high,
>   Arise, ye more than dead!
> Then cold and hot and moist and dry,
>   In order to their stations leap,
>   And Musick's pow'r obey.

> From harmony, from heav'nly harmony,
>   This universal frame began ;
> From harmony to harmony,
>   Through all the compass of the notes it ran,
>   The diapason closing full in man."

These are poetic representations of a great philosophic thought—the theory of the origin of the worlds in atomic substances or forces. It therefore deserves special consideration. A comprehensive study of original or atomic movement includes, 1. The existence of the atom ; 2. The character of the atom ; 3. Its capacity for motion ; 4. The genesis of its impulse to motion ; 5. Its selection of form ; 6. Its development and history.

If it can be scientifically settled beyond doubt that the worlds were originally atoms, or that the original forms of matter from which worlds have issued were atoms, the mystery of the dance is considerably simplified. It is, however, at this point that the trouble begins. The hypothesis of the atom is a good " working hypothesis" for the materialist, and, for that matter, for the theologian also, but the data for such hypothesis are not the most assuring. The assertion that the universe is the product of evolution from star-dust, or atomic centers, is easily made, and such words as " protoplasm," "germs," " units," "ultimates," and "atoms" may be used with a confidence that will inspire respect; but the assertion of atomic origin is not equivalent to the demonstration. " The genesis of an atom," says Spencer, " is no easier to conceive than the genesis of a planet."

Perhaps it should not make against the theory that no one ever saw an atom, for the greatest forces are invisible; nor should it be charged in derision that atoms do not now exist, for existing worlds have taken the place of atoms. It should not be forgotten, also, that if the existence of original atoms be established, our reverence for the Creator must be intensified, for if *he* built the worlds, so magnificent in structure and equipment, from beginnings so marvelously small and unpromising, he is a most wonderful being, quite as marvelous in his doings as the most devout Christian ever supposed him to be. Religion can apostrophize the atom, since it magnifies the Creator, a result the materialistic atomist did not foresee, or he had been slow in adopting it.

It is not sufficient to inspire faith in the theory to know that it is both ancient and modern ; to be told that Democritus expounded it with great enthusiasm, and Epicurus indorsed it as if it were a conviction of his own; or to be reminded that Leibnitz reduced original matter to monads, every one of which was potentially a mirror of the universe. But when such a metaphysician as Lotze insists that the real world of nature should be considered "under the form of an infinite number of discrete centers of activity," we are compelled to treat the atomic theory with the highest respect. He discusses in his "Metaphysic" the "antithesis between atomism and the theory of a continuous extension in space," and because he can not accept the latter he proceeds to vindicate the former. "The sharp edge of a knife, when placed beneath a microscope, appears to be notched like a saw, and the surface, which feels quite smooth, becomes a region of mountains," is his illustrative argument against "continuous extension;" but it is not clear that atomism is the polar extremity of such extension. Mountain peaks, apparently standing apart, may be joined at the base; "discrete" forms may be lost in underlying unity. Atomic separations may be consistent with a basal continuous extension. This involves relation, correlation, interaction, and the system of inter-dependence in the universe, into which it is not necessary to go.

For us, it is not so important to know who subscribes to the atomic theory as it is to know on what basis the theory rests. We are not disposed to assail it on the ground of prejudice, for we have no prejudice to serve; we can believe in the atomic idea with as much enthusiasm as any student of truth, and without any fear of danger to the Biblical exegesis, so soon as the proof, or even the probability, of the existence of atoms is furnished. At present, however, the atomic idea is a conjecture, the proof indefinite and imaginary, and faith in it must be at our option. It does not suit our purpose to deny the theory; on the contrary, anxious that it may be fully understood and thoroughly investigated, we proceed to inspect its contents and listen to its explanation of the evolution of the worlds.

A mystery confronts the inquirer before he takes the first step. It is not proclaimed with sufficient clearness by the advocates of the theory just what the original atoms were, that is, whether they were solids, liquids, or vapors, or whether they had fixed forms or were formless, or where they came from, or whether they were eternal or made themselves. Some of these questions have been overlooked in the eagerness to trace worlds to revolving points, inscrutable in their origin, and potential in their contents, adaptations, and prophecies. The settlement of some of them, however, is necessary to the existence of the theory. Belief in atoms presupposes a knowledge of their origin, content, purpose, power, relation, form, or acting principle. Touching some of these things, the atomist can not be wholly in the dark; hence, the duty of revealing what he knows. Democritus was somewhat specific in his description of atoms, conjecturing that they were infinite in number, assumed mathematical figures, were divisible, and propelled by an inherent law of motion. Epicurus, an enthusiastic supporter of the theory, gave particular attention to the forms of atoms, describing them as square, spherical, and triangular, and that these forms were unchangeable. He also maintained that, by combination, secondary forms were produced, but that the original or primordial atoms were indestructible and entered into all things.

Without controversy, it is conceded that an original atom must have been physical or natural in character or essence; that is, it was in no sense supernatural, for, had it been supernatural, the product or development had been a supernatural world. Inasmuch as the universe is the resultant of the atomic movement, the atom could not have differed in character from the universe. The fig-tree does not produce thistles; the atom produced a world after its kind. This is logically, genetically consistent, and science takes no exception. Natural atoms may be divided into two kinds: atoms of ether, and atoms of solid matter. Over the latter the law of gravitation exercises its influence; the former are independent of it. But this division introduces a vexing problem, for the law of motion affecting a solid can not affect a vapor; hence, two laws of motion are required.

Again, if the atom was the prophecy of the "becoming," then it was potentially the becoming. As the acorn contains potentially the oak, so the atom contains potentially the universe. Evolution is in proportion to involution. The miner gets out of the mountain only what is in it. To allow that one small planet like ours was once an atom is to concede a great deal; but the theory requires that all the solar systems, the nebulæ unresolved, the whole firmament, the astronomic heavens, were at one time nomadic atoms, wanderers in the spatial sea. The magnitude of the universe is not quoted as an embarrassment to the theory, for the theory is tenable if based on the theistic conception, the very thing, however, which the materialist is anxious to overthrow. The fact that the world was built at all, that it exists, is as great a wonder as any process by which it came into existence. Any process of world-building will excite reverence in the thoughtful mind.

A striking peculiarity of the atom is its tendency to motion or capacity for development. Without such capacity, the universe had not appeared. All forms, both of organic and inorganic matter, are the results of the internal disposition of the atom to development. In speaking of the capacities of the atom, we should speak cautiously, since very little has been demonstrated; but, speaking speculatively, we may be bold in statement and even heroic in theoretical suggestion. Granting that the atomic theory is possibly tenable, one is compelled to allow that the atom shall have certain attributes and functions, without which its task can not be performed. Granting it one function, another must be conceded, and still another, until it is sufficiently endowed to project worlds from its center.

Its chief characteristic is the power of motion. Scientists agree that motion is a principle in the universe, and not a few suspect that it is the essence of things, or, as it has been demonstrated that heat may be converted into motion and motion into heat, the conclusion that all things are but the expression or types of motion has been advocated with a logical plausibility. If motion is a universal principle, primarily it must have belonged to the atom; but how the atom came in possession of the impulse is yet an undecided question. Was the atom a center of motion, with independent power of self-motion? or was it an inert thing, incapable of motion until acted upon by some external force? This is the dilemma of philosophy. To admit to the atom the capacity for motion explains nothing. With this embarrassment in view, many scientific thinkers intimate that the atom had an inherent power of movement. Lotze, no less than Hartmann, representing the opposite poles of philosophic thought, substantially agree in conferring upon the atom the function of elementary force; but Lotze accepts the theistic conception, and so is consistent. He does not regard atoms as the final elements of matter, but looks upon them as complex data, behind which science can not go, but from which a divine creative act may be inferred.

The materialistic atomist has no solution for his difficulty except scientific superstition.

Epicurus, atheistic in theology, advocated the theory of spontaneous motion in atoms, explaining their nature and activities by a purely materialistic hypothesis. In his judgment, the atom is an eternal substance and has always been in motion. In itself it is nervous, restless, eager, aspiring, and will not lie still. He attributes weight to it, which presupposes external influence, or the doctrine of the mutual relation of atoms. Its incipient movement is in a straight line, but suddenly and of its own accord it may deviate in any direction, going diagonally, turning around, rising up, or falling down. Independent of all control, it may act soberly or wildly, it may behave itself or appear as if intoxicated, it may walk alone or waltz through space with kindred atoms; it gives no account of itself, except as it pleases. This is a pretty fair biography of the atom, but it is necessarily incomplete.

Leucippus, Democritus, and Epicurus, the ancient fathers of the atomic theory, not always clear in conception or conclusive in statement, do not differ respecting the endowments of the atom which qualify it for independent activity and the power to produce cosmical systems. Leucippus, attributing an infinite standing to atoms, conceived that, under the natural principle of like attracting like, similar atoms approached one another, combined their interests, and grew into the mammoth proportions of the stars. By "ceaseless repercussion," the atoms in the progress of their development assumed all the "possibilities of forms," which took the names of mountains, oceans, trees, birds, animals, and men. Even man is traced to the atom! Clearly enough, the old philosophers were not afraid of the consequences of their theories. Atomism and atheism joined their interests, and materialism was triumphant. To such a conclusion an anti-theistic atomic theory necessarily leads, for the atom is dependent or independent, derived or primary. Its status once settled, and a conclusion is inevitable.

The genesis of atomic motion is the conundrum of the atomists.

The spontaneity of atomic motion the materialist must accept, or resort to the delusion of the eternity of matter. Spontaneous motion, however, is as mythological as spontaneous generation. Motion is implicit with antecedence. It goes back, ever pointing to a single source. Motion implies a mover—so taught Plato; and his account of creation in the *Timæus*, through atomic movements, is superior to the modern materialistic conception, because it involves the presence of an organizing and directing mind. Motion implies antecedent preparation, begetting, touching, imparting, or it is self-begotten. Without pressing this distinction far enough to verge on the necessity of a personal being as the author of all motion, we observe that motion, as now understood and explained, is the result of law, and is in no instance spoken of as spontaneous. Motion is the product of a system of laws, the chief of which is gravitation, and without which motion would be impossible. The revolutions of the solar system are not attributed to any spontaneous force in matter, but rather to the influence of the law of attraction, and every other motion is explained by reference to the same general influence. Is gravitation the law of atomic movement? Sir Isaac Newton denies that the "force of gravity" resides in the atom, leaving it a forceless, motionless thing, and dependent upon an outside power for animation and movement. He was emphatic in the rejection of the idea that gravity is "innate, inherent, and essential to matter." Faraday likewise pronounced the dynamical theory absurd. McCosh repudiates the idea of self-acting matter. Either this conclusion must be accepted, or the dynamical theory of matter, the theory of inherent force, or self-moving matter. Few theists subscribe to the latter, for it is full of danger; it points to pantheism. The old atomic theory of Democritus is too materialistic for Anglo-Saxon or modern theologians; but theistic metaphysicians are found supporting both Sir Isaac Newton in his denial of inherent force, and the dynamical theory, or the theory of innate power. As yet, there is no standard by which to determine whether one's view is orthodox or not, for if he accept the theistic government of the world, he can accept any philosophic theory of matter.

As there is no motion known to science that is not due to attraction, it is consistent to affirm that the atom was governed in its initial movements by the law of gravitation, which had its source, not in the atom, but in the supervising and endowing will of God. This certainly is the genesis of motion in the atom. In itself, the atom had no power of motion; that is, it did not originate motion. Unless moved, it remained motionless. Inertia was, therefore, the primal condition of the original atom.

Nevertheless, the atoms dance—what music thrills them into motion? What voice do they hear and obey? What impulse overcomes the inertia of the atom? Heraclitus held that all nature is in a perpetual flux, forever but silently changing, its constituents passing away to be replaced by similar constituents; perpetual change is the order of phenomena. The law of change however, does not explain the origin of the dance. Geoffroy Saint Hilaire refers all forms of matter to certain "elective affinities of the organic elements," but this is a rhetorical statement, not a philosophic explanation. Whence the organic elements? Whence the affinities? The affinities of matter are the attractive forces of matter, expressed by the generic word—gravitation. If atoms exist, and are endowed with "elective affinities," by which they are drawn together and combine in an aggregation of worlds, dispute ends; but to assume such endowment and then build up the theory on the assumption is a strange way of getting at the truth.

Spencer, compelled to account for these things, suggests the natural instability of the homogeneous as the fundamental cause, but it is a superficial explanation; it explains nothing. Suppose the homogeneous were unstable, what caused the instability? Were the atoms of uniform size, function, and power, or were they of diverse sizes, and did they possess various and dissimilar functions, and were there jealousies and rivalries among the atoms, producing discord of feeling, instability of friendships, and actual hostility, resulting in wars and aggressions? The doctrine of instability implies general commotion, and commotion is proof of motion; but Spencer conducts us no nearer the beginning than Hilaire.

Granting that motion is implicit with the law of gravitation, it must be understood that it includes a variety of laws, without which atomic movement can not be explained. Inertia is the primal state of the atom; motion is communicated; attraction begins here; repulsion is felt there; equilibrium or neutrality is maintained yonder; and so in the general movement centripetal and centrifugal influences become clearly manifest. As these are more or less positive, adhesion, cohesion, chemical attraction, crystallization, condensation, combustion, reaction, interaction, and specific forms follow. To explain all these by the dynamical theory is quite impossible; to explain them as variations of the initial law of motion is not absurd, provided the law of motion is accounted for. If one is undertaking to explain atomic movement, one is bound to explain the *first* movement as well as the last; in fact, if one will explain the first movement, one can be excused from explaining any thing else. The atomic theory is burdened with this unanswered and unanswerable disadvantage that, whatever the explanation of the movement, whether " elective affinity," " instability," " inherent force," or any thing else, it fails to account for the "affinity," "instability," " inherent force," or any thing else that it uses as an explanation. Its explanation always requires another explanation which it can not give. The theory is proof of the limitations of human thought, and shows that matter, movement, and law must have an outside explanation, or a theistic source.

The difficulty is not ended. Granting the power of motion to the atom, according to the theory, it is perplexing to understand the variety of forms matter has assumed, or to explain its transmutableness. If the atom has the power of motion, has it the power of choice in its development, or is the development an accident? Darwin does not explain the introduction of forms, but this explanation the theory must make, or it is valueless. The original atoms were of uniform size, functions, and aims, or they were not; if they were alike in every particular, if they believed alike, so to speak, and danced in the same way and to the same music, it is difficult to account for differentiation in result; if they differed, who or what made them to differ? If like produce like, then uniform atoms should produce uniform results, but the " becoming" is a panorama of infinite variety. It is necessary therefore to allow difference, contrariety, and a menagerie of functions to atoms.

But how account for contrariety of purpose in atoms? What established the difference of aims? Did they hold a convention, and agree on separate idiosyncrasies, or did they inherit from a common parent a multitude of diverse qualifications for their future history? Uniformity of aim in atoms is inconsistent with variety of result; contrariety of aim is indicative of wisdom, a supervising agency, which means more than the materialistic atomist can understand. No knowledge of the universe is at all possible that does not account for difference of aim in nature. Verily, as Herschel suggests, the atom, with its power, functions, aims, and forms, begins to look like a manufactured article.

The form of the original atom is still undetermined. If a solid, its physical shape might be conjectured; if a liquid or vapor, it was without form. Plato in the *Timaeus* represents the original elements as shapeless, and from the shapeless the shaped universe proceeded, but the result is explained by the participation of divine ideas with matter in its progress toward forms. Moses writes that the earth was without form, but was shaped by a Shaper; so the atom may have been formless, but took form in the hands of a Former. From the theistic standpoint the forming process is one of ease and accountability; from the standpoint of the atomist it is in vain that we seek for the power of form, unless it is insisted, like motion, to be inherent; but if the one is absurd, so is the other.

Whence, then, the propensity to form in matter? The relation of motion to form is conspicuous; that is, without motion, form is impossible. With a predisposition to form, an atom must be stirred, moved, excited, and whirled before it will reveal its preference for a particular form. Why the final preference? Why the circular form? Why the octahedral? Why the triangular? Why all the simple and compound forms of matter? Atoms might have danced themselves into a few simple forms, and these by combination have solidified into complex forms, but so soon as the dance was over, each atom, if it had any respect for itself, would seek to preserve its identity, and a return to original simplicity had been unavoidable.

It is time to consider whether the original atom was a simple, unorganized substance, or a concrete receptacle of co-ordinate powers and substantial elements. The validity of the atomic theory, as well as the present question of the origin of forms, is involved in this inquiry. Spencer intimates that germs are homogeneous, or simple substances, without signs of organization; but Mr. Tyndall suspects that the most simple is complex, that the microscopically small is mysteriously large, and that it is impossible to "grapple with the ultimate structural energies of nature." Spencer proposes simplicity, unity, as an underlying fact; Tyndall proposes complexity. The two may fight it out, but observers of the spectacle have something to say while it is going on. If Mr. Tyndall is correct, the atom is a complex substance, which Lotze really implies; but whence the complexity? If Spencer is correct the atom is a simple substance, but whence the simple content? The problem is not reduced by Spencer, it is not magnified by Tyndall; it is as great, it is the same problem whether a germ is simple or complex, for the problem is, not *how much* is in the atom, but is there any thing in it? Tell how the atom came to be loaded at all, and the size of the load will then receive consideration; and until the origin of content is settled the origin of form can not be settled.

The permanency of natural forms also provokes inquiry, compelling the atomist to explain or retreat. With divergence of form there is stability and a basis of classification. Mathematics is grounded in the construction of the universe. Not only architectural ideas of order and proportion obtain in nature, but mathematical principles are easily traced in the organic and inorganic realms. Geometry is the mathematical spirit of matter. Creation proceeded by its rules. The Duke of Argyll emphasizes the belief that creation was by law, as evinced in its order, in its fixed types, in its gradations, in its adaptations; but he might have added that the specific law of creation, however manifold the types, orders, adaptations, and adjustments, is mathematical. Plato lays the universe in triangles. Pythagoras projected his philosophy of number as the secret of the universe, the interpretation being that mathematical proportion, order, and forms constituted the principles and archetypes of the divine mind in the development of the astronomic worlds. Astronomy is the crystallization of geometry. Mineralogy is geometry as a fine art. Chemistry is geometry on wheels.

As geometrical principles are decisive and fixed, so are the forms of matter in which they have illustration. Hence no new mathematical forms have been discovered; the concrete owes its concreteness to the limitations of applied mathematics. Spheres, angles, squares, cubes, polyhedrons, and their cognate forms, constitute the essential manifestations of matter; while straight lines and curved, with their variations, are the tape-lines by which to measure the forms.

We insist upon the permanency of matter-forms, but in so doing the atom may be interrogated for a history of the facts. Left to itself, would it seek any particular form? Would it especially settle down to one form? In the mad dance in space, aroused by inequalities of endowments, would not the atoms assume a thousand different attitudes, and take as many forms as there were groups or individuals? What would restrict the selection of form? Would not each palpitating atom, through sheer jealousy, adopt a form for itself, as the old families of Europe had each its coat-of-arms? Evidently the atom, however inclined to independence, felt its limitation, and stepped into the dance under command of a very embarrassing restriction, compelled to adopt a form it neither invented nor possibly preferred; yet it obeyed. Itself formless, yet endowed with a propensity to form, it found it must regard certain principles which limited its products to a few visible manifestations. Doubtless, as the dance proceeded, the atomic world groaned under the restriction of geometrical ideals, but there was no way to avoid them. These ideals, these geometrical restrictions, the materialistic atomist can not explain; they point to divine wisdom, and are proof of the necessity of a divine personality in creation.

The future history of the atom, or its development from the atomic condition to a world-state, it belongs to us to read. Whatever makes against the theory itself we waive, for materialistic science is inclined to accept it. Let us concede to the atom an unquestioned reality, endowed with capacities unmeasured, if not infinite; let it contain potentially the universe; let there dwell in it the power of self-motion; let the propensity to form be ever one of its animating impulses or thoughts; thus dowered, it starts upon its course. Two questions arise: What is its actual development? What becomes of it?

Look!—a universe greets us. From the atom to the universe is an immense, a magnificent, development, proving that the universe was potentially in the atom, if it prove any thing, and that under no circumstances could it have developed into any thing but the universe. This restriction, in its development, overthrows the suspicion of the element of chance, or even of self-guidance, in its history; it establishes the presence of supervising mind. The universe is not an accident, but the orderly progress of atomic movement, and the result of the concurrent and forefixed agreement among the atoms, which safeguards the divine factor in creation. Now, if the potentiality of the universe reside in atoms, it resides in a given number of atoms, or in a single atom. If in a single atom, why other atoms at all? If in a single atom, does every other atom contain potentially a universe? If so, why are there not other universes? On the supposition that a single atom is the germ of the universe, atoms disappear, and the atomic theory is the theory of an atom; on the supposition that the universe is the development of an indefinite number of atoms in various combinations and relations, the incompetency of any single atom to produce the universe is foreshadowed. But so soon as the imperfection of a single atom is discovered, suspicion is raised against all atoms, whatever their number or relations. If every atom is deficient, or insufficient to produce the universe, it is difficult to understand how any number of atoms can produce it. Deficiency added to deficiency a thousand times does not give value to the other side of the equation. Zero multiplied a million times by zero is zero. Deficiencies multiplied by as many times as there are atoms will not equal potentiality. In this view the atomic individuals are potentially inadequate to the universe.

To assert that the universe is the result of a combination of atoms is not to add a new meaning to the theory. A combination of atoms is not essentially a new production. New forms may appear by combination, but not new constituents of matter ; but it is new constituents that are required to help the infirmities of the original atoms.. In this view a new atomic theory is required.

If it is alleged that imperfect atoms are competent to evolve an imperfect universe, and, in order to justify the atomic theory, it be added that the universe is imperfect, we take issue at once, for, instead of evolving an imperfect universe, the imperfect atom could not evolve any universe at all. An inadequate atom will not satisfy the demands of any atomic theory.

Thus, from whatever view the atom is considered as an original, independent, self-existing, self-endowed source of power, it turns out to be a lamentable failure. To give it the required efficiency ; to endow it with the heritage of omnipotence ; to clothe it with selective affinities ; to stimulate it with an infinite energy, and to circumscribe it with restrictions that prevent it from becoming the sole Infinite, supplemental agencies, forces, or personalities are required. The atom needed for the theorist probably never existed, and it is certain that the atom described by the atomist is only the atom of his imagination. In the development of the universe the atom, therefore, becomes extinct.

To conclude : The atomic theory of the universe is philosophically incompetent to account for it. It satisfies no inquiry respecting the genesis of things. Phenomena can not be explained by phenomena. An atom is a phenomenon requiring explanation.

The atomic theory, eliminating the influence of a governing mind, is self-destructive, since it involves the absurdity of self-originating functions and powers in matter without mind. Given a Creator of atoms, and the atomic theory is tenable. In that case the Creator may have to be explained, which involves other questions, but, what is all-important to the student of genesis, the atom is explained, and a cosmological basis satisfactorily settled.

The dance of the atoms, as the materialist describes it, is the dance of darkness and death ; as the theist would gladly describe it, it is the movement of God over the face of the deeps.

# CHAPTER VI.

## THE GROUND OF LIFE.

"THE word Life still wanders through science without a definition," says Henry Drummond. The failure to define is not the result of scientific indifference to the subject, for it has been thoroughly investigated by the thinkers of all the schools, but it is rather the result of a pronounced mystery that envelops it. Scarcely a solution or provisional hypothesis presented is satisfactory from the inner sanctuary of things; not a theory has been urged that has not been modified or overthrown; and it is confessed that, from the philosophical standpoint alone, the mystery is quite as profound as ever.

The principal theories of life, as announced by biologists, naturalists, physiologists, and scientists in general, may be designated as follows: 1. Spontaneous Generation; 2. *"Omne Vivum ex Ovo;"* 3. Pangenesis; 4. Development; 5. The Physical Basis; 6. Biogenesis; 7. Creation.

The theory of spontaneous generation is a short cut to results without adequate causes; but at one time it was supported by distinguished scientists, and in lieu of something more specific or satisfactory, received general though hesitating assent. It was apparently demonstrated by such learned experimenters as Prof. Wyman, Dr. Bastian, and Prof. H. J. Clark, that the reproduction of infusoria by spontaneous generation had taken place, and even Dr. McCosh considered the announcement not entirely void of truth. Without detailing the experiments adduced in support of the theory, it is sufficient to notify the reader that amœbas, bacteriums, vibrios, and monads were said to be produced from liquids heated to such a degree that all infusorial life originally in them was destroyed, and that, of their own accord, or by spontaneous activity, many of these reappeared.

The experiments were repeated by others who doubted the results, and Prof. Wyman's conclusions were disputed; and, while materialistic science would gladly accept spontaneous generation if it could be established, it has been rejected by Huxley, Tyndall, Darwin, Dallinger, Prof. Tait, and M. Pasteur. As a theory of the origin of life, it is now virtually defunct.

Scientists have also come to the conclusion that the old formula, *"Omne Vivum ex Ovo,"* is not exactly true, for, while the egg plays an important part in the life of the world, certain it is that life is produced without the egg, and so often that it is a question whether the egg condition is not an exception rather than the rule. Anemones and hydras, insects and fishes, originate by budding and self-division, processes entirely independent of parental generation or the egg condition. Allowing, however, that in vertebrates in particular the egg is a necessity to life, one might ask, whence the egg? To accept the egg theory is not to solve the genesis of life.

Mr. Darwin is the exponent of the theory of pangenesis, which has been completely shattered by Mivart and Prof. Delphino. He held that each organism consists of an incalculable number of organic atoms, which had the power of reproduction. These atoms he called "gemmules," in order to be original in the creation of a term, but the idea he borrowed from Democritus, amplifying it and adapting it to the emergencies of modern science. As a single theory of life, pangenesis has less in it than spontaneous generation, and has been abandoned.

The larger, more comprehensive theory of life is that known as the theory of development, first skeletonized by Lamarck, then clothed by the anonymous author of "The Vestiges of the Natural History of Creation," and finally adopted as the child of Darwin. As its chief expounder and promoter, it bears the name of Darwin, but it must be understood that it did not originate with him. In explanation of the theory we quote him: "I believe that all animals have descended from at most only four or five progenitors, and plants from an equal or lesser number. Probably all the organic beings which have ever lived on this earth have descended from some one primordial form, into which life was first breathed." It is at once seen that this really accounts not at all for life, but only for its development. It does not go back to the source, but contents itself with the method of its successive manifestations. Keeping in mind that the development theory *per se* only proposes to trace the laws or forms of manifested life, it is not so objectionable, even though it may be found erroneous in that particular; but when it is strained to account for life itself, alleging that it too is the product of development, unbelievers in the theory may at least ask for the proof of it. Accepting, if one must, the theory as an explanation of cosmical growth, he is at liberty to reject it, until the proof is furnished, as an explanation of life itself.

Closely related to this theory is that more pronounced hypothesis of Mr. Huxley, which he designates as the "Physical Basis of Life." If all life is the product of protoplasm, or protoplasm is life, as the terms of his theory require us to believe, then matter itself not only had the "potency and promise of life," but is the fulfillment of life;

it is life. All substances, Huxley is fond of asserting, consist of carbonic acid, water, and ammonia; or, to speak more correctly in a chemical way, of carbon, hydrogen, oxygen, and nitrogen. All living organisms, whether animals or plants, in their chemical substance may be reduced to these four elements, but in none of these taken singly is the principle of life. How, then, can they produce it when combined? When combined "under certain conditions," he says, the result is protoplasm, which "exhibits the phenomena of life." This word "protoplasm" is borrowed from the Germans, Max Schultze especially having used it, and Huxley sees in it the "life-stuff" of the world. How far it accounts for life, or whether it is life, is the question. Its deficiencies are many, and the admissions of Huxley are quite fatal to the theory. He does not distinguish between living protoplasm and dead protoplasm, but if there is any difference at all between life and death it must apply to animate or vital protoplasm and that which is not vital. In that living protoplasm is productive, and dead protoplasm is not productive, a difference appears that can not be eradicated; but Huxley fails to recognize it. He is compelled by his theory to state exactly what protoplasm is, inasmuch as it is a physical substance, or the vital property of the world. Finding it, he should describe it. It is at this point that he breaks down, confessing that protoplasm is a product of the vegetable world whose chief property is *contractility;* but in tracing it to the vegetable kingdom he surrenders the issue, for, instead of pointing out a vital, originating substance, he has only indicated a *product,* which implies an antecedent originating cause. This, therefore, destroys the protoplastic theory of life.

Equally fallacious are the theories that substitute *bathybius* for protoplasm, for it utterly fails to bridge the distance between the organic and inorganic worlds. Strauss, pressing the question, whether the living can be evolved from the non-living, was at first embarrassed for the want of an answer, but like Häckel finally accepted bathybius as the connecting link between them. What is *bathybius?* "A sheet of living matter," says Huxley, "enveloping the whole earth beneath the seas." As no one has seen this "living matter," St. George Mivart pronounces it a "sea-mare's nest."

Bioplasm is the latest substitute for protoplasm. It is a shapeless, structureless substance, with power to convert matter into life. A bioplast is a sensitive, generating substance, of a higher order and with more specific functions than at first were assigned to protoplasm. Protoplasm lost caste because a certain kind of vegetable dullness surrounded it; but the bioplasts are a society of *beings,* commissioned to build worlds, with all they contain. The superior dignity of the bioplastic to the protoplastic theory is very apparent; but the one is as objectionable as the other, and even more so, for protoplasm can be traced to the vegetable world, but the bioplasts are independent creatures that are above revealing their origin. How came the bioplasts? is a crucial question; for, until answered, the source of life is still a mystery.

In the same line is the attempt to explain life by the doctrine of the conservation and correlation of forces, which reduces it to a physical force, like light, heat, motion, and electricity. The process of reduction is simple. It is agreed that heat, light, and motion are convertible terms, one being changed into another with perfect ease; and it is affirmed that at no distant day life will be added to the series of convertible terms, so that it will be but another word for motion, or light, or heat. The discovery of its physical character is thus anticipated and prematurely declared. That this conception is only in its rudimentary or theoretical stages ought to restrain its advocates from a too hasty announcement of the far-off conclusion, but science is not given to modest and imperfect statements.

To this thoroughly materialistic conception there is a stronger objection than that it is rudimentary. If life is a purely physical force, in correlation with other physical forces, it ought to be easy for the chemist to produce it. That he has not produced it; that he has not changed the inorganic into the organic, or the non-living into the living, is more than a proof of a present incapacity which may be finally succeeded by an ability to do it; it is a proof that life is not a physical resultant, and in no sense a physical substance.

While the scientist may disorganize living matter, so that it becomes non-living matter, he can not reorganize the latter so that it becomes the former. The analysis of living matter is within his power; the synthesis of living matter he has not accomplished. He may analyze water; he may synthesize water; but he can not produce a living frog, or bee, or fly. This is the more perplexing because science teaches that of the seventy elementary substances, only four are involved in the substance of living matter. Why can not the scientist so combine them that life in some of its stages will appear? The task, stated in terms, does not appear difficult. Given four simple elements, out of an infinite variety of possible combinations, surely that combination which results in what is called life will be found. One might think so, but the key to the combination is still undiscovered. The stupendous fact is that, according to his theory, with all the materials of life at hand, with every physical element, primary and secondary, at his disposal, he is unable to produce the first pulsation of life; and this failure must be taken as the evidence of the supreme folly of his conception and the supreme inadequacy of the theory.

In passing let it be noted that in the inorganic world one substance never becomes another. Sapphire never turns into silver, and clay never turns into sandstone. If inorganic substances never interchange, surely the inorganic never turns into the organic. Materialism may dream of the future discovery of the physical basis of life, but it comports with the dignity of manhood to reject such dreams in the presence of truths that solve the mystery in a more consistent and elevating way.

Ancient philosophy, more excusable than modern, since its discoveries were fewer, drifted into a materialism respecting life that has reappeared in these days, although in a new form. It was held that life is a form of matter, but of a higher kind than ordinary matter; but this did not relieve the subject of embarrassment, for matter is matter, whatever its form. It was also taught that life is in some mysterious way the product of the bodily organism containing it; in other words, that life is a result rather than a cause. This theory some of the moderns have adopted, expressing it thus: there is no life without organization; the organization of matter is implicit with life; organization being effected by self-acting forces, life is a phenomenal result. For this one-sided conclusion materialists are contending with unusual violence, forgetting or failing to see that possibly the truth is the very reverse of the conclusion, namely, that life precedes organization, and is the only explanation of the organic world. In the azoic period of the earth's history, electricity, heat, and gravitation were probably in operation, governed by the same laws under which they now act; matter assumed mathematical forms just as it does now; suns may have blazed in the firmament, as they do now; but matter was unorganized; that is, the vital principle was absent, and the earth was dead. It had form, but organization relates to a principle of life. At this point we see the difference between living and non living matter; the latter is unorganized, the former organized. A stone is unorganized, a bee is organized. Did the bee organize itself into life, or did the life of the bee proceed to incarnate itself in an organized form? Organization signifies life; life is the sign of organization; but it is the extreme of philosophical dullness to proclaim that organization resulted in life. Verily, there is little difference between the ancient and modern schools of philosophy in their teachings respecting the origin of life, and so neither is satisfactory. Epicurus and Häckel, Democritus and Huxley, different in their methods of research, and also in their forms of expression, are not far apart in

their conclusions; all are materialists, in spite of any sentimental re-
cantation of materialism, with which some of them, Huxley especially,
are credited.

The theory of Biogenesis, or that life springs from life, is one of
the recent concessions of Tyndall, and Huxley, apparently abandoning the protoplastic theory, coincides with this latest proposition.
Biogenesis means that the non-living can not produce the living, but
that the living has a life-source. This is the vitalistic theory of life
which promises to crowd out all materialistic views from biology. At one
time Professor Tyndall declared that the laws which produce the crystal
will also produce the entire vegetable and animal world. Materialists
generally reject this bold assumption. A crystal and a lion are two
things, the vitalistic principle being as conspicuously absent from the
one as it is present in the other. *Vitalism and materialism can not
co-exist as explanations of life.* The latter deals with the non-living
as the source of life; the former forever with the living; the latter
must bridge the distance between the non-living and the living, a
feat not yet accomplished; the latter has no bridges to build, but
needs to travel upward to one life-giving source of all things.
Plato in the *Phœdo* discusses the origin of life in death and the origin
of death in life, representing the one as contrary to the other, and
each reproducing the other, from which materialism probably took its
cue; but Plato here teaches the doctrine of the resurrection of the
dead rather than a materialistic origin of life. Resurrection and
biogenesis are different ideas; the one looking forward to the revival of
life, the other looking backward to the beginning of life. It is the
*beginning* of life that now concerns us.

The vitalistic philosophy points in the right direction, but it is deficient in its final utterance. It does not entirely lift the veil. It
still leaves the question of origin unsettled. Another theory is demanded, and without circumlocution we announce the theory of
Creationism as absolutely sufficient in its contents to account for all
the mystery, magnitude, and magnificence of life, whether of animals,
plants, or man, Without a positive creation of the vitalistic principle, and its introduction into the physical universe by a supervising
intelligence, it is impossible to account for any thing, or get beyond a
chain of secondary causes. Given a creating power, and mystery
ceases; given a living God, and universal life is solved. Professor
Agassiz was a creationist from the necessity of the case. The insufficiency of all other explanations compelled him to seek refuge in the
sufficient power and wisdom of Almighty God. Agreed on this, men
may differ concerning the vital development of the world, and not
imperil the foundations of faith, or retard the progress of human

history. Agreed that all life sprang from the one great life, and confusion in philosophy disappears. Agreed here, almost any theory hitherto propounded as an explanation of historical development might be sustained; spontaneous generation is possible with a living God to order it; pangenesis, or any atomic theory, is possible with a living God to endow the atoms with life; even the protoplastic basis might be approved if God is allowed to impart to it its life-giving property; and materialism, vitalized by the divine spirit, and put under divine control, might be radiant with universal truth.

Such are the philosophic theories respecting the origin of life. Until one advances to the biogenetic and creational conceptions of the universe, he flounders in misshapen definitions and complex but incomplete explanations. Outside of this region of dullness and darkness, or inside the realm of religious investigation, one would expect to meet with clearer statements, and more satisfactory conclusions. In this expectation one will not be for the most part disappointed; but occasionally an erroneous view is taken, or a compromising explanation given, even when the highest religion is guiding the investigator into the truth. Dr. Noah Porter translates life into soul, but this is objectionable, since it will apply only to the spiritual nature of man. Vegetable life is not soul-life. Dr. Wythe defines life "as the sum of the activities resulting from the union of mind and matter." In framing a definition a cautious phraseology is required in order to secure accuracy of statement and prevent a misleading influence. To use life and soul as synonymous is a high idea, but it is not broad enough; to say that life is the sum of the union of mind and matter is certainly not discriminating, for it does not concede that mind is independent of matter, nor does it insist that the vital principle is not a property of matter. Life is the sum of mind and matter; therefore, it is not either alone. Applied to the vegetable kingdom, the definition is faulty, for mind is not ascribed to it at all; applied to man, it makes matter as much an essential as mind. Life is more than a sum; it is not a total of activities. The activities resulting from the union of mind and matter are the manifestations of life through an organization, by which we predicate life, but with which we do not confound life. In some particular cases, and applied narrowly, life may appear to be the sum of its own manifestations; but in a large sense this is confounding results with causes. The materialist interprets life to be the result of organization; Dr. Wythe interprets it to be the result of the union of mind and matter, without which life would be impossible. Dr. Wythe is not a materialist but his interpretation is logically materialistic.

Dissatisfied with idealistic and materialistic definitions, it is incumbent upon us to advance a definition, in doing which we confess we run the usual risk of failure. However, our estimate of life is in very general terms that it is the cause of all physical and intellectual manifestation; that it precedes all organization and is separate from all physical forms, having no physical property whatever; that it is invisible, intangible, the supreme force, superior to magnetism, gravity, heat, light and motion, is inconvertible into any thing else, and is eternal. It is the *principle of creation*, the breath of God, and therefore capable of an infinite variety of forms, phases and manifestations. It ranks law, force, matter, every thing visible, formal, phenomenal. It is not a material substance; it is not a combination of chemical elements; neither is it a total of manifestations, or activities.

In particular, *life is spirit*; its activity is the activity of spirit; its manifestation is the manifestation of spirit. Paul says, "The spirit giveth life." This is its origin; it flows from the fountains of the eternal. Life is the stamp of the unseen on the seen. Life is God, the sign of God in the world. The living, whether in animals, plants, or men, is the proclamation of the living God.

The word "life" has now a new meaning; it is the word of words. Inspiration is in its bosom; eternity is in its atmosphere. Defining the word thus, we have escaped the usual dilemmas of the definition-makers, and have accounted for the appearance of life in a way consistent and satisfactory to the reason.

If we consider the kinds of life on the earth, the subject will have a practical complexion, but lose none of its philosophic interest. Indeed, the interest is heightened, for difficulties multiply as the varieties of life are considered in their relation to one another, and in their higher relation to a common source. In ordinary phrase, there are vegetable life, animal life, human life, intellectual life, spiritual life. Is life a unit? Are these varieties the product of one life? Is there a unity in the life of the world? Science answers that the four elements, carbon, hydrogen, oxygen, and nitrogen, compose all kinds of bioplastic material, with sometimes the accidental addition of other elements, and that bioplasm is the same in appearance, whether it be the bioplasm of a geranium, a sponge, an elephant, a dog, a crocodile, a horse, or a man. The microscopic appearance of universal bioplasm is doubtless the same, but evidently the power of the bioplasm in each individual is different, or the result would be the same. The sameness of bioplastic substance is incompatible with variety. The unity of life does not signify bioplastic sameness or similarity. In fact, bioplastic life relates only to the animal and vegetable kingdoms, while the life that includes or accounts for intellectual and spiritual activities is of another kind.

Beginning with bioplastic life, as thus limited, it is profitable to note the difference between it and non-living matter. The distinguishing mark is that inertia belongs to the non-living and spontaneity to the living. A piece of quartz illustrates the one, amœboid motion the other. Self-motion characterizes the bioplastic center; inertia dominates in the inorganic world.

Equally conspicuous is the power of reproduction in the living and its absence in the non-living. The power of identity also attaches to bioplastic life. Living matter, from its law of activity, is like a river, ever flowing, and yet bearing the same name and preserving itself. Forever sweeping on and changing in appearance, its identity is a marked fact in its history. Heraclitus's doctrine of the flux of matter has a constant illustration in the realm of bioplasm. With all the varieties of living matter, the special peculiarities of the original vitalistic substance predominate, and are ever maintained. There are varieties of oak, varieties of roses, varieties of sheep, varieties of insects, varieties of birds; but it is noticeable that the law of identity is not disturbed. Relationship in varieties is easily traced.

This leads necessarily to the perplexing but inviting dogma—if it may be so termed of the stability or permanence of species, a dogma as perplexing to the evolutionists as it is comforting to Christian metaphysicians. Its chief value is its demonstration that life is under law, and yet above natural law; that it has metes and bounds, beyond which it will not pass, and that the life-world has a fixed order, consistent with apparent variations from it. This is a hard lesson for the evolutionist.

The dogma is not difficult to understand. The animal kingdom abounds in species which have not multiplied since the age of man. Varieties, many and singular, have multiplied, but the species are identical; that is, fixed, permanent, unchangeable from age to age. Evolution, if true, would require the occasional, if not frequent, production of *new species*, but the utmost that it can do is to produce new varieties of the same species. If evolution produced species in other ages, why not now? Here the evolutionist stumbles and falls. The changes of evolution result in varieties only. The dog is the dog in all lands; the ox is always the ox; the horse is the horse. The fact is all the stronger when it is remembered that man, with all his skill and genius, and moved by a scientific purpose to break the law, has been unable to undermine the permanence of species in any direction. He has not originated any new species, and none have appeared during his occupancy of the earth. Species may become extinct, but new species are unknown. The relation of hybrids to species in no way disturbs the dogma of the stability of species, for the attempt to produce new species results in abnormal products, stamped with sterility, the sign of nature's protest, and the proof of nature's law in the case. *This means something. It means that life has its appointed channels and limitations; it means the overthrow of the scientific theory of evolution as an explanation of the genesis of life; it compels a reconstruction of the scientific view of creation, and secures the confirmation of the Biblical revelation of the same.*

The introduction of species is quite as mysterious as the stability of species is perplexing. Any natural process of introduction is bound to continue to produce species, while a supernatural process may stop with one exercise. This seems really to have been the case. The creation of one pair for the propagation of one species is the only refuge for the thinker; the sending down the ages of one line of animals, not to be broken by nature or man, but to be preserved amid all its changes and varieties, is proof of a creative will and a supervising intelligence. This is creationism again, the inevitable issue of every fact in nature. Bioplasm is tinctured with creationism; the vegetable kingdom chants creationism; the animal kingdom is alive with it. The speculation that stability is only apparent, and not real, we dismiss as idle. It is proof that there is trouble in the camp of the agnostics, and nothing short of a denial of the dogma will answer their end.

It is patent to the reader that living matter is distinguished by the power of growth and non-living matter by its absence. Iron does not grow; the fern grows. Silver does not grow; the squirrel, the ostrish, man grows. Life signifies enlargement, development, change of form, and final cause. These no one predicates of non-living things.

If, with these distinctions, we stop, where are we? The chief differences between non-living and bioplastic matter are: as to *living* matter, spontaneity of motion, or power of self-motion, power of reproduction, power of identity, power of internal development; as to *non-living* matter, the absence of all these—its negative characteristics, its positive characteristic being *inertia.* The vitalistic principle focalizes itself in a number of concurrent powers, motion, reproduction, identity and development, while the non-living substance may be expressed best by a single word—*inertia.*

From bioplastic to spiritual life is the next step, if we choose to take it. Bioplastic life, as seen in vegetables and animals, and in the physical structure of man is intermediate between the inorganic or non-living world, and the psychological and spiritual life, which distinguishes man from all below him, and allies him to every thing above him.

Not a few scientists detest classification. It interferes with fancy; it hinders speculation. Geometry, algebra, fixed forms, and fixed systems are inconsistent with theoretical science. For this reason Häckel condemned the division of matter into organic and inorganic; it made him pause. The classification of life into bioplastic and spiritualistic disturbs the dreams of the materialist, who would run his biological thread through all the cells and tissues of all the forms and manifestations of life, regarding them all as varieties of one life. He insists upon the unity of life at the expense of ineradicable differences, but classification compels him to recognize these differences, and through them to see varieties of life. His vegetable biology he would transmute into psychological biology, but this is a task he has not yet accomplished. Just as living matter is distinguished from non-living matter, so spiritual life has its differentia, standing out from bioplastic forms with a grandeur peculiar to itself, and independent of all physical relations.

Keener vision will be required to detect the essentia of this highest product of the vitalistic principle, since it is so modest that it often refuses to be seen. Between the psychological and the sensational life of man the materialist affects to believe that there is no radical difference ; but the difference between the non-living and the living is not so great as that between the psychological and the bioplastic. Psychological law may be in perfect harmony with physical law, just as base and soprano in music may be in harmony, but they are not the same. If in the process of thinking the brain seems to resemble the liver in its processes of secretion, it does not justify the conclusion that thought is a physical secretion, and that the mental process is physical. Yet modern materialistic philosophy has confounded the processes and degraded the thinker into a bioplastic machine.

The birth-mark of the soul is its *consciousness*, a recognition of itself as distinct from every thing else. The ego and the non-ego, the subjective and the objective, become distinct realities to the soul, through the avenue of consciousness, and it never confounds them. In its normal moods the soul clings to the idea of its separateness or exclusiveness from all things else. However rapid and extensive its flights through the power of imagination; however retrospective in its thinking ; however distant at times it may seem from itself; it always falls back upon the consciousness of its own individual existence. The operations of consciousness may even be unconscious, as the mind often indulges in calculations which it does not remember; but in either case the fact of consciousness remains. Unconscious calculations, unconscious indulgences, do not interfere with the vice-gerency of consciousness. The mind often determines as to the beauty of an object by an unconscious process; the individual can not explain or express the process by which he reached the conclusion ; but that he reached it he knows. Thus the consciousness is so swift in its ratiocinations, its intuitive conceptions are so electric, its discernment of ratio is so immediate and comprehensive, that the mind can not report the processes, and even loses sight of the data which were employed, rejoicing only in the results, Now, this is not a characteristic of bioplastic material. No philosopher attributes consciousness to a rose, or a wheat-blade. There is spontaneity of motion, but this is not self-recognition. There is identity of species, or self-preservation, but this is not self-knowledge. The law of identity in bioplastic matter is analogous to the law of consciousness in soul-life. In both identity is maintained with this difference, namely, living matter does not recognize its identity, while the soul does recognize its identity. Soul-life is therefore the higher life.

A still more marked difference is the power of volition, or of self-determination in the soul, the analogy to which in bioplasm is its spontaneity or the power of self-motion. But living matter is unconsciously spontaneous ; that is, while its direction is from within, it is instinctive rather than voluntarily intelligent. Even the bee building its cell after the most correct mathematical principles, displays no such intelligent volitional power as the child in determining a moral issue. Right here is the abyss between the spontaneous activity of bioplastic life, and the volitional power of the soul, which has never been bridged. The volitional power in man is exercised with respect to moral problems which bioplastic life is not called upon to consider. He must analyze the moral quality of actions, and he has the power to do it. He must understand the principles of the divinest jurisprudence and know how to apply them to the case in hand. He must know what law is; he must know the difference between right and wrong, justice and injustice, truth and falsehood, sin and holiness. He must be able to choose the right and reject the wrong. He must see differences, and choose between them. This is a high prerogative which bioplastic life never exercises. This prerogative, the power of alternate choice, the soul fully, freely, and responsibly does exercise. This is its highest endowment; this lifts it above bioplasm. In itself, or through external influence, the *soul has power to change its character*, a most wonderful result, and such as is never witnessed in the purely bioplastic realm. Look at it. A soul is deformed by contact with evil ; it is purified by contact with righteous principle. What is lovely in it is obscured or brightened, just as evil or righteousness plays upon it. It is the subject of change in its depths and at its very basis. This change is moral. Now, it is not essential whether the change is the result of its own volition or of some helpful external agency, or of the influence of environment. The fact of change is more important than the agency by which it is produced. Solomon at his anointing was different from Solomon on the mount of corruption. Saul of Tarsus was not Paul in Ephesus; that is, morally. Yet, the singular fact is that underlying these alternative susceptibilities of the soul is the consciousness of its identity, making itself manifest in the actual extremes of moral life. No such susceptibility pertains to bioplasm; no such extremes of nature exhibit themselves in living matter. The law of identity forbids alternation in bioplasm; in soul-life, paradoxical as it may seem, identity and alternation, consciousness and volitional extremes, are compatible, and always abide.

Profounder yet is the characteristic of *personality* that is attributed to spiritualistic life. However defined the word, whether it is regarded as the sum of moral powers, or the equipment of conscious being, one thing is certain, it belongs not to bioplasm. The palm tree is not a person; the lizard wears not the sign of personality; the whale is not a person; the kangaroo claims not the lineage of a person. Personality marks the man; it makes man what he is. By this is he separated from the bioplastic realm and enters the divine. This is not fiction, or a term of flattery, or the exclamation of self-praise. Personality is man's inheritance from God, and he has the right to shout over it.

A complete philosophy will not fail to attempt to account for soul-life as it has attempted to account for the non-living and the living worlds about us. Evidently the soul is not the product of an evolutionary force. As the living does not emerge from the non-living, so the spiritual does not issue from the bioplastic. Higher forms of life were never produced by lower, although chronologically the relation between them may be that of antecedent and consequent. The abyss between different kinds of life is not crossed by an evolutionary bridge. The chain of life does not extend from bioplasm to soul.

What then? The old notion of the pre-existence of souls, advocated by Plato, and taught by Origen, has no lodging-place in Christian circles. It opened the door to transmigration, the bane of Oriental religions, and robbed the soul of individuality. The doctrine of creationism, namely, that God creates the soul at the time the human body is ready for it, is not inconsistent with the larger theory that he created all life, all matter, and all the forms thereof. To account for non-living matter, creationism is necessary; to account for living matter, bioplastic or spiritual, it is equally indispensable.

The theory of Traducianism, namely, that the soul is derived in part from the souls of the parents, just as the body is, has been accepted in some quarters as sufficiently explanatory; but it is a compromise. Indeed, it resembles the theory that organization precedes and accounts for life, which we have rejected.

All life is the product of creative power. This does not involve special creations, except in the case of the soul, for bioplastic life in all its forms may be the development of a single principle; that is, the vitalistic principle may be more or less active all along the line, and the forms be different. But the soul, essentially different from bioplastic substance, can not arise from the vitalistic force as ordinarily manifested in the bioplastic realm; it requires the special exercise of the creative principle. For the bioplastic world the vitalistic principle under divine supervision is sufficient; for the soul-world the creative principle, which is the vitalistic concentered in a special product, working immediately, and not by a process of development, is required. Thus all life is the result of the highest force, whether ordinarily vitalistic or creative. *This force is God.*

## CHAPTER VII.

### MAN; OR, ANTHROPOLOGY.

"MAN," says Kant, "can not think highly enough of man." Of all earthly creatures the greatest, the most commanding, the most magnificent; if an animal only, the most perfect in physiological structure and form; if more than an animal, then a being with an investiture of mystery; his "place in nature" still in dispute; his place in time still a subject of inquiry; his history involved in obscurity; his destiny yet to be revealed or wrought out; surely man is justified in centering his study in man. Darwin extols him as "the wonder and glory of the universe," and a Hebrew writer intimates that he is only a little lower than the angels in the scale of created intelligences.

Whether man is natural or supernatural, or both, philosophy is seeking to determine; for, as related to the physical world by a material body, he appears to be natural, but, displaying an intellective capacity, he appears to be related to the supernatural, also; hence, the inquiry concerning man's exact place is fundamental. In a sense, he seems to stand on the border line between the two, partaking somewhat of both and illustrating the existence of both, and yet belonging wholly to neither. As such he is the connecting link between the natural and the supernatural, or nature and spirit; he is the right and left hands of existence, the right clasping the essential or spirit, the left joining the phenomenal or nature. Midway between them, he is perishable because nature is perishable, and indestructible because spirit is indestructible. The double view seems to be according to the facts, but neither philosophy nor religion, in their strict terms, can accept it. Man must be one *or* the other; he belongs to the domain of the natural or the domain of the supernatural. Materialistic philosophy descends to the natural estimate, while religion foreglimpses man's supernatural character.

Widely divergent as are these two general views, they both recognize man's double relations, accounting for them in harmony with their preconceived estimates, and according to facts which seem to point in both directions. Man's relation to nature is one of the first facts of his existence. What the relation is, or rather what it signifies, is an entirely different question, for, while the relation appears natural, the meaning of it may be supernatural. Materialism interprets the relation just as it seems, and fails to detect its hidden meaning.

Within the so-called historic period, man has in part demonstrated the significance of his relation to nature. He has shown a purpose to subdue nature, and nature is fast yielding to his lofty claim of dominion. Nature, stubborn at first, is beginning to feel the spell of his presence, the token of supernatural power, for it is the supernatural only that can control and subdue the natural. He has ferreted out laws which at one time made sport of him; he has defined the poisonous and the harmless in atmosphere and earth; he has changed marshes into landscapes of beauty, deserts into fruitful gardens, and made the ocean a highway of travel for all nations. At no distant day the conquest of earth's forces will be complete, and she will acknowledge the right of dominion exercised by her new master. Over the vegetable, mineral, and animal kingdoms, he will wave the scepter of power, and they will yield to his authority and minister to his wants. Crystal, insect, bird, reptile, quadruped, flower, fern, plant, moss, tree, and grass, will tender an ovation to the human ruler, and surrender to his government. By this is not meant that nature in its essentia will be changed, but only that the agreement between man and nature will be specific, and the latter will be subordinated to the former.

During the growth of this supremacy over nature, man also has waxed in strength, increased in wisdom, and is working out in his history ends higher than the exclusively natural. Which is the more wonderful, man's command over nature, or his self-development, it is difficult to determine.

Back of man's relation to nature is the inquiry of his origin, in which are involved all the facts of history, all the theories of philosophic speculation, and all the revelations of inspired penmen. None of these can be overlooked if a true account of man's origin is obtained. The field is vast, the theories are many and conflicting, and the facts themselves somewhat discordant or perplexingly difficult to trace and establish. The statement needs no proof that the Biblical and philosophical representations of the subject are in disagreement, and ·indeed at such variance that, accepting one account, the student is obliged to reject the other. This is unfortunate, for the two views ought to harmonize, so that the believer in the Biblical view may rest his faith on a philosophical basis, and the philosophical advocate support himself by the records of inspiration.

The disclosures of philosophy relate to four aspects: 1. The Origin of Man; II. The Character of Man; III. The Antiquity of Man; IV. The Destiny of Man.

Concerning the origin of man, there is wanting a uniformity of opinion among philosophic thinkers, many of whom seem to be impelled only by an antagonistic spirit to the Biblical representation; others are almost in harmony with it. As a whole, however, the philosophical conception is void of the Biblical spirit, and as Rome debased her coin when in the decline, so the philosophic conception is grosser and more materialistic as philosophy itself inclines to materialism. The following theories include the more prominent of those which may be found among the thinkers: 1. The Mechanical theory of the world; 2. The theory of Descent, known as Darwinism; 3. The theory of Transcendence, or that of Strauss; 4. The Teleological view, or man the end of nature. In the mechanical theory, as in a womb, lie all other theories of a materialistic complexion, for it includes all creation from the polyp to man, and accounts for all in the same way. The teleological interpretation of nature has reacted in certain circles, resulting in the elimination of the doctrine of a personal Creator and in a monistic conception of the universe. All reactions from theological conceptions are materialistic in their teachings. Not intending that evolution as propounded by him should furnish the basis for atheistic materialism, Mr. Darwin has been used by Häckel, Büchner, and others, to sustain the attack on the teleological philosophy and the theological conception of the world. Nature has been credited with certain independent impulses to life and order, which in their self-initiated activity produced the worlds which now compose the clusters of the firmament, with all else that exists. Nature is its own creation. By virtue of this predisposition to development, both the organic and the inorganic have resulted; and, according to Häckel, so prominent is the monistic principle in matter that the scientific distinction between the organic and inorganic is a delusion, having no reality in fact. All things are one, or the emanation of a principle of unity that presides throughout the universe. In the face of the fact that the distance between the organic and inorganic has never been spanned, it is asserted that there is no difference between them, and that the cosmical spirit is one and indivisible. To this theory of unity we might subscribe if it were qualified, and if in its application to nature certain facts were not ignored. To a theory of monism that eliminates the teleological principle, and especially that dispenses with intelligent supervision by endowing matter with life propensities, we can not subscribe, for it asks us to believe in a self-acting universe, which is a most stupendous absurdity.

The bearing of the monistic or mechanical theory on the origin of man is quite apparent. It includes in its sweep all creatures—man, bird, beast, fish, and creeping thing. It classifies nothing; it masses creation under one banner. Nature is producer and product; man is involved in nature. Whatever will account for nature as a whole will account for man as an individual of nature; whatever will account for any thing will account for every thing. Man was not created as Moses teaches—his "foundations are in the dust;" he is the result of the complicated forces of a self-acting world, and is as much an accident as a logical product. Certainly, nature did not *intend* to make man, for this is teleology; hence, he was a surprise even to nature. Acting in a different manner, nature's forces would have produced a different kind of being from man, or no being at all. The mechanical theory of the world involves the accidental, and not the intended or inevitable, appearance of man.

The theory of "descent," formerly adopted by Darwin, is a more precise determination of man's origin, and at one time threatened to supersede the Biblical account. It would be premature to announce its overthrow, but certainly the theory has not been sufficiently sustained. In his earlier studies, Mr. Darwin had no intention of excluding the reign of a Creator and Preserver from the realm of nature, and even his latest utterances are not atheistic. He meant not to be materialist or atheist. His original thought was that man is in the line of animal succession, descending—ascending is a truer term—from the animal kingdom, and developing as animals do into his present position in nature. The superiority of man to animals is no proof of a different origin, but proof of a larger development according to the laws of nature. To sustain this theory he pointed out the signs of relationship between man and animals, in habits, in hygienic laws, in structural likenesses, and in common physiological vices and virtues. He attempts to show that "man is constructed on the same general type or model as other mammals;" that his skeleton resembles that of the seal; that he can receive from and communicate to animals certain diseases, as hydrophobia, cholera, variola; that "he passes through the same phases of embryological development;" that he "retains many rudimentary and useless structures which no doubt were once serviceable;" and that he is "descended from some lower form, notwithstanding that connecting links have not hitherto been discovered." The physical relationship is quite fairly sustained.

A psychological relationship is more difficult to establish, but Darwin eagerly seeks for facts to support it. He declares that animals have the same senses as men; "similar passions, affections, and emotions; they possess the same faculties of imitation, attention, deliberation, choice, memory, imagination, the association of ideas, and reason, though in very different degrees;" they are liable to insanity also. It is not certain that Darwin is correct in these statements, for, in order to sustain them, he must abolish well-settled distinctions between instinct and rational intelligence, which his theory compelled him to do. As to self-consciousness, the ingrain idea of personality, Darwin was not bold enough to allow that it belonged to the animal kingdom. "No animal is self-conscious," he says, "if by this term it is implied that he reflects on such points as whence he comes, or whither he will go, or what is life and death;" but self-consciousness does include reflection on the questions of past, present, and future, or life and death. Belief in self is so intense, says Spencer, that "no hypothesis enables us to escape" it. This is the dividing line between a man and an animal: the one is self-conscious in the highest sense, embracing past and future; the other is self-conscious, if at all, with respect to the present. The psychological relationship has not been made out quite to our satisfaction.

The difficulty grows as one looks for signs of moral relationship with the animal kingdom. In no hesitating spirit, however, Mr. Darwin approaches the problem and disposes of it by referring the origin of the moral nature in man to the operation of the social forces; "the foundation lies in the social instincts." According to this view, moral ideas are not instinctive or intuitional, but the result of social development which has been going on from the earliest ages until now. Besides, he discovers the counterpart of moral emotions, or the moral nature of man, in animals; he points to affection, sympathy, shame, remorse, and the family tie, in the animal kingdom. Mr. Huxley relates an incident to show that a gibbon has a conscience. Thus man is a descendant of the animal kingdom, is *per se* an animal.

The theory of "descent" is already stereotyped in science and philosophy. Karl Vogt has sketched man's pedigree from the ape, and Darwin contrasting monkeys and savages, concluded that descent from the former would be more honorable to our race than descent from the latter. In a coarse and vehement style Häckel vindicates the theory, pointing out twenty-two stages of development from the lowest form of animal life to man, and apparently connecting them without any missing links; but scientists have shown the error of the stages, proving that some of them do not exist in nature.

The tracing of man's genealogy is an imperative requirement of evolution. Darwin himself accepted such a task, but met with some difficulty when it became necessary to pass from invertebrates to vertebrates. The passage between the ascidæ and the lancelet fish was easily traced; from fish came amphibia; from the amphibia the reptilia; these developed into marsupialia; these developed into lemurs or half-apes; from these a variety of apes issued; then the gibbon and the gorilla; then *one link more;* then man. But this schedule of development is by no means complete, as others have shown, and it fails just where demonstration is the most imperative.

Huxley espouses "descent," tracing the development of the animal kingdom through man-like apes or anthropoids until its consummation is reached in man. For his purposes, he exposes the physiological likeness of the gibbon, the ourang, the chimpanzee, and the gorilla to the human skeleton, affirming in the end that structural similarity establishes physical relationship or genealogical descent. He insists also that "the mode of origin and the early stages of the development of man are identical with those of the animals immediately below him in the scale," and concludes that "secondary causes" are sufficient to account for the phenomena of the universe, man included.

As the Athenians who boasted that they sprung from the earth wore, as a symbol, a grasshopper in their hair, so those moderns who espouse the animal theory of the origin of man should engrave an anthropoid on their coat-of-arms.

Darwin did not intend that "descent" should undermine the theistic notion, and Wallace still later insists that they are compatible; but Häckel and Huxley crush out the idea of a personal Creator in the development of the universe. We do not assume that a theory which carried to the extreme invalidates a fundamental religious idea is to be rejected but it is a suspicious theory, and can not be fully accepted without further proof.

Against the theory of "descent," as a whole, we offer the following consideration or two, which make it difficult to accept it; indeed, until certain facts shall have been discovered, the theory is absolutely null and void. As it is, it has only a tentative character. No geologist claims that fossils have been found that indicate a passage from lower organizations into man; it is the great grief of materialistic scientists that a "missing link" is still missing between the gorilla and man. To assume that such a link will be found is unphilosophical. Until it is found, "descent" fails of its purpose.

Inasmuch as a wide intellectual and moral gap exists between man and the animal kingdom, some geologists are disposed to refer man to a "distinct kingdom in nature." Sir Charles Lyell quotes approvingly the "reasoning of M. Quatrefages" on this proposition. Man constitutes a kingdom himself, the kingdom of improving reason, of intellectual activity, of spiritual life. This certainly is an independent view, destructive of "descent," and in harmony with the Biblical interpretation.

The character of the "primitive" man is usually employed in defense of the "development" theory, inasmuch as it is taken for granted that he was but a little in advance of an animal. Professor Whitney, however, insists that man, whether found in pliocene or post-pliocene or recent formations is *nothing but man.* Sir J. Lubbock has certainly made out a case against savages or barbarians, but his volume of facts goes not back of historic times and only proves the degeneracy of man, *not what he was originally.* The man of the "stone age" was probably less civilized than the man of the "bronze age," and the latter was behind the man of the "iron age," but who claims, unless he is a materialist, that the palæolithic man was the original man, or even a type of him? After the "ice epoch" was a long "watery epoch," or between the glacial period and the stone man—between the original man and the post-diluvian man—was the age of a splendid race, followed by a degenerate people, or the savages who, beginning with or constituting the stone age, remain until the present time.

Of the primeval inhabitants no remains have been found, unless language, the family institution, and the religious idea make up a portion of their legacy. Of monuments there is none; of works of art, of philosophy, poetry, there is none; but language, home and religion are the imperishable mementoes of that early race, inherited by savages, and transmitted to all nations, civilizing and elevating them. Concerning language it must be said that like the hieroglyphs of Egypt the oldest are the best, that is, the first languages have needed no improvement. The perfection of the primitive languages speaks loudly for a perfect people who used them, and overwhelms the theory of evolution in complete ruin. The historic course of the early languages shows a descent, or degradation, and the historic course of mankind shows also a similar descent or degradation, which is contrary to the germinal idea of Darwin, who means by descent the *ascent* of the race. But the palæolithic man was not an ascent; he was a descent, like his language; he was a savage, preserving language, home, and religion, but in the grossest forms, the purification of which has required the work of many generations. "Descent" *breaks down in language, the family institution, and the religious idea;* and in the same way it breaks at a vital point in the history of man. It is a guess, not a fact.

The transcendental theory of Strauss is essentially materialistic, a modified evolutionary process resulting in man. He speaks of the "ascending evolution of nature," and intimates that the scientist conceives of the possibility of the development of the organic from the inorganic, but he confesses "enduring ignorance" of the origin of consciousness. Evolution can not explain self-consciousness. It explains man, as a whole, however. He says: "As nature can not go higher, she would go inwards"—man is the limitation, the end of evolution. Again he says: "In man nature endeavored, not merely to exalt, but to transcend herself;" and, rising in spite of his materialistic preferences, he shouts, "do not forget for a moment that thou art human; not merely a natural production." Is man a "natural production," like a tree, or cloud, or bird, or frog, or flower? According to the mechanical theory of the world, and according to the theory of "descent," as manipulated by the atheists, he is a "natural production," nothing more; but, according to Strauss in his highest mood, he is "human," implying, if it mean any thing, something more than a natural result. Nature transcended herself in man; she could go no higher, and hence turned "inwards." The highest expression of evolution or creative force is man. This much Strauss means; and, notwithstanding his infidelic spirit, we accept him as an intermediate teacher between Häckel and Owen; or, in broader phrase, as a step from rank materialism to theism. He did not intend to occupy this middle ground, but the first step toward a true conception of man is his relation to nature—just the step Strauss took. In his effort to abandon the Biblical account of miraculous creation, he swings to materialism, but finds in his last analysis of man an element that materialism can not explain, and leaves it without explanation. This is the weakness of scientific theories in general, that the human element in man, entirely different from the natural or animal element, they can not explain; or, if they attempt explanation they refer it to a secondary cause, which may account for man as an improved descendant of the kingdom of nature.

The last view claiming notice is teleological in spirit and scientific in form. Louis Agassiz expresses it thus: "Man is the purpose toward which the whole animal creation tends from the first appearance of the first paleozoic fish." By this he does not mean that man was the last in a series of natural developments, partaking of the spirit of the whole, and the inevitable outgrowth of it all—this were but the mechanician's view over again; but he means that *nature was planned with reference to man;* that the earth was prepared for his abode; and that, beginning back in the early ages, the purpose to adjust the world to its future inhabitant is evident. This is a broad view of nature, and a broader view of man than the materialists can allow. It is the teleological view of creation which excites Häckel, and convulses him with rage. He can not for a moment consent to it. He says that "since the awakening of human consciousness, human vanity" has insisted that man is the main purpose of terrestial life, but it is a baseless presumption!

The teleological view of creation is inspiring; at least it is more elevating in its effect to think that man is the *end* or *purpose* of nature, than that he is the *product* of nature. Richard Owen, preferring the former, exclaims: "Man, from the beginning of organisms, was ideally present upon the earth." The ideal aim of nature, under the intelligent supervision of a personal Creator and Ruler, was preparation for an inhabitant it could not produce, but who would in time appear through the intervention and by the appointment of that Creator and Lord. This waiting of nature for its master, to be introduced by a higher power, is a finer conception than that of the effort of nature to produce man as a higher organism than brutes. Between the two theories or conceptions, whether man is the product of nature, or the end of nature; whether he is in the line of animal succession, or independent of it and appointed over it; whether he developed, as Häckel insists, or was ideally present from the beginning, as Owen finely phrases it, one must choose, or have no conception at all. The four theories here considered are reducible to two : man is *the product of nature*, or *the purpose of nature*. These two theories are the height and depth of philosophic and scientific conclusion respecting man; they vibrate between a materialistic, atheistic, monistic conception, and an ideal or teleological theory of his origin, the latter being in harmony with the theological conception that will have consideration later in the volume. The gospel of monism, as preached by Häckel,

Huxley, evolutionists in general, or the gospel of ideal teleology, already foreshadowed in the scientific hypotheses of Agassiz, Owen, and Rudolf Schmid, will be the scientific gospel of the future, with the probabilities in favor of the latter.

Our next duty is to ascertain the interpretation put by philosophy upon the intellectual and moral nature of man, to know whether, even allowing that the physical man has an animalic basis, his higher nature is the resultant of animalic agencies, or has an independent basis. Man's greatness is a supreme fact. Plato affirms that the mind is the man, and Hamilton declares there is nothing great but mind. *Man's greatness, therefore, is the greatness of mind.* Exactly what mind is, under what laws it exists and operates, we consider elsewhere, while here we must consider it only in connection with those materialistic theories which propose to account for it. It may be supposed that the theory that will account for man at all will account for the whole man; that his character is so involved in his origin that one theory only is required to explain both. We shall not insist that two origins are demanded, one for the body, and another for the intellectual and moral nature; one origin is sufficient. The cause that produced man produced all there is of him. If he is a descendant of the animal kingdom, then whatever he is is a development of an animalic nature; otherwise he is not such descendant, and another history must be invoked. As we have seen, Darwin undertook to explain the higher nature of man in harmony with the theory of "descent," but the proof is not conclusive that intellect, conscience, volition, self-determination, and self-consciousness, are the products of development, or are natural states evolved through natural processes. The physical man may consist of solid matter held in solution in about six pails of water, but the intellectual and moral qualities of man can not be reduced to chemical proportions or physical affinities.

The unity of the higher nature is a troublesome fact to the materialists, for it requires that the theory that will explain the intellectual nature will explain the moral also; but while they persuade themselves that thought is the result of molecular action, or mere nervous force, they find it difficult to explain conscience and moral self-determination in the same way. Hence, they are driven to manufacture two theories, or, in the language of Strauss, confess "enduring ignorance." Hartley and James Mill heralded the theory that thought is the product of brain organism, while Bain elaborated it into a nervous result; but none of them explains consciousness, or memory, or imagination in that way. However far the psychologists go, they always stop before they reach the end. True, in mere terms, the

12

psychical character of man has been reduced by the empiricists to a physiological basis, but it is a theoretical reduction only. Thought is a physical play; mental and nervous action are interchangeable terms; affection, fear, hope, joy, sorrow, are chemical results, the product of altered molecular conditions. T. Starr King, commenting on the sublimated theory, said: "When a lady scolds, a man has to face only a few puffs of articulate carbonic acid, but her weeping is liquid lightning." If thought and feeling are physical states, superinduced by sensation, or the interaction of the molecular forces, it is not far, so the psychologist imagines, to the explanation of the moral states, which may be also the play of differently directed nervous sensibilities. This is only an inference, however; the proof is still wanting.

For an explanation of the moral attributes of man we have: 1. The Principle of Association, enunciated by Bain; 2. The Law of Social Development, proclaimed by Darwin; 3. The theory of Evolution, adopted by Spencer. Differing as these do in details, they are closely related, and possess the same value, since they all reject the notion of an independent basis for the higher nature of man. It makes little difference whether the moral nature originated in intellectual exercise, or bloomed from the social instincts, or was evolved by physical processes, the result is the same, the materialism of human nature. In none of these theories is there room for providential endowments, or special creative forces, or the need of divine interposition in equipping man for rightful sovereignty, or clothing him with a noble dignity. Against all these theories we present the plausible conjecture, supported by religious revelation or teaching, that man's moral nature was in him *ab initio*, and its presence can not be accounted for by any theory of development whatever. Sir J. Lubbock, it is true, asserts that the lowest savages seem to him to be "almost entirely wanting in moral feeling," while Mr. Wallace points out that our civilized populations, progressing intellectually, "have not advanced beyond the savage code of morals, and have in many cases sunk below it." Lord Kames is of the opinion that the moral sense is native to man; Prof. Winchell speaks of it as intuitional. This is all that we now care to claim. Whether the primitive inhabitants of the earth had a profound or native sense of the divine sovereignty, or believed in the immortality of the soul, does not belong to the simple inquiry concerning a moral sense in man; and even were they involved in the inquiry, Lubbock's instances of atheism, or rather ignorance of God, only prove the extinction or reduction of the moral idea, and not that it did not originally exist. Nothing has been adduced and no example cited, to disprove the conjecture that the moral idea did not dominate in the earliest inhabitants of the globe. If it was a reigning idea as far back as history can conduct us, then it is difficult to establish that it is a development. Its refinement may be the result of a developing process; its *existence* is another thing, and is implicit with a miraculous suspicion. What are the conclusions of philosophy respecting the character of man? *It traces his physical body to the ancestry of apes; it converts intellectual processes into nervous irritations; it represents the moral faculties as the outcome of intellectual and social interactions; and contentedly suspends its investigation with the play of secondary causes.*

No study of man is complete that omits a searching inquiry into his *antiquity*, since the fate of many theories is involved in it. His appearance on earth was the beginning of a new lordship, and a new life on the planet. Could it be ascertained about when he appeared, controversy over correlated hypotheses would end, and the traditional account would be overthrown or confirmed. It is a singular fact that the Biblical account can be readily and consistently adjusted to a brief or long antiquity, while a short antiquity would be utterly and ruinously subversive of all materialistic and evolutionary suppositions, since they require indefinite periods of time for the accomplishment of their tasks. Take the *conscience* alone—a million years would be none too long for its evolution, even from a potential to the actual state. The stone-wall fact is, that if man first appeared seven thousand years ago, then the web of materialism is torn into threads. Merely as a religious problem, the Bible has been interpreted to settle in favor of a short antiquity, but no violence would be done either its chronology or history to lengthen it. As a scientific question, the antiquity of man has been pushed back into the misty periods of the fossiliferous ages, because on that hypothesis other hypotheses depend for vitality. Unfortunately, the subject has not been considered except in its bearings on some heretical scientific notion, and the result has been a false interpretation of the facts, as they were discovered, or a mere conjecture of facts when none were found. A Biblicist should have no anxiety either way, for it is immaterial whether the scientific antiquity be overthrown or not, except as it tends to support evolution. In any event, and whatever the final discovery, the Bible will be found in happy concordance with it. The scientific spirit may be hostile to the Biblical interpretation, but the scientific *result* can not be contrary to the Biblical truth. The Bible will stand, whatever science may find; philosophy can not stand if science finally reduces man's antiquity to a very short period. This being the case, the defenders of the Biblical account are disposed quietly to wait until scientific exploration and research have submitted all the facts, for this is a question of fact, not of opinion. On the other hand, philosophy, seeing its fate depends upon the specific favor of scientific elaboration and deduction, is in no indifferent mood when new facts are announced, for it lives only as they are propitious.

What, at this stage of research, are the scientific facts touching the antiquity of man? Are they bulwarking philosophic speculation, or buttressing the Biblical interpretation? If the final verdict of science should be opposed to both the current philosophical and theological interpretations, asserting a middle view, would not the gods rather laugh than weep? Precisely to such an overturning, science seems, however unwillingly, to conduct us. Within fifty years past a scientific revolution concerning man has taken place, leaving us the option of accepting an interminable antiquity, or a modified Biblical interpretation. Within this period the geologists have not been idle, but in an enthusiastic spirit they have gone to the extreme of belief in the age of man, supporting it by discoveries that for the time appeared authentic and declaratory. That the prehistoric antiquity which they avowed for man was contradictory of religious traditions, and might unsettle faith in all religious teaching, did not concern them; with consequences they had nothing to do. Vulnerable as are the inferences drawn from the facts, the geologists deserve credit for their persevering industry in searching the fields of nature for testimony to the age of the human race, and they have enriched our knowledge by their discoveries. Carried forward by a scientific enthusiasm that knows no quenching, scientists began explorations in geological fields for ethnological purposes, gathering facts from all quarters of the globe and turning nations into fact-seekers. Caves were explored; peat bogs were upturned; tumuli were sifted of their contents; even the bottoms of the oceans were dragged; deserts were crossed; river gravels were analyzed; every climate, every zone, and every geological stratum was inspected, and the crust of the earth was struck with a hammer as if it would ring back the answer of the antiquity of man. The results were wonderful, and, as the range of investigation was no " pent-up Utica," the inferences ought to have been decisive.

What are the results of the scientific travail? Are they philosophically anthropocentric, or do they vindicate the standard Biblical interpretation? The answer to these questions can not be given in a word. The discovery of facts is one thing; the inference from them is another; and the process by which a conclusion is reached, or the rule of inference, is still another, and indeed the vital feature. The general *geological rule is to estimate the age of fossils by the relative age of the stratum in which they are found;* for instance, whatever is found in the Silurian stratum must be much older than what is found in the Post-tertiary. This seems like a safe rule, but it has led to extravagant calculations. M. Mortillet, by this rule, has figured that man appeared 240,000 years ago! Sir Charles Lyell estimated human relics in the valley of the Somme to be 800,000 years old! Mr. A. R. Wallace estimated the age of some flint implements found in a cavern at Torquay, at 500,000 years! The weakness of the rule is, that whatever conclusion is reached, it is only *relative*, not absolute. There is no starting-point for a mathematical calculalation. It has not been ascertained how old any particular stratum is, nor can it be, for nature has not dated its works. Hence, the conclusions are suppositions and have only a relative value.

Geologists are fond of alluding to what they call the stone, bronze, and iron ages, periods when the inhabitants of the earth manufactured their implements after rude patterns, and advanced slowly toward civilization. Mr. Southall believes that these ages were largely contemporaneous, and not historically successional. He goes so far as to deny the existence of a bronze age, regarding it as merely imaginary. Especially is there no proof of a bronze age in England, Switzerland, Russia, and other parts of Europe. In proof of the contemporaneous character of the Ages, he cites the fact that the tumuli of Russia abound in stone, bronze, and iron implements, and that while one race was using stone, another at the same time was using iron. Dr. Schliemann, in unearthing layers at Troy and Mycenæ, found stone implements in the top layers and bronze in the fourth stratum below, showing that bronze preceded stone, or the stone age was last instead of first. This shows the unreliability of this kind of argument. The Stone Age, in fact, still exists. Finding human implements in strata, or caves, or bogs, whose age they thought they knew, the Swiss geologists especially began the work of calculation respecting the antiquity of the people of those periods ; and M. Morlot concludes that the stone age represents five or six thousand years, and the bronze age three or four thousand more. If contemporaneous, they may represent three thousand years. It is not very difficult to demonstrate that the Palæolithic man so-called, was an average man, if the size of the skull is an indication of character ; and when it is remembered that he used a needle and thread in making his clothing, loved song, and made instruments of music, manufactured implements out of wood as well as stone, and reverenced the memory of the dead, he must not be too harshly judged in this day. At all events, it is clear that he himself is not a proof of even a prehistoric antiquity of any great length. Another estimate has been made in Egypt, inasmuch as pottery and even works of art, have been found that, measured by the geological rule, point to a civilization that must have existed thirty thousand years ago; but Sir Charles Lyell considers the "chronometric scale" unsatisfactory. No absolute "chronometric scale" for the measurement of strata has been found; this is the difficulty.

Much has been made of relics found in the peat in the Somme Valley in France, but Mr. Southall points to the fact that *Roman bricks* have been found below the peat, proving that it is a modern, instead of an ancient deposit, as was claimed. In certain alluvial deposits, hatchets, knives, and the bones of extinct mammalia have been found, showing that the people who made the hatchets were contemporaneous with the extinct mammalia; and, as it is assumed that the latter became extinct thousands of years ago, so man must have been living then. This is a safer rule of inference than the other, but our confidence in it is shaken by the supposition, justified by the history of man, that the mammalia became extinct by virtue of man's opposition; he destroyed the wild beasts as they interfered with his progress; and, instead of showing that he is as old as they were, it shows that they disappeared when he appeared, and that his antiquity is much less than theirs. The theory has been disturbed recently by the discovery that many supposed extinct animals are not extinct, as the elephant, lion, bear, hyena, etc., so that an argument founded on the remains of these extinct (?) species needs reconstruction. "There are more false facts," says Cullen, "current in the world, than false theories." We have here an example of "false facts." Besides, Prof. Winchell points out that extinctions of species have occurred within the historic period, as the great birds of New Zealand, proving that the argument from "extinct species" is of little account to the antiquarian. Prof. Southall adds that the "extinct" reindeer was found in Germany in the time of Cæsar and that the cave horse still exists. Of a similar character is the argument drawn from megalithic monuments and tumuli, scattered all over the globe, which the geologists have interpreted to indicate an extravagant antiquity; but Mr. Southall reduces the argument to very small proportions by pointing out, historically, their origin, the names of their builders, and the purposes of many of the monuments and tombs. Mr. Worsade assigns twenty-five hundred years to some woolen garments found in the cromlechs in Denmark, but it has been shown that they date from the fifth century!

Still another and, as it seems to us, fatal objection to the two geological rules above mentioned, is the paucity of human remains in the strata, caves, and glacial layers, relied upon to establish a great antiquity for man. When it is remembered how abundant are the remains of reptiles, fishes, and mammoths in these strata, the absence of human remains provokes astonishment, and is not easily explained except on the hypothesis that man was the latest arrival on the earth, and has not been here long enough to become a fossil, or to crowd the crust with his remains. This fact troubled Sir Charles Lyell, who attempted to account for it in part by the dissolution of human skeletons into dust; also by cremation, a mode of disposition of the dead among the primitive inhabitants, and by destruction, by fishes and animals, who devoured bones and digested them. It seems not to have occurred to him that such causes, if sufficient to destroy human remains, would be sufficient greatly to limit animal remains, but they are found in abundance. Struggling with the fact he admits the "extreme imperfection of the geological record," but "confidently expects" that the "older alluvium of the European valleys" will in due time exhibit human remains in such quantities as to satisfy the demands of the advocates of a long antiquity! This is pure conjecture.

Are there no human remains at all? Sir Charles Lyell dwells at length upon the age of the "fossil man of Denise," and, from a human bone found on the banks of the Mississippi River, concludes that man's antiquity dates back to the "mastodon and megalonyx." Some remains were exhumed near Maestricht, but he saw no evidence of antiquity in them.

Geologists refer to an old skull found in a cave near Düsseldorf in proof of the antiquity of man; but it is not certain whether it is the skull of a man or an ape. If of a man, as the forehead would indicate, it does not establish antiquity; for it is the skull of an old man, or not of a man at all. *The proofs required to establish the existence of an old man are different from those required to establish the existence of an old race.* Neither from the few human skulls nor from the many human implements found in the crust of the earth is it possible to construct an argument in favor of a high antiquity for the race. On the contrary, the geological evidence seems to indicate a brief antiquity, which can be lengthened only by a torture of the facts. Huxley says that the evidence that assigns the first appearance of man anterior to the drift period is of a very "dubious character," and Nicholson designates a post-glacial period for that appearance. The geologists have well-nigh established the conclusion that the Ice Period began six or seven thousand years ago, *and if man appeared at the close of the Ice Period,* his presence on the earth is reduced to about six thousand years, a figure singularly coincident with that of the Biblical interpretation. Mr. Southall has calculated that the Glacial Age closed in the north of Europe about thirty-five hundred years ago; archæologists say six or seven thousand years ago.

Prof. Capellini recently submitted some proofs looking to the existence of "pliocene" man, which Prof. Dawkins has overthrown, the latter maintaining that no traces of man appear until the "succeeding stage, or the pleistocene." Other geologists agree with Prof. Dawkins, but use the word "quaternary" instead of pleistocene. The significant fact in this connection is that "living species of mammalia" begin to abound in the "pleistocene," and the cereals first display themselves in the "quaternary;" that is, in the period or stratum denominated pleistocene or quaternary. When man's first appearance is detected, the cereals and living mammalia also make their first appearance. Equally serviceable is the conclusion of Prof. Blake that no flint implements have been found in England that bear evidence of an antiquity earlier than the Post-glacial period. Prof. Winchell bravely but inconclusively argues for man's origin in the middle Tertiary period; and Prof. Geikie, from a single bone, *not known to be human even*, claims it as "direct proof that man lived prior to the last *inter-glacial* period!"

Principal Dawson, whose scholarship needs no defense, exhibits the proof of man's post-glacial origin, and assigns him a history of six or seven thousand years. In an address delivered before the American Association for the Advancement of Science, of which he was the president, he said: "Since the comparatively short post-glacial and recent periods apparently include the whole of human history, we are but *new-comers* on the earth, and therefore have had little opportunity to solve the great problems which it presents to us." He further and promptly intimates that "the cessation of glacial cold and settlement of our continents at their present levels are events which may have occurred not more than 6,000 or 7,000 years ago."

Thus science, running wild for a time, and extending its hallucinations to every hint, or fact, or skull, or ax, is at last swinging to the support of the theory of a limited history of man, as interpreted by the Bible defenders. All along the latter have been unaccountably disturbed over the radical scientific variations from the traditional standard, which has been vindicated rather than overthrown. The caverns, indeed, throw up no proofs against the old faith; the seas, dredged and sounded, speak not against the accepted account; not one skull or a hundred, not one implement or a thousand, invalidates the theory of a short antiquity. If finally, abandoning its pretentious inferences from a few skulls, and the contents of geological strata, science should settle down to the acceptance of the validity of the orthodox antiquity, then indeed human history might finally be compassed, and its unwritten chapters be deciphered, but the thought of a remote antiquity fills history with vagueness ; it blots out history.

With the geological evidence thus interpreted, the historical and monumental records of men are in perfect harmony. Grote has shown that the first Greek Olympiad dates seven hundred and seventy-six years before Christ, and Sir Charles Lyell admits that Roman and Egyptian monuments carry us back no farther than fifteen hundred years before Christ. Hindu history is mythical back of thirty-six hundred years ago.

The proof from the lake dwellings in Switzerland, so often referred to by geologists as pointing to the Neolithic Age, is utterly overthrown by the fact that pile villages, as primitive as those of the early Swiss, are still established on many Oriental coasts, the people building them being in an advanced stage of civilization.

History, monuments, and geology agree with the Biblical interpretation of a short antiquity, the overthrow of which belongs to those who, infatuated with the superstitious idea that man sprang from animals, are determined to have a long enough period to bring it about. Prof. Dawson frankly admits that the value of a long antiquity is its bearing on evolution, while a short antiquity is in the interest of human history, as known. The drift of science at this time, however, is toward the Biblical interpretation.

In connection with the origin and antiquity of man, scientifically considered, other questions might be brought forward, such as the plurality of races, the different departments of ethnography, and the common bond of humanity, or the unity of mankind. Prof. Winchell, with a scientific boldness peculiar to the times, is disseminating the theory of a pre-Adamite race, in order to vindicate the early geological supposition of a fabulous antiquity. At this stage of the discussion it is not important whether or not there was a race of pre-Adamites, only so far as it tends to invalidate the Mosaic record, and give countenance to the evolution theories of the materialists.

A race of pre-Adamites may have consisted of beings half animals and half men, or centaurs, who through evolution finally produced Adam, with which the Bible concerns itself. But this is as unscientific as it is unscriptural, and in no way disposes of any existing difficulty or throws light upon any ethnic problem. A pre-Adamite was a man or he was not. If not, he is outside of our inquiry ; if he was, the same questions arise to perplex the ethnologist, as Adam himself suggests. Besides, if the last scientific word on anthropology should favor a short antiquity of man, confirming the Mosaic revelation, the pre-Adamite would disappear quite as suddenly as he has appeared.

Touching the plurality of races, some inquiry is pertinent at this time, inasmuch as it is in conflict with the doctrine of the unity of the race, or its foundation in a single pair. The origin of the races, as a scientific problem, is as perplexing as the origin of man himself. Whether he has a monogenetic pedigree or a polygenetic history, ethnology is making debatable. For it has been demonstrated that climate, food, and temporal conditions alone are not adequate causes of the ethnic lines of separation, and, to involve the matter in increasing mystery, outside of these physical causes others have not been enumerated. The student is in a painful dilemma, for he can proceed no farther until the door to another explanation is opened. What is also most singular is that, as in the animal kingdom the race-types—that is, the species—are fixed, so in human history the race-types have not changed, and give no sign of change. The race-types of the one can not be the product of development any more than the species-types of the other are the product of development.

The fixity of race-types is not at all inconsistent with the varieties of individuals, or the unity of the races, for the law of fixity admits of innumerable extensions and modifications, without compromising its character or influence. The diversity of the races is a fact no one will deny; but this should be expected, as, whether outside influences are sufficient or not to modify man, he is sufficient to modify himself, which he has done. With variations occurring constantly in the race, it must not be forgotten that they are no greater than the variations in animals having a common origin, and so the fact makes not against unity.

Physiologists concede that the structure of the skin of the negro and the white man is the same, and the brains and the nerves of the lowest races do not differ structurally from those of the highest. The languages of the races, under thorough analysis, exhibit in their roots a similarity that is suggestive of a common origin. The Aryan, the Semitic, and the Allophylian group of tongues, with all their variations, point to a " primitive identity;" and the same intellectual aspirations actuate all alike. Even the same moral problems are discussed with more or less intensity by all. With marked diversities there is a wonderful unity among the races, a physical, moral, and intellectual unity. The several race-types prove to be compatible with one race idea, a very satisfactory ethnic conclusion, which, however, is not favorable to " descent" or evolution, since the latter must have changeable types and a disunion of races in order to illustrate its meaning and maintain its position. The unity of the race, as a fact of anthropology, is more than a thorn in the theory of evolution; it is the death-knell of materialism.

Perhaps no phase of anthropology is more captivating than the future of man or the destiny of the race, a subject that follows in the wake of the former discussions, and is really as philosophical as it is religious. What is the philosophic prospectus of man's future? It will be agreed that pessimism—a form of philosophic hypochondria—is without inspiration; it dims the eye as one looks forward, and fills it with tears. The fear of J. S. Mill that man may reach the limit of knowledge or achievement in music, is not productive of energy in musical pursuits. The belief of Schopenhauer that the government of the world is as bad as it possibly can be, with no assurance of change, strips life of all eagerness, and paralyzes human effort for progress. The denial of freedom to man, as made by Häckel—that is, that he is a part of the autonomy of nature, subservient to its conditions, and that development and responsibility are idle words—is a discouraging aspect of life, the correction of which is both a duty and a necessity.

Has philosophy nothing more to offer than a series of discouragements? Is there any philosophic hope of the race? The general theory of development is an inspiration in itself, but that it has not inspired man is proof that it is wanting in a vital element, or, if not thus deficient, that it is self-hindering or self-destructive, by virtue of other elements, or associations and relations.

The weakness of the doctrine of development is its prostitution to the service of materialism. Make it a Christian doctrine—that is, turn it to the service of humanity—and the stars in their courses will fight for it. It has been suspected more than once that the philosophic interpretation of the doctrine implied the retardation of the race; hence it lost its glow. If "development" means only the improvement of man as an animal, there is no inspiration in it; but if it means the progress of man towards his Maker, the supremacy of the spiritual over the animalic, the world will shout in its favor. Deny freedom, banish the idea of moral responsibility, suppress the personality of man, reduce thought to nervous action, and conscience to a social impulse, and the future of man loses its attraction as a subject of contemplation.

If the interpretation of some evolutionists be considered, the "development" theory signifies too much, more than we can ask, for, carried to its logical conclusion, the theory promises, not the future development of man, but his disappearance from the earth, being succeeded by a still higher organized being, as superior to man as man is superior to the gorilla, but retaining traceable signs of relationship to man. This goes too far, as the other interpretation goes not far enough. Unless development stops with man, centering itself in his upbuilding, he must become a fossil in the future; and such a fate philosophers have assumed as possible, and really ventured to predict its probable fulfillment. Thus the "development" theory is dangerous, however applied, resulting, on the one hand, in the dwarfishness and degradation of man, or, on the other, in his extinction, either view being repugnant to that Christian hope of the race which involves an increase in knowledge and the gradual moral elevation of all mankind.

The hypothesis of Christianity, which involves the development of man in the image of God, the enlargement of his moral and intellectual possibilities until he is a hundred-fold greater than he now is, has in it a propelling influence that makes progress both a delight and a certainty. Häckel, dispensing entirely with Christianity as an uplifting force, foreshadows a future for man on the lower basis of mechanical development; but in dispensing with religion, or that form of it which Gustave Jaeger pronounced the "best weapon" in the struggle of human life, he disqualifies man for the largest and truest development. Humanity can not be run on steam-engine principles, or played like an Æolian harp. Precisely this is the religion of materialism, the religion of mechanics or mechanical development. Man is the product of environing forces, and will be developed by them.

In our conception of the future man, we are not loaded with philosophic dead-weights, or embarrassed by clouds of pessimistic darkness. The development we foresee is along the line of the higher nature, resulting in the suppression of the animalic spirit and an extinction of those signs of relationship to the animal world that Mr. Darwin was very successful in pointing out. The social nature, the intellectual faculties, the moral powers, we see blooming in the radiance of a light that shines from above; they are developed, not by mechanical processes, but, in spite of environment, in spite of physical economies, by the aid of religious influences, always the most potent and the most effective in the intellectual and moral regeneration of man. The ideal man is not the mechanically developed, but the religiously developed, man, for the reason that mechanical forces are the lowest, and religious forces the highest. Nor, on the hypothesis of Christianity, is there any reason to suspect that the race is marching on to extinction, to be succeeded by another race still more highly organized and endowed. The higher race is sure to come, but it will be human; *it will be our race perfected along the religious line.* In this there is inspiration; along this avenue of hope we walk.

Even a careless reader can see how closely related to the question of the eternal life of man are these philosophic conjectures, on which alone immortality can not be predicated. "If a man die, shall he live again ?" is quite as philosophic as religious, but philosophy is uncertain in its answer. Emerson, reaching into highest things, rests faith in immortality chiefly in the desire for it, a beautiful but rather provoking kind of transcendentalism, for it is wanting in persuasive sufficiency. The doctrine of immortality is a stumbling-block to materialism. No mechanical or evolutionary theory that attributes instincts, emotions, aspirations, faculties, moral powers, to natural processes, will readily affiliate with a system that allows immortality to man. The argument that makes out man's immortality will also make out the immortality of the animal kingdom, according to the mechanician; we regret that Prof. Agassiz conceded this much to those who differed with him.

Thus we see what robbery materialism has made of one of man's cherished hopes! It has struck at his nobility, allied him to animals, threatened him with future extinction, and quenched the fires of immortality.

Ours is quite another faith, which, turning the laws of development into another channel, foresees another future for man, and intrenches itself in the truth-girdled teachings of Christianity.

## CHAPTER VIII.

### MIND AN INTEGER.

BY insisting on certain limitations to human inquiry, and the proofs of traditional dogmas, modern science has permanently checked the spirit of assumption which more or less characterized the psychology, and especially the theology, of the past. It refuses to believe on the ground of authority alone; it demands evidence of every proposition, and virtually suspends its faith even in axiomatic or primary truths until they have been demonstrated. An axiom can not defend itself behind the assertion that it is incapable of demonstration, or by the bolder announcement that its truth is self-evident. Convicted of granite stubbornness in its position, science nevertheless maintains opposition to so-called self-evident and necessary truths, requiring their logical exposition, and asking at least for a show of syllogistic sympathy in their framework and functions.

Defensible to a degree as is this position, it is indefensible just so far as it overlooks the distinction between assumption and conclusion, the former being the latter without evidence, the latter being the former with evidence. Pure assumption is unevidenced conclusion;

pure conclusion is evidenced assumption.   Of the former, superstition is an example; of the latter, axioms, primary truths, established deductions, rational results, or the results of rational processes, are sufficient examples.

In the study of mind, a subject by no means transparent, we must be on our guard against the influence of old theories, and those prepossessions which have been handed down from generation to generation; but at the same time the conclusions of history must be accepted at their full value.   One of these, and lying at the foundation of this discussion, is the fact of mind itself, which, until philosophy raised its inquiring hand, was accepted without dispute or hesitancy. At the very threshold of the inquiry, the fact of the mind's existence as a separate and independent entity, and entitled to recognition as a *prima facie* force, must be established.   Hitherto accepted without controversy, science designates the traditional and popular belief in its independent existence as an assumption, requiring its demonstration just as it requires the demonstration of the existence of God. We are forbidden to assume the existence of mind; it must be proven.   Prof. Ferrier says: "Matter is already in the field as an acknowledged entity—this both parties admit.   Mind, considered as an independent entity, is not so unmistakably in the field.   Therefore, as entities are not to be multiplied without necessity, we are not entitled to postulate a new cause, so long as it is *possible* to account for the phenomena by a cause already in existence ; which possibility has never yet been disproved."   In another form, Alexander Bain attempts to demolish the doctrine of the two substances, mind and matter, asserting that the so-called differences between them can not be longer maintained.   Even Dugald Stewart raised the suspicious question, whether consciousness adequately testifies to the existence of mind, thus aiding the empirical psychologists in their work of destruction. He says: "We are conscious of sensation, thought, desire, volition, but we are not conscious of the existence of mind itself."   The sensationalism of Locke is here reproduced, or its effect on the philosophy of Stewart is manifest.   The untenableness of the position of Stewart is in allowing consciousness of thought, but denying consciousness of the thinking power, faculty, or sense.   A consciousness of an act of memory is a consciousness of memory; at least the separation between them can not be drawn.   To be conscious of one and not of the other is impossible.   To be conscious of the mind's activity and of its results implies a consciousness of mind ; not a consciousness of the nature of mind, but of the fact of mind.   Thought is proof of mind, as sight is proof of the eye.   The *fact* of mind is therefore a conclusion, and not an assumption.

What is the mind? To this question, so easily asked, a confusion of answers has been returned, each in itself an exploring line of thought, each a contribution to the solution of the philosopher's enigma. Prof. Bain observes that, "the drawing of too sharp a line between sense and intelligence has been the fruitful source of confusions in philosophy," but it might also be remarked that the attempted blending of sense and intelligence has been the fruitful source, not only of confusion, but also of error and despair, in philosophy. The sharper the line between the two, like the channel between England and France, the clearer the characteristics and possessions of each. To undertake to convert the figure two into one, Mr. Bain assumes, is the duty of philosophy; to others, it seems like a destruction both of philosophy and religion.

The task of analyzing the mind is not so easy as the task of dissecting the body. Mind is invisible, eluding physical grasping and physical analysis. Veiled and unseen, however, it shines as did Moses' face through the veil, illuminating the tabernacle of flesh and proclaiming somewhat of its hidden nature. Manifestation of mind is a proclamation of mind, and in sympathetic hands it is a key to its nature. Oxygen is invisible, but it will burn, the lungs will inhale it, and both its existence and character are demonstrated. In the activities and results of mental operations, there are the adumbrations of the character of mind.

Is it possible to contemplate the mind, apart from its physical associations and connections? Can it be insulated, studied as an independent entity? Philo, the Jew, remarked that the mind is like the eye, which, seeing other objects, can not see itself; and Prof. Draper concludes that it can not judge of itself. Prof. Bain discourages self-study by remarking that, "we are not allowed to perceive a mind acting apart from its material companion;" and again, he says, "in removing the body we remove our indicator of the mind, namely, the bodily manifestations, as if in testing for magnetism we should set aside the needle and other tokens of its presence." Here he broaches the doctrine of the identity of mental manifestations and physical states, an instance of the *petitio principii* not infrequent in his writings. His illustration is not exactly pertinent. Magnetism may be contemplated without the needle, and color may be studied independently of objects; that is to say, even physical properties may be insulated from physical objects and studied apart. If so, much more may the mind be made an exclusive subject of investigation. As the Nilometer marks the rise and fall of the Nile, so the body, to a degree, may denote the activities of the intellect; beyond a certain stage of interaction, the mind disengages itself from bodily control or interference, is set free like oxygen from water, or chlorine from salt. and stands out an insulated fact, a spiritual entity. Plato insisted that the eye, by means of a mirror, can see itself, and taught that the soul, as if abstracted from the body, can shut itself up within its own limits and think only of itself.

The habit of studying the mind in its relations with the body, and determining its limitations by the law of interaction, has led the psychologists into the error of believing that the mind, separate from the body, can not be rationally expounded, and that a knowledge of it as an independent substance is impossible. If the body can be studied as an independent instrument, and physiology be interpreted as the science of the instrument, the mind can be studied as an independent agency, and psychology be interpreted as the science of such agency. The blending of the two, or the creation of a physiological psychology, is the attempt of such thinkers as Ferrier, Bain, Spencer, and others; but it is irrational, confusing things that are essentially independent. The connection of body and mind is an indisputable fact, but the identity of the connected parts remains to be established; it must not be assumed. Bain, speaking of the connection, pronounces it "an unaccountable, because an ultimate, fact," but it is unaccountable, as it seems to us, because of the dissimilarity of the two substances, and hence the expression of the union in language is a "puzzle." The union of oxygen and hydrogen in water is expressible, because they are similar substances; the union of mind and matter is not expressible, because they are not similar substances. The great difference forever forbids expression, and proves independence.

Recognizing the mind as an independent substance, it is our purpose now carefully to consider the different interpretations put upon it by the speculating philosophy of modern times, since it is the ruling philosophy of to-day. At least *eight interpretations*, each represented by a distinguished name, must be considered, if we do justice to the scientific and philosophic attempts at the solution of mind. Let Locke, Leibnitz, Hegel, Reid, Hobbes, Mill, Spencer, and Bain represent the manifold interpretations, to which others might, indeed, be added, but without additional gain. In a general sense, these interpretations may be characterized as *sensational, idealistic,* and *materialistic,* showing the fluctuations of philosophic thought and the instability of its conclusions.

To Locke's interpretation we so frequently allude that it is unnecessary to reproduce it in this connection in detail. It is sufficient to remind the reader that, having projected the theory of sensation as the source of knowledge, Locke deprived the mind of all nascent ideas, or intuitional knowledge, leaving it a perfect blank, a capacious but unfilled reservoir, into which truths might be poured. His theory of knowledge defined his interpretation of mind. Later sensationalists have not agreed with Locke as to the necessity of a complete expurgation of original ideas from the mind, in order to sustain empirical psychology, since sensation may be as necessary, to a certain extent, to a mind stored with ideas as to one empty. In the one case, it opens the well-stored mind; in the other, it fills it. Sensationalism does not, therefore, require a vacant mind.

The inner deficiencies of Locke's interpretation are all but apparent. It is destructive of the intuitional sense or the intellectual contents of the consciousness. Locke attempts an explanation of those constitutional ideas and primary truths usually attributed to man by referring their origin to the teachings of the nursery, the instructions of parents, and social education in general. An investigator tracing inborn ideas to servants and grandmothers! This theory assumes that servants and grandmothers teach constitutional ideas, when, if any thing is certain, it is that such ideas do not result from teaching, but precede it, and that children are taught nearly every thing else but constitutional ideas. Intuitional ideas spring up in us like fountains in Athens; they can not be explained from the nursery. Locke compels the mind to begin its housekeeping without any furniture, or begs it seek the aid of hired servants. In itself it is destitute, powerless, helpless.

The interpretation does not provide for intellectual expansion. Such a mind as Locke describes is receptive, not creative. An infinitely receptive mind is not necessarily a growing, expansive mind; its materials multiply, but itself does not enlarge; its capacity may be filled, but the mind itself remains unchanged.

Moreover, Locke's interpretation is contradicted by consciousness; that is, by the mind itself. No man is conscious of being born with a blank mind any more than with blind eyes. Blankness is idiocy, as the closed eye is blindness. In the earliest stages of conscious existence the mind exerts a self-determining power, which grows with the life of the individual, and establishes itself as an inherent and original function, underived from sensational experience, and often commanding and generating experience.

The ethical tendency of the interpretation is toward materialism, which is its most unfortunate aspect. The doctrines of immortality, human responsibility, regeneration, and the highest religious truths were involved in the determinations of Locke, who, discovering the natural significance of his interpretation, attempted to modify it, but in vain.

The interpretation of Leibnitz is the theory of an idealistic philosopher, and an advance over that of the empiricist. In the general he held that the mind is a mirror of the universe, reflecting all things, and containing the types, forms, and ideas of universal existence. Locke held that the mind receives the images or impressions of things, is an image-bearer, a reflector; Leibnitz assumed that the mind threw back, like a mirror, universal truths as its original contents, and also germinated ideas and the forms of truth. The difference between the two philosophies is radical. Locke's image-bearer was originally empty; Leibnitz's mirror is full. Locke's reflector reflected what was cast upon it; Leibnitz's reflected its own depths. One is an external mirror; the other internal.

Contrary to Locke's, the idealistic interpretation recognizes the intuitional character of mind, assigning to it universal ideas, and proclaiming the independence of mind from sensation and experience. This extreme view is objectionable, but as a reaction from the experience philosophy, it has some justification.

The interpretation is also a reaction from the pantheistic doctrine of Spinoza, who reduced all things, including mind, to one substance, which compromised immortality and the divine existence. Leibnitz, therefore, introduced the doctrine of the monads into his system of thought, designating each monad as a world in itself, or a soul, thus going as far in one direction as Spinoza had in the other. Spinoza shouts one universe, one substance; Leibnitz shouts myriads of worlds, myriads of substances. Spinoza unified all things in a logical pantheism; Leibnitz separated them in the difference of substance, and redeemed the divine existence. Spinozism was intensely centripetal; Leibnitzism intensely centrifugal. In so far as it was an attempt to turn back the tide of pantheism, idealism must be approved; but the monadic doctrine is as unwarrantable as pantheism itself, for it tends to undermine the great fact of unity observable in the universe, and which unmistakably points to one Father, the Creator of all things.

The ethical character of monadism is in harmony with orthodox teachings respecting immortality and responsibility; it acknowledges the individuality of mind, and insists upon individual righteousness as the condition of happiness.

The theory of Leibnitz is unsatisfactory, in that it does not define the mind, or even clearly denote its functions. The idea that the mind is a mirror in any sense or of any thing is inconsistent with its nature. It is not a reflector—that is, throwing back what it receives or what it contains—but a reflector in the sense of *thinking*, which implies an active, creative process; it is not a mirror, but a meditator; not a thrower back of ideas, but an originator of ideas; not a panorama of existing thoughts, but a *creator of thought*. Proclus, a Neoplatonist, asserted that a knowledge of the mind is a knowledge of the whole universe; that is, the knowledge of the universe is in some way reflected upon human consciousness through the mind. This extreme Leibnitz seems to have absorbed, for it is his interpretation in a statelier form. The mind is something more than a passive substance, something more than a recipient of thought; it is not a sponge.

The philosophy of Hegel introduces a new idealistic interpretation of mind. Quenching the empirical spirit at its birth, he rose to the contemplation of the highest truth, and attempted to restore it to its rightful authority and influence. Transcendental in his conceptions, bordering even on mysticism, it is not always easy to extract his meaning from the encumbered language he employs to represent his ideas. The light does not shine through him as it does through a diamond. He is penetrative and suggestive, however, to those who plunge into his obscurities.

In discoursing upon the philosophy of mind he divides it into three classes: 1. The *subjective* mind; 2. The *objective* mind; 3. The *absolute* mind,—a classification intended to include all departments of the mind's activities and relations. The "subjective" mind is the internal mind, the rational, thinking power, the intelligent ego, that which contitutes personality, identity. This mind Hegel regards as enslaved, subject to sloth and passion, and that it must experience emancipation before it can be what it was intended to be. In union with nature the mind is individual; when free from nature it is consciousness or ego. In its individual state mind is a theoretical fact, probably what Aristotle calls "potential;" it is intelligence but undeveloped; in the ego state it is practical, developed, represented by the will—it has become "actual," as Aristotle would say. When it has passed from the individual state—a state of nature—to consciousness or will-power—a state of supremacy—it has realized emancipation.

Passing to the "objective" mind, it has respect to the person, but not to personality; that is, it regards the rights, the ethics, the conduct, of the person. The subjective mind relates to personality, thought, spirituality; the objective mind to personal rights, conduct, government, social conditions. The subjective mind is represented by the philosopher, theologian, metaphysician, poet, thinker; the objective mind by the statesman, ruler, legislator.

The "absolute" mind, abandoning an objective form, becomes ideally subjective, expressing itself in art, religion, and philosophy. The highest mind is not subjective, that is, personal, or objective, that is, ethical and governmental, but absolute, that is, æsthetic, philosophical, religious. Religion is the expression of the "absolute" as government is the expression of the "objective," and consciousness the expression of the "subjective" mind.

This three-fold conception of mind, as framed by Hegel, is not without its merits. In the acknowledgment of the enslavement of the subjective mind or will-power, he is in harmony with the writers of the Scriptures, who affirm the debasement of the mental constitution. Upon the objective mind he imposes the duty of erecting States, devising ethical and governmental systems, and of providing for the protection of property, the peace and order of society, and the sanctity and perpetuity of the family institution. More than all, he emphasized the relation of religion to the individual, styling the religious mind as the highest type of conscious intelligence, and vindicated its universal necessity.

Hegel's interpretation, suggestive as we have allowed, is not altogether satisfactory, for it fails at a vital point. He classifies mind with reference to its activities, or manifestations in consciousness, society, and religion ; but these are the results of mind, indicative of the nature of mind, we admit, but an *a posteriori* method of getting at the mind itself. Indeed, Hegel stops with the functions of mind, and leaves the problem of mind unsolved. To say that a knife will cut is not a definition of knife. The only approach to a definition that Hegel makes is that mind involves intelligence and will ; but it is unsafe to admit the word intelligence into the definition. Mind and intelligence are not identical ; mind is power, intelligence is result. No less vulnerable is the statement that the mind is the will in its practical form, since that is defining the whole by a part. The will is a department of mind, and to identify it with the mind is like identifying the War Department with the United States Government.

The classification of Hegel, comprehensive as it appears, is incomplete. Imagination and memory, quite as much as the will, are powers of the mind ; but they, as well as the intuitions, are omitted, or merged into the general contents of consciousness.

The three minds of Hegel, or the three phases of mind, are alike enslaved, requiring emancipation; but Hegel limits enslavement to the subjective mind. In its governmental products, in its ethical systems, in its domestic institutions and regulations, the objective mind betrays imperfection and unfitness for great achievements. Despotisms, oligarchies, monarchies, are the creations of the objective mind, proving its corruption, cruelty, and instability. In the spirit of caste, the artificial distinctions of society, and race-prejudices, we see again the incapacity of the objective mind for its tasks. In the enslavement of races, in the feudal system, in intolerance, persecution, and barbarism, we discover the objective mind in positive debasement. Emancipation is its necessity.

The absolute mind drags a chain. Look at the religions of the world; heathenish, abominable all, save the One, high over all. Hegel admits that the Oriental religions but crudely represent the absolute mind; the Judaic religion is an improvement; Christianity is its best exponent. Christianity, however, is not a product of the human mind; it is the religion of Revelation; pagan religions are man-made, the products of the absolute mind of man. It needs, therefore, purification, yea, emancipation from superstition, idolatry, mysticism, and ignorance. The three minds are in chains, the enslavement of one is the enslavement of all. Necessity is upon us, therefore, to pass on in our search for a true theory or conception of mind.

The interpretation of Reid we next submit for examination. Reid prides himself on taking a common-sense view of things, even of mysteries, which if they can not be solved he justifies as mysteries; but we must beware a little of the "common-sense" philosophy of this Scotch thinker, for this term is sometimes used as a cover for inexcusable ignorance, an obstacle to further investigation. The common, that is, the ordinary, sense of mankind might brand with folly the attempt to ferret out the hidden facts, to solve the insoluble secrets of the universe; and unfortunately Reid sometimes shackles and paralyzes investigation by the employment of this prejudice. The dictum of modern philosophy that God, mind, and matter are unknowable, Reid accepts so far as it relates to mind, agreeing with Hume that the substantive nature of mind is beyond knowledge and insists that common sense requires the acceptance of this conclusion. In like manner he maintains that perception and reflection, as states, are knowable and analyzable, but perceived objects and the perceiving mind are unknowable; in other words, he draws the limitations of knowledge around perception and reflection.

Affirming that the mind is unknowable, Reid nevertheless assures us that it is a perceiving and reflecting somewhat; that it observes, discriminates, discovers, for this is the idea of perception; that it combines, judges, compares, analyzes, for this is the total of reflection. Whatever may be said of this finally, Reid has rendered service to philosophy in the assignment of these two functions—*perceiving and reflecting*, to mind; for, while they are the terms of Locke, he meant more than Locke, because he was more than an empiricist. The original mind, according to Reid, was not empty; and if we comprehend not its nature, we apprehend its faculties or functions. The theory, however, abounds in antinomies, and is as unsatisfactory as Hegel's, and that of Leibnitz. Insisting that the mind is unknowable, he declares investigation of its nature useless, and so paralyzes intelligent endeavor, relieves mental aspiration of purpose, and directs meditation merely to the results of mental activity, without solving activity itself. Without asserting that the mind may know itself, we are strong in the conviction that Reid has not declared all that is possible to be known of mind. If it can not be fully known, we may know more of it than that it has certain functions. Moreover, he is contradictory in the statement that mind is unknowable, for he makes mind somewhat known to us through its functions. One knows in part what paper is when told that it is made of rags; one knows something of mind when told that it perceives and reflects. Like Hamilton and Spencer, Reid is guilty of philosophic inconsistency. Hamilton declared the Absolute unknowable, but spoke of it as the Infinite. If the mind is unknowable, one can not know any thing of it; one can not be certain that there is such a thing as mind; but Reid affirms its existence, and attributes to it two high prerogatives, proving knowledge of it. Evidently then, he was looking in the right direction, but stopped when he ought to have proceeded. He limited his observation when the field of vision began to extend. This is the common fault of philosophic investigation, especially of modern inquiry, as we shall often see.

Of the historic interpretations of mind, the *materialistic* is perhaps the most imposing, as it is the most daring and destructive. Hobbes, who was neither a sensationalist, like Locke, nor an idealist in any sense, represents elementary materialism in the department of metaphysics. Having studied Francis Bacon and Descartes, he departed sufficiently from both to justify his claim as an original thinker, and original thought, even though erroneous, is apt to command attention. Hobbes had a mathematical mind, which prepared him to deal with the sophistries of speculation, and enabled him to construct a philosophy of his own. Prof. Morris contends that the poetical mind sustains a vital relation to the philosophical, is propædeutic in its influence, since he finds in Shakespeare traces of philosophical genius. Plato extolled geometry as the preparatory gateway to philosophical study; and Galen, the ancient physician, declared that geometry saved him from Pyrrhonism. Roger Bacon pronounced mathematics the "alphabet of philosophy." In Plato we discover the poetical as well as the mathematical; in Shakespeare the poetical only; in Galen and Bacon the mathematical; so that it would appear that mathematical studies, rather than poetical, prepare the mind for the grasping of those sturdy and abstruse problems which metaphysics ever thrusts before us.

Hobbes was not poetical; he was mathematical; this is the key to his character, and the opening vein to his philosophy. As he advanced in mathematical knowledge, he was led to believe that reasoning is a mathematical calculation, an example in arithmetic. With this explanation, he assumed that man is "a calculating, computing, ratiocinative machine," the mind is an arithmetic in itself. This is Hobbes's first interpretation of mind, as dangerous as it is plausible.

What his second view is may be arrived at in a similar manner. The physical sciences exerted a peculiar fascination over him; he studied every thing from their stand-point, mind no less than matter; and in the progress of his studies he reached the conclusion that physical phenomena are merely *modes of motion;* but he did not stop with this announcement. Like a philosopher who wishes to extend law to the widest bounds, he soon began to assert that mental phenomena were likewise modes of motion ; that is, that life is the "mechanical play of sensation and passion." Here are two views of mind, the second supplemental of the first. The first is, that the mind acts, thinks, reasons, *mathematically;* the second is, that the mind acts, thinks, reasons, *mechanically ;* and, combining them, the whole view is that the mathematical mind is mechanical in its operations.

That Hobbes was influenced by Pythagoras can not be doubted, for the ancient mathematical philosopher held that "the world is a living arithmetic in its development, a realized geometry in its repose;" and all Pythagoreans, including Plato himself, conceived that the universe was built according to mathematical principles, represented by the generic word *number.* A mathematical conception of the universe was not, therefore, original with Hobbes, notwithstanding his claim to originality. The application of the mathematical, or rather, the mechanical, principle to mind, was a daring attempt, and introduced into philosophic speculation the materialistic tendency. Schwegler tells us that Hegel aimed to prove that the world is externally what the mind is internally, while Spencer asserts that the mind is internally what the world is externally. Either view is a participation in the mechanical principle of Hobbes, derived in part from the Pythagorean conception of the universe.

Without controverting the mechanical principle, does it throw light upon the nature of mind? Hobbes regards the mind as a *reasoning power; it calculates, computes; its chief office is to reason.* No one will dispute the verity of this discovery, or attempt a reduction of its value. Incidentally, too, Hobbes demonstrates not only the value of mathematical studies, but their relation to the development of the mind—a hint to educators that ought not to be over-looked.

Lifting the veil a little, however, the interpretation is seen to be radically defective and ethically dangerous. It involves a too precise and limited view of man. He is more than a *reasoner*. To think is the noblest characteristic of man ; to think correctly the badge of his greatness ; yet he is more than a rational, ratiocinative, calculating animal—he is a loving, sympathetic, charitable, emotional being, having a moral as well as an intellectual nature. To discard the spiritual element and exalt the intellectual at the expense of every thing else, is to degrade man in the very attempt to ennoble him. Man is complete only in the relative development of the spiritual, intellectual, and physical qualities and functions of his being. Hobbes overlooks the difference between spiritual and. intellectual, reducing the activity of man to a mechanical rationalism. Good grounds also exist for doubting that mental phenomena are modes of motion. Whether physical phenomena are modes of motion we shall not now discuss; but when Hobbes undertakes to explain the opera-tions of mind by analogous operations in the physical world, we are at liberty to question the attempt, and ask for the proof of the con-clusions. Mental action, that is, the ferment of mind in the process of thought, may partake of the character of motion ; but if so, it is motion, *sui generis*, without counterpart or even resemblance in nature. Poetically speaking, the rush of thought may be likened to the flow of ocean waves; philosophically speaking, it would be incorrect to apply the laws of one to the other. Fancied resemblance must not be resorted to in vindication of philosophic interpretation.

Hobbes's theory is, in its essence, merely a statement of the method of the mind's activity. It is a *mode* of motion. False or true, it gives the method, not the nature, of mind.

Ethically, the interpretation does violence to the doctrine of moral responsibility ; and, religiously, it is prejudicial to the doctrine of im-mortality. A mechanically acting mind, governed by unchangeable mathematical principles, is relieved of that responsibility which a mind free from a fixed government must assume ; and it is equally clear that, mechanically acting, the mind may be mechanical, that is, material in its nature ; hence, it can not be immortal. In its last analysis Hobbes's interpretation is materialistic, and suggestive of all those dreary conclusions which more recent philosophers, like Häckel, Mill, Spencer, and Bain, have affirmed.

John Stuart Mill, inheriting the materialistic prejudice, threw out upon the world an interpretation of mind which, like an attractive waif, has been picked up, housed, and adopted as the child of the latest schools. Slightly, or at least apparently, less materialistic than that of Hobbes, because edged with idealistic phrases, the interpretation is as barren of positive results as Sahara of trees. His definitions of mind, scattered throughout his works, are not at all engaging or assuring, nor explicit, definite, broad, coherent. At one time he writes that "mind is the mysterious something which feels and thinks," recognizing its reflective and emotional character; at another time he speaks of it as "a permanent possibility of feeling," indicating, perhaps, that it consists in permanent consciousness; then again he refers to it as a "series of feelings," drifting away from the position that it is that "mysterious something which feels and thinks;" lastly, he refers to it as "an inexplicable tie."

What is the value of these definitions? In the definition that mind is something that *thinks*, there is a great philosophical truth; in the definition that it is something that *feels*, there is an equally important psychological truth. The mind is the thinking and emotional center of man, according to these definitions.

Looking at the other side of this interpretation, and following Mill so far as he ventures to go, we find we have allowed too much to his definitions, and given them an overstrained and unintended meaning. Mind is a "mysterious something," an "inexplicable tie." Of its nature, he holds that we know nothing. That mind thinks, he admits, but thinking or thought does not indicate the nature of the thing that thinks. Thought is a superficial manifestation of mind, utterly non-reflective of its character. The definition that mind consists in a "series of feelings" is, according to his own confession, narrow and inconclusive, for memory, imagination, hope, can not be explained as a series of feelings. Thought itself is more than a feeling. Hobbes defined it a mode of motion; Mill, a feeling. Between thought and feeling there is a chasm that Mill's definitions do not bridge; the two may be coupled—they will not coalesce into unity. Thus Mill's interpretation consists in elegant words, fraudulent phrases, superficial explanations, and despairing admissions. It is in the line of fatalism.

The interpretation of Spencer is the theory of evolution, a modern theory in the form of its statement, yet a conglomeration distinguished rather for many-phased conceptions than singleness of view. Evolution is the talismanic word of the nineteenth century, explaining all things, God excepted, whose existence it in no sense recognizes. In the hands of a scholar, such as Herbert Spencer is conceded to be, the word has been transposed into doctrine, or brought forward as a revelation of the secret processes of mind and matter, supplanting idealism in philosophy and theology in religion. If any one, however, approach evolution with the expectation that he will know any thing more about mind when he has exhausted Spencer than before, he will meet with disappointment, for, while Spencer is voluminous, he is not conclusive; while he is always dogmatic, he is not always clear; while he assumes to be an oracle, he is of doubtful interpretation.

The initial thought of the evolutionists is that mind did not make its appearance in the early stages of the unfolding world, but toward its close; that it did not manifest itself at all in the beginning, but dawned at the end of the task of upbuilding; that it is, therefore, a development, and not an original force or guiding power; in other words, mind has been evolved just as the race has been evolved, its beginnings poor, feeble, unpromising, and rising into greatness with its opportunities. Evolved mind, not original or created mind; a mind that has grown from a germ; a mind that was almost nothing at first, and became something afterward, plodding through the stages of impulse, instinct, desire, aspiration, perception, and conception, toward intellectual self-assertion; this is the theory of evolution respecting mind. Plato believed that mind was first, not last, and that the earliest races were no less endowed with memory, imagination, volition, cognition, and all the mental faculties, than the Greeks. It is singular, if Spencer's theory be true, that he can not point to a race deficient in memory, imagination, or will power, and that history furnishes the account of no such a race, or in whom the development of mind from one faculty to another can be detected. The historic man shows no deficiency of mind; the prehistoric man exhibits the mental traces quite as explicitly as the modern man. *Mind shows no evolution of faculties.* Nevertheless, the evolutionist, in violation of historic facts and the antecedents of the race, assumes that mind is the product of an evolutionary process, still manifest in history.

The second step follows the first and is consistent with it. Dr. David Hartley, after many physiological experiments, began to suspect that mental action is due to vibrations in the white medullary substance of the brain, a theory as insufficient as that which would explain electricity by the trembling wire. Conceding that mental activity must inspire corresponding activity in the brain, it no more explains mental action than muscular movement explains volition. Such a theory is a complete reversal of the accepted order of facts in mental history. Until Hartley, it was believed that thought causes cerebral vibration; he announced that cerebral vibration produces thought.

Spencer, influenced by the physiological determinations of Hartley, turned them to the support of the evolutionary hypothesis of mind, and with the aid of associationalists, Bain in particular, the popular conception has been well-nigh wrecked. The step is a short one from Hartley's physiology to Spencer's account of the origin of mind, namely, in the physical organization of man. De la Mettrie expresses the theory thus: "We are what we are by our organization in the first instance, and by instruction in the second." Hartley's theory that the brain produces thought, Spencer transformed into the larger theory that physical activity results in mind. The theories differ only in their extent. In keeping with the theory of the origin of mind, Spencer teaches that it is subject to an evolutionary process of development resulting from a "redistribution of matter and motion," agreeing exactly with Mr. Bain, who, as a psychologist, completes what Spencer begins as an evolutionist. With Spencer, nerve action is the basis of mental action, the Hartley theory in a modified form. Hume also speaks of thought as a *little* agitation of the brain, showing the influence of the mechanical philosophy.

Reducing the mind to a physical product, and explaining its operations by nervous excitements, Spencer declares the nature of mind unknowable, leaving the student of the subject just where he was in the beginning. There is a science of mind, says Spencer, but not a philosophy of mind. Mind is "static, not dynamic."

Not intending now to analyze the evolutionary theory, it is important to remember that the evolutionist finds it exceedingly difficult to account for the self-acting, *self-determining* power of mind, which distinguishes it from the body. Practically, the body is the instrument of the mind; evolution must pronounce the mind the instrument of the body, but it hesitates to do so. The body may be compared to a ship—the mind is the pilot. Sometimes it happens that a ship in a storm is uncontrollable even by a skillful pilot, but the pilot ordinarily is in control. Under certain contingencies, the body may usurp control of the mind, as when it is diseased, but that is not the natural relation. Except the involuntary processes of nature, such as breathing, assimilation, circulation of the blood, pulsations of the heart, the mind will determine the movements of the body; but this is not the chief function of mind. It *determines for itself* as well as for the body; it regulates its own thinking and decides on moral conduct—is master of itself. This proves independence of the body, or, at the least, superiority to it.

Contrary, also, to Spencer, it may finally be demonstrated that the body does not produce the mind, but the mind the body. Organization is the basis of mind, according to the evolutionist; mind is the root of organization, according to a well-founded supposition. The weakness of evolution in its wholeness is that it produces the higher from the lower, when in point of fact the *higher produces the lower.*

Chronologically, the lower often seems to precede the higher; but actually, the higher is present and working, making its appearance later, because it is more elaborate and permanent. The lower, superficial, temporary, accidental, is first visible; the higher, refined, forceful, is invisible until a later stage of the development of the lower, but it has been in movement all the time. The body, gross, material, a finally vanishing substance, is visible; the mind, a positive and perpetual force, is invisible. It is the invisible that produces the visible; the laws of the invisible become the laws of the visible; but Spencer teaches that the laws of the visible control the invisible, or body both organizes and controls mind. Evolution reverses the historic and organic order of the two substances.

Mr. Bain is the representative of the school of associationalists who, evolutionists as they are, conduct their interpretation of mind to the rankest materialism. In their conclusions they go no farther than Mr. Spencer, who himself was an associationalist, but they are more specific in details. From the connection between body and mind they conclude that they are identical; but the connection establishes relation only, interaction only, not identity. Because the body affects the mind, as in disease, or grief or age, there is no warrant for concluding that the mind is material; such effects prove relation and interaction, which no theologian will deny. Mr. Bain presses the claim of identity by describing a mental fact as a double-faced somewhat, being mental on one side and physical on the other, obtaining the distinction from Aristotle. A thought has both a subjective and objective face, but, as it is one thing, so the two faces are a double view of the same thing. Even this strained statement proves nothing more than relation and interaction, for the two faces involve difference, and difference precludes identity. In the fact that thought exhausts nervous substance, Bain discovers the origin of thought in nerve-action, but it only proves dependence, not origin; relation, not identity. "No phosphorus, no thinking," Moleschott declared. This is the same materialism. Intellectual action is a nervous shock, according to Bain; but this proves that the reason employs the nerves in thinking, just as the volition employs muscles in lifting a weight. Why not style Bain's theory the *shock philosophy?* It shocks both reason and faith. Dr. Hammond speaks of the mind as "a force developed by nervous action." It may be true that for every mental action there is a nervous response, but it by no means establishes the identity of the action and the response. When he asserts that mental and physical states correspond; that the mental series and the physical series are exactly alike; that physical feeling reflects the mental; we must ask for the evidence. The most that

Mr. Bain has established is that mind and body are related and interact, and that possibly the law of mental activity controls the physical life. Earnestly does he teach that the law of the physical life may be the law of the mental life; this is materialism; he will be surprised to learn that possibly he has demonstrated the reverse, if he has demonstrated any thing. The law of lower is not the law of the higher, but the law of the higher is molding, and will explain the activities of the lower. This is spiritual government extended to the physical universe. The Associationalists make much of the laws of association by which they affirm the mind is governed in its processes of thought; but it should be remembered that all such laws explain the method of the mind's action, not mind itself. To describe the rotation of the planets according to law, does not explain the nature of the planetary substance; and a knowledge of association, as a law of the mind's processes, is not equivalent to a knowledge of the mind itself. By the law of association Bain explains the method of the memory, not the memory. Mill said he could not understand the memory; Bain does not explain it. To show how the mind thinks is one thing; to show what the mind is, is quite another. Bain has been credited in the *International Review* with tracing mental action to its source, but if he has done any thing he has announced the method of mental action only; yet not the only method, for associational thought is the result of the law of association. Outside of associational thought is *original, intuitional thought*; and beyond is *creative thought*, independent of association and intuition. The law of association results in thought in harmony with itself; intuitional thought must result from another law; creative thought from another still. Associationalism, the last outburst of philosophical definition, tested by thought itself, is deficient as a law of mental activity, and reveals nothing of the nature of mind. Bain himself, while insisting that our conscious states may be analyzed by physical law, confesses of pure mind he knows nothing.

Neither sensationalism, idealism, nor materialism, besides specifying some of the contents and processes of mind, afford a distinct knowledge of its nature, compelling us to seek elsewhere if we ascertain what is mind.

Beginning where associationalism leaves off, we wish to express belief in the great fact that the mind, like the body, like the universe, is under law, and that the key to its nature is in the supreme law of its being, or the laws of its activity. Matter is not alone under law, nor is it under the influence of lower law; it is under the mind's law, so modified as to act without friction and in harmony with its nature.

Contrary to scientists in general, Mr. Huxley agrees with Descartes that "we know more of mind than we do of body," to which we add that a knowledge of the body is possible only as we know the mind. Scientists prate of physiological psychology; a true philosophy points to psychological physiology. The Duke of Argyll, repudiating phrenology, declares its error to be "that physiology can ever be the basis of psychology;" related as the two are, "it is not true that psychology is subordinate to physiology." Psychology may explain physiology; physiology can never explain psychology. *The explanation of matter lies in the explanation of mind;* but materialists have essayed to explain mind by a study of matter. Even Spencer has admitted that there is no "perceptible or conceivable community of nature" between the two sciences, and yet persists in identifying the laws that govern in the processes of mind and matter. Any resemblance between the processes, or any parallel that may be shown between mental and physical laws, must be interpreted as the evidence of the descent of the mental into the physical, and not of the ascent of the physical into the mental; and identity can be predicated only on the supposition of the former. It has been assumed on the basis of the latter; hence, the destruction wrought by materialism.

Many are the laws of the mind, all of which have not as yet been discovered; but the more conspicuous may be indicated, paralleled to some extent by laws observable in the realm of matter. In general terms, it may be conceded that the mind acts at times involuntarily, even unconsciously, as in dreams, absent-mindedness, and other states, just as the involuntary processes of digestion and the blood's circulation go on constantly but without conscious direction, prompting, or interference by the person; and then it acts voluntarily, directing commanding, perceiving and conceiving, just as walking and talking are under the voluntary control of the person. This parallelism of voluntary and involuntary activity between the body and the mind is suggestive of relation, and community of the lower with the higher. Mental activity is under specific government, expressing all its results in harmony with transparent or occult laws, the investigation of which may require patient study, but the rewards thereof will be sufficiently compensative and enduring.

In its historical aspects, the mind displays a tendency to development from incipient stages of thinking to robust reasoning habits, and from ignorance to the facts of knowledge. It is a growing substance; in its constitution is the prophecy of growth; so that among the conspicuous laws of mind must be placed the *law of growth*, paralleled by a similar law in the realm of matter. In what manner the mind realizes enlargement, both history and experience make known, that is, by growth from within to without, and from without to within; in other words, by sensations and reflections, or again, by appropriation of the facts of the outer world, and by independent self-action, or communion with itself. Its growth is exosmose and endosmose. But if the contents of the law of growth are not accurately stated, the fact of growth will not be disputed, and at this stage of the inquiry the fact is quite as important as the law. Growth is a condition of mind; this implies activity, the constituent fact of mind.

In its activity the law of association is very manifest, accounting in many cases for thought, conduct, and character; but the guilt of the associationalists is the claim that the entire history of mind may be reduced to the single principle of association, as if it had no independent power, and especially no intuitional sense. The law of association we accept as one of many, and not as the all in all of mental activity.

Almost as conspicuous, at least as dominant in tendency, as the preceding, is the law of congenital influence in the structure, if not in the methods, of the mind itself. The law of heredity certainly manifests itself in the bodily organism of man, which is proof that it obtains in mental character; but to what extent it obtains has not been fully determined. Robert Burns inherited the poetic instinct, as Charles Darwin inherited the scientific, inquiring mind. Mental tendencies are transmitted, as are physical tendencies. It is not our purpose to inquire as to the origin of the mind, but merely to indicate the reign of parental influence over it, yet so as not to interfere with its legitimate functions or self-evident possibilities. Neither the law of association nor congenitalism can rob the mind of its individuality or responsibility. The law of association is a method of activity; congenitalism is a hint of character.

In many of its processes, the mind is under the law of causation, or cause and effect; in fact, the order of thought is the order of antecedent and consequent. Pure logic is pure causation. If, as Aristotle says, the active reason is "something divine," it is because it is orderly in its processes, either *a priori* or *a posteriori* or some other order in its premises and conclusions. Admitting so much, we do not mean that the mind is under inexorable necessity to one method in its thinking, for this would reduce it to a machine; but we do mean that, in certain processes, it observes the necessary order of causation, without, however, compromising its freedom or independence. It is free to think or not to think on a given subject, but if it choose a particular subject, as, perhaps, the facts of astronomy and geology, it must have respect to a fixed order of thought, which in these cases we denominate the law of causation.

In the largest sense, the mind acts under the law of freedom in perfect harmony with the preceding laws, and, in fact, is reflexively their inspiration and sanctification. Without freedom, the laws of growth, association, congenitalism, and causation would be inoperative, or at least unproductive of a responsible development. Whatever else the mind is, it is *free;* not free from motives, but free to select one motive from a number and act accordingly, and free to reject all motives and not act at all. To a degree, it is under the law of motive in its choices and achievements, but even the motives it respect, it sometimes originates within itself, demonstrating its independence and self-acting character. The mind is free; not free from intuitions since they are a part of itself; hence, it is under intuitional law but neither motives, having an external source, nor intuitions, being internal, arrest the free action of the mind in its determinations. Motives persuade, intuitions command; the persuasion is not irresistible, the command is that of the mind itself. While philosophers have considered the law of freedom in activity as chief in the realm of mind, we submit that its greatest law has been overlooked, namely, the *law of power*, or the measure of the mind's activity. Freedom refers to the ease of the mind in activity; power, to the extent of its activity, and hence is a key to its nature. Identifying mental and physical action, as the associationalists are striving to do, it is being recognized that the brain acts only as it is acted upon, is purely passive, like the eye or ear, while the mind *self-acts*, and is therefore independent. A great difference, this, and the measure of mind and matter. One is passive, the other active; one is inertness, the other energy. The self-acting power of mind implies originating power, which can not be assigned to matter. It originates ideas; it weaves thought out of physical materials, or, like the spider, *out of its own substance; it creates.* In a lower sense, it subordinates all things to itself; it is making nature tributary to it; it changes nature's forms, subordinates nature's laws to its own purposes, and exercises dominion in the realm of matter. This is its power: self-acting, originating, and subordinating all things to itself. This makes it supreme, and defines it by differentia and essentia from every thing else.

What, therefore, is mind? It is something to say that it is an immaterial substance, differing from phenomenal substance, not so much in its laws as in its qualities: but this difference has either paralyzed the materialist or led him to identify the substances. Identity of laws does not imply identity of qualities; but identity of substances requires identity of qualities. The difference between the substances is the difference of qualities; of matter, divisibility, extension, density, color, may be predicated; of mind, volition, cognition, perception, desire, may be affirmed. The parallelism or identity of the laws governing them must not blind one to the ineradicable difference in substantive qualifications.

Immateriality is not a definite term. It takes one away from matter, but it does not clearly translate itself into an intelligible form or utterance. What is immateriality? Kant really demonstrated the existence of a dynamic self-consciousness, or the consciousness of independent, self-acting, self-regulating spirit-power. This, as a definition of immaterial substance, is so nearly complete that it needs not more than brief expansion to accept it. Mind is not to be defined from its qualities, for, while they illustrate its nature, another key must be used in analyzing the mind itself. By qualities we mean faculties, but, strictly speaking, there are no faculties. Locke's decision against faculties is impregnable. The mind is a unit, a single substance, acting in various ways, but always in complete harmony with itself. Dugald Stewart's enumeration of ten faculties is an exhibition of a very faulty analysis of mental operations, because such an exaltation of faculties is at the expense of unity, and it is a question if certain so-called faculties in his list are functions of the mind at all. Not by faculties alone may the mind be interpreted. It is immateriality; it is consciousness; but what kind of consciousness, the faculties do not intimate. The key to the nature of mind is its laws, not its qualities.

By virtue of the law of mind, the law of activity, of power, of freedom, it is evident that mind is *conscious activity*, or the activity of consciousness; or, to reduce the definition to a single word, *mind is power*, it is force. The measurement of mind involves the measurement of its power, but as the power refuses to submit to measure, or even regulation, so the mind is beyond measure and stands above well-defined limitation. The word power, however, is slightly ambiguous, since it may be separated from personality; and power may be latent or inactive; but mind is not an inactive power, or blind, irrational force. To free the definition from ambiguity, it is better to say that mind is conscious activity, or the activity of consciousness. Spinoza attributed to the mind three potencies, knowledge, action, reason, to which we raise no objection, since it is clear that the activity of consciousness is according to its intuitions, and its reason; that is, consciousness is governed by its own laws. Without such laws there is no consciousness, and without consciousness no activity.

If the definition of mind as above given is held to be objection-

14

able, the objection must lie against the form in which the definition is expressed, rather than against its essence, for that mind is activity is certainly a fact. Whether we say it is the activity of consciousness, or the activity of spirit, is of no consequence; spirit is life, activity, power—and consciousness is the same thing. Consciousness and spirit are identical; activity is the normal state, the essential condition of spirit; hence, the definition must retain the idea of activity; indeed, it is sufficient if it contain nothing else. James Mill says that consciousness is nothing but feeling; but, if this is true, it is the feeling of power, of activity. To feel implies the consciousness of something. Feeling is impossible without a consciousness of something created for it or by it. The mind feels its power, is itself the feeling of activity. Whatever the definition of consciousness, it resolves itself into a recognition of existence and activity; self-consciousness is the recognition of self-activity. This is mind.

Bain's classification of the intellect into *discrimination*, or consciousness of difference, *similarity*, or consciousness of agreement, and *retentiveness*, or consciousness of acquisition, is in harmony with our conception. To discriminate is to act; to agree is to act; to acquire is to act. Discrimination, agreement, acquisition, the three functions of intellect, are the processes of consciousness in activity. This is mind.

---

# CHAPTER IX.

## THE AREA OF HUMAN KNOWLEDGE.

ANCIENT Pyrrhonism has been reproduced in the agnosticism of modern times, with the difference that the recent error is worse than the first. Pyrrhonism doubted and waited; agnosticism denies every thing and concedes nothing. The Pyrrhonist walked in the twilight, uncertain that he saw any thing distinctly; the agnostic walks "late at night in Ægina," certain that he sees nothing. The one bruited the doctrine of uncertainty; the other proclaims the dogma of ignorance.

To know or not to know is as important as Hamlet's aphorism, "to be or not to be." Does man know any thing? What is it that he knows? How does he know what he knows? What are the boundaries of the intellect, and how are they indicated? Is the intellect a circumscribed power? What is the value of knowledge? These and cognate questions the inquirer is bound to consider, since philosophy itself, no less than religion, is dependent on the validity of their solution. The assumption that man knows nothing and can know nothing; that his estate is one of pitiable and unending darkness; that so-called light is a delusion, and faith in it a superstition; that the expectation of progress is a courageous but profitless vanity; that supposed consciousness of truth is only a form of self-flattery; involves so many incongruities and absurdities, and so strikes at the root of things, that in righteous self-defense the mind must declare its prerogatives, and assert its possibilities in the realm of what is called the knowable.

At this stage of the discussion we are prepared to make several important admissions, all the more necessary in order to simplify the treatment of the subject, and avoid unnecessary conflict with the agnostic. It is admitted that man does not and possibly can not know all things; that as infinity transcends the finite, the finite may find it impossible completely to know the infinite, or things that are exclusively and unrelatedly infinite. It is admitted that, owing to defective methods of human inquiry, many facts, truths, laws, and relations are unknown that are not necessarily and absolutely unknowable, and which will probably be discovered as improved methods of inquiry are adopted. It is admitted that man's preferences for truth are so vitiated by natural tastes for lower things, and so inactive in assertion that he can rise but slowly from darkness into light, but the ascent is gloriously possible, as Plato's men emerged at last from their caves. It is admitted that special truth labeled "supernatural" often meets with obstructive disfavor among those who profess to be in search of all truth, and that this cherished prejudice forbids the immediate ascertainment of the highest truth, especially by those seeking it. It is admitted that the exact value of truth has not been philosophically determined further than that a knowledge of it would prove a convenience, but is not esteemed a necessity. It is admitted that such are the physical necessities of men and the time required by their occupations in supplying them, that few can devote themselves sufficiently to the investigation of the highest problems of truth; hence, the race's rapid advance in knowledge is hardly to be expected.

These admissions, and many others of a similar nature that readily suggest themselves, imply an imperfect state of human knowledge, and the need of advancement all along the line of speculation and inquiry. From such admissions, frankly offered, agnosticism has hastily inferred the necessary ignorance and the non-improvability of man, and settled down into that bliss which is supposed to spring from intellectual know-nothingism. The inference of agnosticism—a wild bird in paradise—has not a single premise on which to rest its feather-plucked and eyeless form, and not an inch of ground where its bleeding and tangled feet may stand. On the contrary, the assumption of human knowledge, the certainty of its facts, the trustworthiness of its deductions, and the infinite scope of its possibilities, may be proclaimed from evidences alike entertaining and assuring. The task of the vindication of man's inheritance to a realm of knowledge, not measurable by words, we now assume.

The foundation of this assumption is in the mind itself, its capacity and aspiration, the two conditions of knowledge, both of its nature and limitations. The measure of mind is its capacity, as the measure of a river is its basin or banks. The spirit of mind expresses itself in a capacious yearning for knowledge, in a subtle hostility to ignorance, and a persistent seeking after truth. The mind is that vital something that prompts to inquiry, demands explanations of mysteries, laughs at fables and superstitions, and mourns over denials of its requests. The truth-prompting factor of the mind is proof of its ability to know and understand truth. Equipped with mind, it is as evident that man is related to the realm of knowledge as that, furnished with eyes, he is related to physical things or the realm of observation. Only by a denial of mind, or a rejection of those faculties we denominate mental, and which distinguish man from the mastodon, can the possibilities of agnosticism be entertained. The ground-work of the subject is the intellectual fitness of man for knowledge, not how much he has acquired, or whether he has acquired any, nor whether his methods for arriving at truth are consistent or inconsistent, but whether in his mental constitution there is an irrepressible aptitude for knowledge, any receptive or open-door faculties seeking knowledge, any spontaneous affinities with truth, any unquenchable purpose to find the truth. Without this inbred predisposition to knowledge, this inherited and dominant familiarity with the kindred forms of truth, knowledge is impossible. If mind is mere nerve-force, and mental action a physical throb, agnosticism may be true; but if it is a divinely illuminated entity, a spirit-acting force, agnosticism is false, for the realm of knowledge may be entered by such a force. Mind admitted, knowledge is possible.

Assuming the possibility of knowledge from the fact of mind, we proceed with our inquiry in the form of a fourfold analysis: I. The source of knowledge. II. The subject-matter of knowledge, the real or the phenomenal. III. The limitations of knowledge. IV. The methods of acquiring knowledge.

The source of knowledge is a philosophical problem over which the greatest thinkers have bent their energies, pronouncing results neither wholly satisfactory nor totally unsatisfactory. Does the knowing, perceiving, thinking mind know by an intuitional power, or by immediate revelations of truth through supernatural agencies, or does it strive for knowledge through physical avenues? One is not compelled to make choice here, for it is possible that the mind arrives at knowledge in the three ways indicated, depending not on any single source or method for a sufficiency of truth. Philosophers have been guilty of advocating single sources or methods; hence the confusion, the utter irreconcilability of their theories with the facts of psychological history.

The old theory of sensationalism, that sense-perception is the foundation of mind-conception, or knowledge derived through the senses, which has corrupted philosophy from the days of Aristotle until now, bears the mark of the common deficiency; it is too exclusive as an explanation of the mind's activities and resources, and fails to account for knowledge.

Among the Greeks, according to Cudworth, the intellectual states which had a purely internal origin, were named *noemata*, or thoughts; while those of external origin were called *aisthemata*, or sensations. By virtue of the sensations the external intellect is developed; by virtue of thoughts the internal intellect unfolds. But the empirical psychologist knows no difference between thought and sensation; sensation is thought, and the external is the internal intellect. This is a blending of things entirely separate.

Aristotle, though not the first teacher of empiricism, gave it philosophical form, and must be charged with the responsibility of its introduction. Plato began with ideas; Aristotle with things. Plato's starting-point was the ego; Aristotle's the non-ego. In elucidation of the mind Aristotle classified it into two parts—the Passive or Receptive Intellect, and the Active or Creative Intellect—a division, if properly qualified or expressed, not specially objectionable; but it has wrought incalculable mischief in that the empirical schools of philosophy, ignoring the creative character of intellect, have constructed an argument from its purely receptive character for the rankest materialism. The mind may be both passive and active, says Aristotle; the empiricist says it is passive only; the truest philosophy will pronounce it *active* only, and never passive. The condition of mind is activity. The passivity of mind opens the way for sensationalism as the source or theory of knowledge. Locke, taking it up, found it convenient to deny to mind not only activity, but inheritance, or possessions. It is an empty thing, ready, like a cask, to be filled with whatever is poured into it. Passivity, emptiness, empiricism—these are logical steps; and Locke took them, since whose day a large brood of sensational theories have hovered over the psychological realm. The French philosophers carried Locke's conjectures to the wildest extremes, denying immortality and responsibility, with a plausibility that threatened the extinction of the moral foundations of society.

Is there no truth in sensationalism? Is it all an absurdity? Was Locke entirely mistaken? Was Aristotle misunderstood and perverted, or is there some truth in the theory of empiricism? It must be conceded that the senses are avenues of some kinds of knowledge; that is, many streams of truth seem to flow along the channels of the senses, and at least alphabetic or symbolic knowledge is the result. An ox looks upon the landscape that attracts the eye of Landseer; a dog may hear the organ whose keys Beethoven fingers to the delight of thousands; but there is a difference in the results of seeing and hearing, and it is this difference that makes for the immortality of man, and which is singularly overlooked by materialists. The ox is not affected by beauty, or botanical structure, or laws, or the relation of part to part; he can not analyze the flower or interpret the meaning of the plains and the mountains; he can not measure the dimensions of a field or calculate the age of a tree. Nor can the dog explain the process of hearing, or distingnish the notes of the organ, or separate the melody from the discord of the instrument. Sense-knowledge, or knowledge by sensation, must be superficial. Eyes and ears are the gateways of the streams—nothing more. They do not know any thing; they report only what passes through them. Back of these reporters must be something that distinguishes in the reports the true and the false, the beautiful and the deformed, the right and the wrong. It is the *classification of the reports of the senses that constitutes knowledge*, and it is this power of classification that distinguishes man from the ox. He sees more than form and color; from these he goes to structure, law, growth, beauty, inferring scientific principles, and fashioning at last the sciences themselves. Sense-knowledge stops with the outline of things, a mere recognition of their existence, without the recognition of their properties, laws, harmonies and functions. It furnishes materials, but can not combine them into truth, or even index their meaning. It may spell out the words, but can not pronounce, much less define them. Evidently, then, to assume, as does James Mill that all our knowledge of objects is the sensations they produce, or that sense-perception, is the sole inspiration of human thinking, is to assume what is objectionable on the ground of its superficiality, for it does not include all the facts of knowledge.

In man's present state he is somewhat dependent on empirical sources for knowledge of physical things; but this dependence must not be confounded with origin, a distinction that philosophy has not recognied. Malebranche insisted that the material world can not impress itself upon the immaterial soul, that our ideas of things are not derived from the things themselves, a reaffirmation, as the reader will remember, of the dualism of Descartes; but this is as extreme as dualism itself. The defect of the Cartesian teaching is its complete separation of mind and matter, whereas they sustain mutual relations, and exhibit interactions in their history and manifestations. Sensationalism is defective in holding that the external world is the source of knowledge; dualism is equally defective in teaching the absolute separation of mind and matter; while with Beneke we believe that the " without " stimulates the mind's activity, and yet, differing from him, that it has an independent power, which enables it to create thought and arrive at truth without the influence of any empirical auxiliary whatever.

To notice this independent power is now proper. In the natural order of the mind's development the intuitions make themselves felt first, having authority over sensations, conduct, and the outward life, and constitute the fiber of original experiences and history. Intuitional knowledge, or the contents of the consciousness, are of the highest, purest, and simplest kind, being different in this respect from sensational knowledge, which is always complex and somewhat delusive. From a sensation arises a complex notion, as the touch of a piece of marble suggests more than the idea of hardness or whiteness; from an intuition emerges a single, simple, decisive idea, as self-existence, identity. The complexity of sensational ideas led Locke to speak of them as chimerical, as the centaur is a complex but chimerical idea. Consciousness, or an intuitional idea, always suggesting necessary truth, presents it in simplest form, from which combinations and complexities may arise, but in no case are they chimerical. A chimerical sensation is possible; a chimerical intuition is an absurdity.

According to Hume, the consciousness is panoramic, reflecting images, ideas, facts, but it is also dynamic; that is, self-impelling, or a reservoir of self-contained, immutable truth. Not only are images or impressions of truth seen in the consciousness, but truths themselves, imbedded, as it were, in the very constitution of the moral nature. Intuitional truth is necessary in its very nature, but Spencer repudiates the theory of necessary truth; but if intuitionalism can be destroyed only by the sacrifice of the contents of consciousness, or the primary ideas of the intellect, it will endure until the end of the race. Zeno the Stoic agreed that the mind entertains ideas not derived from the senses; that they are connatural to us; that they belong *prima facie* to the mind; that they are intuitions. Reid, in framing his theory of " original suggestion," protested against the Lockeian formula of a barren mind, and insisted that the mind drew from its mysterious depths ideas which not only were regulative, but constitutive in essence and function. Among these ideas are those of self-existence, identity, space, time, unity, number, causation, accountability, right, and wrong. Jacobi said we see God through the intuitions. These are necessary truths, beliefs independent of experience, primary conceptions, the *noemata* of the Greeks, the internal intellect acting and originating for itself.

The theory of the intuitional source of knowledge is as old as sensationalism, Plato having held that the human mind contained ideas not derived from experience, and that they were connatural to it. This conception of the mind, or idealism, drove Aristotle into sensationalism, and the two doctrines have clashed in the conflicts of the ages. The existence of the intuitions or intuitional faculties is not now in dispute ; we accept them as the facts of our mental nature, a part of our intellectual furniture, by the use of which certain truths, called primary or axiomatic, we recognize. That an effect must have a cause is a rational, an intuitional truth. The belief in the existence of God, the notions of right and wrong, the haunting sense of responsibility for conduct, the correlated ideas of finite and infinite, unity and multiplicity, and quality and substance, and all those instincts which guide in morals, relationships, occupations, and religions are classed among those truths denominated intuitional. Certain mathematical axioms or principles also belong here. Locke is mistaken when he says they can nct be pointed out. In a sense, they are born in the mind without scientific influence, aid, or regulation.

Intuitional truths are those formerly known as " innate ideas," against which the sensationalists aimed their thunderbolts ; but certain it is that such truths exist, or the mind is not a spiritual entity. It is either a perfect blank, a reservoir of emptiness, or it possesses inherent truths. Between the doctrine of innate ideas, as Plato teaches in the *Phædo*, and the *tabula rasa* conception of Locke, one must prefer the former. Accepting Plato on this point, we do not accept his doctrine of reminiscence as the explanation of knowledge or the explanation of intuitional truth, for that involves his doctrine of the pre-existence of the soul. Intuitionalism does not necessarily involve pre-existence, as pre-existence does not involve intuitionalism. The connection between them is the result of a philosophical strain which philosophy can not bear.

What is the mind ? Is it any thing ? Is it a waxen tablet for receiving impressions, or has it the power of making impressions? Has it knowledge of itself, or only the capacity for knowledge? Of steam it may be said that it is not only capable of power, but also it is power, and when employed it is power in exercise. Latent power is power. Latent knowledge is knowledge. The mind possesses knowledge in itself, is full, not empty; hence education is literally a drawing out of the contents of the mind, and not putting into it, any thing from the outer world. It is not a citadel of darkness, but a center of light. The mind goes not to the world for knowledge, but the world goes to the mind for truth. Intuitional truth precedes sensational truth, and is the test of it. No truth can be accepted that contradicts the intuitions; but truths may be received that contradict the sensations. Intuitional truth arises from the constitution of the mind, is primary, fundamental, to be received without challenge; sensational truth arises from the fluctuating reports of the senses, and needs to be carefully scrutinized before being adopted.

Kindred to the contents of the consciousness are the products of the spontaneous reason, as materials of knowledge, to be appropriated and used in the grand march of the ages. By the spontaneous reason is meant neither intuition on the one hand, which is not reason, nor reflection on the other, which is directed reason, but a midway functional force, an intellectual rational conviction, consistent in essence, and self-vindicating in its final form. There is in man a spontaneous, unreflective reason in contrast to that which reflects, syllogizes, analyzes, synthesizes. Often in the unlearned there is a clearness in the apperceptions of reason that, being wholly spontaneous, without any premeditated analysis, astonishes the learned. The natural philosopher and his servant reach the same conclusion respecting the agency of fire in the economy of nature; both agree as to its relation to life; the one frames complex notions, the other simple, but the conclusions are the same. In a simple way the spontaneous reason conducts to a knowledge of substance, power, being; gives tokens of a true ontology, while the developed reason fashions them into formulæ.

Kant was fond of saying that knowledge takes the form of the mind, one of the mischievous errors in his philosophy, since it is fatal to uniformity of knowledge of truth. If the mind give form to knowledge, as the color of a vessel appears to give color to the liquid in it, then intuitional knowledge will be individualized, and each man, as Protagoras taught, will be the measure of all things, and all truths as well. Reid well says, " When we have an idea of some object as round, we are not to infer that the mental state is possessed of the same quality; when we think of any thing as extended, it is not to be supposed that the thought itself has extension; when we behold and admire the varieties of color we are not at liberty to indulge the presumption that the inward feelings are painted over and radiant with corresponding hues." Clearly, knowledge is not governed by the form of the mind; truth is not mind-molded, but mind-assimilated, mind-received, mind-projected.

If the spontaneous reason is a source of knowledge, Reason itself, or Reflection, must be allowed a place also in the category. Hegel once taught that the acquisition of knowledge is possible through pure thought, a position which contemporaneous philosophy unanimously condemned. Is pure thinking a possibility? May mental absorption be so complete, so uninfluenced by any thing but mind, that new truth will be the product of its soliloquies? The Athenians held their assemblies at night that they might not be disturbed by visible things—can the mind retire within itself, or shut the doors of the visible and in itself contemplate the great problems of theology, psychology, and ontology? The rational power, exercised exclusively upon invisible things and guided by its own categories of thought, must succeed in the acquisition of intellectual truth; pure thinking under such circumstances must result in pure knowledge. By reflection, however, we do not mean pure thought in the Hegelian sense but that faculty which in possession of facts and truths is able to generalize them, and combine them into systems. The reflective reason could not exercise if there were no objects of reflection. It moves out, therefore, from its own domain in search of reprisals in the form of truths and facts, unfurling its flag upon the widened seas of knowledge, and running down the piratical crafts of error, and fraternizing with all truth. Reason may occupy itself with nature searching for its laws, or with man probing mind, or with God bringing him nearer to the view. In whatever direction it goes, it will find the path broad, long, perhaps thorny, but it has a goal, the discovery of truth in some of its myriad forms. Reason is dialectic in form, substance, authority.

Not all truth is attainable through sensation, intuition, or the double reason; there is a realm of knowledge that sense-perception can not invade, and which the intuitional power can not fully command. If a realm of truth is beyond the invasion of the senses, the intuitions, and the reasons, then the source of knowledge must be beyond these instruments of inquiry. In both cases the supposition is correct. There is a realm of truth beyond the sensational, the intuitional, the rational; there is therefore a source of knowledge not yet mentioned.

Such truth is wholly supernatural, supersensible; the source of knowledge, inspiration and revelation. The difference between inspiration and revelation is very like the difference between the spontaneous and the reflective reason, both essentially the same, but in form and extension different. Revelation is written inspiration. Inspiration, as a source of knowledge, is treated with indifference by modern philosophy, but Plato in the *Ion* speaks of a divine power moving men, which he compares to magnetism, and also to the influence of a god on the priestesses of Bacchus, which enables them to draw milk and honey from rivers. If poets and musicians and priestesses may be influenced by the gods, why may not the magnetic power come upon men in search of truth and help them to find it? This is inspiration, a purely philosophical doctrine when thoroughly understood.

In the theological sense, inspiration is the impression of the divine Spirit upon the human mind conveying positive knowledge, or so illuminating the understanding that its conceptive power is intensified to that degree that it easily discovers and readily discerns the truth. In another form, inspiration is a divine sensation, the counterpart of physical sensation. Both have external sources, the one material, the other spiritual. Inspiration is as valid as sensationalism; *it is sensationalism refined.* The only ground of assault upon it lies in the results of the higher sensation, which, however, are in keeping with its sphere of action and influence. Pure or physical sensations result in external knowledge; refined or divine sensations result in supernatural knowledge. In the one case, matter impresses mind, and mind becomes acquainted with matter; in the other, God impresses mind, and mind becomes acquainted with God. Sensation is Nature rapping at the door of the intellect; inspiration is God tapping on the windows of the soul.

It should be remembered that if God is what he is supposed to be, a personal, all-wise, merciful being, he will be as eager to communicate himself to man as man will be to receive the communication. If he is the universal mind, the mind of minds, himself the All-thought, it is inconceivable that he would not impress himself upon mind wherever he found it. Nature, hard, mindless, characterless, touches us at five points, speaking by signs and symbols and in a language we partly understand; is the mighty God, mind of minds, unable to reach us? As Prof. Bowne puts it, "If God is finite we can reach him; if he is infinite he can reach us." Inspiration is God reaching us. The Duke of Argyll phrases faith in inspiration in the following manner: "That the human mind is always in some degree, and that certain individual minds have been in a special degree, *reflecting surfaces,* as it were, *for the verities of the unseen and eternal world,* is a conception having all the characters of coherence, which assure us of its harmony with the general constitution and the common course of things." The mind is a *reflecting surface for eternal truths*—this is inspiration, and as philosophical as to say that the mind is a reflecting surface for physical truth.

What are the truths derived from inspiration? The truths of inspiration, like the truths of sensation, intuition, and reason, are in harmony with their source, the Artesian principle being as applicable in the one case as in the other. Truth rises no higher than its source. From sensation a knowledge is obtained of material phenomena; from intuition, mind-truths; from reason, rational truths; from inspiration, inspired or supernatural truths. God in his attributes, eternal, infinite, omnipotent, omniscient, immutable, holy, merciful, just; God in his relations to the world as Creator, Preserver, Upholder; God as Redeemer, Judge, Rewarder; the eternal world, the immortality of man, the character and possibilities of the soul in the future state; these and many other truths are valid subjects of inspiration, without which, indeed, they can not be known. Granting the necessity of inspiration as a means of knowledge of supernatural truth, it has been alleged that it is difficult to discriminate between truth professedly acquired by inspiration, and that which mysticism, fanaticism, and superstition have endeavored to fasten upon the world as from God; that is, the line of difference between inspiration and superstition is not clearly drawn, hence the latter often imposes itself for the former. The objection rests upon historic data, and is admitted to be forceful. The Neoplatonists, as sincere as any religious-philosophical sect, plunged into the excesses of mysticism, claiming inspiration for their utterances, and divine direction for their deeds. What was the claim of Pope Pius IX. to infallibility but the assertion of inspiration? Errors, false doctrines, misinterpretations of Scriptural truth, and fanaticism in all forms, have been sustained by the assumption of divine support, discrediting the doctrine of inspiration by teachings subversive of it.

Allowing that the doctrine has been perverted, misused, and credited with unworthy associations, it must still be maintained that inspiration, that is, the in-breathing of spiritual knowledge by the divine Spirit, is a probability, a certainty; and it is for man, by the right use of reason, so far as it will apply, to separate between the true and the false, the human and the divine—a task attended, we admit, with no little embarrassment.

Owing to these embarrassments, there is need of a supplemental, or final and satisfactory source of knowledge, which is found in *revelation*, or the written form of inspired truth. The value of the written form is that it remains the same through the ages, and can be tested by one age as well as another; it varies not, hence it is a standard of truth.

The integrity of the alleged revelation of truth we do not now consider, but mention it as one of the accepted sources of knowledge to millions. How a truth can be revealed in the way claimed involves a study of supernatural methods which for the most part are mysterious, but which are as reliable as natural methods, which are no less mysterious also. Familiarity with empirical methods does not enable us to explain them; and intuitional processes are as obscure to us as the miraculous. Sense-knowledge is as mysterious as inspired knowledge. Whether knowledge come to us from the world through the senses, or from God through the mind alone, the mystery is as great in the one case as the other, and philosophy, accepting one, must finally accept the other.

The necessity of the revelation of higher truth is also as conclusive as the necessity of knowledge of it at all; and the alternative is, either not to know it at all, or to know it by the supernatural method of revelation. Accepting revelation, what a realm of truth is open to human vision and to the possession of faith! St. Aquinas used to remark that the beginnings of knowledge are the morning walks of faith, but it is equally true to say that the beginnings of faith in revelation are the morning walks of knowledge. Not that the knowledge thus furnished is complete, but it is a key to openings in the vast realm of supernaturalism, a knowledge of which is desirable. By the sense-method our knowledge of the physical world is painfully incomplete, and were the mind to rely upon eyes and ears alone we should walk in a blacker than Egyptian darkness. The intuitional process reports a limited number of truths, without explanation, imposing them upon our recognition by the great weight of their authority. So revealed truth may be wanting in that thoroughness and completeness which belongs to the other methods, and still be a revelation. Concerning revealed truths, we are emphatic in the assertion that, since they are of God on the supposition that there is a revelation at all, they are more reliable than either the intuitional, which is of man, or the sensational, which is of matter. Revealed truth should have the greatest authority, sensational truth the least. The one brings us nearer to realities, exposes the invisible foundation of things, makes the universe transparent, and sounds like the voice of God; the other acquaints us with phenomena alone, and points to forms. That which philosophy rejects should have the first, and that which it accepts the last, place in the category of sources of human knowledge.

It is not our intention to vindicate the Scriptures in any theological sense, but to consider them philosophically as a source of knowledge. Fitche boldly acknowledged the necessity of a revelation; Schelling, though prejudiced against the Bible as a whole, adopted Johannean Christianity as the best exponent of the highest truth; Hegel regarded Christ as the "self-externalizing idea;" Locke reverently read the Scriptures, and was a Christian believer.

Turn to Revelation, and what are its teachings respecting fundamental problems? In the writings of Moses, as throughout the Bible, the existence of God is assumed but not proved. Is the assumption unphilosophical? Is it an instance of a *petitio principii?* Philosophy, failing for the want of a proper starting-point, has invariably ended in fog or drift; Revelation, beginning with the First Cause, the principle of principles, the being of beings, explains all things. The beginning must be mind or matter, but matter is an effect of mind. Philosophy, contemplating the effect, has attempted to find its way through the *a posteriori* method back to cause; Revelation, contemplating the cause, has gone *a priori* to the manifold effect. In method of procedure one is the reverse of the other. Beginning with the Beginner, Revelation is a narration of God's unfolding in the universe of matter and his presence in human history, accounting for worlds, races, and destinies; beginning with effects, philosophy tediously essays to climb to summits beyond its vision, lighting its pathway with sparks of its own kindling. Revelation is a descent of truth; philosophy an attempted ascent to truth. Revelation is explicit where philosophy is vague; full, where it is incomplete; certain, where it is in doubt; knowing, where it is ignorant. In revelation we attain to a knowledge of God; in philosophy he is the great unknown.

In respect to man, his character, the account of his moral weakness, the possibility of his restoration to moral greatness, Revelation speaks a specific truth. Plato, acknowledging the impurity of the race, prescribed intellectual discipline as the chief means of purification; Gautama prescribed penances and transmigrations; Spencer foresees the natural evanescence of evil; the Bible preaches regeneration and sanctification.

In respect to Nature, origin, character, and destiny, the Bible is equally definite and satisfactory; the universe is the effect of the creative impulse in a personal deity. Man is as much bound to consider the teachings of Christ, Moses, Isaiah, and Paul, as he is to heed the oracles of Plato, Kant, Hamilton, Hume, and Spencer. On intellectual grounds, not more can be claimed for the latter than for the former; on spiritual grounds, the former must be preferred to the latter.

Human knowledge, as we have seen, has a six-fold source, to wit:

*sensation, intuition, spontaneous reason, reflection, inspiration, revelation;* but these may be reduced to three: Nature, the source of sensation; Mind, including the intuitions, the reason, and reflection; and Revelation, including inspiration. The first is the simplest, the commonest, the rudest; the second, more refined, but limited; the third, divine. Nature, Mind, Revelation—these three, but the greatest of these is Revelation.

The next step in the inquiry is that which concerns the *subject-matter* of knowledge. What do we know? Is knowledge of the real, or of the phenomenal only? This is a broad and profound question, to be answered, if answered at all, in the spirit of carefulness and humility, for the agnosticism of the day is persuaded that absolute knowledge is impossible. Some things all men think they know, and they would repudiate the philosophy that denied to them such knowledge. They know, as they think, the difference between a square and a circle, not so much as mathematical statements as forms of matter. Granted, then, that men understand the differences in the forms of matter. This is a beginning, and, as knowledge, is valuable. It involves magnitude, extension, figure, a great many mathematical ideas applied to planets and objects on the earth. No one would say this is complete knowledge; no one should say it is knowledge respecting the object at all, as the form of a thing is not the thing itself. Form and substance are by no means the same. Glass may be shaped into a bowl, or cup, or ball—the form different, the substance the same. Hence, we must advance a little, that is, know something more than the form of matter to know what matter is.

Many men believe they can name some of the laws of matter. They know the difference between inertia and motion, attraction and repulsion, cohesion and adhesion, chemical affinity and gravitation, and understand the late doctrines of the conservation and correlation of forces. Granted that our familiarity with nature is on the increase, in that its laws are being discovered and understood. This is a great gain, for by such knowledge we may explain the rotations of the planets, calculate their distances from the sun, and apprehend the commonest activities of the natural world. But should one ferret out *all* the laws of nature, and comprehend thoroughly the government of the physical universe, one could not affirm that he had complete knowledge of things. If there is a difference between the form of matter and its substance, there is even a greater difference between a law of matter and its substance. Prof. Bowne, the gifted metaphysician of Boston, insists that a knowledge of the law of a thing is a knowledge of the thing itself; and it is admitted that, in the light of his elaboration, the statement seems unobjectionable; but we can afford to pause before accepting it fully. Theoretically speaking, the substance might exist without the law and without the form; it might be formless, it might be lawless. Law is no part of matter, is not the key to the substance of matter, although it is a key to the explanation of matter. To know the universe, he must needs know more than the laws which produced the universe; they explain the *how*, do they divine the *what?* Is the how the what? Can one know any thing beyond law?

Here is a bar of iron—what can one know of iron? That it is malleable, ductile, hard, non-transparent, heavy, solid, durable, useful. This is an enumeration of some of the properties of iron, a complete list of which would seem to broaden our knowledge of this very useful metal. Here is a branch of cedar, or there a block of marble, the properties of each being distinct and clearly defined. This is a knowledge of the properties of matter, an approach to a knowledge of its substance, and an advance over a knowledge of the forms of matter. Without this knowledge, it would not be possible to use matter. We must know that coal is combustible in order to use it in our stoves, grates, and furnaces. To understand properties is apparently akin to an understanding of substance.

The serious question is now at hand: *Is a knowledge of properties complete knowledge?* Do we know the substance when we enumerate qualities? Do we know a leaf when we say it is green, rectangular, sweet? We are in trouble at this point. No one will say that a knowledge of one property of an object is a satisfactory or complete knowledge of it; and it is a question if a knowledge of all the parts is equivalent to a knowledge of the whole. Between properties and substance there is a wide gulf; is it impassable? If not impassable, what is the bridge? Can we go back of properties or beyond them in the direction of the real? or must we stop with properties? The delicate threads or cables extending from properties to substance are invisible, ambiguous, anonymous, difficult to trace, since they do not break out in concrete forms, or in visible points or knots. We say we are in trouble. Give us one thread, and we will pull our way through to the Real. Is there any *real?* or is our knowledge of the phenomenal a knowledge of all that exists? Is not this idea of a real, as distinguished from the phenomenal, a mere fiction, a dream of the philosopher? or is it a substantive, whose manifestations are the properties, forms, laws, and whatever is visible? We can not part with the idea of the real; we can not think the phenomenal to be the all in all; but how to connect or trace the connection is a task which many assume can not be accomplished. Let us assume there is such a connection; let us assume the reality of the real; let us plunge from the phenomenal toward the real, whether we alight in darkness or on the solid granite of reality. Our track is along the line of law. The *connecting link between phenomena and reality is law. The explanation of all things is law.*

Is law the great reality? Is law substance? Actually, substance without law is impossible; law is the producing agency of substance; law is the explanation of substance. By this we do not mean general laws, or the category of laws as enounced by science, but the particular law by which a particular thing is produced, the law of its existence, or the law of its activity. In this higher sense law is substance, and a knowledge of one is a knowledge of the other. The highest knowledge is not of forms, nor of properties, nor of general laws, but *of the law of forms, the law of properties, the law of the unity of substance.* Under this transformation the world is but the effigy of the creative principle, the outline of the law that produced it. Plato's definition of law, that it is the *discovery of what is,* surpasses any thing ever framed, and justifies Bowne in claiming that a knowledge of law is a knowledge of the thing it produces and sustains. *The only real in nature is law;* this is the thing-in-itself which Kant said is undiscoverable, but it is now made manifest. The Eleatics denied the existence of the phenomenal world, but failed to point out the underlying reality. The reality of the Eleatics was the ego; but law is the non-ego, or the real of nature. Knowledge of the phenomenal centers at last in the knowledge of the real that produced it.

To what extent may the mind know itself? Is self-knowledge a possibility? This is a root-question, sinking itself deeper than the other. The French Leroux denies the existence of the *me* or ego, and denies that man can know himself in the consciousness. Can he know himself at all, then? Does he exist? Locke was driven by his empiricism to deny that the mind can know itself, and sensationalism generally espouses this conclusion. Drawing a distinction between subject and object, it is asserted by the empirical school that the mind can not be both subject and object, or the perceiving and the perceived, the knowing and the known. If, however, the mind can not know itself, certain it is that mind can not be known, for it can only be known by knowing itself. Sir John Davies held to man's capability of self-knowledge; Lord Herbert believed in innate ideas, but innate ideas imply self-knowledge, or knowledge of the contents of the mind. The intuitional spirit is the self-knowing spirit. The mind that knows any thing must first know itself, for there must be a mind to know before any thing can be known. A knowing mind must be a conscious mind; if conscious, it is conscious of itself before it is conscious of any thing else; so that self-knowledge is first,

15

chronologically. The source of original knowledge is not sensation, as some schools affirm, but consciousness. Knowledge postulates consciousness; that is, self-knowledge precedes sensational knowledge. The experience-philosophers reverse the order, and make the former the product of the latter. A false philosophy is always disposed to torture facts, but facts must govern. Self-knowledge is consciousness opening, widening, reporting to itself, is subject and object, an indivisible unity, a stupendous reality. Self-knowledge is real, sensational knowledge phenomenal. As in nature the real is back of the phenomenal and takes the name of law, so in self-knowledge the real is back of the sensational, and is located in consciousness, or in being itself, postulated by the fact of knowledge.

The greatest Real is God. Is he knowable? Pushing the phenomenal far from us, and going out of ourselves, does the soul scent the atmosphere of the infinite? Do the shadows of the infinite deepen and lengthen toward us as we attempt to approach it? Surely the going toward the highest Real is not an impossible experience. Repudiated by Spencer, the approach to a personal Real is in the highest degree a possibility, a matter of fact, a fact of experience. What is the Real? Let us not deceive ourselves with a jugglery of words. The Real, remote from all manifestation, must include the essence of power, and wisdom, and the integers of goodness and justice. It must mean the first source of all that we see, hear, and know. It must suggest a producer, an organizer, a Creator. In a correlative sense, the perishable must suggest the imperishable, the deformed the beautiful, the formal the artificer, the phenomenal the absolutely unphenomenal or the original real. The real must be mind, thought, personality, God; all else is temporary, fugitive, deceptive. He is the great Real in the universe, the one source of all things, knowable because he is reality. The phenomenal is less knowable than reality. God is more knowable than the universe, since it fadeth, but he abideth forever. The great, genuine Real is God; the lesser Real is man; the only phenomenal is the world, its reality being hidden in the law by which it is made. *Law, mind, God*—these three are the only reals, but the greatest of these is God.

The subject-matter of knowledge is the history, the functions, the prerogatives, the relations, one to another, of the *reals*; a vast field, imperfectly surveyed, slowly conquered. The incompleteness of human knowledge is frankly admitted; it has always been incomplete; the conclusion of philosophy is that it will always be unsatisfactory.

This suggests an inquiry into the limitations or boundary lines of human knowledge, how far it is possible to go, and what are the probabilities of pushing the frontier lines a little beyond their present indications. This involves not so much a critical investigation of the subject-matter of knowledge as a critical study of the power of the human mind to comprehend such subject-matter; it requires a criticism of the thinking, knowing mind, and not a criticism of the subjects to be known. Is the mind under fixed limitations, as the associationalists insist, preventing it from a research of all reality? The metaphysical theory is that a barrier like a Chinese wall surrounds the mind, checking its advance; the vision of the intellect is bounded by a horizon; and these limitations are fixed, immovable, permanent, final. Knowledge is relative, not absolute, according to Hamilton; phenomena, not substance, may be known, according to Kant; being, power, mind, God, are forever inscrutable, according to Spencer. In contrast to this law of fixed limitations, we shall affirm that the mind is under a law of *movable limitations*, whereby its progress, however difficult, is assured, and can never be permanently impeded. Whatever limitations confront the speculator and truth-seeker, they are apparently, but not unchangeably, fixed; they are movable, yielding to persistent advance. If there is a horizon, it always recedes as one approaches it. The mind is on the march, is incessant in its going, and never stops because it can go no farther. It moves by its own impulses, and knows no latitude or longitude. The universe is not large enough for its activity.

Are there any limitations which estop farther advance? Paul writes, "We see through a glass darkly," but *we see*. The sight is obscure, uncertain, but it is sight, certainly. "We know in part," he also writes; but *we know*. Along this line we may interpret the limitations of knowledge, or at least admit vaguely-defined limitations, since Paul himself does not name them. Partial but not complete knowledge, the apostle affirms, belongs to our present state. We will illustrate his meaning. Ordinary sight is sufficient for practical life, but it is often embarrassed by limitations, and makes a great many mistakes. On the prairie it will decide, unless trained to measure distances, that a hill or house is distant not more than five miles, when it is fifteen miles away. Respecting magnitude it makes failures equally humiliating. Distances, magnitudes, densities, the untrained eye can not accurately determine. Some things, too, as the gases, as animalculæ, enterely elude the searching gaze of the eye. We do not quote these facts so much as incidents of a defective apparatus, as to show how it is possible to see and know in part, and not see and know in whole. We know in part, just as we see in part.

Of the phenomenal world we know not the whole, and it may be that it will never be entirely known ; but of this we are not certain. As a field of investigation and discovery, it is rich in forms, relations, laws, and principles, rewarding the diligent inquirer by opening the passage-ways to its mysteries, and declaring its grandeur and purpose to him who seeks to know it. In his intense search for the real, man is continually stumbling over the phenomenal, which is full of truth for his guidance and illumination; and so slothful is the mind in its present environment, that it has tardily discovered the physical facts it most needs to know. For ages the race breathed the air without knowing its composition. Oxygen at last was sighted, and has a name. What is true of the air, is true of water, the metals, the rocks, the trees, the stars. Even nature invites the largest genius and covets the presence of the investigating spirit of man. Much remains to be discovered; the forces and laws of nature are still in obscurity; gases are but feebly understood; electricity is a runaway power that needs to be harnessed, controlled, directed; all the properties of matter have not been divulged. Some properties, it is true, may be so exceedingly fine and delicate, so invisible even with the aid of the most powerful instruments, and serve such occult purposes in the economy of nature, that for ages to come they may escape detection, and man, ignorant of them, be subject to accident or danger, which he might otherwise avoid.

Very few laws are known with absolute certainty. Even Newton at one time lost faith in the law of gravitation, which he announced. The scientist may discover the fact of a law, but not the law itself. Gravitation, as a fact, was known long before it was discovered as a law. Magnetism is a fact, but the law of magnetism is another thing, and a mystery. The facts of nature are within easy reach ; the laws of nature may be beyond immediate grasp. Facts are accumulating; laws are the invisible influences that connect the phenomenal and the real; verily they are the real in the phenomenal, and must be sought out by labor, research, comparison, application. What we call principles of science, or the basis of scientific procedure, the phenomenalists themselves—a class of thinkers who veer toward agnosticism—are disposed hesitatingly to use, because of a suspicion against their reliability. Prof. Clifford declares that we have no right to assume that "the laws of geometery and mechanics are exactly and absolutely true, and that they will continue exactly and absolutely true forever and ever." This casts suspicion, if not odium, on the whole fabric of science, linking phenomenalism to agnosticism, and giving us for a footing nothing but "sinking sand."

What, then, can be known? If the principles of science, otherwise the laws of nature, are not fully established, or established beyond the possibility of a doubt; if men are still groping in darkness respecting the fundamental principles of the government of nature; and if scientists themselves suspect the reality or integrity of the laws they have taught others to respect; it is evident that man's knowledge is ignorance, and the prospect of enlargement is lost in the saddening and hopeless limitations of his own anarchy. To this dreary conclusion phenomenalism conducts us; but this conclusion we reject.

That the present state of knowledge is one of deficiency and difficulty, it is freely confessed; but the main question is, whether the deficiency is absolute, and the difficulty insurmountable, or is the discovery of phenomena, properties, laws a rightful expectancy? The ascertainment of law is not an impossibility, and faith in mathematical principles may be grounded in their absolute correctness, as tested in life's history. Forms, properties, laws, as proper subjects of inquiry, will be scientifically apprehended more and more, and so formulated as to be easily understood. If our knowledge now of these things is of a doubtful character, it is proof that man is in the transition state between suspicion and certainty; he is on the way to positive revelation and "much assurance."

If difficulties confront us as we inquire into phenomena, or natural facts and conditions, what may we not expect when realities are the subject-matter of search? Of mind itself what is known? If we study matter by its properties, may we study mind by its attributes? Memory, imagination, judgment, conscience, will, and affection belong to mind, as malleability and ductility belong to iron. But if behind the properties of matter is the real, so behind the attributes of mind must be the mind itself, a thought that compels the consideration of mind separate from its faculties, which is absurd; or its consideration as a mere aggregate of faculties, which is as objectionable as the idea that matter is a combination of its properties. In psychological inquiry we separate the faculties, and discuss them separately; but in point of fact, the mind must be considered in its wholeness, undivided and indivisible.

The fact of mental operation appeals for solution; it taxes ingenuity to its utmost tension. This is a field for the most persistent inquiry, in which superficial methods of study will avail nothing. Mental processes, an act of volition or judgment, an effort of the imagination, the dictatorial voice of the conscience, the proceeding of the memory, the exercises of affection, elude superficial search; but a search profound and prolonged must be made. Self-knowledge, or the mind knowing itself, which is something more than consciousness of existence, is an achievement which includes a knowledge of faculties, their relations and processes, the spirit of reality itself. The attainment of such knowledge is not "too high;" it is not beyond us. If it has not been acquired by this time, its acquirement belongs to the early future, possibly to our own day.

The great Real, or God, is still a problem. He is infinite, man finite. On these premises the unknowableness of God might be predicated, but it would be insufficient. Infinite things the finite mind may, to some extent, apprehend, as space, time, right, justice, purity. An infinite being, or combination of infinite qualities, such as spirituality, omniscience, omnipotence, immutability, and eternity, the finite being may not completely define, but it is a question if human ignorance of God must forever remain as it is. Herbert Spencer is emphatic in the belief that the infinite is beyond any anthropomorphic conception, and can not be reduced within our psychological limitations; but if correct in the assumption that the finite can not find the infinite, it remains to be proven that the infinite can not reveal himself to the finite. The break-down of the finite is repaired by the revelation of the infinite, which religion provides in its book of truth. Revelation is not anthropomorphic ; the very idea of revelation is that it is God showing himself, and not that it is man expressing his view of God. Anthropomorphism and revelation are antipodal ideas. The revelation of the Real is the sure source of knowledge of the Real. As we study matter by its properties, finding its reality in law, and the mind by its attributes, locating its reality in consciousness, so we study God in the light of his manifested attributes, discerning his only reality in spirit, or conscious being.

"We know in part," but we know all along the lines and in the direction of the three-fold realities of law, mind, and spirit, and if there are limitations they are not the limitations of the reals, but arise from the subjective inabilities and hindrances of the mind itself. Like a heroic and advancing army, the mind is pushing on its conquests into the interior of the enemy's country, assailing the castles of ignorance, and really threatening to invade the realms of the infinite. Surely it is extending its base-line toward the summit, and will some time shout the word of triumph from the apparently inaccessible heights of celestial knowledge.

In this faith we announce that the mind in its struggles after truth will finally demonstrate its power to remove all limitations to advance, and will compass all knowledge. Acting for a time under the law of movable limitations, it will finally act as if under a law of removable limitations, breaking down all barriers, and contented with its knowledge of truth. The law of movable limitations is in harmony with the history of the race; the law of *removable limitations* may be judged a mere speculation, but it is the real law of progress, it is the law of mind, of God, and is the opposite of the philosophy of ignorance. It implies that the boundaries of knowledge are infinite; that is, there are no boundaries; the universe of thought, being, substance, personality, reality, is knowable, and if knowable the mind is not piratical in seizing it. The soul that keeps house in the universe of God must at last be at home anywhere in it, with a right to all that it seeks and finds, with a freedom that no hindrance can disturb. Under such a law ignorance is contraband in the universe, and has no sure abiding-place.

With these two laws before us, we see the mind in two aspects: first, the mind as it is, crippled but pressing on; second, the mind as it must be, unembarrassed by limitation. Respecting its limitations, we see them, first *moved*, second REMOVED. This is infinite progress in knowledge. In keeping with these laws we may classify the mind, and designate the contents of knowledge. There is the *spatial*, or longitudinal mind, which is bounded by space and time, and affected in its activities by their contents. Within these boundaries it moves, driving back the limitations of knowledge with its own advancement, and acquiring a familiarity with things beyond, by which it is lured onward. It unmasks nature, it tears the bandage from its own eyes, it walks, it flies, it seeks, it finds; but it flies with broken wing, and seeks the truth only at short range. The spatial mind is the walled mind. Then there is the *ecumenical* mind, which, acting in harmony with the law of removable limitations, smiles at the toyish boundaries of space and time, overleaps all barriers in its aspirations, is allopathic and universal in its conquests. The elasticity of mind has been admitted, but it has been supposed to be like a bow, which would bend only so far without breaking; but the ecumenical mind is mobile, divinely tempered, avaricious of knowledge, runs the blockade of phenomena, and sails into the ports of universal truth. It is exceedingly familiar with some truths, and has a bowing acquaintance with all. Fitche said the non-ego is a hindrance to the ego; it is a temporary hindrance to the spatial mind; to the ecumenical mind limitations are invisible, unknown. Modern philosophy deals with the spatial mind, fixing unalterably its limitations; a true philosophy must accept the law of removable limitations, under which the mind becomes ecumenical.

The conquest of truth, hitherto interrupted by the sloth, the passions, the natural blindness of man, is under the operation of the law of illimitable progress, an admitted possibility, and will eventuate in glorious certainty. God is better known to-day than at any time in the past; man is slowly resolving his own mysteries; nature is yielding her secrets, disclosing her laws, and revealing origin and destiny. The excavation of hidden truth, the solution of trigonometrical problems, the dissolution of metaphysical nebulæ, must go on until the mind is satisfied with its achievements, and glories as an acknowledged monarch in the vastness of its kingdom. Hamilton admitted, in the following declaration, that both the ego and the non-ego are knowable: "We may therefore lay it down as an undisputed truth, that consciousness gives, as an ultimate fact, a *primitive duality*—a knowledge of the ego in relation and contrast to the non-ego, and a knowledge of the non-ego in relation and contrast to the ego." This, though contradicted afterwards by Hamilton's assertion of the law of relativity, is, to our thinking, an exact, but perhaps not final, statement of possible intellectual attainment ; the ego is self-knowing; it knows the non-ego; it knows God.

The extension of knowledge in the direction of absolute realities implies an improvement in the methods of research, a revisal of existing methods of reasoning, and the adoption of short-cut processes to realities. It may be that the syllogistic methods of Aristotle, the Baconian system of induction, and the Kantian antinomies should be accepted as final, and that an entirely new method of inquiry, in which the old style of reasoning will be incidental, or at the most only auxiliary, can not be devised ; but certain it is that the highest truth can not be ascertained, or the instrument of inquiry is faulty and insufficient. Considering the sources of knowledge, we affirm that a knowledge of truth is attainable; *truth exists only to be known*, and if not known, the method of introduction and acquaintance is at fault. Perhaps the old methods, seemingly inadequate and certainly insufficient, may not be rudely set aside, but be incorporated with more efficient methods of inquiry, occupying subordinate but useful relations to the highest results. No one method is at present supreme. Neither induction nor deduction, neither the *a priori* nor the *a posteriori* method, is complete in itself. Each is wanting in something to make its last word infallible. The scientific method of inquiry, embracing the four steps of observation, analysis, classification, and conclusion has flooded the world with inharmonious theories, and arrayed science against itself. Touching geological questions, the age of the world in particular, the scientific method has been singularly fruitful of contradictory results, and especially prolific of error when applied to religious truth, showing the necessity of a revisal of the method.

Metaphysical theologians not a few have conceded that the demonstration of the existence of God by the *a priori* method is impossible, while the materialists ridicule the *a posteriori* method when applied in defense of the theistic idea. The assault on these various methods by different thinkers, and the unsatisfactory results obtained, justify the belief that a new method, retaining the excellences, but relieved of the deficiencies of the old, by which the gateway to truth will be opened, will some time appear.

The greatest stumbling-block to intellectual progress is perhaps Kant's "antinomies;" that is, if the mind, in its struggles, is bound by these contradictions, as laid down by the German philosopher, there can be no progress. His first antinomy admits and denies a "beginning;" his second antinomy assumes and rejects simplicity of origin; his third antinomy joins freedom and necessity in the mind's deliberations; his fourth antinomy accepts and rejects the idea of a necessary being, or cause of all things. How can the mind ascend under such a load of contradictions? Yet philosophy stands in awe of this Kantian environment, refusing to proceed beyond it, and succumbing to the adversity of ignorance within its bounds. Evidently, escape from the environment is the next duty of the mind; freedom from the reign of the "insoluble contradictions" must be the cry of a true philosophy.

The weaknesses of the present methods of reasoning is that in many respects they are artificial, the framework of metaphysicians, who, instead of discovering from the mind itself the method of its activity, have invented a method and imposed it upon the mind. Reasoning must be conducted according to reason; reflecting must be governed by the reflective faculty; the mind must make its own method. Discoverers, not inventors, are in demand.

New methods, freedom from embarrassments, persistence in claiming the possibility of acquaintance with all truth, a rejection of the philosophy of ignorance, must characterize the attempts of the human mind in the future, if its progress toward reality be real itself.

Aristotle, Bacon, Kant—who next?

# CHAPTER X.

## THE LAW OF CAUSALITY; OR EFFICIENT CAUSE.

IN the early morning an Arab saw the foot-print of a camel near his tent-door. It made no impression upon him, because he was not unacquainted with the quadruped that made it; but the stranger whom he lodged was all-anxious to see the camel. Empiricism studies the foot-print, and is unaroused from its monotonous stupidity; philosophy ought to flame with a desire to find the camel. Empirical psychologists, evolutionists, associationalists, all heroically assert that there is no camel; *the foot-print made itself*; it evolved from prior conditions of soil and climate; or, if a camel is conceded, he is pronounced altogether unknowable.

We have chosen to present a great philosophical principle in this fable form, in order to bring it out in its clearness, and to fasten the mind upon the differences that subsist between being and non-being, or between cause, as an originating influence, and effect, as its legitimate result.

Is there a dividing line between cause and effect? Is there a difference between phenomena and noumena? Either phenomena must explain themselves—that is, possess the principle of reality, and stand as self-existences—or they must be referred to some external principle competent to produce them. The choice is between the foot-print and the camel. It is pleasant to sojourn in the region of phenomena; it is not easy to climb rays of light, or go toward the sun with opened eyes. But the philosopher's vocation compels him to go back of phenomena to sources, back of effects to causes; and he is not a philosopher who does not strive to do it. If unsuccessful in his search, he can console himself with the reflection that he attempted to break through the network of phenomena, or scale its bold heights, but was unable to do so.

The problem of efficient cause has a bearing on the fundamental questions of philosophy and religion; hence its importance, and the demand for careful investigation. The discussion of the problem we shall conduct under the following heads: 1. The Basis of the Law; 2. The Spirit of the Law; 3. Objections to the Law; 4. Value of the Law.

If the doctrine of efficient cause can stand upon its own merits— that is, if it can be separated from other " causes," and be viewed independently—its basis will be made manifest, and its vindication will be supreme. Philosophy can not be charged with a spirit of simplicity, either in the distinctions it makes, the terms it employs, or the systems it constructs. So great sometimes are the systems it builds—for example, Hegel's and Kant's—that one wearies in trying to remember them, and often loses sight of the main issue in the superabundant dress with which they are clothed. The doctrine of causation has suffered from philosophical padding until it has staggered with its load. The generic idea of cause, simple enough in itself, has been expanded with the aid of refined distinctions into four different kinds of causes, only one of which is essentially a cause. Would one sweep them out of the circle of investigation, as a servant does the cobwebs from the ceiling, the voice of criticism would be heard; but the problem would be simplified, and the task of solution relieved of embarrassment. Newton advises against the multiplication of causes without necessity.

Plato, in the *Statesman*, distinguishes between "co-causes" and "causes" as follows: "Such arts as do not fabricate the thing itself, but prepare instruments for the fabricating (arts), without the presence of which the proposed work could not be effected by each of the arts, these are co-causes; but those which fabricate the thing itself are causes." Co-causes are secondary causes; but the efficient cause is that which produces the thing itself; it stands to the result in the relation of a creative power.

Neither Aristotle's famous four-fold division of causes nor Plato's "co-causes," nor any secondary causes, belong to a study of the creating or originating cause of things. Separating the latter from all other causes, however related they may be to it, its basis can the more clearly be ascertained. The basis of the law—that is, its existence—may be predicated by either the *a priori* or the *a posteriori* method; but the *a priori* method is little less than an assumption. To reason from cause to effect is possible only by assuming the cause, unless the existence of cause can be demonstrated without any reference to effect, but effect is involved in cause. The idea of cause is implicit with the idea of effect, and neither can be considered as if the other did not exist. The *a priori* method, therefore, involves an assumption.

To reason from effect to cause requires no assumption whatever. Effect is a fact, and is not in dispute; *cause* is in dispute. To enforce the doctrine of causation by first assuming it is not the truest way of defending or defining it. The basis of the law of causality is in the *a posteriori* method of reason. Given an effect, the first inquiry relates to what produced it. "We pick up a round pebble from the beach," says Balfour Stewart, "and at once acknowledge there has been some physical cause for the shape into which it has been worn." The color of a leaf, the sides of a crystal, the fins of a fish, the velocity of the wind, the approach of the seasons, are suggestive of cause. The inquiry raised is usually simple, not complex, and the answer expected is not complex, but simple. The cause, not causes, we seek to know. Examination and reflection may lead to the consideration of co-causes, but the mind's first inquiry is for a single cause. The basis of the law is in the intuitional structure of the mind, acting in the *a posteriori* manner for the ascertainment of truth. There is nothing stronger than an intuitional law or truth. Gravitation is not an intuitional law; it must first be observed, then verified by experiment. Intuitional laws or truths require no independent verification. The *criteria* by which they may be determined are as follows: 1. Self-evidence; 2. Logical priority; 3. Universality; 4. Necessity.

By these criteria, the law of causality, or its basis in rational intuition, may be discovered. A noise is heard in Indianapolis at six o'clock every morning. A stranger will inquire the cause. A savage, an Egyptian, a Chinaman, if in the city, will make the same inquiry. The great cannon at the arsenal is fired at that hour, and the whole city hears it. The stranger's inquiry for the cause is based upon the following conditions: it is *self-evident* that there is a cause; the idea of cause *antedates* every thing else; his inquiry is the inquiry of all who hear it for the first time, and is in a sense *universal*; and he finds it absolutely *necessary* to make it. The idea of cause is an intuitional idea. It finds expression, therefore, in all languages, it is the underthought of all science, it is the leading factor in all history, and the essential element in all religion.

When Mill attributes the idea to the habit of "association," he makes no explanation of it at all; for it may be asked, whence the habit of associating a cause with an effect, if there is no absolute connection or relation between them? Comte denies that *cause* may be known; but the denial is compatible with a faith in the existence of the principle of causation. One may not know cause, but believe in cause. That is a narrow view of universal history which limits the interpretation of the order of things to a mere succession, which reduces natural phenomena to a series of antecedents and consequents without any known connection, which denies a *nexus* between historic events, and emphasizes the visible progress of the ages as an accidental and undesigned order. "We think things," says Kant, "in the relation of cause and effect;" we can not think otherwise. The idea of mere succession in nature and history is objectionable, because it contains not the key to an explanation of things; it can not even explain itself. If nature or history is a succession of events without causal order, there will be some difficulty in tracing the succession; but even allowing succession and that it can be traced, the tracer, going back, will finally reach a time when there was a *first* event. A first event in the line of succession is inevitable. No difference what it was, it occurred; and, occurring, the mind comes forward with its demand for explanation. Admit that both nature and history are *successions*, from which the causal order and the law of causality have disappeared, the beginning of nature and history was not a succession. There was an antecedent that did not follow a consequent, but there never was a consequent that did not follow an antecedent. Whence the first antecedent?

Advocates of succession are embarrassed by a dilemma, as difficult of solution as any thing presented in philosophy. Dr. Carpenter insists that scientists confine themselves to the *order* of nature, and theologians study the *cause* of nature. This is a division of labor which, observed by both parties, will result in the discovery of both the order and the cause of nature. Order and cause are two things. Mill, Hume, and others have reduced the order to succession, but this is unsatisfactory; and theologians, not a few, have assumed the cause, which is equally unsatisfactory.

The mind demands a cause; its rational activities are grounded in the principle of cause, and can be explained on no other principle. The idea of cause is a rational intuition; it may be urged as a religious precept and a philosophical principle, but its foundations are in the consciousness, or the rational exercise of mind. An inquiry may be raised at this point. Will a phenomenon father its cause? Will an event point unerringly to the particular influence that produced it? What causes dew, frost, hail, snow, rain? Intuitionally, we decide at once, as the snow falls, as the rain pours, that it has been caused; the idea of cause is irresistible; but what the cause is, the intuitions do not decide. There is need, therefore, of other faculties, or the exercise of other mental powers. Reason now exerts itself to find out the particular cause, but is inactive until the intuitions first suggest that there is a cause. Intuition originates the thought of cause; reason seeks to know the cause. The basis of efficient cause is, first, *intuitional*, and second, *rational*. We go one step farther, and affirm that the law of causation has a reliable basis in *experience*. Hume opposed miracles on the ground, as he alleged, that they were contrary to experience. In his judgment, experience is a standard or the ultimate test of the reality of a thing. Unwilling to concede so much, for it savors of sensationalism, we are quite willing to submit the law under consideration to so severe a test. For, if it is contrary to universal experience that effects are caused—in other words, if events occur without being caused—it will be difficult to convince men of the operation of the law of causation in nature, or win their faith in it as a principle. If required to point out the *nexus* between an effect and its cause, in order to establish faith in the connecting link, it can be done in cases without number; but no argument can be made against it in cases in which the *nexus* is concealed, for many of the processes of nature are hidden and can not be announced. To conclude that, since a process is hidden, there is no process, is as reasonable as to conclude that, since the *nexus* is unknown, there is no connection. So far as experience is worth any thing, it establishes that an effect without a cause is impossible. The savage recognizes this principle; a scientist is necessary to explain it. But it is the *fact* of the principle, and not its explanation, that must first be ascertained. The proof of the principle is in the mind's structure and the necessities of thought, or in the intuitions, the reason, and experience.

Accepting the law of causality as established, we inquire more particularly now into the content of the law itself, or the processes of its exhibition both in nature and history. With Dr. McCosh's definition of cause we can not express unqualified satisfaction. "Cause," he says, "consists in the mutual action of two or more bodies; that is, their action on each other." This is a limitation of the arena of cause to physical existences, precluding the operation of cause outside of the physical realm, and preventing it where one body only exists. This limitation is not warranted by the facts. It is true, we deal with cause as we see it in the natural universe, but it is not true that the idea of cause involves "mutual action," or a "duality or plurality in causation." If two bodies must exist before cause can operate, if the two must influence each other before an effect is possible, one body is powerless to do any thing in an independent way, or by virtue of its laws. To admit this is to pluck up the law to its very roots. The idea of causation is not *mutual action*, but single, independent action. Regarding causation as the primary law of creation, or as the underlying principle of cosmical order, it implies God's independent action. Creation was not the "mutual action" of God and matter, but the single, independent action of God. If the root-idea of causality is opposed to the idea of "mutual action," its application throughout nature must be grounded in the single, independent action of cause. Mutual action of bodies and forces may subsequently occur, but it is co-operation, it is combination; it is not *causation*.

With Herbart's conclusion, that every action is due to several causes, we can not agree, since it involves the idea of plurality in causation, whereas the idea of causation is simple, and the root of causation is single and independent in creative power. The expression of the principle of cause in the universe, or just how the law of causality maintains itself in the phenomenal world, is a problem over which the strongest minds have pondered with enthusiasm and anxiety. While various explanations of its activity have been framed, they may be reduced to two general propositions, each in content opposed to the other, and each advocated by brilliant and distinguished thinkers: 1. Materialism, atheism, pantheism, and evolution virtually subscribe to the same interpretation, in that they more or less eliminate the divine presence from the universe, assuming that it is self-acting, self-centered, and self-sufficient. 2. Theism asserts divine control, and insists upon the divine presence in the universe. Whatever form the interpretation takes, it is the old question, Is God in the world?

Prof. Tyndall affirms that matter received at the time of its formal organization a quantum of energy sufficient for its purpose until the end; hence, there is no need of divine supervision. Prof. Huxley regards force as a manifestation of something unknown, but which he suspects is a material phase of the 'Deity; but Deity is only present through force. Cudworth suggested the existence of a plastic nature, on which the Creator works, by which to sustain the phenomenal world. Dr. Laycock attributes to nature an organizing intelligence. These represent the different phases of the materialistic conception of the universe in its sustained forms and activities. They are consistent with a theistic conception of the origin of the universe, but in running it on independent principles, or by self-guiding forces, an atheistic world is the result. It now runs itself. The laws, forces, forms, and activities imparted to it in its atomic state are sufficient to preserve, guide, and develop it. The world retains the impelling cause or force communicated to it in the beginning. It is as if one would say that a top, being set in motion, would acquire and retain the impelling motion forever.

Theism, both scientific and Christian, introduces the divine presence everywhere. Lotze represents the scientific side, Dr. B. F. Cocker the Christian idea. *Causation is the direct manifestation of the divine will in phenomena.* God is everywhere present, and in every thing. He personally supervises all things, small and great, in the universe. Force is the energizing spirit of God. He is in nature, not outside. He is in law; he is law. Joseph Cook, expounding this idea and subscribing to the doctrine of divine immanence, says: "We talk of matter as if it were a hand, and not a glove with a hand in it. So far as matter is inert, it is glove only. This glove may be taken off; the supersensible reality at the core of it—the spirit—is God, and is indestructible." Even more explicitly does he express himself: "In a better age science, lighting her lamps at that higher unity, will teach that although he whom we dare not name transcends all natural laws, *they*—the natural laws—*are through his immanence literally God.*" Dr. Cocker glories in the thought of the divine immanence, supporting it on Scriptural grounds, and is as conclusive as Joseph Cook and Lotze in the use of the scientific method.

The danger of the doctrine of the Divine Immanence is its pantheistic complexion, which, however, is guarded against by the accompanying doctrine of the Divine Transcendency. God is in nature, but above it. He dwells in the universe, but is superior to it, preserving, guiding, and developing it. He not only authorizes phenomena, but he produces them. He is the causal spirit in the universe. He not only originated the universe, but he also sustains it. He is not only the First Cause, but also the present Cause. *He is Cause.* To this conclusion both science and religion must come. God is not an outsider or spectator of his works. He is in his works, and yet different from them. One of his ancient names was "mover;" he is the mover, the originator, of all changes, of all activities. Believing in the principle of cause, it has its embodiment in personality, manifesting himself in law and phenomena.

The *objections* to the law of causality must receive attention. In these pages we seek the truth, and if belief in the law is a result of education, or if it have no foundation in fact, it is well to know it. If valid objections can be raised to the principle, they ought to be candidly reviewed. Alexander Bain declares the doctrine of efficient cause unimportant; but if this is true, we are at a loss to know what is important. The doctrine implies a going to the root of things, just what he has been trying to do by the materialistic route, but without success. It can only be unimportant in the sense that some other doctrine is more important; practically, the social and moral questions of life may be more important; metaphysically, it is the only important question—there is no other question. The correct interpretation of the law of causality includes the correct interpretation of God and the universe.

The standing objection of Hume, Mill, and Comte, that the phenomena of causation, or the phenomena of succession, may be recalled for examination. The constancy of succession, or the uniformity of like results from like conditions or causes, has been overlooked by the objectors. Why is there never a break in the royal line of succession? Certain effects always follow certain so-called causes. Why no disturbance of this fact if there is no connection between antecedent and consequent? The uniformity of result demonstrates the existence of law, for law is the expression of uniformity.

One might venture to ask, What is meant by succession? Hume could only mean antecedent and consequent, without relations; for the admission of relations is implicit with order, and order is implicit with law, and law is implicit with intelligence. But materialistic philosophy points with pride to the law of relativity, by which it hopes to demolish the idea of the Absolute and Unconditioned; hence the idea of antecedent and consequent without relations is philosophically absurd. So soon, however, as the idea of relation is introduced, the idea of order, implying the reign of law, imperatively appears, and this compels recognition of causality as a principle in nature. Succession is involved in causation. Without a regular, uniform succession the theory of causation can not be maintained; without causation, succession is impossible; for the process of things would be irregular, if there was any process at all. Succession is the proof of causation, and causation the *raison d'être* of succession.

It has been supposed that causation is a word that refers to a mere coincidence of events, and can not rightly be applied to an established order; that is, since certain results have happened when certain contemporaneous influences were recognized, it has been inferred that the two were in inviolable association, from which the law of causality has been framed. For example, Sirius, or the dog-star, was observed to appear when the Nile began to rise, and the Egyptians surmised that the star caused the river to swell and overflow. This is the theory of coincidence. Coincidence and causation are as different as time and gravitation. Coincidence may occur without any connection or relation whatever between the facts; it can not in any sense belong to the category of cause. Coincidence is a sham; like the rebels at Manassch hoisting the Union flag, it appears in the camp of causation, and attempts to capture it. It is a rebel against the truth.

It has been pointed out that what is called Cause is only another word for effect; that is, nature is a circle of forces or influences, each of which is the effect of something preceding, and becomes in turn the agency of something following. Natural phenomena are the products of an endless repetition of forces, interchanging as causes and effects, whose scientific classification is resorted to for the better understanding of nature. No denial is made that nature's programme appears like a rotation of causes and effects; but since a cause becomes an effect, and an effect a cause, the law of causation is not imperiled, but the rather established. The repetition of causes points to the influence of the principle, and the conversion of effect into causes is proof that it is in power. That a cause becomes an effect is proof that as cause it has served its purpose; it does not show that cause did not exist. The classification of causes and effects is in accordance with the facts of nature, and therefore not imaginary.

Against the association of personality with causation, the doctrine of the equivalence of effects and their causes has been urged; but the doctrine itself is still in dispute. In a certain sense every cause must be equal to its effect, and the total of causes concerned in the origin of the universe must be equal to the phenomena of the universe. If these causes are sufficient for effects, there is no room, as there is no necessity, for personal agency, and cause is left as a self-managing something, without personal form or spirit. This not only empties it of power, but reduces it to a shadow that can not be traced. In the scientific sense, causes and effects are not equal; but science is slow to learn this great truth. If the doctrine of the equivalence of cause and effect can be maintained, then, indeed, there is no need of going outside of a particular cause for a particular effect. But effects sometimes far transcend the cause. In many cases there is a great disproportion between causes and effects, for, as saith the Scripture, "Behold, how great a matter a little fire kindleth." Hermann Lotze, admitting that the idea of the equality of causes and effects obtains in philosophy, pronounces it an error, and explains its origin in loose conceptions. "It would in itself be an inexactness to try to establish an equation between the ' cause,' which is a thing, and the effect, which is a state or an occurrence," says the German metaphysician. He denies that the " effect must be the precise counterpart of its cause," and sees no ground for identifying in kind and degree the cause with its effect. To insist on identity, resemblance, or equality between cause and effect is philosophically absurd, according to Lotze. The idea of causation implies divine sovereignity, or a supervision of forces for the production of given ends; and this may require the combination of forces or causes, so that the smallest fact in nature may be the result of a number of forces or causes in operation. In this sense there is " duality or plurality in causation;" but plurality is possible only because there is personality behind it.

Mr. Mill, speaking of the seventy chemical elements, observes that they exhibit no evidence of being *effects*; there is nothing in them to prove that they were created, and if they were not created, the universe of which they are composed was not created. Such a statement must have been projected for the purpose of compelling the believer in causality to declare what constitutes an effect, for if one is ignorant of the nature or evidence of an effect, one can not found an *a posteriori* argument for Cause. The proof that oxygen is an effect, he thinks, is wanting. Is this because of its simplicity? Is it a simple element?

Until it is fully demonstrated that the primary elements are not complex in constitution, it can not be affirmed that they have not the appearance of effects.

Granting, however, that the primary elements are simple, it is as inconceivable that they were produced without cause as that the universe itself was uncaused. This means the eternity of the elements, if it means any thing. But if the elements have existed eternally, there was a period when they were organized into worlds, and organization required the intervention of Cause. Even in this aspect of the case the idea of Cause is not eliminated from the history of the universe, for if Cause was not involved in the existence of atoms or elements, it was involved in the organization of the universe.

The eternity of the elements is a serious inference if the facts justify it, and a brazen assumption if they do not. The statement that an element does not appear to be an effect suggests a question or two. What is an effect? That which is produced by a cause, says Webster. This definition does not meet the present emergency, for as yet it is not certain that there are any effects. An effect, in order to establish the fact that it is an effect, must contain the proof of it in its own nature, as in its functions, or adaptations, or possibilities; there must be something in it which goes to show that it was produced. Take oxygen. What can be said of it in proof that it is an effect? In its original state it is a gas, but it is generally diffused, entering into combination with the solid earth, and constitutes about one-half of the entire mass. In its acriform condition it is capable of almost illimitable expansion, and remains unchanged, no difference how great the temperature or pressure applied to it. Prof. Cooke affirms that "twenty tons of pressure on a square inch are not sufficient to reduce oxygen to a liquid condition." Recently, however, it has been reduced to a liquid. It maintains its *identity*, whether as gas or liquid. Then oxygen is the well-known supporter of combustion, and indispensable to life. Without analyzing the element, or considering its character further, it is clear that in its expansive tendency, in its ability to combine with all other materials, in its self-preservation, and its relation to combustion, it sustains its reputation as the most useful element in the economy of nature, and bears the image of an effect. Go through the list of primary elements, analyzing each and all, and the same conclusion will be reached; they are effects; they contain the proofs in themselves of having been produced. To deny the appearance of effect to the elements is a stepping-stone to a denial of effect in the universe, which means the banishment of Cause. As the first step can not be taken, so the second is improbable. The fact of Cause still remains.

The admission of the law of causality in the realm of nature is fatal to the mechanical hypothesis of the origin and development of nature; on this account materialism denies its existence. The law presupposes the presence of a superintending mind, which the materialist feigns not to discover anywhere. To oppose the doctrine of causation because it hypothecates the doctrine of the divine existence is proof that prejudice is the substance of the opposition. The law is not urged in these pages with reference to a theological tenet, but solely because it is a self-evidencing primary law of nature, the fundamental content of which appears to be the divine presence. The philosophy of the law is one thing, the theology of the law quite another; but it is true that, given its philosophy, its theological bearing manifests itself. For this, however, no one is responsible, the law itself predicating a divine idea.

The law of causality is a stumbling-block of no mean magnitude in the path of the fatalists; hence, one pronounces it unimportant; another reduces phenomenal order to an unconnected succession; another affirms that cause is entirely unknowable. All sorts of definitions, explanations, guesses, and theories, have been proposed to escape the alternative of theism or atheism, but the issue is plainly along this line. The fact of causal order is a demonstration in itself of the Infinite; hence, it must be impeached, and the absurdity of an uncaused universe reiterated until philosophy will wonder if it may not possibly be true. The animus of the assault on the law of causality is its inherent support of the theistic hypothesis.

This prepares the way for a brief consideration of the doctrine of efficient cause in its relation to general truth. By virtue of the causal idea the world appears as the product of law, and exists under and is sustained by law. Science has strained itself to establish that nature is under the dominion of law; but it must be understood that law is universal, because the principle of causation is supreme. Causation is law—the first law. Law is the content of superintending wisdom, and nature is its theater or receptacle. Every thing, even the wind that blows, is under the surveillance of law, as the Signal Service Bureau of the United States has ascertained. But law, or the expression of order in nature, is impossible except as the principle of causation underlies and precedes it. Causation is the explanation of universal law.

The doctrine of efficient cause is the key to the highest philosophy. In order that the mind's activities may be reliable, it must be governed by certain primary principles, of whose existence there is no dispute. The astronomer does not halt in his calculation to consider or prove that a circle involves three hundred and sixty degrees. If he can not rely on this conclusion, he can not be certain of the truth of any calculation. In geometry there are a multitude of axioms the truth of which is not contingent on repeated demonstration; they must be accepted, or the mathematician can not proceed. Likewise in philosophy there must be axiomatic truths requiring no further elucidation, if philosophical inquiry can proceed. Among the axioms of the highest philsophy is this of efficient cause. Without it, there is neither starting-point nor landing-place. Materialists have floated in a sea of doubt, because they started from nowhere and were making for no headland. *The best cure for a false philosophy is the orthodox doctrine of cause.* Schopenhauer and Hartmann accepted the doctrine, but, stripping it of personal features, and resolving it into impersonal force, or an unconscious activity, they sunk it to the level of a physical agency, and pessimism was the result. One may assent to *a* law of causality, and be fatalistic; if he ascertain *the* law of causation, he becomes theistic.

It is patent to him who reads that the doctrine of efficient cause justifies faith in the doctrine of final cause; in other words, the two causes are related like two brothers. They rise and fall together. A final cause, as we shall hereafter show, is often the key to an efficient cause; and an efficient cause, as we now declare, is often a key to a final cause. If the principle of design is existent in nature, it must be the fruit of the principle of efficiency in nature. Design carried out implies previous executing force. Teleology is one of the paths to the law of causation. If effect is proof of cause, design is proof of efficiency. The two links are inseparable, and opposition to one is opposition to the other. Hostility to the law of causation means a broad attack on all the "causes" in philosophy—a shipwreck of efficient means the shipwreck of final cause.

The value of the doctrine of causation will appreciate as its relation to the theory of development is disclosed. Not disputing that the natural universe is a gradual development from germinal or atomic forms, through manifold stages, into final and fixed forms, it is difficult to understand the system of development which it exhibits without the pre-supposition of the causative principle. If nature's development is a *system* of development, it implies causal order; if it is not a system of development, it is a question if there has been any development. Development signifies system; system is pregnant with law; law is the sign of Cause. Dr. McCosh represents development as *organized causation*, a strong putting of the truth. Any development without directing cause, or independent of law, would be the development of irregularity; but it is agreed that nature is a regular development of order, beauty, adaptation, proportion, and utility, which can not be accounted for in the absence of the causative spirit. Thus the scientific theory of development, if true, is a corroboration of the law of causality.

The doctrine has its practical features. We sometimes speak of the stability of nature or of the universe, meaning that the natural order of phenomena will continue without a probability of disorder or wreck. Business, commerce, navigation, travel, manufacturing and agricultural interests, are conducted without much anxiety, so far as nature's order is involved in these interests. We expect no change of law. The seasons will come and go as in the past, the laws of atmospheric phenomena will abide, chemical principles may be trusted to-morrow as they were yesterday, and mathematical truths will not deceive. The stability of the universe is insured through the presence of the principle of Cause, which, establishing nature's order as the best, will perpetuate it until its mission is accomplished.

In the truest sense the principle is the foundation-stone of the truest religion. The greatest question of religion is that of a personal God. The mind readily espouses the idea of a Supreme Power; but to apprehend the Power as a personal being, to understand his character, to formulate his dispositions, to catalogue his attributes, and express his relations to all things, involves the highest thought; it is, indeed, impossible to the highest human thought. Philosophers from the time of Thales until now have agonized over the problem of the supreme power; they have sought to know if there is a personal being, endowed with infinite faculties, or if Force inherent in matter constitutes the sum of infinite cause, or if there is a principle of life impacting nature, yet derived from an underived source, too remote for human discovery. At this point the law of causality affords not a little relief. Either the universe created itself, or it was created; but as the idea of a self-made universe is absurd, the other idea of creation may be maintained on the Platonic dialectic of refutation or contradiction. Creation once admitted involves the truth of the causative principle. Mysterious it is, but it is not absurd. Causation points to the First Cause. All causes, mediate and immediate, become multiples of the First Cause.

If causation points to an absolute Cause, it is a safe principle on which to build a religion. It goes back to original power. Causation is the autograph of the Deity. In the light of such a revelation all objections to the principle must vanish; a true philosophy and a true religion should shake hands over it, agreeing fully with Paul that "the invisible things of him from the creation of the world are clearly seen, being understood by the things that are made, even his eternal power and Godhead."

# CHAPTER XI.

## THE CONTENT OF FORCE.

PROFESSOR TAIT'S survey of advances in the physical sciences justifies the conclusion that force is only a name, the thing represented by it being unknown. Is the scientist only a name-maker, or a dealer in substances? Is philosophy a barren nominalism, or is it the discovery of realities? This Adamic habit of naming things, powers, and manifestations, is a great convenience, and indeed the first step in progress, but entirely unsatisfactory if one must stop with it. Wrapped up in names are problems, facts, laws, principles; at least we fancy they mean something; if they do not, they are of no more value than Plato's "wind-eggs." In this chapter we treat of the name and the thing, the sign and that which is signified. The name is the index to the reality, in quest of which men are consuming their lives.

What is Force? In the *Parmenides* Plato represents force as "the sudden," or that which has the power to change. "For the sudden," he says, "seems to signify some such thing as changing from it to either. For there is no change from standing, while standing; nor a change from motion, while in motion; but that wonderful nature, 'the sudden,' is situated between motion and standing, and is in no time; and into this and from this, that which is moved changes, for the purpose of standing still; and that which stands for the purpose of being moved." Every translator of this passage confesses that it is ambiguous; but we introduce it to show that Plato's conception of force was that of an influence which affected motions and changes, or is the cause of both stability and instability in the universe. He names it "the sudden" because it is the unexpected, the unknown. While this definition is indefinite, it is as comprehensive as any that modern science has succeeded in inventing, and in some respects less objectionable, for it points to the theistic notion.

Any observer of nature must conclude that in, through, and over all its departments or kingdoms is an influence to which every thing is more or less obedient, an influence originating, controlling, perpetuating, and voicing supreme governmental ideas, which, the more they are studied, seem to reflect the presence of a single governing mind. Nature is the theater of motion, activity, growth, decay, and revival. Over all its processes, variations, and developments, through all its history of appearances, a dominant influence has been felt, and is clearly recognizable. To that influence, supreme, lofty, incessant, science has given the name of Force. The selection of the name we do not criticise, since from a scientific view of nature, it is as appropriate as any. The word, as applied, does not contain all the facts; but so far as it means anything, it means the dominant idea in nature, as understood by the inquirer.

The relation of force to matter, which involves either their identification or a statement of their differences, has provoked not a little discussion in philosophic circles, the earlier opinion being an affirmation of their differences, while the later borders on a qualified identification. The common observer resents at once as fictitious, and in a sense impious, the suggestion that force, or the propelling influence of nature, is to any extent identical with nature; but the philosopher does not consult the common observer, who, he imagines, sees with veiled face, and therefore reports incorrectly concerning nature. Is force identical with matter, or are they two empirico-physical principles, with properties and functions entirely unlike? Ludwig Büchner is fond of distinguishing force *and* matter as two eternal elements; but he has been overruled by others, who insist that matter is the product of force; that force is the essential fact, while matter is a shadowy, phenomenal issue. The relation of force to matter in a philosophic sense, may be expressed in three forms: 1. Force is identical with matter; 2. Force is inherent in matter; 3. Force is an independent element. As to the identity of force and matter, the proof is wanting; besides, the pantheistic complexion of the theory must condemn it. Identification is confusion of things essentially separate. Muscular force is not muscle; a crystallizing force is not a crystal.

The Dynamical theory of matter, or the residence of force in matter, has been employed in vindication of the supposition of the identity of the two; but the supposition itself is grounded on the generally admitted belief of the inherency of force in matter. The advocates of "inherency" are numerous, embracing both theistic and materialistic thinkers, who assume it from different motives. Prof. Huxley says, "Matter is all-powerful and all-sufficient;" Minark holds to the theory of "innate forces;" and Büchner divides the forces of matter into physical, chemical, and mechanical. Spencer, employing the word "gravity" as generic, asserts that it manifests itself as heat, light, electricity, magnetism, cohesion, affinity, and gravity, or in seven different forms; but, whatever the form, it belongs to, and inheres in matter. There is but one force, and its forms are convertible into one another. The old division of forces into kinetic or active, and latent has been, or should be, abandoned, for there is no such thing as latent force; but whatever the division, or how numerous the forms, it is a prevalent assumption that force inheres in matter.

The word "inherent," however, is misleading. The materialist means by "inherent," not a quality, but the essential element, the thing itself, and so blots out the distinction between force and matter. Force is inherent in that it is intimately associated with matter, but the association has its limitations. Force is necessary to, but is not the quality of, matter. Force is a necessary *condition*, but not a necessary quality, of matter. The relation is one of condition, but not of quality.

If not identical with matter, and not a quality of matter, Force must be external to matter, and can be understood only as it is separated from matter. The difficulty of separating the two, the materialist magnifies into an impossibility; but the union of force and matter has an analogy in the union of soul and body, which we are aware is to the materialist not only inexplicable but absurd. His opinion aside, force is the soul of matter, to be interpreted as the acting and interacting influence, separate from that on and with which it acts, and as having independent qualities, functions, and purposes. This is going beyond the name to the thing, but an expression of the relation of force and matter involves a definition of terms used. Force is not matter; matter is not force. Force may be inherent in matter, if "inherent" be explained; it is not identical with matter.

As there is a distinction between force and matter, so there is a distinction between force and law, which in some philosophies are regarded identical; hence, the confusion in thinking, and the failure to understand phenomena. Matter is the theater of force; law is the regulation of force. Force acts not only within the limits of space, but also within the limits of law, but is not to be confounded with either. The law of force, or the methods by which force is communicated and conducted, are not as clearly expressed in philosophy as the inquirer might desire. How force acts at all is really a leading question. Hermann Lotze decides that the element of time is not involved in the communication or transmission of force, and also that force can act only at a distance. Accepting these conclusions as correct, they point to certain characteristics of force which do not belong to matter; but the law of transmission yet lacks expression. Certain laws, as the law of gravitation, the law of reflection and refraction, the law of cohesion and adhesion, and the laws of light and sound, are intended to express the methods of activity in the physical world; but while they furnish a clue to the presence of force, they do not strictly define it. The revelation of a method of activity is not equivalent to a revelation of the thing that is active. Hence, law and force, harmonious and suggestive of each other, are distinct and individual.

A still closer distinction will disclose more fully the isolation of force. Force must not be confounded with its manifestations, some of which seem to be forces themselves. The usual classification of forces is a classification of the manifestation of forces. The old terms, "centripetal" and "centrifugal," and the later terms, "vital," "physical," "chemical," "mechanical," which abound in science and philosophy, express only the manifestations of force, and do not convey any idea of its nature. A "centripetal" force is a form of speech intended to represent the *direction* in which force extends itself; a "moving" force is that which produces motion; "vital" force is that which produces life. Motion is a result, and must not be confounded with that which produced it. When force produces force, we can only speak of the latter as secondary and mechanical; for it as inconsistent to confound a secondary or resultant force with the original or producing force, as it is to confound any effect with its cause. When Kant speaks of the forces that occupy space, he can only mean the secondary or mechanical forces inherent in matter, the resultant of the primary force that rules everywhere. Force must be distinguished from forces. Force is not the aggregation of forces. Forces are those manifestations of activity that science denominates physical, chemical, vital, mechanical; force is the parent of forces. Distinguishing force from manifestation or forces, we approach the thing itself.

Matter is the *theater* of force, therefore not force itself; law is the regulation or *method* of force, therefore not force itself; forces are *manifestations* of force, therefore not force itself. Separating it from all its relations and incorporations, we are compelled to deal with force in the abstract, or as the transcendental factor in the universe. Mivart attributes all existences to an "internal force," which he styles a "single form of force," implying that the parent force is capable of transmutations; but it is not a *form* of force we seek, it is force itself.

The necessity of assigning to force some attributes or properties is imperative, if an intellectual conception of it be entertained. The first condition of a conception of any thing is *attribute*. A knowledge of attributes is not a knowledge of substance or reality, but they afford standing-room for thought; and in this case standing-room even is desirable. The difference between an intellectual concession to the existence of force and an intellectual conception of its nature, must be kept in mind, in order to advance beyond a dreamy or imaginative conclusion respecting it. Wanted, manifestations of force—these we have in forces; wanted, the laws of force—these have been named; wanted, the theater of force—this has been pointed out; *wanted*, the *attributes* of force—these we seek.

It is a superb fact that, going out of phenomena, or merely observing the play of things, there seems to be the manifestation of but a single force; that is, the unity of force, notwithstanding its varieties, may be proclaimed. This is important, beyond all question; it simplifies the problem of attributes; it harmonizes the secondary or derivative with the primitive or original force. From a superficial observation of nature, one might conclude that force is suicidal, so incessant is the conflict or antagonism of secondary forces. To preserve the balance or sustain the equilibrium, however, the observer soon discovers that action and reaction are equal, and that, however violent and aggressive the destructive tendencies, the recuperative powers of nature are equal to any emergency or distress. Counter-irritation is also a principle in nature, intended to preserve its order and insure its stability. Gravitation draws downward, but the blade of wheat overcomes it and shoots upward. Here is the victory of one force over another, the resultant being, not destruction, but the conservation of a benevolent end. On the other hand, the majestic oak graces the hill-side, but a thunderbolt demolishes it. This is a victory of a destructive force, but it is not always in operation. Benevolent forces are in constant operation; destructive forces only occasionally manifest themselves; so that, by a just balance of the facts, it is clear that the conflict of forces is in the interest of benevolent ends, reflecting the teleological principle, and pointing to a wise supervision of nature.

Besides, the fact must not be overlooked that the conflict in nature is the conflict of purely secondary forces. Original force is not in conflict with secondary forces, but the secondary forces themselves, as gravitation and cohesive attraction, are in antagonism. The conflict is the result of the variety of forces and the variety of ends to be accomplished by them; hence, it is more of a seeming than a real conflict. It is a conflict for the best ends, or a combination for the execution of the purposes of nature. Taking this view of the complex forces of nature, it points to an underlying unity, a unity of idea, and a unity of force.

The modality of force in no wise contradicts the hypothesis of the unity of force. Herbert Spencer now regards all imponderables as modes of one force. The variety of mode in the expression of force is no greater than the variety of color into which a ray of light may be dissolved. Colors do not invalidate the conclusion of one light; modes of force do not invalidate the conclusion of one force. The unity of light is no truer than the unity of force. As electricity is one, but is called by different names as its manifestations differ, so force may be chemical, physical, mechanical, or vital in manifestation, and be the same. Science has drifted into the doctrine of the unity of a supreme force; there is no polytheism in science. Spencer speaks of an "infinite force;" Faraday, Helmholtz, Carpenter, Liebig, and Meyer stand as sponsors for the scientic dogma of unity of force.

Scientific minds quote approvingly the doctrine of the correlation and conservation of forces, or the convertibility of forces, as the proof of the relationship of forces, or the final unity of force. To the doctrine itself we make no objection; to the materialistic conclusion that the sum of these forces constitutes the entire force of the universe, we demur, for no number of secondary forces will equal the supreme force from which they are derived. Mr. H. C. Carey is inclined to reduce all forces to electricity, even insisting that it closely resembles brain power; but this is carrying the deduction to an extreme. Whether the atomic unit is hydrogen, and the supreme secondary force is electricity, we care not, only so that the supreme force is not confounded with either. Reference is sometimes made by scientists, especially by Spencer, to *persistence of force*, by which is meant the preservation of force in one form or another; that force itself never is lost; that it will reappear in new forms if its old manifestations cease to exist. This is an index to the character of force; it is one and unchangeable in essence forever.

Chemistry has been defined as the identification of the one in the many, or unity in the manifold; and, so far as it distinguishes the one from the many, it is a very concise and expressive definition; but so far as it confounds the one with the many, it is a learned support of pantheism, and must be rejected. From the apparent conflict of secondary forces, from the modality of forces, from the correlation and conservation of forces, from the persistence of forces, and from the definitions of science, the conclusion of the unity of force seems scientifically warranted. In the highest sense, there are not two forces; *there is one only*. This is simplification; this is progress.

Let us advance to another conception of force. The word itself conveys the idea of resources, and includes possibility, sufficiency. When one speaks of the power of a government, several things are signified, as naval and military equipments, wealth, patriotism, religion, and the common intelligence of the nation. The word "force," taken in the abstract, is suggestive of a complex idea; it suggests resources, possibilities, reserved powers. It means accumulation, exhaustless energies. In the sense now considered, the universe stands as its product, the masterpiece of its work; no conception is too great for its capability, no execution too small for its notice. The relation of force to the universe is the relation of creative power to its product. Force is the spirit of creation, the spirit of rule, guidance, preservation. It is competent both to create and rule.

Creation involves, presupposes omnipotence, and omnipotence has been regarded as a credential of personality. Schopenhauer's idea of the ultimate principle is *will,* or blind, unregulated, and therefore capricious *will-power.* Whether the "infinite force," as Spencer styles it, is the force of will or the force of anything else, its omnipotence points to an omnipotent personality, and yet is not conclusive of it. Again, whatever the force is, it is invisible; it lies back of phenomena. It is all around us; it is in every thing; it propels every thing; it breathes life and death everywhere; it is ceaseless, and slumbers not. The invisibility of force is consistent with the universality of force, and both make for an invisible, universal personality; at least they raise the suspicion of personality. Even science proclaims the invisibility of reality; the visible is a sham or a shadow. The hiding of his presence is as potent as the hiding of his power.

Thus far we have ascertained the *locus* of the activity of Force— the universe of space and time; the *method* of its activity—law; the *products* of its activity—phenomena; and necessarily some of its *attributes,* or conditions of existence, as unity, power, invisibility, and infinity. Shall we stop here?

Stopping at this point, we should conclude for an all-powerful, invisible, impersonal Force. As yet, there is no absolute proof of personality, for all these attributes or conditions might co-exist, co-operate, and unite in a single force, which would be wanting in other evidences of personality.

Strictly speaking, if Force is a Personality, it must possess other attributes than these named, for a materialist may agree with our conclusions thus far and be a materialist still. Are there other attributes?

The revelation of nature or the universe is the only book whose pages the scientist will consult, and if the imprint of a Personal Force is not on the first page he is not inclined to believe in such a force. Looking through the volume, he would be compelled to admit what at first he indignantly rejected.

Keeping in the background the idea of personality as the goal of investigation, we proceed, by a purely scientific method, to inquire for other attributes of the infinite force, regardless of what they shall teach on the subject. The suspicion grows into conviction, as one makes a tour through nature, that the omnipotent and impersonal force, the spirit of creation, is conscious of itself. Neither gravitation nor crystallization makes an impression of self-consciousness, because they are secondary forces or results; but the supreme force, in its government of nature, makes the impression that it knows what it is doing. If it is ignorant of itself, or insensible of its activities, it is inexplicable how it acts with uniformity under similar conditions, and equally difficult to explain its unity. To admit consciousness to man and deny it to the supreme Force is to raise man above the supreme Force; but this involves absurdity. Absurd or not, man is the supreme Force, or the infinite force is conscious of itself. Consciousness, however, is the capital attribute of personality.

Secondary forces are without self-consciousness, and without regulation, direction, and control, they would wreck the universe. Let electricity have a chance, and it would burn up the cosmos. Gravitation unrestrained would shatter the firmament. Fire unbridled would reduce the earth to a cinder. Something controls. Natural, secondary forces are under restraint, embarrassed by the presence of a superior influence, and order prevails throughout the dominions. On the whole, nature is calm because of a supernatural presence. The subserviency of secondary causes to the First Cause, the restraining hand upon nature's erratic and rebellious dispositions, is proof that the Force above nature is conscious, understanding not only what it is doing, but what ought to be done to preserve the peace of the universe.

If the supreme Force be conscious of itself, it follows that order, peace, masterly rule, and development are ends contemplated and sought by this Force. The activity of Force is in some way allied to its results. This alliance is not only chronological, which is all that materialism has hitherto allowed, but it is causal, which implies a contemplation of results, or thought and purpose embodied in activity. This is teleology! We know it. The omnipotent, self-conscious Force is, *per* necessity, a teleological Force, acting with something in view, seeking certain ends, and, at all events, promoting order, stability, and development. It certainly conducts itself as if it had these ends in view.

Were it indifferent to ends, it might sleep or violate the conditions of order, or it might withdraw itself entirely from the world of matter. If it is foreign to matter, as we had heretofore conjectured, what is the bond of association with matter but the ends it consciously seeks to secure? As nature is the embodiment of order, beauty, adaptation, and development, these must be the ends of the supreme

Force; and if man is its highest product, then intelligence and holiness must be added to the designs according to which its activities are regulated. For if order, beauty, adaptation, intelligence, and holiness were not designed by the supreme Force, it is difficult to explain their existence. Dr. J. W. Dawson affirms that the science that rejects the divine principle in creation is "impotent to explain nature." So we think, and add that nature is not explained at all unless it was designed, and design establishes personality.

Governed by the reasoning indicated, the infinite Force appears to be a self-conscious, thinking, rational force. On this ground man is justified in becoming a worshiper. Beyond this philosophical outline, or preparation for the theistic affirmation, we need not now advance.

What is Force? Kant says it is an endowment of God. John Fiske, a disciple of Spencer, says, if he must choose between the expressions, "God is a spirit" and "God is a force," he will choose the latter. In the philosophical sense Force is a name, and not a definition. Even the philosophers are suspecting that it is an insufficient name for the thing it pretends to represent, and they are therefore quietly substituting the word "energy," as more expressive of the spirit of creation or matter. After another decade "energy" will be outlawed, and another word proposed. What word? What is the imcommunicable, the unnamed word yet to be spoken by the philosopher? Thomas Carlyle said: "Force, force, everywhere force! Illimitable whirlwind of force which envelops us; everlasting whirlwind, high as immensity, old as eternity—what is it? It is Almighty God!" Force—Energy—God. The first a name; the second a definition; the third a Personality. To this philosophy will come. Weary with its materialistic phraseology, it will consult the language of religion for the Unnamed, and find it in—*God.*

---

## CHAPTER XII.

### THE FIRST CAUSE.

SCHLEGEL affirms that the idea of God is the only idea, all others being derivative and subordinate; and Lotze teaches that the "absolute, living and creative Spirit alone *is*," all else being secondary, and the effect of one all-sufficient cause. The study of this Idea is the imperative of all preliminaries.

The problem of the First Cause is the problem of the universe.

Given the First, and the descending series through infinite gradations and to an infinite number may be traced, arranged, explained. Without it confusion reigns in inquiry, and conclusion is the merest conjecture. A Beginner and a beginning—one or the other is required; one implies the other; to find one is to find both; to find one or the other is the object of the mysterious searchings of philosophy. To accept either without demonstration is contrary to the function of philosophy; to reject both until demonstrated prevents demonstration. The problem embracing the questions of self-existence, the essentia of being, the attributes of absolute spirit, and its relations to phenomena is too large to be confined to a single aspect; to be understood it must be grasped in its magnitude, and every feature receive exhaustive analysis. Philosophy, tireless in its purpose, but changeable in its methods, has undertaken to reduce the idea of God to a concrete form; but its results have been far from satisfactory.

We shall examine the different schools of thought which three centuries have produced in the attempt to solve the first and final problem, namely, the *original causer of the universe*, observing that up to this hour the problem is unsolved. Varying in methods of reasoning, these systems have a single aim, and when closely studied reveal an inner bond of connection, as if leagued together in a destructive purpose, which they propose to accomplish each by methods of its own. In the nineteenth century, or the latest philosophy, the student discovers a reproduction or imitation of the philosophical fabrics of the ancient Greeks, Schopenhauer, Hartmann, Spencer, and Häckel having advanced but a little beyond Democritus, Heraclitus, or the Ionics in general. They often whistle the old tunes of Greece, but palm them off as the original melodies of the modern musician. If, however, these systems exhibit an originality of thought in the investigation of the problem of problems, they relapse into the same iconoclastic conclusions which the old Grecian materialists foretold. Nothing essentially new, certainly nothing striking in results, may be anticipated from a study of the materialistic phases of modern thought.

In what manner philosophy has considered the problems, what processes it has adopted, and what conclusions reached, we are now prepared to learn. To exhibit these inquiries and their results, we set in tabular form the leading philosophies of modern times, or those which have exercised a superior influence in the field of investigation.

I. The creed of Sensationalism or Empiricism, namely, knowledge is derived from sensation, necessarily precludes by its limitations any knowledge whatever of the First Cause.

II. The embryonic philosophy of Positivism, which teaches that knowledge is limited to material phenomena, and that the principle of causation is irrational, is inadequate to the interpretation of a First Cause.

III. The Common Sense Philosophy, heralding ultimate facts, but unable to explain them, affords no ground for belief in a great First Cause.

IV. In Pessimism, the melancholy wail of atheistic conviction, there is no foundation for faith in a Supreme Being.

V. Idealism, an ebbing and flowing tide, rising betimes to supernatural heights, sinks back into unsatisfying sentiment, leaving the mind bewildered rather than contented respecting the character of the First Cause.

VI. The philosophy of *Relativity*, imprisoning knowledge within the walls of the phenomenal, opens no trap-door into the mysteries of the Infinite.

VII. The theory of Associationalism, anchoring itself in the correlation and conservation of forces, sinks lower than any in ignorance of the First Cause.

VIII. The philosophy of Evolution, or Spencerianism, instead of carrying the mind to starlit heights of vision, sinks it into the tertiary depths of impenetrable nothingness.

These let us consider in their order.

Beginning with Sensationalism, its failure to discover the Infinite, with both its process and object understood, is not surprising. Turning its back upon the Infinite, it never wheeled around faceward toward God. Aristotle, having declared that knowledge is derived from sensation, not only disturbed the thinkers of his age, but also suggested a theory that the moderns appropriated, building upon it a materialistic philosophy, damaging both to intellectual research and the religious spirit. Bacon, wedded to the physical sciences, and Hobbes, dealing with metaphysical as if they were physical problems, paved the way for Locke, who came forth as the champion of the theory in his explanation of the laws and operations of the human understanding, that sensation is the source of knowledge. Logically, empiricism must maintain that the condition of knowledge is *a posteriori*; it is derived from without, or at the most from experience, and the mind has no *a priori* power to discover truth, or reflect upon it when presented. Sensationalism, therefore, is experience-philosophy, or the theory of *a posteriori* knowledge, which is essentially atheistic.

To produce an overflow of materialistic sentiment, there must have been in Locke's theory of the mind, or of the origin of knowledge, something that naturally and logically led to it. Atheism is not an artificial result of sensationalism. Locke's starting-point was the denial of innate ideas, or the emptiness of mind until it began

17

to fill up by impressions from external sources. Self-knowledge, or the power to originate ideas, does not belong to mind, as it first manifests itself; it is a mirror, reflecting what is cast upon it. Such a theory allows to the mind no spirituality, no independent, original, self-acting, or self-determining power; it does away with the immaterialism of man at a stroke. Locke meant not to go so far; but the skeptics engineered sensationalism into the camp of materialism without any difficulty. If the human mind is not immaterial, is there any immaterialism? Who will affirm that God is spiritual, if man is not? Accordingly, knowledge consists in the perception of sensations; consciousness is "static, spectacular, sensible;" the soul is mortal; death ends all. Empirical psychology could reach no other conclusion.

What, now, of its relation to the Causer? Evidently, the same method of argumentation which disposes of mind, disposes of God also; and even Locke was compelled by his philosophy to teach that, as knowledge is the product of sensations, man can know nothing of substance, being, or God. Man must float in the world of sensations, like an insect in the atmosphere, impressed by the flow of its currents, without the power of self-direction, or control of impressions. Sensations we know; but substance, being, God, we can not know. From admissions or conclusions so unfortunate, Condillac, Hume, and others were justified in proclaiming a materialism not at all foreseen by the founder of empiricism; and afterward, Bentham and the elder Mill, the one in elaborating his utilitarianism, and the other his materialism, only completed the destructive work that Locke so innocently forged. Indeed, the sensationalism of Aristotle, amplified into a system by Locke, is one of the pillars of modern philosophy, especially English philosophy. Huxley has affirmed that "our sensations, our pleasures, and our pains, and the relations of these, make up the sum total of the elements of positive, unquestionable knowledge." Spencer, as is well known, is an advocate of the experience-philosophy; and, as an evidence of the materialistic character of such philosophy, it is not contrary to fact to state that these latest and living exponents of it affirm that God is unknowable. The First can not be known through the sensations, and as sensation is the sole source of knowledge, there is no possible hope of ever knowing the Divine Cause. Strangely, these advocates spurn the charge of being materialists, though they support materialism, on the ground that they do not deny the existence of a Supreme Being, but affirm he is beyond us, indiscernible, inaccessible, beyond all knowledge, beyond all thought. What is the difference between a being that can not be known or conceived of, and a being that does not exist? As between them, there is a possible preference, for to say that God does not exist is absolute atheism, but to say that we know nothing about him is only a confession of the feebleness of our powers to grasp a being so infinitely great as the Uncaused must be. The one extinguishes the Uncaused; the other enshrouds him in an inaccessible gloom. The one blots him out; the other says he can not be found. In the latter view he is the Charles Ross of philosophy, believed to exist but forever undiscoverable. Such is the conclusion of Sensationalism touching the problem of the First Cause.

II. What is the interpretation of Positivism? In one respect it is kindred to sensationalism, as, in its affirmation that knowledge is confined to the phenomena of the material world, it can never rise in its apprehensions above phenomena; it can never discern substance, or penetrate being. Comte is the author of this school of philosophers, a man less fearless of consequences than Locke, less systematic in his system, and more eager to overthrow existing religious ideas of God than to establish the truth. Locke searches the laws of mind; Comte, the laws of matter. One is an internal thinker, the other an external thinker. Locke's internal philosophy in its last analysis became external; that is, from the laws of mind he could not predicate subjective existence, or substance back of phenomena. From the laws of matter, cognition of whose phenomena is the sum of knowledge, Comte undertook to establish the same conclusion. Reversing the method, he emerged into the materialism to which empiricism had conducted its friends. Locke was the right hand, and Comte the left, in the movement against immaterialism.

Adequately to establish his conclusion, Comte arrayed his forces against the principle of causation, as recognized by consciousness, and as inductively observed in nature; and refused to accept the Aristotelian category of causes, which has been regarded as almost complete. The notion of cause seems native to mind; it is that from which the mind is led to a conception of the order of the universe, and the existence of the cause of causes. An apple falls from a tree; the mind inquires the cause in the belief that there is a cause; and so strong is the belief that one can not be educated out of it. The force of the idea of cause and its relations to, and proof of, a first cause, Comte could not escape; hence, his effort to annihilate it. He says: "The inevitable tendency of our intelligence is toward a philosophy *radically theological*, so often as we seek to penetrate, on whatever pretext, into the intimate nature of phenomena." That is, a recognition of the phenomena of nature in their relations as causes and effects tends to *establish the theological conception of God*—a conclusion that he proposes to overthrow because his theory requires him to do so. The Idea of God and Positivism can not co-exist; one or the other must go.   After a Spencerian fashion, he does not deny causation, but he pronounces it inscrutable, unknown, unknowable, unthinkable.   What a hiding-place for philosophy is the word "unknown!"  If God is in question, concede his existence, and then blot him out of sight by saying he is unknowable ; if the principle of causation is under consideration, say it exists, but pronounce it unknowable. Phenomena may be known, but not their causes.   What *is* may be studied, but not *why it is*, or what produced it.

Hume varied from this in holding that by causation is meant only a succession ; that is, events are a series of successional facts where legal connection can not be established.   As regards creation he asserts that no one is competent as a witness to testify that causation, as understood to imply cause and effect, was involved in the process. John S. Mill espouses a similar view, reducing causes and effects to mere sequences, or successive acts.   Sir William Hamilton likewise trends toward that *ignis fatuus* by saying that " we have no perception of the causal nexus in the material world."   If the principle of causation be reduced to an appearance of successional movements, without connection, or whose connection can not be established, or on no *a priori* grounds admitted ; if the natural world displays no connectionalism ; if causality, hitherto relied on as invulnerable, is an inductive hallucination ; then the argument for a First Cause has received a blow from which it can scarcely recover.   To eliminate the lurking theology from the principle of causation, to overthrow the principle, as the physician destroys disease, was Comte's great aim. What Locke ignorantly achieved, Comte purposely wrought out, the elimination of the idea of a First Cause.   What deadly, destructive criticism is this?   Sensationalism, beginning with mind, ends in materialism ; Positivism, beginning with matter, pronounces the theology of causation inscrutable, and ends in a godless universe.   The former says God is unknowable ; the latter, that he does not exist. The one names itself a guarded materialism ; the other is atheism.

III.   Next in order, is the philosophy of "Common-sense," its name being suggestive of fair dealing with intuitions, consciousness, historic facts, and metaphysical truths.   Surely, Reid, who represents this phase of speculation, and who discovered the dilemma of his predecessors, will not fall into the same, or an equal error, but point out a way of escape from destructive conclusions.   Let us see.   Reid enunciates the doctrine of ultimate facts, which, in its phraseology, is the core of a great philosophical utterance ; for there must be basal truths, foundation-stones of belief, on which human history may rest.   With Reid, however, these corner-stones are not what philosophy demands ; they are, in short, not basal facts, but intermediate facts which require solution. An initial fact presupposes no anterior fact; it is the end of speculation, solution, inquiry. To such a final fact Reid does not conduct us, for his finals are sensation, memory, imagination, the ordinary operations of intellection, which the common sense of mankind accept as real, and against which it would be useless to contend. Quite vigorously, but really unnecessarily, he makes a defense of these common-sense facts, requiring belief in them, as they are related to life, society, government, and religion.

Back of these, however, we must go if the problem of philosophy be solved. On none of these can the final fact be predicated—the quest of philosophy. Furthermore, the value of the theory is destroyed by Reid's own confession that, going back and recognizing the initial facts as given, no explanation of them is possible—the very thing the truth-searcher demands. The idea of an original fact is self-explanation. A noise occurs in the orchard; the original fact is, not that *something* made the noise, but that a pear fell to the ground, the cause being thus ascertained. Not generals, but particulars, not something, but the *exact somewhat*, the searcher must find, or he is in the dark. A so-called first fact, without explanation, implies that causes are still remote and obscure; but in a true philosophy the distance to the remote must be blotted out, and the obscure must become transparent. According to Reid, a sensation is an original fact which common sense forces us to believe; but the first cause of the original fact, he declares, can not be discovered. In what is this superior to Positivism? Not denying the principle of causation, the theory of Reid implies that it can not be investigated, which advances the inquirer no farther than the dogma of Positivism. As Locke did not intend to furnish a foothold for materialism in his empiricism, but did open the way for philosophical disasters, so Reid, unwittingly, furnished an argument for the most virulent assaults of Positivism.

Respecting the problem of being, or God, Reid stands upon the platform of Locke, Hume, and Kant, none of whom, through their philosophies, ascended the mountain of vision, and from its summit beheld the Cause of the universe. Kant's "phenomena," Locke's "images," Hume's "impressions," and Reid's "beliefs," differing slightly in character, sustained a uniform relation to the problem of problems, echoing a nescience of the character of the Supreme Power, and virtually banishing the Creator from the universe.

In the "Common-sense" philosophy there is the breaking out of a doctrine which, though characteristic of the earlier modern systems of speculative thought, is more patent in Reid, and becomes the shibboleth of the latest apostles of philosophy. According to Locke, sensation is the source of knowledge, which signifies original emptiness of mind, and a qualified imbecility of the mental powers; according to Comte, causation is inscrutable, which signifies mysteries that can not be solved; and now, in the assertion that such mind-facts as memory, imagination, and will, can not be explained, Reid prepares the way for that final accusation of mental imbecility which characterizes Spencer and his followers. Had he contented himself with denying to man the power to comprehend the infinite, he had occupied high and unimpeachable ground; but, in addition thereto, he denies to mind a knowledge of itself, or allows only an acquaintance with its powers and functions, which even the untutored readily admit. Evidently, in Reid, we go not below the surface.

IV. Advancing in our analysis of these systems, we approach a form of philosophy which, icicle-like, has no recommendation other than that it exists. Without heat, without light, it is rigid and comfortless, and goes farther in its surrender than any of the preceding. Pessimism is no longer an abstraction, no longer a stray possibility, but an actual conjecture, the pillar of a philosophy that claims for itself a rational basis. Its earlier exponent was Schopenhauer, a man who hated his mother, and interpreted the universe from a dyspeptic standpoint; its present advocate is Hartmann, a young lion of Germany, eager, bold, self-sufficient. These two thinkers, assigning to others the question of the operations of the mind and the origin of knowledge, saw that the problem of the existence of a Supreme Power is chief, and devoted their energies to its solution. Neither in sensationalism, nor in positivism, nor in the "common-sense" philosophy, is the problem the subject of direct contemplation, its appearance being due to other problems with which it is associated. Contrariwise, the pessimists of Germany discerned the supremacy of the problem of the First Cause, which, instead of ignoring, they sought to explain; but the explanation is an Arctic blast, withering the flowers of faith and hope which hitherto have flourished in the warmer latitudes of religion. Schopenhauer sees everywhere the manifestations of an iron will-power; not an intelligent personal will, but a blind, impersonal force, nature speaking the words of a characterless mover and governor. Force is omnipresent, an idiotic runaway, building up and tearing down with fiendish delight, and creating disorder and misery for the mere pleasure of it. In his view, the world is badly managed, its government being rather one of chance than of purpose, and the hope of improvement is a delusive anticipation. To this pessimistic representation of the world Hartmann does not take exception, but he has attempted to define the will-power of Schopenhauer by adding to it the faculty of reason, and endowing the Somewhat with the powers of being, for will and reason certainly indicate being. Here is ontology; but Hartmann perpetrates a strange paralogism by insisting that this ontological power is unconscious, and that will and reason, though acting in concert, act unconsciously. Hence, God, in the latest pessimism of Germany, is the *Unconscious*. Reason governing and will enforcing, nevertheless the Supreme Power acts without knowing that it acts. Hartmann's God is a somnambulistic creature, *a walking sleeper in the universe*, moving according to the dictates of a rational intelligence, but meanwhile unconscious. Between an unconscious deity and no deity at all, there can be no choice; one is as destructive of worship, faith, prayer, religion, as the other. According to Schopenhauer, God is a wandering idiot; according to Hartmann, he is a sleeping monster. Of both we are equally afraid.

According to the systems previously considered, the First Cause is unknowable; but, excepting the evident atheism of Comte, they impliedly agree that there is a First Cause, which, however, is beyond our investigation. Pessimism lifts the veil, and touches our eyeballs with flashes of celestial light, inviting us to behold what was unknowable to Locke, Hume, Reid, Kant, and Hamilton, and what did not exist, according to Comte. And what is the what? A divine majesty, in truth; but a blind rover, without a throne, a sleepy-head, or a prostrate being, drugged into perpetual unconsciousness by the poison of the universe, or by the tireless vibrations of his own nature. Enough of pessimism.

V. In Idealism philosophy attained a regeneration. From the days of Leibnitz, the idealistic stand-point has been occupied by many noted thinkers, among them Kant, Berkeley, Wolff, Fichte, Schelling, and Hegel, all of whom perceived the reality of subjective experiences, and the superiority of the subjective to the objective in the universe. As contrasted with sensationalism, idealism is as the mountain to the foot-hill; as contrasted with positivism, it is as faith to unbelief; as contrasted with the "common-sense" dogma, one fathoms the ocean while the other skims the surface; as contrasted with pessimism, the one is an unlit tunnel, the other is a sunrise. Idealism is the summit of modern philosophy. Either on that summit stand the philosophers, or on the slopes of sensationalism, positivism, pessimism, associationalism, or materialism.

From the heights of idealism, a clearer view of the divine majesty, a more rational explanation of the universe, is taken; nevertheless, we have somewhat against thee, O Idealism! Not that thy works are evil, but that they are insufficient. Passing Leibnitz, Berkeley, and Wolff, we begin with Kant, as, perhaps, on the whole, the best representative of the earlier idealism, than which the very latest has surpassed it in few particulars, or a wider grasp of the facts involved. The theory of Kant respecting knowledge, though not essentially sensational or empirical, is not an advance, for he held that the world, owing to the intervention of space and time, can not be known as it really is. Phenomena alone can be known; being, substance, must forever remain unknown. With this limitation, a knowledge of God, from the evidence of external signs, is absolutely impossible. The step from phenomenon to God can not be taken. Seeing the destructive tendency of the theory, and its kinship to empiricism, Kant did not press it as the conclusion of philosophy, but as a speculation, from which he emerged into an all-sufficient idealism. Between empiricism and idealism there is a wide difference, but Kant escaped the one and settled in the other through the avenue of the Reason. Of the Pure or theoretical and the Practical Reason he affirms that the former deals with abstract or metaphysical notions, the latter with common principles or facts, or the higher problems in a common manner. As against this division, it may be urged that the same powers exercised by the theoretical reason are employed by the practical; wherefore it is difficult to understand why the one reason will reach conclusions the other will not approve. As evidence of the unfitness of the classification, it will be noted that Kant himself declares that, by the Pure Reason, the doctrine of the immortality of the soul, the moral freedom of man, and the existence of God—the three greatest facts—can not be demonstrated. If the theoretical reason, dealing with psychological, cosmological, ontological, and theological ideas, finds itself unable to demonstrate the necessary and the true, then is it essentially weak. Either these great ideas must be abandoned, or a new instrument of defense and demonstration must be found. In the Practical reason, Kant finds a sufficient sustaining force. It disposes of paralogisms; it unties Gordian knots; it disperses fogs; it lifts the darkness; it harmonizes discrepancies, converting discords into concords; it restores the unities, sees the infinite in the phenomenal, and at last demonstrates the existence of God and the immortality of man. Thanks to the Practical Reason!

Again, Kant taught that the practical reason is the source of pure *a priori* knowledge, which was in contrast with the *a posteriori* condition of knowledge as affirmed by Locke, and is a safer theory.

With its weaknesses, the Kantian scheme is elaborate and strong. It served as a breakwater against the sensationalism of Locke, and resisted the destructive tides of materialism, which for a long period threatened to sweep away the bulwarks of religious faith. After Kant, idealism was modified by Fichte, Schelling, and Hegel, three names usually linked together; but that it rose any higher, or that more satisfactory results were reached, may be doubted.

In Hegel we have the consummation of idealism, as in Liebnitz its beginning. Fichte advocated subjective idealism; Schelling, objective idealism; Hegel, *absolute* idealism. Prominently unfolded in Hegel's logic are the doctrines of being, of essence, and of notion, all of which are conceived in a transcendental spirit and discussed in an obscure and subtle manner. As to being, it is *per se;* it is the one, but the one is as truly the manifold. Though a variation from Spinozism, it can not be called an improvement or a purification. "What kind of an Absolute Being is that which does not contain in itself all that is actual, even evil included?" asks Hegel. God is this Absolute Being. God is not a "motionless, self-identical, unchangeable being, but a living, eternal process of absolute self-existence"—a developing being, including all development. This is the ideal of idealism.

In his treatment of the doctrine of Notion, the divine being appears in another light. The Notion is subjective, objective, and the Idea. The Idea is the highest logical definition of the Absolute; the Supreme Notion is the Absolute Idea; therefore the Supreme Notion is the Absolute. God is a being of ideas, supreme, lofty, controlling, which is a Platonic conception in a new guise.

Hegel also finds it convenient to ornament his idealism with Christian truth, for he affirms that Christ is the internal idea externalized; in other words, that Christ is externally what God is internally; or, as Paul phrases it, Christ was "God manifest in the flesh." Perhaps Hegelians will resist this interpretation of their master, as being entirely too Scriptural and over-theological; but certain it is that the three advocates of idealism herein mentioned made an exhaustive attempt to harmonize it with Christianity; hence, the theological bias of the highest idealism.

But idealism, even in its refined form, failed of its purpose; it did not unite with Christianity; it did not reveal God. According to Kant, God is indemonstrable by pure reason; according to Fichte, he is the infinite subject; according to Schelling, the infinite mind; according to Hegel, the process of absolute being. None of these is a demonstration; none even a satisfactory definition of the Absolute, or the Eternal God.

VI. The philosophy of Relativity was inaugurated by Sir William Hamilton, who, expounding it with singular clearness and force, and yet in a contradictory way, conceived that the Absolute is unknowable. Reasoning from the law of causation, he demonstrated the existence of a First Cause; reasoning from the law of relativity, he concluded the First Cause is unknowable. The law of relativity is, substantially, that knowledge is conditioned upon relations, and therefore no object or being aloof from relation can be known. Respecting physical objects, we know them in their relations, as a tree is known to exist in its relation to the earth, gravity, moisture, sunlight. We do not consider any object separate from fixed or accidental relationships, for outside of relationship we find nothing. Now, is God related or unrelated? If it is shown that he sustains relations, which are recognized by finite minds, then he too is knowable; but if he is outside of all relation, then he is outside of human knowledge. Hamilton's Deity is an unrelated, unconditioned being; therefore, unknowable. But God certainly exists in relation to cause and effect; the universe is the image of his thought, the work of his hands, the effect of his causative agency; he enters into relations, because he acts, thinks, wills, creates, preserves, and governs; and thinking, acting, preserving, and governing imply close relationships. An unrelated God is a do-nothing God, an inglorious idler; a related deity is a necessary postulate of any deity at all. An unrelated deity is, indeed, unthinkable; but such a *nondescript* deity can only be found in a false philosophy.

In order to strengthen the law of relativity in its application to a nescience of the divine being, Hamilton asserts that thought itself is limited by the conditioned; "to think is to condition," or to roam within limits; but the infinite is beyond limitation, and must be unthinkable. Still Hamilton breaks his unbreakable law by thinking of the Infinite, philosophizing on the unconditioned, and declaring his greatness. To predicate infinity of the unthinkable involves an exercise of thought, and in a particular and logical manner; for, unless one know the difference between the finite and the infinite, one can not predicate infinity of any thing. According to Hamilton, we know that the unthinkable, the unrelated, the unknowable, is infinite; but infinite in what? In extent? in wisdom? in power? In something, surely. If by finite we mean limitation, by infinite we must mean unlimited—unlimited in power, wisdom, goodness. Certainly this is knowledge worth knowing.

Again, respecting the universe, Hamilton maintains with rare strength that it had an absolute commencement, or we must predicate of it an infinite non-commencement; a beginning it had, or eternal existence must be accepted. To assume no beginning is to assume an absurdity. The regression of an infinite series of causes is not only bewildering, but also perplexingly absurd, for it is less difficult to believe in a created than in a self-originating universe. This, however, implies a Creator, which Hamilton foresaw and conceded; but he perpetrated one of those contradictions for which he was famous in alleging that mind, though compelled to choose one or the other, is unable to conceive of either. "The Infinite and the Absolute," says he, "are only the names of two counter *imbecilities* of the human mind;" namely, absolute commencement and eternal existence.

Hamilton's practical and ethical deductions were superior to his philosophy. Urging, in accordance with the law of relativity, that the Absolute is unrelated and inconceivable, he admitted the necessity of faith in the Deity. "We must believe in the infinity of God." Faith in the unknowable is as prominent in Hamilton as faith in the knowable is prominent in Christian theology. Like Jacobi's, it is a faith-philosophy. Without knowing God, we may believe in him! Unthinkable as he is, we may trust him! To those whose faith is founded on a partial knowledge of God obtained from revelation and through regeneration, this doctrine of faith without knowledge has the likeness of a great superstition, which even fetich-worshipers have never entertained.

What is the basal feature of this philosophy? Hamilton was an empirical psychologist, denying the knowableness of reals, of existence, of being, of substance, and confining knowledge to phenomena and their relations. It is the old sensationalism in a new form, made legitimate by philosophical legislation, and heralded as the beacon-light in the darkness of the nineteenth century. The affirmation of the law of relativity is more plausible than the denial of innate ideas; but Hamilton's conclusion is as destructive of theism as Locke's famous proverb. The one philosophy as the other is a denial to the mind of the capability of apprehending or conceiving the Absolute, attributing to man an intellectual imbecility which forbids acquaintance with any thing beyond the visible, the actual, the phenomenal. Hamilton banishes God from thought; Comte went a step further, and banished him from existence.

VII. The philosophy of Associationalism, dealing less with metaphysical problems than pessimism or idealism, renders in its final proclamations an adverse decision respecting the theistic hypothesis. Inasmuch as the mind often acts as by a law of association—*e. g.*, as in memory an object will suggest the scenes that ocurred in its vicinity, as Bunker Hill the Revolutionary contest—it is inferred that the mind's action is wholly governed by this law, that all its thoughts are trains of ideas suggested by association. This being the case, the mind acts mechanically and from necessity, and must be without independence or originality; for, if thought is the result of association, a mental operation, independent of association, is impossible. The thoughts, too, form "a compound in which the separate elements are no more distinguishable, as such, than oxygen and hydrogen in water." This law of association, says Schwegler, has been made as conspicuous in philosophy as gravitation in nature, its chief advocates having been Hartley, James Mill, John S. Mill, and Alexander Bain. Hartley was a physician, who first taught that mental action is explainable by the vibrations of brain-matter, a theory indorsed by Jeremy Bentham and James Mill, who transmitted it to John S. Mill, who formulated it anew, and to Alexander Bain, who heads the list of living psychologists.

Important as other questions are, we will now inquire into its relation to the problem of the First Cause. Its relation is apparent in its theoretical conception of man, which allows him an automatic existence, whose soul is deprived of an immortal nature, whose whole life is purely and exclusively mechanical. As it respects immortality, it is in the line of materialism; as it respects the origin of human knowledge, it is in the line of sensationalism; as it respects the Deity, it is in the line of positivism. A mechanically acting mind is incapable of discerning the relations of things, of probing until their origin is gained, of understanding being or God. To an associationalist the Deity, if not mythical, is inscrutable and inconceivable. The younger Mill held with Comte that the doctrine of causation signified nothing more than a succession of events, in which case it could not suggest a First Cause. Causation is not anticipatory or prophetic of a First Cause. Associationalism, therefore, is metaphysical mechanism, or mechanical metaphysics, robbing man of spirituality, thought of independence, and God of existence. This Bain calls a "guarded or qualified materialism;" this, we admonish the reader, is the quicksand of atheism.

VIII. We approach, now, the last form of materialistic philosophy, namely, Spencerianism, a form of associationalism, and yet distinct from it in that its ground-plan is evolution. Herbert Spencer, like Bain, holds that the laws of thought may be reduced to one law—namely, association—but that the process by which progress takes place is *evolution*. Though Spencer insists that his system makes neither for materialism nor idealism, it is difficult to see how it can be separated from its consequences, any more than a blow can be separated from the bruise it inflicts.

In its relation to the First Cause, Spencer, as if in humiliation, confesses that that is a separate problem, and that God is unknowable and unthinkable. He confounds the unknowable and the unexplainable; he sees contradiction in the idea of the absolute and the infinite, and repudiates the doctrine of self-existence. Unfortunately for the truth, he has been apparently strengthened by Dean Mansel, who declares that God's spirit and God's ways are incognoscible; but the Dean does not mean to be understood in the sense in which he is interpreted. Hitherto, the belief among theologians has been that God is incomprehensible, but not inconceivable or unthinkable. Theology has maintained that God is an intelligent personality, the Absolute Being, incomprehensible because of magnitude, magnificence, infinity, but knowable through the three-fold revelation of a written Word, a divine incarnation, and the outpouring of his own Spirit. Evolution can not evolve God from its materials, finds him not in the universe, declares him not necessary to it, traces not his unseen paths in the fields of existence, and so considers him outside the pale of human knowledge. The trend of evolution is toward atheism. Hamilton recovered himself from the fatal inclination of his philosophy by declaring that the unknowable God must be believed; Dean Mansel pronounces in favor of faith in the incomprehensible God; but Spencer uplifts the Deity first beyond knowledge, then beyond thought, then beyond faith. What is this but atheism? Consistent product of evolution, but impious, withering, soul-blasting blackness; this is the outcome. Spencer is the Diagoras of the nineteenth century. However, he is not a professed atheist; he is better than his system. He gives us a *cobble-stone* philosophy; not the philosophy of the stars; not the philosophy of Being, of Power, of Substance; but the philosophy of stone. Man is a sculptured figure, a piece of marble, not a personality, not a spirituality. God is nowhere; there is no God.

Evolution is the latest form of the philosophy of ignorance, a self-confessed impotent system of speculative thought, unable to find the ground of existence, denying, in fact, that there is any ground outside of itself, making no explanation of the unexplained, offering no conception of the inconceivable, no knowledge of the unknowable. Thus, after a candid survey of eight systems of philosophic inquiry, representing all shades of metaphysical attempts at solving the great problem, we find none adequate to the demonstration of the colossal principle in the universe; none is sufficient to reveal the First Cause, or pronounce the incommunicable name of Jehovah.

Not one system has lifted us to Sinai's top; not one ushered us into the presence of him whose footfalls echo in the storm, whose breath is felt in the hurricane or dew; not one has placed the human hand in the divine and unclasped the grip of power; not one has brought us face to face with the Infinite. Idealism mystified him; Positivism denied him; Hamiltonianism believed in him, but as one believes in the center of the earth; Evolution turned him out beyond space, and bade him never return. The answer of modern philosophy to the inquiry, Is there a God? is yea and nay; yea, but we can know nothing of him; nay, for he does not exist.

Plainly, a mountain of error must be shaken down, or it will bury forever the first truth of God. In opposition to Empirical Philosophy we *proclaim the Absolute from phenomena alone;* in opposition to Positivism, the First Cause *may be predicated on the principle of causation alone;* in opposition to the "Common-sense" philosophy, *faith in God may be grounded in the contents of consciousness* or *rational intuition;* in opposition to Pessimism, a personal, *conscious Will may be affirmed from its historic manifestation in a superintending Providence;* in opposition to Idealism, a subjective Absolute, a *personal God may be declared as the primary truth of religion;* in opposition to Hamilton's unknowable Unconditioned, *we proclaim the knowable Conditioned;* in opposition to the unknowable of Associationalism *we proclaim the knowable of History and Religion;* and in opposition to the unthink-able of Evolution, *we proclaim the thinkable of Reason and Revelation.*

The gravity of the problem increases with the failure of Philosophy to solve it, and the responsibility of those who affirm the theistic hypothesis, and especially of those who accept the Christian idea of the Absolute, is profound and burdensome. It would be legitimate to employ the theistic idea as a working hypothesis in accounting for history and nature; for the scientist, in his searchings, usually begins with hypothesis, and can not deny it to those of an opposite faith; but at once to assume the divine existence or posit it on *a priori* grounds, would be unphilosophical, and virtually a begging of the question. Prof. Samuel Harris teaches that "we can not know *a priori* what the Absolute Being is;" to assume his existence, therefore, would be subversive of rational processes, and destructive of our knowledge of certainties. At the same time, it is confessed that the *a posteriori* method is not entirely unobjectionable; we declare without reserve that the accepted methods for the investigation of the First Cause, as a philosophical problem, are utterly and painfully inadequate, and must some time surrender to an easier and more complete rational determination. "To go from reason to God," says Cousin, "there is no need of a long journey;" but Mansel objects to the method of rationalism, yet offers nothing as a substitute, but declares the theistic hypothesis untenable on rational grounds. Rationalism is defective as an instrument of investigation; so is apriorism; so is aposteriorism; so is intuitionalism; but *rational intuitionalism* is the highway to truth, and he that travels along that road will arrive at the truth. The idea of God, or the fact of his existence, and the character of God, or the fact of his attributes, must not be confounded, since the first may be established, and the second be unknown. To prove the divine existence is not equivalent to proving the divine attributes. Hitherto, one attribute has been used as a key to other attributes; but the process can not be justified, for they do not exist in correlation. One does not imply the others, any more than one property of a circle implies all the other properties. Each must be ascertained in succession.

Mansel yields entirely too much when he attempts to establish that the thought of the Absolute involves self-contradictions, for such an Absolute can not exist. By this attempt he opens the path to atheism, which he rejects; or compels one to suspect the validity of his own rational processes, which we reject. The alternative is, the dethronement of God, or the dethronement of reason; whereas, the enthronement of both is a possibility, a necessity to both. If the existence of the First Cause is indemonstrable by the reason, then there is no place either for the Cause or the Reason in philosophy and religion. That the reason may have projected incompetent and unworthy ideas of the divine Being; that idolatry, pantheism, dualism, materialism are among its products, we make no denial; but this does not invalidate the authority of the rational influences of consciousness or intuition, the certificate of the mind to God's existence. Bad poetry does not make against the poetic product in Homer, Shakespeare, Milton; nor the bad astronomy of Ptolemy against the correct discoveries of Copernicus and Kepler; so rationalism, run to materialism, is not a sign of the incompetency of the reason to frame an incontrovertible argument for the existence of a First Cause.

We readily grant that many philosophical and theological arguments in support of the theistic hypothesis are untenable, being rather the products of faith than of reason, between which the theologian has not carefully enough distinguished, and so he has been vanquished, or humiliated, in a contest with his foe. The argument from faith is tenable only as it springs from the reason, and even then it must occupy relatively a subordinate position. The standing argument, that in the idea of correlation is a proof of the ideal God, is valuable only as an analogy, and not as absolutely unanswerable. The phenomenal may imply the real; the finite, the infinite; the temporal, the eternal; the implication may be one of the necessities of thought, but it appears more like the trick of logic. It is a question if any one thing implies the other actually, especially if the other must be opposite or contradictory. White does not necessarily imply black, high is not the proof of low, except as logic may insist upon it. The conceptional may not imply the actual; the conditioned may not imply the unconditioned; in fact, we deny the implication. There is no unconditioned—it is the vain word of philosophy, the result of the theory of correlation imposed upon the reason. Reason, tortured, traduced, imposed upon, may seem to support a lawful hypothesis, which in the end is found untenable, and then a cry is made against reason. Against many so-called rational arguments, against laws, theories, hypotheses, often used to bolster up the theistic fact, there comes a time when reaction sets in, and they are abandoned. Hence, reason is at a discount in the realm of the highest truth ; but it ought to support the reign of Authority, and it will support it as reason grounds itself more and more in consciousness, and less and less in speculation.

In the preceding paragraph we have denied the existence of what is called the unconditioned; for, believing in the First Cause, in a personal God, it is impossible to conceive of him as unconditinoed. An unconditioned Absolute Being is unthinkable, unknowable—does not exist. More than one pseudo-absolute may be found in the realm of philosophic thought, as the pantheistic absolute, the agnostic absolute, the anthropomorphic absolute, all these and more ; but the greatest of these, the most contradictory, the self-evidently non-existent, is the unconditioned Absolute. Lotze defines *being* to be something that stands in relation, and that out of relation it has no existence. In harmony with this thought, Prof. Bowne demonstrates that, contrary to Hegel, pure being can not exist, but must " stand in relation." Fichte says, " The ego posits itself," but always in relation. An unconditioned being is an absolute impossibility—impossible even to thought, and impossible as an actual existence.

The first thought of the Absolute is of a related Something; the first idea of a First Cause is of an effect ; the idea of cause contains the idea of effect. Reason appropriates and endeavors to interpret the related Cause through the relations, finding in the contents of the relations the content of the idea of God. Existence without relation is non-existence.

A second conception of the First Cause is its unity ; it can not be divided against itself ; it is not self-contradictory, as Mansel affirms, for that involves self-destruction. In what the unity of being, or the unity of the Absolute, consists, whether unity of motion, unity of force, or unity of character, or all three, it is not now important to consider. It is enough to recognize the fact of its unity in the most general sense.

A third conception grows out of itself as cause whose content is activity, energy, manifested force. *Cause is activity.* The condition of being is energy ; hence manifestation. Philosophy is recognizing the law of being in the activity of being, and finds itself capable of explaining being by the law of its existence, which is nothing else than energy in execution. This really is the highest interpretation of Spirit—*activity.* Activity implies manifestation ; manifestation must be totally different from the activity, or resemble it. If totally different, it can not be accounted for; it must resemble it, therefore; that is, the effect of the cause, which is the manifestation of activity, must contain something of the cause. The effect may be spiritual, which is a close resemblance, or physical, which is a rude exhibition of the operating cause. Man is the spiritual resemblance, nature the physical; in both cases the activity has manifested itself.

Spinoza taught that God in activity is under a mathematical necessity, limited by laws which in themselves are eternal; but far easier is it to believe that they are in subjection to him than that he is in bondage to them. The characteristic of man is his freedom; surely the Absolute is as free as his creature. The Absolute as First Cause is free in activity, and the author of all methods of activity.

From this law of activity we determine the Absolute to be Cause. There is nothing in the First Cause to show that it is an effect; there is every thing in the effect to show that it had a cause. So the Cause stands in relation to effect as antecedent, self-impelling, self-existing, and all-sufficient. As First Cause, it must differ from every thing else, except so far as, in the manifestation of itself by the law of its activity, it imparted somewhat of itself to the manifestation. Resembling the manifestation, it must possess differentia or characteristics which lift it above the things which are its products. The philosopher's task at this point is by no means an easy one. Just so long as the Absolute may be contemplated by the aid of fixed relations between cause and effect, or the law of causality in the universe—just so long as the law of activity is predicated as the law of being, and is applied to the Absolute, the task, though difficult, may be performed; but when the word "being" must be changed for Person, in whom centers activity, and from whom proceeds relations and manifestations, the task is almost beyond performance. The designation of the First Cause as a Person materialistic philosophy condemns as the gratuitous assumption of dogmatic theology; but to this it must come. The Scriptures always represent God as a Person, and, as Mansel says, never as a Law; God is not Relation or Unity or Activity only; he is *Personality.* He is Unity in Personality; Activity in Personality. He sustains personal relations to man and the universe, and may be interpreted in the light of them. An unrelated universe is as great a fiction as an unrelated Absolute; neither exists. A personal God is the stumbling-block of philosophy. Spencer, holding to a belief in a Creator, so magnifies him beyond all anthropomorphic relations and conceptions that he can not be known or understood. He advances him beyond the altitude of personality. Personality implies limitation, according to the genius of philosophy, and is inapplicable to the

18

infinite, which is unlimited.   An infinite personality, or rather a personal Infinite, is just as consistent as a personal finite; both are conscious intelligences, both are spiritual activities—the one under limitation, the other beyond.   Tyndall calls the Supreme Activity a Power which refuses in his hands to take a personal form, and slips away from all "intellectual manipulations."   It is a singular faith that allows the existence of a Power and denies the existence of a Personality; yet such is Tyndall's tentative faith.

What is God? is a profound question, even after it has been settled that he exists.   From existence to character the journey is of not inconsiderable length, but he will be rewarded who honestly attempts to make it.   Plato's conception of God as the First Cause in the organization of the world, though far from being complete, may be commended to those who, blind to all the evidence of design in the world's organization, have reduced the Deity either to zero or an impersonal force.   Not at all times clear himself, Plato nevertheless supports the theistic hypothesis with more than a conjecture of its truthfulness.   Modern teachers have descended from the Platonic elevation into bogs and caves, sending forth the most dismal proclamations concerning the world's government and the Supreme Power.

Hartmann conceives the First Cause to be an unconscious intelligence, operating in a causal manner, and dreaming away his eternity. He is an insensible God; he is taking an eternal nap or walking in his sleep.   Spencer concedes intelligence and power, regulated by wisdom, to the First Cause; Hartmann concedes intelligence acting automatically and unerringly.   The concession apparently relieves the conception of an atheistic color.   Ludwig Büchner, reckless in his daring, eliminates the idea of a personal God from philosophy, asserting what he does not prove, that it is obstructive of man's spiritual, social, and political development, and reduces it to the activity of impersonal reason.   His task of elimination is somewhat difficult, but he plunges into it as Pharaoh into the Red Sea.   Oskar Schmidt has no room for the theistic idea in his philosophic meditations.   On the other hand, A. R. Wallace, a Darwinian in belief, supports the idea of a personal God as a necessity to the explanation of the universe.   The Duke of Argyll, it is well known, devoutly recognizes the living God.   The vibration of philosophic belief touching the theistic idea from rank atheism to positive theism is here manifest, showing the unsettled state of philosophic thought, and the need of further inquiry and investigation.

The ground of the theological philosophy is Nature, not Christianity.   To nature let the appeal be made.   What is its testimony concerning the theistic idea?   Cato once said, "That God is, all nature cries aloud." Jacobi has said that "nature conceals God." Both Cato and Jacobi are right: Cato respecting the affirmation of nature, Jacobi respecting the incompleteness of that affirmation. Nature is a revelation, but not a full revelation, of God, and, because of its incompleteness, it has been misinterpreted in the interest of materialism, agnosticism, and atheism. Viewed as a whole, the universe is a proclamation of God, as the author of it, and as in some sense a reflection of his character. It is plain that the universe had a commencement, or it had not. If it had no beginning, then matter is eternal, and its existence is not a proof of God. The eternity of matter displaces the theistic presupposition. If it had a beginning, then something originated it, or it was self-originative, which is absurd. The conception of an eternal universe is even more mysterious than the conception of an eternal being, and the conception of a self-originating universe is far more absurd than the conception of a being who never had a beginning. Suppose the theistic conception is a mystery; the other is an absurdity. Suppose the first is an incomprehensibility; the second is an inconceivability.

Admitting a beginning, Herbert Spencer is not satisfied that nature is a solemn proof of a personal God; the uniformity of nature's phenomena protests against the rule of a personal being; nature rules itself, and is therefore invariable. It is clear that nature does not reveal God to Spencer; it conceals him, as Jacobi said. J. S. Mill, less cautious in utterance, went so far as to deny perfection to "the author and ruler of so clumsily made and capriciously governed a creation as this planet and the life of its inhabitants." Either a personal God had nothing to do with the planet, or he is involved in its imperfections. If nature cries aloud that God is, as Cato said, it cries out an imperfect God, according to Mill.

What, then, is the testimony of Nature? If it is true that the medium through which one sees an object affects the sight of it, interfering with clear vision in proportion as its opaque, then it is important that the medium be transparent or removed entirely, and the object be seen without any intermediary substance, if accurate judgment is finally declared. Looking at an object through glass or water, it may be discolored, distorted, appear broken, larger or smaller than it actually is, and so not be seen truly. If one, then, attempt to observe the First Cause through Nature, it is conceded that the medium will affect the observation; but whether a distorted view or a strictly rational and theistic view will be obtained, will depend upon the medium itself, and upon the thoroughness of the observation. Nature conceals God to the incompetent observer; it reveals him to the friend of God. Whatever may be said of the revelation, it is not anthropomorphic; it is the voice of the physical universe asserting the sovereignty of God, and he that hath an ear may hear it.

The total power of Nature is too immense for measure; and while it may not be infinite, it is above human calculation; hence the nature-Cause is immensely powerful. In like manner the total wisdom of nature, after deducting the facts which apparently point to misrule, appears at least superhuman; hence the nature-God is superhumanly wise. The total benevolence of nature is stupendous, and, notwithstanding Mill's suspicion of its hollowness, it is in keeping with a being who has infinite resources; hence the nature-God is benevolent. The total order of nature—that is, its apparent system of causal procedure—evokes admiration, and justifies faith in it; hence the nature-God is order-loving, order-enforcing. The totalities of nature, without reference to the details, affecting observation of the First Cause, suggest that the nature-God is powerful, wise, benevolent, orderly. The totalities are revelations, so far as they are of any value at all.

The medium is rather a help than a hindrance to observation. If it wholly obscured the object to be seen, the medium only would be seen; but in this case the medium reveals—does not conceal. It is not nature that one sees, but God in nature; not the medium, but the object. Nature qualifies the object just as any other medium would; that is, a medium is obstructive of some light, unless its power of transmission is perfect, which is not claimed for nature. It is claimed, however, that it is a good medium, even though it refracts some of the divine rays. All mediums of observation of the First Cause are open to this objection, and hence a mediumistic result must necessarily be an imperfect result. The First Cause we apprehend correctly in this way, so far as we apprehend it at all, but imperfectly. If God, apprehended imperfectly, appears glorious, how would he appear if apprehended without a medium? Nature is the proof, as Cato says, that God *is*.

By the materialistic philosopher the anthropomorphic conception of the First Cause is regarded untenable, since man is the medium of observation; but, if the nature-medium is a philosophical ground of observation, surely the man-medium can not be ignored. The trend of the nature-medium is to materialism; the trend of the man-medium is to a personal God. This explains the readiness of the materialist to turn from man to nature. Humanity, in its historic development and individual character, exhibits a panorama of attributes that nature does not display, and new ideas of God find utterance in every man. The faculties of memory, conscience, judgment, volition, perception, and cognition, the power of thought and reason, suggest that the First Cause is intellectual, moral, spiritual; for what is in man must be in the Cause. This heightens our view of the infinite God. The nature-God is the God of power, wisdom, benevolence, goodness; the man-God is the God of intellect, having a moral nature, being true, eternal, ever-acting Spirit. If the medium of observation is obstructive, then our apprehension of the First Cause as intellectual, moral, and spiritual, is far below the truth; that is, it is infinitely intellectual, moral, and spiritual. The anthropomorphic conception of God, instead of being limited and unreliable, as is charged by a certain school, is the basis or medium of infinite views of his character and sovereignty. Imperfect as is the view, it is elevating; and limited as is our apprehension of the Infinite, it is progressive and comforting.

A complete philosophic conclusion, however, will not rest upon mediumistic suggestions, but will advance, if it can, to a knowledge of the Absolute without the mesmeric aids of nature and anthropology. Can it go to such heights? Can it rise to a clear, rational perception of the First Cause by reason alone? Homer relates that, when Pallas Athene blew the mist from the eyes of Diomedes, he saw the gods in battle. In a greater book than the Iliad, we read that Elisha prayed, and his servant's eyes were opened, so that he saw the mountains of Samaria full of celestial chariots and horsemen—a real display of the supernatural. Perhaps reason's eye, if opened, might discern, back of all phenomena, back of the visible, the invisible Power that produced all things; perhaps a touch of the eye-ball by a single ray of light might reveal the First Cause in supreme command of all the causes now recognized as operating and controlling in the universe. We believe in the power of the reason, under a spiritual quickening, to recognize the Supreme Power, and, without violence to the laws of thought, to satisfy itself of the existence and character of the personal Absolute.

Including in the Reason the intuitions and all the moral faculties and yearnings of the soul, it proceeds to demonstrate the problem in the following manner: First, it attaches supreme significance to the law of causality as manifested in the universe of matter and being. This is not the place to vindicate or even point out the contents of the law; but, recognizing it in full operation as a universal principle, the human mind, acting under the same law, steps backward through the multiplicity of antecedents and consequents until it reaches an initial antecedent, and then it stops, and stops forever. The alternative is an initial antecedent or an endless series of causes. The latter is absurd, since it finally involves uncaused causes. An uncaused or the First Cause is rational; but uncaused causes are inconsistent with the notion of a First Cause. A non-beginning is not half so satisfactory as a beginning. The law of causation conducts backward to an initial cause, and stops. Mental satisfaction is one result; consistent, effective logic is another; explanation of the universe is another, for, given the First and second causes without number may be marshaled into activity; religion, human responsibility, sacred institutions, Churches, prayers, necessarily follow; a sense of Fatherhood in the First Cause rests upon the world, and darkness flees away.

If the law of causality, as applied to the defense of the theistic notion, involves an endless metaphysical speculation, whose conclusions can satisfy only because based on certain presuppositions which materialism ignores, Reason may employ another method, or other facts too patent to be denied, in support of the common idea. The preservation of the universe, or the law of Continuity, is as great a mystery as, and certainly no less a fact than, its organization, or the existence of the law of Causality. In fact, the law of Continuity, securing uninterrupted duration to the universe, is even more marvelous than the law of causality which produced it. In the search for causes, however, this is likely to be forgotten. In a theoretical sense, it might be admitted that the universe required an originator, but that its preservation is due to the laws imparted to it by the originator, who retired from the government of the world as soon as he organized it, authorizing its future existence by virtue of its own laws and resources, or committing it to some inferior but superhuman power that would look after it. If an organized world require an organizer, a preserved, continuous world requires a Preserver. To establish that the organizer and preserver are one and the same is an advance over the materialistic negation of a personal government in the world. God *was;* God *is.* If compelled to accept the Organizer, the materialist utterly refuses recognition of a Preserver.

The spectacle of the universe in utmost harmony throughout its vast domains, all its forces united in the bonds of cordial sympathy and working for the common end of order and progress, all its kingdoms maintaining their original lines of difference, without trespass one upon another, worlds and systems of worlds traveling noiselessly toward an appointed goal and shining perpetually, must be as wonderful to the higher powers as to men. True it is that imperfection is charged against the cosmic systems; the pessimist reiterates his platitudes of misgovernment, as did Mill, and the materialist protests against the infirmities and struggles of men, as does Häckel; but no one can deny the stupendous fact of the world's preservation. Destruction is not the goal of the universe, or at least the facts are against such a supposition. What this has required, what vast expenditures of power, what constant watchfulness to prevent collisions, what interpositions of wisdom, just how to balance the universe so that it shall not shipwreck itself in the spatial sea, no one can estimate or reveal. Yet, in spite of possible collision of worlds, in spite of possible conflagrations so vast that once started the universe might be reduced to an ash-heap, in spite of possible vacillations of climate that might destroy the human race, in spite of possible relationships to the sun that changed in the least might extinguish the planets or deprive them of light, the world moves on without a jar, and is preserved. So marvelous an arrangement, resulting in the perpetuity of the universe, it is difficult to account for, except on the hypothesis of a present personal superintending agency. Atomism comes not to our relief here. The potency of law is almost a fiction-phrase, unless explained. Law is life, law is power; but only as the law of life, or the law of Continuity, is breathed into the great universal mass, and kept there by the Sovereign who is life himself, can the preservation of the universe be explained. Preservation is the proof of personal agency.

Reason, building up a faith in a divine personality on the impregnable basis of the laws of causality and continuity, or the stupendous facts of organization and preservation, finds additional strength for its assurance in an inquiry concerning the *purpose* of the universe. Lying back of organization and preservation is the stupendous motive governing both; and motive is the credential of personality. It is not so much what the motive is that underlies the universe, as whether it exists by reason of a motive, whether it implies a motive at all. If the spirit of purpose is abroad in the universe, stamped upon every orb, beaming in every law, and bursting out of the ages as they pass along, then the creation and preservation of the universe may be justified; but not otherwise. Materialism scorns the teleological proof of personality, because it is conclusive. The law of design in the universe is as conspicuous as the law of causality and the law of continuity, and the three agree in a demonstration of an Absolute Personality. If reason require a cause for things, it equally demands the end or purpose of things. Just here the distinction, usually clear, between efficient and final cause, fades away, enabling one to see in the efficient the final cause; that is, the final purpose of an act becomes the efficient or controlling cause in the act. Reason requires both; one implies the other. It is not enough to say that cause implies effect; it implies a *designed* effect. Again, the constitution of nature involves a purpose or end for itself; else why its order, beauty, symmetry, harmony? Why not disorder, accident, revolution, disharmony, absence of adaptation? The exceptional disorders are not numerous enough to overthrow the law of design; the law of causality and the law of continuity run the gauntlet of exceptions, but they run it in safety. Suppose the spleen is an organ without a known function; it does not contradict the general idea of end or function in the human system. Even studying final cause as merely a preponderating influence, and not as a universal law, it is true to say that, balancing chaotic evidences with cosmical order, the average is on the side of the latter. For, suppose some things in nature appear to be without design—this is all that one dare affirm; as nature *on the whole* exhibits design, the conclusion must be in favor of the latter. Remembering, too, that it requires more knowledge than man at present possesses to warrant him in assuming that any thing that exists is barren of purpose, any argument built on man's ignorance can hardly have the weight of a rational conjecture. Once it was said the thistle is without an excuse for being; but in recent years it has been converted into paper, proving its utility. The failure to find a purpose in some things is not so much a proof of the absence of purpose as it is a reflection on man's ignorance. We repeat, then, that the constitution of nature involves purpose.

The final step is that nature is the prophecy of a purpose which it is steadily working out, and is making visible to those who have eyes to see purpose at all. Von Baer was fond of saying that nature is *striving* toward an end, as if it is alive with purpose, as if it understands the object, the reason of its being, and is consciously pressing forward to its accomplishment. The expression is strictly philosophical. Nature is rushing on with a speed incalculable to a positive achievement, hindered at times by the apparent antagonism of its diverse forces, but harmonizing at last in the unity of a universal design.

What the end is, reason may not fully discover; but the province of philosophy is in great part fulfilled when it establishes the existence of end. That settled, as we think it has been, in the affirmative, it may seek to ascertain the precise end itself. The precise end of nature even theistic philosophers themselves have not fully indicated; they are not agreed what it is; but any end at all is proof of personal supervision. If the end is that the First Cause may be studied in physical achievements; if it is the expression of supernatural power; if it is to root moral ideas in concrete forms; if it is to establish the idea of God; while these ends may be of different value, they reveal purpose, and purpose is the key to personality. Mr. Mivart so interprets organic nature; but the London *Spectator* denies the sufficiency of design in nature to establish the existence of an infinite intelligence. "Design proves intelligence of a limited kind, not of an infinite kind," says the *Spectator;* but we must distinguish between the design of the details of natural things, and the design of the universe as a whole, a distinction entirely misapprehended by the London writer. An insect's wing, however well formed and adapted to a specific purpose, can not be quoted in proof of an infinite intelligence, for the works of man often eclipse the works of nature in the exhibition of design. The locomotive, the telegraph, the telephone, the steamship, the printing-press, exhibits more design than a thousand things in nature, proving intelligence, but not infinite intelligence; so design in the small things in nature, or in great things taken separately, may only prove "intelligence of a limited kind;" but the *design of the universe as a whole* is very different from the functional uses of organs, or the specific purpose of planets. In the one we see a limited intelligence, which, however, implies personality; in the other an infinite intelligence, implying an infinite personality.

By a rational interpretation of the laws of causation, continuity, and design, faith receives unequivocal support in a personality, self-endowed with all-mightiness, infinite wisdom, perfect benevolence, all concreted in self-existence, without beginning or end. This philosophical conclusion is in accord with the purest theistic conception, and it is only by violence that they can be separated.

But the purely philosophical basis of the theistic conception, conclusive enough at least to those who are in sympathy with it, lacks what one may term vitality or sufficiency of inner force. Granite-like as it is, it is cold, unattractive, without contagious influence. Something more is wanted—the conception needs the baptism of fire. If, obscuring its philosophical form, it assumes to be a semi-religious truth, or exchanges its metaphysical dialectic for a religious teaching, interest in it will increase. The theistic conception is, in its very nature, more than a philosophical theorem. The trend of the latter is to the former. The mind in its outgoing relaxes its grip on the exclusively philosophical, and gently grasps the religious, the whole process being philosophical, for the end of philosophy is religion. This intermediate and progressive state from one to the other arises philosophically from the law of development which obtains in the history of mind, and religiously from the manifestations of Providence, which religion more than philosophy is inclined to appropriate and interpret in its own interest.

The defect in the philosophical basis is its pantheistic view of the universe, including man as well as God, mind as well as matter, and so confounding things that are essentially separate. Its ground, or the content of its theory, is nature, with its forms, forces, and laws; but, incontrovertible as is the argument from nature, philosophy weakens itself by confining its view to nature, as if it were all of existence. Identifying nature with the universe of being, its conclusion is intended to be universal when it is only particular, and so it lacks in completeness and sufficiency.

Development in nature, according to a pre-established order, is a philosophical ground of belief in the Absolute; development in human history, according to a pre-established providential plan, is a religious ground for faith in a Personal God. This is the dividing line between philosophy and religion—evolution in nature and evolution in history. Materialistic philosophy deals primarily with the fixed, the permanent, regarding the variable as an incident of the permanent; hence, nature is its field. The manifestations of life, the variable products of causes, laws, and forces, and the outgrowths of human history, it makes too little account of in its theories, interpreting the whole from the underground basis of matter. Religion pursues the opposite method, viewing the universe from the stand-point of man, and interpreting nature accordingly. Nature explains all, says the materialist; man explains all, says the rational intuitionalist, or theistic advocate. One opens the front-door, the other the back-door; both should meet at the altars of the temple of truth. Philosophy scans natural evolution; religion, historic manifestation. History is quite as much a development as nature; but it is the variable, while nature is the fixed, with qualifications. *The execution of the historic plan, whatever the plan is, with its constantly fluctuating forces, its variable elements, is even more wonderful than the execution of nature's purpose, underlying which are fixed forces and laws.* He who holds the winds in his fists must be as strong as He who brought forth the mountains. The Ruler of such an inconstant thing as Time must be as great as the maker of globes. History is in the stupenduous scale an even balance for nature; the former proves as much as the latter. Nature may strive toward an end; but history is pregnant with a vital, sovereign purpose, namely, the elevation of man. If the doctrine of teleology is at all relevant or tenable, it has strong confirmation in human history, where the resultant of complicated and apparently antagonistic forces is the gradual advancement of the race. This is philosophical in its aspect; for the "survival of the fittest" is but the expression of the historic plan, and the ideal of human life. This plan is all the more wonderful since it is not self-executing, nor the result of an administration of law as in nature; for volitional, that is, concurrent and opposing forces, are vitally related to it, and depend upon personal agency for harmony, development, fulfillment. The nature-plan, the materialist avows, is self-executing, that is, independent of personal supervision; but the historic plan shrivels without personal execution. Hence, historic development is a profound proof of a personal God. The nature-God and the historic-God, the philosophic and the religious God, are one and the same, so proclaimed by religion, but rejected by materialism. The advance of the religious conception over the philosophical is therefore apparent.

The way is now prepared for a discussion of the problem of the First Cause in another aspect, or that which is apparently farthest removed from the philosophic stand-point, namely, the religious representation of God. However, the representation is strictly philosophical; for the religious idea is philosophical in essence, and belongs to the category of particular philosophic primaries. A true philosophical conception of the First Cause has logically a religious termination or accent. In spite of itself philosophy has a religious brogue. "Thy speech bewrayeth thee."

In this tracing of the religious representation we shall not be aided by the dicta of theologians, the opinions of the Christian fathers, or the pronunciations of the Church, for these are entirely outside of the specific view here to be opened. Justin Martyr ascribes shape to God; Clement of Alexandria denies him shape and name; Origen pronounces him an "incorporeal unity." Not on such opinions do we rise to conceptions of the Absolute, but in the study of the royal facts undergirding human existence, which point unerringly to the Infinite.

The first religious intimation of God we notice, is the religious intuition in man. The day has passed when this can be satired out of existence, or reduced to an ephemeral emotion or an intellectual sentiment. Theodore Parker allows an intuitive sense of God, and Spencer can not escape from the intimation of consciousness, which presupposes, logically, the existence of God. Prof. Samuel Harris observes that "the development of man's consciousness of himself in his relation to the world is the development of his consciousness of God." The argument from consciousness, the reason, and the intuitions, is absolutely triumphant over every form of skepticism, and is a standing rebuke of, and a challenge to, agnosticism to proceed. In a religious sense, the religious intuition or reason is God in man. It is the divine idea taking root in humanity; it is the proleptic sign of God, unfolding itself in consciousness and in history. Like language, or music, or art, it is native to man, a primitive datum of the consciousness, the ground of thought, of knowledge, of science, of religion. The divine idea is unmistakably voiced by human nature in its great need of divine help. It is more than a feeling; it is the divine personality awaking man to his own personality.

This is evidenced in its universality, for all men, the illiterate and the cultured, the barbarian and the civilized, the pagan and the Christian, the atheist and the theist, possess the ineradicable mark on forehead and soul, and temples of worship and religious ideas and forms are the product. An explanation of the religious intuition with its entire contents it is not necessary to give; for, as it is fundamental to personality, the first duty of philosophy is to recognize it, and explanation then may follow. Consciousness, or intuition, the mother of the theistic notion, can not be accounted for by evolution. It exists without evolution; hence, the data of consciousness are not dependent for existence on the law of evolution. In this way the Absolute impresses the thought of himself in a permanent form upon humanity; it is the only way to do it, and the human mind can sooner annihilate itself than shake off the great conviction. By as much as the historic is in advance over the natural proof of the Absolute, by so much the intuitional is in advance of the historic basis of faith in the Infinite. The proof, therefore, is cumulative.

Interpreting the intuitional anxiety for God by a strictly scientific method, or according to the principle of correlation, which in substance is that a demand of nature indicates a supply, as hunger implies food, and love of truth implies truth, it is evident that the religious basis of theism is as invulnerable as the philosophical. Aristotle declares that the intuitive reason is the source of first principles. Unless the contents of consciousness are entirely misleading, and the intuitional suggestion a piece of self-mockery, in which case philosophy can have no foundation whatever, we may interpret the demands of the moral nature as significant of an adequate supply. Either the intuition is a deceptive play of the emotions, or its meaning must be found in the accepted law of correlation, which points to religion, or the idea of a personal God. The correlative of the religious intuition is a personal infinite, or nothing. It can not be one of many possible beings or realities; it is the highest or nothing. It is not asserted that the intuitional sense looks immediately for gratification to the Christian religion, for that is not involved in the issue, but that it does point to the highest religious conception of God, which is enough to warrant faith in his existence.

Singularly enough, the Bible writers do not attempt to demonstrate the existence of the Absolute, it either being assumed as a rational inference from consciousness, or revealed by direct spiritual communication. One is as authentic as the other. Intuition is as reliable as inspiration.

Neither, taken singly, is the highest or safest source of knowledge, but in combination, the consciousness spiritualized, the intuitional reason quickened, inspired, the resultant knowledge is infallible. *Inspired intuition is the highest form of knowledge of the absolute.* We live in two worlds, the physical and the spiritual: the physical presses upon us, the result is sensation; the spiritual presses upon us, the result is inspiration. The vision of God through the spiritualized intuitions is complete or not, as the spiritualizing process is perfect or deficient. There must be a faculty for apprehending or perceiving the Infinite, or he can not be perceived. This faculty is *consciousness under inspiration.* In its final graspings the consciousness goes beyond truths to Personality, in whom they center, and from whom they issue. It is the soul's vision of God. The purest philosophy stops with truths; *Religion drops on its knees before Personality.* The one points to God; the other goes to him.

The philosophy of the First Cause, however, is not at variance with the religious representations, so far as it concerns the conspicuous attributes of God. Singularly, they are at one touching these, though divided as to method, and as to the fact of a personal Absolute. If there is an Absolute at all, philosophy agrees with Religion in the recognition of certain characteristics, among which we name the following: The invisibility of the Absolute; the unity of his nature; the omnipotence of his energy; the spirituality of his substance; the omniscience of his vision. To be sure, the philosophical conception of these attributes is not exactly the religious conception of the same, but the difference is not one of antagonism. As to spirituality, even pessimism allows that the Supreme Power, whatever it is, is a Somewhat different from organic, material substance—it is Spirit, or Will, or Reason, an intellectual energy, if nothing else. The Biblical conception of God is that of a conscious intelligence, and at all events a Somewhat totally different from the non-ego. Our conclusion respecting the First Cause is reached. Step by step have we proceeded from the lowest philosophical suspicion, to the highest religious or spiritual conception of the Absolute as an eternal Person, clothed with corresponding attributes, the Creator, Preserver, and Ruler of the worlds; and here the task ends. Religion has not framed our philosophy of the First, but philosophy confirms our religion of the First. Nature, Reason, History, Consciousness, and Religion unite in the proclamation of a First Cause, always existing, supernatural, infinite; a Cause adequate to the universe; a Cause *conscious, personal, eternal.* That First Cause we call God.

# CHAPTER XIII.

## THE FINAL CAUSE

LUDWIG BÜCHNER has discovered that the vindication of the teleological principle involves the overthrow of the mechanical conception of the universe, while Prof. Huxley is not certain but that one may be a teleologist and a materialist at the same time; at least, he urges that the one view does not exclude the other. Büchner's position is the more consistent, for teleology and materialism are incompatible, as will appear in these discussions.

Plato did not elaborate a theory of causality or suggest an explanation of nature that is satisfactory to the philosophic sense of modern times. He held that two causes were involved in the organization of world-types; viz., the Necessary and the Divine; but this is superficial, for, while it admits the presence of a creative energy and the fixedness of nature's laws, it does not enter into an exposition of design in nature or reveal the basal motive of the universe. Aristotle censured Plato for ignoring both efficient and final causes, and, taking the subject in hand himself, he formulated a system of causes which for completeness can not be excelled; but it is not clear that it does not include more than properly belongs to it. He reduced all causes, as if there could be more than one, to four: namely, *material* cause, or the substance, or matter itself; *formal* cause, or the pattern, after which a Thing is made or the form which it assumes; *efficient* cause, or the power that produces change or motion; *final* cause, or that on account of which a Thing is, otherwise the end or purpose of a Thing. The words "final cause," he did not originate nor even employ, but he speaks of the "end" of a Thing, or of Nature, which led the school-men to frame and adopt "final cause" as the expression of Aristotle's idea.

It is not our purpose to investigate these distinctions, arbitrarily made as they were, or to dwell upon the relation of each " cause " to the great problems in philosophy and religion; but, separating "final cause" from its associations, to consider its value as an exponent of a creative intelligence, and therefore as a proof of a personal Author of Nature. In order to its full, or at least sufficient, discussion, it will be presented as follows: I. The Principle Stated; II. The Principle Defended; III. Objections to the Principle Removed; IV. The Final Cause or Established End of Nature.

The principle of final cause is simply that nature exhibits evidences of a purpose or end in its forms, functions, and adaptations, and that the idea of purpose or design thus discovered in nature is an infallible proof of a supervising intelligence in, over, and above nature. It is the principle of intentionality in the universe, embracing the largest cosmical plans and the smallest purposes in the most minute objects of nature. It sweeps the whole circle of design on exhibition in the phenomenal realm. To express the teleological character of nature, or the presence of a teleological spirit in nature, philosophers should invent a more adequate and less misleading form of speech than the scholastic term "final cause," and a more definite word than "design," which theology has pressed into service quite beyond justification or necessity. Still, so long as they are understood to refer to an intelligent principle, or the operation of a governing mind in the universe, we shall not quarrel over words and phrases, however inadequate and incomplete they are as representations of the great idea.

Hartmann introduces four elements into the idea of final cause : (*a*). The conception of the end ; (*b*). The conception of the means; (*c*). The realization of the means; (*d*). The realization of the end. This is a larger definition than is required, and involves certain important distinctions in confusion. The end must be distinguished from the means; the means are included in the idea of efficient cause, and do not enter into the idea of final cause. To be sure, the conception of end in the divine mind may have been associated with the conception of means to the end, which is saying that final and efficient causes may be parallel, but not on that account identical, or even always mutually inclusive. In its application to nature final cause must be separated from association with efficient cause, or both will lose their individuality. Each means a separate and distinct feature, requiring, in order to be understood, a separate and distinct treatment.

The necessity of the vindication of teleology as a natural principle arises from several considerations, one of which is that David Hume undertook the wholesale destruction of all causal principles in nature by reducing all events to a series of antecedents and consequents, and denying the causal connection of physical changes and motions. The end he had in view was the annihilation of the doctrine of efficient cause, but it carried with it the elimination of final cause, or the teleological principle. In our day Mr. Darwin utters a caution against "ascribing intentions to nature," but the weakness of the caution lies in the phraseology with which it is expressed. There is a difference between "ascribing intentions *to* nature," and *discovering purposes in nature.* If Mr. Darwin found theistic scientists ascribing intentions to nature, he did well to caution against it; but the work of discovering ends in the economy of nature involves no embarrassment, and calls for no caution.

Quite to our surprise, an attack has recently been made on teleology from a Christian quarter on the ground that it undertakes to prove too much, and fails in proving the very point in dispute, namely, the presence of a supervising intelligence. Prof. Hicks is the new assailant, who coins a word—*eutaxiology*—to express the idea that *order in nature*, rather than the *purpose of nature*, is the strongest proof of divine supervision over nature. Teleology is thus retired to the rear.

The verity of the doctrine of final cause, or its defense and establishment, is incumbent on those who reject the successional idea of Hume, or who refuse to see it retired at the dictum of others, who imagine a better theory in its stead. Preliminarily, we observe that the exposition and proof of the teleological principle is not so easy a task as that which is imposed on the advocates of the doctrine of efficient cause. The existence of any object raises the presumption of efficient cause. What caused the cholera? What caused the American Revolution? Of every thing, every historic event, every disease, every action, we naturally and instinctively inquire the cause. The doctrine of efficient causation is primarily, intuitively, and universally received, except when a perverted philosophy undertakes to overthrow it. The doctrine of final cause does not spring from a law of the mind. It can not be urged on primary or universal grounds. Cause implies effect, but not the *purpose* of the effect. The purpose is an after-thought, taken up, if at all, subsequently to the recognition of both cause and effect. A child may inquire the cause of an action without inquiring if any thing is designed by it. The thought of cause is spontaneous, the thought of purpose reflective. The one involves no rational exercise of the mental powers; the other requires an intellectual act. It is not intuitive to follow out the results of actions, and knit together the observable designs into a concrete or complex system. The first inquiry we can not avoid; the second we can refuse to make. The first, therefore, is necessary; the second optional. If, however, final cause is not an intuitional suspicion, and requires demonstration before it can be received, it is as necessary to the explanation of nature as efficient cause, as either without the other would be insufficient.

In support of the doctrine of final cause we call attention to the relation to it of the theory of development, affirming that if the evolutionary hypothesis of nature be true only in its most general aspects, it is a complete confirmation of the doctrine under consideration. Specific evolution, as advocated by Häckel and others, is essentially materialistic, but in its processes and results it is essentially teleological. If nature is a development at all, it is the development of a fixed order, and, therefore, of a fixed or necessitated and contemplated result. Fixedness of order, process, or result is a sign of the teleological spirit. Dr. McCosh uses the phrase "uniformity of nature" as expressive of the single-eyed purpose of nature; but we prefer to speak of the fixedness of nature's processes and the certainty of nature's results as the constituents of the fact of design in nature. Between chance and design there is no middle ground. Nature bears the stamp either of chance or design. If of chance, then how is development to be accounted for? How are the laws of development to be explained? How are the orderly results of nature to be analyzed and interpreted? How is the "survival of the fittest" to be vindicated? If nature, in her different realms, steadily tends to the preservation of the best and the survival of the fittest, it is proof that the idea of preservation and survival *participates*—to use Plato's word—in nature, and is the inspiration of her energies and the goal of her activities. This is design on a large scale.

Strangely enough, and inconsistently, the development theory has been turned against final cause, because the latter is implicit with the theistic notion. A true evolution theory is implicit also with the idea of God, but since the idea has been eliminated the theory has fallen into decay.

It is affirmed, however, that the development theory, strictly applied, can have reference only to the order or method in nature, and is in no way related to the design or end of nature. It is clear that an argument built upon the methodology of nature—the *eutaxiology* of Prof. Hicks—in favor of divine supervision in the universe must be irresistible; but methodology is one of the strongest evidences of teleology. Why a methodical action, if nothing is intended? Why the regular or uniform rotation of the earth, if it is not intended? Why the seasons, the law of gravitation, the law of chemical affinity? The fact of method, order, harmony, uniformity, regularity in nature, demonstrates not only a controlling agency, but also a designing agency, which supervises nature through harmonious methods for the accomplishment of specific purposes, inwrought in the very fibers of the natural world.

In the same way efficient cause becomes a proclamation of final cause. One is a key to the other, if one will use it as such. Forgetting the mysterious gap that sometimes exists between them, the *nexus* being obscure, the relation of cause and effect is such that, given the one, the other may in most cases be found. In fact, the efficient is the pledge of the final cause; for action is not for itself, but for something beyond itself. Motion is not for motion, but for change. In nature nothing exists or occurs for its own sake, but has reference to something beyond. An efficient cause can not stop with itself; if it does, in what sense is it efficient? It is efficient in proportion as it produces something or effects something beyond itself. An efficient cause is not a species of ventriloquism, a mere appearance of power, a mockery, and a vanity; but a cause capable of achievement, execution, having the ability to go beyond itself; otherwise it is inefficient. The idea of efficient cause carries the idea of final cause, or the terms imply nothing.

The direct or affirmative evidence of the doctrine is in the nature of facts that are difficult of explanation on any other hypothesis than that of final cause. In certain forms of matter we see certain uses and adaptations, a certain preparation for ends; as in the eye the preparation for vision, and in the stomach a preparation for digestion. These preparations, adaptations, and functions are the anticipations of, or sign-boards to, final cause. If this be regarded as a new statement of the old principle that design signifies a designer, no denial will be made; for it is difficult to overcome the prejudice that, wherever there is use or adaptation, it is the result of intention, and, if intended, the personality of the agent intending it is inferred.

At this point not a little warfare has occurred. A discrimination has been demanded between *function* and *end*, or use and design, on the ground that there is no positive relation between them. It is denied that function or use can be inferred from the structure of an organ; and, likewise, that end or design, in the sense of previously contemplated purpose, can be inferred either from structure or function. Quoting Janet's illustrated statement of the denial, "Respiration is performed in one case by lungs, in another by gills; among certain animals it is effected by the skin; among plants by the leaves." Function, therefore, can not be inferred from structure, since the same function is performed by organs of different structure. Such a conclusion is not warranted by the facts, which rather prove that variety of structure is in perfect harmony with singleness of function. Besides, the argument for final cause does not rest in structure, but in *function*. That several organs, as the lungs, gills, and leaves, perform the same function of respiration, is proof that the function-maker employed various instrumentalities for the execution of a common purpose. In these cases there is not variety of function, but variety of structure. Function is the chief thought; function determines final cause; for if, as Janet shows, function is imminent in structure, design or intended purpose is imminent in function. Natural functions imply original design respecting them. There may be perversion of use, or artificial employment of structures, which might seem to contradict the general relation of structure and function; but perverted use must not be confounded with natural use. David selects a pebble, and sinks it into the forehead of Goliah. Here the pebble is used to inflict death; its natural use, its orginal design, is something very different. In the colonial period of our country's history, when metallic money was scarce, tobacco was used in Virginia as a medium of exchange. The *use* of tobacco as money must be separated from the natural *design* of tobacco. Artificial use bears against the doctrine of final cause; natural use supports it. In the physical world, perversion of function is not the rule, but the exception; hence, the argument from natural use is undisturbed. The steps of the argument are, first, structure; second, function; third, design. *Structure points to function; function points to design.*

It is immaterial whether we subpœna physiology, chemistry, astronomy, geology, natural philosophy, botany, or meteorology in defense and illustration of the principle of intentionality in nature; the scientific proof of the principle, taken from any department of nature, is abundant and irresistible. It is a condition underlying human belief that a concurrence of facts reflecting a law or principle strengthens faith in the law or principle. If it were difficult to point to instances of design in the phenomenal world; if the majority of facts were against it; if the evidences of design were not clearly manifest, but must be searched for and explained when found,—the doctrine of final cause would soon retire from philosophy. On the other hand, if the instances are rare in which design is absent; if every science abounds in facts bearing the marks of original purpose; if the exceptions to the doctrine can be explained in harmony with the doctrine; if the evidences of the principle are universal,—it must be received, all other views to the contrary. Design in nature is the proof that it was designed; or, *design was designed.* This we affirm. Plato foreshadows it in the *Timœus*, when he intimates that motion implies a mover, the effect implies a cause. Prof. J. P. Cooke yields entirely too much when he says, " design in nature can not be demonstrated," but that the argument for it is purely analogical. Any thing less than demonstration will not meet the emergency. Unless the principle can be established with mathematical certainty, unless something more than probability can be invoked in its behalf, it will beget a doubt of its own existence, and merely rank as a hypothesis

or presumption, and not as a fact or reality.   To the facts of nature
we appeal in support of the reality of the principle.

First, the "testimony of the atmosphere," which Prof. Cooke regards unimpeachable, is briefly submitted.   Consider the simple fact
of its currents.   We refer not to tornadoes or local breezes, but to
great atmospheric movements, extending from the Equator to the
Poles, and from the Poles to the Equator—currents sweeping from
continent to continent, equalizing the climate of the globe.   Without
these currents, the temperate zone would be almost uninhabitable;
but the warm air of the tropics, in its northward march, bathes the
zone and renders it delightful.   The annual changes in the climates
of Asia and Africa, "the daily alternation of land and sea breezes,"
and the regularity of the principal trade-winds, are due to this atmospheric interchange.   Now, either this interchange was designed,
or it is the purest accident.   If accidental, it may not occur next
year; but that it will repeat itself, and that the interchange is an
established order, all believe; and, if it is a fixed order, the argument
for teleology has something of a basis.   This general fact aside, let
us consider some particulars, more important and more conclusive.
The atmosphere is a reservoir of electricity.   The "electrical machine
of nature" produces electricity in such quantities, and hurls it with
such desperation, that, without some provision to prevent its wholesale discharge upon the earth, man will be in perpetual danger of
destruction from this agency alone.   This is no trifling matter, therefore.   If any arrangement can be detected by which such a danger is
averted, the evidence of design in the arrangement should be granted.
A very important fact in this connection is that the atmosphere itself
is a poor conductor of electricity.   A second fact is, that every rain-
drop and snow-flake will absorb electricity on its way to the earth,
thus limiting the discharge.   A still more interesting fact is, that
every mountain-chain is hungry for the electrical content, and
silently lifts up its hands to receive the descending force.   To complete the arrangement, every tree is a lightning-rod, safely and
quietly conducting electricity to the ground, while every blade of
grass is an absorbent of the descending fire.   Thus, the atmosphere
and the solid earth are so related that it is only when the electricity
accumulates in larger quantities than can be carried off, it becomes a
hurtful force; but even then it is under restraint, showing the presence of a governing and guarding power.   The arrangement may be
accidental, but to one accustomed to perceive relations, or trace the
connection between causes and effects, it appears like a fore-ordained
system of checks and balances, by which benevolent ends may
be realized.

A still more striking instance of a plan in the chemistry of nature is the "diffusion" of oxygen, or its constancy in the atmosphere. The disturbance of the proportion of oxygen would affect sound, sight, breathing, life; whatever changes take place in the atmosphere, the proportion of oxygen must remain. The chemist affirms that the law of proportion is never disturbed. This may be accidental, but it is difficult to understand how an accidental arrangement has the appearance of, and is, in fact, a fixed and unchangeable order.

The arrangement includes the preservation of the equilibrium of the atmosphere; its homogeneity might be disturbed, its volume might be reduced or increased, effecting changes prejudicial to human interests; but the quantity remains the same, and its equilibrium is preserved. Contributing to this end is that delicate provision by which the vegetable world is continually exchanging oxygen for the carbon of the animal world—a process that insures stability, circulation, interchange, and unity in the atmosphere.

Oxygen, too, is odorless and tasteless. Perhaps this is a small fact; but, since the air must be inhaled every moment, what an annoyance it would prove if the olfactory nerve or the sense of taste were affected at every inspiration! This is a part of the testimony of chemistry to the righteousness of the claim of teleology. Is it not sufficient? The alternative is, that the atmospheric arrangement is wholly and essentially accidental, or that it is designed. Order, plans, ends, are the evidences of design, or design is a word that has no meaning, or represents, if it represent any thing, a fictitious idea. The imminency of end or purpose in nature has a satisfactory demonstration in the appointments, laws, and facts of chemistry.

Nor less conclusive is the argument from physiology, or the evidences of final cause in man. Galen, the physician, said the teleology of physiology is the foundation of religion. Janet confines his chapter on "Facts" in proof of final cause to the human body, discovering in its laws and adaptations the evidence he is seeking. "The happiness of mankind, as well as of all other rational creatures," says Adam Smith, "seems to have been the original purpose of the Author of nature." Man the proof of final cause! This is the base-line of the defense.

Look at the human skeleton; a frame-work of uses; an outline of design; a model of purpose. By reason of the bone-form, man is upright, different in this respect from all other animals. This means something; surely it is not an accident. The protection of the vital organs, a most important feature in the human economy, is secured by the arrangement of the osseous system. The skull protects the brain, gives form to the head, and is a distinguishing mark among

the races.   The ribs protect the lungs, and the pelvis the organs of
generation.   In the formation of the knee-joint the idea of a hinge is
patent, allowing one kind of motion, while the shoulder-joint—a ball
and socket—is so constructed as to permit a free movement of the
arm in nearly every direction.   Had accident ruled, the hinge might
have appeared at the shoulder, and the ball and socket at the knee,
and then man had been in perpetual trouble.   The skeleton as it is
is proof of wisdom in its construction.

Passing to the muscular system, it should be observed that the
muscles are attached to the bones, which secures for them permanency
of place.   This is something; it is a fortunate arrangement.   It is
usual to describe some of the processes of nature as involuntary, such
as digestion, respiration, and circulation; they are maintained during
the sleeping as well as the waking hours, and are in no sense dependent on the volition or conscious co-operation of the individual.
Dependent on his co-operation, his life would be a terror to himself.
Asthma, dyspepsia, and palpitation of the heart show what trouble
would be in store were each man under the necessity of watching,
regulating, and prompting the processes now happily involuntarily
performed.   That these processes may thus be performed it is necessary that the muscles involved shall perform their functions without
weariness.   This we find to be actually the case.   The heart beats
for years and never tires; the stomach, unless asked to do more than
it ought to do, will perform its work without fatigue.   It should
be remembered that other muscles, not involved in vital or involuntary processes, do grow weary, and expostulate against continued toil.
The muscles of the legs and hands, though consisting of the same
kind of muscular tissue as the heart, and their method of action the
same, soon exhibit signs of fatigue, and the man must rest.   The difference is indicative of wisdom in the construction of the machine;
the body has been formed with these facts in view.   The vital processes are ceaseless; the voluntary are susceptible of weakness.   If we
should consider separate from the others any single process, or any
muscle whose action is involuntary, it would exhibit the strongest
evidence of design.   As to the heart, the right ventricle is weaker
than the left, for the reason that it propels the blood to the lungs,
while the left ventricle must propel it throughout the system; hence,
the walls of the latter are stronger, tougher, merely adapted to its
purpose.   The doctrine of final cause led Harvey to the discovery of
the circulation of the blood, and properly so.   The valves and general
structure of the heart indicate function.   But we reverse Harvey's
mental process, and declare that the circulation of the blood points to
final cause.   It has an *end*.   From the structure of the heart to its

functions is an easy physiological step; from functions to intention-ality is as easy a metaphysical step.

The involuntary process of digestion is dependent on the gastric juice, the most powerful solvent known. With the exception of mineral and poisonous substances, and living matter, it will dissolve every thing that enters the stomach. All animal and vegetable food at once submits to its power. It is a strange fact that in animals the gastric juice has no such almost unlimited power as it has in man. In animals its power is limited to a few articles, so that some are carnivorous only, while man eats every thing and digests every thing, except as above stated. If the gastric juice in man is such a solvent, why does it not dissolve the stomach itself? Here is another wonder, the explanation of which is another evidence of the law of final cause in his physiological history. The juice will not dissolve living matter; hence, a tape-worm will live in the system; so also other worms. It dissolves *dead* matter only; hence, it can not disorganize the stomach. If this is not proof of design, we know not where to look for proof.

In the respiratory system the arragement for the inhalation and exhalation of air is so perfect that it must have been intended, or intention can not be predicated of anything.

The nervous system is equally wonderful in its testimony to the idea or law of final cause. Admitting that the nerves are the con-necting links between mind and matter, it is well known that the material properties of the nerves are not unlike those of other sub-stances. Again, nerves resembling one another in structure are en-dowed with entirely different functions; as the optic nerve is in no essential different from the olfactory nerve, yet each exercises an in-dependent office. Nervous matter does not differ from other matter; nervous matter composing different nervous tissues can not be classi-fied into different kinds. It is one kind, and similar to other matter. Why these different properties, functions, adaptations of the nerves? Certain physiologists quoted by Janet can not harmonize variety of structure with oneness of function; but here is even a deeper prob-lem, the *harmonizing of variety of function with homogeneity of tissue.* As, however, the one problem has its solution in final cause, so has the other. Both are proofs of the superintendence of wisdom in the world, of ends designed by an infinite mind.

Of the five senses, and the marvelous mechanism of the organs, especially of sight and hearing, a lesson in wisdom may be learned, and a deduction in favor of final cause be made. The eye, the in-strument of vision, is perhaps the most wonderful in construction and the most perfect in its functions of the organs of the human body.

It stands, as Janet says, as the classical argument for design or final cause. Its offices and adaptations have been so frequently described, and all are so familiar with its value, that it would seem like needless repetition to advance here an argument based upon it; but it may be said that the eye is a rebuke of atheism such as no other organ can administer. The ear has been employed in defense of final cause, and why not? To say that the ear may be used in hearing, implying that possibly its chief function may be something else, is to disassociate structure and function, quite impossible in this instance. So the sense of touch, the sense of smell, and the sense of taste, contributing to man's pleasure, preservation and development, may be quoted in proof of intention on the part of man's Maker.

To assume that the organs of the body, the muscles, nerves, bones, viscera, and so forth, have certain functions, without assuming at the same time that they were designed or appointed, is an assumption that falls short of the truth. Even if structure do not indicate or prove function, function indicates and proves design. Human works are interpreted by this principle. A locomotive voices the purpose of the mechanic that made it; a watch—Paley's argument—reflects the purpose of the watchmaker; a statue—Socrates's argument—exhibits the mind of the sculptor; Homer's Iliad—Cicero's argument—must have been written, and, as written, it reflects the genius, the *end*, of its author. Shall it be said that man himself, the most perfect machine ever made, is barren of design? So reason those who distinguish or break the connection between function and design. Folly the most stupendous, this is. The physiological proof of final cause, in our judgment, has never been answered; it is unanswerable.

The astronomical proof which we now examine, although expressive of power and wisdom, has not been considered so affirmative in its impression as the meteorological or physiological, for the reason that astronomical laws are so occult, and astronomical facts so obscure or mysterious as to render full and adequate interpretation impossible. The human mind, too, is not so eager to extend its inquiries to other globes or systems beyond our own, so that the proof from astronomy has not been fully elaborated; it has been neglected. It was Comte, a French atheist, who declared our solar system imperfect, and that it could be improved; but even if this is true, it makes not against the doctrine of final cause. No teleologist insists that the ground of final cause is the perfection of nature, but that structure, function, adaptation, achievement, do together afford a basis of faith in the principle. The demonstration of design in the eye turns not upon the perfection of the organ, but upon the possibility of vision through it. Imperfect hearing does not invalidate the teleological argument from the ear. So an alleged imperfection in the astronomical systems in no way contradicts, undermines, or reflects unfavorably upon the teleological argument based upon the systems. What is the alleged imperfection? It can not lie in the law of attraction, which binds them together, and especially under whose influence our solar system, embracing thirty planets, is maintained in perfect order, every planet pursuing its circular or elliptical course, and at a speed terrific and incomputable, without danger of collision with another, and without variation of one minute in a thousand years from the standard time of its revolutions. Beyond the earth's system are others still more stupendous in their revolutions, embracing worlds that eclipse ours in magnitude, and all revolving around a common center in blissful unconsciousness of the power that controls and the spirit that ordains their movements. Surely there is no failure here.

In the prevention of antagonisms and accidents in the astronomical systems, in the everlasting peace and order of the firmament, there is indisputable proof of the presence of a superintending mind, which regulates the velocity of the planets, and determines the direction of their movements, and calculates the length of their orbits, thus anticipating peace and securing it. Aware that this is a general statement, it is nevertheless sufficient for our purpose; besides, astronomical evidence can not be very, or at least exhaustively, minute. What the final cause of the astronomical system is, we do not now inquire; for it is a separate question. To point out evidences of design in those systems is one thing; to declare the specific design of the systems is quite another, a task that does not belong to the teleologist. However, respecting the earth, it is evident that the design of its revolutions, both on its axis and around the sun, is the perpetual recurrence of day and night, and of the four seasons of the year. So marked results must have been designed; for if not designed, we ask in vain for explanation. If better acquainted with other worlds, one might declare the results of their revolutions in benefits to their inhabitants; but without inquiring for details, or summarizing discoveries in this field, it is apparent that the great design of the astronomical system is in some form the *conservation of life*, an end that justifies faith in the presence of infinite wisdom in the universe. The moral effects arising from a contemplation of the astronomical systems, such as the spirit of humility and adoration, and an overwhelming sense of the greatness of the Creator, the materialist may ignore, nor do we insist upon them; but, confining the view entirely to facts, astronomy, with its wonders, its laws, its harmonies, its beneficial schemes, its security of safety among the worlds, and the spirit of unity which it everywhere exhibits, contributes no inconsiderable argument to the support of the claim of teleology.

The botanical marks of design must be added to the catalogue of proofs of the doctrine of final cause. The vegetable kingdom is, to some extent, a mirror of certain biological forces, working out ends after established patterns under the law of like producing like, and verifying the operation of a fundamental and universal principle. In that the acorn produces the oak, the apple the apple, the grape the grape, it may be claimed that the law of stability of species is in force in the vegetable as well as in the animal kingdom. Law prevails quite as definitely in the vegetable as in the animal world. The habits of plants are as distinctly marked as the habits of animals. In origin, in structure, in development, in function, and in evident design the vegetable world articulates as clearly the law of final cause as the animal world. In the fructification of plants, in the phyllotactic law by which the leaves are properly distributed, so as to secure proportion and beauty, in the uses of fruits as foods, in the variety of forms and colors in tree, fern, and flower, and in the general use of wood as fuel, in house-building, and ship-building, the marks of design are abundant and patent. Even in the decay of the vegetable world, resulting in the enrichment of the soil, or in those vast store-houses of coal, the result of buried forests ages ago, there is proof of a divine purpose to prepare the earth for man, and make it continually contribute to his happiness. Of the beauty in the botanical realm we need not more than say that it is a reflection of the benevolence and beauty of its Maker. European thinkers are almost agreed that beauty is an unknown quality in things having the power to excite the love of the beautiful in man. Beauty is objective. If this be true, then indeed is it a marvelous proof of the final cause of nature. Taking all the facts which the vegetable kingdom brings to us, and interpreting them as they ought to be interpreted, it is difficult not to see that they support the doctrine of final cause.

The zoölogical argument is a complete demonstration of final cause. The Duke of Argyll is emphatic in the assertion that " the whole order of nature is one vast system of contrivance," and while his general argument is in support of the statement, the particular argument is drawn from that provision in the animal kingdom by which *flight* is secured. The machinery by which the navigation of the air is accomplished is a striking evidence of the spirit of contrivance in the world, which adjusts means to ends. Whether one, like Janet, specializes human physiology, or, like the Duke of Argyll, magnifies the machinery of birds, whether man or bird be studied, the result is the same—final cause is proclaimed. Roaming over the field of zoölogy for general facts or evidences of the principle of design, they are soon found in the habits of animals, in the homes they build for themselves, in their care of the young, in their means of self-defense, and in their adaptations to particular modes of life. Here is a spinning caterpillar that resembles the twig under which it has taken shelter—this is its protection; there is a lion with paw strong enough to kill a horse at a single blow—this is his protection. The monkey suspends himself by his tail from a branch of a tree, and sleeps all night, free from the fear of danger; the panther repairs to his jungle, but is alert to see danger, and stands ready to meet it. The squirrel will lay up food for the Winter; the fox will depend upon his shrewdness for his daily allowance. The eagle will train the eaglet to fly; the buffalo rarely imparts instructions to the young, nor is it necessary. Variety of methods, variety of activities, variety of functions, variety of adaptations—these demonstrate the spirit of purpose in the animal kingdom.

*Take nature as a whole; take Maupertius's law of least action, which implies the employment of only a sufficient amount of force for a given end, and forbids a waste of force; take "the law of definite proportions," under which the elementary substances will combine, and combine under no other law; take all the kingdoms of nature, with all their laws, structures, functions, and adaptations, and the conclusion must be that nature is a scheme of ends, breaking out in wonderful variety in all its departments, and regulated by the laws each kingdom reveals.* This is not exhaustive; it is demonstrative, however, and the demonstration is as mathematical as any solution in Euclid.

The duty to consider objections to the doctrine of final cause we shall not ignore or treat with contempt. It is admitted that, demonstrated as is the doctrine, there are those who are not convinced by the "evidences," and require still stronger foundations for faith. Their intelligence we can not impeach, the plausibility of their arguments we can not deny. Justice to truth and a willingness honestly to inspect the alleged weakness of the doctrine require a full representation of the objections in all their bearings, and then an admission of their force, or an exposure of their hollowness. Both sides are bolstered with great names. This should warn the investigator against accepting or rejecting a principle merely because an honored thinker may be quoted on one side or the other. Nor is one's friendship for a doctrine to weigh in a final estimate of it. If the doctrine appeal to fact, then to fact all must go; if to revelation, then to revelation all should go; if to law or scientifically-deduced principle, then law shall be the test; if to reason, there is room for speculation, but logic sometimes is imperious.

In irony K. E. von Baer characterizes teleology as *telephoby*, but the teleological claim can not not be ridiculed out of existence. This, however, is one of the steps a materialist is sure to take, especially if he suspect the principle he assails has any theological bearing, or is difficult to extinguish. Ridicule deserves no answer. An effect follows a cause. Is effect synonymous with end? The anti-teleologist discriminates between effect and end, but the discrimination is no more valid than that of the physiologist between function and end. The effect of the flapping of the eagle's wings is flight; the end is the effect. The effect of the use of the vocal organs is speech; the end can not be separated from the effect.

Schopenhauer was radical enough to assert that, even when design can be predicated from structure, it is not an indication of intelligence, so that the doctrine of ends fully established in no sense justifies belief in a governing mind in the universe. As pessimism will admit the presence of mind under no circumstances in the affairs of the world, it is of little use to contend against it for a principle the proof of which, even though complete, it will not accept.

Comte denied the principle of intentionality, and asserted that nature can be sufficiently explained by the principle of gravitation; but he forgot to acknowledge that the law of gravitation is the law of final cause. Gravitation means order and harmony throughout the universe.

Dropping minor objections, a very forcible exception to the doctrine has been framed out of the apparently useless structures, organs, and objects in nature, to overcome which an adequate explanation of the cases cited in proof must be given. The physiologist reports that the spleen in man is an organ without known functions; hence, it is a useless organ. It should be remembered that Plato considered the bile a vicious secretion. As modern physiology has corrected his error, so future physiology may determine the mysterious uses of the splenetic organ. It is also said that the intestinal canal has a "blind intestine," and the eye a winking membrane, without particular functions, and can be dispensed with without loss; but it is going beyond warrant to assume that any thing is functionless because the investigator is ignorant of the function. The argument from *rudimentary* organs is an extended one, including fish with rudimentary eyes, whales with rudimentary teeth, animals with rudimenatry muscles, worms with rudimentary limbs, and birds with rudimentary wings. The ostrich has wings, but can not fly; true, but they assist in locomotion nevertheless.

Has a grain of sand an end? This perplexed Plato; but the minerologist finds an end for every thing in his kingdom. It is sometimes hinted that as nature is largely composed of ten or twelve elements, it is proof that the nearly fifty elements remaining are almost if not wholly useless, and that the spirit of purpose did not play an important part in the systems of world-building. The question is not so much whether they played an important part as whether they played *any* part at all in the construction of the universe. Essential as are oxygen, carbon, silicon, and hydrogen to the universe, it had not been without the minor elementary substances. Nitrogen, dead as it seems to be, is as necessary as oxygen, the life-giving element. The Duke of Argyll regards the exceptions pointed out by physiologists and materialists as subordinate facts that must be explained by reference to the general purposes of nature. This, we think, is the real solution of the difficulty. Great designs include all the subordinate facts or factors with which they are associated, whether the use of subordinate conditions or structures can be explained or not. The " higher purpose of nature " governs the " lesser," the latter of which it is not essential to understand. If it is evident that a bird's wing is constructed for flight, it is not necessary, in order to vindicate final cause, that the teleologist shall explain the design of the *color* of the wing, which is a subordinate question entirely. If it is established that the eye is designed for sight, the failure to explain the winking membrane is not stupendous, or at all vital. One great purpose may include a score of subordinate purposes. It is a species of presumption in man to circumscribe the purposes of nature by his knowledge of them, or his ability to ascertain them. He assumes that since he does not know the special use of an organ it has no use, when science is loudly proclaiming that by waiting a little we shall know more than we do now. This scientific dictum we accept, and urge investigators not too hastily to employ rudimentary organs in their attack on final cause until they are sure they are rudimentary; and when that is established they must be equally sure that a rudimentary organ is functionless. Both of these conclusions have been assumed; neither has been proved. A materialist looks upon a rudimentary organ as proof that nature attempted to do something and failed, or that, at all events, its work in those cases is useless. But it is not clear in such cases that nature did not accomplish all she had in view, and if she did not it might be pertinent to inquire *if she had any thing in view*, for if she had nothing in view she can not be accused of failing to do something; or it might be asked if she might not yet accomplish purposes not revealed through the rudimentary organs? To assume that a rudimentary organ is functionless, is to assume that it served no purpose in the past and can serve none in the future, an assumption no one is competent to make. *A rudiment is the historic sign of fulfilled purpose, or the prophetic sign of a future purpose.* In this way we dispose of the objection from rudimentary organs against final cause.

The explanation of the details of nature can not be satisfactorily made in the light of a single principle. Many purposes obtain in the phenomenal world to which the great facts may be referred; but the minor works may be obscure or in apparent violation of the great principles or great purposes. Meeting with such contradictions, it is enough if the great principles and purposes can exist in spite of them. Nature is the embodiment of a great plan. Looking at it as a whole, it is pertinent to inquire if the alleged irregularities and useless appendages compromise the plan. Is the discovery of a single unfavorable fact sufficient to cancel the whole plan? Will a broken key in a piano destroy the evidence of design in the instrument? Does consumption destroy the mark of design in the lungs? The whole plan of nature is sufficient to carry all the compromises, irregularities, deficiencies, and rudimentary exhibitions which the busy minds of materialists can invent or discover. In the large view of nature the small disappears.

The next objection is that of Comte, who, on the ground that the ways of the Deity can not be ascertained and have not been revealed, denies validity to our alleged knowledge of final cause. While he preferred not to be ranked with the atheistic school, the atheism of his objection is quite apparent. There are methods of divine action that have not been explained or analyzed; there are ends of the divine government so obscure that one must hesitate in pronouncing them. On the other hand, some ends of his government are fully revealed; or, if not revealed, they may be rationally discovered; and there are methods that are sufficiently transparent, or will disclose themselves to the searching and penetrating spirit. The works of God are not enigmas, in the sense that neither the purposes with which they are pregnant, nor the methods by which the purposes will be wrought out, can be determined. If the mineralogist is baffled in his search for purpose in certain crystals, the physiologist rejoices in the discovery of ends in structures and organs. If the astronomer can not convince himself that a comet has any special end to serve, the naturalist is constantly astounded by the revelations of new designs in the vegetable and animal kingdoms. Nature, dark on one side, may be light on the other. God's ways, methods, laws, purposes, are not all hidden. Because some ends are unknown, it is not conclusive that all ends are unknown. But, if all were unknown, it is not clear that we would be justified in denying the existence of ends. Ignorance of ends is not a valid objection to their existence.

The objection of Positivism, as expressed by M. Littré, that final cause implies supernatural intervention, or an interposing miraculous influence, is a concession to truth not anticipated from that quarter. In order to overthrow the doctrine in issue, the positivist invokes religious prejudice and assails it, not on its merits, but on its alleged theological, or rather supernatural, content, and achieves an apparent victory. The relation of supernatural influence or agency to final cause is such that it is difficult to see how ends can be framed and executed without a supervising intelligence; but the positivist surrenders his position when he recognizes that relation. However, the supernatural element in final cause, or the necessity of a constantly interfering influence in order to accomplish ends, has been misinterpreted by the positivist; hence, his antagonism. He fancies that the supernatural element can express itself only by miraculous method, which compels him to reject it; for the idea of a miraculously sustained universe is repugnant to his sense of order in nature. Any end that must depend upon miraculous aid for its accomplishment, he conceives will never be wrought out. He, therefore, is ready to disown the supernatural element entirely.

One great lesson to be learned is, that the supernatural element, in its interposition in nature, or association with it, through laws, or otherwise, for the attainment of specific ends, acts, not miraculously, but regularly, orderly, and *naturally*. Prof. Newcomb, blind to this distinction, goes over to the mechanical theory of the universe. This is a turning-point in the history of supernatural influence in nature and humanity. It may insert itself in a miraculous manner, but *its ordinary method is natural*. It is a lurking influence in nature, but it is not a miraculously expressed power. Failing to make this discrimination, Positivism has expelled the end-securing influence from its circle.

Descartes denied that a knowledge of ends is possible, but he is sufficiently answered in our reply to the objection of Comte. Bacon eliminated final cause from physics, not because he did not accept the doctrine, but because it belonged, in his opinion, to the region of metaphysics. Forgetting this distinction, others have quoted him in opposition to the doctrine, but unjustly. Conceding sincerity of motive to Bacon, it is not evident that he was wise in the position taken, for final cause has its physical, as well as metaphysical, aspects; it is scientific, as well as theological; and, while the value of the doctrine is theological, the proof of it is physical. Along these lines a great argument might be constructed, showing the interdependence of the physical and metaphysical, and confirming theological truth from a scientific stand-point. Bacon separates the two departments of thought, scientific and metaphysical, in quite a satisfactory manner; but neither is wholly exclusive of the other. He strikes no blow at final cause, but separates it from unnecessary association, as he thinks, and relegates its vindication to the metaphysicians.

Perhaps the strongest objection to final cause is not theoretical, but practical. Of all problems, the problem of evil is the most perplexing both in philosophy and religion. The manner of its introduction into the universe, its possibility in a system of benevolent administration, and the purposes to be achieved through its presence, are alike elusive and unsearchable subjects of discussion. Apparently inconsistent with all optimistic ideas, revolting to all benevolent considerations, inimical to good, it is incumbent upon the teleologist to point out the providential ends involved in the dominion of evil in this world. Evil is the pessimistic spirit that broods over human history. Disease, tornado, accident, death—what the final cause of these?

Janet undertakes to establish that evil is the "accidental consequence of the conflict of efficient and final causes, and of the conflict of final causes with each other." Usually clear in conception and strong in statement, Janet here seems uncertain of his ground, or he would not concede that evil is an "accidental consequence" of any thing. That it implies a conflict of causes is evident; but it is not an accidental issue of such conflict. Far better would it be to say that the conflict is accidental, than that the issue is accidental. Given the conflict, the issue is certain. Besides, evil lies in or grows out of the conflict of causes; evil is conflict. Evil is not the issue of conflict, but the *cause* of conflict. Here Janet mistakes the origin of evil. It is not an effect of antagonistic causes; but the antagonism of causes is the effect of evil. Thus, the origin of evil lies farther back than Janet traced it.

An argument from the methodology of nature in favor of final cause is legitimate; but an argument from the disorders of nature, or want of method, is a little more difficult of construction. However, disorder in the universe is quite as much under law, or the product of law, as order; and until it is admitted that evil is an orderly result, if regarded as a result at all, it can have no explanation. It is either a spirit of order, or the essence of disorder; it is either causally produced, or it is an accident. It can not be an accident, for this implies chaos in the universe; it must be a causal act, procedure, or effect, which implies that it is under supervision. In a competent theodicy there may be a place for evil, and moral reasons may be elaborated in its behalf, confirmatory of the teleological claim, and satisfactory to the theologian; but the philosopher makes sport of them, and pursues his inquiries independently of theology. What then? Is there a break-down here? If evil is a mystery in itself; if its actual benefits can not be portrayed; if its final cause is hidden from view,—it does not follow that it is inconsistent with benevolent schemes, or that it reflects upon the goodness of the Creator. The contraries of good and evil co-exist in the world, and under the divine administration, with some obscure purpose in view. In the present state of knowledge, one is not warranted in arraying evil, with all its difficulties, against the doctrine of final cause.

The feeble attack of Lucretius on the doctrine, that it reverses the natural order of facts by substituting cause for effect and effect for cause, is one of words only, and arises from the unfortunate implication of the terms by which the doctrine is expressed. "Final cause" seems to imply that the design or end of a thing is in some way the cause of the thing. While it is a governing influence, "final cause" is not the essential or producing cause, and can not be substituted for it. Flying is not the *producing* cause of wings, but it is the *final cause*. Lucretius inverted the terms himself, and then attacked his own work, and supposed he had extinguished the doctrine. The terms understood and properly applied, there can be no confusion in reasoning on the subject, and objection to the doctrine must arise from some other source.

Spinoza assailed the doctrine with vigor, asserting that man is ignorant of causes, and that a discovery of ends would compromise the perfections of God. This is a serious charge. As man is not acquainted with all the ends of nature, so he is not familiar with all the causes in operation; but as some ends are patent to his thought, so some causes are evident to his observation and reason. Descartes denies a knowledge of ends; Spinoza, a knowledge of causes. What is left? This conducts to ignorance, the most absolute, of the phenomenal world. To deny knowledge of causes is to invalidate all distinctions drawn respecting the forces in operation in nature, and to reduce nature to an illusion. Granted the imperfection of the human faculties, is the mind unable to distinguish one force from another, one form from another, one fact from another? If so, the denial of the existence of mind might as well follow.

The more serious objection of Spinoza is that the doctrine of final cause implies the imperfection of the Deity. If God acts with an end in view, it is proof that he is not happy in himself, but is seeking happiness in an achievement outside of himself, according to the pantheistic metaphysician. On such a hypothesis the creation of the universe can have no explanation, for had the Deity been completely self-happy, he had not built a single world, and if not self-happy he is imperfect. The objection proves too much, and, there-

20

fore, overthrows itself.  Again, suppose it could be definitely ascertained that God wrought without the inspiration or knowledge of ends—such a God would be an idiot, no better than Hartmann's somnambulistic supreme power.  Of all beings, God must act with the most perfect ends in view, being perfect himself.  He is not an air-builder, nor does he engage in constructing worlds as a pastime; but he has specific ends to accomplish, which are the product of a wisdom that knows no imperfection, and of a power infinite and eternal.  Spinoza's objection, the most elaborate, is the most vulnerable.

The principal objections to final cause have been stated and reviewed; a page only can be given to the fourth proposition announced early in the chapter, namely, the *final cause of nature.*  We have alluded to the necessity of viewing nature in its wholeness, as the only condition or method of understanding the subordinate facts and factors it includes.  The interpretation of nature as one fact, is a large problem, but it must not be set aside on that account.  Janet teaches that *finality* is a law of nature; that is, that nature reflects the teleological spirit, and that *morality* is the supreme end of the universe.  Nature is not for God's sake, nor yet for man's exclusive sake, but for the ends of righteousness, which concern both God and man.  Malebranche, in spiritual mood, declares that the incarnation of Jesus Christ was the motive that led to the creation of the universe; that is, the desire for manifestation by incarnation impelled the appearance of the universe.  According to Plato, the motive of Deity in the organization of worlds, was the love of exercising the principle of goodness infinitely deep in him.  It was not love of happiness, but love of goodness that led the Deity to acts of creation.  A moral principle then underlies the origin of the universe.  This almost harmonizes with Janet's idea, with this difference : Plato held that a moral principle was the efficient cause, while Janet holds that a moral purpose is the final cause of the universe.  Possibly both views are correct; they can not be far out of the way.

To conclude : *final cause is evident in nature*; the final cause of nature is benevolence, goodness, morality.  If not exhaustively satisfactory, it is sufficient for philosophy, and at least helpful in theology.  It contradicts no sound principle in either.  Without final cause, the universe is an enigma.  Without it, God's character would require a new interpretation.  *Teleology or atheism is the alternative.*

# CHAPTER XIV.

## THE BREAK-DOWN OF PHILOSOPHY.

IT is reported that Ulysses, finding his ship yielding to the storm, sought a raft, on which he guided himself to land. He abandoned the great vessel so soon as he saw that its ruin was inevitable. Great ships have been deserted for life-boats, rafts, a single plank, any thing, as a means of rescue from peril, as a deliverance from ruin. Philosophy is Ulysses' ship, a shattered, broken-masted, sinking vessel; Ulysses needs help, a raft, a life-boat.

To inspect wrecks is not a cheerful occupation; to gather up the remains of the dead after an earthquake, or storm, or accident, is not a pleasant task, but such a task is sometimes required at our hands. To this mournful duty we now address ourselves.

In charging speculative philosophy with a break-down, or in speaking of it as a ruin, we must be clearly understood, or be exposed to misunderstanding. It is neither assumed nor asserted that the philosophic spirit has been totally productive of mischief in rational investigation of truth, or that the researches of the philosophers have been valueless; on the contrary, both science and religion have been enriched by their discoveries and strengthened by their teachings. The disposition to undervalue things that do not completely answer their ends has led not a few to reproach philosophy with failure; but its essential work must be recognized, and its worth fairly and honestly estimated.

It can not be disputed that philosophy has securely fastened in the human mind the conviction of the presence of law everywhere, creating the suspicion of a great Law-giver; it can not be doubted that it has excited the human mind to thought, opened paths of inquiry not discovered by the old religions, and led to some results that religion does not challenge. It has not proved all things, but it has demonstrated some truths. We are quite ready to maintain that the scholars it has produced; the systems of thought it has inspired; the principles it has applied to human society and individual conduct; and the daring outreach of its spirit of knowledge into the realm of the infinite, are justifications of the great speculation.

It is neither assumed nor asserted that the introduction of Christianity superseded the necessity of philosophic investigation, and that there is no room or occupation for the philosopher in the presence of revealed truth. This would be going too far, for so long as man is a rational intelligence, he will be interested, and will employ himself, in the discussion of problems which even a supernatural revelation makes plain to his spiritualized consciousness. For it must be remembered that Christianity does not settle every thing, and reveals no truth, after a philosophic method. Revealed truths have a method of their own, so that the philosophic method of inquiry though different from, is yet consistent with, the revealed method of supernatural truth. The mind will philosophize on revealed truth because it is of the nature of mind to philosophize; revelation does not alter the mental structure, or quiet the philosophizing spirit. In the interpretations of the words of God the philosophizing spirit is as helpful as in the investigation of the works of God.

Greek philosophy, in its bearings on or relation to Christianity, can hardly be reproached with failure. In its monotheism, in its doctrine of immortality, in its teachings concerning future rewards and punishments, and even in its perverted conceptions of morality and justice, it prepared the way for apostles and inspired teachers of truth. Measured by its absolute results in ontology, psychology, and cosmology, a different estimate must be pronounced, but it sustained for a time a close relation to practical Christianity.

The break-down of philosophy is a serious, an unfortunate fact. Admitting its services, its heroic labors, its permanent results, and attaching great value to its spirit of inquiry, it is clear that it has not realized its aims in the ascertainment of final truth, nor has it comforted the intellectual anxieties of the race. That it has had sufficient time for trial, that its great systems have been tested both by psychological and religious standards, and that its utter inadequacy to perform the tasks assigned it has been pointed out with every recurring age of thought, must be manifest to all readers and observers of the world's intellectual history. Thales was no greater failure than Herbert Spencer; the latter went deeper into the materialism which the former proposed. In general terms, philosophy failed in what it undertook to do—a failure consistent with valuable services and invaluable results. As Dr. Schliemann has not fully authenticated Homer's Iliad by his excavations in Asia Minor, but has already furnished the materials for the rewriting of Trojan history, so the philosopher has not accomplished his purpose, and yet he has rendered invaluable service to the cause of truth.

It is evident that the problems of philosophy are the problems of religion. Each grapples with their solution by different methods. Religion chants revelations; philosophy deduces truth from observation and reason. The one is a system of truths; the other a system of speculation. The one appeals to the reverent instinct for supernatural truth; the other addresses the rational, inquiring spirit. In their earlier history the two came in conflict, but it was the *conflict of method.* The aims of both were the same, the methods different. Antagonism, instead of fraternity, was the result. One went into superstition—the other into speculation. Neither solved the problems at issue; both demonstrated the need of a religion that, in itself superhuman, would affirm the truth whose scientific development might be left to human reason. However, the philosophic method was chiefly in fault; this was, and is, the occasion of conflict. It is exclusive in its spirit, and independent in its inquiry. The religious method involves the philosophical; but the philosophical abjures the religious, as if it were inimical to a right conception of truth and a successful pursuit of it. The philosophic method and the religious spirit are compatible, but they were early divorced, resulting in inefficient methods of inquiry, and limited and imperfect solutions of problems. This characteristic, and the consequent failure, we shall discover as we follow the track of philosophic investigation.

The sphere of ontological inquiry affords ample illustration of the incompetency of the philosophic method for the ascertainment of truth. Of all questions, that of "being" is confessedly the most mysterious, as it is the most fundamental. It is admitted that there is no such thing as pure being, separate from associations, conditions, activities, and manifestations; but there is absolute, essential being, which *per se* is not a subject of observation. The difference between being and becoming, or being and non-being, or being and phenomena, has been recognized in philosophic circles, but the marks of difference have not been thoroughly indicated or drawn. It is one thing to admit a difference; it is another to describe it. In discussing matter or phenomena, the laws, properties, and forms are certain to be considered; but Kant raised the inquiry if there is not a thing-in-itself, a somewhat that constitutes the essence or reality of matter, of which the forms and properties are the suitable expression. The Eleatic was indisposed to recognize the existence of matter at all, and modern philosophy has limited our knowledge of it to phenomena or property. Over this lower problem of the reality of matter philosophy has struggled from the beginning, vibrating from the "flux" of Heraclitus to the idealism of Emerson, without determining what is the becoming, or the essence of matter. Advancing beyond phenomena, and grasping the problem of being as distinguished from non-being, it makes less progress, for it deals with a mysterious fact. It discusses, but can not define being. It endows it with intelligence, wisdom, power, will, but allows it no moral virtues or convictions. Being is a vague condition of existence, receding, like the horizon, as it is approached, but illuminating phenomena, and is the inspiration of the universe. Between them there is a boundary line, but it is never reached.

In philosophy the idea of the First Cause is enveloped with this vagueness. Spoken of as the Absolute, or Infinite, the terms are almost meaningless for the want of definition. So long as the idea of being is obscure and indefinite, the idea of absolute being, or a personal God, must be intangible and mysterious.

With a singular persistence in perversity, philosophy acknowledges the necessity of being, but denies the possibility of any knowledge of it. Kant affirms the existence of God as a postulate of the Practical Reason, or as a moral necessity of thought, but concedes the weakness of the speculative proof of the idea. Sir William Hamilton insists upon the prerequisite of faith in God, at the same time that he alleges a knowledge of him impossible. Before the Bible can be accepted as a volume of revealed truth, James Mill contended that the moral attributes of God must be proved; but he maintained that the proof had not been and could not be produced. Still later, in Herbert Spencer, philosophy pronounces God "unknowable," precisely the belief of the earlier, and also "unthinkable," the very latest expression of agnostic, belief touching the Absolute Being. Through these different stages of unbelief respecting a personal being philosophy has passed, anchoring itself at last in a radical, atheistic agnosticism, which, while waiting for proof, denies the idea of God as even conceivable. At the very highest point, it fails; where it should be the strongest it is weakest. It is without a theism of any kind; the universe is without a personal presence; the universal power manifested is an impregnable mystery.

To dispense with the idea of God must lead to the subversion of all correlated ideas, and involve the whole fraternity of religious truths in wreck. Without God, religion of any kind is impossible. Not only the death-knell of one religion, but of all religions, is sounded by the philosophic trumpet. Without God, moral distinctions are dreamy imaginations; the Bible turns into a book of fables; and the thought of immortality is a pleasant deception. In overthrowing the foundation the whole superstructure falls. Philosophy may revolt against the impiety of its decisions, and shrink with horror from the darkness of its conclusions, but that its spirit is essentially chaotic, and destructive of eternal principles, can be fairly established against it.

We next notice that philosophy, as applied to the *historic course of civilization*, has misinterpreted its genesis, and the development of the forms of civilization, besides misunderstanding the processes by which its forms were secured. From what does the social and political condition of mankind spring? In other words, what is the warp and woof of history? To confine the reply to the presence and demonstration of certain physical factors or elements would be to exclude the more vital spirit of history. For instance, to say that civilization is the outgrowth of military influence, though war is a staple color in the historic fabric, would be a colossal absurdity. To say that the ambitions of rulers furnish an explanation of the political movements of the world, would be equally fallacious. Deeper than these streams are undercurrents which touch and shake the foundations, involving thrones and peoples in perpetual vibrations. Beneath the visible mutations of an age are forces at work that determine the final results of movement on the surface, and fix the order of progress for the remotest future. No student of history can fail to see that these under-forces may be classified as material and moral, co-operating for the assertion of a given purpose, and the evolution of a predetermined plan. By "material" forces we mean that aggregation of influences that, beginning with purely physical agencies and conditions, such as climate, food, and soil, ascend until they include the purely secular agencies, such as pursuits, governments, ambitions, armies, and every thing potent outside of the still higher, or purely moral and intellectual agencies of society. By "moral" forces we mean the aggregation of all the religious, artistic, æsthetic, and rational influences which may be summoned into the conflict for human elevation.

The line is clearly drawn, the propelling forces of civilization are at once recognized. One might intelligently suspect that all these regenerating forces had entered into the composition of a civilization so complex as ours, but philosophy refuses so broad a generalization, since it involves a concession to religion, which she is resolved not to make. Besides, it is frequently hinted that religious truths and institutions are rather the products of civilization than its fountain-head, which implies the transfer of the problem of origin from civilization to religion. The relation of civilization to religion is the philosophic form of the problem; the relation of religion to civilization is the theologic form of the problem. It is a question of antecedence, which, until settled, will not allow the reign of the religious idea in history. Without attempting to settle the order of relationship between these forces, it is enough to state that history is indebted to one or the other, and, in fact, to both, as instrumental elements in its development. That physical agencies, such as climate, language, nationality, soil, food, and the like have affected man's social condition, and initiated political governments in all their variety, it were vain to dispute. The torrid zone must produce a different race of people from the temperate zone, and the frigid zone a people still different in national impulses and social habits. As a result of climatic and material conditions, there are different races, with physical peculiarities distinguishing them from one another, and with social impulses, which have found expression in different forms of government and different religious faiths. Taking up the subject at this point, Buckle, Grote, and others carry it forward until they pretend to demonstrate that all history is the result of the interaction of material forces, which are in themselves sufficient to account for the highest types of government and religion.

Admitting material agency in civilization, its limitations must be made transparent. To interpret history by the materialistic principle alone would be very like interpreting Washington's monument by the amount of stone it contains. The *materials* of the monument are one thing ; the *idea* of the monument is another. The materials of history and the material forces of civilization constitute one class of facts, not by any means to be inconsiderately passed over; but the *idea* of history, and the intellectual forces in harmony with it, constitute an entirely different class of facts, which can not be ignored or impugned except at the risk of making a false interpretation of the whole. The lordship of man over nature is his prophetic destiny. He assumes the position of lord, not because the Scriptures foreshadow this relation, but because his superiority fits him for dominion. His commission requires him to subdue the natural world, to chain and guide the natural forces, and to rise from a servant of nature to the position of master. If history is but the outcome of material forces, then nature is master, and man is servant. In proportion as he breaks with nature—that is, controls natural forces—and is conqueror in the dominion of the natural, does he attain to his rightful position as lord. Instead of material agencies producing civilizations, one should expect the spirit of civilization to exercise dominion over material agencies. This reverses Buckle's materialism, but a pyramid looks better to stand upon its base than its apex.

The truth is, man has been struggling for supremacy ever since he was delivered to the world, or the world bequeathed to him ; he has been anxious to understand his relations to nature ; he has inquired concerning the laws by which she produces her forms ; he desires a knowledge of her forces : he is a student of her plans ; and it can not be denied that he is gradually extending his authority throughout the entire realm. Instead of the material conquering him, he has conquered the material, and natural conditions are the product of man's presence and sovereignty. The material has not dictated history, but history is a revelation of the dictating power of man. Buckle reads history with blind eyes.

The *philosophic conception of government and education is from the same materialistic stand-point;* that is, governmental policies and educational systems must be determined by the united facts of geography, geology, meteorology, and physiology, a low basis for lofty structures. Creeping like reptiles on the ground, the materialists can not look up; the philosophic basis of the best institutions must be dust, or, as Carlyle roughly phrases it, it is a "Gospel of dirt" that these materialists preach and enforce. Mill says the end of government is public good, but as he does not define the word "good," the statement is ambiguous. Grote has accepted the associational or evolutional principle as an explanation of the governmental idea, but it is materialistic in essence, and quite as inadequate as a theory as Buckle's more pronounced physiological hypothesis. In whatever direction we turn we encounter materialism in one form or another as the active principle, and fatalism as the silent spirit in history.

That another explanation is possible; that another spirit controls in historic manifestations; that other elements conspire in civilization, we hesitate not to affirm, and immediately submit the proof. Since the beginning of history the moral forces have played a conspicuous part in government, education, reforms, and social movements, and it is not too much to say that they constitute the core of all the processes of civilization. Because of irreconcilable differences between the moral and the material, history presents the sad spectacle of irreconcilable conflict between the higher and the lower, or the natural and the intellectual. Both can not be dominant; like Castor and Pollux, one can live only when the other is dead. The conflict of forces has never been rightly estimated by the materialist or physiologist, nor is it quite certain that the moral speculatist has comprehended the significance of the issue. The ebbings and flowings of human history have been the rising and falling of the material and the moral, sometimes alternately, but never contemporaneously, for the two can not co-exist, except in hostile relations. When the material has been in the ascendant, grossness of national life has been the result. Infidel France is a striking illustration of this statement. When the moral has been triumphant there has been advancement toward a national ideal, and public good has been conserved. History is a vibration between the material and the moral, philosophy allying itself with the descending, and Christianity with the ascending, forces.

In this hand-to-hand conflict the moral, less obtrusive than the material, has nevertheless been visible, or its presence has been detected, and moral progress may be affirmed as the result. Steadily, moral forces are triumphing; revolutions, quickened often by the material spirit, end in moral victories; and the swing of the world is toward a universal moral conquest. For the future, then, we may confidently anticipate the regnancy of the moral forces over the material, whose subordination, however slowly wrought out, will finally be complete.

In its *interpretation of the government of the world*, philosophy has exhibited more than its usual bigotry of spirit or inability to comprehend all the facts included in the problem. Pessimism is a corner-word in philosophy. Deeming the world under a system of misrule for which there is no remedy, the pessimist cries out against it and condemns the cruelty which has inspired it. The banishment of God from the universe, and the false interpretation of the historic momentum, naturally prepare the mind for the pessimistic conception of government. Without a thinkable and knowable God; without a system of moral forces in operation; the government of the world appears to the pessimist like the merest accident, and disorder is the natural result. Without a supreme power intelligently and mercifully guiding the lives of men, they must run into danger and be enveloped in darkness. Pessimism is the inevitable product of materialism. Schopenhauer, dismantling the theistic idea, and reducing the divine sovereignty to an imbecile will-force, drifted into a hollow and nerveless conception of Providence, which invalidated all hopes, enervated all desires, and spread gloom over his whole life.

One of the weaknesses of the pessimist is his habit of observing and magnifying the admitted evils of the world to the exclusion of the good that is equally manifest, and his inability after comparing the evil and the good, to perceive an excess of good in the divine administration. He it is who raises the question, "Is life worth living?" Recently Mr. Mallock, a Roman Catholic writer, has taken up the pessimistic question in a semi-philosophical way, and answered it in the negative. Schopenhauer said it is better "not to be" than "to be." In this question all men have a vital, because it is a personal, interest, yet it can not be solved summarily or imperatively. It is a question of *comparison of facts*; neither side can be ignored. We dwell amid shadows, and we know only in part; we see only the smallest openings through the dark-browed clouds that fill the sky. Human life is a pent-up mystery; the world at times is refractory and dull. Through feeble, if not a perturbed, vision we do not see things as they are, and are prone to misjudge the ruling spirit, and pronounce against the decrees of the throne. Considering by themselves the evils of life, Buddha taught the mischievous and hopeless doctrine of *nirvana*, or that release from the world and absorption with the supreme Good will be most fortunate. The idea of death awakens music in the soul; the idea of life produces a monotone of despair. Consistently he authorized the means of death, such as disease, crime, self-murder, any thing to secure the release of the soul from its bondage to matter, any thing that would conduct to eternal freedom, though it involve eternal silence or annihilation of conscious existence. This was the philosophy, not the religion, of Buddha. In any form whatever, Paganism substantially accords with this interpretation of life. It degrades it into a hopeless ruin; it robs it of the possibilities of development; it points to a future of uncertain existence or substantial annihilation.

Is pessimism a factor of civilization? It is not, but its shadow falls occasionally on the thinker, who finds it difficult to account for the sway of evil in this world, who sees that man is handicapped with heredities, mortgaged with infirmities, and doomed to a grave; and he pauses to wonder at the apparent insensibility of the divine ruler, who might order a different state of things. There is at times a seeming undervaluation of life, of its swelling significance, of its growing possibilities, of its world-wide relationships, and of its final adjustments. Even those not disposed to bad dreams, men who never have the dyspepsia, who never see the world going to pieces, philanthropists who are never exhausted or discouraged, and statesmen who are never disheartened and never grow weary, sometimes indulge in gloomy forebodings touching life, the human race, and the great world. The spirit of sin menaces every human being; storms bewilder every pilgrim; misery is universal; the invisible ruler of the nether world strikes like an invisible Gyges whomsoever he will; God seems impassive and impersonal; and the suspicion that possibly life is a mistake gnaws like a vulture at human hopes, and men are afraid. The disadvantages of the present life are too many to be unobserved, and too severe and debilitating to be estimated as trifles. Man enters the world, helpless, dependent, exposed to forces he can not control, under laws he does not understand, the victim of an environment he did not originate. Physical evils are so abundant as to fill him with fear, and often so terrible as to prostrate and destroy him. Earthquakes, volcanoes, water-spouts, electrical discharges, atmospheric commotions, famine, pestilence, heat and cold, all the vicissitudes of the natural world, seem in league against him, oppressing and taxing him beyond his power of endurance.

To none of these things is a denial made; but, granting the presence of evil, is there ground for pessimistic inferences? One is not compelled to choose between optimism and pessimism, the two extremes respecting the government of the world, for it is neither the best possible nor the worst conceivable, but it is in a transition state from a crude form to that which is absolutely perfect. It can not be that the present government is the best, but it is becoming the best through discipline and the subordination of evil to righteousness. If the Captain of our salvation was made perfect through suffering, then the world-life of man, which includes the government *over* him as well as that *in* him, by a similar process may be developed and be made to harmonize with the highest ideals of order and perfection. Struggle, discipline, conflict with evil, fear of danger, liability to overthrow, are steps to a higher condition. When the purpose of life and the fruits of discipline are weighed, the mixed government of the world has an explanation, and pessimism retreats like an owl into a cave.

Besides, the comparative range of evil, or the *excess of good*, in human history is sufficient to cancel the force of the pessimistic declaration. As one surveys the universe the conviction spontaneously arises that it is framed according to a benevolent idea, working itself out by manifold methods in benevolent results; and, looking at the course of history, one is impressed that the idea of good is dominant in human affairs, and that the presence of evil is an accident some time to be overcome and removed. This large view must precede any study of details, or the study will be valueless. The idea of the world must first be understood before its complex movements can be analyzed or a single discordant feature explained. Of physical evils how great the sum, but they are counterbalanced by the flowers, the valleys, the landscapes, the cataracts, the mountains, the fruits and grains, or the beauties and the blessings of nature. A judgment accustomed to the discernment of occult differences, and expert in comparing facts, must at once discover the excess of good in the natural world, and this excess is the representation or sign of the benevolent spirit that underlies the providential administration over man. It is good in itself, and good in its provisions, adaptations, and possibilities.

Passing from untoward external evils, it is contended that man's condition in itself is one of pitiable and helpless embarrassments and restraints, of which no denial is made. His natural ignorance, his feeble physical powers, his limited intellectual acquisitions, and his uncertainty touching the future, are proofs of man's ignoble state, justifying the pessimistic conclusion. Additionally, the condition of those more unfortunate than the majority, in the partial or total loss of reason, and incurable infirmities and deformities of the body, may be used in resistance of the idea of a benevolent government of the world. The insane, the idiotic, the blind, the deaf, the dumb, the walking skeleton, the invalid of inherited maladies, speak loudly against the present order of life. Even the social and industrial conditions of life are under influences that imperil society, and, unchecked, will degrade man. The point is made, that the structure of man's world-life, which he did not create or frame, is such as to admit of the social and industrial oppression of man; whereas, in a wise, and especially a perfect, government, there ought to be no room for despotism, disease, or sin. The poverty of the race, the unequal distribution of riches, the hardships of the laboring classes, the degradation arising from pauperism and slavery to toil, the suffering that such conditions entail, and the hopelessness of relief, declare against the justice and goodness of the divine administration, and furnish weapons for the pessimist.

Nor is the list of social evils yet complete. By reason of ignorance and selfishness, nations are led to differ respecting their rights; the difference appeals to the sword; war ensues, and nations grieve. The tramp of the soldier has been heard in every land; the roar of cannon and the flash of cimeter are not new to any people. War is the staple of history, and one nation is often the product of the ruin of another. Why this antagonism of man to man? Why the absence of harmony in the world?

With all these evils as his inheritance, there is the appalling fact of the inevitable brevity of life, which haunts every man and pursues him until it can pursue no longer. As he begins to shake off the nightmare of evil surroundings, and to ascend into better conditions, life reaches a termination.

Adding these facts together, the pessimist seems to have found a footing for his dismal proclamation. Under the pressure of affliction, Job complained that he had been born, and was ready to surrender his life. Elijah, estimating his work a failure, prostrated himself beneath a juniper-tree, and solemnly wished for death. Jonah, troubled over the turn of affairs at Nineveh, sat within the shade of a gourd, and was eager to push out of the world. Under the touches of religion, the antidote for despair, these good men were revived and renewed their calling; but the suicide and the ungodly, unrestrained by the absence of religious convictions, push pessimism to its fatal conclusion. Pessimism is the suicidal view of the world, and philosophy is responsible for it.

Another view of the world, or man's relation to it, is possible. The idea of life is sweet to the mind; the word itself is musical to the ear of the soul. To live at all; to have a heart that can beat, a brain that permits thought; to have hands, feet, eyes, ears, nose, mouth—a body that answers the soul; to be able to communicate with the outer world; to hold relationship to the inner realm of being; to know that we *partake of the universal life*,—is, as it is studied, a source of profound gratification. With all the mystery that impends over existence, with its liabilities to misfortune, with the supposed misrule of affairs, with the certainty of dissolution, life is an inspiration. Life is a divine product, a divine substance, and the earthly friction which it experiences diminishes not the sacredness of its character, nor affects its eternal value. Looking deeper than this general estimate, that is, inquiring into the nature and possibilities of human life, the pessimistic teaching of Schopenhauer is more than counterbalanced; it is overthrown. The marble bust of Shakespeare is without possibilities; but the living Shakespeare was a prophecy of illimitable development. Aristotle was once an infant; the Duke of Wellington once weighed fourteen pounds. In infancy life is only a promise, but it is a promise which eventuates in realization. The underrating of possibilities, the forgetting of the germs of power in man, and the overrating of the frictions, hindrances, and disturbances that environ human history, have led to a gloomy interpretation of individual life. Keeping the eye on toils, low wages, persecutions, infirmities, all of which are external and no essential part of man, and neglecting the essential prophecies within us, the gravitation toward the despondency of pessimism is easy and natural. Solomon says, "a living dog is better than a dead lion;" which, being interpreted, is, that life in its lowest stages is better than extinction. Life is essential possibility; death is extinct possibility.

The weakness of pessimism is its omission of God in its calculations and interpretations. The philosophers of Greece and Rome discussed with earnestness the old problem of God's relationship to the world, and divided in their conclusions; some asserting that he is insensible to man's dangers, needs, and sufferings; others, that he regards only the great and vital issues of the world, while there were few who comprehended the great truth that not a sparrow falls without the Father's notice. Without God, without his constant interposition in human affairs, without his superintendency of the world, there must be friction, collisions, darkness, death. With God as the Father, Ruler, Benefactor, Redeemer, man lives in hope, and lifts up his head in every storm. Religion reveals God's juxtaposition to the world. Religion explains the difficulties of man's temporal life. *Religion is the cure for pessimism.*

In no department of inquiry is the break-down of philosophy more conspicuous and more complete than in its exposition of the *genesis of life and the origin of the universe,* or its attempted settlement of the whole problem of being, and its manifestations in the organic and inorganic spheres of the phenomenal world. Certain facts must be admitted, *ab initio*, as the conditions of discussion—the facts of the world, life, phenomena. Whence life? Whence matter? From among the multitude of answers given to these questions, we select two as expressive of nearly all that can be said on the subject, two answers that are directly opposed in their contents to each other. They are the religious or theological, and the scientific or metaphysical. The theological account of the world involves the exercise of the creative power of the Almighty, while the philosophical account is a theoretical attempt to trace things back to an alleged self-originating propensity in matter, dispensing entirely with the divine principle. Overwhelmed with defeat, the labors of the theorists have not been altogether fruitless; for, in addition to the discovery of the properties, forces, laws, and functions of matter, they have unintentionally rendered the theological conception impregnable. The strongest defense of the theological idea is the breakdown of the metaphysical.

Without analyzing the mechanical notions of the theorists, it is sufficient to state that the problem of origin is practically unsolved, and that no light has been thrown upon it. When Helmholtz and Sir William Thompson announce that organic germs were originally distributed over the earth from other planets by means of aerolites, what explanation of the origin of things is given? It shifts the origin from one planet to another, but does not explain the origin; in fact, it makes it more mysterious than ever, for this places it beyond our reach. When Huxley declared that *bathybius* had in it the potency of life, it was supposed a great discovery was made; but when it was proved that bathybius is nothing more than gypsum, even the scientific world smiled at the foolishness of the professor. Had his discovery been genuine, it had revealed nothing on origin. When the theory of atoms is urged as a sufficient starting-point for existence, the problem is simplified, but it is as inexplicable as ever; for, if atoms contained the principle of life, it is imperative that the origin of life in them be explained. How came an atom in possession of any power, any principle? How came there to be an atom at all? Conceding that the development theory, if true, partially explains the method of the growth of the world, it fails to account for the origin of the principle of growth, or for a beginning. If it account for the development of species—a matter not yet fully substantiated—it does not account for the origination of species. The "development theory" is the key to development only, not the key to origin.

From the mechanical theory of things the history of man or his origin presents the same immovable difficulty. The theory of descent may account for certain historic courses, or certain racial characteristics or human customs, but it is incompetent to explain the first appearance of man. The gulf between man and the animal kingdom has not been spanned. Even if the physical man were evolved from physical antecedents the difficulty of explaining his intellectual and moral character would be as great as ever, and require another and essentially different exposition. Evolution can not explain the conscience, or judgment, or will, or memory. The primitive races were endowed with intellectual and moral faculties, and prehistoric man was as intellectual as the modern man. *Evolution has added no new faculties to the equipments of the race.* It has introduced nothing new, either in species, which have had fixed types from the beginning, or in man, who is to-day a development only of what he was in the prehistoric ages.

Back of all these attempts at world-building without the divine energy, back of evolutions and revolutions, back of all theories respecting life, is the profounder problem of life itself. What is it? Its *origin* is one phase of inquiry; its *development* is another; its *nature* is primary and fundamental. It will be observed that some theories are applied to an exposition of the history of life, or its unfoldings in permanent forms; others boldly assume the task of ferreting out the beginning or origin of life; but the nature of life—more mysterious than its origin or development—no theorist has been able to make transparent, or even define, with any approximation to truth. Bichat's definition that life is the "sum of the functions by which death is resisted," is no definition at all, for it reduces life to a function or purpose. Life is a *cause* with functions, and not a sum of functions. Coleridge defined life as "the principle of individuation;" but a tree has individuation. The definition is incomplete. The difference between organized matter and inorganized forms has been thoroughly specialized, but the materialist would strike at the indestructible barriers, and reduce the organic to a differentiation of the inorganic. Herbert Spencer says, "The chasm between the inorganic and the organic is being filled up;" but it is one thing to make a statement and another to prove it when it is called in question. The bridge between the organic and inorganic is yet to be built, for the chasm still exists. Häckel fancies that organic matter is an "albuminous carbon combination," while Du Bois-Reymond interprets it as the mechanical principle of atoms.

With these statements, definitions, and fancies, the student is as distant from a proper conception of life and of the world as he was at the beginning. Ponderous systems and theories of high-sounding names have been framed in explanation of phenomena, and the inorganic world has been searched for a clue to the organic; and the result has been a number of hypothetical accounts, which, with their limitations, are unsatisfactory and tentative only. This is a monstrous failure. Besides demonstrating the limitations of human knowledge, it has demonstrated the incompetency of philosophy to settle these inquiries, and has prepared the way for Christianity as an explanation of all things, which introduces God as the author of life, and fills creation with the splendors of his glory.

Thus far we have traced the philosophic disclosures respecting the lower problems, with occasional hints of the higher, and have witnessed in every instance, whether the origin of the world or its government was in question, its complete ignorance of both, and its failure to account for either. We pronounce these "lower problems," inasmuch as they relate chiefly to material principles, forms, connections, and results, and to distinguish them from the moral and religious problems in the sphere of which philosophy is dumb, as it is our purpose soon to show. If in the lower it has proved a failure, we can anticipate nothing better in the higher, where, indeed, it comes to a stand-still, and makes no progress whatever.

The theories respecting mind and intellectual operations; the theories of knowledge and their application to both infinite and finite, have been almost exhaustively considered in these pages, and need no recapitulation here. Herbert Spencer and Alexander Bain are the dead-weights in this department, for the one declares God unknowable, and matter unknowable, save in its phenomena, thus branding the intellect with imbecility; and the other predicates mind as the product of organization, and ventures to explain its activities on mechanical principles, robbing it of immortality, and man of any great destiny. According to both, man is involved in the mechanism which produced the universe, and is himself as much a mechanically acting organism as any thing within the realms of space and time. Mind is the flower of matter. Philosophy has transformed itself into physiology—this is its failure.

A more practical phase of philosophic inquiry is its discussion of the *ethical element*, involving the construction of systems of morality, or the presentation of rules and principles for the government of the social and moral relations. The inquiry includes two points: 1. The origin of ethical or moral distinctions; 2. The value of ethical instructions. Touching the origin of moral ideas and discriminations, there is a great diversity of views among the philosophers, with little approach to uniformity except among the grosser materialists, who resolve ethics, as they do every thing else, into mechanical products. Adam Smith's famous doctrine of "sympathy," as the explanation of the moral sentiments, is peculiar in form, and immature as a theory. The intensity of the sympathetic instinct is admitted, but it is no stronger than other instincts, and it furnishes no secure basis for morality. It makes every man the measure of his morality. It does not recognize a uniform outside standard of right, but permits the sympathetic faculty to make one of its own, by which each man becomes the independent judge of what is right and what is wrong.

Hobbes taught that the moral idea is the artificial product of law, reversing the historic order of the two principles, for law is the effect of moral principle, or of the idea of right and wrong. The enactment of law implies the antecedent idea of right and wrong. Law is the expression of that idea. Again, inasmuch as civil law is changeable, the moral sentiments dependent on it must be changeable also ; hence, the stability of moral ideas, and the permanency of moral distinctions might be disturbed by every new enactment, and finally be destroyed altogether. The safety of the moral idea is in its independence of law, or the caprices of men.

Mandeville resolved all morality into the efflorescence of the spirit of self-love, which in its coarser form is selfishness. In this there is no innate love of right and no constitutional abhorrence of wrong, but a determination to right or wrong as the interests of the individual are promoted or restrained. This is only another and perhaps better form of the utilitarian theory of Hume, who held that the virtue or vice of an action must be determined from its beneficial or hurtful tendencies. James Mill, ignoring a moral sense in man, and renouncing all allegiance to moral sentiments, measures an action by Hume's law of utility.

The most recent exponent of moral ideas is Herbert Spencer, who theorizes at length both on the data of ethics and the contents of a scientific, as opposed to a supernaturalistic, morality. In the foreground is the doctrine of altruism, which is nothing else than absolute selfishness. From this beginning Spencer advances to the suggestion that moral systems are the result of evolutionary processes, which must insure with the passage of the centuries a fixed and possibly complete system of ethics. Ethical systems are still in a transition state, undergoing silent changes, and ripening slowly with the intellectual advances of the race. Originally there were no ethical ideas, but they were invented or formulated as the necessities of the social condition required, at first being crude and often inimical to public good, but, as human relations were more thoroughly considered, the ideas of right and wrong took more definite form, and were appropriated as guides in social life. Moral convictions are, therefore, the products of evolution. In his "Data of Ethics" Spencer makes a broad distinction between absolute and relative ethics, and attempts to show that an ideal or absolute system of ethics can not arise from a knowledge of, or relations to, the unconditioned, but must be the product of relations suggested by the conditioned, which robs the moral idea of its divine origin, and reduces it to a result of human adjustment of relations. Conduct is the product of the adjustment of man to his condition. Divine principles are not involved in this adjustment; it is a human effort to establish harmony between inner and outer conditions. If one succeed in perfecting the adjustment his ethical life will be blameless; but if he fail he goes down under the wrath of the stronger outer conditions. The idea of absolute morality is foreign to all philosophic schemes. What is called " Occamism " is an approach to it, but Mansel objected to it, and, pointing out the apparent weaknesses of the moral faculty, he announced his belief in a *relative* morality only. This strikes at the doctrine of inherent rightness. If right is a relation, or the expression of a relative condition only, the standard of right can not be fixed or uniform, for relations and conditions vary. Right is absolute, or its authority is gone.

Ethical naturalism is as defective as evolutionary ethics. Häckel, maintaining the mechanical conception of the universe, includes man in the mechanical arrangement, which implies his want of freedom. If man is not free, but a cog in the wheel, he is not responsible, and ethical distinctions vanish. To this conclusion Häckel goes at a bound, and rejoices in it. It means the overthrow of the ethical government, and the correlated ideas of future responsibility and the possibility of future punishment. Mr. Darwin was reproached for the ethical weakness of his theories, but it is allowed that his disciples carried the destructive work farther than he anticipated or desired. Rudolf Schmid affirms that ethical naturalism means the dissolution of all moral principles.

Separating these philosophic suggestions, or aggregating them, what is their significance? What becomes of the ethical spirit? If the moral idea is the product of law, or arises from an observed utility of action, or from the indulgence of self-love, or the practice of selfishness, or is evolutionally produced, or is a feature of the mechanism of the universe, what sacredness can attach to it? What authority has it? How can it be enforced? As it is not supernatural in origin, it may not be imposed from supernatural considerations; and as God is not behind or in it, it is only a prudential rule of conduct, to be observed as necessities or conditions may suggest, in which event it is without authoritative character. To be effective, however, the moral sentiment must be obligatory; and it can not be obligatory unless grounded in superior authority. Systems of morality framed according to these conceptions must be defective in representation, and as powerless in influence as the conceptions themselves. As a result, human concepts of sympathy, utility, legal justice, and equity will be dominant, while the divine ideas of benevolence, virtue, truth, and holiness will be absent, except as they are dragged down to the level of the human or mechanical, in which case they would be as powerless as mechanical ideas themselves.

Other theories, half philosophic and half religious, and in advance of the preceding, concerning the rise of the moral idea, have appeared, bridging the distance from philosophy to religion. Lord Shaftesbury pronounced in favor of a moral sense in man, by which he is able to detect the virtue or vice of actions, a conception that was previously elaborated by Hutcheson. Clarke traced the moral idea to the intuitions, giving it a psychological basis. Cudworth, believing that an ethical decision involved a rational perception and comparison of motives and facts, attributed the final moral discrimination to the *reason;* while Butler rose still higher in attributing it to the *conscience.*

The superiority of these views to the utilitarian and evolutional theories must be apparent without discussion. If the latter are correct, fixed and invariable ethical standards are out of the question; if the former obtain, uniform and authoritative ideas of right and wrong may be installed in the activities of the world. Grounded in the intuitions, the reason, and the conscience, there can be no variation, and they may be enforced by sanctions which can not be disputed. Moreover, while the philosophical systems, inasmuch as they spring from external conditions and relations, are *conditional* systems of morality, the intuitional systems, taking their rise in the moral and intellectual nature of man, are *unconditional,* and therefore uniform and universal.

Yet, that the ethical notion has for its sole or chief source the moral nature of man, we are not prepared to affirm. This is an advance over the conclusions of the materialists, but we can not stop here. The ethical idea has its root in the divine being, or is the offshoot of the theistic influence, which, descending into the conscience and reason, makes itself felt in intuitive affirmation of right and wrong. This is its highest source; it is too high, however, for philosophy. In the interpretation of the moral instincts, in its systems of morality, in the character and authority of its ethical instructions, philosophy has completely failed. The total of its teachings is that every man should do the best he can for himself in given conditions, being governed by considerations of utility and self-interest.

Plainly, too, philosophy, pretending to reveal the secret of things, has failed in pointing out the *secret of true happiness*, and in suggesting methods for the satisfaction of the holiest aspirations of the soul; and, were it to be judged by its own principle of utilitarianism, it would be summarily rejected. The conviction that the principles of philosophy are not sufficient, when enthusiastically espoused, to produce abiding contentment, unless cold resignation to fate be honored with this distinction, is abundantly sustained by the principles themselves, and by the lives of philosophers, many of whom have been pessimists, fatalists, and materialists. Ignorance of God, the theory that the world is misgoverned, the hope of immortality reduced to a myth, thought pronounced a secretion, mental activity substantially a nervous impulse, and man a descendant of the animal kingdom—these and such ideas are not calculated to relieve the world of gloom and pain, or introduce sunlight into the abodes and pursuits of the race. By such teachings one is not made strong for temptation, nor is he comforted when trial comes, nor enlightened as the shadows lengthen. Fate, Cæsarism, disease, chains, are not inspiring words, yet they are the pass-words of materialistic philosophy. Epicurus, denying immortality, pledged his life to pleasure, but it was a hollow mockery, and fruitless of good. That man who bought the earthen lamp of Epictetus, in the hope that he could get wisdom from it, was not more foolish than the man who would buy the cup of Epicurus in the belief that pleasure is hidden in it. Adam Smith asked, "What can be added to the happiness of the man who is in health, who is out of debt, and has a clear conscience?" What of the majority of mankind, who are without health, and are poor and in debt, and ignorant, and with consciences unenlightened? Something more is wanted than health, riches, and a conscience. Schopenhauer hated his mother, despised womankind, and drew dark pictures of life. J. S. Mill was a proverbial example of unhappiness, the victim of an inherited and enforced philosophy. Aristotle held that the life of pleasure, the life of ambition, and the life of knowledge, constitute the life of happiness; but pleasure sought for its own sake is a failure, ambition has often resulted in ruin, and culture even has its drawbacks. Consider any scheme of happiness formulated by philosophy, and essential elements will be wanting. Thus the break-down is patent.

The review of philosophy as a failure requires at least an incidental allusion to the insufficiency of its reflections and teachings concerning essential religious truth. Since philosophy must not be confounded with religion, any estimate of the one from the standpoint of the other may seem unwarranted; but it must be remembered that the avowed purpose of the philosophical teacher is to supplant the religious teacher, which implies that he has something better to offer than religion. James Mill looked upon religion as a social force, and Herbert Spencer tolerates it as a myth. The ultimatum of philosophy is the abandonment of religion, but it offers nothing in exchange for atonement, inspiration, resurrection, immortality, heaven; it offers nothing in exchange for the world's Creator and Governor, the holy Sabbath, the doctrine of moral responsibility, and the pleasing thought of man's creation in the image of God. It demands much, but gives nothing in return. Aristotle said the philosopher is a devotee of fable. He was right. What fables are pessimism, utilitarianism, Epicureanism, altruism, materialism, atomism, and the whole brood of evolutionary hypotheses! Religion is not a "cunningly devised fable," but the truth, and nothing but the truth.

The field of philosophy is a field of ruins. It reminds us of Baalbec, with temples in decay, with pillars broken, defaced, and scarred, with worshipers absent, and music and sacrifices wanting. Sensationalism, Idealism, Positivism, Pessimism, and Associationalism are the prostrate pillars in the garden of the world; the temple of worship is without an altar; and the world's throne is without a Ruler. For this decay, this ruin, this break-down, there is a cause; and it is either in the nature of philosophy itself or in the perverted aims of the philosophers. Philosophy itself is a legitimate child of thought, but the philosopher is a prodigal, wasting the substance of the Father in riotous demonstrations, and mocking at the heavenly visions with which he is sometimes favored. He needs to turn his head upward, to ride on Ezekiel's wheels or Zechariah's horses until he reaches the azure heights, or ascends John's mountains, from whose summits he may catch glimpses of the ineffable glory of the celestial sphere. A new phase of philosophy, or an independent grappling with the great mysteries of ontology, psychology, and cosmology must occur before its redemption from materialism is possible. It has sight—it needs insight; it has perseverance—it needs power; it has mechanism—it needs life; it has nature—it needs God.

In the contemplation of the various systems of speculative thought, in their relation to human interests, scarcely a satisfactory result has been obtained. In the study of ontological truth, mystery, vaster and deeper than the supernaturalism of religion, is proposed to our acceptance. Inquiring for biological results, life is presented as an atomic mechanism ; seeking psychological principles, the mind turns out to be a mechanically-derived and a mechanically-acting Thing ; studying nature, causation is reduced to succession, and final cause is denied an existence ; and as for man, his origin is obscurely derived from animals, and his destiny is involved in that of the universe.

For the greater part these conclusions are denials of facts, beliefs, and principles, which, from the earliest periods, have been accepted by the popular judgment of the race as correct, and as being rooted in consciousness and the developments of history. Yet this negative philosophy calls itself positive ; this azoic philosophy styles itself protoplastic ; this severe philosophy calls itself benevolent ; this *antagonistic, undermining, pillar-throwing, soul-blotting philosophy* dares to claim that it is progressive ! Evidently, there is something wrong somewhere. These systems are comets, not stars ; revolutions, not reformations ; novels, not Bibles.

The root-defect of such speculations is seen in the difference between the organic purpose of philosophy on the one hand, and the organic purpose of religion on the other. *The ultimate of philosophy is*—FUNDAMENTALS ; *the ultimate of religion is*—PERSONALITIES. *Fundamentals embrace principles, laws, facts, agencies, forces*; PERSONALITIES INCLUDE BEINGS, INTELLIGENCES, CONSCIOUS EXISTENCES. Philosophy, roving among the fundamentals, does not rise to the personalities of the universe ; hence it talks, but can not explain. It eulogizes gravitation, as did Comte ; it bows before the uniformity and unity of law, as does Huxley ; it creates an unconscious, impersonal First Cause, as do Schopenhauer and Hartmann ; but it knows nothing of the living, personal, omnipresent Jehovah, or of man's relation to him. Philosophy reveals facts, laws, methods, principles ; *religion reveals cause, intelligence, being, personal authorship.*

The reconstruction of philosophy is imperative, as it stops short of triumph. Its achievement is that of the chemist, who can decompose and recompose crystals, but who can not compose life. *Personality is the only ultimate of thought, the original source of all things.* Philosophy has concerned itself with relativities, not with absolute truth ; with phenomena, not with primary cause. It must go beyond fundamentals ; it must advance toward the great Personality ; then its reconstruction will be complete.

During the reign of the Thirty Tyrants in Athens a law was enacted prohibiting conversations on philosophical themes in the city. Tyrannical was the decree ; better far an order that it shall take a broader view ; that, dropping fables, it shall embrace truths ; that, heralding fundamentals, it shall march upward to personalities.

Neither atheism, nor pantheism, nor pessimism is productive of enthusiasm, generosity, social order, or the elements of a progressive civilization. Materialistic philosophy is the incubus of the age.

Clearly and sufficiently has the necessity for a religion that includes the highest truth, concreted in personal intelligences, been demonstrated; and since philosophy, even in its best estate, has failed to furnish the required truth, we turn with confidence to that form of religion which, rising to heights illuminated with celestial light, or descending from summits burning with a supernatural glory, proposes to answer the universal question, namely, *Christianity.*

---

## CHAPTER XV.

### THE RELATION OF PHILOSOPHY TO CHRISTIANITY.

IN a classification of contributing elements to religion, or in an attempt to do justice to auxiliaries in the development of religious truth, philosophy should be accorded a conspicuous place. As a tree is indebted to soil, moisture, light, heat, and the atmosphere, so the best system of religion has derived its character and strength from a multitude of forces and influences, not one of which should be forgotten in the final estimate or historic conception of religion. Far too common is it either to ascribe to Christianity an exclusive Jewish background, regarding the pre-Christian idea as the root of the Christian system, or to discern in it only the supernatural factor that gives it its high value. The intimate relation of other things not essentially religious to religious truth will be acknowledged more and more as an impartial tracing of the origin of Christianity is conducted, and the useful elements of outside systems of thought are properly recognized.

Outside of the accepted preliminary religious influences that aided in the introduction of Christianity, philosophy performed a service in the interest of the true religion, both in its preliminary work and its radical teachings, that should not be despised. What that work was, what its revelations and teachings were, and so what the debt of Christianity to philosophy is, we shall attempt to disclose. Philosophy is not religion, and sometimes it has lacked the religious spirit, being bent in the pursuit of ends strictly special to its calling; but it has opened many a door, parted many a cloud, and held in its hands some truths that we now see were antitypes of things to follow. It is not ritualistic in form, sacrificial in spirit, mediatory in method, or merciful in its aims; yet has it pointed out the religious factor in nature, history, civilizations, and religions, Hegel going so far as to include in it nearly every thing good or worth having, and making it the basis of civil, political, and moral life.

The relation of philosophy to Christianity is indicated very definitely in the *stubborn resistance it offered to the mythologies and idolatries that preceded and accompanied the introduction of Christianity*, thus preparing the way for the assertion of some of the greatest truths of a true religion. In this preliminary work of demolition it had no intended reference to Christianity, nor perhaps to the establishment of a different or better religion than any that prevailed; its work was philosophical, and its effect on the popular religions was incidental. Nevertheless, the process of undermining was as effectual as if it had been instituted for no other purpose, and in Greece the old Homeric and Hesiodic theologies declined, while in Rome Cicero was made to laugh at the augurs, and statesmen winked at one another when the gods were worshiped. In far-off Persia, Zoroaster, climbing to the heights of a monotheistic conception through philosophic visions, dealt sturdy blows against idolatry, and left on record a very satisfactory testimony to the power of religion based on philosophic instead of revealed truth.

It may be stated, as a fact, that the philosophers were first to break with national religions as they were the first to see their absurdities; then followed the poets, the historians, the common skeptics, and, at last, the people. The poetic spirit was too sympathetic with religious impulses to inaugurate preliminary assaults upon old faiths; indeed, the poets were the founders of fabled religions, as the philosophers were their destroyers. Historians could only record the initiatory work of the poets, and the iconoclasm of the philosophers. By these back-handed strokes—strokes in the dark, for with the overthrow of the prevailing religions there was no less a need of a right religion, which philosophy was unable to provide—resulting in the extinction of public faith in mythology, idolatry, superstition, and ignorance, the service of philosophy was incalculable.

One of the accusations against Socrates was that he did not believe in the gods, and that in disseminating his infidelity, he was corrupting the youth of Athens. Theodorus, the disciple of Aristippus, ridiculed the idea of the existence of gods, and abandoned nearly every teaching of mythology. Plato proclaimed the existence of one Supreme Being, doing for the Grecians what Zoroaster did for the Persians, and Moses for the Jews, though under less religious conviction and with less spiritual illumination than either. Seneca likewise espoused the idea of one God, bridging the distance from paganism to Christianity, and preparing the way for a Pauline demonstration of the highest truth in theology. In this preparatory work of laying monotheistic foundations neither Gautama, the exponent of Hindu philosophy, nor Lao-tzŭ, the representative of Chinese philosophy, seemed to share, for neither had conceptions of a personal God; but Greece, Rome, Persia, Palestine, Assyria, and Egypt, in their philosophers, swung from idolatrous notions toward faith in one God, the Creator of all things and Preserver of all men. Crude and indistinct was this philosophic faith, consisting at first only in a denial of the gods, but later in an affirmation of a personal Ruler, and so striking a fatal blow at polytheism, and co-ordinate religious teachings. The accomplishment of the ruin of the pre-Christian mythologies was largely due to the infidelity of philosophies, which, differing from one another in other things, joined hands in an assault upon the polytheism of the nations, awakening them to a sense of unity in the Supreme Power, or at the least preparing them for its inculcation and reception.

The preparatory office of philosophy, or its actual work in pioneering the human mind through the darkness of speculation into a state of receptivity for religious truth, may be inferred from the fact that nearly all the founders of religions have been philosophers; that is, that religion, true or false, has a philosophical basis, resting primarily on the reason, and secondarily on revelation. The exception to this statement is Christianity, which is primarily the religion of revelation, and, secondarily, the religion of the reason. The philosophic spirit is an inquiring and reflecting spirit; it refuses to accept any thing on authority; it demands evidence instead of assumption; it requires reason instead of faith. Hence, it often doubts when another spirit believes. It is not to be denied that the old philosophic doubt of the old religions was a step in advance, and that philosophic inquiry led to the abandonment of errors, both scientific and religious. That Arcesilaus of the Middle Academy doubted too much may be granted, for he even doubted the possibility of knowing any thing; but even this infidelic, Pyrrhonic way of dealing with all truths, sacred, historic, and scientific, disadvantageous as it seemed to order, harmony, and progress, was productive of inquiry which, with the aid of other influences, resulted in the dethronement of the old faiths. Bacon was a doubter; Descartes was a doubter. Not Pyrrhonists were these, but investigators of truth, and found it after much searching.

One looking into the old religions will find certain philosophical forms of truth, or religious dogmas, grounded in philosophical statements. Many of the errors of the antagonized religions are these philosophic forms of religious dogmas. On no moral problem has philosophy expended more ingenuity than that of the existence of evil,

but in every instance the religion that adopted a philosophic explanation was embarrassed by it, and never recovered from it. Neither
Manes, nor Zoroaster, nor Gautama, nor Confucius, nor Epicurus,
was able to frame a satisfactory theory of evil, but each uttered a
little philosophy, which went forth as the dictum of the reason, to be
afterward contradicted and overthrown by the doctrines of Revelation.
At the head of all outside religions there have stood both priests and
philosophers, ready to philosophize on religion, or breathe a religious
tone into philosophy ; and the result has been neither pure philosophy
on the one hand, nor an incorruptible religion on the other. Whether
we consider Lao-tzŭ, the Chinese philosopher, or Gautama, the establisher of Buddhism, or Zoroaster, the Persian priest, or the unknown
composer of *Bhagavad Gita,* or the Norse system of theology, or the
early Germanic religions, a philosophical spirit is prominent in all
their teachings, and is the secret guide in all their developments. In
one religion philosophy produces Pantheism ; in another Eclecticism ;
in another Pyrrhonism ; in another Manicheism ; in another a
Platonic spirit ; in another Idealism ; in another Materialism. When
philosophy assailed the old religions, it purified or extinguished them ;
when it incorporated itself with them, it corrupted and prepared the
way for their overthrow, doing equally valuable work in both
directions.

In this *quasi* invasion of religion by philosophy, or the attempted
reduction of religious truth to a philosophic form—an outgrowth of
their relations—we discover the weakness of the one and the independence of the other. The philosopher could not accompany the
priest all the way from reason to revelation, nor did the priest suspect the thunder-stroke of the philosopher. They parted company so
soon as one detected the spirit of the other, but often it was too late,
either to save religion from a downfall, or philosophy from ridicule.
In most cases a philosophical cry gave way to a religious song, or a
religious dogma was lost in philosophic formula. The character and
career of Scholasticism is a conspicuous proof of these statements.
If, as Prof. G. S. Morris observes, it " was in some sense the balance-
wheel of mediæval life," still it was incompetent to purify the life or
restore the supremacy of Christian sentiment to the age which it was
impressing. That it toned the intellectual spirit, gave direction to
research, held in check the rapid march of vice, and advertised the
necessity of a public reformation, must be conceded by all who are
familiar with the epoch of its authority. Its great weakness was not
its method of expression, or the character of its purpose, but its inherent rationalism from which it could not extricate itself. From
Anselm, its founder, to William of Occam, who inflicted upon it a

final death-stroke, there is a constant fluctuation of conceptions, a change of faiths, an unsettled conviction of truth, a philosophic spirit that tantalizes the religious life to death ; and reason paralyzed surrenders the field to those more capable of adjusting the differences between the formalism and false ideas of speculation and the realities and mysteries of religion. Insufficient, either as a philosophy or a religion, it was followed by something more definite in both departments of thought, not without, however, illustrating the distinctness of sphere of each, and teaching the lesson needed in these times as well as then, that wherever philosophy exalts itself into a religious form, or attempts to dictate the highest truth, or explain revealed truth by its rules and methods, a collapse of power is the result. Both go down in the wreck.

Notwithstanding the usurpations of philosophy, or rather its attempted exposition of religious dogma, or the substitution of itself for religion, it gave expression to religious truth, especially in the early period of the Christian Church, in such a way as to confirm the revelations of religion. A sufficient example is the relation of the Alexandrian philosophy to Scripture truth, or the attempt, under the leadership of Philo, to unite Hellenism and Orientalism. Admitting the Bible to be true, it was subjected to an interpretation that reduced some of its revelations to absurdities, and exalted others into a refined state most satisfactory to the mystical or idealistic mind. As a consequence, Christianity was Platonized ; in other words, Biblical truth was transmuted by a philosophical exegesis into philosophical truth, losing its spiritual meaning, and raising a suspicion of its verity. In this transmutation, the spirit of infidelity is conspicuously absent ; faith abounds, but it is under the guidance of the speculative reason. The weakness of mysticism, as a philosophical interpretation of religion, is of the nature of a false and imperfect interpretation, and as such it could not long endure. Whether, as between Alexandrian speculation or mysticism, and scholasticism, there is ground for preference, certain it is that the former in due time subsided, as did the latter. Christianity was compelled to separate from both, and stand in its true position as a religion from God, to be interpreted rather by spiritual than philosophic methods.

A more direct relationship between philosophy and religion may be traced in the *harmony of their teachings respecting fundamental religious ideas;* for, as philosophy broke away from mythology and idolatry, it was more inclined to substitute semi-religious suggestions of its own, which in many respects were corroborative of the more distinct truths of revelation. While the Gospels brought many truths into light, without which they would not be apprehended at all, it was, in a sense, to make transparent what was only obscure ; to make plain what already existed, and was supposed to exist, but had not been articulated. Harvey did not originate the circulation of the blood in the human system, but gave the fact a physiological expression. No one will assert that the thought of immortality had no existence, and that it did not cheer the race, before the advent of the great Teacher; but it is quite true to say that his presentation of it was of the nature and authority of demonstration; he illuminated it, and changed a philosophic suspicion into an inspiring reality. In the philosophic uncertainties of Christ's times were the roots of many religious truths that grew into fullness of meaning in the light of the Sun of righteousness.

By this statement is not meant that Christianity is indebted to philosophy for germs of truth, for the highest religious truth has always been in the world, and preceded all philosophies. Obscured, corrupted, one age would lose sight of it, and another would recover it. It found its way into philosophy, as a stray light, through which it shone, and from which it may seem to have come; but philosophy is indebted to religious truth—that is, the universal idea of truth, as imbedded in the consciousness of the race—and should not assume to be the fountain of truth. In a certain sense, it was the pioneer of positive religious ideas, the pioneer of positive religions; but back of positive philosophy was the Judaic religion, which, owing to the distribution of Jews throughout the East, took root in all countries and flourished among all peoples, affecting their philosophies as well as their religions. It is believed that Plato acquired a knowledge of Moses and the prophets through Egyptian priests, and it is not a disputed fact that Daniel and the Jewish captives made known the Jewish cosmogony, laws, and institutes, throughout the Babylonish Empire. While granting to philosophy a propædeutic office, it must be understood that it was not without connection with antecedent religions; like a satellite, it shone with borrowed light, and was in no sense original or inspired. That is a pregnant statement of Dr. B. F. Cocker, that "Greek philosophy was unquestionably a development of reason alone," a statement accepted with a qualification or two. If the Hebrew Scriptures were unknown to the philosophers of Greece, certain religious conceptions, and certain fundamental religious ideas, were not unknown to them. Even in the dreamy mythology of the poets were positive religious ideas, which were wanting in a proper presentation to be true. Overthrowing mythology, as they did, they did not overthrow fundamental religious ideas adumbrated by mythology, but appropriated them, as spoils from a wreck, and made them philosophical. Besides, the Holy Spirit brooded over the philosophic mind of Athens, inspiring to intellectual activity, but not to spiritual revelation. Admitting the pre-existence of religious ideas as fashioning forces, and the agency of the Holy Spirit as a directing and quickening influence in the development of Grecian philosophy, it is true that Reason exercised itself to its fullest extent in the solution of the problems committed to it, and did not wholly fail. If, therefore, religion is indebted to philosophy for rescue from superstition and mythology, *philosophy is indebted to religion for religious influence* and the contents of the religious idea.

We shall now briefly examine the *theological elements of philosophy*, in order to ascertain its relation to Christianity, or the final religion that followed the early philosophy. The first necessary idea of a correct religion, whether supernatural or not, is a true conception of God. Without this, the superstructure must be baseless. Monotheism is the radical element of a permanent or absolute religion. This was the basal idea of Judaism; nor was it less a primal conception of Christianity, although other ends engaged its contemplations. Twelve hundred years before Christ, the idea of one Supreme Being was dominant in the religion of Zoroaster, who was as devoted in its promulgation among the Persians as was Mohammed, six centuries after Christ, in its enforcement in the countries of the Levant. It has been represented that Brahminism was the original religion of the Persians, but under some influence—the penetrating, if not universal, influence of the Judaic spirit—the masses revolted against it, and the unity of God became the leading and impulsive doctrine of the new religion. Under the sway of the monotheistic idea, the Persians were delivered from idolatry, and became worshipers of the true and living God. Ahuramazda was his sacred name. He differed in no essential attribute from the Jehovah of the Hebrews. Through the influence of a superstitious spirit, and unable to settle the problem of evil, Zoroaster compromised his monotheism by the admission of a dualistic principle or spirit in the nature of God, which wrought mischief in both philosophy and religion, and which prepared the way for the gradual decline of the Persian faith. However, the monotheistic principle, pure and simple, was recovered and made triumphant in the later religion of the Nazarene. In Greece, the monotheistic idea was antagonized by a very prevalent polytheistic sentiment, which existed down to the time of Paul, who, seeing an altar in one of their temples to the "Unknown God," vindicated the theistic hypothesis, and shattered the lingering faith in the gods of Greece. Prof. Draper intimates that the Oriental conception of God was primarily adopted by the Platonists, or that monotheism was the accredited faith of the Platonic Christians or Mystics of Egypt. In one way and another, monotheism, struggling for supremacy in Persia, Greece, Egypt, or elsewhere, and contending with dualism, polytheism, or Brahminism, succeeded early in planting itself in the philosophies and religions of the world. It was a great victory, and Christianity found the way prepared for it by these triumphs over the old superstitions.

Involved in the monotheistic conception is the doctrine of the government of the world, and the reign of Providence in human affairs. According to the old legends, Zeus reigned in the heavens, Poseidon in the sea, and Hades in the invisible or under-world, while all shared in the government of the earth. This polytheistic government subsided so soon as polytheism itself fell under the blows of the rational monotheism of Judaism, philosophy, and Christianity, but the adjustment to the idea of unity in the divine government was as difficult as the previous adjustment to the idea of unity in the divine Being. One government was as difficult to comprehend as one God; but both ideas, involved in monotheism, first maintained by Judaism, then by other religions, then by philosophy, passed into Christianity as among its fundamental truths, and are now universal.

Respecting Providence, or the reign of divine influence in human affairs, all religions and all philosophies have been in doubt as to its extent, and some have even questioned the fact of divine supervision at all. Cicero held that the important events in terrestrial affairs might receive divine attention, but that divine supervision is not minute or individual. The errors, crudities, sophistries, and uncertainties of the old faiths, and the skepticism or suspicious interpretations of the old philosophies adopted in a reactionary mood of mind, were not without value in preparing the religious mind for the more comforting doctrine of Christianity, which represents that not even a sparrow falls without the Father, implying the most careful superintendence of human life and sympathy with it.

Fundamental, therefore, as these double ideas of the divine unity and divine government are to Christianity, philosophy, by its vigorous protests against the errors of false religions, and by its own errors touching the same truths, opened the way for the transparent and authoritative promulgation of the truth, as it is, by Him who is the truth and the life.

In the struggle for the assertion of human rights, that is, in the final religious estimate placed upon man, philosophy, though not uniform in its teachings, nor wholly consistent with the revelations of Christianity, played no inconsiderable part, and has aided in generating a much-needed enthusiasm over humanity, in its rights and interests. Hindu philosophy, prescribing caste, asceticism, and an inhuman eschatology, can not be wholly condemned, for it has nourished the religious instinct, and kept it alive, even when it was perverting it and stupefying it into permanent lethargy and dullness. Hindu eclecticism, as represented in the *Bhagavad Gita*, elaborates the caste system in an attractive form, basing its discriminations on a supposed existent differentiation in humanity, which is a contradiction of the doctrine of the unity of the race; but it leads to the doctrine by a perverted discussion of it. In the Yoga philosophy man's bondage to evil is explained as the result of five causes; viz., ignorance, egoism, desire, aversion, and love of life; and "the means or accessories of Yoga," by which emancipation or restoration is secured, are eight; viz., *restraint, obligation, posture, regulation, abstraction, devotion, contemplation, and meditation.* No one can read this philosophy without feeling that the diagnosis of man's condition is approximately good, and that the complex remedy is beneficial. The analysis of the disease does not include all the symptoms; the remedy is not atoning or redemptive; but both the analysis and remedy are suggestive, and the reign of that philosophy is a preparation for the truth as it is in Christianity.

Seneca, representing the Stoical philosophy of Rome, advocated human rights with a fidelity and a conscientiousness not excelled by Christian writers. He declaimed against gladiatorial sports, savage customs, and cruelty of all kinds, and exalted the rights of man into a doctrine of political faith. He believed in the brotherhood of man. This was a step in the right direction, and Roman Stoicism may be credited with a propædeutic office in its relation to Christianity.

Grecian Stoicism, dimmed by the spirit of the age, but feeling its way along the lines of human thought, rather inclined to broad views of the natural rights of man, and was less friendly to systems of caste, slavery, and oppression, than the petrified religions of the East. In its larger vision of what man is, and of his rights, relations, and obligations, Grecian philosophy was a ray of that light that was so soon to dawn upon the world, and drive away the darkness that had enveloped it from the beginning.

In its *ethical* teachings, philosophy prepared the way for the supernaturalistic morality of the New Testament. It taught morality from different motives; its standards of right and wrong were defective; its application of ethical rules to the social condition of man was loose and ineffectual; and it is a question if philosophic morality was ever reduced to practice, or elevated human society in its practical administration. In spite of these deficiencies no one can read Cicero, Epictetus, Seneca, Socrates, and Plato, without recognizing the intense earnestness of these teachers in their searching for a moral base, and without being convinced that they desired the moral elevation of their respective nations. What learned disquisitions they have written on patience, fortitude, benevolence, patriotism, temperance, the chief good, the true, the beautiful, filial love, and the parental relation, and the virtues and duties suggested by man's relation to himself, his family, his country, and God! It may be doubted that modern philosophy has gone beyond the ancient in the value of ethical suggestion, or in the construction of ethical systems. Surely Adam Smith, in his theory of "sympathy," and Herbert Spencer, in his theory of altruism, and James Mill, in his abnegation of the moral sense, may not claim superiority to Seneca or Socrates, who thundered against vice with apostolic fervor and apparent inspiration. By virtue of the ethical spirit of philosophy, sufficient or deficient, humanity was prepared for the revelation of a fixed, uniform, and universal standard of morality.

A glance at Assyrian philosophy, as the preparation or virtually the embodiment of the Assyrian religions, leads to the same conclusion. According to the discoveries of George Smith in Assyria, the religion of the Accads embraced such ideas as magic, gnosticism, sorcery, diabolism, solar influences, good and evil spirits, and many other curious and erroneous teachings; but they were related to the philosophy that then prevailed, and to the Jewish religion that followed; to the one in that practically philosophy and religion agreed in teaching the same things, to the other in that they prepared the public mind for a religion of a higher order, with the supernatural factor in it. Whatever the philosophy, whether as diagnostic as Hindu Eclecticism, as discriminating as Roman Stoicism, or as superstitious as Assyrian Gnosticism, in every instance it has pioneered the mind toward a better condition, or prepared it for a better religion.

As prominent as any thing in Christianity are the two doctrines of incarnation and atonement, the one pertaining to the birth, the other pertaining to the death of its founder. So radical are these truths that without them the proclamation of Christianity would be a failure. Did these doctrines have any foreshadowings in the national philosophies, or did Christianity appear unheralded in these respects? As to incarnation, Brahminism was already full of examples, and Judaism had predicted the birth of a son from a virgin as the world's Savior. But these were the anticipations of religions; what, if any, were the anticipations of philosophy? As in Assyria, so in India, the popular religion was the popular philosophy; what was taught by one was assumed by the other; the distinction between philosophy and religion was not clear, therefore. The doctrine of incarnation was a Brahminical doctrine, quite as philosophical as religious, pre-

22

paring the Oriental mind for one incarnation not included in their prophecies or expectations. Even the grotesque and fabulous stories of Brahminical incarnations, baseless and foolish as they were, would qualify the mind to consider a supernatural incarnation, or an event so lofty and divine that, instead of being rejected, it must be accounted for and received. The philosophical religions prepared the Eastern mind for the new doctrine of incarnation.

Pure philosophy, revolting from mythology and superstition, never expressed itself directly on the subject; at least, no philosopher turned prophet, like Isaiah or Micah, and announced the advent of the great Teacher; but philosophers, historians, poets, and people lived in anticipation of the arrival of a Revealer of truth in the person of a Messiah. The expectation was general, created for the most part by the Jewish prophecies, but also by that philosophic preparation, perhaps not fully recognized, that preceded it.

As to atonement, the *principle is as philosophical as it is religious*, and the fact of atonement is as historical as the fact of death itself. All religions, barbarous and enlightened, have acknowledged the necessity of suffering, both as a penalty and remedy for sin. The sacrificial system of Judaism was the ordained typical system of atonement, completed in the voluntary death of Jesus Christ. The religious idea of atonement by sacrifice pervaded all schools of thought, as it had all systems of religion, only it was clouded by superstition, and enforced without proper guards and restrictions, leading often to inhumanity and cruelty without procuring the ends in view. Just before he drank the hemlock, Socrates ordered the sacrifice of a fowl to Æsculapius, recognizing the duty of sacrifice, and that it in some way atoned for sin.

In these particulars philosophy, crude in its conception of the relation of sacrifice to human redemption, and superstitious in its faith touching religious duties, laid the foundation for a belief, first, in the incarnation of the Son of God, and, second, in a sufficient sacrifice for sin by the death of the Great Master. Less reliance, however, should be placed on these foreshadowings which relate more particularly to Christianity than on those which relate to religion in general; for, in its broadest scope, philosophic truth is a finger-board to the great principles, such as monotheism, human responsibility, and eschatology, that underlie religion, rather than an index to the particular tenets of Christianity. It may be added, however, that in proportion as it points to religion at all, it must point to Christianity, which embodies all the virtues and truths of the religious idea.

Viewed in this general aspect, philosophy is the *best antecedent perspective of eschatological truth* that ancient literature affords. The doctrine of immortality, dimly apprehended, did not go begging for support among the philosophers. It was questioned, analyzed, suspected, but not often, except by the materialists, rejected; influenced by the superstitious spirit of the age, it was associated with errors, such as transmigration, but it was not pantheistic, and so was an improvement on the fatal dream of the Buddhist. In fact, as between Grecian philosophy, with its echoing discord of announcements touching the future life, and those Asiatic religions that fostered pantheism, transmigration, nirvana, and all such uncongenial dogmas, the former must be preferred. While Cato mused on immortality, Socrates, under condemnation, talked of meeting Orpheus, Homer, and Ajax in the other life, gleams of immortality irradiating from his prison couch. Did Stephen talk more confidently when stoned? Epicurus, a materialist of the lowest grade, advanced arguments against a belief in the immortality of the soul, showing the decadence or uncertainty of faith in the later period of the philosophical era of Greece, but as a whole Greek philosophy may be quoted on the side of the great doctrine.

As to the abode of departed spirits, the standard by which rewards and retributions will be administered, and in what the rewards and retributions consist, philosophy theorized freely, and was more rational than some of the old religions. The old Homeric theology, popular with the masses, was not without influence in philosophic circles, but it was resisted as it was subjected to analysis, and in the later days only unconsciously recognized, if recognized at all. As the apostles were infected with the Judaizing spirit and carried into the new dispensation some of the features of the old economy; as Protestantism still exhibits the impression of Roman Catholic teaching; as Buddhism is not entirely free from Brahminism; so Greek philosophy was not entirely emancipated from the theology or mythology of the poets.

In respect to eschatological truth, it may be said in favor of the poetical theology, that it was far more rational and accorded better with Scriptural teaching than it did in its cosmology or ontology. Its perspective of the future was more vivid, just, and truthful than its historical conception of the genesis of matter and man, or its theological notion of God. Even this concession to the merits of the poetical theology must be understood with the qualification that it applies only to generic principles, and not to the details of the eschatological conception. Concerning the doom of the wicked and the happiness of the righteous, this theology is outspoken, reciting at length the horrors of *hades* and the glories of the abode of the gods, and impressing upon the Greek mind the necessity of righteousness as the condition of entrance into that elysian abode. Its purpose was legitimate; its details of description provoked in the philosophic mind a doubt of the existence of such worlds. The poet located heaven and hell with all the confidence of knowledge, which added to the impressiveness of his teaching, but philosophy questioned the locations.

Heaven was located above the sky; hell sometimes in the interior of the earth, sometimes not far below the surface. This is specific, but not more specific than the remorse that must fill the cup of woe of the vicious and ungrateful. A judgment-seat, judges, degrees of suffering, degrees of reward, were revealed by Homer as if he were inspired; and to these general principles of immortality, judgment, rewards, and punishments, no exception can be taken. The philosopher—Plato, in particular—rejected Homer, not because of the inherent absurdity of these principles, for he adopted them himself, but because of the superstitious excrescences that had gathered around them. In the statement of doctrinal principles Homer was clearer than the inferior poets who followed him, and who, instead of enforcing the principles, buried them in a mass of foolish crudities. The poet fore-glimpsed the truth and announced it; the philosopher stripped it of mythology; the Apostle Paul amplified it on Mars' Hill, revealing the doctrines of immortality, resurrection, and judgment, as Athens had never received them from poets or philosophers. It was all in the same line, however; the poetical, the philosophical, and the apostolical, were *three successive stages of revelation*, the last being complete and authoritative, because divinely inspired, as the others were rationally conjectured.

Thus the old philosophy sustained an intimate relation to Christianity. It reflected its teachings and prepared the way for the apostolic proclamations to such an extent that Prof. Draper says: "Christianity was essentially a Greek religion." This conclusion, plausible because of the relation, is not justified by the facts, nor is the conclusion of Prof. Lindsey, that Christianity is the offshoot of Judaism. Neither Greek philosophy nor Judaism can be ignored in an estimate of Christianity; both contributed to it, the one a philosophic spirit, the other religious truth; but it contains elements, truths, a spirit not found in either, derived from a source not common to them. The bearings of philosophy on religion, and its missionary work, must be prominently recognized in a just historic account of the introduction of Christianity; but the special, differentiating truths of Christianity, however anticipated by the old religions or the old philosophies, had for their source a Messianic character unknown to both, the reformer of all religions and philosophies, the Teacher of all truth, and the Savior of all who would believe in him. In its highest position, as in its last analysis, *Christianity stands alone, supreme, intended for no creature but man, indebted to no source but God.*

In this survey the relation to Christianity of the ancient Oriental philosophies, more particularly the Greek and Hindu, has been considered, but modern philosophy sustains a missionary relation that it may be profitable briefly to study. A visitor from Jupiter to the earth might be impressed with the hostility of modern science and philosophical research to religion in general, and to Christianity in particular; but a protracted stay and a close view of what is going on would lead him to suspect that modern materialists are doing a great work for the religion they would overthrow. The Bible has been assailed by every scientific weapon that could be manufactured; every new science has been developed into a force against it; geology, chemistry, psychology, biology, and physiology, have been employed against revealed religion, and at times with telling effect, staggering the faith of the elect, and creating rejoicing at the gates of hell. The attitude of modern philosophy, embracing the scientific spirit of the age, to Biblical truth, is one of opposition, but it is one of support also, not cordial, fraternal support, but, by virtue of its discoveries and concessions, a bulwark of defense for a truer Christianity than was bequeathed us by the former ages. For, while its questionings of certain religious announcements have led to the abandonment of certain fossilized interpretations, as that concerning the antiquity of the earth, it has also led to a verification of the more essential truths of Christianity, as atonement and responsibility.

If Christian theology has erred at all, it has erred in the scope and magnitude of its undertakings, rather than in its hostility to physical research and discovery. Undertaking to settle all questions, scientific as well as religious, it failed, and under the papal *régime* it obstructed pure and undefiled scientific venture, paralyzing aspiration, and limiting the area of knowledge. The modern spirit, free from papal bondage, has entered upon an exploration of facts on its own account, and in its progress of discovery it has been compelled to differ with standard ecclesiastical systems of chronology, and with geologic and astronomic theology in general; and, emboldened by its success, it is not surprising that it has at last assailed the spiritual side of Christianity. Aiming to correct the scientific notions of theology, it has gone to the other extreme of trying to overthrow its spiritual teachings. This is another task, however, and of quite different proportions, and it will fail, just as theology failed in its attempt to teach science. It can not monopolize all questions any more than theology.   While philosophy, through scientific agency, is correcting the scientific weakness of religion, Christianity is slowly injecting religious truth into philosophy.   At all events, this is the drift of the struggle for supremacy at the present time between the two forces.   Certain it is, that the spiritual truths of Christianity, assailed in every possible way, remain unchanged and unharmed, and, indeed, in a sense confirmed, by philosophic investigation, so far as philosophy can confirm things spiritual.

One evident effect of the modern struggle is that the theologians have been aroused to a strong defense of the citadel of Christianity. This was necessary, on the ground of dissatisfaction with old statements of truth, and with uncertain and scientifically inconsistent interpretations of fact and doctrine.   The cry of heresy, the spirit of loyalty, the power of the creed, and the influence of Church polity had held the multitudes to a uniform acceptance of all the forms of truth, and prevented independent inquiry and rational proof.   While this spirit of quietness reigned  there was no original searching for foundations, except at the peril of penalty ; but a general attack on the line, even querulous and acrimonious as it was, incited to calm, heroic, profound response from the other side.

The final result has not been announced ; but thus far the struggle has established a difference between religion and philosophy, that each has its sphere, and that mutual invasions are no longer justifiable.   This is a gain for both, especially for religion.   As in Wesley's time, the bad odor of the philosophy of Hume, Hobbes, and others drove the religionists to prayer, study, and conflict for the truth, so now the infectious spirit of philosophy excites to a thoughtful comparison of the two systems, and the relative position of each as a factor in the civilizing processes of mankind.   Without doubt scientific philosophy will win laurels in the field of ideas, and discover principles essential to and underlying human progress ; meanwhile Christianity will demonstrate its separate and divine origin, acquiring in our world-life a conquering influence, and at last exercising indisputed dominion over the ages.

## CHAPTER XVI.

### THE RELIGIOUS CONCEPT.

M. THIERS is on record as saying, " Whether true or false, sublime or ridiculous, man must have a religion." The necessity for religion, or satisfaction of the moral nature, is as imperative as the necessity for food, or the maintenance of the physical life. The ground-plan of religion is the religious idea, or the religious bias of humanity, the study of which will reveal it as one of the intense and differentiating peculiarities of man.

To the statement that the religious idea is universal, or that one of the contents of consciousness is a religious concept, exceptions have been raised by Sir J. Lubbock, Prof. R. Owen, Hooker, Moffat, and others, who cite barbarous tribes, altogether twenty-eight in number, who, in addition to living without a religion, have no knowledge of God, and from whose minds a sense of the supernatural has entirely faded away. Accepting these statements as correct, an argument of no inconsiderable force may be raised against the common view of an innate recognition of God in the race, and of the integrity and force of the religious convictions of men. So direct an assault on an established theological proof of the existence of the moral sense, and the citation of instances against it, compelled a re-examination of the alleged instances, with the following favorable results, as tabulated by Prof. A. Winchell : As to seven tribes, the information is superficial and insufficient ; as to nine tribes, the information is contradicted by overwhelming evidence to the contrary ; as to nine other tribes, the religious life is nothing, but the idea of the supernatural is recognized as fundamental to existence ; as to *three* tribes—the Gran Chacos of South America, the Arafuras of Vorkay, and the Andamaners—the mind is a religious vacuum. Of the vast number of tribes, nationalities, peoples, and tongues composing the human family, *three* small tribes have been found in whom not a solitary religious idea, feeling, or affection seems to exist. Perhaps an exhaustive attempt at the discovery of the religious principle in them might be rewarded with success.

The exception granted, the general statement that the religious concept is universal remains. Wherever man is, there is a worshiper, or a thinker of supernatural things. Superstition, gross, carnal, cruel, is an index to the existence of a religious faith, which, in its unenlightened and perverted form, is a demonstration of its power. Superstition is a bad definition of religion, but it is the proof of the religious principle. Nothing can be made against the idea itself by quoting the irregularities, complexities, barbarisms, and cruelties which it has provoked; on the contrary, a *wrecked religion is the evidence of the religious principle.* The natural appetite for food and drink may be perverted into gluttony and intemperance, but the folly and excess of appetite furnish as strong proof of its existence as its moderation and proper exercise.

Going back as far as history will take us, and then reading the proceedings of the prehistoric ages in hieroglyphs, and on cuneiform tablets and the tombs of sages, it is easy to conclude that religion has been a dominant influence in all the centuries, and that all peoples have subscribed to certain forms of worship, and paid homage to the deities understood by them. The universality of religion is proof of the universality of the religious idea, and, according to a canon of philosophy, whatever is universal is native to man. A universal conscience proves that it is natural to man, just as universal speech proclaims it as a characteristic of man. The religious idea may be assigned to the category of universal ideas, the exception noted having no more value than idiocy, if quoted against man as an intellectual being, or dumbness, if quoted against language as his characteristic.

Putting it on a level with other universal ideas, it must be as authoritative as others, and entitled to the development and satisfaction which its nature solicits and requires. But, at the risk of seeming to exaggerate its significance, we go a step farther, and affirm that it is *more authoritative than any other*, and should be developed and satisfied, though all others suffer hunger, dwarf, and die. Back, beneath, over all instincts, intuitions, natural and rational principles, is the religious concept strongest, the most vital, the only eternal, principle in man. The greatest idea in man, it is the most liable to perversion, and is, therefore, the greatest source of danger, as well as the greatest source of development. Perverted, man is a wreck; developed, man is a sovereign. Other universal ideas operate in a well-defined, limited sphere, but this idea ranges through all the spheres of human thought, and expands by contact with the greater thoughts of God. Moreover, in the developed or undeveloped man other universal ideas are subordinated to the religious idea, which is always supreme, unless smothered, starved, paralyzed. The religious idea speaks, and appetite is restrained, the thought of responsibility is awakened, a rule of right is sought, the conscience is courageous in its impelling power, the judgment is clear in its discriminating decisions, and the soul bows in prayer before its Maker. Other ideas may suggest moral duties, or moral obligations may arise from an observation of the relationships of men, and a sense of right may seem to originate in the midst of social conflicts; but the religious idea is supreme in its germinating, discriminating, and impelling power, and commands the whole life.

The *producing capacity, or the spontaneous growth of the religious concept, is marvelous,* indicating a high mission, and establishing the claim of its superiority. It is crowding the world with religious institutions; it builds altars and temples; without a knowledge of the true God, it will make gods for itself; without the true Bible, it writes religious documents of its own; without true prophets, it raises up those professing to be the inspired servants of the Most High; without the Cross, it induces sacrifices for sin; and in its lowest form it fails not to impress itself on the customs, laws, beliefs, and moral life of a people. The religious idea is the source of the religious *ideas* of the many religions to which history points, and which still exist. Brahminism is a religion of ideas traceable to the religious idea. Buddhism is a religion of ideas; Taoism, Parseeism, and Shintoism are religious ideas, born of the idea. In these we see a perverted development of the idea, which, however, is not extinguished in the development, but exists as the controlling influence, waiting for right development in the order of time. The religious norm is Christianity, to which the old religions will finally accommodate themselves, and religious ideas will yield to the exactions of the true religious idea.

This concept is not on the way to extinction. Religious ideas, expressing themselves in the tortured types of paganism, may wither and expire, but the idea is imperishable. Strauss asks, "Have we still a religion?" The more important question is, *Have we the religious idea?* Given the Idea, and Religion follows. The idea is not a latent force; it never was, it never can be, inactive; it must always be producing. It may be misdirected; it may be at variance with modern thought; but it is on hand everywhere and at all times, producing religions, and ready for the right religion. Other ideas, active, growing, intelligent, conserving, are yet neither so omnipotent nor prolific. The love of order, liberty, and fraternity, the instinct of patriotism, breaks out in various forms of government; the spirit of sympathy rears philanthropic institutions; but Churches, Bibles, priesthoods, prayers, sacrifices, songs, faiths, stand forth as the peculiar witnesses to the power of an idea dominant throughout the ages.

If, therefore, the religious concept is universal, authoritative, and productive, it is entitled to a consideration which no other idea may invoke. Rising above others, like Mont Blanc above surrounding peaks and ranges, to its height we propose to go, and from its summit survey the inalienable characteristics of the idea, and its relation to manhood, civilization, and destiny.    Not a little difficult is the task, however, first to take the idea out of its relations, to isolate and examine it and describe it, and then portray its relations, with their significance and value.    This must be done, if the idea itself receive a just philosophic treatment.    The universality of the religious concept has been affirmed.    No account of the fact, no history of the origin of the fact, was given.    The only explanation of the statement is, that the religious idea is *constitutional*, an inalienable characteristic of man.    It belongs to him alone.    Animals are not equipped with it.    It is his glory, and is the key to his possibilities.    It is the measure of his strength and the index to his immortality.    It opens up the supernatural to his vision, and clothes him with supernatural power.    The constitutional idea links him with the constitution of all things, by virtue of which he sustains a pantheistic relation to the universe and God.    Under the direction of the idea, he has his hands on every thing, and his eyes continually open upon the unseen. That its objective point is God, no one will deny; that it postulates immortality, all must admit; that it echoes the thought of personal responsibility, all by experience know; that it enjoins prayer, faith, sacrifice, humility, honesty, history attests, and individual life fully corroborates.    The religious idea, swinging out into eternity, brings back eternal things to the soul.    This is its purpose, or it is purposeless.    The establishment of relations between man and God is the end of its administration, its only function.    The religious idea is, therefore, not only the basis of religion, but also the root-idea of humanity, the key to character, the source of possibility.    To know man adequately, more than his religion must be known; his religious nature, or the religious roots of character, must be analyzed and under-stood.    Back of religion is the idea that produced it, as back of the steamship are Watt and Fulton.

Auguste Comte, a positivist, examining the historic growth of the race, propounded, as its explanation, the "law of the three stages," through which, according to his judgment, it had passed.    The first stage is *theological;* the second, *metaphysical;* the third, *positive* or scientific.    While he hoped to demonstrate that the intellectual growth of the race, beginning with theological conceptions, is toward a positive or scientific affirmation of truth, and ultimately away from the religious, it is singular that he concedes the theological spirit to be the earliest historic human force, the foundation of the first social, political, and moral institutions in the world.    History compels this acknowledgment, for it is a fact that the idea of the supernatural appeared among the earliest manifestations of human activity. Comte interprets it as a superstitious or fictitious idea, the outgrowth of ignorance and fear; but its *existence* he frankly acknowledges. As to his interpretation, it does not concern us; for even fear could not excite it if it did not exist, and ignorance of the supernatural would not likely lead to it if there was nothing in the nature of man to correspond to it. The theologic spirit is primary, antecedent, and constitutional.

Strauss discusses his question, "Have we still a religion?" for the purpose of annihilating the religious instinct, and proceeds to explain the rise of religions, or the reign of the supernatural idea among men, by attributing both the idea and its expression to natural causes. He quotes Hume to the effect that man adopted religion, not from a "disinterested desire of knowledge and truth," but because he fancied it might aid him in his material conflicts, or from a spirit of selfishness. This falls short of the truth. Oppressed by a sense of want and helplessness, man was driven by his religious nature out of himself to form an alliance with the Supreme Power, that he might conquer in conflict and reign as a sovereign. It was a sense of need that drove man to God; but the sense of need is the religious sense awakened or in power, and the impulse to seek God is the prompting of the active religious idea. The thought of self-interest thrives in the presence of the religious idea; it is legitimate; it is the thought of deliverance, development, eternal happiness.

Strauss, looking at the early religions, sees in them the play of ignorance and the sway of a supernatural fear of nature. Polytheism was not an unnatural type of religious faith. In the intellectual progress of man, and as his acquaintance with nature increased, the polytheistic sentiment weakened; and, as he reflected on the unity of the world, as he did in Greece, or, as he claimed the attentions of a personal Ruler, as did the Jews, the drift of thought, both philosophical and religious, was toward the "serried form" of monotheism. Polytheism is the religion of ignorance; monotheism is the religion of reflection; but it is "only an ancient Christian-Hebrew prejudice to consider monotheism the higher form of religion." It is evident that Strauss means that, if one religion is superior to another, of which he is not certain, all religions are the products of human fears, or human reason, and barren of divine elements, and, therefore, without any authority.

The supernatural character of religion is not now in question; but, if Strauss is correct in his analysis of religions, he confirms the position taken in this chapter, that the religious idea is constitutional. Polytheism and monotheism are proofs that it is an organic idea of human nature.

Strauss undertakes at some length to expose the anthropomorphic origin of the concept of a personal God and the doctrine of a future life, two fundamental conceptions of any religion; and, having satisfied himself that these doctrines are the result of philosophic speculation, religious hopes, and rational fears, he concludes that the world is without a divine religion. To contest this conclusion is not now our purpose. The alleged discovery of an anthropomorphic origin or center of great religious doctrines, is substantial proof of the constitutionality of the religious idea. It is in man to think supernatural things, and to project supernatural conceptions. We do not say supernatural *truths*, for the religious idea needs enlightenment; without enlightenment, it runs into superstition; but, enlightened or not, it exhibits in its highest activity a supernatural animation, and issues religions, superstitious or otherwise.

That this concept is constitutional, is more a question of fact than speculation. To testimony we appeal. Of South African tribes, ignorant, debased, vicious, Dr. Livingstone says: "There is no necessity for beginning to tell even the most degraded of these people of the existence of a God or a future state—the facts being universally admitted." Mungo Park represents the Mandingo Africans as in possession of the same beliefs. Says Adolf Pictet: "If there ever had been, or if there still anywhere existed, a people entirely destitute of religion, it would be in consequence of an exceptional downfall, which would be tantamount to a lapse into animality." Sir John Ross reports the sense of a personal God in the Arctic Highlanders. Dr. McCosh says: "The idea of God, the belief in God, may be justly represented as native to man." Ritter holds that the idea of God is original to the mind. Herbert Spencer says: "Religious ideas of one kind or another are almost, if not quite, universal."

Darwin asserts the existence of "numerous races who have no idea of one or more gods and who have no words in their language to express them." Sir John Lubbock says, "It has been asserted, over and over again, that there is no race so degraded as to be entirely without a religion—without some idea of a deity. So far from this being true, the very reverse is the case." Both Darwin and Lubbock have been disputed, and the instances they report have, upon further examination, been turned against them. Dr. W. B. Carpenter declares that the attempts made by some travelers to prove that some nations are destitute of the religious principle have been "based upon a limited acquaintance with their habits of thought and with their outward observances;" and Herder asserts that "traces of religion, however different its garb may be, are found even among the poorest and rudest nations on the verge of the earth." The weight of authority is against the disputants; the cases cited by them have been overthrown; and the conclusion that the religious idea is constitutional is buttressed by historical, scientific, ethnological, theological, and philosophical proofs not easily demolished or answered.

Dissection of the constitutional religious idea will disclose a framework of co-ordinate facts, principles, and ideas that will aid materially in our comprehension of man's religious nature. What, then, does the religious idea include? What does it exclude? In summarizing man's natural equipment, we must remember all that belongs to it. There are, besides the religious idea, the exponent of religion, an intellectual idea, synonymous with the intellectual nature, and an emotional idea, synonymous with the emotional nature. Does the religious concept include or exclude the intellectual and emotional? To claim that it excludes them is to leave it to itself, with independent functions capable of producing religion without them; to insist that it includes them is to reduce them to subsidiary elements in the human constitution. The religious idea is great, so overshadowing all other constitutional forces that no injustice is done in including them within its own territory and within the sphere of its operations. Human nature, like Ezekiel's wheels, is a combination of ideas, one included in another, and each sufficiently different in peculiarities to be easily identified. *Intellectual activity is pre-supposed in moral activity.* One without the other is impossible. Moral distinctions, moral issues, moral acts require the intervention of intellectual discrimination and intellectual purpose.

The Will is the central faculty, the sign of personality, and is involved in every moral act of man. The power of self-determination is a constitutional power; a volitional exercise is a constitutional exercise; and responsibility can be predicated only on the possession and exercise of a will free, independent, and conscious. Under the direction of such a Will the mind thinks, plans, decides, acts. Primarily, it may be spoken of as an intellectual faculty, but such is its relation to moral character that it may be elevated to the rank of a moral faculty. Its chief function is moral, not intellectual. The decisions of the Will are in most cases the decisions of the moral nature. It must, therefore, be included in the religious idea.

The Judgment the psychologist will mark an intellectual faculty, yet it deals with moral questions, determines moral choices, and exercises all the functions of a moral faculty. It belongs to the religious idea.

The Imagination may play in the æsthetic realm, or roam over the fields of thought, but it takes the moral nature with it, and impresses it, either elevating or contaminating it.

The Memory, crowded with evil impressions, may reproduce them to the consternation of the moral principle and assail it with the sharp edge of unholy remembrances.

It is not asserted that every intellectual faculty is a religious faculty, or religion-inspiring, but it is asserted that every intellectual faculty is closely related to the religious constitution of man, and in its exercise is tributary to moral character. The religious idea is not without intellectual foundations ; the religious constitution is in a sense the intellectual constitution ; a religious act is an intellectual act ; *religion is the human mind in worship.*

In like manner it may be established that the *religious concept has emotional foundations*, or sustains a direct relation to the emotional structure and the active life of man. By emotional structure we mean the affections, appetites, passions, the whole range of human feeling as by the intellectual structure we mean the whole range of human thinking. Both in their highest and lowest activity, the affections take a moral complexion and the result of their exercise is always apparent in the moral nature. In proportion as the affectional nature inclines to worthy objects the moral nature is strengthened ; as it lingers in the vicinity of base objects the moral nature is weakened and contaminated. Love of truth, and preference for error, are affectional as well as intellectual exercises. Love of the beautiful, love of order, proportion, harmony, unity, and aversion for their contraries are more nearly exclusive affectional acts, while love of the pleasures of appetite is a purely affectional exercise. The malevolent affections, such as jealousy, revenge, envy, hatred, as well as the benevolent, such as sympathy, the forgiving spirit, humility, and benevolence, are strictly affectional and religious.

In whatever direction the affectional nature goes, or to whatever objects it attaches itself, whether intellectual, æsthetic, social, passional, or moral, it affects the religious principle and produces religious results. More even than the volitional, the affectional nature is an adjunct of the religious idea, since its activities spring directly from the moral character or result in molding and transforming it.

The religious concept is grounded in feeling as well as thinking, in affection as well as reflection. Its emotional character philosophers concede, but are wont to deny its intellectual character. Religion is an emotional, not an intellectual condition ; it is a fluctuating, superficial thing, like the emotions themselves. It is a mistake to regard religion as an exclusive emotional or affectional state ; and it is equally erroneous to suspect that it is unsound or unsafe because of the presence of the emotional element. The appetites and passions swing back and forth, or rise and fall, while the affectional nature remains the same in spite of the variety and fluctuation of its manifestations. The benevolent affections often change with objects and conditions, but the benevolent nature abides in its intensity and integrity. So the emotional or affectional element of religion, varying in intensity, and expressing itself in superstitious or refined ritualisms, exists always and in all men. Lake Erie, with all its storms, its shallows, and its deeps, is Lake Erie still. The emotional foundation of religion is not its weakness, but its strength.

The claim that the religious concept rests on religious foundations, or is the outgrowth of certain religious elements in human nature, as distinguished from the intellectual and emotional, is consistent in itself, and requires special recognition. The *religious in man is the foundation of the religion of man.* That great moral faculty, commonly denominated *conscience*, speaks for the religious principle as nothing else in human nature. It is, in a sense, the religious principle, for without it religion is impossible.

The origin of conscience baffles the evolutionist, who can not explain it by the theory of development. Conscience *per se* is a structural principle, an original and necessary moral function of man. Without conscience he is not man. The pagan, the savage, the Hottentot, exhibits proofs of its existence, in whom, however, it is found in an imperfect and undeveloped state, requiring enlightenment, education, training before it will act in harmony with an infallible standard of righteousness. The function of conscience is religious, but it will not create a religion absolutely right; it does not originate the ideas of right and wrong, but enforces them as soon as taught or discovered. · The religion of conscience may be the religion of superstition; but in such an event the conscience needs enlightenment. It supports religious ideas; it supports religions; it is religious in its impulses, promptings, and enforcements. In its undeveloped state, however, it will turn to one religion as quickly as to another; hence, the need of education.

To affirm that the religious notion is intuitional is nearly the same thing as to affirm that it is constitutional; but the thought is reproduced here briefly to note the strength of the intuitional idea in its relation to religion. Prof. Bowne designates innate ideas as the "raw rudiments of consciousness," or undeveloped but original concepts in human history. This quite agrees with our thought that the native religious elements in man are undeveloped, whether we mean by "religious elements" the intellectual, emotional, or the purely intuitional, or the contents of consciousness, or the authority of conscience, It amounts to this, that the religious concept, fundamental, universal, intuitional, is in a "raw" state, and requires enlightened development to perform the specific functions assigned it.

One has only to examine the religious intuitions, or trace the history of their development, or the development of religious ideas, to be satisfied that in their original, primitive condition, they are undeveloped, but prophetic of final authority. The faith-principle is intuitional, which, in its original state, will attach itself to superstition as readily as to supernatural truth. Under guardianship and training it may become a heroic characteristic, as in Abraham and Paul. The sense of responsibility to a Supreme Power is intuitional, but is in a "raw" state in the undeveloped man. He is oppressed with the thought that he will be called to an account, and he trembles in view of the future; hence, he is ready for a religion that either quiets that sense of responsibility, or shows how one can prepare to meet all the demands against him both now and hereafter. To refer this sense of responsibility to religious education will not do, for it precedes religious teaching, and leads to it. It is in man to believe; it is in man to fear the higher powers; it is in man to acknowledge responsibility; it is in man to suspect that he will live after death. Immortality is an intuitional suggestion; all religions are full of it, but they have perverted it. It is in man to suspect the existence of one Supreme Being. Human nature is theistic in its intuitional outgoings, but in the undeveloped condition they may embrace polytheism or pantheism; theism is the sign of trained intuitions.

The ideas of faith, responsibility, duty, sacrifice, prayer, immortality, and God, are the output of the religious idea; they are proofs of its existence. With or without revelation, the religious nature will run to these things; without revelation the ideas will appear eccentric and irregular, and religions will be superstitions; with revelation, Christianity will supplant every superstition.

Superstition is a perversion of the religious concept; Christianity secures its proper development and fulfillment. Incidentally it may be observed that Christianity itself is a development of religious ideas, as the monotheistic and Messianic ideas are suggested and revealed in the Old Testament, but brought out in their vivid relations more clearly in the New Testament. If Christianity, or the religion of divine ideas, is a development, it is not strange that the religious concept should itself be subject to a like process; and this we find to be the fact. Both the religious idea, and the religion that satisfies it, have been under a law of development in their unfoldings and enlargements. Imperfect in the beginning, they have developed into perfect conditions, the one as an intuitional conviction, the other as a system of truth.

An analysis of the religious idea shows it to be, first, universal and authoritative; second, intellectual; third, emotional; fourth, religious; fifth, intuitional; sixth, imperfect, "raw," undeveloped.

We proceed to notice the *value* of the religious concept, or its power to produce a true religion. Distinguishing between the idea and its products, we now pass from one to the other, discussing the product abstractly rather than concretely. If the ground-work of a true religion is not in man, then it must be external to him, or he must abide in darkness and death. It is conceded that the religious idea will evolve into religion; but will it evolve into a *right* religion? In the study of this question, foreshadowed by previous paragraphs, we must not forget the Artesian principle, which allows water to rise no higher than its source. Religion will not exceed in value or character the source from which it springs. Within the limitations of the religious idea will be found the essentials of a religion; the religious product of that idea will consist of rational principles, intuitional suggestions, theistic and eschatological ideas, all of them valuable, all essential.

For the most part, all the old religions partake of these ideas, and have prepared the way for a religion truer than themselves. In addition to the theistic idea, coupled with eschatological considerations, many of them have inculcated some of the virtues that belong to the better religion, and all of them profess to be supported by a philosophic foundation. Theories of creation, both of man and the universe; hospitality, benevolence, honesty, virtue, truth; responsibility to the Supreme Ruler, and the doctrine of future rewards and punishments, find a place in Brahminism, Buddhism, Mohammedanism, Shintoism, and all the religions of the pagan world. Even of deism, pantheism, naturalism, the same observation is true in a qualified sense. Responsibility, virtue, immortality, echo from the temples of such religions. The test-question is, are these the best the religious idea can produce? Without revelation, the religious idea, acting alone, has evolved into these various types of religion; and, as specimens of its power or tendency, they are valuable. Evidently, the religious idea has done its best in these religions. It has had time, opportunity, favoring conditions to do better; the necessity for a better, that is, a right religion, began with man's religious decline. But the religious idea, weak, though fundamental, imperfect, though universal, has at no time produced a right religion; never has it satisfied the religious demand of the world. Neither the intuitions, nor emotions, nor intellectual faculties, nor the absolutely religious instincts combined, have suggested an adequate religion; they have demanded it, but could not produce it. We have written of the break-down of philosophy; we now write of the *break-down of the religious idea.* Man is not a successful religion-maker. Even the philosophic Kant grovels on a low level of religion when he says that its chief purpose is to sanction moral duties. Philosophy has no right idea of it. A religion not of man is the world's necessity; a religion from man's Maker is the imperative need; a religion of revelation, and not of discovery or human invention, is the cry of the hour.

In this extremity, Christianity may be presented as a religion adapted to the religious nature of man; a religion, though not the product of the religious idea, great enough, flexible enough to meet the demands of that idea. In a general sense, it may be said that Christianity, properly studied and lovingly received, stimulates the religious nature to growth and development far beyond what it would attain by self-motion or self-activity. The religious nature, vital and eternal, is susceptible of eternal development. What shall touch it, uncoil it, and send it out into the eternal realm? Its tendency to self-development is often arrested by obstacles seemingly superior to it; its area of growth is seemingly within the horizon of one's natural view; and it often grows into deformed shapes, and with limited resources at its command. For a proper and healthy stimulus it must look to an outside source. Christianity is a stimulating religion. As the sun pours its light and heat into the vegetable world, giving life, form, and beauty to it, so Christianity enlightens, warms, and develops the religious nature into life, activity, and moral beauty. It stimulates the whole being by its truths, adaptations, provisions, promises, supports. It is the source of religious revivals, which result in the opening of the religious nature, or the restoration of moral life to man. Other religions are wanting in this power. Mohammed enforced his religion, not by its *inherent stimulating property*, but by the sword, or the law of force. Other religions depend on external aids—Christianity depends upon its inherent vitalizing spirit.

Other religions, developing what they find in man, bring nothing new to man; Christianity *adds* to man's religious resources and inspirations. It is a stimulus to activity; it is an addition to his possessions. The contents of the religious concept in its natural state do not include all religious ideas; there is much beyond it. Messiahship, atonement, reconciliation, resurrection, judgment, justice, and mercy; a Savior, a divine Friend—the religious concept is barren of these notions. These notions Christianity brings to men, and presents them as necessary truths, the basis of a religious life, and as they are accepted other religions perish.

Nor is this the total of the contributions of Christianity to the religious nature. It makes clear to the consciousness what was accepted before with some uncertainty, or was liable to perversion. Natural as is the theistic notion, other religions perverted it; it could not take care of itself; it needed something; Christianity purified it, organized it into a fact of belief, revealed God, and settled the question. As to a future life, other religions have assumed it, but loaded the belief with superstitions dark, repulsive, painful, false. A ray of light shines from the upper world through Christian revelation, and man is satisfied.

In bringing to men truths they do not have, revealing God as they have not known him, revealing the future as it has not been discerned, and revealing redemption as it was only foreshadowed, but never defined, Christianity may claim to be a new religion. More, it may insist that it is a religion from God. In addressing man at all, it may claim his attention; in invigorating his nature, it is entitled to his gratitude; in adapting itself to his condition, it should be embraced by him without delay; in saving his soul, it deserves his consecration, and the service of his life.

Christianity is the supreme religion. Its origin, its truths, its philosophy, its ethical system, its claims, its progress, its power, must be considered in detail if its real character be understood. What Christianity is, what it proposes to do, what are its relations to other religions, and how it conserves human interests, it will be pleasant to attempt to ascertain. Its history is marvelous, a splendid record of contests with the dragon; it knows what fire is; it has met death, hell, and the grave. Its influence is ever widening; millions believe in it as the power of God unto salvation; millions would die for it in opposition to paganism and materialism.

---

# CHAPTER XVII.

## THE APOSTLE PAUL.

IN his lecture on "Numbers," that noted English thinker, Mr. Matthew Arnold advances the theory that the multitudes are corrupt, selfish, and ignorant, and that the hope of the world's progress and regeneration is in the genius, the leadership, the providential work of the "few," or the "remnant," to use the expressive word of the Scriptures. Plato himself discovered this fact, but Christ announced it in laconic form when he said, "Many are called, but few chosen." To the few, chosen of God, chosen by reason of natural fitness, chosen because they would perform the divine tasks, the world is indebted for inventions, discoveries, governments, philanthropies, reformations, moralities, inspirations, and religions. The one "chases," controls, instructs a thousand; the one is on the throne, the many are subjects; the one foresees, the multitudes follow; the one orders, the others obey; the one inspires, the majority keep step to his music.

Paul takes his place among the "few," ranking with them in nobility of character, persistency of purpose, severity of method, and range of achievement. He is not of the "many," either scaled by his aspirations or weighed in the balances of the divine ideals. From the "many" he stands apart, rising higher, as Mount Tabor rises above the plains. He is one, not two; he is not lost in the multitude.

The opinion of Chrysostom that Paul is little understood and imperfectly known in the Christian world is proof of the general indifference which usually obtains among the multitudes respecting the greatness of their heroes and the value of their labors and achievements. Out of this obscurity Paul is sure to come, for, next to the Son of Man, he is the world's greatest religious teacher, if not the world's greatest moral hero, and history will gradually recognize his relations to all religious movements, and necessarily to the world's civilization. As no other man, he is the representative of Christ's truths; as Plato stands for Philosophy, so *Paul may properly stand for Christianity.* So many-sided was he in character, so versatile in endowments, so wise in the selection of methods, so energetic in the execution of plans and purposes, so forcible a teacher of truth, and such an example of the system itself, that as an exponent of religion he eclipsed his brethren of the apostolic college, and has inspired the Church of the ages by his example of heroism and devotion to the mission of the Master. To know this representative as he actually lived, toiled, and died; to understand his original relations to the old faith and his adopted relations to the new system of truth; to trace his career through its vicissitudes of labor and suffering; to observe his environments, what effect they had on him, and what impression he made on them; to study his adaptations to the different spheres in which he is found, his skill in meeting emergencies, his courage in the presence of danger, and his patience and calmness in trial and darkness; to comprehend the designs of his life, the great religious plans committed to his keeping, and the faith that stimulated him while working them into historic results; to reveal his personal experiences of salvation, and the ground of his Christian life—are matters of no little importance, and deserve our most careful consideration.

Over the question of his birthplace it is needless to indulge in speculation; for while Jerome reports that he was born at Giscala, there is every reason to believe that this is an unfounded conjecture, and that Tarsus, a Roman city of Cilicia, was the place of his nativity. The most convincing evidence of this fact is that Paul himself alludes to it in his defensive address from the steps of the fortress of Antonia. Owing to negligence in preserving genealogical records, Homer's birthplace has been in dispute for ages, no less than seven cities claiming the honor; but the Jews were careful to record their family history, and were able to trace their ancestral lines back to the patriarchs. More than once, Paul prided himself as having descended from the tribe of Benjamin as proof of his Hebrew relationship, and when his life was in jeopardy he referred to his Roman citizenship as proof of being foreign-born, and that it entitled him to the protection of the Roman Government.

In the double sense, therefore, he was a Jew and a Roman, a Jew by parentage, a Roman by birthplace; a Jew descended from one of the tribes, a Roman citizen because in some way his father had obtained the rights and liberties of such citizenship, transferring them to his son, who never forgot them in his holy zeal for another kingdom, whose interests he sought to conserve.

The city of Tarsus was one of the ancient cities of Asia Minor. It was situated twelve miles from the Mediterranean coast, on the bank of the Cydnus, its veritable site being now occupied by a Turkish town called *Torsoos*. An Assyrian king founded it about one hundred years after Solomon, from which time until long after Paul's day it continued to flourish as one of the important commercial centers of the East. Cicero resided here during his governorship of the province. Augustus reorganized its government, and Mark Antony, with the approval of the Emperor, made it "free," or instituted "home rule" in the province; but it was long afterward before the people were endowed with the rights and immunities of Roman citizenship. In referring to Tarsus Paul speaks of it as "no mean city," implying distinction as a city of the Roman Empire, and also implying the commercial enterprise and general public spirit of its inhabitants, the educational pursuits and privileges of young and old, the elegant taste and artistic zeal of its upper classes, and the prevailing love of progress, virtue, and truth in the mixed population of the Cilician capital. He meant to honor it; he did not defame it; he spoke of its bazaars, its schools, its temples, its synagogues, its palaces, its statues, its ships, its soldiers, and its eagles. In such a city of wealth, splendor, equipage, and culture he was born, and many a year he spent within its limits, engaged in the common occupation of tent-

making, and quietly prepared himself for the providential career that
he finally began and so brilliantly completed.

According to trustworthy suppositions he was born A. D. 3, or
at least during the first decade of the Savior's life. The one is born
in the obscure village of Bethlehem; the other in the splendid city
of Tarsus. The one sleeps the first night in a manger; the other in
a palace; but the manger and the palace are alike in the sight of
the Lord. Paul is a chosen vessel to bear the treasures of grace to
the households of kings, and distribute the gifts of salvation among
the poor and the lowly. He is not called to make atonement for
sin, as was Christ, but he is called to teach the truth as it is in Jesus.

What was his preparation for the providential mission? In physical appearance he was not prepossessing as a man, nor calculated to
impress men that he could speak with authority, or act with courage.
Small of stature, bald-headed, afflicted with strabismus, without a
pleasing voice, evidently without oratorical accomplishments, he was
not apparently fitted for the high office of the apostleship. If chosen
at all, it must be for other than physical reasons. Paul himself
draws no very complimentary picture of his person or his speech in
his Epistles, and we are bound to believe that possibly irritable in
temper, repulsive in manners, and imperious in conduct, he was,
Plato-like, somewhat disagreeable in the exercise of authority, and
not very congenial as a companion. After his conversion he was a
different man, patient, obliging, attractive. Of his boyhood life there
is no special report further than that he fished in the streams, roamed
over the hills, practiced horseback riding on the plains, and indulged
in the sports, festivals, and associations common to the times and to
the city in which he lived.

The early years of his life were spent in his native city. What
were his educational opportunities in Tarsus? What did he learn in
her schools, from her people, from the prevailing religion, and what
was the measure of parental influence upon him, and what direction
was given in those days to his future? Like Socrates, he exhibits
no love of nature, being absorbed with higher thoughts, and anxious
to know rather the origin of things than things themselves. He is
not a student of nature; he inquires not for facts, forms, phenomena;
he is not in the fields gathering flowers; he hammers not the rocks,
forcing them to tell their secrets; he is not an observer; he can not
be an empiricist. All this is evident in the Jewish youth of Tarsus. During the play-hour he mingles with his school-mates; but when
alone he meditates, not on things, but on *truths.* Neither plain, nor
sea, nor sky; neither the earth, nor the mountains, nor the stars, arrest the gaze, or capture the thought of this wretchedly built phys-

ical pupil of the Cilician schools. He is introspective by nature, quietly thoughtful from habit; he seeks subjects, not objects.

If he did not spend years in the schools of Tarsus, it was not because of any deficiency of scholarship in their teachers, or because of a limited curriculum of study, or because it was not honorable to graduate from any of its numerous halls of learning. The colleges of Tarsus were not excelled by those of Alexandria, Athens, or Rome. Here, then, for a brief period, the provincial Saul is a school-boy. Certain it is, that, after acquiring a knowledge of the alphabet, he seeks a knowledge of mathematics. He is a born mathematician; his Epistles are mathematical truths. In these days he develops the logical faculty, perhaps disputing with professor and student, and triumphing in every intellectual contest. He studies metaphysics, poetry, and art, for the youth of nineteen centuries ago was limited to mathematics, metaphysics, poetry, and art. He studied the Greek language, which was the language of the people, and may have become familiar with Greek authors, Greek systems of philosophy, and Greek ideas of life. This probability Canon Farrar disputes on the general ground that his Epistles contain no allusions to such authors or such subjects, forgetting that just as he ostracized himself from nature, so also he may have cut loose from Grecian influence. If he was sent at thirteen years of age to Jerusalem to complete his education, it is certain he did not master these authors or subjects before going; but, as he spent several years in his native city after his graduation in Jerusalem, it is more than probable that he familiarized himself with Grecian and Roman literature, inasmuch as no other was accessible, and because a knowledge of it was necessary fully to prepare him to meet sophist, philosopher, or teacher in public discussion or private conversation. He is dialectical, like a philosopher; he alludes to the wisdom of the Greeks; he quotes their poets, and on Mars' Hill confounds Stoic and Epicurean. He denounces science, " falsely so-called," and cautions the Colossians, lest any man spoil them through philosophy; that is, by sophistical reasonings, such as a Gorgias might impose, with which he had become acquainted in Tarsus. These sufficiently indicate that Paul's philosophical education at Tarsus followed, if it did not precede, his religious instruction at Jerusalem.

The parental influence in the Jewish family was usually exclusive and supreme. It decided the occupation, the marriage, and the religion of the children. These decisions, it is true, were in harmony with public customs, orders, institutions, and laws; but the preparation of a child for such decisions was a part of the home-training, and relieved the grown-up son of some embarrassments. In no family, perhaps, was the governing influence more patent or more potent in the education of the children than in Saul's childhood home. Tarsus was a pagan city, tolerant of the Jewish religion because it was a "'free" city, but enforcing pagan ideas in the schools and encouraging the superstitious worships of the times, so far as it enforced any worship or religion at all. From such religious influences Saul's parents were anxious to rescue their only son. There is nothing on record that they objected to the Greek language, or to the courses of study in the schools; but the religious atmosphere of the city was poisonous, and the public religion repulsive to their taste and faith. On this ground, if on no other, they determined that their son should go to Jerusalem, where his education might be completed in a school equal to any in Tarsus, and his religion be uncontaminated with pagan teaching and example. At thirteen years of age he enters Jerusalem, a student excited by the glowing descriptions he had heard in his home of the city of God, and a devout believer in the faith of Abraham. The turning-point in his life had come, or was now passed. Both his education and religion are guaranteed. He is not a pagan; he is a Hebrew. He is not a Greek; he is a Jew.

During the college life of Saul in Jerusalem it is difficult to determine which exerted the controlling influence in the development of his character, the educational environment or the religious spirit, or whether they were co-equal in power and relation. In intellectual endowment the young man had few superiors, and soon exhibited an aptness to study, a facility in acquiring knowledge, and an original and persevering habit of inquiry that, while astonishing his instructors, revealed to them the man of the future. In the school of Gamaliel he early took the highest rank, both as a student and a dialectician, often engaging with Gamaliel himself in the discussion of the most abstruse problems, and reasoning with such penetrating force and sublime reverence, that it was generally believed a mighty advocate of Judaism was being raised up in the person of Saul. His was a large brain; his intellect seemed avaricious for truth; and, stimulated in its pursuit by parental teaching, by profound discussion, and especially by the natural bent of his genius, it is not surprising that he excelled the disputants of the school, and emerged as a young giant. In these days his logical, that is, philosophical, powers, acute as those of Socrates, soonest appeared, and were more prominently developed; he was usually inductive in his methods of inquiry, but a lurking deductive tendency finally displayed itself, and became the ruling principle of his mental action. Attributing to a process of revelation the great doctrinal truths of his Epistles, he was as ready to *settle fundamental questions by logic as by revelation. In him-*

*self he was philosophical;* as an instrument he was a revealer; but his revelations are philosophical in content if not in form.

In religious opportunities Jerusalem was in advance of Tarsus. The Hebrew religion was the public religion, paganism being confined to the public functionaries, of whom the majority were appointees of the Roman government. In fact, the religious condition of the two cities was reversed. In Tarsus paganism was the public religion, the Jewish faith being tolerated; in Jerusalem, Judaism was the religion of the people, while paganism was confined to limited official circles. In Tarsus a superior secular education was possible; in Jerusalem a superior religious education was certain. Hence, Saul's religious education is assured, because he is in Jerusalem. He is "brought up" in Jerusalem in the faith; what is commenced in Tarsus is completed in the Holy City; acquiring the Greek in Tarsus, he acquires the Hebrew in Jerusalem, and emerges as a scholarly rabbi, a defender of the Judaic religion, and hostile to the rising faith of the Redeemer. Paganism in Tarsus; Judaism in Jerusalem. Behold in Saul the scholar, the rabbi, the advocate, the religionist. The two schools have done their work.

Saul's real preparation for the apostolate, which is his final historic position, is by no means complete; but his preparation as an apologist for the old faith has been sufficiently indicated in these lines to justify a glance at his work as such apologist. Passing the preliminary period of birth, youth, and education, therefore, he stands before us an equipped advocate of Judaism, and almost without an equal. Prior to his day Jewish teachers, in defending their faith, were compelled to assail different forms of paganism, with the different instruments of their religion, for single errors must be combated with single or specific truths, and not with all that religion teaches. Idolatry must be met by monotheism; the immorality of the Roman Empire must be met by the ethical laws of the Mosaic economy; Sabbath desecration must be counteracted by the Sabbath law; and general sinfulness must be condemned on the ground of individual responsibility to God in the last day. The idea of an attack on a single error by a single truth is philosophical, and the method is usually successful. In the time of Gamaliel, however, the defense of Judaism implied an attack on an entirely different form of religion; more, it implied a conflict with a *supremely new idea* of religion; it implied a conflict with a new religion, one not pagan in its dogmas or practices, one not inferior to Judaism in its claims or teachings, one above Judaism in its tone, purposes, and agencies. Fighting with paganism was like cannonading pebbles; fighting with Christianity was like an attempt to pull down the stars on one's head.

It is significant that in that period of history, until Saul's appearance, Judaism had no logical or heroic defender, and Christianity no positive or dialectical assailant. Herod haughtily ridiculed the Christ, and Pilate ordered his execution, but these were social and civil acts, and not in the interest of any religion. Saul is the exponent of Jewish hatred, in logical form, of Christianity, and stands as its philosophical opponent. It is noteworthy that he is usually represented as a persecutor of the new religion, employing the brutal weapons of cruel opposition to limit, if not prevent, its threatening ascendency in the Jewish world, and that he is quite willing to go far and near to accomplish his purpose. This is the lowest aspect in which his early apologetic career can be viewed. It requires neither genius nor courage to be a persecutor; any depraved man can be such. Saul was more than a persecutor. He was the philosopher of Judaism. His opposition to Christianity was neither from depravity of nature nor cruelty of impulse, but on grounds religious in form, but philosophical in principle. His was the persecution of the philosopher; it was logic reduced to stones or kindled into fire. Educationally, he was fitted for just such opposition; and, religiously, he was bound to the extreme of self-defense.

Yet, scanning his career as a high-toned persecutor, it does not appear that he employed educational means in defense of the old or resistance of the new faith. He never engages in forensic discussions with the apostles on the differences of the two economies; he never issues parchments in explanation of the two faiths; he never apparently examines that which he assails, for believing in the old it is impossible that the new religion can be true; he attacks the new by violence, and means to stamp it out by personal force and legal advantage. The *ground* of his persecution is philosophical; the *method* of his persecution is physical, brutal. Any method may be employed to accomplish the philosophical purpose, so thought Saul; but this is unphilosophical. If a project, purpose, or end be philosophical, the method by which it is promoted must be philosophical. This was Saul's break-down, *the break-down of method.* Under the influence of Judaism, and reckless of method, he could imprison helpless women without compunction, and sanction the murder of devout disciples without a thought of wrong. Saul's personal attitude is the attitude of prejudice, because his religion is insufficient to deliver him from it, and because his method of activity is such as to keep it alive and give it edge and power. The need of another religion might be founded on Saul's relation to the old faith, and its effect on him.

Saul's career as the antagonist of Christianity is of short duration.

He meant to make short work of the new faith, little thinking that his zeal, his genius, his spirit of leadership, and the dialectical habit of his mind, would be employed for twenty years in the defense of that which he seemed ambitious to destroy. He was permitted to exercise his powers in the wrong direction, as a prophecy of what he could do when he should turn in the right direction. Viewing his conversion as a providential event, it was a strategic move to deprive Judaism of its chief advocate, and reinforce Christianity by the very agency which threatened to extirpate it. The conversion of Gamaliel would not have been of so great service to the rising faith as that of Paul. Education, scholarship, genius, logic, religious faith, and religious zeal, may be regarded as a legitimate and absolutely imperative part of the equipment of an apostle; but, with these and nothing more, Saul's preparation had been markedly incomplete. His religious attitude toward Christianity must be changed before he can proclaim or defend it; his moral nature must undergo the transforming power of Christianity before he can define or recommend it. No change is required in his education; the change required is religious. No other school must he needs attend but the school of Christ.

The conversion of Saul, like any case of conversion, was a most wonderful event in its character, circumstances, processes, and extent of results. There is in Scripture no other conversion so fully reported, and human history furnishes no instance that parallels it. It stands alone, and properly; for, as Saul had represented Judaism, so thereafter he must represent Christianity, both as a system of truth, and as the source of regenerating power. This he can not do without positive experience. It is imperative that he pass through Christianity, or rather that Christianity pass through him, that he may know what it is and what it can do. No such necessity is imposed by any other religion. An intellectual acquaintance with its truths, or with itself as a system of truths, and a belief in them, is all that religion required until Christianity, which, in addition thereto, required a spiritual apprehension of its truths, and a spiritual experience of their meaning and power. Conversion, according to Christianity, is not merely an intellectual change, or a change of belief, or a change of sentiments, or a change of truths. Important as such change is, and involved in conversion as it is, it is not conversion. Nor may it be defined as a change of relations to religion; for, while such change is a condition, it is not the essence, of the religious life. Regeneration, involving external relations or conduct, and internal relations or the intellectual attitude, is richer in its spiritual content, and more comprehensive in its spiritual range, than either. It has reference to a new life in man; it is an organic spiritual life that did not previously exist. When it occurs, it equals a new birth, so great is the change in character. The old life dies; the new life begins. With its occurrence, every thing changes; the man is new—new in his sentiments, new in his faith, new in his external relations, new in his intellectual apprehensions, new in his spiritual life. Language can not adequately portray the change; it can only declare· that it has taken place.

This change Christianity requires of its subjects; it never required any thing less; it did not require less of Saul. In his case, however, the order of change is the reverse of that which usually takes place in one who fully accepts the Lord Jesus Christ as the Savior. Frequently, the external change, or change of relation, and the internal change, or change of sentiment, belief, appreciation, precede the spiritual change, or change of nature wrought by supernatural power. It sometimes happens that intellectual conversion takes place long before spiritual conversion, and, as a rule, the former precedes the latter. Saul, however, was spiritually converted before his intellectual judgment of Christianity changed or conformed to the spiritual ideal of life. His intellectual, that is, philosophical, attitude toward Christianity made it impossible for him calmly and thoroughly to examine the spiritual truths of the new religion, and without examination he could not receive it. In his case, therefore, there is no attempt on his part to inform himself of the essential meaning of Christianity, and no providential agency employed to arrest his thought or convince his judgment. Hence, the suggestion of a *psychological explanation of his conversion* made by Pfleiderer is unwarranted, for not a single precedent psychological condition is involved in it. There is no previous examination of Christianity; there is no previous change in the mental attitude of Saul respecting Christianity; there is no psychological conversion antedating the spiritual revolution in his life. The psychological conversion is subsequent to, and the result of, the spiritual conversion. The primary change occurring first, secondary changes immediately followed. The external relation of Saul to the new religion at once conformed to the new life begotten in him by the Spirit of God. Separation from Judaism was the inevitable result of a change of affection toward it, or an absence of attachment for it. An inward preference for Christianity seizing him, he was bound by the expulsive power of the new affection to abandon the old faith and declare for the new. Christianity, rooting itself in the soul-life, does more than manipulate the sentiments; it molds the affections, and wins the subject in spite of mental remonstrance or social resistance. Saul found himself a changed man; as a result, his relations to Judaism and Christianity regulated themselves, and his intellectual attitude harmonized with his spiritual experience.

Sometimes the conversion of Paul is referred to as a miracle, but, as it seems to us, in forgetfulness of what constitutes a miracle, and of what conversion is, its purpose in this case, and, in the larger sense, its design in the economy of Christianity. Unless every conversion is a miracle, this particular conversion can not be explained as a miracle. In its important features, it does not differ from conversions in general; in the order of preparation for conversion, Saul's experience differs from the majority; in the "accessories" of the event, there are some unusual, if not miraculous, signs or displays, but these must not be identified with the event itself. Pentecost, or the great spiritual baptism of the infant Church, was in no sense miraculous, though the appendages of the occasion were very striking, and even miraculous. Saul was converted by the Holy Ghost, just as every human being must be who is converted; his apprehensions of Christ were changed as Christ manifested himself to him; and, surrendering immediately, and accepting without debate the entire truth of Christ, he was converted. The divine agencies employed in the conversion of others were likewise employed in the conversion of the man of Tarsus. There is no difference in agency; it is the same power, the same wisdom, the same glory. The difference between his conversion and that of others is the difference of antecedent preparation, or order of change, and the difference in the method of spiritual manifestation and attendant paraphernalia. The conversion itself was the spiritual change wrought by the divine Spirit, with only a difference of order in preparation and method in manifestation. The differences are minor; the event itself is the principal thing.

Of this conversion, three accounts are given in the New Testament, substantially agreeing to the most minute particulars. Luke relates it quite fully in the ninth chapter of the Acts of the Apostles, and Paul himself reports it in detail, first, in the temple in Jerusalem, and, second, before Festus and Agrippa in Cæsarea. The salient points are discovered at a glance. Embittered because of the rapid progress of Christianity, and fearing its future ascendency in the world, the Rabbi resolves upon an immediate and decisive inauguration of agencies for its suppression. It does not appear that this movement against the disciples of the Lord is prompted by a concerted action of the school of Gamaliel, or by any consultation with the priests of Jerusalem. Saul is originator of the scheme of opposition. All he asks is a commission from the authorities to proceed. Obtaining the requisite letters, and selecting his body-guard, he hastily and joyfully departs from Jerusalem on his way to Damascus, with the avowed purpose of rescuing Judaism from its new and dangerous environment, of extinguishing the new religion. The journey is a difficult one. The crossing of the Anti-Lebanon range is wearisome, because slow and unattractive. At last the party begin to descend the eastern slopes, from which the wide-extended plain in which Damascus is situated is plainly visible. Practically, the journey is ended; a ride of three hours, and the gates of the embowered city will open to the footsteps of the arch-oppressor. The jaded horses are spurred, for the leader of the company is anxious to suppress the religious revolution, the head-quarters of which have been transferred to Damascus. They ride rapidly, and without solemnity. It is a ride of victory. Over that road the writer himself has traveled, and halted where Saul halted about the noon-hour. Just beyond is the city.

Human calculations sometimes fail, human endeavors sometimes are for nought. In a moment the city fades from Saul's sight, the mountain journey is forgotten, and all earthly things are unknown to this ringleader of persecutors. He falls as if the mountain behind had rolled upon him; he hears a voice, but it is not that of man; he sees a face, but it is not that of one who belongs to the earth. Helpless, blind, reserved, and calm, Saul is a prisoner of the higher powers. Helpless as a child, he is conducted into the city slowly and with reverent step. The hilarity of one hour ago is superseded by a solemnity that the body-guard themselves share; the malicious scheme of their leader withers in his hands like poisonous flowers, and is forever cast aside; and on he goes to the appointed house of Judas, on the street called Straight, to receive instruction. What a change! Expecting to enter the city with a shout, he goes with prayer on his lips; thinking to enter the gates with delight, he enters as a blind man, not knowing whither others may lead him; intending to slaughter the disciples, he is at once ushered into their company, and is dependent on them for comfort and instruction. Ananias, living on one of the crooked streets of the city, was deputed by the Holy Ghost immediately to proceed to the house of Judas, where, finding Saul, he laid his hands on him, and he received his sight and also the Holy Ghost. Here is a double vision; temporal sight restored, and spiritual sight fully given. Saul is numbered with the disciples, and known thereafter as Paul.

The inquiry as to the time of Paul's conversion is pertinent, since some writers hold that the work of regeneration was performed and completed on the plain, and that the subsequent baptism received at the house of Judas was a second or distinct spiritual work; while others insist that regeneration in its initial stages occurred at the noon-hour, and was completed at the end of three days on the visitation of Ananias to Saul. There seems to be no sufficient reason for doubting that conversion actually took place on the plain, for Saul surrendered to Christ, and became obedient as a child. By that act he renounced Judaism, abandoned his mission to Damascus, and desired at once to enter upon the service of the Master. As Dr. W. M. Taylor expresses it, "the spiritual crisis was over before Ananias appeared," and the Christian life was already a reality to Saul.

Believing this position invulnerable, it remains to interpret the spiritual baptism at the house of Judas. What was it, or what did it signify? It signified either a second work of the Spirit, commonly called sanctification, or a *special spiritual preparation for the apostolic office;* the latter seems the more rational interpretation. To be sure, if regeneration was experienced on the plain, it might seem as if sanctification was the after-experience in the city. This is possible, and, within certain limits of view, probable; but when it is remembered that Paul was a chosen vessel to bear the great Name to the Gentiles, and that he must suffer many things for Christ's sake, it is natural to infer that the baptism was a preparation for apostolic life. It is true that sanctification will prepare the minister for ministerial life, as it does the average Christian for the Christian life; but beyond these religious conditions is that peculiar state or prerogative which inheres in the apostolic or ministerial office, for which special education is required. If, then, we teach that the ceremony at the house of Judas was the induction of Paul into his apostolate, and that the spiritual baptism then received was the full and final apostolic equipment of the candidate, it is because the record of the event will bear the interpretation without doing injustice to the other.

The effect of the spiritual transformation on Paul was as deep and radical as the transformation itself. It was all-important that he should recognize the supernatural character of the change through which he had passed, or its loftiest benefit had not been appropriated. Judaism did not emphasize the doctrine of regeneration as the condition of entrance into the kingdom of God. The old administration was content with its elaboration of the doctrine of the Fatherhood of God, and imposed upon men those duties that grew out of faith in divine providence. Spiritual change, as formulated by the New Testament teachers, was but dimly apprehended by the old economists, many of whom, in particular Joseph, Moses, Elijah, Samuel, and Daniel, were as saintly in their lives and as enthusiastically devoted to religion as Peter, James, and John, of later times. But the Jew of Paul's day, darkened by traditions, and stunted in his growth, had no correct conception of what is known as spiritual regeneration.

Saul himself was a bigoted Pharisee, a zealous formalist, and a heroic guardian of the old faith; but his was not a biogenetic faith. He must experience regeneration; he must not only be converted by supernatural power, but the inward change must be supernatural. The change occurring, it separated him from the old faith, as restored health separates from diseased conditions. The new faith became his life.

In this change the beginning of *Paul's relation to Christianity* is apparent. He did not embrace it from a previous knowledge of its merits, or from a long-standing conviction of its truth; he had not discussed it with Peter, as Luther and Dr. Eck discussed the two phases of the Christian faith, and, being vanquished, had yielded the old and accepted the new faith; he had not been persuaded by friends, or even warned by Providence that any truth of Christianity was vital to his happiness or usefulness; but he is changed by the power that makes for righteousness, and he would sooner have denied himself than deny the Lord who mercifully overwhelmed him with light. He recognized the supernatural character of his transformation.

Its more manifest effect was the reconstruction, not only of certain temporary plans, but also of his entire *life-plan*, which hitherto had been devoted to the maintenance of Judaism. From the moment of his equipment for the apostleship he entered upon it, severing the ties that bound him to the Judaic dispensation, and renouncing allegiance to those duties which he had voluntarily assumed. Paul is more than a disciple—he is henceforth a preacher of the religion he aimed to destroy. By his education and general training; by his knowledge of Judaism and his acquaintance with the Jewish nation; and by his relations to the Gentile world, he is fitted for a public career, and at once engages in public tasks and duties. By his conversion, so deep and so thorough; by his obedient and trustful spirit; by his heroism and consecrated zeal, he is qualified to proclaim Christianity to all the world, and begins to preach in Damascus, the very city that was to witness the extinction of the truth that now filled his heart. He does not wait to be examined, licensed, or put on probation, but goes forth to declare the revelation of Christ to him. It was always the boast of Paul that he received his call from the Lord; that he preached not by the will of man, and that what he taught was that which he received from God. This made him confident in spirit and invincible in argument. He preached, not his sentiments, nor the traditions of others, but what came to him through the channels of regeneration and revelation. No other such instance is known to the Church. As to the ministry, *vox ecclesiæ* is considered supreme; but no Church votes him a license, and no apostles ordain him to the sacred office.

In a sense he is above organizations, orders, institutions, for he is in charge of the Christ whom he persecuted. He stands pre-eminently above the apostles, and is the noblest, because the truest, exponent of Christianity.

It is not surprising that so complete and radical a change in his character and conduct should give rise to various explanations of the alleged conversion; nor is it surprising that, since it was a genuine conversion, all explanations that eliminate the supernatural element utterly fail to satisfy the inquirer. Baur says that "in his sudden transformation from the most vehement adversary into the most resolute herald of Christianity, we can see nothing short of a miracle." It was not a miracle, for conversions are occurring constantly; but it impresses scholarly men as something wonderful, as *catastrophic* in human history, to be explained only by supernatural intervention, and is therefore of the nature of a miracle. The *fact* of the conversion can not be denied. It is a matter of record in profane as in sacred history, in Jewish as in Christian writings. *It must therefore be explained.* Several theories have been propounded for the clearing up of the profound mystery which is involved in the historic event.

The "scientific" explanation excites interest. If the event has any natural ground, or was a purely rationalistic process, and can be made so to appear, then the supernatural feature will disappear; but, even if such a solution is possible, it does not alter the stupendous fact of Saul's *changed attitude* and *career*. The career of Paul is marvelous, even if the offspring of the naturalistic spirit. Rénan, espousing the suggestions of Baur in particular, and assuming to believe that Luke's account and Paul's as well, of the conversion-scene, is a mythological narrative, clothes the event with natural drapery, and transposes it into an effect of atmospheric conditions and physical environment. He assumes a thunder-storm in progress on the plain. Saul, now across the mountains, with city in sight, is bewildered with expectation of victory; his head is turned; the sun pours down its heat upon his excited brow; he babbles like one with fever; he reels on his horse as if sun-struck; the lightnings flash and his ophthalmic eyes suffer and start with tears; the thunder roars, and he falls to the ground. All this is possible. These, however, are external conditions; these are physical states, to obtain which Rénan drew on his imagination, for the Scriptural account does not contain them. It makes no reference to a storm, or that Saul was bewildered, or sick, or sun-struck. Besides, if the atmospheric conditions were such as he describes, the men with Saul must have suffered likewise, or been affected in a similar way; but, while he fell to the earth, they *stood;* while he saw Jesus Christ, they "saw no man;"

while he talked, they were *speechless;* while they heard a voice they understood it not. It is at least strange that no one is affected as is Saul.

If Saul's condition was the result of physical causes, then a physician would have been called so soon as the party arrived in the city; but it seems that physical remedies were not sought either by himself or his friends. Saul understood himself, and preferred the *remedy of discipleship.*

A singular feature of the proceeding on the plain is the conversation that ensued between Saul and his invisible interlocutor. A " voice " is heard by the men with Saul. They did not pronounce it thunder, as does Rénan. " Who ever heard the thunder," asks Dr. Schaff, " speak in Hebrew or in any other articulate language?" Thunder, lightning, sun-stroke, ophthalmia, these are natural phenomena; but the " voice," the conversation, the obedient purpose, the changed attitude, the *extinct rebellion* in Saul, the spiritual preference, the love of discipleship, and the new life of that hour, are signs of a spiritual phenomenon, not to be explained by the legerdemain of a storm, or the heroic vacillation of a feverish sinner.

The unsoundness of the physical theory of Saul's conversion being discovered, the Tübingen school of rationalists have proposed a pyschological explanation of it, which, superior to the other in that it interprets it as an intellectual or subjective process, is as inadequate as the other, and to be abandoned as quickly and as rationally as one abandons the other. Holsten is the principal defender of this theory. It is alleged that Saul, all his life-time, was subject to visions and delusions, which prepared him for the great hallucination to which he finally submitted. On his way to Damascus he was reticent, introspective, meditating on the testimony of Stephen, and absorbed with the great designs of the crucified Christ, as they had reached his ears. In this self-forgetting state of mind, wondering if, after all, the new Master might not be the promised Messiah, and silently, but perceptibly, gravitating toward such a belief, he found himself within sight of the oldest city in the world ; and, instinctively and religiously revolting against the mission he had planned respecting the Lord's disciples, he swooned as if sun-struck, but was really stunned by his conscience and overcome by remorse of guilt. During the swoon, or trance, he had a supposed vision of the Lord, and heard his voice and conversed with him, the result being a permanent modification of religious belief and a new direction to his subsequent life.

The difference between the physical and the psychological theories is that the former attributes the conversion to external causes, while the latter attributes it to internal conditions. The one is objective, the other subjective; the one refers the event to the influence of *nature*, the other to human or *mental activity*. Neither attributes it to the supernatural, or involves a single supernatural element. The event is a natural or human, and not a supernatural, event. If, however, the conversion was a purely subjective event, it establishes that Saul was the victim of his own delusion, and not the victim of another's hallucination. He was self-deceived, others did not deceive him. He saw a form, a face, but it was unreal, it was the invention of a highly excited imagination; he heard a voice, but it, too, was unreal, it was the echo of his own thought. Saul must, therefore, be viewed as an unbalanced heretic, erring by reason of his imagination, drifting suddenly into mysticism because unable to restrain the activity of his idealistic faith,—all of which is contrary to the temperament, education, career, and profession of Saul, who is understood to have been a man with little or no imagination, with no poetic fervor, with no training in mystical lore; a man disciplined by danger, cool in emergency, and never given to delirium, either in his religious or social life. To establish the theory will require a new portraiture of Saul, a blotting out of his well-known characteristics, and the invention of a man entirely different from the Apostle to the Gentiles.

Equally fatal to the theory is the consideration that had Saul in a moment of excitement abjured Judaism, from the temporary belief that Christianity is the final religion, he would afterward, when reason was again installed, have reviewed his hasty action and returned to the embrace of the old faith. If, when in a delirium or dream, Christianity appeared to him true, when rational and self-restrained it might have appeared false, in which event he would have abandoned it. But it seems that in his rational moments, as in the delirium, he declared for Christ on the ground that he had both seen and heard him; and there was no disposition, after his examination of the two religions, to confess haste or error in turning from one to the other. Even if it could be granted that the conversion, being psychological, was a delusion, it can not be said that the *subsequent rational judgment of Saul respecting Christianity was a delusion*, or the error of his imagination.

Prof. Reuss, of Strassburg, detecting the weakness of the psychological theory, pronounced the conversion an " unsolved psychological problem;" but it is not a psychological any more than it is a physical problem. It is a *supernatural problem*, lifted out of the circle of the physical and the psychological, the only solution of which is the actual manifestation of Christ to Saul, and the work of his Spirit in the heart of the Hebrew. If Paul's testimony to the event is insufficient to establish it, his career in defense of it is unanswerable; his after-life is an irresistible argument for the truth of Christianity. Behold the scholar and the Christian; behold the educated and the converted man! Education and religion are his special equipments for his life-work, which is foreshadowed in the revelation to Ananias that Saul is chosen as the Apostle to the Gentiles.

In addition to these equipments Paul's endowments, or his temperamental and natural heritage must be catalogued, in order fully to comprehend the adaptation of the man to his providential assignment. He was not chosen wholly on the ground of his scholarship or conversion, but also because of certain natural forces or qualities which, independent of scholarship and religious training, constituted the elemental man, but which, refined by culture and restrained and directed by religion, constituted him the incessant toiler, the invincible hero, and the unrivaled apostle in the Christian Church. Of the moral qualities native to the man, none is more conspicuous than his *sincerity of conviction and transparency of purpose*, which always governed him, whether as a Pharisee or a Christian. He wore no mask, and, free from self-deception, scorned to deceive others. He was not an enigma, working in the dark, and with an unsettled purpose in life. He had a distinct duty before him, and proclaimed it everywhere. He was known as the sincere and positive defender of what he believed and taught as the truth. Such a man could not be negative or neutral, but was always on one side or the other in every issue. Outspoken, honest, and conscientious, he struck heavy blows for his cause, and defended it from conviction. If he aroused antagonism, he also was honored for the simplicity of his aims and the earnestness of his methods. In his plans, labors, discussions, and aggressions he would refer to the approbation of his conscience as proof that he worked from a high motive, and with a desire to promote the reign of righteousness in the world.

He, however, was more than the moral man; he was sincere, honest, transparent, and tremendously in earnest; but his religious spirit eclipsed the moral side of his life. He went beyond the ethical into the positively religious. None was more scrupulous in the observance of the Jewish festivals, in the repetition of the Talmudic traditions, and in the use of the Jewish rituals, than Saul. In his self-defense before his countrymen and before magistrates he boasted of his constant obedience of Jewish law, of his practice of benevolence under the tithe system, of his manifold works, sacrifices, and prayers, as prescribed by the temple party, and of his intense appreciation of Judaism. As his moral impulses expressed themselves in a sincere and transparent life, so his religious spirit expressed itself in and through the national religion of Palestine, to which he was more devoted than the rabbis of the schools. To be sure, he was only ceremonially, and not therefore sufficiently, religious; but he was devout, reverent, truth-loving, the antagonist of error, and the hater of wrong. He believed in holiness, as Moses taught it; in fraternity, as Abraham exemplified it; in justice, as Joshua enforced it; .in repentance, as David illustrated it; in wisdom, as Solomon used it; in foresight, as the prophets exhibited it; in courage, as Elijah demonstrated it; in consistency, as Daniel lived it; in monotheism, as Habakkuk taught it; in worship, as Nehemiah enjoined it; and in the *coming* Messiah, as Isaiah and Micah had foretold the fact. Saul was the old dispensation over again. *He was the incarnation of the patriarchs, the judges, the kings, and the prophets.* His was the religion of the fathers in human life again. Saul was moral, he was religious by nature. This was a strong point in his character, and biased him in the choice of a life profession.

Intellectually, it is not enough to say he was superior to John the Baptist, who may have been his school-mate in Jerusalem, or superior to Gamaliel, who was the professor of law in the University of Jerusalem, or superior to the men of his age; he was a giant, without a rival in his day, without an equal since his time. His was a broad-gauge mind, apprehending truth in all aspects and relations, and coveting knowledge as if it were his individual inheritance. A truth-seeker, the weakness of error soon disclosed itself under his analytic process, and retired from his presence; half-truths yielded to his logic, and quit the field without a conflict. Severely logical, he was uncompromising when the truth was found, and, with the aid of revelation, he was always sure to find it. What Paul was in his apostolic life, as a logician and teacher, he was in an embryonic state in his youth and early manhood. He was the logical youth, the mathematical man, the intellectual teacher, the doctrinal apostle.

His national spirit, or love of his people, was rare in its integrity and ungovernable in its expression. It is altogether probable that Palestine, like Cilicia, was without the power to affect him, for the æsthetic sense either did not exist or was never awakened in him; but his *people* aroused his patriotism, their history kindled his pride and enthusiasm, and their religion received his reverence and devotion. His is not the attachment to country, but love for a people. In this one-sided patriotism was his special fitness for the apostolate, which required him practically to forsake his country but not his people. His love of locality was not strong; hence he itinerated without regret; he longed not for particular spots or scenes; he was at home everywhere—in Rome as in Damascus, in Athens as in Antioch, in Ephesus as in Jerusalem. Palestine did not charm; localities did not fascinate. But in all places he met his "kinsmen according to the flesh," to whom he was eager to preach Christ and him crucified. Even when he turned to the Gentiles, shaking from his feet the dust of the cities of Israel, he never forgot the Jewish race, but prayed for their repentance unto life. Still, remembering that the last shall be first, and the first last, he devoted his energies to the indoctrination of the Gentile world, which, however steeped in heathenism, was more susceptible to spiritual influence, and really anxious for the light of the new truth.

In a very eminent degree Paul was possessed of the genius of leadership, another qualification for his apostolate. It is trifling with his career to accuse him of ambition, and discreditable to his history to impeach him of a love of place; for, while able to meet the requirements of exalted station, it does not appear that place was sought, or that he was unhappy when dispossessed of it. As a Pharisee, he occupied the highest rank; socially, he was admitted into the most refined and cultured households; and as a religious teacher, none was more respected, and none received larger emolument or nobler honor. Recognition, place, honor, estate, all were his so long as he was a Pharisee. All were lost so soon as he professed faith in the Messiah. Recognition, except in the form of persecution, is denied him; honors are withheld, and the position he occupied declared vacant; estates collapse at his feet, and the world recedes in his presence. It has nothing to offer him, and robs him of that which it formerly conferred. Surely ambition dies when it has nothing to feed on, and love of place perishes when it disappears from the vision of man. It was not innate ambition that qualified Paul for leadership.

The energy of Paul was *sui generis*. It was the *energy of personality*. It was not the expression of animalic force, but the outburst of his intellectual and religious life in consolidated action. One sees it in Elijah, Luther, Cromwell, Mohammed, Knox, Hildebrand, Cæsar, and Charlemagne. It is the *inside life turned into outside events*. It is the substance of the heroic, the guarantee of achievement. Paul was surpliced with heroism. His was the energy of lightning; his the enthusiasm of fire. Dr. Schaff reports that "he combined Semitic fervor, Greek versatility, and Roman energy." In him centered the aristocracy of power, the royalty of courage, and the generosity of light.

One may sometimes arrive at a knowledge of physical forces by a study of them from two stand-points. For instance, one may determine the beneficence of electricity by the destruction it is able to accomplish; that is, the useful or helpful power of electricity may be suspected from its power to do harm. In like manner, one may also predicate the utility of fire from its ability to destroy. In such cases destruction is the measure of the conservative value of force. By such a rule men may sometimes be judged; that is, their power for mischief is the measure of their power for good, their evil life affords a basis of calculation of what their righteous life may become. The actual in one direction is the suggestion of the possible in the opposite direction, as the swing of the pendulum on one side indicates the possible, if not certain, ascent on the other. Constantine, a pagan ruler, then a Christian king; Luther, a Catholic, then a Protestant; John Bunyan, a prisoner in the cell, then a writer of Christian allegory; Peter, the fisherman, then an apostle,—illustrates the rule by which one kind of life is the key to another possible kind of life. The most conspicuous example of history is the apostle Paul, who, in his Pharisaical life, was courageous from conviction, shrewd in schemes of destruction, despotic in their execution, self-reliant in emergencies, and usually triumphant in his purposes. The fragmentary biography of the Pharisee indicates a persevering, resolute, iron-clad, and successful man. Such a record is the key to his possibilities as a Christian. Given to leadership in the one sphere, he is competent for it in the other. The very qualities that rendered him a terror to the infant Church, qualified him for aggressive movements in its behalf, and rendered him an object of dread to the temple party. The Jew knew that a leader had gone when Saul became a Christian. Of his weaknesses few are recorded against him, though it is allowed that he partook of imperfection and grieved over it, as other men grieve over their infirmities. He was a man of temper, as is evident from his treatment of Peter and his quarrel with Barnabas; but the weakness of the man was the measure of his strength. Temper is personality on fire. No hero equals the Son of man in moral perfection. Abraham, Moses, David, John, Peter, and Paul are eclipsed by the Sun of Righteousness. Granting imperfection to the hero of Cilicia, no one will question his fitness for leadership or his adaptation to the apostolate.

In a previous paragraph we say, Behold the scholar and the Christian! we now say, *Behold the man!* His preparation for the high office of apostleship is now complete; complete because he is a scholar; complete because he is a Christian; complete because he is a *man.* His future is assured, because there are poured into it the rich treasures of scholarship, the eternal forces of religion, and the plenary glories of a model manhood.

The revolution in Paul's history was twofold in character; it was religious, arising from spiritual regeneration, it was intellectual or doctrinal, arising from the new experience and the new revelation. The religious revolution, already reported, preceded the intellectual revolution now to be considered. A psychological conversion did not antedate or prepare the way for the spiritual conversion; the reverse actually occurred. Hence, Paul's ideas of the Christian religion were primarily shaped by his unexpected religious experiences; his thoughts are religious because his experiences are religious; his doctrines are spiritual because he first apprehended the truth in its relation to himself. In studying Plato one is constantly impressed that his "Ideas" are supreme and constitute the essence of philosophy; so in studying Paul one can not escape the conviction that his "Ideas" are the ground of Christian thought and constitute the essence of the truest theology. Paul's Ideas, therefore, must be sought out, separated from all other ideas, and indorsed as the contents of the religion of the Master.

No injustice is done others in claiming that Paul's intellectual work stands alone, is unequaled by that of any other apostle, and must be regarded as the all-sufficient exponent of the mind of God in the revelation of truth. He was set apart, not merely as an apostle, to be a herald of messages or worker of miracles, or as a missionary of the new faith, but also as a theologian, a teacher of truth, an expounder of mysteries, and a revealer of the wisdom of God in his religious plans respecting this world. Others wrought miracles; others preached; others wrote; but he was commissioned to formulate the divine truth-ideals in theologic form, for the use of the Christian Church and the enlightenment of the unsaved world. In this direction he went farther than any other sacred writer, holding up the light a little higher, and calling with a still louder voice to mankind to believe in the Lord Jesus Christ. The characteristics of the Pauline theology; the merits of his interpretations; the harmony of his views with those of the Master; the range of his intellectual vision, and the spiritual truths that he unfolds, making clear what was obscure, strengthening what seemed to be weak, and defending what was liable to attack; are enough to engage the closest thought of the profoundest inquirer for a life-time.

Paul's ideas are divine ideas. He affirms as much when he says, "The Gospel which was preached of me is not after man. For I neither received it of man, neither was I taught it, but by the revelation of Jesus Christ." This affidavit, conscientiously made, is important; for it clearly signifies that he was not educated or disciplined into a belief of Christianity, or that he had received it second-hand, or borrowed it in any sense from man. The apostles were not his principal instructors; *he had no primary teachers.* He acquired a knowledge of the truth in no circuitous way, in no school-like way, in no alphabetical way; nor had he imbibed it as a popular sentiment, but received it as an inspiration from God. Not by laying on of hands, not by any physiological process of communicating spiritual things, did he enter into sympathy with the truth or an honest adoption of it. Nor does it appear that by a rationalistic process he wrought out the truth, or planned to discover it, or found it as other men find the truth. To him the truth unsought came; upon him it fell as light falls upon the earth, as rain falls upon the grass. In this respect he is alone. No philosopher obtains truth except by seeking it; no human mind receives spiritual truth except through sympathy with it and ardent searching for it. Paul is authoritative, not as a discoverer of truth, but as the *receiver* of truth; he is the echo of the divine voice; he is the truth. Less than this can not be granted; more than this is not required.

However, the inspirational attitude of Paul, as a teacher of truth, must be understood as including all those complex influences which joined in his education and prepared him to be a receiver of truth. Not every man can receive as much as Paul; not every mind can comprehend as much as Paul. A gulf is larger than a rivulet; Paul's gulf-mind took in more than the creek-mind of Jude. Paul was intellectually prepared for revelations. Certain other influences, doctrinal and otherwise, also entered into his preparatory life, which, not recognized perhaps at the time by himself, contributed to that large theological grasping so noticeable in his later utterances and writings. Among these unrecognized forceful influences may be placed the theologic teaching of Stephen in his address for his life before the Sanhedrim, Saul hearing it and excited to wrath by it. The address, as a literary performance, was masterly; as an argument, it was unanswerable; as a revelation of truth, it was full of surprises, and provoked the bitterest resentment in the minds of those educated in Judaism. It is altogether probable that Saul, then about thirty-five years old, reviewed the address in his own mind, and saw for the first time the radical difference between the faith of Christ and the religion of the Sanhedrim. The knowledge of this difference, instead of leading him to further inquiry, only infuriated him the more, and really provoked his contemplated massacre of the Christians in Damascus. Too much preparatory influence, however, has been attributed to Stephen in Saul's conversion. Augustine declared that if Stephen had not prayed, Paul had not been converted; and Pressensé holds that Stephen made so powerful an impression on Paul that he inaugurated a system of persecutions in order to quiet the tempest of his soul. This is conceding far too much; the concession is a speculation. There is no evidence that Stephen's address influenced the psychological attitude of Paul, and indirectly led to his conversion ; but it is plain that, conversion having taken place, Stephen's theologic influence on Paul begins to be felt, as he recalls his testimony and remembers his martyrdom in its behalf. The truth reported by Stephen, Paul now believes and adopts. In his missionary addresses to the Jews, in his doctrinal epistles to the Churches, and in his prayers everywhere, Paul draws on the phraseology of Stephen, or employs some of the religious ideas of his address, showing that, while uninfluenced by him at the time, he recognized in his converted state the majesty of Stephen's utterances and the inspiration of the truths he then announced. Not denying the influence of Stephen, it is proper to insist that it had no educational, no theologic, power on Paul until after the revelation of the Messiah to him at the time of his conversion. Abraham Lincoln's addresses on the rights of slaves, or the inalienable right of all men to freedom, in the years 1856–1860, fell on dull ears in our great South-land ; but after the abolition of slavery even the South perceived the great truths that had been previously uttered, and accepted them as basal thoughts of the nation's life. Truth does not always have an immediate effect on an unprepared mind ; it rarely has any effect on such a mind, except to inflame it with hostility against it. Stephen's thoughts reappear in Paul's Christian theology, and yet not to the extent or in any way to compromise the original claim of the apostle that he received the truth from Jesus Christ. Stephen's thoughts or truths, though heard before the trip to Damascus, came to Paul as influencing thoughts after the trip had been concluded, and were rather confirmatory than suggestive of the original revelation.

Paul's claim to original revelation from Jesus Christ is sustained by the fact, which he himself relates, that, after a brief sojourn in Damascus, he retired to Arabia, where it is altogether probable he spent nearly three years in seclusion and meditation upon his new and great life-work. Just where he went, and whether or no he communicated during that period with any human being, are matters to which he does not allude, nor any one else ; but the inference is that he spent the time in a review of the Hebrew Scriptures in their Messianic features and references, and in a study of his new experiences and of the preparation required for his new position. Evidently, he knew but little of the Scriptures in their references to the birth, works, career, and death of the Messiah, or he had discovered their fulfillment in Jesus of Nazareth. That he devoted himself in his solitude to the thorough examination of the Scriptures on these points is all but certain, as such knowledge was absolutely necessary to his future career as an apostle. Moreover, it is not extravagant to claim that, during the period of seclusion, the Lord Jesus again visited him, not as a reprover or to discuss the question of duty with him, but as the glorious revealer of truth, and communicated to him many of the doctrines so elaborately presented in Paul's Epistles. To be sure, the facts of the incarnation, the baptism, the transfiguration, the miracles, the crucifixion, the resurrection, and ascension of Christ, may have been reported to Paul by the disciples of Damascus; but the doctrinal interpretations growing out of such facts, such as regeneration, justification, atonement, faith, love, and redemption, may have been *inspirations*, or the result of personal fellowship with Christ. Arabia proved to be a theological school to Paul, in which the only teacher was the Master himself. In Jerusalem, Gamaliel taught him Judaism; in Arabia, Christ taught him Christianity. The proof that the Arabian influence was helpful, whether the result of personal meditation or divine revelation, or *both*, as we judge it to have been, is in the improved tone of his preaching, or rather the positive affirmation of the Messiahship of Christ after his return to Damascus. To him Christ was the Son of God, not only because the prophecies of the Old Testament were fulfilled in him, but also because Christ revealed himself as such to Paul, both at his conversion and while he was in Arabia. From careful study of the sacred books, Paul concluded the doctrine must be true; but by revelation he *knew* it to be true. *The theological education of Paul is constantly improving, because the revelations are continually increasing.*

The human element in Paul's education thus far is insignificant. Grant that Stephen's influence was considerable—it came later in life; grant that the disciples of Damascus poured into his ears some of the truths of the new dispensation—his time with them was short, and he occupied most of it in preaching; so that he makes good his claim that the truth came to him directly from Jesus Christ. If any human influence made any impression upon him, and if any divinely called teacher was instrumental in his theological instruction, such influence was felt when he returned to Jerusalem a Christian man, and such instrumental teacher was the apostle Peter. Even his relationship to Peter must not be exaggerated; for Paul abode in Jerusalem only fifteen days, spending part of the time in securing recognition among the Christians, some of the time in visiting with James, the Lord's brother, and not a little of the remainder of time in disputing in the synagogues, and publicly affirming that Jesus is the Christ. Apparently, Paul must or might have learned much from Peter, James, Barnabas, and others in the Holy City; he might have visited Gethsemane, and listened to its story of sorrow; he could have gone to

Calvary, and heard in his heart the dying shout of the Redeemer, and lingered long enough at the sepulcher to see the Victor rise; he could have walked over to the Mount of Olives, and witnessed by faith the ascension of the Lord; and, retracing his steps, he could have tarried on the Pentecostal site until the holy baptism had been repeated in him. Paul may have been a sight-seer in Jerusalem, and Peter may have been his dragoman! We shall not insist that this is the case, because there are sufficient reasons for believing that the reverse is true. What Peter taught him, or whether Paul received any thing from him, or from any other in Jerusalem, or whether *Paul enlightened Peter and the infant Church*, are questions not settled in the Scriptural narrative. Naturally, one would suppose that Peter would communicate to Paul a full account of Christ's birth, ministry, and death; and yet there is no record that the interview of the two apostles had any religious significance. Perhaps Paul impressed upon Peter that Christianity was larger in its intent than Judaism, and that both should bear it to the Gentile world; perhaps Paul related his conversion, his revelations in Arabia, and the plan of his life-work as an apostle; perhaps Paul declared the independence of his apostleship, and his amenability only to Jesus Christ. During this visit, it is not clear that Paul is particularly instructed by any body, but merely comforted or confirmed in his faith, while he may have instructed Peter and the Christians of Jerusalem in the broader things of God.

The providential fellowship of Paul and Luke was, in the religious sense, more advantageous to the latter than the former, though, from the social stand-point, it was mutually helpful and comforting; and, inasmuch as Luke was a physician, and Paul, especially after his encounters with mobs, was physically dilapidated and ever on the border of a break-down, the services of the former were as necessary as they were refreshing. The religious alliances of Paul with Timotheus, Aquila, Luke, and others, should not be so interpreted as to convey the impression that he was to the smallest extent indebted to them for spiritual knowledge or the revelation of truth, for he was the Gospel father of many of his friends, and the instructor of those who had been longer in the faith than himself. His religious experience developed a social hunger, which was appeased only by Christian fellowship, which he ever sought and only rarely obtained. From all the data on the subject, the conclusion is warranted that Paul was not inducted into a knowledge of the Christian religion by man, but received religious truth, as he had spiritual experience, from Jesus Christ. The proof that Paul's ideas, whatever they are, are divine, is complete.

To ascertain just what he received, or to state the contents of the

Pauline theology, is our next business. In order to a complete triumph in his day, Christianity was compelled to contest the rights, teachings, and purposes of three organic religious ideas, because they were out of harmony with its spirit, and incapable of union with it on the grounds of rational, not to say revealed, truth. The necessary threefold conflict of Christianity with the opposing forces in human society is a key to the revelation made to Paul, and an explanation of his apostolic career. These conflicts were with—

1. Judaism, a divinely ordained religion.
2. Paganism, in its multiform organisms, or Gentilism.
3. Philosophy, or Culture, religious and otherwise.

The conflict of Christianity with Judaism has the appearance of a conflict of the supernatural with the supernatural, for the inspirational element abounds in the one as in the other; and that the one had a divine mission is as evident as that the other is ordained for the accomplishment of a divine purpose. Why the conflict, then? The relation of Judaism to Christianity it is not at all difficult to define; but the Jew, because of perversity of judgment, never would recognize the relation, and has obstinately opposed that form of religion which in its inmost spirit is but the fulfillment of his holiest faith. In Paul's case, the religious revolution, otherwise his conversion, did not consist in a mere exchange of religious dogmas; it was really less an abandonment of certain Judaic sentiments, than a right interpretation of them and the discovery of their fulfillment in the new religion. Uninterpreted, and especially misinterpreted, Judaism in the hand of the Jew became a weapon of self-destruction; rightly interpreted, it opened the way to the Lord Jesus Christ. Fortunately, Paul was impressed to put a right interpretation upon it, and began immediately after conversion to declare its propædeutic office and relation to Christianity. It was none the less divine because it was not a final religion. John the Baptist was none the less an inspired herald because Christ succeeded him. Judaism was the preliminary form, or advertisement, of the final faith, and dropped out of sight so soon as it was fulfilled.

This was Paul's dictum everywhere, on account of which he was persecuted in every city, and suffered many things for Christ's sake. Because of this definition of Judaism, the Jews of Damascus organized to slay him, and he departed by night from the city, escaping by being let down "by the wall in a basket." Because of the espousal of Christianity on this basis, the Jews of Jerusalem determined to kill him, and he again fled to another place of safety. In Asia Minor as in Syria, and in Macedonia as in Italy, the Jews exhibited toward him a malicious spirit. Judaizing teachers insisted on the observance of the Mosaic ritual as a condition of salvation, and obstructed the work of the apostle by tantalizing methods and false devices. The priests and elders were far-seeing enough to discover that in proportion as the new faith spread the old faith must decline, and so were violent in their denunciation of Jews who passed from the tutelage of the one into the experience of the other. When it was impossible to prevent the defection of their own people, or the Gentile multitudes from embracing the Messianic religion, they were ready to compromise on the basis of a *mixed* religion; that is, the Christian must be a believer in some of the Mosaic traditions and an observer of some of the Judaic ceremonies.

A conflict on these lines was inevitable. It must be settled once for all to what extent the Judaic spirit shall affect the Christian life, or whether it shall not entirely disappear, giving place to the higher truth of Christianity, which shall be supreme in its authority over man. The Jews were troubled; Jewish Christians, reverential in feeling toward the old dispensation, were agitated; Gentile Christians, recognizing no obligation to Judaism, were aroused; and the apostles themselves, eager perhaps to unite the two faiths, or bridge the distance between them, were anxious for a settlement of the difficult problem. After many triumphs in Gentile fields, Paul hastens to Jerusalem to report to a council of apostles and elders the work of grace among the Gentiles, and to discuss the necessity of the circumcision of Gentile converts, and how far Jewish laws and usages should prevail in the Christian Church. It was a remarkable council, both for the character of the disputants and the decisions finally reached. *The fate of Christianity was involved in the issue.* The council was divided in opinion in the beginning, but was harmonious in its conclusions, affirming the position of Paul, who denied the necessity of the circumcision of the Gentiles, but did not object to it in the case of Jewish Christians. He had taken Titus, a Gentile convert, with him, and demanded his exemption from the barbarous rite of the Jews. In this new position Peter loyally and fervently supported him; James indorsed, but with no enthusiasm; and the council, by a large majority, decreed the exemption of Gentile converts from circumcision and all other Jewish obligations. Christianity broke with Judaism on a fundamental point, and was relieved of future embarrassments. We see in Paul no compromising spirit, no jutting out of "liberal Christianity" when an essential principle is involved, and no disposition to yield what had been gained. Clearing the Christian Church of Jewish influence, which was Paul's open purpose, he intended that it should rest on a Christian idea, to which all other ideas, laws, and usages should fully conform. The concession of circumcision to Jewish Christians, which was agreed to by the apostles, was for the purpose of obtaining the favor of the Jews; but Paul knew that if it did not involve them in future trouble it would soon expire. He himself agreed to it on the ground of expediency, and because it did not sacrifice the main principle.

The dominant idea in the Christian Church, according to Paul, is Messiahship. This appeared in his experience, and it must be authoritative in the Church. The idea itself meant separation from, because it was the fulfillment of, Judaism. Paul knew Judaism. He knew its heartlessness, its lack of spiritual power, the insignificance of its barren forms, the intellectual limitation of its highest truths, and the inertia of the whole economy. None knew it better than Paul. None was more anxious to save the Gentile world from it than he. It was the leaven of hypocrisy, the ministration of death. The Messianic idea is inspiration itself. As a truth, it is the key to all other religious truth; as the central fact of Christianity, it is the illumination of all it teaches or contains. Paul knew the meaning of Messiahship, and was anxious that it should prevail. In breaking with Judaism, therefore, he severed a vital relation. In preferring Christ to Moses, he eschewed the formal type of religion for a life-saving system; he abandoned ceremonies for truths, and a dull faith for a triumphant experience; he emerged from darkness into light. The primary idea of the Pauline theology is Messiahship, with its cognate truths.

In his religious advances he found it also necessary to break with Gentilism, or with its organic religious systems, which, unlike Judaism, were not fulfilled in Christianity. The conflict, therefore, was not a conflict of interpretation, but a conflict for mastery involving the destruction of the one and the vindication of the other. It involved not the oppositions of truths, so-called, but the opposition of truth and error. It meant the surrender of the one to the other. Paganism, with its organic systems, its effete ideas, its forlorn hope, confronted the apostle everywhere, and stubbornly and irrationally disputed the truth he proclaimed. He must needs introduce new ideas into the public thought of the Gentile world, and compare the old worn-out systems of religion with that of the Son of God. New ideas must demolish old ideas; a new system of truths must entirely subvert the old systems of error. The antagonism is direct, because the difference is immeasurable. Long before Paul preached the sermon in Antioch of Pisidia, he had revealed in divers places the subject-matter of Christianity, as a system of truth; but as this discourse is quite fully reported, it may be quoted, along with others, as reflecting the Pauline conception of Christianity in its relation to the Gentile world. In addition to the positive affirmation of the Messiahship of Christ, supported by indisputable proofs, Paul distinctly enounces and logically elaborates the doctrine of justification by faith and the forgiveness of sins, founded on the atonement of the crucified Lord. Though the sermon was formally preached to the Jews, many Gentiles heard it, and before Paul quitted the city he repeated it, or amplified the great doctrines to the Gentiles, assuring them of eternal life and an equal right to all the provisions of the divine kingdom if they only believed in Christ. Here is an advance in theology. In the conflict with Judaism Paul brings prominently into view the Messiahship of Christ; in the conflict with paganism he brings forward the doctrines of atonement, justification, forgiveness, just what no Gentile religion had taught or foreshadowed. But these did not constitute the sum of Christian doctrines employed by Paul in conflict with and for the overthrow of the Gentile spirit. At Lystra, in particular, he discusses *theistic* truth as if it were all-important, and yet secondary to others. In his various epistles other doctrines are emphasized, *such as man's helplessness or sinfulness, spiritual freedom or deliverance in Christ, repentance toward God, the available efficacy of prayer, the leadership of the Spirit, the resurrection of the dead, the judgment-seat of Christ or human responsibility, the immortality of the soul, and eternal rewards and retributions.* All these are prominent, not in any one epistle, because neither the Gentile nor Jewish Christians needed instruction in every thing, but according as a Church or people were unenlightened along these lines, or were in dispute over these doctrines, Paul wrote and preached. The Messiahship of Christ is the center to which Paul ever points the Jew; but the other doctrines constitute the circumference of religious truth, which he exposes to the view of the Gentile world. This is enlargement, this is progress, both for Christianity and the world.

Another conflict awaited Christianity, for which it seemed quite as well prepared as for those through which it had passed. Judaism was firm and self-reliant, because it was in a sense supernatural; Gentilism was pliable, because it was ignorant and weary with itself; but philosophy was obstinate, because, regarding religions as superstitions, it recognized no special merit in Christianity, and attempted to ridicule it out of existence when its babbling defenders first announced it. In Macedonia, Epicureanism, gone to seed in Atheism, disputed the great doctrines of the resurrection and the judgment; in Rome Stoicism, pretentious in its love of virtue, co-operated not with Christianity in the suppression of crime or the moral education of the people. With both systems of philosophy, or with the cultured classes throughout the Roman Empire, Paul came in contact, and was required to defend his religion, not by an appeal to prophecy, as was his wont among the Jews, nor by showing the worthlessness of prevailing religions and the adequacy of the new religion, as he did to the Gentiles, but by a rational exposition of the truth, and a demonstration of the facts on which his religion rested. Logic, not prophecy; facts, not traditions; truths, not beliefs, are wanted in a strife with culture. For such a conflict Paul was prepared; for he was familiar with the philosophical thought of the times, and was the man to preach to Epicureans, Stoics, Platonists, or others wherever he found them. The philosophical method, no less than philosophical thought, influenced Paul not a little, the traces of which are on exhibition in his Epistle to the Hebrews, and in that wonderful sermon he preached at Athens. The influence of Alexandrian philosophy on Paul, Canon Farrar fully concedes; the influence of, or acquaintance with, Grecian and Roman systems of thought, is quite as apparent.

In this conflict with philosophy, what is the instrument that Paul handles the most skillfully? what is the idea with which he pushes his way into the cultured thought of the East? It is not Messiahism; it it not atonement and justification through Jesus Christ; it is monotheism first, but finally it is the great doctrine of the *resurrection of the Lord Jesus Christ*. To the Corinthians, Athenians, and others tinctured with philosophic wisdom, he expatiates more on these two truths than on any other; he is as strong as Moses in the defense of the theistic notion; but, as the Christian religion rests on another idea, he gives less attention to the one than to the other. In the presence of the philosophers of Athens, he dwells at length upon the doctrine of the resurrection as fundamental, and insists at all times that Christianity stands or falls as this doctrine is true or false. Messiahship is a *prophetical* question—hence, talk to the Jews on that line; atonement is a *religious* question—hence, talk to the Gentiles about it; resurrection is a legal question, a *philosophical* question, a question of facts, arguments, logic—hence, talk to the philosophers about it. Messiahship is a Jewish question; justification is a Gentile question; resurrection is a philosophical question. In this order Paul's ideas grew, were revealed, and developed, the first gradually losing its importance in the practical value of the second, and the second being valuable only as the third had final demonstration. *The initial truth of Christianity is Messiahship, but the basal truth is Resurrection.* From its introductory phases Paul rapidly passed to its fundamental excellences, as separating from the Jews he mingled with the Gentiles, and discovered the relation of the doctrine of the resurrection to final triumph.

Nature's kingdoms or systems, however complex in their development and extensive in their variety, seem to rest upon single truths

25

or simple facts. Far-reaching, mysterious complexity is but the evo-lution of a, perhaps, not distant original simplicity. As in California, the *Sequoia gigantea*, or mammoth tree, springs from a seed no larger than the mustard, so nature everywhere unfolds from small to great, exhibiting in its ever-varying modes of life, and in its transfigured expressions of beauty, the existence of a single purpose, and in its myriad-typed phenomena illustrates well the simplicity of its begin-nings. With all its endless manifestations of form and growth, chemistry declares that the conspicuous element of nature, found in every thing and vitalizing every thing is *oxygen;* or, following Mr. Huxley, we should be compelled to say that the base of nature is protoplasm, thus reducing the universe in its last analysis to a single germ. Botany's sign-manual is a leaf; the index of geology is a grain of sand; of astronomy, a fixed star.

In like manner, the base of the highest religion known to man is a single but sublime truth. Notwithstanding the truths of religion, embracing as they do the mysterious problems of the Infinite, relat-ing to all things past, present, and future, and including all the per-manent necessities and strange possibilities of the human soul, are many, and glisten with celestial light, and are sources of comfort and inspiration to the sons of men; yet faith in them is dependent upon a prior faith in one truth which underlies the whole system of religion.

So Paul instructs us in these words that "if Christ be not raised, your faith is vain;" that is, that the resurrection of our Lord is the ground-work of all Christian faith; that while other truths are radiant as the stars, all-quickening and all-inspiring as the angels, possessing an acknowledged loftiness of grandeur, they rise and fall with one truth, and their destiny, their future power as truths, depends upon the glory of the resurrection.

At Baalbec, Syria, the traveler will observe the ruined Temple of the Sun, once a structure of granite and marble, the mystery of masonry and architecture, still a lesson-teacher in its dilapidation, still artist-ically beautiful in its fragments, and reflecting perfectly the strength and design of its ancient builders. In defiance of Time's cruel touch, six noble columns, majestic in form, heroic in purpose, bearing the marks of antiquity, dare to stand. The temple would have been in-complete without them; but, though necessary, they are not the foundation. Resting upon these broad-shouldered columns are capi-tals, massive, ornamental, essential to the grandeur of the pagan temple; but they are not the foundation. A part of the wall, too, remains, consisting of stones so immense in size that the moderns are puzzled to know how they were elevated to their places; but the walls and these stones in them, resisting all attempts at destruction, are not the foundation. Columns, cornices, walls, all essential to the beauty, dignity, and strength of the temple, and yet all dependent upon the solid, unseen, well-proportioned masonry under ground.

So the temple of religion, consisting of doctrinal walls, buttresses, columns, friezes, and niches, rests upon the all-supporting foundation of one underground truth.

Let us contemplate this one truth from this stand-point—the stand-point of Scripture. The resurrection of our Lord furnishes adequate proof and sufficient support of a religion professedly divine. To a philosopher or theologian a blade of grass may demonstrate the existence of a Creator; but to each a planet, in the regularity of its motions and the solidity of its framework, is a more definite demonstration of his existence. So, while there are other truths that have convincing power, and are really the available and working facts and hypotheses of Christianity, this one truth is the granite rock beneath all, and the inspiration of all. An examination of, or an inquiry into, other truths, as to their sustaining or weight-bearing influence, will satisfy this Pauline conclusion.

Is not prophecy a pillar of Christianity? It is. Does it not demonstrate the inspirational character of revealed religion? It does. Daniel in Babylon and John on Patmos, with prescient sense opened, give us the keys to the world's greatest movements, from before the appearance of a Redeemer to the end of time, unqualifiedly proving their familiarity with the purposes of the divine wisdom. On such a rock as prophetic truth, surely Christianity can establish itself, challenging all opposition. Prophecy is a pillar, but not the foundation, of the temple. Jesus himself frequently assumed a prophet's rôle, delivering his teachings in prophetic forms; but the fate of religion and the faith of Christendom do not rest upon prophetic truth in general, nor in particular, except on that one which Christ uttered in reference to his resurrection.

We pass, then, to miracles, the splendid attestation of divine power, the scintillations of the divine enthusiasm in manifold forms of beauty and benevolence. He that by a word quelled stormy Galilee; he that gave sight to blind Bartimeus; he that spoke Lazarus back into life,—must be the Son of God; and surely Christianity may quietly repose upon these tremendous facts and awe-inspiring events of the Master's life. We can not, nor would we if we could, underrate the value, or misunderstand the motive, in the use of miraculous power on the part of Christ, for it is confessedly supernatural; and, besides, the Savior himself referred to his works as the conclusive evidence that his Messiahship was not an unwarranted assumption. Yet upon no miracle of his miraculous life, save the last, does the fate of Christianity turn. Not to the blasted fig-tree on Olivet; nor to Nain, where the widow's son was raised; nor to Gadara, where the demon-possessed man was set free,—do the finger-boards of the Gospel point us, but, as Paul shouts, *to the sepulcher!*

The incarnation of Jesus is the initial mystery of the New Testament, appealing to faith's mysterious recognition. The birth of our Lord, heralded by angel's song, is indeed a startling event, essential to all that followed. "God manifest in the flesh"—this, says the searching mind, is the basis of all belief. No, even this initial fact of the Gospel becomes a worthless and transparent myth, without persuasive power, unless the alleged resurrection was a literal achievement. The fate of religion, according to Paul, lies not in its origin, but in its *end;* not in incarnation, even as a proven fact, but in resurrection as its terminal glory, as a Joppa orange-tree is tested, not by its flourishing roots, but by its oranges. The manger of Jesus is nothing to the world if his grave is not empty on the third day.

What a marvelous scene is that at the Jordan! Hastening from Galilee, the Master receives baptism at the hands of the weird preacher of the wilderness, the Father speaking approval as by a voice in the over-hanging cloud; the divine Spirit alighting in the form of a dove upon the Master's head; and the Son of God is thus glorified in the sight of men. In that baptismal scene the Trinity appears on exhibition, a pantomimic type made visible. On this scenic truth, potent with affirmation, may religion securely stay itself; this is foundation enough. "No! no!" says Paul, and he points to the sepulcher, saying, "If Christ be not raised, your faith is vain."

See the Son of man in fierce struggle with the world's Adversary on the rugged heights of Mount Quarantania, the conqueror of the first Adam striking death-filled blows upon the head of the second. How heroic the Master! How patient; how submissive! In the end, how defeated the foe! How paralyzed is Satan! Surely Christianity will plant itself upon this matchless victory, proclaiming the sinless character, the perfect humanity, of Jesus as the corner-stone of all truth, the key to his godhead. *Go to that sepulcher first,* says Paul.

But we will gather at the foot of Hermon, catch a glimpse of the transfigured face of the Carpenter's Son, listen to the echoing words of Moses and Elias, and then say: Religion has its foundation in supernatural things. Hermon is its source. Again, the apostle brings us back to the sepulcher, where glows a light and shines a glory eclipsing that of Hermon.

We have found the indestructible support of the Christian religion, suggest others, in the martyrdom of Christ's friends and followers, in the pitiless death of John the Baptist, in the crushed but crowned life of Stephen, and in the decapitation of Paul himself. Martyrdom, furnishing a bloody page in the world's history, is considered a glorious and almost irrefutable testimony to Gospel truth; but it must be remembered that error has had its martyrs, and, besides, martyrdom has this weakness, that it is the testimony of the martyr to what he *believes* is true, not necessarily to what is true.

Martyrdom is the expression of one's *faith*, not necessarily the certificate of truth. But, if the martyrdom of Christ's followers is an unsatisfactory foundation, it may be supposed, and it has been affirmed, that the self-sacrifice of Jesus is all that could be desired for a basis of religion. And did not Paul himself write: "But God forbid that I should glory, save in the cross of our Lord Jesus Christ?" What glory! what power! what redemption is symbolized by the cross! No tragedy so mournful, so pathetic; no death so heroic, so sublime. Religion without Calvary is religion without redemption. Is *this* not, then, the one truth necessary to religion? We answer by an illustration. The river Jordan rises, according to one writer, at Dan; according to another, its fountain-head is at Cæsarea Philippi. The first writer intends to be correct; the second writer *is* correct. The two sources are only four miles apart, the fountain at Dan being supplied by water from the mountain spring at Cæsarea Philippi. So Calvary and the sepulcher are within sight of each other, and are equally related, and it is not surprising that one Christian will shout the praise of Calvary as Salvation's source, while another, going back of it, piloted by the apostle, will discover that the fountain-head of power and glory is the abandoned sepulcher—in other words, the fact of the Lord's resurrection.

Let us stand a moment on the southern shoulder of the Mount of Olives; let us hear Jesus' last earth-words; let us behold him as he spreads his open palms in blessing; listen, and we shall hear angel wings, and soon see the beatific forms of angels themselves; look, and we shall witness a descending and an ascending cloud, bearing away the deathless body of our Lord. Event unrivaled! Pageantry uneclipsed by that of Elijah's ascension! Here on Olivet's heavenly brow, where the prismatic colors of eternity are playing, will we lay the foundation of our faith. No! No! No! shouts Paul; the sepulcher! the sepulcher! "If Christ be not raised, your faith is vain;" your faith in all the occurrences, teachings, life, and death of Christ is vain, a self-deceiving hope, a misery-producing thought, unless he vacated the tomb on the third day.

So not in any event in that manifold and exceptional life; not in his birth; not in his baptism or temptation; not in his transfiguration or ascension; not in Calvary's awful fate,—is the corner-stone of our religion to be found. These all add beauty and dignity to the temple, which is indeed incomplete without them, but these incomparable and unapproachable truths are nothing without the one all-supporting fact of the resurrection.

In keeping with the preceding thought, it is clear to all that the resurrection of the Lord must be viewed as the *final* proof of his mission and religion. In the inspired records, we reach a limit to almost every proceeding, human and divine; we view the last act in the drama of history, prophecy, creation, and redemption. With the creation of man, the creative work of the Almighty ceases; with the destruction of the first-born in Egypt, the miracles of Moses before Pharaoh are suspended. In these and like events in Scripture, the last act is the greatest, the highest water-mark of power and wisdom is reached. So in the establishment of Christianity in the work and person of Jesus Christ, the last miracle is the greatest; the last picture is the most beautiful; the last event is all-powerful and highest. Not even the ascension, though glorious enough, had any such glory, any such demonstrative excellence and power, as the resurrection. Other events, other miracles, are *efficient* in the line of evidences; but, adopting a word of Joseph Cook, the resurrection is *sufficient*. Hermon is *efficient* in its display of celestial beams; the resurrection is *sufficient* as an output of upper-world glory. The baptism is *efficient* as a temporary approval from God; the resurrection is Christ's *everlasting vindication* before man. Calvary is *efficient* as an atonement; the resurrection *sufficient* for all there is of religion.

Paul's ideas are not indistinct or unknown. In the attempt to catalogue them we have been impressed with the range of his thought, which is as wide as the Gospel itself, embracing all the idiomatic truths of the new religion. No sacred writer equals him in the completeness of his revelations. The synoptists are narrators, not expositors or interpreters. They construct nothing, they add nothing to what they know or have heard. They are reporters, expressing no opinion of sayings or doings. In his gospel, John breaks away from this historical position, and utters as profound thought as ever Paul entertained, but he shrinks from a venture into mysteries so soon as he discovers his inability to grasp them. In the Apocalypse he is favored with visions of the future, by which he is distinguished from Paul, who was not a seer, or vision-monger, but a dealer in facts and the foundation-truths of the new kingdom of God. Paul sees truths, not visions. He is intensely individual in this truth-telling, system-building task, turning all the currents of his thinking into divine channels, and standing for truth against the world. Appointed as the truth-teller, he thunders it until the stars quake, and flashes it until its light fairly consumes the errors of opposing systems. He roams in the fields of revelation, gathering up all that has been spoken, studying all that has been written, seeking for all that has been withheld, and communicating all to mankind, from Cæsar's household to the mobs of Lystra and Ephesus. In the exegesis of divine wisdom he addresses the individual, as in letters to Timothy and Philemon, and the Churches, as in the Epistles to the Thessalonians and Philippians; in discourses, as in that before Agrippa and on the staircase in the tower of Antonia; in conversations, as in that on the wrecked ship and with the brethren at the Three Taverns; in songs, as in the jail at Philippi; and in prayers, as he bids adieu to the disciples at Ephesus. Addressing all classes, and speaking on all occasions, he applied truth as it was needed, always prescribing it in the old form if adapted to existing conditions, or submitting it in an entirely new way, which either provoked inquiry, aroused antagonism, or issued in repentance and reformation. No subject related to his mission, whether philosophical, ethical, moral, social, or religious, escaped his hand, but was developed with a surprising boldness, and enforced with the authority of a teacher from God. It was God's truth, not man's, as it fell from his lips or dropped from his pen; it was God's business of which he was the representative; hence the fullness of his revelations, the equipoise of his purposes, the consummate skill of his applied logic, the transparency of his courage, the steadfastness of his faith, and the tragic tone of his life.

Hence the *career* of Paul, both as a teacher and a missionary, a brief survey of which can not be avoided. The converted Pharisee was not a dreamer, a sentimentalist, a mystic; his religion was not the religion of the beautiful, or the religion of the reason, but the product of supernatural influence in his soul. It was *fire*, of which enthusiasm, tremendous activity, and heroic achievement were the outward signs. Religion is not alone introspective, it has external relations; it is a religion of service, of doing, of conquest. Paul was not, could not be, a silent force, a neutral disciple, a negative Christian. He was positive, self-assertive, and armed with the despotic power of truth. Naturally a man of energy, of which his career as a Pharisee is proof, when he espoused the Christian movement he gave to it all his possibilities, augmenting himself by the supernatural endowments suddenly conferred, and became a conspicuous leader and the chief apostle in the early Church. Not often do the logical and the emotional faculties cohere or unite in a single mind; but in Paul they happily combined, so that it is a question which was the stronger, the keen, logical faculty, which enabled him to answer all opposers and extinguish all errors, or that pathetic and energetic spirit which often terminated in the holiest courage, and at times resistlessly bore him on to the destined result. If, as the author of "Ecce Homo" intimates, *enthusiasm* is the key-note to the life of Christ, certainly it is the undertone of Paul's vivid and successful career for Christ; for so great was his passion for man that, as he spoke, the idols on the Acropolis trembled, and Felix's and Nero's household were made to pause and consider. Such results are not the proofs of eloquence or genius, but the signs of an inspired enthusiasm, which the face of kings could not repress, nor the mobs of Jews at all silence or overcome.

The apostolate of Paul was to the Gentile world. Not refusing to declare the new Gospel to his countrymen, but the rather anxious that they might be saved, he nevertheless was commissioned as the apostle to the Gentiles, differing in this respect from the original apostles, who, except Peter, were limited in their labors, until Paul's proclamation of independence, to the "cities of Israel." It required not a little logic to convince the apostolical college that the grace of life in Jesus Christ should henceforth be offered to all men; and, had it not been for the *logic of events*, it is almost certain that the *logic of truth* had not then prevailed. Peter was for a season the representative of the new idea, but was superseded by Paul, who championed a "liberal Christianity," and discerned the greatness of the redemptive idea in its relation to the race. Paul's enlarged Christian idea produced a momentary convulsion throughout the Church; it was the rending of the veil again; it was tearing it into pieces. But this idea of the world's emancipation was Christ's idea, which the Church but dimly understood. Revealed to Paul, he must declare it; he can not be narrow or exclusive; and, while willing to recognize the authority of the brethren at Jerusalem, he would have broken with them and gone his way as an independent apostle, had the divine programme been curtailed or the powers of his commission been abridged. *The world shall have the Gospel.*

Henceforth he bears a world-wide Gospel to a sin-weary race. He is an evangelist of the highest type. He is not a settled pastor, but an itinerant, by the terms of his commission, traveling from country to country, entering new provinces and old cities, planting Churches everywhere, and organizing Christian communities throughout the vast Roman empire. He was a trained organizer; he was methodical in his pursuits, knowing how to divide his time, appropriate agencies, and accomplish tasks not possible to one of less regularity and habit. He was qualified to superintend the largest missionary operations, and upon no one could the "care of all the Churches" have rested so safely as upon him. His vision was open to the most distant fields, and his resources seemed equal to all emergencies. Other apostles labored and died in foreign countries for the faith, but the missionary journeys of Paul eclipse the united efforts of the twelve.

For an account of the missionary work of the apostle we are obliged to depend upon "The Acts of the Apostles," as recorded by Luke, which Rénan appropriately designates the "second idyl of Christianity," the first being "furnished" by the "Lake of Tiberias and its fishing barks." In the time of James, or before the dispersion of the apostles, Jerusalem was the capital of Christianity; but as Paul rose to supremacy Antioch in Syria virtually became the head-quarters of the Christian Church, or, as Farrar says, the "second capital of Christianity." Not that Jerusalem was abandoned by Paul, for he visited it no less than five different times, but, as a historic fact, it lost its prestige as a Christian center, and divided its importance with other cities. Jewish Christianity recognized Jerusalem as its center; Gentile Christianity, drifting away from Jewish influence, centered itself first at Antioch, where the Christians received their name, and later at Ephesus, as Antioch declined.

Antioch is the misssonary center, the birthplace of the missionary enterprise, of the early Christian Church. From the Syrian City, as Rénan observes, Christianity "launches out into the wide world," instinct with a purpose to conquer the race and mold it after its likeness. Two men, Paul and Barnabas, after much prayer, initiate the task ; for, bidding adieu to the disciples, they start westward, trusting only in Him who commanded them to go. Rénan does not ridicule the small beginning, but credits these men with sincerity, and acknowledges a solemnity of ideal in their lives, however much he may doubt the success of the movement they have inaugurated. Tracing them in their voyages and travels, he affirms that they followed the "road of Jewish emigration ;" but this is only partly true, for in Asia Minor they traveled often where there were no roads, and among cities without inter-relations or communication. Paul was an original missionary, not building on other men's labors, but organizing new movements, and going where he had not been preceded by religious teachers.

In this apparently wandering but providential life he usually traveled on foot, supporting himself by the labor of his hands, especially by the trade he had learned when a youth, and was not dependent on Churches or communities. This gave him influence, for he could not be accused of mercenary motives in the preaching of the Gospel.

The first missionary tour, consuming about one year and a half, was largely confined to the cities of Asia Minor, in which Churches were organized, and the breach between Judaism and Gentile Christianity was greatly widened. From Antioch they proceeded to the island of Cyprus, where, after preaching in the cities of Salamis and Paphos, they embarked for Perga, and without delay hastened to Antioch in Pisidia, Iconium, Lystra, and Derbe, meeting with fierce opposition at every point, except at Derbe, from which they returned to Antioch in Syria.

The significance of the tour is not in the results achieved. These were small enough, and secured at the hazard of life. Paul's work was introductory; it was a trial, not of himself, but of Christianity in contact both with the Judaic and Gentile spirit. He felt his way into the conflict, and came out satisfied, though he had been stoned nearly to death at Lystra. Commissioned to the Gentiles, he preached at first in these cities to the Jews, in order to convince them that Jesus is the Messiah; but, arriving at Antioch in Pisidia, he threw of the mask, and, as the Apostle to the Gentiles, assured them of the same Gospel privileges he had offered the Jews, and urged them to unite in Church fellowship, and accept Jesus as their Savior. He did not condemn the Jews, but he had reached the point when he was no longer under obligation to preach to them, or neglect the Gentiles in their behalf; henceforth, we shall see and hear him as a Gentile preacher. His personal separation from the Jews was religious, and not on ethnic or national grounds, and this separation was a marked product of this missionary tour.

More striking still was the *actual opening of the Gospel to the Gentile world.* The intermittent efforts of Peter must be recognized as providential indications of a purpose to confer upon foreign nations the Gospel rights which were supposed primarily to belong to the Jews; but under Paul that purpose steadily and rapidly evolved into actual results, and finally became the great aim of the Apostolic Church. As the Master had said, "The first shall be last, and the last first," meaning that the Jew should *hear* the Gospel first, and the Gentiles last, but that the Gentiles would *receive* it first and the Jew last, the time had come for the fulfillment of the statement. In Christ's time the Jew was treated as the heir of the kingdom of God; in Paul's time the Gentile was promoted to the same heirship, and entered upon the Gospel inheritance, and, as a consequence, the Churches that were organized were Gentile Churches, and the leavening power of the Gospel spread more and more throughout the Gentile world. The actual Gentile movement toward Christ begins after Paul strikes the shores of Asia Minor, the Jew receding in importance with the progress of the tour, and finally disappearing altogether.

Perhaps the turning to the Gentiles was the exasperating cause of Jewish hatred to Paul. His conversion, his declaration of Christ as the Messiah, and his renunciation of Judaism was interpreted in no friendly spirit in Jewish circles; but that he should aim to undermine Judaism and install Christianity as the religion of all mankind, inviting all nations to the enjoyment of the same divine rights, was an offense tenfold more aggravating, and whetted to intensity all that hostility that broke out against him in his work of religious propagandism. But as the Gentile world was larger than the Jewish world, so the Gospel economy was better than the Jewish economy, and Paul dared every thing in publishing it, first to the Jews, and then to the Gentiles.

Five years intervene between the first and the second tours of Paul. Leaving Antioch, he proceeds by the shortest route to Derbe, beginning the second tour where he closed the first, as if it were his intention to carry forward the work from that point eastward until he had explored the whole country, and proclaimed the Gospel in every city. But as his "goings" were under the superintendence of the Holy Spirit, he soon found that effectual doors were opened to him in other and entirely new fields, and that he must be ready to enter them. From Derbe he revisits Lystra, and then plunges into Galatia, a province inhabited by a wild and superstitious people, to whom he discourses of Christ, and whose hearts he wins, and then hurries to Troas on the western coast. A new programme is now suggested to his thought. He is impressed that he must introduce the Gospel into Europe; Gentile Christianity exercises its controlling influence upon him; and so he sails as the first Gospel message-bearer to the continent of Europe. Now he is at Neopolis; then at Philippi; anon we find him in Thessalonica; suddenly he turns his steps to Athens; and for two years Corinth listens to the religious zealot, quite as much impressed by his eloquence as astonished at his doctrine. The tour is completed by a stop at Ephesus and a direct journey to Jerusalem.

In its extent, and in the character of the work performed, the second tour was even more remarkable than the first. Hitherto the Gospel herald had confined his ministry to Asia; now Europe seemed as anxious to hear the divine message and greeted the apostles, not with stones, but with arguments and more apparent consideration. In this respect Europe was a more promising field than Asia, and Paul's report of labor in the Macedonian cities was doubtless as thrilling as it was encouraging, and the results were as stimulating as they were providential. Greece and the south-east quarter of Europe were renowned for art and culture. Philosophy still dominated the public thought, and statues still graced the temples and adorned the palaces of their chief cities. Asia Minor obstructed the apostle's progress with Jewish prejudices and pagan vices; Southern Europe offered the resistance of culture to Christianity. *Paul is on Plato's ground at last, and must contend with him.* At Lystra stones; at Ephesus beasts; at Athens philosophers. In Antioch Christianity contested with pagan religions; in Damascus and Jerusalem with Judaism; in Asia Minor with pagan corruption; in Europe with *scholastic thought.* These contests were necessary to exhibit the nature of Christianity and indicate its claims.

What was the result of the European tour? In Philippi a jail, but finally a Church; in Thessalonica and Corinth large Christian Churches; in Athens confusion among the philosophers and the conversion of a number of people. *Mars' Hill is more famous than Plato's Academy.* The latter has disappeared; the former, a huge rock, with its chiseled steps, still remains. Its situation is remarkable, and afforded Paul a splendid opportunity, which he improved, for pointing out the errors of philosophy and explaining and defending the great truths of Christianity. To the right of Mars' Hill rises the Acropolis, on which the Parthenon and other temples dedicated to gods and goddesses were standing and still exist in a ruined state; to the left is the Pnyx, where Demosthenes thundered his philippics, and where the multitudes grew patriotic; in the rear is the market-place; in front, and at his feet, was the city of Athens, containing perhaps one-half million of people. Not far away is the temple of Theseus; beyond is the old cemetery; and one mile to the north is Plato's Academy.

This was Paul's environment in Athens, amid which he pronounced the sermon that made him famous as the apologist of Christianity, and to which Athens never replied. Idolatry and philosophy were vanquished on Mars' Hill. Athens did not respond with stones, as did Asia Minor; nor with a jail, as did Philippi; nor with beasts, as did Ephesus; nor with arrests, as did Jerusalem; but with intellectual vanity and a promise of investigation. Philosophy is investigation. Asia *persecutes* the Gospel; Europe *investigates.* In these behold the Asia and Europe of to-day!

Paul's third and final missionary tour is made from Antioch, rather for the purpose of confirming his work than of extending it. He visits Asia Minor and the Churches in Europe, explaining doctrines and mysteries, instituting forms of discipline or Church order, settling theological differences between Jews and Gentiles, and organizing Christian communities into active forces for the propagation of the Gospel. New Churches spring up in his path, and new cities are visited and instructed in the Gospel, but his principal work seems to be *supervision, establishment, organization, centraliza-tion, and indoctrination.* In this sphere of labor he was not less active or less successful than when engaged in the more aggressive conflicts with the opposition to the Gospel. He now appears as the administrator, the Church parliamentarian, the episcopal head of Christendom, responsible only to Jesus Christ, and yet concedes the nominal authority of the original Church. In this tour, of which the central point is Ephesus, where he remains three years, he seems to have gathered up the fragments, reduced disorderly and ignorant societies to subjection, instructed them in doctrine, usages, and duties, and crystallized the Christian spirit within the confines of two conti-nents. As distinguished from the other tours, the chief products of this last missionary journey are *Church order* and *Church life.*

On to Jerusalem to observe the feast of Pentecost is Paul's next ambition, and thitherward he tarries at Troas, Miletus, Tyre, Ptole-mais, and Cæsarea, listening in Philip's home to the ominous prophecy of Agabus respecting what should befall him at Jerusalem, but with-out discouragement he proceeded and arrived in the Holy City in time for the great celebration.

Another journey is before Paul. It is a missionary tour also, but unlike the others, it is a journey to death; he rides on his coffin from Jerusalem to Rome—a victor nevertheless. Mobbed by blood-thirsty Jews, arrested at the instance of the high-priest, and hurried to the fortress of Antonia, it seems that the end has suddenly come; but he has a chance or two for his life. He is tried before the Sanhedrim, more as a heretic and blasphemer than a violator of civil law, and, just when sentence might have been pronounced upon him, he providentially divides the legal body, bringing the Pharisees to his defense and rescue. Forty men, infuriated by the result, bind themselves with an oath to kill Paul; but this plan is circumvented by the Roman officer, who immediately arranges for the transfer of his prisoner to Cæsarea. Here he is tried before Felix who reserves judgment; and Festus, his official successor, delays a settlement, which leads Paul to appeal to Cæsar, which is the determining point in this crisis. To Rome he must therefore go. During the voyage he is shipwrecked at Malta; but this is only an incidental obstruction, perilous at the time, but in no wise a fatal hindrance. On he goes, and at last arrives in the " Eternal City." From the " Holy City to the Eternal City!" One step more, and the " Celestial City " will open its gates to the hero.

Paul's imprisonment in Rome; the law's strange delay in his case; the time improved in preaching to both Jews and Gentiles; his sup-posed acquittal on legal grounds; his hasty journey to Macedonia and

Asia Minor again; his more rapid visit to Spain; his re-arrest and return to Rome; the death sentence passed upon him and its bloody execution just outside the city,—are matters not historically established, but the probabilities are that these events occurred. Curiosity would be satisfied if the missing pages in the biography of so illustrious a toiler could be found; but the incomplete record, as we have it, is the key to a very complete life, which, after all, is the important point to be remembered.

Our preparation for an estimate of Paul in the varied aspects of his character and life, as a thinker, a writer, a worker, a martyr, an example, and an influence, is sufficiently extended to justify an immediate attempt in that direction.

It is needless to remind the reader that, on the whole, and notwithstanding critical opinion has endeavored to deprive Paul of his true historic position, and has either underrated or overrated his relations to Christianity, the general verdict of the centuries is an appreciation of his apostleship and a widening of his fame as the hero of God. In eulogy of him Monod pronounces him "the greatest benefactor of our race," while Rénan discovers only an ordinary man in the apostle to the Gentiles. Canon Farrar says that men did not "recognize his greatness," nor is it certain that he is yet fully recognized in his leadership of thought and in his influence in the world. The Jew is his vilifier; the skeptic is his critic; the philosopher is his investigator; the Churchman is his historian; the theologian is his interpreter; the Christian is his admirer and believer.

From these various sources, religions, skepticisms, histories, philosophies, and theologies, varying opinions and inferences might be drawn; but it is gratifying that the preponderance of testimony is in complete harmony with our own opinion that Paul was the greatest man that ever lived.

As a *thinker* he has been fairly considered in previous paragraphs; but a slight reference to his scholarship, his logical powers, his intellectual vision, and psychological constitution is imperative at this point, since so graceful a writer as Rénan has impeached his intellectual standing by declaring him "unlearned," unpoetical, as having "injured science," and as incapable of becoming a "man of learning." This is a criticism born of that general prejudice to Christianity which has actuated the French writer in all his assaults upon Christian truth, and which blinds him to the recognition of those qualities which constituted Paul the marked man of his age and the chief apostle of the Church. A Jew might join Rénan in depreciation of Paul, but an honest student of Paul's writings must accord him, not only genius, but inspiration, not only acute perception of truth, but supernatural knowledge of it. When Rénan asserts that Paul's revelations were his own "whims," he means to strike at the revelations and at the apostle, implying that the two stand or fall together: and they do; but he is the first critic to reduce truth to a *whim.* The revelations of Paul, deprived of inherent supernaturalism, and viewed merely as the original products of his inflamed imagination, in which Rénan says he was deficient, or of his profoundest psychologic research, which every epistle establishes, are accepted even in rationalistic circles, of which Baur is a leader, as stupendous announcements and superior to the average discoveries of philosophic thought. The theism of Paul; the doctrine of Messiahship; the law of Atonement; the theory of justification; the explanation of sin; the certainty of resurrection; the penalties and rewards of the Judgment,—are not *whims,* or all the sacred writers were whimsical, and Christ himself may be pronounced a whim. Rénan might have recognized Paul in his intellectual greatness without compromising his final opinion of the place he should occupy in history.

In natural order Paul appears as the *writer,* different in style or rhetoric, as he is different in thought or substance, from all inspired penmen. Recalling the fact that he was a *truth-teller,* one might suppose that he would employ the historical style, but he was not a narrator; hence the style is not historical. He was not imaginative; hence the style is not poetic. He was not seer-like; hence the style is not prophetical or apocalyptic. He deals not with scientific facts, except incidentally; hence the style is not of the schools, or scholastic. He writes not for sensational effect; hence the style is not oratorical. He writes not to protect any supposed weaknesses in Christianity; hence the style is not sophistical. What is left? He is set for the *announcement* of truth; hence the style is declarative; he must *explain* the truth; hence the style is didactic; he must *defend* the truth; hence the style is logical. Paul's commission was to *prove,* as well as *preach,* the Gospel. *Preaching is proving.* Of all Bible writers, Paul is the chief logician, importing reason into religion and abstracting superstition from it, thereby refuting the common suspicion that Christianity is unfriendly to reason. The Pauline idea of religion is superlatively rationalistic. Prior to Paul, religion is a narration, a history, a catalogue of facts; *under* Paul, religion is logic, order, reason; *in* Paul, religion is spiritualized perception, it is the divine reason. *First,* historians, reporters; *second,* the logician; this is the order of the sacred writers. Hence, in Paul's fourteen epistles we find arguments for all the truths of the Christian religion, and a methodical attack on all the errors of philosophy, idolatry, and sin. "The world by wisdom knew not God," is his text against philosophy; "What agreement hath the temple of God with idols?" is his text against idolatry; the "wages of sin is death," is his text against sin. In Paul we have an instance of the *inspiration of reason*, while in others there is the inspiration of memory, or the inspiration of affection, or courage. Inspired reason is superior to academic reason; hence, Paul is superior to Plato. He did not dream, or speculate, or inquire; he *knew*. This accounts for the brevity of the Pauline Epistles, the equal of which no literary annals furnish. Logic needs few words, truth fewer. History, poetry, science, philosophy, requires a vocabulary. Truth clothes itself in monosyllables. Paul is brief, but incisive; compact, but full; his words, like himself, are short but perpendicular.

For the preservation, as well as the dissemination, of truth, Paul chose the epistolary, as Plato chose the dialogistic, style. "The epistolary form," says Canon Farrar, "is eminently spontaneous, personal, flexible, emotional." That the apostle took to this form of composition because it suited his mental taste, is not clear; but that he adopted it because it was the common method of communication, and because it admitted of a certain freedom which the scholastic style prohibited, seems reasonable enough. Into these "encyclical epistles" he pours profoundest convictions, and through them reveals the highest and holiest truths, but always so as to impress the heart while he storms the mind, and compels the submission of both to the ideal idea he is unfolding. Luther regarded his utterances as "living creatures, with hands and feet," which is only another way of saying that Paul's words are life-words.

The authenticity and genuineness of some of the epistles ascribed to Paul have been called in question, not by one writer only, but by several, as by the critics of the Tübingen school, and by skeptics like Rénan; and not for one reason only, but for many, among which may be noted certain internal deficiencies of style, or incoherency or aimlessness of argument, and the external impossibilities of their composition at the time and by the apostle. Little general objection is made to the Epistles to the Romans, the Corinthians, and the Galatians; Hilgenfeld is also willing to accept the First Epistle to the Thessalonians, and the Epistles to the Philippians and to Philemon, holding in doubt all the others; Rénan accepts the Second Epistle to the Thessalonians and that to the Colossians; so that, of the fourteen bearing the apostle's signature, even the critics, rationalists, and skeptics concede the Pauline authorship of nine, and resist the claims of the others on grounds not at all historically, philosophically, or doctrinally sufficient.

According to Rénan, the epistles of the apostle were edited after his execution by unknown hands, and suffered materially in the process, the editors determining what was Pauline and what was not; and he declares that they re-arranged the contents of some of the epistles, presenting them, not as Paul actually wrote them, but as the editors *believed* he wrote them. He insists that the Epistle to the Romans, under such editorial supervision, is objectionable; but waiving the objection, he admits the general authenticity of the epistle. The same remark applies to the eight other epistles, whose authenticity he does not dispute.

Slight technical objections might be urged against these accepted epistles, such as the theory of anti-Christ in the Second Epistle to the Thessalonians, and the apparent Gnosticism in the Epistle to the Colossians; but Rénan does not urge them, because the ingrain thoughts of the epistles are Pauline.

As to the Epistle to the Ephesians, Rénan suspects that it is a perverted copy or imitation of the Epistle to the Colossians, since the Gnosticism in the one appears in the other; and he affirms that, as it is addressed to converted heathen, it was not designed for the Church at Ephesus, which was largely composed of Jewish Christians; but this, in part, is speculation, and can not weigh against the reputation of the epistle.

The two Epistles to Timothy, and the one to Titus, Rénan pronounces "apochryphal." They are fabrications, full of "Latinisms" and ecclesiasticisms; the language is not Paul's; the hierarchical spirit is not Paul's.

His chief objection to the Epistle to the Hebrews is, that, while traditionally attributed to Paul, and containing, as he admits, Paul's *ideas*, the *style* is not Paul's, and, therefore, the document must be rejected.

Reduced to briefest statement, the critical opposition of Rénan to the authenticity of five of Paul's epistles may be expressed by such words as *editorship, technicality, imitation, fabrication,* and *rhetoric. Editorship* does not invalidate authorship—it really implies the genuineness of the epistles; *technicality* makes not against any of them, since it implies only a speck on the mirror of truth; *imitation* is only a confirmation of the original epistle; *fabrication* is a serious word, but, as applied to three epistles, it is without foundation. Timothy and Titus were Paul's disciples in Christ and companions in travel, to whom it would be natural to write when separated from them, and the "ecclesiastic spirit" of these epistles is in keeping with the ministerial relations both these sons in the Gospel sustained to the Church. The *rhetoric* of the Epistle to the Hebrews is its fascination; its *philosophic Christianity* is an exhibition of the advanced state or

26

knowledge of Paul, which found its fittest expression in Alexandrian allegory or hyperbole. None of the objections seems fatal to the claim of the Pauline origin of the fourteen epistles.

Accepting them as genuine, what a writer was Paul! To the *Romans*, he writes like a theologian; to the *Corinthians*, he writes like an archbishop and a philosopher; to the *Galatians*, he writes like an earnest teacher; to the *Ephesians*, he writes like a self-composed advocate; to the *Philippians*, he writes like a joyous Christian; to the *Colossians*, he writes like a philosophical Christian; to the *Thessalonians*, he writes like an eschatological Christian; to *Timothy*, he writes like a father and Church parliamentarian; to *Titus*, he writes like a beloved pastor; to *Philemon*, he writes like an affectionate brother; and to the *Hebrews*, he writes like a scholar and a philosopher. What variety of style; what variety of truth; what variety of purpose; what variety of result!

Considering Paul as the *worker*, he is as remarkable for his devotion to duty as for the sincerity of his religious convictions, and quite as successful in one sphere of labor as another. When the first ray of light penetrated his darkened mind, his first inquiry was in relation to service, in the words, "What wilt thou have me to do?" No sooner did the scales fall from his eyes in the house of Judas than he began to proclaim that Jesus is the Christ, and this principally to the Jews in Damascus; and, until life's tragic close, he was the faithful and obedient apostle, striving to lay foundations that others might build thereon.

He is the incessant preacher of "Christ and him crucified;" he is an itinerant, a Christian traveler, a flaming evangelist, spreading the news of the Gospel from continent to continent, and anxious to offer life to the isles of the sea. His, as we have observed, was not a settled pastorate; he could not settle. His longest pastorate was at Ephesus, rounding out in three full years; but the city was the headquarters or capital of the Christian Church for Asia Minor and Europe, on which account he deemed it advisable to tarry longer there than elsewhere. In a certain sense, the Gospel must anchor on the shores of time; but John reveals an angel *flying* with the Gospel through the heavens, and shouting to the earth to hear the message of the Lord. Others, like James, may settle in Jerusalem; but Paul, like the angel, will fly from nation to nation to declare the tidings of salvation. What religious histories, written and unwritten, are embalmed in the words, Jerusalem, Antioch, Ephesus, Corinth, Philippi, Athens, and Rome! These cities represent Paul's life, the Gospel's conquering march, and are the prophetic land-marks of its triumph in all the world. Rénan intimates that the success of Paul in Asia Minor was largely owing to the religious credulity of the people; but his explanation of success is very like Gibbon's, in that, recognizing the effects, the causes are only obscurely or remotely apprehended. That the inhabitants of Galatia, in particular, were superstitious, must be believed; but not more superstitious, nor more wedded to mythological and traditional stories, than the Athenians; and yet Galatia received the Gospel, while Athens, on the whole, did not. Nor must it be forgotten that it should add to the credit of the Gospel, if it can relieve a gross, ignorant people of their dull and heartless superstitions; for the philosophic spirit did not pilot Athens into liberty therefrom, nor is it in the power of civilization to extinguish religious error; but the Gospel rescues a people from religious barbarisms, and enlightens them in ethical duties, and saves them from sin. Granted that the Gospel will deliver from these things, and we shall not trouble ourselves with the skeptic's explanation. Wanted—facts, not explanations; wanted—effects, not causes.

Whatever may be said of Paul's work in other directions, he will always be recognized as the principal *Church-founder* of his day. Churches were not built, but Christian societies were organized, disciplined, and supervised, by the apostle; and his interest in them never ceased, for, absent from them, he communicated with them by epistles, and, in his third journey, devoted himself specially to confirm them in the truth. Again, Rénan exhibits his inability to recognize the merits of Paul, by declaring that "his Churches were either slightly substantial or denied him," and that they soon fell to pieces, and their founder was forgotten. Yet the Pauline Churches of Asia Minor introduced new elements into Oriental life that have never disappeared; and, because they were established, we have not only Paul's epistles, but John's addresses to the "seven Churches of Asia." The Churches do not exist, but the epistles they evoked constitute the substantial documents of Christianity. The outcome of Paul's Church-planting, Rénan seems to forget. Let the Churches go—the epistles addressed to them are our inheritance.

In studying Paul as a worker no allusion has been made to the miracles he wrought, or their relation to his mission, for the reason that the miracle was an incidental factor in his history, and employed only in emergencies. His first miracle, which occurred at Paphos, a city of Cyprus, Rénan ridicules and rejects, but he rejects all miracles. Elymas is stricken blind, and the people are stricken with fear, and the Word of God prevails. In Philippi a maniac girl is relieved of the incurable trouble, and consternation follows; the people believe in God. Paul's equipment for missionary work was not the miracle-working power. His equipment was educational and religious; the gift to work a miracle was exceptional, and only occasionally granted. He could not exercise it at pleasure; he could not cure Epaphroditus of his illness; he could not extract the thorn from his own flesh. He was a poor miracle-worker; he was not called to work miracles, and the few recorded of him arose from necessity, and were possible because of immediate supernatural endowment and immediate divine direction to proceed. Hence, the apostle is not presented as a miracle-performer, nor is his career or success to be explained on that basis, or by any thing kindred to it. He is the spiritually equipped worker, and sufficient for all things.

Just when Paul assumed the title of "apostle," or whether it was conferred upon him in an informal way by the brethren, are matters not of record; but it is evident that after the council in Jerusalem, which decided the emancipation of the Gentiles from Jewish thralldom, Paul's ascendency was recognized. His discipleship had been fully established, Barnabas vouching for it in the beginning; and now his apostleship seems to be fully approved, yet not without some embarrassment and possibly resistance. Perhaps the secret reason for the separation of Barnabas from Paul was the growing jealousy of the former respecting the growing power of the latter; for it was about this time when Paul, flushed with his victory at Jerusalem, quite willingly consented to do independent work. The positions of Paul and Barnabas are, therefore, reversed; Paul is master, Barnabas is co-operator or follower of others. Rénan complains of this usurpation on the part of Paul; but it is an instance of the survival of the fittest. Paul was a born leader; Barnabas was a good worker, but not an original superintendent.

Rénan also grieves over the exaltation of Paul, and the diminished or fading splendors of Peter, who he declares was the greatest of apostles. Paul is nothing; but, "talk to me of Peter," says the Frenchman, "who bends the heads of kings, shatters empires, walks upon the asp and the basilisk, treads under foot the lion and the dragon, and holds the keys of heaven." Peter wrote two epistles of comparatively minor value; Paul wrote fourteen epistles, every one packed with supernatural truth. Peter labored chiefly in Syria; Paul in Syria, Asia Minor, and Europe. Peter was a bigot after conversion; Paul a philanthropic Christian from the moment of his *new* birth. Peter was a Jewish Christian until Paul opened to his vision the world-wide, world-embracing ideal of Jesus Christ; Paul was a Gentile Christian from the beginning, broad-gauged, humanity-loving, race-saving. Rénan, influenced by Catholic tradition, shakes the bones of Peter at the Christian Church; we, influenced by a Protestant faith, point to the crown of Paul as the inducement to walk in his footsteps.

Paul, as the exemplar of Christianity, is a very interesting study. Human at all times, even under inspiration, he is not to be thought of as faultless, but it is small business to dwell on his deficiencies to the exclusion of his excellences. An artist might discover some slight defect in one of the figures in the dome of St. Peter's, but such defect would not overthrow the reputation of Angelo as an artist. Imperfection in human character, refined by grace, is not a demonstration of the failure of Christianity to effect its blessed work. Acknowledging, without detailing, supposed weaknesses in Paul, he is nevertheless an exemplar, not eclipsed by any contemporary or by any modern saint. Even the sun has its ecliptic, or more nearly analogical, its black spots, but it shines and enlightens the world. When Rénan disputes Paul's saintship, and charges him with being harsh, severe, and repelling, he exhibits his prejudice, and advertises an evil purpose in blackmailing so illustrious a character in the Christian Church. Few men have so often quoted the conscience for the regulation of conduct as Paul, who in his wildest moods 'of persecution verily thought he was doing God's service. Thus reasoned he, showing that he aimed to have reference to a standard of righteousness, even before his relations to the old faith had been dissolved. In later life he had reference always to the Gospel order and the Gospel ideal of life, and as his conscience was educated in Christian responsibility he obeyed its signals or communications with unfailing persistency and a steady purpose.

But as a conscience-governed man is not the highest type of human character, inasmuch as the conscience is not infallible, so Paul is seen, not at his best, until he is the subject of spiritual leadership, and is a divine instrument for the fulfillment of divine purposes. He is the righteous man who is under the sovereignty and regnancy of the divine Spirit. He is a God-governed man. Paul belongs to this class. It is as a religious man, divinely guided, divinely used, performing the duties of a divinely called and a divinely endowed man, that he is man's example. It was bold in him to say to the Philippians, "Those things which ye have both learned, and received, and heard, and seen in me, do." He appealed to his life as an example of Christianity.

Rénan, disposed at least once to do his subject justice, recognizes the man of action in Paul, comparing him to Luther, and also discovers in him that "peculiar characteristic" in a great soul to "grow great and expand without ceasing," comparing him in this respect to Alexander. This is the limit of his recognitions. Luther resembles him; Alexander is like him. He is the man of force, he is a conqueror, he is a commander. Because he is Alexander or

Luther over again, Rénan might have placed him above Peter and the other apostles, but he reduces him below them. Paul was the man of his age, the man of character, the man of conscience, the man of Christianity.

Paul, as a *martyr*, is a tender subject, full of inspiration. His death is an argument in favor of his religion. Death brought no terror to his great soul. When stoned at Lystra; when mobbed in Jerusalem; when shipwrecked in the Bay of Malta; when a prisoner in Philippi; he could say, "None of these things move me." No danger appalled him; no prospect restrained his enthusiasm; no suffering quieted his activity. Believing in the sanctifying power of tribulation, he expected it to come, and submitted to it with all humility and grace. When, therefore, under sentence of death, he could write, "I am ready to be offered up." His life-work finished, he calmly waited for the heavenly reward. Suffering the martyr's fate, he received the martyr's crown.

His *influence*—will it ever die? If, as Rénan concedes, he is the representative of a "marching and conquering Christianity," and if Christianity continues to march on and conquer, the name of Paul will have a fixed place in history, and his influence will abide in the heart of the world. Determined, if possible, to uproot that influence from Christian nations, the French critic represents that, until the Reformation, Paul was well-nigh forgotten, but that Luther rescued him, Protestantism championed him, and a "new era of glory and authority" for him ensued; but that the reign of Paul is now drawing to a close. It is true the Reformation superseded Peter with Paul, and the highest type of Christianity has since prevailed in the world; and if Paul is declining we are not aware of it. Rénan is anxious for his decline, and imagines that it has taken place. When Jesus shall decline, then Paul shall decline.

Paul is more than the representative of *apostolic* Christianity, which, in its original terms and purposes, was Jewish, and, therefore, inferior to that which the Master taught and designed to perpetuate. He stands apart as the representative of all the revelations of the divine Teacher, and as the expounder of all the truths which the Christian religion is supposed to embody. From the original apostles a *historic* Christianity emanates; from Paul, a *vital* Christianity. From the twelve, a *synoptic* Gospel; from Paul, a *systematic* religion. From the one, a *miscellaneous* Christianity; from the other, a *doctrinal* Christianity. Rénan suggests that Paul is responsible for bad theologies, and that he imported metaphysics into religion. The Gospels are alphabetical schools; Paul is a theological university.

Paul introduced the Gospel to the Gentile world, opened the door that had always been shut, and laid the foundation for a universal Christian civilization. Sectional or race religions were as common as the reeds on the banks of the Jordan. A universal religion was not even a conception or abstraction. Christianity revealed the conception; the apostles disputed over it; the Jews pronounced it heretical, fanatical; while Paul embraced it, and put it into execution. Peter did go to the house of Cornelius, but Paul invaded the Roman empire with it, and turned the world "upside down." *The Gospel to the Gentiles meant new government, new customs, new social and moral ideas; it meant the destruction of paganism, and the uplifting of the sons of Japheth into a Christian civilization.* Hence, in calculations respecting the forces underlying the world's progress, the Gospel can not be omitted, and Paul can not be forgotten.

Paul built the bridge between Judaism and Christianity. No apostle so grieved over the defection of the Jews, and their inability to appreciate the Gospel, as did Paul. Loving them, he preached to them, and predicted that, recovering from their deception and extinguishing their prejudices, they will at last embrace the rejected Messiah. On Paul's prophecies, teachings, and suggestions, and affectionate remonstrances, may be based the hope of their return into the kingdom of God; and then shall the end come. Paul stands midway between Jew and Gentile, to unite both in the love of Christ; and, when it is accomplished, he will be acknowledged as the chief instrument in the consummation.

Paul gives to the Christian Church the key to Gospel propagandism, and reveals the plan by which the world will be brought to Christ. Christ's commission is "Go." Paul's life was an execution of the commission. Christ commands; Paul obeys. Christ gives us *orders*; Paul gives us *methods*. From Christ we learn *what* to do; from Paul, *how* to succeed. The itinerating plan of conquest, which gave Asia Minor and Europe to Paul, will conduct the world to the Savior. Is not Paul the exponent of Christianity?

## CHAPTER XVIII.

### THE PROVINCE OF CHRISTIANITY.

CHRISTIANITY is the *philosophy of the divine activity* expressed in governmental relations to the universe and the creatures who inhabit it. It is not a speculation touching these relations, but a revelation, supported by all-sufficient testimony, both internal and external, addressed to the intelligence of the human race. According to its own terms, it is more than an inquiry concerning the truth; it is the truth. Its specific purpose is the revelation of truth, or the mediation between reason and truth. Its province is the province of mediated, necessary truth, in which it proposes solutions for speculations, and revelations for discussions. It states and settles the questions of the ages, taking them up where philosophy lays them down, and unfolds them by methods peculiar to itself, and satisfactory to the human mind.

In a preliminary sense, it is necessary to determine if Christianity includes all truth, or truth of a peculiar kind; for if restricted to one truth, or one kind of truth, our duty will be to separate such truth from all others, and then consider it in its fullness and relations. To define the limitations of religion, or to prescribe the inquiries of Christianity, involves a knowledge of Christianity itself, to which no one has perfectly attained. Of Christianity we think we know something; but, as its stretches out into the infinite realm, including the contents of divine wisdom, and glorying in supernatural wonders, it is not certain that the human mind can properly mark its boundaries, or even declare its purposes. To affirm that Christianity is the religion of the illimitable is to open the door to mysteries without number, and to put it beyond human understanding; to affirm that its province is clearly defined, requires one to point out the boundary lines, which in some directions are either obscure or too distant to be observed.

Recognizing the difficulty, we dispose of it by announcing that there are at least two fields of inquiry proper for religion to occupy. The one is the field of the natural or phenomenal world; otherwise the physical universe. To what extent Christianity may undertake to interpret nature will be shown in succeeding pages; it is enough now to state that a religious interpretation of nature is justifiable, and that Christianity is supported by the natural world may be made apparent. The two are so related that one may be turned to the defense of the other. The mutual relations, the differences, and the resemblances between natural and spiritual truth have escaped discovery or acknowledgment, both in scientific and religious circles, involving them in needless controversy and hopeless disunion. Truth is without limitations, but the scientific relation to truth is one aspect, and the religious relation to truth is another. The difference is not in the truth, but in the relations of science and religion to it.

Studying nature in its lower aspect, as the region of facts, together with its laws, forms, forces, uses, systems, and adaptations, the sciences are established; but the scientific view of nature is not a complete interpretation of its spirit or end. To ascertain the spirit and purpose of nature it must be viewed from another stand-point; and as Christianity interprets the spirit of nature, so nature is found to reflect Christianity. Paul declares that the invisible things of the Godhead are indicated in the visible creation; that is, nature is a demonstration of the theistic hypothesis, and of infinite truth. Hence, the theologian may inquire of nature for testimony to Christian truth, as well as the scientist for the facts of science. If chemistry, geology, physiology, zoölogy, botany, meteorology, and biology issue from nature, as scientific truths, so do theism, depravity, regeneration, atonement, immortality, resurrection, heaven, and hell as religious truths. Christianity, as well as science, has a *physical basis*, which, however, must be sought to be found.

To establish its truths Christianity invades the natural, demanding a knowledge of its facts, laws, and forces, and appeals to the mind through the natural in proof of its revelations of higher truth. This process is in the interest of religion, and not in the interest of science. Nature is tributary to religion, as it is to science, but each has its own interpretations, inquiries, purposes. These inquiries establish the limitations of the scientific and religious interpretations of nature. The limitations of Christianity are the limitations of its inquiries, which concern religious truth; the limitations of science are the limitations of its inquiries which concern physical truth. Neither invades the other; there is no collision of inquiry; both co-exist in the same field, are supported by the same facts, and establish one truth in its two-faced variety of matter and spirit.

The other field of inquiry is the supernatural, or the *spiritual universe*, of which Christianity is the purported revelation. It is a vast, unbounded empire of realities, distinct from the natural, but whose spirit often strikes, invades, is incorporated with, the natural, illuminating it and explaining it. The peculiar province of Christianity is to reveal the spiritual, not only in its connections with the natural, but also in its independent character and eternal essence.  Purely religious truths are essentially superhuman, having their roots in the unseen or spiritual universe, and descending, in their growth, into human history, according to man's needs and sympathies.  As the spiritual is associated in mysterious ways with the natural, justifying an interpretation of the natural from the spiritual stand-point, so the spiritual is associated with the human, justifying an interpretation of man from the stand-point of Christianity.

Christianity, in the lowest sense, is the religion or philosophy of the natural, but in the highest sense it is the religion or philosophy of the supernatural.  As, however, it has its limitations when applied to the natural, so it has its limitations when applied to the supernatural.  It does not reveal all the supernatural.  There is a *vast un·known* in the spiritual universe.  Questions without number, with reference to eternal things, Christianity does not answer ; it is beyond its province even to attempt to answer them.  The existence of a supernatural world, of supernatural truth, of a supernatural spirit, Christianity makes known, but it does not define the boundaries between the natural and supernatural, nor does it indicate the processes of supernatural manifestations, nor the exact differentia of the supernatural.  The doctrine of regeneration is a revealed truth; the instrument of regeneration is the Spirit of God; the process of regeneration is unknown and unknowable.  In like manner the truths revealed relate to doctrines, experiences, instruments, purposes, and results, while *processes* are hidden, or, at the most, only inferred.  The supernatural is revealed with limitations.

The circle of Christianity is not large enough to include all truth, except in the subsidiary sense that it includes all revealed truth.  Its relation to the natural and supernatural is a *relation of limitation*; its purpose is neither wholly natural—that is, scientific—nor supernatural—that is, altogether religious.  It includes both and differs from both.

Christianity is the only truth ; it is more than a single province of truth.  *The province of Christianity is, in the very highest sense, the province of truth.*  There are truths not in themselves definitely religious, as there are religions not definitely true, both of which sustain relations to the truth of truths, and must be estimated in an interpretation of Christianity.  What, then, it may be asked, is the relation of Christianity, as the truth of truths, to other truths, other religions, other systems?  In the discovery, explanation, and announcement of truth, have philosophy and Christianity agreed, or is there any relation whatever between them as systems of similar truths?  In its attitude of hostility to Christianity, materialism has held very little in common with religion; but as to fundamental truth, theistic, ethnic, and eschatological, philosophy might readily, and without stultification, accept the teachings of Christianity, because they are not incompatible. From Thales to Herbert Spencer the great problems of creation, being, mind, and the future have engaged the most serious philosophic investigation, as also they constitute the most serious revelations of Christianity. In this respect the province of Christianity and the province of philosophy are one and the same. In method of discovery, development, and presentation of truth the two systems are radically different; hence the hostility, which is primarily a hostility of method only. The oneness of Christianity and philosophy is the oneness of pursuit; the difference of Christianity and philosophy is the difference of method. Out of the difference of method grows the difference of result.

It is precisely this difference of method that accounts for the failure of the one and the success of the other. Respecting the greatest truths, philosophy has failed in its explanations and declarations, producing as monuments of its incompetency the wretched and ghostly forms of materialism and agnosticism, while Christianity, pulsating with a divine energy, announced the sublimest doctrines with a faith born of knowledge, and a fullness that proves it to be a revelation from God. The province of Christianity is philosophical in the sense that, taking up philosophical truth in its nakedness and wretchedness, it gives it a new body, clothes it with a supernatural beauty, and breathes into it a supernatural life. Under this transforming process whatever is absurd in philosophy is cast out, and its truth passes over in a new and true form into the religious realm. Philosophic Realism, absurd in its very nature, is lost in the rational conception of the existence of absolute ideas, or inherent ideals of mind; that is, the separate existence of ideas, outside of mind, is supplanted by the doctrine of inherent ideas of absolute mind. Epicurean atheism is succeeded by Christian theism; Pythagorean transmigration is given up for revealed immortality; Alexandrian mysticism fades into Gospel spirituality; evolutionary ethics is replaced by supernaturalistic law; and the truth of a personal, providential superintendence of worldly affairs roots out pessimism and the whole troop of philosophic falsehoods and errors.

Christianity is philosophical, not only in its truth, but equally in its consistency and certainties. Mansel objects to the attempt to support religious truth by rationalistic foundations, which is the same as saying that he denies to Christianity a philosophic consistency and certainty. He is not the first who would deprive religion of a philosophical basis, nor the first to concede certain contradictory elements in the Christian notion of the Absolute and Infinite, and that religious truth must be accepted on other grounds than that of philosophic coherency and rationalistic transparency. So far forth as it is a statement of truth, Christianity is a revelation; so far forth as it demonstrates its truths, whether by an appeal to the natural, experimental, historical, archæological, or to the inner consistency of truth, it pursues a philosophic method, and is so far a philosophy. The truth of revealed religion is supposed to rest upon, and to be vindicated by, moral evidence, while the application to it of philosophical tests or principles, by which a mathematical certainty may be reached, is considered presumptive, and the attempt pronounced a failure. Yet it is clear that Christianity may submit to such a test without danger to it as a whole, or to any part of it. The concession that the proofs of Christianity are moral, and can not be philosophical, is damaging in the extreme. Dealing with philosophical truth, it may be exposed to philosophical tests; and, as philosophical truth demonstrates itself to a mathematical certainty, abjuring moral evidence, so Christianity may demonstrate itself to a mathematical certainty, employing moral evidence with reserve, and then only incidentally. The truth of revelation is as open to demonstration as the truth of philosophy. *Revelation itself is a demonstration.* Christianity is the demonstration of the supernatural, as philosophy is the demonstration of the natural. One is as complete as the other; one is as mathematically certain as the other. Christianity teaches this view, or it would not be taught here. In his introductory word to Theophilus, Luke says he writes his Gospel that he might "know the *certainty* of those things wherein thou hast been instructed." Christianity is a certainty, a consistency, a rational, philosophic, supernaturally demonstrated system of truth. It is truth revealed; therefore, of unquestionable certainty, more reliable than any mathematically demonstrated truth. Incarnation is as well established as any historical event recorded by Gibbon or Macaulay. Atonement may be demonstrated as clearly as any problem in Euclid. Independently, however, of historical tests of the historic data, and of logical or mathematical proofs of the doctrinal truths of Christianity, the whole is addressed to human intelligence on the superior ground of a supernatural revelation, which has in it every element of certainty and every assurance of absolute verity. On common philosophic grounds, the truth of Christianity may be fully demonstrated; on its own ground, it makes itself transparently true, and is above all suspicion. This is the highest achievement—to make truth transparent, to make it appear what it is, to relieve it of all illusion and error, to fasten it upon the mind as incontrovertibly and eternally true. In its philosophical relations and demonstrations,

Christianity undertakes to accomplish this work, adding the supernatural proof of its claim as a revelation.

In the same spirit, Christianity disposes of the truths that other religions claim as their exclusive property, appropriating them when in harmony with itself, fulfilling their own predictions respecting the appearance of divine teachers, and uprooting the errors and superstitions that have characterized them, and unfitted them for the very purposes for which they were established. The old religions were prophecies of the new, in that they contained many truths or suggestions, which, like those of philosophy, required elaboration, transparency, systematic and orderly development into unity, before they could exercise the native power in them, or before they could be accepted at their full value. Gold in the ore is not as valuable as gold minted. Truth in the ore, such as it was in the old religions, is not as valuable as truth cleansed from error, and lifted out of its crude environment into a stately attitude of independence and beauty. Christianity brought to light the hidden truths of the old religions, and introduced them in new forms to the attention of the world. In this work it revealed the value of truth, but it was quite as distinct a revelation as had it revealed the truth directly from God. *To reveal, explain, and elaborate old, existent, but hidden and misunderstood, truths is as necessary as to reveal new and entirely unknown truths.* In either case the result is truth, and the method is the same—*revelation.*

Brahminism, a system of religious dreams, furnishes a striking illustration of this statement. Among its essential teachings are those respecting gods, incarnations, trinities, sacrifices, and divine teachers, the whole a crude prophecy of the leading doctrines of Christianity, for the latter proclaims Incarnation, the Trinity, Atonement, and Messiahship, as fundamental ideas, as essential facts, without which religion is impossible. Brahminism is an antecedent religion, of which Christianity is a full revelation or development. The Persian prophets predicted the birth of a divine child from a virgin, and the Athenians in Paul's day erected an altar to the "Unknown God," the prophecy of the one and the altar of the other pointing to two great truths of Christianity. In the one, these truths are in an embryonic state ; in the other, they are developed. The old religions were the forerunners of the new. Christianity was a reformation of old forms, as well as a revelation of new ideas. It was a development of old truth, as well as the announcement of new truth. The aim of all religions is the same, as the anxieties of the world in all ages have been the same. The same problems, the same hopes and fears, the same ideas, more or less clear, have interested the race from the beginning; and the religion that solves the problems, satisfies the hopes, and evolves the ideas into great transparent realities, must finally reign in the world until it ends. The early religions undertook to pilot the race in the dark, but hoped for the morning, and announced its coming. Trench observes: " These dim prophetic anticipations, the dreams of the world, so far from helping to persuade us that all we hold is a dream likewise, are rather that which ought to have preceded the world's awaking. These parhelia do not proclaim every thing else to be optical illusions, but announce and witness for a sun that is traveling into sight."

The relationship of religions is an acknowledged fact. Holding to similar truths, one prepared the way for another, or gave birth to another, as Brahminism to Buddhism, and all prepared the way for Christianity, which, recovering old truth from its superstitious environment, joined it to new truth as it descended from heaven. The relationship of religions does not imply the necessary unity of religions, only so far forth as the characteristic of truth is its unity. The unity of religions is the unity of the truth in them. James Freeman Clarke speaks of Christianity as " one of the good religions," and W. H. Channing alludes to it as " one of many religions, all essentially divine." These are misleading statements, for the independent and supernatural character of Christianity is a great fact, and must not be ignored; nor must other religions be permitted to occupy the rank of divine religions, else in what respect is Christianity any better than preceding religions? Christianity is a development of the old; it is also a revelation of the new. As a development, it is superior to the old; as a revelation, it is independent of them.

However, it is clear that the province of Christianity is, in its broadest sense, the province of all religions, undertaking nothing not common to them, but succeeding wherein they failed. It is a new religion in doing that which other religions, having the same ends in view, could not realize or accomplish. The province of Christianity is definitely the province of religion.

It has been stated that its work is limited, both in its revelations of the natural and supernatural; that its relation to philosophy is fraternal and helpful, its purpose being the recovery of truth from philosophic uncertainty, and its assertion in transparent and divine forms; and that its relation to religion is the same, its purpose being the development of all the truths they contain. In addition, it has been hinted that Christianity is a revelation of truths not found either in nature, philosophy, or religions, and that it has special functions, or a special mission. With this specialty of Christianity it is important to become acquainted.

Christianity, separated from other religions, is the religion of supernatural truth, or of necessary spiritual truth, made known, not by philosophic methods, nor by ordinary religious methods, but solely by revelation. The province of paganism is *the province of superstition;* the province of philosophy is *the province of speculation;* the province of Christianity is the *province of revelation.* This is its distinguishing feature; this it is that isolates it from philosophies and religions, notwithstanding their oneness of aim and points of agreement; this it is that places Paul above Plato.

The method of revelation, for it is a method only of communicating truth, justifies itself by the singular and stupendous fact that what is called necessary spiritual truth can be found only in the Book alleged to contain a revelation. The question of revelation might be waived, if the truths of the book were accepted as genuine; but a denial of revelation is implicit with a denial of the truths supposed to be revealed. Practically, there is no difference between faith in revelation as a method of communicating truth, and faith in the truths alleged to be the result of revelation. Faith in the method and faith in the result are one and the same, and a defense of the one is equal to a defense of the other. Whether the Book may be said to *contain* a revelation of truth, or is the truth itself; whether it is plenarily, dynamically, or mechanically inspired, or inspired only so far as the truth is concerned; whether it is substantially or in every particular true,—it is not important to decide. The main point is, that Christianity is a revelation of necessary spiritual truth; this is its province—a province not occupied by philosophy or other religions.

To the method of revelation it has been objected that it refutes itself by an alleged want of transparency in the truth it undertakes to reveal, and that obscure truth, or truth obscurely presented, is inconsistent with truth alleged to be revealed. The objection arises from a mistaken view of the method itself, or the function of inspiration. Revelation is not synonymous with full disclosures, explicit explanations, and perfect illuminations of truth. That is a revelation, in a Biblical sense, that serves to open the way to knowledge, or furnishes the key to a limited knowledge of supernatural truth. The Bible is a glass through which one sees the truth; it is a telescope which he points to the spiritual universe, and through which he sees the universe; but he sees it not perfectly, although he sees it.

Again, a revealed truth may be so obscurely expressed, or hidden from view, as to require no inconsiderable effort to find it, or to recognize it when found; it is nevertheless in a *state of revelation.* Oxygen was not discovered until within about a century, but it was in the atmosphere when Plato was inhaling it in Athens, and when Abraham snuffed the air in Chaldea. Prophetic truth, wrapped in symbols; Messianic truth, hidden in poetic metaphors; monotheistic truth, unseen in the ashes on patriarchal altars; eschatological truth, opening its gates but a little in the metaphysics of apostles; soteriological truth, adumbrated in types and shadows and services of prophets and disciples; all necessary spiritual truth is in the great book, hidden or obscure perhaps, but *it is there,* to be found, unfolded, appropriated, used. If it were not there, the claim of revelation would be false; no difference how it is there, hidden like pearls in the deep, or blazing like suns in the firmament, as it is there, the claim of revelation is true.

Moreover, some truths of revelation are declared as mysteries, never to be explained; *they are to be known as unknowable,* and they are revealed as such. The secret thoughts of Deity; the processes of spiritual work; the doctrines of atonement, immortality, resurrection, heaven, and hell, are involved in mystery. As the working facts of Christianity, they are powerful and sufficient; as the mysteries of revelation, they are accepted, and the soul is silent in their presence. In respect to mysteries, revelation leaves us in ignorance; a paradox not difficult of explanation when all that it includes and excludes is remembered. For instance, Christianity is a revelation of the monotheistic idea concreted in a personal God, but in such a way that, while it enlightens, it also darkens. The revelation of God is incomplete. He is known and unknown. "Verily, thou art a God that hidest thyself," is consistent with "he that hath seen me hath seen the Father." A hidden and a visible, a seen and an unseen God, is revealed in the sacred books. All other doctrines are mingled light and darkness, because of the one purpose of religion.

The limitations of Christianity are not in contradiction of, but rather in harmony with, the idea of revelation There are necessary spiritual truths, which it is the province of Christianity to disclose, but back of these there are supernatural truths, equally necessary to God's ideal purposes, but not necessary to man's existence, development, or destiny, that Christianity does not disclose. *Truths in no way related to human interests find no place in revelation.* Such truths may address the intelligence of redeemed souls in the next life, but, having no reference to redemptive or providential purposes in this life, they are not revealed, and Christianity is in no wise weakened by not revealing them. Only the absolutely necessary spiritual truth can be the subject of revelation.

If this is the province of revelation; that is, if it is circumscribed by necessary truth, the province of Christianity can not be larger, different, or superior, for the province of one is the province of the other. Whatever is consistent with the idea of revelation, whether limitation, obscurity, or imperfection, is consistent also with Christianity as the religion of revelation. If revealed truth is true, then Christianity is true; if one is false, the other is false. The two are identical in substance, and share the same fate of ill or good.

Now, as the necessary spiritual truths of revelation are supernatural, or such as are beyond the intellect to discover, originate, or explain by natural or scientific principles, so the truths of Christianity are supernatural in character, and must rank above all other truth either in philosophy or religions. The necessary truths of Christianity may be classified as follows: I. Theistic; II. Governmental; III. Anthropological; IV. Soteriological; V. Eschatological. This list may not include all that belongs to the religious concept, but it comprehends the vital and sovereign facts of Christianity, with which we are more immediately concerned.

Respecting these necessary truths, it may be asked, Are they truths? Are they sufficiently revealed? Assuming that they are truths, revelations, inspirations, we can proceed; otherwise, the whole system of Christianity as a revelation must be defended, which is beyond our present purpose. The defense of revealed truth is not so much required as a statement of what is revealed truth, or its separation from all other truth, and its own exaltation. Theistic truth occupies the first place in the category of necessary or primary supernatural truth, since, without a personal God, the universe is inexplicable, and, without a knowledge of God, religion is impossible. Atheism, agnosticism, positivism, and materialism, rise up in frenzied horror against the theistic conception, which has its roots both in human consciousness and in supernatural revelation. Aside from these, it is supported by ontological, cosmological, and psychological arguments, which have never been answered, except as speculation seems to answer truth. To abandon such a conception, grounded in consciousness, science, philosophy, and revelation, can not be done, except as one abandons all tests of truth, and, therefore, all truth. Our statement of theistic truth does not require an investigation of the proofs of the existence of God, but merely that the fact of the divine existence is a part of the subject-matter of revelation, and fundamental to the religion based upon revelation.

The theistic idea is not the sole product of Christianity, for it

27

existed in the world long before the advent of the incarnate Teacher, and, with all the superstition that environed it, it exercised a controlling influence on the old religions, if it did not produce them. Tracing the career of the idea until Christianity appropriated and ennobled it, it appears like a homeless and fugitive idea, the skeleton of a great truth, without plan, or a historic purpose, left to itself to do a tentative work, and then to be taken up finally by a religion that would honor it, and give it a crown and a throne. Many truths now credited to Christianity were floating ages before the Messiah taught them in the public mind, like seeds in the wind, which, dropping here and there, took root, grew, and bore fruit in worships, ceremonies, and religions. The idea of God, prayer, sacrifice, resurrection, immortality, judgment, and eternal settlements, were not unknown prior to Christianity, but they were dreams, superstitions, speculations, eventuating into truths through the reality of inspiration. Occasionally a strong-minded teacher would arise, as if touched by the divine hand, and commissioned to do something new, and a religion, embodying these ideas, would be framed; but the teacher himself ignorant, they were sure to be clothed with absurdities, fantasies, and cruelties. Hence the need of a clear revelation of truths whose existence had been inspiringly suspected for ages. Dreams, suspicions, speculations, and superstitions before Christ; afterward, truths no longer in shadows, but sunbeams striking within the horizon of human vision.

The theistic idea must be interpreted by this historic plan or rule of the development of Christian ideas. Its history is the history of dreams ending in realities, of superstitions converted into facts, of speculations metamorphosed into truths. Scarcely a tribe of men, however barbarous, or stupid even to religious insensibility, has been found that has not entertained the idea of a Supreme Power and the correlative idea of worship. All nations, however thick their moral darkness and all-pervading their superstitions, have quarantined their coasts, so to speak, against the infection of atheism, and have worshiped either man-made idols, the sun and stars, or the objects of nature, meanwhile waiting for a divine teacher, or a revelation of the true God. Neither the old religions, fastening themselves to the theistic idea, nor the old philosophies, speculating on the probabilities of a First Cause, were able to take the idea, strip it of vagueness, vitalize it with the eternal breath, decorate it with divine beauty, and present it to the race as the holiest of supernatural truths. For this consummation of the idea the race anxiously waited for ages; every ceremony was a prayer, every sigh a hope, and every thought a desire for revelation; but priests and philosophers made no response, or only such response as sunk them deeper in the pit of ignorance. The anxiously sought truth Christianity at last disclosed, shooting its light like early morning rays over the Oriental world, and revealing not only God, but also the universe and its infinite contents, to the joy of a race of men sometime to become the sons of God. This was the function of Christianity, its specialty, the revelation of God, and all that the idea carried with it. It revealed him by appropriation and assimilation of the idea of God, so long in the world; it revealed him by a close and particularizing enumeration of his attributes; it revealed him in the character of an infinite personality; it revealed him as the First Cause, Omnipotent Ruler, Universal Benefactor, and gracious Redeemer; it revealed him as absolute and unconditioned being, and in anthropomorphic relations and characteristics, that he might the more readily be apprehended. It sounded his name throughout the universe, and turned the pessimism of the ages into the laughter of eternal praise.

We say this is a revelation; philosophy can explain its presence in the world on no other hypothesis. The pre-Christian idea of God has surrendered to the Christian idea, which now dominates as the true and only idea in civilization. It is the theistic representation of Christianity that is quenching the superstitions of the old religions, and piloting philosophy out of its speculations into the region of reality. This is a necessary spiritual truth, for the particular revelation of which the world must forever be indebted to the great religion of the Nazarene.

As an adjunct of the theistic conception, the governmental idea of the world, or the *reign of a providential spirit both in nature and human history*, deserves special consideration. Its truest representation belongs to Christianity. Viewed from the stand-point of philosophy, the government of the Supreme Power is a centralization of weakness, imbecility, indifference, and cruelty; philosophers themselves in their opinions swinging between fatalism and pessimism on the one hand, and pantheism and deism on the other. Herbert Spencer concedes to the unsearchable, indiscernible, and unknowable God, a benevolent spirit working in the universe for the attainment of the best ends; but the attribute thus philosophically framed or conceived is different from the attribute of infinite goodness which the Scriptures declare to be the glory of God. The evolutionist interprets the government of the world as strictly of and within itself; it is under a system of law, self-instituted and self-administered. The reign of personal authority in nature is disputed and scorned. Hartmann, accepting the existence of a Supreme Power, regards it totally unconscious, both as to its own existence and as to the world's government, implying the reign of a most absolute and undeviating fatalism in human history. Schopenhauer went farther in eliminating rational impulses from the intellectual or personal center of the universe, turning the eternal throne into a play-house for the ghost of an idea, and robbing the universe of a much-needed personal ruler. Materialism, positivism, agnosticism, pessimism, and atheism, in single attempts or unitedly, have failed to frame a satisfactory theory of the government of the world; and yet this is a necessary truth, quite as necessary to philosophy as religion.

The old religions, imbibing the spirit of the old philosophies, did not advance much beyond them, and if they posited a bolder conception, it was so involved in superstition as to fail of recognition as a new truth, so that neither from the one nor the other emerge comforting views of divine Providence, or accurate representations of the divine government.

To Christianity one must go for the truth, or be without it. According to its tenets, God's government is both general and particular, having in view the development of man and the execution of the divine ideal in the universe. Tyranny is not found in Christian theology as the exponent of the divine administration. As reflected by Christianity, among the first notions one receives of the divine government is its paternal character, or the divine interest in the human family, or the alliance of God with man. This general truth, comforting and inspiring, has illustration in the history of the race, which, with all its vicissitudes and apparent lapses and uncertainties, is a history of progress toward definite ideals, a proof that God is directing the world, a proof that the Father cares for his children. This idea of progress is as scientific as it is Scriptural, as philosophic as it is theologic; and, accepted as Scripturally interpreted or defined, man's entire history becomes an illumination of a divine project, is seen to be the fulfilling of a divine ideal. This, however, is not its chief glory. Its general purposes, however honorable and electrifying, are lost to the view when the relation of the divine government to individual lives is detected and emphasized; in other words, the special providential government of God, as it is unfolded, is seen to transcend the general, world-wide, age-long government of the throne. This distinction modern philosophy is incompetent to recognize; as to the two facts or governments, it denies one at the same time that it rejects the other. To Christianity alone is man indebted for the supreme thought of a personal government, and a special providential spirit in human life.

This is set forth in the Scriptures in a threefold manner: 1. Providence respecting the call and mission of the prophets;

2. Providence respecting the assignments of particular men to different spheres of usefulness; 3. Providence respecting individual life in all its details. As one of the pillars of Christianity, prophecy still stands unshaken and unharmed. The mystery of the prophetic gift, equal to the mystery of the miracle-working power, has never had, nor can it have, any philosophical explanation; the root of the gift, or the process of inspiration, is not in psychology; the only explanation of the power to announce future events is that it is an endowment of the Almighty. Daniel, looking down the ages from a palace in Babylon, first sees and then portrays the rise and fall of kingdoms in a certain historic order, which, as time moves on, is fulfilled to the letter; Isaiah, with eyes opened upon a particular event, announces the day when the reign of the Messiah shall begin; Micah designates the humble place of his birth; Daniel foretells the tragedy of his crucifixion; and David sings of the glories of resurrection and ascension. To attempt to explain these prophetic disclosures by psychological methods would be very like an attempt to explain the trade-winds by the same methods. There are natural things that can not be explained by psychology; there are supernatural things in whose presence philosophy is dumb, and prophecy defies the ingenuity of the evolutionist to solve it on any other than a divine hypothesis.

In some subtle way God took possession of the prophets, opened their eyes, and, unfolding to their gaze a panorama of events ages distant, commanded them to write that the world might know, not so much what would happen, as that God is present with men, as ruler, inspirer, and friend. This is personal providence on a grand scale, the like of which is not seen in the annals of philosophy, and of which philosophy can give no rational account. Christianity, the religion of inspiration, refers the prophetic impulse to a divine source, appealing to the prophetic parchments and their contents in proof thereof.

The divine government is equally personal in its superintendence of the special vocations of the great moral heroes of history. Moses, divinely called to be leader of the Israelites, towers like some great mountain, conspicuous for the handwriting of God upon his brow; Joshua, hearing the divine voice, when others imagine the wind is blowing, steps into his shoes, a worthy successor of the great lawgiver; Elijah, in cave or mountain, commissioned by the angel of the Lord, flames through Syria as a herald of the divine administration, awakening terror in royal palaces, and then ascends by a new route to the skies; Zerubbabel, of forecasting genius, chosen by the directing Mind in the heavens, rebuilds the temple in superior glory, on the sacred summits of Moriah; Paul hears a voice near

Damascus, obeying which he is prepared for the shipwreck in the Mediterranean, and the loftier hurricane in the tribunal of Nero; John, charmed by the sweet invitation of the Master, is ready for Patmos, Ephesus, heaven; Peter, leaving the fishing smack at the command of the divine One, emerges on Pentecost, shakes Jerusalem, and suspends, head downward, from the cross. Supernatural calls these; supernatural lives; supernatural histories. No divine call is heard in the porch of Zeno, or rings through the vaulted chambers of the Academy of Plato; not even the Peripatetics, with faces toward the sky, see visions, or hear the echoes of heaven. Special inspirations to duty are unknown outside of Christianity.

Of still more importance to the race, Christianity teaches the most minute providential care of the individual life, enforcing it by an exhibition of the divine regard for smaller things than human interests, and then representing every providential plan as intended to promote those interests. Not a sparrow falls to the ground without your Father—men are of more value than many sparrows; the hairs of one's head are numbered—a trifle this, but typical of that which is not a trifle; the steps of a good man are ordered by the Lord; he will guide by his counsel into truth and into life everlasting. By such revelations the idea of divine providence is imbedded in the heart of humanity; and the governmental truth of Christianity, unique, merciful, fascinating, rises into view as a fit corner-stone of a religion designed to satisfy human aspiration and to quiet the pessimistic forebodings of an otherwise irreligious world.

The anthropological truth of Christianity, isolated from philosophic representations, is special in its content, and of the nature of an independent revelation of self-knowledge and self-interest. It includes the *genesis of man*, with the cognate questions of his antiquity and relation to the natural world, or the physiological aspects of the race; all *psychological problems*, as the nature of mind, the processes of intellectual activity, the laws of cognition and perception, the relation and interaction of soul and body, and the immortality of the soul; all *moral problems*, as man's positive moral state, the genesis of depravity, the origin of ethical relations and duties, the nature and extent of human responsibility, and the historic resources of human restoration to greatness and perfection. No inquiry, raised by philosophy concerning man, is ignored by the new religion; on the contrary, all its inquiries, physiological, psychological, ethical, ethnical, and religious, are espoused by it and answered in its own way and with sufficient fullness for its purpose. In these respects its function is intensely scientific; that is, it asks for facts, and must have them; it goes where evolution goes; it may be found in company with geology, chemistry, botany, physiology, and psychology. Concerning God, it is *philosophically theological;* concerning the government of the world, it is *theologically philosophical;* concerning man, it is *scientifically anthropological,* and *anthropologically theological.* Christian anthropology and scientific anthropology are the hemispheres of the same globe of truth; they fit together, one is necessary to the other.

Of necessary spiritual truths, which it is the province of Christianity to unfold, none are of greater moment or more nearly related to human interests, than those which pass as soteriological, or such truths as include atonement and regeneration as the sources of recovery from the effects of sin. Ethical systems, for instance, Aristotle's, Hegel's, Spencer's, have an honored place in philosophy; but philosophy is without the soteriological spirit, and is incapable of devising a soteriological system. Such a system, the content of which is the redemptive purpose and project, belongs to, and must come from, religion alone, and the best system can emanate only from the best religion. In a pessimistic mood the philosopher may point to the evils of life, but he can provide no remedy for them; he may sit down in ashes and mourn, but he can not rise with songs in his mouth, and shout deliverance from all his troubles; he can go down into dungeons of despair, but he can not ride Ezekiel's wheels of light, or ascend into Paul's third heavens of vision. Stoicism, educational purification, social ostracism, the pursuit of philosophy—these have been suggested as remedies for sin, but a trial of them has demonstrated their utter inadequacy. Nor have the old religions succeeded any better in soteriological suggestions, although they have prescribed more definitely for the healing of the soul's infirmities. Penances, sacrifices, ceremonies, ablutions, avail nothing. To Christianity alone the race must turn, not only for a remedy, but also an adequate remedy for sin. An explanation of atonement, an analysis of its process, and the manner in which it is applied and made effective in human salvation, are questions that must finally be studied; but at present it is sufficient to declare atonement as the primal force in the world's moral regeneration. In the life and death of Jesus Christ; in his teachings and miracles; in his example and institutions; in his agony and triumph; in his resurrection and ascension; the remedy for sin is complete. It is the only remedy that has justified itself in human history, the only remedy that puts hope into the heart, and brings salvation to the soul. *The specialty of Christianity is atonement for sin,* or the redemption of man from sin. It is a revelation of the redemptive idea, the redemptive process, and the redemptive result, crowning its purpose with achievement, and lifting the earth into the heavens.

Among the necessary spiritual truths which Christianity must make known, if they are known at all, are those relating to the future, commonly denominated *eschatological.* Death is a grim fact. To live again is a hope ; the ages echo with the song of immortality, and reveal it as a conviction of the race ; all religions avow belief in another life, but cloud the faith with superstition. The idea then is in the ages, and in the heart of man. As usual, philosophy treats this most vital question with indifference, or, in its more positive form, rejects the thought of conscious existence after death. Epicurus argued against it, while Socrates was inspired with a touching faith in its certainty. Emerson presents immortality as the guess of the soul, while the materialists announce the probability of the dissolution of the spiritual fabric with the body. Enveloped with the uncertainties of philosophy and the superstitions of religion, the Gospel dawns upon the world, bringing immortality to light, and opening a way into the other life. It relieved the old idea of superstition and made it a truth, it relieved it of uncertainty and made it a fact.

In natural order the great truths of resurrection, judgment, heaven and hell follow ; they, too, are brought out of darkness into light, out of mystery into transparency, out of uncertainty into reality. Christ speaks, and the eternal world opens to the gaze of man ; Paul speaks, and the dead live ; Peter speaks, and the world is in ashes ; John speaks, and hell's lake of fire flashes its heat into the future, and heaven's gates of pearl open to receive the martyrs of God. The eschatology of Christianity is of the nature of a divine revelation of facts, events, and destinies, impossible to be foreknown except as they are communicated. The communication of such truth is one of the functions of the new religion.

The province of Christianity is now sufficiently foreshadowed to warrant a discussion of its truths. It is the province of the natural and the supernatural, with limitations ; of the natural, chiefly as it reflects the supernatural, and of the supernatural, chiefly as it reflects the divine purposes in their relation to the universe and the creatures who inhabit it. In its more definite undertakings it *assumes the solution of the theistic problem, the presentation of the divine administration in its providential aspects, the settlement of all anthropological questions, employing scientific helps when necessary to such settlement, the discovery of the soteriological resources of the race, and the announcement of a future life, with rewards and punishments conditioned upon man's present life ; in other words, it undertakes to furnish an* ABRIDGED HISTORY OF THE DIVINE ACTIVITIES *in the creation of the world, the introduction of man, the recovery of man from the moral lapse of his early career, and the final disposition of man and the universe.* Great problems these, to solve which it invokes the aid of inspiration, and presents its truths in their final form, not as philosophic speculations nor as religious superstitions, but as revelations of the truth-giving God.

---

# CHAPTER XIX.

## THE TWO CHRISTIANITIES.

IS there in form or name more than one Christianity? Narrowing the question to one line of thought, does the New Testament reveal or contain two Christianities? Some Jewish writers contend that the religion that Jesus drew up, originated, or imposed, was only an improvement or purification of Judaism; that he contemplated only the reform and not the extinction of the Hebrew system; and that, judging by the synoptists, there is no evidence that he went beyond this design. They, therefore, speak even friendly of his work, styling his religion "Jewish Christianity," and go so far as to say that in the first century the Jews and Christians, understanding that the differences that separated them related to the Messiahship of Christ, were not hostile, but mutually helpful in the propagation of the essentials of both faiths. They assert also that the early Christians embraced many of the teachings, observed many of the ceremonies, and held sacred and inviolable all the laws of the Jews, and that had it not been for the perversions of Paul the breach between them had never occurred. Paul's Christianity they contemptuously style Pauline, Hellenistic, or Gentile Christianity, in opposition to original or Jewish Christianity.

Here, then, is an issue, based upon an alleged difference between religion as taught by Christ and religion as taught by Paul. Is Pauline Christianity a perversion of original Christianity? Did Paul or the apostles institute a religion derived in part from and suggested by the great Teacher, but in many essentials original with themselves? Is Paul the original teacher, the fountain-head of what is popularly known as Christianity? Has the Church drifted away with Paul from what Christ revealed, taught, and established? Paul's fourteen epistles, written in less than thirty years after the death of the Master, make up the greater portion of the New Testament, and are explicit in their statements of truth; they are literary marvels, and as professed inspired documents contain supernatural truths that place Paul beyond those who, like him, addressed epistles to the Churches; and it goes without proof that, next to the Master himself, Paul is highest in authority, as he is of all the apostles most definite in his experience, and the clearest and fullest in his theology. We would not detract from him as a teacher, theologian, exemplar; his life was a sacrifice for the truth; his death the grandest of martyrdoms; and his memory sacred on earth and vital in heaven. Called out of due time, he stands forth the conspicuous head of the apostolic Church, teaching more, suffering more, accomplishing more, than any other of the illustrious band.

But did he originate Christianity, or any part of it? Did he supersede Christ, or do his epistles abound with truths contradictory of those taught by the Master, or different in any sense from them? We are quite as much interested in the settlement of the problem as the Jews themselves, for it involves more than the reputation of the apostle; it involves the integrity of the Christian religion. If Pauline Christianity is a fungus growth or an antagonistic system, or original with Paul, we desire to know it, for the popular supposition is that it is merely an expansion of original Christianity.

The scope of the problem is such that we must first understand what original Christianity is before we can ascertain if Pauline Christianity is a perversion or no. Was Christ's religion, or system, Jewish in complexion, in essential truth, and in final design? Was he the founder of a new system of religion, or a reformer of the existing religion? In heralding him to the Jewish nation, John, the forerunner, said, "Now also the ax is laid at the root of the tree"— not at the branches, but at the root; he is not a pruner, but a destroyer. It is true he came not to destroy the law, but the gross paraphernalia of Judaism and the inadequate parts of the system he was quite ready to overthrow. As a religion he was disposed to supplant it. Nowhere is he denominated a reformer or purifier of the old faith. The other John says, "The law was given by Moses, but grace and truth came by Jesus Christ." The two religions were different, as their two personal exponents were different, and if conflict between them was not intended and was unnecessary, it grew rather out of the perversions of Judaism than out of the perversions of Christianity. If Christ did not array himself against the old systems, and disclaimed a hostile motive for his career, its defenders antagonized him to the death, and so compelled their own overthrow. Without such antagonism it is possible that Judaism would have been transformed into the new faith, but it resisted transformation, reformation, and purification, and destruction was the *dernier ressort* of the Master. Jesus, therefore, pursues his career independently; he teaches with authority; he reveals truth according to his own wisdom and pleasure; he demonstrates his power by occasional miraculous displays;

he institutes a ministry, founds a Church, commits his message of redemption to the world, and retires to wait until his soul shall be
satisfied with the fullest achievement.

Now, at his death, what truths do we find controlling the minds
of the apostles? What is the system of religion that appears after his
three years of itinerant ministry? Do we find every thing in it that
is taught by Paul? Is it a complete system of religion? Was Paul
needed at all? No one can understand fully the merits of Christianity without canvassing these questions, as they bring to light some
facts which must forever hush the cry of antagonism between Paul
and Christ.

What Christianity was at the ascension of Christ we can only
know from the four Gospels, written by Matthew, Mark, Luke, and
John. We can not accept suggestions from Jewish writers, nor will
we infer any thing from the record of the epistles of the apostles
themselves. Confined to the four Gospels, what was Christianity?
No one will pretend to affirm that these Gospels are more than mere
fragments of history, or that they contain more than the briefest report of the sayings and doings of Christ. Christ himself wrote
nothing, save once on the ground, and that was never read, and what
we have as his utterances came through others. We do not doubt
the genuineness of the Gospels, but it is well enough to remember
just what they are and what they teach. They are fragments, or the
framework of Christianity. Besides this, they reveal no system of
religion, no theological plan, no formal creed. We are prone to talk
of systems and plans and theologies, but the Gospels are only suggestive of them—they are innocent of a system. The truth is from
God, but the system of arrangement is always man-made. As in
nature, so in religion. Scientific facts, truths, and principles are
found in irregular masses and confused heaps and fragmentary forms
everywhere—this is nature's method; but sciences, as systems, are
man-made. Take botany. Flowers, ferns, trees, are distributed over
the globe promiscuously, but the botanist constructs the science of
botany out of them. So zoölogy is a human structure, while the
animals abound in all latitudes. In some such way, divine truths
are imbedded in the Bible. They are without system or order of arrangement. In the Gospels, especially, there is no development of
truth. Hints, scanty revelations, mere statements, great fragments—
these are numerous, and very suggestive of what is beyond or underneath. At the same time, there are occasional complete, clear-cut
statements, that are satisfactory and comprehensive.

Now, it is out of this disorderly array of truths, these great hints,
these fragments, that a consistent and orderly statement of what Chris-

tianity is must be made. Theology is the gathering up of this mass of truths, and putting them into order, and labeling them with definite names. The relation of theology to Christianity is the relation of zoölogy to the animal kingdom, and of botany to the flora of the globe.

Paul was the first Christian theologian who undertook, under divine direction, to shape the utterances of the Teacher into a consistent whole, to form a Scriptural theology, and to employ terms and indicate relations that were in advance of what seemed to be inherent in Christianity as laid down by the Founder. This grew out of the nature of the task itself, and was inevitable. But, as we shall see, between Christ as the Teacher, and Paul as the theologian or interpreter, there was no divergence, but a oneness of spirit and purpose that rather relates than divides them.

Christ originated Christianity; Paul *formulated* it. He took up the fragments, and they multiplied in his hands; he caught glimpses of the unshapely masses of truth, and reduced them to order, and, in the reduction, developed them in all their proportions; so that, in Paul's vision, Christ's truths seem, if possible, a little larger, if not more beautiful, than in their own author's hands. This, too, was inevitable and necessary. Looking into the apostolic ranks, one can see that, of all men to undertake the analysis, development, application, or theological expression, of Christianity, as it came from the Master's hands, Paul was the most fitted, by nationality, education, temperamental constitution, and inspiration. Prof. Fairbairn says, that "God made Paul for the moment, the moment for Paul." Of Jewish parentage, he had inherited the ancestral fervor and intense devotional spirit of the Hebrews; he was also, doubtless, proud of his social connections, and believed in the superiority of the old faith. Born in a Greek city, he came in contact with the Gentile world, and saw its wonderful needs and its wonderful capacities; and as no other, he seemed able to bridge the great chasm between the Jews and the Gentiles. "In his single mind two races and two worlds met"—he was the instrument of both. In this broad relationship, Paul's fitness for the task of elaborating the great and folded truths of the new religion must rest.

Just how great is the indebtedness of the Church to Paul, for his elaboration of doctrine, can not be measured, except by a survey of the particulars of the elaboration. In this it will be discovered that he departed not from the original teachings of the Master, nor suggested any thing that had not been previously taught, and left in a sketchy or fragmentary form. Paul's work was completed in thirty years after the scene on Calvary—his epistles written, his great missionary tours accomplished, his religious assault upon the household of Cæsar effected, and his death outside the city of Rome a veritable fact—a time too short for the introduction of a religion different from that that had been announced; a period scarcely long enough to even corrupt the teachings of the Church, which were well understood even before Paul's conversion. Moreover, Paul's highest interest centered in Christianity as he had received it. His remarkable conversion could have no other effect than to win him over to the support of the religion he had so maliciously opposed, and whose extinction he had sought to accomplish. Converted, saved, the instinct of gratitude would bind him forever to the Savior, and his greatest desire must have been to know more about him, and to glory in nothing so much as in Jesus, and him crucified. This interest would make him a friend, and not a corrupter, of the religion that had redeemed him. To suppose otherwise, or to allow for a moment that Paul undertook to establish a religion himself and supplant Christ, or that he went so far as to modify and reconstruct Christianity, so as to appear as great as the original Teacher, presupposes some things that we should be loath to concede. It implies that Paul was a schemer, a man filled with an ambition to secure both power and fame, and that he would forsake one religion to become the founder of another, whenever opportunity offered. This presupposition is not in accordance with Paul's character, as it is described. The scheming, ambitious spirit is certainly not manifest in his abandonment of Judaism, which entailed the loss of estate, position, endowment, and social influence. Ambition is the source of restlessness and fluctuation of purpose, but Paul is an example of firmness truly admirable. Never does he waver in his loyalty to Christ; never does he change his purpose to preach the Gospel; never does he shrink at sacrifice; never does he hesitate, debate, cringe, apologize, or forsake the divine course before him. In this heroism, equal to that of Moses, and superior to that of the other apostles, there is not the slightest exhibition of ambition.

What is decisive of the question is the fact that his marvelous successes, as an apostle, were along the original line of Christian truth, and because he stood forth as the defender of the character and mission of Christ. On no other ground can his historic career be explained. It was Christ in him that gave him triumph throughout Achaia. What was it that made him the successful antagonist of Judaism? Surely not a religion of his own, but the Christianity of the period. What was it that carried him from the isles to the continents, that led him to brave all danger, and to be fearless in death? Surely not that he might be the founder of a new faith. He disclaims all such pretensions when he says, " Was Paul crucified for you?"

"Who then is Paul?" His great career is built upon his devotion to Christ, and not upon an independent purpose of his own, and the greatest injustice is done him even to suspect him of a purpose to originate a religion himself, to say nothing of the injury done to Christianity by supposing that the Pauline form of it is different from its original form.

We shall now examine Paul's specific elaboration of Christian doctrine, showing that it is in no sense a departure from what Christ himself taught. We begin with the greatest notion of theology, the largest thought of the Scriptures, the being and character of God. Prior to the revelation of God through Christian teachers, the world's idea of Deity was dismal, obscure, unsatisfactory in the extreme. Outside of the Jews, that idea was mythological, and, therefore, unreal. Zeus was a mythological creature. Among the Jews the idea took a personal form, and yet God was banished from or had not taken personal relations. He dwelt in the dark, he was unseen, he was heard on Sinai, or manifested himself in a moving cloud, or through a solitary code. The Jewish people had no intercourse with Deity. They spoke of him as a Father, but distant; as a lawgiver, but severe in enforcement; as a leader, but pitiless and unmerciful. The best Jewish idea was a gross mixture of unpaternal and paternal conceptions. God was far off. In this atmosphere the Jew dwelt, and out of it into a better there was no way until the Christ came, one of whose stupendous purposes was to bring God nearer to humanity and in more sympathetic relations to the race. He was styled Emmanuel, or God with us, and Christ said to Philip, "He that hath seen me hath seen the Father." This revelation of God in Christ was to destroy mythology, and show wherein the Judaic conception fell short of the whole truth, and so bring the world closer to God, as it had brought God nearer to man. The purpose was realized in the incarnate life of Jesus Christ, which should have been recognized by the Jews. That it was not is evident from their crucifixion of Christ. That it was not is proof that so blinded were the Jews to spiritual truths, a subsequent elaboration of the great fact was indispensable. At this point Paul's work begins, and right heroically does he perform it. Nowhere does it appear that he contradicts the assumption of Christ, but everywhere he proclaims him as the Son of God, the power of God, the wisdom of God; everywhere he proclaims that Jesus is Lord, the equal of the Father, to be honored and worshiped as the Father; everywhere he declares that Jesus is the Christ, that by him were all things created, that he is before all things, and that all things are put under his feet. Christ is general, Paul is specific; Christ is universal, Paul is particular;

Christ claims to be Father, Paul asserts that he is Creator, Upholder, Benefactor, Lord, and Ruler.

But in this Pauline amplification of the Deity of Christ there is nothing not implied in and required by the position that Christ assumed for himself. The claim of William to be king of Germany includes all that the title and position imply, without specifying the particulars. Christ intended all that Paul has so minutely affirmed. The apostle was an analyist, dissecting the darkest mysteries, penetrating to the essence of the divinest sayings, unfolding the narrowest promises, and expanding into life-likeness the smallest forms of truth. Who charges that Paul transcended the prerogatives of his position, or gave to Christ's words a meaning foreign to them? In the same methodical manner Paul writes of Christ himself, loading him down, as it were, with new titles, and inventing phrases descriptive of his character and work that could not have been born in a mind not in entire sympathy with its subject. It is along this line that Jewish writers are disposed to urge their strongest objection to Pauline Christianity. They must concede that the Pauline development of the idea of God's character is correct; but in the attempt to demonstrate that Christ is the Messiah and Redeemer, they insist that Paul went beyond what Christ himself warranted. This, therefore, deserves to be noticed, for it is the dividing line between Christianity and Judaism, and it is vehemently asserted that Paul is responsible for the division or breach. What did Christ claim for himself? Did he not assume to be the Messiah? Did he not always represent himself as the Savior? Are we mistaken here? Did not the prophecies receive fulfillment in him? It is a broad question— Is Christ the Messiah in truth, or is he the figure-head, the product of Pauline Christianity? What find we in the Gospels? He forgives sins; he works miracles; he invites men to come unto him for rest; he says he is the way, the truth, and the life; in Nazareth he declares Isaiah to be fulfilled in him; his parables are disguised representations of his Messiahship; he predicts his crucifixion and the atonement; he appeals to his works; he lives, labors, dies, all to to make sure that the world may be saved. It is difficult to take any other view when reading the four Gospels. Now, did Paul go beyond this? Did he not represent Christ in all his offices so fully that no one can charge him with ambiguity or insufficiency, and yet in the elaboration did he draw a single conclusion, or enforce a single statement not authorized by the Gospels themselves? With Paul Christ had the pre-eminence. Wherever he went he was present in spirit, and proved that Jesus is the Christ; that is, the Messiah; and everywhere he was anxious to declare that Jesus Christ came into

the world to save sinners.  It seems to have been given Paul to discern the great offices of Christ as no other had discerned them, and
he dwells upon them with intensest enthusiasm, producing conviction
in the multitudes, and terrifying even the rulers of all countries.  John
exalts Christ as divine, but Paul exalts him as the wonderful Savior.
If, indeed, there is a " plan of salvation," we are indebted to Paul
for the statement of it.  The Gospels reveal Jesus as the Savior, but
Paul expatiates on the method by which salvation is secured.  He is
the great logician of the New Testament, and he often aimed to
prove how God could be just, and yet the justifier of him who believed in Jesus.  *Paul reduced his theology on this subject to a science.*
He not only preached the Gospel, but proved it.  The whole idea
of salvation in Jesus Christ received logical treatment at his hands.
His epistles are burdened with arguments in support of it.  The
necessity of redemption; the inadequacy of the Judaic system; the
prophetic mission of Christ; the divinely sustained character of
Christ; the impregnable fact of the resurrection of Christ; and the
certainty of salvation in Christ, arising from his own unanswerable
experience of it, constituted a few of the points on which the apostle rejoiced to speak and write.  Paul amplified, but did not originate,
modify, or pervert Christian doctrine.

If we consider Christ's teachings concerning *man*, his natural condition, his spiritual possibilities, his depravity, and the necessity of a
regenerating change, and then study Paul on the same line of
thought, we shall find perfect harmony, the latter but the echo of
the former.  Christ knew what is in man, and taught his greatness
when he asked the famous question, " What shall it profit a man if
he shall gain the whole world and lose his own soul?"  He showed
his estimate of humanity by himself taking its form and living among
men for a generation.  " The word was made flesh and dwelt among
us."  The incarnation, on one side a humiliation of the divine, was
on the other a glorification of the human, and declared to the universe the infinite worth of man.  Then his death for man, and atonement for his sins, is proof that in the mind of Christ man is inex-
pressibly valuable, and must be redeemed, even if it cost the treasures
of heaven.  We affirm that the life and death of Christ, without
mentioning particular acts or particular teachings, demonstrate quite
as much the loftiness, majesty, and dignity of human character as the
benevolence and virtue of the divine character of Jesus.

In this estimate of humanity does Paul surpass Christ?  Does he
teach any thing different, any thing contradictory?  Or do we not
find that he repeats, only in another form, just what Christ himself
had taught?  The Pauline exaltation of man is not mythological, is

not exaggerated fancy, is not different from that of Christ. If he does write that man was made a little lower than the angels, that Adam was formed, not generated, it is because he truly anticipated the "development" theory eighteen hundred years in advance of it, and blocked its way by the announcement of the high-born origin, the creation of man. If he writes that " when I was a child I spoke as a child, I understood as a child, I thought as a child ; but when I became a man I put away childish things," it is because he saw the evolution theory true as applied to man's development in knowledge. As to man's origin, he was a creation ; as to his history, he is a development. Evolution is false as applied to origin ; true, as applied to history. But is this anti-Biblical? Is this new to Christianity ? Is this Pauline construction of man singular and apostate? Nay, rather it is in keeping with Christ's ideal of humanity, both as to origin and character.

So, when we pass to man's dishonored moral condition, the two teachers are in perfect accord. Surely no one will insist that Jesus misunderstood this condition, or misinterpreted it, or failed to reveal it. It was he who said, " The Son of Man is come to seek and to save that which was lost." The ground of his coming was the fact that man was not only in immediate danger of perishing, but in a sense had already perished ; that he was not liable to be lost, but is lost. His mission was not to prevent destruction, but to deliver from it. This of itself indicates a want of righteousness in man too appalling to be fittingly portrayed. In all his teachings, plannings, and works the underground thought seems to be the painful recognition of the moral disabilities of men, the shipwreck of the race. It is not the ship in the storm, *but the ship gone down in the storm.* This is the picture, and it saddened the heart of the Son of Man as he contemplated it.

In announcing the mission of Jesus to Joseph the angel said, " He shall save his people from their sins." Sin is in the way, salvation is a necessity, and Jesus is the Savior. The great fact of sin is revealed by the biographer of Christ as the burden that he would roll away, and he often forgave sin to show his power and indicate his mission. One sick of the palsy he both healed and pardoned ; to the woman taken in adultery he extended forgiveness; and to the woman who entered the house of a Pharisee he offered the word of pardon. He cast out devils frequently, illustrating his purpose to cast the evil spirit out of the hearts of men. He lived and died that he might reveal and perfect the way for man's rescue, and restoration to a normal spiritual condition.

The Pauline epistles are not more specific touching these things

than the Gospels themselves.  Paul, however, discourses on depravity, or the ruin of man, revealing human helplessness to a degree
startling and decisive.  He declares that men are " dead in trespasses
and sins," and in his Epistles to the Romans and Galatians he shows
the antagonism of the spirit and the flesh, proving how completely
man is under the dominion of sin until he is brought under the dominion of grace, and even then how the flesh lusts against the spirit,
until, through the sanctification of the truth, man has complete rest
from its power.  Expatiating on this condition, he turns to the necessity of a Savior, and finds that Jesus Christ came into the world to
save sinners.  Over this he rejoices, and declares he will glory in
nothing save the cross of the Lord Jesus Christ.  Paul does not
originate the doctrine of depravity, nor does he promulgate the attitude of Christ as a Savior for the first time.  These are facts fundamental to the biographical Gospels, and are the authentic testimony
that they were taught by Christ, and they would remain even if Paul
had not alluded to them.  Both recognized man as a sinner, and both
proclaimed Christ as the Savior.

Concerning the doctrine of *regeneration*, or Christian experience,
and the witness of the Spirit, Christ precedes Paul, as he does on every
other doctrine.  In his conversation with Nicodemus, Christ declares
for regeneration, and this by the Spirit.  In his Epistle to Titus, Paul
speaks of the " washing of regeneration, and renewing of the Holy
Ghost."  Both teach spiritual regeneration.  Christ promised the
Spirit that he would come and guide unto truth, convict men of sin,
and dwell in his disciples, revealing the things of Christ to them.
Paul writes of a spiritual religion, saying that " the Spirit beareth
witness with our spirit that we are the children of God."

It is here that Christianity divides with Judaism, and, indeed,
with all other religions.  In its intense spirituality, in its independence of material machinery, in its spiritual truths, spiritual precepts,
spiritual experiences, and spiritual destiny, it is lifted far above other
religions.  Breaking away from ceremonies, feast-days, and all the
visible display of Judaism, Paul entered into the spiritual conceptions
of Christianity, enforcing them upon the attention of the Jews by sacrifices, by zeal in their behalf, by benevolence, by tenderly uttered
sympathies, by unparalleled services.  It was this change from the
visible to the invisible, from the physical appendages or externalism
of religion to its spiritual essence and power, that the Jews did not
understand, and that irritated them to the last degree.  Paul emphasized the spiritual elements ; he saw that every thing else in religion
must be subordinate to its spiritual aim ; and hence, crude enough as
Christianity appeared in the hands of the fishermen, under Paul it

assumed a spiritual tone, and rose at once into a spiritual religion. But this was its appointed function, as it was spiritual in nature.

Earlier, when the apostolic mind was slow to apprehend spiritual ideas, Christ did not develop them. He, however, deposited them, and they afterward germinated under Pauline cultivation. The acorn had become a tree, but not a different tree from what the acorn indicated. Paul, as a teacher of Christianity, had an advantage over the apostles, and made large use of it in his advocacy of the religion of the Master. One may embrace Christianity as a system of truth, and defend it on logical or rational grounds, without an experience of its power, or a knowledge of its possibilities. He may finally acquire an experience, but it is better to begin with an experience and advocate from that standpoint, than to begin with logic and end with experience. The apostles had their experience last, and Paul had his first. To them Christianity was a new religion, doctrinal, personal in that it had a recognized founder, but more of a philosophical system that had to be tested and proved. To Paul, it was from the beginning an experimental religion, spiritual, personal, persuasive, powerful, adapted to human needs, and sufficient unto salvation. They preached the truth, he preached an experience. He is the only apostle who relates his experience, and he relates it to governors and priests and officers and the multitude, and great is the power that attends it. This is just what Christ contemplated, an experimental, spiritual Christianity, eclipsing the material religions of the times and drawing men into the refinement and purity of something better. But in this we do not see that Paul is a usurper, or that he teaches what Christ did not contemplate, or that Christian experience is not an essential doctrine of the Scriptures, nor the blessed privilege of the believer.

Passing into *eschatology*, we have no reason to believe that the Pauline epistles contain any thing not warranted by the Gospels; or, that their author pretended to be an independent reader of things future. On the contrary, we discover the utmost harmony between them, and are thankful for the additional light Paul has shed on some of the problems that must finally confront all men. Touching the resurrection of the body, Christ announced it, not as an entirely new thought, for the Pharisees already held to it, but he made it more prominent as a doctrine than it was in Judaism. Martha expressed belief in the resurrection of Lazarus at the last day. This was Phariseeism, and this also was Christianity. Both to substantiate his power, and to foreshadow the possibility of a general resurrection, Christ raised three persons from the dead, Lazarus being one of them. He sometimes spoke of persons coming up out of their graves, and promised to raise the disciples at the last day. Resurrection! If it did not seem like an original doctrine with Christ, it was because the people were already familiar with it. But Christ did not explain the resurrection, nor relieve it of mystery, nor answer the difficult questions it raises. The only mystery growing out of the resurrection that he shed light upon was with reference to the marriage relation in the future state in answer to a question by the Sadducees; but that had reference to the resurrection-life, rather than to the resurrection itself. From Christ we also learn that the resurrection will occur at the last day, and yet he is not specific. Whether it shall be the event that shall close up the present dispensation, or signal the end of the world, or whether there will be a period between the resurrection and the end, he does not intimate. And concerning two resurrections he is equally silent. How it is to be accomplished, whether it will be gradual or instantaneous, and with what bodies the dead shall come he does not discuss, he does not reveal. Perhaps all these questions were satisfactorily disposed of in dialogue with the apostles, so that they declared the resurrection with understanding wherever they went, but the Gospels are barren of information.

Evidently the Church craves information in all these directions, whether wisely or not is another question. In all ages of the Christian era men have asked questions, and in Paul's time there was a disposition to deny the resurrection. This denial Paul had to meet, and providentially it led him into a discussion of the subject in many of its phases, especially with reference to the character of the resurrection body, and the time of the resurrection, the two factors over which the greatest anxiety has suspended. Christ's revelation of the fact of resurrection was all that was necessary; Paul's discussion of the character of the resurrection was opportune and supplemental. For ages the thought of a material resurrection, the natural body reappearing in all its numerical proportions, flesh and blood again revivified, the physical man fully restored, was accepted as the genuine interpretation of the Scriptural idea of resurrection. To this interpretation, however, numerous and cogent objections have been raised, both by those who denied the resurrection, and by those who believed the Scriptures. The drift of the Christian mind in the early centuries was toward crude material conceptions of spiritual truth, and a physical resurrection was the outcome of exegesis, and the instrument of terror or hope as it was applied by theologians to sinners and saints. Out of this fog the Church seems to have advanced, but it is because of Paul's teaching. Christianity is spiritual. *Even so literal a fact as resurrection is spiritual.* The natural body is sown, but a spiritual body is raised. For the soul in this life there is a natural, a physical body; for the soul in the other life there is a spiritual body. Flesh and blood can not inherit the kingdom of heaven. How clear such a statement! The wonder is that any confusion ever existed on a subject that was lifted into transparency by apostolic revelation.

So with reference to the time of the resurrection. Paul takes a small gold leaf, and hammers it out until in its expanded state it covers a great deal of ground ; that is, it makes clear what before was almost an ambiguous hint. He declares that "the Lord shall descend, . . . and the dead in Christ shall rise first." Paul is as definite in eschatological as in soteriological teaching ; he is reliable and invaluable. Without quoting further, it is evident that in the mind of Paul the second coming of Christ and the resurrection of the dead will be simultaneous events ; that one purpose of the next coming will be to raise the dead. This certainly is definite information. Moreover, in his Epistle to Timothy, he says : "I charge thee, therefore, before God, and the Lord Jesus Christ, who shall judge the quick and the dead *at his appearing"*—second coming, resurrection, and judgment here affirmed as events in close order. Other passages are at hand confirming the general revelation on this line ; but as they will be considered later we omit them in this connection. Resurrection and judgment are associated together in this passage. Paul's revelations are like an extensive panorama, which, beginning with hints and promises, opens out into vast vistas of scenery, alike gratifying and complete. Surely Paul has rendered a service to the Church, both by explanation of obscure truth and revelation of things not before revealed.

Concerning *immortality*, there is the same straightforward statement from Paul as is manifest in all his utterances touching revealed truth. Christ, indeed, assured the disciples of another life, and revealed both heaven and hell by parable and direct teaching, so that he should not be misunderstood ; but Paul takes up all these primary revelations and elaborates them into fullness. With him there is no uncertainty. Immortality is a fact. He answers Job's question, "If a man die shall he live again?" by declaring that all men must appear before the judgment-seat of Christ to give an account for the deeds done in the body. In his preaching to Felix and Agrippa, he announced the future in such terms as to strike terror to the hearts of his pagan judges. Contemplating his own departure, he spoke of the joy immortal before him, saying : "To live is Christ, but to die is gain." Then, passing to the rewards and retributions of eternity, he is as outspoken as the Master, and as full in his statements. Christ promises mansions, and Paul speaks of "the house not made with hands eternal in the heavens." Christ promises a reward even to those who are late in entering the kingdom. Paul glories in crowns that shall never fade away. Christ tells of Dives and Lazarus, the beggar; while Paul discloses the banishment of the wicked to the horrors of Tartarus, and the triumphs of the righteous in the Paradise of God. The two teachers are one on immortality, and agree concerning the judgment-seat, and the final issues of the judgment. One looks as far into the future as the other. Christ restrains himself in revelation, foreshadowing the whole by parable and teaching; Paul is palsied in utterance, telling all he can; and in the end both stand on the same level as teachers of the same truth, as comforters of the children of men.

In this brief survey of Paul's work we see how true he was to the Master's teaching on all subjects. He derived what he taught from original sources. He never appears as the supplanter, but as the *supplemental teacher.* We see, also, how much the Church is indebted to him for faithful exposition of truth in itself beyond human delivery, and dark until made transparent by him. We see how unjust the insinuation that he in any sense intended to become the founder of Christianity, and finally see that Paul without Christ was impossible.

---

# CHAPTER XX.

## PHILOSOPHICAL GERMS IN CHRISTIANITY.

NOT a few agree with Wolf, that religious truth, however occult in itself, or from what source obtained, should rest on a philosophical basis, and meet the philosophical tests usually applied to all truth. Understanding Christianity, the most zealous dogmatist will not object to so reasonable a proposition, for it gives no undue advantage to philosophy and involves no concession on the part of religion. Religion and philosophy are so closely allied in their aims, and are so similarly affected by final results, that one may expect to find religion in philosophy and philosophy in religion. Diverse in method and form of statement, they are not antagonistic systems, intending to destroy each other.

In a very broad sense, it may be affirmed that religion, even in its crudest form, is philosophical; for the idea of religion is truth, and truth implies those fundamental questions with which philosophy has concerned itself since the human mind began to think. If truth is philosophical, it is also religious; and so soon as it is contemplated its religious and philosophical character appears.

In a different sense, religion is philosophical in its adaptation to the moral necessities of the race; that is, its greatest truths are so formulated as to be of efficient service in moral emancipation and spiritual discipline. For example, the existence of God is so expressed in the sacred writings, that man rises to the conception of God as a Father, a Protector, a Guide, a Helper, a Teacher, which is an improvement over the single conception of God as a Creator. The single conception of philosophy of a Supreme Power as the inaugurator of cosmical order and life, expands in the Bible into a complex conception of that Power in all its manifold and personal relations to the children of men. In this enlargement of conception, religion is still philosophical; for the conception of causality involved in world-building is philosophical, but its development into a personal form involves religious revelation. The genesis of the conception is philosophical; the consummation of the conception is religious, and of practical value to human life. In its philosophical form, it is morally useless; in its religious form, it is inspiration itself.

To the claim that Christianity is philosophical in content and purpose, an objection or two might be noted, more to vindicate the claim than to silence the objection, although the latter disappears as the former is established. Philosophy proceeds on the assumption that, as its data are wholly within the realm of the natural, the methods of investigation pursued must also be natural, and the results, therefore, will be natural; while Christianity, compassing the supernatural as well as the natural, assumes that its methods of investigation may be supernatural as well as natural, and the results will correspond; in other words, one largely proposes natural methods and natural truths, the other, supernatural methods and supernatural truths. One opposes the supernatural as a method, in proportion as the other insists upon it.

Christianity is a religion of inspiration, of supernatural truth; it comes not forth as the product of human inquiry, research, or discovery. Without the same ground, all religions profess to be more than human, incline to the claim of supernatural content; so that the objection makes against all religions, if it makes against any. It strikes at the foundation of all. If, for the ascertainment of truth, the supernatural method is ruled out as unphilosophical, it remains that a knowledge of supernatural truth is impossible, which leads to agnosticism or open infidelity. By natural methods, we arrive at a knowledge of natural truths; by supernatural methods, we obtain a knowledge of supernatural truths. The method and the truth which it seeks are mated. A natural method and a supernatural truth would be unequally yoked together.

Insisting that inspiration is essential to the communication of religious truth, it must not be forgotten that such truth has a human as well as a divine side ; and the human phase of religion may be as philosophical as the human phase of philosophy itself. Leave out the highest truths, the supernatural phases of Christianity, and it will appear that the human elements are as philosophical in character as the same elements in philosophy. Much of the geology, chronology, astronomy, botany, and zoölogy, or the science of the Bible, belongs to the human phase of revelation, or constitutes its natural elements, in contradistinction to those spiritual truths which constitute it a moral guide to the race. This division of truths into human and divine, or scientific and spiritual, while germane to outside religions, and an aid in explaining their errors, we shall not urge with reference to Christianity, since its spiritual truths are scientifically true, and its scientific truths sustain spiritual relations that will be manifest before the end of this volume shall have been reached. Accepting both kinds of truth, as constituting the inspired record, and one kind as inspired as the other, it is evident that, if the inspirational method is unphilosophical as applied to one truth, it is unphilosophical as applied to the other. If unphilosophical at all, the whole record goes—the scientific as well as the spiritual, the spiritual as well as the scientific.

The difficulty will be very much reduced if the distinction between method and truth be observed, for, even if a supernatural method be objectionable to philosophy, a supernatural truth may be very acceptable ; that is, an inspired truth is not necessarily an unphilosophical truth, even though an inspired method for its ascertainment may be rejected as unphilosophical. Truth is truth, supernatural or natural; truth is truth, method or no method, supernatural method or natural method. Truth is not philosophical in proportion to its natural content, but in proportion to its trueness, whether the content be natural or supernatural. All objection, therefore, to truth is unphilosophical; supernatural truth, as such, is as philosophical as natural truth.

To the objection made against the supernatural method, we might be indifferent, since it is immaterial how one gets the truth, supernaturally or otherwise. The only duty is to get the truth. However, the supernatural method is as legitimate as the natural method, and, in the sphere of religion, more legitimate, for it is the only method by which a knowledge of truth can be obtained. Seeing that supernatural truth is not the subject-matter of discovery, but must be made known by revelation, if known at all, the inspirational method becomes legitimate, and the whole system of religion deduced from it philosophical. If, then, revelation is not unphilosophical, the terms in which Biblical truth is formulated are not unphilosophical. We shall see this in a moment. Philosophy is given to logical processes, the analysis of inquiries, the details of proofs, and inferences from facts; and, if these fail, it resorts to rationalistic speculation and metaphysical hypothesis. Many of its conclusions are, therefore, conjectural; some of them are inharmonious with the axioms of religion; a few are incoherent and absurd. At least in method, Christianity stands alone, reaching its conclusions without any circumlocution of speculation, and even without the framework of a syllogism. *Religious truth is the conclusion of the divine mind,* without the intellective processes by which it is reached. The Bible is not a book of reasons, but a book of truths; it is not a book of speculations, but a book of conclusions. It states truth, without the analysis of truth, without pushing off into latitudes not real. Christianity is not speculative, it is not rationalistic, it is not metaphysic; it is truth, it is light, it is the sun. Whatever it is, the method by which it is what it is rises or falls with it. The two at last are inseparable. To strike at one is to strike at both; to vindicate one is to vindicate both.

Equally futile is the objection that Christianity, as found in the New Testament, is not a system of truth at all, but a medley of moral teachings or rules, and, therefore, violative of all philosophical order and unity. The charge that New Testament Christianity is unsystematized truth, we admit; the inference that, on that account, it is unphilosophical truth, we deny. For systematic theology, we must go outside the New Testament; for systematic Judaism, we must go outside the Old Testament. Neither Judaism is reduced to system, nor Christianity, in the Book that reveals it. This is not unphilosophical, for the *idea of philosophy is not system; it is truth.* Truth is one thing, system another. Any system is legitimate, provided it is the framework of truth; but let truth come, even if it come without any system at all. System ranks with method, and both are below truth. Plato had no system; at least no one has discovered it. Emerson is without system. Philosophy is systemless from beginning to end. It can not be otherwise. Truth precedes system, is the content of all system, and must first be given or found before system can be formed. Plato was after truth, not after system. Paul was after truth, not after system. The sum of philosophic investigation since the time of Plato is a number of half-truths, fragments of thought, arcs of ideas, and certain hints, that, taken altogether, might constitute a system. The New Testament writers have done more than the philosophers, for all the truths necessary to a complete system they have revealed; all the doctrines, all the ideas, all the thoughts, necessary to the circle of Christian thought, are declared by them. What is wanted is

assortment, combination, a theologic structure out of the materials at
hand. It is like building a pyramid with the stone on the ground.
Unfortunately for philosophy, it not only lacks system; it also is
wanting in the material necessary to an orderly, rational, and comprehensive system of the highest truths. The chief question, then,
is, not whether Christianity is a *system* of truth, but, is it *truth?*

The answer to this question involves a brief analysis of the philosophic content of other religions, by comparison with which not only
the difference between the true and the false will appear, but also the
character of Christian truth will be made manifest. Beginning with those
religions that antedate Christianity, or contemplating those that arose
at a later period, we shall see that they grappled with philosophical
problems even more than with those that are distinctively religious.
Their aims were philosophical, not religious. This is true of Brahminism, Buddhism, and the early Persian and Egyptian faiths. The
diagnostic of the later pagan religions, such as Hindu Eclecticism, is
almost exclusively philosophical. The impressive inference to be
drawn from this patent fact is, that, because these religions dealt so
largely with the philosophical aspects of truth, they failed as religions. If this is a correct inference, it points out clearly the path
religion is to pursue; it declares that religious truth has a mission of
its own, and that the philosophical aspect must be subordinate. Religion makes shipwreck of itself if it is more devoted to philosophical
experiment than the fulfillment of religious functions. The Hindu
race took up very early the questions that Plato and his successors expounded more rationally and beautifully, but why should the religious
mind take to the philosophical investigation of religious truth? In
the case of the Hindu this was a necessity, for what passed for truth
was error; it did not satisfy the intellectual demand; it did not
awaken the religious nature; hence, the scholarly Hindu, wrecked by
religion, sought the life-boat of philosophy.

In its philosophical ventures, however, Brahminism was as complete a failure as it was in its religious teachings. Its mood toward
truth of any kind was altogether unsatisfactory. It solved nothing;
it finished no intellectual undertakings; it dissipated no darkness,
either as a religion or philosophy. Its incarnations and regenerations
are but scaffoldings of ideas, standing alone, without relation to genuine truth, except as all fragmentary conceptions may be considered
adumbrations of final truth, as contained in the Christian religion.
In its gropings it so often stumbled that at last it fell into the embrace of an intense superstition, without self-illumination, and but
slowly disposed to yield to light from outside.

To the average Brahmin the Vedas are the source of inspired

truth. He can not be persuaded that the Bible is superior to the sacred writings of his fathers; he persuades himself that the Vedas preceded the Bible, and are the original sources of all truth. Many truths in the Vedas are found in the Bible. This is not a coincidence, but to unbiased minds a proof that the truths of the Hebrew writings early dominated Eastern thought, and impregnated the most superstitious religions. Without doubt the Vedas borrowed from the Bible; the Bible borrowed nothing from the Vedas. Because of the borrowed divine truths in the sacred writings of the Hindu race Brahminism has survived the ages; truth is a living force, and has maintained more than one erroneous religion. Pure error would immediately die, but, mixed with truth, it seems sometimes to be as immortal as truth itself. The divorce or separation comes at last, error fleeing, truth triumphing. Thus it will happen that truth will gradually separate itself from all error in paganism, and false religions will be no more.

Indebted to the Bible as the Vedas are for religious truth, they are not indebted to it for philosophical suggestions. Not that Brahminism is barren of the philosophical spirit; on the contrary, it is excessively philosophical, and is original in its philosophical suggestions. This relieves the Bible of a load of responsibility, which a true religion can not afford to carry. In their highest conceptions the Vedas descend to an undisguised pantheism, confounding creation with the Creator, blotting out all the distinctions between an independent, uncaused, eternal personality, and the physical work of his hands, and leaving the world destitute of personal rule, and without a federal government. The universe is God; God is not *in* nature, but is nature. Brahminism means this as its ultimate teaching, no difference what metaphysical distinctions it draws respecting Deity, no difference what personal functions it allots to Brahma, Vishnu, and Seva. In its philosophy Brahminism is pantheistical. In this form it explains nothing and confuses every thing. It unites what forever should be separated, and separates what forever should be united. It demolishes the distinction between cause and effect, overruling all laws of order, introducing all the liabilities of chance, or the still more revolting consequences of fate in the government of the world.

The weight of objection to this doctrine is that what is true in the philosophical sense is also true in the religious sense; that is, if pantheism is philosophically true, it must be religiously true. It can not be true in philosophy and false in religion. Hence, Brahminism is pantheistical in the religious sense; but a pantheistic religion is virtually a self-contradiction, as a pantheistic philosophy is an absurdity. Pantheism and prayer are incompatible; pantheism and atonement can not co-exist in any religion ; pantheism and forgiveness are foreign to each other ; pantheism and providence are unrelated ideas ; pantheism and revelation are inharmonious terms ; pantheism and spiritual influence can not be made to agree; pantheism and redemption are impossible. Pantheism is destructive of the connatural elements of religion, and, therefore, can not stand for the religious idea; it can not represent that which it subverts.

In its teachings concerning matter Brahminism is as curiously involved in absurdity as it is in its teachings concerning God. Briefly, the Brahmin holds that matter is an illusion ; it does not exist ; it is without substance. In this conclusion it is the parent of that form of modern philosophy known as transcendentalism, of which our Emerson is the exponent. The illusion theory is the cardinal doctrine of a form of idealism, adopted by the Eleatics, and accepted in these days by a coterie of thinkers around Boston and London. Thus the old has become the new, modern thought worships an idea that had its birth on the banks of the Ganges three thousand years ago, and the Brahmin rejoices in the vindication. This philosophical interpretation of matter, applied religiously, leads to the rankest atheism ; for, if nature is God, and nature is an illusion, then God is an illusion or nothing. Pantheism on its religious side does not symbolize atheism, but on its philosophical side it can not avoid it ; it, therefore, is even more dangerous to the religious idea than any other known form of religion.

Its teachings respecting the soul are equally incredible, and unfounded in history or experience. The soul is supposed to be a fragment of the Deity, to whom it returns when separated from the body, and in whom its individual consciousness is forever lost, or by transmigration it is permitted to assume new types and conditions of existence, from which it finally passes into the state of Brahm himself. Religiously, this is repugnant to the moral sense ; philosophically, it is without foundation, either in reason, experience, or observation. History records no such transmigrations, and in the nature of things they are impossible. Even if possible, they are inconsistent with the natural dignity of human character, and are out of harmony with the highest destiny of man. It is not our purpose to philosophize on the Vedic revelations, but rather to state them, believing that the inconsistencies of the Brahminical religion will appear in these revelations, and that when Paul says the " world by wisdom knew not God," we may refer to this and all other false religions for illustration and vindication.

The same conclusion will be reached if we turn to Buddhism, a later religion of the East—in fact, a *protesting* religion against the vagaries of Brahminism. It was announced by Gautama in the tenth century before Christ, coming forth as a reformation or trans-migration of the religious idea, and with seeming providential guar-antees, and in the name of a divine authority. Brahminism was unsatisfying; it was irrational; it was wanting in inspiration; it was a load. In his protestings, recommendations, and religious reve a-tions one would suppose that Gautama would substitute activity for inertia, establish new methods of religious service, declare truths adapted to human necessities, ordain new religious forms and institu-tions, inhibit old, worn-out customs and practices, introduce new mo-ralities and philanthropies, and elevate moral life to a higher level.

Here, again, disappointment is the result. What truths did it announce and what evils did it suppress? What is the fruit of Bud-dhism? With higher aims, is it certain that its uplifting power was any greater? Recognizing the superiority of some of its teachings, the total impression that this religion makes is that it did not disturb the moral inertia of history, or tend to the religious development of the race. The rule we apply in determining its historic place among religions, and its relative value as a religion, is not to inquire the specific value of any single truth it may have espoused, but to take the sum of its historic impression. It must be judged as a whole, and not by its parts. By this rule it ranks little above that against which it protested, and falls short of meeting the religious demands of the race. *Though not quite so tortuous as that of Brahminism, its course was equally narrow and shallow; though more refined, its conceptions were as confused and perplexing; though more energizing in action, its final effects were relapses into insipidity and lethargy.*

The theistic notion it dealt with summarily by robbing the Su-preme Being of consciousness and personality, leaving only a Supreme Force, omnipresent and eternal, in possession of the reins of the world's government. It quickly sunk to the atheistic level, and is the parent of that scientific dictum of modern times which reduces all existences to the vibrations of force, and elevates it to supreme command in the universe. If the transcendentalism of modern times may be traced to Brahminism, the scientific hallucination of modern times concerning Force may be traced to Buddhism. Modern errors are the newly dressed dogmas of Oriental nations.

In respect to matter, Buddhism put itself in a dilemma from which it has never been extricated. It proclaimed the eternity of matter, but was inclined to doubt the reality of matter. The Bud-dhist desired to break with the Brahmin at this point, but did not know how to do it. The theory of illusion is irreconcilable with the theory of eternity. Holding to the latter, the ancient Buddhist could easily have disavowed the former, and completed his separation from the Brahmin ; but he was not independent enough in thought to take the step, and so did not advance beyond the established religious tradition.

The Buddhist conception of man is as vulnerable as the Brahminical conception, for it recognizes in him only a temporary individuality, to be lost in the life of the Infinite Force, which is regarded as the chief boon of mortals. Accepting the old doctrine of transmigration, the Buddhist looks forward to a period when re-embodiments in various forms shall cease, and conscious being be swallowed up in the greater activity of the Supreme Power. Individuality shall lose its crown in eternal self-forgetfulness.

Philosophically and religiously, what is the value of Buddhism ? It settled no philosophical question ; it threw no light on the aged darkness of truth ; it opened no new path to mystery ; it was a blind guide, leading the blind into errors as great as those it aimed to correct. As a religion its aim was purer than that of its rival, but it revealed no new truth ; and if it awakened new desires, it was as incompetent to satisfy them. The hopes it raised turned to ashes, and its music became a dirge.

Forgetting the pagan faiths, and turning to other religions, with different aims, the investigator will find temporary relief from the nightmare which the former provoked. *Temporary* relief, we say, for all religions, except Christianity, are essentially false, notwithstanding their relation to the true religion, and the spiritual contents of their revelations. This is certainly true of Mohammedanism, which, far from being pagan in spirit or purpose, is as far from being Christian in content, design, or method. Measured carefully, it is as much inferior to Christianity as it is superior to paganism ; but its superiority on one side is more than balanced by its inferiority on the other. It is, therefore, an untruth, in that it is not more than a half-truth. As to its philosophical solutions, they are repugnant to the scientific sense, and contradictory of scientific fact ; and if, in any respect, they are an improvement on the Hindu conception of the universe or of matter, it is proof of the influence of the Hebrew Scriptures and of the spirit of the age on the mind of the great prophet, who was inaugurator of the new religion. The science of the Al Koran is " science falsely so-called," as it teaches that the earth is balanced by the weight of the mountains, and that shooting-stars are red-hot stones thrown by angels. If these were minor or incidental teachings, they would not be quoted ; but they reflect the character of the geology and astronomy of the sacred book of the Mohammedan, who is as much required to accept its science as its religion.

The strong or essential doctrine of Mohammedanism is its exposition of the theistic idea, showing at this point its superiority to all pagan notions of the Supreme Being. Fortunately for the Oriental nations, Mohammedanism was a complete break from all the old religions touching this fundamental truth, for Mohammed accepted the Old Testament as his guide, and represented God in his true character, as a personal being, endowed with all the attributes enumerated by Moses. This gave him advantage as a leader, which he was not slow to improve. The theistic idea was an improved idea, and had inspiration in it ; and under its influence the multitudes joined him in his attacks upon idolatry, idealism, pantheism, and all the fancies of the old religions. It brought the East to its knees before God, who governed all nations, who observed human actions, who would punish all wickedness, and reward all virtue.

Persistent in the enforcement of this conception, as was Mohammed, the conception itself, as finally formulated, was compromised by an excess of anthropomorphic elements introduced into it ; it was lowered to gross human standards of what God ought to be, and not what he is, as taught in the Scriptures. Determined to break with Christianity, as he had broken with Paganism, Mohammed rejected the doctrine of the Trinity, and stood out as an independent religious teacher, accepting only a few truths from the sources around him. He gained on the old religions by the doctrine of monotheism, but fell back from the new by his anthropomorphism and denial of the Trinity ; and to-day, as in his time, the faith he instituted is quite as much opposed to the new as to the old.

If in like manner we should analyze the old religions of Egypt, or question the ancient systems of belief in China, as to particular teachings respecting God, nature, and man, we should find that, holding to some truths that might be approved, and exhibiting a sincerity that ignorance always creates, they were defective in those truths that are essential to a perfect philosophy and a redemptive religion. All religions, ancient and modern, would repeat the same story of imperfection, inadequacy, and incompleteness.

The sum of this survey of religions is that *religion is instinctively philosophical*, in that it grapples with philosophical problems, or, in better form, its connatural ideas are *per se* philosophical. The two can not be separated ; *to be religious is to be philosophical.*

The conclusion is also warranted that, whatever their value as religions, they have failed in their philosophical departments, partly owing to want of data, partly to irrational methods, partly to explain the mysteries, or state exactly what pertains to such departments. This failure is universal. No uninspired religion has developed a competent philosophy; not one has solved one philosophical problem in a philosophical manner. From the philosophical departments of religion have come the idealism, transcendentalism, pantheism, materialism, pessimism, atheism, and those scientific heresies which modern science has appropriated and palmed off as its own.

We finally conclude for the necessity, either of another philosophy, or another religion which shall philosophically succeed where others have failed, and demonstrate that man must go to that religion for his philosophy, rather than to outside philosophy itself.

This brings us to the consideration of the *philosophical character of Christianity*, the only religion that meets the requirements of philosophy, and the only philosophy that suggests a true basis for religion. Before analyzing the radical elements of this religion, it will be necessary to take a general view of its relation to philosophy, that its exact position may be understood. First, Christianity is in its contents a system of religious truth; *it is a religion;* it is not a philosophy. We say this just as we say water is a liquid; it is not a gas. Philosophical truth abounds in Christianity, but in itself it is a religion; its purpose is religious, its methods are religious, its effects are religious. Second, Christianity is a *philosophical religion;* it is the only philosophical religion among men. As we have seen, the metaphysical researches of other religions have been fruitful of deep-seated errors, involving unjust misconceptions of God, nature, and man, and have prevented moral and intellectual progress. Christianity holds not a religious truth that is not philosophically true; its highest truths accord with the highest reason; its philosophy harmonizes with its religion. Christianity harmonizes its elements as nature harmonizes gases, liquids, and solids; the result is order, stability, development. Third, Christianity disposes of philosophical problems as it disposes of religious problems, namely, *by revelation.* Its religious truths are not more inspired than its philosophical, and its philosophical not more than its religious truths. The truth relating to the origin of the worlds, the creation of man, the range of the flood, and the final conflagration of the planets, is as much inspired as the truth relating to regeneration, prayer, faith, immortality, marriage, and the Sabbath. The difference is in the class of truths; the source is the same. Hence, the infallibility of the philosophical revelations of Christianity. By these philosophical revelations the religious revelations stand or fall; for, if it can be shown that the one is uncertain and unreliable, discredit is also thrown upon the other. Fourth, Christianity is the *final test of all systems of philosophy.* There must be a final court of appeal, or truth is at the mercy of prejudice. Either Christianity must be tested by philosophy, or philosophy must be tested by Christianity. If religions may be weighed in her scales; if all religious truth may be judged by her ideal standard of truth; if its own philosophy may be tested by its own religion; surely philosophical systems, pretending to investigate that which primarily belongs to the domain of religion, must submit also to that religion whose tests are ideal and final. In another form it might be added that the final religion must originate, dictate, and enforce the final philosophy; and then the two will perfectly agree, and Christian philosophy will be the synonym of the Christian religion.

With this general understanding of the relations or kinship subsisting between philosophy and Christianity, it will be interesting to search for those final forms of philosophical truth that are concealed or disclosed in the Book of Revelation.

Among the common-place truths of Christianity is that which relates to cosmological history, or the creation and development of the universe. Without exception, the sacred writers reveal God as the philosophic ground of all existence, and explain the worlds by the principle of causality in association with personality. They recognize will, purpose, and power, in conjunction in the creation of matter and its organization into systems of worlds. This principle of cosmology is the rubric of the Christian religion. Accepting this principle as the key to cosmological history, the Christian thinker has a starting-point; he starts from God, the all-sufficient source. Immediately, he opens the door on one side into geology, and on the other into astronomy, arranging the facts of these sciences in harmony with the principle of causality, and explaining physical development by law ordained by the Establisher of all things. Neither philosophy itself, nor any pseudo religion, began at this starting-point. All began with nature and aimed at God. Christianity begins with God and aims at the universe.

This principle of cosmology involves the incidental factor of chronology, carrying us back to a period when, atomless, non-existent, and unanticipated by any antecedent, the worlds were made by the power of God. Millions of years do not disturb the principle. Any chronology, long or short, doubtful or positive, may be asserted without shaking the principle. At one time the conservatism of Christian thought, or rather the importance attached to cosmological chronology, was such as to disallow this interpretation; but Christianity is as scientific in its science as it is religious in its religion, and it sinks the lower question into the higher, regarding the principle of creation more important than the chronology of creation. Over the chronology of the birth of the worlds there can be little contest between the friends of religion on the one hand and the friends of philosophy on the other, since it is a subordinate question. In its narrow sense, world-birth is a geological question; in a larger sense it is astronomical; in the whole sense, it is theological, implying God himself and his relation to matter. Settled in any sense, however, it is settled in all; for truth is a unit, and, given a key to the origin of any world, it will unlock the mystery of all worlds.

An outside or secular philosophy, disregarding the theistic hypothesis, has sought to explain the cosmic systems either by independent processes, or by self-executing laws, or by the operation of "second causes," or at all events by a Power, impersonal, unconscious, and synonymous with the forces at work in nature. It is not charged that the nebular hypothesis and the "development" theory exclude the theistic idea, but they fall short of a full recognition of divine intervention in world-building, involving the subject in deeper mystery than is possible in the light of the Christian principle of cosmology. Christian belief has insisted on the exercise of creative power in the origin of matter, and the exercise of wisdom in the planning of the solar systems, and has been unfriendly to a compromise with scientific hypothesis along these lines. The difference involves on the one side the reign of personality in the universe, and on the other the self-potency and self-sufficiency of matter in the process of world-building. The issue compasses two extremes, or the opposite heights of the pendulum of human thought, from one of which we look upon all things as from a throne, and from the other of which we behold the universe as from a polar point. Scientific thought, recognizing the cheerlessness of the atheistic assumption, is rapidly veering toward the Christian principle of cosmology, and adapting its "development" theories to the Biblical revelations.

Descending to the smaller questions of science, such as the Mosaic order of creation, the time of man's appearance on earth, the origin or introduction of language, and the law of heredity, as it affects the race, similar battles have been fought, but in a less violent spirit and without permanent disaster to the truth, for the settlement of the greatest problem signifies the settlement of all other problems. *A theistic triumph is the triumph of all truth.* Viewing the conflict over the lesser questions, one is impressed that the outside scientist has been assailing ecclesiastical interpretations rather than Biblical truths, and that neither ecclesiastic nor scientist has intelligently considered what those truths are, or at least has not sounded them to their depths, and has mistaken the direction of their currents. It may, therefore, be assumed that, as the old dogmatic interpretations are modified, and scientific theories are molded in the light of facts and

Biblical hints, a reconciliation between philosophy and Christianity will take place, and the true result will be secured, namely, the Biblical stand-point of creation will have amplest vindication. Until this is realized, the chasm must remain, and unbelief touching the higher verities of religion will boast of its intrenchments and point to its victories. Contention over Biblical truth there will be; but, as the testing of truth means the testing of error also, so an analysis of revealed truth will be followed by an analysis of all other so-called truth, by which error will at last be made transparent and the truth be set apart from it. The conflict is in the interest of truth, and it ought to go on until the true shall be victorious over the false. Error can not long resist the truth, nor long abide after a defeat.

As an example, it has been affirmed in certain circles that the geology of the Pentateuch is incomplete in detail and incorrect in its substantial facts; yet no theorist proposes entirely to dispense with the Mosaic manual. This manual has been interpreted so variously that one is obliged to conclude that it is not a superficial document, or it would be interpreted in one way only, or be entirely rejected. The effort of the scientific mind is so to interpret the geological revelation as to harmonize with scientific discovery, the product being at least six theories, which are here noted: 1. The theory of Literal Agreement; that is, the chief geological divisions of the globe are supposed to agree with the six divisions of Moses. This is straight, clear, definite. 2. The Restitutionary Hypothesis; that is, the geological material existed before the inaugurated movements of the six days, and was arranged, or *restored* to order, beauty, and system during that period. The Mosaic "week" was a week of organization and reconstruction. 3. The Diluvian Hypothesis; that is, the present geological order must be referred to the Deluge, the original order having been entirely subverted. 4. The theory of Ideal or Substantial Agreement; that is, the Mosaic account is true as a general representation, but is not scientifically accurate. 5. The Epochal theory; that is, the Mosaic "day" refers to an epoch in geologic movement. 6. The Allegorical theory; that is, the Mosaic account is the idea of development in a picture, the idea being more important than the facts, the picture more beautiful than the frame; hence, the account is the narrative of an idea, and not the relation of facts.

It will be observed that none of these theories, however widely they differ from one another, seriously antagonizes the Biblical account, or eliminates the Mosaic idea of creation; as experiments at interpretation they are valuable, since they show that a truth may be looked at from many sides and not suffer from the inspection. One might accept any of the above interpretations, and be in harmony with

Moses. Many German thinkers take kindly to the theory of Substantial Agreement, because of its elasticity, but this is the chief objection to it; the Bible is never speculative, suggests no tentative theories or working hypotheses, does not state truth substantially, but *positively* and *absolutely*. If its geology is substantially true, its spiritual teachings may be regarded as substantially true, which would open the door to speculation, fanaticism, superstition. Revelation, like mathematics, must be one thing or another.

Whatever objection may be raised against the other theories, they are free from this weakness; they are positive, even if defective. But it is not so much to discuss theories as to show that the Pentateuch has given rise to the prevailing philosophical explanations of the geological movements, or of the order of the creative week and its results. *The Pentateuch is the source of geological truth.*

Passing from origins to destinies, Christianity is as prophetic as it is historic; it points to the end as well as the beginning, surpassing philosophy in the one respect as it does in the other, and yet is strictly philosophical itself. Ordinarily, philosophic inquiry confines itself to the ascertainment of causes or beginnings; rarely does it consider effects or ends. A whole philosophy, however, must range from one to the other, and explain one as well as the other. Christianity foresees the end of all things, declaring that the earth shall be burned up, reduced to a cinder, or purified and transformed by fire. This is a definite revelation, sustained, too, by nature itself, and, therefore, is doubly true. The earth is a store-house of combustibles, waiting for the torch of the last day, when the conflagration of the mountains and oceans will be immediate and universal. Oxygen is the great promoter of combustion, and is found in combination with the solids and liquids of the globe. The greater portion of substances consists of this gas. Water needs only to be resolved into oxygen and hydrogen, when the oceans can be converted into roaring seas of flame. Besides, the interior of the earth is supposed to be a raging furnace of fire, sending out its forked tongues through volcanic craters and heated springs in testimony of its existence. The earth can burn; its constitution affirms its possible destruction by fire. Astronomy records several instances of the conflagration of stars. Will it not by and by add to its record the conflagration of the earth?

This is the revelation of Christianity; this is the *prophetic possibility of nature.* Does science accept it? In some quarters, the destiny of the earth has been under consideration, various theories having been presented, and all agreeing on the probable destruction of the globe. One theory is to the effect that the earth will freeze to death, the sun failing to supply it with heat; another is, that the earth is slowly approaching the sun, or the sun the earth, and in time the earth will wheel into the orbit of the sun and be consumed. Some have predicted its destruction by collision with comets or planets, and others that the laws which regulate its activities and secure its preservation will be suspended, and the earth fail with age and infirmity; but its destruction, whether by one method or another, is now a conclusion of science as well as religion. Christianity reveals more than the *fact* of *destruction;* it declares the *manner* or instrumental cause of the destruction, which science now recognizes as probable. In this Christianity does not sustain science, but science sustains Christianity.

For a true philosophy of the cosmical system, which includes the genesis of matter, the origin of worlds, and the destiny of the universe, or for a key to geology, chemistry, and astronomy, the investigator must first and last acknowledge his indebtedness to the revealed truths of Christianity, which, in their scientific content, are as rational as in their spiritual content, and, therefore, as serviceable to science as to religion.

A turning-point is now reached. As the sphere of philosophy extends beyond the physical domain, so the philosophical in Christianity embraces more than a category of physical truths. As nature is the key-word to all physical truth, so man is the key-word to all intellectual, if not spiritual, truth. Man stands for higher truth, as nature stands for lower truth; and, by so much as he is greater than nature, by as much is the truth he represents greater than the truth of nature. Man thinks; he has a conscience; he recognizes moral distinctions; he determines the difference between the *me* and the *not-me.* All the differences or idiosyncrasies, which distinguish human from brute intelligence, all those achievements which prove the superiority of man, and all those graces and virtues that lend dignity to human character, are proper subjects for the contemplation of the theologian and philosopher. What is man? asks David. The answer of modern philosophy has been given in this volume. It strikes at the divine in humanity. The answer of Christianity is, that man is a twofold being; he is constituted with a body which is physical and will perish, and a soul which is intellectual and spiritual, and, therefore, immortal; and these are mysteriously united for all the purposes of a brief time-life, and then separated, that the soul may enter into everlasting relations with another life. Such a view of man invests him with sacredness and nobility, and points to unlimited possibilities of development and achievement. On this foundation, man's place in nature, in the spiritual realm and in eternity, can be fixed, and a philosophy, building up on these premises, will abide. A true philosophy must recognize the intellectual in distinction from the physical, and the immortal in opposition to the mortal. Epicurus denied the immortality of the soul, but Paul emphasizes it as one of the first principles of religion. Nor is this a religious truth only, to be accepted because revealed; it is also a philosophical truth, which Plato demonstrated, and *to be accepted because demonstrated.* Immortality is as inherent as memory, imagination, conscience, or will; it is not a conferred gift, but an essential attribute of soul. The genesis of soul is the genesis of immortality.

*The philosophic spirit of Christianity is manifest in its recognition of the reign of evil in the universe, and in the revelation of a positive method for its extinction.* Homer does not use the word "sin," or any equivalent, in the Iliad, for, to the ancient poets, and the fable-makers, wrong-doing was a trifle, in some instances it was *godlike,* for did not the gods commit crimes? While philosophy struck mythology from history as a baseless fabric, and condemned its ethical notions as absurd and injurious, it can not be said that philosophy occupied a safe ethical ground, or that it comprehended all that is involved in the existence and reign of evil. If to the ancient philosopher mythology was fiction, to the Christian thinker of to-day Manicheism and Gnosticism, as philosophical explanations, appear equally untrue and inapplicable. What then? Christianity reveals the philosophy of evil, not in a mythological way, not as a speculation, but as it reveals all truth, by the declaration of its character, as the opposite of holiness, and by the declaration of its origin in a spirit of disobedience to the law of righteousness. It does not locate evil in matter, but defines it as the abnormal condition of mind, as *enmity to law.* As an act, evil is the voluntary flow of mind in a forbidden channel; as a result, it is the disorder consequent on disobedience.

The ethical remedy of Christianity is atonement, forgiveness, and regeneration; a remedy as philosophical as it is religious, because available and sufficient.

Christianity is philosophical in its *biological principles.* The principle of life is a profound secret, the scientist being as ignorant of it as the average theologian. Life is invisible; its manifestations we alone can observe and know. Still we know there is such a something as Life, or something that we call Life. Now, it would be dogmatic in the Christian thinker to announce that Christianity makes a full exposition of life, or that it resolves its chief mystery, and dissipates all the darkness which invests it; it does not clear the subject, but it throws a halo around it; it does not explain its essence, but it conducts to its source.

Christianity is not azoic in any sense; it is Life, because its Founder is Life. To him all life may be traced, and from him all life has come ; but the mystery of life still remains. The universe is the embodiment of a principle of life, which is called Energy ; the human race is the embodiment of a principle of life, which is called Salvation ; and one is as philosophical as the other. Philosophy recognizes the one ; Christianity imports the other. The law of bio-genesis, or life from pre-existent life, or lower life impregnated with higher life, reigns in the physical universe and accounts for its development ; the same law reigns in religion, accounting for Regeneration, and all the mysteries of spiritual development. Physical development and spiritual development are under the same law of life. Hitherto spiritual life has been interpreted by the scientific thinker as a sentimental condition, independent of natural laws, and secured, if at all, by supernatural influences which science knew nothing about and whose existence, therefore, it was inclined to impeach. But biogenesis is as much a law of the spiritual realm as of the natural ; regeneration is as natural as it is spiritual ; and the life of the universe is only the symbol of the life of the eternal world. *Christianity is the true philosophy of biological law.*

In like manner, it may be shown that Incarnation, Atonement, Justification, Sanctification, Faith, Joy, Liberty, and Prayer, are philosophical principles, or philosophical conditions, realized by philosophical methods, and manifested in a philosophic order in the Christian life. That is to say, whatever Christianity is, it is philosophical ; whatever Christianity does, it does philosophically ; whatever mysteries it withholds, they are philosophical mysteries ; whatever revelations it submits, they are philosophical revelations.

If nature is the key-word to physical truth, and man the key-word to intellectual truth, *God is the key-word to spiritual truth*, to all truth, physical, intellectual and spiritual. God is the key-word to nature, man, and himself ; the key to the secrets of the universe, the key to the treasures of the spiritual world. Philosophy has sadly erred in trying to open the doors without the key ; it has not opened them. Christianity opens all things, explains all forms, reveals all laws, and is the sum of all truth. As in philosophy the greatest problem is God, so in Christianity the greatest revelation is God. Christianity is the revelation of God. It is not a problem ; it is a revelation. It is not a theory ; it is a truth. As a truth it is more philosophical than a theory, for, while philosophy runs to theory, it ought to be grounded in the truth, which truth is Christianity. The theistic truth of Christianity embraces all other truths ; hence, the revelation of one is the revelation of all. On this highest truth a philosophy is possible ; on this highest truth a religion is possible ; on this highest truth the unity of philosophy and religion is possible.

Philosophy without Christianity is uncertain, and its discoveries must be partial and accidental; Christianity without philosophy is truth without theory, and must abide forever. *Christianity is philosophy.*

---

# CHAPTER XXI.

## CHRISTIANITY THE KEY TO THE PHENOMENAL WORLD.

GIORDANO BRUNO, an Italian philosopher of the sixteenth century, represented the world as a "living being," with reason as its regnant faculty. Gorgias, the ancient Sophist, imbibed the Eleatic notion of the non-existence of matter, declaring that nature is without reality. Horace Bushnell, adopting the etymological suggestion of the word "nature," as something *about-to-be*, speaks of it as "that created realm of being or substance which has an acting, a going on, or process from within itself, under, and by its own laws." Pascal affirms that "nature is an image of grace;" and Henry Drummond undertakes to establish the identity of natural and spiritual laws, or that the Religious and Natural realms are under the same code of laws.

These differences in opinion respecting the physical world make it clear that a purely philosophical explanation of matter will be unsatisfactory, and also, that a religious theory, unless fully buttressed by revealed truth, can not hope for recognition. It is not sentiment, it is not theory, that is wanted. It is truth, and truth only, that will satisfy the rational mind in its search for explanation of the phenomenal world.

To assume that the phenomenal world may be understood does not imply that any direct revelation of its character, purpose, and destiny has been made, or that an understanding has been fully wrought out; but it does imply that by searching, comparing, asking, and prompting nature to respond, a satisfactory schedule of its contents and purposes may be framed. The certainty of explanation lies in the possibility of explanation. Chemistry, astronomy, geology, and physiology were all scientific possibilities long before they became trustworthy systems of truth. So the whole realm of nature, like any department thereof, may, under analysis, or by the application of principles used in the testing of higher truth, be interpreted or be induced to reveal all that it contains. It is here assumed that in the light of Christianity the phenomenal world may be properly understood; but the assumption is not made without qualifications. Believing that philosophy has failed in its attempt to explain nature, it must be admitted that by its aid many mysteries have been simplified, many laws discovered, and human knowledge has been increased. To that source the debt of the thinker is not small. Philosophy must not be reproached for not doing what it is unable to do.

If the task of explanation has been committed to Christianity, it is not because its prophets and apostles were, as men of genius, scholarship, and wisdom, superior to philosophers and scientists, but because they were the instruments of the divine Spirit in revealing the hidden truths of the ages. The ground of the claim here set forth is not the superiority of the sacred writers, but the superiority of the truth itself. Even in this respect our claim must not be extravagant. Science is very imperfect in its contents ; it reveals facts, but accounts for nothing ; it discloses the composition of things, but does not explain the things themselves. It tells the properties of oxygen, but does not tell how oxygen came to be, or what it is. It eulogizes chemical affinity, points out its uses, but does not define it. Of crystallization as a law it says something ; as a force, it says nothing.

Now, if philosophy stops short of explanation, though it expounds laws and principles ; if science scarcely goes beyond the facts, though it is enthusiastic in its search for them ; does not Christianity, discarding the instruments of philosophy and science, essay a task far beyond its power and range when it proposes to illuminate the phenomenal world, and declare the secrets it has contained since its foundations were laid ? To guard against disappointment it should be stated that the revelations of Christianity touching the phenomenal world are by no means complete ; they fall short of what curiosity requires, and even Reason complains of the apparent paucity. Ignorance, therefore, prevails even in the circles of Christian thought. This leads us to observe that the light of Christianity is a peculiar light ; like the light of the sun, it is a mystery, but, like that light, it is light to those who have eyes. Science gives facts without explanations ; Christianity is an explanation without the facts. It is one thing to take knowledge of the facts ; it is another thing to take knowledge of the explanation. One may see darkness ; it is not always certain that one may see light. Science can not explain Christianity ; Christianity explains science—that is, its facts.

It makes nothing against the explanation that it is imperfect, so long as the imperfection lies chiefly in the want of details, or in its application to single objects. It grapples with the whole, with magnitude, not with atoms. It comprehends the All, not a single point. It explains not the pebble in which there is all of geology, but it explains the heavens, out of which all science, all philosophy, all religion must come. It explains not the leaf, which is botany, but the globe, which is universal truth; not the insect, which is "natural history," but the human race, which is divine history. Dealing seldom with single facts, but always with broad principles; omitting the details of the total result, but comprehending the total result, the interpretation of Christianity at first appears imperfect, but at last it is sufficient.

First, touching the genesis of the physical universe, Christianity speaks a definite word on which it rests its scientific character. Over this question what contests have occurred! What solutions have asserted themselves! How the philosophical eye has strained itself to catch a glimpse of the beginning! What ponderous theories, what pessimistic hypotheses, what materialistic statements, what agnostic settlements, have appeared, each and all to be succeeded by others less objectionable in form, but quite as deficient as explanations! Listening to the babel of scientists, we hear of monads, atoms, spontaneous motion, eternity of matter, germs, laws, forces, protoplasm, bioplasm, evolution—words suggestive of tension, perplexity, atheism, materialism; words with the mildew of night upon them. The elimination of a Divine Power from the universe, or the endowment of nature with a self-creating energy, dispensing entirely with the necessity of personal superintendence, impious as it may seem to the devout, has been attempted by materialistic philosophy; indeed, the Nebular hypothesis, as propounded by Laplace, and evolution, as expounded by Spencer, seem not to require the mediation of a personal Creator. When Napoleon inquired of Laplace why he did not recognize God in his *Mécanique Céleste*, his reply was, "I have no need of such a hypothesis." However, it must be confessed that the Nebular Hypothesis and Evolution are not in themselves incompatible with the theistic notion; they seem to be atheistic, and are employed as supports of the atheistic sentiment, but as methods of the divine working in creation they are not *per se* atheistic. As a "working hypothesis," no objection is made to the Nebular theory, or any other theory apparently contrary to the theistic conception, provided, when the experiment of solving mysteries by it has been honestly made, the result shall be honestly declared.

Materialistic philosophy, in its eagerness to interpret nature, begins with the atheistic assumption, to which no objection is raised, provided it will reject the assumption when required by the facts so to do. Christian thinkers, quite as anxious to read nature, begin with the theistic assumption to which materialists should not object, provided its friends will agree to abandon it so soon as its unavailability is discovered. Truth gains a double advantage by the double assumptions; it will be vindicated finally by both, and as truth is more important than any theory, every theorist should be encouraged to press on to a conclusion, for truth is waiting for a settlement.

How the worlds were made is a mystery, more because God is a mystery than that matter is mysterious. Understand God, and his works and methods are understood. It is because he is in shadow that his methods are still obscure. However, the method of world-building may finally be known, since he is becoming better known; it " doth not yet appear," we may now say. We stand ready to accept any theory or method, whether the Nebular hypothesis or any other, that is compatible with the theistic notion, for Christianity reveals the Maker of the world, even though it does not reveal the method of the Maker's activities.

If the method of creation is obscure, incomprehensible even to the scientific mind, the *order of creation* is transparent, and, as given in Genesis, is almost complete. No scientist has improved on Moses in the discovery of the plan of creation, which, beginning with light, terminates with man. Without extending this thought, it may be stated that Christianity is both a key to the authorship of the world in a personal Creator and to the order pursued by him in creation. This is the dawn of day; this is an *approximate settlement of the fundamental problems*.

As lower problems are always involved in the higher, and as the solution of the lower is determined by the solution of the higher, we may now proceed to the lower and specific questions arising from the fact of a phenomenal world, remembering that its authorship and order have been defined in the terms of the Christian religion.

The phenomenal world is a great mystery. He who undertakes to define the essence of matter, or report all her secrets, will be overwhelmed by the magnitude of his task, and probably be willing to surrender it to others before he shall have concluded it. Between a property of matter and the spirit of matter, or the law of its being, there is a wide difference; and it is not understood that philosophy, while successful in detailing the one, has thrown any light upon the other. Forms of matter may be described; many of its laws may be enrolled in our categories; the beauties of the physical dress of matter may be discovered; the curiosities and combinations of matter may be exhibited and preserved; but matter itself, the idea of matter, the being of matter, separate from its concrete types, eludes the gaze of the most intrepid explorer of nature, and refuses to acquaint man with its mystery. Does matter exist? If so, what is it?

In the presence of this question philosophy is either dumb or divided and confused.

Nor let us hastily conclude that the Christian thinker is free from embarrassment as he is asked this question. Confronted at the gateway of the phenomenal world with the becoming, or non-being, he can not speak with any more assurance or perceive with any greater delicacy of vision the essential spirit of matter; but Christianity is the pass-word to the inner sanctuary of things, and by this he may enter and declare the secrets of the hidden world. Perhaps not all the secrets; but such as are essential to intellectual comfort he may understand. Christianity leaves us not in total darkness, nor is nature in an eclipse when the Sun of righteousness shines upon it. In its light we see deeper than forms, we see more than properties, we apprehend more than laws, we comprehend nature as the idea of God reduced to physical conditions and impregnated with his lofty purposes. Nature is a panorama of divine ideas, or the reality of divine thought, cognizable in visible form. As Christianity is the divine idea itself in spiritual form, it is not unreasonable to anticipate that the divine idea in physical form will agree with it. Agreement may be predicated on the assumption that the divine idea is not self-contradictory, but self-luminous and self-harmonious; hence, the divine idea in nature must agree with the divine idea in Christianity, or Christianity and nature are one. This is the same thing as saying that the theology of nature corresponds to the theology of Christianity, and that what one is in essence the other is also, the only difference between them being the frame-work which supports them.

Now, if this view is correct, Christianity will have a strong defense in nature, and nature will have a satisfactory explanation in Christianity; but it is not the value of the view that at this moment concerns us. We are impressed to know if the representation of the relations of Christianity and nature is true; if the supernatural and the natural are one; if either exists without the other. Bishop Butler's remarkable treatise on "The Analogy of Religion to the Constitution and Course of Nature" is suggestive of the harmony, the kinship, the identity of the two kingdoms of God. His "Analogy" has never been answered, because the facts employed can not be disputed, and the argument founded on them is remorselessly logical. In the analogy is a path to the explanation of nature. We shall, therefore, walk therein. Shakespeare speaks of "sermons in stones," but there are sermons in the stars, sermons in the trees, sermons in the oceans, sermons in every thing. Nature is the great sermon or expositor of Christianity, as Christianity is the great sermon or expositor of nature. Christianity is the apocalypse of natural religion.

By nature is meant the phenomenal universe, which includes space, time, motion, law, and force, as well as the solid forms of matter, or that concrete realm of non-being which is the outward expression of being. Phenomena are illustrations of Christian truths; this is the thought.

Consider *space*. Like God, it can not be adequately defined; like God, it is without parts; like God, it is everywhere, occupied or unoccupied. Space, then, is a mirror of the Infinite so far forth as it is a suggestion of certain qualities we attribute to the Infinite. It does represent to human thought the idea of omnipresence, and also the idea of bodiless spirit. Though it does this imperfectly, it does it. Space is the allegory of an infinite idea.

Consider *time*. The reality of time is an independent philosophical question; as a moral factor, or as related to any truth of Christianity, it is the exponent of the eternity of God, for a limited duration is possible only because there is an unlimited duration from which it is derived. Time is the reflex of eternity. This may not be satisfactorily conclusive, but it is the weakness of analogical argument in general that it is not equal to demonstration.

Consider *motion*. Dispensing with the laws of motion, the fact of motion is a sign or proof of the existence of some definite characteristic of the divine Being. It is inconceivable that there was a time when motion was not, for a motionless universe implies universal inertia, which is absurd. If there was a time when God only existed, our conception of him requires us to believe that he was active for and in himself, for a motionless Deity is as inconceivable as a motionless universe. In this view motion is eternal. It belongs to the nature of God, and a universe is impossible without it. This, however, is not exhaustive. Motion is everywhere perceived or unperceived, felt or unfelt, representing not only the ceaseless activity of the Deity, but the omnipresence of the Supreme Power. It is in space; every star quivers with motion; every atom is a reservoir of motive forces; the universe is *in* motion, it is *a* motion. This is the foreshadowing of the universality of the divine Presence.

Thus space, time, and motion join in suggesting the attributes of spirituality, omnipresence, and eternity, as belonging to one who is above all things, who is God.

Likewise, if we consider some of the laws and forces of nature, we shall find adumbrations of the attributes of the Infinite, or revelations of the divine intelligence and the divine government, such as the preceding did not suggest. Whether law is the method of action, or the course of a process, or the sign of a purpose, certain it is that the laws of nature are singularly uniform in action and always conducive to specific results. The laws of nature are not failures. Interfered with, they may not accomplish what otherwise would follow, but they never break of themselves.

Gravitation may be overcome, but, unrestrained, it honors the center of the earth by bowing to it as if it were in authority. So stable is law, and so reliable are the forces of nature, that calculations based upon them are not likely to deceive, unless the calculations themselves are erroneous. The stability of law points to the immutability of the divine character, and is an assurance that the divine promises will be fulfilled. The laws of nature have their counterpart in the promises of the Gospel.

Another analogy or suggestion springs up at this point. The law of crystallization results in crystals; the law of attraction and repulsion in planetary motion; the law of capillary attraction in growth; the law of cohesion in solidity; and every other law fulfills itself in a product consistent with its governing influence. This secures order in the universe, and it expresses the wisdom of the mind that devised it. Law is wisdom. A divine order, or a beneficent arrangement, is as much a reflection of the divine wisdom, as power in nature is expressive of the divine power, or motion of the divine activity.

Equally expressive of some divine attributes are the *forms of matter*, which to us are antecedent signs of ideal thoughts; but which in themselves are the products of the divine idea respecting matter. That matter should assume any form at all is significant of a former; but when it seeks a variety of forms the spherical, triangular, and rectangular, the thinker is compelled to pause and inquire the meaning thereof. Either matter at its own instance selects a particular form, or an unseen hand puts it in shape, and sends it forth on duty. Why the drop of water prefers the spherical, no one has explained; why a star has center and circumference no one knows. Matter runs in molds, and reappears in all the splendid forms of the natural world.

It is the idea of Thomas Hill that these forms are after geometrical ideals, which borders on the Pythagorean conception that geometry is the content of nature. To this suggestion, rational and explicit, we subscribe. Nature is the crystallization of mathematical principles; the phenomenal world is an algebraic equation. Whence the principles or ideals? Account for these, and the mystery is dissolved. Plato, in contemplating the genesis of matter, held forth the doctrine of "ideas" as the pre-existent condition of matter, worlds, and being; that by ideas the Deity was governed, and incorporated them in all existences; that he is the great Idea himself, and conformed all things to that idea; hence, unity, beauty, adaptation, and utility, as the constituents of the universe. The thought of Plato is magnificent, its value is incalculable. Ideas imply mind, and executed ideals imply intellective action. If nature is a concreted ideal, or a reduction of thought to physical form, it implies intellectual activity on a stupendous scale; it implies infinite mind. Thus the forms of matter, less important than the fact of matter, or the reality of being, have their explanation in the Christian doctrine of the activity of eternal thought, which is the sign of an infinite mind.

The lesson from *color* is a confirmation of the same doctrine. What is color? Is it a variation of light? Whence light? God said: "Let light be; and light was." As this is the origin of light, so is it the origin of color, for without light color is impossible. Color is not without its uses, is implicit with a divine idea. Form is one source of beauty; color is another, addressing and refining the æsthetic sense in man, and pointing to the æsthetic attribute in the divine character. Given one color only, and the physical world would be unendurable. Given seven colors, and it is beautiful.

The distribution of color in nature must have been made according to a law in harmony with the æsthetic sentiment, or according to æsthetic law. For instance, the firmament is *blue;* the forests in the Spring-time are *green*, and in the Autumn turn *brown;* the snow is *white;* sunsets, landscapes, mountain scenery, the fields of grain, and gardens of flowers, exhibit color in all its variety and combination, addressing the eye, and ministering to the taste of man. *The æsthetics of nature signify the æsthetics of the divine character*, revealing the beauty, perfection, and harmony of God.

Surely the relation of natural and revealed religion is not an accidental, much less an unmeaning, relation. Christianity reflects its doctrines in nature, and nature, like a mirror, gives them back again; this is fellowship, this is unity. The two are one. In space, time, and motion, we catch a glimpse of spirituality, omnipresence, and eternity; in laws and forces the foreshadowings of infinite wisdom and a providential government are manifest; in the forms of matter, burnished with living colors, there are the reflections of wisdom, beauty, and perfection. Nature is a confirmation of the theistic hypothesis on which Christianity rests, on which all philosophic thought must eventually rest.

Admitting that nature furnishes a chapter of facts for the support of the theistic idea, it is sometimes hinted that it throws but little if any light on the spiritual doctrines of Christianity; or, that what constitutes it a separate and independent religion has no confirmation in the analogies of nature. To this suspicion let us at once give attention. The argument from analogy is worth nothing in this discussion if it does not establish faith in the idiosyncrasies of Christianity, or give support to those truths not found in other religions. However, to be effective analogy must not be pressed too. far, nor be made to include every thing. It is not now affirmed that nature is a reflection or confirmation of every spiritual truth in the New Testament, much less of all its facts, although an elaborate analysis of the contents of natural and revealed religion might result in a vindication of certain truths supposed hitherto to stand upon an independent basis, and without any support whatever in nature; but it is affirmed that *nature, as a whole, is an arch beneath Christianity, as a whole.* The one is not contrary to the other; the one is the secret defender of the other. Bishop Butler did not support every doctrine by analogy; nor is it necessary. If it can be shown that the drift of natural truth is toward spiritual truth, or one is the index to the other, the point is gained.

As we have seen, nature drifts toward the theistic hypothesis. As we shall now see, the constitution of the world is the index to the doctrine of a moral government, with all implied in it, in the universe. A drifting of human government toward moral government is discovered in the general approval of virtue and the general condemnation of vice among men; but the drifting of natural law toward moral law is seen in the fixed sanctions of virtue and the unchangeable condemnation of vice in the constitution of things. Man's attitude toward virtue and vice may be arbitrary, arising from self-interest, while nature's attitude on ethical principles is unpartisan, universal, and eternal. The spirit of justice is in the world, regulating, or suggesting the regulation of affairs, according to the principle of equity. Whence came it? Back of education, back of governmental policies, back even of religious impulses, must the searcher go for the genesis of the spirit and principle of justice. In spirit the government of the world is a picture of exact justice; it is the perfect adjustment of relations or conformity to an ideal of order. Justice, as a principle, is as inherent in the constitution of things as is the ethical idea itself. It is as fundamental to nature, to the reality, the regularity, and order of the physical universe, as it is to the religious spirit, that is to say, religion. What is justice? Defining it with reference to men, Plato says *it is non-interference with other men's affairs,* which is deeper than it seems. It implies abstinence from wrong, which in its inner content implies the doing of right. Justice is right-doing, but right-doing involves liberty, order, fraternity, equality, humanity; but this is the ethical concept transferred from nature to society. Nature abhors wrong-doing; it never does a wrong. Nature is the synonym of right-doing, involving the concrete ideas of the ethical concept. Likewise, truth is one of the symbols of nature. Mysterious nature is, but never deceptive. It is not a huge lie. Its laws are the images of truth; its forces are truth-conserving forces; its forms are the truthful representations of divine ideals. Nature is reliable. Nature acknowledges responsibility to a Supreme Ruler, and obeys every mandate. Hence, the idea of government springs from the faithfulness and integrity of nature.

In like manner, virtue, courage, honesty, and goodness, are thoroughly portrayed in the unwritten constitution of the world, suggesting the primary ideas of authority, honor, sobriety, and righteousness, in the moral government that is seen to prevail.

This analogy, the natural foreshadowing the moral, is one of the most formidable the materialist confronts. Everywhere the proclamation of justice, truth, and righteousness rings in his ears; everywhere the terror of penalty rolls across the path of the wrong-doer; and continually the thought of responsibility weighs down the heart of the obdurate, and checks him in contemplated crime. It is the voice of nature speaking through her laws, forces, and forms, the moral truths of God; it is nature certifying to the double doctrine of rewards and punishments in the moral realm. If a natural world suggests a moral world, and a natural government a moral government, then natural penalties and blessings suggest moral penalties and rewards. If the analogy is worth any thing, it is worth this much; but if it is worth so much it is a conformation of just what Christianity itself foretells as the issues of moral government.

Another great doctrine of Christianity is *the removal of evil by redemptive agencies,* the chief of which is the personal influence and power of Jesus Christ. Does nature reflect this doctrine? Here the analogy has its limitations, but it is not wanting in satisfactory elements, or in direct reference to the Christian idea. The trend of nature is toward the doctrine, even the method of removal being foreshadowed in the course of its development. If it does not point to Christ as underneath all things, it does sustain the idea of sacrifice as the condition of growth, prosperity, life; if it does not foreshadow a person on the altar, it points to altar and executioner; if it does not proclaim atonement by law, *it practices it as the essential of its history,* and prepares the way for its holier exhibition in religion. Herbert Spencer insists on the evanescence of evil through evolutionary processes; declares that nature proposes, by methods entirely its own, to expel evil as an incumbrance; and believes that righteousness will some time prevail. This is the objective ideal of the Gospel, to be realized, however, not through natural agency, but by Gospel agency. By its evolutionary process, entirely inadequate in itself, nature typifies the redemptive process, which is all-sufficient for the purpose. Evolution is the promise, or the sign of redemption in Jesus Christ.

Christianity posits the extinction of evil on the vital influence of the personal sacrifice of the Son of God. Is this the doctrine of nature? Sacrifice is a doctrine of nature, so vital to nature that it could not survive without it; hence its religious bearing. Without light, atmosphere, and soil, the vegetable world must perish, which is the same as saying that the vegetable world lives at the expense of other worlds. Without sacrifice neither tree, nor flower, nor grain, nor fruit had been, nor will be. In like manner the animal world either preys upon itself, or upon the vegetable world; every animal lives at the expense of some other animal, or some other form of life. To a still greater extent man is dependent on all the worlds around him. He can not live alone. He is not independent of any world. He lives because other worlds lie at his feet *dead*. Every living thing is indebted to some other living thing for life. There is nothing that is adequate to life alone. Life means that something has died. *The thread of sacrifice runs through nature, is found in every department, and links the kingdoms together.* An evolutionary system of redemption, without sacrifice as its chief corner-stone, would not be in harmony with nature. The redemptive system, as wrought out in Jesus Christ, harmonizes with the sacrificial order of nature; in one a Thing is sacrificed; in the other a Person; in one physical blessings result; in the other spiritual life.

So far, Nature is in accord with the teachings of Christianity. The two agree touching fundamental truths, and this is all that is necessary. Agreement or non-agreement on other lines will not affect the analogy herein exhibited, or the argument drawn from it. The agreement established is almost equal to a demonstration, for it is cumulative, gathering strength as it is unfolded, and substantiating the last truth with more certainty than the first. Beginning with the theistic hypothesis it confirms the Jewish faith; ending with atonement in Jesus Christ it confirms the Christian faith. By virtue of these analogies, nature has a *moral explanation* in Christianity, as by virtue of the theistic notion it has a *philosophical explanation* in Christianity.

If it is suggested that the so-called analogies or teachings of nature were not observed in other ages, and have not impressed the scientific thinkers of modern times, and, therefore, the inferences deduced are to be received with reservation, it is sufficient to reply that this does not destroy the force of such teachings or contradict the analogies. The pulpit sometimes alludes to the common fact of day succeeding night as a fair illustration or hint of the resurrection, and it makes not against it that Solon and Cicero never drew such an inference from the fact. The rejection of an analogy must be grounded in something better than the rejecter's ignorance of the matters involved. It is confessed that the interpretation of nature is not easily made; without the light of Christianity it is questionable if it can be understood in any true or lofty sense. The discovery of an analogy is due to an acquaintance with both nature and religion, and can not arise from a knowledge of one only. Analogy, like comparison, implies two objects, and it can not be drawn except as the person drawing it understands both objects. If Solon did not see any analogy in the unfolding of the butterfly from the chrysalis to the resurrection; if Cicero saw no hint of it in the re-appearance of day after night, it chiefly proves that while they were familiar with one set of facts they knew nothing of the other; that is, they knew the physical facts, but were ignorant of the resurrection. Hence, they could not draw an analogy. Given both sides and analogy is possible, pertinent. As an equation is possible with two sides, so analogy is possible when both objects are understood. The analogy of nature to Christianity must, therefore, remain an indubitable evidence of the truth of the latter, and a key to the secrets of the former.

A more specific study of the phenomenal world is now required, and is possible in the light of Christianity. Let us contemplate the universe as a whole. There is one universe, and one only. Worlds many, systems of worlds complex, laws governing them numberless, but after all one universe, identical in subtance, motion, spirit, purpose. Astronomy is a wilderness of facts, but order reigns throughout the vast domain of the firmament, and points to a single organizing mind, and to a single fulfilling purpose. The larger the realm of the worlds the more amazing the thought of its unity, but it grows upon the mind as the proofs of it become conspicuous. How unity is consistent with such far-reaching complexity; what the idea of unity comprehends or foreshadows; what general laws contribute to the fulfillment of the single programme evidently being carried out in the universe; in what unity actually consists; these are phases of the subject that press themselves forward for attention.

What is the unity of the universe? It is a *unity of substance.* The proof is from chemistry. Of the seventy elements of which matter is composed, the chemists report not more than twelve which are common, and of the twelve only three or four are universal, and even these they are disposed to reduce to one. The one may be, must be, complex, but it is one evidently. If the universe is the procession of one substance, so divided, energized, and manipulated by divine wisdom as to produce the heavens and the earth, and it is found in all organic and inorganic bodies, the interpretation of nature is simplified and the theistic notion of Christianity scientifically confirmed.  To this conception of unity any objection founded on the variety in nature must be regarded superficial, for variety is compatible with unity.  Carbon is the principal element of diamond, graphite, and charcoal, substances so different as seemingly to contradict the notion of unity, but not different after all.  Fixing the mind on the varieties of the human race one must pronounce against unity until one learns that in instinct, blood, social impulse, and religious desire the human family is a unit.  "Of one blood," says Paul, all nations were made.  The unity of the race is a unity of blood, a "physiological unit," to quote Herbert Spencer.

If variety makes not against unity, it may be supposed that the absolute differences between the kingdoms of nature can not be reconciled with the theory of the "unit;" as the animal kingdom is apparently in no wise related to the mineral kingdom; an elephant can not be one with the emerald.  To undertake to reconcile differences between specific objects might be entertaining, but it is unnecessary, for if it can be demonstrated that all nature, with its subdivisions, kingdoms, ranks, originated from one substance, the problem of difference is settled with it.  Difference is another word for variety. Nature had a beginning; if a single beginning, then it is proper to speak of a physical unit containing the possibilities of the universe. Chemistry inclines to a physical unit, and has gone far enough to intimate that hydrogen is that unit.  This is getting back to a first principle, to the "beginning."

If hydrogen is the *substance-unit* of the physical universe, all things, theoretically at least, must be resolvable into hydrogen, or into elements kindred to it.  This will explain the emerald and the elephant, the eagle and a grain of sand.  Inquiring into stellar conditions the idea of unity has received such encouragement as practically to be indorsed by all thinkers, materialistic and Christian. Hydrogen is a constituent of the earth, the sun, and all the stars. Sodium enters into the composition of all the worlds.  Iron, magnesium, and calcium abound in all the orbs.  "The dust of our streets," says Winchell, "is ignited to starry suns in Arcturus and the Pleiades." The scientific proclamation of the substantial unity of the worlds is an advance step toward the resolution of the problem of the origin of the worlds, for one in substance they must have had a similar origin.

Passing to the harmony of forces in nature, the observer will be justified in assuming a *unity of purpose* in the universe, which has some bearing on Christian truth, as we shall shortly see.  Storms, earthquakes, accidents, and diseases, in the judgment of the pessimist, are proofs of a disorderly government, of a government without ends. If the world has a ruler, he is a tyrant, remorselessly crushing the majority, and delighting in the agony of his subjects. Pessimism is dyspeptic philosophy ; it looks at one side only, and does not see that clearly. Admitting friction as the result of a play of forces, the total result is harmony ; admitting suffering in the realm of nature, its beneficent use is moral elevation ; admitting conflict, the stability of nature is assured. Nature exists for ends ; either for itself, or for man, or for its Maker. Descending to the lowest mechanical view of nature, that it exists for itself and is unrelated to man, here is the idea of purpose, not high purpose, but purpose surely. To accept such a teleology, however, one must know first that nature is conscious of such an end, otherwise the end is valueless. Nature is beautiful, but if beautiful for herself only, she must be consciously beautiful, which can not be admitted. The ends of nature are beyond herself ; she exists not for herself. *Nature is because man is, because God is.*

The relation of nature to man is a teleological relation ; otherwise nature is absolutely dumb, barren of interest, a clod. In the spirit of self-flattery man will insist that the earth was made solely for himself ; but he remembers that the first man, representing the race, was commanded to conquer the earth and exercise dominion over it. It is beneath him ; it is his footstool ; it is his servant ; it is to minister to him. Its beauty and bounty are for him ; the mountains rise and the oceans roll for him ; the sun shines and the earth rotates because he is here ; the soil yields its harvests and the trees bear fruits because he desires them. The subordination of nature to humanity, or the ministry of the phenomenal world to the development of humanity, is one of the revelations of Christianity, placing man and nature in right relations and for worthy ends.

Nor is this a full expression of the teleology of nature. Every man is related to some " district " in nature, as Emerson intimates ; that is, one being a botanist in spirit, he will find botany in nature ; another being a zoölogist, he will find zoölogy ; one a chemist, chemistry will appear. Whatever the mind is there will be a field in nature to correspond to it and minister to it. In this sense man is a representative of nature, or nature is but humanity concreted in another form. Nature is the symbol of mind ; it is the exponent of thought. Without mind, nature is impossible. The two are counterparts ; one fits the other because one is the mirror of the other. Nature stands for man ; man stands for nature. Humanity emphasizes itself in nature, as Christianity reflects itself in the laws and forms of matter.

To stop here, however, would fall short of an exhaustive teleological interpretation of nature, which exists not for man alone. Related to him as nature is, the exponent of his being, as we have seen, nevertheless nature's highest end is the glorification of its divine author. If it represent human thought, it also represents divine thought; if it is the symbol of the human mind, it is the counterpart of the divine mind. Nature is the outcome of a divine plan framed in the beginning, and working for divine results. The vast universe is rushing on in fulfillment of a stupendous plan—one plan harmonious and consistent throughout its labyrinth of details; one plan that embraces the stars and protects the sparrow; one plan that belts Saturn, turns the Euphrates from its channel, and pricks Vesuvius into flame; one plan that guides a leaf in its fall, gives Niagara its brim, and tosses the rain-drop from the cloud. God is in nature; nature is the arcana of divine thoughts. Nature stands for God; God stands for Nature. In its ambassadorial capacity Nature is human and divine, representing the character of the one and the will of the other.

In world-building the ideals, whether of forms, laws, or constituents, were few, perhaps reducible to one, just as all substances are one and all purposes but developments of one purpose. A *unity of ideal* is, therefore, next in order. To explain: We cite the form of a planet, which is spherical. This is the form of all the worlds, the asteriods, the comets, the firmament itself; it is likewise the form of their orbits; motion itself is largely circular; and even small things, as a drop of water, the human eye, a tree, a flower, observe with some variation the regulation form. Even the laws of nature conserve the spherical tendency, as falling lead turns into shot. Evidently the mathematical idea of the divine mind is the spheroid, which involves orbits, attraction and repulsion, distances, harmonies, all that astronomy contains, all that the multiplied sciences can reveal.

Another ideal is the stability of species under which the animal kingdom has grown up with definite limitations, as to number and distinct lines, as to difference and separation. One species can not merge into another; it either dies or remains forever separate. God's ideal can not be broken or obscured; it stands out plainly in the history of the animal creation. Going back no further than the infusoria, animal life has evolved in a regular and undisturbed order, according to law and within its originally prescribed limitations. Scientific efforts to break down the barriers have resulted in failure, and established the reign of law. So the vegetable kingdom is an evolution, according to the law that like shall produce like, as the oak must produce oak. The fig-tree can not produce olive berries; like can not produce unlike. *Evolution is nothing but the ideal work-*

*ing itself out in the law of like producing like, securing stability, order, and progress in the different realms of nature.*

In the generalization of the universe, a specific ideal of form governed the divine mind; and in the particularization of earth-life, a specific ideal of law was in operation. Development is wholly after ideals—can not proceed without them. In any event, unity is the result. Of this unity in the manifold, a unity toward which all development tends, and which embraces all things, we must make something, because it means something. Perplexed a moment over it, Christianity comes to our relief, interpreting it in a beautiful and religious way, and solving all the problems growing out of it without complications or tedious processes. On all its pages it proclaims the existence of one God, the Maker of all worlds, ascribing to him all power, wisdom, and goodness, and revealing him in his personal relations to the smallest things that exist. Now, if the universe were made to reaffirm this doctrine—if its specific teleological aim were to establish the divine existence, it seems that it succeeds perfectly. The unity of the universe, whether considered as to substance, purpose, or ideal law, is a vindication of the monotheistic conception of the sacred Scriptures. Everywhere in the empire of nature, the impression of a master mind is visible. Whatever the variety of forms or complexity of forces; whatever the details of organic and inorganic manifestations; however mysterious the laws of activity and growth,—the intelligent observer always concludes on the unity of the supreme or presiding genius of creation. Polytheism he rejects, because nature nowhere teaches it. Nature is the Testament he reads, and, reading, he believes in one God.

The unity of substance—of stars and specks of granite, of suns and shells and blades of grass, of Neptune and the earth—how was it possible if gods many were on thrones? From one God came one universe, and one universe from one substance; this is harmony, this is truth. Equally decisive is the unity of purpose in the manifold, for from a many-centered source must issue many-formed plans; but oneness of mind is compatible with oneness of purpose. The unity of ideal, or the organized development of the universe, according to a single ideal—how was this possible if two supreme powers were in command? Either the universe is mindless, or one supreme mind dictated the phenomenal world. Were the former true, we should be sorry to know it; were the former true, it could not be known, for the appearances of nature are against it. *The unity of the universe is the phenomenal sign of the unity of God.* From this conclusion there is no escape, either in religion or philosophy; to this truth both must forever cling.

Next, the beauty of nature has a very satisfactory explanation in Christianity. The relation of the sublime to religion, or of religion to the beautiful, is acknowledged; but the explanation of the relation is, as heretofore given, philosophical, rather than religious. The word "beauty" includes the total effect of order, form, proportion, harmony—every thing that goes to make up the idea itself, or contributes to the impression of the sublime. An object may be beautiful in form only, or grand from its magnitude, or attractive from its delicacy and minuteness. Yosemite Valley turns the traveler into a worshiper; Niagara Falls subdues the visitor into silence; an Autumn leaf speaks eloquently of approaching age, and mellows the spirit into sobriety and humility; a rose inspires a botanist to classify it and an artist to paint it; and unæsthetic minds can hardly resist the charm of a sunset, or the loveliness of a landscape, or the grandeur of the heavens. Matter, through its form, or qualities, or relations, addresses the æsthetic nature of man and satisfies it. The æsthetic faculty in man is proof of the æsthetic world external to man. Thomas Starr King regarded materialism as vicious, in that it brushes the halo from nature and shaves the twinkle from the stars. If the idea of God is repugnant to materialism, it is not surprising that any striking evidence of that idea is also repugnant to materialism. This is the turning-point in the thought: materialism shuts its eye to the beautiful, or rather, has no eye for the sublime in nature, while Christianity appropriates it, discovering in a decorated universe an additional proof of the mighty God. Jesus saw in the lily more beauty than in the gorgeous vestments of Solomon.

The idea of the grand, the sublime, is congenial to Christianity; it glows with the supernatural; now and then a miracle bursts forth from its mysteries, and wonders multiply with its revelations. The beautiful in nature is matched by the beautiful in Christianity; the wonders of nature, by the wonders of Christianity; the sublime of the natural, by the sublime of the spiritual and heavenly. The beautiful in the one is the key to the beautiful in the other.

The interpretation of nature is not complete. In these pages we have frequently referred to the laws and forces of the phenomenal world, as if they had an independent existence—as if they stood apart from matter, but were incorporated with it as the condition of physical government. Given an explanation of natural laws, and nature itself, so far forth as it is worth considering, is explained. One thing is certain, that a knowledge of these laws has been but slowly obtained, and not all are yet understood. Perhaps the future will bring to light laws of which we now have no thought. Whether new laws will be added to the list or not, it is a singular fact that the laws now recognized were discovered by believers in God, and not by infidels, atheists, rationalists, or materialists. This is a triumph of Christianity in a new field, and in a new and unexpected way. This statement may be denied or be regarded as too exclusive, but we challenge the materialist to overthrow it by proof of the contrary. Newton discovered the law of gravitation; Franklin gave us electricity in bottles; both were believers in God. Materialists and scientists opposed to Christian theology have discovered facts and announced theories; but we are now speaking of *laws*. Prof. Tyndall never discovered a law. Darwin suggested the "law" of the survival of the fittest, but it is a *theory*. Häckel constructs theories, and offers them as laws. Looking at the list of those who have revealed laws, the names of atheists and materialists will be conspicuously absent.

Now, this means something. It looks as if it means that Christianity qualifies the scientist for discovery, and materialism disqualifies for such work. It looks as if God has committed the revelation of the secrets of his universe to those who are in sympathy with himself, just as he committed the truths of his spiritual kingdom to those who believed in him. Nature, opaque and reserved to those who see not the divine foot-prints in her paths, turns lovingly to those who believe in her divine authorship, and pours forth into their hands the hidden treasures of her kingdom. If this be true, then Christianity and nature are on intimate terms, the precise character of their relationship being hitherto a matter of conjecture, but now the subject of revelation.

Socrates, discerning the intimacy of the natural and spiritual worlds, said that the laws below are *sisters* of those above; Bacon, more practical, but keen-sighted enough, said that nature and truth are like print and seal; and Swedenborg, mystical to the extreme, and seeing in things terrestrial the symbol of things celestial, invented a system of correspondences intended to express the hidden relationship; and recently, Henry Drummond has sought to establish the identity of natural and spiritual laws, or that the spiritual was projected into the natural, and rules all phenomena. In common with the above, Fourier, a French socialistic, styles social force as Passional Attraction, and regards the "Newtonian principle of attraction applicable to the social and mental worlds." In these theories, we see a disposition to link the natural and the spiritual, and to explain one by the other. To explain the spiritual by the natural might land us in materialism; to explain the natural by the spiritual will surely open up Christianity to our contemplation; and, so far forth as these theories are an attempt to explain the lower by the higher, they deserve approval, and, perhaps, should be adopted.

The theory of the identity of natural and spiritual laws, as propounded by Drummond, can not be dismissed by materialism as conjecture, or by theology as revolutionary, for it is of the nature of a revelation. The ground-thought of the theory is the naturalness of the supernatural and the supernaturalness of the natural, or the unity of the natural and spiritual worlds, which is a great if not a true thought, and to be candidly considered, whether accepted or rejected. If natural laws are "blood relations" of the spiritual laws, the mystery of the universe disappears, or deepens into the supernatural, which, as Christianity is supernatural, must tend to confirm it. "Law in the visible," says Drummond, "is the invisible in the visible." The spiritual world existed first; the natural world was created in its image; the laws of the higher were let down for governmental purposes into the lower, Hence, while the higher explains the lower, the lower may be the key to the higher. Gravitation, biogenesis, growth, death, and life, have their counterparts in the spiritual world; more, they are spiritual laws transferred to the natural sphere. Drummond resists the suggestion that possibly natural laws are analogous to spiritual laws, by saying "it is not a question of analogy, but of *identity.*" The entire code of natural laws, embracing chemical affinity, crystallization, capillary attraction, action and reaction, reflection, refraction, and combustion, is a transcript of laws that obtain in the spiritual world, or were initiated into existence in the realm of the supernatural.

Such is the theory. Much may be said in its favor; it is on the side of Christianity and a thunder-blow to materialism. If the theory is true the natural and spiritual worlds are one, and need not be considered apart; they are one in their government, one in law. Materialism admits the unity of the physical universe, but according to this theory and under the principle of continuity the natural and spiritual are one. The two are hemispheres; the seen and the unseen are one world.

Prof. Drummond urges that in this view religion has a new "credential," a "new basis," being supported scientifically as hitherto it has been supported dogmatically. This, we think, is true, and is good reason for accepting it. While religion can thus be made to rest upon a scientific basis, science will be compelled to be reconciled to religion. Science will assail the dogmatic basis; *the scientific basis it can not disturb.* At present this view of nature is not championed by theology, but science opposes theology because it refuses an explanation of spiritual truth from a scientific stand-point. However, as the spiritual world is understood to be a world of order, governed by law, and as spiritual truth is understood to be adumbrated by natural truth, so spiritual law will be made amenable to natural law, and spiritual methods be made to harmonize with natural methods. This conclusion will be reached without any detriment to revealed religion ; it will vindicate it and extinguish all traces of materialism in the thought of the world. The drift is toward a scientific explanation of religious truth. The Duke of Argyll fears that the natural is casting out the supernatural, but the fact appears to be that *the supernatural is casting out the natural.* Bushnell declares the supernatural to be compatible with the natural, and that God governs the world by a supernatural method, which is the same thing as saying that the natural is supernatural. Paul settles it when he says, "The things which are seen are temporal, but the things which are not seen are eternal." The eternal rules the temporal, is incorporated with it, and will exist after it has passed away. The identity of natural and spiritual laws establishes the reign of the supernatural in the universe, and the subordination of matter to spirit.

The danger at this point is the tendency to idealism, which reduces matter to nothing by exalting law, spirit, personalty, or something to dominion over it, but this kind of idealism is the idealism of Christianity. The unseen, whether law or spirit, is eternal.

As Christianity is unfolded and its principles are applied to the natural world, the problem of explanation of its relations and activities is emancipated from many difficulties, and the solution rendered more probable.

Nature and Christianity harmonize in their *moral lessons*, which is proof of a very intimate relationship, and that they are under one government and are endowed with similar functions and purposes. The perishability of the phenomenal world is an appalling fact to be explained only on moral grounds, and as having moral ends in view. Globes cease to revolve ; comets burst ; nature decays ; and terrestrial life is on a march to the tomb. The delicate flower fades, the ripest fruit perishes, and the stateliest work of God is reduced to dust. What is the explanation? Materialists run off into pessimism, saying the world is misgoverned and wrong is on the throne ; fatalists say it is the natural order, and must be borne with patience and without regret ; but the one walk as in the night, the other amid arctic blasts. Christianity relieves the scene of darkness and cold. It explains the inevitable destiny of nature with a clearness that is satisfactory, and with a dignity that is assuring. The divinest philosophy of matter is that of Paul, who pronounces things " seen " " temporal," and things unseen eternal. Matter is phenomenal, perishable ; the invisible is real, eternal. The moral lesson is to cling to the eternal.

Emerson defines the end of nature to be moral ; that is, its economy is adapted to discipline man, and, as discipline is the condition of development, it is adapted to the highest purposes of humanity. The moral idea of nature is grounded in its constitution and exhibited in its relations to man. But this transcendental notion harmonizes with the orthodox representation of the present life that it is a probation, or a moral trial, all its sufferings, frictions, and oppositions having in view the moral discipline and spiritual culture of man. *The becoming is the grindstone of being;* the phenomenal is turned to the refinement and spiritual sharpening of the intellectual and moral; the visible burnishes or brings to light the invisible.

Dropping to a practical level, or at least emerging from the mysticism of philosophy, we quote with approval the sentiment of Adam Smith, that nature is organized in "benevolent wisdom," having for its chief purpose the promotion of human happiness and the suppression of misery. Averaging the works of nature, and recognizing an evil bias in physical government, still there is an overbalancing propensity to good which in the fullness of the ages serves to secure happiness and repress misery. This is a check to pessimism, which sees a preponderance of evil in the universe, or, failing to strike the average, fixes its thought exclusively on evil, the disciplinary compensations and the all-sufficient counteractions not being recognized. Too much is made of evil as an argument for misgovernment; it is a proof of benevolent wisdom that good may be wrought out through suffering, and that the highest ends may be secured through the opposition or instrumentality of evil. The objective interpretation of nature, discovered in its relationship to ends, is a subject of vast interest, since it involves both religion and philosophy. Thus far it is on the side of religion.

Pantheism interprets nature philosophically in the interest of itself as a religion. Let us look at the interpretation of a false religion in contrast with that of the true religion. The study of its origin carries us back into the misty periods of Asiatic history, for the Eastern mind has always been given to mythological conceptions of nature, God, and man, resulting in systems of religion and philosophy that are marvels as mere systems, but of relative value only as truths. Looking into the phenomenal world the Eastern mind saw the presence of a governing spirit, apprehending it in its exhibitions of power and wisdom; but instead of separating the Ruler from the world, the two were united and pronounced one. Personality was lost in phenomena. Nature is God, is the pantheistic creed. Outside of nature, there is no power; nature is power, nature is wisdom; nature is justice. The blindness, the stupidity of this centralized conception is so apparent that one wonders if it could control a thoughtful mind; but it is both a religious and a philosophical sentiment. Pantheism is still an interpretation of nature, closely allied to the scientific interpretation which reduces the world to the mechanism of law. In fact, what is the mechanical view of the world, which eliminates God, but a form of pantheism? Häckel says the religion of the future will be the religion of nature, which is saying that there is no God but nature. Pantheism, therefore, is the legitimate fruit of mechanism as advocated by the materialists.

The Greeks had a way of looking at nature that rivals any modern attempt at sentimental expression, and if Christian theism were to be abandoned, or the Christian exposition of matter were superseded, the mythology of the Greeks would be as satisfactory to us as any thing yet suggested. Nature's forces were deified and worshiped, so that while a supreme god—Zeus—was acknowledged, the universe was apportioned to gods many, as Jupiter had the earth, Neptune the sea, and Pluto the infernal regions; there was also a god of agriculture, a god of war, gods representing all of nature's forces, and human conditions. This polytheistic interpretation inspired a reverence for nature which pantheism can not inspire. To be sure, it had its disadvantages, and was superseded, but it recognized nature as the product of godlike force, and saw a deific influence in superintendence of nature. Whether polytheism is to be preferred to all anti-theism is a question which we should not be long in deciding. The issue, however, in these days is not between an outgrown philosophic conception and a religious view of nature, but rather between anti-theistic philosophic conceptions, and the theistic apprehension of the world. To the latter both religion and philosophy now tend, and all religions and philosophies in conflict with it must subside. *The final cause of nature is moral, theistic.* To teach man the wisdom and power of God; to illustrate to him the divine goodness and the divine love of order; to impress upon him the certainty of retribution for violation of higher law and the expectation of reward for fidelity to truth; to *wean his mind from temporal things*, and *awaken in him a love of the eternal*; this is the *colossal explanation of nature* found in Christianity and found in no other religion or philosophy. With this explanation, we must be reverent in the presence of nature; we must worship in her temples, but avoid worshiping the temple; we must believe in her teachings but avoid making them the sole truths of religion; we must at last look away from nature to the religion she reveals, emphasizes, and proves, to him by whom and for whom all things consist.

# CHAPTER XXII.

## THE THEODICY OF CHRISTIANITY.

BÜCHNER is sponsor for the charge that Christianity has originated more crimes than it has hindered, a charge akin to that which makes liberty responsible for slavery, and life responsible for death. The implication is that the prevalence of the Christian religion contributes to human misery, notwithstanding its pretense of ability to relieve it, and that God, as revealed in the Scriptures, is in some way seriously involved in the existence and dominancy of evil. On the contrary, it is conceivable that the actual state of the world is not inherently depraved, and that whatever imperfection exists is quite incompatible with the known designs of the great Ruler, who in his own time will extinguish it, and demonstrate the ascendency of his reign in the universe. Just what is conceivable is actually the fact, as we shall discover.

Christianity is an explanation of evil, as respects its origin, nature, purposes, and destiny, and equally an explanation of man's moral condition, as affected by evil, and as it may be improved by religion. It relieves God from responsibility for sin; it relieves humanity from a traditional opprobrium which has long paralyzed its self-effort for moral elevation; it relieves theology from falsehood and crudity; it relieves Christianity from any voluntary participation in human degradation and sorrow. If it is assumed that the existence of evil can be vindicated from the revelations of Christianity, and that its mission is related to the progress of the world, according to the intent of religion, some of our readers will doubtless be startled, and imagine that a problematical reason for evil has been discovered. We shall not assume so much; we shall assume nothing. The awfulness of evil can not be overrated, its existence can not be palliated; but, *inasmuch as it is,* if it can be shown that it is in the power of God to employ it in divine purposes, and as an auxiliary force in the development of his kingdom, a reason for its being may be announced. Its origin is bad, but its instrumental mission or uses may possibly be made under the divine control subservient to divine ends.

A superficial view of man's environment or of his natural character as inherited, and debased by a wrong development, is not likely to captivate the senses, or satisfy the thinking of an honest soul. A close scrutiny of his environment, inherently deficient in means of alleviation, has produced the extremes of pessimism and atheism. No thoughtful or sympathetic mind will deny any fact of evil, any want of adaptation, any dissonance in life, pointed out by the pessimist or observer. We are quite willing to admit the history of evil and even to add to what he has angrily declared to exist. It is useless to hide the facts, as glaring as day, and to regard them as temporary blemishes, for they are deep-rooted, universal, and as painful as the intensity of life will permit. Even the blind see crookedness in the ways of the world. Smoke eclipses the sun, and the race walks on edges in darkness. The earth rocks like a ship in a tempest and reels like a drunken man in the mountains. It almost shakes itself out of its orbit, so wide-spread are its convulsions. Peace is on a visit to another planet. War reigns here; war with the elements, war with law, war with disease, war with ignorance, war with death. Underneath the apparently fixed order of things there is a kind of nihilism at work, if not to destroy, at least to torment, and render abortive the best attempts of the race to rise to nobler things. Irregularity, confusion, distress, failure, are the common items of human experience. Cæsar is on the throne, Job sits on an ash-heap; Dives is in his palace, Lazarus is in rags at the gate. Exaggeration of human experience in its distressful content is impossible. Let the pessimist paint the picture dark—we shall undertake to add a darker shade. Let him write gloom on the ground—we will engrave it on the stars.

But what of it all? What of midnight? Is there no day? Facts first, then explanations. The origin of evil is a problem by itself; the uses of evil, or its possible helpfulness in the world's upward movements, may be made to appear in the light of its history. It is the *uses* of evil that now concern us. The origin of evil is the subject-matter of explanation; but, if its uses can be made clear, man's unhappy lot will have a partial explanation. Let it not be supposed, however, that Christianity is obscurely silent on the original problem, for, if its revelations are not transparent, they are more satisfactory than any thing propounded by philosophy. What, forsooth, does philosophy propose as its theodicy? Does it point to the laws of heredity as the cause of vice? *Heredity is only a method of transmission of the evil tendency;* it is not an explanation of the origin or nature of the tendency. M. Caro, of the French Academy, contradicts the theory of heredity as explanatory of the passage of the sinful tendency, insisting that personality or individuality can not be inherited, but temperament and physical types only may pass from generation to generation. If evil is the taint of personality, and the origin of personality is not in heredity, then the origin of evil is not *via* heredity.   This is a new idea in philosophy, but it is invulnerable, and disposes of heredity as the genesis of sin.   The broader theory of evolution is sometimes summoned to account for the introduction of evil, but it applies only, if at all, to the development of the vicious nature, and not to its beginning.   Pitiful, indeed, are the attempts of philosophers to reveal the foundations of the evil government in the universe, and equally insufficient their account of its historic convolutions.   To Christianity the inquirer must turn for explanations of the first appearance of diabolism in the universe; if disappointed here, the hope of explanation must be abandoned.

For the Bible explanation of evil, it is not claimed that it is altogether complete or transparent, since it is wanting in certain data that belong to the initial stages of its history, or, what is more important, it is wanting in specific statement concerning the original impulse to evil.   Carlyle says original sin is the vanishment of the conception of God from men's minds.   God is absent from human thought—this is the beginning of sin.   Given the source, and the stream follows.   Christianity is a revelation of such facts as are absolutely necessary to individual redemption; it does not seek to satisfy curiosity, or make known that which, however important to intellectual development hereafter, is not important to moral living here. For this reason, the explanation is allegorical, incomplete, hintful, but not a revelation that satisfies.   However, evil had a definite beginning, a point of departure, in the earth's history.   That at one time it broke out in heaven, is proof that its possibility has run parallel with eternal righteousness.   Theoretically, it may do to say it has always existed, as the opposite of the idea of right, and this without any blemish on the divine government.   If, as Dr. Whedon says, the power to sin implies no imperfection in character, so the possibility of evil, inherent in the constitution of things, inherent in the idea of existence, implies no imperfection of government or things. Possibilities are without moral qualities.   *The possibility of evil is not an evil.*   Evil, as a possibility, is eternal.   From possibility it descended into reality, heaven first feeling its touch when it undertook to despoil the throne of the great King, but, failing in its purpose, it began its destructive work in the earth, where it still abides to torture the innocent and wreak its vengeance on the family of God.   Its introduction to our globe is related in the Scriptures, of which various interpretations have been given; but, however understood, certain it is that, from the hour when Eve coqueted with the serpent, evil has been the tremendous fact in human history.   The account is true in essence, and a solemn satisfaction is the product of faith in it.

The more vital problem is the relation of evil to human life.

Whether the universe, all worlds, all creatures, are corrupted, or are the victims of an evil spirit, we know not; it is enough to know that humanity groans and waits for deliverance. Human history is the joint product of good and evil forces in ceaseless operation, the one now, and then the other, apparently in the ascendant, but together working out the one magnificent result of human progress, and the reign of the divine principle in the world's affairs. As the ocean tide includes both ebbing and flowing, so human history includes retardation as well as progression. History is the arena or play-ground of antagonistic forces, each bent on the exactly opposite idea of the other. One is good, the other is evil. To explain the relation, interaction, and counteraction of these forces, or the presence of evil in history, the framer of a theodicy is under obligation. In essaying such a task, it is not incumbent upon us to explain every incident of evil, every fact of suffering, every accident or injustice; but rather to consider the whole in the light of certain principles, under which the details of life may be grouped. Without these principles, it will be impossible to explain any thing; with them, it may be difficult to explain a particular incident. But, as gravitation explains all falling bodies, so these principles, it is believed, will explain evil as a whole. If they do not, we shall have to surrender the task and settle into the ignorance of mystery.

Of the mission of evil, inferred from the uses to which Providence devotes it, we submit a tentative explanation. The word "evil" we use in a generic sense, including in it all the irregularities, disorders, incongruous complications, and chaotic conditions of man's natural life, arising from his environment, as well as the ignorance, falsehoods, oppositions, cruelties, bad governments, false religions, and sins justly chargeable to himself. It signifies the aggregate of disorders in man's world-life, the physical, intellectual, and moral obstructions to his happiness, development, and destiny. By the mission of evil, in this largest sense, we mean its moral ends, or the providential employment of evil as an instrument in the securing of moral results, possibly not attainable by other methods.

In our observations of God's government of the world, we are apt to overlook the fact that evil is under the restraints of law, or, to express it in another form, that *evil is the product of law*. This is a perfectly safe proposition, when examined in the light of its supports. Acknowledging the existence of God and the reign of a providential government, the idea of chance is inadmissible as an explanation of any thing. Accident is unknown in a providential government. No event happens that is not the result either of direct divine supervision or of the operation of fixed and beneficent laws. Evil, therefore, must be the decreed result of divine Providence, which is a rejectable hypothesis, or the natural product of laws and forces, and, therefore, both in bondage to them and an orderly produced result, which approximates the truth if it does not declare it wholly. Nature's irregularities or disorders do not happen except in harmony with law, and are the products of law. The inconstant wind, sweeping over a prairie, is as much the product of law as the trade wind, which has a meteorological mission. The tempest at sea is as methodical in its procedure as the tides. Nature's laws will produce poisons, as well as agreeable and nutritious fruits. Zoölogy points out monsters of the forest; ichthyology tells of fishes without eyes; and natural history reveals insects with a stinging apparatus. All these are as much the products of laws as animals that are useful, as fishes with eyes, as insects that are harmless. Calamities, resulting from a supposed violation of nature's laws, are in the line of nature's order, and as lawful as her benedictions. To say that the explosion of a steam boiler is the result of violated law is a very superficial explanation, for, while it may involve the carelessness of the engineer, the explosion occurred in obedience to law. It is not an anti-lawful result. The Ashtabula bridge disaster was the result of the law of gravitation.

Approaching a little nearer the line, the diseases from which man suffers are not chance results, but the products of law, a study of which enables the physician to master them and rescue the patient. The diagnosis is along the line of causation—the track of law; the prognosis is along the line of effects, recognized through the lens of law. Fever has its laws; consumption, rheumatism, neuralgia, ague, all occur in obedience to law. Intermittent heart-beats result from law, quite as much as the regular pulse.

Evidently, the disorders, the sufferings, the irregularities in human history are the consequences of law, and not of lawlessness. This does not involve God in close partnership with evil, but is an evidence that he is on the throne, and that evil is under divine restraint. It has the bandage of law about it. Evil, as the result of divine caprice, would be intolerable; but evil, so-called, as the result of law, does not invalidate the benevolence of the Deity. Evil is not arbitrary, therefore; it arises from the constitution of things, and can not well be avoided.

Many of the sufferings of mankind are due to natural environment, which consists of, or abounds in, disorders and irregularities, that issue in a regular succession from the operation of fixed laws, and are inevitable. They constitute a part of human history, from the necessities of the situation, a situation divinely ordered and pre-arranged.

If the foregoing is at all rational, one may be justified in suspecting that evil, in its broadest sense, as a constitutional disorder, has a place assigned it on the divine programme of the world.

Let us see how far the suspicion is correct. The teleology of evil can not be expressed by fatalism, or Calvinism, or by any short-hand method. If evil is the result of law, it anticipates an end, for law strives toward an end and always means an end. It is a scientific theory that progress is an end of nature ; its rule is the " survival of the fittest;" it proclaims that through gradual processes, intricate and long-continued, and even obstinate and persistent, the world will arrive at an improved condition. Nature, history, man, unite in proclaiming the end of the world-life to be progress. To this theory we subscribe in full faith. Now, does evil in any wise interfere with the execution of the historic idea or plan of progress? In still narrower yet stronger, phrase does evil successively check the natural, historic providential program of progress? We do not ask if evil retards human progress, for it does retard it, as we see it, or if it would not entirely prevent progress, were it not overcome, for it undoubtedly would stay the world's march. But evil as a friction or retarding obstacle, and evil as the extinguisher of progress, are quite different things. The former, evil is ; the latter, it is not. Notwithstanding the obstacles to progress, history on the whole reports progress ; the gains exceed the losses ; the friction movements are overcome by the radical progressive currents; and the world rises slowly, comparing with joy its present with its past. What does this signify? That the designs of Providence can co-exist with evil and evolve into success : that in spite of it and by its aid God's purpose will triumph ; that the divine idea of the world will round out in complete and concrete beauty, notwithstanding evil, like a mountain, stands in its path and disputes its success. *Evil is not a hindrance to the execution of the providential idea.* This is the broad view of evil. If not a final or fatal hindrance, it may prove to be a co-operating force in the progress of the world.

The particular view is almost personal. What is the relation of evil to the individual? To what uses may it be applied in the prophetic development of human character? If evil will not prevent the fulfillment of the providential idea respecting the world as a whole, will it interfere with the providential idea respecting the individual? The development of the individual is a wholesome possibility. He has a mind that may be expanded, a soul that needs cultivation. To secure his development two methods suggest themselves: 1. By an uninterrupted flow of truth into the mind ; 2. By struggle. The first method God has not ordained ; the second method is universal. Being universal, we are moved to say it is providential or natural, arising from man's environment, and his own inherited deficiencies of sloth, passion, ignorance, and depravity. Either the environment must be changed, and man's nature be different, or struggle with the environment, and struggle with one's self must surely follow. Struggle is the logical necessity. But struggle implies a world of evil, so-called. Ignorant, a struggle for knowledge is imperative; environed with laws, forces, solid forms of matter, a struggle for acquaintance with laws and mastery of forces is indicated; possessed of passions and appetites anxious for excessive gratification, a struggle for self-control and purity is foreshadowed. Education, righteousness, order, life, signify struggle. Bread, health, society, government, all mean struggle. The condition of man is the condition of discipline, the thoroughness of which is made to depend on the strength and acuteness of the forces summoned against him. The use of obstacles, the virtue of discipline, is conceded in some departments of life. Poverty is pronounced a blessing when it leads a young man to self-effort, developing independence, integrity, courage, faith, genuine manhood. Webster was indebted to his obstacles, and Jesus to his temptations. Stones in one's path often prove to be stepping-stones to the heights.

If the general principle is true, then its application must be true. If poverty, opposition, persecution, are the conditions of development, then suffering, temptation, sickness, and sorrow may open the life in its manifold possibilities. If discipline or development be the end of evil, it in a sense justifies evil as a providential instrument in human history.

Another general fact which has not had full consideration in theology is the *self-destroying power of evil*, or the providential restriction imposed upon it, and the providential provisions for its extinction. Satan is in chains, and within the range of the chains his power is tremendous, and its exercise is dreadfully apparent. But we mean more than a general circumscription. Among the divine plans for the upbuilding of the world in righteousness not one is more conspicuous than that which in the long run arrays evil against evil, and produces its destruction. In this way error dies amid its worshipers. Evil destroys evil, as one nail drives out another. War is organized barbarity, a type of evil, but the American war of 1861–1865 resulted in the extinction of slavery. Great evils arise, rooting themselves in customs, legislation, and social forms, and even take a religious name and threaten the subversion of our ideals of government, and we wonder how they will be circumvented and overthrown. Sometimes by righteous methods, sometimes by the peaceful exercise of civil authority; but often mammoth evils go down by the resisting power of other evils, as the pirates' ship goes down in the storm. Purgatives may be evils, but they expel disease ; counter-irritants may be severe, but they draw enemies from the vitals. The French revolution was a dreadful evil, but it was a remedy for a worse evil. This providential method we may not fancy, since it involves suffering, but it is a providential method, and often explains the rise and fall of evils.

In still another aspect evil will appear as a providential instrument for beneficent ends. Let us take the world as it has been, as it is, full of wicked men, plotting for empire, the subjugation of the races, and the conquest of the hemispheres. Who or what can resist the surgings of political evil, the tides of ungodly ambition, that carry the Neros and Napoleons far toward success? The frame-work of villainy is visible in the schemes of statesmen and rulers and warriors. What can overthrow them but Providence, by methods that may entail suffering, and at the same time conquer the lusts of men? Evil may not only be employed in resisting evil, but in resisting evil men. It was an evil that chained Napoleon on St. Helena, and rid Europe of its enemy. Caligula went out by the assassin's blow. The sword was drawn, and Belshazzar and his drunken lords perished. The fatal cup of intemperance was drunk, and Alexander, who had despoiled the eastern hemisphere, was himself a corpse. The worms seized him, and Herod was dead. The winds blew, and the Spanish Armada was no more, and England was saved. If there must be evil, God can use it in the restraining of the wicked, in the punishment of the guilty, and even in the extinction of the gross evils that afflict mankind.

Looking again at the world as it is, with false religions in the ascendency in the East, and bad governments in power, it is evident that Providence has his hand upon them, and is turning them to advantage in the execution of his purposes. However evil may have been introduced, it was introduced, and contaminated the springs of human history. The natural man is ignorant, selfish, cruel, without the capability of self-government, without apprehension of spiritual truths. The lower forms of government, such as despotism and aristocracies, grew out of man's natural condition, and were inevitable ; and, without the Bible, false and superstitious religions were equally inevitable. It would be presumption to deny to these political forms of despotism any virtue or mission ; it would be the extreme of bigotry to deny even to false religions a place in the divine program. Despotism and superstition, with all their crimes and cruelties, have been providentially linked with the world's destinies, and have been used in the preservation of the religious idea amid ages of darkness, and in preparing the world for the reception of the Gospel, and of democratic ideals of government. God's truth has had partial embalmment in superstition, and heathen sages have piloted the heathenish millions through the uncertain past to the hopeful present. Thus in these things God's hand is seen, and his plan is visible.

From this brief survey of the empire of evil, we conclude it is under the dominion of divine law and restraint, and that disorder, irregularity, disease, suffering, poverty, persecution, war, slavery, intemperance, assassination, crime, superstition, and despotism; yea, all evils are reckoned in the category of divine instruments for the accomplishment of divine purposes, the fulfillment of which is as certain as that God rules. The world exists for a purpose which is ripening every hour, and evil, restrained and divinely directed, but adds to its unfolding and perfection. Through the lenses of history, Scripture, observation, and experience, we conclude that evil, however originated, has now a providential mission, and is in haste to perform it, and in the performance itself will expire.

In the foregoing analysis or explanation the direct reference is to natural evil, as if it were the supreme and solitary fact in the universe, while theologians devote their theodicies to moral evil, the reign of which is as conspicuous as the reign of natural evil. The question then is relevant: is there any difference between natural and moral evil? If a difference, what is the relation of the one to the other? Evil is evil, whether it be physical, intellectual, or spiritual; it differs not in essence, but in intensity only. The distinction between the two evils is one of convenience only; it is not founded in any difference between the evils themselves, so that an account of one will serve as an account of the other. Natural evil is only the grosser form of the wrong spirit in the universe, and attaches itself to physical objects, while moral evil is the refined type of the same spirit, afflicting the minds and souls of men. If natural evil is under law and the product of law, so is moral evil. If there are uses to which natural evil may be devoted, there are uses to which moral evil may be devoted. As showing the intimate relation of the two, natural evil is often employed to serve moral ends, and moral evils sometimes are made to contribute to natural ends. It is believed that cholera visits civilized countries once in seventeen years for moral ends; that commercial panics are affected by the spots on the sun; that comets are the vanguard of trouble; that earthquakes are intended to shake the people into a recognition of moral principles; and that nature often disturbs the race in order to impress it with the thought of God. Trenching on superstition as these views may seem to do, it can not be resisted that natural evil is often the source of moral evil, and that the two are indissolubly related. The ancient theologian was disposed to attribute all evil, both natural and moral, to the forensic sin of Adam; and Milton, adopting the sentiment, echoed it in lofty phrase until it became the current doctrine of the Church; but is not the truth exactly the reverse, namely, that moral evil is the result of natural evil, and that natural evil is the result of the constitution of things? *Evil is the constitutional disorder of the universe.* Moral evil is the contagion of natural evil, the outgrowth and reality of constitutional possibilities.

There was a time when it was important to vindicate the goodness and holiness of God in the presence of evil, for it was assumed that in some way it compromised the perfections of the Deity. Dr. A. T. Bledsoe, seeing the inconsistency of the implication, defends the attributes of God in a masterly exposition of the principles of the divine government; but it occurs to us that such vindication is no longer necessary. A mistake is made in involving the divine perfections in the problem; the problem can only include the divine ideas or purposes in reference to the human race. Eliminating the perfections, and including only the divine purposes, the relation of evil to the universe has an explanation, and that explanation is God's vindication.

If, instead of regarding evil as the result of broken law, it is regarded as the result of *executed* law, its explanation will be still more definite. Evil is sometimes a penalty and sometimes a discipline. As a penalty, it is always the result of enforced law. A murderer violates law; the violated law does not punish him; if the punishment is the sting of conscience, then a moral law is executed; or, in other words, an executed rather than a broken law is the source of his affliction; if he must suffer capital punishment, it is not by virtue of the law he violated. Another law, which he did not violate at all, hangs him. Wherever evil is suffered as a penalty, it is by virtue of executed law, which implies the authority of the law-maker in the land.

As a discipline, evil must be considered on other grounds. The earlier Calvinian schools were inclined to interpret evil only as a penalty; but evidently this is too narrow a view of it, since infants, not having sinned, and animals, not having violated any law, are the subjects of suffering, the explanation of which can not be referred to the word penalty. The final causes of evil are not penal but moral. Suffering has a mission. It is not inflicted always as a punishment. Advocating it as a penalty, the theologians had to rescue God from ungracious imputations, and save the world from pessimism; but the task was too great. Evil as a discipline, or with moral ends in view, makes a theodicy possible. It is the turning of the immoral into moral uses, as night is made to serve certain benevolent purposes in nature.

Following the course of evil in its assaults upon the Church, or the movements of Christianity, one is astonished at the beneficent result. As an organized agency for the spread of Christianity, the Church has been the target of enmity since the days of the divine Founder; its pathway has been marked with blood, and its history is full of flame and suffering. Even in the days of its greatest conquests, paganism resisted its advances with defiant contradiction, and its progress has ever been over obstacles so numerous and so great that one wonders that the Church is a living institution to-day, and can account for it on no other ground than that it is stronger than evil. Think of the martyrdom that occupies so prominent a place in the world's history, of the cruel laws against Christians, of mobs, fagots, dungeons, and gladiatorial sports, all directed and employed for the extinction of the rising faith and the suppression of the Church. Evil, in its historic relations to the Church, is seen on a stupendous scale; organized and palpitating with hate, it undertakes to destroy the only institution whose chief object is the salvation of the world. To explain evil as a penalty will not explain its assaults upon Christianity or the Church, any more than it will explain the sufferings of animals and infants. To assert that God builds his Church for high moral ends, and then engages evil to try to destroy it, as a punishment for sins it never committed, is so palpable an absurdity that it is mere trifling to notice it; and yet certain old-time theologians embraced the absurdity with as much sincerity as if it had been a truth.

The explanation of the illicit relations of evil with the Church is in the moral ends finally wrought out by Christianity itself. The testing of Christianity as a system of religion was at stake in these historic oppositions; they were permitted in order to prove Christianity, and they did establish it as true in the eyes of the world. Polemical discussions of Christianity were insufficient to vindicate it from aspersion and misconstruction; logical abstractions and analytic definitions of truth did not overcome the doubt and rancor of the opposition; even the saintly lives of Christ's followers were robbed of their force by false report; but *the survival of Christianity in spite of the malice and trial of eighteen centuries is the refutation of all opposition, and the prophecy of its future.* The use of trial in the establishment of religion is therefore justified.

On a smaller scale, but with the same purpose in view, the Christian is the subject of trial, and ripens only as he is disciplined. The Christian hero is impossible except in a world of conflict. Patience is possible only amid an irritating environment. Virtue is possible where vice is possible also. Right character is possible only in proportion as wrong character is possible. The afflictions of the righteous are intended to establish him in the faith, to test his integrity, to prove to him the truth of what he believes. The whole brood of evils, from martyrdom down to the slightest ridicule, from flames to a finger raised in derision, from death to the smallest slander, is intended to make strong the believer in God, and to build up the Church with *fire-proof material*, that it may stand throughout all ages. Discipline explains temptation, affliction, ignorance; it explains man's pitiful lot and his hopeful future. Drummond calls the evil in man a "retrogade principle," to overcome which even more than atonement is necessary. Atonement by Jesus Christ is the initial and fundamental support of the Christian life; but in a sense the human subject must atone himself for sin and work out his own salvation by the discipline of suffering. *What we call evil, therefore, may be atonement for evil, as it certainly is discipline by evil.* In one of his voyages Captain Cook landed on one of the Friendly Islands, whose inhabitants were so ignorant of the nature of animals in general that on seeing the sheep and goats in the ship they called them *birds*. We smile at their ignorance, but our ignorance of what are evils and what are not may be as dense as was theirs of the animal kingdom. Disciplinary events, or trials, helping men to holier living, may not be evils at all, as sheep are not birds.

In the attempt to explain evil as a discipline, we almost pass beyond the border-land of evil, and find ourselves in another region of fact. Suffering is not necessarily an evil. Darkness is not light, but it may be as useful as the light. Death is not to be compared with life, but death is not an unmixed evil. An extremist might deny the existence of evil, but as a disciplinary instrument it overcomes the evil intent and contributes to the world's progress and happiness. Considering evil as a penalty it is just, and, therefore, no compromise of the divine government; as a discipline, admitting its existence as evil, it vindicates itself, and requires no further explanation.

The relation of evil to the theistic hypothesis is of more importance than its relation to the divine perfections. Is evil consistent with the idea of Deity at all? One studying the world from the materialistic standpoint might conclude that it is in anarchy and without a moral ruler; but the reverse is the truth. *That evil follows the track of causation is proof that a higher power has imposed upon it the restraints, and given it the direction, of law.* With this view the theistic hypothesis is easily maintainable. But this is not the all-important point at this time. Evil exists as an apparent disturber of divine plans and ideas. This is the *evil of evil.* So far forth as it succeeds in effecting a collapse of a divine idea, it is evil; but so far forth as it fails to undermine a divine idea, evil does not result, although the conflict with it may be painful and protracted. If divine ideas are working out their lawful results, it is proof that a divine being is at the helm of the universe. As these plans broaden and eventuate in reality, evil is circumscribed, defeated, and destroyed. The shadow of the Infinite presses hard upon the darkness of sin, and ever drives it toward its last resting-place. The conflict of evil and righteousness is apparent in all history and attested by all experience; but, as it goes on, the turning of victory on the side of righteousness is visible, and God comes out of the shadows and dazzles the eyes of men with the brightness of his glory. In these triumphs over evil the reign of divine authority is as conspicuous as the virulence of the enmity that disputes it. Looking at the general trend of human history toward righteousness and the perpetual tendency of the world, so to speak, to right itself, the conclusion of divine rule is satisfactory, and the hope of the final triumph of truth is well-grounded in those probabilities which the providential government continually inspires.

Evil has its hour, its apparent triumph, but its destruction is foretold by the sacred writers, and is one of the animating purposes of Jesus Christ. He came to destroy the works of the devil. Wide as has been the desolation of evil, infectious and self-propagating as it is by nature, it has been circumscribed, and its progress stayed. Its future disappearance is one of the predicted certainties of Christianity. A true theodicy has only to recognize the purposes of God respecting its manifested power in order to escape metaphysical inconsistencies and justify its presence in the world. If it is God's purpose utterly to destroy it, leaving no trace of its existence in the universe, he is exhaustively vindicated from all reproach, and stands before his creatures as guiltless of all sin. *The framer of a theodicy must confine himself to divine purposes, as the key to the divine character; but the early theologians felt that the divine character must on a priori grounds be first studied and supported; hence, the weakness of theodicy in general.*

If it is one of the divine purposes to extinguish evil, as Christianity affirms it is, a bold thinker might wonder why it takes so long to do it, especially when the infinity of the divine resources is considered. This reflects somewhat on the tardiness or inefficiency of the divine methods, and calls for explanation. No theodicy is possible that attempts to build itself on the divine administration alone or on

God's relation to the world. Man is an important factor in the great problem, is as essential to it as God. *The freedom of man is the explanation of the slow evolution of the world into holiness.* Man is responsible for present sin. With the divine agencies at his command and the lessons of human experience as inspirations, he might remove evil from the face of the earth. Freedom invests man with wonderful power and corresponding responsibility; it is for him to say how long evil shall continue its ruinous work in the world. This goes back to the constitution of things, and raises the question, Why is man free if freedom involves not only the possibility of evil, but its certainty? Before the divine mind there was the alternative to create a race, holy in nature and restrained from sin, and, therefore, mechanically constrained to righteousness, or to create a race with a free-will, implying all the possibilities and certainties of evil, with the ability through grace to overcome it, and stand before their Maker as the voluntary subjects of holiness. The divine Ruler preferred the latter; hence, man is free; and, being free, he sins, and, sinning, he delays God's idea of holiness, and, that idea delayed, man suffers and death reigns. God is responsible for making men free; men are responsible for abusing their freedom to their own degradation.

Further examination enables us to conclude that evil, understood in its relations to time and eternity, has a bearing on one of the most dreadful doctrines of Christianity, namely, that of hell, or future retribution, against which materialism has spoken with fierce and angry tones, and in evident revolt against the truth. That the doctrine is Biblical, it goes without saying Is it a true doctrine? The scientific method of proof would require its vindication from natural religion, or the teachings of nature; for, if nature foreshadows the principle of retribution, the Christian religion can not be impugned if it teaches it openly.

No scientist doubts the orthodoxy of nature respecting the law of suffering and punishment. The physical world, with its unchanging laws, is regarded by materialists as a testimony against the doctrine of a benevolent Ruler; for these laws are never suspended in the interest of man, and his history is one of incessant struggle with them. On the whole, nature is declared to be against man. He, therefore, suffers. Whether this be a true view or not, it should prove to the materialist that, if the God of nature has so arranged the physical universe as to produce suffering, it makes not against the God of the Bible if it is proven that he has so arranged the spiritual universe as to be productive of suffering also. If the natural world is ceaselessly active in inflicting suffering, the spiritual world may be ceaselessly active in inflicting it also. The grim testimony of nature is not, therefore, against the doctrine of future retribution, and the God of the Bible can not be condemned any more than the God of nature.

The fact of evil in this life may be suggestive of evil in the next life. What is the evil of this life? Natural evil, or the evil of environment, the cause of untold suffering from the cradle to the grave; moral evil, or the evil of personality, the cause of subjective misery and death. The evil of condition and character here may portend the evil of condition and character there. If the eternal condition has in it the possibility of evil, it has also the possibility of hell; and if it involves the certainty of evil, it involves the certainty of hell.

If personal character, once formed, is irreversible, having in it the potency of evil, what is to hinder hell from becoming a personal experience? "Myself am hell," says Milton's Satan.

What are the conclusions?

1. Christianity fully recognizes the *origin, potency, and influence of evil in the universe.* Emerson makes little of sin, but Jesus Christ makes much of it.

2. Evil is the *possibility of the constitution of things,* without involving the divine government in imperfection or reproach.

3. As a constitutional disorder, *evil is under law,* and is the product of law.

4. The distinction between natural and moral evil is puerile, and can have no place in a true theodicy.

5. A constitutional disorder, its final cause is a providential purpose, and, instrumentally, it serves a providential mission.

6. Employed as an instrument, God's character is not involved in its activities or results. The basis of theodicy is not God's character, but *God's purposes.*

7. Evil has a place in the category of realities as a *penalty,* and, as such, it is just; it must be viewed also as a *discipline,* and, as such, the gains from it have exceeded the losses; it is also a partial *atonement* for sin, which, joined to the atonement of Jesus Christ, affords an adequate remedy for the world's inclination to wrong.

8. The history of evil furnishes proof of the existence of God, and its gradual extinction is evidence of the reign of divine wisdom, and the authority of a divine purpose.

9. The continued existence of sin is no reflection on the character of God, but is proof of the freedom of man. Man, not God, is responsible for sin.

10. As evil is the possibility of the constitution of the universe, so *hell is the possibility of the constitution of evil.*

# CHAPTER XXIII.

## THE IDEAL SOCIETY; OR THE RELATION OF CHRISTIANITY TO SOCIETY.

TO the thought of the historic Greeks, the millennium or golden age of mankind had, long before their day, arrived and departed, never to return; it was participated in by their godlike ancestors, who were a superior race, and specially favored by the supreme powers. As to the future of the world, they anticipated stagnation of political forces, decay of the best civilizations, degradation of social order, arrest of individual development, and the appearance of an inferior race of human beings, whose history would end in colossal convulsions and final and exhaustive exterminations. The tone of Grecian prophecy is leaden, sepulchral, uninvigorating.

Taught by a truer inspiration, the ancient Jew reversed the dark anticipations of the Greek, holding that the Past was the age of inferiority, limitation, incipiency, while the bow of promise spanned the future, and illuminated the eye-ball of nations. The tone of Jewish prophecy is sanguine and assuring, and, by its incorporation into Christianity, it has become the stronghold of faith respecting man and the future—a view that sweeps away pessimism, stimulates philosophy to right thinking, quickens the indifferent energies of slow-going peoples, and floods the world with optimistic thoughts of the race's development.

It is not our purpose, at this moment, to describe the future man, or indicate the peculiarities of future civilizations, under the operation of either philosophy or Christianity, or both, as this will appear in the later and larger discussion of the subject; but, first of all, to consider if an ideal state, in an experimental or absolute form, is at all possible, and whether it may be realized sooner and more permanently through Christianity than by any philosophical system or basis of life. In other words, must systems of sociology rest upon a purely philosophical or theological basis?

Whether naturalistic or supernaturalistic agencies must be chief in social reconstructions, we shall learn in this review. No less than *eight* distinctive theoretical or experimental ideas or bases of human society, a brief notice of which can only be given here, human history furnishes for our instruction and guidance.

I. Perhaps as prominent as any, and certainly more forceful

than many, is the *ecclesiastical idea* of human society. To this, in the
general, and so far as it partakes of, or borrows its spirit from, apostolic ideals, no exception can be taken ; but, in searching and following the historic development and application of the idea, we come
in contact with strange ecclesiasticisms, embodying centralization, intolerance, and stagnation, and appearing in our day as the monumental forms of bigoted force. Three such ecclesiasticisms readily
occur to us. The Roman Catholic conception of human society
concreted in the eleventh century in Hildebrand, than whom a more
aggressive and successful exponent of papal ideas and papal policies
never lived. Long before he assumed the miter, he was the acknowledged influence in the circles of the Church, and began even early in
his monastic career to meditate upon a scheme for the consolidation
of political and spiritual power that has not been paralleled in human
annals ; and, under his own administration, the consolidation was
virtually effected. He conceived that the pope should be the ruler
in temporal, no less than in spiritual, affairs ; that he should be the
head of the Church, infallible in his ecclesiastical judgments, and that
all temporal rulers should pay him homage and tribute, and that the
whole world should regard him as its lawful potentate and as God's
vicegerent on earth. The scheme was magnificent in outline, and
plausible as a proclamation. It meant the priority of the Church in
all things, temporal and spiritual ; it meant the heroic domination
of Christian ideas in civil governments ; it meant one source of authority and uniformity of rule throughout the world ; *it meant unity
of civilizations, unity of social structures, unity of religious worship, unity
of human responsibility.* Vast, heroic, magnificent, as the scheme was,
it was not without serious internal weaknesses, which manifested
themselve, like incurable diseases, as it was unfolded and executed.
It possessed heterogeneous elements, which interfered with its application ; it wrought out its anticipated unities, not by spontaneous and
natural methods, but by force, which alienated instead of cementing
them ; aggressive in its purpose, it became oppressive in its plans ;
unyielding to circumstances, it awakened resistance, and, instead of
giving peace, it produced war. For a period accepted, human society
degenerated under its authority ; the Bible was unopened to the
masses ; ignorance was a virtue ; absolution from sin became pur-
chasable ; martyrdoms multiplied ; kings and parliaments violated
compacts with Rome ; kings were unkinged ; parliaments were dissolved ; human legislation was rebuked, and legislators were defied ;
and such were the tumults, frictions, conflicts of authority, general
degradation of the people, poverty, crime, social disorders, persecutions, and bigotries that it produced, that a protest of the nations

was made against it in the form of a Reformation. The Roman Catholic idea of religious centralization has demonstrated its unfitness and inability in its historical trial.

Under Henry VIII. the ecclesiastical idea tended to a similar result, but being narrower in its range, and avoiding some of the conceded errors of the papal scheme, it never rounded out in complete development. However, in its thought of the centralization of religious power; in its selfish conception of one visible Church, the sole ruler in religious affairs; and in its claim of antecedent connection with the apostolic or original Church, it was not less vehement than its predecessor, the Roman Catholic hierarchy. As to the supremacy of ecclesiastical authority in temporal governments, and the subjection of the people to its social order, the Episcopal scheme is less objectionable than the other. Still, wherever the consolidation of the temporal and spiritual has been at all a possibility, as to some extent in England, the result has been religious proscription, a heterogeneous civilization, and a divided government. Not under this milder type of Hildebrand's scheme is a reconstruction of society desirable, for in effect it means the same thing.

In the American colonies there appeared a peculiar ecclesiasticism, different from the preceding in some particulars, but kindred to them by a common idea, namely, *Puritanism*. Without recalling our colonial history, it is sufficient to report that the Puritanic idea was for a season in power in the New England portion of the country, and that its chief purpose was to secure unity of civilization by conformity to enacted religious and social ideas and methods, all of which had to be accepted at the peril of one's life. It is not denied that Puritanism bore fruit. The claim that our civilization is indebted to it we care not to dispute. What we now affirm is that the Puritanic idea can not be the final or *beau ideal* idea of society; that its very intolerance was suicidal; that it was a political and religious scheme which in the long run had to be exchanged for something better. What it did with Roger Williams it would do with all dissenters. Hence, it was illiberal, and denied to man the right of private judgment, and the free exercise of all God-given privileges. Bancroft speaks of it as "the reign of the visible Church," but it was the political rather than the religious reign of the Church. Of the theologic aspects of Puritanism we shall not speak; nor of its philosophic bearings on human society; but, as a political and social force, it failed as utterly as the ecclesiasticisms heretofore mentioned. Indeed, it actually perished, while the others still maintain an appearance of life, but under very paralyzing conditions.

These three ecclesiasticisms in their recognition of the unity of the race, the unity of the Church, and the unity of civilization have a justification; but the weakness common to them all was the attempted enforcement of centralized political and religious power under the sacred guise of the doctrine of unity.   Both religion and philosophy agree touching unity; but these ecclesiasticisms secretly plotted for political unity, or civil power, under the name of religious unity. Of the theology and the philosophy of the ecclesiastical establishments we have not spoken adversely; it is the social and political results that we enumerate as evidences of their unfitness as social and political forces in the world's civil regeneration.

II.   If not on the ecclesiastical idea, may not society be reared on the *political idea*?   What the political idea is, history defines, and concerning its adaptation to the social state history is equally positive. Certain political ideas must enter into the constitution of the public state, as the duties of reciprocity, the laws of political economy, the equality of civil rights, and the distribution of political favors, but what political form of government will promote these and other political ends must not be determined too hastily.   An appeal to historic political forms, the illustrations of the political idea, will aid in the solution of the problem.   At least three separate political results will reward our search after historical examples.   In the early stages of human society the political idea took a barbarous complexion and built itself up in despotic and monarchical forms, the remains of which appear in modern Asiatic and African tribal governments.   The authority of might had its final illustration in the splendid civilizations of Babylon and Egypt, which after a sturdy existence suddenly passed away.   Earlier than these were the crude political fabrics of savages and pagans, whose ideas of human relationship were subordinated to the one thought of dominion, self-preservation, and self-gratification.   But neither the coarse nor the refined political barbarisms of the ancient days; neither men who fought with clubs nor those who gracefully cast their spears, are true types of government or manhood.   As far as the animal kingdom of to-day is in advance of cephalopods, so far are our political forms beyond the barbarian's idea of social government.   Study these forms, however.

The royal political idea, the rule by divine right—what is this but a political deception?   The test of a political system is not exactly its power to endure, for the old pagan civilizations endured many centuries, but at last succumbed to the attrition of forces more inherently pregnant with life than they.   By virtue of the royal political idea, kingdoms vast and civilizations magnificent have been the product; and it is idle to deny that many of them have seemed to perform a providential mission, having fostered the great ends of government: viz., the education of the people, the establishment of religious worship, the reduction of temporal evils, and the promotion of individual rights. Conceding the superiority of the royal to the barbarian policy, both in its purpose and achievement, it is not clear that the one any more than the other is the ideal of human government. It is clear that the royal idea must be finally displaced, as one stratum is by another, in the great future of the world. *Asia and Africa furnish monuments of the barbarian's political idea; Europe points to the reign and ruin of the royal political idea.* The latter has been on trial in every European nation, to the final disadvantage of all; for ignorance, pauperism, crime, irreligion, and revolution are all but universal. At this very hour, such is the outcry against the modern political idea of government that thrones are shaking, kings trembling, and revolutions are imminent. Nihilism and Socialism are mocking the royal idea. Neither the authority of might, nor the authority of divine right, as crystallized in a governmental form, furnishes a sufficient basis for the political and social structure.

The third political idea is different from the others, both in its nature and extent. Napoleon conceived the mammoth project of extending the boundaries of the French Empire to the European limits, of consolidating a continent under one government, thus securing political unity and uniformity of social order. That in his thinking he went beyond this scheme, which he vainly endeavored to realize, and mused over the consolidation of all kingdoms into one, can not be questioned. The conception of such a consummation may be due to Napoleon's genius for the entertainment of great ideas; but, as a political project, put in motion, and for a time marching on to success, it is perfectly astounding. Hildebrand's scheme of consolidation was *quasi* spiritual and for spiritual ends; Napoleon's scheme was political and for political ends. Both were magnificent; both were in process of execution; both excited the fear of the world; both failed. Force was the method employed by both—a lesson that the unity of the world in ideal conditions can not be secured by the coercive method. In these we reach the antipodes of the idea of governmental unity, the one assuming spiritual unity and the other political unity, as the ideal of human condition.

The dream of one civilization, or the centralization of political power in one headship, was not original with the French ruler, nor was his attempt at its realization the first made by political dreamers. No less a conception than universal rule and the conversion of continents into provinces of the Macedonian Empire was the palpitating hope of Alexander the Great, who, like the "he-goat" of Daniel, waxed strong and pushed in all directions, conquering all nations, and wept when there was none to reduce to submission. At his death the massive kingdom fell to pieces, a proof that the experiment was artificial, and the cohesive spirit inanimate and dead. A more serviceable illustration of a world-wide political unity, or conformity to one governmental idea, is that of the Roman world under Augustus, who made Roman citizenship a coveted respectability, and Roman arms a terror to the most distant foes. This political achievement is more nearly the analogue of Hildebrand's conception of the universality of spiritual authority under one headship than Napoleon's brilliant, but unsuccessful attempt. Though enduring for centuries, at last, from internal enfeebling causes, it perished like Alexander's short-lived and more nominal universal sovereignty. Neither the colossal experiment of founding a spiritual headship for the world, nor the oft-repeated attempt at organizing all nations into one kingdom under one political authority, has had permanent success, or demonstrated the feasibility or necessity of either. While, however, these failures have been conspicuous, it should not be forgotten that in the ideal society the idea of unity must have a place, and that the scheme of unity, in order to achievement, must be in perfect harmony with the idea of unity. Both Hildebrand and Napoleon failed in their *schemes; the idea still remains.*

III. To what extent shall the *philosophical idea* dominate in human society? Is there a philosophical idea around which government may grow? We must lose sight of the theological ideas of the philosophers, since, so far as they are theological, they belong to the domain of religion, and will be considered as such at the proper time, as the atheism of Epicurus, the moral code of Seneca, the mythology of Socrates, and the ethics of Spencer. But the philosophical systems of ancient and modern thinkers, so far as they relate to the regulation of human life, and contain suggestions touching the governmental order of society, we may investigate with reference to their fitness as social and governmental forces.

One example from the ancients, and one from the moderns, will be quite sufficient for our purpose. More than all others of his day, Plato undertakes to describe the ideal society, insisting that it will be under the influence of the philosophic spirit, that the governors will be philosophers, and that laws will be enacted in accordance with philosophic considerations. A "philosophic race," he observes, "must have the government of the state," or miseries will never cease.

To this view, then, let us appeal. In his *Republic* this philosophic social system is revealed in all its details, with much of beauty in description, and not a little virtue in suggestion. In his *Laws* the reader will find, indeed, laws covering human conduct to its minutest acts, and regulating life to its smallest obligations. Taking the two together he will find Plato's system entire, with its virtues and blemishes, which have been enumerated in the first chapter of this book.

The admirers of Plato's scheme have been many, but attempts to reduce it to practical operation, or to institute a society in conformity to certain supposed ideal conditions, have been fruitless, except as they demonstrated the unwisdom of the scheme itself. Sir Thomas More's Utopia, like Plato's Republic, was a suggestive ideal, but never reduced to experiment; on the other hand, the Harmonites, a pious people under the leadership of Mr. Rapp, located in Indiana and organized a community under the inspiration of a Utopian conception. Far more commendable was the experiment than Plato's speculative republic; for it maintained the family idea, divided labor, and exercised a common and equal care over all its subjects. The despotism of leadership, the unity of interest, the absence of individual ambition, the repression of religious inquiry, and a forced social conformity were the weaknesses to which it finally yielded under the more pretentious superintendence of Mr. Owen.

According to Josephus the Essenes were a sectarian organization, dominated by the spirit of self-abnegation, and having in view only the larger weal of the whole in place of the development and happiness of the individual. Provisionally, too, it may be allowed that the early Christians adopted, and for a brief period observed, a Utopian plan in the surrender of their wealth to a common fund, and in the recognition of the equality of each in the social inheritance. Whether the philosophical suggestion of an isolated or communistic organization has been accepted and observed in a religious or purely political way, the result in all cases has been the same—the decline of individual character, the withering of the social functions, and at last the decadence of the social system itself.

Very different, if not the opposite, are the philosophical recommendations of Herbert Spencer touching the problems of sociology. The author of evolution affects to see in it the key to the development of a perfect social structure from which all evil will be eliminated, and in which the individual will attain his largest consciousness. He recommends no isolated organization for the trial of his suggestion; he recommends no trial at all of his theory, but points to history itself as both an illustration and a vindication of the evolutionary process in the expulsion of evil and the regeneration of the social order. With skillful hand he traces the slow evanescence of vices, diseases, and disorders in human history, and the natural working of better agencies for the elevation, education, and improvement of man, and on the historic basis of progress, whether the agencies to be employed be enumerated or omitted, he justifies faith in future progress until the social structure will contain more of good than evil, and frictions and hindrances be reduced to the smallest number, without power to prevent in any individual life the attainment of its true destiny. As this view of the future is in accord with the prophetic purpose of Christianity, it can not be resisted; but in the consideration of the agencies that must promote the purposes Mr. Spencer is singularly out of harmony, not only with theologians, but with statesmen, and thinkers of all schools, except those of his own. Evading the religious influence in the culture and development of man, it is fundamental with him that the law of life is such as in its very nature to produce aspirations and ambitions for better conditions, and that, as there has been an evolution of physical structures, so there will be an evolution of social structures, the last always superior to that which preceded it. By means of natural agencies, therefore, there will finally appear a social system, perfect in morals, perfect in industrial energy, perfect in the culture of men, accomplishing ideal ends in an ideal way, the whole the result of the evolutionary order inaugurated from the beginning. Conscience, mind, and soul will by evolutionary processes become perfect mechanically operating forces, as by similar processes the human body and physical organisms have attained their present harmony and beauty.

To other philosophic theories respecting society we must omit all reference; and of these mentioned it is quite enough to say that, as Plato's never was reduced to practice in all its details, so Spencer's has never had, and never can have, an independent trial, for even if the evolutionary process be recognized, it must include the religious factor, to which modern society, if it be superior to the ancient, is indebted more than to all other agencies combined. Evolution without religion is as speculative as materialism without God.

IV. The *scientific idea* of society is quite as specific and individual as any of the preceding. An examination of what it teaches or proposes is, therefore, next in order. Mr. Buckle is chosen as the exponent of the materialistic interpretation of civilization, for the reason that, though not its original advocate, he has applied it with more distinctness and made it more plausible than any previous writer of his school. According to this apostle of materialism, civilization, whether massive, as in Egypt; refined, as in Greece; vacillating, as in Spain; or vital and vigorous, as in Scotland, is the result of material forces, to which both pagan and civilized must yield dominion. Man is not above nature. His " conquest of nature " is a flattering phrase, whose interior meaning is that he has put himself in harmony with nature. Nature's laws may be discovered, used ; they are never conquered ; nature's forces are not overcome, but turned to the production of ends. By virtue of obedience to laws, forces, and material conditions, mankind rise, since they all portend progress, if obeyed, and destruction, if disobeyed. Civilizations have originated in conformity to material forces, and disappeared in contention with or violation of such forces, leaving their wrecks to tell the mournful story of their non-adjustment to environment as the secret of their downfall. No difference what the civilization, or social structure, or governmental form, its true test is this of material force, or the relation of material energy to governmental vitality. Culture and religion, or the ideas of divine providence and intellectual force, are subordinate to the universal laws of natural order and development. In this view the lower explains the higher ; the higher is the slave of the lower. The dominion of man, as lord of creation, is surrendered to the dominion of nature, as the primal force in all things. To this kind of materialism, reversing the historic order of national development, and eliminating religious agency, the most potent of all, does the scientific idea in Buckle's hands conduct us. The refutation of the materialistic hypothesis of civilization is the history of civilization itself, which points to the decay of all governmental institutions, whose elemental strength was in material force, or which, among the instrumental causes of growth and apparent stability, was sovereign. *Not a civilization exists which grounded itself exclusively in the lower forces.* What is true of materialistic civilization is also true of civilizations mixed, or those in which, while other elements were apparently constitutional, the vital force was physical, or, at the least, neither intellectual nor religious. No institution or government, without the religious force, can overcome the gravity of the lower forces. Buckle reduces the problem of national greatness to a problem of geographical conditions ; but no nation can stand long on a little geography.

Dr. J. W. Draper handles more astutely the scientific idea in its reference to the problems of civilization, marshaling an army of facts in support of it, but arriving at a conclusion almost as unsatisfactory as that that follows Buckle's generalization. Human society, in his careful estimation of its history, seems to observe a physiological law of development, passing through various stages from the beginning to the end, as an individual passes from one period of life to another until his mission is accomplished. He compares national life to individual life, assigning to the former : 1. An Age of Credulity ; 2. An Age of Inquiry ; 3. An Age of Faith ; 4. An Age of Reason ; 5. An Age of Decrepitude,—which correspond to infancy, childhood, youth, manhood, and age in the latter.  That this physiological interpretation of civilization has its justification in the history of society, must be admitted; for the exceptions to this general order of initiation, progress, and decadence in national life are rare and unimportant.  We make nothing in Dr. Draper's interpretation of the omission of Christianity as a vital principle in civilization; for, granting that without Christianity all great civilizations have decayed, and national forms have existed only for a period, it furnishes proof of the need of a new principle of national existence, which shall have the power to perpetuate a civilization until the end of time.  His interpretation reminds one of the Spanish navy, whose ships could not endure the recoil of their own guns.  Out of his physiological law emerges the conclusion that civilization is in need of a higher principle, which shall arrest the tendency to decay, and promote national immortality.  Evidently this principle is Christianity itself.

V. Still another view of human society, foreign to the Christian hypothesis, is itself under the reign of the *Socialistic idea.*  Two kinds of Socialism John Stuart Mill distinguishes—the one philosophical, represented by M. Fourier; the other revolutionary, represented by the destructionists of all modern systems of organized government.  Of the former he subscribes himself a friend, while confessing that the peculiar opinions of Fourier on marriage were independent of the principles of his industrial system.  The virtue of philosophical Socialism is in its regulation of the industrial interests of a community, or the adjustment of the differences and difficulties that occur between capital and labor; but who will consent that industrial interests are supreme? that they supersede in importance the domestic relations, public education, health, religious discipline, and the social economy?  Mills's Socialism does not grasp the profounder interests of society; Fourier's grasps but to overturn them; so that philosophical socialism is, on the one hand, unadapted to the needs of society, and, on the other, it is a standing menace to its peace and order.

From revolutionary socialism, which proposes to destroy the proprietary rights of the individual, and substitute a central government, which shall distribute the wealth of the nation to the inhabitants thereof, and override all other established institutions, secular, moral, and religious, Mr. Mill turns with horror, and pronounces it impolitic and impracticable.  What, however, is the essential difference between Fourier and Herr Most, the one philosophical, the other revolutionary, it is difficult to discover, as the introduction of the ideas of either into governmental affairs must result in demoralization and denationalization.  A concession to the Socialistic idea can only result in social revolutions, unsettling the settled principles of the ages.

VI. More subversive of the social ideal than any of the preceding is, to use a comprehensive term, the *pagan idea* of human society, human institutions, and human achievements. As one of the reigning ideas in human history, it has been on trial the longest, dominating in more countries than any other, and with every conceivable advantage in its favor; and yet it does not appear to have elevated society from the low level of ignorance, superstition, degradation, and crime, or reformed the wicked masses, or inspired a desire for improvement in the sages and leaders of the people. Under its potential influence the social impulses withered, governments themselves stagnated, and whole nations stood still, a commentary on the weakness of the idea itself. Whether ancient Rome, or ancient Greece, or modern India, or modern China be selected as the exponent of the pagan principle, the facts and conclusions will be the same, notwithstanding some variations in national development and historic relations may be discovered. Pagan Rome, inheriting a national principle, profoundly aggressive and apparently vital, expanded and outgrew its earlier self, becoming a terror to its own provinces, and threatened to absorb what little remained outside of itself. That this mammoth empire should dissolve, separating into fragments so small that not one can be identified, and for the most part itself, once the political absorbent, now absorbed by other national forms, is a standing fact of history. For the detailed causes of its overthrow, correctly given by Mr. Gibbon, the reader is referred to the history of "The Decline and Fall of the Roman Empire;" but for the present it is sufficient to point to two remaining monuments of the social character of ancient Rome as evidence of its internal weakness and certainty of decay, and to warn modern society against the revival of the pagan spirit.

The Coliseum has too often been described by travelers to require any extended reference here; its monumental meaning we alone desire to reveal. A vast structure, an elliptical figure whose external circumference measured five hundred and seventy-six yards, and diameter two hundred and five yards; with arched corridors, one hundred stairways, and four principal entrances; which seated eighty-seven thousand people, and furnished standing-room for twenty thousand more; is in ruins, only one-third of it remaining. Having personally inspected it, the impressions it made upon us, as a sign of civilization happily ended, we can never forget, but we as readily recall them as when, looking down from the disfigured and crumbling galleries into the arena, we fancied we witnessed the gladiatorial scenes of other days re-enacted, and felt horror-stricken and profoundly disgusted. Here the gladiators entered; there the wild beasts sprung from behind the gates; not distant, a passage-way for the dead was kept open; and on butcheries of man and beast, on contests between slaves, and on the higher contests between *faiths*, represented by Christian and pagan antagonists, Rome complacently looked and applauded. Rooms for the emperor and his family, from which the proceedings in the arena could be viewed; seats for the patricians; and accommodations for the multitude, signified the intense interest of royalty and the common people in the brutal scenes of the Coliseum. Let the decaying structure stand for a civilization which had in itself the seeds of decay; let the structure itself be one seed of decay.

Pagan Rome, crystallized into cruelty, exhibited an equally ruinous tendency in another aspect of its social life. The Baths of Caracalla, now a splendid mass of ruins, contrast with the stately signs of Roman coldness and inhumanity in the Coliseum. The one is repulsive; the other, attractive. The one drew the multitudes as well as the nobles; the other was visited only by senators and their families, or those above the plebeians. Built of thin brick, the bath houses contrasted with the rugged stone edifice of the gladiators. Besides rooms for bathing purposes, there were lecture and reading rooms, and picture galleries, and every arrangement and every comfort was made to minister to the voluptuous and luxury-loving spirit of the higher classes. Even the statuary excited the licentious instincts of the visitors. Here tired senators resorted for enjoyment. The sexes bathed promiscuously. Here patricians spent days and nights in forgetfulness of their domestic relations, immersed in the unforbidden pleasures of a higher licentiousness than the polluted masses knew any thing of; but the law of purity was as inexorable in the one case as in the other. A civilization that is the outgrowth of the licentiousness of higher or lower classes is in violation of the divine ideal of the social structure, and can not survive; thus Rome found herself undermined and enfeebled by her own vices, and ready to perish, long before the northern Vandal struck her a blow. The Coliseum represents the coarse and brutal instincts of pagan civilization; the bath-house represents the voluptuous spirit of ancient life, which was even more ruinous than the other.

In the absence of the religious principle, which is ever a restraint on man's cruelty, and a cure for love of pleasure, the old civilizations perished, a fearful warning to modern peoples, who think their happiness can consist only in abjuring righteousness.

The symbols of ancient Grecian civilization, no less pagan in its essential significance, are the Parthenon, a temple of marble, and the Pnyx, the forum of oratory and eloquence; both speaking of a people and a civilization that have perished. The disfigured friezes of the temple still proclaim the name of Phidias; the consecration of the building as the temple of Minerva reveals a religion of gods and goddesses as supreme in Grecian life; the building whose construction was superintended by Pericles speaks of an age of art, beauty, luxury, philosophy, and learning. The Pnyx, with its cyclopean boundary wall, seems almost to echo the eloquence that kindled the patriotism of the Greeks, and certainly impresses the visitor with the greatness of the civilization that produced it.

Perhaps the truth is not so self-evident that art, poetry, philosophy, and eloquence, unaccompanied with a religious life, are as dangerous to national stability, and as certain to result in national overthrow, as the bolder and more cankerous forms of inhumanity and licentiousness. The Parthenon is as great a ruin as the Coliseum; the Pnyx is as vacant as the bath-house. Both social civilizations, the one essentially voluptuous and sense-serving, the other essentially and intellectually aspiring, fell into chaos from insufficient internal vitality, or the absence of a lofty, regenerating, preserving religious principle.

The lesson is the same if the civilizations of China and India be subjected to the same analysis. In China, a principle of order resulting in national perpetuity has undergirded the life of the people; but order has been gained at the expense of progress. Stagnation is the characteristic of Chinese civilization; a fatal condition, and far removed from an ideal achievement. In India the principle of caste has governed so absolutely that, until the rigid protest of another and more vitalizing civilization was heard, the nation was asleep and unconscious of power. Between the two civilizations one can not choose, for stagnation is no more destructive of progress than caste, and both are obstacles to a broad inquiry, to the doctrine of the unity of the race, and to expansion. The pagan idea of society has not in it a single ideal recommendation.

VII. There remains for mention the *Mohammedan* idea of society, or a semi-Christian principle of civilization, which has manifested itself in that colossal government known as the Turkish Empire. In India the friction between exclusively pagan ideas, and the Mohammedan principle of divine sovereignty in human affairs, has prevented the free and full exhibition of the latter; but in the empire of which it is the almost exclusive religion, just how it has affected the social life, and whether it is a sufficiently vital principle for human government, may be the more easily determined. No one traveling in Syria, or the Turkish provinces, would think of preferring Mohammedan civilization to the native Hindu types of society; for, while the sovereign principle of Mohammedanism is divine, it is insufficient from its incompleteness. Moreover, the vitality of this faith is not the divine principle, but a superstitious corruption, which either robs the principle of its legitimate functions, or supplants it entirely with another principle. It is not the thought of God, but *the thought of Mohammed as the prophet of God*, that constitutes the strength, and, therefore, the weakness, of this religious civilization. The divine element, lost in the human, or having only formal acknowledgment, has ceased to invigorate the empire, and effected the prostration of its civilization beyond recovery. A false religion is as completely ruinous of social institutions and political governments, as any form of paganism, or the worst type of socialism. Turkey and Syria, Arabia and Egypt, under the sway of the Mohammedan principle, are as stagnant as China, and as corrupt as ancient Rome, and verify the statement that another religious principle is absolutely necessary to their political regeneration.

After this survey of civilizations, ancient and modern; after the contemplation of societies in which scientific, philosophical, and socialistic principles have been put in practice; in view of the study of peoples governed largely by religious principles, mythological, semi-Christian, and Christian; and carefully considering the force of political ideas, as exemplified among barbarians and the enlightened, what conclusions may justly be announced? Certainly no ideal society, government, or civilization has been found, either in ancient or modern times, in Christendom or in Heathendom. Certainly no ideal principles, taken separately or in their combination, sufficient to restore society to an ideal condition, have been named, for under the operation of whatever is esteemed best there has been decay. Certainly no ideal religions, with power to preserve from impurity and decline, have, amid the heterogeneous mass of faiths and worships we have traced, declared themselves. In vain we seek ideal conditions; in vain we ask for ideal principles; in vain we request ideal religions. Nothing ideal emerges from the true or false, the sincere or the hypocritical, the permanent or transient, the stable or fluctuating, the religious or irreligious, the ancient or modern, the radical or conservative, the stationary or progressive. A search for the ideal is like the search after the philosopher's stone.

Is there no ideal? Is the thought of it a dream, a mockery, a vanity? Must the restless, suffering world roll on, believing in a better state, and even pursuing a higher hope, only to find in the ages to come that it has repeated its history, and not advanced beyond the fathers? We assume there is an ideal; we assume there are ideal principles, there is an ideal religion, there must be an ideal society in the future. Whence the dissatisfaction with social states, as they are, if they are final? Why schemes of reconstruction? Why Plato's republican principles? Why Socialism? Why philosophy? Why religion? Why Christianity? Nations and social structures go down that something better may appear, and the palpitating principle of the universe is progress, apparent in nature, history, civilization, religion, and Christianity. On social dissatisfactions, on human aspirations, on national changes, on philosophic and religious grounds, we predicate the ideal, and insist that already ideal principles are at hand, and an ideal religion is in force, working silently but effectively for the realization of the ideal society. We refer to Christianity, not the corrupt forms, or the corrupt religious establishments which exist in its name, but to those religious truths and principles which, vitally incorporated into the life of the world, will regenerate and preserve it. The relation of Christianity, as the sovereign religious force, to the world's development and the world's fulfillment, must be patiently and exhaustively considered if we shall discover its ideal character, purpose, and possibility.

That the requirements of the ideal state may be apprehended, and whether any thing short or outside of the Christian theory of life is adapted to promote them, it will be necessary carefully to consider the fundamental needs of society as they express themselves in universal history.

First, *the constant recognition of the individual rights of every member of society is imperative, and an inviolable condition of the ideal state.* The very triteness of the suggestion may be in the way of an appreciation of its value; but its repeated and long-continued disregard in all social states, not excepting those supposed to be under the reign of Christian sentiment, is the apology for its insertion here. Fully to comprehend human rights, their nature, number, and expediency of exercise, one must be thoroughly acquainted with certain ethical as well as natural principles, which no religion, save that of which the Divine Master is the inspiration, has completely embodied and magnified. With a knowledge of these principles, the conclusion is unanswerable that a violation of rights is a violation both of nature and ethics, and so subversive of human welfare.

Studying human conditions in the light of these principles, a thorough reformation of social and political ideas is imperative; such a reformation as must result in the subordination of ideas hitherto held supreme. By the terms of nature, and equally by the authority of ethics, war is precluded from the ideal state. Mankind constitute a brotherhood, cemented together by the unity of their origin, and organized into societies for the conservation of justice, equality, and happiness. In violation of the ideal of universal peace, Plato, in his ideal republic, provides for the military, assigning to the soldier a place only a little lower than that of the governor, and dignifying the profession of arms far above that of the tradesman or laborer.  Patterned after a true ideal, no society will need the soldier, whose chief business is to enforce the wishes of his government, regardless of the ethical considerations involved.  The ideal excludes the military, eliminating the spirit of conquest, oppression, and political prejudice from national policies.  Under this teaching standing armies melt into fragments, or disappear altogether, as snow-flakes under the sun ; swords become plowshares, spears are turned into pruning-hooks ; race oppressions and national vituperations cease ; and a millennial peace spreads its white mantle over the whole earth.  Surely this end is not unworthy of the religion that proposes to secure it.

Nature protests against the spirit of caste in society, but offers no remedy.  The differences in men, arising from their creation, upon which ranks and gradations have been founded, we can not wholly ignore ; but we can avoid the extreme and fanatical conclusions, disrupting society, and breeding mischief and misery, of which these natural differences have been made the burden-bearers.  The cure for the caste-spirit is, omitting the differences, to fix the eye on the resemblances, or the common and equal rights of men, under nature and the true religious conception of man.  Life is a common right ; liberty is inalienable and universal ; the end or purpose of life—self-development—ought to be sacred, and interference with it should not be tolerated.  If one have the right to live at all, he has the right to live for the highest ends of life.  Any thing that strikes at the end strikes at the beginning of life, the reason of being at all.  Conceding the idea of equality, how it strikes, not only at certain social conditions, as caste, slavery, and communism, but more forcibly still at certain philosophical principles, the inculcation of which has resulted in the conditions which have proved to be the weaknesses of civilized life.

Caste is the curse of the Orient, the fruit of the old religions and philosophies that knew not the mind of God concerning the race, or the great doctrine of the unity of mankind.  Slavery in the early days was not an artificial institution, but the logical result of such religions and philosophies.  The liberty of man was submerged in the idea of the inequalities of men.  The restoration of liberty belongs to the religion that, looking deeper than differences in men, discerns equality and unity as the superior factors in the consideration of the interests of the human race.  Under the domination of an ideal idea, caste and slavery must quietly or forcibly be ejected from the ideal state.

In other directions the rights of man have been unjustly curtailed on philosophical grounds, while nature and religion unite in a repudiation of the justifying argument. The range of individual rights, as defined in the Gospel, is broad enough to include both sexes; but no philosophy or religion has gone so far as to concede to woman an equal share in natural rights; hence she has suffered, and society has never risen to its proper height. By an evident providential arrangement, which is perplexing to the materialist, it so happens that in the matter of births of human beings the proportion of males to females is 106 to 100; that is, a slight majority of males preponderates, since they are more exposed to climate, hardship, and war, showing that the divine design is to preserve the sexes in equal numerical proportions. By no system of marriage—by no enforced violations of nature's suggested order—must this proportion be disturbed. Both polygamy and celibacy go down beneath the order of nature; but of all religions Christianity alone appropriates nature's hint, or "Dorically harmonizes" with nature's teaching, discerning that monogamy is the inexorable law of God. With Plato's community of women this idea comes in direct collision. Under the philosopher's perverted conception woman lost her marital right, and home its divine sacredness. Such is the relation of the family to government, individual character, and social progress that, if it lose its solemnity, or compromise its unity, immorality will abound, the safeguards of public virtue will be reduced, and society will become a nest of iniquity. In the ideal state, Plato's community, the polygamy of Mohammedanism, and the celibacy of the Roman Catholic priesthood can have no existence, being repugnant to the law of monogamy, founded in the fact of the equal proportion of the sexes.

*Summarizing individual rights in the light of an ideal principle, or arranging them under the co-operating proclamations of nature and religion, it is easy to see that war, caste, slavery, polygamy, and celibacy must be expelled from society, and peace, unity, equality, freedom, and monogamy must be everywhere installed.*

In an ideal society, the *problem of education will have definite and satisfactory solution.* The woful ignorance of man, not only of real being, but of phenomena, or the manifestations of being; not only of things, but of forces likewise; not only of effects, but of causes,— is at once acknowledged. He is steeped in ignorance, incessantly violating law, right, duty, and self-interest. He is blindfolded, yet walking toward the sun. He is the heir of darkness and all its fruits, of which crime and calamity are the most universal. He is the sport of laws he does not understand, the victim of penalties he can not foresee. He needs truths, knowledges, vastness of vision, magnificent illuminations, eternal revelations. Until every man's eyes are opened to the truth until all know universal law and its penalties; until nature and the supernatural, being and non-being, are grasped by the intellective forces; until the mind arrives at the summits of philosophical research and moral wisdom,—there will be room for the play of ignorance, which may prove to be the fly in the ointment, or the spark in the magazine. Danger lurks in ignorance. Plato is the advocate of education, as a moral restraint, the means of reformation, and the basis of a well-ordered society; but his educational system is not of public utility, for he confines it to the guardians of the state, and limits acquirements to gymnastics, music, the military art, and philosophy, a curriculum that a modern university would pronounce inadequate to self-culture and self-development. For artificers, agriculturists, and tradesmen, Plato provides no education at all, deeming it quite unnecessary to skill, efficiency, or success in their pursuits. Thus education, in his estimate, is for a class, and that the smallest, only! This is Platonism, which is the key to all philosophical systems of education, the chief objection to which is a *limited curriculum, confined to a limited class.*

The opinion has gained currency that universal education is not desirable, since neither the industrial pursuits nor the commercial interests of society demand it. The error of the opinion lies in the estimate of education as a mere instrument in matters of acquisition or worldly pursuit, whereas education is self-development, having respect wholly to the internal life of man. As an instrument, it is useful; as a development, it is essential. The man requires education, whether his pursuit can be prosecuted with or without it. *Co-education, compulsory education, and universal education, are the triple ideas that must enter into any great or effective system of education;* for an ideal state is impossible in which ignorance and intelligence co-exist in about equal proportions, or in which the multitudes walk in darkness, while the guardians alone walk in the light. For fear of misguiding, it must be added that education alone is not a sufficient remedy for the afflictions of the Christian state, for it may obtain with a perversion of morals and spiritual blindness, and be inoperative as a regenerating force. Nana Sahib, an incarnation of cruelty, was broad-brained and a cultured gentleman. Voltaire was educated; likewise, Gibbon; but education saved neither from spiritual imperfection. These admissions or hints are of force in showing that other agencies besides those named will be required for the fostering of the purposes and ends of the best society.

The *industrialism* of society must have recognition and regulation, according to nature and the dictates of a Christian philanthropy. The majority of men are engaged in agricultural, commercial, and mechanical pursuits, developing the physical resources of their country, and making the blind forces and agencies of matter tributary to human happiness and destiny. By his industries, man is obeying the commandment to subdue the earth, and acquiring dominion over every created thing.

Shall man's environment subdue him, or shall he subdue his environment? Such a question he can not escape; its issue is in the line of personal supremacy or personal degradation, and, therefore, intensely religious. That this problem involves difficulty, no one acquainted with it will doubt. Dangers, prolific and threatening, attend the acquirement of personal authority, or the reign of mind over matter. What means shall be adopted to avert disaster or shock during the processes of development, is no small question. No subject more profoundly stirs the masses than that of national industrialism, or the relation of labor to civilization, requiring genius, philosophical discernment, and statesmanship perfectly to settle it. For among the discontented masses of the nation is a volcanic spirit, whose mutterings of a cruel purpose are distinctly heard, and which, thoroughly aroused and in action, may engulf wide-spread interests, and even involve in peril the national life.

In the settlement of a problem so far-reaching in its consequences, and in the adjustment of relations, hitherto strained, between capital and labor, there will be opportunity for the exercise of justice, patience, a spirit of philanthropy, and a regard for religion. In the Old World, the oppression of the laborer has been degrading in the extreme, the only escape from it being in emigration to free America, where labor has dignity and remuneration. This is not the greatest evil of low wages—emigration—but it has engendered a dissatisfaction with society, whose pillars rock with the commotion of a general indignation against further outrage and oppression. Communism, socialism, nihilism, a brood of evils, reduced from theoretical conceptions to practical experiments, are the logical reactions of an exacting age, and menace the age itself. Either the social structure, as constituted, or nihilism, is wrong; the animating spirit of one or the other needs purification. In its present organized form, social structures of the most liberal type are not altogether favorable to the laborer. Injustice, with seeming parade of justice; lines of division between the upper and lower classes, so-called, becoming more distinct; hereditary titles and official honors confined to the patricians; wages graduated according to the caprices of wealthy proprietors; the mechanic deprived of social privileges; the hours of labor extending into the night; Sunday desecrated by mercenary requirements—all these are indications of a perverted social order, and the causes of an impending conflict that may rend the social structure that tolerates divisions, oppressions, and violations of right.   In America, socialism has been under restraint, manifesting itself only in occasional " strikes," haughty discussions, and proposed reckless legislation, which, however objectionable and un-American, are the deep foreshadowings of a chronic complaint with industrial regulations.

It is not our province to propose a cure for these evils, a matter that more properly belongs to the political economist; but, recognizing the disorders of society, we shall be justified in appealing for relief.   In this emergency, philosophy has nothing to offer, or what it offers is, as has been more than once proved, insufficient.   It is settled that communism can not enter the ideal society, but how to keep it out is the question.   Plato's teachings are communistic; John Stuart Mill is a conservative socialist; Fourier is a most fanatical socialist; but, from the refined and philosophic communism of Plato and Mill to the revolutionary socialism of Europe is but a single step.   The theory of the one is the practice of the other; the ideal of Plato is the real of Europe.   In the construction of an ideal state, therefore, it is not clear that either ancient or modern philosophy can help us.   Herbert Spencer's social system is an evolution, *not yet evolved*—a growth toward supposed ideals, but not the realization of them.   But are there no industrial ideal principles that can at once be adopted?   Must society tardily grow into true ideas of justice, benevolence, philanthropy, and as tardily outgrow the tendencies to nihilism?   Verily, the radical cure of these disorders is in the principles of the Christian religion, the adaptation and efficiency of which for the purposes required will hereafter be portrayed at length.

Next, it is incumbent on us to give place to the *moralities*, or a working and producing ethical system, in the ideal state.   On wrong, injustice, and moral misrule, the State can not long exist.   Between the public life and the ideal ethical order, there must be concord; the relation must be musical.   In the people there must be a love of the right, so that wrong will create friction, disturbance, and convulsion.   In such a society, resistance to wrong will not be theatrical or simulated, but intensely aggressive and victorious.   The chief good will be sought in the direction of righteousness.   Immorality, coarse or refined, is as destructive of the State as ignorance or communism, and to be extinguished quite as speedily.   If education must be confined to the minority, morality must be universal; the lowest classes must be as moral as the highest, or irreparable mischief is inevitable. To prevent an increase of criminals, and a new troop of dangers, a higher standard of moral life must be raised.   In devising or seeking a system of morality, it is not so important that it be philosophically perfect and adapted to master minds, as that it shall be universal in its application, restraining iniquity in whatever form it appears, and inculcating righteousness in all classes of society. Ethics for the multitude; ethics for the *élite*. Philosophy devises ethics for the latter; but a broader system must be reared, which shall be adapted to both, as, morally, there is no difference between them.

In need of a broad and efficient system of morality, where shall it be found? In need of ideal standards of right, who will proclaim them? Philosophical or naturalistic morality runs to low definitions of right, justice, and truth, and frames narrow-minded views of duty and human responsibilty. Zeno, more penetrating than his contemporaries, declared that rightness and wrongness inhere in actions; but so profound an idea did not prevail in the academies of his day. Epicurus determined the morality of human action by its power to produce happiness; and Aristotle suggested that virtue consists in the observance of the mean between extremes, which is the theory of temperance or moderation in life. No swinging to excesses, no fanaticism, but a well-balanced purpose or action, avoiding excess on the one hand and deficiency on the other, is moral or virtuous, and entitled to reward. Generosity is neither extravagance nor parsimony, but the middle point between them. In ancient philosophical circles the Aristotelian definitions, succeeded by the Epicurean system, had for a long period full sway, and a molding effect on teaching and practice. For the wider circle of the multitude the metaphysics of ethics was not required; but an incorporation of principles to which the common mind could respond was a necessity.

Not less delusive and incapacitated are the modern philosophical suggestions touching the ethical problem. From his definition of justice as a mere conformity to local legal ideas, James Mill rose to the conception of the essential element or secret bond of all moralities, seeing in them only a conformity to the idea of utility, or a serving of self-interest in the performance of the so-called duties of life. Hume's conception of morality entirely agrees with this of Mill. Utility is the ideal of life, the test of all virtues, the standard of all actions. Herbert Spencer's ideal morality is of a purely naturalistic, as opposed to a purely supernaturalistic, type, consisting of growths rather than revelations. It is scientific morality, as distinguished from spiritual or religious morality, realized as the issue of social collisions, compromises, and final co-operations. Altruism, the core of Spencerian ethics, destroyed Rome, Egypt, Persia, and Greece; and it is difficult to avoid believing that, if adopted, it will destroy modern civilizations. Morality reduced to utility, or whose chief idea is centripetal, *i. e.*, personal selfishness, must go outside of history and human experience to justify itself to this age, for under the sway of such systems the old civilizations tottered to their ruin. In Christianity alone will one find an ethical system that elevates while it restrains, and preserves while it prohibits.

In this schedule of the necessities of the ideal state, no reference has as yet been made to the form of government, or the civil and political complexion which it must finally assume for the security of the ideal ends before it. Evidently, the form of government must be in harmony with the purposes to be accomplished by it. Legislation and politics must have reference to the conservation of individual rights, the extension of education, the regulation of the industrial interests, and the authority of ethics, overlooking which the government must fail of a vindication of its existence.

What, then, shall be the form of government for the ideal society? Of existing or superseded forms of political authority, none is perfect, none ideal, if that be necessary. A tyranny is at once rejected, being incompatible with all the ends of government. Oligarchy, the government of the rich, is the reign of a class who are oppressive in spite of a purpose to be considerate, and must, therefore, be rejected. The fate of the aristocracy, the government of the few, is the same. Monarchy, the most popular old-world form of political government, we can not eulogize as ideal, since it is proscriptive of the ruled, and tends to a too ambitious exaltation of the rulers. Virgil taught the Romans to salute Augustus as divine, an early illustration of the idea of the divine right of kings. If divine in person, they must have divine authority. From such an extreme a recoil was certain, and it has come, royalty occupying a much reduced position in the estimation of men, and no longer receiving celestial honors. Government is of God—governors are men. Plato stoutly opposes pure democracy, which is always in danger of anarchy. Historic governmental forms are not ideals.

What then? What is the *beau ideal* of the civil power? Is there such a thing as ideal politics? If our ideal society is not to be a picture of the imagination, but a reality on the footstool, its principles must be moral, its virtues human, its methods available, its form tangible. Not an airy, sentimental, aristocratic form, weakened by Platonic effeminacies, but a republican, or representative form of government, cohering by the virtues of its citizens, and perpetuating itself in the world's life, as its greatest moving force, is that for which we now appeal. It is not a philosopher's government that is suggested; nor is metaphysical statesmanship advocated; nor can political æstheticism rule in this ideal. Face to face with the basal idea of the ideal, we submit the proposition that the *Christian State is the ideal*

*State;* in other words, that *essential Christianity is the elemental life of the ideal society.* Going immediately below the surface, this means that religion shall be the principal exponent of the social order and the outward sign of its inward life. In Plato's republic religion is not an apparent feature, since not more than two or three religious allusions are made, and more to appease popular faith than from a recognition of its value. In no philosophical system for the improvement of society is religion, except in the broad sense of a morality, regarded as vital, or so much as important. In social structures, barren of religious essentials, the moralities and philanthropies occupy conspicuous places, but rather as instruments of comfort and progress than as ideal experiences and achievements. The difference between the philosopher's ideal of society, and that here formulated, is the difference between the presence and the absence of religion.

The extent to which Christianity shall enter into the life of the State, and whether it shall be regnant, giving complexion to jurisprudence, education, manners, morals, industries, and dictating the 'tone of civilization, or become a silent but reflective influence, are fundamental considerations, the vital points of the subject itself. To make a general declaration of faith, or political policy, in answer to the above, we submit that Christianity will introduce to the notice of the State all the institutions, ideas, moral forces, and moral benefits embodied in the word *Church*—a word foreign to philosophical systems. In its final workings it will be evident that it will be aiming to convert the State into the Church and in a sense to convert the Church into the State ; that is to say, *Christianity will Church the world.* This is a definite purpose, requiring and providing all reformatory and redemptive agencies, and laying foundations as strong as the everlasting hills for the future society of man. Christianity has a twofold object, as its permanent aim : 1. The inward, relating to the regeneration of man ; 2. The outward, expressing itself in an organized Church. With the second only have we now to do. The authority of Christianity, and how it shall be exercised, whether distinct from State forms and State ethics, and, therefore, a rival or twin power, or in unison with them, forming an iron and clay combination, deserves careful consideration. It is the old question, never satisfactorily solved, of State Churchism, or a free and independent Church. Monarchies prefer Church establishments, and maintain them at vast expense ; but very much is lost to the Church itself by the secular association. In England the Church is more of a political institution than is consistent with its design, working out political rather than religious schemes, and enforcing religious teachings by machine methods, which are always inimical to spiritual elevation and

intelligent living.   The dissenting spirit is strong, making itself felt
in the organization of independent religious societies, which for
activity and efficiency have already eclipsed the moss-bound Church
orders of the kingdom.   What is true of England is also true of
Germany, and will be true of Roman Catholic countries when independent action shall be tolerated.

The evils of State Churchism are greatly to be deplored.   Whatever the advantage to the State, the Church suffers inevitable loss in
vigor, spirituality, and activity.   The State secularizes the Church;
the Church fails to regenerate the State.   Thus it was in the days of
Constantine, when, notwithstanding the splendor of his reign and the
apparent advance of Christianity, it lost in moral tone, and society
became as a turbid pool.   In the ideal State the Church must be free
and so separate from the civil power that the functions of each may
be performed without the interference of the other, both conserving
by independent methods the common idea of unity, progress, and
happiness.   Shall there be two influences in power?   Shall both
Church and State rule?   Rule they can not if united—can they rule
if separated?   Each is an organism, blending in the pursuit of the
public good, but working towards it by machinery of its own.
*Given a republican government and a free Church: the* PRODUCT IS AN
IDEAL SOCIETY.   The double reign of Church and State is paralleled
by the double rotation of the earth, the one around its own axis,
the other around the sun.   The magistrate is not the priest—the
priest is not the magistrate.   No monarchy, no theocracy, no State
Churchism—a dual government, whose politics is ethically sound,
whose religion is politically democratic; this is the ideal State and
none other.

That Christianity is vital to the ideal society has been more than
once intimated, and little needs to be added in proof of it.   Whatever is vital to the State, Christianity promotes and preserves.   What
is the great fear of nations?   Internal decay, external opposition;
strife within, assault from without.   The former is the greater peril.
Niebuhr says, "No nation ever died except by suicide."   Political
intrigue, public corruption, the loss of individual virtue, the decline
of the family institution, the love of vicious luxuries, and variation
from righteousness have been more effectual in national overthrows
than organized external war against a people.   National immorality
is the prelude of national extinction.   The Grecian cities united were
invincible; divided, they were conquered.   From internal decay and
external assault; from national vices and foreign wars, Christianity
will save the State.   Were the world a Church, the sword would be
a relic, for war is not a Church force, or a Church condition.   Where

the Church is, there is the holiness of peace, and the peace of holiness. To this ideal condition the world is slowly drifting; nations even from the low level of economic reasons are considering the expediency of abolishing standing armies and submitting international differences to arbitration. Both Kant and the elder Mill favored an international code for the guidance of international affairs, under the nfluence of which they anticipated the elimination of international evils; but, like other philosophical schemes, the code was never adopted. Christianity is in force, working out its legitimate and beneficent suggestions in the world's advance toward peace. Saving the State from external or foreign assault, it saves it from internal gloom and decay by the repression of popular vice, and the introduction of virtue. In these respects Christianity is vital to the ideal State.

In the very nature of the organization of society, the liberty of the individual, or the sovereignty of personality, is an essential of its growth and preservation. The freedom of vocation; the sacred right of marriage; the choice of religion; the possession of property; the exercise of suffrage; the right to public office; all these and more belong to free men. But the assertion of individual rights is inconsistent with caste, slavery, despotism, polygamy, and the "inhumanities" of man. However, Christianity is the assertion of individualism; one of its magical words is "brotherhood," as opposed to the world's word—"bondage." Christianity is emancipation, unity, freedom, development. Under it man is the heir, not the slave, of the race to which he belongs.

In the matter of industrialism the necessity for harmony between capitalists and laborers is self-evident. Harmony or communism—one or the other. Christianity casts its vote in favor of harmony. Favoring justice, curbing the greed of men, instilling patience, invigorating human sympathies, and sanctifying human toil, it prepares the way for reconciliation between classes, mutually jealous and hostile, undermining the communistic spirit by its sweet ministry of love. Divorce religion and labor, and the latter sinks into materialism. Without religion, labor deals with matter as a *thing*; religion inspiring, it deals with matter as an expression of God's power and wisdom, and the laborer rises ever into thoughts of God.

Practically, Christianity will have an influence in determining the rewards of labor, and international policies respecting international trade. In the Christian state man's toil will have just remuneration, wages being assessed according to the principles of political economy, which considers the welfare of the whole rather than the advantage of the few. Monopolies will not flourish; the poor will acquire property; and life will be agreeable to all.  Home trade, such as agriculture, mercantile business, and the manufacturing interests of communities, will be regulated by the moralities of the ordained religion of the state, which will promote good will, the harmonious adjustment of conflicting enterprises, and an orderly progress in all departments of civil life.  As to foreign trade, or the law governing exports and imports, a partisan spirit will not dictate free trade or protective tariffs but the conflicting doctrines or policies will be harmonized on the basis of a large philanthropy, which regards other peoples besides one's own, and the world as well as one's own section of it.  Equalization of international rights touching trade, or philanthropy rather than a local patriotism, which sometimes degenerates into systematic selfishness, will have larger consideration in the future than it is possible to have now among partisans; and to that future we refer the whole question.

That Christianity is the friend of education none will hesitate to admit, except those who confound the Roman Catholic religion with the divine system of the Master.  Christian governments are favorably disposed to popular education, proving that Christianity is something more than a religion, or that, as a religion, it stimulates to high and intellectual achievement.  This stimulation it effects by the force of its truths concerning God and man; by its eternal law of righteousness; by its system of laws; by its detail of duties; by its visions of destiny.  In Christianity itself, its revelations of being, cause, order, life, and ends, is the ground-work and inspiration of education.  It makes the *ideal man*, without which the ideal state is impossible, for it is only an aggregation of ideal units, of ideal human beings.  The fact, too, must not be obscured, that the ideal state does not produce the ideal man, but the ideal man produces the ideal state.  With him, the State is certain.  The primary object of Christianity is not the production of Christian communities and nations, but Christian men and women, of whom Christian communities and nations may be organized.  It deals with the individual.  It enjoins the moralities; it approves and fosters the philanthropies; it ordains religious regeneration, or religious character.  This is the summit of idealistic manhood, reached through the divine stepping-stones of Christianity.  The ideal man, sustaining a divine relation to the universe, becomes in society the center of the moralities, the philanthropies, and the spiritualities.  He is grounded in God, and God in him.

Naught but Christianity produces such.  Produced, he makes the State, the community, the family, the Church.  The ideal State concretes in ideal men made real by the Christian forces.  Had J. S. Mill discerned the ideal in the real of the Christian religion he had never despaired of the world, and never proposed a philosophical reconstruction of it.

In the presence of those who see the approaching day of the Christian State, under whose sway moral, social, and political evils will retire, and a heavenly life of wisdom, justice, purity, and development prevail, pessimism dwindles into absurdity, materialistic theories vanish like a nightmare, and Christianity arises as the force and inspiration of the actualized social ideal. Hasten, the new day! Welcome, the Christian State!

## CHAPTER XXIV.

### THE PERFECTION OF MAN THE IDEAL OF CHRISTIANITY.

IT is reported from Liberia that some of the natives are able with unaided eyes to behold the satellites of Jupiter, so marvelous is their power of vision. A vision equally acute is required to descry the distant or future man in his harmoniously developed character and life, as it shall appear under Christian rule and in complete subserviency to the will of God. As a human description of the future man as the result of the natural order of things, must partake to some extent of conjecture, and be based upon inferences from empirical, historical, and philosophical studies, it is important that the best helps, and even divine assistance, be invoked if the ideal man be truly prefigured. Looking upon him through the telescope of Christianity, and knowing that its revelations are accurate, and conclusions therefrom will be reliable, the task of description will be simplified, and faith in the attainment of the ultimate purpose of Christianity will be strengthened.

If Christianity has an ideal object of pursuit, or is controlled by a single supreme purpose, however manifold its incidental and collateral purposes may be, the inference is that, as indicated by its teachings and as already manifested in its history, its ideal purpose is the moral perfection of man. At the present moment it is sufficient to know that it has before it an ideal idea without knowing definitely the contents of that idea. Speaking philosophically, the teleology of Christianity is a theme worthy of the philosopher's consideration, for it is high enough for his vision, deep enough for his plumb-line, and moral enough for employment of his conscience and intuitions. Without risk we assume that it is inspired by the thought of achievement, that the motivity of religion is the realization of the ideal in human history, and that its inner life is in some way adapted to promote it.

Possibly it is assuming too much when we affirm that its ideal purpose relates to man, but if it relate to other beings only it can not concern us. Man is interested in it only as it is interested in him. If it relate to others, rather than to himself, he may admire its beauty, and, discerning the hidden wisdom of its truths, be ready to eulogize it as a divine product; but he can not be interested in it. *The fascination of Christianity arises from its relation to the race, its adaptation to human needs, its moral helpfulness in extremity, and its delivering power from the bondage of sin.* That Christianity is a revelation of God none must deny; but it must be something more. Primarily, its function is both to reveal God to man, and to conduct man to God; it is to create a Godward impulse in humanity, and leaven it with a heavenly life. Its work is for man and in man to the glory of God in Jesus Christ. Whatever other ends it promotes, or seeks to make known; however much it contributes to the ascendency of other ideas and truths; its chief end is the elevation, development, and perfection of man.

This view magnifies man as the creature of God, and magnifies Christianity in proportion as its ideal end relates to man. If man is not included in the mission of Christianity, if his development is not the chief end of Christianity, Christianity is worthless. Perhaps this assumption of man's exalted position in the universe is owing to that vanity which humanity, even in its degradation, has always arrogated to itself, but which it will overcome as it is more enlightened. The evolutionist, renouncing the tendency to self-flattery, takes an entirely different view from the above, regarding man as very low in the scale of being, and destined to disappear. His is not a comforting revelation to the race. Quoting history, he informs us that the scientific thinker in the splendid days of Egyptian supremacy conceived that the earth is the center of the astronomic universe, and that all the planets revolve around it, and in a sense exist for it. Even Greece and Rome accepted the flattering astronomy; but Copernicus extracted the romance from it, and pointed out that the earth is one of the smallest of orbs, and that it probably ministers to others, and will some day expire. Without emotion the evolutionist also informs us that the vanity which places man at the head of creation, eulogizing him as the first creature of the Almighty, destined to development and dominion, will be punctured by and by, and man will see himself as he is, an atom, a worm, a clod, with no destiny but decline, with no future but oblivion. Between the cold, forlorn, non-progressive assumption of evolution, and the warm and inspiring teaching of Christianity, one must make choice. Is the thought of man's greatness a vanity? Is the hope of progress an idle sentiment? Is man at the head or foot? *Christianity places him at the head; evolution, at the foot.*

Christianity is the only religion that foresees for man the development of his moral and intellectual possibilities, prescribing the method of such development, and providing the means by which it may finally be attained. It is the only religion that is committed to the doctrine of progress; that looks forward, not backward; that sings of millennial days, and plans for the triumph of order and the reign of wisdom. Contemplating the world in sin and darkness, it comes as the breaker of the yoke of sin, and as a light shining in darkness, a purpose no other religion ever espoused, a work no other ever performed. No one who reads the pages of the New Testament will deny that its first principle—regeneration—is a preparation for progress, and that its last eulogy is pronounced upon the man who has risen from the dust to the throne. The teleology of Christianity, therefore, relates to the development of man into an ideal character.

Nor is this among the final recitations of Christianity, but really its first; or, representing it otherwise, the creation of man was the prophecy of his history, as it has unfolded into complex characteristics, and as it now points to an unending development and refinement of his possibilities. Studying the account in Genesis, it appears that man was *last* in the series of creative acts, and then suddenly it appears that he was *first;* in other words, there are two accounts, apparently contradictory in their chronological relations, to be explained only on the ground of two authorships, or rejected entirely. It falls not within our province to attempt a reconciliation of these accounts, further than to state that, viewed from the standpoints from which they are given, they are the same in substance, and consistent as a revelation of a historic act. The difference in chronology makes not against the authenticity of the record, but, on the other hand, adds to its value. Considering the double account as written by one hand from opposite points of thought, we see that man was the supreme subject, whom the sacred writer desired to represent in more than one relation. As one may write the history of the United States from A. D. 1620 to 1886, or, beginning with 1886, write backward to 1620, so the Mosaic account concerning man seems to be written in both orders; in the one, man is last, in the other he is first. Whether first or last, however, he is the pre-eminent character of creation, occupying the larger thought of the writer who records the creation. As *last,* man stands conspicuously enough in the series, waiting until the earth is ready for an inhabitant before he appears, and then he comes forth with a commission to subdue all things to himself. Last, he is greatest. As *first*, he precedes all things, as if independent of them, contented with the presence of God. It is not easy to determine whether as first or last he appears the greater, for he is great no difference when made, or how made. He either begins or ends the creative series; introduces the panorama, or gives it the finishing beauty; and is as pre-eminent in the one case as in the other. According to the original account, therefore, man is related to the world's beginning, and the world's beginning in both instances is subordinated to his position and destiny.

The assignment to such a position in the creative series implies not only the greatness of the creature, but also an equally conspicuous future in the development of the series. Representing him, not as an evolved being, but as created and divinely endowed, Christianity continually awakens in man the thought of his high origin, and the hope of a destiny that shall correspond to it. He was created in the divine image because a divine future lay before him. *His creation is implicit with eternal development.* Reasoning from analogy, this is patent from the divine order in the world's upbuilding, both of what we see and what we can not see. According to the theory of evolution, the different kingdoms of nature, ever subject to the laws of growth, exhibit a historic series from preliminary stages to complete or stationary forms, showing sometimes a leisurely development, and then a very rapid march to a given point, but in all cases observing a specific and fixed order of history. From lichens and mosses the vegetable kingdom has evolved into flowers and forests, beautifying the rugged earth, and ministering to the æsthetic element in man. From fishes and reptiles the animal kingdom has developed into mammoths, useful quadrupeds, and all other individuals embraced in zoölogy. Now, the striking fact in these kingdoms is, not merely development after a fixed order, but *development with reference to a final purpose;* in other words, the motive of the development is the end or purpose foreseen from the beginning. At every stage of their development these kingdoms pointed futureward, not aimlessly, not ignorantly, but prophetically of a higher order of life or form. The lichen was the prophecy of the forest, and the reptile of the whole animal kingdom. These prophecies of nature's kingdoms related not so much to general development as to development of a particular kind, and for the realization of a particular end, incorporated with the world's forces, and regulating them from the beginning.

But so manifest a historic development has its limits; almost universal, it does not apply to man; and, since it does not apply to man, another development or order of life must be predicated to account for his place in the universe. According to the Biblical revelation, the work of creation ceased with man; nor does it point to another and more highly organized being, as the result of a development of the original man. Man is the chief product of creative skill and wisdom; he will not become extinct by a natural order, and give place to a superior being. Creation not only stops with man, but centers in him its most delicate workmanship, and the most delightful prophecies of his greatness. He is the masterpiece of divine power and goodness. He is to develop, not out of himself or into another being, but *into himself*, as the rational exponent of God's idea of being. He is to develop, not into a grander being, inasmuch as he is grandeur itself.

In this presupposition we are but following the well-worn path of Bible teaching; but, well-worn as the idea is, it can not be too often reiterated that creation centers and exhausts itself in man.

Besides, the path terminates in the highway of Christianity which confirms and completes the original idea of man's creation. It is the only religion that confirms the history of man's origin and will complete the prophecy of his destiny. Taking him up where creation leaves him Christianity, centering in him all its recuperative forces, undertakes to build him up into a concrete model of life. It has no other mission than to fulfill the original purposes of his creation. *The masterpiece of creation, he will appear finally as the masterpiece of Christianity.* As at the first creation's forces centered in him, so at the last the forces of Christianity center in him, undertaking to do for him what the former failed to do, that is, to furnish him with adequate resisting power against evil and to develop his spiritual nature into perfection. The thought is overwhelming that Christianity focuses its power in man for his development, for it means that all righteous self-effort will be supplemented by divine agency and that the race need not despair; it means the employment of all the supernatural influences of Christianity in the great task of human development. Unaided in such a task, humanity must fail; yea, it will perish; aided by the divine forces, humanity will bloom with spiritual beauty and bear fruit unto holiness. Whatever Christianity is, whatever it can do, the pledge is that humanity shall be the recipient of its favor, and rise to the height of its promises. Not man as the masterpiece of creation, but man under Christianity, more, Christianity in man, guided by it, developed by it, *developed into it*, this is the future man, this is the highest man.

Under Christianity, as under no other system of religion, man is attaining to dominion of the earth and is bold enough to anticipate final and undisputed possession of its forces and facts. That physical dominion is one of the contemplated ends of his creation will be admitted at once by readers of Genesis, and by students of his adaptations, functions, and possibilities. The progress toward dominion it is confessed has been exceedingly slow, not at all in proportion to his capacity for dominion, nor sufficiently satisfying of his ambition or needs. For the most part, nature has had dominion over him, subjecting him to laws he did not understand, and playing with him, as a tempest with a yacht, or the wind with a fly. His intellectual dullness in the presence of nature was as apparent as his spiritual darkness in the presence of God. Until the dawn of Christianity, or until its influence began to be felt on the human intellect, nature was unsubdued, inspiring man with dread which expressed itself in religious superstition ; the stars were worshiped ; fire was deified ; comets were the heralds of evil ; animals and reptiles received human homage ; and in ignorance of the reign of law man subscribed to fate and drifted into pessimistic darkness, or a heartless faith. Nature won the victory ; man was a slave.

With the new torchlight in his hand, man has advanced in his conquest over nature, asserting as he goes his right to dominion, and making it good by a courage that must excite the admiration of the upper powers. He is ascertaining the limits of the empire of nature ; he is anxious to know what are the laws of this empire, and is persistent enough to demand a full revelation of them ; he is acquainting himself with the forms and forces, functions and adaptations of nature ; he has reduced the forests and exterminated the wild beasts that inhabited them ; he has discovered the various poisons hidden in nature's garments and found also an antidote for them ; he is conducting himself as if he were master of the situation.

This is one of his first duties arising out of his relation to the universe, namely, the subjugation of the earth and the acknowledgment of his authority in the empire of nature. By virtue of his creation this duty was imposed upon him, but without Christianity, as the stimulating and guiding force in conquest, he had failed. The idea of dominion is congenial to the new religion ; it fosters it in every way possible ; it dignifies man with a sense of authority ; it promises him royal prestige ; it exalts him to the throne. Hence, discoveries are not accidents, and inventions are not surprises ; they are the natural results of that inspiration which religion induces and of that expectancy which it creates. The revelation of new facts, the discovery of new principles, and the employment of forces in new ways, are in perfect harmony with the designs, and in **perfect** fulfillment of the purposes of Christianity.

If it is imagined that the work of subjugation is external and without relation to man's personality, and can not contribute to its development, it is because the relation of the external to the internal, or, more concisely, the relation of the physical to the spiritual, is misunderstood. Once examined, it will be seen that dominion is impossible without the supremacy of the spiritual over the natural; it implies such supremacy. What is dominion? Is it not the adjustment of man to his environment? Is it not the mastery of the material by the intellectual and spiritual? Does not conquest signify the superiority of man to material forces and laws? Dominion and the want of it is the difference between man, as a barbarian, and man as an enlightened, civilized, Christianized being. The barbaric man is not a discoverer or inventor; the developed man is both, and great in proportion as he is both. Over the former nature has dominion; the latter has dominion over nature. Thus the idea of dominion is significant of the idea of development; in fact, they are the same thing, or one without the other is a solecism. The duty of subjugation is enforced by the imperative condition that either man must regulate his environment, or it will regulate him; he must subdue the external or it will subdue him. The conflict is for single mastery and not for reciprocal dominion; one can not share with the other the title to authority; one must subdue the other. This is necessary to personal comfort and future destiny. Man's first work is along the physical line, external in character, but profoundly related to self-development and salvation.

Widening the view a little, *the relation of the occupations of men to self-culture and the spiritual life is as vital as the relation of the internal and external conditions of the race.* As pursuit is related to character, Christianity unobtrusively but effectually dictates to Christian nations those occupations which in their ultimate effects tend to moral elevation and the supremacy of man. To the superficial observer this may seem more poetic than real, and to the materialistic thinker it may seem grossly heterodox. Upon careful inspection we find that the motive of self-interest exercises a controlling influence in the selection of pursuit, but self-interest implies self-knowledge, and self-knowledge, broadened and refined by Christian truth, ordains just those pursuits which contribute most to human happiness and the general welfare of man.

Studying the occupations of men, one will see that they are the product of human necessities, tastes, environments, and, therefore, the providential result of the general situation. Why agriculture, commerce, art, business, legislation, government, industrial occupation, and the miscellany of pursuits in civilized lands? The explanation is at hand.  As a barbarian, man's wants are few in number and simple in spirit; he scarcely needs a house, clothing is a burden, fish, roots, nuts, and herbs constitute his food.  Turn the barbarian into a civilized man and his wants immediately multiply; he wants every thing; he wants a house, a wardrobe, a pantry; he wants a government and a Church; he wants law and education; he wants the universe and all that it contains.  He is an organized want, incessant in his demands on all existence to minister to him.  This change in aspiration, this march from simplicity to complexity, this demand for every thing, signifies that his barbarism has disappeared and a new life has taken possession of him.  It is this new life, born of Chris-tian thought, that expresses itself in the multiplied pursuits of men, that runs out into agriculture, art, commerce, education, government, and religious activity.

This, however, is not the whole truth respecting the subject.  It can not have escaped observation that the majority of men's pursuits in their aggregate effects do tend to promote that self-development of man which Christianity sets forth as its supreme aim and ideal purpose.  The moral content of human pursuit must not be ignored. Agriculture is a moral promoter of life, prosperity, and peace; commerce contributes something to international comity, and strengthens the doctrine of the unity of the race; the manufacturer or inventor who aids in expelling labor from the earth is fulfilling the command to subdue nature and exercise authority over it; the teacher, the journalist, and the minister, by pointing out the avenues of truth, is turning human thought to its highest possibility; and by all the pursuits of men the world is being lifted out of conservatism, misery, darkness, and delusion.

Another glimpse reveals the fact that those occupations which have for their direct object the supremacy of man are in the ascend-ency, while those are in a decline that oppose the manifest destiny of human dominion.  With the advance of the philanthropic spirit, the cultivation of the æsthetic faculty, and the priority of intellectual callings, the muscular or manual occupations have receded, or occupy the background of human progress.  Barbaric pursuits and barbaric methods had a kind of justification in the periods of savage life or during the pastoral epochs; but, as the earth is subdued, the race rises to philanthropic, intellectual, æsthetic, and religious ideals as the noblest objects of aspiration, and regulates its activities accordingly, From the savage state to the civilized condition the process is purely evolutional; every step is an advance; every age witnesses a ten-dency to an increase of human authority in the realm of nature; and the day is not distant when man will be perfectly adjusted to his environment by the aid of the pursuits which a Christian civilization originates and promotes. Not by Christian institutions alone, but also by the sanctification of the secular pursuits of men, is the ideal purpose of Christianity being wrought out. The plow, the ship, the locomotive, the easel, the yard-stick, the scales, and the pen contribute to this purpose as certainly as the Church, the school, and the home; that is, *the occupations of the race are related to the ideal end of the race as surely as the sacred agencies, divinely authorized to promote it.*

Under Christianity political government is harmonizing with the ideal purpose, in that it is gradually assuming a form consistent with the largest liberty of the individual, and is prompting by its concessions and auxiliaries to the largest development. Where it obtains, or has any reigning or assimilative power the tendency is toward a democratic form of government, which is the ideal conception of government, as revealed in the Scriptures; and so permeating is its influence that it is felt in lands where neither priesthoods nor rulers are disposed to recognize it. Whatever the uses of other forms of government, and however necessary they may have been in the early history of the race, the time has come when the personality of man requires for its self-assertion just that liberty which the republican type of government insures. While under any government genius may thrive, and the scholar secure honorable recognition, under many governments the masses are crushed, and rise only with an increase of liberty. So imperative is the government of liberty that without it progress is slow and degradation is sure. Despotisms, barbaric laws, legal cruelties and oppressions, have characterized the exercise of civil authority from the earliest ages; and, justified as they may have been by reason of the general ignorance, they did not promote culture or develop character. Better forms were, therefore, required. To overthrow the old forms, however, was no easy task, but it was finally accomplished by the agencies or suggestions of Christianity. As Christianity is received the impulse to popular or representative government, or the breaking away from the forms of tyranny, becomes intense and grows until it secures its end in democratic government. The political tendency, apparently at times to disorganization, nihilism, anarchy, is really toward personality, individualism, or the assertion of human rights. Individualism can not have the fullest play in governments, royal or despotic, as witness in Persia and Spain, but flourishes best in those civil conditions which deny to no man any right that belongs to another. This is a hard lesson for rulers to learn, but the people are learning it through the impregnating political enthusiasm of religion. As it prevails, caste and slavery, long the structural elements of society, disappear, and freedom with aspiration rules the heart of man.

It is not claimed that Christianity definitely points out the republican form of government as the ideal to which society in its civil constitution should conform; but it inculcates such political principles and favors such liberties, privileges, and rights, that such a form of government is a condition of their enjoyment; and by this indirect method such a form of government appears to have divine sanction, and to be preferred to all others.

It must not be forgotten that Christianity is the proposed religion of all races; that it is not the religion of a single nation; but that it has in view, without respect of persons, the elevation of all men and the conversion of all nations, going farther in this particular than any other religion or any other project devised by men. It has but one purpose, which includes all races and nationalities. That purpose is to make men free, politically, intellectually, spiritually; to develop the personality of every man; to insure to every man the fulfillment of his greatest possibilities. To be in harmony with such a purpose, political government must be democratic in spirit, guaranteeing the same inalienable rights to all its subjects, and fostering the noblest aspirations of the national life.

As Christianity spreads, taking root in the governmental idea, it will transform it, and the government will become more humane and liberal, and less cruel and extortionate; and the individualism of man, eccentric or orderly, regular or irregular, will have free course and be glorified. This expansion of individual rights; this guarantee of personality; this privilege of personal development, Christianity enjoins, and is enforcing upon the attention of rulers and people. This means progress, and progress means perfection.

The latitude of our vision extends over the *relation of Christianity to social customs, and social and moral institutions.* Do these to any degree feel the impression of Christianity? And to what extent are they involved in the execution of its ideal program? Without question, the social life of man in civilized lands is under the authority of religion, and is in a large degree molded by it. To be sure, acknowledgment of such influence, owing to human pride, may be reluctantly made; but, acknowledged or not, it is evident that customs, manners, institutions, neither distinctively religious nor political, have been under the guardianship of religious teaching, the results being seen in a healthy, moral tone in society and popular approval of refined sentiment and elegant conduct. Coarse, brutal manners, retire in the presence of the Christian spirit. Gladiatorial sports ceased at the command of Christianity. If bull-fighting is a pastime in Spain, to which the multitudes turn with delight, it is because Christianity has not taken root in public thought and does not sit on the throne. Cruel amusements, whether they involve men or beasts, religion condemns and will destroy. As for institutions, slavery went down beneath the righteousness of God; feudalism was consumed in the blaze of a quickened public judgment; and invidious social systems expire in the light of the truth that the Lord is the Maker of all men.

Again: Under Christianity the languages of men are undergoing such transformations, and are so rapidly approaching unity, that belief in a common elevation of the race is no longer chimerical, and the expectation of a universal tongue no longer an idle dream. The refinement of language, the multiplication of words, and the harmony of thought with the ideal purpose of religion, constitute signs of progress entirely due to Christian influence. Before any signal advance in these matters was observable human thought was impregnated with pagan ideas, and human speech was reduced to an exponent of the lower nature of man. We do not fail to remember that the Greek language in the days of Pericles was strong and bountiful, but the paganism of the age was the fountain that corrupted it, and unfitted it for future civilizations. Even current tongues, under Christian thought, are not free from coarseness, blasphemy, and provincialism, and modern literature itself can not claim to have reached perfection; but modern language is an advanced language. It is the representative of modern thought, which in its spirit is Christian and in its purpose progressive. As pagan thought has been superseded by Christian thought, so pagan words, phrases, and sentences have been superseded by Christian words, phrases, and sentences. Refinement in morals and manners has been followed by refinement in speech, intercourse, and conduct. The language of the street is being exchanged for the language of the home and the Church. Language now is the exponent of the higher nature of man, as before the reign of Christianity it was the exponent of the lower nature of man.

Hence, religious words have multiplied, and languages are taking a religious cast. Few there are that do not abound with words relating to the Deity, the soul, worship, and eternity. This is elevation; this is sanctification.

It is a remarkable sign of the times and a proof of the pervasive influence of Christianity that there is a belief in the final universality of one language in the world; that gradually the many dialects will subside or coalesce with one of the prominent languages; and at last all nations will speak one tongue. This is not an unreasonable

34

hope, nor are the probabilities against it, for all the languages are one; that is, they are branches of one trunk, having similar roots and pervaded by a similar life. The kinship is unmistakable, and unity is possible. This hope is like to other ideas that float in thinking circles, such as the unity of the race, the unity of the universe, the unity of history, and the unity of God, being founded on a similar basis, and quite as likely to become a practical realization. Underlying all history, all thought, is the idea of unity, in accordance with which is the expectation of one language. But unity of language signifies a common elevation and the cementing of the nations in a great brotherhood, by whose aggregated enthusiasm and in the light of the great Gospel purpose they will together march on to the higher development prefigured in Christianity.

The possibilities of man under Christianity may be discovered from still another standpoint. The scientific spirit of man is the prophecy of a new development of his intellectual nature to be achieved through the agency of religious influence. The direct bearing of science on the future man and the preparation it affords for the fulfillment of his great ends are of more consequence in this study than any thing that has hitherto received our attention, for, in a philosophical sense, it relates to the reign of mind in human affairs, which supersedes in importance the reign of man in nature. The latter is an external reign; the former, an internal reign. The one signifies dominion of the world; the other, *self-dominion.* Subduing his environment, and regulating his occupations by, and conforming his political governments to, the Gospel ideal, the question remains, what will he make of himself? External dominion is one thing; internal development another. Christianity promises both, insures both.

Through the stimulating energy of religious truth the scientific spirit in man has been wonderfully quickened in modern days, so much so that it has taken the reins in its own hands and is driving at a furious rate, exciting not a little alarm lest disaster happen to the very interests it would conserve. We say, let it go, or as Paul said of the ship in the storm, *we let her drive.* Scientific enthusiasm is not prejudicial to the best results in the Christian sphere. Spiritual truth supported by natural evidences is just as strong as if supported by spiritual evidences. Natural evidence and spiritual evidence must at last coincide in the defense of the highest truth. It is because scientific truth is in perfect harmony with spiritual truth that scientific evidences are as interesting as spiritual evidences, and no danger is possible to either, since both are one.

In these modern times the scientific spirit is as evidently under the administration of Christianity as are the pursuits, governments,

arts, and institutions of men, resulting in the pronounced activity of
the investigator, and in the accumulated facts and principles of the
scientific student.   One might not think so as, looking over the field,
he discovers materialism, pessimism, and agnosticism, in apparent
possession of scientific thought and arrayed against the very religion
by virtue of which their existence is possible.   All these antagonistic
elements were anticipated as belonging to the evolutionary stages of
scientific development; but in process of growth these excrescences
will slough off, and science stand as redeemed thought allied to the
divine.   In like manner the occupations of men formerly included
piracy, counterfeiting, gambling, and other pursuits not legitimate,
but Christianity is trimming human pursuit of its illegitimacy, and
preserving only those occupations which are right in themselves.
Political governments likewise at one time were despotic and inhuman,
but Christianity is modifying and refining them.   Similarly, science
loaded down with skepticism and agnosticism, Christianity will purify
and harmonize its greatest truths with the truths of religion.

Philosophy, seeing the inner content of truth, and anxious to find
out the basis of things, began with a theologic inquiry, but its
answers, always barren of a divine element, fell to the ground, and
yet they were valuable in suggesting the necessity of a theistic creed
as the solution of all mystery and the condition of all progress.
Science did not rise so high, did not see so far.   She dug in the dirt
and found diamonds, but could not properly estimate them.   Discovering facts, she could not explain them.   This is the limitation of
the scientific spirit as the theologic inquiry is the limitation of the
philosophic spirit within which the human mind may find sufficient
exercise for its development.   Just here man needs development.

Under scientific influence and with philosophic problems to solve,
the mind must enlarge, both in capacity and achievement; and as it
enlarges it must become conscious of the still higher destiny that is
possible.   Notwithstanding the superficial antagonism of the scientific
spirit to religious truth, Christianity has appropriated it as an instrument of man's development, seeing that culture is a part of the
property of the future man.   Man's expansion into a cultured and
sanctified consciousness is the primary object, the ideal purpose of
Christianity, for the realization of which it subsidizes every thing.

Such being the ideal end, it justifies the use and sanctification of
every thing, occupations, governments, arts, institutions, sciences, and
philosophies, that it may the sooner be accomplished.   Some of these
auxiliaries are not religious; they seem secular, physical, and incapable of producing religious results or contributing to the religious
ideal.   But the spiritualization of the secular life of man, and the

turning of the natural to spiritual account, is one of the secret virtues of Christianity and one of its methods for the success of its projects. As Jesus rode into Jerusalem on a colt, causing the earthly to carry the heavenly, so he lays upon the material the burden of the spiritual, or appropriates the earthly, the physical, the secular for spiritual uses and spiritual ends.

In view of its resources and adaptations, it is proposed as a fundamental thought that *Christianity has in contemplation the moral perfection of man*, the security of which is guaranteed by the provisions of the Gospel itself. As it is the only religion whose ideal purpose relates to man's highest development, so is it the only religion that provides for the realization of the purpose. With any other religion such a purpose would appear sentimental, dreamy, an idle hope, since adequate power for its execution would be wanting; with Christianity the purpose is the measure of the power, and the power the index to the purpose. By that general rule which limits results to aims, all religions may be judged; and Christianity stands or falls by it also. The results of a religion never exceed its purposes.

Inasmuch as philosophy never contemplated universality, it never provided for it, and never secured it. Brahminism, never dreaming of itself as a world-wide religion, spread but little beyond its birthplace. The internal thought of pagan religions has been that they were national, not international or cosmic religions; hence, they were satisfied with national recognition, and did not seek international dominion. On the other hand, Christianity is gifted with the universal impulse, and *aspires to cosmic honors*; it is not the religion for one people only, but for all; it knows no national boundaries, no race peculiarities, no climatic influences; it is world-wide in its aims, and universal in its adaptations. It reduces its manifold purposes to the central or ideal purpose of perfecting every man in Jesus Christ, and proposes to produce a race which shall be the exponent of the divine idea in its creation. This is its aim, and, as we study its agencies, mark its historic steps, pry into its adaptations and mysterious power, we see that it is practically succeeding, and that it must fully succeed. Its purpose is not Utopian, only as the Gospel itself is Utopian in content, promise, and potency.

Look at the Church as the divinely ordained agency of man's spiritual development. Of all the institutions that have appeared as the product of religion, or as sanctified by it to the welfare of man, the Church deserves the most grateful recognition, and its work the highest reward. Whatever criticism it deserves on account of its imperfection, it is animated by no other purpose than that which constitutes the ideal aim of Christianity; it is one with the Gospel purpose. In the lower sense, Christianity is a leavener of human society, stimulating man's impulse to dominion, directing and sanctifying his occupations, inspiriting and reforming his governments, penetrating and refining social customs and manners; but, in the higher sense, it concretes itself in a visible, organized institution, having as its sole purpose the turning of the eye of the world to its appointed destiny of moral greatness. Christianity has been creeping around and getting into every thing, whether men would or would not have it; but now it comes forth as an organized movement in the Church, announcing definitely its broad purpose, and striving deliberately, being conscious of its power, for its completion in the world's redemption.

The word "Church," so familiar to all ears, implies more than an assembly of people; it implies a *congregation of ideas and agencies in mutual fellowship*, and co-operating for a single result. Among its ideas are those of God, man's relation to God, man's relation to man, man's responsibility and immortality, from which grow the great systems of duty, morality, and religion. The ground-plan of the Church, its impulsive spirit, its instrumental ideas, are just such as must promote the purpose which Christianity has in view. For the diffusion of truth and the enlightenment of men in their highest interests, the agencies employed are entirely adequate and in harmony with the end. In proof, we point to the living ministry, who cease not to proclaim the existence of God, the methods of the divine administration, the moral character and responsibility of man, and the necessity of regeneration and holiness; who declare the will of the Most High, and the method by which "reconciliation" with God has been effected; who emphasize the conditions and reveal the sources of developed, purified character; whose vision is bounded only by eternity, and whose prophecies are only those of God. The Church insists that it is a divine institution, with a ministry to declare its relation to man's development. Its holy sacraments; its Sabbath days; its sanctuaries of worship; its benevolent societies; its Sunday-schools, prove that in many ways the Church has entered upon its specific work of enlightening and perfecting man.

Passing from the institutions and external agencies of Christianity to Christianity itself, it is evident that, great as is the task imposed upon it, its resources, its spirit, and its achievements furnish the guarantee of its future success. In the carrying out of its program it is not defective, or the mere echo of an ideal it can not reduce to practice.

By its own terms Christianity is the life of man, the inherent force of character. Speaking of Christ, John says, "In him was life;" and the Master says, "I am come that they might have life, and that they might have it more abundantly." Life! It is inspiration; it is growth; it is development. To have life "more abundantly" must signify more life, greater enlargement, deeper experience, an ever-widening consciousness of God. *More life* is the promise of the Gospel; *more life* is the cry of the soul; it means spiritual elevation, the opening of the spiritual faculties, the refinement of the spiritual tastes, the mutual indwelling of God and man. This whole idea of life is the product of Christianity, and its abundance is prophetic of new, better, and approximately perfect conditions for man in this world. Life is opposed to stagnation, inactivity, indifference, darkness, death. It has in it the possibility of infinite degrees of moral excellence. It opens the door to the eternal ages. It links thought to eternal truth. If the life promised by Christ is eternal, then the soul receiving it obtains an eternal impulse, a divine preference, a longing for all that is divine and eternal. He that receives Christianity receives a life-giving principle, and he that receives the life itself in its abundance may calculate upon never reaching the limits of growth, or exhausting the possibilities of grace.

The ultimate product of Christianity is the Christian, a new man, with new functions, new visions of life, new views of himself, and an increase of knowledge respecting God. Out of the old, sluggish life of the world, which, reaching a certain low height, falls back into routine and insipidity, the new rises in spiritual beauty and knows no end but that of God. Agesidamus, a Pythagorean philosopher, taught that the perfect man is a "self-sufficient man," but he meant an intellectual sufficiency. The "perfect man" of the Gospels is "self-sufficient;" sufficient because God dwells in him, because he is like God. He is fully equipped with the divine resources; he is not wanting in any good thing; he is full, complete. Such a man Christianity is adapted to produce; it does produce *the self-sufficient man.*

How true it is that "it doth not yet appear what we shall be!" As the barbarian has no pre-supposition of a civilized life; as the infant can not comprehend manhood; so man himself, civilized, Christianized, can not foresee his greatest possibility or his highest grandeur in Jesus Christ. Accepting Christianity, which, gratifying some aspirations awakens others, he finds himself silently unfolding, growing larger, seeing farther, until he catches glimpses of heights invisible from the fogs below. He rushes on, leaping over the mountains, rising toward the stars, gladdened in his journey by the music of another world, but is not satisfied until he has arrived at its open gates, whose keepers welcome him with the refrain, "Man, thou art immortal!"

# CHAPTER XXV.

## THE FRUITS OF CHRISTIANITY.

GROTIUS affirms that " the Christian religion . . . is so far from doing any thing destructive to human society, that, in every particular, it tends to the advantage of it." The value of Christianity is on exhibition in its benefits to human society.

The test of all inventions, discoveries, institutions, systems, civilizations, and religions, is their adaptation to human conditions, their ability to meet human necessities, their tendency to promote human happiness, and the security they give for the stability of promised results.

Truth itself can be distinguished from the false, and safe-guarded in its conflicts with error, by appealing to the *time-test*, by quoting its effects, by rehearsing its history. History is the supreme test of all things. In another form the divine Teacher announced the same principle when he said, " By their fruits ye shall know them." Under the operation of this rule the worth of all philosophies, all political economies, all constitutional governments, and all religions, may be fairly determined.

It may be insisted that many of the principles of the religions that perished, or are in process of extinction, are fundamentally right, but the answer is that what is fundamentally right is productive of good, is a helpful influence to those who accept it. To be sure, the law of gravitation has sometimes resulted in disaster, as notably in the Tay bridge calamity, and the law of combustion has sometimes resulted in injury, as when it laid Chicago in ashes; nevertheless the laws are holy and good; it was a violation of these laws that resulted in evil. These different systems of religion and politics have been productive of evil, not because their teachings were violated, but because they were observed, showing that they were fundamentally wrong.

And this is the *trying test of religion;* that is, the effect of its teachings when observed. Judaism itself, feeling the touch of this imperious test, surrendered on the ground of its inadequacy to conserve the welfare of the people. The law of Judaism received the encomium of Paul, but he reminded the fathers that it " made nothing perfect," and so did not accomplish what it undertook and what was necessary to man's spiritual growth and culture. Christianity, essaying the unfinished task of Judaism, and assuming all the prerogatives of a complete and competent religion, must submit to the same vital test, the rule of advantage to, or effect upon, human society. Admitting that at times and in places the results of its influence have not been satisfactory, it can be shown that superstition, fanaticism, and common ignorance jointly interfered with its designs and methods, and are responsible for any apparent miscarriage of the new religion in its relations to society. Such compromises or failures must be separated from the legitimate and orderly fruits of Christianity.

In both the Old and New Testaments the Christian religion is frequently represented under the similitude of a tree, as having been planted, as being guarded and cultivated by a husbandman, as budding, growing, and finally bearing fruit; in short, as passing through the different stages of growth from the seed to the great fruit-bearing tree. In Eden it is the "tree of life." Conceiving of it in this aspect, the great Teacher compares it to the mustard-seed, which, though the smallest of seeds, germinates and becomes one of the greatest of trees. John saw it in bloom in his old days, and described it as bearing twelve manner of fruits, and its leaves were for the healing of the nations. Christianity a tree! Shall we say a *new* tree, the *sequoia* of theology?

In the days of the Judean kings the religion of Moses was in the ascendency, but in the days of the prophets it was without vigor, it had lost its luster; the old tree that had borne fruit for Abraham, Samuel, and David began to decay; its leaves withered and fell to the ground; the trunk was knotty and worm-eaten; time had girded it with a cut that extinguished its life; and the venerable form, with roots broken, fell under the blast of a hurricane from the upper world, and gave place to another. Judaism, rotten, infirm, pauperized to the last degree, fell with resounding echoes into the arms of a providential fate that crushed it. This is simple history.

Jesus now appears planting a new tree in the old soil, grafting upon it all the divine elements of Judaism, and imparting to it such additional life-forces as have constituted it the imperishable religion of humanity. In careless speech it is sometimes said that Christianity is the off-shoot of Judaism, a position assumed by Prof. Lindsey in the *Encyclopedia Britannica*, but without warrant either in history or logic. Christianity was not derived in part or in whole from the preceding religion; it was adumbrated by the types or ritualism of the once famous faith, but is indebted to it for not one of its distinguishing truths. The passage of the old to the new was the transformation of certain eternal truths, common to all religions, or at least identical with the religious idea, into Christian forms, or the realities of a permanent religion. Holding that incarnation belongs specifically to the one and not to the. other, and that the Messianic content of the one is absent from the other, Christianity can not be accepted as an evolution of a former religion, or the development of a pre-existent truth. The student of the two religions, the old and the new, the extinct and the living, will discover the remains of the one in the other, but as the traveler discovers fragments of the temple of Ephesus in the Mosque of St. Sophia. Building material abounds in all religions, but the temple of Christianity is not a reconstructed edifice, but original throughout in plan, purpose, and achievement. What it has accomplished through the natural force of its truths, by virtue of its inherent tendencies to benevolent expansion, and because of its perfect sympathy with the highest human aspirations, must indicate somewhat its character, resources, and possibilities. We shall consider Christianity in two relations only, the *budding period of its history* and the *fruit-bearing period*, or its positive effects in human society.

The budding period was the period of its beginning, embracing such truths as were announced by the Master, together with the apostolic development they received, and such other truths as logically issued from such development. Embryonic truth may seem to differ from the same truth when developed as a man seems to differ from a child; but the outline is the same, and the substance differs only in degree. Incarnation, as an embryonic truth, was too mysterious to be understood, and was, therefore, rejected; but, as a developed truth, it is readily received; its relation to religion is one of indisputable necessity; its value determines the value of religion. Atonement suffered in its embryonic form, but, developed as a vital fact, it can not be abjured any more than religion itself. The resurrection idea ran the same gauntlet with the same result. With undeveloped truths in their hands the apostles started forth to conquer the world, or rather to enlighten it in those things concerning which there was more or less ignorance. Ignorant themselves of the fullness of these truths, they must have proclaimed them imperfectly; but, assisted by the Holy Ghost, they delivered them with power, and success followed. Embryonic truth has power; any truth, or any form of truth, is powerful; but developed truth needs less the external aid of the miraculous than the other. Hence, at a later period, *truth depended more upon itself*, drew upon its own contents, and was inspired by its own power, dispensing with miraculous supports and credentials from heaven. A religion that thrives by its inherent energy, calling upon itself to enlighten and move the world, is in advance of that religion that trusts more to external, artificial, or miraculous aids in its defense or for its propagation.

Without casting any suspicion on the origin of the Christian faith, or detracting in the least from the excellences of the early teachers, it may be stated that the apostolic period was the embryonic period of religion, requiring miraculous aid, and depending for success upon divine interpositions, such as no subsequent age has called for or desired. The most intimate friends of Jesus misunderstood his teachings; they were slow in apprehending spiritual truth; and without special divine assistance they had broken down in the beginning of their efforts to indoctrinate the nations. Peter succeeded on Pentecost because the Holy Ghost managed him and even directed his utterance. The sermon was not Peter's, but the Holy Ghost's. Under the supernatural developments of John and Paul, especially the latter, Christianity began to take doctrinal shape; but in the early stages it was a chaotic mass of truths—truth in the ore. Without form, it was not without power, but its greatest power appeared when it was reduced to system, and exerted itself through divinely ordered forms, and by the ministry of its own spirit. It is only as the crudities of apostolic teaching are reduced to, and organized into, a systematic whole that Christianity appears in its best light. While it is not the result of evolution from pre-existent religions, it is a self-evolution from apostolic stages to final truth in stable forms. For example, the Trinity, hinted at by the Savior and grasped at last by Paul, was left in a chaotic state by the apostles; and but for the resultant Church which expanded the doctrine into a rational conception, it had remained rather a grotesque or mythological picture than a stupendous revelation of the divine character. The doctrine of justification by faith, unfolded by Paul, did not bloom in all its beauty until Luther shouted it as the basis of the Reformation. The freedom of man, an apostolic truth, was smothered in its unfolding by the more commanding fact of the sovereignty of God, and it never had the fullest theological defense until Arminius raised it as one of the pillars of the temple of truth. The double thought of eternal retribution for sin, or the existence and perpetuity of hell, and of eternal glory and reward for virtue and godliness, or the perpetual duration of the heavenly life, was announced by the apostles, but for expansion, and for full understanding and discovery of the hidden contents of so wonderful a truth, we owe much to subsequent scientific and religious inquiry.

The apostles, as taught by the Master, foreshadowed a complete religion and delivered all necessary spiritual truths to mankind; but many truths they gave in embryonic form. From them the world has received a budded Christianity—a religion whose contents are all-sufficient, but whose development is even yet in its preliminary stages. Hence, not in the apostolic era, nor even in the first three centuries when its spread was violently rapid, and when the heroism of its defenders was never grander, will one find Christianity exerting its most beneficent influence, or displaying all its possible potencies. Courage, martyrdom, joyous experiences, enthusiastic projects, we certainly shall find ; but for the undermining power of Christianity, for its inspiration of the intellect, for its wide-spread and deep-rooted effect on civil government, for its purification of literature, its transformation of civilization, and the elevation of domestic life and social manners, and for permanent and powerful accomplishments in all departments of life, we must track its course along the ages, pausing longest over its career since the German Reformation. In the apostolic age it wrought wonders by the aid of miracle ; since that age it has wrought by the force of its truths. Our inquiry is not, what were the effects of a religion of miracles ? but, what are the *achievements of a religion of truth ?* In modern times Christianity stands by itself, vindicating its right to authority and dominion by its superhuman character, as exhibited in its spiritual program, and appealing to its work as an evidence of its genuineness and ability to do what it claims.

In its broadest aspect Christianity has been productive of a *new, if not model, civilization.* It must be conceded that an advanced civilization exists ; that is, a civilization superior to any thing either Rome or Greece reared and promoted now obtains in the world. Whence came it ? Without denying that other influences besides Christianity have contributed to the progress of mankind, it will appear on examination that in all the forward movements of the race the dominant force has been religious, with certain subordinate forces, of which there are many, working in harmony with it. Much has been attributed to Stoical philosophy as an instrument of the regeneration of the East, but it must not be forgotten that, while it frowned on many vices, it was inefficient in restraining them, and certainly powerless in destroying them. Concede that Stoicism objected to wrong, it did not introduce the right, or even approve of it, as presented by the teachers of the new faith. Equally incompetent to reform the world is the commercial spirit to which philanthropists sometimes have turned with expectancy ; but it has been on trial for ages, resulting, it is true, in a broader and better view of fraternity and unity, as the duty of nations one toward another, but not resulting in moral elevation or spiritual reform.

Buckle's theory of materialistic agency in civilization, instituted in the interest of an infidelity that has become reckless in its attacks on Christianity, loses sight of the highest forces in existence, thus compromising itself by its ignorance, and forfeiting respect by its assumption of causes entirely inadequate for the promotion of modern civilization. Cousin has demonstrated that physical forces are coming to recognize the authority of man, and are ready to contribute to the realization of human purposes, which, in their last analysis, appear to be the ideal purposes of God. Civilization is not the product of nature; nature is under the control of civilization.

Whatever the relation of the material forces to civilization, and granting that they may exercise a controlling influence, it is patent to the student of history that civilizations resting on such forces alone, and in disregard of the moral basis, have died of infirmities and disabilities which, under Christian rule, would have been restrained, if not extinguished. Not a little has been written in praise of the ancient civilizations, particularly the Egyptian, the Babylonian, the Grecian, and the Roman, as the exponents of material ideas; but it is significant that none of them exists to-day. Egyptian civilization represented the idea of force, combined with superstition, both being manifested in pyramids and temples, and the worship of animals and idols. All through it was tainted with slavery, or the subjection of man to cruel and irresponsible authority. Yet this Cyclopean civilization was unable to resist the tendency to decay, to which it so yielded that the relics of the days of its glory are few, indeed. The Babylonian civilization was the highest type of the lust principle, or the embodiment of the base, pleasure-loving spirit of man, and, though it maintained itself for fifteen hundred years, the site of its renowned capital can not to-day be identified; not only its chief city perished, but the whole empire disappeared like a spider's fabric. Of superior excellence in some respects, less brutal and more intellectual, less luxurious and yet not less corrupt, was the subsequent Grecian civilization, representing the perfection of art and the triumphs of philosophy; yet was it a civilization speculating in moral questions without determining their value, and preferring a low level of public life while seeking to know the truth, and so perished. Roman civilization, less philosophical and more practical, sought to represent justice, and enforce it by methods peculiar to itself. Ambitious for universal dominion, and boastful of its history, it pressed on, but wrecked itself on the rocks which lie in the path of nations that disregard the first principles of morality, and center their supreme thought on themselves.

The testimony of history is that a singular fatality has overtaken all civilizations destitute of moral principles. The epitaph of such civilizations may be reduced to a few words: they were born, they grew, they declined, they died. If materialism points with any pride to such civilizations, it should not be blind to the lesson their history discloses, for it makes plain that another basis is required if civilizations are to endure.

Succeeding all these, or at least different from them, is what may be denominated Christian civilization, an order of governmental life that has the promise of perpetuity in it, whose fate is not decay, corruption, and death. No one can affirm that such a civilization has had equal chances with the others, or that it has not met with obstacles in its attempt at development, for, all along its history, it has been resisted from within and without; within, since its nature has been misunderstood by its own subjects; without, since evil foresees its downfall in the triumph of the Christian conception of government. *The ideal Christian civilization is yet future.* Heretofore, as now, and now, as heretofore, material forces and antagonistic influences too largely affect the spirit and purposes of our progressive civilizations; passion, lust, brute force, slavery, caste, ambition, intemperance, and all the lower forces, are at work to prevent the sway of beneficent authority, and the erection of Christian governments among men. Yet such a civilization is the demand of the world. If Rome, in the days of her splendor, needed more than any thing else a new religion, so the world to-day needs, more than all things else, the inspiring touch of the Christian religion. Into our dark world the light of the new religion has shone, but as by broken and refracted rays.

New political governments, having in view the suppression of vice and the conservation of virtue, and especially regardful of the natural rights of man, have been and still are a necessity, but they never arise as a philosophic suggestion, or as the product of the order of things. They come forth, if at all, as the result of the inspiring force of Christianity, although such force may have no definite recognition. Often it works so silently, its truths being gradually diffused throughout empires and nations, that even statesmen are apt to forget their controlling power, and take to themselves the credit of the advances in popular sentiment and political change. Disguised or open in its work, heeded or unheeded in its influence, Christianity is the dynamic element of the best civilizations.

*Christian government is the political ideal of the Gospel.* For centuries this ideal had no recognition, though Christianity was accepted in its true character as a divine religion. It was accepted as a religion only, its political genius being unknown. It was received as a spiritual system, without political bearings or suggestions. It was seen to be fundamental to Church life; but governmental forms, principles, and laws were left to statesmen with political wisdom. Religion and politics were separable. The mistake of ignoring religion in the framework of government was at last discovered; but no sooner did it dawn upon the national mind than the democratic idea began to grow. Political heresies were investigated, condemned, abandoned. The tyrannical doctrine of the divine right of kings was undermined. The trend of society was toward the original ideal. Granting that other influences were associated in the subversion of gross political sentiments, which justified oppression, slavery, and debauchery, still, more is due to the Christian ideal than to all other agencies combined. Without Christianity, other agencies had been ineffectual; with it, they accomplished something, receiving more credit than belongs to them. Buckle's materialism never rose as high as the original ideal; Plato's best idea of government was impossible of realization.

That all governments are not democratic in spirit and Christian in form, and that so-called Christian governments are still politically imperfect, often enacting laws contrary to the public welfare, and refusing to legislate in harmony with Christian teaching, establish that religion has not fully triumphed in the political thought of society. In Christian lands, there are institutions, monopolies, customs, and partisanships, which Christianity does not justify, and which it will overcome as its rightful influence is extended and obeyed. Tyrannies, race discriminations, socialism, oppression of woman, ignorance, poverty, and crime co-exist with the Christian religion in the state. Verily, this ought not to be. The work of correction, assimilation, and regulation is slow, but it is not fruitless, and it will be complete in due time. As a political religion, as the basis of civilization, Christianity is not a failure.

Quite as remarkable as the general effects of Christianity are the special results of its influence in the world. Admitting that, under its fostering care, a broader and a higher civilization has appeared, it is equally noteworthy that, in the narrower fields of human effort, its influence is no less conspicuous, and its power no less manifest. In the lowest sense, it is the inspirer of the *material activity of human society.* While the force of Christianity, as a religion, has been constantly emphasized, other features, and this in particular, have been disregarded. The result is, that the opinion prevails that its effects, outside of religious thought, are incidental and insubstantial. It is time to correct the misapprehension, for the relation of religion to labor, or the occupations of men, is most intimate, and the results of the union have been surprisingly great. The old religions threw no halo around physical toil, but degraded it. Brute force ruled in all the realms of life. The only birthright of man was the birthright to toil. By the terms of the old covenant, he must eat his bread in the sweat of his face; but even so healthful a law the old religions carnalized to the last degree. Man, as an intellectual being, as spiritual and immortal, and, therefore, to be educated, disciplined, redeemed, the old faiths did not comprehend. Hence, man became a slave, a burden-bearer. He was oppressed, robbed of wages, reduced to starvation; impossible results were exacted of him; the consequence was the loss of manhood, the decline of aspiration, the extinction of freedom, the death of hope.

To reverse this state of things, or rather, to extinguish the social order, and raise man from the dust, a new religion was needed. As Christianity asserted itself, a sympathetic religion was perceived to hover over the world, and the millions shouted for joy. Instead of adding to burdens, it lifted them; instead of enslaving, it proclaimed freedom; instead of centering wealth, it diffused it; instead of merging the individual in the State, it defined his responsibility. Under the new religious administration, the rights of property were guaranteed to all; privateering on the seas, and confiscation on the land, were stigmatized as robbery, and punished as other crimes; legislation from the time of Constantine was favorable to the poor man; and it became evident that, so long as the Golden Rule had authority, every man would reap the fruits of honest toil.

This general change of sentiment was followed by other and far-reaching changes in the social structure, that secured to the common people additional safeguards and privileges, such as the right of suffrage, and the right of representation in national councils, especially when taxed. Nor were such legal concessions lost on the laboring classes; for, stimulated by larger privileges, and strengthened by self-respect, they sought to make labor honorable by a new consecration to its offices. It is a noteworthy fact, whatever the explanation, that in Christian lands the spirit of invention characterizes every department of human industry, reducing the difficulties of labor, and multiplying the comforts, not only of the workingman, but of all classes of society. To affirm that agriculture is indebted to Christianity for machinery, ought to be a truism. To affirm that the inventions in Christian lands are the product of the Christian religion, is as true as to affirm that Churches and Sunday-schools are its products also. Even if this is true indirectly, it is true enough for our purpose. Heathendom is not prolific in invention, and can not manufacture the best instruments of labor. The locomotive, the telegraph, the sewing-machine, the reaper, the telephone, and the printing-press must be credited to the Christianity which is the root of the civilization under which such inventions are possible. Ours is a steam-engine civilization, in the sense that the civilization produced the engine, not the engine the civilization. Buckle's material forces did not produce Christian society, but Christianity developed, pointed out, and employed the material agencies by which the world has been lifted out of stagnation and death.

Moreover, famines, which are of frequent occurrence in heathen lands, as in India and China, are impossible in Christian lands. National sympathies are too acute for one-half of a nation to permit the other half to starve. Besides, such is our knowledge of soils and seasons, and the relation of labor to harvests, that a failure of crops is an incident that does not affect the general welfare. The rewards of labor, the motives to steady, persistent toil, in a Christian country, are different from those in pagan countries; and, as a result, in the former, activity is manifested on a stupendous scale, inventions that almost accomplish miracles multiply, the blessings of peace extend, the idle are prompted to achievements, the ambitious are restrained by principles, evils are curtailed by an intelligent, moral, public sentiment, and labor is honorable in the sight of men. In its sanctification of labor, its inspiration of the laborer, its stimulating effect on inventive genius, its condemnation of idleness, and its prevention of the evils usually associated with labor, Christianity commends itself to the students of social science and the statesmen of governments.

The story of the effect of Christianity on, or its relation to, literature and education, is most wonderful, whether considered only in its general aspects, or minutely, *and must answer all objection to its power to direct the thinking of the world.* With the opening of the Dark Ages the Bible compulsorily retired as an inspiring agency, or was imprisoned in a cell, from which its light did not shine upon the outer world. At the call of Luther it came forth, never to return ; it spoke, and a listening world heard. Long prior to the Reformation an attempt was made to break the spell of dullness which had held in thralldom the whole civilized world, but it was only partially successful, and finally failed. The age of the schoolmen will be remembered as an age of scientific inquiry under the leadership of Roger Bacon, of philosophic investigation under the patronage of Duns Scotus, and of unsettlement of theologic dogmas under a host of thinkers ; but, marked by spirit, and promising in the beginning, it was only preliminary to the literary eagerness which became contagious throughout Christendom after Luther broke his chains. Before the Reformation Europe was without a practical or intense intellectual life ; since that period, which secured the right of private judgment touching truth, and emancipated the intellect from all dogmatic grips, mankind have advanced in knowledge to a degree almost incredible. Science, some of whose advocates have had the temerity to charge that religion is hostile to its pursuits, never flourished, never discovered so much as since it was given a *cärte-blänçhe* to ransack the universe for facts and reveal the laws under which the present physical order exists; philosophy, piloted into the realm of mysteries by Christian teachers, has apprehended as never before the juxtaposition of all truth to the central idea of Christianity; poetry turned to the Bible for epics and songs; and the whole range of literature has been electrified by the presence and inspiration of the new religion. Geology has had its expounders in Chalmers, Whewell, Hitchcock, and Pye Smith, honored Christian names; mathematics has been represented by Isaac Barrow, Roger Coles, Matthew Stewart, and others, all defenders of the Bible; and in a general way it is enough to mention Faraday, Samuel Clarke, Carpenter, Fleming, Sir William Thompson, Abbé Picard, Priestley, and Bradley, Christian thinkers all, as the exponents of scientific truths and discoveries, to establish the indebtedness of scientific thought to religious influence. The same is true touching poetry. Neither Milton could have written "Paradise Lost," nor Dantć his "Inferno," had not the Scriptures furnished the facts and suggested the purpose to use them. Cowper, Montgomery, Toplady, Heber, and Charles Wesley, the authors of sacred hymns, were less indebted to their genius than to the Scriptures for subjects, experiences, truths, and melodies. The same may be said of Coleridge, Tennyson, Longfellow, and Willis; and even Byron wrote best when under the inspiration of the Hebrew spirit. Strike Christian sentiment from modern poetry, and it would be equal to expelling oxygen from the atmosphere.

All literature has equally shared in inspirations from this common source, though the debt is more obvious in some departments than in others. Let it be philosophical, historic, ethnic, religious, or scientific, the department has been affected more or less by the commanding truths of Christianity, either modified by them, or vainly attempting to modify them; but whether resisting or accepting them, whether harmony or struggle be the result of contact with them, the effect is marvelous and usually visible. Skeptical literature owes its possibility to that which it assails. Voltaire was possible only because twelve apostles lived and died; Rénan had written nothing had not Christ and Paul lived and taught; Hume never had discussed miracle had not the miracle-worker first appeared; Matthew Arnold writes because there was a Christ.

Again, the incidental effect of the truths of Revelation in lit-

35

erature is quite as impressive as the more direct and positive influence. The majority of books not religious relate to subjects which it has suggested and it is difficult to write on things entirely outside of it. Even the novelist gives a Christian tinge to his stories, or impregnates them with Christian sentiment as the means of commending them to public opinion. One lays down "The Tale of Two Cities" by Charles Dickens in tears because the hope of the resurrection is mingled with the execution of a doomed man. "Ben-Hur" by General Wallace is but a tale of the Christ. The thought of God, as developed in the Old Testament; the character of Christ, portrayed in such simplicity in the Gospels; the thrilling ideas of inspiration, miracle, prophecy, retribution, and immortality find their way into public thought, crowd the magazines, fill the newspapers, and multiply volumes without end.

On the other side, what libraries have issued in defense, exposition, and elaboration of Christianity! Since the invention of the printing press pens have been busy with the discussion of the great Biblical problems, in an attempt to elucidate their mysteries or find the limits of human thought, and the treatises on such subjects are practically inexhaustible. At one time the drift of thought is toward the historical evidences of Christianity; at another it turns to the philosophical phases of religion; yesterday it discussed miracle; to-day it is hermeneutical; once it was doctrinal; now it seeks the practical elements of religion; once it considered heaven and hell as eternal states; now it mutters purgatory, an intermediate world, and a second probation; hitherto the mode of baptism was a subject of interest; at present the meaning of *Sheol* is of more consequence. Thus the discussion of truth goes on, the Christian thinker having gone beyond Calvin, Edwards, and Luther to clearer visions of the divine revelations.

For the *preservation of the Anglo-Saxon language*, the world is indebted more to the Bible than to the ordinary agencies believed to be sufficient to insure the stability and purity of a living language. Containing idiomatic English, and being read by the people as no other book is read, the Bible holds them to a common speech, and tends to create a universal language, thereby aiding the slow-growing doctrine of the unity of the race. The great objection to the Revised Version of the New Testament is that, while it is faithful to the original Greek, it violates the idiomatic Saxon with which the public mind is familiar, and from which it is unwilling to depart, showing a disposition to make the Saxon the standard of correct language. Careful linguists inform us that while fully one-third of Gibbon's books consist of words not Anglo-Saxon in form or origin, and while Shakespeare derives one-sixth of his words from foreign sources, and Addison one-eighth, only *one-twenty-ninth* of the words in the Bible have a foreign complexion. This speaks much for the purity of the English tongue and is a guaranty of its future stability and growth.

In the matter of *popular education* Christianity must be credited with an influence so promotive of it that in its absence, or where it is resisted the masses are in ignorance and without mental aspiration. In reply to this position reference is occasionally made to the universities of India and China, whose curricula, it is claimed, equal those of the universities of the United States; but this is not true; besides, the masses of those countries are in the chains of an ignorance harder to be broken than the physical chains of slavery. Popular education is unknown in the Orient. With shame it must be said that Christian countries have been slow enough in providing for universal education; that in our land the illiteracy is extensive and threatening the safety of our institutions; and that in Roman Catholic countries it is still more appalling. This unhappy condition, however, is the result of a narrowness not born of Christianity, of a prejudice that a false religion or a blind judgment would sanction, but which the new religion is bound to overcome. In Christian lands, where religion has half a chance, colleges and schools do flourish, ignorance is being limited, education is regarded as the sign of manhood, and a general intellectual desire obtains among the people. In England, Oxford and Cambridge are the fruits of the Christian religion. In the United States, Yale, Harvard, Princeton, Dartmouth, Amherst, Ohio Wesleyan, DePauw, as universities, and hundreds of seminaries and academies, were born of Christian influence. Perhaps all our colleges, save Girard College, are the direct result of Christian benevolence and teaching.

In the matter of public schools Christian nations lead, Prussia standing at the head, with the United States second, and England and Greece not far behind. Such fruits indicate the worth of the tree that bears them.

Nor in this category of effects would it do to omit the *influence of Christianity on Art,* for its divinest achievements have been realized under the inspirations of the true religion. Long before the Master walked the earth the fine arts flourished in the East, and, so far as genius directed, they were developed to perfection. In the age of Pericles sculpture reached the limit of beauty and finish; beyond the models of the artists of that day no nation has gone. Egypt, too, devoted herself to figures of stone, chiseling them rather out of granite than marble; and Rome, ever imitative of the colossal and the beautiful, endeavored to excel her masters, and painted what she could not chisel.

But, applying a supreme test, what was the effect of pagan or pre-Christian art on society, government, and religion? In a single sentence, pagan art was the source of the corruptions of social life that obtained throughout the East, and justified the terrible description of Rome as given by Paul in his Epistle to the Romans. Dr. John Gillie states: "It is unnecessary to crowd the picture, since it may be observed in one word that the vices and extravagances which are supposed to characterize the declining ages of Greece and Rome took root in Athens during the administration of Pericles, the most splendid and the most prosperous in the Grecian annals." If asked how ancient art became so debasing, and what was its relation to the public life, the answer is, that it appealed to the sensual in man, developing the lower life, and debauching the public taste. Designed to minister to the æsthetic, it forgot its mission, or confounded it in a ministry to the lustful and baser elements in humanity. The love of the beautiful, divinely inwrought in human nature, was supplanted by an expressed preference for the carnal, resulting in licentiousness, degradation, and national overthrow. Besides, the range of ancient art was exceedingly limited, its subjects coming more frequently from mythology than from nature, biography, or history. Bacchus, Venus, Apollo, Ceres, and Juno engaged the sculptor's chisel oftener than the heads of generals and rulers. Neither poetry nor philosophy had any elevating effect on art. In the midst of pagan ideas, it rose no higher than their level, and at last, sinking beneath that level, drew all down to its depths of degradation.

Turn we now to Christian art, whose range is as extensive as history, whose subjects are as numerous and various as biography, nature, and the Bible can present. Pagan art largely devoted itself to sculpture; Christian art, to painting. The best products of Christian art are representations of Bible scenes, and from the hands of masters who have lived within the last three or four centuries, or since Christianity has taken a modern aspect and been endowed with a modern energy and purpose. As specimens, and as indicating the spirit of art since the Reformation, we need only mention Leonardo da Vinci's "The Last Supper," Raphael's "Transfiguration," and Michael Angelo's "The Last Judgment." That the galleries of Europe are adorned with paintings of the Temptation, the Baptism, the Crucifixion, the Resurrection, and the Ascension, is proof of the sacredness of art; and that the Old Testament furnished such subjects as Creation, Eden, the Flood, the Ark, Abraham's Sacrifice, the Tabernacle, and the Temple, for the painters' pencils, is evidence that art has discarded mythology, and preferred the facts and events of Bible times and history.  Even Gustave Doré, who was not Christian in faith, regarded his artistic Christ as his masterpiece; and certainly his representations of New Testament events were not below par.  Take Christ or the Bible out of modern art, and it shrivels like a wrinkled parchment.

To be sure, other subjects than the religious have engaged the thought and skill of modern artists; military scenes, historical events, landscape views, and fancy sketches, occupy the entire time of many celebrated painters; but it must be allowed that, on the whole, art is predisposed to the Christian idea, and is consecrated to the moral elevation of the race.  This is the difference between ancient and modern art, the former degrading, the latter ennobling man.

Yet this difference can only be allowed with qualification, for Christian art is not entirely free from pagan influence; and so far forth as pagan ideas have infected modern art, it has lost in moral power; while so far forth as it has confined itself to its legitimate mission of moral instruction, it has promoted the objects of religion.  It must also be conceded that those nations that have fostered Christian art the most are more corrupt than Protestant nations that have not considered it the handmaid of religion, a fact that needs explanation.  Germany is the nursery of socialism; France, of infidelity; Italy, of Roman Catholicism; *they patronize the fine arts.*  Neither England nor the United States pays a premium on the arts, and yet both are advanced in civilization and religious activity beyond Germany, France, and Italy.  What account can be given of these facts?  Is it a credit to Christianity that it fosters the fine arts at all?  We think it is.  The evils we speak of are not inherent in art, or inevitable products; some of them are political in their nature, others are social, others intellectual, and some religious, and might or might not exist with or without the fine arts.  Pure art is possible, and has a mission.  That it has not been in the ascendant is because Christianity has been corrupted by paganism and enfeebled by the Papacy, all its products being more or less modified by the spirit of one or the other.  In its Protestant form, Christianity has rarely expressed itself in art, resigning its interest to the Roman Catholic monopoly of the æsthetic ideals.  For it must be remembered that the great artists of modern times have been, and are, Roman Catholics, men who like to paint Madonnas, angels, and martyrdoms, and who, going to the Bible for their subjects, pervert it in the interest of their own faith.  But if while in bondage to Roman Catholic teaching it has suggested the masterpieces in the Louvre and the Vatican, what would it not do under the purer guidance of Protestant thought and liberty? If Christianity has any duty to perform respecting art, it is to rescue it from the superstitious grasp of mediæval thought, and clothe it with the nineteenth century beauty and aim.

Passing to *architecture*, Christianity, as in other departments, has exerted a prominent and wholesome influence, traceable from the days of Constantine down to the present time. Religion has always dictated temple architecture, the structures built in its name being the expression of some dominant thought, or the embodiment of some divine purpose. Christianity has been the originating or suggesting cause of the historic and current styles of Church building in Europe, as it has been the world over where its presence has been recognized. Granting that the Ionic, Doric, and Corinthian styles of columns had a pagan origin, and have not been eclipsed for beauty by any modern discovery or invention, it is true to say that Byzantine architecture and ecclesiastical edifices constructed after the Greek or Latin cross were possible only because Christianity was the dominant religion, and the Church sought to express that religion in the forms of its edifices. Church architecture owes little to pagan models. Back of the Christian period, the temple was patterned after a divine suggestion, and it is noteworthy that all succeeding temple structures are but modifications of the original ideal given to Solomon. From the dawn of the Christian era the different styles of Church building, the Roman Christian, the Byzantine, the Romanesque, the Gothic, and the Renaissance have appeared as the products of Christian ideas, representing to the outside world the principal factors of the Christian religion. It is not claimed that Christianity has influenced the styles of dwellings as it has those of basilicas and tombs; but that it has contributed to the improvement of architecture, and that in Christian lands the dwelling-house has been beautified, are among the facts that establish the helpful influence of religion in the common spheres of life.

Eagerly we proceed to notice the relation of Christianity to *reformatory movements*, or its aid in the removal and extinction of mammoth public evils, for its power must be felt here if anywhere. As an operating force Christianity is apparently slow, working with almost careless interest in human affairs, but its purpose is never obscured or unknown, and its final declaration is always executed. It stands in open hostility to all illegitimacy, whether political, social, or religious; it is in alliance with no evil; it is on fraternal terms with no wrong. At the same time it is not a direct antagonist, or violent opposer of wrong in the sense of a persistent and immediate destroyer of it. It does not precipitately array its forces against evil and overthrow it by a single blow, but it is an undermining force that, like sappers, requires time for its work. Witness the long reign of Mohammedanism in the Orient, a single providential order, a single divine movement would extinguish it; recall the weary despotism of feudalism, it might have been speedily overturned had God's hand interposed; observe the slow decadence of slavery in the world—such a gigantic evil had subsided long ago had the providential purpose ripened fast; see how polygamy has dominated the Oriental nations—it ought to give place to the Scriptural idea of marriage; observe that intemperance has invaded society and shaken the altars of religion; and the inquiry is pertinent, Does God reign, or is Christianity able to cope with the great evils in the world?

This, however, is a very superficial statement of the case, or at least is not a broad view of the methods of God's government and of the agencies he employs for the reduction of evil. To the remark that Christianity is an undermining religion must be added another, and that is, that it is an *inspiring* religion, propelling to just that activity required for the final extinction of the evils that afflict the world and demonstrating by this method its positive inclination to righteousness and its purpose to extinguish all forces opposed to it. For the evils that infest human society, disturb its peace, and threaten its safety, mankind are for the most part directly responsible and must themselves organize for their removal. God sends the cyclone, the lightning, the sirocco, the tempest; against these we may pray, asking that the divine hand be stayed; but he never sent intemperance, or slavery, or Mormonism, and, therefore, is not to be invoked to put them away. *That belongs to men to do.*

Let us be understood. Moral evils originate with men and must be abandoned by men. The relation of Christianity to such evils is not that of a destroyer, but that of an inspirer, quickening the reformatory spirit in man, and prompting him to abolish evil. As the destruction of evil is in man's hands, its long reign in the world is explained. Had the Almighty assumed the prerogative of Destroyer, evil had disappeared long ago; but as man must be destroyer he dallies, hesitates, debates, reluctantly puts evil away, and sometimes after advancing against it backslides and returns to his idols. This explains the rise and fall of evils. By its undermining processes, and its inspiring influences, Christianity aids in the extinction of evil, the amelioration of human ills, and the moral elevation of society.

What has been the result? The annals of the Romans abound in gladiatorial scenes, cruel in themselves, and debasing of the common taste; slaves, prisoners, culprits, and Christians were compelled to fight with wild beasts or with one another in the Coliseum or in the theaters; emperors, nobles, and patricians regarding the spectacles as amusements for their benefit, and encouraging them by their patronage. In vain Constantine endeavored to suppress them; in vain were the denunciations of moral teachers; in vain did pure-minded philosophers condemn. For four centuries after the Incarnation the bloody exhibitions continued with the connivance of royal authority and the support of the higher classes of the imperial cities. How were they finally suppressed? Read the story of the victory of Alemachus, an Eastern monk, in the Flavian theater, and learn that the extinction of the gladiatorial spirit was due to the courage of a Christian. Even so feudalism went down under the reformatory demands of the Gospel. Likewise slavery, though now not an unknown evil on the face of the earth, has been banished from Christian and civilized lands, never to return, for it is a historic sign of providential progress that when a national evil is overthrown it is never restored. To be sure, it cost something to expel it from the United States, as the expulsion of any evil means a struggle and suffering, but its going was a victory for the Gospel. Through the benevolent spirit of Christianity reforms in prison life have been instituted; wretched punishments have been abandoned; tortures have ceased; and a new idea of penalty has modified criminal legislation. The spirit of feud, so rampant in the days of chivalry, and which had something to do with the establishment of the order of knight-errantry, no longer broods over the social circle; the duel is rare and under ban; and so rapid has been the growth of the philanthropic spirit, and so universal the desire for peace, that arbitration is being resorted to as the best method for the settlement of international differences and difficulties. Surely these are no small results, effected largely by the presence of the peace-inspiring religion in the world.

The *Christian home is the fruit of the Christian religion.* Outside of Christian lands, or where other religions prevail, the basis of the family institution is tyrannical and unsafe, domestic habits and customs are corrupt and profligate, superstition prostrates individual energy and purpose, and domestic sweetness and beauty are unknown. For the model family or the ideal home one will not go to India, China, or Japan. In Siam many of the Chinese live in floating houses, and are as nomadic as the Bedouins, or as the men who in primitive times clothed themselves with skins and dwelt in caves. In pagan and Mohammedan countries the social position of woman is incompatible with a refined and elevated condition, her capabilities for a larger and more helpful life are unrecognized, her instincts are smothered, her rights denied, and the home of which she should be the center and pride is little else than a nursery of vice. Brahminism and Buddhism shut the women up in their zenanas, cover their faces with veils, screen the windows of their apartments with lattice-work, and teach them that they are degraded and without souls. What sorrow fills a household when a girl is born! No wonder that polygamy, with all its related vices, is authorized in such countries, and that woman is a toy or beast of burden. Even the Koran takes this view of woman, sanctioning the believer's right to at least four wives, though the sheiks of the desert often have many more. In polygamy, female degradation, and domestic cruelty, the homes in pagan lands have had their birth.

As enunciated in the Scriptures, the true basis of marriage is monogamy, but, like every other good principle, this doctrine has come down the ages, opposed by malice and ignorance, and has run the gauntlet of sophistry, paganism, superstition, and crime. As a Christian principle, it confronted the social corruptions of Rome in the days of Paul and Seneca, when, indeed, vice was on the throne, and innocence was a barren ideality. Stoicism was absolutely power-less to check the reign of the social vice among the aristocratic classes, who lived only for pleasure, and sought it in their own degradation. To no lower depths of corruption could society go, when, as Uhl-horn represents, "friends exchanged wives," and, as Tertullian re-marks, "they marry only to be divorced." This is enough. To turn the tide of infamy, to condemn the public licentiousness, to restore the idea of purity, to establish the home in its ideal aspects, was an un-dertaking all other religions shrank from, as being absolutely un-promising of any good. In this emergency Christianity assumed the task, entered upon it with vigor, demolished the altars of shame, raised woman from the pit, and restored to man his lost manhood and virtue. The change in the social life of the State was immediate and unequivocal.

Thus has it ever been when the true principles of religion have been announced, and the sincerity of the conscience invoked. Against the domination of these principles polygamy, bigamy, and lust have protested with lecherous voices, asserting their priority in the social institution, and even defending themselves as inviolable and legitimate. In vin-dicating Mormonism, Joseph Smith declared that four-fifths of man-kind believed in and practiced polygamy, while only one-fifth held to monogamy. So extravagant a statement has not gone uncontradicted, but it is confessed that the monogamous principle of Christianity met with obstruction from a majority of the races and peoples of the globe; hence its triumph is all the more conspicuous, and indicative of its power in the regulation of the domestic life of the world.

Insisting that the model home must be founded on the Gospel

idea of marriage, and that this idea is in the ascendant, it is as notorious as it is painful that in many of the States of Christian America divorce laws are so numerous and so elastic that the marriage relation can be dissolved without effort, and illegitimate combinations thereafter formed.   This is one of the evils incident to the reign of the higher principle of marriage, which must be combated until checked and overthrown.   However, bigamy and polygamy have no countenance in law or custom in these lands, and exist, if it all, in violation of law.   Here, if anywhere, the model home may be found ; here woman is the helpmeet of the husband, and the mother is the ruler of the household ; here God is worshiped at the domestic altar, and purity makes sacred both conjugal and filial relations.   Lyman Beecher's and Martha Washington's homes were the products of the Christian idea.

This is the beginning of Christian society, with its contents of order, fraternity, unity, liberty, and philanthropy.   *The great though: that of one blood God made all the nations of the earth is of Gospel origin,* signifying the unity of the race, and necessarily the equality of man before God and under the Gospel.   In its historical development society drifted away from the fundamental principle ; as a fact, it never was organized on this principle, and left to itself, it never voluntarily would adopt it as the prime element of governmental order and life.   In the legendary period of Greece the theory was advocated that men were composed of gold or silver or iron, as they represented different virtues, and that dissimilarity of character established a difference of origin, which prevented the recognition of unity and equality of rights.   Such a spirit has always and everywhere prevailed, except where Christianity arrayed itself against it, and breathed the doctrine of "one blood" into the veins of human thought.   In India the system of caste has exercised a tremendous power in retarding the growth of the Gospel doctrine, and in degrading the people below the level of a common heritage, imposing upon Christianity in its attempt to uplift and reorganize society a task no other religion ever encountered.   In Judea, in Peter's time, it was difficult for the Jew to recognize the Gentile as superior to a dog in rights or privileges, the moral distance between them being too great for any religion but Christianity to bridge.   At the present time heathendom is infected with the suspicion that different men are made of different kinds of clay, entitling some to lower and others to higher stations, which suspicion receives the sanction of the popular religions.   Hence the indoctrinating the heathen nations on this subject implies antagonism to prevailing religions, as well as honeycombing the entire social structure with the truth.

In Christian lands, ostensibly committed to this paragon of philanthropic doctrines, a work remains to be done before the millennium shall have dawned, for a spirit of oppression, akin to caste, still menaces the peace of society, debasing the sensibilities and corrupting the fountains of justice. In England and Ireland the oppression of the poor by land-owners and general misgovernment of the lower classes is crushing out the life of the people, who, in resistance thereto, are employing dynamite and studying the tactics of revolution. In the United States the spirit of monopoly is the great danger to civil liberty; the rights of the masses are ignored; and the cry of the socialist, whose incentive is less a moral than a physical want, is heard from the mountains to the sea. This is in contravention of the Christian idea, to which society must return if it escape disorganization and the terrors of nihilism. Recognizing the unity of the race and the equality of man, caste will disappear from heathendom, and oppression no longer curse Christendom; society will rest securely, because on a Christian basis. Christian society is one of the perennial fruits of Christianity.

In Christian lands, too, as nowhere else, there is a genuine and *popular enthusiasm for morality*, the evidence of the working of the ethical spirit of the Christian religion. In heathen lands the moral condition of society may be likened to a stagnant pool, sending forth corruption and death; the commonest virtues have little sway over the multitudes, and are discarded by the aristocracies; truth is at a fearful discount in China and Egypt; honesty is rare; theft is a breach to be punished when discovered; murder is justifiable for causes without number; and as for patriotism, benevolence, humility, patience, brotherly kindness, and the forgiving spirit, they are seldom seen, and even then are usually the fruit of the Gospel. Paganism is the nursery of immorality; its ethical standards are without practical virtue; the popular ethical notion is the subject of ridicule and satire. Mohammedanism, apparently more careful in ethical discriminations, presents a one-sided and distorted picture of humanity molded by its influence.

How different the condition in Christian lands! The ethical notion is at the basis of public life; it constitutes the root of individual character; it is the standard by which all transactions and events are judged. There is a tendency to moral order, a growth of the moral sentiments, a repression of criminal pursuits, and an inculcation of the highest virtues in communities dominated by the Christian idea. Truth, honesty, benevolence, and patriotism are held in such repute that he who does not practice them goes without recognition or reward. Even in circles in which Christianity is not formally acknowledged in its religious character, the claims of ethical righteousness are authoritative, and considered the indispensable condition of happiness and progress.

In a very congratulatory way we may refer to Christianity as the source of the *multiplied benevolent agencies and institutions* which have been established for the comfort and relief of the unfortunate, and for the recovery of the fallen and the outcast. Asylums for the blind, the insane, the deaf and dumb; poor-houses, children's homes, and hospitals; reformatory schools and homes for the diseased and vicious; soldiers' homes, and pensions amounting to millions annually, tell not only of misfortune and the reign of disease and poverty in this world, but also of that benevolent spirit that, taking its inspiration from the sympathetic Christ, provides relief, comfort, education, and salvation for the needy. Such institutions are almost unknown outside of Christendom. It is reported that an asylum for the unfortunate among the priesthood exists in China, and we observed a lunatic asylum in Judea; but it can not be denied that the benevolent asylum is the special product of Christianity. Were blind Bartimeus living in Ohio he would not sit long by the wayside, but be taken to Columbus, and clothed, fed, educated, saved. The deaf and dumb would also be transported thither, and even the leper would be housed and cured. For these and all other such benefits the world is not a little indebted to the religion of the Nazarene.

Going still higher in the scale of beneficent enterprise, Christianity has impelled the *Christian Church, within a century or two, to organize for the redemption of the world*, concreting this purpose into missionary societies, which are only prevented from turning the earth into a paradise again by the unwillingness of Christian people to sacrifice sufficiently for the attainment of the purpose. By so much as the Gospel is world-wide in its provisions, truths, and benefits, by as much the Church is bound to spread the tidings of salvation to the uttermost parts of the earth; and this it will do in the years to come. First relieving mankind of temporary evils and supplying the temporal wants of the race, the Church, as it is fully enlightened in the Gospel, turns its endeavor to the positive spiritual enlightenment of the nations, demonstrating the adaptation of Christianity to all peoples, and paving the way for its universal dominion among them. Its Churches and Sunday-schools planted everywhere; its teachers and missionaries going to the ends of the earth; the Gospel proving itself to be the power of God unto salvation on the banks of the Ganges as on the banks of the Mississippi, and in Peking as in Cincinnati; a child buried with Christian rites on the Sandwich Islands as in America; the Sabbath-day observed in Japan as in England; the Christian secular school opened in Damascus as in Cleveland, constitute a few of the many items of the history of the Gospel in this world, and are proofs of a divine plan to redeem all nations, and to let heaven descend to the earth. If we speak of the universal conquest of Christianity through these agencies, predicating faith for the future on the history wrought out in evangelization, one may suspect us of Utopianism, or charge us with being the promoter of a fanatical and impracticable purpose; *but Christianity is practical Utopianism;* it is realistic optimism.

In the highest sense, Christianity is a religion. Whatever its achievements in the human realm, whatever the inspiration it lends to human activity in the realization of its aspirations, its greatest power is as a religion, and its inexhaustible possibilities are in the religious realm. To trace its influence outside of that realm is profitable and assuring. We have seen its effect on civilization and the industrial pursuits of men; we have observed its impregnation of literature and refining tendency on art; we have witnessed its initiation of reforms, and its sovereignty in home-life; we have noted its teachings of morality, its organization of the benevolent spirit into societies for the relief of the needy, broadening out into a world-wide project for the salvation of the race; but its chief excellence is in its effect on human character, its effect as a spiritual religion. It is the religion of regeneration, the religion of faith, the religion of revelation, the religion of atonement and salvation. By its converting power, it demonstrates its divine origin; by its revelations of truth, it establishes its supernatural character; by the satisfaction it affords its adherents, it proves its sufficiency; by its ability to deliver men from sin, to support them in death, and open immortality to final vision and expiring life, it may claim to be from God.

If a religion may be tested by its fruits, *Christianity is the eternal sentiment of God.*

---

## CHAPTER XXVI.

### THE NEW IN CHRISTIANITY.

WHEN Roger Bacon pushed his scientific inquiries into the secrets of nature, revealing facts that astonished the ignorance of his times, and laid the foundation for a broad philosophy in the future, it was believed that he was in league with Satan, the retribution for which was ten years in a dungeon in Paris. In a later day, and for the still milder offense of publishing a treatise on logic in English, Sir Thomas Wilson likewise suffered incarceration at the hands of the papal authorities—a proof that the spirit of progress was considered heretical, sinful, and hurtful, and should be quenched in its incipiency, and by the punishment of its advocates.

The present is a different age, imbued with a different purpose, branding ignorance, instead of knowledge, as the foe of happiness, and rewarding instead of decapitating those who open doors hitherto shut to explorer and thinker. Golgotha now stares conservatism in the face; it stands no longer in the path of the truth-finder. Zeal for knowledge is wide-spread, and is the key to the progress of the nineteenth century. The demand everywhere is for the new, arising from a dissatisfaction with the old, because of its imperfections, its traditional burdens, its inconsistent teachings, and its degrading power. Lord Bacon said, truth is the daughter of time, not of authority. Time is the bearer of new truths; authority is a tyrant in the realm of thought. Truth, not tyranny, is the cry of the hour. Outside of religion, especially in science, history, and philosophy, investigation has not only been rapid, but it has succeeded in crowding into outer darkness many errors almost sacred from age, and establishing faith in nature on entirely new foundations. In the circles of religious thought, despite the conservative tendency, a change is apparent in opinion, touching the necessity of a re-opening of questions, and a larger exploration of fundamental truth.

With the purpose to ascertain all there is in Christianity, to expose its hidden foundations, and examine its rare claims, so well attested by historic evidence, we are in entire sympathy; and this sympathy is grounded in the general fact that Christianity, as yet, is substantially an *undeveloped* religion. Neither exhausted on the one hand, nor completed on the other, it remains for this or succeeding generations to fathom its depths, gather the unseen pearls at the bottom, and report all the glories of the invisible.

It is easy to believe there is a thousand-fold more in Christianity than has been produced or discovered. It is any thing but small or effete; its magnitude has never been measured; its volume of power has never been calculated; its range of influence has never been surmised. To those who, through spiritual curiosity or intellectual aspiration, covet a knowledge of the new in religion, it is enough to say, that it is not necessary to seek a new religion so long as there is so much that is new in Christianity. The suspicion that Christianity has nothing new to offer mankind; that, because its book of revelations is complete, a knowledge of new truths is impossible,—can only be maintained by those who fancy they have exhausted the meaning of religion, or reached the bottom of the great ocean of thought with their measuring lines of inquiry. If it is imagined that the world will outgrow the doctrines of monotheism, providence, incarnation, Messiahship, crucifixion, atonement, regeneration, prayer, resurrection, and immortality, it must be on the supposition that it will advance beyond present interpretations of them ; for, until the doctrines themselves are exhaustively understood, they must remain as subjects of thought and investigation. Going beyond an interpretation is not the same as going beyond the truth to which the interpretation is fastened.

The spirit of change is in the world. Death is the prophecy of birth. In keeping with this order of things, governments have passed through all varieties, from despotism to democracy ; institutions have appeared and departed, being succeeded by purer forms, as the feudal system gave place to enlarged freedom in Europe ; philosophies, too, rise, make their obeisance, and die ; and all religions are undergoing modifications, presaging their extinction. Will Christianity be an exception to this order ? Will its old truths survive age ?

The natural tendency of Christianity, amid the environment of change, is to perpetuity. Error, sin, physical forms, may perish, but truth is immortal. Truth, philosophical or ethical, husbands its vitality for future conflicts, and comes out of the depths of the ages, scarred by opposition, but ready to inflict a paralytic stroke upon error; and it must attain, by virtue of its nature, the highest place as a governing element among the forces of progress. The decadence of Christianity will be the decadence of truth, a result that can not be contemplated with composure. The relation of Christianity to truth, or the assumption that Christianity is truth, is involved in the preliminary consideration of the subject, justifying the statement that the fortunes of the one are the fortunes of the other.

Religion, or the idea of religion, is old ; the great question is, is there any thing new in it? Is the old consistent with the new ? *Is the old sufficient?* Is it exhaustive ?

Religion is old ; this is its glory. It bears the imprint of the Almighty upon it ; it dates from the beginning ; its ark is fringed with the leaves of Paradise ; its music is that of the early morning ; and its message is embalmed in the innocence and purity of the first day. Creation and Religion are the twin products of Eternal Power and Wisdom. The one carries us into the region of the other ; both exhibit the marks of the same paternity. Recently, a few travelers entered an immense cavern, unlighted by sun or candle ; it was dark, deep, and wide ; soon a red light was kindled, and it illuminated floor and roof, showing the broken forms of stalagmite and stalactite, and making visible what was unknown to the outer world. Religion is the inextinguishable torch, the ever-burning light, that illuminates the retreating Past, that gives us the key to history, indicates the plan of creation, and writes out the secret of the universe and the story of its beginning.

But is religion nothing more than a mausoleum? Is it the tomb of truths? the alcove of ancient dust? or is it a modern, vital force, as quickening in its influence to-day as when it first chanted the glory of God? Is it not the only genuine Janus, looking into the past and future at the same time? Surely, the old alone does not constitute all of religion; but, like a speck of gold in the sand, it must be the sign of larger treasures and more inexhaustible riches. New wonders eclipsing the old, new truths explanatory of the old, new prospects surpassing even prophetic visions, are all possible under the reign of a religion that opens its doors wide to the advance of mortals. Satisfaction with the old has blinded the vision to the new, and impeded the march to conquests over error.

Underneath the form of a verbal religion, there are things new to philosophy, new to theology, new to human wisdom, that must be brought forth and declared as the central and inspiring truths of God. We have been coasting along the shore, content with bays and rivers, and picking up a few shells; we must "launch out into the deep," where Omnipotence has room for its displays, and where storms turn out to be the amusement of an hour. He falls into error, who fancies that Religion has expressed itself in every possible form, or that Revelation is insusceptible of other interpretations than those predicated at Nice or framed by Athanasius.

Revealed religion, as a historic system of moral truths, has observed the general law of development, being in this respect in perfect harmony with the theory of the universe as a development; and under a similar law of evolution it will continue to expand until its mission shall be fully accomplished. If we study the evolutionary aspects of religion we shall see that it has developed in proportion to the intellectual capacity of the race, the light shining more brightly as man confessed his need of it, until it burst forth in a blaze of supernatural splendor that time has not been able to extinguish. "The light brightens," says Newman Smyth, "as the world is prepared for its shining." In distinct phrase, Revelation has been progressive, not given in a lump, but rather by piece-meal, given as a panorama with ever-changing scenes, suited first to childhood, then to manhood, and finally to age. From Abraham to the Messiah religion is a clear development under divine auspices of monotheistic and Messianic truth, reaching an apparently fixed condition in the judicial proclamations of the Master. In the patriarch's time how crude every religious idea—an altar, a sacrifice, a worshiper? Abraham felt that this was not all of religion, but it was the best possible in the primitive condition of society. Whether it is said that religion keeps pace with society, or is the pioneer of civilization, they seem to occupy contiguous positions, and are adapted to each other, all history certifying to their relative interaction. In primitive times, a primitive religion—in later times an advanced religion. From the tabernacle to the temple; from Elijah's musings under the juniper-tree to the full-voiced preaching of Peter on Pentecost; from the angels who saved Lot to those who ministered to the tempted Christ; from Solomon in all his glory to Christ in his transfiguration; from the raising of the Shunammite's son to the resurrection of Lazarus; from the sacrifice of David on Moriah to that of the world's Victim on Calvary; was a series of advancing steps in religious unfolding, of new developments all the way, of changes in the very structure, spirit, and design of religion, a complete remodeling of the old, a final crowning of the new. Until its culmination in the great Teacher, religion was in outward appearance as changeful as the kaleidoscope, a marvel of surprises, adapting itself to the changed conditions of man, and all tending to and preparing the way for its final incarnation. Sinai, with its terrific splendors, is a monumental mile-post in religion; Carmel, with Elijah's victory, signifies another measured advance; Solomon in Jerusalem, Jonah in Nineveh, Daniel in Babylon, each unrolled the scroll which contained secret things from the foundation of the world. By its prophets, true and false; by its kings, loyal and disloyal; by its phalanx of teachers in the motherhood and fatherhood of Israel, religion sent out, as from a sun, myriad rays of light, giving the world in a regular order of development, monotheism, sacrificial worship, temples, a priesthood, songs, incarnation, resurrection, immortality, and judgment; and these not as experimental or speculative ideas, but as primary, fundamental, essential facts, teachings and certainties.

Treating of the progressive method of Revelation, Newman Smyth affirms that " the general formative truths of the Old Testament were progressive forces in early history," and that they were adapted to the moral education of the race. With this thought as a starting-point he specifically discloses the " pedagogical intent " of the Judaic system and shows a " plain progress of doctrine in the Bible from without inward, from external restraints to inward principles, from law to love." Waiving the educational purpose of the Judaic administration, it is patent to all who examine it that it is a gradually developing system of truth, glorious in its advancement, and more

36

glorious in its culmination in the new administration of the Spirit. Dr. Smyth sees the educational purpose in the law of sacrifices, and the law of the Sabbath, while also he as readily discovers a development of the monotheistic conception, the hope of immortality, and the idea of atonement. In his view the development of revelation is a development within limitations; not all of truth has been revealed; not too much or too little, but enough for pedagogical and probationary purposes.

Agreeing that Revelation is circumscribed by limitation, it must be remembered that mankind in their discoveries, researches, and interpretations, have not reached the limits. Much of Revelation is still unknown; it is an undiscovered and an undeveloped region. As there is a development within limitations, so should there be a *development as far as limitation.* But even the limits are unknown. While religious truth grows larger under development, and requires two dispensations to exhibit it fully, Christianity must not be regarded as a mere development. The development of truth is the process of its unfolding; truth itself is more than the process, it is not in its nature a development. *It is a revelation, and development is a method of revelation.* It is a supernatural thing unfolding by a particular method, which must ever be distinguished from the thing itself.

As Christianity appears in the Bible in larger forms or newer types as it is developed, so in its historical growth it has passed through a variety of forms, the more prominent of which are Gnosticism, Mysticism, Roman Catholicism, Oriental Sectarianism, and Protestantism, each a progressive type, each just what might be expected of a religion in process of unfolding. Biblically, Christianity developed from obscurity toward transparency, or from a few to many truths; historically, it has been affected by its environment, absorbing errors, and suffering therefrom, so that its development, as spiritual truth, has been impeded by the compromising presence of false interpretations and interpolated doctrines. In this error-impressing form or Christianity obscured by theological interpretations, it stands out before the world at the present time, misunderstood from necessity, and sometimes rejected because it seems irreconcilable with itself. The next advance must be a development from error toward truth, its independence from the creed-maker, and an exact portraiture of its legitimate character. Just as truth is developed in the Scriptures, so must it be developed in history and in practical life.

Has religion lost its progressive character? Has it reached its growth? Has its development been arrested, and are we shut up to the familiar forms of truth, the tabulated series of doctrines, and to a revelation marked by distinct limitations clearly pointed out by the theologians? Or will development go on as long as man develops? Will it progress as he progresses? To suppose otherwise implies a misunderstanding both of man and religion, for both as they appear to us are undeveloped, a long future being required to fully mature the one and unfold the other.

In what respect will religion appear new? However ancient in form, it will always exhibit new phases in the developments of Christianity, producing advanced conditions of society, satisfying the most complex aspiration for truth, and even ministering to that devout curiosity which sometimes casts its innocent spell over believing and inquiring souls. *Down in the old is the quiet, sleeping spirit of the new.* It is a palpable error into which many fall, that the old truths of religion are fully understood, and that their power has been fully tested, and that a definite conclusion as to their value may be pronounced. The conceited advocate sometimes deludes himself with the belief that because he is familiar with certain truths, or rather with the manner in which they are uttered, he is also familiar with their nature, he knows their origin, and is capable of answering any question respecting them, when a little examination would convince him that he really knows nothing about them. The sage of Athens inhaled the atmosphere, but knew nothing of oxygen—not any more, at least, than the insect that floated over the Acropolis. The Norwegian slaked his thirst with water, and dipped his oar in the cold stream, but was ignorant of the latent force of steam. In the days of Queen Elizabeth lightning flashed in every storm, as it did in the later day of Morse, but what did she know of the power of electricity? Who knew that sunlight would stamp the picture of a face upon glass, or a metallic plate, until Daguerre said so? How long were mankind familiar with water, light, air, gravitation, cystallization, chemical affinity, polarization, yet knew nothing about them, were ignorant of the forces and possibilities in them! How much of nature still remains *incognito!* Who declaims on the uses of the thistle, or the beauty of the dandelion, or the virtue of dogberry? Yet there lurks in every poison a medicine, in every fruit a food, in the most worthless member of the vegetable kingdom a specific use, and all nature is but a store-house of beauties, uses, virtues, and forces that must have final recognition, application, and relation to civilization.

May it not be so with respect to higher things? May it not be that, as new powers and new laws were found in, or in association with, the old forms of matter with which men were long familiar, so in the oldest forms of religion, especially in Christianity, may be found new truths, new moral distinctions, new ethical forces, and new spiritual possibilities, not suspected even by those who live within the shadow of altars, and are acquainted with the historic forms of religion? That *the new is in the old* we are fully persuaded, and that Christianity, as taught and understood and applied, is still a folded germ, ready to sprout and grow under congenial conditions into something different from what it is, we must believe. Is any one ready to assert that the great problems of inspiration, prophecy, miracle, regeneration, spiritual dynamics, incarnation, Providence, and immortality, have received adequate treatment at the hands of the Christian teacher, or are competently explained, or have been exhibited in their true character and in all their relations? So long as Paul's cloak (II Timothy, iv, 13) is considered inconsistent with inspiration; so long as Jonah's prophecy concerning the downfall of Nineveh is quoted against the infallibility of prophecy; so long as Pentecostal influence is interpreted as moral enthusiasm generated by a moral purpose in human hearts; so long as miracle is reduced to legerdemain; so long as immortality is poetized as a dream, or a doubt, or a perhaps, or a possibility, there will be need of re-investigation, yea, *deeper* investigation, of the commonest bulwarks of our holy religion.

A great question like that of the government of the world, or all that is involved in providence; a great duty like that of prayer, or all that is involved in fellowship with God; a great doctrine like that of regeneration, or all that is involved in relationship to God; a great fact like depravity, or heredity, or all that is involved in the lapses of human history; and a great hope like that of atonement, resurrection, and immortality, or all that is involved in human destiny, can not be wrapped in superstition, or given out in fragmentary form, or settled by incomplete statement, or passed over with apologetic silence. "More light" is reason's cry; "more light" is the heart's agony. The solution of these questions is in the truth given; the light is in the darkness; the new is in the old.

In these oldest questions the newest discoveries must yet be made. We say nothing of schools of theology, with their conflicting interpretations; nothing of private and speculative beliefs in outside circles; nothing of skepticism touching religion in general; but, so long as religion itself as a system of truth is a complex inconsistency, or an architectural absurdity, or its disciples are ignorant of the nature of the truths that enter into its composition, there will be the necessity for repeated exploration, adoption of new definitions, and ventures on higher achievements.

It is significant that the Bible is composed of an *Old* Testament, embracing the old laws, old forms of worship, the old spirit, and a *New* Testament, breathing a new spirit into the world, presenting a new character, a new model, a new worship, and a new life to men.

It is the pledge of the new in Christianity, or, rather, that Christianity is the new in religion, and will forever remain so. Of all that is obscure in religion, taxing human wisdom beyond its ability to interpret correctly, is the great Personage who is its inspiration, and who is the center of Christianity—Jesus Christ. Understand him, and miracle, spiritual energy, and immortal existence, have an easy explanation. Christianity is illuminated in the person of its Founder, and is obscure only as he is enigmatical. Who fully comprehends him? Have not all read of his incarnate birth, his benevolent deeds, his marvelous life, his elevation upon the cross, and his resurrection from the dead? Yet the realities of his history rise like mountains that have never been scaled; his words are more than Austerlitz battles that shake errors to their foundations; his deeds more than the thunderbolts of a brigade of gods, yet few there be who comprehend their import. Who has grasped all there is of that character? Who has found the key to the supernatural in him? Who has touched the umbilical cord that connects the human with the divine and makes him what he is? The tremendous fact is that Jesus Christ is yet the newest character of history, possessed of elements never yet analyzed, exerting a power never yet comprehended, planning a purpose appalling to genius, and accomplishing an end that, when understood, will link his fame to the stars. After eighteen centuries of study, comparison, and inquiry, mankind see in him a grandeur that words can not express, and a loftiness that human wisdom can not measure. *The great central figure of Christianity is still an uninterpreted or a misinterpreted character, obscure because sublime, distant from the human sphere because divine.*

Now, it must not be assumed that religious problems, from their very nature, must remain unsolved, and that Christ, from his nature, must be out of human reach—this is an indirect apology for our ignorance. A reverent spirit must acknowledge the limitations of finite knowledge, but these limitations may be artificial, the result of moral infirmity, to be removed so soon as man's disability is overcome. Christianity is more than a moral influence; it is an intellectual force. In it is the secret of holiness, and the key to knowledge, and under its inspiration all mysteries should dissolve, all questions should be answered, all doubts be overthrown, and mankind know the truth as it is revealed in Christ. Christianity is divine wisdom; and, studied, comprehended, known, all problems will have an adequate solution. Hence, *in the old of Christianity is the new of religion*—new solutions, new principles, new powers, new certainties.

Christianity is the representative term of the occult in the spiritual sphere, the *sign-word of mysteries of a very high and complex order.* Among the Greeks the Eleusinian mysteries, half religious and half philosophical, involved more properly the processes of vegetation, and the deification of nature's powers and methods. The Greek disciple confined his study to the *material.* The disciple of Christianity has a wider field, and begins at a higher altitude. Indeed, *the material is not at all to be explained by the material.* Nature will not explain itself, and a deification of nature's energies removes the problem to the background without throwing any light upon it. Mysteries abound both in nature and in that which is above nature, and a religion, sinking its roots deep in the one or the other, or in both, as Christianity does, will necessarily present a mysterious side to the world. Mystery is the scientific side of nature ; much more the philosophical side of religion. Robert Hall has said that "a revelation without mystery is a temple without a god." The sky has its milky way; Christianity, its constellations of surpassing beauty. If it is the province of religion to deal with fundamental or primary truths, then must it deal with things hard to be understood, and even revelation itself may need interpretation or a hyper-revelation. But a religion that would reject the supernatural and confine itself to the natural would not be a religion at all; it might be philosophy, but nothing more. The essence of a comprehending religion is the supernatural, as the essence of philosophy is the natural. From the one to the other is the distance from the tangible to the intangible, from the seen to the unseen. By virtue of its remoteness, its intangibility, its eternal perspective, the supernatural is a cloud-land, mapped off only in outline, with the great landscapes of truth intervening, unexplored, undefined, and unknown ; and the more of the supernatural in religion, the larger its mysteries and the more numerous its problems.

Now, it is in keeping with fact to assert that Christianity is the only religion that has joined itself completely to the supernatural; or, being still more exact, that out of the supernatural has issued but one religion, namely, Christianity. It has attempted a materialization of itself in the religion of the New Testament, through the great Teacher, and in the many-voiced truths of the entire volume. As a consequence Christianity partakes of the mystery of the supernatural, and is an open field for the discovery of new forms of truth. Possibly, within the circle of the supernatural, there are truths concerning which the human mind must forever remain in ignorance, or know them imperfectly at best ; and yet of this we are not quite certain. At all events the supernatural is as legitimate a field for inquiry and exploration as the psychological, biological, chemical, and physiological, and must yield some of its contents as it is invaded and inspected. If there is a supernatural at all, it can not be fenced from observation or buried out of sight. Especially may the minor mysteries, the superficial truths of Christianity, be explored throughout their borders, and be relieved of any superstitious complexion piety may have given them. The Master was continually teaching truths in parables, astonishing the Jews, and purposely throwing over them the veil of obscurity, yet to the disciples they were made transparent; and when asked why he spoke in parables the Master replied, "Unto you it is given to know the mystery of the kingdom of God," but not "unto them that are without," implying that the key to knowledge is discipleship. Christianity is the *parable of the supernatural, to be interpreted by and through the experience of discipleship,* and to be revealed in proportion to the spiritual capacity of the recipient. Intimacy with the supernatural, acquaintance with the profound truths of God, is a part of the programme by which spiritual mysteries may be resolved into realities. We do not, therefore, concede the necessary obscurity of the spiritual, for, as Audubon drew birds to his hand, so the spiritual mind will draw the supernatural to itself, extract its meaning, measure its power, compass its relations to time and space, and discern the eternity of things supernatural.

Spiritual knowledge, or an advance into the supernatural, is as possible as it is imperative; an opening in the clouds and a discernment of what is beyond, or an upheaval of truth, freed from grossness, and transparent as light, may be expected, as the ages come and go. Is the soul forever to remain a mystery? Is the ego, self-conscious, to be self-ignorant? The inside must be as visible as the outside, spirit must be comprehended as well as matter, as the condition of comprehending the significance of the divine utterances respecting immortality and the future life. Science is the material phase of world-life; religion is the spiritual phase. Shall one reveal its secrets and the other withhold them? Shall physiology be triumphant, and psychology confess defeat? Soul-life must reveal itself, or be revealed by religion.

Atoning influence is a theological mystery, which must succumb to the reverent inquiry of souls, steeped in love divine; and, as its power is understood, so will it be coveted and appropriated. It is not difficult to show that the idea of atonement is not inconsistent with nature, or with the universal order of things, for nature is an atoning system; and if the basis of nature and religion is atonement, it may be preached without prejudice. More than an agreement, however, between the truths of Christianity and the facts of nature must be pointed out; for the method by which religious truth is applied to men is not always paralleled by the course of nature. The fact of atonement has its vindication in nature ; the application of atonement stands unrepresented in nature.   Here is need of a new revelation, or a new discovery.

The doctrine of the resurrection, comforting as it is understood, but absurd as it is sometimes taught, needs to be redeemed from vagueness and crudeness, and clothed with celestial charms, while the hope of immortality must be transformed in the presence of faith into a certainty of the future.

The greatest mystery of religion is God.   Inaccessible, invisible, yet omnipresent and all-loving, it is the world's anxiety to know more about him, and, according to the Scriptures, it is God's anxiety to be fully known.   This double anxiety will eventuate in new revelations of God, the shadows of the Infinite being succeeded by the open presence of the Everlasting Substance in the world.   This additional light, however, will not dawn through the medium of a new Bible, but by the illumination of existing truth through human research and divine agency, or the mutual approach of God and man in the devout study of the Word.

With progress in these directions, all other subjects will receive elucidation ; angelic life will no longer be dark and impenetrable ; miraculous force will be seen to be spiritual, not material ; regenerating force will be recognized as superhuman, not natural ; inspiration will appear as a supernatural influence ; providence will be interpreted as the personal supervision of the supernatural ; prayer will be esteemed a supernatural instrument, and man will make the natural his foot-stool and the supernatural his dwelling-place.

The revelation of the supernatural through intellectual sympathy, and by contact with spiritual sources of truth, belongs to the possibilities of religion.   The order of revelation and advancement will be gradual and rapid—rapid enough to startle the world out of its lethargy, and graduated according to the receptivity and sympathy of the race.

Progress in religion, or development in spiritual knowledge, may be at the expense of old-time beliefs, and involve the sacrifice of certain creed-forms of truth ; but the eager, truth-seeking mind, unfettered by antiquity, authority, or forms, alone will find the new contents of Christianity.   The investigator must not be a bondman, except to truth already known.   For him aspiration is inspiration, and let him fly with the freedom of God.

Conquest in the highest sphere will be followed by achievement in the lower ; that is, the supernatural, not only vindicated, but also disclosed, *exposed*, and explained, the natural will yield up its contents, and declare mystery to be a fable of the past.   The realm of

Greek thought was the material; even the gods, according to the Greek, were natural forces deified. To his mind the spiritual is in an eternal eclipse. In our day the supernatural is the chief factor at bottom of every thing, explanatory of all existence, the secret of all force, the ultimatum of transcendentalism no less than Christianity.

Deriving all things by a true Christian philosophy from the omnipotence of the supernatural, the solution of the mystery of the physical universe, not yet wrought out, must soon be proposed. What with Moses, and the nebular hypothesis and evolution, and the spectroscope, and a thousand other sources of knowledge yet to be opened, the mystery of the creative art will be disclosed, and the fiat of the Almighty will have its sublime vindication, not alone in the sincerity of a cherished faith, but in the results of scientific and religious achievement. How far Christianity may contribute to the discovery of the secret of the physical universe; whether the Biblical writers furnish any clue to the origin of things or their final destiny; whether cosmical systems, physical laws, mathematical facts, scientific orders are foreshadowed to any degree in Revelation; or whether the Book is exclusively a revelation of spiritual truth, carrying along in its stream of light not one grain of physical dust, are questions that have been discussed by all schools of thinkers with varying opinions and conclusions. The one opinion that the Bible is a revelation of scientific truth is as untenable an extreme as the other, that it is entirely barren of such truth. One looks in vain for zoölogy, botany, chemistry, biology, psychology, physiology, meteorology, and the other sciences as such in the Book; for that matter, it is a question if certain *theologies* may be found there; but there are scientific intimations, scattered through the Book, which have a certain value, and possibly, like Theseus's thread, may lead the *savants* out of Dædalus's labyrinth of difficulties into the open fields of knowledge and safety. Some stress must be placed upon these scientific allusions, as little things have been the preludes to great discoveries. A piece of glass suggested the telescope; a falling apple pointed to the law of gravitation; Franklin's kite taught the tamableness of lightning; the boiling tea-kettle was the forerunner of the steamship and locomotive. A partial or obscure revelation of scientific facts is consistent with a full revelation of spiritual truths; and the Bible is made up after this fashion, containing scientific hints, not even yet fully discerned, and revealing great spiritual truths, not yet adequately realized. Is the earth globular? So recent science has demonstrated, but Isaiah, twenty-three centuries ago, spoke of " the circle of the earth "—a scientific hint of its sphericity that science has been slow to recognize, but which it has at last accepted as prophetically true. Has air weight? Torricelli established that fact, but long before his day Job announced that God made "the weight for the winds"—another scientific hint that slept for ages, waiting for confirmation by discovery. Of the ancient theories concerning the earth one was that it is a plain, another that it is a triangle, another that it is a seven-storied house, another that it rests on the back of a tortoise; no intelligible, and certainly no correct, view of its place in the planetary system being taken. But Job, quite as astronomical in vision as Herschel by study, proclaimed that God "hangeth the earth upon nothing," relieving it of gross relations, and suggesting the reign of an invisible law in the universe of worlds. What shall be said of Moses, whose cosmogony, chronology, and scientific order of the creative processes and results have occasioned more investigation than Darwinism or any modern scientific proposition? Is Moses in error touching any point? Archbishop Usher's chronology, long acccepted by the Church, conveys the impression that Moses taught that the earth was created six thousand years ago; but it is found that, according to Moses, the creation of the earth occurred "in the beginning," which may mean millions of years ago thus harmonizing with the most radical conjectures of geologists. Does geology establish the order of creation by the strata of the earth's crust? That order is Mosaic throughout. Likewise the astronomy of Moses, in its intent if not in its terms, is strictly scientific, and a key to a correct astronomy and geology. Time demonstrates Moses to the letter. This is all the more striking, since the scientific teaching of the days of Moses was at variance with all modern conclusions, and since modern science itself turns out to be lame only where it is contrary to Moses, Job, and Isaiah. Respecting the destiny of the globe Peter especially declares that it shall suffer conflagration and be reduced to a cinder, and, corroborating this possibility, science has already shown that the earth in its gases and solids is one vast combustible store-house, ready for the match of the world's destroyer. Surely Christianity has something to offer to the consideration of thinking men besides spiritual truths; it is a *scientific hint-book*, a key to science, the study o° which will lead to scientific truth.

This obviates the objection made to its scientific character, that a revelation of physical facts, laws, and systems, will prevent research, that man, ever prone to intellectual inertia, will not examine, inquire, search for laws and orders if they are revealed to him, for the scientific allusions in the Bible are incomplete revelations; they are hints only, keys, fore-glimpses requiring searching and examining just as much as if they were not there.

It is sometimes alleged that the scientific language of the Bible is unscientific, but this grows out of the fact that the nomenclature of Bible times was not scientific, and that inspiration employed language that could be understood by the people to whom it was addressed; and, further, English translators have been as careless in their work as the Jews were incorrect in their conceptions. In order to eliminate the scientific spirit of Christianity from Revelation—a task undertaken to accommodate the querulous spirit of materialism—Dr. J. H. McIlvaine insists that the Hebrew writers were totally uninformed in science, and that the Bible, therefore, is unreliable in its scientific allusions and statements. He holds that the geocentric system of the physical universe is fairly maintained in the Bible; that the sacred writers "conceived of the earth as a solid, immovable body, with a plane or perhaps a slightly convex surface;" that, in their minds, the sky was likewise a "solid substance;" that also above the firmament or solid sky there was a great body of water, from which rains descended, just as under the earth there are waters from which issue springs, rivers, and wells; that in small zoölogical matters Moses is in error, as when he speaks of the coney and hare as ruminants when they are rodents; and thus he lays the foundation for a suspicious attack on the scientific elements of revealed religion. To this it may be replied that, as has been shown, the scientific allusions to the air's weight, the sphericity of the earth, and the chronology of the earth's creation, are precisely and scientifically correct; that, while the Bible writers may have not been learned scientists, and spoke in an uninspired way, just as the people would speak, yet, when they wrote a scientific hint by inspiration, it was infallibly reliable; that these same Bible writers must not be loaded down with the errors of translators; that our inferences of the knowledge of the Bible writers may not be sufficiently supported by the facts; and that apologies for the supposed deficiencies in scientific knowledge of the sacred writers not only discredit the scientific spirit of the book, but the entire book, for it at once compels a discrimination between the scientific and spiritual, which the majority of mankind will not undertake to make. The overthrow of the scientific in Christianity opens the gate to the invaders of the spiritual in Christianity.

Superficial reviewers of the scientific revelations of the Bible reach unfavorable conclusions; but a close student of the same will be surprised at certain underlying facts or principles, fundamental to the Bible, and distinguishing it from all other pretended religious documents and revelations. The absence of mythological conceptions, and of religious and scientific myths, prevalent in the early ages, from the Pentateuch, is a remarkable fact, to be accounted for on no other ground than inspiration. Why no gods, no myths, no centaurs, no half-human and half-animal creatures in Genesis? The earth comes from the hand of a Creator, a personal Being, not from gods; and is peopled, not with gods, or half-human creatures, but with animals and men. The science of Genesis is not mythological.

Again, the " optical accuracy" of the Old Testament writers is an unmistakable evidence of the scientific verity of the Bible. Newman Smyth and Prof. Dawson employ this fact in support of the scientific virtue of Christianity, insisting that, with few exceptions, the scientific references, if taken literally, have been or will be confirmed by modern investigation. The first chapter of Genesis Dr. Smyth calls a " religious and scientific primer," or, as we term it, a pedagogical manual of creation, revealing in narrative form the creative process, or world-building by development.

Creation was not an instantaneous act, but a development, even according to Moses. The theory of development originated with Moses, from whom Darwin borrowed it. Dr. Smyth assumes that the alphabet of science is in revelation. So we believe.

If, then, Christianity is accepted as a scientific hint, what new discoveries may yet be made in the regions of matter under the pilotage of religion! The faith is thrilling that religion may yet be the torch, not alone through the spiritual realm, but for the guidance of the explorers throughout the visible universe. The modern spirit is opposed to such guidance; the lines between religion and science are being carefully drawn, the light of one being considered useless in the other; but it remains, and will forever remain, that true science is the auxiliary of religion, and true religion is the auxiliary of science. The cessation of conflict between them is not in their separation, as has been proclaimed, but in their unity; not in their divorce, but in their marriage. If truth has two faces, the one is spiritual and the other physical; they do not contradict; they are not in opposition; they look in the same direction; they may boast of the same divine lineage; they are one. Like parallel lines, they run along side by side; only the physical must end, while the spiritual must go on forever.

In still another realm the new in Christianity will have demonstration. Its profoundest effect will be on exhibition in man, and to man must one look to discover its possibility. Christianity, in expanding forms of truth, in the application of its oldest teachings to social conditions, in the flood-tide of light it pours upon supernaturalism, and in its graduated disposition of physical problems, will ever claim attention; but its greatest work will be on man himself. Christianity is for man, his enlightenment in duty, his understanding of truth, the molding of his character into a divine likeness, the development of his moral possibilities into genuine qualities, the reclamation of the waste of the soul by the fertilizing processes of the Holy Spirit, the impartation of immortal energy to his awakened powers, his establishment on a fixed moral basis, and the security of his future beyond the fear of loss by apostasy.

All truth is for man, to make him what he ought to be, what he can be, to make him a new man, and, therefore, a new subject for his own contemplation. In its ordered operations religion works by different methods, producing results somewhat uniform in appearance, but with marked diversity in the underlying stratum of soul-life. To all the same Spirit is given, but there are manifold operations productive of manifold results, bearing a common likeness, and yet exhibiting a distinct functional end or object. To one, Paul says, is given the word of wisdom; to another, faith; to another, the working of miracles; to another, prophecy; to another, discerning of spirits. It is the self-same Spirit that worketh in all, but the products are distinct, and original in certain moral peculiarities. By this process Christianity is precipitating upon the world new men and women, lifting them above the common level of others, endowing them with new and unanticipated functions, and inspiriting them with a new and divine mission. We are too slow in perceiving the outcome of the religious operation, too dull in inquiring into the nature of the regenerating accomplishment, and permit the Christian to pass before us almost unnoticed when he carries in his soul the new design of the Master's workmanship, even the ideal of God respecting man. We pause over the conversion of Paul, so dramatic in its scenes; we read with vivid interest the life-work of George Müller, or Madame Guyon, or Fletcher, or Zwingli, the principal feature of which is the divine halo that encircles it; but forget that in the converted miner, or in the evangelized creole, or in the reorganized neighbor, there has been felt the moral power of the universe, and that whoever is converted is a "new creature." By the mouth of Ezekiel the Lord promised to "put a new spirit within" man; and, according to Paul, such a man is new; new, in the sense that he is different from his former self, and new in that he is different from others. Not new truths alone then, not new forms of religion, not new developments of supernaturalism, not new explanations of physical facts, will alone issue from and through Christianity; but *new men*, in whom religion will have its brightest displays, and exhibit the extreme of its power. The fact of creation is in matter; the doctrine of providence is in events; the *summum bonum* of Christianity is in man.

If Christianity is the source or fund of things new as well as old, it is evident that a pursuit of the new is legitimate; if the new is necessary to the completion and development of the old, it is clear that a knowledge of the new is essential. What is it that stimulates discovery, exploration, invention, like the hope of finding something hitherto unknown? Over the old half-truths, disordered facts, conflicting principles, ideas, and achievements, the sluggish world falls asleep, and is only aroused by necessity or inspiration. Given some new field of research, a prospect of overthrowing an error, or establishing the truth, a hint of new methods, new systems, new laws, new forces, a supposition that more lies beyond and can be found, and men will toil and sacrifice, suffer and die, in their searchings and achievements. A new asteroid thrills every astronomer; a new flower charms the botanist; the north pole draws the navigator; a new discovery in physics leads to multiplied inventions; and a new law sometimes changes the face of civilization. If in all departments of life—physics, science, history, social movements—the quickening influence of the new is felt, and operates as a stimulating motive, what must be its effect in the higher spheres of knowledge and research? Indeed, should we not expect that it would conduct to greater ventures, and inspire to the greatest possible intellectual stretches in fields practically illimitable, and where the results are so intimately blended with man's noblest well-being and destiny? In this view Christianity, with its prophetic new truths, is the *religion of inspiration*, not alone "given by inspiration," but prompting the intellectual energies of man to endeavors, inquiries, and attainments impossible without it.

Again, the observing student is profoundly impressed with the incoherent teachings of philosophy, science, and external religion, concerning fundamental religious truths; in other words, a conflict of ideas is raging over these truths. What is truth? may well be asked. The antagonism of conflicting systems has resulted in agnosticism, as fatal to religion as skepticism and atheism combined. Disagreement concerning truths is proof that all of truth has not been obtained, and unity is impossible except as new truth, or the remainder of truth, is sought and found. What shall reconcile science and religion? More truth, we answer, which means new truth. What shall reconcile philosophy and religion? More truth. What shall reconcile Christianity and Mohammedanism? More truth. *The cure for difference is truth—new truth.* On truths as now known, whether speculative as in philosophy, fragmentary as in science, superstitious as in religion, unity between conflicting systems is out of the question. On old truths conflict is as inevitable in the future as it is now. On the new in all departments of knowledge, as a basis of unity, sciences, philosophies, and religions will approach for conference, negotiation, and the establishment of friendly relations. It can not be otherwise. Old truth is insufficient, as a basis of unity, because of its incompleteness ; new truth, embracing all there is to be known, removing the shadows from the contents of revelation, and bringing forward the supernatural in right relations to the natural, must be sufficient as a basis of unity for science, philosophy, and religion. Christianity is, therefore, the bond of unity among the irreconcilable so-called truths of religion, science, and philosophy.

Another fact must not be omitted in these calculations. Christianity is not exerting its full working power; its resources, especially its reserve forces, are not employed in redeeming the world. It is not true that it is accomplishing its purpose, with its mysteries still mysterious, with the world ignorant of what is in it, with its greatest truths slumbering within reach of man. Religion is an undeveloped giant, and is working with the disadvantages of infancy. Perhaps, with these drawbacks, it will finally be able to save the world, but all must agree that under the present methods redemption is a slow process, and the highest efficiency of Christianity is yet to be demonstrated. Christianity is redemptive in its aim, redemptive in its work, redemptive in its spirit ; *but an unworked Christianity will not redeem any thing.* Its past is a history of redemption, of the shaking of the nations by its power, as in the time of Constantine, and then of a long lapse into darkness and barbarism ; of revival again and reverses, of controversy, antagonism, uncertainty, and infidelity ; meanwhile the world slowly rising because of its undergirding by religion. In spite of fanaticism, superstition, and great misunderstandings ; in spite of theological differences and false interpretations of doctrine, Christianity is a saving power ; it is the instrument of redemption, and has demonstrated its capacity for conquest. The internal weights removed, the differences canceled in the unity of knowledge, and Christianity apprehended in its length, depth, and breadth, all the sooner will its world-wide and exceptional task be accomplished. The new in Christianity, as the source of internal unity, is indispensable to the largest and speediest success.

To the acquisition of the new, however, there are obstacles steadily persistent in their assertion, and penalties that threaten every pursuer after that which is hidden from the common observation. Forward movements in religious thought are too much under ban, and *prohibition of a new idea has been carried to an extreme.* The new in Christianity will not be the product of another revelation, but of *illumination of the revelation given.* The new is at hand ; it is here in Revelation, to be sought out and proclaimed by those who have a genius for finding things, and who are under a promised inspiration in search of truth; it is within reach of the mind that is in Christ. Through the faith that overcometh all things, there may be progress in the acquisition of spiritual knowledge such as has not been anticipated. Not through a new revelation, therefore, is the new to be had, but through new labors, guided by the divine Spirit, and expended on the rough material of the old.

To this kind of effort there is the obstacle of an innocent sectarianism, which forbids a change of base, or a new formula of belief, in the fear that the whole superstructure will fall if a single stone be removed. The prejudice that attaches to one form of truth is the root of a vigorous defense of it, and, so far, so good ; but it is in the way of a broad vision, and militates against enlargement. Education, ancestral influence, the utterances of creeds, and the strength of Christian organizations, oppose any very liberal inquiry in new directions, as unnecessary, speculative, and injurious; and earnest souls step cautiously, and walk, like the gods, with feet shod with wool. Excommunication is sometimes the result of too much boldness in attempted discovery. Over a peccadillo in expression, a conflict has ensued, that has resulted in estrangement of advocate and opponent, and almost rent the respective organizations to which they belonged. The cry of heresy has sounded in the ear of the independent investigator, fettering his movements, padlocking his speech, and severing his ecclesiastical relations : yet, in spite of derision, he has modestly gone on in his work for the truth. Nor can it be said that Roman Catholicism is alone guilty in this respect; for our beloved Protestantism has its spies, heresy hunters, and defenders of the old faiths, innocent souls who mean to contend for the truth as it has been delivered to them. However righteous the opposition to error, and justifiable the proclamations of truth in the narrowest aspects, it is apparent that ignorance, prejudice, passion, sectarianism, and superstition, rather impede than assist in discovery and interpretation.

Even more obstructive than these is that spirit of contentment with revealed truth as a mysterious system which has cast its spell over Christendom, disturbed only now and then by an attempt to shake it off. The many seem unaware that the word mystery is a reproach ; and, blindly accepting the leadership of those as confirmed in the faith as themselves, they dream of no increase of knowledge, and are ready to frown upon any masculine attempt to resist the reign of mystery. The enchantment of ignorance must be broken, the spell of satisfaction must be disturbed, and Christian spirits must have the right of way into obscurity, darkness, and speculation, that they may overshadow it with light and victory. As David, when transporting the ark of God from Kirjath-jearim, set it upon a *new* cart, so Christianity may ride on new wheels, over new roads, into new regions, causing the race to shout over its new revelations, and rejoice in its brighter achievements.

---

# CHAPTER XXVII.

## THE ESCHATOLOGY OF CHRISTIANITY.

W. R. ALGER says: "The Hereafter is the image flung by the Now. Heaven and hell are the upward and downward echoes of the earth." Rivaling Elijah's translation, is the Greek account of the destiny of Empedocles, who, "after a sacred festival, was drawn up to heaven in a splendor of celestial effulgence." According to the New Zealanders, the souls of nobles are immortal, but the Cookees perish utterly. To the Indians of the Oronoco, the Great Spirit, on his departure from them, said, "Ye shall never die, but shall shed your skins." A philosopher once reported: "Strange that the barrel-organ, man, should terminate every tune with the strain of immortality!" Another thinker says, "The very nerves and sinews of religion is hope of immortality."

That there is a future life for man, is a concession, if not an affirmation, of all mythologies, superstitions, and religions. Without inquiring into the origin of the universal conviction, it is important to study it as one of the cherished hopes of humanity—what it really means, what it excludes and includes, and what is its philosophic and theologic value. The range of the problem is quite as extensive as any in theology or philosophy, and quite as embarrassing as any, if studied only philosophically, historically, or even religiously. The whole field of eschatology is cloudy, distant, and unspeakably mysterious. Of beliefs, traditions, concessions, guesses, hopes, there are an abundance; of facts, experiences, probabilities, certainties, the number is much less. Profound is our embarrassment, since our individual interests, as well as those of the race, are involved in it. As to the creative process, as to the essence of being, as to the nature of matter, as to the destiny of matter, we may waive the desire for knowledge; for, desirable as such knowledge may be, it is not so important that we everlastingly perish without it. This is true of the majority of problems, both in religion and philosophy. Personal interests are not at stake in our knowledge of chemical affinity, or gravitation, or the ecliptic, or in the questions why Jupiter is

37

attended with moons, and Saturn is enveloped with belts; but they are promoted or damaged, as the eschatological outlook is definite or vague, positive or ambiguous, authoritative or conjectural. The future! the future! is the cry of every earnest spirit, the hope of every honest mind. To be or not to be hereafter, is of more value than to be or not to be here; *the Hereafter is of more consequence than the Here.*

Faith, anxious with desire, and pathetic with hope, is intoxicated with delight whenever she remembers that no religion, however debased or ignorant, has ever stared vacantly and blindly into the future. The glazed eyes of paganism are fixed on Elysian glories. The perturbed vision of false religions sees open doors beyond the grave. The howl of Tartarus roars in the ears of mythology, and the melody of Hades awakens joy in the breast of Mohammedan and Hebrew. Defined or undefined, all religions peer beyond the gates of the eternal, and all souls shout across the abyss of ages, *we live.* But man's acutest instinct, his intensest hope, his profoundest desire, in a matter of so great moment, is an insufficient foundation; it may be confirmatory of faith, but the origin of faith must not be grounded alone in hopes and desires. Questioning such hopes, Plato affirms immortality; but Epicurus rejects it, and advances plausible proofs against it. Philosophy, compelled to deal with the psychological proof alone, has reported a confused mass of affirmative and negative accounts, and, being unsettled in its conclusions, it can settle nothing for inquirer or traveler.

In this dilemma, driven out of ourselves, and away from the oracles of philosophy, and looking with suspicion on the *data* used by religions in general, the only thing to do is to turn to a religion that speaks with authority, and reveals what man can not discover. The true and final source of information is *revelation.* If the future state can not be rationally, that is, scientifically, demonstrated, and if Christianity is a divine religion, it belongs to it to make known the truth touching the future, with all the clearness and authority with which it proclaims the truths pertaining to redemption. If eternity is a myth, what is redemption but a myth also? If it fail on so vital a subject as the future, suspicion must rest upon the religion in every other aspect and undertaking. If it is a revelation, it must certify to truths in which men have a vital, personal interest, especially if they can not discover them themselves, and will never know them unless they are revealed. In this study, we feel perfectly helpless without outside aid, without a revelation. Like fishes in the Mammoth Cave, we have no eyes for the beyond. The light must shine upon us, or we shall not see at all. Dependent for information on revelation, and Christianity proclaiming itself to be the religion of revelation, the heart turns to it with a quiet joy, anxious to accept its teachings, and ready to embrace the truth, if it is made known therein.

It is not denied that the great doctrine of the future life impregnates other religions, but it is so associated with legends and superstitious accounts, and the rewards and retributions foreshadowed are so rationally improbable, that the disclosures can not be accepted as truths, much less the superstitions accompanying them. The Homeric theology is just as reliable on this subject as Brahminism and Buddhism. The old Persian faith, and even the dreary Egyptian doctrine, are as authentic and as valuable in this particular as the teaching of Confucius and the dreams of Mohammed. Verily, the leading thought of these religions loses its character in the midst of the errors that encrust it, and calls piteously for help from a religion whose basis is inspiration, and whose sole content is truth. The vindication of the doctrine of the future life, as espoused by other religions, is contingent on the verity of the one religion now under consideration. If immortality is not a revealed truth, then it can not be a philosophical, rational, or religious truth ; but, if revealed, it is philosophical, rational, and religious. That religion that authorizes faith in another life must be so consistent in all its teachings, and so primary in its truths, that, while one truth may be tested by experience, another demonstrated by observation, another established by philosophic processes, another vindicated by history, others may be taken as revelations. Such truths, multiplied and compatible, Christianity contains, and submits them to all the tests required. Its experiential truths, or the hidden contents of the religious consciousness, have been analyzed and verified in multiplied thousands of cases; its historical truths are open to the inspection of sacred and profane eyes, and seek the light to show their transparency; its philosophic truths, containing the mysteries of the ages, unfold their meaning to those *en rapport* with truth itself; its *revealed* truths, calm in conscious potentiality, and rich with divine splendors, are only the consummation of the philosophic, historic, and experiential, and challenge error to immediate conflict for sovereignty. Christianity turns not back when it gets beyond the depths of the human mind. It reveals when man can not see for himself; it makes known when he can not demonstrate; it speaks when he must be silent. A valuable religion, indeed, is that which travels along the beaten paths of philosophy, history, and experience, and weaves its story out of the fruitful materials of these fields; but more valuable that religion, which, overleaping the boundaries of time and sense, and rising above earth-thoughts, can pluck fruit from the trees on the shores of that other land, too distant for mortal sight, and drop it into our hands as readily as it does the other. Christianity has its time-side, its philosophy, history, and experience, and its eternal-side, or the other life. It does open doors, whose hinges human hands have vainly endeavored to remove; it does fore-glimpse the eternal world, not one of whose gates stood more than ajar until the Son of God commanded them to be lifted up. With Christianity as our guide into the future realm, superstition will be succeeded by knowledge, a beclouded faith will be transformed into a rational affirmation, and probability will emerge into certainty.

Let it be primarily observed that the revelation of the future life is authentic and to be accepted without dispute; second, it is free from superstition, such as haunts the old religions, and may, therefore, be taken in its fullness; third, it is in harmony with itself, all the truths of Christianity mutually agreeing, and addressing the reason as a whole or as one truth. This is a decisive test of the value of any truth, and of the value of any system of truth—the inter-harmony of the whole or the proportion of its parts.

Conceding authenticity, sufficiency, and harmony to revelation, the eschatology of Christianity is under the limitations that belong to the entire system and to all parts of it; that is, as revelation in its wholeness is an indistinct presentation of truth, so its teachings concerning the future partake of the general limitation, indistinctness, and character of the whole. Revelation is light; it is darkness also. The revelation of spiritual facts, such as atonement, regeneration, the baptism of the Holy Ghost, is incomplete and question-awakening; results, not processes; facts, not explanations, are revealed. Incarnation is a fact, but shrouded in mystery; miracle-power is on exhibition in Christ, but explanation of it is not given; divine sovereignty and human freedom, supposed by some theologians to be incompatible, are taught in the Scriptures without any attempt at reconciliation; how Christ can be divine and yet the subject of temptation are facts also, but mysteriously perplexing to those who are troubled with the difficulty. In like manner the eschatology of the Scriptures, authentic and sufficient, is the region of light and darkness; the shadows of mystery fall upon us as we enter it. It is only a partial revelation of facts, conditions, estate, and life. The limitations, however, have respect to those conditions concerning which curiosity would prompt us to inquire, but a knowledge of which is not necessary to our inspiration or salvation. Frequently, the contents of revelation are overlooked in the belief that the truth is only incompletely set forth, and is by virtue of these limitations unreliable and without value; but, instead of settling into a suspicion that too little is revealed, one will find as he goes forward in his searching after truth that more is revealed than has been imagined, careful study being required to bring out what is in revelation. If the statue is in the block of marble, so is the truth in the volume of inspiration. If beauty is in the Apollo Belvidere, so is the truth in revelation. The duty to "search the Scriptures" rests upon the fact that they contain the words of this life and of that which is to come.

In accurately determining the eschatological truth of Christianity, as distinguished from similar teachings in the old religions, we shall be embarrassed by the historic interpretations of the Church, which are the inheritance of mankind, but which interfere at least slightly with independent investigation. By this it is not insinuated that such interpretations are erroneous, and that the Church is an unsafe guide in these things, and yet Christian faith has a dogmatic environment that sometimes has been permitted to overshadow and eclipse the faith itself. Of the presence and power of dogmatism we should certainly beware. The dictum of Roman Catholicism is a leaven from which the honest thinker must separate himself. But dogmatism is not confined to a corrupt form of Christianity, Protestantism sharing the tendency if not exhibiting the very spirit it condemns in such religions as it opposes. In Roman Catholicism the seeker runs into purgatory; in Protestantism he confronts flesh and blood resurrections, intermediate abodes for the dead, and semi-physical conditions in the future state that are quite as Quixotic as any thing he finds in mythology; in corrupt forms of Christianity he hears of soul-sleeping, annihilation, the Swedenborgian idea of the resurrection, a mixed or a progressive heaven, and the hope of a final abandonment of hell. Evidently, the Church, including the heterodox and evangelical branches, is at variance with itself in its teachings respecting the condition of the dead, and the final disposition of souls. Nor is there any seeming prospect of reconciliation of conceptions so divergent, or of unity of view touching these supreme subjects; on the contrary, the antagonism has but commenced, a tornado of heterodox beliefs is sweeping the world, and will continue its destructive work until old faiths have expired, and the truth of the Gospel has been confirmed. The spirit of inquiry is almost wild, but in its very recklessness it will go far toward the settlement of things, which means the extinction of error, and the affirmation of truth. We are called upon, therefore, to separate between the deliverances of Christianity and the utterances of creeds, councils, and man-made forms or expositions of truth, as the condition of rescuing the eschatology of Christianity from the superstitions of Christendom. If, however, the variant conceptions of Christendom seem rooted in the Gospel, or may be traced to

Christianity, is it certain that it is uniform in its revelations? Why this piebald product if the Gospel is unmistakably clear in its teachings, if it is a revelation? It must be remembered that the eschatology of Christianity is not on the surface, but in the depths; nor is it always clothed with the strait-jacket of literalism, but often appears in the beautiful robes of allegorical forms; and seldom is it discoursed or discussed, but hinted, hyperboled, reflected, and imbedded out of sight. Hence, the need of searching. Here, then, is our guide, or rather our *dictum;* not the Church, but Christianity; not theories, creeds, but the profound revelations of the divine Word.

What does Christian eschatology include? We answer: I. The Immortality of the Soul; II. An Intermediate State; III. The Resurrection of the Dead; IV. The Second Coming of Christ; V. The Final Judgment; VI. Heaven; VII. Hell. And whatsoever is more than these may be regarded as non-essential, or as explanatory of the seven great truths involved in eschatology. If the Scriptures reveal on these seven subjects any light at all, it ought to be followed; if the light is sufficient for the purposes of religion, there ought to be uniformity of faith, and the joy that comes from the ascertainment of truth. To the consideration of these momentous subjects we at once address ourselves.

The foundation-truth of eschatology is the *immortality of the soul.* The existence of another, or the eternal world, so-called, is not implicit with the idea of the immortality of the soul, but the immortality of the soul presupposes the existence of an immortal world. It is not enough that God's eternity be demonstrated or revealed; it is not enough that the angels are immortal; it must be shown that man is immortal. Will he live after he is dead? Does Julius Cæsar still live? Is Nero still a conscious being? Does Paul see, talk, remember, know? and will he forever live? Is Luther only a memory in this world, or a person in the other world? Is Charles Sumner an intellectual giant in another sphere? To such questions what is the answer? Who will undertake to answer? Assuming that Christianity heroically reveals the answer, is it sustained by outside proof? May the doctrine of the immortality of the soul refer to philosophy for vindication? If, after the revelation of the doctrine, no rational ground for faith in it can be discovered, and it must be accepted, if at all, only and wholly because it is revealed, faith itself may stagger at the duty required of it, and fall beneath the burden imposed upon it. If reason, or the philosophic sense, does not support the doctrine after it has been declared, then it is in jeopardy. The philosophic sense may not discover the truth, but it may confirm the revelation of it. That the doctrine is rational *per se;* that its philosophic basis is as impregnable as the philosophic basis of any other doctrine requiring revelation to bring it from darkness; that its philosophic verity is unimpeachable, because its divine verity is the subject-matter of revelation, we devoutly believe and urge others to believe. The philosophic grounds for faith in immortality may now be stated.

The intrinsic difference between soul and body constitutes a confirmatory proof of the Christian doctrine of the immortality of the one and the mortality of the other. The difference is not superficial, as it is the difference of essence, whereby one can not be immortal, but the other may be. No one thinks of attributing immortality to the body; many do think of attributing it to the soul and are unembarrassed in so doing by any rational objection. Only a confused philosophy will confound matter and spirit. Unfortunately, the attempt to blot out the differentia of soul and body, or to identify the two substances, has recently been made by Bain in England and Häckel in Germany, but the attempt has been unsuccessful. Without elaborating the differences between matter and spirit, but only reminding the reader of them, it is certain that one is justified in believing in the antecedent *probability* of immortality. It is not improper to frame probabilities from facts, or to invent inferences when they are in harmony with revelations. Immortality is not, however, an invented inference, but occupies on philosophic grounds the rank of a probability, and on Christian grounds the high position of a certainty. We re-affirm that no one espouses immortality for the body. Its final resolution into the common mold is apparent from its constitution; but it is philosophically absurd to predicate mortality of the soul upon the same ground as it is predicated of the body. If the soul is wanting in immortality, it lacks it for a reason that the body does not lack it. In other words, in our predicating we must have two bases; in our reasonings and conclusions we must have two sets of premises. This grows out of the essential difference of the two entities with which we are dealing; and, while this does not establish immortality for the soul, *it prevents the affirmation of its mortality.* To predicate mortality of two unlike entities, one must find two unlike conditions of mortality, which has not yet been done; and the improbability of finding the other or unknown condition of mortality becomes greater as the difference between the two entities becomes more apparent and irreconcilable. So far forth as mortality is a condition of the body, it is *not* a condition of the soul. In proportion as they approach a common likeness, or may be referred to a common origin, the probability of the immortality of one diminishes; but in proportion as they are unlike in constituent elements and different in origin, the probability of immortality increases. It is at this point that Christianity adds immensely to the presumption of the soul's immortality, on the ground of its difference from the body, pointedly affirming that the soul is the breath of the divine life, and will return to God, while the body, dust-made, will return again to the dust.

The philosophic questionings of the philosophers are not of inferior consequence in a discussion whose end is truth. Such questionings are the gleanings of the teachings of human nature, or the bountiful harvest from instincts, intuitions, and religious sentiments; or, viewed in another form, they are the deep soundings of consciousness, showing the drift of natural faith and fear. Cato mused over his soul as the painter muses over the product of his art. Plato and Socrates do not soliloquize; they dare affirm what they believe. "Catch me when I am gone, if you can," was the defiant assurance of Socrates's faith in the future before he drank the hemlock. Seneca, Cicero, Epictetus, and Marcus Aurelius, no less than Hegel, Descartes, Leibnitz, Cousin, and Lotze, discovered a satisfactory ground for faith in a future state, and join philosophic testimony to the revealed truth of this doctrine. *If there can be faith in immortality without revelation, it is evident that there can be such a faith with it.* If such a faith Socrates triumphantly held, it was because there was a philosophic basis for it—he could hold it on no other ground. The ground of his faith was in himself. *Every man is the proclamation of his own immortality;* every soul has the warrant of its eternal existence written on its very face. If immortal, it must say so, or by its silence deny its own condition. We place infinite stress upon the verdict of the soul, even if it is not as disinterested testimony as we might desire. The testimony of the soul, being in harmony with the teachings of Christianity, must be the testimony of truth, even if without Christianity such testimony may be discredited.

Another probability of immortality arises from the necessities and capabilities of the soul, or the *demand of another world for the full expansion of soul-life.* Continuous existence will insure ample opportunity for the development of capabilities, supposed to be exhaustless, and for the refinement of those virtues that constitute the image of God after which man was created. His time-life is a brief period of distress, misfortune, humiliation, and embarrassment; he goes through the world consciously undeveloped, a giant sunken into the proportions of a dwarf, with no opportunity of becoming what is possible. Man is not the great creature foreshadowed in his creation. The diamond has turned to carbon; the star is an orbitless comet. The intellectual imperfection of man, coupled with the painful fact of his moral apostasy, speaks loudly for a life of unclouded days, and a world of unsullied purity, in which he, breathing its atmosphere, and conforming to its order, may celebrate his possibilities by transforming them into powers, and employing them in achievements all too great for dwarfs here, but what might be expected of free and holy spirits there. Immortality is the antithesis of ruin, and restoration to greatness in another life is the only atonement for wreckage in this world.

Recently, a new conception of life has been advanced by Prof. Weisman, a German scientist, which, if correct, may be used as a scientific argument for immortality that materialists can not ignore or invalidate. He asserts that life in its very nature is unending, and that death in no sense is natural to life. Death occurs as an accident to life, and not as the *inherent product* of life. The proof adduced is in the history of the protozoan, which dies only as it is killed, or suffers accident. The division of the protozoan by which two individuals are produced occurs without any cessation of life, and life only ceases as it is interfered with by an outside force. Left to itself it will continue forever. In this view of the case, even physical life seems to be immortal; but, as it is environed by death-producing causes, it perishes. If, then, physical life is immortal in itself, surely soul-life is immortal, and, unless an outside cause inflicts death upon it, it will continue forever. It is not in the nature of life to die; and, as soul-life can not be destroyed by a physical cause, physical death, or the death of the body, does not affect the life of the soul. The death of the soul can only be effected by a cause equal to the soul or superior to it; a divine power only can destroy it. This practically and in a new way furnishes ground for scientific faith in immortality. The position of the German philosopher is scientifically correct, and the inference is in harmony with the Scriptures.

The especial character of the soul may be referred to in proof of its immortality, an argument that is of philosophic weight, if of any weight at all. What the soul is, or in what it differs from matter, has engaged the thought of all the schools, both philosophic and theologic, with varying conclusions, and an approximate settlement of the subject. Hermann Lotze does not find a ground of belief in the soul in the fact of its apparent freedom of action, or that its substantiality is different from that of matter because psychical processes are apparently different from physical processes; but he does discover the character of the soul in the *unity of consciousness*, a something that can not be predicated of matter or physical life. Establishing its character by this phenomenal mark of a single and identical consciousness, he proceeds to define the soul by its activity, that is, by its manifestation. "The soul is what it does;" "every soul is what it shows itself to be, unity whose life is in definite ideas, feelings, and efforts;" "to a certain extent the soul shows itself to be an independent center of actions and reactions;" so says Lotze. This is a key to the study of its character; and, inasmuch as it differs in the fact of its consciousness from matter, Lotze affirms that it is a "pre-mundane substance," and "that in no changes of the world, whatever they may be, can either an origin or an end be ascribed to it." This is immortality, or a supplement of Prof. Weisman's conclusion, that the death of the body can not affect the soul.

The common grounds, outside of the instructions of religion, for a belief in immortality are semi-philosophical, and of historical value; as proofs they are circumstantial rather than direct and conclusive. The existence of faith in immortality, on the account of its genesis and universality, is given an importance none too large in polemical discussions of the subject; for whether religion originated such faith or has maintained it, or whether it is a natural instinct, the fact remains that faith in immortality is world-wide and supreme in the thoughts of men. The universality of belief in a future life can not be dismissed as the product of authority or the result of education alone. *It is grounded in man himself.* If it is supposed that the natural love of life and the horror of annihilation have joined in the production of faith in another existence, it must be admitted that these are powerful incentives, and they show that such faith has its roots deep in humanity, and must not be ruthlessly plucked up and destroyed. Again, the effect of this faith on man himself in promoting self-development, self-purity, and in restraining the vicious tendency, is an incidental proof of a second life of no mean value. The sense of responsibility gains in force as it is impressed upon men that they must give an account to God, and they regulate themselves and order their lives in harmony with righteousness as they understand that the next life will be determined by the facts of this life. Even the analogies of nature, sometimes used as arguments, are not to be despised, since it is more comforting than if they were on the other side, or opposed in their suggestions to the idea of immortality. If nature by any of its processes counterfeits immortality, or attempts its realization, it helps one to go farther and suspect an actual immortality in another sphere. Suggestions from history, nature, science, psychology, and astronomy are eagerly appropriated by believers in immortality and turned into arguments in favor of the belief; and these taken in connection with fundamental and philosophical truths impress man most profoundly with the conviction that another life succeeds the present.

To this rational, historic, and philosophic conclusion more than one objection has been raised, and the inspiring hope of immortality has been bartered for a contrary hypothesis. Goethe expressed his belief in the future as follows: "The conviction of continuous existence suggests itself to me from the conception of activity; for if I am unceasingly active to my very end, nature is bound to assign to me another form of being, if the present one is no longer capable of fulfilling the requirements of my spirit." Acknowledging the beauty of this sentiment, Strauss assails it as only the special form of the common belief, and ridicules the idea that "nature is bound to assign" any body another form of being. He also declares that Goethe had "lived out his life" and needed no other world for his development, striking in this conclusion at the common supposition of the infinite capacity for development of the human soul. Admitting that Schiller died before his full development, he yields so far as to say that if another life is needed for those who have not reached their maximum, they also must perish when the maximum is attained, and that a "life extending interminably" can not be inferred from the premises, or from what he hesitatingly allows. Most manifestly his argument is reactionary in its assumption and concession. The assumption that Goethe had exhausted himself can not be explained, except on the ground of special pleading, for the mind testifies to itself of an ever-widening consciousness; and if Strauss ever had the feeling of Victor Hugo, that God is in him, he would be ready to believe that he had scarcely begun to develop in this life. Said the Frenchman: "I feel in myself the future life. I feel I have not said the thousandth part of what is in me. When I go down to the grave I can say, like so many others, 'I have finished my day's work,' but I can not say, 'I have finished my life.' My day's work will begin again the next morning." *The future is in us*, unending development is before us. No human being can say of another, nor of himself, that he has exhausted his capacity and developed all his possibilities to their full proportion of growth and fruitfulness, and that henceforth, should he live longer, he could not advance beyond his present achievement. This assumes a complete knowledge of the human mind and the discovery of certain fixed limitations that even an eternal existence will not remove. Strauss pronouncing Goethe complete, finished, exhausted! He did not know him; Strauss never knew himself.

The concession that Schiller could develop more with a continued life, and that, therefore, there may be another life, is a surrender to the advocates of immortality, for all that they philosophically claim is that the soul enters upon a second life, which in its very nature is eternal, and that the soul attains its full development in it. Given a life suited to the development of the soul, and the prob-

ability of immortality is assured, for in such a life *the soul will develop into an immortal condition*, even if it were not inherently immortal before its entrance into the eternal state.   The eternal world
will breathe its  eternity into  newly admitted  souls  and adapt them
to its unending duration.  Given existence at all after death, and eternal
existence ensues.   The belief in  immortality has been  suspected
of including  by  the arguments  it employs entirely  too much, or
more than it originally intended, for it is alleged that the argument
that makes out the immortality of man will also establish the immortality of brutes.   Annihilation is unknown to science; matter is
immortal.

If matter in some form must ever exist, then it is not incredible
that soul in some form will exist, nor is it at all incredible that
brutes, as such, or in other forms, will occupy the eternal spaces
and spheres.   It is no argument against the one that it proves the
other also.   Both brutes and men co-exist here; analogy might suggest their co-existence there.   However, we can not permit ourselves
to avow faith in the immortality of brutes, but, giving full force to
the objection, it is evident it does not invalidate or even touch the
question of man's immortality.   Brutes may or may not be immortal,
we are not concerned.   That which is of interest is to know if man
is immortal.

Of even less weight is the scientific objection that the universe is
the representative of a fixed amount of energy, and that its continuance in any form is contingent on the retention and activity of the
total energy.   The soul is the source of the highest energy, and contributes its possession to the great mass of the universe.   Now, it is
claimed if the soul is taken from the physical universe and contributes its energy to another universe, the equilibrium of the physical
universe is disturbed, and its existence is in peril.   Immortality is,
therefore, a menace to the peace and welfare of the universe.
Scientists are not prone to consider all the facts; they are specialists,
and notice only what is within their departments.   The physical system
is only one-half the universe; the other half is the spiritual universe.   The whole universe is a double-faced system, being physical
on one side and spiritual on the other, but correlated and interpenetrating, the energy of one passing into the other, and each under
control of the other.   The passage of energy from the physical to the
spiritual results in no loss of energy or disturbance of the equilibrium,
since there returns from the spiritual to the physical a counter-current
of influence that makes for order and stability.   The passage of souls
is equated by the transmission of spiritual energy in another form.

Our speculations must cease.  Going outside of Revelation, we find *the belief in immortality supported by the old religions, by the difference between soul and body, by the character and aspirations of the soul for something beyond, by the necessity of another life for development, by the tender musings of philosophy in its robust periods of thought, by scientific discoveries touching the question of life and death, by the common historical grounds of universal faith, and the analogies of nature, and is not overthrown or even shaken by objections, scientific, philosophic, or superstitious, arrayed against it.* The issue of this survey is the *probability of immortality.*

The certainty of immortality, or the positive assurance of another life, is derived from Revelation. Given Revelation, and the foregoing arguments, hints, and suppositions, are confirmations of the great truth, and appear relevant in a discussion of it. The outside adumbrations of immortality are fulfilled by the inside revelations of it, which we are ready to examine. Christianity, as understood, is the religion of the New Testament; but a larger view includes the Old Testament, in which are found the germs or roots of religious ideas, that assume a developed form in the new economy of Christ. Both the patriarchal and prophetic dispensations related to a future religion, and prepared the way for it by forecasting its contents and losing themselves in its loftier manifestation. The eschatology of the new had its antecedent signs in the old religion, or, as it is conceded, the Gospel brought immortality to light from the darkness of the Judaic administration. It is an extreme to assume that the ancient Judaic faith was barren of immortal hope, and that patriarchs, judges, kings, and prophets walked in the deepest shadows, without a single ray of light illuminating their pathway. They lived in the twilight age of the world, when truth was obscurely presented, but they discovered it in its obscurity; they had eyes and could see; they had intelligence and could know; and they were awake to all that has ever concerned man, and studied his destiny with an interest as profound as that which animates those who walk in the clearer light of the Gospel. At the same time, the Old Testament is not a manual on immortality, nor does it excite in the student that anticipation of another existence, which it is the business of a final religion to inspire; it awakens hope, but it does not reveal knowledge; it suggests faith, but permits doubt to accompany it; it makes immortality probable, but not certain. Prof. Tayler Lewis finds in Judaism a number of "scanty intimations" of a future life, over which the "veil of a solemn reserve" has been thrown, because, in the age of its glory, "there was danger of more evil thoughts coming out of the doctrine than good ones." In his judgment, the obscure doctrine had a "higher moral power" than a clearer doctrine could have had, inasmuch as, in its reserved form, it did not excite the fancy or lead to super-stition. This is not a satisfactory reason, for, if valid, the doctrine ought not to be revealed in the New Testament, since it has led to the most extravagant conceptions, and to just such dangerous opinions and heresies as he imagines it would have produced in the days of Greek and Roman ascendency. The "reserve" in the Old Testament is in accordance with the evolutionary plan of revelation, divine truth being made known as the world progressed in intelligence, and as the religious need of men required additions to their knowledge of divine things. The old economy, having an educational function, and intended to fore-shadow the brilliant disclosures of the new, stepped forward slowly, and revealed its hints and aspirations, only to retire when the actual truth swallowed up all hints and apparitions in itself. Speaking of the "void left in the Jewish mind," Dean Stanley ob-serves that, "the future life was not denied or contradicted, but it was overlooked or set aside, overshadowed by the consciousness of the living, actual presence of God himself." The idea of Judaism was monotheism, and eschatology was an incidental factor of it. This explanation is drawn from the spirit and purposes of Judaism, as contained in and revealed by its history from the days of Abraham until the advent of Christ, and is unobjectionable.

In the New Testament, the doctrine of the future life occupies no obscure place, but is as prominent in the teachings of the Savior and his apostles as the pillars of the Parthenon in Greek civilization. Immortality in parables; immortality in histories; immortality in biographies; immortality in laws; immortality in rewards and pun-ishments; immortality in ethics; immortality in epistles, visions, doctrines, counsels; immortality in Churches, elderships, magistracies, and governments; immortality in conduct, life, labors, and death-scenes; immortality at the grave, and written on the tomb-stone of the ages—Christianity is full of it, and breathes it into the world. The proverb passed from lip to lip in the early Church that Christ had "*abolished death*," and John wrote from Patmos that Christ held the keys of death, hell, and the grave. It was Christ who re-minded the thief of Paradise, and who, in one of his parables, spoke of "Abraham's bosom" as the abode of the righteous, and of *gehenna* as the abode of the ungodly; it was Christ who declared to his disci-ples, "I go to prepare a place for you, . . . and I will come again and receive you unto myself;" and who also said that, in the great day, he would banish from his presence those who had not be-lieved in him; it was Christ who declared that the righteous shall go into life eternal, but the ungodly into everlasting punishment. He "brought immortality to light," and his apostles proclaimed it wherever they went, recorded it in all their epistles, and left it as the inheritance of the Church for the ages to come. It is true we write under the spell of our faith in the doctrine, and, if this is a disqualification for impartial searching, we can not help it; we desire the doctrine to be true; we believe it is true, first from philosophy, second from revelation. Believing it to be true, it has magnetized us, and led us to appropriate in its support every argument, every fact, every allusion, found in history, science, religions, philosophy, and Christianity, and nothing is clearer to our vision than that man is immortal.

What is his title to immortality? The only being who is essentially immortal is God; the angels are immortal by endowment. It is as possible for God to deprive them of it as it was possible for him to confer it. Man is immortal by the same voluntary power and goodness; his immortality is an endowment—it is the gift of God. It is possible for God to extinguish the immortality of any of his subjects; the soul can be annihilated, just as angels might be destroyed forever. As an abstract proposition, this is perfectly defensible; as an event that has occurred, or will ever occur, it is without proof. Immortality guaranteed by creation, or in any other way, it must ever remain; annihilation will never be enforced against a human soul. At this point thinkers divide, some contending that annihilation will be the portion of the wicked, while immortality will be the reward of the righteous. Certainly a forfeiture of immortality would be an incalculable and irreparable loss, so great that it is a question if an unforgiven soul would not prefer eternal existence in hell to absolute non-existence forever. The preference in the matter, however, is not urged as an agument against it; the possibility of annihilation is not urged as an argument in favor of it.

Others contend that immortality is not a natural endowment, but the special gift of Christ to all who believe in him, so that unsaved men are not immortal, and perish forever because they are not immortal. This depends upon our knowledge of antecedent facts involved in the creation of man and his loss of life by sin. When Adam was created, he received the spirit of immortality, being made in the image of God; when he transgressed the first prohibition ever given from the throne, *he lost divine favor, but not immortality.* Holiness, not immortality, was involved in the fall; the recovery, therefore, is a recovery to righteousness only. This is a brief statement, but it comprehends all the facts. It does not admit annihilation, since the question of existence is not involved. It does not admit the idea of immortality as a gift, since it was not affected by the fall. Sin or no sin, death or no death, the soul is immortal.

Besides, the condemned angels are not doomed to annihilation, but to conscious punishment and degradation, which implies continued living. By analogy, we reason that the punishment of unpardoned souls is not the loss of immortality, or annihilation. To accept the other view requires us to distinguish some souls as mortal and others as immortal, or two kinds of souls, whereas all souls are alike in their origin and constituent facts, the final difference between them being moral, and not constitutional. The thought of mortal souls is in harmony with false and skeptical science, and it is in the direction of a false and perverted religion. The distinction between soul and body can not be maintained if immortality be regarded a gift, and that the wicked naturally go into annihilation. Immortality is the inalienable fact of every soul, and it will be an abuse of the divine power for any cause now known or conceivable to quench or modify it.

Not the most serious, but the most uncertain, problem of eschatology, and of commanding proportions, is that of the resurrection of the dead. It is a theological problem, since it is associated with final religious events; it is metaphysical, as it involves philosophical conditions, relations, and suppositions; it is less important than others, since an understanding of it is in no sense a condition of salvation; and one can not be accused of heresy in holding to any particular view of it, since many views obtain in the Christian Church, not one of which is regarded standard or the fixed view of believers. The most that can be said respecting it is, that it is a revealed doctrine of the Scriptures; the best doctrinal exposition of it is that given by Paul; and the clearest idea one gets of it has not yet satisfied the Church at large that it is the true and only idea to be adopted. Theologians, philosophers, all, are in a cloud, or in the sea, respecting the great doctrine.

As to the fact of a resurrection, there are few who doubt that it is contemplated in the Scriptures, and that it is intimately related to the consummation of Christianity, even those who, like Hymenæus, charge that it has taken place, agreeing that it occupies a position in the history of the new religion. The agitation rages over the character of the resurrection, and the time when it shall occur. It is not asked, Will there be a resurrection? It is asked, What *kind* of a resurrection will there be? Summarily, *What is the resurrection?* Are we certain we understand it? Misunderstandings certainly do exist, and have always existed, respecting the doctrine, Paul himself having been interpreted differently, and confusion being the total result. Certain interpretations have been dominant in the circles of Christian thought, but not one is considered supreme in itself, or superior to others, or satisfactory to the majority.

Preliminarily, the theories of the resurrection must have recognition, inasmuch as they are held and advocated by thoughtful minds, and possibly one of them may satisfactorily explain the fact of the resurrection; or, in the combination of two or more, a pathway to the actual fact of which we are in search may be opened.

I. The common or the most widely accepted interpretation of the doctrine is, that the natural body which suffers death will be raised by the power of God from the grave, be fitted by virtue of spiritual processes for the eternal condition, and be reunited to the soul as its partner forever. It is not difficult to build around this interpretation a great many passages of Scripture, and to offer defensible arguments in its behalf; but the drift of metaphysical thought is in other directions. This is known as the "literal" theory.

II. Origen, he of the third century, advanced the idea that the identical natural body will not rise, but a body composed of natural properties, and exactly resembling the old body, will appear as the resurrection-body, *produced by the power of the soul to organize for itself a body* suited to the various spheres of its existence. This implies the creation of a new body.

III. The Germ theory, or that advocated by Samuel Drew, is in substance that, in the human body, there is a "certain principle of future being," which "shall form the rudiments of our future bodies." It is indestructible. The old is the nucleus of the new body.

IV. Still another is Swedenborg's conception that the soul is clothed with a spiritual body, which, at the death of the natural body, enters the spiritual body, where it abides forever. The resurrection is the rising of the soul at death with its spiritual body into the eternal state.

V. Again, it has been suggested that the resurrection is the rising of souls out of *hades* on the great and notable day of the Lord, when they shall appear before him to render an account of their earth-life and receive judgment. Mr. Alger supports the theory, and turns some Scripture in its behalf.

VI. An *evolutional resurrection* has been surmised from Paul's illustration of the seed producing its kind; so the resurrection-body will be after the pattern, though not of the substance, of the natural body.

VII. The resurrection-body, Bishop R. S. Foster supposes, will be a "suitable body," devised by the Creator for the soul; it will not be a "reproduction of the old body."

That these so-called resurrections have a Scriptural basis, and that they may be vindicated by intensely and cogently rational arguments, is clear to one who listens to their advocates; but, after listening to all, we inquire, which is the correct theory? or are they all correct?

38

The seven theories, apparently different, are not altogether mutually opposed; one is not exclusive of all the others. The literal theory, the germ theory, and the evolution theory are not so far apart as to be radically antagonistic; but, agreeing as to the relation of the natural body to the resurrection-body, they should harmonize on lesser features, and vindicate the resurrection from the single stand-point of the transformation of the natural into a spiritual body. The theories of Origen, Swedenborg, and Bishop Foster should coalesce, each conceding unimportant points, and uniting on the main point of the appearance of a spiritual body as the resurrection-body. The theory of Alger stands alone. We have, therefore, but three theories of the resurrection: (*a*) That theory that *involves the natural body,* more or less, in the event of the resurrection; (*b*) That theory that eliminates the natural body, and *involves a spiritual body,* in the event of the resurrection; (*c*) That theory that eliminates both a natural and spiritual body from the resurrection, *involving only the deliverance of souls from the intermediate world,* as the condition of entrance into final everlasting abodes. Prizing distinctions as stepping-stones to truth, we once more characterize the theories as (*a*) natural, (*b*) spiritual, (*c*) soulical. The natural or literal resurrection has been supported by Bishop C. Kingsley, Bishop D. W. Clark, and recently by Dr. R. J. Cooke in a masterly exposition; the spiritual or anti-natural resurrection is ably maintained by Swedenborg, Bishop Foster, Dr. Newman Smyth, and others; the soulical resurrection has countenance from W. R. Alger and others of mixed faith.

The arguments, both rational and Scriptural, employed in the defense of these theories, and the manner in which objections to them are removed or answered, would furnish a chapter of interesting reading; we can not more than notice a few, in order to indicate the general support that each receives. As to the natural resurrection, Dr. Cooke insists that there can be no other than the literal reproduction of the "material fleshly" body; any other kind of a body would not be a resurrection-body. A created body, or a body resembling the natural body, or a body evolved from the natural body, can not be the resurrection-body; that is, the *resurrection is the standing again of the natural body.* This is not an ambiguous statement, nor a double-faced definition; but it is very like the definition of baptism urged in some quarters, that it is immersion, and nothing else; resurrection is the reappearance of the natural body, and no other kind of a body can be substituted. The definition of the word is, then, regarded as a support of the natural theory. Bishop Foster does not accept the definition or its application. "The word resurrection," he says, "is strained when it is insisted that it is

equivalent to the statement that the exact body is to be restored."
Quoting again: "The resurrection is the standing again of the person
in a body, or after his severance from the gross body." Substantially,
Dr. Newman Smyth agrees with this conception, for he says: "Our
resurrection shall not be  .  .  .  simply a setting free from the
bonds of the flesh of a finer spiritualized form,  .  .  .  but it shall
be  .  .  .  the assimilation by the living energy or soul of these
bodies  .  .  .  of the material of the unseen universe," or " the
gathering, around the vitalizing principle, of the materials of a more
spiritual body from the heavenly places." Paul alludes to the question that some will urge, "With what body do they come?" implying
that it was an undecided problem in his day as to what the resurrection-body will be. At the same time, the apostle does assure his
readers that Jesus Christ will "change these *vile bodies*, and fashion
them like unto his own glorious body," apparently implying that the
natural body is the subject of the resurrection.

Again, it is urged that, as the body is united with the soul in
this life, so must it be united with the soul in the next life, to share
either the rewards or punishments that may finally be decreed by the
unerring wisdom and faultless justice of the great Judge. Growing
out of this thought is that other, that before the resurrection the soul
only is immortal, but after the resurrection *man*—body and soul—is
immortal. For the natural theory, the three supports are, the *definition* of the word, *Scriptural passages* in apparent harmony with it, and
the *necessity* of a literal resurrection to restore man to his completeness, and to involve all there is of him here in the awards of all that
may be possible in a future life. The threefold argument is plausible,
and, in the absence of rebutting testimony, is well-nigh conclusive;
but it is not certain that it is unimpeachable.

The definition itself needs reconstruction. Etymologically, it is
not certain that it refers to the natural body. The application of it
to the natural body for nearly fifteen centuries has led many to believe
that any other application is indefensible, and that a denial of the interpretation will be fatal to the integrity of Christianity as a system of
truth. The "resurrection of the body" is not a Scriptural phrase;
the "resurrection of the dead" is Scriptural. The former phrase, expressive, perhaps, of the belief of the early Christians, was not coined
or embalmed in creed-form until the fourth century; nevertheless, it
probably represents the Christian idea. Little allusion is made in the
Scriptures to the resurrection of the *body;* frequent allusion is made
to the *resurrection of the individual,* or the resurrection of personality.
For example, the Savior says (John vi, 54), "and I will raise *him* up
at the last day." It is a question if the resurrection of the body is

equivalent to the resurrection of the person, and it is equally a question if the arguments employed in the defense of the one are not as available for the defense of the other.

Scripturally, the believer in the natural theory must not be over-confident that all the apostles, including the Master himself, are on his side, for Paul says: "Flesh and blood can not inherit the kingdom of God; neither doth corruption inherit incorruption." One would conclude, from reading the advocates of the three great theories, that Paul favored all of them, for he is quoted, explained, and referred to by all, as the unanswerable defender of their faith.

Likewise, the arguments touching the natural theory are not all on one side, nor are those framed with special reference to it exhaustively complete, or inwardly satisfactory. It is clear that the body is not necessary to *conscious* existence hereafter; it is not so clear that it is necessary to a *perfect* existence hereafter. Respecting the materialistic view, Dr. Newman Smyth observes: "The body which shall be is not fashioned of matter of the same kind as these earthly bodies. It is not of the earth earthy. The earthliness in which the seed is buried does not appear in the flower. . . . Our science leaves us no tenable support for it. Any proper physiological conception of the human body precludes it. Is it necessary for any one, at this late day, to spend time in clearing the simplicity of the Biblical doctrine of the resurrection of the dead from the cumbersome additions of the traditional teaching of the resurrection of the flesh?" This is in the right direction. If the conditions of the future life are different from those of the present life; if the employments of spirits are different from the employments of mortals; if the resources, agencies, and objects of the immortal life are different from such as obtain in our time-life,—it is incredible that the natural body, even glorified, can have any functions or prerogatives in the other life. Plotinus rejoiced that his soul was not to be tied to an immortal body.

Dr. Cooke traces the "hyper-spiritualistic" ideas of the resurrection, which have more or less infected Christian belief from the days of Origen, to the influence of Gnostic philosophy, which looked upon matter as inferior to the soul, and as the residence of evil; and a class of Christian thinkers appropriating the philosophy gradually and philosophically ignored a material resurrection. While the Gnostic principle is antagonistic to the resurrection of the natural body, it must not be forgotten that it contributed toward relieving Christianity of certain phases of materialism that are incompatible with its character, and would be fatal in these days to its progress as a spiritual religion. Christianity is a spiritual religion; nearly all its doctrines are spiritual; and so far forth as any doctrine is reduced to a material form and urged as such, it compromises the religion and mantles its spiritual character. Immersion is a materialistic phase of baptism, which the Church will finally outgrow; transubstantiation and consubstantiation are materialistic interpretations of the Eucharist; the pre-millennial reign of Christ on earth is a materialistic conception of Christ's spiritual government in the world; *and the natural resurrection is a materialistic type of the spiritual resurrection that occurs at the end of the world.* In this materialistic age we must abandon materialistic ideas of religion.

As to the soulical theory, taking it out of its order in the discussion, since it can not be amplified or vindicated, it is almost enough to say that it is not at all contained in the word resurrection. It implies a resurrection of *souls*, whereas the resurrection of the New Testament involves a resurrection of *bodies*. It is true, as Mr. Alger shows, that the author of the Epistle to the Hebrews speaks of "the *spirits* of just men made perfect in the heavenly Jerusalem," but the word spirit may mean the conscious life or the whole personality, as found *after* the resurrection, or it may mean the spiritual body of the soul in its perfected form, as it appears in the heavenly Jerusalem. If it has any reference whatever to the resurrection, it must imply the spiritual *body*, which is the subject of resurrection, and not the spiritual *being* after the resurrection. A resurrection of souls from the under-world, or the intermediate abode, doubtless will take place; but it is straining the word, perverting the Scriptures, and invalidating nearly all the arguments used for either a natural or spiritual resurrection, to apply it to the deliverance of souls from *hades*. This is not a resurrection at all.

The spiritual theory is in its very terms antagonistic to the natural theory. It may be objectionable, but it can not be abruptly dismissed as incompatible with the idea of resurrection. The word itself will allow either the natural or spiritual theory, and the arguments for one are as indisputably strong as those for the other. With many it is a question of choice which to adopt, one being as plausible as the other; with others it is a question of conviction, the spiritual being the preferred view. In general terms the resurrection is intended to be a deliverance of the soul from the reign of matter, or the extinction of its bondage to corruption. Death alone, or the separation of soul and body, does not accomplish this end, for full deliverance from evil also implies complete equipment for good. Disembodiment must be followed by re-embodiment, or one body, mortal and corruptible, must be exchanged for another body, immortal and incorruptible. The decisive argument in favor of the spiritual body is Scriptural. Without a Scriptural basis the theory would be not only untenable, but revolutionary and infidelic. Its ground is in the Scriptures, both in the Old and New Testaments. The resurrection is alluded to more positively in the Old Testament than the doctrine of immortality, and is a powerful argument in its favor. Job declares that in his flesh he shall see God; David asserts his flesh shall rest in hope; Isaiah announces, "Thy dead men shall live, (together with) my dead body shall they arise;" Ezekiel prophecies the resurrection of the body by the resurrection of the dry bones in the valley; and Daniel decrees that "many of them that sleep in the dust of the earth shall awake, some to everlasting life, and some to shame and everlasting contempt." Now, without controversy, the resurrection in the Old Testament is materialistic or natural, but it is on that account no proof of the materialistic type of the actual resurrection. Mr. Alger finds a materialistic resurrection in Zoroastrianism, which he affirms gave birth to the Jewish doctrine, and the Jewish became in turn the mother of the Christian idea, or materialistic conception of the resurrection in the Christian Church. For this opinion we care nothing, because it does not settle the question of the character of the resurrection body. To say that a Christian doctrine has its roots in Jewish teaching, and that Jewish teaching borrowed itself from Persian sages, does not invalidate it; it may be a *true* doctrine, whatever its source.

It is all-important to know, however, what is the significance of the flesh-and-blood resurrection of the Jewish economy. Is it *per se* the resurrection of the new religion, or only the materialistic type of a spiritual event to occur at the end of the world? The atonement of the old economy was materialistic; the atonement of the new is spiritualistic. The religion of the old was ceremonial, physical, legal; the religion of the new, spiritual altogether. *The resurrection of the old was materialistic, the resurrection of the new is spiritual.* The old idea was glorious, but it has lost its glory in the "glory that excelleth." So the analogy of faith teaches and requires. The New Testament doctrine of the resurrection is the fulfillment or development of the Old Testament doctrine; but if the one resurrection is the same as the other, there is no development, there is repetition. Is the New Testament, in its monotheism, atonement, and spirituality, a development of the Old Testament, but as touching the resurrection, is it but a repetition? Because Christ and the apostles used the same words for the new resurrection as were used by the Jews for the old idea of it, Dr. Cooke argues that they must have meant the same resurrection. This is very inconclusive, and violates the relations of the old to the new. The word Sabbath in the Old does not signify the day that it represents in the New, except when so mentioned.

The word sacrifice in the Old has a different application in the New. The word atonement in the Old Testament means one kind of sacrifice—in the New Testament another kind of sacrifice. Likewise the word resurrection in the Old Testament means a different event in the New Testament. To the New Testament let us turn.

Paul intimates what the resurrection body will be when he says, "For in this we groan, earnestly desiring to be clothed upon with our house, which is from heaven." If the natural body can be spoken of as "our earthly house of this tabernacle," the spiritual body can be spoken of as "our house which is from heaven." The natural resurrection body is the "earthly house;" the spiritual resurrection body is the "heavenly house." That is, it is a *heavenly* and not the earthly body. This is conclusive. Again, when brought before the Sanhedrin, Paul opened his defense with the exclamation, "Of the hope and resurrection of the dead I am called in question." He affirms the resurrection of the *dead*, but who are the dead? When it was reported that "General Grant is dead," it was meant that *he* had separated from his body. *He* is dead—not his body. "The dead" are the living individuals; they are not putrefying bodies. The dead — that is, the conscious individuals — shall stand in living bodies again; in this life they stood in corruptible bodies; in the next they stand in incorruptible bodies. So seems to say the great apostle.

Dr. R. J. Cooke assumes that the Greeks understood Paul on Mars' Hill to preach a "literal corpse resurrection," and hence were infuriated and disgusted; but this does not establish that he did preach it. It establishes that they construed the spiritual resurrection into a gross, carnal resurrection, just what Dr. Cooke has done, just what the naturalists and materialists do, and are led to renounce it, just what the natural mind is prone to do whenever the Gospel is preached. It is easy to paraphrase the spiritual into the physical, and to speak of the incorruptible as the corruptible. Reducing the spiritual teaching to a physical idea, it becomes foolishness to the natural mind, and even a stumbling-block to the fleshly and the ungodly. It by no means solves the problem, or throws any daylight upon it, to be told that the Greeks understood Paul to mean a particular thing; the question is not what the Greeks thought he meant, but what did he mean? That he employed Jewish terms when he addressed the Jews, and Greek terms when he addressed the Greeks, only proves that he undertook to represent the great doctrine in the language of the people whom he addressed, without graduating the truth to their preconceived ideas of it, or conforming the doctrine to any existing notion by running it in the language-mold of the people. Employing their language, the doctrine was not their doctrine. Sameness of language is not equivalent to sameness of doctrine.

The fundamental chapter on the resurrection of the dead is that which composes a part of Paul's First Epistle to the Corinthians. It is singular that this chapter has been so often perverted in the interest of the theory of a natural resurrection, while the whole is unmistakably a revelation of the spiritual resurrection. "There is a natural body and there is a spiritual body." Here the existence of the two kinds of *bodies* is affirmed. "It is sown a natural body, it is raised a spiritual body." Evidently the *sowing* is not the resurrection; the *raising* is the resurrection. Now, if a spiritual body is raised, then the resurrection relates to a spiritual body. The natural body is sown, but it is not raised. In keeping with this distinction Paul affirms that "as we have borne the image of the earthy," or natural, "we shall also bear the image of the heavenly," or spiritual. This distinction is also illustrated by the sowing of grain and the product thereof as follows: "That which thou sowest, thou sowest *not that body that shall be;*" that is, the natural body shall not be the future body; "but God giveth it a body as it hath pleased him, and to every seed his own body." The revelation is that *God will give to the soul such a body as shall please him,* which can not be the natural body, because "thou sowest not that body that shall be," but it will be a "spiritual body," of which Paul speaks.

Paul's seed-thought is pregnant with another suggestion. The seed is planted; the hull dies; the vitalizing principle re-appears in the grain. The seed is man, physical and spiritual, or body and soul; the hull is the body; the soul is the immortal principle that re-appears after the dissolution of the body, waiting until the resurrection for the spiritual body, or to become the perfect grain; that is the perfect man again. To us the apostolic argument is transparent, elaborate, and unanswerable in its revelation of the resurrection-body as spiritual and incorruptible.

The Lord's resurrection might be studied, and a conclusion in harmony with the Pauline revelation be drawn; but we have not space to analyze that event. Bishop Foster concedes too much when he asserts that Christ's body is not a pattern of our resurrection; for, while it may not be a pattern, it sustains the spiritual quite as freely as the natural theory, and should not be eliminated from the discussion. At one time Christ's body seems natural, human; at another, spiritual, immortal. He assumed a natural appearance to convince his disciples that he was alive again; and a spiritual appearance, to suggest to them the resurrection-body. The true resurrection-body manifested itself in spiritual phenomena which they recognized;

but, as their chief concern was to be assured of his power over death, the spiritual body worked temporarily through the natural body, which, as an exception to the general order, may possibly have ascended on high and become assimilated with the spiritual body, to reign with it forever.

The most satisfactory revelation from Christ touching the resurrection life appears in his conversation with the Sadducees, who, disbelieving in the resurrection, propounded to him a question which they imagined would confuse him. His answer we give (Matt. xxii, 30) : "For in the resurrection they neither marry nor are given in marriage, but are *as the angels of God in heaven.*" The resurrection-body is as an angel-body, which is spiritual, heavenly. "As touching the resurrection of the dead," he says, " God is not the God of the dead, but of the living ;" that is, the resurrection relates to the living souls, and not to the bodies in the graves. He is not the keeper of dust, but he is the preserver of souls, and giveth each a body as it pleaseth him.

Accepting the spiritual theory on Scriptural grounds, it may be enforced on rational or scientific grounds, but their elaboration is unnecessary. Evidently, the scientific spirit is antagonistic to a physical resurrection. Reason is against it; faith only can conquer reason, because it must if the natural theory is accepted. No such embarrassment environs the acceptance of the spiritual theory. Reason pronounces it tenable; revelation assures us that it is certain. A "spiritual body" for the soul is not an unscientific thought, since such a body is in essential sympathy with the soul, as indeed it is of the same eternal constitution. A belief in the spiritual body is as rational as a belief in the soul. One agrees with the other. Again, the necessity of the spiritual body is a scientific necessity. The law of continuity, which has its fittest illustration in life, requires the association of the spirit-body and the soul, as co-partners in the life of the soul from its beginning through all eternity. When the natural body falls, the continuity of life is broken and paralyzed; but, inasmuch as the continuity of real life is not a physical resultant, nor dependent on physical conditions, it is secured by conscious spiritual existence in another world. The spiritual body takes the place of the natural, and secures continuity; it secures it by anticipation of the spiritual body; it secures it by an actual realization or possession of the spiritual body.

With the manner in which the spiritual body is provided, whether the soul organizes it out of its own materials, or transforms the surrounding elements of the spiritual world into a suitable body, or whether God prepares one independently of the soul's agency and activity, or whether it abides with the soul in this life as an undeveloped or unused body, and remains quiescent until the great day, when it assumes an active relation to the soul, we have nothing to do. The *fact* of a spiritual body is all that must engage our attention. That the resurrection, or the standing again of the soul in a spiritual body, will occur at the end of the world we sincerely believe. We must, therefore, repudiate every theory that holds that the resurrection takes place at death, and every theory that has not for the subject of the resurrection some kind of a body. Touching the doctrine *we follow no teachers, save Christ and the apostles;* touching revelations, *no document has any authority save the New Testament; and,* touching theories, *they all vanish in the presence of the monumental representation of the great truth made by the apostle Paul.*

Between death and the resurrection a period of unknown length elapses, during which disembodied souls are in a state of conscious existence, and engaged in occupations either congenial or otherwise, patiently waiting for the re-embodiment which the resurrection will confer. Where are the disembodied souls during this period? Are the righteous in heaven, and the wicked in hell; or, do they occupy an *intermediate place,* which is neither heaven nor hell, except in spirit and indications? This is the next problem.

Prior to the study of the problem, the existence of an "unseen universe," or a world back of, different from, and productive of the visible universe, must be noted. The immortality of the soul and the resurrection of the dead conjoin in the affirmation of another universe. The New Testament is the testimony to its existence. It is a sphere of angels, fallen and unfallen, of spirits redeemed and punishable, and it is the theater of God's infinite enterprises of grace, wisdom, and power. In that universe he dwells, and it will endure forever. "The things which are seen are temporal, but the things which are not seen are eternal." Out of it come the angels who minister to the heirs of salvation; out of it come the devils who seek a dwelling-place in men; out of it came the Son of God, and into it he returned; out of it came the voice that was heard at the baptism of the Savior, and from it comes the Spirit that reproves the world of its iniquity; into it looked the dying Stephen and the holy martyrs, and the race in its swift march to the tomb gazes wistfully toward it. That unseen universe embraces heaven and hell; the intermediate world, if there is any, and the final world, of which no doubt can exist.

Not a few theologians hold to the idea of an immediate entrance at death of the sanctified soul into the highest heaven, and of the unrepentant soul into the deepest hell. Nor can it be denied that some passages of Scripture easily and naturally incline to that view of the future state. To the doctrine of an Intermediate World there are some objections that, though not necessarily fatal to it, must be removed, or explained, before it can be fully accepted by all the readers of the Scriptures. The doctrine itself is the foundation of many errors in theology, or the root of heresies and fancies not at all compatible with an intelligent Christianity. Granted an intermediate world, and the Roman Catholic may plausibly preach his doctrine of purgatory; the Spiritualist may proclaim his idea of progression and moral discipline and preparation in the future life; the Universalist can apparently prove the final salvation of all mankind if he is allowed an intermediate, half-way place of preparation; the New Theology can flourish its dogma of a second probation, and transfer Gospel conditions to the disembodied life of man; and so the most pernicious errors are possible from the assumption of an intermediate world. Let it be understood that the soul at death ascends to heaven or descends to hell, and there is no room for any of these errors. This would be a great gain to theology. But, in investigating a truth, the probability that error may spring out of an interpretation, or theology may be more or less affected by it, can have no positive influence on the honest seeker after the truth. No doctrine of the New Testament has failed to awaken criticism, or suggest objections, or produce positive errors in interpretation. From the doctrine of the Incarnation have emerged Monophysitism and Eutychianism; from the Eucharist, transubstantiation and consubstantiation; from the Foreknowledge of God, predestination, denial of human freedom, and denial of contingencies; from the Atonement, election and reprobation; from the Trinity, Unitarianism, Swedenborgism, and infidelity. Objections to doctrines revealed, and to be known by revelation only, are of little weight with minds who discern the truth of revelation.

It may be made against the doctrine of the intermediate world that it partakes of the materialistic spirit of the Homeric theology and the Judaic revelations. The ancient Jew, while intending to be spiritual, was practically a materialist, and clothed truth in physical forms. By him the future was conceived under material aspects, from which he could scarcely deliver himself, even when the spiritual view was exclusively enforced. To him *sheol* was as literal a place as the grave; the one for the body, the other for the soul; and the one remained in its place so long, and no longer, as the other in its place. Both the grave and sheol are intermediate abodes, from which both body and soul will be delivered. Naturally enough, this view found its way into the theology of the Christian Church, and even Christ and the apostles in their teachings employed the terms that represented the Jewish thought, and gave countenance to it. It is certain, also, that the Homeric theology contributed its terms and teachings to Christianity to such a degree that it has been surmised that the under-world idea is Greek or pre-Christian, and not definitely the product of inspiration. Both the Jews and the Greeks had an eschatology of their own, different in important particulars, and yet agreeing in those things that constitute the essential ideas of a theologic view of the future. Both pointed out the immortality of man; both indicated the happiness of the good and the wretchedness of the ungodly in the next life; both foreshadowed an intermediate world of disembodied spirits; and both prophesied final rewards and retributions through a judicial process at an eternal tribunal. This shows that the truth had been *partly* revealed even to Homer as well as to Moses; but Christianity was needed to bring these partly revealed truths to light. Hence, a similarity of teaching between Christ and Homer, and between Christ and the prophets. From the materialism of the Greek and the Hebrew conception of the future state Jesus immediately separated himself, emphasizing the spiritual character of future rewards and punishments, and dissolving the connection between *sheol* and the grave. In Christianity the grave disappears; *sheol* is transformed into *hades*; and *hades* fades finally into a fixed eternity. This is the progress of thought in the Scriptures, or a passing from materialistic views under the old dispensation to the exclusively spiritual under the new. It can not be maintained, therefore, against the Christian idea of an intermediate abode, that it is essentially Homeric and Jewish, and therefore ought to be abandoned; for it is Homeric and Jewish preliminarily only, and not essentially.

Sometimes it is suggested that the Intermediate World in its social conditions and relations can not be different from this world, for it seems to be the abode of joy and sorrow, and of mixed phenomena of life; but if so there is no necessity for such a world. If the world-life there is a reproduction or continuance of the world-life here, it must be a life of alternate hopes and fears, of liabilities and surprises, of progress and discovery, without any positive settlement of those religious questions that engage the anxious thought of the race here. Such a view arises from a misapprehension of the intermediate world, which is represented in an entirely different aspect in the Scriptures. It is nowhere declared to be a reproduction of this life. It is everywhere represented to be the beginning of heaven to the righteous and the dawn of hell to the wicked; it is heaven to the one and hell to the other.

The positive Scriptural arguments for the intermediate world are almost complete. The Old Testament scarcely gets beyond the intermediate world; this is in harmony with its character as an incipient revelation. When Saul disturbed Samuel, the old prophet shouted,

"Why hast thou disquieted me *in bringing me up?*" The meaning may be that he was in a state of satisfaction in the *under-world*, and did not wish to be connected again with earthly scenes or events. The word *sheol*, used sixty-five times in the Old Testament, can have no other meaning than that of the intermediate abode of souls waiting for the resurrection. It has been displaced in the New Testament by the word *hades*, which it is impossible to believe refers to any other than an intermediate place of the dead. David says (Acts ii, 27), "Thou wilt not leave my soul in *hades;*" here he looks to a deliverance from the intermediate abode. Paul asks (I Cor. xv, 55), "O, *hades*, where is thy victory?" Victory over, or rescue from the under-world, is the meaning. John represents Christ (Revelation i, 18) as saying, "I am alive for evermore; and have the keys of *hades* and of death." He proposes to unlock the gates of the intermediate world and bid all come forth. The final disposition of *hades* is thus (Revelation xx, 14) indicated: "And death and *hades* were cast into the lake of fire." This is extinction of *hades*.

The intermediate world must necessarily consist of two departments, the one for the righteous, the other for the wicked. So we find it in the Scriptures, Paradise standing for the former and Gehenna for the latter. Dr. L. T. Townsend speaks of the one as Paradise-Hades, and of the other as Gehenna-Hades, a division clearly justified by the New Testament. Jesus (John xiv, 2) said unto the disciples, "I go to prepare a place for you," intimating that the final heaven is not yet ready for saints, and possibly will not be ready until the resurrection. Peter (Acts ii, 34) said in his Pentecostal sermon, "For David is not ascended into the heavens," intimating a waiting for the heavenly life. To the thief on the cross Jesus said, "To-day shalt thou be with me in Paradise," or *hades;* and in his parable of the rich man and Lazarus he pictures the latter in Abraham's bosom and the former in gehenna in torment. "Abraham's bosom" can only be understood as a temporary resting-place of the saved, while gehenna is the temporary abode of the unforgiven. In that wonderful description of the judgment-scene (Matt. xxv, 31–46), we read of final rewards and punishments, but it does not take place until *the end of the world*, or "*when the Son of man shall come in his glory.*" According to this scene, heaven and hell will not be opened until after the judgment at the end of the world. This is more decisive than any thing else in the New Testament that in their disembodied state the dead are in an intermediate world.

Less elaborate, but hardly less explicit, are other passages relating to the temporary character of gehenna and the final passage of its inhabitants into lower conditions of suffering and punishment. Peter (II Peter ii, 4) writes, "For if God spared not the angels that sinned, but cast them down to *hades*, and delivered them into chains of darkness, to be *reserved unto judgment*," etc.; and Jude, sixth verse, rehearses the same fact; both implying that the fallen angels and wicked spirits are held like prisoners for judgment, and will be brought forth from the prison-house, or gehenna, at the last day to receive sentence of punishment that will never be revoked, and to be suffered in hell or the deeper abode prepared for the devil and his angels.

The revelation of an intermediate abode is satisfactory; the necessity of such an abode is involved in the revelations themselves. The relation of the resurrection to *hades* is conspicuous; the one involves the other. The disembodied soul, waiting for its spiritual body, remains in *hades*, until clothed with its house from heaven, a building of God, and enters its final abode when so clothed and prepared. If the disembodied soul, represented as "naked," is fitted for heaven, and has been there since death dissolved its connection with the body, there is no need of the resurrection; but if the disembodied soul is in an imperfect state, and must be clothed with a spiritual body before it can enter heaven or hell, its occupancy of an intermediate abode, or waiting-place, is a necessity.

Moreover, the Judgment-day presupposes an Intermediate World. If souls at death enter their final abode the necessity of the judgment at the last day is overruled; but if they remain in waiting for a spiritual body and for judgment the necessity of final judicial decrees is apparent. Whatever may have been the views of the Christian Church touching these matters, certain it is that an intermediate world exists, and man's relation to it is as has been indicated above.

In a previous paragraph incidental reference is made to the theory of a second probation, or probation in the next life. We pronounced it an error, and shall now assign the reason therefor. Neither in the Jewish nor in the Christian Church has the thought of another probation been regarded otherwise than as heretical, as contrary to the fundamental revelations, and, therefore, to be rejected and denounced. In both the Jewish and the Christian Church there have been, as there are now, those who for one reason and another feigned to foresee, as they glanced futureward, renewed chances of escape from the consequences of sin, and additional opportunities of salvation. Universalism has pressed this feature of eschatology with enthusiasm, but not with ability, upon the attention of the public mind. In these days such thinkers as Canon Farrar, Dr. Dorner, Newman Smyth, Henry Ward Beecher, and others of Protestant and orthodox tendencies, have espoused the theory, and are setting it forth with that skill that characterizes their theological work in general, and creating a suspicion that it may possibly be well-founded in the Scriptures. It is not, as a dogma of Universalism, that it deserves notice; but, *as a theory of Protestant thinkers,* it can not be ignored.

It is alleged in its favor that infants, dying as such, have not passed through a probation, and, inasmuch as probation is related to character, they must undergo its liabilities and discipline in the next life. This is pure speculation; it is not revelation. It is faulty in that it requires the intermediate world to be essentially in its moral conditions what the present world is, for probation involves just such conditions as environ human life here. The intermediate world is nowhere represented as a probationary world. This remark also applies to the suggestion that the heathen have not had a Gospel chance in this life, and it must be afforded them in the next life. No one is on probation there, either infants because they were taken from probation here, or heathen because the Gospel idea of probation was unknown to them. Paul shows that the heathen, ignorant of the Gospel here, shall not be judged by it there. No Gospel probation here, no Gospel responsibility there; this is the Gospel. The Apostle Peter (I Peter iii, 18–20) is considered by Farrar, Dorner, and others, as a second probationist, whereas in the passage referred to it is evident that even if another probation should be granted to the antediluvians it would avail nothing in their behalf, and would result in no improved chance of salvation. Let it be granted that Christ preached the Gospel in the intermediate world, and that it was heard throughout *hades* by all the inhabitants thereof; what avails it? He never went there but once on such a mission, and it failed; he has not instituted a ministry to proclaim the Gospel in his name to the intermediate world; the Gospel he preached was one of comfort to the righteous, and of condemnation to the wicked, and no change was produced in that world by his temporary ministry. If the passage is of worth in this connection it proves that a second probation to the ungodly will be as ineffectual as the first, and hence there is no sound reason for another probation.

Consulting the Scriptures, which bear directly upon the subject, they are clear in their repudiation of a theory that in its ethical aspects can not promote human welfare or the prospects of eternal salvation. Paul (II Cor. v, 10) affirms that "we must all appear before the judgment-seat of Christ, that every one may receive the things done in his body, according to that he hath done, whether it be good or bad." The decisions of the judgment-day will be based on the *first* probation, and not on any subsequent probation, if there is any.  In that judgment-scene recorded by Matthew (xxv, 31–45) the decisions are based wholly on the events of this life, and no reference is made to an intermediate probation.  These alone are sufficient to dispose of the heresy of another probation.  The intermediate world is not probationary like the present world, but it is a type of the eternal world into which all finally go.  It is not like the present, but like the *eternal*, world.  It is the eternal world.

Closely associated with the doctrines of this chapter thus far considered are others of no little importance and bound up in the miscellany of the "last things."  We refer to the Millennium, the Second Coming of Christ, and the expiration or consummation of the Christian dispensation.

That there will be another advent of the Lord, most, though not all, Bible interpreters concede.  Among the majority of believers, the certainty of a second advent is no more held in suspense than the fact of a first advent.  Indeed, from *a priori* considerations, there were more improbabilities of the first advent happening as recorded, than that a second advent should take place in the manner and for the purpose specified in Holy Writ.  But, while most accept that interpretation which allows a second visitation of our Lord to the earth, all are not agreed as to the time, manner, significance, or purpose of the event, and therefore it can hardly be expected of us to furnish an interpretation which will reconcile all differences and unite all in one opinion.  Still, we venture to lay before our readers an understanding of the Word which seems to contain less difficulties than any other, and, on the whole, that which satisfies us.

It might be remarked in passing, that there are those who have eliminated all Second Adventism from their creed, on the *ad captandum* ground that the Scriptures do not indicate the thought of Christ's return to the earth in the future, for any purpose whatever.  There are others who construe the Scriptures bearing in this direction in a figurative sense, denying the personal reappearing of our Lord, and contending that his spiritual presence is a sufficient fulfillment of the prophetic advent.  Contrary to this position, Swedenborg has taught that Christ is to come again into the world in his Word, as he once came in the flesh.  But the word-coming of the Lord—no less than his spirit-coming—fails to satisfy believers in a personal advent; and it is questionable if any other than a literal, visible, bodily, personal coming of the Lord is a coming at all.  A spiritual, or word-coming, can not be any thing more than a qualified, representative coming, which is very different from a personal coming.

Much, perhaps the greater, interest centers in the chronological aspects of the question, and this because all correlative questions are dependent upon the settlement of its chronology.

Respecting the chronological phase of the subject, two theories have prevailed in the Church since the apostolic age, each eloquently advocated by peerless men. The theory of pre-millennianism, or the advent of the Lord prior to the millennium, and for the purpose of introducing it, is very ancient, and has for long periods of time been in the ascendant in the conception of Christian people. Having the right of way in the realm of Christian thought, its authority has not been strongly disputed and has been almost silently accepted as the only possible construction of the Scriptures, by the Church at large. Singularly enough, the theory has been traced back to the Jews, who, taught by the prophets, entertained a belief in the future glory of the earth, and, along with it, the cognate doctrine of the millennium. Among the early Christian fathers, Justin Martyr, Irenæus, and Tertullian held to Chiliasm with a firm grasp, and suggested the thought that Christ would have a residence at Jerusalem and reign over the earth. Chiliasm bore in the earliest times a materialistic stamp, growing out of the disposition of the fathers to read the Scriptural representation of the Advent in a strictly literal manner. They did not hold to a spiritual-coming or a word-coming of the Lord, but to a personal coming, and affixed the time for his appearance at some point this side of the millennium. While later Christian thought has stripped the doctrine of its materialism, such modern men as Christlieb, Lange, Olshausen, Van Oosterzee, Chalmers, Alford, Horne, Trench, Ellicott, McIlvaine, Bedell, and Winthrop, adhere to the adventism of their fathers, and join in support of a pre-millennial faith. John and Charles Wesley have been likewise summoned as witnesses to the Scriptural soundness of the theory of pre-millennianism. With this array of authorities, ancient and modern, supporting, and with this chandelier of lights illuminating the theory of pre-millennianism, it may seem presumptuous to contend for another view, or assume the possibility of another construction.

On the other hand, there is the theory of post-millennianism, or the return of the Lord *after* the millennium, at the close of the world's history, and for purposes entirely disconnected with the millennial state.

It is the statement of Dr. Nast that post-millennianism is popular in the Methodist Episcopal Church; and, excepting a few honored names, our standard writers are on this side of the question. Dr. Whedon says, "The millennium first, and then the second advent." Dr. Raymond holds the same conclusion. Bishop Merrill likewise contends for it in a masterly monograph.

Without further stating the differences between these theories, or invoking the approval of Christian authorities, we propose to examine the relation of the advent to the millennium, which will involve two questions: 1st. What is the Millennium? 2d. What is the Advent? If these questions can be answered satisfactorily, or rather, if we can read the Gospel between the lines, it will require but a moment to assign the advent its chronological place in the history of time.

1st. What is the Millennium? The answer to this primary question involves a few intermediate considerations, such as those respecting its manner of introduction, the signs accompanying it, and its duration. It may be well to remember that the word "millennium," like the word "sacrament," and other Church words, is not in the Scriptures; but, unlike those other words, it rests upon a single passage for its authorized use. Etymologically, the word is derived from *mille*, a thousand, and *annus*, a year; and, when taken together, it signifies a thousand years. It implies simply a definite duration, without involving the events or conditions of the period; and yet, because John in the Apocalypse alludes to a millennial bondage of Satan, and a millennial reign of martyrs, the fascinating doctrine of a millennium, in which Christ will personally reign on earth, has been constructed and popularized in every conceivable form. But if it can not be supported by parallel passages, as no one will pretend it can be, he must not be subjected to criticism who says that such a millennium is a fiction. To this conclusion the post-millennialist is logically carried.

But, waiving any etymological exception, what is the millennium in the apocalyptic sense? For, without controversy, the millennium of John, the thousand-year period of the exile of Patmos, is regarded as the most definite of any of his statements on the subject. Turn to the twentieth chapter of Revelation, the only millennial chapter in the Book, and these particulars are noted: 1. Satan is confined in the bottomless pit for a thousand years; 2. Beheaded ones live again and reign with Christ a thousand years. Study the chapter as closely as one will, and these are the net particulars, the only allusions in it touching the millennial state.

We will be pardoned if we express surprise at the omission of certain statements which should have been made, if the personal reign of Christ on earth were involved in the millennium. It is not stated that Christ reigns on earth, nor that he descends to the earth, nor that the beheaded ones, now alive again, who reign with Christ, reign on the earth. The most liberal, and at the same time the most literal, rendering of the enigmatical chapter foreshadows the resurrection of the martyrs in advance of the general resurrection of the race, and that they reign with Christ, *where Christ is*, a thousand years longer than the other pious dead. Christ is in heaven, and has been reigning there since his ascension; and that class of worshipers, beheaded for the testimony of Jesus, enter sooner upon the eternal reward than the majority of Christ's followers. This is the first resurrection, and blessed is he who has a part in it, because it is in advance of the general resurrection. Christ does not reign with risen martyrs on earth, but the *risen martyrs reign with Christ in heaven.* Thus the millennium of John has a heaven-side to it.

The earth-side of the millennium has respect to the bondage of Satan, and in this we are greatly interested. In fact, we are to deal only with the millennium as it affects the earth or human condition upon it. Satan is in chains; the earth has unexpected, uninterrupted rest from his reign. Sin measurably disappears, it being under Heaven's ban. What is left of it is the utterance of unexpelled, innate depravity, the moving of the pent-up sinful tendencies of the soul, like the fires of an active volcano. But these fires will at last subside, and every crater will be cold. There can be sin without Satan, but the great instigator of sin, the great leader of the world's mischief and the great progenitor of the world's sorrow will be absent, unrepresented, save by Christ-abandoned souls; sinful enterprises will lag, sins themselves will decay; tribes of men will covet the best civilization, and the hemispheres will echo with the voice of love—a grand opportunity for extending the sway of the Gospel.

It will be extended; the hindrances will disappear before the heralds of the cross; nations will be born in a day; peace will be universal; skepticism will retire to a cave; Bacchus will seek some other planet to ply his vocation of ruin; heathen idols will fall from their shrines; heathen temples will be vacated forever; Christendom will embrace the whole earth; all hearts will pulsate with Christian joy, and all lips tremble with Christian praise. Such a period of moral supremacy, of the authority of moral law, the prevalence of Gospel influence, and the disarmament of Satanic rule will come and continue for a long period. If this is the millennium of the Apocalypse, as it seems to be, then is it in harmony with the millennium of the entire Bible, and equally in harmony with the post-millennianism of some of the ablest thinkers of the day.

To make sure, however, what this millennium is, let it be analyzed. 1. It signifies a political millennium. By this we mean the disappearance of all obnoxious and despotic forms of government, and the substitution of all noble and conserving exhibitions of civil power. Monarchies, aristocracies, nobilities, tyrannies of every sort shall subside, and a democratic form of government will obtain everywhere.

This is not a dream, for a millennium that would not regenerate civil authority, and give to the nations the most approved forms of government, would be sadly deficient in its influence on rulers and public men. Besides, the tendency of every enlightened government is toward a republic, and the world anticipates the subsidence of all oppression and all tyranny. The millennium must be *political*.

2. There will be a *scientific* millennium. By this we mean the spread of knowledge and the reign of truth among all peoples. Ignorance must vanish. The mind of man must expand, and mystery must no longer be the apologetic word for ignorance. The laws of nature must be known, and the flag-staff of light must be planted on the highest summit of truth. The world must not ask a question in the realm of the Finite which it can not answer. Science is to have a millennium, a great perpetual triumph in its own field of existence. Astronomy, geology, philosophy, chemistry, putting off their swaddling clothes, will become giants and tread the earth in conscious power, subduing all intractable things to themselves, or, like new-made suns, career through the heavens and illuminate the world.

3. It implies a *religious* millennium. Of this we have spoken, but let us not forget that the Gospel will not be surpassed in the broadness of its triumphs by either government or science. It will be preached everywhere, believed everywhere, and reign everywhere, changing the moral complexion of the race, touching the dead heart of humanity into life, and breathing into the souls of men the impulses of heaven. The Gospel will be supreme in the world, and the promises of the prophets will be realized in the regeneration of the family of man. We can not over-state the extent or comprehend the glory of the triumph of the Gospel in the period of its unresisting progress.

What is the relation of this millennium to the others? These three millenniums are one, and are to occur simultaneously. One can not exist without the other. They are not independent, but co-existent, millenniums. We have been in the habit of emphasizing the religious aspect of the millennium, and regarding other conditions, political and scientific, as incidental, or the outgrowth of the Gospel reign; but certain it is that if not synchronous in their existence, the millenniums are so related that they can not be far apart. Each assists the other, and each shares the glories of all. It is trinity in unity, applied to the millennium.

Guided solely by the apocalyptic chapter, we should say that this three-fold millennium compasses in its duration the period of a thousand years. We are sorry to say it; we prefer to say it will have no end, and that it will continue until Gabriel shall announce the termination of time. But John plainly intimates a *limited* millennium, which, we think, is in accordance with the duration of the Bible millennium in general and with post-millennianism in particular.

Accepting a millennial condition limited to a thousand years, the decisive question now is, What has the Second Advent to do with *such* a millennium? Is not such a millennium, transcendently glorious as it must be, possible without the intervention of Christ's personal presence on earth? Are the two inseparable? Let us give heed to the reasons that may be urged against the necessity of the advent at this juncture of the world's history.

Such a millennium as we have described, consisting of perfect forms of civil government, of the dawn of universal science, of Gospel successes and illuminations, is the *ultimate purpose* of the Gospel. This new condition of earth-life is just what the Gospel promises shall exist and what it proposes to secure. The triune millennium will be launched upon the open sea of human life by the Gospel, and will be a result of the Gospel. Nowhere is it stated that it is to be introduced by the appearing of the Lord, or by his reign upon the earth, but rather by the aggressive and assimilating power of the Gospel. Micah says: "But in the last day it shall come to pass that the mountain of the house of the Lord shall be established in the tops of the mountains, and it shall be exalted above the hills; and the people shall flow unto it." The prophet here alludes to the universal triumph of the Gospel through the Church. Jeremiah says: "And they shall teach no more every man his neighbor and every man his brother, saying, Know the Lord; for they shall all know me, from the least of them unto the greatest of them, saith the Lord." Here is universal knowledge of God through the Gospel. Habakkuk says: "For the earth shall be filled with the knowledge of the glory of the Lord, as the waters cover the sea." This is always interpreted to signify the triumph of Christianity in the earth. But it is needless, in support of this opinion, to quote from a Book with which all are familiar.

If these millennial conditions can not be produced by the Gospel, or if it does not tend to establish them, then its mission is a failure, or its mission is not what we have assigned it. If the ultimate of the Gospel is not the millennium, it is something else. What is it? It must be something short of it, for it can not be any thing beyond it, or any thing that will parallel it. Conceiving that the ultimate of the Gospel is any thing less than a millennial condition, its mission is tentative, insignificant; its hold upon us must be feeble, and our hold upon it exceedingly light.

But it must appear to all that, finally realized or not, the tendencies of the Gospel are in the direction of the millennium, and it is preparing the world for a better condition. Prophets sing of an age of peace, apostles tell it is forthcoming, and Christ saw triumph from afar. It can not be denied that the Gospel, as an operating factor in the world's progress, has changed governments, and is in its very constitution opposed to oligarchies, despotisms, monarchies, and all forms of power which oppress men. The Gospel is the Guy Fawkes under tyranny, and as it explodes doubtful forms of government, and its teachings are incorporated in the civil life of man, democracy must prevail. It will prevail. France has yielded to the millennial impulse already, Spain is in perpetual ferment on account of it, and Europe is on the verge of a continental republic.

In the realm of science, its effect is no less significant. It tells of light chasing away darkness, of midnights sinking out of sight in the meridian glare of perpetual day. It tells of the dawn of knowledge, prophesying the period of emancipated intellects and the wide-spread reign of truth.

Religiously, its power has always been supreme. It melts the chains of sin, and then transforms the sinner into a believer and the transgressor into a worshiper. It molds unmolded characters, and saves unsaved souls. These are its tendencies and these its works.

Now, if the millennium be the ultimate of the Gospel, then must it be reached by the Gospel, or it is attempting an achievement on an insufficient basis, and contemplating a result which, however much it may promote, it can not realize, in which case it must be set down as a failure.

Still greater and more shameful must be the failure, if the millennium is the ultimate of the Gospel, and Gospel agencies are sufficient to produce it, and yet some other agency must finally be employed to precipitate it on the world. We can not resist the conviction that the Gospel has inherent power to accomplish its own purposes, that *it gravitates toward success*, and that Omnipotence alone can turn it back from its appointed destiny. This is different from, it is not even kindred to, that transcendentalism of Germany which allows to truth a self-propagating and self-operating power, and that it is independent of external agency for its triumph. The Gospel will not propagate itself; it must be preached. But its agencies, we are constrained to say, when set in motion, are directed by an inspiring hand, one certainly sufficient to accomplish its ultimate purposes.

How has it been in the past? We are prone to attribute the disappearance of great evils, such as slavery, feudalism, barbarous punishments, to the commanding power of the Gospel. Will it not do as much for the world in the future as it has in the past? Has it lost its power to cope with evil, its skill and cunning in extinguishing vice, or may we not rightfully expect that its long experience and struggle with gigantic evils has prepared it for broader aggression and wider triumphs? If so, if the Gospel will measure up to our expectations in the future, if the edge of its sword is all the keener for the conflicts it has engaged in, and is wielded by more skillful hands in the future,—the long delayed millennium will arrive, and turn the noise of a sinful world into the echoes of the Redeemer's worship.

We do not understand from the Scripture that the millennium is to be introduced on short notice; that the world, retiring in wickedness at night, will awake the next morning in the blaze of a millennial day. Such a thing might happen, inasmuch as great Scriptural events have happened as suddenly, as the destruction of Sodom, and, perhaps, the flood, and it is taught that the general resurrection and the second coming of Christ will likely break upon the world as a surprise, though not without antecedent signs. But it is not probable that the millennium will astonish the world by a sudden revolution in its condition, or its introduction be distinguished by unexpected phenomena, by the sudden collapse of error and the elevation of truth. Introduced by the Gospel, it will dawn as the rising of the sun, gradually folding up the curtains of the long night of darkness, and flooding the earth with its beams of glory. Every thing will point in the direction of a new day; but it may be difficult to tell just when it has begun, and the world may enjoy it a score of years before it is aware of its presence. This silent leavening power of the Gospel, this quiet approach of the millennium, will be in keeping with Gospel methods, and in harmony with its ultimate design.

In contrast with this moral quietude of the millennium, note the noisy, earth-rejoicing and heaven-shouting manner of the *second coming* of Christ. He comes to disturb the existing order, introduce confusion in mundane affairs, and, by the suddenness of his coming and its judicial purpose, frustrates the first condition of the millennium, which is that of peace and glory.

Now, if the millennium of the Apocalypse is the ultimate of the Gospel; if it can be produced by Gospel agencies; and if it is not a revolution, but the moral product of the Gospel,—the conclusion is irresistible that, as yet, there is no necessity for connecting Christ's next advent with it.

To be added to these considerations is this, that in this millennial chapter of John there is not the slightest allusion to Christ's personal coming in connection with the events described. John does not say that Christ will come at that time. He does not even say that the chaining of Satan is by Christ, but by an appointed angel from heaven.

The reigning of martyrs is with Christ after the resurrection, and, it may be inferred, after their ascension into the upper kingdom of Christ. They go to him—he does not go to them; so that the mysterious connection of Christ's second coming with the millennium of the Apocalypse is the gratuitous work of the imaginative theologian, rather than the utterances of the inspired writer.

This enigmatical millennial chapter suggests a problem, which, if satisfactorily solved, will be decisive of the validity of pre-millennianism. Does it not plainly intimate what shall occur at the expiration of the thousand years of universal peace and of the reign of righteousness? We are in no doubt as to the certainty that the millennium expires; we are in less doubt as to what follows it. Satan is unchained, and roams again through the earth, devouring, desolating, as before, and involving the nations in battle. Satan's authority is regained, and Satan's kingdom has recognition. We dislike to concede such a lapse from the millennium, but John teaches it, and we must account for it, if we can.

How explain this disappearance of the millennium? If the Gospel introduces the millennium gradually, we can conceive of its decline gradually, or, for that matter, speedily; for it is not an uncommon thing for the Gospel to lose its grip on the nations, and for countries once Gospelized to relapse into heathenism. What is Asia Minor to-day? Few are the Christian Churches within its borders. Yet Paul planted the Cross in its cities, and John addressed seven Churches there seventeen hundred years ago. The Gospel has almost disappeared, and with it its influence. Has it not also lost its influence at Jerusalem, where the apostles received the Holy Ghost, and from which they went forth to conquer the world for the Master? The whole Roman Empire was once won to Christ, but, after Constantine, it was well-nigh lost to him. Great apostasies may succeed great triumphs, great defeats supplant great victories. The millennium, introduced and fostered by the Gospel, may be succeeded by apostasies, far reaching and universal, blotting out all remaining Gospel influence in the earth. The Gospel reign ebbs and flows, rises and falls, in this world, and it may suffer an eclipse, a decline, after a thousand years of joyful triumph. Like a candle which has burnt itself out, the millennium expires. The explanation is not embarrassing, and all may accept it as definite.

But, on the supposition that Christ comes in person to set up a millennial kingdom, the post-millennial apostasy can not be easily explained. He reigns a thousand years—what then? Does he leave the world again, ascend to heaven, and, without a struggle, permit Satan to resume? Or does he have a struggle with the arch-fiend, who drives him off the field and raises his banner in triumph in spite of Christ's power? We can not think so. If Christ retires from the earth at the close of the millennial period, then must he come again at the end of the world to close up its history, in which case he would have a third advent, which no one will recognize as taught in the Word. He can not come to establish a millennium and then permit it to fail in his hands, nor can he come before the end without coming again at the end of the world, which involves too much adventism.

The conviction grows on us that when he comes it will not be for the purpose of establishing a millennial kingdom on earth, or to conserve any millennial purpose whatever.

What, then, is the object of Christ's second coming? Negatively considered, the purpose of the next advent is not to assist the Gospel in evangelizing the world; it has no reference to the spread of the Gospel. His first advent had this in view, and contemplated victory without the intervention of a second advent. He came as a Savior; he was the incarnate God, offering to men in his own person the fruits of redemption. He does not come again to repeat his first work. His second errand has reference to objects distinct from those which engaged his attention when he sojourned among the Hebrews. In so far as the Gospel kingdom may be vindicated by Christ at his second appearing, the two advents will be related; but he comes not to organize redemption, but to gather its harvest, and deliver the mediatorial throne to the Father. *His first coming was the introduction of his kingdom; his second coming will witness its termination.*

Keeping in mind a discrimination warranted by the Scripture, the fogs which have gathered about the subject will rise and be gone, and we shall have no difficulty in understanding the order of the events of the future: 1. The Gospel and the millennium are associated together in the inspired volume, the one as instrumental cause, the other as processional effect. 2. The second Advent and the events connected with the closing of the world's history, such as resurrection, conflagration, and judgment, are associated together as occurring almost simultaneously, or, at least, not far apart. Looking beyond the millennium, after its traces have disappeared, and its blessings have been submerged in the vices of an apostate race, when sin seems to have usurped authority in the earth, we see coming in glory the Son of God to administer on the affairs of the world and deliver it over to the Father for final disposition.

If this is the object of his coming, the Scriptures must certainly foreshadow it, and to them let us at once turn.

Concerning the resurrection, Paul, the best sacred eschatological writer, in his first Corinthian epistle says: "But every man in his own order; Christ the first fruits, *afterward they that are Christ's at his coming.*" Here is resurrection at his coming. In his letter to the Philippians he says: "For our conversation is in heaven, from whence also we look for the Savior, the Lord Jesus Christ, who shall change our vile body that it may be fashioned like unto his glorious body." Here is resurrection again in connection with his coming; and, without multiplying references, it must be clear that one object of Christ's coming is to raise the dead.

After the resurrection, what then? Again confiding in the apostle of the Gentiles, we hear him say, as he addresses Timothy: "I charge thee, therefore, before God, and the Lord Jesus Christ who shall *judge the quick and the dead at his appearing.*" He affirms that judgment takes place at the second coming—no millennium here. Again, it is recorded: "For the Son of man shall come in the glory of his father with his angels, and *then* he shall reward every man according to his works." Here are the two events, Advent and Judgment, connected in the same passage. Paul likewise asserts that "when the Lord Jesus shall be revealed from heaven with his mighty angels, in flaming fire, taking vengeance on them that know not God, and that obey not the Gospel of our Lord Jesus Christ; when he shall come to be glorified in his saints in that day." Here it is affirmed that when Christ shall come he will punish the wicked and glorify the obedient. This is not millennium—this is judgment.

In close connection with these events, Peter tells us that the conflagration of the world, a terrific catastrophe, is to occur and close up earth's history.

Now, if Christ's second coming shall occur simultaneously with resurrection, judgment, and conflagration, as it undoubtedly will, according to the above Scriptures; and if it is established that these three great events occur at the end of the world, the post-millennial feature of the advent is sustained. Matthew (xiii, 36–43), besides other writers, teaches that resurrection and conflagration are among the events of the last day, and that Christ's return to the earth is to accomplish these changes in its history.

THEREFORE, *the second advent will occur at the end of the world*—not before the millennium; but, perhaps, ages after it. Pre-millennianism is the dream of piety; post-millennianism one of the "certainties of religion."

The end of the world! The end of time, of the intermediate world, and the dawn of the resurrection life, the judgment-day, and the opening of the heavens and the hells! What a period! What events! What a future! The Judgment! Our time-life reviewed;

our eternal choices ratified; human character evolving into eternal destiny. In the face of the Scriptures declaring that the Judgment shall occur at the end of the world, it is supreme folly to insist that it is revealed at death, for while eternal destiny is shaped by this life, and it is irrevocably fixed at death, the judicial sentence will not be heard until the great day of the Lord, the day of reckoning with the universe. Then all shall know that the Lord is King and the Judge of all mankind.

Heaven! The soul, clothed with a spiritual body, its house from heaven, builded by God, enters to go out no more forever. Angels are there; the good of the ages past are in the fadeless mansions; there is the fruit of the tree of life; on golden-paved streets the saints forever walk; no trouble disturbs the endless peace of the soul, and no discord is heard in the endless songs of the redeemed. Yonder is the great throne, white with the light of Him who made the universe; and sitting on it is the form of One who once was nailed to the Cross. Redemption is complete; heaven is gained.

Hell! The word is crowded with all the repulsive words of all the languages of men. It means darkness, obloquy, banishment, failure, tears, sorrow forever.

These are the doctrines of Christian eschatology. They are consistent in themselves, in harmony with the highest human interests, calculated to hold men in check, and inspire them with awe and a love of right. In these revelations Christianity proves itself to be from God.

---

# CHAPTER XXVIII.

## THE DYNAMICS OF CHRISTIANITY.

JAMES WATT told George III. that he was dealing with something that kings coveted. Pressed for an explanation of his statement, he answered with one word—*power.* Steam power is great; the power of gravitation is greater; but the power of Christianity, or the secret force of religion, is greatest. This is the power that kings should covet, for it is the safety of thrones; the power that all men should seek, for it is the salvation of character.

The reappearance of Christianity from age to age, since its Founder was crucified, is not only a historic fact, but is also significant of certain indwelling forces, or sources of perpetuity, the consideration of which must necessarily be included in any just estimate of its nature and history. There have been times when the death-knell of the Christian religion has been sounded, but invariably it has revived and survived, and gone on its way as insensible to the attempts made upon its life as though they had not been made. Fires, persecutions, legislative obstacles have threatened the extinction of the apparently helpless cause, and united in an endeavor to overthrow it, but the fires are extinct, and its enemies have been consumed by their own flames.

In this chapter we shall not trace its historic career, or seek to explain it as a historic movement; but it is our purpose to discover, if possible, its inherent power, or those internal elements which constitute it the vitalizing and imperishable product it appears to be. If, as Gibbon undertakes to prove, the causes of its historic successes, the recognition of which can not be avoided, are largely external, or may be credited to the enthusiasm of believers, then it must be regarded as a religion of sentiment only, or superstition.

Allowing that ecclesiastical machinery may have something to do with the propagation of religion, and that it often attracts when the truth is apparently powerless, it is clear that unless religion itself is in a sense self-propagating, all the machinery in the world can not preserve it from ultimate decay. *The motive forces of religion are so far from being mechanical that, without any mechanism whatever, it will live and assert itself.* If the Church were not in existence, and no organization espoused Christianity as the end of its being, Christianity would still possess all that inherently belongs to it, and it is in its *inherent characteristics*, and not in its mechanical relations, that its power may be detected.

It may be a little circuitous, but evidently in the right direction, to suggest that there is in Christianity the absence of what other religions have regarded as essential, which they finally outgrew, or which was the cause of their decline. The old Greek paganism was a stiff kind of philosophy after all, with little of spiritual elevation in it. Love of nature, or natural religion, was the basis of the religious cultus in Athens. The personification of nature's forces was in regular order both religious and philosophical; but when the philosophical personification ceased the religious deification ceased also. Their legends, fables, histories, and worships were the outgrowth of a philosophical desire to recognize in nature the source of all things, or a self-begetting principle in the universe; hence the forces were clothed, deified, and received the homage of the people. Instead of personifying that which is the proper subject of deification, namely, *personality,* they personified that which in no sense is the exponent of being. Non-being can not be the figure of being; hence its personification was a piece of philosophical absurdity, which in due time was exposed, and the religion based upon it declined. The form of religion, however, long obtained after its vitality had been exhausted and its inconsistency was made manifest.

Not to nature did the Roman go for his religion. Less philosophical than the Greek, he was more religious, and in the absence of divine direction he turned to humanity for the ideal statue of worship, as the Greek had turned to nature. He fell to worshiping deceased ancestors, and in his long communion with their virtues he transfigured the departed and gloried in the invisible. The Greek worshiped nature; the Roman humanity. The Greek adored the visible; the Roman the invisible. The Greek personified force; the Roman deified human spirits. The religion of the Greek was the religion of beauty and power; the religion of the Roman was the religion of human sentiment and dreamy spiritualism. Both were without vitalizing properties; neither was a biological religion; both decayed.

Equally, the spinal cord of the Oriental religions is as defective in strength and as feeble in sensibility as were the paganisms of ancient Greece and Rome. Brahminism still preaches the doctrine of the transmigration of souls; Buddhism shouts *nirvana* as the end of existence; and Mohammedanism loads itself with sensual and superstitious conceptions of the future life. Meanwhile the evidences of internal decay and the absence of the biological principle are patent to the students of these religions, which in the future will be regarded as relics of religious history, having disappeared as active religious forces from the world.

Whether personified force, or ancestral worship, or transmigration, or nirvana, or a lustful heaven be the spinal doctrine of religion, enforced by political, social, or military power, Christianity embraced none of them, and is incompatible with all of them. The deification of nature is blasphemy; its forces are the forces of Him who made the worlds; its laws are those of the Supreme Law-giver. Personification signifies the idealizing of character, not the idealizing of force; and Christianity proposes, as a subject of idealizing, the personal character of Jesus Christ, the express image of God. Such an idealizing no other religion ever attempted. More repugnant in a theological sense is the Roman idea of religion, or the worship of the departed. Not even the angels receive worship. John fell down in adoration before a communicating spirit, but was rebuked for his idolatry, and commanded to worship God. As to transmigration and nirvana, they are the offspring of diseased imaginations and perverted beliefs, having no foundation either in reason or revelation. In its conceptions of the future life Mohammedanism is a fountain of iniquity to be sealed by the religion it has sought to extinguish. Christianity repudiates all religions grounded in philosophical absurdities, rooted in metaphysical errors, springing from superstitious soils, or bursting forth from the fires of sensuality. What it is not, and especially what it has not in common with other religions, it is important to know, and may be ascertained by quiet inquiry.

Freeing it from things common to other religions, we are prepared to consider the "thing-in-itself," or Christianity in its simplicities rather than its complexities, in its principles rather than its details of operation, in its magnitude and wholeness rather than in its parts.

I. Christianity is the *substance of religious truth.* When Hegel calls it "absolute religion," he means that its essence is absolute truth. By substance or essence we mean the underlying basis, the essentia of religion, without which religion is impossible, and with which religion is power. Physical objects have their substance in oxygen, hydrogen, nitrogen, and carbon, the four primordial elements, with the addition of some of the other elements in small proportions. The four are the essential elements, and constitute physical substance. So Religion, dropping its specific name for the moment, must have its substance in imperishable truth, or truths, such as divine personality, providence, theistic administration, soteriological principles, and eschatological facts. These are the *essentials* of religion. Some of them may be found in all religions, but in curious combinations, in contradictory relations, in traditional masks, and in unrecognizable forms, and so without vital influence or sovereign power. They are like the wheat in the mummy-case, vital during the ages, but without growth until rescued and given the sunlight and a true soil. In Christianity, religious concepts are rescued from non-development, and appear in all their vitality and sovereignty, as the substance of truth.

In addition to the essentials of religion, there are other ideas, related to the primary truths, as the sixty-six elements are related to the four principal elements of oxygen, hydrogen, nitrogen, and carbon. In Religion, monotheism is a basal idea, reflecting an intelligent conception; that is, it differs from the Mohammedan idea of the unity of God, which is a by-word of religion rather than its power, and from the Jewish conception, which, incipiently correct, had its fullest and stateliest manifestation in the dispensation of Christ. The early Jewish monotheism was exclusive as a religious faith, Jahveh being the God of the Jews only. In the progress of the ages, or with the arrival of Christ, the Jewish conception was enlarged, so that Jahveh was the God of all nations; the exclusive faith was succeeded by a universal conception of the common fatherhood of God.

It was a great reach in religion to step over the primordial bounds of belief; but Hebrewism was always insensibly, and yet gradually and surely, making advances toward a higher order of things; but, when prepared for the consummation in the highest truth, it unfortunately collapsed, and is still defunct.

In like manner, the ideas of government, law, providence, atonement by sacrifice, and the future life, initial and germinal in the elder Hebrewism, became, under the cultivating and manipulating influence of Christianity, forceful ideas in the religious realm, and the very substance of a definite and final religion. If Christianity, with its inherited, transformed, and revealed truths, is not the "absolute religion," and has not the substance and essentia of truth, the world is without, and must be ever without, such a religion.

II. In its exponential character, Christianity is the *incorporation and crystallization of religious truth.* Substance alone, however essential to being, to truth, to reality, is insufficient; truth must have objective form, visibility, reality. Religion, as an invisible truth, must emerge into religions, or into a particular religion, chosen for the expression of the substance-idea; and this has happened in Christianity. It stands as the re-embodiment of invisible truth, as Judaism was its original embodiment. For instance, in the latter, God dwelt in light inaccessible; in the former, he comes to the front, manifesting his personality in a tangible form, voicing his will that the world may hear him, teaching truth that the world may know it, and promising salvation that the world may be of "good cheer." In Christianity, *religion passes from substance into form*, or substance identifies itself with form, the invisible rushing into the visible,—a unique relation unknown to other religions. In other religions, substance and form are entirely incongruous; they are paired merely, not fitted to each other. Christianity is the form of the essentia of the divine substance of truth, as Jesus Christ was the form and image of God. Philosophically, it is the religion of substance and form, with an indissoluble expression in Jesus, the Teacher and Savior.

What the contents of the form are, it is needless to recapitulate, since our readers are supposed to understand what are the general doctrines of religion; and yet, all along from incarnation to ascension, including miracles, prophecy, atonement, forgiveness, regeneration, sanctification, heaven, hell—all that he taught, or left to be taught by his apostles—there is the outcropping of the invisible substance of truth. Variety in form, that is, in teaching, is consistent with unity in substance; the form, complex or simple, is the product of the substance. Divine ideas of law, providence, and redemption, hidden in the substance, composing the substance, become concrete in the form, or the masterpieces of Christianity. Knowledge of divine realities, divine programs, divine ideas, the world obtains alone through the exponential office of Christianity. It is the only religion in which the divine is transparently and exclusively on exhibition, the only religion that rises above or sinks behind phenomena, the only religion that manifests the spiritual through the empirical, the only religion that makes the unknowable knowable. The process of the revelation of substance in form, or the essentia of truth in religion, is divine; it is enough that such process takes place; it is enough that the result is known. This, in part, is the secret of its power; it is, in part, the power itself.

III. The *evolutionary spirit* in Christianity is the sign of its vitality, and the guarantee of its propagating efficiency. The scientific word "evolution" is here employed to express the continuous development of religious truth from its incipient character in Hebrewism to its completed state in the apostolic dispensation. That Christianity is the *religion of revelation by evolution,* that is, by gradual unfoldings, is a cardinal doctrine of the book called the Bible. There is no religion *so* evolutionary as Christianity; there is no religion that *is* evolutionary, save Christianity; for, while other religions appeared at once in a completed form, like Minerva from the brain of Jupiter, and have from the first declined and are declining, Christianity was, in a sense, a growth from a previous stock, and is in process of development still, with the promise and potency of growth that insures its indefinite expansion in the future. Evolution has fewer illustrations of itself, as a law, in nature than in Christianity, for nature has its limits, and evolution stops. Nature is what it was ages ago. Nature's laws are those imposed upon, or incorporated with, the huge physical frame-work called the universe at the beginning. Nature knows no change of law, no progress of forms, and repeats its phenomena within well-defined and well-known limits. In the zoölogical department of nature, the stability of species very early arrested or abruptly terminated any tendency to evolution, and has been a stumbling-block in the path of the evolutionist ever since. Nature is not the playground of evolution. History is evolutional; race-life is evolutional; Christianity is evolutional. Nature-evolution is only a figure of the greater truth-evolution embodied in Christianity. It is conceded that, laying aside the subject of the authorship of the sacred books containing the oracles of God, and even forgetting their contents, the great book grew like a mammoth tree, requiring at least three thousand years for its completion. From Genesis to the Apocalypse is the path that truth, in its evolutionary stages, made for itself. This striking historic development is eclipsed by the evolutionary development of the truths themselves, which, faintly adumbrated in the earlier worships and teachings, emerge into settled facts and doctrines, and become the axioms of the Christian faith. This process is so marked, and the truths that have passed through the chrysalis state into vital and sovereign forms are so many, that it will repay the effort made to glance at them.

The allusion in a preceding paragraph to the growth of the monotheistic idea may be quoted with force in this connection. The first Jewish ideas of God were remote from the completed Christian idea, to which they bear only the faintest resemblance. The first Pentateuchal representation of God is that of the Creator, or a being of indefinite and illimitable power. Such representation, however necessary to religion, was preliminary to the riper disclosures of the Mosaic administration, and inferior to the hypothecated evidences of the divine existence as furnished by Paul to the philosophers of Athens. The revelation of a Creator was first in the order of evolutionary revelations; as a starting-point it was simple, but the Creator stands before us in the majestic utterance of inspiration, like a distant mechanician, or worker of matter. Another revelation is needed, to relieve the first of its distant and frigid aspects. He comes forth as the Ruler, both in heaven and in earth, having all authority, as he had all power as Creator. The idea of rulership is suggestive of government, law, dominion, and subjects, the latter involving relationship. As Ruler, he is still afar off, and another revelation is required. It is given, and God approaches in the form of a Father. To the patriarchal mind he was a local deity, as Jupiter to the Greeks, and Diana to the Ephesians. The idea that he is the *world's* Father was a late growth. From local limitations it swung loose, taking to itself an international complexion, and resulting in the proclamation that he is the God of gods, or above every other in heaven and earth. This was progress, but there was more to follow. The growth did not stop with the extinction of localized or national relations. He must be the world's Creator, the world's Ruler, the world's Father, communicating with all his children, which signifies progress in revelation. To the multitudes, the early God of the Scriptures communicated nothing; to the Gentile nation, nothing; to the Jews something, but only through their leaders or the priesthood. To the great majority of his children, even after they accepted him as the Father, he appeared distant as ever, distrustful of individual relationship, and cold as an ice figure. He had an austere bearing, and remained away from his creatures, or spoke to them only with the voice of thunder.

In the new dispensation God is Creator, Ruler, Father; but in Jesus Christ there is a Mediator by whom the individual's approach to God is secured, and the distance between the Creator and the creature is completely bridged. An immense advance this, but not equal to the still later steps of the new dispensation. To the Jewish mind God embodied the idea of inexorable justice, without a break or flaw in his holy disposition, without the first element of compassion for his morally infirm subject. That he was paternal in his care was not denied, but for a violated law there remained only the penalty. Nature established no bureau of pardon, and Sinai only gleamed with fire. Authority, obedience, penalty—these were the awful words of a dispensation that they accepted as divine, and under which they grew into a disciplined and vigorous people. While in the new dispensation these words are not replaced by others, they lose their harsher features, and are accompanied by such words as repentance, pardon, mercy, and salvation.

The change or growth in human conceptions was even greater than in the nomenclature of the dispensations. God himself, in a sense, was growing all the time; that is, the human conception under revelation of the truth was a development toward the reality of God. So long as he manifested himself in angel-form, or came in thunder and flame, or lingered unseen over the mercy-seat, or bivouacked in a moving cloud, it was difficult to apprehend any thing more than that he was an invisible guide, friendly to men. Even the names of his attributes as they were pronounced were almost unmeaning words, scarcely symbolical of his mysterious qualities and virtues. Through the ages the race walked amid these shadows, and was locked up with these ambiguous voices and words. With the dawn of Christianity God comes forth as a Spirit, not more bodiless than space and time, uttering words that have a meaning, scattering truths that abound with life, and shouting to the race to approach the throne.

In this quiet but effectual way, by this evolutionary process of the growth of the divine idea of God in the human mind under the influence of spiritual teaching, not the Jew only, but mankind have inherited an approximate understanding of the character, relations, and purposes of the Supreme Being. Our present knowledge, however in advance of the earlier revelations, is still inadequate, because incomplete. Agnosticism, science, philosophy, are quarreling over such knowledge. Other evolutions in knowledge through a larger discernment of revealed truth may therefore be anticipated, until agnosticism will have no room for its feet, until science will proclaim the divine being with as much assurance as Christianity has always proclaimed him, and until philosophy will concede all that religion demands. God will develop more and more before our eyes in the mirror of the Scriptures, and in his handiwork in the universe.

*The evolutionary process in the Scriptures is very apparent in the growth of the Messianic idea which they contain.* This is so plain that a lengthy tracing is unnecessary, but it is as marvelous as it is plain. Beginning with the promise in Eden that the seed of the woman shall bruise the head of the serpent, the idea successively appears in all the sacrifices of Israel's migratory life, in all the religious institutions of the national period, in the gloom and sunshine of every prophetical announcement, and had exact fulfillment at last in Jesus of Nazareth. To the earliest Jew, as to the latest, the idea itself wore a cloudy dress, and was dimmed still more by the romance that enveloped the political hope of the nation; to one, as to the other, the spiritual content of the idea of Messiahship was unseen or unappreciated, and upon the national life it was evidently powerless. The poetical and political Messiahship of the Jew was all-powerful; the spiritual Messiahship came forth like a root out of dry ground, and he would have returned it to the ground. Notwithstanding the insensibility of the Jewish mind to spiritual ideas, the Messianic idea enlarged with the growth of the national idea, and ripened in the mildew of the old faith and bore fruit before their eyes in a personal and divine Messiah. Looking back over the route of the idea in Jewish history, it is not difficult to follow it through all its wanderings; it left its track in the wilderness; it was engraven over the doors of temple and synagogue; it was written in the heart of the Pharisaic nation; it conducted itself step by step through the centuries, until it made a royal assertion of its meaning on Calvary. Its consummation was a personal manifestation; its spiritual content found a dwelling-place in the heart of the Son of Man.

The Messianic idea, as such, or amplified in the personal character of Jesus Christ, is traveling still; the Messianic plan is on the march; the Messianic hope is still evolutionary, having in it the talismanic purpose of progress, and will develop more and more, until all generations shall discern its content and appropriate its power. Messiahism is a divine growth. Its purpose is not yet fulfilled; it is still misunderstood; it must be understood and it will be, for the eternal years of God are before it for development and sovereignty.

*The eschatology of Christianity is under the same law of development,* exhibiting it in even more marked aspects than the theistic and Messianic ideas previously considered. The door to speculation is open in this region of truth. If clear revelation or specific teaching is needed at all, it is needed here; if the motives used from the thought of the future life are to be effectual, the teachings of religion respecting it should be definite, and free from possibility of misconstruction. In the absence of positive and unequivocal knowledge, other religions took up superstitious conjecture, and loaded themselves with visionary and degrading conceptions of the future state. The religion of the Bible does not plunge immediately into the depths of the subject, or enlighten the truth-seeker with early and satisfactory announcements concerning the life beyond, but proceeds slowly and cautiously with its hints, turning them gradually into probabilities, and finally opening out into well-assured certainties. Important as a knowledge of the future life seems to be, the Hebrew religion advances hesitatingly, enshrouding even its final testimony with a sacred vagueness that allures the soul on, and forever excites its curiosity to know more. With the Old Testament alone it has been supposed that one would find it difficult to pilot himself safely into the eternities. He might, indeed, drift into the protected harbor of the Beyond, but his voyage would not be under intelligent guidance, or have any more inspiration than that of a sacred dream. He needs to know something more than that he must go into eternity. He needs to know that definitely; and, while not sharing the view of Edward Beecher, that the Old Testament does not establish immortality, and that the ancient Jew had no hope at all, we confess that the fore-gleams of it in the old dispensation are rare and feeble, and yet, taken together, give ground for faith.

The doctrine of the immortality of the soul is as fundamental to character as it is to religion. If a fact at all, it is a tremendous fact, and religion should echo it in the depths of consciousness until the soul, catching the inspiration of the thought, will feel the thrill of its immortal being. Judaism, paving the way for a more explicit affirmation of the doctrine, is eclipsed by Christianity, which brought life and immortality to light. In the ancient Hebrew faith the doctrine of immortality was as black as the robes of a funeral priest; if seen at all, it was seen by twilight; in the new faith it is a full-orbed sun, illuminating human history, and pointing to the everlasting destiny of the human race. As in the Old Testament the existence of God is not demonstrated, but assumed from the beginning and all through the oracles, interpenetrating them with its spirit, so in the New Testament immortality is not logically established, but assumed and expanded as if known, and on the assumption of its truth are built the certainties of future rewards and punishments. In this way the doctrine, vaguely taught in Hebrewism, has come to light, clearly and sufficiently, in Christianity.

Concerning the general resurrection, there is the same uncertainty in the Old Testament as envelops other eschatological truth. It is unsatisfactory, and creates an uneasiness, and sometimes a suspicion that the early Hebrew faith was devoid of the doctrine of the resurrection. More is wanted than the reader finds in the dusty pages of patriarchal history, or in the unrolled parchments of the prophets. If Christianity settles any eschatological problem with emphatic assurance, it is this of the resurrection, which carries with it the sovereign proof of immortality. The resurrection of Christ is the cornerstone of Christianity, employed always by the Apostle Paul in proof of Christ's divine character, and upon the truth of which Christ himself based the future of his religion. Establishing the resurrection of Christ, the final resurrection of mankind Paul demonstrates in syllogistic form, insisting upon it not more because it may be demonstrated than that it has been revealed. It is both a demonstration and a revelation, and the Church has accepted it with an irresistible persuasion of its verity. The distance from Abraham to Paul is great, but it has been traveled, and the shout of the last day re-echoes in the ear of humanity. Out of the tomb of Machpelah sprang no flower of of hope, or at least it sent no fragrance down the ages; but Paul's death-cry shook the sleeping forms of the dead, and with his dying hand he wrote resurrection on the gateway of their tombs.

The doctrine of the resurrection is a mystery; the *fact* of resurrection is one of the accepted as it is one of the revealed doctrines of Christianity. Of the event itself, its real character, process, and purpose, we need to know more, and through evolutionary processes it will doubtless be better understood in the days to come than now.

As to the doctrines of rewards and retributions, or heaven and hell, the same evolutionary process of revelation is observable. From dimness, suspicion, and wonder, we grope into transparent conceptions, and industrious statements of truth. Judging by the record, it is not evident that Cain had any knowledge of another life, much less any suspicion of hell; but Felix, under the preaching of Paul, which was a revelation of judgment to the sensual governor, trembled. From Cain to Felix is a long path, but it marks the unfolding of truth, and its power on the conscience. Jacob dies, but the death-bed scene, beautiful and pathetic, has in it no supernatural glimmer, while Stephen sees the heavens open, and Jesus sitting at the right hand of God. From Jacob to Stephen is a dusty march, but visions of eternal glory break upon the traveler at the end. In the Old Testament *sheol* casts its shadow over the mortal, and finally overtakes and overwhelms him; in the New Testament *hades*, *gehenna*, paradise, heaven, hell, are the magic words that inspire hope or thrill with horror. Two definite termini of life are marked out, the one enticing, the other forbidding, the one perennial in its joyousness, the other unending in its gloom; and to these Christianity is ever pointing in its promises, appeals, invitations, and threatenings. Respecting the termini Christendom is not in doubt.    Some may be in doubt respecting the exact character of the double-headed future as revealed by Christianity; but that there is such a future is the unequivocal testimony of Christianity.

In like manner we might pursue the development of every Christian doctrine, from its incipient state through manifold stages, to its final exhibition in a completed form in Christianity; but this is unnecessary.

One or two questions closely associated with the evolutionary character of Christianity require a moment's consideration.   We have traced the evolution of truth in the Old Testament, but not in the New Testament; but it is susceptible of proof that the evolutionary process in the latter is even more direct, positive, and assuring than in the former.   No more attractive or intelligent theme is propounded by Christianity than the progress of doctrine in the New Testament, or the growth of truth in the inspired forms of the New Testament. The assumption of immortality, the ground-idea of all eschatology, is so illustrated by the Savior, and so enforced by apostolic argument, that naught remains but to proclaim the last words of our religion as the truth of demonstration and revelation.

Christianity is still an evolutionary system of truth, or is yet under the law of evolution, and ever will be, in its growth and influence.   Many of its truths are still beyond us.   Like Hebrew poetry, the spell is upon us when we read them, but the key to their secret seems to be lost.   That key the future must find.   Take the doctrine of the second coming of Christ, a thrilling, moving, helpful, but, at the same time, a much misunderstood and perverted doctrine.   Resurrection, too, needs illumination.   *The whole field of eschatology needs to be plowed again.*   It will be.   Lost keys will be found; hidden meanings will be uncovered; and truth, stately and transparent, will be welcomed as it is recognized.   Physical science, questioned as to the origin of the universe, and the descent of man, quietly replies that if its explanation is not valid it will furnish an explanation hereafter that will be accepted.   Physical science, compelled at times to confess its failure, promises success in the future.   It is *scientific*, therefore, to promise success hereafter.   In this spirit, but with a basis for faith in the evolutionary history of doctrinal Christianity, one may expect that the future will disclose many of the secrets of truth, and that future ages will be witnesses of truths and sharers of revelations now either unapprehended or unknown.   Supernaturalism is exhaustless, and, given the ages for its development, it will stand out clearer than ever, and supreme in its dominion over the thoughts of men.   The secret propagating power, or the *dynamical element of*

*Christianity consists, therefore, in its evolutionary character,* in its exhaustless tendency to development, in its supernaturalism, which eschews the common conditions of time and space, and in its inheritance of all that is divine.

IV. In the conception of Christianity as a *geometric ideal,* or the perfect illustration of the mathematical spirit, is also the key to the discovery of its dynamical character and power. We shall speak guardedly here, since we may be misunderstood. Physical science in its generic content is mathematical; it embraces geometry, algebra, and arithmetic. Upon these, or by the aid of these, chemistry, astronomy, physiology, botany, and geology are built; that is, the laws, principles, and conclusions discovered or established by science, are established by mathematical methods and in harmony with mathematical principles. Both botany and crystallography are mathematical sciences; that is, botanical forms are geometric, and the laws of growth, of symmetry, of proportion, observed in trees and crystals, are mathematical laws. The formation of the topaz and the sapphire, the phyllolactic arrangement of leaves on a tree, the elliptical orbits of planets, the laws of reflection and refraction of light, the mathematical proportion of gases in liquids and solids, demonstrate the spirit and authority of the geometric principle in nature. The physical universe is an epitome of mathematical principles.

Is the geometric principle purely physical, or limited in its application to physical objects? Is it the property of physical science only, or will it explain, support, and defend religious truth? Is physical truth the attempted realization of a geometric ideal, and does revealed truth fall short of it? In other words, may Christianity be vindicated from a mathematical standpoint? The elder theologians, or those known as the fathers, were averse to any thing like a demonstration of divine truth, and denied the application of the mathematical test to the dogmas of Christianity. Again and again has it been asserted, with a painful and pitiful regularity, that the evidence of Christianity is moral, and not mathematical, and that, therefore, the certainties of religion are moral and not demonstrated realities. In this day of physical science and philosophic inquiry, the mathematical test is being applied with unsparing energy and frightful haste to all kinds of truth, so that some have trembled for the result. To such a test Christianity must submit itself, as the condition of its acceptance, and as the surer condition of its triumph, for nature is only an approximation to a geometric ideal, while Christianity is its perfect embodiment or illustration.

We have waited too long for the acknowledgment of the relation of religious truth to the geometric spirit, or the evolution of the geometric ideal in Christianity, and, therefore, the mathematical demonstration of its certainty; but the time is at hand to proclaim it. It is a singular fact that materialists and evolutionists deride the notion of the algebraic principle in matter, the only explanation of their derision being the discovered relation of that principle to Christianity. Geometry is the key to the universe and the key to Christianity. According to the materialist, physical forms are the result of environment; according to a strict knowledge of fact, it is the result of mathematical law. Mathematical law is suggestive of supervising intelligence, and in its remote bearings presupposes the theistic principle; hence the virulence with which the geometric idea of nature is persecuted. *The geometric idea of nature is also the geometric idea of Christianity*, as we shall now see. *Spiritual truth is as geometric to the core as any natural truth;* and both stand or fall by this supreme test.

The most perplexing doctrine of the Scriptures—the Trinity—is an ample illustration of the geometrical idea in Christianity. It includes three things: (*a*) Substance; (*b*) Form; (*c*) Influence. The Father is the Substance, or invisible essence; the Son is the Form, the express image, of the Substance; the Spirit is the Influence, or procession from the Father through the Son, or from the Substance through the Form. Precisely these three, and no more, co-exist in every created thing; the Trinity is the geometric figure of the universe. Here is a geranium. Its substance is the gases of which it is composed, and which is, therefore, invisible; its form is that which we see; its influence is its fragrance, delighting the sense, or its beauty, addressing the æsthetic element in man, or its uses, appealing to the needs of man. Instead of a dogmatic or theologic conception of three persons in one, compelling men to exclaim as did the great Webster, "I do not understand the arithmetic of heaven," reveal it in its geometric character, and its truth will be conceded.

To other doctrines the same observation will apply, and the same mathematical principle will aid in determining their validity. God is infinite, omnipresent, without body or parts; but, mysterious as is this statement as a theologic utterance, it evolves into a clearly expressed reality under the pilotage of the geometric ideal. Time and space are bodiless conditions, omnipresent, and really infinite to the human mind; they are the geometrical figures of a bodiless and infinite omnipresence. Equally representative of the divine being in his bodiless condition is oxygen, a substance without parts, and as universal as air and matter. As to the unity of God, scientists are engaged in rehearsing the great fact that the universe is a unit, and matter is reducible to a single atom, forgetting that the unity of the universe is the mathematical figure of the unity of God. On such geometric pedestals the existence, character, and attributes of God may stand, natural truth being the figure of spiritual truth.

In like manner the Incarnation, an apparition in religion, may be reduced to a simple geometric ideal, having its illustration in the incarnation of gases in solids, such as trees, rocks, flowers, mountains, and seas. *The visible is the incarnation of the invisible.*

Atonement, or antidote for sin, has its counterpart in the antidotes of nature for poison, disease, accident, and pain; and resurrection is typed by the day succeeding the night.

In the facts, forms, laws, and principles of nature are the adumbrations of spiritual truth, or, to express the thought less metaphysically, *Christianity is the counterpart of nature.* The laws of one are the laws of the other; he who understands one must understand the other, for the one is the figure of the other. Christianity is natural religion, or the religion of nature in its geometric ideal. The secret thinker now holds that religious truth can be demonstrated by mathematics, or that the evidence of such truth is as mathematical, as positive, as certain as the evidence of scientific truth. Cousin speaks of thought as having a geometric form, implying that the root of psychology is geometry. Poetry is a mathematical product. *Intellectuality is geometry in motion.* Dante's "Inferno" is a species of mathematics. Relying upon the geometric character of Christianity as explained, the conclusion is justified that the dynamic force of nature is the dynamic force of religion, or that the life of the higher is also the life of the lower. Its dynamical character, however, is not fully manifested in its analogy to natural force. In fact, its highest force is of a higher kind.

V. A truer conception of the real character of Christianity as a religious force arises from a study of the *benevolent spirit* which seems hidden in all its truths. Christianity is the incarnation of benevolence in its teachings, in its projects, and in the methods by which it communicates itself to the world. Its great principle is love, the power of which can not be estimated. Taken in its lowest form, as charity, it represents the relieving and helping power of religion, which has stimulated the establishment of asylums, hospitals, and alms-houses, and led to prison reform, the abolition of slavery, and the mitigation of the evils of poverty. Not that charity had no existence in the world until the Master taught it, but it found an advanced expression in his teachings, and an exhibition of it in his life and self-sacrifice that has ever since made the word beautiful, and the thing itself sacred. In the same spirit it offers liberty to mankind; freedom from oppression, liberty to worship God; freedom from slavery. It is emancipation as well as love; it is the religion of char-

ity and the religion of liberty. These two are words of power. *Love
and liberty are stronger than a pair of steam-engines.* Preach these, and
religion triumphs. These the needy, suffering world can appreciate,
while the metaphysical content of religious truth is overlooked, and
its power unfelt. Mathematical it is—this is the guaranty of its orderly working, and the pledge of its perpetuity; benevolent it is—this
will arrest attention, and draw the needy world to its embrace.

VI. In a most emphatic sense Christianity is a *biological religion,* or
the religion of life. It is the only life-imparting religion ; its highest
force is biological. In the preceding pages of this volume Christianity has been discussed as a system of truth, and its power has been
represented as the power of truth. We are now compelled to draw
a distinction between truth and life, or allow that life is one of the
contents of truth, or truth is one of the contents of life. Is there
any difference between truth and life ? The dynamical character of
truth must be conceded ; it has power, the power of knowledge ; but
is there not something in religion besides its truth ? Truth may be
the instrument of life, but is it life ? Is truth a biological force, or
is the biological force of Christianity something else ? Truth-power
and spirit-power, however related in the accomplishment of redemption, are different ; both belong to Christianity, but the latter is the
sovereign and final power. By spirit-power we mean the power of
the divine Spirit working in the human heart for its salvation, as
truth alone can not work. Truth enlightens ; the Spirit kindles the
soul into a living fire. *Truth points out the way to life; the Spirit imparts life.* The Spirit-force of Christianity is the life-force of religion,
and this is its greatest power.

We must also distinguish the truth respecting power from power
itself. The atoning force of Christianity is one with its spirit-force,
for without atonement salvation is impossible. But the truth of
atonement is not the power of atonement, or the fact is not its power.
Atonement-truth is not atonement-power ; back of the truth is the
power which is spiritual, or the power of God in Jesus Christ, manifested by the Spirit. The supreme dynamical elements of Christianity
are not, therefore, its revealed truths, but its spiritual forces in Atonement and Spirit-presence, for in these alone are its life-giving tendencies and its life-imparting agencies. It is a biological religion,
not because of its truth, but because of the spirit of God operating
through and by the truth upon the hearts of the children of men.

VII. Christianity is the religion of *realities,* having power in proportion as it is inherently real. Philosophy may be reduced to a catena
of abstractions on subjects the illumination of which may be found in
religion. Physical science is compelled to deal with abstractions, and

to deal with them as if they were true. In geography the equator is treated as a definite something, whereas it is defined as an *imaginary* line; so it is. The lines of longitude and latitude are imaginary, but geography treats them as if they have an absolute existence. Geometry begins with a point, an indefinable nothing that has the appearance of being something. Higher mathematics even presumes to make use of the following most extraordinary *imaginary fact*: The mercury in a thermometer, it is agreed, must be above zero, below it, or at zero; but it may be necessary to suppose it is somewhere else than at any of these points. Impossible that it be anywhere else, yet science works with the mercury at an impossible place, and treats the imaginary fact as if it were a reality. Nothing like this or equal to it obtains in Christianity. It is without abstractions, imaginary facts, impossibilities. It works from realities, many of them supernatural, but realities full of power. Abstractions may be useful; realities are powerful. Theism, incarnation, inspiration, regeneration, and resurrection are not abstractions; they are realities; hence they are powers.

VIII. Christianity is a *plan*. To say that it is a "plan of salvation" would be speaking theologically; it is such a plan, but it is more. It is not the plan of history, as known to us; it is not the plan of the Church, as manifested in its purpose; *it is the plan of God for the universe of matter and men, for earth and heaven, for time and eternity*. It is broad, deep, high, divine, eternal. It comprehends all things; it includes all history; it touches the springs of causation, and turns the wheel of universal destiny; it organizes the enterprises of grace, and makes a kingdom for the reign of truth; it originated with God, and is adapted to man; it is the power of God, and, therefore, the power of the universe.

If this conception of Christianity be correct, its power is no longer a mystery. If it is substance; if it is evolutional; if it is geometric; if it is reality; if it is the only plan of God for this world and all world's,—its future is as God's.

# CHAPTER XXIX.

## THE MAGNETISM OF CHRISTIANITY.

CERTAIN citizens of Thessalonica, in describing the effect of apostolic preaching, said unto the rulers that it had "turned the world upside down," than which a more accurate concession to the radical power of Christianity never was rendered. No more potent influence has the world felt than that which the Galilean teacher has exerted. Wherever his Gospel has been declared, the effect, whether instantaneous or gradual, has gone out into all conditions, and has been as permanent as it has been impressive. In heathen or civilized lands, the results of Christian truth have been the same— governments have been reconstructed, religions dethroned, evils disturbed, checked, and rooted out, and a new order of civil and social life has been introduced and fostered. In conflict with pagan religions, tumults, uproars, and excitements have sometimes occurred, and prejudiced historians have not been slow to attribute to it a seditious tendency, provoking revolutions, strifes, political commotions, and unnecessary frictions and antagonisms in the social machinery of the world. Without controversy, it has the peculiar faculty of developing a strange enthusiasm for salvation; it has a genius for effecting large reforms, a spirit that promotes the philanthropies, a propelling power that aids the moralities; it does inflame the public mind against caste, slavery, intemperance, polygamy, idolatry, mammon, murder, Sabbath-breaking, theft, inhumanity, infidelity, and atheism; and wherever it lifts its voice it agitates, disturbs, and awakens the evil-doers, and unites in organized effort the energies of the virtuous and the good against the influence of the wicked and the reign of the ungodly.

What is the agitative force of Christianity? What is its magnetism? Is it a visible, tangible somewhat, or the occult influence of the supernatural and invisible? Is its power the result of mechanism? or is Christianity a vital force, pushing itself to the surface, and overturning as it goes the lawless organisms and impure agencies and institutions of the world?

Replying in a general way, it is clear that the exciting power of Christianity is not in the methods employed for its propagation, or in the use of any carnal or secular force whatever. In this it differs from all religions that preceded it, and from those that still exist and oppose its progress. Scanning the history of Mohammedanism, the student is pained on account of the methods which it adopted for its extension, and the excess of violence to which it resorted. The religion of the prophet was, and is, the religion of the sword. Whole countries have been thrown into consternation by the presence of priests, who were the advance guards of a bloodthirsty and fanatical army, bent quite as much on religious persecution as on political power and territorial aggrandizement. Empires have been devastated by the soldiers of that faith, which advanced, never by the voluntary recognition of its inherent adaptations on the part of peoples, but by military processes, and thrived only in soil nourished by blood. A religion of terror, it excited the fears by suppressing the hopes of millions whom it forced into obedience and punished into loyalty.

The record of Christianity is not a record of blood. We do not disguise the fact that, at important epochs in its history it has worn a military complexion and essayed its tasks through the aid of force, as under the brilliant administration of Constantine, and later under the gigantic imposition of the Papacy; but the dashing Christianity of the fourth century lost its spirituality by contact with the secular power, and the cruel Christianity of Hildebrand and his successors is paying the penalty of its apostasy by a slow and marked decay.

Outside of the barbarism of method, and independent of the ecclesiastical structures reared for its safety, Christianity, in a spirit of peace, has agitated, shaken, and surprised the world out of its stupor more than all things else, the surprise being all the greater as its methods have been unwarlike and apparently inadequate. It is not new to compare Christianity with light, working silently in expelling darkness, or with leaven, permeating civilization by a slow and graduated process, or with salt, preserving the world from moral decay. It is the glory of Christianity that it is light, it is leaven, it is salt, but it is more. *It is fire, it is a hammer, it is wind, it is resurrection.* It is not the hiding of power merely, like electricity in the cloud, or like an army sleeping; but it is power at work, like electricity shooting athwart the sky, setting fire to the stars, and shaking planets in their orbits; it is like Napoleon's army at the Pyramids, or like Barak's in Esdraelon, accomplishing its task under the inspiration of the past and the future. It is the religion of active force, guided by the spirit that originated it, and for the conservation of spiritual ends. Gibbon, who was somewhat elaborate in his analysis of the causes of the progress of Christianity, discerned not the motive power of the religion itself. He saw in the zeal of the early Christians, the simple ecclesiastical plans of the Church, and the miraculous claims of the apostles and fathers, a source of enthusiasm, communicating itself to multitudes, and resulting in the multiplication of. Christian societies; but he failed to explain the origin of the Church, and why there are Christians at all. While Gibbon's *résumé* is a partial explanation of the spread of Christianity, it does not reveal the spirit, the essence-power, of Christianity; it does not exhibit the agitating, overturning, progressive, and magnetic elements of the new religion. To these let us now devote attention.

In its *doctrinal character* lies its secret propelling force. A doctrine is a principle or truth fundamental to the system to which it is accredited. A religion of doctrines is a religion of primary principles, indicating its character, temper, tone, strength, and possibility of success. A continent made up of rivers, prairies, and plains would be inhabitable; but it would be wanting in the solidity, variety, and grandeur that mountain chains would give it. A religion of speculations, or commonplace truths, might be accepted in the absence of any thing better; but it would be inferior to a religion of revealed truths. Dogmatic Christianity, or the religion of doctrinal truth, is a primary necessity. A religion without revealed truths would be like astronomy without stars, botany without plants, and geology without rocks. Christianity is a revelation of truth; it is a mountain chain of doctrine; it has its Alleghenies, Rocky, and Sierra Nevada ranges in the great doctrinal teachings that are so prominent in it; they hold it together, weave it into form, combine to give it sublimity, and are the sources of its power. From their altitudes a vision of God, man, life, being, and eternity may be taken, and in the atmosphere that sweeps around the summits the soul learns to be still, and takes its first lessons of life. In a very pronounced way, Paul exhibited religion in its doctrinal form in Thessalonica and Asia Minor, and idols fell from their pedestals, and the niches of temples soon emptied their statues in the dust. Exhibited doctrinally anywhere, it strikes at evil, whether moral, social, political, or commercial, arresting attention, provoking inquiry, and leading to changes in the manner of the public and the individual life.

What specific doctrinal truths have an arresting and agitating power? In his summation of "causes" Gibbon announces the eschatological elements of Christianity as supreme, asserting that the doctrines of the immortality of the soul, of the millennium, and of the end of the world, were potent factors in arousing the fears and securing the faith of the multitudes, to whom they were presented. It is undoubtedly true that Christian eschatology, unfolded in its breadth of meaning, will awaken inquiry, reverence, reformation, and worship; and if the apostles and Christian fathers urged with vehement interest the consideration of the great truths of resurrection, immortality, and judgment, it was because pagan religions had only obscurely and indefinitely, if at all, reminded their subjects of them, and because a knowledge of such truths was imperative, and to be acquired only by revelation. With faith in immortality the Greek sages loaded it with a mythology quite as dreary and repulsive as superstition had ever invested it; and the old religions were too sensual or material in their horoscope of the future life to satisfy reason or justify faith. No distinct answer to the problem of life after death had been given by philosophy or religion, except as it was involved in mythology or superstition. Into that night of intellectual darkness Christianity shone like a new sun, clearing up the midnight scenes of paganism, and extinguishing even the twilight of Judaism in the broader and fuller revelation of the Gospel of the Son of God.

The doctrines of the pre-existence of souls, of transmigration, of incarnations, of Tartarus, of the river Styx, and of the abode of the gods surrendered to the clearer teachings of immortality, resurrection, hades, final judgment, and ultimate heaven and hell, as they fell from Christ and those who went forth as heralds of the truth. *Sheol* was supplanted by *hades*, *hades* was divided into *gehenna* and *Paradise*, and beyond both were seen the open gates to final destiny. The "last things" of religion in the hands of the apostles stood out as the *bas-relief* teachings of religion, which had immediate recognition, and which impressed men with fear if sinful, and with hope if godly. Christianity was a *clearing-up religion* in the field of eschatology; it reaped the truth and plucked up error by the roots.

That it excited all classes to inquiry, and satisfied both the reason and the faith, is not surprising; that it does not excite a deeper demonstration of interest now than then is surprising. In the passage of the centuries Christianity has not abandoned its eschatological truths, but rather insists upon them as truths underlying a correct religious faith, and as all-important motives to a religious life. If it threw the shadows of the last day, the gloom and terror of the grave, and the certainties of judgment, over the souls of men in early times, it does so now; if Felix and the Philippian jailer trembled in the presence of Paul as he reasoned of eternal things, so now rulers quake in view of judgment; if Paul's sermon at Athens, Peter's on Pentecost, and Christ's parables relating to the judgment-day and its final decrees, impressed multitudes in their day, the same truths have the same power to-day. Such truths compel men to pause in their career of ungodliness, insincerity, and degradation; such truths are the magnets of Christianity, influencing men to reflection, repentance, and a new life; such truths will turn the world upside down.

Christianity did not depend alone upon the spell of the future for its power. It had other resources, it had another mission, and so intent on present achievement was it that the thought of the future was often lost in immediate undertakings and revelations. Neither philosophy nor the pagan religions had sufficiently represented the infirmities, weaknesses, and moral disabilities of the race, nor, acknowledging the power of evil, were they able to invent a satisfactory explanation of its origin, or acquaint mankind by what means it might be overcome. In its own way Christianity undertook to throw light upon the dark subject, explaining the introduction of evil into our world, its transmission under laws of heredity from generation to generation, its fatal influence on the body and the soul, and the impossibility of its extinction by human or natural agency. At the same time, revealing iniquity in all its hideousness, it proposed an adequate method for its suspension and final extinction.

The appalling fact of evil, as a universal burden, has never been denied either by philosophy or paganism; but its appalling nature has never been declared by either, and a gracious remedy never foreshadowed until the dawn of Christianity. The root of evil is in matter, thought the philosopher. Natural evil was the subject of discussion and the object of assault. Christianity, however, declares itself the antagonist of moral evil, which has its root in voluntary disobedience of right. Remove moral evil, and natural evil will cease to disturb or annoy. *Philosophy bombarded natural conditions; Christianity assails moral conditions.* Philosophy condemns God's physical government; Christianity condemns man's moral life.

A modern type of transcendentalism apologizes for sin in affirming that it is not criminal; it affirms that it is a misfortune, a blunder, a mistake; it is this, and it is more. Transcendentalism, or Unitarianism, needs enlightenment quite as much as philosophy or paganism. Out of the shadow of darkness Christianity conducts the inquirer into a region of knowledge, in which the nature of sin is exposed, its ruinous tendencies exhibited, its dreadful penalties, both natural and judicial, announced, and the antidote for the poison prescribed. Teach the doctrine of human sinfulness, as it is portrayed in the Testaments; represent human helplessness as it appears on the pages of the Gospel; declare the doom of the obdurate and unforgiven, as the same Gospel warrants; and then preach the hope of deliverance through Jesus Christ, as he has authorized in his own words, and a city like Athens, a ruler like Agrippa, an officer like the centurion, a bigot like Sosthenes, and a worldling like Dionysius, will weep, repent, and rejoice, or, alarmed and impenitent, will become enraged, and sink all the deeper in sensuality and despair. Either truth of the Gospel—human infirmity or divine rescue, or both—will excite the emotions of the multitude, and arouse from sleep the nations that hear the Gospel.

These double-edge truths are the magnets of Christianity. This is the practical side of the Gospel, and it is as effectual in awakening the world as the eschatological previously noted. What the Gospel can do for men here interests them quite as much as what it proposes to do with them hereafter. The present helpfulness of Christianity is as attractive as the promise of future deliverance from eternal condemnation. Present deliverance is the condition of future deliverance. Insisting upon its present adaptations, men are drawn to it.

The theistic element of Christianity constitutes a prominent doctrinal characteristic, and in apostolic times it was especially contagious of disorder, excitement, and revolution. In its teachings respecting God, perhaps, it antagonized the old religions more violently than by its eschatology or atonement, for monotheism and polytheism can not co-exist in the same religion, or enter into the same civilization and social conditions. Polytheism, though in a state of decline, had yet its advocates and altars in the days of Paul; and where it did not obtain there idolatry of another type was in vogue. The condition of the introduction of Christianity, as emphasized by the Christian leaders, was the subsidence of polytheism and idolatry. Between the two religions there could be no fraternity, not even the look of recognition. God, not gods; Jehovah, not Jupiter, was the cry of the apostles wherever they went. Diana of the Ephesians must retire; Neptune and Minerva must be dethroned; and Pluto must surrender the keys to the lower world. In its theism Christianity was not a compromise with polytheism, but rather a challenge, like that of Elijah on Carmel, to all religions to prove themselves or sink into nothingness. This attitude of the teachers of Christianity provoked the opposition of all classes; business men, polytheists, rulers, priests, the whole city and the whole country, arose in indignation against the enemies of their religion and their faith. The theistic idea is magnetic, and in proportion as it settles down upon the heart of humanity, it draws it upward toward God. The existence of God is a fundamental truth, necessary not more to religion than philosophy. When proclaimed it requires from men more than honest reverence; it imposes the obligation of immediate repentance, correct habits, pure feelings, holy worship; it arouses the thought of dependence and responsibility, and has a restraining effect on the disposition to wickedness and profligacy. In the presence of the great truth, false religions withered away; the violent were restrained; and nations were disturbed. Christian theism promotes the reign of conscience in morals, and the reign of God in the soul.

The Biblical representation of a personal God contains the correlated idea of divine providence, or the rule of God in the affairs of men.  On this point the world has always needed instruction, and needs it now quite as much as at any time in the past, for the materialist is undertaking to banish the divine administration from the universe.  Ancient philosophy removed God from any friendly interest in human affairs; modern philosophy predicates a universe so constructed as to manage itself, not only doing away with the miraculous, but precluding the intervention of God by the ordinary avenues of fixed law; in other words, the universe is independent of God.  Such a view is cold and comfortless, and contrary to the teaching of Him who knoweth our frame, and numbereth our steps.  The fatherhood of God, the protection of human life and the supply of its wants, the guidance of human steps and the ordering of human ways, the unseen leading of individuals into positions of usefulness, and the conservation of individual happiness, are among the beneficent results that follow the providential administration of God.

The doctrine of divine providence, special and general, as taught in the Scriptures and illustrated in the lives of the eminent saints and heroes of the Church, is magnetic in its power over the hearts of the children of men, and insures Christianity a welcome when it is understood.

*The core of Christianity is the three-fold doctrine of monotheism, involving providential relations to man, of atonement, involving human sinfulness and divine rescue, and of the future life, involving an eternal heaven and an eternal hell.*  On this three-fold basis Christianity in its doctrinal character rests, challenging the world to overthrow it, and agitating and attracting mankind as they comprehend its significance, and discern that the highest self-interest requires personal acceptance of it.  *Doctrinally, it does not appeal merely to the fears of men; it enlightens the judgment and extinguishes errors, preparing the mind for a rational study of truth; it dethrones idols and enthrones a personal Creator, giving one an inside view of the divine government, and pointing out the necessity of harmony with the divine will; it reveals human helplessness to an alarming degree, creating a desire for rescue, and then provides an available remedy for sin, urging all to appropriate it as soon as presented; and, to enforce the duty of volitional surrender to God, and the necessity of a new life, it points out the fearful guilt of delay and the awful consequences of rejection, at the same time enticing the soul into immediate obedience by the promise of rewards, as fascinating as they are wonderful, and as divine as they are imperishable.*  The three-fold doctrine of Christianity is the great magnet of the new religion.

Even more powerful than doctrine is the *personic* element in the foundation of Christianity, or the character, offices, and influence of the Master himself. Truth sometimes seems cold and distant, but personality is a center of interest, inquiry, and enthusiasm. Christianity is more than a system of truths, it is the divine personality crystallized in humanity, chiefly in Jesus Christ. Mankind are prone to judge of systems of religion by their authors or founders, inquiring into their parentage, education, physical appearance and habits, social connections, worldly advantages, and secular positions, and especially are they anxious to know the origin of the religious idea which dominates in their lives, and to which they are striving to give outward reality. This is natural, and every religion should satisfy the demand for historical explanation. Christianity came forth, not with a fabled character as its founder, or with a hermit as its introducer, but as the outgrowth of one who dwelt among men, but surpassed them in the perfection of his human qualities, and in the possession of powers not less than superhuman and supernatural. The story of his birth is weird-like and of rare celebrity; the obscurity of his life in Nazareth, and its relation to his after-work, have not been fully explained by historian or theologian; the brief public career that followed, filled with deeds that still live in the memory of the world, and illuminated with teachings that constitute the life-blood of the best civilizations, is calculated to excite the thoughtful and arouse even the stupid; while the melancholy fate that overtook him, and the sufferings with which he sealed his mission, still touch the heart and force the flow of tears.

The results of his presence in the world are as potent as the facts of his history. *Living*, he was the attractive source of the religionists of his age, shaking the foundations of old faiths to the ground, and subverting false social orders and customs, as easily as light expels darkness; *preached*, he became the disorganizing element in all communities, robbing paganism of its charms, and disarming all religions of their power of propagation; *crucified* and *RISEN*, he has become the corner-stone of civilization and the inspiration of the world's progress toward an ideal condition of morality, industry, and happiness. Christ is in every thing, the omnipresent factor of history, the omnipotent force of the ages, the guiding spirit of the race. Literature teems with thought concerning Christ, either to acknowledge his authority and enlarge his influence, or to criticise his claims and deny his place in religion; without him, modern art would be barren and uninteresting; without his teachings, civilization would degenerate into barbarism; without Christ, society would decay. No other religion has such a Founder; no other a comparable personic force behind it or in it. Supreme moral excellence, immaculate purity, unquestioned veracity, transparent humility, universal benevolence, sympathetic helpfulness, boundless faith, illimitable knowledge, and infinite affection, are the personal adornments of Jesus Christ.

The sinlessness of the Son of Man is a proof that he was more than man; or, as Horace Bushnell phrases it, "the character of Jesus forbids his possible classification with men." Whether he maintained his sinlessness by miraculous means, or by inherent love of righteousness; whether the theory of his perfection is a theory only, without justification in the presence of his full history, or to be maintained until positive proof to the contrary is furnished, are questions that thinking men sometimes discuss. Mr. Hennel, in asserting that Jesus is an "imperfectly known character," insinuates that if all the facts of his life were known it might be found morally defective where we least suspect it; but Paul says he "knew no sin." Sometimes it is declared that, even if his external life was blameless, we have no means of knowing what his internal life was, and that it may have been imperfect. This is only a supposition, without force or value beside the testimony of those who were eye-witnesses of his majesty, and the companions of his life. The supreme fact of his sinlessness gives him supreme power as a teacher and exemplar of his religion.

The Messianic character of Jesus Christ is also a magnetic element in his history. As the Son of Man he was perfect; as the Son of God, he was the Messiah, establishing the kingdom of God, or the eternal rule of religion in men. In the one aspect he is an example, in the other an authority; in the one a teacher, in the other a king. A new moral government, with new laws, new aims, new plans, and new results, is contemplated by the presence of the Messiah. This means the overthrow of old moral governments, or their transformation into the new; it means a radical change in the moral life of the world, and a conformity to the new standard of conduct as set forth by the exemplar himself; it means regeneration, sanctification, and eternal glory. In himself different from all men, his mission was no less different from that of all teachers of religion. He is the promised Messiah, and, therefore, the hope of man. Without him, as perfect man, Christianity can not be; without his mission or Messiahship, Christianity can not redeem or triumph. The root of Christianity is, not theism or eschatology, but Christ. From the region of theistic thinking have issued polytheism and mythology; from eschatology have come the brood of pagan futures that have paralyzed the races; from Christ comes Christianity, with its light and power. Singularly enough, Gibbon does not discover the relation of Christ to the great system of religion, or that he is its inspiring character, or the vital influence which the world everywhere is feeling. To overlook Christ is to overlook the essentials of Christianity. He is the magnet of magnets, the only source of power.

The great purpose of his religion is conquest, not conquest in the political or military sense, but in the sense of universal supremacy as a religion ; and this purpose, not common to religions, it seeks to promote through efficient organized agencies. To trust to the inherent leavening power of truth, without co-operating instrumentalities for the spread of truth, is folly indeed, for the ungodly world does not mean that truth shall prevail. To overcome its opposition, truth must organize its forces, and array them in human instrumentalities. The human mind takes not kindly to abstractions. Abstract thought is powerless over the multitudes. An abstract philosophy will not extend beyond the circle of the philosophers. An abstract religion is equally powerless; it must concrete itself in visible forms, and employ visible agencies for its work. An abstract ship is one that exists in the mind of the builder—a concrete ship is one that rides the seas. The Christian religion is both abstract and concrete ; abstract in its great doctrinal structure, concrete in its supernatural Founder, in its institutions and instrumentalities.

The Christian Church is the exponent of the Christian religion, organized not merely to gather in one those who receive a common faith, but more particularly for the vindication of the oracles of God, and the extension of Christianity by systematic and organized means. It was intended to be more than a brotherhood, or close corporation of similarly affected souls ; it was established as an aggressive force, for the purpose of invading the haunts of sin, and crushing out by methods singular and effective all the Protean forms of error, and enriching the world with its possessions of truth, wisdom, and salvation. With this end before it, the Church could not be in any community a merely latent influence, or a quiet and accommodating organization ; it must be a correcting, reforming, stimulating, consuming influence, putting itself at the head of all social changes, demanding just legislation on all vital subjects, and resisting by positive efforts the encroachments of vice, until it is stripped of its power to do harm. Such is the mission of the Church, but in executing it, it necessarily comes into antagonism with all that is opposed to Christianity, and creates consternation, hatred, hostility, and persecution.

In its missionary character the Church is an exciting instrumentality, a disturber of old foundations of misbelief, of the false security of the world, and bears the odium that attaches to Christianity itself. The Church is not Christianity, but the two are inseparable in their fortunes, and the latter succeeds, if at all, only through the aggressions of the former. Gibbon recognized the Church as the propagating instrumentality of Christianity, and perceived that through its councils and the devotion of its members it was a compact force hard to resist, and its success could not be stayed. The Church is not a secret organization, nor dependent on secret methods for the accomplishment of her task; the doors of her temples are wide open, and, entering, we may inspect her altars, listen to her teachings, catch the melody of her songs, and see her in her beauty and glory. Her agencies are as simple as her institutions, and her customs as venerable as they are attractive. See how sacredly she keeps the Sabbath, and how she enforces the hebdomadal rest on natural as well as spiritual grounds! Witness the tender observance of the Eucharistic feast, and how carefully she guards the memory of Christ by the monumental sacrament; follow the living ministry as they go forth into all lands, declaring the same Gospel to all peoples, and thrilling an unsaved world with the tidings of redemption; listen to the ten thousand songs in the home and the sanctuary, bearing religious truth to human hearts, and proclaiming the graciousness of Him who sits on the throne; observe the Sunday-schools gathering in the unnumbered children of earth, and teaching them the lofty ideal of life in Jesus Christ; listen to the pious prayer of Christendom from prayer-meeting and family altar for baptism of strength and victory in conflict with evil; examine the benevolent movements of the Christian Church, having in view the publication of the Gospel among the nations, and the redemption of all peoples; and the conclusion must be that the Church is the best organized agency for the spread of Christianity that can be devised. Its purpose known, wherever it commences its work, evil arrays itself against it; the result is public commotion, and the display of the magnetizing power of Christianity. The Church is the magnetic instrument of the new religion.

*The internal claim of Christianity, or its assumption of a divine origin, is pregnant with enthusiastic influence.* Almost all religions trace themselves to God, or, at all events, to superhuman authorization. None, we believe, claims a purely human origin, for that would at once invalidate its right to authority. To satisfy the higher wants of man, ever expressing themselves in religious acts, there must be in religion something that man can not himself originate or suggest. All religions, the spurious as well as the genuine, recognize the fundamental necessity of a superhuman element, growing out of human conditions. Hence Greece and Rome ascribed a divine source to their religions. Paganism, receiving religious instruction from priests, supposed them to be related to supernatural beings, or to be superhuman beings themselves. The Christian religion, overleaping all interme-diary agencies, ascends higher than any other, centering itself in the authenticated will of God as revealed in Jesus Christ. Its initial claim is not that it is god-like, but that it is from God.

From the initial claim grow others as imperious in nature, and really accessory to its vindication. If divine, it follows that it must be the only religion for man, and can in no sense fraternize with lower religions, or allow them the least room in this world. It pushes out in every direction with the avowed purpose to crush out of existence all other religions ; it means "disintegration and absorption" of all others. Intolerant in its aims, the claim has providential proportions ; the purpose is really majestic, and grows sublime as it becomes des-potic ; but its execution is attended with serious difficulties and many apparent uncertainties. As it rises to view, crushing out other faiths, or absorbing them, as the sun extinguishes lesser lights, and marches on, conforming this world to the moral idea of God, it awakens the enthusiasm of the race, and nations join the upward movement with the glee of conquerors. Such a religion can not be narrow ; its pur-pose relieves it of a single restricted view ; it is ocean-broad, sky-deep, infinite as God. A religion with such a claim, enforced con-tinually by providential interpositions, and heralded by inspiring agencies, is calculated to arrest attention, and draw the thought of men to itself.

Authoritative and uncompromising as Christianity is, it displays credentials of origin, character, and purpose that sometimes mock human wisdom, and certainly compel careful investigation and cool judgment in determining their integral value. The origin, growth, structure, and unity of the documentary records of Christianity, or the harmony of Biblical truth, constitute a marvelous fact in the his-tory of the development of religious truth. It is noteworthy that a book written by more than forty authors, at periods remote by cen-turies from one another, and under circumstances opposed to consec-utive and harmonious work, should yet be pervaded by one spirit, and combine in the presentation of one truth. *The sixty-six books of the Bible are one—one in the idea of right, one in the idea of religion, one in atonement, or method of redemption, one in resurrection, one in the standard of eternal judgment.* Such a unity of ideas, coupled with a oneness of purpose, is most astounding, compelling recognition from the devout and explanation from the unbelieving. The Christian re-ligion has but one book ; the Christian religion is the revelation of a single idea, with manifold branches, and a many-sided development.

Gazing at the one truth, its manifoldness is at once apparent. Monotheism, the single element of the earliest patriarchal theology, rings on the ear like a note from Paradise; the Hebrew cosmogony, or a revelation of the scientific order of world-building, stands out as a stately, divine panorama of facts; the origin of man and the introduction of evil, as narrated by Moses, constitute two chapters found nowhere outside of Revelation; the record of the deluge and of the multiplication of tongues must be added to the pages of revealed Biblical science; Sinaitic thunder is still heard by mankind, and the mountain summit rules in the justice of all civilizations; the pious odes of David continue to reverberate their mysterious echoes of experience into human hearts; the Son of God still atones and still forgives sin; the Church flourishes throughout the world as it never did, even when apostles proclaimed Christ, and kings protected the sacred name from reproach; mankind are catching the rays of John's apocalyptic vision, and dreaming of the dawn of a so-called millennial day; and Christendom marches on with swift tread and jubilant feet to the music of the Gospel. Running parallel with the science, the law, the poetry of the divine religion, are the monotheism, the atonement, the music, and the millennium of Revelation. The two, the lower and the upper strata of religious truth, are one in their import, and signify the moral education, the spiritual development, and the final redemption of the race.

What are the credentials of Christianity? Just what we have mentioned: its science, its law, its monotheism, its atonement, its music, its millennium. These are magnets of wonderful power; these are " evidences " that convince.

Among the evidences usually quoted in support of the integrity of divine revelation, the strongest are supposed to be prophecy and miracle, the first being proof of supernatural wisdom in the prophet, and the second certifying to the supernatural power of the performer. These two pillars of Christianity appear sufficient to support it; but evidences so supernatural in themselves, and so exclusively relied on by theologians, have created a suspicion of their genuineness by their very character, and by the difficulties which attend an examination of them. As to prophecy, it is a demonstration of the inspiration of the prophet; as to particular prophecies, it is difficult to ascertain when some of them were uttered, the meaning of not a few is ambiguous, or susceptible of a variety of interpretations, the usual application of some of them to certain events is considered strained and unwarranted, and the prophetic spirit, the genesis of the impulse, is involved in the thickest mystery. These objections to the prophetic credential unbelievers have urged with vehemence and apparent plausibility.

Miracle likewise suffers repudiation at the hands of those who reject Christianity. To deny the possibility of divine intervention in physical affairs is easy enough ; to relegate authenticated instances of such intervention to mythology is a cheap and ignorant way of disposing of them. To say with Hume that a miracle is contrary to experience, means nothing ; to study it, as does Huxley, from the stand-point of the naturalist, is as reasonable as to study regeneration from that stand-point. To charge that miracle is a disturbance of the "order of nature," an order supposed to be fixed and unchangeable, is a play of words, for believers in miracles make no such claim, and, as a matter of fact, the order of nature, as Mozley shows, is *not* disturbed by miraculous interposition. Nature proceeded in its accustomed order after a miracle had been performed, as though insensible to the interposition that had taken place. If the sun stayed a little its march in behalf of Joshua, it soon resumed its stately movement, the inhabitants of the earth unaware that any thing had happened. Gibbon assails the credibility of prophecy and miracle by the statement that some eminent men of the early Christian centuries were unaffected by them, as if that demonstrated any thing more than their own blindness and skepticism. Some "eminent men" reject the evidences now, but the Gospel goes on in spite of such rejection, and will never lose its power. "Eminent men" once denounced Harvey's discovery of the circulation of the blood, and Jenner's theory and practice of vaccination, and Galileo's idea of the rotation of the earth, and Copernicus's solar system; but it only established how perverse is ignorance, and how ruinous is prejudice. However, Gibbon concedes that the miracle had much to do with the introduction of Christianity, as it fed the appetite for the marvelous, and held the ignorant masses in fear, the two conditions of the reign of superstition.

Indispensable as prophecy and miracle are to Christianity, there are other evidences in its favor quite as forceful, certainly as complete, and more adapted to win modern thought, that its advocates should hasten to employ, and substitute, if necessary, for the antiquated proofs of other days. If the scientific world proposes to test the integrity of revelation by its scientific statements and anticipations; if it is insisted that the purity of revealed truth must be determined by the character of its ethical system or supernaturalistic morality ; if it is urged that, as a religion, it can stand only as the character of Christ is relieved of all moral impeachment; if it is asserted that, as a religion, its monotheism and system of atonement must submit to the closest investigation ; and if, as a religion, it must be judged by its history, and by what it still proposes to accomplish,—it may joyfully accept such tests, and present its science, its laws, its doctrines, its Founder, its history, and its projects, as the credentials of its divine character, and as affirmative indications of its future ascendency. Not alone by miracle and prophecy, *but by the truths of Revelation in their modern aspects and relations*, must the religion of Revelation be interpreted, as the condition of its progress in these times, and of its victory over skepticism.

If Christianity, in its apostolic order, phases, and works, is incompetent to satisfy the requirements of the reason, and fails to magnetize the world, let an appeal be made to nineteenth century Christianity, freed as it is from the miraculous, but abundant in proofs of the divine genius that still animates it, and of the Providence that still guards its hopeful and expanding life. If the old credentials no longer excite man's interest, if the past no longer stirs the anxious heart, the new proofs can not fail to arouse the sluggish spirit of the unbelieving, as well as to quicken the trembling faith of the followers of Christ. There are in Christianity besides those mentioned other sources of enthusiasm, other instruments of power; but it is needless to refer to them, as it is apparent that Christianity is practically exhaustless in its influence, and without bounds in its range of power.

Has Christianity lost its magnetism? That depotisms, paganisms, mythologies, social structures, inhuman legislation, and public vices have felt its restraining hand and surrendered to its presence, is true as applied to the past; what is its present power, and what is its hope of the future? It is not uncommon in these days to hear that Christianity is obsolete, that it has lost its power over the intellectual classes, and that its chief supporters are the priests, women, and children. He who settles into this conclusion, and will not open his eyes to all the facts, is like the man who, denying the existence of Jupiter's moons, refused to look through the telescope lest he might observe them. The mathematical progress of Christianity in these times—its undermining of great evils, its purification of public sentiment touching public conditions, and its stimulating effect on all the philanthropies, to say nothing of the increasing number of its adherents and their high social standing—contradict the assumption that it has lost its hold upon the intellect and conscience of man. Were it merely a historic religion, without adaptation to modern conditions; or did it array itself in any wise against the highest physical, intellectual, social, and religious welfare of man; or did it result in superstition, fanaticism, or mental or moral stagnation,—resistance of it would be justifiable. *It is magnetic, because it is theistic, scientific, ethical, and eschatological; it is magnetic, because it is adapted to man; it is magnetic, because it is from God.*

As a divine religion, the decadence of its exciting power is not a possibility. Its mission is to arouse the sleeping world out of its dream of security; to interrogate governments as to their legislation, and peoples as to their moral habits; to question the family as to its unity and purity; to test the Church by suffering and discipline; and to administer rebuke to all who will not obey the Gospel of the Son of God. In the execution of its projects, it will clash with selfish interests, political prejudices, secret vices, and an independent spirit, resulting in disturbance and antagonism. The power of Christianity may be measured by the antagonism it develops, as well as by the graciousness it exhibits. Let the doctrines of monotheism, incarnation, atonement, regeneration, resurrection, immortality, and future retribution be declared, and an agnostic storm ensues; let the duties of worship, faith, prayer, benevolence, and the forgiving spirit be announced, and resistance is raised; let the ministry hold up the Son of God as the Teacher, the Model, and the Judge, and infidelity croaks and seeks revenge; let the virtues of patience, humility, veracity, temperance, and peace be taught, and war breaks out and sin riots in the sun; let an assault be made on the heathen world, with no other purpose than to lift it up into the light, and false religions will contend, dictate, squirm, and die in maddened haste and rebellion; let Messiahship, miracle, and prophecy be vindicated, and the floodgates of rationalism will open wide, and vainly essay to stem the rising tide of truth; let the sacredness of the Sabbath and the sanctity of the moral law be urged, and ranting defenders of personal liberty will be multiplied; let evil be restrained and condemned, and evildoers will go insane with rage over restriction. In the work it undertakes to day, Christianity will meet with opposition as hateful in spirit, as agnostic in character, and as revengeful in purpose, as that that confronted it in Paul's time, or in any subsequent period of its history. Opposition, however, awakens its energies, stimulates its magnetic power, and leads to spiritual achievement.

It is not enough that Christianity be true; it must have the power of persuasion, of contagion, of generating and perpetuating moral enthusiasm for the sake of truth. In the exercise of this power it is not unlikely that fanatical outbreaks and superstitious movements may occur, as in the past the Crusades, papal extravagances, and sectarian institutions appeared as its fruit; but in the future its power should be the internal heat of truth, confined in its expression and development to the accomplishment of its specific mission in the world. Instead of relaxing its hold upon the intellect, it must tighten its grasp; instead of polishing the social virtues, it must purify them; instead of coquetting with "eminent men," it must elevate them to its height of vision; instead of submitting to governments, it must teach them their responsibility to God; instead of withholding its purposes, it must publish them to the ends of the earth, shaking it into loyalty, reverence, and harmony with God. The Christianity that captured the Roman Empire has the power to dictate religion to all nations, as it has the purpose to save them. If the zeal of its first disciples carried it to the isles of the sea, and planted its banners on three continents, the zeal of Christ's followers to-day, with the multiplied agencies of a Christian civilization in their hands, and with a sense of ever-widening responsibility to Gospelize the nations speedily, should introduce the millennial condition, and give victory to all of Christ's dearest hopes and divinest aims. Let Christianity become epidemic.

## CHAPTER XXX.

### THE PSEUDODOX IN CHRISTIANITY.

STRAUSS characterizes the resurrection of Jesus Christ as a historical humbug, and his ascension as a symbol, or a mere "satire." Rénan traces the story of the resurrection to Mary Magdalene, rejecting all the evidences of its credibility. Häckel repudiates the Biblical notion of a personal God as a piece of ecclesiastical fiction. Büchner boldly declares that "Christianity has but injured the spiritual and material progress of mankind," and Schopenhauer pronounces it a "pessimist religion." Of all religions, Christianity is the worst, because its falsehoods are the greatest, its misrepresentations the most fascinating, and its direct influence the most baneful. It is pessimistic, satirical, symbolical, fictitious, irrational, and oppressive. The sum of skeptical critscism is that Christianity, in its constituent elements, is a tissue of falsehoods, some so deftly and obscurely presented as to escape the detection even of those who are anxious to know the truth, while others are so transparently self-inconsistent and self-refutatory that one is amazed at the honorable reception accorded them. Its greatest so-called truths, as its theism, its incarnation, its atonement, its resurrection, its immortality, its heaven and hell, are its greatest deceptions. Christianity is thus set forth as a monstrous error, having originated in the pious imagination of Christ's followers, but perpetuated in after ages by the ecclesiastical organization known as the Church in the face of the exposure of its stupendous falsehood. The *false* in Christianity is, therefore, the subject of our inquiry.

It embraces not only the errors of creeds, but also the essential weaknesses of organic or revealed Christianity. It embraces not only the frailties of Christian organizations, but also the imperfections of Christian believers, which are persistently quoted as an embarrassment to its acceptance, and as evidence of its darkening and degrading influence in the world. Christianity is not only bad ; it is also *false*. Christianity may be viewed as *orthodox*, or, as it is popularly accepted, as a system of revealed truth ; as *heterodox*, or a variation from the orthodox ; and as *pseudodox*, or essentially and internally false, and therefore a variation from both of the preceding.

It is not at all difficult to point out defects in human religions, or errors in systems of philosophy. The Assyrian religions, embodying certain revealed truths, or truths that seem as sacred as any in the Hebrew Scriptures, were yet preliminary, and inadequate to the accomplishment of their purpose. Absorbing mythological notions— the tendency of human religions—they easily glided into fanaticism or superstition, and rather degraded than elevated their subjects. Brahminism, more stately in form, was less free from mysticism, mythology, and erratic suggestion. Buddhism, protesting against pure Brahminism, and advancing in its teachings, was as religiously enervating as the religion it opposed. Mohammedanism, superior to both, because including in its category of doctrines certain divinely accepted Christian tenets, renders itself obnoxious to the Christian world, by its surplusage of irrational and superstitious revelations. In all religions of human origin the pessimistic, the irrational, the unphilosophical, the pseudodox abound.

Likewise every philosophical system from Plato to Spencer partakes of the general debility of human speculation, and is religiously both pessimistic and pseudodox. Blemishes in human religions, weaknesses in human institutions, insufficiency in human philosophies, errors in all, we are not surprised to find; but will a religion not human in origin exhibit similar weaknesses, and be equally irrational and unphilosophical? Is Christianity a system of pseudo elements? Is it a crude, narrow, speculative religion, inadequate on account of limitation, insufficient from want of power? Or is it so manifestly perfect in its doctrinal structure, so transparently pure in its spiritual influence, so obviously divine in its origin, and so magically omnipotent in its energies, that criticism is absurd, and questioning entirely wrong?

For a religion so notably high-born as Christianity no exemption from inspection is claimed, and assertion of perfection should not be made unless it can be demonstrated. Investigation is in order to satisfy its friends, and a necessity to answer the objections with which skeptical thought has assailed it.

Much confusion has arisen in the public mind from the failure to recognize the radical difference between Gospel Christianity and Theologic Christianity, the former consisting of the essentia of the New Testament, while the latter is the human presentation of it. The one is absolute *truth*, the other absolute *belief*; and so far forth as truth and belief may be radically different, so far may original Christianity and formulated Christianity be radically different. It is clear that what passes for Christianity may be something else entirely, just as the Ptolemaic teaching passed for centuries as true astronomy.

It must also be taken into the account that the difference between the several types of Christianity is as great as the difference between any single type and Christianity itself. Papal Christianity is a single type; Protestant Christianity is a different type; and quite possibly the objections urged against the one will not at all apply to the other. The iconoclast who assails theologic Christianity might be brought to acknowledge the beauty and to discern the truth of original Christianity; and the scientist who attacks Papal Christianity, as did Prof. Draper, might be disposed to look with favor upon some Protestant form of religion. It is imperative that these distinctions be kept in mind, for the Gospel idea has been jeopardized in the confused assaults upon theologic and Papal representations of it. If all the Christianities—Gospel, Theologic, Papal, Oriental, and Protestant—were in perfect harmony in spirit, working by different methods for a common end, differing only slightly in form, and none whatever in structural elements, room for criticism would be indeed small; but the differences among them strengthen the suspicion that Christianity itself, at its very roots, is a multiplex religion, sending forth a variety of branches, bearing an endless variety of fruit, without unity of nature or the possession of common qualities. *The number of Christian religions is a standing reproof of the Christian religion.* History reveals a sectarian Christianity in opposition to original Christianity, the Roman hierarchy pointing to the former as an evidence of its departure from the truth.

Is the conglomerate religion known as Christianity identical with the revelations of the New Testament? What explanation can Protestantism, Roman Catholicism, and Oriental Sectarianism give of themselves as offshoots of Christianity? That Christianity in its development has assumed these historic forms, and that they are mutually antagonistic will not be denied; but one should be slow to infer any thing to the prejudice of Christianity on that account. The educational idea has produced Voltaire, Calvin, Shakespeare, Pollock, Latimer, Diderot, George Eliot, Byron, Ingersoll; but with all its variety of product the idea is right *per se*, and should be encouraged.

From the bosom of democracy have come treason, secession, slavery, socialism, as well as the ripest fruit of the highest civilization; democracy is nevertheless politically sound.

Carefully distinguishing between what Christianity is, and what has seemed to grow out of it, or what has been erected in its holy name, the suspicion raised against the true religion subsides. Theologic Christianity is the product of Church councils or theologians; Papal Christianity is the product of a single ecclesiastical organization; Oriental Christianity is the blossom of Eastern sectarianism; Protestant Christianity is the exponent of a revised and progressive order of religious faith. On these broad historic divisions no argument against the unity of Scriptural Christianity can be maintained.

If, however, we should consider these four-fold divisions as constituting ecclesiastical Christianity in contradistinction to original or New Testament Christianity, and should seek the marks of difference between them, we might find in the former an exaggeration of non-essential particulars, and possibly an omission of fundamental truths that would justify the charge of the false in what passes for the Christian religion. Remembering that theologic structures are the work of human builders, such a result might also be expected. Even in framing a revealed religion into form, the imperfection of human handiwork will be visible, and religion may possibly suffer by its passage into a human structure. Imperfect as the instrumental manifestation may be, it is nevertheless indispensable, both to faith and an intellectual understanding of its contents. Dogmatic Christianity is as necessary as experiential Christianity. Religion without truths is like a science without laws; and Christianity without the New Testament would be like physiology without the human body as its content and illustration.

Over Dogmatic Christianity the great historic controversies were waged, and necessarily so, for they were the violent and persistent seekings after exact truth. Certain schools, interpreting the Gospel by cast-iron rules, issued certain documentary declarations of truth; and pulpit, press, song-book, and prayer-circle have reflected these declarations, and fastened them upon the public mind. In this way theologic truth found a lodgment in human thought, and insensibly was substituted for Gospel truth. One school proclaims the sovereignty of God; another the freedom of man; another declares both to be compatible, while a fourth discovers them to be irreconcilable. Theology is thus reduced to fractions instead of wholes, and Christianity seems divided against itself. Unitarianism exalts one truth to the exclusion of other essential truths, while Trinitarianism offends the mathematical spirit of certain precise theologies. Rationalism accepts truths that may be rationally discerned, while Pauline followers appropriate those that are "spiritually discerned." Universalism removes the bars to the heavenly life, while evangelical Christianity requires a soul-fitness for the enjoyment of the delectable abode. Touching the great doctrinal truths of religion, as espoused by theology, there is no uniformity of belief, and hence no bond of union. Must theology continue to dress like an Ishmaelite? So long as the theological spirit, or the school-idea of religion is dominant, the Gospel idea of Christianity will be superseded, or at the least fail of the exalted recognition it deserves.

In another aspect theologic Christianity is at war with itself. Concerning the ordinances of the Church, there is as much division as concerning the doctrines of the Gospel, while the strife for their observance is even greater. For example, the Christian rite of baptism has been the innocent cause of much controversy and the source of feuds and alienations in Christian circles. While one ecclesiastical body concedes the validity of three forms of baptism, another recognizes the Scriptural character of but one, and goes so far as substantially to unchristianize all other bodies not in harmony with it. Is the Gospel ambiguous in its teachings, contradictory in its examples? Or is the theologic spirit in the ascendency in Church life? Concerning abstract truth one can imagine a ground for speculation, discussion, difference; but that an ordinance should provoke difference is a mystery. Yet as it was a breach of etiquette at Ems that brought on the Franco-Prussian war, so whether immersion is only a *mode* of baptism, or the *only* baptism, has convulsed Churches, nations, continents. The same spirit appears in the interpretation of the Eucharist, one ecclesiastical body insisting on the doctrine of consubstantiation, another shouting transubstantiation, another rejecting both, and interpreting the sacrament as a monumental institution with moral purposes in view. One might suppose that in a matter of so little positive value there would be no difference of opinion; but it was great enough to divide Luther and Zwingli, and it is a dividing line between Protestantism on the one hand and Roman Catholicism on the other. Over the small matters of whether the Psalms should be sung or omitted at public worship, whether one should stand or kneel when one prays, whether a musical instrument should be introduced into a church, or be cast out as offensive to pure devotion, a spirit of antagonism has been developed, and the spirit of amity, unity, and progress has been suspended. If these were questions of taste, expediency, or ecclesiastical mathematics they would not have mention here, but in the conflicts they excited an appeal was made to the Word of God, the use of an organ or a song, or a form of worship becoming a profound theological question. Christianity itself was invoked to decide.

The origin, organization, and purposes of the Christian ministry have also passed into the theological arena for settlement, and must be determined by Christian dialecticians according to exegetical rules and the genius of the interpretative spirit. This were well if the design were the protection of the sacred order from imposition; but one ecclesiastical body ordains that the Christian ministry, outside of the alleged line of apostolical succession, is illegitimate, and its pulpits are not open to such uncalled and unrobed shepherds of the flock. Even this narrow and self-centered conception, wrung from supposed Scripture, is the basis of a Churchly organization, just as the doctrine of election, equally untenable, is the basis of another, and as baptism by immersion is the corner-stone of still another. We are not writing in defense of a particular doctrine of belief, or of a particular method of ordinance-observing, or of a single method of worship, but showing how in the hands of devout men Christianity has been distorted, and even prostituted, in support of doctrines, methods, and ceremonies quite incongruous to its spirit and design. If the world must judge of Christianity wholly by its theologic aspects, it is not surprising that criticisms have arisen and are multiplying; indeed, the theologic spirit will provoke the critical spirit. If we must decide as to the nature of Christianity by the result of the attempts of Christian men to pry into the secret councils of the Almighty on the one hand, or by the quantity of water used in an ordinance on the other, then it must appear too large on the one hand and entirely too small on the other, as a religion for this world. If baptisteries, genuflections, clerical robes, mathematical reprobations, and sacramental superstitions are the outward signs of the inward religion, or the essential contents of religion, then it can hardly hope for a long future among a civilized people. The religious mind demands more than the externalism of religion. Yet the history of Church controversies reveals the deplorable fact that small matters, the anise and the cumin, have provoked as violent an agitation, and led to as unreasoning a division, both of religious sentiment and organization, as the weightier matters of Christianity. In a sense, therefore, theologic Christianity has been the source of the pseudodox in religion, as it has exalted out of all proportion those docrines and ceremonies which are by comparison with others non-essential to the purposes of religion; and by such exaltation it has given a false coloring to true Christianity and occasioned a grievous misunderstanding of its character and objects.

To even greater lengths of absurd interpretation has Papal Christianity gone in its appropriation of the Gospel, presenting it in a form scarcely recognizable by those supposed to be familiar with the teachings of its Founder. In addition to its exegetical work, it imposes traditional teaching upon its followers, and occasionally exercises the right of revealing doctrines not at all contained in the Word of God. By a varying exegesis, by old traditions, by new revelations, Papal Christianity poses as a religion as different from original Christianity as evolution is different from the Mosaic creation. According to its canons the Church is the true interpreter of the Bible ; the right of private judgment respecting revealed truth is forbidden ; and new truth must be received with the same unquestioning faith as old truth. This prepares the way for false teaching, fanaticism, intolerance, and organized assault upon opposing faiths.

The history of Roman Catholicism is in conformity to this anticipation. By virtue of its prerogative to interpret the Bible and to add to it, it has produced such doctrines as auricular confession, the Immaculate Conception, prayers for the dead, purgatory and deliverance therefrom, priestly absolution, and the infallibility of the Pope. The last is the extreme of Papal claims, the highest notch of absurd pretensions on the part of religion. The Papacy itself, with its alleged foundation in the assumed primacy of St. Peter, and its attempted exercise of divine rights from Hildebrand to Leo XIII., is a standing demonstration of the hypocrisy of Christianity, or the monstrous stupidity of Roman Catholicism. The sovereign claim of the Papacy to temporal power, by which it would appoint and depose rulers, frame the form of governments, dictate laws, and compel the subjection of nations to the Church, is a misrepresentation of the radical idea of Christianity, or Christianity is defective in its first principles. The equally supercilious claim of the Papacy to enforce its spiritual doctrines on believers and unbelievers by the threat of excommunication in this life and eternal torment after death, is pregnant with mischief as a doctrine, and has wrought dismay throughout the world. What persecution has it not authorized ? Who kindled the martyr's fires? Who established the Inquisition? Who inaugurated the massacre of St. Bartholomew? The record of that organization against so-called heresy and liberty of thought ; against civil government, popular education, and scientific research ; against the rights of conscience, and the rights of religion in general, is such as to make one tremble as one reads it, to make the Christian heart thankful that its power is broken, to make humanity ashamed that in some sense it still stands for Christianity.

Is Protestant Christianity a pseudo-religion in any respect ? Does it also partake of the liabilities of the preceding types, or is it a model exponent of Gospel elements? Considering its origin, and that uninspired men molded it into its present shape, and that the best religious minds differ from one another in exegetical construction, it is not surprising that even Protestantism is burdened with weaknesses, and supports errors which in the future it will abandon.

In breaking away from the dominion of the Roman Catholic power, Luther naturally broke away from the human authority it exercised, and held to many of the doctrines it presumed to teach. While the Reformation anchored itself in the thought of personal liberty, at the same time it inherited from the Church the spirit of its truths, many of which were Scriptural, and others only traditional, or additional to the old revelations. The inheritance was inevitable, both because Catholic teaching was not erroneous in every particular, and the dissolution of Luther's relation to the old Church had quite as much reference to authority as to doctrine. Similar instances, with similar results, have occurred elsewhere. John Wesley transferred to Methodism many of the teachings of the Church of England, whose moral reformation he strenuously sought to accomplish, but whose doctrinal character was in great part unobjectionable. Luther could not forget all that the mother Church had taught him; hence, it was natural that even by those things which he repudiated he was insensibly affected in his feelings and beliefs. From palpable errors in doctrine, and detected or authorized evils in practice, he separated himself by a distance too great to be retraced; but in matters concerning which there was room for doubt, he was somewhat under the discipline of the old life. In its early stages Protestantism showed the taint of Catholicism, and it is questionable if the Christian Church is yet entirely free from that pestilential influence. To be sure, none of the open absurdities of the corrupt religion, such as auricular confession, the legend of St. Peter, or the infallibility of the Pope, has taken root in the advanced faith; but certain superstitions made sacred by age still attach to it, whose origin is rather papistical than inherent. For instance, the dogma of "baptismal regeneration," and the doctrine of consubstantiation, are relics, so to speak, of the days when the one religion broke from the other. The observance of special days, as Palm Sunday, Easter, and Whitsuntide, not at all objectionable, is of Roman Catholic origin, and here mentioned as an illustration of the influence of the one faith on the other. The intolerance that has characterized the history of the Papal Church is reproduced in the disposition of certain Protestant bodies to ostracize all Christians from the fold of Christ who have not become members thereof by their prescribed methods, and the acceptance of their form of faith. The custom of Lent, and the clothing of ministers in robes for the duties of public worship, have been transmitted to Protestantism. While in essentials Protestantism has been successful in its separation from Latin Christianity, and the divergence is constantly growing wider, the influence of the latter upon the former is not entirely extinct; on the contrary, it is believed by many that that influence is too potent in our religious customs and forms of worship. Perhaps this relationship of custom, doctrine, and form, so objectionable now, may serve in the future as the basis of a union of the two antagonistic types of Christianity, and so justify what is now understood to be the infection of Romanism in the Christian world.

By virtue of the antagonism of these types of religion, Christianity is unfairly represented; it is supposed to be self-contradictory; it stands out as divided against itself, which can only be true of error. The union of these rival religions, which can only take place by the abandonment of traditional teaching and superstitious dogma on the part of Roman Catholicism, and a pledge of fraternity on the ground of oneness in faith touching the essentials of truth on the part of Protestantism, will do much toward correcting the popular misunderstanding of what Christianity is and what it proposes. Until the two factions come together in the spirit of harmony, each will pursue its way as if it were a different religion, and as if Christianity were also a different religion from what it is, endangering both them and it.

The exhibition of the defects of Theologic, Papal, and Protestant Christianity must now end, its purpose doubtless being apparent to the reader. Christianity is known to the world by the forms it has assumed, the fact being forgotten that the form may be false, while the original may be true. Theologic Christianity may be an error; Papal Christianity may be inherently a superstition; Protestant Christianity may be a borrowed and approximately correct religion; while original Christianity is essentially and eternally true. *The pseudodox of Christianity is the pseudodox of its various types, while the antitype of religion, or Christianity, is invulnerable in its constitution, and without a discoverable error of fact or teaching.* Herbert Spencer refers to the "Hebrew religion," meaning the entire Biblical system, as a "pseudo-religion," but Gospel Christianity, as distinguished from its types, we shall see is entirely destitute of *pseudo* elements. Separating it from the types by which it is known, it may be studied in its original character and contents, the only way, indeed, by which to discover its weaknesses, if there are any, and its excellences, if at all inherent or prominent. Is it in itself a superstition, or a truth? Does it abound in falsehoods, crudities, obsolete elements? Is it crowded with ambiguities, moral impossibilities, spiritual delusions? Is it a mystical rhapsody, an ideal hallelujah, a sentimental touchstone?  Is it religious magic?  These questions reach in all directions, bringing into the discussion the truths, the personages, the institutions, and the projects of the New Testament; for Christianity includes them all, and stands or falls with them.

What is original, or Gospel Christianity?  On opening the Bible, two religions at once are discovered, the one commonly called the Jewish, the other commonly known as the apostolic religion ; yet are they so related that the best elements of the one are reproduced in the other, and both constitute the single religion which passes by the name of Christianity.  Original Christianity is that, therefore, which, beginning with patriarchs, lawgivers, and prophets, was completed by Jesus Christ and his apostles; or, with Jesus Christ as its corner-stone, it is that religion which, including all truths made dimly known before his advent and by revelation, unfolded all essential truth from himself and by revelation, through chosen apostles, evangelists, and teachers.  Christianity is the truth, or the religion of the whole Bible, in other words.  It is this religion that is pronounced mythical by Strauss, and "pseudo" by Spencer.

In this investigation of Biblical Christianity, it is important to keep before us only its fundamental truths, for these determine its character, and are the proofs of its divine origin.  The attempt has been made to turn the incidental communism of the apostles, the single instance of feet washing, and the custom of the "holy kiss," into an argument against the Christian religion ; as well employ the fact of the existence of insects against the existence of God.  Christianity is not to be judged by the religious customs, the social states, the political ideas, or the domestic habits and private beliefs of the apostles ; it is a system of religion, founded on *revealed truth*, by which alone it can be judged, and any other judgment of it is irrelevant and superficial.

Is Christianity *philosophically false?*  No believer in the Scriptures will assert that they reveal a complete philosophical system, or that a philosophical system is at all conspicuous in the sacred volume ; but it is claimed that the philosophical revelations of the Scriptures are unqualifiedly and inherently true.  We have nothing to do with the incompleteness of such revelations; it is only important that they are *true*.  In pagan and other religions, the philosophical spirit is dominant, while the religious spirit is secondary ; in Christianity, the religious spirit is supreme, and the philosophical spirit is subordinate.  Without exception, the Hindu religions, the Druidic worship, the Persian faith, the Egyptian rituals, and the Grecian and Roman mythologies, abound in philosophic speculation concerning matter, the creation of the world, and providential government, all seeming more anxious to solve these problems than to determine man's relation to God and the conditions of a future life. In all, speculation is the rule; in Christianity, revelation is a fact. As philosophic speculations, the old religions are a failure; as a philosophic revelation, Christianity is unquestionably true.

The origin of the universe is rather a philosophic than a religious problem, yet do the Scriptures reveal it so definitely that the purest philosophy is compelled to bow to its truthfulness. Strauss sees " childishness" in the first chapter of Genesis, and reproaches Moses with ignorance of the Copernican theory; but for all that the Mosaic astronomy, the Mosaic geology, and the Mosaic cosmogony, have survived all other astronomies, geologies, and cosmogonies, and show no signs of decay and no disposition to retire. Materialistic evolution, finding Moses disputing its authority, began an assault upon his history of creation, but expired before it finished its task; while theistic evolution supported Moses, and shouted the verity of his records. Dr. McCosh, as a Christian evolutionist, sees no inherent inconsistency in the Mosaic account, and no incompatibility in it with a true idea of evolution.

Such philosophical problems as the origin of man, the origin of languages, the nature of the soul, and the existence of God, as profound as they are dignified, and as absorbingly interesting as they are comprehensive, the Scriptures determine with an exactness that astonishes the philosopher and with a fullness almost sufficient. That man is physical and spiritual, or earthly in body and divine in soul, the Scriptures teach; and what philosophy has eclipsed the teaching? Interpreting man thus, he is understood; by any other theory, he is a greater mystery than ever. The Bible does not reveal the origin of language, except as the natural property of humanity; but it does reveal the origin of the diversity of tongues. The linguistic faculty is as native to man as memory or imagination; speech is as natural as walking or seeing. But the diversity of languages is the enigma of the etymologists; yet it ought not to be. The diversity is a " confusion," a barrier to unity, the result of violated law, and the penalty of outraged justice. The philosophical fact has a moral hue, as every philosophical fact is more or less surrounded by a religious halo. Incomplete are these philosophical revelations, but, as hints or guides to truth, they are correct. *In not a single instance is a falsehood apparent.* Even if the miraculous is sometimes invoked, as an explanation of an event, as the standing still of the sun, or the dividing of the waters of the Red Sea, the philosophical spirit is not at all offended, for a miracle is a philosophical possibility, on the supposition that there is a divine sovereign, and really the temporary proof of his dominion in the natural world. Miracle is philosophically consistent with Christianity, which characterizes the creative act as miraculous, and which reveals redemption as the supernatural purpose and power of God. In its facts, in its miracles, in its projects, it is philosophically self-consistent, and absurd only to those whose infidelity is of a cast that resists truth, whether rational in form or not. Christianity is philosophically true.

Is it *doctrinally true?* Even in its doctrinal aspects, it may seem short of completeness; but, as a theological revelation, it is far in advance of itself as a philosophical revelation. Touching many things—as the nature of God, the process of regeneration, the abstract idea of immortality, and the method of the resurrection—the curious may ask questions, to which satisfactory answers are not returned by the sacred writers; but, if the revelation on these subjects is not full, it is not false. Christianity is a revelation of truths, but not an explanation of truths. Revelation is not explanation. Revelation pertains to facts; explanation pertains to processes, analyses, unfoldings, and developments. Revealing facts, it withholds explanation. The mystery of Christianity is not so much the mystery of its facts, or the mystery of what it reveals, as it is the unknowableness of what is not revealed. Revelation, so far as it goes, is not mysterious; it is the unrevealed that is mysterious and unknown. Often the charge of mystery in religion belongs only to the unrevealed, and not to the revealed. What is revealed, however, is not false.

The crucial point relates to the content of revelation. What truth is revealed? According to Dr. W. Robertson Smith, the truth of the Bible is rather a natural development than a revelation, an unfolding from simple, uncertain, and yet prophetic, forms in the earlier history of the Hebrew people, to the complete and stately proportions of New Testament doctrinal declarations. It is not incumbent upon us even to attempt to determine if Biblical truth is revealed or naturally developed truth, only so far as the claim of revelation is inseparable from the claim of truth. For, if the truth of the Bible can not be naturally developed truth, it must be revealed truth, or it is not truth. In the very nature of things, incarnation, the root-thought of Christianity, can not be an outgrowth of previous truth, except as the fulfillment of prophetic truth; but the actual fact of incarnation is not a development, but a revelation. Likewise, the atonement can not be a mere development of previous and similar truths; the fact had no predecessor, and the fact is the essence of revelation. The resurrection is not a developed truth, but a revelation. Some truths of the Bible may be accounted for by a process of development from previous seed-truths; but other truths are the product of revelation, and, while it is valuable to rescue the developed truths from the imputation of being contradictory or false, it is especially required of us to deliver revealed truths from the slightest suspicion of inherent antagonism.

In the general, it may be assumed that doctrinal truth, whether developed or revealed, involving God, the divine government, the soul, and eternal destiny, is absolutely free of inherent weakness and error. In its monotheism, in its incarnate basis, in its Messianic features, in its redemptive plan, and in its eschatological forecastings, it is invulnerable on the ground of error. Whatever the rationalist may affirm of the Old Testament, and whatever changes in interpretation the new school of Biblical critics may require, the Old Testament will remain unimpaired as the volume of truth. Mansel may apply rationalistic rules to revealed truth, and Strauss may insist that, by such rules, the whole superstructure is overthrown; but, while it changes color by the rationalizing process, it does not lose its substance or change its nature. Truth, even in apostolic hands, suffered somewhat by their inability to comprehend it. Let it be admitted that the apostles were mistaken in their views respecting the second coming of the Lord; it does not prove that the doctrine of the second advent is false. Strauss makes the mistaken apprehension of the apostles a ground of objection to the doctrine itself; but, as usual, he fails to discriminate between the truth itself and the apostolic understanding of it. Equally ignorant were the disciples of the spiritual nature of Christ's kingdom; hence, they clamored for the restoration under divine leadership of the old Israelitic kingdom; but this mistake does not make against the spirituality of the religion of Christ. In the New Testament, side by side, are mistaken notions of Jews, Greeks, Romans, disciples, and apostles, and the truths of which the mistaken notions are entertained. The notions may be false; the truths themselves are still unassailable.

Contradictory doctrines are supposed to be taught in the Biblical documents, and are explained on the ground that Biblical truth is a development, which, in its various stages of unfolding, and affected by its environment, occasionally reversed itself and even turned a somersault, but, recovering itself, went on, and in its final form appears substantially and honestly correct. A developed truth may exhibit the scars of the developing process; a revealed truth can not be self-contradictory. Self-contradiction is destructive of the idea of revelation. Such ideas as the sovereignty of God and the freedom of the human will; the omniscience of the Deity and the doctrine of foreordination; the goodness of God and the reign of evil; divine knowledge and human prayer; personality, or human identity, and regeneration, faith, and rationalism,—are supposed to be among the contradictory teachings of Christianity. Because of apparent irreconcilable elements in such and similar truths, Schleiermacher proposed the Compromise Theology, or the suggestion that, by mutual concessions on both sides, the truth would be found in a moderate opinion of the great mysteries. Truth, however, is positive or negative; it is not a compromise between mysteries. Tholuck struck the key-note of a settlement when he said that, "truth is not in the middle, but at the bottom." It is always at the bottom, at the foundation of things. The foundation can not be true and false; contradiction is impossible; mystery is possible. If, then, these truths are apparently antagonistic and can not be reconciled, it is a proof that they have not been clearly revealed; they are revealed so far that we know them to be truths, but so dimly revealed are some of them that, like cathartic and emetic, they pull in contrary directions. In such a dilemma, no one would be justified in proclaiming either truth to be false; he would be justified in saying he did not quite understand them.

By a like process other doctrines or teachings are brought into conflict, and the unity of Christian truth is sought to be disturbed. Consciousness after death and soul-sleeping; eternal punishment and annihilation of the wicked; one probation only, and a renewed chance hereafter; baptismal regeneration and the "new birth;" Unitarianism and Trinitarianism; Predestination and Universalism; Prescience and Contingency,—these, supposed to be supported by the Scriptures, are submitted as evidences that the Scriptures themselves furnish the proof against their own inspiration, and that they do not reveal truths.

To this presentation of contradictory ideas in the New Testament the reply may be brief but definite, and in substance the reply to the apostolic misunderstanding of truth. *What the truth is, and what the human understanding of the truth is, are two different facts* ever to be remembered in the study of Christianity. More than once the Bible has been employed in defense of polygamy, slavery, war, intemperance, and Sabbath-breaking, when, without controversy, its unit idea is monogamy, freedom, peace, temperance, Sabbath-keeping, and salvation. More than once has it been turned to the defense of two Sabbaths, two resurrections, two or three regenerations, three or four forms of Church governments, a multitude of Church worships, and many ecclesiastic creeds. The Bible is quoted by every body to sustain every thing, as if it were on all sides of all questions, showing the wealth of its revelations, but the almost universal misunderstanding of its truths. The apostles misunderstood and prepared ascension robes; the Athenians misunderstood and laughed at

Paul; the Pharisees misunderstood and crucified Christ; the Papacy misunderstood, and what errors flowed; Pusey misunderstood, and Sacramentarianism followed; Calvin misunderstood, and predestination sat on a pedestal at the front door of the Church, smiling at the few, frowning upon the many; Socinus misunderstood, and the Unitarian germ grew; Orson Pratt misunderstood, and polygamy flourished; Luther misunderstood, and consubstantiation ruled at the altar, and converted the Eucharist into a semi-cannibalistic feast. The misunderstandings respecting the Scriptures are the misunderstandings of men; the supposed contradictions of the Scriptures are the contradictions of the human mind in its effort to explore mysteries not revealed; and the errors of Christianity are the errors of theology. The truths of Christianity, separated from the errors of theology, are truths still; and, even allowing a want of harmony among its mysteries, its revealed facts can still resist the imputation of being false.

Is Christianity *religiously* false? The estimate that forgets that Christianity is a religion, and not a philosophy or a theology, is narrow, and falls short of a true appreciation of its internal spirit. Even if true in its philosophic revelations, and harmonious as a theologic system, it is of little value if it is false in its religious teachings and revelations. True as a religion, if proven false as a philosophy, no great harm is done; but prove it false as a religion and true as a philosophy, and the world sinks hopelessly in darkness.

As a revelation of religious truth, complaint has been made that it is utterly unsatisfactory, even if trustworthy, by reason of the reserve it maintains respecting the problems in which the human mind has the highest interest. It reveals some things, but is silent touching other things equally important. It veils the truth quite as often as it exposes it. It pretends to make known, but withholds at the critical point of interest. This is an old complaint with a good foundation; that is, it is true that Christianity is far from being a complete revelation of truth. Touching spiritual processes, the nature of God, the ministry of evil, the state of the dead, and even the final condition of the race, there is not a revelation such as satisfies the curious, or knowledge such as can dispense with faith. The reason for the silence of the Scriptures on these subjects, as given by Dr. A. P. Peabody, namely, that it is because of the poverty of human language to express the divine thoughts, and that they are " beyond the range of any teaching of which we are susceptible," we regard insufficient; for the human mind is capable of a much larger understanding of truth than it is possible to possess under the present limitations of revelation. We can know more if permitted to know.

The limitation of revelation is not so much owing to the imbecility of the human mind as to the wisdom of the divine Mind, which must regard further knowledge as unnecessary to the purposes of the present life.

Not a few critics have been disturbed by the apparently borrowed character of many New Testament truths, such as the Logos of John, the Law-Gospel of Paul, and the Rabbinical traditions of Christ, compromising, as they allege, the inspirational character of the truth, and so implicating it in hypocrisy. Speaking of John's Gospel, Mr. Alger says: "There is scarcely a single superhuman predicate of Christ which may not be paralleled with striking closeness" from the "extant works" of Philo, a "Platonic Jewish philosopher." It is true that Philo employs such words as "Logos" and the "first-begotten" in his writings, and it seems as if John had appropriated them, but the appropriation of phrases, popular words, proverbs, and teachings in no sense affects the question of the inspiration of John's Gospel, or of the New Testament. Paul resorts to Jewish idioms to express Christian ideas, and Christ turns to the Greek language for the most striking words to convey the truths that constitute the substance of religious teaching; but because philosophers, poets, mystics, Gnostics, Jews, and Greeks furnished words, phrases, and even sentences for the conveyance of Christian truth, it does not follow that Christianity is derived from Philo, Plato, Homer, or others, who may have coined the word thus appropriated. The doctrine of inspiration is compatible with the use of any word that properly expresses the truth, whether the word be pagan or otherwise.

If it is meant that the doctrines of the New Testament are plagiarized from the philosophers, and, therefore, can not pose any longer as revealed truths, a more serious aspect envelops the inquiry. Such a supposition is likely to arise from a superficial comparison between Philo and John; but when it is remembered that John's aim in part was to counteract the prevailing Gnosticism of the age, and in part to exalt Christ to his true position as the Son of God, the use of terms and ideas prevalent in philosophical circles is at once explained. But to assume that John's Logos is Philo's Logos is an inexcusable assumption; to assume that incarnation, atonement, regeneration, resurrection, and immortality are borrowed doctrines, can safely be met by denial or a demand for proof. As the ark of the tabernacle was carried about in carts, so divine thoughts were conveyed in human vehicles wherever found, and without loss of their original character.

Strauss intimates that many of the so-called virtues of Christianity belonged to previous religions and philosophies, as compassion to

Buddhism, and assistance of enemies to Stoicism, as if it made somewhat against Christianity as an original religion, to find it inculcating the same. None but a dotard will claim an entire destitution of moral principle in other religions; they had a mission; they taught some truths and illustrated some virtues; but it is the glory of Christianity that it magnified the obscure virtues of other religions, and added truths of which they had no types or foreshadowings. The virtues of Christianity, however, are not borrowed virtues; they are such as human nature in its best mood authorizes, or such as spring directly from the teachings of Christ. It is remarkable that if the Christian virtues are culled from other religions, only the true and exalted virtues were selected, for suicide, falsehood, murder, theft, and even parricide are justifiable under certain conditions in other religions. The omission of such virtues from the Christian religion is proof of the inspiring influence that guided in the selection of those which it inculcates.

It has been observed, too, that what are regarded as honorable worldly virtues are not enumerated among *religious* virtues in the New Testament. Rénan points out that heaven is not promised as the reward of military glory, and that religion has been impeached for its alleged silence touching the virtue of patriotism and the glory of political fidelity. Christianity is a religion; its virtues are religious; it does not exalt worldly achievements, or those earthly conditions and honors to which the ambitious aspire. It is a misapprehension, however, that it does not enjoin faithfulness in civil life and loyalty to civil government, for Christ said, "Render to Cæsar the things that are Cæsar's," and Paul ordered obedience to the powers that be. Worldly duties, however well performed, can not be substituted for religious duties, and the worldly spirit can not stand for the religious spirit; this is the lesson of the New Testament.

Strauss has a routine way of disposing of the truths of Biblical Christianity, as if they were literally false. The "so-called" fall of man he pronounces a "didactic poem;" the ascension of our Lord is a symbolical representation of an idea, but to speak of it as an "actual occurence is to affront educated people at this time of day;" and all the so-called truths of the religion are symbols of ideas which admit of a "moral application." Even if the Gospel, as a whole, is pure symbol, it represents something, which must be literally true. If the symbol is not the truth, the truth is back of it, or the symbol itself is false.

Admitting that the Gospel is a symbol, the next step is to find the truth which it symbolizes, but Strauss goes not so far back. He denounces the truth, and thinks to reduce the Gospel to a shadow by reducing it to a symbol; but in the name of honesty we demand to know what it symbolizes if not the very truth he denounces. The idea of a symbol is that it is a representative of something, but if the existence of the something is denied, then it is a solecism to use the word symbol at all. Strauss is driven into a corner by his jugglery of words.

Christianity is the religion of mysticism, it is affirmed, and, there fore, unreal in its contents. Let it be said that it is a religion of spiritual forces, acting on the spiritual nature of man, and the origin of the suspicion of its mystical character is revealed. It is invisible force which the natural mind can not comprehend; it is by experience a renovation of the consciousness which unspiritual minds do not realize, and, therefore, it is pronounced whimsical and erroneous. In the days of Plotinus Christianity took the form of mysticism, but it is as improper to brand it a mystical religion on that account as it would be to define it a system of rationalism because Cousin, a Christian believer, was a rationalist. There is no more mysticism in Christianity proper than in the transcendentalism of Emerson or the evolution of Spencer.

Is not Christianity an *ambiguous system* of religion? If so, ambiguity may be found in its teachings, purposes, and agencies, the search for which must be immediately made. Ambiguity implies want of clearness, and allows double interpretations, which signify uncertain meaning and possible contradictions. Not a little effort will be required to establish such a charge against the teachings of Christ and his apostles. The doctrine of the Trinity, more mysterious than any other in the New Testament, and apparently based on a violated mathematical principle, is free from ambiguity, except in ambiguous minds. It has no double meaning; it does not mean one of several repugnant alternatives. It implies the mystery of relation, but is not a self-contradiction. Neither the atonement, nor the resurrection of Christ, can be overthrown on the score of ambiguous meaning. Even the incarnation, with its unnatural process, is unambiguous; it is overwhelming because of its magnitude. Running through the category of doctrine we would find that, mysterious as some teachings are, they are unlike the pagan oracles, whose answers admitted of every possible construction, and whose glory was their obscurity of form.

As to its purposes, Christianity is as transparent as day. To redeem the world from sin is its supreme object. Unambiguous in doctrine, unambiguous in purpose, it is equally unambiguous in its resources and agencies. Said the Master to his disciples: "All power is given unto me in heaven and in earth;" "go ye, therefore, and teach all nations." Heavenly and earthly power join in the prosecution of the purposes of Christianity. There is no ambiguity here. Is not Christianity *optimistic*, utopian, dreamy, a *self-deceived*, and *deceiving, system* of religion? Is it not a visionary, fanatical, superstitious system, and doomed to defeat? That its undertaking is superhuman, requiring resources that are inexhaustible, a patience that knows no intermission, and a hope that is everlasting, can not be doubted; but what would be fanaticism in other religions is reality in Christianity. It is not the religion of false hopes, but of prospective triumph through the aid of the higher powers. It is the outlook of Christianity that answers all insinuations of utopianism, and turns slowly into history the impossible.

*The pseudodox in Christianity is yet to be found. It is not in its philosophical revelations; it is not in its doctrinal revelations; it is not in its religious revelations; it is not in Moses, Paul, Christ; it is not in the Old Testament, and it is not in the New Testament;* if anywhere, it is in the forms of Christianity, which will do well to take heed to themselves, and return to the fountain-head for healing, purification, and blessing.

---

# CHAPTER XXXI.

## THE DIAGNOSTIC OF CHRISTIANITY, OR EXPERIENCE THE PHILOSOPHIC TEST OF RELIGION.

WHEN the Emperor Trajan was passing through Antioch, Ignatius seized the opportunity of advocating in his presence the Christian religion, well knowing that it would end in his martyrdom. He explained his title—*Theophorus*—as meaning a person "who has Christ in his heart," and, when pressed for a more definite statement, confessed in specific terms that he carried the Deity with him, or partook of his nature and life. For this strange confession the holy man was condemned to the amphitheater of wild beasts in Rome, and joyfully suffered a martyr's death in expectation of a martyr's crown.

The religion of Ignatius is the religion of Christianity—the religion of experience, or the new reality of consciousness, a study of which involves an inquiry into its origin, processes of development, contents, or categories of facts and laws, and relation to character and destiny. That Christianity, either as a truth, or as a life-imparting power, may be incorporated with individual history, becoming its inspiration, regeneration, sanctification, or its guiding and redemptive source, the Scriptures certainly teach, and teach it as the vital and final test of the truth of religion.

To make clear this statement, as well as to enforce it, we must distinguish between the tests applied to other religions and philosophies, and this exceptional and sufficient test of Christianity. The common test of religions is their history in their relation to civil government, domestic life, individual pursuits, and literary achievements of the people adopting them, together with the moral life produced by them. The historic test is the time-test of all things, of nature as well as religion, of God as well as man. In its light we may read of Brahminism and Platonism, of theocracy and democracy, of civilization and barbarism, of skepticism and Mohammedanism, of all religions, all philosophies, all beings, all things. To this primordial test Christianity must likewise submit. Its history of facts, relations, incidents, truths, and effects; its prophecies, miracles, methods of growth, and plans of conquest; its adaptations, powers, promises, and certainties, make an argument of irresistible strength in its own defense. Tested by history Christianity is a surviving and fulfilling religion.

Another common test of religions is the character and number of their followers. If the cultured classes accept a form of religion; if the thinkers of the age, scientists, poets, historians, and philosophers, may be quoted as the friends of a particular religious faith; if kings and queens are its honest promoters and defenders, then it may boast of an influential, though by no means a conclusive, argument. On this estimable ground Christianity may appeal with great confidence for the world's favor. Its followers are not only numerous and increasing every day, but they are also from the best classes and the highest ranks in human society. Christianity is the religion of the school, as well as the street; it is the religion of culture, as well as ignorance; in palaces as in hamlets, in the homes of luxury as in the dwelling-places of poverty, are those equally ready to die for Immanuel. The martyr-spirit is still in the Church and the world.

A more specific test of the vitality of religion, to which all religions prefer more or less to appeal, is the supernatural character of their teachers, or teachings; that is, the religion must appear to be supernatural. Never has a religion gone forth as purely, or exclusively, of human origin. In a sense it must appear to be from God; it must expose a supernatural stamp. For this reason every religion, however incongruous in its teachings, abounds with the marvelous, the naturally impossible, the miraculous; the *supernatural is essential to religion.* If the religion is essentially false, absurdities, crudities, superstitions, and hypocrisies are employed to meet the demand for the supernatural; it must introduce the supernatural in form or by pretense, or perish.   As might be expected, while the historic test is exposing the hollowness of the supernatural claim of many religions, the supernatural character of Christianity is becoming more luminous with the passage of the centuries; as others expire, it survives and unfolds.   Claiming to be strictly supernatural in its Founder, teachings, mission, and results, it is demonstrating itself with the lapse of time, and stands or falls as this claim is maintained.

Neither history, social support, nor supernatural claim, nor all together, furnish unanswerable testimony to the truth of Christianity. To such proofs other religions resort; such proofs Christianity employs; but they now begin to diverge, Christianity employing a proof not possible to other religions, and standing alone in its appeal to it.   *The proof of experience is the philosophic proof of Christianity.* When a German thinker assumes that religion "is nothing more nor less than a belief in conflict with experience," he exhibits an ignorance both of what religion is as a system of truth, and of what it is by experience.   When Spencer alleges that the "subject-matter" of religion is that which passes the "sphere of experience," he exhibits the same ignorance.   When Hume objected to a miracle on the alleged ground that it is contrary to experience, he was ignorant of what he was saying, and misunderstood both miracle and experience.   His argument, refuted as often as it has been repeated, is valuable only for the single thought that experience is a test of particular truths, or, comprehending more than Hume intended, the test of religion.   If the test of miracle is experience, then the religion which miracle supports may also be tested by experience.

The experience-philosophy of modern times can not object to the application of its particular dogma to ascertain the validity or soundness of religious truth, or religion.   A philosophic treatment of religion requires that it be submitted to the philosophic test of human experience.   Galen, the physician, regarded experience as the source of knowledge.   In accord with the physician, we affirm that an experience of Christianity is the key to a knowledge of it, and the means of its verification, and that if it is impossible to experience it its claim to a supernatural origin is invalidated.   If its addresses to the soul awaken no response; if its attempted reconstruction of character turns out to be superficial and delusive; if it does not become a fact of consciousness; then it must surrender its claims, and yield to other religions.   By the one test it rises or falls.

Before deciding upon the nature of religious experience, or determining the categories of religious consciousness, it is important to understand what it is that experience proposes to test and establish. Without reviewing religions, it is evident that "natural religion," and the "religion of humanity," justify themselves partly on the ground of their alleged harmony with experience, and that, if the test of experience is supreme, they must be accepted as genuine religions. So far as natural religion is based upon the facts of nature, such as the unity of the universe, the laws governing planetary motion and life, the correlation of forces, and the conservation of energy, it is a legitimate religion; and, so far as the religion of humanity is in harmony with the highest intuitions of the soul, it is a legitimate religion. It is not clear, however, that natural religion is within the sphere of experience, or that even the so-called religion of humanity, which may include æsthetics and morality, enters into consciousness, and becomes the subject-matter of the inner life. The facts of natural religion are within the scope of observation, or objective experience. They lie outside the inner life, and are foreign to a subjective experience. Christianity belongs to the subjective realm, addresses the spirit of man, and takes root in the invisible life within. Natural truth may be tested by objective experience; supernatural truth, by subjective experience ; and one is as reliable as the other. If the fact of gravitation may be tested by the objective experience, or objective mind, the fact of regeneration may be tested by the subjective experience, or subjective mind. As the highest experience is subjective, so the highest truth which it tests must be supernatural. The province of experience, as a test of truth, natural and supernatural, is, therefore, clearly defined, and its application to Christianity in its supernatural character is certainly admissible.

As a system of religious truth, Christianity may be tested by experience. This does not mean that every truth of the Bible may be subject to the same test, for the scientific order of creation, as given by Moses, the miracle at the Red Sea, the fall of Jericho at the sound of horns, and the victory of Elijah on Carmel, are not within the range either of our objective or subjective experience; they may be vindicated, however, by other and adequate tests. But the religious truths of Christianity may be comprehended, tested, and sustained by subjective experience; in other words, revealed religion may be vindicated by the subjective, as natural religion is vindicated by the objective, experience.

Nor is it meant that Christianity, in its wholeness as truth, may not be defended and maintained by other methods than that from experience. Either of two methods of reasoning, or both, have been and may be employed in the investigation and development of religious truth, and in a rational exposition of Christianity they can not

43

be ignored. Inductive reasoning, or that method which Bacon applied in the investigation of physical facts, and which led him from particular facts to universal truths, and deductive reasoning, which implies the application of a universal principle to a particular fact, may be employed in the ascertainment of the fundamental truths of Christianity. By these methods, explanations, defenses, and vindications without number of revealed religion are possible.

While Christianity is a truth, it must not be forgotten that, according to its own teaching, it is a *revealed* truth, and therefore is not a first or primary truth. Some of the truths of revealed religion, as the monotheistic idea, are primary; but Messianic truth is not primary, it is revealed. As Christianity is a revealed system of truth, the usual criteria of truth, in reasoning or otherwise, can not be applied to it. Leibnitz insists that a characteristic of fundamental truth is its *necessity*. Necessity looks out of a mathematical axiom; but internal necessity does not belong to Christian truth. Self-evidence is another supreme characteristic; but many truths of Christianity are not self-evident. They require illumination, analogy, explanation, before they can be believed, and even then many reject them. The ball is round—this is self-evident so soon as one observes it. Immortality is not a self-evident truth, nor atonement, nor incarnation. They need to be demonstrated or revealed. According to Dr. McCosh, "*universality* is the tertiary test" of fundamental truth. All men believe in such truth. Revealed religion can not bear this test; it is not a summary of fundamental or first truths. By these criteria Christianity is not to be judged. It is a revelation; inductively and deductively, it may be vindicated, but its supreme test or criterion is *experience*.

The test of revelation or supernatural truth is its involution in experience. Truth is clear only as it is apprehended by the consciousness. An intellectual perception of truth is incomplete, being preliminary to further unfoldings and analyses; but one may be deluded by the belief that a mathematical or intellectual study of supernatural truth is all that is required. A skeptic may apply intellectual tests, with mathematical precision, to such truth, and seem to detect error in its substance and to its very center. He may be in the neighborhood of truth, and not find it, as one may sail over the ocean, ignorant of the pearls in its depths. Supernatural truth takes a concrete form in the Scriptures, but they must be searched, studied, analyzed, if the truth be found. The truth is there, but hidden like law in matter; it is there, but flashes as a mystery, and requires searching; it is there, but like oxygen in the atmosphere, and ages may come and go before it is known. Abbé Winkleman, in his exhortation to students of art to study the Apollo Belvidere as a model of beauty, observed that at first they might not discover any beauty in it; but they must study it again and again, "for," he said, "I tell you there is beauty there." The traveler stands in the presence of the pyramid of Cheops, disappointed at first with its apparent want of magnitude; but, as he walks around it, enters its labyrinthine passages, and ascends to the summit, he is overwhelmed with its proportions, and pronounces it the greatest architectural pile of man. Thus Christianity, as a system of truth, does not impress the soul at first as supernatural; or, if supernatural touches are felt, they are not comprehended; the whole is seen in diminished aspects; but, as one becomes receptive and sympathetic, *en rapport* with truth, it unfolds, enlarges, and begins to carry him beyond himself, until he gazes upon things not possible to describe, and is finally lost in the mysteries of the eternal.

In its process of development the greatest truths are glimpsed, appreciated, and determined, as Monotheism, Providence, Messiaship, Regeneration, Responsibility, and the Future Life. They stand as the central facts of religion, and are appropriated by the intellectual investigator as the key to all else that may be found. Revealing truth, Christianity emphasizes itself as an intellectual religion; it satisfies the aspiration of mind for truth; it quickens intellectual inquiry, and leads human thought through the mazes of mystery and obscurity into the clear sunlight of the highest truth. An intellectual religion, or a religion that conducts the mind to truth, or flashes the truth upon the mind, must be true; a religion that reveals God, with all that belongs to the one great idea of God, must be from God; a religion that reveals a Messiah, with all that grows out of Messiahship, must be divine; a religion that is new to man, pointing out the way of restoration to intellectual greatness, can not be of man, but must have an eternal or supernatural source. Such a religion is Christianity.

An intellectual or truth-revealing religion, however valuable, is not altogether sufficient. An experience of religion involves more than an intellectual knowledge of religion; that is, there is a difference between an intellectual and a spiritual apprehension of the truth. Christianity is not only truth; it is also *life*. As truth, it appeals to the mind; as life, it quickens the soul. As truth, it is light; as life, it is power. Embracing religious truth, the mind is enlarged, and reaches at once into the infinities; receiving supernatural life, the soul opens its gaze upon God, and expands into God as the ages roll and eternity dawns. The former is a necessary experience; the latter is the greater experience, as life is better than light. A more prominent contrast arises between the exclusive nature of

Christianity as an intellectual religion and its exclusive nature as a spiritual religion. As an intellectual religion it does not include itself as a spiritual religion; as a spiritual religion it does include itself as an intellectual religion. One may accept Christianity in the intellectual, and not in the spiritual sense; but if one accept it in the spiritual, he must also in the intellectual sense. The intellectual does not include the spiritual; the spiritual includes the intellectual.

A spiritual experience of truth, or a deep, inviolable instinct of religion, Christianity begets, and demonstrates itself by its spiritually begetting power. Other religions may inspire intellectual reverence for truth, but they are incapable of negotiating spiritual relations with God. Philosophy asserts truth to be the objective end of its pursuit; but of spiritual truth it has no conception, and really denies its existence. As explained by the modern philosophic teacher, religious experience is a refined state of the emotional life, or a regulation of the sentiments by certain religious principles, which may be pronounced mystical, fanatical, or superstitious, as the investigator is inclined. Intellectual experience or intellectual perception of truth is granted; emotional experience, or the emotional assent to religious truth, is possible; but spiritual experience, or the sympathetic union of the soul with truth by which it is regenerated and sanctified, is held to be an assumption, requiring proof.

Is spiritual experience a fiction or a reality? This is a root-question, determining the validity of Christianity as a spiritual religion. The genuineness of so-called spiritual experience is sometimes questioned on the supposition that it is exclusively emotional in its character, and that vacillation and superficiality, characteristics of an emotional religion, are not the appropriate signs of a supernatural religion. Matthew Arnold pronounces the spiritual state as exclusively moral in character, but intensified by emotion in action. It is granted that Christianity is an emotional religion, but it is believed that that which belongs to it as an emotional religion invalidates its claim as a spiritual religion. The two are held to be incompatible; they can not co-exist in the same soul at the same time. As an emotional religion, Christianity is trustworthy, because the emotional nature of man is trustworthy. The spirit of fear that seizes one when in danger and leads to an escape from it, is not a disadvantageous spirit; the spirit of hope that leads one on through reverses until one wins again, is a most helpful spirit. In their relation to character, the emotions are fundamental, and if religion works in and by the emotions, or interacts with the emotional nature, it has quite as strong a hold upon man as when it interacts with his intellectual nature. Without the emotional nature man would be as cold as a marble statue, and without religion the emotional nature would involve man in moral anarchy. Buckle has said that "the emotions are as much a part of us as the understanding; they are as truthful, they are as likely to be right. They have their logic and their method of inference."

Now, if Christianity works itself into the emotions, eliminating all carnal tendency, and subjects them to spiritual discipline and transformation, a government of self-control is at once installed over the life, the advantages of which can not be computed. What is life? Is it thinking, or feeling, or both? What is thought but a state of consciousness? What is sensation but an expression of consciousness? Christianity, as thought, finds its way into the thinking of men, and is an intellectual religion; Christianity, as life, finds its way into the sensibilities of men, and is an emotional religion. Perhaps its greatest work is on the emotional nature, which, even more than the intellectual, is in need of repair and purification. It touches first the springs of life, and careers through the hopes and fears, the desires and affections, the appetites and lusts of men, casting out, restraining, refining, and regulating, until the emotions are as obedient to spiritual law as the restless seas to physical law. Religion, says Julius Muller, is affectionate communion with God. It is the alliance of the affections or the emotional life, purified and renewed, with God! The sources of life are corrupt, the thinking, feeling, and acting of men bearing witness to the corruption. Christianity strikes for the center of being, involving radical changes in the intellectual and emotional natures, bringing the one into harmony with truth, and the other into sympathy with purity.

Spiritual experience, involving both the intellectual and emotional, is higher than the one and deeper than the other; it is more profound than intellectual conviction and more permanent than emotional assertion. It is a transformation of the inner life, of which thought and feeling are reliable exponents; it is more than knowledge, it is more than emotion; it is the essence of life, of which spirit-power is the best exponent. Adequately to understand spiritual experience, its categories or the contents of spiritual life must be enumerated and so placed that it will stand as a separate experience, both from the intellectual and emotional states which religion superinduces. Truth apprehended spiritually appears differently from the same truth apprehended intellectually or emotionally. In the latter, the forms of truth only are perceived; in the former, the essence of truth is cognized and appropriated.

The foundation of experience is consciousness. By consciousness we mean, using Leibnitz's suggestion, the central monad, or the unit

of being with psychical predicates, or the permanent sensation of
life.   Within the life-center, or upon the psychical unit, a spiritual
work is excited and performed, resulting in the spiritual intensity of
being and the purification of the life-ground.   As the spiritual work
is within the realm of life, so its first recognition will be by the life
itself, or consciousness.   The source of spiritual knowledge is not intellectual inquiry or emotional states, but the introspective search
of consciousness, *the affidavit of life to life.*   Sir William Hamilton
defines consciousness as a "comprehensive term for the complement
of our cognitional energies."   Dr. James Rush employs consciousness
as "a term to signify the knowledge which the mind has of its own
operations."   Dr. Porter says, "Natural consciousness is the power
which the mind naturally and necessarily possesses of knowing its
own acts and states."   Consciousness is the region of spiritual life,
and the source of spiritual knowledge.   As it embraces the whole
life, it also embraces changes in the life, and an apperception of the
changes as and when they are wrought.   The first revelations of
spiritual life are to consciousness; afterward, to the various mental
faculties and the various emotional conditions of being.

The degree of revelation of spiritual life to consciousness can not
be fully stated.   The Roman Catholic Church holds that the soul is
not conscious of spiritual regeneration, which it teaches is effected by
the manipulation of the priesthood, and must be accepted by faith on
the part of the subject.   This is the doctrine of *unconscious* spiritual experience, which so infuriated Luther that it not only drove him from
the old Church, but also led him to proclaim the doctrine of a conscious salvation and a conscious union with Christ.   The recognition
of spiritual life by the consciousness is the testimony to its existence,
and an absolute necessity in the nature of the work involved.   All
the contents of consciousness may not be recognized by the understanding, but so radical a work as the regeneration of the consciousness can not occur without the consent of the understanding, and
without the knowledge of the subject in whom the work is wrought.
Experience is the outgrowth of consciousness, as consciousness is the
ground of experience.   Schleiermacher taught that "religion is not a
system of dogmas, but an *inward experience,*" which is the same thing
as saying it is the experience of consciousness.

This goes to the roots of being; this gets into the depths of life.
Behind consciousness, one can not go; as far back as consciousness,
religion must go, or its work is superficial.   The sinfulness of human
nature, or the recognition of an internal evil principle, in man is
one of the categories of religious experience.   To establish the fact
of the reign of evil in the world, it is not difficult; but to establish

the reign of evil in personal life, some proof is required. Prior to his departure, the Master assured his disciples that, after his separation from them, the Spirit would come and "reprove the world of sin," conveying the idea that, through the Spirit's ministry, sin would be fully recognized. To "reprove" means to lay bare, expose, demonstrate. The Master meant that the Spirit would demonstrate to human consciousness the fact, nature, processes, and effects of sin, and powerfully incline the mind to its contrary, holiness. Philosophy failed in its knowledge of the nature of sin. In ancient times it knew not what sin is, and in modern times it apprehends not the nature of the world's irregularity. Falsehood, jealousy, revenge, murder, suicide—these philosophy has sanctioned, because evil as evil was not properly discovered. To assume that evil is the friction between matter and spirit, or that it emerges from the struggling character of spirit, is not fully to define it. A demonstration to the consciousness of what sin is in essence, in its relation to God, in its bearing on the divine government, and in its effect on character, is required if it be understood; and Christianity furnishes the demonstration in the offices of the Holy Spirit and the revelations of the Sacred Word. In this respect, Paul eclipses Plato, and John Wesley reveals more than Emerson. Religious experience, or the passage into spiritual life, involves the full recognition of the character of sin, with its consequences and relations.

To the problem of sin is annexed the problem of atonement or redemption, and a demonstration of the one is accompanied by a revelation of the other. Spiritual recognition of sinfulness is followed by a spiritual recognition of atonement. Christianity reveals both the fact of sin and the remedy for it. One's spiritual eyes opened, the Cross is as quickly discerned as the Pit. The dreadful thought of ruin is succeeded by the exhilerating hope of recovery. First apprehending the atonement as a historic fact, the consciousness admits it into personal relations, and feels its uplifting power. From that moment the atonement is no longer a historical event, but a personal fact; no longer an external achievement, but an internal experience. The transformation of the external fact into internal character, or a historic event taking root in human consciousness, or truth converted into life, is a most wonderful event in human experience. It is the crisis of eternity respecting the individual, or the crisis of the individual respecting eternity. Yet atonement is a category of spiritual experience.

The full accomplishment of the redemptive agency of Christianity terminates in the holiness of the subjects in whom it has unrestricted operation. *Holiness is the chief characteristic of the Christian, as it is the*

*central idea of revelation, and the exalted grace of Deity.* It is the outcome of Christianity. Constantine clothed himself in a white garment
for baptism, and in his last years slept on a white bed, in token of
the holiness which religion required, and to which he sincerely
aspired. Religion is holiness; holiness is religion. Christianity is the
one only as it is the other. In that mystical spirit for which the
Pythagoreans were famous, they symbolized righteousness by the
number three, some say by the number five, and others by the number nine, intending that, whatever number was used as the symbol,
it should represent the idea of completeness, harmony, and unity.
Righteousness is spiritual harmony with spiritual things; it is the
ground of spiritual unity in the universe; it is the source of completeness in mankind.

It is regretted that the theological schools do not agree touching
righteousness as a fact of experience, for one insists upon the doctrine
of "imputed righteousness," as contrary to the idea of inherent
righteousness, and another, more rationally and Scripturally, upon
the doctrine of "imparted righteousness," or an inwrought experience
of holiness as the condition of final salvation. A unity of view on
the basis of experience is certainly desired. Imputed righteousness is
an object of faith; imparted righteousness the subject-matter of experience. Both are consistent; the former may exist without the
latter; the latter can not exist without the former; hence, it is more
comprehensive and just as personal on one side as it is divine on the
other. A personal divine righteousness or holiness, the glowing factor
of the divine nature, concreted in human personality, is the possible
heritage of a believer in Jesus Christ. This is the consummation of
religion, the flower of experience.

In this connection, the following question seems to be relevant:
Is the supernatural element in experience the root or the crown of
the moral life? Does religious experience originate in a supernatural
impulse? or, springing out of a religious germ within man, does it
terminate in its development in a supernatural character? Dr. Martineau assumes that the supernatural is the crown of the religious
life; we assume that it is the *root* of all religious experience. Without a supernatural beginning, religious experience is wholly impossible; without the root, there can be no crown. The attempt to separate root and crown, or distinguish between the religious elements in
the initial stages of experience and the consummation in holiness, is
likely to involve one in a misunderstanding of the whole subject, as
it is an attempt to separate similars and disjoin the essential extremes
of a developed religious life. The inception of experience is the
prophecy of its fulfillment; the beginning is the root of the develop-

ment; and the consummation is the completion of what existed in the earliest stages of experience. The beginning is holiness in an embryonic state; the consummation is holiness completed. The root is holiness; the crown is holiness. *Holiness, root and crown, is a category of experience.*

As the play of Hamlet is impossible without Hamlet, so Christianity is impossible without Christ. Christianity is Christ. Any consideration of the one presupposes the consideration of the other, and any religious experience, rooted in or related to the one, bears a corresponding relation to the other. One of the categories of experience must be Messiahship, the spiritual center of religion. Without Christ, incarnation, atonement, resurrection, immortality, are fables; with him, they are living truths, to be preached to all men. The vitality of religious experience wholly depends on its connection with Christ, as all religious truth depends upon him as the truth. Intellectual opinions, beliefs, creeds, superstitions, are possible without Christ; but experience of truth is only possible as Christ is experienced. The experience of Christianity is the experience of Christ, or the reproduction of his life in the soul. It is the spiritual procreation in man of what is in Christ, or of what Christ is in nature. The Christian is a new incarnation of Jesus Christ. He is God manifest again in the flesh. In this highest sense, Christianity is the life of the world, imparting to it the God-given life of its Founder, and building it up in his likeness, so that the angels in heaven and human beings on earth may appear to be, and are, the children of one Father.

Into this experience are crowded thoughts of the future life, involving the immortality of the soul, the resurrection of the body, and final rewards and punishments. Heaven and hell arise before the spiritual vision as the final facts of religion; they are the last truths, as creation, sinfulness, atonement, regeneration, and holiness are the first in the system of religion. Heaven with its glories and hell with its horrors are apprehended in their vividness, and affect the religious life in the growing stages of spiritual experience. Experience is the cure of skepticism touching the final truths of religion. No doubt clouds the eye as it gazes into the future. Spiritual experience is a demonstration of the truth of all the Scriptures teach as to the final disposition of the righteous and the wicked, and the divine government never appears so firm and so holy as when it moves forward to the execution of its plans respecting the future of its subjects. One of the categories of religious experience is a clear-sighted view, according to the Scriptures, of the justice and holiness of the divine administration in its settlement of human affairs, awakening the sense of responsibility and inspiring carefulness in life, as but few other truths are able to do.

Spiritual experience is so comprehensive, both in its truth-contents and in its relation to Christ, that an exhaustive list of its categories must not be undertaken; we, therefore, stop with those given. To such experience belong all there is of Christianity in its theistic, Messianic, redemptive, and eschatological revelations, which become the root and ground of the Christian life. *The complete Christian life is Christianity completed in the life.* Alexander Bain attributes character to pigment; we attribute Christian character to Christianity. Herbert Spencer makes "complete living" possible as it conforms to naturalistic standards and laws; we see that it is possible only as it is a supernaturalistic development of a supernaturalistic principle of life implanted by Him who is Life and hath promised it to all who desire it.

The perplexing part of the subject is the *process* by which Christianity is reduced to a spiritual experience. Intellectual assent to Christianity, or an intellectual perception of its truth, is less mysterious than the spiritual appropriation of truth; indeed, it is a question if the former is a mystery at all. Intellectual changes, involving reversal of sentiments or adoption of new truths, are psychological facts within the range of analysis. A change from atheism to theism, or from Unitarianism to Trinitarianism, is or may be purely intellectual, important enough to be worthy of notice, but not profound enough to stand for Christian experience. An intellectual regeneration may be accomplished through psychological laws, with which we are familiar; spiritual regeneration is more than a psychological change, and can not be explained as yet even by spiritual laws known to us. A Buddhist may pass over to Christianity by the intellectual process, but he is not a Christian except in name. The spiritual process is independent, different, and unknown.

Intellectual changes are vital, but as perilous as they are vital. As an intellectual view of Christianity is incomplete, so an intellectual regeneration, or change in religious sentiments, is incomplete and unsatisfying; and, without spiritual experience, Christianity will seem to him who accepts it on intellectual grounds only, as incompetent to fulfill its promises, and he turns against it. Honestly accepting it through an intellectual process, he has honestly abandoned it by a similar process. The intellectual root does not hold—he needs spiritual grappling-hooks. A sentimental religion or an intellectual experience may be beautiful, but it is not life-imparting; it may be magnetic, but it is not powerful; it is not a dynamical, but a mechanical, religion. Christianity is life, not truth only.

The impartation of the vitalistic principle is one of the secrets of religion, and its enjoyment is one of the experiences of human history. On the supposition that the soul is in a state of spiritual death, as the sacred writers represent, it is a mystery that by any process at all it can pass into a state of spiritual life. How can the non-living become living? It is a scientific as well as religious teaching, neither science nor religion having answered it. Prof. Tyndall has urged that under the operation of the laws of crystallography all vegetable and animal life may be produced; but so bald a proposition has been overthrown by experiment. Crystals are not known to grow into vegetables or animals. So under no laws, physical or psychological, thus far discovered, is it possible to explain the initial appearance of religious life in man. To attribute it to an evolutionary process or natural development would please Herbert Spencer, but the religious life had a beginning, in which evolution played no part. The religious foundations are divine—not natural and evolutionary. Religious teachings, religious customs, and religious temples may result from the domination of the religious idea; but religious life is not evolved from the religious concept, or from any thing human. Religious life is the antecedent or normal condition of the soul, to be explained by no preliminary natural condition or force. It is preliminary; it is first. Evolution never produces the first; it may account for the second. It can not explain the beginning of the world, or of religion; it may trace its development, but nothing more.

Only two theories of spiritual life are possible—the theory of spontaneous regeneration and the theory of biogenesis, or the introduction of life from antecedent and external spiritual life. As the theory of spontaneous generation, as applied to physical things, has been abandoned and pronounced unscientific, so the theory of spontaneous regeneration, or spiritual life springing out of spiritual death by the action of the latter, is repugnant on scientific as well as religious grounds, and must be abandoned. Henry Drummond pronounces it an "impossible Gospel." Life from life is the only explanation of life. Spiritual life in man points to its antecedent in God. Regeneration is a biogenetic fact. Regeneration is a new generation, not a development of nature. As the lower order can not pass into the upper, the inorganic into the organic, unless the upper breathes into the lower, unless the organic touches the inorganic, so the natural never becomes the spiritual unless the spiritual touches the natural, imparting its life to it, and assimilating it into its own likeness. This is the law of biogenesis—this is regeneration or the law of spiritual life.

If, then, the religious life is not the evolution of a natural existing principle in man, it can not be the product of an evolutionary force without him. He did not catch the religious idea from his environment, nor did he find it in the forces of nature. Neither in himself, nor in nature, does he discover it. The religious source is elsewhere; the religious life is not derivative from a human or natural root, but is from outside and beyond the human and the natural.

The mystery of spiritual change lies in the fact that it is not the result of voluntary mental action, but of the energy of a force quite independent of the mind or the individual. *In intellectual changes man is active; in spiritual changes he is passive. In the one he works; in the other another works.*

As an objection to spiritual experience it is alleged that character is indestructible, and does not admit of change, and, therefore, the representation of change must be understood in an allegorical, and not in a literal, sense. The indestructibility of character is an admitted fact, and regeneration not only respects it, but also aims both to conserve and perfect it. Regeneration is a transformation of indestructible character, effected through the operation of the divine spirit without extinguishing a single faculty or destroying a single function of the soul. The young man of Nain is dead; Jesus Christ speaks the body back into life, not by destroying the body, but by imparting to it that which it had before death. Regeneration is a similar act with reference to the soul; it is rebuilding what is in ruins; it is repairing the damaged walls of the spiritual palace; it is perfecting the imperfect. The blind eye is opened, a restoration to normal functions; diseased conditions are banished, and health is stamped upon the whole system. The work is beneficent, normal, healthful, redemptive.

The fact of an internal transformation of elemental character is fully taught in the Scriptures, and the instrument by which it is effected is as clearly revealed, but the generic process of change is so hidden that it can not even be inferred. Nor is an explanation needful either to faith or satisfaction. *God reveals results, not processes.* Botanical mysteries are as conspicuous as spiritual mysteries, and pregnant with similar lessons. The revivification of nature after the Winter's cold has passed over it is a sublime spectacle, adumbrating a similar fact in the spiritual hemisphere, of which it is the truthful counterpart. Sun-heat and sun-light are poured into apparently lifeless and denuded forests, which in brief time exhibit all the signs of life again, clothing themselves with their accustomed foliage, and ministering to the earth as the earth has ministered to them. Even this familiar re-blooming the materialist must recognize without an adequate knowledge of the process that effected it. Likewise the divine influence is poured into a spiritually lifeless soul, in which germinates a new life, whose peculiar manifestations are moral beauty, superhuman strength, divine impulses, and gaspings after holiness. In the new condition the soul reaches after the divine nature as the divine nature reaches after it, and one merges into the other, so that, as Peter affirms, the soul partakes of the divine nature. The fact is patent, the process is unknown.

This is not mysticism. The doctrine of spiritual experience has been misunderstood by the materialistic thinker as a reproduction of the mysticism of the Neo-Platonists, or the fanaticism of the schoolmen, with which neither intellectually nor religiously is it at all connected or related. The mystery of the spiritual process, and consequently the mystery of spiritual experience, is acknowledged ; but mystery is not mysticism, mystery is not fanaticism. Plotinus is not the best exponent of Christianity ; Thomas Aquinas is not the truest interpreter of the doctrine of experience.

The secret of regeneration is the secret of the soul. The soul is an unknown quantity, refusing to be interviewed to any great length ; it will not turn " informer," and tell all it knows. God is even more inexplicable. The two come in sweet contact ; the Highest overshadows the Lowest, and the latter is born into the former. A divine operation, this ; it is more than an intellectual throe ; it is the divine sweeping over the soul, like the eagle over its nest, and at last settling down upon it as its own, and warming it with its own life. The soul is the nest of God.

To produce this change philosophy is utterly incompetent ; it may introduce and produce intellectual regeneration. Plato addresses the mind ; Paul reaches the heart. The one transforms the thinking ; the other transfigures the life. Great is intellectual purification ; greater is spiritual sanctification.

The ground of these statements is, besides the experience itself, the teaching of the Scriptures, to which one must always turn for final truth respecting religion. Mr. Spencer declares God unknowable and unthinkable, and religious experience, predicated on a knowledge of God, impossible. What saith the Scriptures? John says: " Beloved, let us love one another, for love is of God ; and every one that loveth is born of God and *knoweth God*." " He that believeth on the Son of God hath the witness in himself," says John also ; and to the agnostic Jews Jesus said : " If any man will do his will, he shall know of the doctrine, whether it be of God, or whether I speak of myself." In these passages it is clearly evident that a knowledge of God, grounded in relationship to God, is affirmed as the substance of religious experience. The anticipations of Christianity include a revelation of God to believing souls, and such a revelation as will constitute a fundamental experience. In harmony with these passages are others quite as explicit in their teaching, and significant of the same inference, but it is not necessary to quote them. No one will deny that the doctrine of experience is the doctrine of Christianity.

Mr. Lewis teaches that "mathematics is an empirical science." Christianity is an *empirical religion*, justified and established as truly by experiment, observation, induction, and deduction as mathematics or any physical science. It is the religion of experience, and experience is as authoritative as an axiomatic truth. Respecting the reliability of experience, Leibnitz says: "If our immediate internal experience could possibly deceive us, there could no longer be for us any truth of fact; nay, nor any truth of reason." Experience is the positive test of truth; truth is not the test of experience. The standard of philosophy is alleged truth; the standard of Christianity is positive experience. The clash is between truth and experience. Philosophy precipitates a collision; Christianity seeks a harmony. Truth must conform to experience, not experience to truth. Truth is truth only as it is one with affirmative experience; that is, all truth is empirical. The test of experience is supreme, final. With alleged truths materialism may make war; in the presence of positive experiences it is powerless, it is harmless.

As the religion of truth and life Christianity is without a rival. As a religion of truth it opens doors hitherto closed to the unsandled feet of sages; it reveals God as Plato never apprehended him; it defines world-building as the materialist has never conceived it; it points back to the beginning, and its last rays carry one to the end and beyond. A truth-religion it is.

As a religion of life all men need it, for all are dead in trespasses and sin. Its words sound in every cavern of despair, and its flower of hope blooms over the door of every sepulcher. My words, says the Savior, "are spirit and life."

Christianity is the real of the soul.

# CHAPTER XXXII.

## COMMON GROUNDS OF PHILOSOPHY AND CHRISTIANITY.

THE conception of Heinrich Lang that the realm of religion is distinct from the realm of science is beautiful in outline, but as he regards the contents of the scientific realm as richer and vastly more important than the contents of the religious realm, and that they have nothing in common, one will wonder to what extent the conception of difference is true, and will desire to analyze it before accepting it. It is like saying that England and China, because distinct as countries, are without mutual interests, and that the stronger may wage war against the latter at its option and for its own benefit.

It is this conception of difference that has led to irreconcilable antagonism between the theologic and philosophic interpretations of truth in its physical, ethical, and religious aspects and relations. A survey of the field we have traversed shows two giants in hostile or strained relations, two movements of thought opposed in their methods of research and discovery, and two investigating systems at variance on points of vital worth. That this is an unnatural attitude is self-evident; the strife is very like the "War of the Roses" in England or the war of the North and South in America; it is the strife of truth with truth, brother with brother.

Anciently, religion was a philosophical principle, and philosophy was a religious principle. Pantheism was as philosophical as it was religious, and as religious as it was philosophical. All the earlier religions, save the Jewish, partook of a philosophical spirit, and, inquiring most profoundly into the nature of things, framed expositions, however superstitious and erroneous, that for ages satisfied the intellectual life of the races who received them. Such religions, not fulfilling the idea of religion, immediately sought the aid of philosophy, but in their philosophical work they were as ineffectual as in their more appropriate religious work. Thus the blind led the blind, with the usual fatal result.

The Judaic religion proposed from the first to stand on an independent basis, and taught truth, not by rationalistic processes, not in the form of speculation, not as an inquiry, but as exact truth, so far as the human mind, in the days of its authority, was able to apprehend it. Never was the strait so great that any of its law-givers or prophets degenerated into philosophical discourse, but they always set forth Judaic truth as religious in content and purpose. To a still greater extent Christianity stood out as a *bas-relief* religion, with nature as its background, asserting religious truths for religious purposes, as though it had nothing else in view; it avoided the circumlocutions of philosophy, the demonstrations of mathematics, and the licensed prodigality of poetic symbolization. Intended as a revelation, it took the shortest route to the truth, and made it known quickly.

If credit must be given, it belongs to the Bible religions that they drew the line between religion and philosophy, assigning each a special sphere, bounded by walls that can not be broken down, and affirming the authority of each in its sphere. This was necessary, since the old religions united the two in unnatural bonds, and without benefit to either. It was a union of iron and clay, and had to be dissolved, the result being on the one hand an independent philosophy, and on the other an independent religion. Developing its genetic elements in their natural order, it is not strange that Christianity appears as the exclusive religion of the supernatural, while philosophy, pursuing its independent course, arrays the natural against it. In the one miracles, Messiahship, faith, repentance, regeneration, ethical laws, prophecy, prayer, immortality, and resurrection challenge investigation, and are urged in opposition to the findings of philosophy; in the other, pessimism, evolution, natural selection, atheism, mechanism, atomism, and all such are urged as the essentials of philosophy, without regard to the demands of religion. One concerns itself with things spiritual, ethical, immortal; the other with things physical, psychological, sociological, and temporal. The dividing line is distinct.

Christianity meant that it should be drawn, though it seemed like the drawing of a sword to declare the division, but unintentionally hostility has been the result. It meant that truth should be apprehended from the double stand-point; that at first the natural should be interpreted by natural methods, and the supernatural by supernatural methods; that afterward the natural should be interpreted by the supernatural, and the supernatural by the natural, to the end that it would appear that all things are one, and God is over all. The program of Christianity is broad and comprehensive, looking to unity through methods diverse and even antagonistic, purposing to provoke harmony between the ego and the non-ego, and allowing to philosophy the widest range of thought, yet going beyond it in its province of revelation. This purpose, misunderstood or not discerned at all, has been made responsible for the actual variance between the two systems of thought, and many like Lang divide them inseparably.

His conception of difference is the real cause of hostility ; the Bible's conception of difference is the basis of final unity and harmony.

The more specific alienation has occurred within the last fifty years, during which science has made prodigious progress in its proper field of discovery, being emboldened, as it explained some things in a new yet hypothetical way, to declare that it could explain all things in a similar way, or at least differently from religion. Its apparent preliminary successes deepened its unintended prejudice toward religious truth and the religious method. In advance it announced the downfall of religion ; not that it had grounds for the announcement, but, in a self-confident, partisan spirit, it was ready to believe that it could undermine the solid truths of religion as easily as a few workmen had pared down the rocky cliffs of England's coast. Upon the task, so serious, and so herculean as well, it entered, demolishing some presuppositions of theology, compelling a restatement of some beliefs, and a remodeling of some definitions, and, in a way, threatened the bulwarks of Christianity. Under the circumstances, the fears of the ignorant were aroused ; the attention of Christian thinkers was secured ; original inquiries were re-asked ; and a battle, without the spirit of compromise on either side, began, which has raged with an arbitrariness that promised an endless contest.

The conflict continues, but indications of a truce are visible, and the preliminaries of an agreement have been discussed. There are leaders on both sides, who, recognizing the suicidal result of the struggle, are quite willing to concede some things heretofore regarded as fundamental, but now ascertained to be incidental, and who believe that, however necessary the conflict in itself, the important ends aimed at have already been secured. So soon as a willingness to consult upon the situation is manifest, there is hope of reconciliation ; but it is no easy task to bring together in amicable relations two such colossal belligerents ; but he renders service to both sides who, instead of inflaming the relations, contributes by wise words to a peaceful settlement of the matters at issue. Peace is absolutely necessary to both. The "peace relation," as Rudolf Schmid calls it, is the condition of further truth-development.

In suggesting the possibility of reconciliation between philosophy and Christianity, we do not mean that either side shall compromise itself by unfounded concessions to the other, or by any experience of self-stultification, or by an abandonment of any essential principle, discovery, or truth, for such compromise is not at all necessary. Whatever truth the one may have discovered, it will be of benefit to the other to know it. Instead of compromise of truths, let there be unyielding independence. Nor is it necessary to harmonious relations

44

that the two abandon their distinctive peculiarities, forming an entirely different system out of materials common to both, for philosophy is functional in the natural sphere, and Christianity is functional in the spiritual sphere. Any suggestion that proposes to weaken either, or compromise their character, or alter their functions, or blot them out as integral systems, can not be the basis of an enduring reconciliation, or even of temporary mutual sympathy. Nor is the proposed reconciliation to grow out of a mere correction of mutual misunderstandings, for these give way on other grounds; but the basis of harmony lies deeper, rather in an *understanding of fundamentals* than in an overthrow of misconceptions and superstitions. No one is prepared to say that either science or religion is overthrown; no one can rationally believe that either will be overthrown; and no one religiously desires the overthrow of either. To secure friendly recognition of the inner merits of each; to allow both as wide a sphere as they can occupy; and, at the same time, to unite them in a common pursuit, or to make one tributary to the other in the carrying on of its special work, is a result devoutly desired by many on both sides.

What basis of mediation is, therefore, possible? The short answer is, not a basis of disagreements, which must forever keep them apart, but a basis of agreements or common possessions. The secret of Paul's missionary triumphs was his observance of this general rule—as, at Athens, in order to win the pagan mind to a consideration of the truths of Christianity, he pointed to the agreement of *certain* pagan teachings with these fundamental truths, and did not assail their errors. He avoided arraying the religions against each other, but insisted with tremendous force upon their agreements, capturing their assent if it did not result in their conversion. The "unknown God" of Athens is the known God of Christianity, said the apostle, and they listened without prejudice. So elsewhere he did not widen the breach between Judaism and Christianity by contrasts and exposure of disagreements, but referred to truths common to both, and attempted thus to unite them. Even when he must speak of symbols or ceremonies that had passed away, he was careful to point out their fulfillment in Christian usages and teachings, showing their preservation in a transposed form and in new relations in the new religion. In this manner, philosophy and Christianity may be harmonized, or the differences between them overshadowed by the larger agreements; not entirely harmonized, we confess, for there are some differences that are essential and must remain; but the agreements are so many that, if emphasized, held up to the gaze of both sides, the result will be a higher mutual appreciation, and a shortening of the distance between them.

HALLUCINATIONS OF SCIENCE. 691

The first agreement we propose relates, not to the contents of either religion or philosophy, but to a willingness on both sides that such contents may be investigated, tested, proved. The scientist may smile at this basis, since he may fancy that the trouble all along has grown out of the alleged refusal of religious truth, having clothed itself in mystery, to undergo critical inspection, while scientific truth has been open-hearted and always ready for examination. It is at this point we must pause. The claim of science that its truths are self-transparent is a trifle delusive, and the charge against religion is not exactly in accordance with the facts. Not a little parade has been made over certain discoveries in the scientific field, but it is not certain that science has desired a close investigation of its discoveries. It has really forbidden a re-examination by the boldness of its announcements, ridiculing a want of faith in them, and imposing acceptance of them by its *ipse dixit*. There was a time when it was imprudent, a sign of ignorance, to question any of the supposed facts of science, and to revolt against any of its deductions was revolution against knowledge. In this way science repressed, not investigation generally, but *investigation of its own doings*, which prepared it for crime against the truth, and which it frequently committed. In this independent mood, it announced facts that later investigation has destroyed; it framed systems that mature reflection has overthrown; it inaugurated *sciences* that recent facts have canceled. Early geology with its eighty anti-Biblical theories was a false science. Häckel's twenty-two animalic stages preceding the appearance of man, Darwinism in its prostituted forms, natural selection, the nebular hypothesis, an immense antiquity for man, and such theories, were supposed to rest upon inviolable facts, but they were the presuppositions of science, without value except as presuppositions. The hallucination of science was seen in its purpose to put these forward as discovered facts or truths, which the Christian thinker resisted. He demanded that science, as to its methods and results, should be investigated; that it should be responsible to truth for its deliverances; and that, until its reputation for veracity should be established, it should be without the *ipse dixit* in the realm of nature.

This put a check on high-handed burglary of facts, on scientific iconoclasm of religious truth. Darwinism has been investigated, and "natural selection" is exceedingly modest, even as a theory; evolution contracts with new data, and is on trial for its life; the distance from the organic to the inorganic has never been shortened; the prehistoric man, back of sixty centuries ago, has not been found; the mechanical view of the universe requires a theistic undergirding to be at all tenable; and finally science has taken off its shoes, for it has learned that the universe is holy ground. In compelling science to submit to investigation, many errors have been corrected or are in process of correction, many facts appear in their true proportion, theories pass at their true value, and rarely is any scientific statement fully accepted without the accompanying demonstration. The gain to truth, to religion, to science itself, has been incalculable.

On the other hand, Christianity, at first guarding its sacred truths from profane touch, has at last submitted them all to critical, historical, scientific, and philosophical tests, which has resulted in great gain to itself, and demonstrated the intimate relation of natural and supernatural truth. In honest guardianship of religious truth, the early Christian thinker construed all outside attempts at investigation of it as irreverent in spirit and infidelic in purpose, and felt justified in rebuking it. The thought of applying natural tests to supernatural things was, in his judgment, a proof of a depraved impulse, which should be suppressed, and he suppressed it.

Further objection to a rigid scientific examination of religious truth was made on the ground that the method of examination appeared to be incongruous, and, therefore, the result could not be exact or reliable. As well attempt to test the law of chemical affinity by the hydraulic ram as to test supernatural truth by a natural principle; so thought the pietistic believer. If Christianity, as a religion, is to be investigated, it should be investigated, not by a philosophic or scientific method, but by a religious method. Matter is the test of matter; mind the test of mind; science the proof of science; religion the proof of religion,—thus reasoned the religionist. From the objection of Christian thought to the supposed unnatural method of investigation, the conclusion was drawn that there must be something in Christianity that can not bear investigation; hence, a reaction against Christianity was the result.

In the refusal of the pietist to open the doors of the temple of truth to the world, he placed religion on the defensive; he seemed to shield it at a time when it ought to be known; he guarded mysteries that needed no protection; and in objecting to the scientific method he objected to the only method the profane mind can or will apply to truth. This was not merely a breach of propriety, but the position was false; false scientifically, false religiously. To the philosophical mind, the scientific method is the only method; he knows nothing of the supernatural method, and should not be asked to bow to it. The chief objection that philosophy proposes to the religious system is the method it requires for its examination; and, on the other side, the chief objection that religion proposes to philosophy is the method it has adopted for the discovery of truth. Philosophy says to religion, your method is false; religion retorts, your method is not sound. Reduced to final terms, it is a *conflict over method*, arising from a misunderstanding of the functions, claims, and agencies of the contestants.

Evidently, Christianity may propose its method of expression and its method of vindication. It has done both, and on examination it will be found that it is friendly to any or all methods, natural or supernatural, which guarantee the discovery of truth. Peter exhorts the Christian to be ready to give a *reason* for the hope that is in him; this is the *rationalistic or philosophical method.* Under certain conditions, the Master said, the disciple might know whether the doctrine he taught is divine or not; this is the *supernaturalistic or experimental method.* The indorsement of both methods by the Gospel should end the conflict and lead to the highest truth.

To what extent the two methods may be applied to Biblical truth must be determined in part by the specific character of the truth itself, and its relation to the entire system. It will be going too far to assure the scientific investigator that he will be able to demonstrate the integrity of every spiritual truth by the scientific method, but he may apply the method so often as to persuade himself of the truth of Christianity as a whole. To the historical data of the Biblical documents he may apply the rules of historical criticism; to the scientific hints therein found he may apply scientific proofs; to the poetical products of inspiration he may apply the laws of prosody; for the verbal frame-work of the documents the laws of language may be consulted; and for the general structure of the volume of Truth the usual analytic and synthetic rules may be employed.

Possibly this is all that philosophy can fairly undertake or succeed in accomplishing, for the mysteries of the spiritual side of Christianity can neither be explored or explained by any of the above rules or principles. Incarnation, regeneration, atonement, miracle, prophecy, immortality, and resurrection are beyond these scientific rules; but if there are any other rules by which even these truths may be analyzed, no objection should interpose. *All that is required is the rule.* Investigate to the remotest bounds of the truth-area, but the rule of investigation must first be known. There should be no ecclesiastical barrier to the scientific pursuit of mystery; hunt it down, expose its content, tell its hidden life, and reveal its hidden glory; and if any barrier at last is found, it will arise from the truth itself. *An open door to science; an open door to religion: this shall be the common law.* On this basis there can be progress.

The corollary from this general position is that philosophy must recognize the appropriate sphere of religion, and religion must recognize the appropriate sphere of philosophy. Philosophy is a hemisphere; Christianity is, under certain qualifications, a hemisphere also; it requires both to make the globe. Hitherto philosophy ranged throughout the universe of being and becoming, intrenching at times on the particular domain of religious truth. If, however, there are limits to religious thought, there are limits to philosophical thought also. Granted that the physical realm, with all the problems it can suggest, belongs to the philosopher, it must be granted that the spiritual realm, with all the problems it can suggest, belongs to the Christian thinker. If the spheres are distinct, they must be recognized, and the laborers confined to one or the other; and limited to the laws and methods appropriate to the sphere. With such recognition collision will be avoided and peace will be assured.

In military phrase, these, however, are only the preliminary conditions of a truce; they are not the basis of an enduring friendship. Philosophy and Christianity, mutually repugnant on the ground of difference, may be drawn together in defense of common interests, and mutually support each other in the presence of a common danger; that is, *mediation is possible on the basis of agreements.* One who looks over the field of conflict can not fail to see that, distinct as the belligerents are, occupying separate spheres as they do, and pursuing certain definite aims peculiar to their spheres, they have common interests, and are so related to fundamental truths that they can not afford to be divided. There are errors, theories, and misbeliefs to which philosophy is as constitutionally opposed as Christianity, and both are striving to circumvent, curtail, and extinguish them. In this category we include that latest form of intellectual mischief-making known as agnosticism, or the apologetic system of ignorance now offered as a substitute for all philosophical speculation. In its content it is old Pyrrhonism reproduced, implying now, as anciently, a denial of knowledge and of the possibility of knowledge. It does not deny truth, but affirms that we know nothing about it. Man is a know-nothing from necessity, by virtue of the limitation of his faculties, and must forever dwell in darkness. His intellectual aspirations are the mockeries of his nature. Blindness, uncertainty, the fatalism of ignorance, must paralyze all his attempts at inquiry. The hope of emancipation from such a thralldom is delusive, or at the most sentimental; emancipation can not be realized. The agnostic is the apostle of midnight.

Now, it is important to consider the relation of philosophy to agnosticism, especially to inquire if its tendency is to this extreme form of unbelief, or if it is not essentially and radically opposed to it. In determining this relation we meet with embarrassment in the fact that some philosophers are agnostics, and philosophy itself has veered toward a general agnosticism. When it is recalled that philosophy has denied the possibility of knowing God, since he is indiscernible, and that he is unthinkable, since he is entirely beyond the conditioned; that anthropomorphic conceptions of the supernatural are not tolerated in some philosophic circles, and therefore the supernatural is banished from thoughtful inquiry; that the essence of being confessedly eludes all successful searching; that matter still refuses to disclose all its secrets; that man is self-ignorant, and hopelessly so; and that some of the great questions of history are still unsettled, it is easy to believe that philosophy has been coquetting with agnosticism. Verily, it is only another instance of Saul seeking the witch of Endor for information, the result being the report of things not pleasant to hear.

The alliance of philosophy with agnosticism is proof of degeneracy, but it can not last long; it is an illegitimate alliance, and will dissolve of its own accord. For a true philosophy is based on the opposite platform, having for its purpose the elimination of the unknown, or, what is the same thing, the solution of all mysteries and the reign of all knowledge. Hence its penetrating spirit, its inquisitorial energy; hence its goal must be universal knowledge, not universal ignorance. It proposes to lay bare all truth, to illuminate all darkness, to conduct mankind out of Plato's cave, to gild every peak with sunlight, and to dissolve the nebulæ of history into related events and a systematic order of development. It proposes to knock at the door of nature until it shall be opened, and to seek her gems until they shall be found. It proposes to look up into the face of the Infinite Intelligence, and inquire with immortal calmness concerning the origin and substance of being, and its relation to non-being. Its purpose is as broad as " being " and " becoming," which includes all things.

This is not the goal of agnosticism. The two are irreconcilably opposed; there is no common ground where they may meet; there is no bond of union between them. Already the different directions they are taking are apparent in the different results they are announcing.

Philosophy is on the track of truth, scenting the highest laws, gathering the most resourceful facts, and widening the sphere of knowledge, to be sure in a crude way, and often adopting palpable errors and rejectable conclusions, but constantly adding to the sum of the world's knowledge, and ministering to the intellectual wants of the race. Agnosticism is a contracting, enervating spirit; its pulse is slow, its step tardy, its walk backwards. There is no elasticity in it. It beats a funeral march in our ears.

In proportion as philosophy and agnosticism are essentially opposed, philosophy and Christianity are essentially agreed touching the limits of human knowledge and the province of human thought. Christianity is the revelation of man's right to the domain of knowledge, going so far in that direction as to aid him by supernatural fore-glimpses of those truths he can not discover by the scientific process, and so laying at his feet those facts, laws, systems, and principles necessary to his happiness and advancement. It is not the religion of ignorance, but *prima facie* a revelation, and therefore the source of knowledge. It adds to its value also that it purports to be a revelation of those truths of which the agnostic confesses he knows nothing, and can learn nothing from any source open to him, and in which the philosopher is most profoundly concerned. The existence of God, the reign of providence, the origin of the worlds, the character of man, and the destiny of all things, while enigmatical subjects to the agnostic, are the common truths of revelation, the exposition of which belongs equally to the sphere of philosophy. At this vital truth-point agnosticism separates from Christianity and philosophy, and philosophy and Christianity unite. *Agnosticism is the foe of both—of philosophy as a truth-hunter, of Christianity as a truth-revealer.* Forgetting their differences in the broader purpose to defend common interests, and agreeing that truth must be protected at all hazards; the two, though differently equipped for the task, will seek to serve the same end, and share the glory of a common victory. A cold observer may pronounce this the selfish basis of union—a union prompted by the instinct of self-preservation; a union without an inner bond; but a formal union, perhaps, is the pre-condition of absolute organic union, and at all events the pre-condition of a suspension of hostilities. Both are in danger from a common foe, both must provide for the common defense.

The idea of common defense is relieved of its selfish character by the identity of many of their truths, a number of which are as vital to the existence of one as to the other. Take that refined form of philosophic speculation known as idealism, which in its functional relations is closely allied to certain Biblical truths, and can not be easily separated from them. Interpreting matter as non-existent, the result is contempt for nature; but, while Christianity emphasizes its reality, it equally emphasizes its perishability, and ever strives to wean human affection from it. The result is the same in both cases—*contempt.* Philosophy goes off into hyperbole, but the hyperbolic is the shadow of the truth of religion. The one raises the question if matter exists; the other treats it as existing; but both lift *being* above it, and are substantially at one at this point. It should not be forgotten that the materialists, pricking hyperbole to its center, are exalting matter to a high position of responsibility, even endowing it with the power of procreation, and with the potency of all life. It looks as if the deification of matter will be proposed as the opposite pole of idealism. To this exaltation of matter, or raising gods out of the dust, Christianity will unite with idealism in protesting, and will raise up barriers against the surging tides of materialism.

Nor is this the only point of contact between them. Respecting natural evil, or the evil environment of man, the two are not sufficiently far apart to provoke remark. Tribulation, affliction, disease, and death, the idealist looks upon as the conditions of moral development; Emerson interprets moral evil in this way; and Christianity is not in disagreement with the interpretation. Without using the word "probation," idealism interprets life as a probation, attaching moral significance to every trial, and relieving moral friction of its edge by assigning it a disciplinary function. To both, therefore, pessimism is unknown. Both interpret alike, leaving the religion of melancholy to Schopenhauer and his followers, The spirit of idealism is the spirit of Christianity. The latter is ideal in its inmost function and character; it is spiritual, supra-sensible, holding the material at arm's length, and centering all in God. If the former has not gone up to such heights, it is looking in that direction; they can not fall out by the way; they are friends.

The theistic notion, or the problem of the Unconditioned, is the enigma of metaphysics, and the summit-truth of inspired revelation. Agreement touching this greatest truth must result in the extinction of disagreement touching all lower or subsidiary truth. Interpretations of natural phenomena, containing the germs of atheism, have been framed by the Häckel school of investigators, but the majority of philosophic thinkers prefer to be in harmony with the theistic hypothesis, and express dissatisfaction with their proposed expulsion from the ranks of believers. Philosophy must break with atheism or monotheism; it can not serve both, nor can it be indifferent to either. It leans to the monotheistic idea even when confessing that it is unexplainable and unthinkable.

More than once Mr. Darwin grieved that his theory was construed into a support of atheism, for in the early stages of his career he had not lost faith in the existence of a personal God. In his "Origin of Species" he affirms that the views therein expressed should not "shock the religious feelings," as the development idea is in perfect harmony with the theistic hypothesis. As to "natural selection," K. E. von Baer condemns it is as "scientifically indefensible, but not anti-religious." Oskar Peschel vindicates Darwinism from anti-religious tendencies, holding that creation by development is nobler than creation as an instantaneous product by catastrophic power. Among the living thinkers may be mentioned Herbert Spencer, who insists that, so far as his evolutional teachings have any theological bearing or value, he has been misunderstood, for he spurns all atheistic sentiment. He holds to the existence of an absolute Intelligence, without personality in the anthropomorphic sense, but as a conscious, self-governed, eternal *power*, to whom the universe is responsible. He further conceives of the divine Intelligence without conditional relations, and so completely infinite in all functions as to eclipse any finite conception, so that it is impossible that man should know any thing of him beyond the mere fact of his existence. The Christian thinker just here discovers the need of a revelation from God to supplement human knowledge, and points to the Bible as such revelation; but Spencer holds that the revelation compromises itself by its anthropomorphic conceptions, which is an objection to finite conceptions altogether, for all thought is necessarily and vitally anthropomorphic. Truth is visible only to anthropomorphic eyes, and a revelation of God not anthropomorphic would be unintelligible. The position of Spencer is that of the Athenians, who believed in God without knowing any thing about him. If the so-called revelation of the Infinite is valuable at all, it is valuable as an accommodation to finite thought, but must not be taken as an actual representation, or as containing a positive enumeration of the qualities of the Infinite. He is too great to be known; he is not small enough to be even apprehended. With the theory of the divine greatness we are in entire sympathy, it being but an echo of the Biblical truth that he is "past finding out," he is "unsearchable," he is eternal, all-wise, immortal, and invisible. Spencer's supreme exaltation of the Infinite is not equal to the lofty revelation of the eternal throne and its holy occupant. Spencer is not the peer of Isaiah, or of Habbakuk, or of Job, or John. He says nothing that they have not forestalled and did not originate. He says nothing new when he writes: "If religion and science are to be reconciled, the basis of reconciliation must be this deepest, widest, and most certain of all facts—that the Power which the universe manifests to us is utterly inscrutable." To this the Christian thinker assents, not because Spencer demands it, but because it is true. Sir Wm. Hamilton and Mansel likewise assert the same thing, going farther, however, than Spencer in requiring faith in the Infinite.

Whatever opinion one holds of Spencer's basis of reconciliation, one will not condemn it as intentionally atheistic, but will concede that it is reverent and perhaps useful. The weakness of the Spencerian theology is that it embraces too much or not enough as truth, and it is either too high or too low, as a working hypothesis for the unearthing of truth. It embraces too much in that it assumes to explain all things, being and non-being, from the single point of incomprehensibility, when it is utterly impossible to explain any thing from that stand-point; it embraces too little in that it assumes that its representation of the Absolute is exhaustive, when it is not more than inceptional; it is too high, as a working hypothesis—for no one can walk far on stilts—its view of God is entirely out of the anthropomorphic range; it is too low, for, abandoning the high level of investigation, it prostrates the worker in the dust, requiring at his hands a mechanical explanation of the universe. Spencer's theology is a perversion of the truth, or an error dressed in metaphysical robes.

The descent from evolution to rank materialism is rapid and precipitate, but the materialist may be as honest in his desire for the truth as the evolutionist, and may have rendered not a little service to the religion he is anxious to overthrow. He is not shy of atheism, since he does not apprehend the necessity of the divine presence in the development of the world, and since nature is the only Teacher he feels bound to respect. The work of the materialist is not irrarational—it is his deduction that contradicts faith. The facts he furnishes are such as Christianity can appropriate in its own behalf, although he has not the remotest intention that it shall be bolstered by any thing he seeks or finds. It will surprise him, doubtless, to learn that he has not, as yet, shaken a single stone in the temple of truth, and when he becomes fully aware that his iconoclasm has been absolutely harmless, he may see things in their right relations, and subscribe to that which he can not subvert. The origin of matter, or the old problem of the genesis of the universe, is his hobby, which he rides in all kinds of weather and in all the fields of literature and human thought. To the facts he discovers we have not the slightest objection; indeed, on the basis of ascertained facts we propose reconciliation between Christianity and philosophic materialism. As to world-building, whenever it is proved that "fire-mist," or "star-stuff," or atoms, were original sources, or the beginnings of the universe, we shall accept them without the slightest fear to Christianity; *but presumptions must not be presented as proofs.* On presumption alone reconciliation is out of the question, since the science of the future may overturn it, and presume some other origin. Let the origin be established; let materialism establish it, and Christianity will not contradict it. This is not a concession to materialism, but the proof of the broad-gauge character of revealed religion, which is broad enough to concede that creative power might have exercised itself in a thousand ways, whether atomically, protoplastically, germinally, or otherwise. Reconciliation is possible on broad-gauge truth.

We must keep in mind all the time that Christianity locates the creative influence, whether it acted instantaneously, *once for all*, or gradually, consuming millions of years in the development of its designs, in a personal God; while philosophy, somewhat estranged from the theistic hypothesis, is disposed to confine itself to an examination of the modalities of creation, or the plan of the universe. We frankly confess that it is immaterial to the defense of Christianity what method of creation philosophy may finally approve, as any method, plan, or order, or even a *methodless method*, can scarcely be detrimental to the theistic idea, or the reign of God in the universe. If Christianity goes to philosophy for the modality of creation, philosophy must come to Christianity for a knowledge of the creative force—the Creator. To recognize the specific work of each system is to lay the foundation for an organic union of the systems, which is fast approaching.

As regards the antiquity of the worlds, evolutionists and theologians have differed not a little, the latter holding to a limited antiquity, the former to a practically endless one. In the advocacy of their interpretations the theologians were all too stubborn and without supporting facts, which they had to acknowledge in the final determination of the question. Science has pronounced against a short antiquity. The Bible leaves it an open question, to be ascertained in a scientific way, for its great assertion—"In the beginning, God created"—will allow the removal of the creative period back even too far for the searching gaze of scientific inquiry. Now, it is of no moment whether the materialist puts the "beginning" back so far that the figures pass beyond finite comprehension or computation, or brings it forward so that it almost grazes the historic period; it is immaterial whether the earth was created twenty millions of years ago or only one hundred thousand years ago; Christianity can accept any scientific interpretation of the "beginning." It is a curious commentary, however, on scientific vacillation that, having announced various antiquities for the universe, stretching out into the numerical infinities, it has recently reduced the age of the earth to the brief period of three million years! We accept this reduction with a sense of relief, but with the understanding that should the figures be changed hereafter, either increasing or still further reducing the antiquity, the "age" will be in perfect harmony with Moses. On the pledge not to disturb the "figures" of philosophy the two systems certainly can agree to suspend hostilities; we go further, and say that even fraternal relations may be established between them.

If the friendship thus suggested appear a trifle cold and distant, or not more than formal, the two systems will throw off all social reserve and rejoice together on another ground, namely, on the doctrine of the unity of nature. On the hypothesis of a world-unity Christianity enforces its doctrine of monotheism; the unity of the universe is proof of the unity of God. Nature manifests the presence of a single mind, the evolution of a single plan, and the reign of a single will or power. Theology approvingly quotes this unity. Does science contradict it? Before modern materialism lifted its sepulchral voice against Christian theism, scientific thought was unanimous in the declaration that nature is a panorama of unity. Humboldt avowed it with convincing proofs, and regarded it as the key to scientific generalization. The German materialists, especially Häckel and Büchner, proclaim it, founding upon it the religion of nature, as the substitute for the religion of revelation. Christianity suggests monotheism; materialism adopts monism. What is the difference? Both are intensely perceptive of that spirit of unity that pervades the universe, recognizing but one order of development in its history, and the single law of continuity in its progress. They are brothers in defense of the great family truth. They can not divide on this ground; but the inferences they draw are different, repugnant, antagonistic. Again and again has the proof appeared that the conflict between the opposing systems is the *conflict of inference.* Honest investigation is securing an agreement touching the facts; but to infer correctly from the facts involves reason, intelligence, skill, and a devout purpose. St. George Mivart agreed with Darwin as to facts; he differed with him as to the inferences. The inference-maker speculates, reasons, turns prejudice into an argument, foresees conclusions before they logically appear, and at last tortures facts out of complexion, character, and relation, to justify the result he prefers. Often facts are made to do the bidding of the inference-maker when he should in homage submit to the decree of fact.

An instance of perversion of fact in support of inference is at hand. Christianity, detecting the physical unity of the universe, rises to the conception of one God, as the logical teaching of the fact; materialism, honoring the fact by recognizing its existence, dishonors it by attributing to the universe a self-producing and self-sustaining power; it does not rise out of the fact itself to any thing beyond. The fact is the all in all. Strauss says: "We demand the same piety for our cosmos that the devout of old demanded for his God." No greater homage shall be paid to the personal God than to the cosmic God. Christianity runs on the track of facts to personality; materialism on the same track to cosmical character. The facts are the same—the inferences are opposite poles. On the common ground of unity both may stand; on facts, laws, and principles, they harmonize; the agreement of inference must be left to time. They are the husbandmen of the same fields, and are equally interested in the products of those fields; and, diverse as are their methods of plowing them, they reap the same ground-facts, upon which they will finally pronounce the same value.

A closer agreement is still possible, even on the basis of fundamental truth. "The fundamental truth of all philosophy," says Herbert Spencer, "is the persistence of force." Modern science means by this doctrine that the total quantity of energy in the universe, however employed, and however manifested, neither increases nor diminishes, but remains the same forever. Spencer declares this to be fundamental to philosophy. Though not fundamental to religion, religion has no reason for suspecting its unsoundness, and will grant it a place among the dogmas of science, so soon as science itself demonstrates it to be a verity. When Spencer said reconciliation between religion and science is possible on the basis of the inscrutability of the supreme power, religion accepted it; and now, when he says persistence of force is fundamental to philosophy, religion accepts the truth, as not at all dangerous to itself, or harmful to any projects it has in view. As yet we have not asked philosophy to accept what is fundamental to religion, but in the best of temper religion accepts what is fundamental to philosophy.

*Equally safe footing is found for both antagonists in a common view of man,* a subject that has hitherto divided them beyond all supposable hope of reconciliation. Time and again theories of descent, laws of heredity, and morphological ideas of the race have been declared and so supported by facts, as absolutely and entirely to render incredible the Scriptural account of man. He is a descendant of the animal kingdom; he is the product of evolutionary forces; his ancestry were gibbons, chimpanzees, and gorillas. If the philosopher insists on this ancestral history of man, the Christian thinker must bid him adieu, for it is not fundamental to anthropology. In the extemporaneous period of the evolution theory some unique statements—the temporary hallucinations of enthusiastic scientists—were undoubtedly made; but the sober, thoughtful, scientific evolution of to-day is reconsidering the grounds of its faith, and recasting the terms of its theory, and at all events it is not as demonstrative as it was in the beginning.

It is a significant fact that the Pentateuch furnishes in immediate succession two apparently contradictory accounts of the appearance of man, the first assigning him the last place, and the second the first place, in the creative series. Over this historic dilemma the evolutionists have perplexed themselves not a little, regarding it as an inner contradiction, irreconcilable on any hypothesis whatever. The accounts, however, as we have heretofore seen, are one, related in inverse order for a special purpose. In the first account the regular scientific order of creation is given, man being reserved to the last, not because he was the masterpiece, but because the earth was not in scientific readiness for him; while in the second account he is placed at the head, not because he was first, but because he was *best.* It is as if one writing the history of the Christian Church should begin with apostolic times and carry it down to the present day, or beginning now should write backward to the apostles; the history would be the same. The fact of man's creation is not disturbed by the order of the account.

This, however, is the dividing line between theology and evolution. The evolutionist magnifies the *order* of the creation; the theologian magnifies the *fact* of creation; the one dwells on the system or *method* of the creative work, the other on its *results.* Both may be justified in their positions, but it must be clear that the facts themselves take precedence of the order of facts; that is, it is proper first to consider what the facts are, and then to establish the order of their succession. Theology precedes evolution. In one account in Genesis man's relationship to the world is announced; in the other his independence of the world is as clearly set forth. As the last in the series, he is in the line of animalic succession; as the first, *he begins a line, not of animals, but of rational intelligences.* As he is the end of one so he is the beginning of another line.

The evolutionist, appropriating the first account, heralds the idea of descent, which is a phase of truth; but, ignoring the second account, he is ignorant of the true character of man, and reminds us of the eagle with one wing, or a boat with a single oar.

The double account, favorable to evolutionist and theologian, may be accepted as common ground, or as the basis of a general agreement. It is not conceded that the first account is suggestive of materialistic Darwinism, but no principle of interpretation is compromised, no fact is in jeopardy, by allowing that it is evolutionary in the historic sense, that the creation of man belongs to a series of creations, whether by development or otherwise is immaterial, terminating in the finished work of God. Christianity will accept evolution as a historic fact, even if it can not accept the scientific interpretation of the historic fact. Here agreement is possible again on the basis of facts; the disagreement pertains to inferences.

If evolution has any standing at all in the realm of thought, it ought to have a standing in history, religion, and physical order and government. We have already indicated faith in evolution as a historic feature of world-life, as the only explanation of history. It is not without its disadvantages as a "working hypothesis," for historic movements sometimes resemble the flow and ebb of tides, or the motion of a swing, forward and backward, with no perceptible progress. The Dark Ages illustrate the historic motion without advance. This makes against the scientific view of evolution, whose germinal idea is progress, but not against the historic law of evolution, which allows for the play of regressional forces, and so for backslidings in history. In such an emergency the evolutionist may find room for lapses in the historic movement in his collateral theory of "struggle," which implies retreats as well as advances; but the theory of struggle is a temporary expedient, a plank in a storm, and does not insure safety.

In the historic, but not scientific sense, Christianity is an illustration of evolution. According to its own account, four thousand years of preparation passed away before the incarnate Teacher appeared; the Messianic thought itself is a development, and the Messiah in the human sense was the product of the evolutional forces of history. As, however, this statement may be misconstrued, the Messiah must be lifted out of the evolutional program, and the historic preparation for his appearance only be considered evolutional.

History itself, under the manipulation of a providential spirit, is an evolution, having for its end the elevation of the race, and is slowly accomplishing it.

Man's lordship over nature is evolutionary, implying a slow conquest of its forces, a slow discovery of its laws, nevertheless a conquest, a discovery, a triumph in the world of matter.

Nature itself, or, rising higher, the universe is an evolution from primary stages and conditions to its full form and magnificence as we now behold it. Christianity can not consent to the theory of a self-originating, or self-subsisting world, but it can consent to an evolved universe, evolved by law even from atomic sources, provided the existence of atoms is credited to the divine Being. Thus Christianity is evolutionary in its history, in its interpretations of the cosmos, and of time itself, with all its wondrous products, forces, and issues. With this conviction, we can not agree with Dr. B. F. Tefft that evolution is "wicked," "atheistic," a "denial or abandonment of revelation." This is an extravagant arraignment of a theory which, while scientifically inaccurate, is historically sustained, and can not be overthrown by religious denunciation of it. Such denunciation estops union, quenches the spirit of fraternity, and violates the canons of truth. On the basis of a limited, historic evolution, the two antagonists may harmonize, adjusting the theories of the one to the dogmas of the other, thereby all the sooner arriving at the truth. If evolution is an attempted revolution against truth, it is wicked, and there can be no reconciliation; but it is difficult to see an opportunity for conflict on the historic basis as here presented.

Thus, whether philosophy be considered in its most ideal aspects, or in the lowest form of scientific materialism, it may harmonize through the medium of its facts with Christianity, as also a system of facts.

In still other particulars an agreement between philosophy and Christianity is possible. The doctrine of teleology is scientific; it is also theological; it may, therefore, be presented as a basis of peace between metaphysic and religion. The materialist is expending his phosphorus in an attempt to eliminate the proofs of design from the realm of nature and, as usual in such cases, he has fore-announced the accomplishment of his work; he has eliminated the idea of design from his thought! That is all. This is not a surprise, for the teleological idea is subversive of materialistic science. Many of the German philosophers are hostile to the idea; but the idea is unconquerable, and will ever occupy a place in the category of scientific truths. The Duke of Argyll indorses it as an irreproachable proof of the divine personality. It is a scientific idea; theology appropriates it because it is scientific. The doctrine of the unity of nature, or the "unitarianism" of nature, points with unerring finger to the doctrine of teleology. The evolution of nature, or its development according to plan, is implicit with the doctrine of teleology.

Still stronger support is underneath the idea. Nature is a supposed causal series; scientifically speaking, it proceeded in its development after a fixed order of antecedents and consequents, otherwise known as the product of causality. Causality is the sign of teleology. Cause is the anticipation of effect. Admit the one and the other appears. Materialism striking at one strikes at the other; and, as it can not break the bond between them, it has rejected both causality and teleology from its vocabulary.

The better philosophy, recoiling from the consequences of these eliminative attempts, approves the law of causality in nature and the reign of the teleological idea. K. E. von Baer, uninfluenced by religious conceptions, points out that nature is striving after an end, and almost endows it with a hidden purpose of its own. This is scientific teleology of a refined and wholesome cast, on the basis of which the Christian thinker can make peace with the philosophical thinker. As teleology is fundamental to Christianity, and apparently fundamental to philosophy, there is no reason for further conflict between them.

Lastly, the two may agree on the *ethical* basis. A system of morality, embodying correct ethical distinctions, and adapted to promote the happiness of all races, is demanded both by religion and

45

science, and it is not surprising that certain ethical schemes have been formulated and recommended by both. The contention is as to the authority of the ethical scheme. If, as is claimed by the theologian, the Biblical scheme is of supernatural origin, its code of laws enacted by a personal Law-giver, to whom a personal account must be rendered, its authority will be supreme and final; but if the ethical system is without supernatural force, and is the growth of man's ideas and expedients, an attempted adjustment of his relations to environments, as Herbert Spencer is inclined to think, then the system is not authoritative and man is not responsible. More than one investigator has discovered that an evolutionary morality is changeable, and not necessarily progressive; therefore, it may be no better in a thousand years than at the beginning. Mivart demands an *authoritative morality*; we demand a *fixed, unchangeable ethical system*, for scientific morality makes it uncertain whether there are such things as right and wrong; that is, it abolishes moral distinctions, or recognizes them only as products of relations.

That conduct may be scientifically regulated we believe, but scientific regulation is implicit with ethical regulation. Scientific morality must agree with supernatural ethics. The agreement is slowly taking place in that the scientific thinker is beginning to discern the scientific character of supernatural ethics, and that the attempt to regulate the world without primordial ethical distinctions is absurd and impossible. Human nature echoes the virtue of supernatural ethics. Among nations unblessed with Christian teaching, the strong and imperative ethical ideas of the New Testament have prevailed because they are identical with the demands of human nature. The ancient Persians punished falsehood with extreme severity. Seneca eulogized many virtues of the Christian religion. Mohammed extolled the practical duties of hospitality, repentance, and forgiveness. *The common thought of man is in harmony with the higher moral thought of the New Testament.* Scientific moralists, recognizing the priority of the ethical system of the sacred writers, and that it is founded on human nature, as well as in divine revelation, will not much longer either dispute its authenticity or deny its supremacy in the regulation of human conduct.

In closing this chapter, reference may be made to the reciprocal relations existing between Christianity and philosophy.

1. *Religion is necessary to Philosophy.* The philosophical thinker is dependent on religion for data. He may not think so, but he can not solve any great problem without invading the circle of religion for facts. He can not interpret nature without the aid of Christianity; he can not explain conscience, volition, mental operations, or hu-

man experiences, without the aid of some of the truths of the Christian religion. He needs religion.

2. *Philosophy is necessary to Religion.* Clement intimated that philosophy "guided the Greeks toward Christ." It is a schoolmaster teaching primary truth, and pointing to its richer development in religion. Philosophy is thought; religion is truth; and as thought is related to truth, so philosophy is related to religion.

*The conclusion is that one is not independent of the other; each needs the other. Plato said philosophy is the love of God. Christianity is also the love of God. Philosophy is Christianity; Christianity is philosophy. Lactantius must not again say philosophy is "empty and false;" Büchner, Häckel, Spencer, and Huxley must not again deride religious truth and sport with immortal things. God is the philosophic center; God is the spirit of revealed religion.*

---

# CHAPTER XXXIII.

## THE PROSPECTUS OF THE FUTURE OF CHRISTIANITY.

HABAKKUK wrote: "For the earth shall be filled with the knowledge of the glory of the Lord, as the waters cover the sea." Leroux, the French thinker, declared that Christianity is a "natural stage in the progressive development of man," and will be superseded by a superior religion, just as it has superseded inferior religions. The one pronounces the prophetic triumph of Christianity; the other assumes its natural dissolution. As the two views are irreconcilable, it will be interesting to inquire which view is correct, or at least to search the ground on which the views rest, that an intelligent conception of the future of religion may be entertained. If Christianity is a mere development from preceding religions, and subject to the general law of evolution, which would require its disappearance in a larger and richer form of religion, it will be well to know it; but if it has a law of its own which will insure its perpetuity, universality, and supremacy, it is equally important that we understand it.

Geologists tell us that in some parts of the world there is a gradual elevation of land through the operation of forces beneath, and that the tendency of such activity is to equilibrium of geographical conditions. The Christian thinker is inclined to the belief that a moral upheaval of the world is going on through the operation of moral forces from above, and that the design of it is the moral stability and salvation of the race. No well-informed reader of the Bible will dispute that in its prophetical outlines the future of the new religion is represented as triumphant in its influence and unassailable in its authority. Habakkuk is one of many who foresee the dawn of a day when the Gospel shall reign throughout the world.

Yet prophecy is only a starting-point. The promise of Christianity to succeed in enthroning itself in the world as the only religion for man, is matched by its potency to fulfill its promise. The promise is inspiring because it can be believed; the potency is assuring because it is supernatural, and, therefore, sufficient. Without the potency, the promise were nothing. Without the promise, the potency would seem to be acting aimlessly. The ground of all faith, therefore, is in the promise and potency of Christianity.

To assume a triumph on the ground of promise and potency is to assume some things by no means inconsequential or irrelevant. Such a triumph as is foreshadowed implies more than a temporary exaltation of the Christian religion, and more than its political recognition in the world. Its great triumph will be permanent; it will not be succeeded by a collapse. Once in authority it never will surrender it, unless the race return to the rule of the Dragon. It will be the religion of the world; a religion that shall have overcome all other religions; a religion universal, because it will meet universal demands; a religion whose triumph can not easily be disturbed. This is a broad outlook, but none too generous, if the triumph is worth anticipating, or shall be worth celebrating when it is realized. In this prevision of its future conquest we must be governed less by speculative inquiry than by those logical indications which warrant the inference of faith and the inspiration of prophecy.

The prophetic conception, however pleasant to the Christian thinker, and however inspiring to activity in the people of God, is not accepted in certain outside circles as any thing more than a hallucination, or at the most as the generating cause of the religious enthusiasm in the world. But aside from its prophetic cast, it is difficult to see what can properly make against the conception itself, which, if it shall actualize in future history, will turn the earth into paradise, and every man into a son of God. If the conception mean sobriety, justice, philanthropy, temperance, honesty, veracity, virtue, order, law, civilization, everlasting progress, and the reign of supernatural sentiment, surely he is in league with the archfiend who can object to it. In its outward form, in its lowest aspect, the triumph must mean this much, or it can mean nothing. In its narrower phases, and including all that it contemplates by the reign of the Spirit, it means ennobled manhood, a spiritual race, a divine family on earth, to which only demons can object. The conception itself is invulnerable.

Escaping one gauntlet, it must, however, run another. Such words as "impracticable," "impossible," "revolutionary," "Utopian," and "fanatical," are applied to it, and the methods which it proposes for its execution are pronounced hopelessly incompetent and injudicious. We shall not shrink from looking at the proposition of the Gospel from the stand-point of the objector, and consider just what he says, what he means, and what weight belongs to what he alleges.

Is it true that the proposition to conform the world to Gospel ideals is Utopian, extravagant, delusive, and destructive of the practical ends and responsibilities of life? The triumph of the Divine religion is implicit with the triumph of one ideal, or one system of ideals. It admits of no contradictory ideas; it refuses admission to foreign elements, except by that process of transformation which identifies them with itself; it stands alone in its greatness, is imperious in its authority, and bows all other ideas out of existence. Irrational as this seems to be, it is the most positively scientific procedure which religion has adopted. In the natural world one system of laws is in authority, ruling everywhere, and conserving the order and stability of the whole. Two systems would result in interminable confusion and disastrous collision. Gravitation is universal, ruling the small and the great, and is of one kind or knows but one law. So far as crystallization obtains in nature, it constitutes a harmonious idea, because it is the same everywhere, and operates according to one law. Of vegetable growth the laws are the same, whether observed in China, Brazil, or California. Chemical affinity is not one thing in the Eastern and another in the Western Hemisphere. If Christianity conceives of a universal conquest, or its supremacy in the hemispheres, she caught the idea from Nature, whose underlying thought is unity forever. As there is but one natural government, so Christianity foreshadows but one spiritual government, co-extensive with the race, co-eternal with God. If the lower thought of the unity, universality, and supremacy of the natural government is stupendous and affecting, what may not be said in eulogy of the higher thought of the unity, universality, and dominion of the spiritual government of God? The higher is no more Utopian than the lower.

It will assist the reader properly to estimate the prophetic idea of Christianity by reminding him that it is original, deep-seated, and constitutional, and that the program of the Church is in strict accordance with it. The idea of universality is a part of the productive endowment of the new religion. It is an underived, and therefore independent and untrammeled idea; it is not germane to other religions, and is, therefore, without ancestral antecedents or affiliations; it is not an after-thought, but a primary fore-thought, of the sacred writers, and is, therefore, an inbred element of the divine religion. Max Müller enumerates three missionary religions, because they are active in themselves and aggressive in extension, but only one anticipates a world-wide reign. In a political sense Mohammedanism is a missionary religion, but it would be truer to style it a *military* religion, for its method of conquest is military, and the changes it has wrought have been usually rather political than religious. It is not a religiously missionary religion. Its triumphs, too, far from resulting in the extinction of opposing religious ideas, have been very meager and incomplete. It triumphed in Syria, but Judaism exists within its borders; it triumphed in India, but Brahminism still disputes its authority; it has not triumphed over Buddhism in the East or Christianity in the West; and as for taking the world, it has not the slightest idea of doing it. This is not because it considers such a project undesirable, but from its stand-point it is impossible, and its prophets have fore-declared its final overthrow and the ascendency of Jesus of Nazareth.

Buddhism is a missionary religion, but it does not avow for itself universal authority, and is content with dominion in Asia.

None of the old religions of the East contemplates any extension of authority or a new lease of life, or the subjugation of new lands to its influence. Mohammedanism is the religion of *motion*, as Mr. Maurice shows, but it is of motion, not toward the aggrandizement of the world, but *towaad the center of its own realm of life*. It is active within, but not without, its circle of thought; Brahminism, as he also points out, is the religion of *rest*, but it is the *rest of death*. Neither the motion of the one nor the inertia of the other indicates future growth, elasticity, or conquest. These and all other Old-world religions were and are exclusive, confining all activity to a single people or country or continent, and, so far as they fail to include all peoples, all countries, and all continents, they must fail in securing universal dominion. At the present time all religions save Christianity have abandoned the expectation of a larger influence in the world than they have already acquired; they are not preparing for extended conquests, because they do not believe them possible. They are *race* religions; they can not, therefore, be universal.

Regarding Christianity as only one of a number of religions, it may seem to savor of presumption in its teachers to suppose a world-wide triumph possible; and perhaps it is fanatical to plan for such a conquest. But presumptuous or not, fanatical or not, the Christian Church is inspired in its plannings by the vision of just such an ideal triumph, and is putting forth in these days a herculean effort to secure it. Impossible to other religions, Christianity ventures to assume such a possibility to itself. This assumption, it will be allowed, is not the result of human designing, nor is it a late scheme of certain religious leaders, who hope to profit by the enthusiasm it has awakened; its *origin is in Christianity itself.*

Other religions derive impulse to activity from man; Christianity obtains its authorization to take the world from God. Other religions depend for preservation upon human methods, often resorting to carnal weapons to aid in propagandism, and in the end always exhibit the feebleness of human systems; while Christianity depends upon its supernatural influence and its unaided power to impress the world that it is from God. In the former the inspiration to activity is earthly, hence intermittent and ineffectual; in the latter it is heavenly, hence permanent and efficient.

It is sometimes urged that the introduction of a foreign religion into lands regulated by a native religion, long intrenched in the public thought and life of the people, will be attended by disorder, tumult, and resistance, and be promotive rather of injury than benefit, and that the proposition of Christianity to subvert such religions is revolutionary, iron-clad, and will be destructive of the rights of religions and nations. Granting that this representation is correct, the purpose of the new religion is nevertheless legitimate, and its success will be its vindication. If these conflicts among the religions were reduced to a mere question of *might*, Christianity would be at liberty to test itself in foreign fields, for other religions have not been careful to observe the laws of neutrality in this respect, and are not entitled to exemption from invasion or trial. Mohammedanism did not confine itself to the country of its birth, or among the people for whom it was designed; but it entered India, Persia, Palestine, and at one time threatened all Europe, and to-day points to a thousand mosques on the continent. Buddhism, reaching out beyond home, made its way into China, and rooted itself in the isles. Surely Christianity may contend for the balance of power in this world without an infraction of the law of reciprocity. If, however, these conflicts may be reduced to a question of *right*, then Christianity has no favors to ask and no conciliations to offer, but is bound from its stand-point to undertake the suppression of all other religions, or rather to secure the conformity of all peoples, irrespective of former religious affinities, to its standard of truth and justice, and its order of righteousness and life. If its mission is not so broad and world-wide, it may be doubted if it has any mission at all, for it is the only redemptive religion of history; the world needs it quite as much as any single people, and it can not prove itself divine except by being universal. It is universal or nothing; it is for all nations or it is for none.

With the question whether it can execute its mission peacefully— that is, save the world without a struggle—or whether the execution will involve revolution, disorder, overturning of social conditions, and new political organizations, it has nothing to do. *Mission and method are two things.* The settlement of the mission of religion is primary; the selection of method must be left to events, or to the nature of religion itself. If the spread of the Gospel can not be accomplished without some noise; if, when Diana falls to the ground, a little dust is raised; if, when King John signs the *Magna Charta*, he tears his hair and wrings his hands in rage; if the sight of the Cross infuriates the infidel and the heathen, as it will; if rebellions must follow the missionary; if the footfalls of the Christ in this world shake the thrones of lust and civil power; if progress must be by the sword, and divine covenants be proclaimed with the thunder of cannon, and enforced with the majesty of providential authority, so be it. Better that the Ganges be turned into a river of blood than that India should not have the Gospel; better that Foochow be bombarded and the Soudan be invaded with armies than that Christian civilization should not progress in the Oriental world. Many worldly methods we do deprecate, but the Gospel must find its way into the heart of the nations. Its mission is peace; its method may be *war*. Its spirit is love—love of order, love of righteousness; its method may be antagonism, frenzy, disorder.

A consideration of Gospel methods is imperative only so far as to distinguish them from other methods employed for the realization of the ends of the Gospel, for it has sometimes happened that political methods, and particularly ecclesiastical methods, have been at variance with well-defined Gospel methods, and deserve reprobation rather than commendation. For instance, when St. Cyril leads a mob of monks against Hypatia, and quarters her body, and rejoices over the bloody work, we can not see that he adopted a divinely ordained method for the suppression of Neo-Platonism. Again, when Constantine, ambitious for renown, supported Christianity with the sword, extending the reign of the Gospel by military means, it is not certain that he was acquainted with the Gospel idea of its own propagation. Again, when the Roman Catholic Church ordered inquisitions and martyrdoms for heretics, so-called, streaking its history with human blood, and exhibiting more intolerance than pagans ever showed toward their adversaries, it is certain that the Gospel was not ruling in that Church, and that the idea of religion was well-nigh forgotten by its priests and leaders. Nor are we quite sure that modern methods are in every respect in harmony with the plainly prescribed methods of the Gospel, for violence, intolerance, and iron-cladism too much characterize the modern Church to insure the rapidity of progress possible to it, although its superiority to the mediæval Church must be acknowledged, and its conformity to the Gospel idea is approximately secured. The greatest victories of the New Dispensation have been the result of means the most peaceful, but at the time estimated as the most inadequate, illustrating that Providence "hath chosen the foolish things of the world to confound the wise, the weak things to confound the mighty, base things, and things which are not to bring to nought things that are, that no flesh should glory in his presence." God's methods are supreme, and will be successful.

If the Reformation under Luther was born in a whirlwind, its leaders were calm, and the events inaugurated by it were governed by calm-producing agencies, which are still in force, and which are diffusing the spirit of the religious revolution throughout the world. It must be viewed, not merely as a violent reaction from Papal oppression, but also as a grand providential movement for the recovery of the world. The violence apparent in its progress was the violence of form, or the extreme of enthusiasm, but its spirit was orderly, peaceful, and conservative. During Luther's lifetime, it was to his credit, and was a sign of the providential character of the movement, that it provoked no wars, either in its favor or for its suppression. In like manner, Methodism inaugurated the religious revolution of the eighteenth century in England, accomplishing its mighty task by Gospel methods; but it excited animosity, and mobs, sacrifices, and sufferings mark her path, and make up no inconsiderable portion of her history. The effect of a religious movement, however, must be distinguished from its principles, which must be studied in their ethical contents, and determined to be legitimate or illegitimate by their adaptation to the moral elevation of man or an utter inadequacy to promote it. The effects of a religious movement may be natural, logical, and in the order of the principles underlying it, or artificial and antagonistic to the principles that govern it. The natural effect is legitimate, since it is the fruit of the principles; the artificial is illegitimate, since it takes the form of mobs and divers oppositions. The natural effect of Christianity is—*redemption;* the artificial effect may be—a *mob.* Athens roared its ridicule over the preaching of Paul; Ephesus went mad; Lystra stooped in the dust for stones; but such tumults were not the intended or natural, and, therefore, legitimate, effects of the Gospel.

Distinguishing Christianity, so far as its purposes are independent, from the results that sometimes follow it, and keeping in mind that a Christian method may not be a Gospel method of propagation, we are prepared to consider more fully just how Christianity proposes to execute its purposes and secure a world-wide triumph.

First, *its relation to other religions, and its facility for turning them to account in its own interest, deserves most careful consideration.* The conquest of the world implies the disappearance of all opposing religions, for, so long as a rival religion exists, it must be uncertain which will finally displace the other. Just what to do with other religions, or whether to do any thing with them; how to assail them, or whether they will decay from internal maladies, or die from old age; what estimate should be placed upon them, and whether, if permitted to exist, they can render incidental service to mankind,—are problems that can not be hastily solved. In Christian lands, the chief work of Christian people is evangelization of the masses, or destruction of sin; in heathen lands, war is made upon religions, or time is spent in proselytism from pagan faiths. That the latter is necessary, no one will doubt who has visited heathendom or knows any thing of pagan religions; but, as one studies the great historical religions of Asia, one is inclined to think that, in the settlement of the relation of the divine religion to these human systems of faith, a more excellent way might be devised.

It is conceded that the Asiatic religions are philosophical in their spirit and religious in their aims; neither profoundly philosophical nor safely ethical, it is true, but disposed both to philosophy and religion. Their inquiries are as broad and deep as humanity, but they are unable to answer them. Neither their philosophers nor sages nor priests can satisfy the thoughtful mood of the East, unravel the mystery that broods over life, disclose an effectual method of salvation, or point out the certainties beyond the grave. They inquire with outstretched hands; they are anxious for truth; but the truth-revealer is not among them.

To say that the Gospel will answer the inquiries of the pagan world, is true; but in what form or manner shall the Gospel send its answers into those regions of moral darkness? Shall it go as a torch shining upon their path, or as a glistening bayonet piercing the old systems to death? Is it by friction, attrition, antagonism—that is, *enforced* conformity to the divine will, that the Eastern world will learn what the Gospel is, and what it requires? or is there not a better way, by which to lift heathendom to the Gospel level? Are the old systems so worthless that they should immediately be put to death and be buried out of sight? or do they not, even though dimly, foreshadow some of the cardinal truths of Christianity, which entitle them to a place in the Christian system? The old religions, incompetent, deficient, and even pernicious, as they are, are not wholly valueless, and have served a purpose which the grateful thinker will recognize. Wanting in specific redemptive power, they are, nevertheless, the vehicles of certain divine ideas, which, under the transforming influence of the Gospel, may become potent and beautiful, and enter into the very constitution and life of the new religion. Students of religions are quick to discover verities common to all, or teachings so fundamental that religion in any form is impossible without them. In some religions the common principle is theistic, polytheistic or monotheistic; in others it is an incarnation, gross and crude, but the germ of a common faith; so that all religions are half-brothers, or cousins, or bear some relationship to one another.

It is this relationship, near or remote, but at all events fundamental, that is the key to fraternity among the religions, and, if one absorb all the others, it will amount to an absorption, rather than an annihilation, of relationship. The conquest of Christianity does not imply the dissolution of the verities of other religions, but their emphasis, purification, enlargement, and adaptation, with other more helpful truths not found in them, to the needs of men. After this manner Paul proceeded in his attacks upon paganism, acknowledging the resemblance or points of agreement between the old religions and that of Christ, and ignored the differences so long as the truth would permit. Antagonism was not his aim; reconciliation and victory were the ends he sought. At Athens the basis of agreement was the theistic idea, which he evolved into Christian monotheism, and the philosophers listened to him. In his conflicts with the Jews, he continually referred to the incorporation of certain laws, truths, and usages of the old economy with the Christian dispensation, winning along that line when open rupture would have followed a direct attack. Brahminism, without understanding the significance of its own teaching, urges that man must be born again, that is, he must separate himself from the crowd, commune with the great unseen Intelligence of the universe, and be filled with the spirit of Brahm— a doctrine in its essence akin to the purer Christian doctrine of regeneration, and on the basis of which reconciliation between them is possible. The Hindoo, misapplying his principle, builds up a caste, or creates a circle of men pronounced to be better than others because they have given themselves to spiritual meditation, which is the shadow of the Church idea, needing purification and direction. How really to be born again the Hindoo does not know, except that he must strive to rise into this *caste-experience;* he must become a member of the caste; but Christianity will teach him that such a birth is from God, and that the truest caste consists of regenerated and spiritual souls. At this point the two come in contact, and reconciliation, or the transformation of the Brahminical idea into the Christian doctrine, may, under certain educational rules, be accomplished. In like manner the Yäma of Hindu mythology may be transformed into the Satan of Christianity, and difference and conflict cease. The Christianity in Brahminism must be rescued from superstition, and the Brahminism in Christianity must at least be recognized, if the union of the two systems, that is, the virtual triumph of Christianity, be guaranteed.

Quite as striking is the resemblance of the incarnation idea of Buddhism to the true incarnation doctrine of Christianity, on which future mediation may be predicated and a future triumph made altogether probable.

Christianity does not more clearly vindicate the monotheistic principle than Mohammedanism. The chief business of the latter is the proclamation of this principle. The coalescence of the two religions on the acknowledgment of so fundamental a truth should not be longer delayed.

Without continuing the thought, it is evident that in one religion Christianity discovers a principle of regeneration, in another a doctrine of incarnation, and in a third the truth of monotheism, on which union with them is not impossible, and final victory over them a sometime certainty. In this fraternity or union, Christianity can not surrender any thing vital to itself, nor be lost in any other religion, nor compromise with superstitions; but it may accept their truths, refine their ideas, and gradually disclose their fulfillment in itself. *Christianity is the fulfillment of all the truths of paganism,* which is to be made so clear to the pagan mind that it will suffer no humiliation in agreeing to it, and will not long delay in abandoning the one for the other, just as the shipwrecked mariner abandons his leaky craft for the ship of rescue.

More important still, and to be reiterated until time shall end, *the chief glory of the triumph of Christianity will be the universally acknowledged authority of its greatest principle.* By virtue of its redemptive element, which discriminates the new religion from the old faiths, Christianity alone will succeed, and bases its future anticipations on its power. It is not its monotheism, or decalogue, or ordinances, or priesthood, or Sabbaths, that either constitute it a separate religion or insure its dominion in the future; but redemption from sin through Jesus Christ is its radical doctrine, its original starting-point, and the inspiration of its mission in this world. So constitutional is this soteriological element that it should be preached, if necessary, at the expense of every other Gospel idea. All other ideas are auxiliary, transient, incidental, compared with this idea of salvation. But the one idea includes, or is able to carry with it, all the other ideas of the Gospel system. Doctrines, ordinances, Church government and usages, are easily regulated and placed if the leading idea of redemption is in authority. The future triumph of the new religion implies the redemption of the world, or the triumph of its greatest principle in the children of men.

Let us consider what is meant by redemption, or the magnitude of the triumph of this great principle in human affairs. The word "redemption" is not a particular word for a particular spiritual state, but the key to the largest results of the influence of Christianity on the human race. It includes all that is possible through Christianity within the area of human life; it includes physical, social, ethical, and intellectual, as well as spiritual, regenerations and achievements; it comprehends in all its aspects the *constant elevation of man.*

First, *its influence will be more largely exercised in the domain of political government,* dictating laws in the interest of righteousness, suppressing evils of long standing or of recent origin, and regulating, without infringement on his natural rights, his political and civil life. The redemption of the governmental idea from oppression, which is the same thing as its conformity to the Gospel ideal of government, is as imperative as the redemption of science from fiction, or of medicine from quackery. Under its fostering care in its new form, the spirit of crime will disappear, the best civil institutions will prevail everywhere, and order, sobriety, stability, and esteem of the public good will characterize the administration of authority in all lands. History is a record of the struggle of the Gospel ideal with the governmental notion in its despotic and inhuman forms, recounting occasional victories, the gradual growth of humane ideas, and presaging the final elimination of every political heresy and governmental tyranny from the activities of the world. The Coliseum, a relic of pagan barbarism, is not possible now. Slavery is well-nigh a memory. The humanity of the race embodied in civil institutions is on the increase. Law accords with righteousness. Despotisms are crumbling. The idea of self-government is contagious, wrecking in its development the strongly built ideas of royalty, and pointing with unerring certainty to the enthronement of the individual in his natural rights. Civilization, not what it ought to be, is Christian in form, and is approximating the Gospel idea in spirit and impulse. The East dwells in the shadows of superstitions, but the West is rising toward God. As to the Gospel spirit must be attributed the improved changes in law, government, and civilization, so to the same spirit we look for speedy modifications in governmental forms which shall place them in harmony with God's idea of rulership, and lift up man to the enjoyment of every right to which his creation entitles him. In the future progress of the race, the redemption of government will occupy no inconspicuous relation to the final purpose of Christianity.

Second, *under the influence of the new religion the social life of man, as important as his political, will undergo an equally conservative transformation.* In the apparently small matters of dress, etiquette, manners, social customs, and domestic ideas and relationships, Christianity is revolutionizing the world, and must continue its regulating work until all peoples conform to its wholesome hints and suggestions. In China, where the paternal idea is venerable and strong, Confucius having insisted on its sacredness, and constituted it a part of religion, there are no such homes as in England and the United States, where the Christian idea of marriage and domestic life prevails. In Mohammedan lands polygamy is not only authorized by law, but also solemnized by religion, and exists in its most corrupting forms, debilitating the domestic idea, and destroying the national life of the people. It is not surprising that in such lands woman is without character as an immortal being; she is regarded as soulless. Nor is it surprising that the birth of a girl produces sadness, while the birth of a boy is the occasion of a great demonstration of joy. In Christian lands, inasmuch as polygamy does not prevail, woman is honored as the equal of man, and the birth of boy or girl is welcomed with eager pride. Evidently, it is a part of the mission of Christianity to redeem the *home*, or the domestic institution, from the vice of polygamy, and to elevate woman in the esteem of mankind.

The etiquette of pagan lands is as debasing as their religions are enervating, and needs the reformatory touch of Christian teaching. Asiatic dress is in violation of the purest ethical standards, and needs the Christian pattern. In India and Egypt the burial ceremony, usually Mohammedan, is repugnant, without solemnity, and so dreary as to deprive breaking hearts of all thought of a future world; while in Christian lands it is beautiful, tender, significant. The home, the life, the tomb, will appear in their holier aspects under the teachings of Him who is the way, the truth, and the life. *Social regeneration will be one of the benefits of the new religion.*

Third, *Christianity proposes to exert its healthful influence on the artistic sentiment of the race;* in other words, it proposes to purify the *fine arts*, more particularly sculpture and painting. There are those who object to these arts from the fact, not here questioned, that they have fostered the licentious spirit, and led to the general corruption and degradation of the nations patronizing them. It is too true that many sculptors and painters have acquired fame for genius at the expense of morality and purity.  Idolatry and corruption have thrived where these arts have flourished.  Athens decayed in the presence of its statues; Rome perished in the flames of the canvas.  That the artistic idea is as native to man as the governmental or social idea will not, perhaps, be disputed.  It has its functions, therefore; and the religion renders mankind a service that will purify the idea, regulate its functions, and make it instrumental in the public education and elevation.  This service Christianity proposes to render the fine arts, under whose influence man's love of the beautiful will be idealized in actual forms.

Thus far we have grouped the future work of Christianity in governments, institutions, homes, social customs, and artistic products; it is *external*, therefore; but it performs an *internal* work more profound, because more vital, and really the source of all external results. It is related to the thinking forces, the ethical ideas, and the spiritual lives of men quite as intimately as it is related to the homes, governments, and arts of society.

Fourth, *in its proposed regulation of the thought of mankind, or the government of the thinking forces, Christianity undertakes a work fundamental in character and permanent in result;* it is, therefore, a superior and supreme work.  In its contests with philosophic thought, its purpose has been, not the annihilation, but the purification of thought, and the harmonization of the various systems of speculative inquiry with the idealities of Christianity.  When harmonization was impossible, the old system disappeared and never revived.  Whatever truth was imbedded in such systems passed over into the religious category, but the system from which it was derived perished.  Thus Christianity has rescued the vital principles of the ancient systems from obscurity, and adopted them in the family of imperishable truths which constitute the Gospel system of religion.

In its contests with modern philosophic thought its object is the same, but the method is different.  While the aim is the rescue of truth from the incrustation of fiction, it also includes the annihilation of error, which is intelligently supported by modern thought.  According to the conception of Christianity materialism, which includes the atheistic tendency of psychology, cosmology, and the various phases of evolution, is a monstrous error, to be destroyed like any Sadducean heresy or contradictory and ruinous opinion.  From want of internal force the ancient speculations perished; but materialism, assuming a rational form, and appealing to intelligence, must be assailed, and its error eliminated from thought.  Ancient thought inquired for the truth; modern thought denies the greatest truths. The former sought the eternal cause of things; the latter denies the personification of the eternal cause. Hence, Christianity not only assumes the defensive, but is compelled to inaugurate an aggressive campaign against the offensive errors of modern thought. It must conquer in this domain, or lose what it has already gained. Thought is the source of life, activity, progress, salvation. Right thought is as imperative as right conduct; it precedes and regulates the conduct. The battle of the hour is, therefore, for supremacy in the realm of thought.

Fifth, the improvement of the *moral life* of the world may be justly inferred from the presence of Christianity in it, for it is reformatory, educational, and disciplinary. Its cry is against injustice, oppression, and inhumanity; its appeal is for law, order, sobriety, temperance, and righteousness; its warnings and retributions are urged in the interest of progress and happiness; its decalogue encourages every virtue and condemns every vice; its spirit promotes unity, hospitality, veracity, " peace on earth and good will to men." Under its influence the moral life of the race is quickened and the tendencies to evil restrained.

Sixth, *its greatest influence on mankind, however, is, not governmental, social, æsthetic, intellectual, and moral, but spiritual.* Its highest purpose is the procreation of a spiritual race on the earth, the elimination of sin as a dominating element in the world, and the rehabilitation of the old sin-cursed globe in the beauty and glory of Paradise. It means more than a millennium; it means the never-ending reign of Jesus Christ in the race begotten by the spirit of his love. A millennium ends; but the spiritual reign once established will go on forever. To spiritualize men; to destroy the carnal impulse; to introduce the saintly spirit in human life; to rule over the race so completely that birth by generation will be equivalent to birth by regeneration, or *the natural birth will be also a spiritual birth*; this is the ultimate idea of Christianity

*The universal sway of Christianity in the world signifies the existence of ideal political governments, the development of a perfect social life, the purification of the æsthetic sentiment, the government of the intellectual activities of man, the reign and elevation of perfect ethical principles,* AND THE SUPREMACY AND AUTHORITY OF THE DIVINE IDEA OF LIFE, OR THE SPIRITUAL REGENERATION OF THE RACE. *This is the outlook from the observatory of the apostles.*

On what grounds may an expectation of the universal triumph of Christianity be based? If it is any thing more than a hallucination, a pious hope, or a devout and dreamy sentiment; if it is a *rational expectation* grounded in the philosophy of things, or the nature of truth, or the trend of human history, it will be inspiring to consider it; otherwise it is without value. The expectation of such triumph, we are happy to write, has a philosophical ground, which appears in both a historical and statistical form, and complete enough to be assuring to those who are timid in faith or vacillating in hope.

The historical argument for the final supremacy of Christianity can not be overthrown, unless history itself is a delusion and without significance. The argument is two-fold in character, relating to the *tests* of Christianity by *historical science*, and to the integrity, and, therefore, the *proofs*, of Christianity by *historical events*. As a historic system Christianity must submit to the historic tests usually applied to other systems. To this it does not object; indeed, it covets a historical investigation conducted according to the canons of historical science. Such investigation has been made by critics, rationalists, exegetes, and theologians, the preponderance of evidence being largely in support of the integrity of the sacred books. The rationalists of Germany and Holland, under the leadership of Edward Reuss, reject the supernatural character of the Pentateuch, and deny its authorship to Moses. Another class of critics, known as Conservatives, of whom König, of Germany, and Robertson Smith, of Scotland, are representatives, accept the supernatural character of the Pentateuch, and attribute its important revelations to Moses. The contest thus far is largely one between radical and conservative critics, the one striking at the inspiration and authorship of the Pentateuch, the other carefully considering both, and modifying, without materially rejecting, accepted views. The historical criticism raging around the Pentateuch illustrates the historical attack made on all the Biblical records and the theologic interpretations of the Church. Rénan assails the authorship of some of the Pauline epistles. John's Gospel, too, has suffered a severe but harmless examination from skeptical inquirers.

While these one-sided investigations have been going on, leading to unexpected discoveries of proofs of authorship and credibility of the sacred records, others, among whom is George Rawlinson, have applied the historical tests in a purely scientific manner to these same records, and have overwhelmingly sustained them in spite of the denials of their radical opponents. Laying down four indisputable canons of criticism, Mr. Rawlinson applies them vigorously to the Old Testament, establishing in particular its historical portions from geology, physiology, ethnology, and geography so completely, that he has not been answered. Respecting the Pentateuch, he says it is "a history absolutely and in every respect true." The same conclusion is affirmed with respect to all the revelations of the Old Testament.

It may also be observed that the subversion of the historical integrity

46

of the New Testament has been found an utter impossibility, for as historical criticism has taken the shape of science, and has announced itself in the terms of law, it has been intelligently applied to historical truth ; and applied to the historical contents of the documents of Christianity, they have been sustained. The historical ground of Christianity has been established. That ground is the *philosophical prophecy of its stability and supremacy.* Tested by historical science, it has had incarnation in historical events. In a limited sense *Christianity is the history of mankind.* The activities of the race, the intellectual inquiries for truth, the seeking of ethical ideas and standards, and the conflicts and struggles of all generations, are the inspirations of fundamental religious ideas, which found final expression in Christianity. History is the manifestation of the religious idea; it is the result of a religious, that is, a divine plan. The plan has been obscure, is somewhat obscure still ; the idea is either unrecognized or undefined ; nevertheless history is the evolution of Christianity.

In its direct evolution, or, more particularly, in its specific relation to mankind as a religion, the historic results have been as manifest as the spirit that produced them, and as numerous as could well be tabulated. In the apostolic period of Christianity the development of the religious life of Oriental nations was marked and permanent. In the Constantine period the authority of the Christian idea was extended over the Roman Empire, and superseded pagan influence forever. In the Papal period the new religion, corrupted by traditions, asserted itself with enthusiasm, and acquired indisputable dominion in new lands. In passing, we write, given the missionary zeal of Francis Xavier, and Protestantism will be universal in a decade. In the days of the Lutheran Reformation the truth, separated from error, waxed mightily and prevailed in the greatest of Teutonic nations. In the Wesleyan era it saved England from despair, and transferred a Christian civilization to the Western hemisphere. If its internal history is the proof of its inspiration, its external history is the proof of its supremacy. Beginning at Jerusalem, it went forth to take the world, and it is on the march still, conquering wherever it goes, and promising to overturn all things in its way until it shall have delivered all kingdoms unto the Father. The task is difficult, the spectacle sublime, the result sure. *The law of evolution must break, or triumph can not be prevented.* Opposition is nothing. Infidelity is as the grain of dust on a chariot wheel.

If the historical argument is of the nature of a philosophical prophecy respecting the future of Christianity, the *statistical argument* is of the nature of an absolute revelation confirming the prophecies, and indicating further fulfillment. The statistical argument is **a** *mathematical truth,* or a revelation in philosophic form, and, therefore, entitled to more than ordinary consideration. Prophecy inspires hope; history quickens faith; revelation is of the nature of knowledge, and answers expectation. To include the details of the argument, or the items showing the relative progress of Protestantism and Roman Catholicism, and the comparative growth of Christianity and Moham-medanism, or of false religions in general, is unnecessary. It will be sufficient if we indicate the steady progress of Christianity from the beginning in all its forms throughout the world, as an evidence of its persistency toward the consummation, or the attainment of final su-premacy. The following are regarded as the approximately correct statistics of the number of Christians in the world at the end of the different periods given :

| | | | |
|---|---|---|---|
| First Century, | 500,000 | Eleventh Century, | 70,000,000 |
| Second " | 2,000,000 | Twelfth " | 80,000,000 |
| Third " | 5,000,000 | Thirteenth " | 75,000,000 |
| Fourth " | 10,000,000 | Fourteenth " | 80,000,000 |
| Fifth " | 15,000,000 | Fifteenth " | 100,000,000 |
| Sixth " | 20,000,000 | Sixteenth " | 125,000,000 |
| Seventh " | 25,000,000 | Seventeenth " | 155,000,000 |
| Eighth " | 30,000,000 | Eighteenth " | 200,000,000 |
| Ninth " | 40,000,000 | 1880, A. D. | 410,900,000 |
| Tenth " | 50,000,000 | | |

Under the Papal *regime* the progress of Christianity was stayed, and came almost to a stand-still in the thirteenth century; but under Protestant direction it now controls the civilization and development of fully one-third of the populations of the globe.

This, however, is not the strongest way of putting the case, for Dr. Schem has figured it out that in 1876 nearly *seven hundred millions of people,* or quite one-half of the world's populations, were under the dominion of Christian governments, showing a gratifying extension of the governmental ideas of Christianity. "One hundred and eighty-years ago," says Dr. D. Dorchester, "only 155,000,000 of the earth's population were under Christian governments."

In an equally striking manner it can be made to appear that, while the territorial area of the globe is about fifty-two millions of square miles, Christian governments exercise legitimate control over thirty-two millions of square miles, showing that their authority is on the increase, and exceeds that of all other religions combined. The argument from statistics points to an ever-widening domain of Christian influence, and the final supremacy of Christianity as a religion.

If any thing more is needed to confirm this mathematical view of the future, we might draw on what we are pleased to style the *retributive argument,* or the argument of facts which portend the doom of all other religions. " Mohammedanism," says Ram Chandra Bose, " has proved a failure." It is too late to reconstruct it or purify it; it must go; it will be absorbed and disappear. " Mere secular education," says Dr. T. J. Scott, " would wreck Brahminism;" but as it would fail to " reconstruct India morally," he adds, "the Gospel is pulling down the stronghold of Brahminism with irresistible effect, and in its stead is rearing the temple of God." Dr. J. M. Thoburn reports of Parseeism that, " as a religious system, like every thing else which ' decayeth and waxeth old,' it must soon vanish away." He asserts that education alone will demolish it. Buddhism is, perhaps, the most difficult religion to subvert, but Dr. E. Wentworth observes that, " half the difficulty of a grand undertaking is accomplished when we know what we have to contend with." The old religion is a mountain in our path, but " faith, prayer, and sacrifice vanquish devils and overturn mountains." Taoism, according to Dr. V. C. Hart, " is sere and ready to decay. Its weird and grotesque growth stands palsied in the presence of true education and religion." "Shintoism," says Dr. R. S. Maclay, " has lost much of its individuality and self-assertion;" and, " like many other systems of a similar character, it is gradually moving to take its place in the silent chambers of the past." As to Confucianism, it can not properly be enumerated among the religions of the East; nevertheless, granting it a religious rank, Dr. S. L. Baldwin affirms, that the " awakening intellect and conscience of China can not be satisfied with the negative character of Confucianism." It must, therefore, finally be displaced by a positive religion.

From these estimates of missionaries, it is evident that the old religions are enfeebled by their own corruptions and superstitions, and are on the way to extinction, public education being sufficient in many cases to entirely overthrow the nation's faith in them. Time alone will visit with destruction these hoary-headed faiths; but education and religion will undermine their foundations and reduce them to chaos.

In the Vatican gallery is a prophetic painting of the fate of paganism. It represents a broken column, prostrate, partly covered with sand, and partly hidden with rankest weeds. Thus paganism, hydra-headed and old as the ages, shall fall and be buried out of sight.

The prospectus of Christianity contains a recital of the overthrow of paganism, the universal sway of Christian civilization, the sanctification of political government, and the spiritualization of the human race, or the elimination of evil from the abodes of men.

# CHAPTER XXXIV.

## CHRISTIANITY A PHILOSOPHIC AND RELIGIOUS FINALITY.

PLATO'S allusion in the *Republic* to a "torch-race on horseback" was founded on a beautiful custom that obtained in the Panathenæan festivals, in which the contestants, seizing torches lighted from the altars of sacrifice, ran for the prize, he securing it whose torch did not expire in the race.

Of another torch-race, which began in Plato's time and still continues, we moderns are witnesses. It is the race of ideas, of which religion and philosophy are the representatives; both have drawn their light from sacrificial fires; and both have run along the pathway of the centuries, sometimes with fatiguing steps, but usually with a hopeful enthusiasm and a belief in final victory. Perhaps it is too early in the race, long as it has been going on, to prepare wreaths for the victor, not knowing which it shall be; but, judging from appearances, relative achievements, and future prospects, the lamp of philosophy, already nearly extinguished, must grow dimmer with the coming years, while the light of Christianity, like that of the sun, is as bright as the day it first shone upon the earth, with no indications of a decline and no signs of extinction. The verdict of history is in favor of Christianity; the voices of prophecy, of evolution, of the impulse of progress, and of human hope, are musical with the strains of a jubilee over its final vindication in the world.

To speak of a final religion, or of a stereotyped religious idea, superseding all others and governing all men; to speak of one religion absorbing all others and conforming the race-life to its ideals,— may savor of strong prejudice in its favor, but such prejudice is rooted in the reason of things. It is a philosophical, not a religious, prejudice that justifies the extreme faith here uttered. One school of philosophers, materialistic in their sense of things, may pronounce such faith inconsistent with the spirit of progress, which, while it uproots some things and establishes others, does not point to final settlement of any thing, or at least to *final things*, in this period of the world's history. It should not be forgotten that the best idea of progress is a *tendency to finality in all things*. A drifting universe, either of thought or matter, is contrary to the highest conception of order, stability, and progress. A final religion, a final philosophy, a final Bible, a final God, a final eternity, are things which the human mind craves, and to which progress tends.

Again, the votaries of the old religions, indisposed to accept the solution of the supreme problems according to Christianity, will be slow to embrace the idea of a final religion for man, since they understand that the universal, that is, the final, element is wanting in their own. They prefer the present state of conflict to the extinction of their ancestral and traditional faiths, and the enthronement of what they regard as a foreign religion. From their stand-point, Christianity is as defective in the universal element as their own religions, and they pretend to see no benefit in the exchange of their faith for that of another people. All talk, then, of a final religion strikes the materialist and the traditionalist as the acme of absurdity, as the outburst of that bigotry which religion is always supposed to inspire.

Nevertheless, there is a finality in the most literal, as well as in the highest accommodated, sense in both philosophy and religion, to which we do well to take heed. Gravitation is a finality in physics; memory is a finality in psychology; the circle is a finality in mathematics; the circulation of the blood is a finality in physiology. In like manner, there are certain religious finalities, which constitute the frame-work of Christianity and make it the final religion. These we shall proceed to emphasize.

We affirm, first, that *Christianity is a philosophic finality, or the finality of all philosophic truth*; but we do not so affirm in a dogmatic, but rather in a philosophic, spirit. It is not meant that Christianity will supersede a true philosophy, for the two are as consistent as mathematics and astronomy; but it will extinguish false philosophy respecting truth, and become the end and explanation of a genuine philosophy in its treatment of the highest truth. In itself, it will prove to be the true philosophy of all truth, without assuming a philosophic form, or usurping the prerogatives of philosophy as a distinct realm of thought and investigation. In *essence*, Christianity is philosophy; in *form*, it is religion. As to its *ends*, Christianity is philosophical; as to its *ideals*, it is religious.

In their methods of arriving at truth, secular philosophy and the Christian religion have widely differed, the method of the one being rationalistic, the method of the other being supernaturalistic. The ends, however, are the same. As one may travel from New York to San Francisco by water and another by railroad, the difference in these cases being the *method* of travel or the *routes* taken, while the end is the same, so one may seek the truth by the philosophical, and another by the Biblical, method, each having the same end in view. The same truths are before philosopher and inspired writer. One seeks to discover, the other proposes to reveal. One asks questions, the other listens to answers. One is an interrogation, the other is an echo. Philosophy is an anxious inquirer after truth; Christianity is a calm revealer of truth. The methods are exactly opposite, but the results, if the one could go as far as the other, would be precisely identical. Häckel would throw himself into a rage to be told that the philosophical method must result in the establishment of supernatural truth, but it is difficult to account for the glorification of that method if it breaks down when applied to the highest truth. To this Häckel might reply that it is the truth that breaks down, which would be very like an astronomer condemning the stars because his telescope did not reveal them. If there is any failure in the application of the method to the truth, it is the failure of method, and not the failure of truth. All along in these discussions we have lamented the break-down of the philosophical method at vital points, implying the necessity of the purification of the method whereby supernatural truth may be discerned and approved. Besides, the unity of truth, the oneness of the natural and supernatural, justifies the application of the philosophical method to the supernatural, and the supernatural method to the natural; that is, an interchange of methods is not at all impossible, since the truths to be ascertained belong to both spheres of thought and inquiry. The theologic thinker is quite willing to submit revealed truth to philosophic analysis, but the materialist is quite unwilling to submit philosophic truth to spiritual introspection. Yet to this one must come as well as the other.

In the hands of its friends the philosophical method has been prostituted to the support of wretched theories, as Darwin urged natural selection, Häckel the mechanical theory of the universe, and Bain the mechanical process of thought, showing either an awkward use of the instrument—reason—or a false report of the results, or both. Is theory or fact the issue of the philosophic method? Is opinion to be maintained or truth to be sought by its use? Hitherto scientific fictions, heresies, theories, opinions, and philosophic falsehoods have been sustained by the philosophic method, just as superstitions, traditions, mysticisms, and fanaticisms have been apparently justified by the religious or supernaturalistic method. The time has arrived not only for the purification of method, but its rescue from perversion and its legitimate application to truth. A philosophic method, a rationalistic process, must terminate in the support of the ultimate truths of Christianity, otherwise Christianity is vulnerable at its strongest point. Supernatural truth is as philosophical as natural truth, and the method applied to the latter may also be applied to the former, so far as the method itself has been developed or perfected. As the algebraic method of to-day is an improvement over such method of yesterday, so the philosophic method is developing, and must be adapted finally to test all truth, and will establish the highest truth. This is the purport of that method, this is its use in the realm of thought, and this foreshadows its relation to religion.

Granting that the philosophic method has been turned against highest truth, it is evident that such truth has received its strongest vindication at the hands of that method. With its predilection for atheistic sentiment, by virtue of its method philosophy has been compelled to declare in favor of the fundamental *idea* of God. We do not say it has declared for God, but it supports the *idea* of a Supreme Power as a condition of thought, as a condition of existence. Hamilton, Darwin, and Spencer, of the moderns, and Socrates and Plato, of the ancients, demonstrated the *idea of God* as an ultimate fact of philosophy. In order to save Darwinism, evolution, and kindred theories from a total wreck, it has come to pass that their founders have proclaimed their compatibility with the theistic hypothesis. Foreseeing the utter impossibility of blotting out the divine name from the universe, the friends of evolution bolster it up by assuming that it was the *divine method* by which the Supreme Power inaugurated the universe. Here is a philosophic theory transformed into a divine idea for self-preservation. Thus it may happen that, in order to self-existence, nearly every philosophic theory will clothe itself in divine garments, and walk the earth as a divine idea, sovereign at last in the thought of man. To this we have no objection ; this is what we expect. The drift of philosophy is toward a demonstration of ultimate truth ; that is, the philosophic method, rescued from its corruptions and misapplications, is at last reaffirming the truths first made known by the supernaturalistic method, and justifying them on its grounds and in its own way. In natural order the supernaturalistic method preceded the philosophic method in the ascertainment of religious truth, but the philosophic method is now that by which religious truth is confirmed. *The supernaturalistic method for revelation; the philosophic method for confirmation.* Confirmation is as valuable as revelation ; confirmation *is* revelation ; the philosophic *is* the supernaturalistic method, applied later in the historic order for the demonstration of revelation. Hence it is not too much to say that Christianity is a philosophic finality, because the philosophic method conducts to its ultimate truths.

Again, *Christianity must be accepted as a philosophic finality, or final solution of all philosophic truth, on the ground that its own truths are essentially philosophical, rational, and of the highest utility to man.* Christianity is a philosophical religion ; it is a philosophy of truth in its fundamentals and a philosophy of knowledge in its revelations. In making this statement we do not forget the great mysteries of religion, but they are the mysteries of philosophy as well, and without religious illumination must be utterly inexplicable. Being, generation, life, matter, God, immortality, and man are stupendous mysteries, taxing philosophy beyond its ability, and reducing religion to a fabled mass but for its supernatural revelation. This is our relief in the investigation of these mysteries, and the only relief. To dispense with the mysteries by calling them absurdities will not do; they are truths, a knowledge of which is essential to human welfare, human hope, and human faith, but such knowledge is not attainable through philosophy alone. Christianity is the key to final or ultimate knowledge of these subjects, and, therefore, superior to philosophy, which, aiming at such knowledge and anxious for it, falls short of acquiring it. In this respect, while Christianity is strictly philosophical, it can not be said that philosophy is strictly religious. The two are *half*-brothers, both exhibiting a natural likeness, but only one a supernatural image. As the supernatural is the end of the natural, so Christianity is the end of philosophy.

Then it must be remembered that the truths of Christianity are not only ultimate; they are also rational. An ultimate truth is not necessarily rational in the sense that it may be apprehended as rational; it must be rational, however, in its content or essence. Frequently not a few of the sublime revelations of Christianity are ridiculed on the ground of an alleged disharmony with reason, the skeptic failing to recognize the difference between the *rationale* of the truth he assails and the *rationale* of his apprehension or assault. The incarnation has been the subject of ridiculous interpretations, because human reason did not recognize the divine reason of the truth. Yet incarnation is as rational as generation; both are great mysteries.

The so-called irrational truths of the Bible are on a par with the so-called irrational truths of natural theology; in many instances the truths of one sphere are the truths of the other, and both must be allowed or both rejected. Truth, natural or supernatural, is rational. Philosophy appropriates natural truth, discerning its rationality, while Christianity appropriates supernatural truth, pointing out its inner consistency and beauty. To many minds the rational character of spiritual truth is more patent than the rational character of natural truth, since the latter reaches a limit and solves nothing, while the former knows no limit and solves every thing. Verily, the reason that solves or discerns the highest truth is the highest reason. To those whose reason is spiritualized or dominated by the divine wisdom, and whose interior sense enables them to penetrate through all seeming irrationality of form to actual rationality of essence, and so discern the sublimity of truth, a knowledge of infinite things is not impossible. Because Christianity is a philosophical ultimate on the one hand, and a rational religion on the other, it may truly claim to be a finality.

It might well be observed that the mysteries of Christianity, as well as its demonstrable truths, are philosophical and rational, without reproach in the realm of thought, without discoverable weaknesses in their inner relations. That these mysteries amaze and often perplex the thinker, we shall not deny ; but a mystery is not a contradiction. Neander says all contradictions are reconciled in Jesus Christ. To this may we add that all mysteries are *solved* in Jesus Christ, because they all emanate from him. One thing is certain : Biblical truths do not outrage the reason like Kant's Antinomies, nor do they confound the inquirer like many philosophical theories; but grow in proportion as they are studied, and demonstrate their high-born character as they are investigated. The atomic theory of creation, with the divine element eliminated, is more mysterious than the Mosaic revelation, while the evolutionary theory of the origin of man requires more faith than any miracle recorded in the sacred Gospels. Speculative philosophy never had so many embarrassments to meet as now, for in the ancient period truth was not in its way, but in these days, its theories, its suggestions, its teachings, are immediately subjected to that final test of all things—the *religious canon.* Unwilling to admit the test, nevertheless the test is applied, and error is exposed. There are no antinomies in Christianity ; there are mysteries. There is no speculation in religion ; there is philosophic rationality. Speculation assumes to be the criterion of truth, but truth is the criterion of speculation.

The stones, the trees, the oceans, the mountains may test gravitation, but in a broader sense gravitation tests the whole earth. In a narrow sense philosophy may test Christianity, but in the final verdict it will be seen that Christianity has tested philosophy. In the fourth pair of his antimomies Kant supports a belief in God, and then contradicts it by a contrary supposition, leaving the thinker to work himself out of the logical dilemma, and creating a doubt as to the value of reason and the integrity of knowledge. In like manner, in the third pair of antinomies, he advocates both necessity and liberty, requiring escape in order to ascertain the truth. In such follies and to such extremes of absurdity Christianity does not indulge. It is one thing or the other. It affirms the existence of God, and never compromises the affirmation. It declares human liberty, basing thereon the doctrine of human responsibility, and never intimates the reign of the fatalistic spirit in human affairs. Kant proposes the singular justification of his antinomies that they are essential to knowledge; that is, the knowledge of truth lies along the pathway of these contraries, or within their boundaries. On no such cast-iron logical regulations is Christianity dependent for its settlement of the questions of truth; it has a logic of its own at once fascinating, complete, irresistible; it is the *inherent logic of truth.* Its mysteries belong not to the common categories of thought, and are not strictly amenable to the standards of Aristotle and Bacon. However, they are not inimical to philosophic reason, since they are rational in their inmost contents and in harmony with truth not mysterious. Mysterious truth is not in antagonism with transparent truth. Miracle, prophecy, inspiration, regeneration, and redemption, considered as exclusive religious truths, are as rational as the more exclusive philosophical doctrines of creation, providence, biogenesis, and the conservation of forces. To the natural mind, however, the former seem like abstractions, or borrowed and refined superstitions, while the latter appear as concrete facts within the domain of observation, analysis, and utility. The higher truths seem all but unreal, while the lower advertise their reality. The conflict of the spiritual and the material is the conflict of the apparently unreal and the real; the antagonism of philosophy and Christianity is the antagonism of lower and higher, of sense and spirit. Christianity is spirit-philosophy, of which its mysteries, the greater realities, are the proofs. The rational content of Christianity is the solution of all philosophic truth.

We dare also to hazard the assertion that Christianity is a very practical philosophical scheme, adapted both in its spirit and purposes to the present life, and, therefore, destined to be final. Who does not wonder at the endless stupidities, the "insoluble contradictions," and the abstruse vagaries with which the tomes of philosophers are filled? Much of it, aside from its relation to some exploded theory, is wholly useless. The wordy discussions of nominalists and realists, of idealists and sensationalists, of evolutionists and materialists, have a place, doubtless, in the progress of thought, and are mile-posts along the weary way to truth; but the average man knows nothing of their existence, could not understand them if reported to him, and lives in another realm entirely. The "dirt philosophy" of the day is not vital to human history. Atomism is destitute of ethical influence; Herbert Spencer's scientific morality is an unapplied fiction; Häckel's constructive ethical system is without inherent strength or adaptation.

On the other hand, Christianity is vital in its philosophical relations, or it is nothing; it imparts life to human history or infects it with spiritual insensibility. In its adaptations to man, in its power to promote his welfare, to pilot him in darkness, and create in him immortal hope, its philosophical character is clearly revealed. *It is a philosophy of life; it is a philosophy of the universe; it is a philosophy of man;* IT IS A PHILOSOPHY OF GOD. Of life, it reveals not only the origin, but also the Originator; of the universe, it reveals the primordial, the Platonic, plan and its execution. Of man, it is a complete revelation, both as to his possibilities and certainties. Its laws, its promises, its truths, its mysteries, whose edges wear an eternal hue, have in them an inspiring force that he feels, a guiding influence that he obeys, a redemptive power to which he submits. Of God, it is decisive, revealing him in his unity and proclaiming him as the world's Lawgiver, Benefactor, and Deliverer.

Perhaps right here the dividing line between Christianity and Philosophy proper is more conspicuous than at any other point. Christianity is more philosophical than philosophy, because it is more rational, because it is more useful. The uplifting, guiding, redeeming power of the one finds no counterpart in the other. The revelations of the one are not at all matched by the conclusions of the other. Häckel, Darwin, and Spencer have rendered no such service to the world as Moses, John, and Paul. It must also be confessed that Christianity, for its revelations, is in no sense indebted to philosophy; it did not borrow its truths, it originated them; it does not work out its truths, it states them. Truth may be the end of philosophy, but *Christianity is the end of truth.* While Philosophy has been working toward the end, Christianity has reached it. Christianity is truth, the end of truth, beyond which philosophy can not go, as far as which it has not yet come. If Christianity is the end of truth, it must also be the end of philosophy; hence, philosophy must finally be absorbed by Christianity. If ultimate truth absorbs all related or intermediate truth, and the highest truth includes the lowest, then philosophical truth at last must be lost in the broader truth of Christianity, which is the same as saying that *Christianity is the final philosophy.* As such we proclaim it. Final in its truths, it must be final as a philosophy of truth.

As Christianity is the final philosophy, so is it the *final religion.* It is not only the supreme religion, it is the only supernatural religion, and therefore *the only religion.* All others in their sober contents are mere adumbrations, reflections, or imitations, to be fulfilled, and, therefore, to be lost in that which shall endure forever. Except among those who, dissatisfied with certain theologic phases of Christianity, are prophesying great structural changes in the religious concept, the world is not anticipating a new religion, nor are there any signs of preparation for another. An entirely new religion, embodying the principal features of all religions, and supplanting all, because superior to all, is not a possibility. Such eclecticism has been mooted in certain quarters, but the expectation of a religion made up of eliminations, combinations, and additions, is theoretical. Even should such a religion appear, just so far as it contained the truth, it would be nothing more than Christianity under a new name, and in a disguised form, aiming at the very ends it proposes, and by methods, just so far as they would prove effectual, in harmony with its agencies and revelations. In a sense not applicable to any other religion Christianity is the purest eclecticism, or a revelation of the absolute truth of all religions, and filled only with the highest and holiest inspirations both from earth and heaven. Improvement on the eclectic plan is impossible. Hence, Christianity is a religious finality.

What, it may be asked, is meant by religious finality? It is not intended to mean that the Christianity of the future will be unchanged in its particulars, nor that its truths will not seem larger, richer, fuller, than they do now, nor that it will be unantagonized by ideas apparently religious and contrary to itself. As we have shown, there is the "new in Christianity" that must be brought to light; there is an unexplored realm, a vast deep, of truth that must be entered, and report made of its contents. The anticipation of the new is an inspiration to faith and labor, but the new will not be inconsistent with the old; it will be more glorious; it will be broader, higher, deeper; it will be a fathomless ocean. The discovery of the hidden realms of truth will be a part of the joyous labor of the future, resulting in the relief of Christianity from its accessories of error and superstition, and its enlargement of just such revelations which up to this time the human mind has been too timid to anticipate, and too sluggish to desire. Man's ability to apprehend Christianity in its larger aspects is by no means exhausted. His studies of its truths have but begun. He must search more and more; he must go into the depths. In his deep-sea soundings he may find pearls that the fathers never saw; he may bathe in waters that, unlike Lethean streams, will revivify his intellectual aspiration, and produce a widening consciousness of existence that he never before felt. Neither Eusebius, nor Luther, nor Knox, nor Wesley, nor all the religious teachers of the past fully disclosed the divine mysteries as taught in the holy oracles. Future generations will have something to do if they comprehend the majesty and magnitude of the world of truth.

Speculation, however, on the probable developments of Christianity must cease, lest we forget the important point that whatever the development, and larger as the Christianity of the future will be, it will be the old Christianity of Christ, and John, and Paul, the Christianity we ourselves have received. In its unfolded character, the old better known, and the new in strictest harmony with it, it will be as it is now, the final announcement of God to man, and accepted, where accepted at all, as the only religion worth having or protecting. For this belief or anticipation several reasons may be stated.

First, Christianity is a religion of *positive affirmations.* Emerson insists upon affirmations, and that they be as strong and loud as cannon balls. There is nothing so empty, so powerless as a negation; it is a fuse without powder. Agnosticism is the crater of the extinct volcano of Pyrrhonism. In religion one affirmation is worth more than a thousand negations, one truth is more valuable than all the errors of the centuries. Light, not darkness; knowledge, not ignorance; certainties, not dubieties; are wanted in the realm of religious thought. Is it answered that in nothing can man be less positive in belief, less sure that he is correct in thought, than in religion? that he must deal with traditions, superstitions, legends, theologies? that religious truths so-called are the products, not of the brain, but of the heart? and that Christianity, in assuming to be supernatural, deprives itself of a rational basis, and must appeal to credulity for support? Some things are not to be denied, even though they compel an abandonment of some supposed truths, and a change of theological position. It is true that the current of religious thought, following it in its course down the ages, appears at times like a muddy stream, in some places more like a stagnant pool, and so frequently it flows on like a turbid river. Of the mythological religions the heart grows sick in recounting the oppressions, the idolatries, the sacrifices, and the benumbing influence which under their reign were everywhere sure to exist. Of the great historical religions in the East more can be said in their favor since, in a preliminary sense, they were related to that which followed, and to a degree their old teachers, ignorant of truth, were yet stirred by the deepest religious impulses, but if they fore-glimpsed the necessities of the race they were unable to provide for them, and so man, in their hands, was as helpless as ever.

In Mohammedanism, a religion on crutches, a religion lame in one foot at least, we see an advance, but only in one direction. The truth here gained is shrouded in superstition as distressing and in darkness as dense as that which preceded it, showing that the core of a helpful religion can not be any one of a number of great truths, but it must be the central truth of the kingdom of God.

The need of another religion, without superstition, without an enervating aim, without a depressing effect, has its demonstration in the weaknesses of the world's religions. Such religion is Christianity. Is tradition a weakness in religion? Jesus condemns tradition. Is fable a positive infirmity of religion? Jesus says, "I am the truth," lifting his religion above fable. Are other religions barren of a majestic purpose? Jesus says, "The Son of Man is come to seek and to save that which was lost." Neither Gautama, nor Confucius, nor Mohammed centered their activities in a purpose so philanthropic or exhibited a spirit so divine. Separating Christianity, as Jesus warrants us in doing, from superstition, fable, mythology, and tradition, its superiority to all religions is apparent, and its positive character is the more readily apprehended. It deals neither with negations nor superstitions, but consists of the most positive and coherent affirmations on the sublimest truths ever addressed to man. Its great and growing power lies just here. *It affirms the existence of God, the origin of the worlds, the creation of man, the moral degeneracy of the race, the authority of supernatural ethical distinctions, the eternal wages of sin, the nature and necessity of holiness, the hope of redemption in Jesus Christ, the certainty of death, the promise of resurrection, the final accountability of man at the judgment-seat of Christ, and the eternity of the rewards and retributions pronounced upon the last day.* On subjects so vital Christianity is transparent; it utters no uncertain sound; it misleads no honest inquirer, for if the Gospel be hid it is hid to them that are lost; it inspires every truth-seeker, being truth itself. On many themes the Bible is not as explicit as curiosity might desire, nor as clear as some of its teachers have wished; but such themes are oftener scientific than religious. Religious truths, which concern human character and are related to human happiness and destiny, are positively, strongly, repeatedly affirmed, so that the wise student thereof may sufficiently apprehend them. Affirmed truth is not necessarily explained truth, God's existence is affirmed, but not defined. Regeneration is an affirmed necessity, but the process by which it is secured, except that the Holy Spirit is the instrument, is not explained. Truths, not explanations; theorems, not solutions; affirmations, not negations, constitute the substance of the divine revelations, the strength and frame-work of Christianity. On this ground we predicate, not only the solidity of Christianity, but also its perpetuity and finality as a religion.

Again, the *vital principle* of Christianity is a guarantee of its future and its finality as religious truth. The continued reign of a religion is dependent upon the inherent vitality of its sovereign or predominant principle. External forces, usurpation of rights, and public misinstruction, may enthrone a false religion and perpetuate it many centuries; but its decadence is certain and its overthrow final. Time is long enough to work its revenge on error. False religions must perish, because falsehood is perishable in itself. Equally uncertain are those religions whose great truths, drawn from divine sources, are enshrined in superstition, because superstition is doomed. Mohammedanism, with its one underlying truth, will not be able to save itself, first because the one truth of the unity of God is not sufficient for a religion, and, second, because, if sufficient, its incrustation of superstition quenches its vitality and reduces its activity to a routine movement of blind and helpless faith. In time, therefore, it must be a religion of history.

Monotheism, as a sovereign principle, is fundamental to Christianity, but monotheism alone is not Christianity. From the great doctrine of the unity of God issue many great truths, facts, and elementary teachings, all essential to religion, as the ideas of authority, will, law, obedience, homage, and duty. The idea of God's sovereignty projects into the world the thoughts of government, providence, justice, equity, force, order, and stability. However sovereign these thoughts, however essential to religion, they do not constitute the highest religion. More is wanted than *sovereignty.* Religion does not reach its highest altitude in *law* or force. This was the supreme weakness of Judaism, as it is the religious infirmity of Mohammedanism. The Judaic God was intensely personal, a ruler; but decay smote Judaism like drought the king's garden. The personality of God was sounded by Mohammed, and it echoed over the continents, and paganism turned pale, and atheism sought a cave; but it has proved insufficient.

For a like reason Brahminism has suffered an almost total eclipse, and is bound to go out in the blackest darkness. It is not enough that Brahm is intelligence or light, since the world has need of something more than light. Besides, the average Brahmin, worshiping Intelligence, does not receive knowledge, and inquiring for Light he never finds it. He worships emptiness, and is empty in return. He waits at the altar for revelations, but they never come. He prates of wisdom, but he has it not. He speaks of light, but ever walks in darkness. Buddhism, dissatisfied with a distant or abstract light, incarnates the divine intelligence in one of the race, a child or man, whom it styles Lama or the priest, but from whom the worshiper receives nothing. With this incarnation Buddhism stops, and the Buddhist stops, without relief from sin, inspiration to holiness, or encouragement to activity.

These are variations of the monotheistic principle, sovereign in the Eastern religions, proving how incompetent any religion is for the highest tasks without another or the life-giving endowment. It is at this point that the great difference between Christianity and the historical religions is manifest, a difference as wide as that between life and death. Its vital principle is not the sovereignty of God. While the fact of the divine existence is as prominent and as potent in Christianity as in any other religion, it is not the supreme fact; it is rather the initiatory step toward the religion whose central truth is something else. The difference between the sovereignty of God and the incarnation of God measures the difference between the divine and all human religions. The latter are rooted in sovereignty; the former begins with the incarnation of Jesus Christ. *Incarnation, not monotheism, is the vital principle of Christianity.* Jesus Christ is the chief corner-stone of the new religion. Recognizing law, sovereignty, government, providence, justice, and force, as the preliminary ideas of religion, Christianity presents salvation from sin, atonement by Jesus Christ, regeneration by the Holy Ghost, and future rewardability on the basis of the temporal life, as the essential elements of a better religion. Judaism and Mohammedanism announced that the world had a Creator and man a Law-giver; Christianity, reiterating these announcements, lifted up its voice and proclaimed a Savior. This is new; this is the vital principle of Christianity. Superseding all other principles, it does not seem possible that any other can ever supersede it, and, therefore, the religion based upon it must be final.

Furthermore, the settlement of the future of the divine religion is partly determined by the providential fact that the greatest truths of the historical religions find their counterparts in Christianity. It is not important to ascertain just how certain truths are common to all religions, nor how it happens that such truths, relieved of grossness and incapability, crystallize in strength and beauty in Christianity. He who denies to Hindooism, either in its philosophic or religious utterance a trace of truth, needs the opening of his eyes, for, deficient both as philosophy and religion, it is neverthless the exponent of great religious ideas, and has wrought in man a hunger for things divine that must always precede their attainment. All the old religions excite an intolerable craving, but they do not satisfy it. Religions that have stood like great pillars supporting the ages must have in them some truths that Christianity can appropriate, or which are identical with the truths of the divine Teacher. The substance of what is good in them, the final elements of the old systems, may be transformed either into primary or final elements of the new religion, and so will be preserved forever. The sovereignty of God, the authority of law, the reign of providence, the manifestations of

47

the divine presence, all essential divine truths, must pass from the old into the new in order that the followers of the old may lose nothing essential in embracing the new. Many superstitions, many false interpretations of the facts of life, many vagaries in traditional forms, corrupted during the lapse of time, they will abandon; but of the unity of God and of the facts of creation, providence, and government, they will have all the brighter conception, since it is the province of the new to emphasize, illustrate, and enforce these ideas as it was impossible for the old to do. Christianity contains all the essential truths, the sovereign ideas, the vital teachings and principles of the ancient faiths, rescuing them from a barbarous environment, and assigning them their true position in the final system of religious truth.

This is not its greatest virtue, however; for what better is it than they if it is only a conglomeration or reproduction of the old faiths? Christianity has its specialties, doctrines that separate it from all other, even the most kindred, faiths, and which declare it to be from God. That other religions in their primary elements resemble Christianity, is a sufficient reason for their absorption by the latter; that the latter is unlike any other in specific truths, is sufficient ground for its perpetuity. Many religions, animated by common sovereign principles, can not be as promotive of general righteousness as *one* religion, containing all the sovereignties, owing to the frictions and irritations which the many are likely to provoke, while the one can fight its way along a single line. Brahminism, Buddhism, Mohammedanism, Shintoism, and Taoism, are reproduced or preserved in their essentials in Christianity. The difference between them and the one religion standing out against them is that what is vital, supreme, essential in these Eastern faiths, must occupy a subordinate relation in the Christian faith, parting with their authority as religions, and sinking out of sight as divine systems. From supremacy to subordination is a step down, but it has reference, not to annihilation, but solely to a change of position in the religious conflict. The truth of the old is a truth of the new, but with less influence in the latter than in the former. What is absolute in the old is relative in the new; what is fundamental in the one, becomes auxiliary in the other. The ascendency of Christianity is the ascendency of its specialty, namely, the Incarnation, and the subordination of all other sovereignties in religion.

Too much stress can not be laid upon the fact that Christianity is proving itself to be the final religious answer of God to man by its *abundant and exhaustless revelations*. It is a canon of faith that the inspired Scriptures are sufficient in themselves, as sources of truth, and that new revelations are unnecessary and will never be made. This is not startling to those who reflect that the revelations already given contain within themselves new and unknown, but not unknowable, truths, to be gradually unfolded as man's spiritual preparation for their apprehension and use is completed. Inspired truth is a wheel within a wheel; one revelation is a key to another revelation; one truth is the vestibule to the palace of treasures. As, ascending the Rocky Mountains, the summit of one peak enables the traveler to discern still other peaks, higher and greater, that he did not recognize or anticipate from the valleys below, so, ascending the mount of revelation, one truth after another, not foreshadowed by any thing below, breaks upon the vision and enchants the beholder with its celestial charms, bidding him go forward forever. The human race has not gone up to the summits, but it is going. The great ranges of truth in the Scriptures but few men, explorers, the vanguard of a mighty host, have descried, ascended, and measured. Occasional flashes of light have suggested their existence, and the devout student has kindled into rapturous enthusiasm as he gazed upon the outlines; but he hesitates to scale the dizzy heights, or waits until the divine Guide invites him upward.

This view of Christianity has not received the attention it deserves, and really has encountered no little opposition from those who are the guardians of the oracles of God. Creed-makers, with fine and pious assumption, have hedged in what they declare to be the essentials of Christianity, and have been fierce in denunciation of those who saw a little beyond the hedge-line. More than once the charge of heresy has been nailed on the student's door; and not infrequently the suspicion of moral dishonesty has been raised against one whose chief offense consisted in a purpose to find out the lurking-places of truth; and so investigation had been under ban, and freedom of thought a most perilous exercise.

Our age is on the eve of a new departure in regard both to the importance of truth and the right of discovery, or of the use of that which may lead to the truth. Dissatisfaction with antiquated creed-forms has led to the suspicion that they do not accurately report Christianity, and that there is more in the supernatural revelations than has been imagined or declared, and hence inquiry without restraint and without responsibility is legitimate, and to be encouraged. The disposition to break away from the discipline and leadership of the creed-monger does not imply a purpose to disown the verities of the new religion, but rather a purpose to find out what they are, and not to be satisfied until they can be defined and apprehended. We are on the borders of the new revelations of Christianity, revelations which shall dissociate truth from superstition, which shall harmonize truth with the philosophic idea of it, which shall envelop the profoundest mystery with a rational atmosphere, besides contributing to the theological repository of the Church new truths, which ages ago were not within the realm of speculation, but which the present age is intellectually and spiritually prepared to receive, and which are necessary to the harmonization of truth with itself. If our own age is unprepared for the reception of a broader and deeper revelation of truth, then the preparation will go on, age after age seeing a little farther into the mysteries of the supernatural, each finding what its predecessor never dreamed of, and conveying to its successor the new forces and the new inspirations which it has received. In all this development the spirit of Christianity will remain the same, for it is a development of form only. It is the struggle of Christianity, not only how best, but how fully to express itself. Reaching full development of form, in which its spirit will have the freest activity, Christianity will then appear to be the connecting link of the ages, from the sunrise in Eden to the days of the great and universal conflagration, and the only truth from which all error has sprung, and to which all truth has returned.

Christianity may safely depend upon its methods to secure its perpetuity, and to become the only, that is, the final, religion of man. Carnal weapons it does not seek or employ. By availing itself of the sword the Swiss reformation lost its glory, and Zwingli, its promoter, lost his life. Christianity, majestic and heroic under Constantine, compromised itself by association with the secular power, losing more than it gained, and almost lost its identity as a religion. Results gained by such combinations are usually at the expense of religion. To insure certain success, such as it prophesies of itself, the mode of conquest must be spiritual. To observation it may be slow, but it is solemnly providential, and will finally be irresistible. It wins, it does not force.

In vindication of the proposition that Christianity will be the final religion no appeal has been made to the prophecies, which are all-assuring and all-enlightening on this subject, because *our ground of faith is in Christianity itself.* Some look to prophetic visions; we prefer to consult the truths of the religion, study their foundations, examine their adaptations, and then determine if the thought of a future triumph has a rational basis, if the truth itself foreshadows its universality. This method of determination is strictly philosophical. Prophecy begets songs, inspirations, gladness, faith; truth quickens thought, reveals knowledge, undergirds faith with reason, and gilds the future with the halo of millennial supremacy.

# CHAPTER XXXV.

## PRESENT TASKS OF CHRISTIANITY.

THE Gospel of Christ is *true;* it therefore has something to do in this world. A true religion has a mission; a mission without limitations, since truth is without bounds; a mission that shall know no end, since truth will never cease, and will always be a necessity. The work of Christianity, except in its remote or purely incidental effects, is in no sense temporary; nor, as we have learned, is it confined to one age, or people, or country. It is the religion of the ages, the religion of all peoples, the religion of the globe. As algebra, chemistry, and geology are universal sciences, without national characteristics, so Christianity is the universal religion, without local or national peculiarities or elements.

Nevertheless, its relation to the present age, and the special tasks imposed upon it as the result of this relation, are sufficiently important to justify special elaboration. In these days of intellectual inquiry, of dissatisfaction with old forms of truth, and of agnostic tendency, and positive disquietude in the world's moral life, the revelations of Christianity need to be more distinctly emphasized, its assurances more rationally reiterated, and its absolute verities more frequently demonstrated. The relation of religion to society, civilization, and government, its unavoidable conflicts with scientific pursuit and philosophic thought, and its acknowledged vitalizing tendencies in the realm of human activity and spiritual progress, require that it recognize existing conditions, present necessities, and the character and extent of current influences in the world's development.

Its tasks are two-fold: (1) Tasks respecting itself; (2) Tasks respecting philosophy.

In submitting the work the new Religion must do with respect to itself, it may be suspected that the writer is under the influence of Christianity, and therefore is blinded to its deficiencies, and disqualified to indicate the purification it needs, and the enlargement possible to it if redeemed from certain supposed errors and superstitions. It is true the spell of religion is upon us; but Plato was influenced by Socrates, Locke by Descartes, Hamilton by Reid and Kant, and Spencer by Hartley; we are influenced by Jesus Christ, and Paul, and John, and by Christianity as a whole, but are not ready to acknowledge any disqualification on this account. If we are settled in any special opinion, it is that which relates to the self-purification, enlargement, and future achievements of Christianity. We are interested in its future; and, that it may not disappoint the ages, it is all-important that its present status be understood, that present duties be performed, and that its present hindrances be eliminated.

The attitude of Christianity with respect to the present age must be one of *deep, extensive, and penetrating observation.* It must not close its eyes to modern life, or be deaf to the demands of this modern age. It must not take for granted that obstacles are retiring as it advances, and rest in the recognition of its own supernaturalism as the guarantee of its own safety. It must discover its enemies, observe their critical assaults on its foundations, familiarize itself with their plans and purposes, and study how to circumvent their schemes, answer their arguments, and repair their damages. In dealing with skepticism, three methods may be pursued: (*a*) Ignore it; (*b*) Persecute it; (*c*) Answer it. To ignore honest doubt, and to fail to enlighten it, is high treason against individual liberty, and is the sure way to strengthen such doubt. To ignore dishonest doubt is also one of the steps toward converting it into an honest suspicion of the truth. Ignoring doubt, honest or dishonest, it grew until it stalked into the presence of Christian thought a full-grown and formidable giant.

In many instances, recognition of the skeptical tendency has been followed by artful persecution, or a spirit of intolerance guised in the form of truth has undertaken to demolish it. Departure from certain ecclesiastical standards of faith has been visited with excommunication and the threatened terrors of perdition. Independent thinkers, anxious to separate truth from error, have been characterized as blasphemers and heretics, and driven by ecclesiastical tormentors into positions they did not care to assume, and into final abandonment of what once they supposed was true. Intolerance of inquiry is always baneful, always prejudicial to the discovery of truth.

The more excellent way is to ascertain what is going on in the world, what questions men are asking, what problems are agitating the thinkers, what amount of truth there is in agnosticism, what errors science claims to have discovered in the Gospels, what is the trouble with the world, and what is the trouble with Christianity. Recognition of doubts, inquiries, false reasonings, false sciences, false religions, and a willingness to hear all sides and patiently to consider all claims, must now and hereafter characterize the advocates of Christianity as the condition of its progress in the circles of those who philosophically reject it. *It is because Christianity is true, that we insist on the largest liberty of those who have rejected it to point out its want of internal veracity.*

There is no need that Christianity make special effort to save itself, but there is need that it *explain and purify itself.* Lamartine says, "God alone is strong enough against God." If Christianity is a divine religion, it can be overthrown only by divine means and divine agencies. Intrenched as it is, and supported by divine resources, nevertheless it needs defense, explanation, vindication. Its truths are peculiar and stand in peculiar relations to the world, and in order to be effectual in impressing the world, they must be presented in a peculiar way, and as having peculiar authority and influence. Many of its mysteries are impenetrable and jar on the reason; they must be simplified, explained, and illuminated. Many of its truths require rationalistic support before they can be accepted, and many of the events recorded in the Gospels must stand the test of historical criticism before they can be regarded as real or true. The whole system of truth calls for a system of defense.

This, however, does not imply that truth is in danger, or that its supporters must grow frantic or become fanatical in upholding it. The effort sometimes made to save God, or save the Bible, is useless. God is on the throne, and will maintain his sovereignty; the Bible is a self-demonstrating revelation, and, differing from all other books in the inspirational origin of its contents, it will take care of itself. The defense of Christianity must lie along the track of its own truths. The best defense is to preach it; the best answer to skepticism is to proclaim the truth. But preaching the truth implies a knowledge of the truth, and requires a careful study as to the best manner of presenting it. It is a philosophical Gospel; it must at times be preached philosophically, that is, the philosophic base of truth must sometimes be exposed. It is an intuitional Gospel, that is, many of its truths harmonize with intuitional conclusions; it must, therefore, be proclaimed as an intuitional truth. It is a spiritual Gospel, that is, its highest truths are essentially supernatural, and accomplish their effects by supernatural means; it must, therefore, be proclaimed as a religion from God. Its philosophy, its rationality, its spirituality, and its supernaturalism constitute it the religion that it is, and are the sources of its power, and so long as these features are exhibited and urged, it will stand, and overcome the oppositions brought against it.

Ecclesiastical Christianity needs to save itself from some things that are essentially no part of original or Gospel Christianity, but which have gradually grown up with it, and sometimes have passed for the truth itself, to the great injury of true religion. Among the excrescences or natural outgrowths of ecclesiasticism is *cant*, which, whether regarded in its aristocratic or vulgar sense, is a hindrance to the rapid progress of truth. Johnson says, " Clear your mind of cant."

There is no book so absolutely exempt from the spirit of cant as the Bible, and no religion with less of it than Christianity. The cant of the Eastern or Oriental religions is their chief peculiarity, which may be accounted for from their want of truth. In the absence of truth, cant or superstition, or both, is likely to result. But a religion of truth is able both to discard superstition and suppress cant. Spiritual truth may be as positive in content, as free from superstitious forms, and as truly sincere and transparent in the expression of its aims and methods, as physical truth; and both may be clear of all hypocrisy and hollowness. The truth of the existence of God should not be molded into a cant-phrase any more than the law of gravitation. Regeneration is not a cant-word any more than light or heat. Of the words and phrases of the Bible we are not afraid or ashamed, for they express great realities, and are the very best for the revelation of such realities. They are *inspired* words, and, therefore, truth-words. In the selection of its words or terms for the expression of ideas, philosophy has been less fortunate, for it deals with abstractions, and uses words in any sense, if by so doing it believes it may reduce the abstract to a concrete conception. The word "idea" is really a cant-word in philosophy, for it means one thing in Plato, another in Aristotle, another in Reid, another in Hamilton, and another in Cousin. It has no fixed or established meaning, and expresses an abstraction rather than a reality. This is the most refined kind of cant, of which philosophy furnishes abundant examples. Kant's "antinomies," in which stock words are used in a double sense, are the stately forms of philosophic cant. Except as its language is evidently figurative in meaning, the Bible declares its truths in simple speech, creating little confusion in the mind of the reader, and is so direct in its revelations that it is surprising that double or uncertain meanings have ever been inferred. In the use of such words as "world," "heaven," "hell," and "angel," a figurative meaning is sometimes discoverable, but in no case is the truth which these words represent compromised or invalidated.

Cant is the joint product of abstraction, ambiguity, superstition, insincerity, and irrationality. It should have no place in religion, therefore; but, unfortunately, there is a suspicion that Christianity is the religion of cant. This "cant" is of two kinds: (*a*) What the scientific world calls cant; (*b*) What the common world calls cant. The materialistic scientist pronounces such words as God, eternity, incarnation, atonement, justification, regeneration, faith, prayer, resurrection, heaven, and hell as cant-words, representing imaginary ideas, or alleged facts that have no existence. It is easy to retort that such words as atoms, force, correlation, mechanism, matter, protoplasm, law, order, cause, and effect are the cant-words of science, representing misconceptions, or the wildest fancies of the thinkers, and no more entitled to regard than the ideas of mythology. The word "atom" is far less intelligible than the word "creation;" the word "unknowable" far less satisfactory than the word "God;" the word "force" more inexpressive of a reality than "being." The terms of science are recondite, superficial, experimental, yet necessary and useful. The scientific charge of cant in religion rebounds with slaughtering effect on science. Both religion and science must have a nomenclature, a vocabulary, expressing truths, facts, laws, and principles peculiar to them, and the words of religion, expressing its realities, are not any more objectionable than the words of science, expressing its supposed facts.

The common charge of cant in religion is one of the subterfuges of the race, a sign of indisposition to accept the truth. The average man does not rise to a proper conception of what religion is, either as a system of truth or as an experience of realities, and such words as repentance, faith, humility, forgiveness, and salvation sound to him like the phraseology of a new superstition, which, without examination, he is inclined to reject.

The Christian teacher must employ the terms of religion as the exponents of stupendous realities, thereby silencing the suspicion that they are empty forms of speech, and express only the excited sentiments and convictions of the heart.

It is incumbent on Christianity to *reconcile its alleged contradictions and satisfy its respect for consistency.* Truth is self-consistent; divine truth should be above all suspicion of internal contradiction. Considering the range of Revelation, the various modes in which truth has expressed itself, and the supernatural mysteries with which the Christian religion has loaded itself, it is not surprising that discussions with reference to the integrity of some of its truths have arisen, and that differences of opinion have been established. Because of mysteries that have not been scientifically explained, they have been scientifically condemned; and because of imperfect revelations, the whole has been charged with imperfection and insufficiency. In a general way, it is alleged against Revelation that it is faulty in its scientific reports and allusions, incorrect in its historical data and connections, unsound, and therefore unsafe, in its ethical teachings and examples, and so at variance with itself in the details of its soteriological scheme that the claim of its inspiration is rendered worthless. Rev. R. Heber Newton expresses the critical objection to the Old Testament in the following words: "The Old Testament historians contradict each other in facts and figures, tell the same story in different ways, locate the same incident at different periods, ascribe the same deeds to different men, quote statistics which are plainly exaggerated, mistake poetic legend for sober prose, report the marvelous tales of tradition as literal history, and give us statements which can not be read as scientific facts without denying our latest and most authoritative knowledge." This broadside is a challenge to investigation which the Christian thinker is bound to notice. Indifferent to the author of the above criticism, the criticism itself must be answered, or remain as a proof of the weakness of the so-called revelations of the Old Testament.

What renders the allegation the more deserving of notice is that, without a thorough investigation of the historical contents of the Pentateuch in particular, the reader might be led to some of the radical conclusions of Mr. Newton; in other words, the criticism is, in certain respects, *apparently* true. Not a few theologians have conceded an inaccuracy of statement in its scientific postulates, which has strengthened the suspicion that possibly its history is likewise inaccurate, and that, if the Book is infallible at all, it is only in its revelation of spiritual truths. But, if its science is a delusion and its history is admitted to be false, the step to a denial of the truth of its spiritual revelations is a short one, and many will take it. Either the Book as a whole is true, or it is false. Its scientific truth must be as genuine and authoritative as its spiritual; the first chapter of Genesis must stand or fall with the first chapter of the Gospel according to John; the Flood and the Resurrection, Babel and Pentecost, the Fall of Man and the Atonement of Jesus Christ, must be believed or rejected; the one class of truths stand or fall with the other class of truths. The science, the history, and the inspiration and revelation of the spiritual truths of the Bible, can not be separated, the one being pronounced fallible and the other infallible.

No more troublous problem has arisen in these days in connection with Biblical interpretation than that which the authorship of the Pentateuch has provoked. A majority of theologians and Biblical scholars hold with unquestioning faith to the long-accepted view that Moses wrote the five books bearing his name; but schools within as well as without the Christian Church have assailed this view with no little vehemence, and propounded disturbing questions to the other side. Within the Church such writers as Dr. G. T. Ladd, of Yale College, and Prof. C. A. Briggs, of Union Theological Seminary, have seriously questioned the Mosaic authorship of the Pentateuch, and have compelled a reinvestigation of the proofs. Prof. Briggs holds that the Pentateuch is the product of four different writers; that it is somewhat legendary in its details, and without the supernatural authority usually attributed to it. Robertson Smith, of Scotland, grants that Moses wrote the Ten Commandments, but is uncertain that he wrote more of the Pentateuch. Prof. Ladd, advancing a theory of inspiration, which excludes a portion of the Bible as inspired, denies to Moses the authorship of much of the Pentateuch. Thus a direct attack on the doctrine of inspiration itself is made within the Church, the motive being, without doubt, the purification of human views of truth, and the destruction of errors and superstitions which age has made sacred and piety beautiful. Here, then, are grave problems for the Christian critic and thinker to study; problems that can not be solved by raising the cry of heresy against those who propose them, or by the expulsion from his chair of a professor striving to solve them, or by quietly forgetting that they are related to progress and to the future. Truth is the end of all seeking. *The Bible, as the book of truth, can stand the fires of investigation; let them burn.*

Inasmuch as the scientific and historic accuracy of the Bible is in question, and the authorship of several Old Testament books is in dispute, the task of explanation, defense, and settlement of these questions must be undertaken by the Christian thinker with the same enthusiasm which govern the so-called errorists, and be prosecuted until it shall be finished.

If Christianity is proclaimed as a religion, standing beside other religions, and taking its chances with them, it is likely to succeed, even if the doctrine of its inspiration must be abandoned; but if it is proclaimed as a *divine* religion, superior to all others, and intended to extinguish all others, then the question of its inspiration is paramount, and alleged contradictions and inconsistencies must be explained and reconciled.

The concession of historic and scientific errors in the Bible must be withdrawn, but in withdrawing it the supposed errors must be shown to be distortions of the truth, or to have arisen in a way that does not compromise the integrity of the documents containing them. It must not be forgotten that the original manuscripts of the sacred writers are not before us; we read copies, or translations of copies, the infallibility of which no one is justified in asserting. Errors of translation, difficult to detect and equally difficult to correct, have rendered ambiguous or uncertain some paragraphs or chapters of the Book, but these are not numerous, and do not affect or change the accepted meaning of Revelation. It must be remembered also that the original languages of the Bible were ancient and Oriental, differing in idioms, grammatical construction, and provincial character from modern languages, and especially from the Anglo-Saxon or English tongue. Employing the Hebrew and Greek in their purely native sense, it frequently happens that the sacred writers have contradicted the Occidental conception of things, and the modern notions of truth. To understand the Bible, therefore, it is necessary to understand the languages in which it was written.

Nor must it escape attention that the customs and manners of the Bible-making period were exclusively Oriental, a knowledge of which is absolutely necessary to a correct interpretation of the Bible. In their salutations and ordinary speech, in their dress and occupations, in their etiquette and domestic customs, in their social ideas and habits,. the Oriental nations differed, as they do to-day, from European nations, the Bible writers recognizing the Oriental customs, and not infrequently presenting the truth in an Oriental frame-work. So far as it is an Oriental book, it can be understood only as Oriental ideas are understood.

As a matter of fact, the Bible is better understood to-day, in the light of archæology, geography, and Orientalisms, than at any period of Biblical study and investigation. As an instance of progress, consider that until recently the subject of the antiquity of man has perplexed both evolutionist and theologian, the former having been anxious to establish a long antiquity, while the theologian was equally anxious to cut it down to sixty centuries. Geology, at first wild and eccentric, has under discipline become sober and inquisitive, and practically settled the dispute in favor of the theologian. Dr. Southall concludes that man's first appearance on the earth was about 6,600 years ago; Principal Dawson dates the appearance from 6,000 to 8,000 years ago; and the Septuagint version of the Scriptures places it 7,290 years ago. As another instance, consider that recent investigation of monuments in Syria, Egypt, and Mesopotamia has demonstrated the truthfulness of the Biblical account of the dispersion of the races from the plains of Shinar at the time and in the manner indicated. One more instance : Infidel scholarship has regarded Ur of the Chaldees a mythological city, but the modern geographer has identified its site on the river Euphrates, and thus supplied a missing link in the biography of Abraham. If, then, geography, archæology, and the monumental and geological records are establishing questionable facts, or solving the enigmas of the Bible, is it unreasonable to infer that whatever is still in dispute may finally be sustained or disposed of in the same scientific and philosophic way ? One thing is certain, and that is that *scientific research, when completed along a given line, has in not a single instance overturned or even shaken the Biblical account, but, on the other hand, it has triumphantly vindicated and explained it.* The conclusion is that the so-called scientific errors of the Bible are *errors of interpretation*, errors of ignorance, errors of limited investigation, and not *errors of fact.* The duty of the Christian thinker to submit the science of the Bible to scientific research, and the history of the Bible to historical tests, is plain enough. In this way its scientific and historic character will be established.

One of the chief duties of Christianity is to *define itself* with greater perspicuity and simplicity. A transparent definition, not of dogma, nor yet of single truths, but of Christianity as one truth, is a demand that must be met if the public mind shall be relieved of confusion and embarrassment. In the absence of such a definition the misunderstanding of what Christianity is or proposes to do has been fruitful of strife, of wasteful expenditure of energy in behalf of creeds, and of serious resistance on the part of many to the just claims of religion. Taking advantage of the misunderstanding, the creed-builder went to work rearing an architectural frame in which the simplicities of the Gospel have occupied an obscure place. The Athanasian creed is a wonderful structure, a fine specimen of theologic architecture, but has it saved the world from death, or is it what the world needs? The imposition of creed-forms of truth, the penalties inflicted upon those who could not philosophically accept them, the dissensions of ecclesiastical bodies over them, and the trail of the heresy-hunter in the Christian circles of thought, have been a disgrace to Christendom, an obstacle to religious progress, and an unpardonable stain on the pages of human history. As Rome spent more time in conquering a province in Italy than was necessary after she controlled the Mediterranean to subdue the whole earth, so the Christian Church has consumed the ages in the defense of peccadilloes of expression, when long ere this day she might have conquered the world.

It is not against a creed *per se* that we are writing, for a formulated article of faith, embracing the fundamental truths of Christianity, is proper enough. As in mathematics, certain axioms are necessary ; as in chemistry, certain laws must be accepted ; as in physiology, the existence of certain organs and functions must be recognized, so Christianity may be represented by certain truths, which, taken together, constitute the creed or the axioms of religion. It makes not against this position to affirm that no specific creed or articles of faith are recorded in the New Testament, for faith in the Lord Jesus Christ is required as the condition of salvation ; and faith in Christ includes all the truths of Christ, or Christianity. The objection to the creed is its elaboration of details, and its attempt to reduce religion, in all of its peculiarities and mysteries, to formal statement, belief in which is regarded necessary to admission in the Christian Church, and to the benefits of the atonement of the Son of God. By so much as it elaborates beyond essential truths, the creed becomes a burden to faith and a stumbling-block to inquiring souls. Real faith acts intuitionally. It sees the truth in a moment; it needs no architectural or Gothic form. Give it the truth, not as an ideality, or a fiction, or an abstraction, or as a dogmatic affirmation, but as a reality, and in the simplest form, and the mind will harmonize with it. In religion, as in science, the *fundamentals are the simplicities.* We do not deny complexity to religion; its truths reach into the eternities; but man may spare himself the trouble of going so far for his knowledge of saving truth. The undertaking to define the details of all mysteries, or to project a Scheme of Faith which should include revealed and unrevealed truth, instead of defining Christianity as the supernatural instrument of the world's salvation, has been productive of serious misapprehension and not a little intellectual perplexity. The world must first be taught what Christianity is *not* before it will truly apprehend what Christianity is; that is, there is quite as much to unlearn as there is to learn. Men must learn that Christianity is not a system of sacraments, or a theory of the priesthood, or a set of dogmas, or a series of ethical truths, or the constitution of ecclesiastical bodies; but that while sacraments, priesthoods, dogmas, truths, and laws are in some sense the products of religion, they do not constitute the essential ideas of Christianity. On its negative side Christianity is complex; on its affirmative side, simple. The affirmations of religion, the yeas of divine truth, are in demand, and must be given to the world.

In the same spirit *Christianity needs explicitly to set forth its purpose in the world,* to characterize its mission in such terms that organized resistance will diminish, and a glad welcome be accorded it. Its mission is three-fold: (*a*) Moral; (*b*) Philanthropic; (*c*) Spiritual. Its moral purpose appears in the re-enacted Decalogue, and in the ethics of the New Testament. Unobjectionable as is the moral code of the new religion, and elevating and restraining as is its moral spirit, it meets intellectual criticism on the one hand and practical rebellion on the other. Its injunction of self-denial is interpreted as ascetic; its virtues are alleged to be borrowed from the pagans; its inelastic requirements are considered too ideal for practical life. Civil governments enact laws, violate treaties, and engage in war, in violation of the principles of equity, as taught in the New Testament; while individuals commit crime and trifle with right as if moral laws were not in operation. This condition of things Christianity proposes to remedy by the incorporation of moral principles in the constitutions of governments, and into the beliefs, habits, and activities of individuals and communities, guaranteeing the sovereignty of man and the reign of the moral idea in this world. To magnify the ethical principle, and insist upon conformity to it, is one of the first duties of the Christian worker.

The philanthropic purpose of Christianity is sufficiently misunderstood to provoke opposition and excite depreciation, yet is it the beautiful exponent of the graciousness of the divine scheme. Our religion looks with sympathetic yearning upon the degradation, ignorance, and wretchedness of the human race, and comes with pitying eye to relieve, and with open hand to help and rescue. It comes not with the sword, but with balm for wounds already made; it comes not as a tyrant to crush out the remaining life, but as a Samaritan, with oil and money to assist the unfortunate world; it comes all-benevolent in spirit, pointing to schools, asylums, homes, churches, and is anxious to lift up the fallen and make glad the whole earth. To such a mission what objection can be raised? The skeptical pronounce its benevolence the outcropping of ecclesiastical selfishness, and its works the fruit of a culpable sectarianism! This is proof that the philanthropies of the Gospel are misunderstood, and that the only cure for such misunderstandings is the wide-spread sway of the Gospel.

*The spiritual purpose of Christianity is its highest purpose.* It proposes to deliver men from the thralldom of sin, to make them saints, to equip them with immortal functions, to make them messengers of light and children of God. Such a purpose no other religion embodies in its teachings or efforts; it belongs exclusively to Christianity. To the spiritualities of the Gospel, the most important of all, the most formidable objections have been raised. To the moralities and philanthropies of the Gospel the opposition will be easily overcome; but the triumph of the spiritualities implies and will require patience, discipline, culture, intellectual purification, enlargement of moral capacity, and the intensification of the moral pursuits of life. The first need of man is *spirituality.* Given the spiritualities, and the moralities and philanthropies bloom; given the latter, and it is not certain that the former will flourish. The divine order of development is, first, spirituality, then morality and philanthropy; the world's attempted order is the reverse; hence, the failure. The true order of development, or the three-fold mission of Christianity to the human race must be explicitly stated and enforced as the condition of moral and spiritual progress; otherwise morality will be scientific instead of spiritual, and philanthropy will be philosophical instead of divine, or morality and philanthropy will be divorced from religion, with no power except that derived from their own mechanical working, and with no assurance of triumph except that which the general law of evolution will inspire.

While it is the duty of Christianity to take care of itself, correct its weaknesses, repair its infirmities, and eliminate its inadequacies, *it must not forget its relations to philosophic thought*, and that the task growing out of such relation is one of magnitude, and should receive immediate attention. The adjustment of the differences between Christian thought on the one hand and the philosophic pursuit on the other, is so necessary to the purity of the one and the freedom of the other, that its postponement can only result in widening the breach and possibly effect a permanent alienation. From the stand-point of Christianity, certain views have been entertained which, however justifiable in spirit, may, in their practical workings, have impeded the work of reconciliation. It has been supposed that the scientific thinker will finally discover the harmony of the facts of nature with the truths of religion, and that this discovery will open the way to agreement and unity without any special negotiation between the parties concerned. In a sense this is true, and doubtless reconciliation will finally be forced by the logic of events, or the self-evident harmony of all kinds of truth. Truth is a unit, however many-sided it is, and it will agree with itself. In mathematics there is no conflict among the squares, triangles, and circles; without them mathematics is impossible; yet there is no apparent likeness or kin-ship among them. Nor can there be any conflict among forces, laws, causes, doctrines, cosmogonies, miracles, prophecies, and spiritual facts when fully apprehended, for, different in form, presentation, and use, they are not antagonistic, but are essential to a religion that professes to emanate from God, and comprehend the universe of thought and being. That there is seeming conflict now is no evidence of an inner irreconcilability; it is proof of the perversion of truth so far as discovered, or of ignorance of truth yet to be known. If owing entirely to the latter, the future will take care of it and secure the harmony needed, for an increased knowledge of truth will certainly result from additional investigations, and remove grounds of differ-ence. If, however, the antagonism is owing to any degree to a dis-torted view, or a perverted use, of truth, then the duty of a re-exami-nation of our knowledge and of the ends to which it is applied, and the motives that have governed in the use of it is imperative, or truth itself must for a time suffer. Prejudices, distortions, rebuffs, imperfections, and hypocrisies have without doubt interfered with an honest adjustment of the antagonism between the religious and intel-lectual forces, but the time has come for a close and fearless attempt at reconciliation.

Perhaps it is not too much to say that Christianity, conscious of its strength, or at least satisfied that it can not be overthrown, has been too indifferent to the nature of the attacks made upon it, and to the motives that have impelled agnosticism and materialism to join their forces against it. Surely it is time that Christian thought should recognize the animus of the opposition and strive to overcome it.

Again, it is assumed in certain Christian circles that philosophic thought, goaded into a false attitude by the scientific thinker, is responsible for the antagonism now existing between itself and revealed truth, and that it must work out the problem of reconciliation. As a historical fact this will not be disputed, but it is a question if philosophic thought, however honest in its purpose, can, unaided by inspired truth, solve the difficulty and bring itself into right relations with such truth. The task is a great one, too great, we fear, for philosophy. It is asking the lower to put itself in right relations with the higher, when perhaps *the higher ought to put itself in right relations with the lower.* The stars can not adjust their relations to the sun, but the sun may establish relations with the stars. Left to itself, philosophy runs into pessimism, atheism, materialism, and agnosticism; what hope is there that, unaided by divine truth, it will some time grasp the theistic conception in its wholeness, and embrace Christianity as the final utterance of God? In this dilemma the Christian thinker can not haughtily refuse to consider methods of reconciliation or initiate the steps to be taken in order to secure it. His supreme duty is to advance toward philosophic error, not as a Cæsar to strike it, nor with the threat of penalty if an immediate surrender is not made, but in the spirit of a counselor, setting forth the truth in its brightest colors, and quietly shaming error out of existence. The cure for materialism is the intellectual and spiritual truth of Christianity; properly applied it will not fail. Philosophy can not harmonize itself with revealed truth; Christianity, undertaking the task of harmonization, can affect it. Instead of placing the burden of reconciliation upon incompetent philosophic thought, let Christianity boldly assume it and proceed to discharge the duty required. Herbert Spencer concedes that the "central position" of religion "is impregnable," meaning that certain central facts or teachings addressed to the conscience, the intuitions, and the reason will be recognized as authoritative, and homage and obedience must follow. In a larger sense we may affirm that, in its central position, in its fundamental truths, *Christianity is absolutely invulnerable,* and is demonstrating its stability of character and permanence of conquest by its progressive history and its efficient every-day work in human life. If religion is impregnable, if its truths can not be overthrown, instead of relapsing into a quietistic state, content with the belief that it will finally subdue all things to itself, it should be intensely

48

active in the work of illumination, and ceaselessly aggressive against sin, that the holy and universal triumph may be all the sooner achieved.

The Christian thinker has delayed the inauguration of an aggressive campaign against the materialistic metaphysician because of a fancy that science and philosophy, by their interminable quarrels, will possibly destroy each other, or end the strife by a willing surrender to Christianity. It is well known that the scientific theorists of the age are quite put out with one another, and that they differ among themselves touching the great questions quite as much as they differ with the theologians. As regards the age of the world, the nature of light, the origin of matter, the essence of mind, and the cause of things, a discordant cry comes from laboratory, hall, grove, and the study. St. George Mivart and Darwin can not agree; Huxley and Tyndall dispute; the evolutionists are at war among themselves; Häckel is frantic; English thinkers tremble as they discover the foundations of morality quaking under the fearful tread of materialists; John Fiske, disciple of Darwin, at last pronounces in favor of a personal God; and the whole brotherhood of scientists and philosophers are disturbed, divided, and ensnared in their own dilemmas. Confusion is on the increase in the circles of the materialists, atomists, sensationalists, atheists, psychologists, and pessimists. Greedy in their love of facts, they hoped to be justified by facts in turning Christianity out of doors and banishing God from the universe; but the facts have well-nigh expelled the metaphysicians. The furnace was intended to destroy Daniel, but it burned his persecutors; the gallows was built for Mordecai, but Haman hung therefrom. However, it will not do to trust entirely to the reactionary result of discovered facts, or to the confusion and division among the fact-seekers, for a final vindication of revealed truth. The truth itself must be introduced into the conflict, dividing the scientists more and more, and troubling them as mere theories have never troubled them. Hitherto, the bone of contention has been *theory*; hereafter, let it be *truth*.

Just what we mean by reconciliation may be readily inferred from the general discussion in preceding pages of the standing differences between Christianity and philosophy. They are not at one touching central or fundamental truths, such as the existence of God, the Mosaic account of creation, the inspiration of the Bible, the origin of man, the origin or introduction of evil, the possibility of miracles, the incarnation of Jesus Christ, the doctrine of atonement, the significance of regeneration, the immortality of the soul, and all other vital teachings of religion; and so long as they are at variance, the one holding them as speculations or superstitions, and the other as *revealed truths,* there will be conflict, there will be confusion of judgment, there will be loss of souls. As to how these primary truths shall be defended and taught we have indicated elsewhere, but we may here point out the stages of the conflict, or the work that must be performed before reconciliation shall have been fully established. The stages of the conflict are three: (*a.*) Positive Antagonism; (*b.*) Transition Period; (*c.*) Reconciliation. Of antagonism the world has had enough; philosophy can not desire more; Christianity has had all that is necessary. In many quarters the antagonism is still going on; the battle rages; the smoke rises; banners fly or fall; the slain, alas! are many. But the antagonistic age is nearly ended; the spirit of virulence has almost spent its force; a calmness of inquiry is on the face of the thinker; and prejudice is dying amid its worshipers.

That we are in the transition period, emerging into better conditions and into final settlements of differences, let us fondly hope. Philosophy is less presumptuous in spirit; evolution in its early scientific form is waning; materialism is losing its grip on faith and thought; the Absolute has appeared; the face of God shines through the storm; and the thick-armored hosts of force have halted and can not advance.

The next step is *reconciliation,* which will be not complete touching details at first, but gradual, certain, satisfactory, embracing all things at last. When philosophy prostrates itself before God, the battle is won, and won forever. The idea of God once accepted will make room for every other Christian idea in the realm of philosophic thinking, and sway the nations as completely as does the sun the planets.

In its relations with philosophy Christianity must not forget to respect the *rationalistic principle* in man. It often appeals to the affectional nature, since its own spirit is affectional, but the rational principle is vital and to a degree sovereign in the life of man. So imperious is it that it compels him to reject what it condemns, and to receive what it approves, becoming the criterion of truth and the arbiter in all disputes between truth and error. Nor is this prerogative of the reason a mere conceit or presumption; it is its endowment or function which is intended to protect the truth from fanaticism, superstition, and radicalism. It is not assumed that religion violates the reason, or that revelation is irrational in content or purpose; but a misunderstanding of the function of reason on the part of religion, and an alleged irrationality in the truths of religion on the part of reason, have produced painful and unnecessary conflicts, without any special compensations, or advantage to the truth. The rational power of man must be understood, and the rationality of revelation must also be apprehended. **Human reason is not always the sole umpire** in the settlement of differences between religious truth and error, but in many cases its final decision is authoritative, and must be respected. *The rational side of Christianity must be submitted to the rationalistic principle of the thinker in order to obtain a rational judgment in its favor.* Channing says, "Christianity is a rational religion." The theologian has said it is a mysterious religion; a supernatural religion; a miracle-sustained religion; a prophetic religion; a redemptive religion; all of which is true, and, being true, it has appealed with force to faith, love, fear, instinct, desire, and self-interest in the awakening of men to spiritual thought and activity. We do not question the sincerity or sufficiency of motives to activity that take their rise in the affectional or emotional nature, but contend for a place for the exercise of reason in the spiritual life. The rationality of Gospel truth; of supernaturalism as an idea; of miracle as a metaphysical possibility; of regeneration as a philosophical process; of immortality as a scientific result, can be made to appear, along with the usual theological defenses of the same. The doctrines of Christianity are as rational as the laws of the natural world, to be studied from the same stand-point, and to be accepted with as little hesitation or misgiving of faith. *Christian teachers must present religion to men as the most rational idea in the regions of human thought.* It is not necessary to make it irrational in order to prove it supernatural, or show that it is so mysterious that it can not be understood in order to impress men that it is divine. *Its supernaturalism lies along the track of the highest and purest reason.* A presentation of revealed truth as supremely logical in itself will destroy the challenge of infidelity, which heretofore has invoked the aid of reason in its defense as against the supposed irrational dogmatics of religion. In this way also the sympathy of all truth-seekers with revealed religion will be secured, for, posing as a rational religion, they can not consistently oppose it until, having examined it, they shall find that it is not the truth; but investigation by rational methods will result in a rational judgment in its behalf.

This is what we mean when we insist that Christianity shall respect the rationalistic principle, or that it shall appeal to the reason; we mean an appeal to the *methods of reason* for the ascertainment of truth. Reason, disciplined and schooled to close work, usually resorts to one or all of three methods of expression in the execution of its tasks: (*a*) The *a priori* method, or reasoning from cause to effect—a mode of reasoning legitimate, forcible, and within limitations sufficient; (*b*) The *a posteriori* method, or reasoning from effect to cause— a mode of reasoning regarded even stronger than the preceding;

(c) Reasoning from *analogy*, or the discovery of the bearing of physical truth upon religious truth. With these instruments at hand the reason works vigorously on its great problems in the lower realm, often discovering physical truth and proclaiming it, not in mere joyousness of words, but with all logical assurance, and is satisfied.

To change the phrases, the reason works according to the *inductive* method, or the method of physical science, reasoning from parts to the whole, from particulars to generals. Bacon introduced the inductive method into modern science, and employed it as an all-sufficient method in his realm of investigation. The method of *deduction*, or the going from generals to particulars, is considered a safer because it is a larger and more self-evidencing method than the former; yet the two taken together constitute the final forms of rationalistic expression.

Without question Christianity should appeal to these various methods of logical inquiry for the vindication of its truths. As a religion of truth it should not shrink from the methods of truth, but appropriate them as the methods by which it shall be communicated to the minds of men. As to the monotheistic conception, inasmuch as it is a doctrine of revelation, the *a priori* method will support it, and when it can be assumed as an *a priori* fact, all the other truths of religion can be assumed, and will be received. The *apriorism* of Christianity needs to be enforced with the commanding assurance that *a priori* truth inspires. In the hands of the theologian the monotheistic idea has been ably vindicated by the *a posteriori* method; but as philosophic thought has sometimes questioned the adequacy of the method, the other may as surely be employed in defense of the same truth. To be sure, not all of the truths of Christianity can be as clearly demonstrated by one method as by the other, but *there is no revealed truth that will not yield to one of the methods of the reason.* If the *a priori* or the *a posteriori* method fail, or the thinker fail in using them, then, like Joseph Butler, he may resort to the *analogical* method, and be sure of some kind of discovery. All that the reason can legitimately ask is that its methods have recognition in the investigation of revealed truth, and the least that Christianity can do is to grant the request.

Within recent years Christianity has submitted itself to the limited methods of rational investigation, and with advantage to itself. The world begins to recognize that it is a scientific as well as spiritual religion, a philosophical as well as supernatural revelation of truth; it finds that *it is as rational as it claims to be*, and deserves intellectual homage as well as the veneration of faith.

It belongs to Christianity to *urge and encourage both science and philosophy to push on in their work of investigation, that final results may be established.* Hitherto there has not been, from the Christian thinker, the warmest welcome for the discoveries of science or the honest conclusions of the philosophic inquirer; on the contrary, a spirit of hostility has too frequently been manifested toward those who were toiling in the lower realm of matter, and were anxious to ascertain its laws and contents. The most expeditious way to reach finalities is to press on through the thick darkness toward them. There must not be imposition, or hypocrisy, or presumption in science, any more than in religion. The task of finding truth is a serious one, and the methods adopted must be sober, and the results announced must be genuine. The cure for agnosticism, materialism, and pessimism is partly to compel the investigator to go on in his searchings, denying him rest until his work is completed. *The danger to truth is in unfinished investigation of it.* From the constitution of things there is evidently a limit to the physical universe, which when found will distrain the thinker from further inquiry. Spatial and temporal conditions environ it; its history is the history of change; and limitation is the law of its existence. Predicating density, weight, color, utility, and relation of things, is the same as predicating limitation, for these are the terms of limitation. In like manner, physical forces, laws, orders, processes, and agencies operate within conceivable, if not within defined, limits, the searching of which is incumbent upon the philosopher. We may spur the philosopher on, we may shout him to his work. *To the limits! To the limits!* Go on, friend, until you can go no farther. What then? From the "limit" to the "limitless" is but a single step, which the thinker will then eagerly take; his difficulties will then be solved in the full revelation of truth; and at last, with all doubts removed, all fears quenched, and all aspirations satisfied, he will rejoice in the abundant visions of God. To this consummation Christianity may contribute not a little by its quickening and encouraging influence on the minds of the thinkers of the race.

Especially is it the duty of Christianity to remember that, as it is adapted to all ages of the world, *it has special adaptation to the nineteenth century,* or the times in which we live, and should therefore employ its resources and agencies to the utmost in the spiritual culture and elevation of the world of to-day. In its ethical teachings, as well as in its spiritual ministrations, and in its philanthropic spirit as in its redemptive purpose, it is the religion the humanity of our times needs. Without it our governments become corrupt, the family institution disorganizes, social life falls to a vicious level, and divine ideals are forgotten. It is a *developing* religion, developing the people who receive it, and developing itself into a richer form as they receive it. It is the priceless heritage of the nineteenth century, let it not be trodden under foot; it is the light of the world, let it not be extinguished; it is the truth of God, let it not be buried or forgotten. *Christianity is Truth.* Of all sacred or religious teachers, *Christ was exceptional in this that he was not a truth-seeker;* he sought it not, *because he was the* TRUTH. The stars may seek the light, the sun only shines. Christ is truth ; he is *philosophic and theologic truth;* he is *natural and supernatural truth;* he is *ethical and eschatological truth;* he is *governmental and æsthetic truth;* he is *personal and impersonal truth;* he is *rational and spiritual truth;* he is FINAL AND ABSOLUTE TRUTH ; he is VISIBLE AND INVISIBLE TRUTH ; he is JUST AND HOLY TRUTH ; he is KNOWN AND UNKNOWN TRUTH ; he is CREATIVE AND UNCREATED TRUTH ; he is the *Alpha and Omega of truth;* he is the *strength and illumination of truth;* he is the *crown and glory of truth;* he is the *immutability,* the *omnipresence,* the *everlasting goodness,* and the ETERNAL ESSENCE OF TRUTH.

*Christianity is Truth.* Its mission is the propagation of truth, its inspiration is the inspiration of truth, its success is the success of truth. Let error tear down, the truth must build up; let the one agnosticize the world, the other must illuminate it; let the one materialize the thought of men, the other must spiritualize it; let the one drive the race into Plato's cave, the other must draw all men into Christ's kingdom; let the one actualize an anarchy of letters, the other must establish a republic of immortal truths.

*Christianity is Truth.* Nature is at one with its solemn proclamations, and in its development is a re-assertion of all that religion unfolds or enforces. Every spiritual truth has a physical basis, and every physical truth has a spiritual basis. The natural is the spiritual, the spiritual is the natural. The universe of non-being is the advertisement of the universe of being. Nature, with its myriad voices of power, wisdom, and goodness, stands for God, and for all that Christianity is, or is doing in the world. History, too, is the mirror of the ideal purposes of religion, the panorama-like representation of divine ends in process of fulfillment. Nations, governments, and civilizations are the concrete forms of divine ideals, imperfectly wrought out, but speaking loudly in their imperfection of the divine movements among men. Man himself is the sublimest proof of Christianity. He distances every opposing argument, and silences every skeptical suggestion. He is truth incarnate. He is immortality on foot; he is God in human form. Christianity is truth ; *the truth of nature, the truth of history, the truth of humanity,* THE TRUTH OF THE EVERLASTING GOD.

*Christianity is Truth.* Assailed it will be, but its defenders need not be afraid; misrepresented it will be, but believers need not be alarmed; struggles with error it will have, but its friends need not sink into despair. "Ye believe in God, believe also in Me." The hope of victory is engraved on the brow of truth; the strength of victory is in the sword of truth; the pledge of victory is from Him who is the author of truth. Sooner will the firmament fall than one jot or tittle of divine truth fail in its appointed task, or become weary with its solemn work. *Victory!* The earth will sound it; the heavens will echo it; man will sing it; eternity will celebrate it. VICTORY! This is the end of truth.

*Christianity is Truth.* So the patriarchs believed; so the law-givers declared; so the prophets foretold; so the apostles proclaimed; so the martyrs assumed; so the sons of God everywhere have affirmed.

TRUTH! Let the poets recognize its eternal beauty; let the historians record its stately marches to conquest; let the rulers remember Him who judgeth the nations according to its holy and unimpeachable standards; let the scientists toil in its sunlight, and rejoice in its abundant and ever-increasing testimonies; let the philosophers, abandoning speculation, embrace the wondrous revelations of the divine Master, offering to him that meed of honor that belongs to the original discoverer and the authoritative teacher; let the religionists of the world join in praises to Him who was the incarnation of blessed, immortal truth, and who ever liveth to enlighten our wayward and ignorant race with the thoughts, the wonders, the ideals, and the achievements of the eternal King, unto Whom "be glory in the Church by Christ Jesus throughout all ages, world without end."

# INDEX.

## A.

PAGE.

ABERCROMBIE, . . . . . . . . . 92
Abstractions, . . . . . . . . 634–635
    Powerless, . . . . . . . . . 645
Accads, Religion of . . . . . . 337
Acropolis, . . . . . . . . . . . 396
Addison, Anglo-Saxon of . . . 547
Advent, The Second, . . . . . 608
    Associated Events, . . . . . 617
    Disturbing Features, . . . . 615
    Misunderstanding, . . . . . 664
    Object of . . . . . . . . . . 617
    Time of . . . . . . . . . . 618
Æsthetics, . . . . . . . . . . 463
Agassiz, Prof., . . . . . . . . 160
    Argument for Immortality, . 189
    Teleological Position of . . . 176
Age, The Bronze, . . . . . . . 181
    Glacial, . . . . . . . . . . 183
    Golden, . . . . . . . . . . 493
    Iron, . . . . . . . . . . . 181
    Stone, . . . . . . . . . . . 181
Agesidamus, . . . . . . . . . 534
Agriculture, Moral Spirit of, . . 526
Agnostic, The . . . . . . . . 210
Agnosticism, . . . . . . . . . 212
    Objection to . . . . . . . 694
Algebra, . . . . . . . . . . . 741
Alemachus, . . . . . . . . . . 552
Alexander, . . . . . . . . 485, 498
Alexandrianism, . . . 332, 334, 385
Alger, W. R., . . . . . . . . . 577
    Theory of Resurrection, . 593–597
Al Koran, Science in . . . . . 446
Altruism, . . . . . . . . . . . 513
Amusements, Cruel . . . . . 529
Analogy, Argument from . 463, 464
    Conditions of, . . . . . . . 467
Anaxagoras, . . . . . 79, 105, 136
Anaximander, . . . . . . . . 105
Anaximenes, . . . . . . . 76, 105
Andamaners, The . . . . . . . 343
Angelo, Michael . . . . . . . 548
Angels, . . . . . . . . . . . 601
    Condemned, . . . . . 592, 606
Annihilation, Doctrine of . . . 591
Anselm, . . . . . . . . . 87, 221
Antediluvians, . . . . . . . . 607
Antinomies, Absurd . . . . . 730

PAGE.

Antinomies, Kant's . . . . . . 233
Antioch of Pisidia, . . . . . . 383
    In Syria, . . . . . . . . . 393
Antisthines, . . . . . . . . . 110
Anthropology, . . . . . . . . 422
Anthropomorphism, . . . . . 230
Apes, . . . . . . . . . . 173, 179
Apollo, . . . . . . . . . . 15, 51
Apostasy, Post-millennial . . . 616
Apostle, . . . . . . . . . . . 404
Aquinas, Thomas . . . . . 87, 685
Arabia, Paul in, . . . . . 379, 380
Arafuras, The . . . . . . . . 343
Arbitration, Method of . . . . 552
Arcesilaus, . . . . . . . 105, 330
Architecture, Church . . . . . 550
    Pagan, . . . . . . . . . . 550
Argyll, Duke of . . . . 152, 206, 219
    Final Cause, . . . . . . . 298
    The supernatural, . . . . 475
Aristotle, . . . 26, 82, 83, 105, 207
    Classifications of . . . . . 213
    Theory of happiness, . . . 325
Aristophanes, . . . . . . . . 22
Armada, The Spanish . . . . . 485
Arminius, James . . . . 103, 538
Arnold, Matthew . . . . 353, 545
    Interpretation of religion, . . 676
Artists, Modern . . . . . . . 549
Arts, The fine . . . . . . . . 547
    Christian . . . . . . . . . 548
    Pagan . . . . . . . . . . 548
    Patrons of . . . . . . . . 549
    Purification of . . . . 718, 719
Ascension, Christ's . . . . . 389
Asia, . . . . . . . . . . . . 396
    Minor, . . . . . . . . 393, 396
    Minor, Churches in . . . 403, 616
Associationalism, . . . . . 204–206
    Relation to First Cause, . 267, 268
Assyria, Philosophy, . . . . . 337
Astronomy, Moral impressions
    from . . . . . . . . . 296, 297
Asylums, . . . . . . . . 556, 633
Athanasius, . . . . . . . . . 560
    Creed of . . . . . . . . . 749
Atheism, . . . . . . . . . . 697
Athenians, The . . . . . 218, 665
Athens, Paul in . . . . . . . 396

761

PAGE.

Atmosphere, Weight of . . . . 570
Atoms, Capacity of . . . . . . 146
   Contents of . . . . . . . 151
   Dance of . . . . . . . . . 143
   Development of . . . . . . 150
   Difficulties of . . . . . . . 145
   Epicurus's explanation of . . 147
   Form of . . . . . . . . . 151
   Genesis of . . . . . . . . 144
   Inertia of . . . . . . . 149, 150
   Kinds of . . . . . . . . . 146
   Leucippus's explanation of . 148
   Lotze's view of . . . . . 143–147
   Purpose of . . . . . . . . 150
   Theory of . . . . . . . 79, 154
Atonement, Nature's teaching
   on . . . . . 465, 466, 567, 633
   Necessity of . . . . . . . 423
   Philosophic . . . . . . . . 338
   Recognized, . . . . . . . 679
Audubon, . . . . . . . . . . 128
Augustine, . . . . . . . . . 377
Augustus, . . . . . . . . 357, 514

**B.**

Baalbec, . . . . . . . . . 326, 386
Babylon, . . . . . . . . . . 540
Bacon, Francis . . . . 88, 106, 558
   Roger . . . . . . . . . 87, 557
Baer, K. E. Von . . . . . 280, 697
Bain, Alexander . 100, 126, 141,
   . . . . . 191, 204, 205, 210
Bancroft, . . . . . . . . . . 495
Baptism, Christian . . . . . 656
   Christ's . . . . . . . . . 388
Barbarian, The . . . . . . . 526
Barnabas, . . . . . . . . 393, 404
Barrow, Isaac . . . . . . . 545
Bastian, Dr. . . . . . . . . . 155
Bathybius, . . . . . . . . . 157
Baur, . . . . . . . . . . . 369
Beauty, . . . . . . . . . . 472
" Becoming," The . . . . . . 138
Beecher, Edward . . . . . . 628
Being, Defined . . . . . . . 272
   Problem of . . . . . . 309, 310
Beneke, . . . . . . . . . . 215
" Ben Hur," . . . . . . . . 546
Bentham, Jeremy . . . . . . 100
Berkeley, . . . . . . . . 93, 106
Bhagavad Gita, . . . . . 331, 336
Bible, Affirmations in . . . . 735
   Anglo-Saxon in . . . . . . 546
   Contradictions in . . . 664, 665
   Developed, . . . . . . . . 663
   Errors in, explained, . . . 748
   Human elements in, . . . 440
   Infallible, . . . . . . . . 746
   Investigation of . . . . . 693

PAGE.

Bible, Languages of . . . . 747, 748
   Man's origin recorded in . 702, 703
   Manuscripts of . . . . . . 747
   Misunderstandings of . . 665, 666
   Oriental spirit of . . . . . 748
   Pedagogic character of . . . 628
   Rationalism in . . . . . . 729
   Sealed, . . . . . . . . . 544
   Symbolized, . . . . . . . 668
   Tested, . . . . . . . . . 673
   Unity of . . . . . . . . . 647
   Unscientific, . . . . . . . 571
Biogenesis, Theory of . . . 160, 683
Biology, Christian . . . . 454, 455
Bioplasm, . . . . . . . . 157, 162
Births, Law of . . . . . . . 509
Blake, Prof. . . . . . . . . 184
Bledsoe, A. T. . . . . . . . 487
Blood, Harvey's discovery, . . 294
Boehme, Jacob . . . . . . 88, 106
Botany, . . . . . . . . . . 427
   Mysteries of . . . . . . . 684
Bowne, Prof. . 103, 111, 141, 219, 223
Brahm, . . . . . . . . . . 736
Brahminism, . . . . . . . . 345
   A failure, . . . . . . 442, 736
   Pantheistic . . . . . . . . 443
   Prophetic . . . . . . . . 413
Briggs, Prof. C. A. . . . . . 746
Brown, . . . . . . . . . 92, 106
Bruno, Giordano . . . . . . 456
Büchner, Ludwig . . . . . . 170
   Charge against Christianity, . 478
Buddha, . . . . . . . . . . 314
Buddhism, . . . . . . . . . 345
   Evils of . . . . . . . . . 445
   Its priesthood, . . . . . . 736
Burns, Robert . . . . . . . 207
Bushnell, Horace . . . . 140, 456
   Natural and supernatural, . 475
   View of Christ, . . . . . 644
Butler, " Analogy " of . . . . 460
   Ethics of . . . . . . . . 324
Byron, . . . . . . . . . . 545

**C.**

Calamities, . . . . . . . . 482
Caligula, . . . . . . . . . 485
Calvary, . . . . . . . . . 389
Calvin, John . . . . . . 103, 666
Camel, Footprint of . . . . . 234
Cant, . . . . . . . . . . . 743
   Kinds of . . . . . . . . . 744
Capellini, Prof. . . . . . . . 184
Caracalla, Baths of . . . . . 504
Carey, H. C. . . . . . . . . 252
Carlyle, Thomas . . . . . . 255
Caro, M. . . . . . . . . . 479
Carpenter, Dr. W. B. . . . 237, 348

PAGE.

Caste, . . . . . . . . . . . 336, 508
Castor, . . . . . . . . . . . . 313
Catholicism, Roman . . . . 581, 654
Claims of . . . . . . . . 658
Causation, Aristotle's division, . 235
Basis of . . . . . . . 235, 237
Comte's denial of knowledge
of . . . . . . . . . . 236
Doctrine of . . . . . . . 31
Hamilton's interpretation, . 260
Herbart's interpretation, . . 238
Hume's rejection of . . . . 260
McCosh's definition, . . . . 238
Mill's interpretation of, . 201, 236
Objections to . . . . . . 240, 244
Plato's co-causes, . . . . . 235
Relation to theory of develop-
ment, . . . . . . . . . 245
Value of . . . . . . . . 244, 246
Cause, Efficient . . . . . . . 234
Final . . . . . . . . . . 286
Argument from atmosphere, 292
Argument from botany, . . 298
Argument from five senses 295, 296
Argument from function, 290, 291
Argument from nervous sys-
tem, . . . . . . . . . . 295
Argument from the sciences, 291
Argument from zoölogy, . 298, 299
Bacon's objection, . . . . . 303
Comte's objection, . . . . 302
Darwin's Caution, . . . . 287
Development theory a con-
firmation, . . . . . 288, 289
Hartmann's conception, . . 287
Hick's objection, . . . 288, 289
Hume's objection, . . . . . 287
Idea not intuitional, . . . . 288
Janet's facts, . . . . . . . 293
Littré's objection, . . . . . 303
Relation of efficient to . 289, 290
Spinoza's objection, . . . . 305
Causer, the Infinite . . . . . 116
Causes, Aristotle's . . . . . . 286
Plato's . . . . . . . . . . 286
Celibacy, . . . . . . . . . . 509
Channing, W. H. . . . . . . 414
Character, Sources of . . . 682, 684
Chemistry, Definition of . . . . 252
Cheops, Pyramid of . . . . . . 675
Chiliasm, . . . . . . . . . . 609
China, Religions of . . . . . . 447
Choice, Alternate . . . . . . . 166
Christ, Ascension of . . . . . . 652
Deity of . . . . . . . . . 431
Magnetism of . . . . . . . 643
Millennial reign of . . . . 610
Paul's relation to . . . . . 438
Personification of . . 621, 640

PAGE.

Christ, Resurrection of . . 629, 650
Sinlessness of . . . . . . . 644
Uninterpreted, . . . . . . 565
Christianity, Absolute religion,
. . . . . . . . . . 622, 388
Affirmations of . . . . 734, 735
Antagonisms to . . . . . 351
Anthropology of . . . . 422, 423
Apriorism of . . . . . . . 757
Background of . . . . . . 328
Benevolence of . . . . . . 633
Büchner's opinion of . . . 352
Budding period of . . . . 537
Channing's opinion of . . . 756
Chronology of . . . . . . 449
Contempt, A doctrine of . . 396
Core of . . . . . . . . . 542
Cosmology of . . . . . . 449
Credentials of . . . . . . 548
Creed form of . . . . 749, 750
Decalogue of . . . . . . . 720
Defended, . . . . . . . . 746
Defensive, . . . . . . . . 342
Development of . . 413, 418, 562
Dogmatic, . . . . . . 638, 655
Dynamic elements, . . . 631, 633
Effects of . . . . . . . 636, 638
Empirical, . . . . . . . . 686
Enemies of . . . . . . . . 742
Eschatology of . . . 424, 579
Evidences of . . . . . . 531
Experience the proof of . 572
Finality, A religious . . . 732
Finality, A philosophic . 726, 728
Form, A . . . . . . . . 523
Forms of . . . . . . . 562, 554
Founder, The . . . . . . 565
Gentile, . . . . . . . . . 425
Geometric, . . . . . . . . 534
Historic periods, . . . . 722
Inherent logic, . . . . . . 731
Inspiring power, . . . . . 574
Intellectual, . . . . . 673, 382
Jewish, . . . . . . . . . 425
Life, A . . . . 533, 534, 654 675
Limitations of . . . 410, 415, 416
Magnetism of . . . . 642, 650
Material benefits, . . . 542, 543
Methods, . . . . . . . . 637
Military support, . . . . . 712
Modern proofs of . . 649, 654
Mysteries in, . . . . . . 566
Necessary truths of . . . . 417
New in . . . . . . . . . 563
Opposed to Agnosticism, . 694–696
Papal, . . . . . . . . . 654
Philosophic basis 412, 439, 448, 455
Physical basis, . . . . . . 409
Plan of . . . . . . . . . 635

| PAGE. | | PAGE. |
|---|---|---|

Christianity, Platonized, . . . 332
  Political . . . . . . . 542, 668
  Practical . . . . . . . . 731
  Prophetic Basis . . . . . . 708
  Province of . . . . . . 411, 424
  Pseudodox in . . . . . 660, 670
  Purpose of . . . . . . 408, 410
  Rationalism in . . . . 756, 757
  Relation of Church to . . . . 515
  Relation of Greek Philosophy
    to . . . . . . . . . . 308, 340
  Relation of Judaism to . . . 536
  Relation of Paul to . . . . 429
  Relation of Present Age to. 741, 742
  Relation of Reforms to . . . . 550
  Relation of Society to . 507, 515
  Religion of Realities . . . . 634
  Revelation the Source of . . 448
  Revelation of the Supernat-
    ural . . . . . . . . 409, 410
  Root of . . . . . . . . . 644
  Soteriology of . . . . . 423, 575
  Specialty of . . . . . . 423
  Sphere of . . . . . . . 688
  Spiritual . . . . 434, 596, 597
  Standard, A . . . . . . . 448
  Statistics of . . . . . 722, 723
  Stimulating Property of . . 354
  Supreme . . . . . . . . 355
  Tasks of . . . . . . . . 741
  Tendency to Universality, . . 532
  Triumph of . . . . . . 708, 709
  Truth, . . . . . . . . . 634
  Undeveloped . . . . . . 358
  Unitarian Idea of . . . . . 414
  Unsystematized, . . . . . 441
  Utopianism of . . . . . . 709
  Virtues of . . . . . 667, 668
Chronology, Usher's . . . . 570
Church, Controversies in . . 555–557
  Idea of . . . . . . . 533, 545
  Instrument, An . . . . . 346
  Interpreter, Bible . . . . 658
  Mission of . . . . . . . 345
  Program of . . . . . . 709
  Reign of . . . . . 515, 516
  Supervision, Paul's . . . . 397
Church-founder, The . . . . 403
Churchism, State . . . . . 515
Cicero, . . . . . . 136, 335
Circumcision, . . . . . 382
Civilization, Asiatic . 496, 505, 540
  Buckle's Theory of . . . 312
  Christian . . . . . . 541
  Corner-stone of . . . . 643
  Draper's Theory . . . . 501
  European . . . . . . 497
  Forces of . . . . . . 311
  Historic Development of . . 31

Civilization, Model . . . . . . 539
  Unity of . . . . . 497, 498
Clark, Bishop D. W. . . . . . 594
  Prof. H. J. . . . . . . 155
Clarke, James F . . . . . . 414
Classification, Scientific Objection
  to . . . . . . . . . . 165
Cleanthus, . . . . . . . 84
Clement . . . . . . . 283, 707
Clifford, Prof. . . . . . . 228
Cocker, Dr. B. F. . 100, 239, 240, 331
Coincidence, Doctrine of . . . . 241
Coleridge, . . . . . . . 64
Coliseum, Significance of . 503, 504
Colleges, Christian, . . . . . 547
Color, . . . . . . . . 463
Comets, . . . . . . . 486
Coming, The Second . . . . 437
Common-sense, Philosophy of,
  . . . . . . . 89, 92, 197
Common-sense, Objections to. 260, 261
Comte, . . . . . . . 99, 106
  Positivism of . . . . 259, 346
Communism . . . . . 499, 517
  Apostolic . . . . . . 661
Concept, Analysis of . . . . 353
  Emotional Content of . . 350
  Religious . . . . . . 346
  Value of . . . . . . 353
Condillac, . . . . . . 91
Confucius, . . . . . . 331
  Religion of . . . . . 724
Congenitalism, . . . . . 207
Conscience, . . . . . . 351
  Origin of . . . . . . 179
Consciousness, A Birth-mark, . 165
  Definitions of . . . 677, 678
  Mansel's Objection to . . 122
  Mill's (James) Idea of . . 210
  Needle-points of . . . . 120
  Unity of . . . . . . 585
Conservatism, . . . . 575, 576
Constantine, . . . . . 637
Consubstantiation, . . . 656, 666
Conversion, . . . . . 363, 573
  Paul's . . . . . . . 365
  Philosophic . . . . . 327
Continuity, Law of . . . 278, 279
Cook, Joseph . . . . . 239
Cooke, Prof. . . . . . . 243
  R. J. . . . . . . . 594
Copernicus, . . . . . . 520
Cosmology, Jewish . . . . 333
Council, Church . . . . . 382
Cousin, Opinions of . . 81, 86, 109
  Plato defended by . . . 35
  Rationalism of . . . . 270
Creation, . . . . . . 142
  According to Law, . . . . 152

PAGE.

Creation, Man's, . . . . . . . . 521
  Modality of, . . . . . . . . . 700
  Order of . . . . . . . . . . 459
Creationism, Theory of . . . 160, 167
Creed, Christian . . . . . . . 749
Creed-maker, The . . . . . . 739
Cromwell, . . . . . . . . . . . 128
Crystals, . . . . . . . . . . . 683
Cudworth, . . . . . . . . . 213, 239
  Ethics of . . . . . . . . . . 324

D.

DALLINGER, . . . . . . . . . . 155
Dante, . . . . . . . . . . . . 545
  Inferno, . . . . . . . . . . . 633
Darwin, Charles . . . . . 155, 156
Darwinism, . . . . . . . . 691, 697
Davis, Henry . . . . . . . . . 22
Davies, Sir John, . . . . . . . 143
Dawkins, Prof. . . . . . . . . 184
Dawson, Prof. . . . . . . 184, 255
Dead, The . . . . . . . . . . 599
Deduction, . . . . . . . . 674, 757
Definitions . . . . . . . . . . 26
Delphino, Prof. . . . . . . . . 156
Deity, The Unconscious . . . . 122
Democracy, . . . . . . . . . . 528
Democritus . . . . . . . . . 78, 105
Descartes . . . . . 88, 89, 106, 206
Descent, Theory of . . . . . . 171
Development, Theory of . . . . 156
Dickens, Charles . . . . . . . 546
Diderot, . . . . . . . . . . . 91
Diogenes, . . . . . . . . . . . 108
Dionysiodorus, . . . . . . . . 44
Diseases, . . . . . . . . . . . 482
Dispensation, The New . . . . 626
Dogmatism, Theologic . . . . 89
Dorchester, Dr. D. . . . . . . 723
Doré, Gustave . . . . . . . . 549
Dorner, Dr. . . . . . . . . . . 606
Doubt, Philosophic . . . . . . 116
Draper, Prof. . . . . . . . . . 334
  Physiological Law of Civiliza-
    tion . . . . . . . . . . . . 501
Drew, Samuel . . . . . . . . . 593
Druidism, . . . . . . . . . . . 661
Drummond, Henry . . . . . . 155
  Identity of Natural and Spirit-
    ual . . . . . . . . . . . . 474
Dryad, The . . . . . . . . . . 136
Dryden, John . . . . . . . . . 143
Dualism, . . . . . . . . . . . 89
Dual, The . . . . . . . . . . . 552
Dynamite, . . . . . . . . . . . 555

E.

EARTH, Antiquity of . . . . . 700
  Astronomic Center. . . . . . 520

PAGE.

Earth, Conflagration of . . . . . 452
  Destruction of . . . . . . . . 453
  Globular . . . . . . . . . . 569
  Subdued . . . . . . . . . . 524
  Theories Respecting . . . . . 570
Earthquakes, . . . . . . . . . 486
Easter, . . . . . . . . . . . . 659
Eclecticism, . . . . . . . . . . 733
Eden, Promise in . . . . . . . 627
Education, Christianity the In-
    spiration of . . . . . 518, 547
  Nations leading in . . . . . . 547
  Oriental . . . . . . . . . . . 547
  Plato's Curriculum . . . . . 510
  Problem of . . . . . . . 509, 510
  Relation to False Religions . . 724
  Remedy for Evil . . . . . . 49
  System of . . . . . . . . . . 510
Egypt, Religions of . . . . . . 447
Eleatics, The . . . . . . . . . 77
Electricity . . . . . . . . 131, 292
Elements, Chemical . . . . 131, 157
  Proof that they are Effects, . . 242
Elisha, Prayer . . . . . . . . . 277
Emerson, R. W. . . . 21, 189, 469
Emotionalism, . . . . . . . . 89, 95
Emotions, Religious . . . . 676, 677
Empedocles, . . . . . . . . . 70, 105
  Translation of . . . . . . . . 577
Empiricism . . . . . . . . . . 89
Energy, Amount of . . . . . . 588
  Tyndall's Theory of . . . . . 239
Ephesus, . . . . 393, 396, 397, 402
Epicurus, . . . . . . . . . . . 105
  Philosophy of . . . . . . 84, 147
Equivalence, Doctrine of . . . 242
Erigena, Scotus, . . . . . . . . 87
Eschatology, Christian . . . . . 582
  Development of . . . . . 627–629
  Effect of . . . . . . . . 638, 639
  Homeric . . . . . . . . . . . 604
  Jewish . . . . . . . . . . . 604
  Revision Necessary . . . . . 630
Essenes, The . . . . . . . . . 499
Ethics, Evolutionary . . . . . 101
  Intuitional . . . . . . . . . 324
  Natural . . . . . . . . . . . 706
  Origin of . . . . . . . . . . 321
  Supernatural . . . . . . . . 706
Etiquette . . . . . . . . . . . 718
Eucharist, The . . . . . . . . 603
Europe, Paul in . . . . . . 395, 396
Eutychianism . . . . . . . . . 603
Evil, An Atonement . . . . . . 489
  Apology, for . . . . . . . . 640
  Condemned, . . . . . . . . 640
  Defeated, . . . . . . . . . . 490
  Defined, . . . . . . . . . . 489
  A Discipline . . . . . . . . 487

PAGE.

Evil, Divine Perfections In-
    volved, . . . . . . . . 487–489
    Future Possibility of . . . . 492
    Man's Duty Respecting . . . 551
    Method of Extinction, . 454, 465
    Mission of . . . . . . . . . 481
    Moral . . . . . . . . . . . 486
    Natural . . . . . . . . . . 486
    Penalty, A . . . . . . . . . 487
    Presence of . . . . . . . 315, 479
    Principle of . . . . : . . . · · 33
    Product of Law, . . . . . . 481
    Relation to Hell, . . . . . 492
    Relation to History, . . . . 483
    Relation to Man, . . . . 483–488
    Self-destroying . . . . . . . 484
    Teleology of . . . . . . . . 304
    Test of . . . . . . . . . . 488
    Unrecognized, . . . . . . . 679
    Uses of . . . . . . . . . 478, 479
Evolution, . . . . . . . . 89, 101
    Breaks in the Law of . . . 704
    Christianity an . . . . . . 722
    Condemned, . . . . . . . 704
    Defined, . . . . . . . . 470, 471
    Example of . . . . . . . . 624
    In History, . . . . . . . . 282
    In Mind, . . . . . 201, 202, 320
    In Nature, . . . . . . . . 282
    Kinds of . . . . . . . . . 704
    Relation to First Cause, 268, 269,
        . . . . . . . . . . . . . 626
    Relation to Scriptural Truth, . 433
Evolutionists, Disagreement
    among . . . . . . . . . . 754
Experience, Brahminical Doc-
    trine of . . . . . . . . . 715
    Criterion of Truth, . . . 672, 674
    Eschatology an . . . . . 681
    Holiness an . . . . . . 680, 681
    Misunderstood, . . . . . . 685
    Reliability of . . . . . . . 686
    Religion an . . . . . . . . 435
    Processes of . . . . . . . 682
    Schleiermacher's Opinion . . 678
    Spiritual . . . . . . . 676-678
    Unconscious . . . . . . . 678

F.

Fables, . . . 37, 41, 55, 57, 326, 735
Faculties, Mental . . . . . 209, 349
Faith, Justification by . . . . 538
Fairbairn, Prof. . . . . . . . 428
Famines, . . . . . . . . . . 544
Faraday, . . . . . . . . . . 148
Farrar, Canon . . . . . . 359, 606
Ferrier, Prof. . . . . . . . . 190
Feudalism, . . . . . . . . . 529
Fitche . . . . . . . . . . 96, 106

PAGE.

Finalities, . . . . . . . . . . 726
Fiske, John . . . . . . . . . 255
    Theism of . . . . . . . . 754
Force, Attributes of . . . . 250, 251
    Buddhistic Origin of Doctrine
        of . . . . . . . . . . . 445
    Centripetal . . . . . . . . 250
    Electricity the Content of . . 252
    Ends of . . . . . . . . . . 254
    Internal . . . . . . . . . . 250
    Manifestations of . . . . . 250
    Modality of . . . . . . . . 251
    Persistence of . . . . . . 252, 702
    Personality of . . . . . . . 253
    Plato's Definition of . . . . 247
    Relation to Matter, . . . . 249
    Self-consciousness of . . . . 254
    Transmission of . . . . . . 249
Forces, Classification of . . . . 248
    Conservation and Correlation
        of . . . . . . . . . . . 158
    Cousin's View of . . . . . 540
    Secondary . . . . . . . . 251
Foreknowledge, Divine . . . . 603
Fossils, Age of . . . . 180, 181, 183
Foster, Bishop R. S. . . . 593, 594
Fourier, . . . . . . . . . . 473
    Socialism of . . . . . . . 502
Franklin, Benjamin . . . . . 473
Fundamentals . . . . . . . . 327

G.

Galatia, . . . . . . . . . . 403
Galen, . . . . . . 198, 293, 672
Gamaliel, . . . . . . . . . 360
Gautama, . . . . . . 330, 331, 445
Gehenna, . . . . . . . . 590, 605
Geikie, Prof. . . . . . . . . 184
Generation, Spontaneous, . 155, 683
Genesis, Man's creation, . 521, 703
    Non-mythological, . . . . . 572
    Strauss's opinion of . . . . 662
Gentiles, Gospel among the . . 394
    Paul's mission to . . . . . 392
    Rights of . . . . . . . . 382
Gentilism, Conflict with . . . 383
Geologists, Labors of . . . . . 180
Geology, . . . . . . . . . . 741
    Pentateuchal . . . . . . . 451
Geometry, . . . . . . . . 20, 152
Geranium, Geometric . . . . . 632
Geulinex, . . . . . . . . . 90
Gibbon, Anglo-Saxon of . . . 546
    Objections to Christianity, . . 649
    Progress of Christianity ac-
        counted for, . . . . . 637, 638
Gillie, John . . . . . . . . . 548
Gnosticism, . . . . . 337, 401, 562
    John's attack on . . . . . . 667

PAGE.

Gnosticism, Traces in eschatology, 596
God, *A priori* conception of . . . 120
  Argument from correlation, . 271
  Author's position, . . . . . . 270
  Barbarians' ideas of, . . 343, 348
  Belief in . . . . . . . . . . 119
  Büchner's objection, . . . . . 274
  Conceptions of an absolute, . 272
  Development of the idea, 625, 626
  Existence assumed, . . . . . 222
  First act of . . . . . . . . 142
  Geometric fulfillment, . . . . 632
  Hamilton's alternative a proof 125
  Hamilton's idea of the uncon-
    ditioned, . . . . . . . . 266
  Hartmann's idea, . . . . . . 263
  Involved in evil, . . . . . . 487
  Key-word to truth, . . . . 455
  Knowable, . . . . . . 226, 685
  Lotze's idea, . . . . . . . . 255
  Necessary, . . . . . . . . . 143
  Personal . . . . . 226, 273, 285
  Philosophic idea of . . . . . 728
  Schopenhauer's idea, . . . . 262
  Spencer's interpretation, . . 698
  Spinoza's idea, . . . . . . . 273
  Testimony of Nature, 275, 281, 470
  Testimony of Psychology, 276, 277
  Tyndall's idea, . . . . . . . 274
Goethe, . . . . . . . 104, 134, 587
Good, Contents of the . . . . . 48
Gorgias, . . . . . . . 80, 105, 456
Gospel, Benevolence of the . . . 751
  Figurative in . . . . . . . . 744
  John's . . . . . . . . . . . 667
  Millennial teachings in . 613, 614
  Paul's . . . . . . . . . . . 376
  Philosophical. . . . . . . . 743
  Reign ends, . . . . . . . . 616
  Spiritualities of . . . . . . 751
  Supreme, . . . . . . . 612, 614
  Triumph prophesied . . . . 613
Gospels, Fragmentary . . . . . 427
Government, Bad. . . . . . . . 485
  Christian . . . . . . . . . 541
  Divine . . . . . . . . . . . 419
  Necessity of good . . . . . 527
  Philosophic idea of . . . 313, 314
Grasshopper, an Athenian em-
    blem, . . . . . . . . . . 173
Grau Chacos, The . . . . . . . 343
Gravitation, . . . . 148, 297, 473
  Newton doubted . . . . . . 228
Gravity, Spencer's idea of . . . . 248
Greece, Birthplace of philosophy, 71
  Systems of philosophy in . . 72
Grote, . . . . . . . . . . 18, 185
  Associational principle, . . . 313
Grotius, . . . . . . . . . . . 535

Grove, Sir W. R. . . . . . . . . 130
Growth, Law of . . . . . . . . 206

**H.**

Häckel, . . . . . . . . . . 126, 165
  Animalic stages of . . . . . 173
Hades, . . 54, 335, 339, 597, 604–606
Hall, Robert . . . . . . . . . 566
Hamilton, Sir William . 106, 123, 125
  Doctrine of relativity, . . 265, 266
  Paralogisms, . . . . . . . . 267
Hammond, Dr. . . . . . . . . 204
Happiness, Sources of . . . . . 325
Harmonites, The . . . . . . . 499
Harris, Prof. S. . . . . . . 270, 283
Hartley, David . . . . . . . . 100
  Mental action explained . . . 202
Hartmann, . . . . . . . . 99, 106
Heaven, . . . . . . . . . 340, 619
Hegel, . . . . . . . . . . 97, 106
  Classification of . . . . . . 196
  Doctrines of . . . . . . . . 265
  Philosophy of mind, . . . . 195
Hell, . . . . . . . . 491, 492 619
Helvetius, . . . . . . . . . . 91
Helmholtz, . . . . . . . . . . 319
Hennel, Mr. . . . . . . . . . 644
Heraclitus, . . . . . . . . 78, 105
Herbart, . . . . . . . . 106, 140
Herbert, Lord . . . . . . . . 225
Herder, . . . . . . . . . . . 348
Heredity, . . . . . . . . . . 479
Heresy, . . . . . . . . . 576, 739
Hermon, Mt. . . . . . . . . . 388
Heterodox, The . . . . . . . 653
Heterodoxy, . . . . . . . . . 581
Hilaire, St. Geoffroy . . . . . 149
Hildebrand, . . . . . . . 494, 637
Hinduism, . . . . . . . . . . 737
Hippias . . . . . . . . . . . 80
History, Gibbon's . . . . . . . 503
  Product, A . . . . . . . . . 481
  Providential development, A . 483
  The test, . . . . . . . . . 535
Hobbes, . . . . . . . . . . . 198
  Ethics of . . . . . . . . . 322
  Indebted to Pythagoras, . . . 199
  Interpretation of mind, . . . 199
  Interpretation of phenomena, .199
  Materialism of . . . . . . . 200
Holiness . . . . . . . . . 679, 680
  Philosophic, . . . . . . . 52, 53
Holsten, . . . . . . . . . . . 370
Home, Christian . . . . . . 552–554
  Pagan . . . . . . . . . . . 718
Homer, Incident from . . . . . 277
  Plato's condemnation of . 50, 340
  Sin not portrayed in . . . . 454
Homology, Argument from . 132, 133

PAGE.

Hooker, . . . . . . . . . . . 343
Humanity, Roman Worship of . 621
Humboldt, . . . . . . . . . 130, 135
Hume, David . . . . . 91, 106, 203
  Theory of consciousness, . . . 215
Huxley, Prof. . 131, 155–157, 206
  . . . . . . . . . . 239, 248, 258
Hydrogen, . . . . . . . . . . . 132
  Substance-unit . . . . . . 468
Hypatia . . . . . . . . . . . 712
Hypothesis, Diluvian . . . . . . 451
  Nebular . . . . . . . 137, 450
  Restitutionary . . . . . . . 451
  Substantial agreement . . 451, 452
  Theistic . . . . . . . . . . 450

I.

IDEA, Meanings of . . . . . . 744
Idealism, . . . . . . . . . 89, 92
  Christian . . . . . . . . . 139
  Decline of absolute . . . . . 98
  Relation to First Cause, . 263–265
  Weaknesses of . . . . . . 265
Ideals, Geometric . . . . . . 152
Ideas, Innate . . . . 216, 225, 351
  Pseud . . . . . . . . . . 102
  Religious . . . . . . . . . 344
Identity, Law of . . . . . . . 163
Ignatius, . . . . . . . . . . 670
Immanence, Doctrine of divine . 240
Immortality, . . . . . 53, 339, 424
  Argument for brutes, . . . . 588
  Certainty, . . . . . . . . . 589
  Developed, . . . . . . . . 588
  Endowment, . . . . . . . 591
  Gift, . . . . . . . . . . . 591
  Goethe's faith, . . . . . . . 587
  Hugo's faith, . . . . . . . 587
  Judaic Intimations, . . . . . 589
  Lotze's idea, . . . . . . . 586
  Moral effect of belief in . . . 586
  Necessity, . . . . . . . . . 584
  Objections . . . . . . . . . 588
  Pagan doctrine of . . . . . 579
  Paul's idea of . . . . . . . 437
  Personal . . . . . . . . . 582
  Philosophical . . . . . . . 584
  Physical, impossible, . . . . 583
  Probable . . . . . . . . . 583
  Revealed, . . . . . . . 578, 579
  Strauss's unbelief, . . . . . 587
  Testament, The New, on . . 628
  Testament, The Old, on . . . 628
Incarnation, Geometric, . . . . 633
  Relation to the Universe, . . 306
  Value, . . . . . . . . . . 388
  Vital, . . . . . . . . . . . 737
Incarnations, Brahminical . . . 337
  Buddhistic . . . . . . . . 716

PAGE.

Indians, The . . . . . . . . . . 577
Individualism, . . . . . . . . . 527
Induction . . . . . . . . . 674, 757
Industrialism, . . . . . . . . . 510
Inertia, . . . . . . . . . . . 164
Infinite, Definition . . . . . . 120
  Related, . . . . . . . . . 121
  Super-rational, . . . . . . 123
  Unrelated . . . . . . . . . 121
Inquisitions . . . . . . . . . 712
Inspiration attacked, . . . . . 747
  Defined, . . . . . . . . . 219
  Difficulties, . . . . . . . . 564
  Forms of . . . . . . . . . 15
Institutions, Benevolent . . . . 555
  Social . . . . . . . . . . 528
Intemperance, . . . . . . . . 551
Interpretations, Biblical . . . . 559
Intolerance, . . . . . . . . . 742
Intuitionalism . . . . . . . . 121
Intuitional Truths, Criteria of . 236
  Theistic argument from . 284, 285
Invention, . . . . . . . . . . 543
Iron, Knowledge of . . . . . . 224

J.

JACOBI, . . . . . . . . 95, 106, 216
Jaeger, Gustave . . . . . . . 188
Janet, Explanation of Evil, . . . 304
  Final cause of nature . . . . 306
Jerome, . . . . . . . . . . 357
Jerusalem, Schools of . . . . . 360
Jew, Religious development of . . 627
John the Baptist, . . . . . . . 426
John of Salisbury, . . . . . . 87
Johnson, . . . . . . . . . . 743
Judaism, Conflict with . . . 381, 382
  Defense of . . . . . . . . 361
  Inadequacy of . . . . . 535, 536
  Religious content of . . . . 687
Judgment, Basis of . . . . . . 608
  Day of . . . . . . . . 437, 607
  Scenes, . . . . . . . . . 605
  Time of . . . . . . . . 617, 618
Jupiter, . . . . . . . 37, 477, 645
Justice, Plato's definition of . . . 464
Justification, Doctrine of . . 384, 385
Justinian, . . . . . . . . . . 86

K.

KAMES, LORD, . . . . . . . . 178
Kant, Immanuel . . . . 93, 94, 106
  Antinomies of . . . . . . 233
  His philosophy criticized, . . 264
King, T. Starr . . . . . . 178, 482
Kingsley, Bishop C. . . . . . . 594
König, . . . . . . . . . . . 721
Knowledge, *A posteriori* . . . . 257
  Hamilton's admission, . . . 232

PAGE.

Knowledge, Intuitional . . . 215, 217
Latent . . . . . . . . . . . 217
Limitations of . . . . . . 227, 228
Necessary, . . . . . . . . . 577
Object of Search, . . . . . 695
Possibility of . . . . . . . 212
Progress in . . . . . . 230, 231
Reflection a source of . . . 218
Relational, . . . . . . 118, 126
Sense-knowledge, . . . . . 214
Sources of . . . . . . . 212–223
Subject-matter of . . . 223–227
Superficial . . . . . . . . 223

**L.**

Labor, . . . . . . . . . . . 517
Lactantius, . . . . . . . . . 707
Ladd, Dr. G. T. . . . . . . . 746
Laertius, Diogenes . . . 22, 61, 112
Lama, The Buddhistic . . . . 736
Lamarck, . . . . . . . . . . 156
Lamartine, . . . . . . . . . 743
La Mettrie, , . . . . . . . . 91
Lang, Heinrich, . . . . . . . 687
Language, Anglo Saxon . . . . 546
Greek, . . . . . . . . . . 529
Origin of . . . . . . . . . 662
Purification of . . . . . . . 529
Unity of . . . . . . 529, 530
Languages, . . . . . . . . . 141
Primitive . . . . . . . . . 175
Lao-tzu, . . . . . . . . 330, 331
Laplace, . . . . . . . . . . 458
Law, . . . . . . . . . . . . 225
Definition, . . . . . . . . 141
Force of . . . . . . . . . 462
International . . . . . . . 517
Knowledge of . . . . . . . 223
Laws, Discovery of . . . . . 473
Relation of natural and spirit-
ual . . . . . . . . . . 473
Laycock, Dr. . . . . . . . . 239
Leibnitz, . . . . . . . . 92, 106
Characteristic of truth, . . 674
Theory of mind . . . . . . 194
Lent, . . . . . . . . . . . . 660
Leroux, . . . . . . . . . . . 225
Idea of Christianity, . . . . 707
Leucippus, . . . . . . . . . 105
Lewes, Criticisms of . . . 108, 109
Lewis, Prof. Tayler . . . . . 589
Liberia, Natives of . . . . . 519
Life, Deathless . . . . . . . 585
Definitions of . . . . . 161, 162
Kinds of . . . . . . . . . 162
Nature of . . . . . . . . . 320
Possibilities of . . . . . . 318
Theories of . . . . . . 155, 320
Lindsey, Prof. . . . . . . 340, 536

PAGE.

Linnæus, . . . . . . . . . . 130
Littré, M. . . . . . . . . . . 303
Livingstone, Dr. . . . . . . . 348
Locke, John . . . . . . . 90, 106
Mistakes of . . . . . . 257, 258
Philosophy condemned, . . . 193
Sensationalism of . . . . . 192
Value of sensationalism, . . 214
Loggia, Raphael's . . . . . . 108
Logos, the word, . . . . . . 667
Lotze, Hermann . 103, 106, 107,
. . . . . . . . . 141, 239, 242
Lubbock, Sir John, . . 174, 178, 343
Lucretius, . . . . . . . . . . 74
Final cause, . . . . . . . . 305
Luther, . . . . . . . . . 538, 544
Papal education of . . . . . 659
Personal salvation taught
by . . . . . . . . . . . 678
Lyell, Sir Charles, . 174, 181, 182, 185
Lystra, . . . . . . . . . 394–396

**M.**

Machinery, Origin of . . . . . 543
Machpelah, . . . . . . . . . 629
Magic . . . . . . . . . . . 337
Magnetism, . . . . . . . . . 228
Malebranche, . . . . . . 90, 215
Mallock, Theory of . . . . . 314
Malta, . . . . . . . . . . . 397
Man, Ancestry of . . . . . . 702
Antiquity of . . 179, 183, 184, 748
Barbaric Idea of . . . . . 526
Buddhist conception of . . 446
Development of . . . . . . 522
Dominion of . . . . . 524, 525
Eulogies of . . . . . . . . 168
Exaltation (Paul's) of . . . 432
Fall of . . . . . . . . . . 591
Flatterer, A . . . . . . . . 520
Freedom of . . . . . . . . 491
Future, the . . . . . . . . 519
Immortal . . . . . . . . . 759
Lordship of . . . . . . . . 312
Masterpiece, A . . . . . . 523
Occupations, . . . . . 525–527
Origin of . . . . . . . . . 170
Palæolithic . . . . . . . . 181
Poor, the . . . . . . . . . 543
Primitive . . . . . . . . . 174
Problem of . . . . . . . . 125
Relation of Christianity to . . 523
Relation to animal kingdom,
. . . . . . . . . . . 172, 173
Relation to nature, . . . 169, 469
Religious . . . . . . . . 349, 350
Rights of . . . . . . . 507, 508
Sanctification of . . . . 531, 532
Scientific spirit in . . . . 530, 531

PAGE.

Man, Scriptural representation
of . . . . . . . . 433, 434, 453
  Self-sufficient . . . . . . . 534
Mandeville, Ethics of . . . . . 322
Manes, . . . . . . . . . . . . 331
Mansel, . . . . 96, 119, 123, 411, 664
Marriages, Royal . . . . . . . 66
Martineau, Dr. . . . . . . . . 680
Martyr, Justin . . . . . . . . 283
  Chiliasm of . . . . . . . . . 609
Martyrdom, Value of . . . . . 389
Martyrs, Resurrection of . . 610, 611
Materialism, Ancient . . . . . 73
  Assailed . . . . . . . . . . 719
  Ionic . . . . . . . . . . . 73
Mathematics, . . . . . . . . . 686
Matter, Brahminical notions of. . 444
  Buddhistic notions of . . . 445
  Co-eternity of . . . . . . . 32
  Definitions of . . . . . . . 141
  Deification of . . . . . . . 697
  Dynamical theory of . . . . 248
  Explanation of . . . . . . . 206
  Forms of . . . . . . . . . 462
  Non-existence of . . . . . . 124
  Organization of . . . . . 33, 159
  Pre-existence of . . . . . . 136
  Spherical tendency of . . . 470
Maupertius, . . . . . . . . . 299
Maurice, F. D. . . . . . . . . 710
McCosh, Dr. . . . . . 103, 348, 662
  Criterion of Truth, . . . . 674
McIlvaine, J. H. . . . . . . . 571
Mediation, Basis of . . . . . 690
Memory, Unexplained . . . . 205
Merrill, Bishop S. M. . . . . 609
Messiahship, . . . . . . . 383, 627
Method, Abuse . . . . . . . . 727
  Biblical . . . . . . . . . . 693
  Boundaries of . . . . . . . 692
  Philosophical . . . . . . . 309
  Psychological . . . . . . . 123
  Supernatural . . . . . . . 439
Methodism, . . . . . . . . . 713
Mettrie, De La . . . . . . . . 203
Military, the . . . . . . . . 508
Mill, James . . . . . . . 177, 214
Mill, John S. . 100, 101, 106, 141, 200
  Interpretation of Mind, . . . 201
  Socialism of . . . . . . . 502
Millennium, Apocalyptic . . . 610
  Definition of . . . . . . . 610
  Gradual . . . . . . . . . . 615
  Greek Idea of . . . . . . . 493
  Jewish Idea of . . . . . . 493
  Limited . . . . . . . . 612–616
  Political . . . . . . . . . 611
  Religious . . . . . . . . . 612
  Scientific . . . . . . . . . 612

PAGE.

Millennium, Subsidence of . . . 616
Miller, Hugh . . . . . . . . . . 128
Minark, . . . . . . . . . . . . 248
Mind, Attributes of . . . . . . 229
  Creating power of . . . . . 208
  Definitions of . . . . . . . 209
  Fact of . . . . . . . . . . 190
  Freedom of . . . . . . . . 208
  Hamilton's opinion, . . . . 177
  Interpretations of . . . . . 192
  Laws of . . . . . . . . . . 206
  Relation to Body, . . . . . 204
  Self-determining power, . . . 203
Ministry, Christian . . . . . . 533
  Ecclesiastical Differences Con-
    cerning . . . . . . . . . 657
Miracles, . . . . . . . . . 387, 403
  Hume's objection, . . . . . 237
  Objections, . . . . . . . . 649
Missionary Center, . . . . . . 393
Missions, Christian . . . . . . 556
Mivart, St. George . . . . . 157, 250
  Ethics of . . . . . . . . . 706
Mohammed, . . . . . . . . . 354
  Methods of . . . . . . . . 637
  Religion of . . . . . . . 446, 447
  Sovereign Principle of . . 505, 506
Mohammedanism, . . . . . . 710
  A Failure, . . . . . . . . 724
Moleschott, . . . . . . . . . 204
Monarchy, . . . . . . . . . . 514
Monadism, . . . . . . . . . . 93
Monism, . . . . . . . . . 135, 171
Monogamy, . . . . . . . . . 553
Monophysitism, . . . . . . . 603
Monopoly, . . . . . . . . . . 555
Monotheism, . . . . . . . 334, 347
  Defective . . . . . . . . . 736
  Jewish . . . . . . . . 622, 625
Montaigne, . . . . . . . . . 116
Monuments, Egyptian and Roman.185
  Scriptures Confirmed by . . . 748
Moon, Size of . . . . . . . . 84
Morality, Christian . . . . . . 555
  Definitions of . . . . . . . 513
  Necessity of . . . . . . . . 512
  Pagan . . . . . . . . . . 555
  Relative . . . . . . . . . 323
Mormonism, . . . . . . . . . 553
Morlot, M. . . . . . . . . . 181
Morris, Prof. . . . . . . . 140, 198
Mortillet, M. . . . . . . . . 181
Moses, . . . . . . . . 142, 151, 333
  Books of . . . . . . . . . 746
  Creation week of . . . . . 451
  Errors of . . . . . . . . . 571
  Geology of . . . . . . . . 570
  Sustained, . . . . . . . . 662
Motion, . . . . . . . . . . . 148

PAGE.

Motion, Kinds of . . . . . . . 34
    Suggestive . . . . . . . . . 461
Muller, Julius . . . . . . . . 677
Müller, Max . . . . . . . . . 710
Musæus, . . . . . . . . . . . 137
Music, Mill's Fear . . . . . . 187
    Pythagoras on . . . . . . . 77
Mysteries, Christian . . . . . 568
    Eleusinian . . . . . . . . . 566
    Solved . . . . . . . . . . 730
Mysticism, Christianity a . . . 669
    Swedenborg's . . . . . . . 134
Mythologies, . . . . . . 15, 74, 639
    Overthrown . . . . . . . . 329

**N.**

Napoleon, . . . . . . . . . . 485
Naturalism, Ethical . . . . . . 323
Nature, . . . . . . . . . . . 127
    Beauty of . . . . . . . . . 472
    Cause of . . . . . . . . . 237
    Christianity the Counterpart of .633
    Common Representation of . 129
    Emerson's idea of . . . 475, 476
    Final cause of . . . . . 306, 477
    Goethe's idea of . . . . . . 134
    Greek interpretation of . . 477
    Häckel's idea of . . . . . . 133
    Idealistic interpretation, . . 139
    Laws of . . . . . . . . . . 473
    Man's place in . . . . . . 703
    Mathematical spirit of . . 138, 631
    Mivart's idea of . . . . . . 133
    Moral lessons from . . . . 475
    Order of . . . . . . . . . 237
    Personified . . . . . . . . 620
    Planck's idea of . . . . . . 133
    Smith's (Adam) idea of . . . 476
    Socrates's indifference to . . 128
    Spinoza's idea of . . . . . 138
    Store-house . . . . . . . . 563
    Swedenborg's idea of . . . 134
    Theism of . . . . . . . . . 701
    Unity of . . . . . . . 130, 471
Neo-Platonism, . . . . . . . . 86
Neptune, . . . . . . . . . . . 477
Newcomb, Prof. . . . . . . . . 303
Newton, R. Heber . . . . . . 745
    Sir Isaac . . . . . . 148, 235
    Sir Isaac, discovery of . . . 473
Niebuhr, . . . . . . . . . . . 516
Nihilism, . . . . . . . . . . . 511
Nile, the . . . . . . . . . . . 241
Nirvana, Doctrine of . . . . . 315
Nominalism, . . . . . . . . . 247
Novelist, the . . . . . . . . . 546

**O.**

Occamism, . . . . . . . . . . 323
Oersted, . . . . . . . . . . . 140

PAGE.

Oligarchy, . . . . . . . . . . 514
Olives, Mt. of . . . . . . . . 389
"Omne Vivum ex ovo," . . . . 155
Ontology, Problem of . . . . . 118
Oppression, Social . . . . . . 511
Ordinances, Church . . . . . . 656
Origen, . . . . . . . . . 167, 283
    Theory of the Resurrec-
        tion . . . . . . . . 593, 594
Owen, Richard . . . . . 175, 176, 343
Oxygen, . . . . . . . . . 131, 191
    Discovery of . . . . . . . 416
    Is an effect, . . . . . . 242, 243

**P.**

Paganism, Claim of . . . . . . 646
    Fate of . . . . . . . . . . 724
    Fulfilled . . . . . . . . . 716
    Greek . . . . . . . . . . 620
Pangenesis, Theory of . . . . 156
Pantheism, . . . . . . . . 90, 687
    Errors of . . . . . 443, 444, 477
    Origin of . . . . . . . . . 476
Papacy, the . . . . . . . 658, 666
Paphos, Miracle at . . . . . . 403
Parables, the . . . . . . . . . 567
Park, Mungo . . . . . . . . . 348
Parker, Theodore . . . . . . . 283
Parmenides, . . . . . . . . . 105
Parseeism, . . . . . . . . . . 724
Parthenon, the . . . . . . . . 504
Pascal, . . . . . . . . . . . . 456
Pasteur, M. . . . . . . . . . . 155
Patmos, . . . . . . . . . . . 590
Paul, Ambition, . . . . . . 374, 429
    Apostle, an . . . . . . . . 406
    Birthplace of . . . . . . . 357
    Career of . . . . . . . . . 394
    Chrysostom's opinion of . . . 356
    Cities visited. . . . . . . 402
    Classical education . . . . 359
    College life in Jerusalem . 360, 361
    Conflict with Gentilism, . . . 383
    Conflict with Judaism, . . 381, 382
    Conflict with Philosophy, . 384, 385
    Conversion of . . . . . 363–368
    Criticisms of his Epistles, . . 400
    Damascus, going to . . . 365, 366
    Defense of Messiahship, . . . 383
    Doctrines of . . . . . . . 384
    Effect of his conversion, . . 368
    Empiricist, not an . . . . . 358
    Energy of . . . . . . . . . 374
    Enthusiasm of . . . . . . . 392
    Epistles of . . . . . . 399–402
    Eschatology of . . . . . . 435
    Exponent of Christianity, . 356
    Farrar's opinion of . . . . 398
    Greatness of . . . . . 405, 406

PAGE.

Paul, Ideas of. . . . . . . . . 376
  In Rome, . . . . . . . . . . 397
  Intellectual temperament, . . 373
  Jerusalem, going to . . . . . 397
  Judaic Spirit, . . . . . . 372, 373
  Luke's influence on . . . . . 380
  Luther's opinion of his Epis-
    tles, . . . . . . . . . . . 400
  Methods of . . . . . . . . 690
  Miracle power of . . . . 403, 404
  Missionary tour, the first . 393, 394
  Missionary tour, the 2d. . 395, 396
  Missionary tour, the third.396, 397
  Monad's opinion of . . . . . 398
  Moral character of. . . . 372, 405
  National Spirit, . . . . . . 373
  Parental influence on . . 359, 360
  Persecutor, the . . . . . . 362
  Peter's influence on . . . 379, 380
  Physique of . . . . . . . . 358
  Preparation for Apostleship, . 367
  Prophecies of . . . . . . . 407
  Psychological  c o n v e r s i o n
    of  . . . . . . 364, 370, 371
  Qualifications for leadership, . 375
  Revelations of . . . 378, 390, 399
  Rénan's criticisms of his Epis-
    tles, . . . . . . . . . . . 401
  Rénan's opinion of . . . . . 398
  Scientific explanation of his
    conversion, . . . . . . 369, 370
  Sermon in Antioch in Pisi-
    dia, . . . . . . . . . . 383, 384
  Specific teaching of . . . . 430
  Stephen's influence on. . 377, 378
  Style of . . . . . . . . . 399
  Theologian, the . . . . . . 428
  Time of his conversion, . 366, 367
  Title of Apostle, . . . . . . 404
  Trial in Cæsarea, . . . . . 397
  Trial in Jerusalem, . . . . 397
  Visit to Athens, . . . . . . 396
Peabody, A. P. . . . . . . . 666
Pentateuch, A u t h o r s h i p  con-
  tested, . . . . . . . . 721, 746
Pentecost, . . . . . . . . . . 538
Perictione, . . . . . . . . . 15
Peripatetics, . . . . . . . . 422
  Path of . . . . . . . . . 21
Persians, Religion of . . . . . 334
Personalities, . . . . . . . . 327
Personality, Man's . . . . . . 167
Peschel, Oskar . . . . . . . 697
Pessimism, . . . . . . . . . 89
  Cure for . . . . . . . . . 318
  Overbalanced . . . . . . . 316
  Relation to first cause, . . . 262
  Suicidal . . . . . . . . . 317
Peter exalted, . . . . . . . . 404

PAGE.

Peter, Relation to Paul, . . . 379, 380
Petitio Principii, . . . . . . . 191
Phenomena, Explanation of . . . 234
Philo, . . . . . . . . . . . . 191
  Phrases of . . . . . . . . . 667
Philippi, Miracle in . . . . . . 403
Philosophers, Ancient . . . . . 105
  Christian . . . . . . . . . 89
  Modern . . . . . . . . . . 106
Philosophy, Alienation of. . . . 689
  Boundaries of . . . . . . 114, 688
  Breakdown of . . . . . . . 307
  Confirmation of Truth, . . . 728
  Conflicts with Christianity, . 755
  Definitions, . . . . . . . . 112
  Disappearance in Christianity,732
  Divisions of . . . . . . . . 110
  Embarrassments of . . . . . 730
  Fundamental truth of . . . . 702
  Greek, a development, . . . . 333
  Inspiration of . . . . . . 16, 334
  Moral . . . . . . . . . . . 81
  Opposed to Agnosticism, . 694, 696
  Province of . . . . . . . . . 108
  Pseudodox in . . . . . . . . 653
  Reconciliation of Christianity
    with . . . . . . . . . . . 689
  Responsible for antagonism, . 753
  Roman . . . . . . . . . . . 74
  School-master, A . . . . . . 707
  Theological tendency of . . . 259
  Transition period of . . . . 755
Phrenology, . . . . . . . . . 206
Pictet, Adolf . . . . . . . . . 348
Pietist, Position of . . . . . . 692
Pius IX., Pope . . . . . . . . 220
Plato, Academy of . . . . . . 20, 21
  Biographies of . . . . . . . 17
  Birth of . . . . . . . . . . 18
  Caste taught, . . . . . . . 57
  Character, moral . . . . . . 18
  Communism, . . . . . . . . 59
  Cosmology, . . . . . . . . 30
  Educational schemes, . . . 49, 50
  Emerson's opinion of . . . . 21
  Esoteric Philosophy, . . . . 23
  Ethics of . . . . . . 45, 46, 65
  Governmental Ideas, . . . 57, 58
  Ideas, Doctrine of . . . . . 35
  Immortality, Doctrine of 39, 40, 53
  Intemperance condemned, . 45, 46
  Knowledge, Limitations of . . 43
  Knowledge, sources of. . . 41, 42
  Language, Philosophical . . . 64
  Lewes's opinion of . . . . 26, 60
  Logos defined, . . . . . . . 44
  Marriage views of . . . . 58, 66
  Method of . . . . . . . . . 26
  Mind, Definition of . . . . . 41

PAGE

Plato, Monotheism of . . . . . 28–30
   Motion, doctrine of . . . . 36, 63
   Mythology, . . . . . . . . . 29
   Originalities of . . . . . . 32, 63
   Philosophy, Influence of . . 62, 67
   Physiology of . . . . . . . 37
   Prayer, Utility of, . . . . . 48, 52
   Prometheus, . . . . . . . 37
   Providence, Doctrine of . . . 51
   Psychology of . . . . . . . 36, 37
   Purgatory suggested, . . . . 55
   Reminiscence, Doctrine of . . 38
   Republic, Ideal . . . . . . 58
   Services to religion, . . . . 68
   Socialism, . . . . . . . . . 56
   Socialism, objections to . . 66, 67
   Socrates's pupil, . . . . . . 19
   Socratic element in . . . . 24
   Soul, Depravity of . . . 39, 40, 47
   Soul, Nature of . . . . . . 39
   Soul, Pre-existence of . . . 38
   Spirituality, . . . . . . . 52–55
   Style, Dialogistic . . . . . 23
   System of . . . . . . . . . 21
   Theology of . . . . . . . . 27
   Transmigration taught, . . . 54
   Travels of . . . . . . . . . 20
   Universals, Doctrine of . . . 36
   Universe, Conception of . . . 34
   Works classified, . . . . . 22–25
   Writer, A . . . . . . . 23, 60, 61
Plotinus, . . . . . . . . . . 86, 596
   Mysticism of . . . . . . . 669
Pluto, . . . . . . . . . . . 477, 641
Pnyx, The . . . . . 396, 504, 505
Pollux, . . . . . . . . . . . 315
Polygamy, . . . . . 509, 603, 666
   Authorized, . . . . . . . . 718
Polytheism, . . . 330, 335, 347, 471
   Extinction of . . . . . . . 641
   Taught by Greeks, . . . . . 477
Porter, Dr. Noah . . . . . . . 161
Poseidon, . . . . . . . . . . 335
Positivism, . . . . . . . . 89, 99
Post-millennianism, . . . . . . 609
Pratt, Orson . . . . . . . . . 666
Pre-Adamites, . . . . . . . . 185
Pre-millennianism, . . . . . . 609
Privateering, . . . . . . . . . 543
Probation, Force of I Peter iii,
   18–20, . . . . . . . . . . 607
   Necessity, . . . . . . . . . 607
   Philosophical . . . . . . . 697
   Second . . . . . . . . . . 606
Problems, . . . . . . . . . . 113
   Christian, . . . . . . . . . 564
Prodicus, . . . . . . . . . . 80
Progress, Idea of . . . . . . . 725
   Law of . . . . . . . . . . 104

PAGE.

Progress, Political . . . . . . 717
Properties, Knowledge of . . . 224
Property, Rights of . . . . . . 543
Prophecy, . . . . . . . . . . 387
   Value, . . . . . . . . . . 648
Prophets, Persian . . . . . . . 413
Protagoras, . . . . . . . . . 105
Protestantism, . . . . . . . . 654
   Tainted . . . . . . . . . . 659
Protoplasm, . . . . . . . . . 157
Protozoan, . . . . . . . . . . 585
Prout, Dr. . . . . . . . . . . 131
Providence, Doctrine of . . . . 335
   Magnetism of . . . . . . . 642
   Methods, . . . . . . . . . 551
   Scriptural representations,.420–422
Psalms, Singing of . . . . . . 656
Pseudodox, the . . . . . . . . 653
Psychology, Relation to philoso-
   phy, . . . . . . . . . . . 111
Purgatory, . . . . . . . . 581, 658
Puritanism, . . . . . . . . . 495
Purposes divine, unknowable, . . 302
Pusey . . . . . . . . . . . . 666
Pyrrho, . . . . . . . . . . 85, 116
Pyrrhonism, . . . . . . . . . 210
Pythagoras, . . . . . . . . 77, 105
   Philosophy of . . . . . . . 138
   Philosophy defined, . . . . 112

**Q.**

Qualifications, Paul's . . . . 375
Quarantania, Mount . . . . . . 388
Quarrels, Scientific . . . . . . 754
Quatrefages, M, . . . . . . . 171
Quotations, Poetic . . . . 89, 143

**R.**

Race, A perfect . . . . . . . 188
   Unity of the . . . . . . . 554
Races, Plurality of . . . . . . 186
Raphael, . . . . . . . . . . 548
Rationalism, . . . . 89, 100, 664
   Mansel's objection, . 270, 271, 411
   Respected, . . . . . . . . 755
Rationalists, Tübingen School of . 370
Rawlinson, George, . . . . . 721
Realism, Ideal . . . . . . . 89, 98
Reason, The . . . . . . . . . 207
   Defective methods, . . . . 232
   Established methods . . . . 756
   Kant's classification of . . . 89, 94
   Spontaneous . . . . . . . 217
   Theistic content of . . . . . 283
Reconciliation, Ground of . . . 699
Redemption, . . . . . . . . . 717
Reformation, German . . . . . 406
   Leadership of . . . . . . . 713
   Swiss . . . . . . . . . . 740

PAGE.

Reformation, Value of . . . . . 544
Regeneration, . . . . . . . . . 434
　Baptismal . . . . . . . . . . 659
　Brahminical . . . . . . . . . 715
　Error concerning . . . . . . 678
　Spontaneous . . . . . . . . 683
Reid, Thomas . . . . . . . . 92, 106
　"Common-sense," . . . 260, 261
　Criticisms of . . . . . . . 198
　Interpretation of mind, . . . 197
Religion, Central position impreg-
　nable, . . . . . . . . . . . 753
　Development, A . . . . . . . 561
　Essentials of . . . . . . . . 620
　Forces of . . . . . . . . . . 622
　Jewish . . . . . . . . . . . 661
　Magnetism of . . . . . . . . 647
　Natural . . . . . . . . 463, 673
　Objective . . . . . . . . . . 673
　Old . . . . . . . . . . . . . 560
　Revealed . . . . . . . . . . 560
　Subjective . . . . . . . . . 673
　Words of . . . . . . . . 744, 745
Religions, Assyrian . . . . . . 653
　Defects of . . . . . . . . . 726
　Disintegration of . . . . . . 714
　Foundation of . . . . . 351, 646
　Hindu . . . . . . . . . . . 442
　Historical . . . . . . . . . 734
　Inspiration of . . . . . . . 711
　International . . . . . . . . 532
　Missionary . . . . . . . . . 710
　Non-evolutionary . . . . . 624
　Race . . . . . . . . . . . . 710
　Rights of . . . . . . . . . . 711
　Spinal cord of . . . . . . . 621
　Strauss's explanation of . . . 347
　Tests of . . . . . . . . . . 671
　Verities of . . . . . . . . . 715
Remains, Human . . . . . . . 183
Reminiscence, Doctrine of . . . . 216
Rénan, Criticism of Christianity, . 668
　Paul's conversion explained, . 369
Resurrection, Alger's theory . . . 597
　Cook's physical . . . . 594–597
　In Nain, . . . . . . . . . . 684
　Jesus' . . . . . . 385, 600, 601
　Nature's suggestions . . . . . 467
　Necessity of . . . . . . . . 386
　Old Testament Materialistic, . 598
　Paul's exposition, . 435, 436,
　　. . . . . . . . . . 599, 600
　Physical rejected, . . . . 595, 596
　Problem of . . . . . . . . . 592
　Scriptural language perverted,
　　. . . . . . . . . . 598, 599
　Seven theories of . . . . . 593
　Spiritual theory affirmed . 597–602
　Spiritual theory, scientific . . 601

PAGE.

Resurrection, Strauss's criticism
　Christ's . . . . . . . . . . 652
　Theories reduced, . . . . . 594
　Time of . . . . . . . . . . 618
　Vaguely taught, . . . . . . 568
　Word defined . . . . . 594, 595
　XVth Chap. of I Corinthians,. 600
Retributions, Eternal . . . . . 54
Reuss, Prof . . . . . . . 371, 721
Revelation, . . . . . . . 219, 221
　Ambiguity of . . . . . . . 669
　Concerning God, . . . . . 222
　Concerning man's purification, 222
　Concerning nature, . . . . 222
　Darkness of . . . . . . . . 580
　Evolutional . . . . . . 624, 625
　Exhaustless, . . . . . 738, 739
　Limits of . . . . . 569, 663, 666
　Necessity of . . . . . . . . 698
　Objection to . . . . . 415, 570
　Philosophical . . . . . . . 448
　Specialty of . . . . . . . . 419
　Stages of . . . . . . . . . 340
Review, *International* . . . . . 205
Revolution, The French . . . . 485
Righteousness, . . . . . . . . 680
Ritter, . . . . . . . . . . . 348
Rome, Corruptions in . . . . . 553
　Pagan . . . . . . . . 503, 504
　Paul in . . . . . . . . . . 397
Ross, Sir John . . . . . . . . 348
Rousseau, . . . . . . . . . . 128
Rush, James . . . . . . . . . 678

S.

Sacrifice, Christian idea of . . . 466
　Socrates's . . . . . . . . . 338
Sahib, Nana . . . . . . . . . 510
Salvation, Plan of . . . . . . 432
Sanctification, . . . . . . . . 367
Sanhedrin, Paul before . . . . 599
Satan, . . . . . . . . . 610, 616
Schaff, Dr. . . . . . . . . . 370
Schelling, . . . . . . . . 97, 106
Schem, Dr. . . . . . . . . . 723
Schiller, . . . . . . . . . . 587
Schlegel . . . . . . . . . . 109
　Idea of God, . . . . . . . 225
Schleiermacher, . . . . . . . 96
　Classification of Plato's Works, 22
　Theology of . . . . . . . . 665
Schliemann, Dr. . . . . . 181, 308
Schmid, Rudolf . . . . . 177, 689
Scholasticism, . . . . . . . . 331
School, Concord . . . . . . . 103
Schopenhauer, . . . . . . 98, 106
　Pessimism of . . . . . . . 314
Schultze, Max . . . . . . . . 157
Schwegler, . . . . . . . . 24, 99

PAGE.

Science, False claims of . . . . . 691
   Limitations of . . . . . . . 457
   Modern . . . . . . . . . . . 341
   Province of . . . . . . . . . 116
Scott, Sir Walter . . . . . . . . 128
Scotus, Duns, . . . . . . . . . . 87
Sectarianism, Oriental . . . . . 654
Selection, Natural . . . . . . . 697
Self, Belief in . . . . . . . . . 172
   Knowledge of . . . . . . . . 225
Self-existence, . . . . . . . . . 113
Seneca, . . . . . . . . . 136, 140, 329
   Eulogizes Christian virtues, . . 706
Sensation, Defined . . . . . . . 219
   Knowledge by . . . . . . . . 258
Sensationalism, . . . . . . . . . 257
   Aristotle's . . . . . . . . . . 258
Sense, a moral . . . . . . . . . 178
Sepulcher, Christ's . . . . . . . 388
Sermon, Nature's . . . . . . . . 460
   Paul's at Antioch, . . . . 383, 384
Sexes, Proportion of . . . . . . 509
Shaftesbury, Lord . . . . . . . 324
Shakespeare, Anglo-Saxon of . . 547
   Philosophy hint of . . . . . 117
   Poetical mind of . . . . . . 198
Shintoism, . . . . . . . . . 345, 724
   Reproduced . . . . . . . . . 738
Sheol, . . . . . 546, 603, 605, 629, 639
Siam, Living in . . . . . . . . . 552
Sin, . . . . . . . . . . 454, 433, 678
   Destroyed . . . . . . . . . . 611
   Original . . . . . . . . . . . 480
   Reproved . . . . . . . . . . 679
   Secret . . . . . . . . . . . . 50
Sirius, . . . . . . . . . . . . . 241
Skepticism, Attacks on . . . . . 742
Skulls, . . . . . . . . . . . . . 183
Smith, Adam . . . . . . . . . . 293
   Doctrine of Sympathy, . . . . 322
   Theory of Happiness, . . . . 325
   George . . . . . . . . . . . 337
   W. Robertson . . . . . . . . 663
   W. Roberston, Authorship of
     Decalogue, . . . . . . . . 747
Smyth, Newman, . . . . . . . . 560
   Pedagogical intent of Old Tes-
     ment, . . . . . . . . . . . 561
   Theory of Resurrection, . 593, 594
Socialism, . . . . . . . . 56–58, 67
   Philosophic . . . . . . . . . 502
   Revolutionary . . . . . . . . 502
Society, Augustus's scheme, . . . 498
   Bases of . . . . . . . . . . . 493
   Episcopal scheme . . . . . . 495
   Hildebrand's scheme, . . . . 494
   Ideal . . . . . . . 506, 515, 516
   Mohammedan idea of . . 505, 506
   Napoleon's scheme . . . . . 497

PAGE.

Society, Pagan idea of . . . . . 503
   Plato's scheme . . . . . 498, 499
   Political idea of . . . . . 496, 497
   Puritanic scheme, . . . . . . 495
   Scientific idea of . . . 500, 501
   Socialistic idea of . . . . . . 502
Socinus, . . . . . . . . . . . . 666
Sociology, Herbert Spencer's . . 499
Socrates, Dæmon of . . . . . . . 48
   Philosophy of . . . . 19, 81, 82
Somme, Valley of . . . . . . 181, 182
Sophists, . . . . . . . . . . . 80
Soteriology, . . . . . . . . . . 716
Soul, the . . . . . . . . . 166, 567
   Brahminical notions of . . . . 444
   Immortality of . . . . . . . 63
   Lotze's definition of . . . . 585
   Resurrection of . . . . . . . 597
Southall, Prof. . . . . . . . 181, 182
   Prof., Antiquity of man, . . . 748
Space, . . . . . . . . . . . . . 461
Species, . . . . . . . 105, 132, 163
   Extinct . . . . . . . . . . . 181
   Introduction of . . . . . . . 164
   Stability of . . . . . . . . . 470
   Variety of . . . . . . . . . . 163
*Spectator,* the London . . . . . 280
Spencer, Herbert . . . . . 101, 106
   "Complete living" of . . . 682
   Ethics of . . . . . . . 322, 323
   Interpretation of mind, . 201–203
   Non-atheistic, . . . . . . . 698
   Opinion of Christianity, . . . 660
   Sociology, . . . . . . . 499, 500
   Theism of . . . . . . . 698, 699
Spinoza, . . . . 89, 90, 106, 194, 209
Spirit, Hellenic . . . . . . . . 114
   Modern . . . . . . . . . . . 341
Spiritualism, . . . . . . . . . 55
   Roman, . . . . . . . . . . . 621
Sports, Gladiatorial . . . . . . 528
   Suppressed, . . . . . . . . . 552
Stanley, Dean . . . . . . . . . 590
Statistics, Religious . . . . . . 723
Stewart, Balfour . . . . . . . . 235
   Dugald . . . . 92, 106, 190, 209
Stoicism, . . . . . . . . . . . 83
   Contributions of . . . . . . 539
   Morality of . . . . . . 336, 553
Strauss, "Have we a Religion?". 345
   Ignorance confessed, . . . . 177
   Object of worship, . . . . . 701
   Symbolical interpretation of
     Bible, . . . . . . . . . . 668
   Transcendental theory, . . . 175
Strikes, . . . . . . . . . . . . 512
Struggles, Life's . . . . . . . . 484
Styx, the river . . . . . . . . 639
Substances, the two . . . . . . 583

PAGE.

Succession, Doctrine of . . . . 241
Supernatural, the . . . . . . 566, 567
Superstition, . . . . . . . . . 352
Swedenborg, . . . . . . . . 134, 473
  Second adventism, . . . . . 608
  Theory of resurrection, . 593, 594
Switzerland, Lake dwellings in . 185
Sympathy, doctrine of . . . . 322
Synoptists, the . . . . . . . . 390
System, Value of . . . . . . . 441

T.

Tait, Prof. . . . . . . . . 155, 247
Talleyrand, . . . . . . . . . . 61
Taoism, . . . . . . . . . . 345, 724
  Reproduced . . . . . . . . 738
Tarsus, . . . . . . . . . . . 357
  Schools of . . . . . . . . . 359
Tartarus, . . . . . 55, 438, 578, 639
Tefft, B. F. . . . . . . . . . . 704
Teleology, . . . . . . . . . . 286
  Astronomy a proof . . . . 296
  Baer's Ridicule, . . . . . . 300
  Cook's, doubt . . . . . . . 291
  Duke of Argyll's indorsement, 298
  Gastric juice, . . . . . . . 295
  Hick's assault, . . . . . . 288
  Oxygen a proof, . . . . . . 293
  Physiology a proof, . . . . 293
  Plato's trouble, . . . . . . 300
  Premature conclusions, . . 301
  Rudimentary organs op-
    posed . . . . . . . . 300, 301
  Schopenhauer's objection, . 300
  Theological . . . . . . . . 705
  Various arguments, . . . . 296
Temptation, Christ's . . . . . 388
Tertullian, . . . . . . . . . . 553
Testament, New . . . . . . . 564
  Ethics of . . . . . . . . . 750
  Evolution of . . . . . . . 630
  Immortality taught . . . . 590
  Old . . . . . . . . . . . . 564
  Old, Assault on . . . . 745, 746
  Old, Immortality taught . 589, 590
  Old, Optical accuracy . . . 572
  Old, Scientifically vindicated, . 721
Thales, . . . . . . . . 74–76, 105
Theater, Flavian . . . . . . . 552
Theism, Argument from de-
  sign . . . . . . . . . 280, 281
  Cato's declaration, . . . . . 274
  Intuitional, . . . . . . . . 447
  Law of Causation a proof, . . 278
  Law of Continuity a proof, . 278, 279
  Magnetism of . . . . . . . 641
  Philosophic basis defective, . 281
  Mohammedan doctrine . . . 447
  Triumph of . . . . . . . . 450

PAGE.

Theodicy, Basis of . . . . . . . 490
  Range of . . . . . . . . . 486
Theodorus, . . . . . . . . . . 329
Theology, . . . . . . . . . . . 27
  Compromise, . . . . . . . 665
  Evils of . . . . . . . . . 655, 656
  New . . . . . . . . . . . 603
  Poetic . . . . . . . . . 339, 579
  Scientific . . . . . . . . . 432
Theophorus, . . . . . . . . . 670
Theseus, Temple of . . . . . . 396
Thiers, M. . . . . . . . . . . 343
Tholuck, . . . . . . . . . . . 665
Thompson, Sir William . . . . 319
Thought, Regulated . . . . . . 719
Thrasyllus, . . . . . . . . . . 22
Time, . . . . . . . . . . . . 461
Titus, . . . . . . . . . . . . 382
Townsend, Dr. L. T. . . . . . . 605
Torch-race, a . . . . . . . . . 725
Torricelli, . . . . . . . . . . 570
Trade, International . . . . 517, 518
Tradition, . . . . . . . . . . 735
Traducianism, . . . . . . . . 168
Trajan, . . . . . . . . . . . 670
Transcendency, Doctrine of . . . 240
Transcendentalism, . . . . . . 444
Transmigration, Doctrine of . . . 444
Transubstantiation, . . . . . . 656
Trench, Archbishop . . . . 414, 609
Tribes, South African . . . . . 348
Trinity, . . . . . . . . . . . 388
  Developed, . . . . . . . . 538
  Errors from . . . . . . . . 603
  Geometric . . . . . . . . . 632
  Rejected . . . . . . . . . 447
Truth, Basis of . . . . . . . . 438
  Christianity is . . . . . 759, 760
  Criteria of . . . . . . . . 674
  Danger to . . . . . . . . . 758
  Difficulties in obtaining . . . 211
  Embryonic . . . . . . . . . 537
  Hidden . . . . . . . . 674, 675
  Intuitional, . . . . . . . . 216
  Nature of . . . . . . . . . 440
  Necessity of . . . . . . . . 574
  Revealed . . . . . . . . . 221
  Self-dependent . . . . . . 537
  Sources of . . . . . . . . . 220
  Theistic . . . . . . . . 417, 418
  Unity of . . . . . . . . . 752
  Unknowable . . . . . . . . 416
Tyndall, Prof. . . . . . 151, 155, 160
  Idea of energy, . . . . . . 239

U.

Uhlhorn, . . . . . . . . . . . 553
Ultimate, Incognizable . . . . . 117
Ultimates, . . . . . . . . . . 327

| | PAGE. |
|---|---|
| Ulysses, | 307 |
| Unconditioned, the | 113, 119 |
| Rejected | 271, 272 |
| Unitarianism, | 640, 655 |
| Unity, Argument from | 471 |
| Nature's | 467, 468 |
| Of the race, | 468 |
| Universalism, | 665 |
| Universe, Eternal | 124 |
| Explanation of | 569 |
| Imperfect, | 296 |
| Materials of | 468 |
| Produced, | 153 |
| Teleological character of | 279, 280 |
| | 468, 469 |
| Unseen, | 602 |
| Upham, | 118 |
| Ur, City of | 748 |
| Utility, Doctrine of | 513 |
| Utopia, Sir Thomas More's | 499 |
| Utopianism, Practical | 557 |

**V.**

| | |
|---|---|
| VACCINATION, | 649 |
| Vatican, Fine arts in, | 549 |
| Vedas, The | 442, 443 |
| Version, Revised | 546 |
| Septuagint | 748 |
| Vibrations, Philosophic | 115 |
| Vico, | 104 |
| Vinci, Leonardo da | 548 |
| Virgil, | 514 |
| Virtue, Aristotle's definition of | 513 |
| Vishnu, | 443 |
| Vitalism, Theory of | 160, 683 |
| Vogt, Karl | 173 |
| Voltaire, | 510, 545 |

**W.**

| | |
|---|---|
| WALLACE, A. R. | 173, 178 |
| Flints, Estimating age of | 181 |
| Theism of | 274 |
| Watson, Richard | 09 |
| Watt, James | 619 |
| Weight, Atomic | 132 |
| Weisman, Prof. | 585 |

| | PAGE. |
|---|---|
| Wesley, John | 659 |
| Whedon, D. D. | 480, 609 |
| Whewell | 545 |
| Whitney, Prof. | 174 |
| Will, Scopenhauer's idea of | 262 |
| William of Occam | 87 |
| Wilson, Sir Thomas | 558 |
| Winchell, Prof., Tribes examined by | 343 |
| Winkleman, Abbé | 674, 675 |
| Wolf | 438 |
| Woman, Mohammedan idea of | 552, 553, 718 |
| Women, Community of | 509 |
| World, Conflagration of | 618 |
| Intermediate | 602–606 |
| Phenomenal | 456 |
| Spiritual | 474 |
| Worsade, | 182 |
| Wyman, Prof. | 155 |
| Wythe, Dr. | 161 |

**X.**

| | |
|---|---|
| XAVIER, FRANCIS | 722 |

**Y.**

| | |
|---|---|
| YALE COLLEGE, | 547 |
| Yäma, the | 716 |
| Yoga, Philosophy of | 336 |
| Youth, Paul's | 358–360 |
| Plato's | 18, 19 |

**Z.**

| | |
|---|---|
| ZEALANDERS, NEW | 577 |
| Zeno, | 83, 105 |
| Ethical notions of | 513 |
| The Stoic | 215 |
| Zenocrates, | 17 |
| Zenophanes, | 77, 105 |
| Zero, | 635 |
| Zerubbabel, | 421 |
| Zeus, | 335, 430, 477 |
| Zoölogy, | 132, 437 |
| Zoroaster, | 329, 331 |
| Zoroastrianism, Resurrection idea of | 598 |
| Zwingli, | 656, 740 |

FINIS.